Maume/Maute/Fromberger

The Law of Crypto Assets

The Law of Crypto Assets

A Handbook

edited by

Philipp Maume
Lena Maute
Mathias Fromberger

2022

Published by
Verlag C.H.Beck oHG, Wilhelmstraße 9, 80801 München, Germany,
email: bestellung@beck.de

Co-published by
Hart Publishing, Kemp House, Chawley Park, Cumnor Hill, Oxford, OX2 9PH, United Kingdom,
online at: www.hartpub.co.uk

and

Nomos Verlagsgesellschaft mbH & Co. KG, Waldseestraße 3–5, 76530 Baden-Baden, Germany,
email: nomos@nomos.de

Published in North America by Hart Publishing
An Imprint of Bloomsbury Publishing 1385 Broadway, New York, NY 10018, USA
email: mail@hartpub.co.uk

Suggested citation:
[Author], in: Maume/Maute/Fromberger,
The Law of Crypto Assets,
2022, § [#] mn. [#]

www.beck.de

ISBN 978 3 406 74396 2 (C.H.BECK)
ISBN 978 1 5099 4594 8 (HART)
ISBN 978 3 8487 8570 4 (NOMOS)

© 2022 Verlag C.H.Beck oHG
Wilhelmstr. 9, 80801 München
Printed in Germany by
Westermann Druck Zwickau GmbH
Crimmitschauer Straße 43, 08058 Zwickau
Typeset by
Reemers Publishing Services GmbH, Krefeld
Cover: Druckerei C.H.Beck Nördlingen

chbeck.de/nachhaltig

All rights reserved. No part of this publication may be reproduced, stored in a retrieval system, or transmitted, in any form or by any means, without the prior permission of Verlag C.H.Beck, or as expressly permitted by law under the terms agreed with the appropriate reprographic rights organisation. Enquiries concerning reproduction which may not be covered by the above should be addressed to C.H.Beck at the address above.

Preface

Distributed ledger technology (DLT) and blockchain are two emblematic examples of innovative technologies that allow new business models and opportunities. Since the introduction of the internet, no other innovations have caused such a stir in the global business community. The current development is remarkable. Before 2017, Bitcoin or initial coin offerings were only known to tech enthusiasts. Only four years later, various countries have introduced legislation regarding the freshly-dubbed 'crypto assets'. Issues such as the suitability of cryptocurrencies for money-laundering as well as their impact on energy consumption and climate change have found their way into the general media. While some countries compete to create a suitable legal 'crypto environment', others react with crackdowns on the fledging crypto scene. The establishment of DLT-based digital currencies seems only a question of time.

At present, the pressing question is how this new technology fits into the current legal framework. Are token offerings subject to prospectus requirements; and if so, which ones? What is the regulatory status of crypto exchanges? Can cryptocurrencies be considered as legal tender? Are crypto assets subject to taxation like 'normal' assets? Where are the gaps in the regulatory quilt?

In this book, we attempt to answer as many of these questions as possible. The focus is on the laws of the European Union. This is not just because of the size of the internal market and the strength of its economies. Although commonly considered as sluggish, EU lawmakers have demonstrated surprising agility in implementing regulation specifically tailored to crypto assets. The 5th Anti-Money Laundering Directive from 2018 was one of the first pieces of legislation that specifically addressed crypto-specific issues. The extensive Regulation for Markets in Crypto Assets (MiCAR) is expected to come into force in 2022. This will be accompanied by a pilot regime for crypto marketplaces. In addition, the existing EU rules for financial markets regulation have proved surprisingly well-suited for tackling the challenges presented by crypto assets. These EU-law based issues are discussed in the first half of this book, including inter alia EU private international law, consumer protection law, financial services and prospectus law, payment services law, data protection law, taxation law and funds regulation.

However, many countries, both inside and outside the EU, have enacted national legislation on crypto assets. Therefore, the second half of the book provides an overview of the development of crypto regulation in various major financial marketplaces. These country reports include inter alia the US, the UK, France, Germany, Russia, the PR of China, Singapore, Australia and New Zealand. It is our hope that these chapters allow further comparisons between jurisdictions and promote the international debate on best practice in the crypto space.

It is our view that we are currently witnessing the 'law of crypto assets' as a distinct area of law. This book is supposed to contribute towards an exchange of ideas and further harmonisation of crypto laws. It is current as at 1 July 2021. We appreciate all kinds of feedback.

Munich/Augsburg, Germany, October 2021

Philipp Maume   Lena Maute   Mathias Fromberger

Table of Contents

Preface V
List of Authors IX

Part A
Introduction

§ 1. Technical and Factual Background 1
§ 2. Economics of Crypto Assets 33

Part B
EU Regulation

§ 3. International Jurisdiction and Applicable Law 69
§ 4. Consumer Protection 109
§ 5. Intermediaries of Secondary Crypto Trade 120
§ 6. Data Protection 146
§ 7. Initial Coin Offerings (ICOs) 174
§ 8. Financial Services Regulation 227
§ 9. E-Money Tokens, Stablecoins, and Token Payment Services 242
§ 10. Anti-Money Laundering 269
§ 11. Market Abuse 313
§ 12. Confiscation 331
§ 13. Value Added Tax 353
§ 14. Accounting 369
§ 15. Crypto Assets & Funds 383

Part C
Country Reports

§ 16. France 429
§ 17. Germany 444
§ 18. United Kingdom 456
§ 19. Switzerland 475
§ 20. Liechtenstein 492
§ 21. Russia 507
§ 22. United States of America 523
§ 23. Singapore 542
§ 24. Australia 554
§ 25. New Zealand 570
§ 26. Hong Kong 583
§ 27. People's Republic of China 594
§ 28. Middle East and North Africa (MENA) 603

Index 619

List of Authors

Iris M. Barsan, Dr., LL.M. (Cologne), Maître de Conferences en Droit Privé (UPEC) and Ancienne Élève de l'ENA (Willy Brandt).

Andrew Dahdal, Dr., Associate Professor at the College of Law, Qatar University and Head of Economic Diversification at the Centre for Law and Development, Qatar.

Marco Dell'Erba, Dr., LL.M. (NYU), Assistant Professor of Law, University of Zurich, Switzerland, and a Fellow at the Institute for Corporate Governance & Finance, NYU School of Law, USA.

Michael Denga, Dr., LL.M. (London), Maître en Droit (Paris), Postdoctoral Researcher at Humboldt-Universität zu Berlin, Germany.

Benedikt Downar, Dr., Postdoctoral Researcher at Technical University of Munich, Germany.

Mathias Fromberger, Dr., Lawyer, Postdoctoral Researcher at Technical University of Munich, Germany.

Christoph Gschnaidtner, M.Sc. (TUM), M.Sc. (Augsburg), Research Associate and PhD Candidate at Technical University of Munich, Germany.

Lars Haffke, LL.M. (Nottingham), M.Sc. (TUM), Research Associate and PhD Candidate at Technical University of Munich, Germany.

Veronica R. S. Hoch, Dr., Postdoctoral Researcher at Ruhr-University Bochum, Germany.

Sebastiaan Niels Hooghiemstra, Dr., LL.M. (VU Amsterdam/Tilburg University), Associate at Loyens & Loeff Luxembourg and Senior Fellow/Guest Lecturer of the International Center for Financial Law & Governance at the Erasmus University Rotterdam, Netherlands.

Pawee Jenweeranon, Lecturer in Law at the Faculty of Law, Thammasat University, Thailand, a Research Affiliate at Cambridge Centre for Alternative Finance (CCAF) at University of Cambridge Judge Business School, United Kingdom, and a PhD Candidate at the Chinese University of Hong Kong (CUHK).

Markus Kaulartz, Dr., Counsel at CMS Germany in Munich.

Mario Keiling, Dr., M.Sc. (Erlangen), Research Associate at Technical University of Munich, Germany.

Jasmin Kollmann, Dr., Senior Tax Consultant at EY Munich, Germany.

Joseph Lee, Dr., Reader in Corporate and Financial Law at the University of Manchester, United Kingdom.

Philipp Maume, Dr., S.J.D. (La Trobe), Professor of Law at Technical University of Munich, Germany.

Lena Maute, Dr., Juniorprofessor of Law at University of Augsburg, Germany.

Tanja Niedernhuber, Dr., Postdoctoral Researcher at Ludwig-Maximilians-Universität Munich, Germany.

Anika Patz, Dr., Senior Associate at YPOG, Berlin, Germany.

Christina Delia Preiner, Dr., LL.M. (Liechtenstein), Senior Associate at Gasser Partner Attorneys at Law, Vaduz, Liechtenstein.

Daniel Schmid, Dr., Postdoctoral Researcher at University of Augsburg, Germany.

Florian Schramm, M.Sc. (Erlangen), Research Associate and PhD Candidate at Technical University of Munich, Germany.

Benedikt Seiler, Dr., PD, Senior Lecturer at University of Basel, Switzerland.

List of Authors

Björn Steinrötter, Dr., Juniorprofessor of Law at University of Potsdam, Germany.

Samantha Tang, Sheridan Fellow at the Faculty of Law of National University of Singapore and Academic Fellow at the Centre for Asian Legal Studies, Faculty of Law of National University of Singapore.

Annabelle Walker, M.C.L. (Cambridge), in-house lawyer in Melbourne, Australia.

Gordon Walker, Dr., S.J.D. (Duke), Emeritus Professor at La Trobe University, Australia, and Adjunct Professor at the International College of Digital Innovation, Chiang Mai University, Chiang Mai, Thailand.

Jan Max Wettlaufer, Associate at lindenpartners, Berlin, Germany.

Corinne Zellweger-Gutknecht, Dr., Professor of Law at University of Basel, Switzerland.

Peter Zickgraf, Research Associate and PhD Candidate at Ludwig-Maximilians-Universität, Munich, Germany.

PART A
INTRODUCTION

§ 1
Technical and Factual Background

Literature: Antonopoulos, Mastering Bitcoin: Programming the Open Blockchain, (2nd edn, O'Reilly Media, Sebastopol, 2017); Barsan, 'Legal Challenges of Initial Coin Offerings (ICO)' (2017) 3 *Revue Trimestrielle de Droit Financier*, 54; Berentsen and Schär, *Bitcoin, Blockchain and Kryptoassets* (Books on Demand, Norderstedt, 2017); Chohan, 'Initial Coin Offerings (ICOs): Risks, Regulation, and Accountability' (2017) Discussion Paper Series: Notes on the 21st Century, available at https://beck-link.de/dcz63 (accessed 8.9.2018); Chohan, 'Tethering Cryptocurrencies to Fiat Currencies Without Transparency: A Case Study' (2018), available at https://beck-link.de/kc2xx (accessed 17.6.2021); De Filippi and Wright, *Blockchain and the Law* (Harvard University Press, Cambridge, 2018); Diffie and Hellman, 'New Directions in Cryptography' (1976) 22 *IEEE Transaction on Information Theory*, 644; Eikenberg, 'Mitgeschürft – Spezialhardware fürs Bitcoin Mining' (2013) 25 *c't – Magazin für Computertechnik*, 140; Ekkenga, 'Bitcoin und andere Digitalwährungen – Spielzeug für Spekulanten oder Systemveränderung durch Privatisierung des Zahlungssysteme?' (2017) 36 *Computer und Recht*, 762; Fromberger and Haffke, 'ICO Market Report 2018/2019 – Performance Analysis of 2018's Initial Coin Offerings' (2019), available at https://beck-link.de/d6zac (accessed 23.1.2020); Fromberger, Haffke and Zimmermann, 'Kryptowerte und Geldwäsche – Eine Analyse der 5. Geldwäscherichtlinie sowie des Gesetzesentwurfs der Bundesregierung' (2019) 19 *Zeitschrift für Bank- und Kapitalmarktrecht*, 377; Haffke and Fromberger, 'ICO Market Report 2017 – Performance Analysis of Initial Coin Offerings (Presentation Slides)' (2019), available at https://beck-link.de/awwh6 (accessed 23.1.2020); Haffke and Fromberger, 'ICO Market Report 2019/2020 – Performance Analysis of 2019's Initial Coin Offerings (2020), available at https://beck-link.de/awwh6 (accessed 23.1.2020) Hoppe, 'Blockchain Oracles – Einsatz der Blockchain-Technologie für Offline-Anwendungen', in Hennemann and Sattler (eds), *Immaterialgüter und Digitalisierung*, Junge Wissenschaft zum Gewerblichen Rechtsschutz, Urheber- und Medienrecht (Freiburg 2018), 59; Kaulartz, 'Die Blockchain-Technologie – Hintergründe zur Distributed Ledger Technology und zu Blockchains' (2016) 36 *Computer und Recht*, 474; Klöhn, Parhofer and Resas , 'Initial Coin Offerings (ICOs) – Markt, Ökonomik und Regulierung' (2018) 30 Zeitschrift für Bankrecht und Bankwirtschaft, 89; Kütük-Markendorf, *Rechtliche Einordnung von Internetwährungen im deutschen Rechtssystem am Beispiel von Bitcoin*, Schriften zum Wirtschafts- und Medienrecht, Urheberrecht und Immaterialgüterrecht (Peter Lang GmbH, Frankfurt am Main, 2016); Maume and Fromberger, 'Regulation of Initial Coin Offerings: Reconciling US and EU Securities Laws' (2019) 19 *Chicago Journal of International Law*, 548; Moran, 'The Impact of Regulatory Measures Imposed on Initial Coin Offerings in the United States Market Economy' (2018) 26 *Catholic University Journal of Law and Technology*, 2; Nakamoto, 'Bitcoin: A Peer-to-Peer Electronic Cash System' (Satoshi Nakamoto Institute, 31.1.2008), available at https://beck-link.de/hh2f8 (accessed 31.1.2020); Noonan, 'Bitcoin or Bust: Can One Really 'Trust' One's Digital Assets?' (2015) 7 *Estate Planning & Community Property Law Journal*, 583; Rivero, 'Distributed Ledger Technology and Token Offering Regulation' (2018), available at https://beck-link.de/cz7x3 (accessed 7.9.2018); Rohr and Wright, 'Blockchain-Based Token Sales, Initial Coin Offerings, and the Democratization of Public Capital Markets' (2017) *University of Tennessee Legal Studies Research Paper* No. 338, 12, available at https://beck-link.de/peh4b (accessed 7.9.2018); Roßbach, 'Blockchain-Technologien und ihre Implikationen – Teil 2: Anwendungsbereiche der Blockchain-Technologie' (2016), available at https://beck-link.de/5mxh5 (accessed 22.01.2020); Rosenberger, *Bitcoin and Blockchain* (Springer Vieweg, Berlin, 2018); Safferling and Rückert, 'Telekommunikationsüberwachung bei Bitcoins – Heimliche Datenauswertung bei virtuellen Währungen gem. § 100a StPO?' (2015) 18 *Zeitschrift für IT-Recht und Digitalisierung*, 788; Small, 'Bitcoin: The Napster of Currency' (2015) 37 *Houston Journal of International Law*, 581; Subcomittee on Commerce, Manufacturing and Trade of the Committee on Energy and Commerce House of Representatives, 'The Disrupter Series: Digital Currency and Blockchain Technology' (Second Session of the hearing before the 114th US Congress, U.S. Government Publishing Office, 16.3.2016), available at https://beck-link.de/tpdc5 (accessed 31.1.2020); Werbach and Cornell, 'Contracts Ex Machina' (2017) 67 *Duke Law Journal*, 313; Witte, 'The Blockchain: A Gentle Introduction' (2016), available at https://beck-link.de/sw7s7 (accessed 31.1.2020); Zickgraf, 'Initial Coin Offerings – Ein Fall für das Kapitalmarktrecht?' (2018) 63 *Die Aktiengesellschaft*, 293.

Part A. Introduction

Outline

	para.
A. The Blockchain Technology	1
I. Introduction	1
II. Blockchain Participants	7
III. Categorization of Blockchains	10
IV. Structure of a Blockchain	14
V. Transaction of Tokens	16
VI. Technical Representation of Tokens	22
VII. Wallets and Wallet Providers	25
VIII. Extension of the Blockchain through Verification	28
1. Finding a Consensus	28
2. Incentive Scheme	33
a) Similarities of the different Schemes	34
b) Proof-of-work Procedure – Mining	38
aa) Technical Implementation	38
bb) Aggregation of Miners and Mining Pools	40
(1) Background and Purpose	40
(2) Modes of Operation	45
(a) Collaborative Mining Pools	46
(b) Non-collaborative Mining Pools	49
(3) Forms of Organisation	53
(a) Managed Mining Pools	54
(b) Peer-to-peer Mining Pools	55
(4) Cloud Mining Services	57
c) Proof-of-Stake Process – Minting	58
aa) Technical Implementation	58
bb) Staking Pools	60
IX. Smart Contracts	62
X. Disadvantages of Blockchain Technology	67
B. Phenomenology of Tokens	68
I. Basic Technical Design	68
II. Currency Tokens	70
III. Investment Tokens	71
IV. Utility Tokens	73
V. Hybrids	74
VI. Asset-backed Token	75
VII. Token-based Financial Products	77
C. The Acquisition of Tokens	78
I. Original Acquisition	79
1. Initiation of a Blockchain	79
2. Mining/Minting	80
3. Initial Coin Offering (ICO)	81
II. Derivative Acquisition	88
1. Direct Derivative Acquisition	89
2. Trading Platforms: Crypto-to-Crypto Exchanges and Fiat-to-Crypto Exchanges	90
a) General Information	90
b) Functional Categorisation	93
aa) On-Chain vs. Off-Chain	94
bb) Central vs. Decentral	97
D. Anonymisation Efforts	102
I. Pseudonymity as Starting Point	102
II. Tumblers	106
III. Privacy Tokens	108
1. Ring Signatures	109
2. Stealth Addresses	110

§ 1. Technical and Factual Background

A. The Blockchain Technology

I. Introduction

The blockchain first appeared as the technology behind Bitcoin.[1] It is a digital, chronologically structured,[2] **decentralised, distributed, and almost forgery-proof register, similar to a database**. 1

This register, commonly referred to as distributed ledger, is managed by a computer network on a peer-to-peer basis.[3] In a peer-to-peer network, data is stored simultaneously on each computer that is part of the network.[4] This distinguishes the peer-to-peer system from a cloud system in which the stored files are distributed over different computers. The **distribution**[5] protects the blockchain from being damaged by local events. If a copy of the blockchain is lost, the network participant that lost it can send a message to the other network participants asking them to resend it. If the stored versions differ, the one that contains the longest blockchain always prevails. This is the version in which the blockchain participants have invested the most computing power.[6]

Every blockchain is based on a source code. This code forms the basis of the respective network and determines the beginning of the blockchain as well as its conditions and features. In decentralised systems, the code is regularly open source, i.e. freely available.[7] The **protocol software** (also called **client**) is based on this code. It connects the respective network participant with the blockchain and gives him the ability to interact with the network. For the Bitcoin blockchain, this software can be downloaded under the name 'Bitcoin Core'.[8] The users of the blockchain have the opportunity to further develop the code. However, the implementation of an update requires a consensus between the network participants. Not every blockchain is per se open source and thus publicly modifiable. In addition, the respective initiator is free to make the blockchain invisible to third parties and to permit only a limited circle of users. 2

The dynamics that the initiation of a blockchain can develop is illustrated by the example of the Bitcoin and the underlying Bitcoin blockchain. This blockchain was the first of its kind. It forms the basis for the development of partly very similar, partly clearly different blockchains. The idea of the Bitcoin is based on a paper published in 2008 under the pseudonym *Satoshi Nakamoto*[9] in which the developer (or possibly a group of developers) describes a digital, decentrally managed register as the basis of an electronic 'monetary system' on a peer-to-peer basis. 3

---

[1] Rosenberger, *Bitcoin and Blockchain* (2018), 63.
[2] Nakamoto, 'Bitcoin: A Peer-to-Peer Electronic Cash System' (Satoshi Nakamoto Institute, 31.10.2008), available at https://beck-link.de/hh2f8 (accessed 31.1.2020).
[3] See also the summary in De Filippi and Wright, *Blockchain and the Law* (2018), 13.
[4] For this and in the following Kaulartz, 'Die Blockchain-Technologie' (2016) 36 *Computer und Recht*, 474 (475).
[5] Therefore, many also call the blockchain distributed ledger.
[6] For further details, see Berentsen and Schär, *Bitcoin, Blockchain and Kryptoassets* (2017), 216; for the Bitcoin Blockchain, see also Nakamoto, 'Bitcoin: A Peer-to-Peer Electronic Cash System' (Satoshi Nakamoto Institute, 31.10.2008), available at https://beck-link.de/hh2f8 (accessed 31.1.2020): 'The majority decision is represented by the longest chain, which has the greatest proof-of-work effort invested in it'.
[7] See De Filippi and Wright, *Blockchain and the Law* (2018), 21.
[8] See Bitcoin Core, available at https://bitcoin.org/de/download (accessed 31.1.2020).
[9] Nakamoto, 'Bitcoin: A Peer-to-Peer Electronic Cash System' (Satoshi Nakamoto Institute, 31.10.2008), available at https://beck-link.de/hh2f8 (accessed 31.1.2020).

Nakamoto[10] calls the units of value in this concept Bitcoins. With the Bitcoin publication, he revealed all aspects of Bitcoin and the underlying blockchain technology. *Nakamoto* thus laid the foundation for the further development of the blockchain in general and the Bitcoin system in particular. After initiation, this system became independent of *Nakamoto*; he does not have a special position – neither in terms of operation nor in terms of further development of the Bitcoin blockchain. It is only the participants of the system that can influence it. As a result, shortly after the article was published, numerous users joined the network and the Bitcoin blockchain developed an impressive life of its own. The price for one Bitcoin developed from USD 0.000764 in January 2009 to over USD 60,000 in June 2021.

4   The storage of digital units of value such as Bitcoins in a blockchain is one application, but the possible fields of application are much broader.[11] A blockchain can mirror the current status of a wide variety of objects and relationships, such as the legal assignment of real estate or movables or the (non-)execution of a contractual relationship. Of particular interest for this handbook is the assignment of virtual units of value to specific users in the respective blockchain network. These units of value are virtual calculation variables to which the users of a blockchain attribute a certain value.[12] They are called **tokens**. Each token can be individualised based on the transactions that have taken place and that have included the token.[13]

5   The publicly accessible register in the blockchain shows which token is assigned to which network user at any time; all transactions ever made are unchangeably contained in the blockchain.[14] Users are able to transfer tokens among each other without the need to use an intermediary. This not only reduces transaction costs,[15] but it also eliminates the risk that an intermediary tampers with or thwarts the transaction, e.g. due to insolvency.

6   The total number of tokens that are available on one particular blockchain can be fixed from the outset or may vary over time. For example, the total number of Bitcoins was defined in the code of the Bitcoin blockchain. Depending on the 'mining' speed (→ para. 38), new Bitcoins will be created until around the year 2140 – until the maximum amount of tokens is reached. At this point, the total number of approximately 21,000,000 Bitcoins will be available.[16] The overall number of tokens can also be made available to users immediately upon initiation of a blockchain or distributed after certain conditions have been met. It is also possible to increase or decrease the number of tokens in accordance with the respective demand situation, similar to the monetary policy of central banks. To reduce the token stock, a so-called **burning** can be carried out. In doing so, tokens are irrevocably deleted from the blockchain.

---

[10] Until today, it is still unclear who is hiding behind the pseudonym; instead of many Rosenberg, *Bitcoin and Blockchain* (2018), 25 et seqq. Since the pseudonym used is masculine, we will use the masculine personal pronoun in the following – without intending to speculate.
[11] Instead of many Kaulartz, 'Die Blockchain-Technologie' (2016) 36 *Computer und Recht*, 474 et seqq.
[12] For details, see below in particular → para. 68.
[13] Each transaction carries a transaction ID.
[14] De Filippi and Wright, *Blockchain and the Law* (2018), 22.
[15] Nakamoto, 'Bitcoin: A Peer-to-Peer Electronic Cash System' (Satoshi Nakamoto Institute, 31.10.2008), available at https://beck-link.de/hh2f8 (accessed 21.6.2021).
[16] Werbach and Cornell, 'Contracts Ex Machina' (2017) 67 *Duke Law Journal*, 313 (329).

II. Blockchain Participants

The blockchain participants are called **nodes**.[17] They can be divided into so-called full 7 nodes (= full-featured nodes) and light nodes (= not fully functional nodes). This distinction results from their different position and function in the network environment.

The blockchain is distributed on the computers of all **full nodes**. Each of them keeps 8 a complete, up-to-date version. Full nodes are comprehensively involved in all transaction processes of the blockchain. Not only do they receive and send tokens themselves, but they also commonly supervise and maintain the blockchain register by verifying transactions. The condition for being able to act as a full node is that the respective network participant downloads the existing blockchain from another full node to his/her computer. For the exact further tasks of a full node → para. 29.

Light nodes on the other hand do not actively participate in the expansion and 9 protection of the blockchain. Their functions within a blockchain are limited. They are mere users of the blockchain. This means that they only send and receive the respective tokens of the blockchain. Thereby, they rely on the honest behaviour of the full nodes.

III. Categorization of Blockchains

Blockchains can be classified according to the access and usage rights of its 10 participants. **Two distinguishing features** are decisive in this regard: **private/public and permissioned/permissionless**.

The distinction between **private/public refers to the visibility of** the information 11 stored in the blockchain. A blockchain is public if it can be viewed by anyone at any time.[18] A private blockchain, on the other hand, is a closed system whose contents can only be accessed by a limited group of authorised network participants.

The distinction between permissioned/permissionless concerns the **participation** 12 **rights** of the network members. A blockchain is permissionless if all network participants have the same participation rights, for example, if all of them can carry out transactions. If the participation rights of the network participants diverge – for example, if only a limited group is authorised to verify transactions – the blockchain is to be classified as permissioned.

These two characteristics can be combined in any way, so that **four different design** 13 **variants** are possible. The Bitcoin and Ethereum blockchains, for example, are public and permissionless, whereas the Ripple and EOS blockchains are public and permissioned.

IV. Structure of a Blockchain

A blockchain is composed of individual blocks. The blocks largely consist of a **bundle** 14 **of transactions** that were carried out via the blockchain. In the vast majority of blockchains, each transaction carried out in the network leads to an extension of the chain.[19] For example, the Bitcoin blockchain bundles about 2,500 individual transac-

---

[17] Nakamoto, 'Bitcoin: A Peer-to-Peer Electronic Cash System' (Satoshi Nakamoto Institute, 31.10.2008), available at https://beck-link.de/hh2f8 (accessed 31.1.2020).

[18] For this and in the following Roßbach, 'Blockchain-Technologies and their Implications – Teil 2: Anwendungsbereiche der Blockchain-Technologie' (2016), available at https://beck-link.de/5mxh5 (accessed 22.01.2020).

[19] De Filippi and Wright, *Blockchain and the Law* (2018), 56.

tions per block. The generated blocks are strung together and form a chain. This process is the reason for the term 'blockchain'.

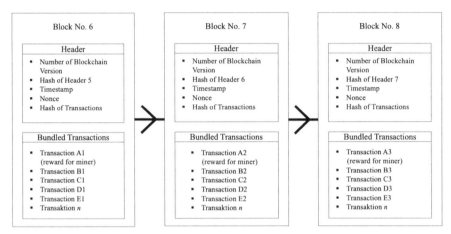

Figure 1: Simplified representation of a blockchain

15   Each block is made up of different components. In addition to the transaction bundle mentioned above, the so-called **hash** is essential.[20] The hash is part of the so-called header of a block. A hash is the output of a hash function. It serves in particular as an alphanumeric checksum – metaphorically speaking as a **fingerprint**[21] – of the underlying data.[22] The hash of a block reflects all data contained in it, especially the bundled transactions. If a transaction within the data bundle is modified, be it with regard to one of the parties or the amount of tokens transferred, the hash also changes. Each block contains the hash of the previous block.[23] This reference of the new block to the previous block always determines the location of the new block within the blockchain.[24] In addition to the 'version number' of the blockchain, the block header contains[25] a time stamp[26]. This stamp proves that the transaction data contained in the block existed at the specified time.[27] In addition, each block has a sequential number.

V. Transaction of Tokens

16   For most blockchains, blocks mainly consist of transactions of the tokens stored in the Blockchain. To assign a token to another network participant, blockchains use the so-called **public/private key concept**. This cryptographic mechanism gives the name to

---

[20] Ibid, 22.
[21] Ibid, 22; Kaulartz, 'Die Blockchain-Technologie' (2016) 36 *Computer und Recht*, 474 (475).
[22] Subcommittee on Commerce, Manufacturing and Trade of the Committee on Energy and Commerce House of Representatives, 'The Disrupter Series: Digital Currency and Blockchain Technology' (Second session of the hearing before the 114th Congress, U.S. Government Publishing Office, 16.3.2016), 47, available at https://beck-link.de/tpdc5 (accessed 31.1.2020).
[23] De Filippi and Wright, *Blockchain and the Law* (2018), 22 et seq.
[24] Rosenberger, *Bitcoin and Blockchain* (2018), 66.
[25] Madeira, 'What is a Block Header in Bitcoin?' (CryptoCompare, 1.1.2015), available at https://beck-link.de/2p44b (accessed 31.1.2020).
[26] De Filippi and Wright, *Blockchain and the Law* (2018), 23.
[27] Nakamoto, 'Bitcoin: A Peer-to-Peer Electronic Cash System' (Satoshi Nakamoto Institute, 31.10.2008), available at https://beck-link.de/hh2f8 (accessed 31.1.2020).

§ 1. Technical and Factual Background

the somewhat imprecise (→ para. 68) label 'cryptocurrencies'. The concept, also known as asymmetric encryption,[28] goes back to two cryptographers at Stanford University.[29] Each participant in the network has two keys – a private key and a public key.[30] The number of key pairs is not limited. A user can create as many pairs as desired and thus carry out transactions under various pseudonyms.[31]

The **public key** is an address within the blockchain to which tokens can be assigned. 17 This address also serves as a pseudonym that stands for a particular network participant.[32] This means that a blockchain is **not an anonymous, but a pseudonymous system**.[33] The public key can be compared, for example, with an account number[34] or an email address – especially if the email address is used to receive Paypal payments. The reason is that a network participant in a blockchain also passes his/her public key on to others in order to receive tokens. In the Bitcoin network, the so-called Bitcoin address can also be used as an alternative pseudonym for receiving tokens. This address is the hash value[35] of the public key.[36]

Tokens that are assigned to a particular public key can only be transferred by the person 18 who knows the corresponding private key. This principle is comparable to the password of a Paypal account or the TAN in online banking.[37] Here, the assigned monetary units can also only be transferred if the remitter knows the account password or TAN.[38]

The **private key** remains exclusively with the user and is used to **sign transactions**.[39] This ensures the authenticity and integrity of the transaction. The private key guarantees that the transaction was actually signed by the owner of the private key.[40] It also ensures that the 'sender' actually 'has' the respective token.[41] The private key enables proof that the user is authorised to transfer the token assigned to the respective public key.[42] The reason for this security mechanism is that a public key can be mathematically derived from the corresponding private key, but the public key cannot be used to infer the private key.[43]

---

[28] For example, Kaulartz, 'Die Blockchain-Technologie' (2016) 36 *Computer und Recht*, 474 (475).

[29] Diffie and Hellman, 'New Directions in Cryptography' (1976) 22 *IEEE Transaction on Information Theory*, 644 (644 et seqq).

[30] De Filippi and Wright, *Blockchain and the Law* (2018), 2.

[31] Nakamoto, 'Bitcoin: A Peer-to-Peer Electronic Cash System' (Satoshi Nakamoto Institute, 31.10.2008), available at https://beck-link.de/hh2f8 (accessed 31.1.2020); Berentsen and Schär, *Bitcoin, Blockchain and Kryptoassets* (2017), 119.

[32] Berentsen and Schär, *Bitcoin, Blockchain and Kryptoassets* (2017), 119.

[33] De Filippi and Wright, *Blockchain and the Law* (2018), 68.

[34] Safferling and Rückert, 'Telekommunikationsüberwachung bei Bitcoins – Heimliche Datenauswertung bei virtuellen Währungen gem. § 100a StPO?' (2015) 18 *Zeitschrift für IT-Recht und Digitalisierung*, 788 (789).

[35] For an explanation of hash values, → para. 15.

[36] Berentsen and Schär, *Bitcoin, Blockchain and Kryptoassets* (2017), 120 et seqq.

[37] Safferling and Rückert, 'Telekommunikationsüberwachung bei Bitcoins – Heimliche Datenauswertung bei virtuellen Währungen gem. § 100a StPO?' (2015) 18 *Zeitschrift für IT-Recht und Digitalisierung*, 788 (789).

[38] See Small, 'Bitcoin: The Napster Of Currency' (2015) 37 *Houston Journal of International Law*, 581 (588).

[39] Nakamoto, 'Bitcoin: A Peer-to-Peer Electronic Cash System' (Satoshi Nakamoto Institute, 31.10.2008), available at https://beck-link.de/hh2f8 (accessed 31.1.2020); Small, 'Bitcoin: The Napster Of Currency' (2015) 37 *Houston Journal of International Law*, 581 (588); De Filippi and Wright, *Blockchain and the Law* (2018), 16.

[40] Kaulartz, 'Die Blockchain-Technologie' (2016) 36 *Computer und Recht*, 474 (475).

[41] See Berentsen and Schär, *Bitcoin, Blockchain and Kryptoassets* (2017), 119.

[42] Ibid.

[43] Kaulartz, 'Die Blockchain-Technologie' (2016) 36 *Computer und Recht*, 474 (475); see also Berentsen and Schär, *Bitcoin, Blockchain and Kryptoassets* (2017), 119 et seq.

Part A. Introduction

It is also possible that a network participant communicates his/her private key within a transaction (so-called **off-chain peer-to-peer transaction**[44]), e.g. to settle a 'token debt'. Using the private key, the recipient can transfer the tokens that are linked to the corresponding public key. The downside of such transactions is that the 'sender' of the private key does not fully lose his/her access to the key and therefore to the respective tokens.

19   For the **transaction** of a token the sending network participant sends a corresponding transaction message to the blockchain using public and private key.[45] This message is not sent directly to the recipient of the token. Instead, it is transmitted to various full nodes which, in turn, forward the message to other blockchain participants until the entire network is aware of the transaction message.[46] By doing so, the qualified users, i.e. the full nodes of the blockchain, check the **integrity and authenticity** with respect to the sending party. For this purpose, the blockchain software installed on the full nodes' computers scans all transactions ever made.[47] If more than 50 % of the full nodes consider the checked transaction valid,[48] it is considered verified and is added to the transaction bundle of a block.[49]

20   Thus, whenever a token on the blockchain is part of a transaction, it is not actually transferred from one blockchain participant to another. Instead, it is **only the assignments on the blockchain that change**, that is, only the assignment of the respective transferred token. In the blockchain, another node is displayed as the last receiver (= assignment subject) of the token.

21   **Example:**
If A wants to send a Bitcoin to B, she needs the public key of B as a receiving address. The transaction message is signed with A's private key.[50] A then sends the transaction message to all nodes linked to her. These, in turn, forward the message to all nodes linked to them until it has been transmitted to all network participants. After the verification process is completed by the full nodes, the Bitcoin is assigned to B's public key. B can now recognise from A's public key (as the sending address) that the transaction originated from A. Using his private key, he can now dispose of the Bitcoin and, for example, transfer it to another node.[51]

VI. Technical Representation of Tokens

22   The tokens of a blockchain each possess an **input** and an **output**.[52] For example, if a Bitcoin is assigned to A, this means that the output of the Bitcoin is free. This output is commonly referred to as **UTXO – unspent transaction output**.[53] If A transfers the Bitcoin to B, the consequence is that B's public key is linked to that Bitcoin's input. Thus, the respective UTXO is no longer assigned to A's public key.

---

[44] On the off-chain operation of trading platforms, see → para. 96.
[45] See Nakamoto, 'Bitcoin: A Peer-to-Peer Electronic Cash System' (Satoshi Nakamoto Institute, 31.10.2008), available at https://beck-link.de/hh2f8 (accessed 31.1.2020).
[46] For forwarding, the classification of the network subscriber as Full or Light node is irrelevant.
[47] De Filippi and Wright, *Blockchain and the Law* (2018), 26.
[48] Respectively checks the software installed at the user's site for integrity and authenticity and sends a (non-) validity signal to the network.
[49] Rosenberger, *Bitcoin and Blockchain* (2018), 18.
[50] De Filippi and Wright, *Blockchain and the Law* (2018), 21.
[51] See De Filippi and Wright, *Blockchain and the Law* (2018), 16.
[52] Newly mined tokens have only one (unspent transaction) output, because they are newly created.
[53] From a technical point of view, a token is the history of all transactions that follow the UTXO included in the Blockchain for the first time. A UTXO is stored in the Blockchain for the first time when a new block is initiated or mined.

B can leave the input unused. Thus, he keeps the Bitcoin. However, he can also transfer it again. This is effected by another transaction message that converts the free input into one or more outputs. A token can only ever become an output in its entirety. This does not mean that B can only assign the token 'as a whole' to another user C. It is possible, for example, that B sends half a Bitcoin to C and keeps the other half.[54] This requires two outputs. Output 1 is 0.5 Bitcoin assigned to C's public key. Output 2, also 0.5 Bitcoin, is re-assigned to B. This means he keeps half the Bitcoin.

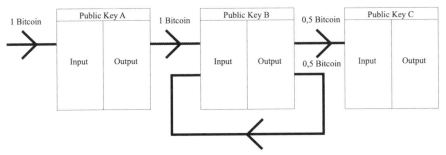

Figure 2: Input and Output

In principle, depending on the respective value of the outputs available to the sender, several UTXOs can **be combined into one input** in one transaction. This combination is done automatically by the blockchain protocol. The number of outputs that are bundled into one input in one transaction message has an effect on the transaction fee to be added (→ para. 36). If a sender intends a transaction consisting of several outputs to be sent as quickly as a transaction consisting of fewer outputs, he/she must increase the transaction fee accordingly.[55]   23

Example:
Three outputs with a value of 0.3 BTC[56], 0.7 BTC and 1.2 BTC are assigned to the public key of A. A now wants to transfer 2 BTC to the public key of B. The corresponding transaction message refers to all three UTXOs and divides them into two inputs. Input 1 with a value of 2 BTC is assigned to the public key of B; Input 2 with a value of the remaining 0.2 BTC is re-assigned to the public key of A. B now has a UTXO of 2 BTC, A has a UTXO of 0.2 BTC.

Each transaction has its own ID (= transaction ID),[57] by which it can be publicly traced – given that the respective blockchain is public.[58] The singularity of each transaction means that each token can also be individualised based on its transaction history. In other words, it is clearly defined and traceable to which pseudonym a particular token is assigned to at any time.[59]   24

---

[54] Nakamoto, 'Bitcoin: A Peer-to-Peer Electronic Cash System' (Satoshi Nakamoto Institute, 31.10.2008), available at https://beck-link.de/hh2f8 (accessed 31.1.2020).
[55] An indication of this is provided by BuyBitcoinWorldwide, available at https://beck-link.de/75ezn (accessed 3.4.2019).
[56] BTC = Bitcoin.
[57] In the Bitcoin blockchain, this is the (double SHA256) hash of the transaction.
[58] See Rosenberger, *Bitcoin and Blockchain* (2018), 22.
[59] See Ekkenga, 'Bitcoin und andere Digitalwährungen – Spielzeug für Spekulanten oder Systemveränderung durch Privatisierung der Zahlungssysteme?' (2017) 36 *Computer und Recht*, 762 (763).

VII. Wallets and Wallet Providers

25   The 'location' where network participants store their private keys is called wallet.[60] The purpose of a wallet is the secure storage of the private key against unauthorised third parties. Depending on the design, a distinction can be made between five different basic types of wallets: If the user stores his/her private key on a USB stick or on a device developed especially for this purpose,[61] this is referred to as a **hardware wallet**. Software installed on a computer with a safekeeping function – the so-called **software wallet** or **desktop wallet** - can also be used for safekeeping.[62] **Online wallets** store the key on a server, **mobile wallets** store the key on a mobile device.[63] If a user prints out the private key in order to manually enter it into the respective interface when needed, i.e. to send a transaction notice, the print out is called **paper wallet**.[64] Some digital wallets also allow to generate a new pair of cryptographic keys for each transaction. Using a new pair of keys for each transaction makes it difficult to trace the transactions (→ para. 16).

26   There is no actual transfer of a token to the wallet. In this respect, the term wallet is imprecise. In contrast to the classic wallet in which cash is actually stored, the wallet only secures the private key and does not store any tokens as such.

27   In most cases, network participants use the services of so-called **wallet providers**, although this is not mandatory. Wallet providers can be divided into **two groups**, custodian and non-custodian wallet providers. Custodian wallet providers, on the one hand, store the private keys for the network participants.[65] Non-custodian wallet providers, on the other hand, enable network participants to store the private keys themselves (e.g. by providing a printable version of it). Wallet providers have to be distinguished from mere providers of user interfaces that enable network participants to communicate with the blockchain, particularly to carry out transactions on the respective blockchain (= **interface providers**).[66]

VIII. Extension of the Blockchain through Verification

1. Finding a Consensus

28   **Consensus building** is an elementary prerequisite for the functioning of a decentralised system. In the absence of supervision by a central party, this principle ensures the integrity and authenticity of the network. Within a blockchain environment, the basis for consensus building is the bundling of a certain number of already

---

[60] On this and in the following Fromberger, Haffke and Zimmermann, 'Kryptowerte und Geldwäsche – Eine Analyse der 5. Geldwäscherichtlinie sowie des Gesetzesentwurfs der Bundesregierung' (2019) 19 *Zeitschrift für Bank- und Kapitalmarktrecht*, 377 (378).

[61] See description in Rosenberger, *Bitcoin and Blockchain* (2018), 22 et seq.

[62] Rosenberger, *Bitcoin and Blockchain* (2018), 23.

[63] Ibid, 23 et seq.

[64] Ibid.

[65] On this and in the following Fromberger, Haffke and Zimmermann, 'Kryptowerte und Geldwäsche – Eine Analyse der 5. Geldwäscherichtlinie sowie des Gesetzesentwurfs der Bundesregierung' (2019) 19 *Zeitschrift für Bank- und Kapitalmarktrecht*, 377 (378).

[66] An example of this is the provider MyEtherWallet. This only allows access to the Ethereum Blockchain. The private key of the user is not stored. MyEtherWallet is therefore not a custodian wallet provider. However, it enables the user to store the private key (e.g. by creating a paper wallet) and is therefore not a custodian wallet provider. Cf. MyEtherWallet, available at https://www.myetherwallet.com (accessed 31.1.2020).

§ 1. Technical and Factual Background

verified individual transactions into a new block. The new block is added to the existing blockchain only after verification. The blockchain is continuously extended by this principle.

Only full nodes participate in this verification process[67] because it is only them who manage the blockchain and have the current version stored on a computer (→ para. 8). They use the block headers (→ para. 15) for the purpose of verification. If a full node considers a block valid, he/she then adds the block to the version of the blockchain stored on his/her computer.[68] Full nodes use the hash of the current block as the basis for generating the next block.[69] If more than half of all full nodes extend their stored version of the blockchain by the new block, the block is accepted. Since a consensus between the full nodes regarding the status of a block is reached at this point, the principle described is also known as consensus building.[70] The light nodes, in contrast, are not involved in this process; they merely use the provided network without actively influencing it. **29**

There is the theoretical possibility that within the network two full nodes simultaneously add different blocks to the blockchain. Metaphorically speaking, this leads to a splitting of the chain, a so-called **fork** is created.[71] The splitting endangers the integrity of the blockchain register, e.g. the **double spending** of a single token could occur. This would mean that the same token was assigned to several users. In order to avoid this, a blockchain contains a security mechanism: all nodes always consider the longest version of a blockchain to be valid (→ para. 2 at the end).[72] This means that the string of the chain is valid and thus continued, to which further blocks are added more quickly.[73] In principle, it is possible that new blocks are added to **different chain strands**. Shorter chain strands are not automatically rejected. Each full node can freely decide which chain strand he/she works on, that means which chain strand he/she intends to extend. Usually, however, the mining activities within the blockchain network are concentrated on the longest chain strand. Theoretically, there is a possibility that a shorter chain strand overtakes the longest one. However, with each additional block added to the longest chain strand, this probability decreases. Conversely, each block added to the longest chain increases the likelihood that its previous blocks will be in line with the consensus among network participants.[74] **30**

If the longest chain strand gains a certain 'lead' of newly added blocks over the second longest chain strand, the longest chain can be considered 'valid'. From this point on, the mathematical probability that the longest chain strand will be overtaken by a **31**

---

[67] Werbach and Cornell, 'Contracts Ex Machina' (2017) 67 *Duke Law Journal*, 313 (328); De Filippi and Wright, *Blockchain and the Law* (2018), 24.
[68] De Filippi and Wright, *Blockchain and the Law* (2018), 24; see also Werbach and Cornell, 'Contracts Ex Machina' (2017) 67 *Duke Law Journal*, 313 (328).
[69] Nakamoto, 'Bitcoin: A Peer-to-Peer Electronic Cash System' (Satoshi Nakamoto Institute, 31.10.2008), available at https://beck-link.de/hh2f8 (accessed 31.1.2020)
[70] See De Filippi and Wright, *Blockchain and the Law* (2018), 2, 21, 24.
[71] Ibid, 24.
[72] Cf. Nakamoto, 'Bitcoin: A Peer-to-Peer Electronic Cash System' (Satoshi Nakamoto Institute, 31.10.2008), available at https://beck-link.de/hh2f8 (accessed 21.6.2021); Werbach and Cornell, 'Contracts Ex Machina' (2017) 67 *Duke Law Journal*, 313 (328); De Filippi and Wright, *Blockchain and the Law* (2018), 24; Witte, 'The Blockchain: A Gentle Introduction' (2016), available at https://beck-link.de/sw7s7 (accessed 31.1.2020); for further details see Berentsen and Schär, *Bitcoin, Blockchain and Kryptoassets* (2017), 216.
[73] Nakamoto, 'Bitcoin: A Peer-to-Peer Electronic Cash System' (Satoshi Nakamoto Institute, 31.10.2008), available at https://beck-link.de/hh2f8 (accessed 31.1.2020).
[74] Werbach and Cornell, 'Contracts Ex Machina' (2017) 67 *Duke Law Journal*, 313 (328 et seq.).

shorter one tends towards zero. The **relevant point in time** depends on the individually designed code of the respective blockchain. With the Bitcoin blockchain, after six more blocks have been added to a chain strand, this critical point in time is exceeded. The same applies to the transactions bundled in a block. If a transaction is six blocks 'deep' in a chain strand, it is considered valid.[75]

32 The individual blocks of the blockchain build on each other. If a full node wanted to change a block at a later date, he/she would have to regenerate not only this block, but all subsequent blocks in the chain.[76] This makes it almost impossible to forge the (transaction) information written in the blockchain. Altering the data would require the infiltration of more than half of the computing power.[77] This means that although it is not impossible to change the data stored in the blockchain, it is practically almost impossible.

2. Incentive Scheme

33 To ensure that full nodes participate in the verification process, blockchains have an incentive system.

34 **a) Similarities of the different Schemes.** The first person to create a new block **receives remuneration**. It comprises the block reward and the transaction fees.

35 The **block reward** consists of newly created tokens in the form of an UTXO (→ para. 22).[78] This UTXO is part of the newly created block for which the block reward is granted. It is disbursed by assigning it to a public key specified by the full node. This is usually an address of his/her.[79] The block reward does not have to be fixed. As with the Bitcoin blockchain, it can be designed flexibly (e.g. its amount can change over time). The initiator of the respective blockchain can define the amount of the block reward in the code. When the Bitcoin blockchain was initiated, the block reward was 50 Bitcoins per block. The reward is roughly halved every 210,000 blocks (approximately every four years)[80], so that there will be no more new Bitcoins created from 2140 onwards.[81] This incentive will then disappear.[82]

36 In addition to the block reward, a full node also receives all **transaction fees** of the transactions bundled in the respective block.[83] Network participants can pay these transaction fees on a **voluntary basis**.[84] Since a full node is free to choose which transactions he/she bundles into a new block, the fee is intended to encourage him/her to process a particular transaction as quickly as possible.[85]

37 The incentive and consensus system can be implemented through various technical procedures. The decisive factor is how the code of the respective blockchain is

---

[75] See Bitcoin Wiki, available at https://en.bitcoin.it/wiki/Confirmation (accessed 31.1.2020).
[76] Nakamoto, 'Bitcoin: A Peer-to-Peer Electronic Cash System' (Satoshi Nakamoto Institute, 31.10.2008), available at https://beck-link.de/hh2f8 (accessed 31.1.2020).
[77] Ibid; see also Rosenberger, *Bitcoin and Blockchain* (2018), 120.
[78] De Filippi and Wright, *Blockchain and the Law* (2018), 25.
[79] Nakamoto, 'Bitcoin: A Peer-to-Peer Electronic Cash System' (Satoshi Nakamoto Institute, 31.10.2008), available at https://beck-link.de/hh2f8 (accessed 31.1.2020).
[80] Werbach and Cornell, 'Contracts Ex Machina' (2017) 67 *Duke Law Journal*, 313 (329); De Filippi and Wright, *Blockchain and the Law* (2018), 26.
[81] De Filippi and Wright, *Blockchain and the Law* (2018), 24.
[82] Nakamoto, 'Bitcoin: A Peer-to-Peer Electronic Cash System' (Satoshi Nakamoto Institute, 31.10.2008), available at https://beck-link.de/hh2f8 (accessed 4.9.2018).
[83] Ibid; Werbach and Cornell, 'Contracts Ex Machina' (2017) 67 *Duke Law Journal*, 313 (329).
[84] Rosenberger, *Bitcoin and Blockchain* (2018), 68; technically the transaction fee is the difference between the inputs and outputs of a transaction.
[85] Ibid.

structured. The initiator of the blockchain is free to choose the principle according to which the remuneration is distributed.

b) Proof-of-work Procedure – Mining. aa) Technical Implementation. One possibility is the so-called **proof-of-work** procedure. The most prominent blockchain that uses this principle is the Bitcoin blockchain. In the proof-of-work procedure, the full nodes which extend the blockchain by adding new blocks are called **miners**, and the block creation is called **mining**. The procedure is based on the miners solving a mathematical task by using hardware computing power according to the **trial-and-error principle**.[86] Metaphorically speaking, the miners, in order to unlock a new block, try to find the key that fits into the lock of the respective block from a large number of existing keys. The solution of the mathematical task, that means retrieving the respective key, is fundamental for the creation of a new block. It depends on the respective transactions and is therefore different for each new block to be generated.[87] The code of the Bitcoin blockchain is designed in such a way that a solution is to be found approximately every ten minutes,[88] thus miners create a new block every ten minutes.[89] This means that it takes at least ten minutes before a transaction is completed (for validity of transactions → para. 28).

38

The first miner that calculates the solution of the block to be created receives the reward.[90] In the Bitcoin blockchain, for example, the mining of a new block in 2020 was rewarded with 6.25 Bitcoins.[91] The probability of being successful in creating a new block is directly dependent on the **computing power** used by a miner in **relation to the total computing power** of all miners in the blockchain.[92] The higher the proportion of computing power, the more likely it is that the respective miner will be successful in creating the new block (for details, → para. 38, figure 3). If the computing power of the overall system increases, the difficulty of the task rises accordingly.[93] If a miner finds the solution to the task for a new block, the other participants in the blockchain network can easily check if it is correct. This is because, unlike finding the solution, verifying the result is a simple mathematical operation, which can be carried out rather easily. To take up the key example again: it is difficult to find the right key for the lock of the block. However, once a miner has found the key, it is easy to find out whether the key fits by turning the key.

---

[86] De Filippi and Wright, *Blockchain and the Law* (2018), 23; Rosenberger, *Bitcoin und Blockchain* (2018), 67.
[87] Werbach and Cornell, 'Contracts Ex Machina' (2017) 67 *Duke Law Journal*, 313 (328).
[88] See the details of the arithmetical problem in the Bitcoin Blockchain De Filippi and Wright, *Blockchain and the Law* (2018), 23.
[89] Werbach and Cornell, 'Contracts Ex Machina' (2017) 67 *Duke Law Journal*, 313 (328); De Filippi and Wright, *Blockchain and the Law* (2018), 23.
[90] Werbach and Cornell, 'Contracts Ex Machina' (2017) 67 *Duke Law Journal*, 313 (328).
[91] Bitcoin Halving, available at https://beck-link.de/ta3xp (accessed 19. 9. 2021).
[92] Werbach and Cornell, 'Contracts Ex Machina' (2017) 67 *Duke Law Journal*, 313 (328); De Filippi and Wright, *Blockchain and the Law* (2018), 24, 40.
[93] For the Bitcoin Blockchain, see Nakamoto, 'Bitcoin: A Peer-to-Peer Electronic Cash System' (Satoshi Nakamoto Institute, 31.10.2008), available at https://beck-link.de/hh2f8 (accessed 4.9.2018); De Filippi and Wright, *Blockchain and the Law* (2018), 24.

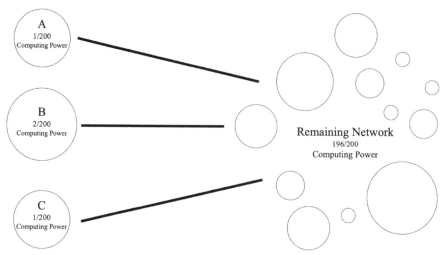

Figure 3: Simplified representation of mining with the significance of the influence of computing power

39   Figuratively speaking, this system can be imagined as a kind of lottery, where the total computing power represents the number of tickets. These tickets are then distributed proportionally among the respective miners, whereby a certain number of tickets is allocated to each miner depending on the computing power provided. The more computing power a miner contributes to the network, the more tickets he/she receives. Subsequently, at certain intervals (when a new block is generated), a lot is drawn and the holder of the winning ticket is rewarded with new tokens – the block reward. As a result of this concept, a higher computing power increases the probability of getting the reward.

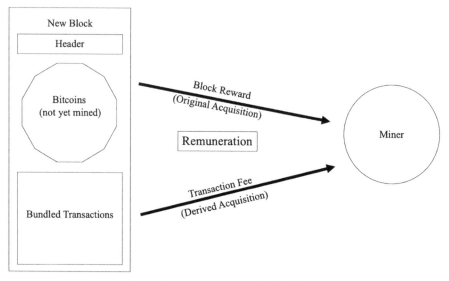

Figure 4: Incentive system of a blockchain

bb) Aggregation of Miners and Mining Pools. *(1) Background and Purpose.* Due to **40** increasing numbers of miners and the resulting higher computing power within a blockchain network, it is becoming more and more difficult to generate a block. If a miner only has a rather small share of the total computing power, it can take a very long time before he/she is able to find a solution to the mathematical task and mine a new block. This can lead to several months or years without remuneration or even to permanent failure. For this reason, miners often cooperate. They pool their individual computing power and thus increase the probability of creating a block.[94]

In some cases, a group of miners is not fixed on a certain blockchain or a certain type **41** of token. Rather, the miners participate in the mining process of a blockchain environment whenever it seems lucrative. Such aggregations of miners are also known as **multipools**. The participants of a mining pool are free to terminate the mining activities for the pool at any time and, for example, provide mining services for another mining pool.

If the participant of a mining pool succeeds in generating a new block, the block **42** reward is shared with the other miners of the pool and, if there is one, the operator (→ para. 54). The allocation formula is regularly determined according to the ratio of the computing power provided by the pool members. For this purpose, see the following figure.

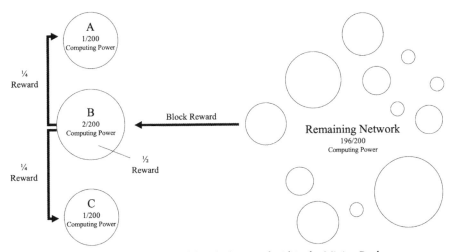

Figure 5: Distribution of the Block Reward within the Mining Pool

In this sketch A, B and C form a mining pool or participate in a mining pool. After B **43** has successfully mined a new block and received the block reward, she distributes to A and C the shares due to them, unless this is done by a pool operator. Since in our case A and C each contribute only ¼ to the combined computing power of the three, their share of the block reward is also only ¼ each. B hermself, however, is entitled to ½ of the reward.

The respective share of the reward is paid out regularly in tokens of the respective **44** blockchain. Sometimes, however, the block reward is also sold directly to other participants of a blockchain. The pool participants then receive their due share in fiat money or other tokens.

---

[94] De Filippi and Wright, *Blockchain and the Law* (2018), 40.

45 (2) *Modes of Operation.* Based on their mode of operation, mining pools can be subdivided into collaborative and non-collaborative pools.

46 (a) *Collaborative Mining Pools.* Collaborative mining pools aim to operate as efficiently as possible when solving the mathematical task required to create a new block. They divide the necessary work steps into work packages and assign them to individual members of the pool.[95] This procedure does not only increase the frequency of getting payments for the participating individual miner. It also boosts the overall probability of the pool participants mining a block and receiving a block reward. The profit of a participating individual miner over a certain period of time increases.

47 **Example:**
Assuming that there are 1,000 different possible results to solve the mathematical problem of a new block. To mine the block, miners have to find the correct solution. They need to try the possible results according to the trial-and-error principle until they have found the correct solution. In the collaborative mining pool, the 1,000 potentially correct results are now distributed among the individual miners, so that each miner only has to try out a smaller number of results. This planned procedure enables the pool to find the solution to the task faster than in a constellation in which the pool participants would try out all the keys each for themselves independently.

48 If the participant of a collaborative mining pool generates a new block and receives the block reward, the reward is allocated to the individual pool members according to their contribution to the collaborative process (if necessary, after deduction of a share for the operator, → para. 54).[96] This contribution will regularly correspond to the computing power used (→ para. 42).

49 (b) *Non-collaborative Mining Pools.* Non-collaborative mining pools are characterised by the fact that the individual miners all try to solve the mathematical task of the respective block in parallel and independently of each other. This leads to efficiency losses in comparison with collaborative mining pools.

50 **Example:**
Assuming that there are 1,000 different possible results to solve the mathematical problem of a new block. To mine the block, miners have to find the correct solution. They need to try the possible results according to the trial-and-error principle until they have found the correct solution. In the non-collaborative mining pool, the 1,000 potentially correct results are not distributed among the individual miners. Each pool member tries out single results from the 1,000 possible ones individually until he/she or another pool member has found the correct result.

51 If a pool member receives a block reward, it is divided (if necessary, after deduction of a share for the operator, → para. 54) in proportion to the computing power used by him/her and the other miners in the pool. Even though the expected total profit of the individual miner does not change as a result of being part of a non-collaborative mining pool, the **frequency with which a block reward is distributed increases**, which leads to greater planning reliability for the individual miner.

52 For an illustration of the effect of non-collaborative mining pools, please refer to Figure 5. In this sketch, A, B and C each act as single miners. The numbers beneath

---

[95] Eikenberg, 'Mitgeschürft – Spezialhardware fürs Bitcoin Mining' (2013) 25 *c't – Magazin für Computertechnik*, 140 (141); Antonopoulos, *Mastering Bitcoin: Programming the Open Blockchain* (2nd edn, 2017), 251; Kütük-Markendorf, *Rechtliche Einordnung von Internetwährungen im deutschen Rechtssystem am Beispiel von Bitcoin* (2016), 83.

[96] See Antonopoulos, *Mastering Bitcoin: Programming the Open Blockchain* (2nd edn, 2017), 28, 251 et seq.

their names show their respective share of the total computing power of the network. As a result, on average A will only receive a block reward every 200 blocks that are created. If A, B and C join forces in a non-collaborative mining pool, the probability for A would increase from 0.5 % (1/200) to 2 % (4/200), of course only in relation to ¼ of the block reward. This increase leads to a more regular pay-out. However, the total pay-out for A does not change within a certain time window.

(3) Forms of Organisation. The aggregation of miners in pools requires coordination 53 and organisation of the participants. Depending on whether this is done centrally or decentrally, a mining pool can be defined as a **managed mining pool** or a **peer-to-peer mining pool**.

(a) Managed Mining Pools. In a managed mining pool, the task of coordinating and 54 organising the mining pool is performed by a central instance, the so-called **pool operator**. The pool operator runs a **pool server**. In a collaborative mining pool, he/she assigns the tasks to be performed to the participants of the pool. These tasks can differ from participant to participant.[97] As consideration, the operator receives a share of the block reward for each block created by the mining pool – regardless of any computing power used for the mining.

(b) Peer-to-peer Mining Pools. In a peer-to-peer mining pool the central instance of 55 the pool operator is missing. The tasks of coordination and organisation, which are also necessary here, are carried out decentrally via a further blockchain. This processing blockchain (= **pool blockchain**) is independent of the blockchain on which the pool participants perform their mining activities. The protocol software on which this pool blockchain is based determines the allocation key of the block rewards. The distribution itself can take place in different ways. For example, a smart contract can be used. After a block has been created by a pool participant, he/she assigns the block reward to a public key of the pool blockchain. The smart contract then distributes the reward. It is also possible that the successful pool participant, after having created a block, assigns the block reward directly to the public keys of all other pool participants. Finally, a 'manual' allocation and splitting of the block rewards by transactions of the successful pool member would also be possible. However, the last two variants are prone to error.

In collaborative mining pools, the protocol software of the pool blockchain also 56 determines the work packages to be completed by the individual miners.

(4) Cloud Mining Services. A characteristic of the described aggregations of miners is 57 that the individual pool members themselves provide computing power. However, it is also possible to participate in the mining operations of a full node without having the required hardware and software. So-called **cloud mining services** enable the use of resources held by a full node by paying a one-off or ongoing sum of money. The income generated by the mining activities of the full node is then distributed among the users.

c) **Proof-of-Stake Process – Minting. aa) Technical Implementation.** A prominent 58 alternative to the proof-of-work procedure is the **proof-of-stake procedure**, which is used by the Ethereum blockchain, for example. In the proof-of-stake procedure, the full nodes that extend the blockchain are called **minter (or forger**, the block creation is called **minting** or **forging**. The decisive factor to be successful in minting a new block is the number of tokens **staked** by the respective full node compared to the total number

---

[97] See Eikenberg, 'Mitgeschürft – Spezialhardware fürs Bitcoin Mining' (2013) 25 *c't – Magazin für Computertechnik*, 140 (144).

of tokens staked by all minters in total. If a minter stakes tokens, these are temporarily blocked; i.e. they cannot be used for other purposes during this time, e.g. they cannot be transferred. As a result, all tokens of an individual minter are divided into two groups – freely available and staked tokens.

59   This procedure can also be imagined as a kind of lottery. In this case, it is not the total computing power that represents the number of tickets, but the total number of tokens staked within the blockchain environment. These tickets are also distributed proportionally to the minters. The distribution depends on the number of staked tokens. The more tokens a minter stakes, the more lots he/she receives. For example, if a minter owns 10 of a total of 100 staked tokens of a blockchain, the probability of generating the block and to receive the block reward is 10 %.

60   **bb) Staking Pools.** Minters also cooperate by forming staking pools (= minting pools). They thus pool their tokens in order to control a higher percentage of all tokens staked in the network. This increases the probability that the staking pool will be able to mint a newly generated block (for details → para. 39). Comparable to non-collaborative mining pools (→ para. 49 et seqq.), this increases the frequency with which the participating miners receive pay-outs. However, in the proof-of-stake procedure – unlike with collaborative mining pools in the proof-of-work procedure – no efficiency gains can be achieved through the aggregation of miners. The overall profit for the individual pool members does not increase over a certain period of time.

61   In contrast to mining pools, staking pools have the pool itself appearing to the outside world via the blockchain. If the staking pool generates a new block, the block reward is divided between the pool participants after it has been assigned to the pool. The allocation ratio is determined by the tokens staked by the pool participants. Staking pools are found both in the form of managed pools and peer-to-peer pools (→ para. 53 et seqq.).

IX. Smart Contracts

62   Smart contracts are **automated mechanisms** based on **if-then-relationships.** They are often used in combination with 'normal' contracts, which can thus be **concluded and/or processed (partially) autonomously** by using the smart contract. This can be illustrated by a comparison with an ATM. The person in possession of a debit card and the corresponding PIN code is automatically paid out the desired amount of money – provided that there are sufficient funds in the account . This is a classic example of an if-then-relationship. **If** the user provides a debit card, the respective PIN code and a covered account, he/she **then** receives the desired amount of money. Vending machines also stick to this principle and use smart contracts. The payment of the respective amount of money leads to the purchase of a specific product. Smart contracts are therefore not a new phenomenon.

63   Smart contracts also play an important role with regards to blockchain technology. In this context, the if-then-relationships are linked to a blockchain to automate transactions.[98] This is, for example, the main purpose of the Ethereum blockchain which is used to process the majority of smart contracts.[99] In addition, if-then-relationships can also be translated into the script language of the Bitcoin network.[100] For ICOs, for

---

[98] See Rosenberger, *Bitcoin und Blockchain* (2018), 98; De Filippi and Wright, *Blockchain and the Law* (2018), 29.
[99] See Werbach and Cornell 'Contracts Ex Machina' (2017) 67 *Duke Law Journal*, 313 (333).
[100] Ibid.

example, a smart contract is used for the exchange of tokens (→ para. 86). If the investor sends tokens (e.g. Bitcoins) to a specific address, other, newly generated tokens are returned automatically.

Smart contracts are also used in the context of purchasing digital goods: anyone who sends a certain number of tokens to a certain public key receives a digital good in return, e.g. the MP3 file of a song.[101] Very often, smart contracts also occur at the stage when a contract is being processed. Contracting parties translate the content of an already concluded 'offline' contract into code.[102] For example, a sales contract can be processed in this way: The buyer pays for the goods via the blockchain using tokens. However, the blockchain does not release the money to the seller until the buyer has informed the blockchain network that he/she has received the respective goods. Once a contract that has been implemented in a blockchain smart contract has been set in motion, further processing of the contract can no longer be prevented by human intervention.[103]

For more complex contract designs, external, 'real world' circumstances can also be included in a blockchain smart contract. So-called **oracles**, third parties or even computer programs that collect and store information from the real world can send signals to the blockchain that certain circumstances included in the contract have occurred.[104]

Example:[105]
A farmer takes out an insurance policy for the case that his harvest will turn out badly due to severe heat and drought. The farmer and the insurer can execute the insurance contract via the blockchain. If an included oracle, for example a digital weather service, detects that the mean temperature of the summer months was above and the precipitation below a certain threshold, the blockchain releases the insured sum to the farmer.

However, unlike e.g. 'normal' vending machines, contracts are also conceivable in which both parties to the contract have machines acting for them.[106] One might think of a self-driving car, for example, which independently handles the refuelling and payment with an automatic filling station machine. Such a constellation can also be processed with if-then-relationships on the basis of a blockchain.

X. Disadvantages of Blockchain Technology

In individual cases, the blockchain technology can come with various disadvantages. This always depends on the respective design of the blockchain code. A particular limiting factor with the Bitcoin blockchain is that a new block with a limited number of transactions is created only every ten minutes. In addition, an increasing number of miners leads to an 'arms race' among miners. This is because they have to use increased computing power to create a new block and receive block rewards. The

---

[101] See Rosenberger, *Bitcoin und Blockchain* (2018), 99; De Filippi and Wright, *Blockchain and the Law* (2018), 28, 76.
[102] See De Filippi and Wright, *Blockchain and the Law* (2018), 74, 78.
[103] Werbach and Cornell, 'Contracts Ex Machina' (2017) 67 *Duke Law Journal*, 313 (332).
[104] De Filippi and Wright, *Blockchain and the Law* (2018), 75; cf. also Team Ripple, 'Smart Oracles: Building Business Logic with Smart Contracts' (Ripple, 16.7.2014), available at https://beck-link.de/vx3e5 (accessed 8.9.2018); Buterin, 'Ethereum and Oracles' (Ethereum Foundation Blog, 22.7.2014), available at https://beck-link.de/2n6v6 (accessed 8.9.2018); see also Hoppe, 'Blockchain Oracles – Einsatz der Blockchain-Technologie für Offline-Anwendungen', in Hennemann and Sattler (eds), *Immaterialgüter und Digitalisierung*, 59, 65 et seqq.
[105] See also the example in Werbach and Cornell, 'Contracts Ex Machina' (2017) 67 *Duke Law Journal*, 313 (331).
[106] Ibid, 333.

consequence of this is a constantly increasing energy consumption of the single miner and the Bitcoin blockchain as a whole (→ § 2, para 85 et seqq.). In the Bitcoin network, it is also very likely that transaction fees will increase significantly once the upper limit of Bitcoin tokens is reached.[107] Otherwise, the incentive for full nodes would decrease drastically. This contradicts the original approach to minimise transaction costs. The increased pooling of computing power in mining pools also counteracts the basic idea of decentralisation.

B. Phenomenology of Tokens

I. Basic Technical Design

68   The generic term for units of value within a blockchain environment is **token**.[108] Inspired by the 'original coin' Bitcoin, tokens that are connected to their own blockchain are also called altcoins (alternative coins) or simply coins.[109] The term cryptocurrency is sometimes misleading, as it suggests the use as a means of payment. However, not every token is used in the sense of a currency nor is it intended to be used as such. At the end of 2021, there were about 11,00 different types of tokens.[110] **According to their respective objective function,**[111] they can be divided into three[112] categories. These are non-legal terms that have become established in practice.[113] The categories do not imply any classification as security, currency, etc. in a particular legal system. There are also tokens that cannot be assigned to any of the categories described.

69   Common to the different types of tokens is that they can usually not only be transferred as a whole, but also in fragments.[114] For example, a Bitcoin can be divided into Satoshis. One Satoshi corresponds to 0.00000001 Bitcoin.[115]

---

[107] De Filippi and Wright, *Blockchain and the Law* (2018), 42.

[108] Fromberger, Haffke and Zimmermann, 'Kryptowerte und Geldwäsche – Eine Analyse der 5. Geldwäscherichtlinie sowie des Gesetzesentwurfs der Bundesregierung' (2019) 19 *Zeitschrift für Bank- und Kapitalmarktrecht*, 377; Maume and Fromberger, 'Regulation of Initial Coin Offerings: Reconciling U.S. and E.U. Securities Laws' (2019) 19 *Chicago Journal of International Law*, 548 (558).

[109] Maume and Fromberger, 'Regulation of Initial Coin Offerings: Reconciling U.S. and E.U. Securities Laws' (2019) 19 *Chicago Journal of International Law*, 548 (558).

[110] CoinMarketCap, available at https://coinmarketcap.com/ (accessed 5.9.2018).

[111] Fromberger, Haffke and Zimmermann, 'Kryptowerte und Geldwäsche – Eine Analyse der 5. Geldwäscherichtlinie sowie des Gesetzesentwurfs der Bundesregierung' (2019) 19 *Zeitschrift für Bank- und Kapitalmarktrecht*, 377; Maume and Fromberger, 'Regulation of Initial Coin Offerings: Reconciling U.S. and E.U. Securities Laws' (2019) 19 *Chicago Journal of International Law*, 548 (558).

[112] This includes Fromberger, Haffke and Zimmermann, 'Kryptowerte und Geldwäsche – Eine Analyse der 5. Geldwäscherichtlinie sowie des Gesetzesentwurfs der Bundesregierung' (2019) 19 *Zeitschrift für Bank- und Kapitalmarktrecht*, 377; Maume and Fromberger, 'Regulation of Initial Coin Offerings: Reconciling U.S. and E.U. Securities Laws' (2019) 19 *Chicago Journal of International Law*, 548 (558); Rivero, 'Distributed Ledger Technology and Token Offering Regulation' (2018), 4 et seqq., available at https://beck-link.de/cz7x3 (accessed 7.9.2018); Klöhn, Parhofer and Resas, 'Initial Coin Offerings' (2018) 30 *Zeitschrift für Bankrecht und Bankwirtschaft*, 89 (101); a distinction into only two categories is made by Barsan, 'Legal Challenges of Initial Coin Offerings (ICO)' (2017) 3 *Revue Trimestrielle de Droit Financier*, 54 (54 et seqq.); Rohr and Wright, 'Blockchain-Based Token Sales, Initial Coin Offerings, and the Democratization of Public Capital Markets' (2017) *University of Tennessee Legal Studies Research Paper* No. 338, 12–26, available at https://beck-link.de/peh4b (accessed 7.9.2018).

[113] Fromberger, Haffke and Zimmermann, 'Kryptowerte und Geldwäsche – Eine Analyse der 5. Geldwäscherichtlinie sowie des Gesetzesentwurfs der Bundesregierung' (2019) 19 *Zeitschrift für Bank- und Kapitalmarktrecht*, 377 (378).

[114] See Maume and Fromberger, 'Regulation of Initial Coin Offerings: Reconciling U.S. and E.U. Securities Laws' (2019) 19 *Chicago Journal of International Law*, 548 (581).

[115] De Filippi and Wright, *Blockchain and the Law* (2018), 21.

II. Currency Tokens

The main function of currency tokens (also referred to as payment tokens) is their **use as a means of payment**.[116] They can be issued by a central instance. However, currency tokens are usually based on a separate, decentralised blockchain without a central counterparty. They are not of inherent value.[117] Yet, currency tokens are traded at a certain price because other market participants assign a monetary value to the tokens – based on the finiteness of the number of tokens written in the code and the counterfeit protection of the blockchain behind it.[118]

III. Investment Tokens

An investment token can grant the right to participate in **future profits** of the issuer, the right to claim **fixed payments** or can grant **voting rights**.[119] If the investment aspect of a token is based solely on anticipated profits on the secondary market (which means: the prospect of selling the token for a higher price than the purchase price), this is generally not sufficient for it to be classified as an investment token. Otherwise, almost every token would be deemed to be an investment token.

Investment tokens can also be actually linked to the shares of a company; they are then called **equity tokens**. Therefore, the shares of a company can be transferred to a third party that holds them in custody. In this constellation, ownership of the token conveys a 'claim' against the custodian third party for 'surrender' of the share and 'assignment' of all rights flowing from it. Alternatively, company shares may be tokenised directly. That means that the company share itself can be held and traded on a blockchain. The viability of this approach depends on national company laws.

If an investment token embodies the right of the token holder to recurring fixed or variable payments and is thus structured in a manner comparable to a bond, it is referred to as a **debt token.** The term **security token** is also used. It describes tokens that meet the legal requirements of securities (for the Security Token Offering → para. 81).

IV. Utility Tokens

Utility tokens embody a **claim or right to a certain performance** to be rendered by the issuer. They are therefore similar to a digital voucher.[120] The holder of a utility token

---

[116] Fromberger, Haffke and Zimmermann, 'Kryptowerte und Geldwäsche – Eine Analyse der 5. Geldwäscherichtlinie sowie des Gesetzesentwurfs der Bundesregierung' (2019) 19 *Zeitschrift für Bank- und Kapitalmarktrecht*, 377 (378).

[117] Maume and Fromberger, 'Regulation of Initial Coin Offerings: Reconciling U.S. and E.U. Securities Laws' (2019) 19 *Chicago Journal of International Law*, 548 (582).

[118] Barsan, 'Legal Challenges of Initial Coin Offerings (ICO)' (2017) 3 *Revue Trimestrielle de Droit Financier*, 54 (57).

[119] Maume and Fromberger, 'Regulation of Initial Coin Offerings: Reconciling U.S. and E.U. Securities Laws' (2019) 19 *Chicago Journal of International Law*, 548 (559); see also De Filippi and Wright, *Blockchain and the Law* (2018), 101.

[120] Fromberger, Haffke and Zimmermann, 'Kryptowerte und Geldwäsche – Eine Analyse der 5. Geldwäscherichtlinie sowie des Gesetzesentwurfs der Bundesregierung' (2019) 19 *Zeitschrift für Bank- und Kapitalmarktrecht*, 377; Maume and Fromberger, 'Regulation of Initial Coin Offerings: Reconciling U.S. and E.U. Securities Laws' (2019) 19 *Chicago Journal of International Law*, 548 (560); see also De Filippi and Wright, *Blockchain and the Law* (2018), 100.

can redeem it with the issuing company for the good or service connected with the token. Goods and services of this type include, for example, the provision of storage space,[121] meals in restaurants or the use of promotional services.[122] The issuer of a utility token is free to choose the structure of the token. Utility tokens can also be the subject of secondary market transactions. However, the tradability and possible expectations of profits do not affect their classification as utility tokens (→ § 7 para. 54).

If a token holder redeems a utility token, the issuer can re-issue the token. Alternatively, he/she can perform a **burning**. By doing so, the token is deleted permanently from the blockchain. The token is then irreversibly unavailable as a unit of value.

V. Hybrids

74 Since tokens can be equipped with diverse properties and functions, hybrid forms occur.[123] In these cases, the categorisation is to be carried out on the basis of the concrete attributes of the individual token within the framework of the relevant legal norm.

VI. Asset-backed Token

75 Within the different token categories, there are tokens which are directly linked to a real object of value. This subcategory is called **asset-backed token**; the linking of the real object with the virtual token is called **tokenisation**. The holder of an asset-backed token regularly has the right to reclaim the linked object – if it is kept in safekeeping – from the party holding it in custody by 'redeeming' the token.[124] It is the token issuer that often acts as the custodian. Sometimes **one** real object is linked to a certain **number** of tokens. In this way, for example, works of art or real estate are tokenised. If a token is linked to the share in a company, it is an equity token (→ para. 72).

76 A special type of asset-backed token is the stable coin. Stable coins are asset-backed currency tokens. For example, the token Tether is linked to the US Dollar. The exchange rate therefore oscillates around one USD without significant fluctuations.[125] It is also possible to link the token to precious metals or other valuable objects. The advantage of asset-backed currency tokens is their relatively low volatility, which makes them particularly suitable as a means of value storage. The problem with such asset-backed tokens is that sufficient coverage of the tokens is often not guaranteed.

VII. Token-based Financial Products

77 Participation in the price performance of tokens can be achieved not only by purchasing the token itself, but also by investing in financial products based on tokens. For example, there are derivatives that are based on a specific token as the underlying. In addition, there are funds that invest in tokens. A sub-form of these are so-called

---

[121] See e.g. the Filecoin, available at https://filecoin.io/ (accessed 31.1.2020).
[122] See e.g. the Friendz Token, available at https://www.friendz.io/ (accessed 31.1.2020).
[123] Maume and Fromberger, 'Regulation of Initial Coin Offerings: Reconciling U.S. and E.U. Securities Laws' (2019) 19 *Chicago Journal of International Law*, 548 (558).
[124] See Chohan, 'Tethering Cryptocurrencies to Fiat Currencies without Transparency: A Case Study' (2018), available at https://beck-link.de/kc2xx (accessed 31.1.2020).
[125] CoinMarketCap, available at https://coinmarketcap.com (accessed 31.1.2020).

ETFs, Exchange Traded Funds. ETFs also reflect the value of one or more tokens.[126] In some cases, the tokens are actually acquired by the respective fund company via the blockchain. However, it is also conceivable to simply represent the value without actually acquiring the respective tokens. Investors do not buy such ETFs on crypto exchanges, but on regular stock exchanges.

C. The Acquisition of Tokens

78 Tokens can be purchased in two ways: originally on the primary market or derivatively via the secondary market.

I. Original Acquisition

1. Initiation of a Blockchain

79 When initiating a blockchain, the first tokens must be stored digitally.[127] They form the basis for transactions, mining/forging activities and thus for the creation of further tokens. Alternatively, all tokens can be made available upon the initiation of the blockchain (→ para. 6). In this case, there is no continuous increase in the number of tokens. Naturally, it is the initiator of the blockchain who has access to these first tokens and can transfer them. Usually, a large part of the first tokens is distributed to other potential participants in the network in order to get the blockchain started as quickly as possible by the blockchain participants making transactions.[128] However, the initiator is free to retain a portion of the tokens – either to keep the price stable at a later date or to make capital gains on the secondary market. Thus, by initiating a blockchain, the tokens that are based on it can be acquired originally. *Satoshi Nakamoto,* for example, holds about 67 Bitcoins under the address 1A1zP1eP5QGefi2DMPTfTL5SLmv7DivfNa since the initiation of the Bitcoin blockchain.

2. Mining/Minting

80 Starting point of the blockchain is a first block – the so-called Genesis block, which is set by the initiator of the blockchain. After the blockchain is set up, mining or forging is the only way to make new tokens available and acquire them originally.[129]

3. Initial Coin Offering (ICO)

81 Initial Coin Offerings (ICOs) are another original way of acquiring tokens. The term is inspired by Initial Public Offering of stock corporations, so-called IPOs. ICOs are also known as token sales. If the tokens to be issued are security tokens, the term **STO – Security Token Offering** is also used. In the context of an ICO, companies can use the issue of newly created tokens to raise capital.

---

[126] Cf. Grannemann, 'Coinbase arbeitet an Crypto-ETF, wird von BlackRock unterstützt' (2018), available at https://beck-link.de/3vtk8 (accessed 31.1.2020).
[127] This is done in the form of unspent transaction outputs.
[128] See also Fromberger, Haffke and Zimmermann, 'Kryptowerte und Geldwäsche – Eine Analyse der 5. Geldwäscherichtlinie sowie des Gesetzesentwurfs der Bundesregierung' (2019) 19 *Zeitschrift für Bank- und Kapitalmarktrecht*, 377 (378).
[129] Nakamoto, 'Bitcoin: A Peer-to-Peer Electronic Cash System' (Satoshi Nakamoto Institute, 31.10.2008), available at https://beck-link.de/hh2f8 (accessed 4.9.2018); Werbach and Cornell, 'Contracts Ex Machina' (2017) 67 *Duke Law Journal*, 313 (329).

Part A. Introduction

82 In 2017, more than 6.5 billion USD were raised worldwide through ICOs.[130] In 2018, the figure was more than 14 billion USD.[131] At the time of the publication of this handbook, there is a decline in the number of ICOs on the one hand,[132] while, on the other hand, established companies plan to raise capital through the issue of tokens. The market seems to 'mature' in some ways.[133] It is therefore very likely that the market volume will continue to grow in the medium term. Besides these immense amounts of money, it cannot be overlooked that there is a large number of issuers that fail to achieve the goals pursued by the ICO and communicated accordingly. For example, 46 % of the 902 ICOs of 2017 can be regarded as having failed in the first six months of 2018.[134] It is estimated that about 10 % of all ICOs are conducted fraudulently.[135] This might be one of the reasons why the ICOs of 2017, 2018, and 2019 were not a success from an investor's perspective. In the majority of cases, investors incurred (high) losses.[136]

83 Before an ICO is performed, the issuer generates new tokens.[137] Thereto, he/she can use a separate, newly developed blockchain or an existing one.[138] Very often the issued tokens are ERC-20 tokens based on the Ethereum blockchain.[139] The reason is that the Ethereum blockchain allows the creation of new, individual tokens with less than 100 lines of code.[140] The ERC-20 smart contract enables the issuer to issue the new tokens and to receive the respective payments automatically. The smart contract also creates a list of token holders and maintains this list even after the tokens have been issued. The ownership of a token can thus be gleaned from the Ethereum blockchain at any time.[141]

---

[130] Haffke and Fromberger, 'ICO Market Report 2017 – Performance Analysis of Initial Coin Offerings (Presentation Slides)' (2019), 8, available at https://beck-link.de/awwh6 (accessed 23.1.2020).

[131] Fromberger and Haffke, 'ICO Market Report 2018/2019 – Performance Analysis of 2018's Initial Coin Offerings' (2019), 9, available at https://beck-link.de/d6zac (accessed 23.1.2020).

[132] Ibid, 12. Haffke and Fromberger, 'ICO Market Report 2019/2020 – Performance Analysis of 2019's Initial Coin Offerings' (2020), 12, available at https://beck-link.de/x2kez (accessed 23.6.2021).

[133] Cf. Burton, 'The ICO bubble is about to burst… but that's a good thing' (Wired UK, 15.12.2017), available at https://beck-link.de/3y8r7 (accessed 31.1.2020); Fromberger and Haffke, 'ICO Market Report 2018/2019 – Performance Analysis of 2018's Initial Coin Offerings' (2019), 23, available at https://beck-link.de/d6zac (accessed 23.1.2020).

[134] 'About Half of 2017's ICOs Have Failed Already' (NewsBTC, 26.2.2018), available at https://beck-link.de/vtpx3 (accessed 31.1.2020).

[135] Chohan, 'Initial Coin Offerings (ICOs): Risks, Regulation and Accountability' (2017) Discussion Paper Series: Notes on the 21st Century, 3, available at https://beck-link.de/dcz63 (accessed 31.1.2020); Rosenberger, *Bitcoin und Blockchain* (2018), 130.

[136] Haffke and Fromberger, 'ICO Market Report 2019/2020 – Performance Analysis of 2019's Initial Coin Offerings' (2020), 34, available at https://beck-link.de/x2kez (accessed 23.6.2021); Fromberger and Haffke, 'ICO Market Report 2018/2019 – Performance Analysis of 2018's Initial Coin Offerings' (2019), 21, available at https://beck-link.de/d6zac (accessed 23.1.2020); Haffke and Fromberger, 'ICO Market Report 2017 – Performance Analysis of Initial Coin Offerings (Presentation Slides)' (2019), 22, available at https://beck-link.de/awwh6 (accessed 23.1.2020).

[137] Maume and Fromberger, 'Regulation of Initial Coin Offerings: Reconciling U.S. and E.U. Securities Laws' (2019) 19 *Chicago Journal of International Law*, 548 (560).

[138] Kastelein, 'What Initial Coin Offerings Are, and Why VC Firms Care' (Harvard Business Review, 24.3.2017), available at https://beck-link.de/h3wws (accessed 31.1.2020).

[139] Fromberger and Haffke, 'ICO Market Report 2018/2019 – Performance Analysis of 2018's Initial Coin Offerings' (2019), 13, available at https://beck-link.de/d6zac (accessed 23.1.2020); Haffke and Fromberger, 'ICO Market Report 2017 – Performance Analysis of Initial Coin Offerings (Presentation Slides)' (2019), 12, available at https://beck-link.de/awwh6 (accessed 23.1.2020).

[140] Rohr and Wright, 'Blockchain-Based Token Sales, Initial Coin Offerings, and the Democratization of Public Capital Markets' (2017) *University of Tennessee Legal Studies Research Paper* No. 338, 21, available at https://beck-link.de/peh4b (accessed 31.1.2020); Zickgraf, 'Initial Coin Offerings – Ein Fall für das Kapitalmarktrecht?' (2018) 63 *Die Aktiengesellschaft*, 293 (294).

[141] Rohr and Wright, 'Blockchain-Based Token Sales, Initial Coin Offerings, and the Democratization of Public Capital Markets' (2017) *University of Tennessee Legal Studies Research Paper* No. 338, 21, available at https://beck-link.de/peh4b (accessed 31.1.2020).

§ 1. Technical and Factual Background

The issuing company then names the new token and determines the issue price. **84**
Before the token is actually issued, potential investors register for the ICO without obligation to actually buy it – usually on the issuer's website. As a rule, the investors then exchange established tokens such as Bitcoin or Ether for the new tokens.[142] These tokens can belong to any of the token categories described above. Sometimes, tokens can also be bought with fiat money. The 'sale' usually takes place via the issuer's website.

ICOs are typically divided into different rounds of sale. Each round is usually limited in time. The conditions of the token purchase can vary considerably between rounds. For example, tokens are firstly sold to 'family and friends', that means to the founders, employees, and investors close to the company at a discounted issue price or as a consideration for a service already rendered (so-called **private sale**). Often, a further round of issuance follows: The so-called **Pre-ICO**, in which the general public can now also purchase the tokens (so-called **public sale**), sometimes at a price considerably[143] below the actual issue price. Instead of a price reduction, additional free tokens are sometimes given out to early investors at a later date (so-called **Airdrop**).

This first round of public sale is followed by the actual ICO and a token exchange at the issue price. The issuer determines the hard cap and soft cap of the ICO. The **soft cap** is the minimum number of tokens to be issued via the ICO. If this threshold cannot be reached, the ICO is not carried out. Tokens that have already been bought are refunded. The **hard cap** is the maximum number of issued tokens.

Sometimes the issuer equips the new tokens with a **lock-up**. This is a technical transfer lock and means that the tokens cannot be transferred to another public key by the investor after he/she has received them. This lock-up can be either temporary or permanent. If the lock-up is temporary, it usually serves to stabilise the price of the issued tokens after their release. Besides that, there are also tokens that are equipped with lock-ups that permanently inhibit their transferability, particularly in the case of utility tokens. If the demand for tokens is lower than the quantity of tokens generated by the issuer, but the soft cap is still reached, issuers occasionally carry out a so-called **burning process**. This deletes the unissued tokens from the blockchain.

Issuers primarily use digital channels, especially social media platforms, to promote **85**
the ICO.[144] For the purpose of information, investors can regularly use a **whitepaper** produced and published by the issuing company. This document contains information about the company, the facts and figures of the ICO, the planned use of the raised capital and the specific characteristics of the issued tokens.[145] The whitepaper therefore provides important insights into the category the issued token can be attributed to. The general framework for the sale of the tokens is often written down in so-called **token purchase agreements**. Their layout and structure is similar to that of general terms and conditions. However, (potential) buyers rarely take notice of them in practice.

Frequently, issuers want to exclude investors from certain countries from participating in the ICO. They hope to circumvent the regulations that apply in the respective jurisdiction. For this reason, **disclaimers** can be found on the websites of the ICOs stating that investors from specific countries are not allowed to take part in the ICO.

---

[142] De Filippi and Wright, *Blockchain and the Law* (2018), 102.
[143] 50 % below the actual issue price is not unusual.
[144] Zickgraf, 'Initial Coin Offerings – Ein Fall für das Kapitalmarktrecht?' (2018) 63 *Die Aktiengesellschaft*, 293 (294); De Filippi and Wright, *Blockchain and the Law* (2018), 102.
[145] Maume and Fromberger, 'Regulation of Initial Coin Offerings: Reconciling U.S. and E.U. Securities Laws' (2019) 19 *Chicago Journal of International Law*, 548 (560).

Furthermore, companies introduce so-called **KYC (Know Your Costumer)** processes – at least for investors that invest a certain amount of money. It is common that investors must identify themselves by uploading the photo of an ID document. The technical specifications and framework conditions of an ICO are often also found in smart contracts (→ para. 62 et seqq.). Issuers can either set up their own, individual smart contract or use ready-made models and standards. The latter ones can be adapted to the individual circumstances of the respective ICO with relatively little effort.

86 In particular, the exchange of established tokens for newly issued tokens is also carried out on the basis of smart contracts (→ para. 62).[146] The investor assigns the number of tokens (e.g. Bitcoins or Ether) that he/she wants to invest to a public key provided by the issuer. The investor then automatically receives the corresponding number of new tokens which are added to the investor's public key. This process has the advantage that no intermediaries are required. As a result, ICOs can be completed faster and more cost-effectively than conventional IPOs.[147] In some cases, the new tokens are also traded on crypto exchanges[148] after a short time.

87 ICO issuers often create a pressure situation with potential investors. They try to suggest through – sometimes aggressive – advertising and lurid market bawling that the tokens to be issued are very scarce, that the opportunity to invest is unique. Issuers want potential investors to believe that they face a once in a lifetime investment opportunity. In this way, in particular private investors are to be persuaded to make hasty investments. Such practices – together with the often very poor price development of the tokens issued – have led to ICOs increasingly coming into disrepute as an investment opportunity. In the meantime, however, it can be said that the ICO market is 'maturing'.

II. Derivative Acquisition

88 If tokens are already in circulation, they can be purchased on secondary markets.

1. Direct Derivative Acquisition

89 The simplest form of derivative acquisition is the transfer of tokens to another public key. This form of acquisition takes place without the involvement of a third party (e.g. a bank) as an intermediary. The direct derivative acquisition of tokens can be compared to a digital cash payment between two parties. However, this transaction between two (non-institutional) blockchain users is visible for all other blockchain participants on the basis of the pseudonyms used.

Sometimes, tokens are not permanently transferred to another network participant. If tokens are only provided for a limited timeframe, this is referred to as **crypto lending**. Temporary crypto lending of tokens is usually remunerated with a fee to be paid in fiat money or crypto tokens.

---

[146] Moran, 'The Impact of Regulatory Measures Imposed on Initial Coin Offerings in the United States Market Economy' (2018) 26 *Catholic University Journal of Law and Technology*, 2 (7); Noonan, 'Bitcoin or Bust: Can One Really "Trust' One's Digital Assets?' (2015) 7 *Estate Planning & Community Property Law Journal*, 583 (593).

[147] Maume and Fromberger, 'Regulation of Initial Coin Offerings: Reconciling U.S. and E.U. Securities Laws' (2019) 19 *Chicago Journal of International Law*, 548 (560); De Filippi and Wright, *Blockchain and the Law* (2018), 100.

[148] See → para. 90 et seqq.

2. Trading Platforms: Crypto-to-Crypto Exchanges and Fiat-to-Crypto Exchanges

a) General Information. Users of the blockchain technology usually purchase tokens on so-called **trading platforms**.[149] These are usually operated online.[150] A user creates an account for the trading platform, which can vary in type and scope of functions. The user account has an interface that is regularly structured in a way comparable to an online banking account.

The services provided by the platform operator are remunerated by appropriate exchange rate premiums or by some other fee. Frequently, trading platforms also issue their own utility tokens (so-called platform tokens) which can be used to pay the transaction fees.[151] If the user of a platform uses the respective platform token to pay the transaction fees, the fees are often reduced.

Trading platforms can be divided into two categories, crypto-to-crypto exchanges and fiat-to-crypto exchanges. **Fiat-to-crypto exchanges** exchange fiat currencies into tokens and vice versa.[152] Currently, the number of tokens that can be acquired in this way is limited. The most common fiat-to-crypto exchanges only exchange into the 15 to 30 different token types that have the highest market capitalisation. This is only a small proportion of the almost 11,000 different types of tokens that are traded on secondary markets.[153]

Many tokens are only available on so-called **crypto-to-crypto exchanges.** These exchanges are characterised by the fact that they allow the exchange of tokens for other tokens.[154]

b) Functional Categorisation. Fiat-to-crypto exchanges and crypto-to-crypto exchanges function differently. This depends on the respective design of the trading platform which was chosen by the operator. On the one hand, there are platforms that enable **trading from user to user**; on the other hand, there are other platforms on which the platform is the user's trading partner in each transaction.

aa) On-Chain vs. Off-Chain. Trading platforms can be divided into **two subgroups**, depending on the **transaction process**. A distinction is to be made between providers that actually settle each transaction via the blockchain (on-chain trading platforms) and those that merely adjust the users' digital accounts according to the exchange (off-chain trading platforms).

On-chain trading platforms are characterised by the fact that the trading activities on the platform are actually carried out on the blockchain. That means that each transaction performed on the platform leads to a real change in the allocation of the involved tokens on the blockchain. The respective tokens are **assigned** to the public keys

---

[149] On the term, see already Fromberger, Haffke and Zimmermann, 'Kryptowerte und Geldwäsche – Eine Analyse der 5. Geldwäscherichtlinie sowie des Gesetzesentwurfs der Bundesregierung' (2019) 19 *Zeitschrift für Bank- und Kapitalmarktrecht*, 377 (378).

[150] Cf. for example the crypto exchange Coinbase, available at https://www.coinbase.com/ (accessed 31.1.2020) and the crypto exchange Binance, available at https://www.binance.com/de (accessed 31.1.2020).

[151] See e.g. the platform token of the Binance platform: the Binance Coin, see Binance, available at https://www.binance.com/de/bnb (accessed 31.1.2020).

[152] De Filippi and Wright, *Blockchain and the Law* (2018), 27; Fromberger, Haffke and Zimmermann, 'Kryptowerte und Geldwäsche – Eine Analyse der 5. Geldwäscherichtlinie sowie des Gesetzesentwurfs der Bundesregierung' (2019) 19 *Zeitschrift für Bank- und Kapitalmarktrecht*, 377 (378).

[153] CoinMarketCap, available at https://coinmarketcap.com/ (accessed 5.9.2018).

[154] Fromberger, Haffke and Zimmermann, 'Kryptowerte und Geldwäsche – Eine Analyse der 5. Geldwäscherichtlinie sowie des Gesetzesentwurfs der Bundesregierung' (2019) 19 *Zeitschrift für Bank- und Kapitalmarktrecht*, 377 (378).

of the acting parties or the platform due to **a blockchain transaction**. This can be traced by means of a blockchain scan of the participating public keys. Consequently, the token accounts kept by the trading platform for the users always correspond to the actual token allocation as it can be seen on the blockchain after the transaction has been completed.

> **Example:**
> A would like to exchange EUR 2000 for one Ether. To do this, she first transfers the necessary amount of EUR 2000[155] to an account designated by fiat-to-crypto exchange operator B. Once the money has arrived, she selects the 'Exchange Euro/Ether' option on B's online platform. B then sends a transaction message to the Ethereum network to transfer an Ether that was previously assigned to his public key to A's public key. After the transaction is processed by the blockchain network, A can see that the Ether has actually been assigned to her public key by checking it via a scan by a blockchain scanner.[156] The same account balance is displayed if A checks the interface of her user account at B's exchange.

96 **Off-chain trading platforms**, on the other hand, do not carry out an actual blockchain transaction when processing exchange activities on their platform; there is no real change in the token allocation on the blockchain. It is only the virtual account balance in the respective user accounts that is updated. Therefore, there is only an **internal adjustment on the accounting level** of the platform. This means that the user only has a 'claim' against the operator to actually assign the respective number of tokens to a certain public key via the blockchain. The advantage of this design is the lower technical effort, since no actual exchange takes place. In addition, such a procedure avoids transaction costs which generally occur with each blockchain transaction (→ para. 36). For the downsides → para. 101.

> **Example:**
> A would like to exchange EUR 2000 for one Ether. To do this, she first transfers the amount of EUR 2000 to an account designated by fiat-to-crypto exchange operator B. Once the money has arrived, she selects the 'Exchange Euro/Ether' option on B's online platform. B then reduces the amount of the Euro account held for A by EUR 2000 and increases the Ether account by one Ether. B does not send a transaction message to the Ethereum network. A has acquired a 'claim' against B for allocation of one Ether. If A wants to use this Ether token, e.g. in an exchange, she provides B with the respective public key. B now assigns the token to the provided public key via a blockchain transaction.

97 bb) **Central vs. Decentral.** A characteristic feature of **central trading platforms**, which are regularly operated off-chain, is the operator's prominent role. The basis for this role is his/her **comprehensive possibility of influence and access**. The operator can exercise control over the transactions processed by the users and over any tokens stored. The reason for this is that when a user account is created, the operator usually generates a new pair of cryptographic keys (public key and corresponding private key) for the user. The user is then only provided with the public key. The private key, however, remains with the platform operator; the user does not have access to it. As a result, central platform operators are regularly wallet providers that functionally store the keys (→ para. 27). The user's password serves as a substitute for the private key. He/she can use it to access his/her user account and carry out trading activities. The tokens assigned to the user's public key are thus exposed to the possibility of access by the platform operator. Additionally, if they are operated on-chain, central platforms generally process trading activities between users 'around the corner'. That means that the 'flow of tokens'

---

[155] Depending on the current Ether rate. Here, the sum is chosen arbitrarily to illustrate the example.
[156] For the Ethereum Blockchain, such a scan of the public key can be done e.g. via Etherscan, see Etherscan, available at https://etherscan.io/ (accessed 31.1.2020).

is always settled via a central public key of the platform operator. The platform acts a central counterparty; it is thus **directly interposed between the acting traders**. Both parties to a transaction therefore assign the tokens to be traded to the public key of the operator. The operator then sends the respective acquired tokens to the exchanging parties after having deducted a fee for his/her service. This gives the operator the opportunity to stop or to delay the transaction.

> **Example: Central crypto exchange (Off-Chain)** 98
> After A has purchased one Ether via the fiat-to-crypto exchange B, she wants to 'exchange' it into 20,000 TE-FOOD tokens. A first transfers the Ether via a blockchain transaction message to a public key provided to her by crypto-to-crypto exchange C. The corresponding private key is not known to A; only C has access to it. Sender of the transaction to the crypto-to-crypto exchange C is A's Public Key at B. As soon as the blockchain transaction is completed, A sees the token in the online interface of C. The check of the public key named by C would not necessarily show a status of one Ether. For example, it is possible that C names the same address to all Ether 'depositing' users. The result would be that a blockchain scan would show, significantly more Ether tokens assigned to this Public Key. A now chooses the option 'Buy TE-FOOD for Ether'. Now she can purchase about 20,000 TE-FOOD tokens from D, a third party unknown to her. In her user account she sees a credit of 20,000 TE-FOOD tokens. However, C only carries out this transaction at the accounting level, without initiating a corresponding blockchain transaction. A's Ether account is decreased in value by one Ether, the TE-FOOD account is increased accordingly by 20,000 TE-FOOD tokens. This means that both D and A have 'claims' against C for the procurement of the respective tokens.

Regarding **decentralised trading platforms**, which necessarily operate on-chain, the operator lacks the influence and access possibilities described above. The transactions of blockchain participants using the platform take place autonomously. In addition, the **platform operator has no possibility to access the users' tokens**. Even with a decentralised trading platform, a pair of cryptographic keys is generated for each user. Unlike central trading platforms, it is only the user who has access to the private key; the operator of the platform, however, has no access to it. The trade of tokens is **always processed directly between the trading parties**. The tokens are assigned directly to the public keys of the parties to the transaction; the operator acts **purely** as an **intermediary**. 99

> **Example: Decentralised crypto-to-crypto exchange (On-Chain)** 100
> After A has purchased one Ether via the fiat-to-crypto exchange B, she wants to 'exchange' it into 20,000 TE-FOOD tokens. A first transfers the Ether via a blockchain transaction message to the public key at platform C. This key was made available to her by C after creating a user account. A has exclusive access to the private key, operator C has no access. The sender of the transaction is A's Public Key at fiat-to-crypto exchange B. As soon as the transaction is completed, A sees the token in the online interface of crypto-to-crypto exchange C. If she checks her public key at C using a blockchain scan, she recognises that the token is actually assigned to this key. A now chooses the option 'Buy TE-FOOD for Ether'. Now she can purchase approx. 20,000 TE-FOOD tokens from D, a third party unknown to her. D has previously selected the option 'Sell TE-FOOD for Ether' in his user account. C brings the two parties together. In her user account, A sees a credit of 20,000 TE-FOOD tokens, which appears there either immediately, or at the latest after completion of the blockchain transaction. If she checks her public key at platform C again, no Ether is assigned to it anymore, but the 20,000 TE-FOOD tokens are.

This different design of decentralised trading platforms is particularly relevant for **the technical security of the user accounts** and any tokens deposited. Central trading platforms are susceptible to **external attacks**, such as hacker attacks, due to the operator's central access and the central storage of data. The use of a central platform is therefore immanent to the risk of loss of the tokens for the users. 101

Part A. Introduction

Furthermore, there is the risk of **internal attacks** by the platform operators themselves – due to their extensive access rights. An operator's insolvency can also lead to serious problems.

D. Anonymisation Efforts

I. Pseudonymity as Starting Point

102   The blockchain in its original form is a **pseudonymous, not an anonymous** system (→ para. 17). It is a register that is accessible by the public. Every transaction ever carried out on the blockchain is traceable, since both sender and recipient as well as the number of tokens transferred are publicly visible.

103   **Example:**
The criminal A maintains a public key to which a certain number of Bitcoins are assigned to. If A transfers these tokens to a public key of B for criminal purposes, this transaction is publicly visible. In addition, all transactions subsequently carried out by B with these incriminated tokens are also traceable. This can provide law enforcement authorities with a comprehensive picture of criminally relevant payment flows and thus information for possible criminal prosecution.

104   Due to the technical design of pseudonymous blockchains (→ para. 24), it is possible to trace the origin of tokens. This is the starting point for the introduction of so-called **blacklists**. A blacklist is a directory in which transaction IDs are listed. These IDs make it possible to infer certain tokens (→ para. 20).

The reason for placing a token on a blacklist is its **potential link to criminally relevant activities**. Blacklists can be maintained by governmental organisations, interest groups, commercial service providers and individuals. The inclusion of a token on a blacklist is intended to **restrict its tradability**. This is because many nodes, in particular trading platforms, do not accept tokens that are included in blacklists.

105   **Example:**
In the context of a hacker attack on the trading platform A, 100,000 Bitcoins are transferred to the public key of the hacker H without authorization. From there, H transfers the Bitcoins to various other public keys maintained by him in order to exchange them for Euros via various fiat-to-crypto exchanges. A reports the IDs of the stolen Bitcoins to all blacklist operators known to it. As a result, all other nodes in the Bitcoin system now know which tokens originate from the hacker attack. This consequently makes it more difficult for H to use these tokens in transactions.

II. Tumblers

106   Tumblers (also known as mixers) are service providers that offer to **disguise transactions** on blockchains.[157] For the user of the tumbler service (= customer), this means that the use of a blockchain, which in itself is pseudonymous, is made anonymous. By **simulating an economic cycle,** it is almost impossible for third parties to trace the origin of the transferred tokens. The **central condition** is to ensure that the tokens paid in by a customer do not correspond to the tokens returned to him after completion of the tumbling process. For this purpose, the

---

[157] See on this and in the following basic explanations at Fromberger, Haffke and Zimmermann, 'Kryptowerte und Geldwäsche – Eine Analyse der 5. Geldwäscherichtlinie sowie des Gesetzesentwurfs der Bundesregierung' (2019) 19 *Zeitschrift für Bank- und Kapitalmarktrecht*, 377 (378).

tumbler maintains numerous public keys and transfers the tokens stemming from its customers back and forth between them randomly and automatically. The amount paid in is also split into smaller partial amounts as it flows through the simulated economic cycle. For outsiders, the blockchain usually does not show which transactions were executed by a tumbler and which originate from 'real' nodes. After completion of the procedure, the tumbler transfers several tokens equivalent to the original amount to a public key designated by the customer. The tumbler retains a fee for this service of up to three percent of the paid-in tokens. Some providers work with a random, variable fee rate. This makes it even more difficult to prove that the paid-out tokens can be associated with the paid-in tokens. Furthermore, this disguises the fact that a tumbling process has taken place.

Example: 107

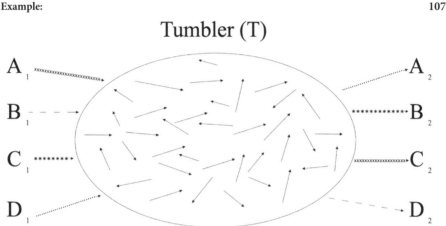

Figure 6: Functionality of a tumbler

A has assigned 10 Bitcoins to his public key A_1. The tokens originate from criminally relevant activities. As he wants subsequent transactions of these tokens not to lead back to this public key A_1, A uses the service of tumbler T. He, therefore, sends the tokens from his public key A1 to a public key T_1 provided by T. He also gives T another public key A_2 that he maintains as the receiving address. T then carries out the tumbling procedure. He sends the tokens received from his customers (here A, B, C, D) back and forth between the public keys he maintains. The tokens are mixed randomly and automatically. After completion of the procedure, A receives the tokens transferred to his public key A_2. The number corresponds to the number of tokens originally sent by public key A_1 minus the transaction fee retained by T. It is excluded that the tokens originating from public key A_1 are transferred to public key A_2. Technically, this means that the **outputs of public key A_1 never match the inputs at public key A_2**. Now A can transfer the tokens that have been assigned to public key A_2 without being able to trace them back to the original public key A_1.

As an alternative to this procedure, A can also give T the public key of a third party. After the tumbling process is completed, T sends the token directly to this public key.

III. Privacy Tokens

Privacy tokens are based – unlike tumblers – on **their own** blockchains. In contrast to 108 the original idea of blockchain, they are not pseudonymous, but **anonymous**. The underlying codes make all transactions anonymous; they conceal the sender, recipient and number of tokens transferred. For this purpose, different mechanisms can be implemented in the blockchain code.

1. Ring Signatures

109 In pseudonymous blockchains (such as the Bitcoin blockchain), a transaction is signed by the private key of the sender (→ para. 18). Anonymous blockchains that use ring signatures take a different approach. In addition to the active signing by the sender, **other random (passive) nodes (= non-signers) also sign the respective transaction**. The automatic inclusion of other nodes as fictitious senders by the blockchain system leads to the actual sender being concealed. This means that no one, not even the recipient of the transaction, can recognise the sender. In addition, ring signatures guarantee that even the original sender of a token cannot recognise whether and when the recipient will resend the token.[158]

2. Stealth Addresses

110 Stealth addresses render the sender of a transaction and the number of tokens sent **anonymous**. If a transaction takes place on a pseudonymous blockchain, a certain number of tokens are assigned to the public key of the recipient. If, on the other hand, the code of a blockchain provides for the use of stealth addresses, **the tokens** are **assigned to these stealth addresses alone**. For this reason, each stealth address is also a newly created **public key that can be used once**. However, this does not change the fact that each node of the blockchain is assigned its own key pair of public and private key.

111 For each token transaction, the sender creates a new stealth address using the public key of the recipient. Only this stealth address appears in the blockchain. The recipient can use his/her **private key** (which is also the **view key**) to **scan** the blockchain for **stealth addresses** assigned to him/her and use them in new transactions. The necessary prerequisite for this is the generation of a new stealth address that can only be used once. As a result, **transactions are only processed from an existing stealth address to a newly created stealth address**. An assignment of the tokens to the public keys of the nodes, i.e. sender and recipient, does not take place. This prevents the traceability of the tokens and ensures anonymisation of the blockchain. Third parties have no way of identifying the respective transactions in terms of sender, recipient, and number of tokens sent.

---

[158] See in detail 'A low-level explanation of the mechanics of Monero vs Bitcoin in plain English' (Monero), available at https://beck-link.de/8kp6a (accessed 31.1.2020).

§ 2
Economics of Crypto Assets

Literature: Adhami, Giudici and Martinazzi, 'Why do businesses go crypto? An empirical analysis of Initial Coin Offerings', (2018) 100 *Journal of Economics and Business*, 64–75; Al-Naji, Chen and Diao, 'Basis: A Price-Stable Cryptocurrency with an Algorithmic Central Bank' (June 2018), available at: https://www.basis.io/basis_whitepaper_en.pdf (last accessed 22.1.2021); Ali, Barrdear, Clews and Southgate, 'Innovations in payment technologies and the emergence of digital currencies', (2014) 54(3) *Bank of England Quarterly Bulletin*, 262–275; Ali, Barrdear, Clews and Southgate, 'The economics of digital currencies', (2014) 54(3) *Bank of England Quarterly Bulletin*, 276–286; Ammous, *The Bitcoin Standard: The Decentralized Alternative to Central Banking* (Wiley, 2018); Athey, Parashkevov, Sarukkai and Xia, 'Bitcoin Pricing, Adoption, and Usage: Theory and Evidence' (August 2016), available at: https://siepr.stanford.edu/sites/default/files/publications/17-033_1.pdf (last accessed 21.1.2021); Back, 'A partial hash collision based postage scheme' (1997), available at: https://perma.cc/2B8F-8ZQN (last accessed 23.1.2021); Bank for International Settlements, 'Central bank digital currencies' (March 2018), available at: https://www.bis.org/cpmi/publ/d174.pdf (last accessed 10.4.2021); Bank for International Settlements, 'Triennial Central Bank Survey, Foreign exchange turnover in April 2019' (April 2019), available at: https://www.bis.org/statistics/rpfx19_fx.pdf (last accessed 21.1.2021); Bariviera, Basgall, Hasperué and Naiouf, 'Some stylized facts of the Bitcoin market', (2017) 484 *Physica A: Statistical Mechanics and its Applications*, 82–90; Behme and Zickgraf, 'Zivil- und gesellschaftsrechtliche Aspekte von Initial Coin Offerings (ICOs)', (2019) *Zeitschrift für die gesamte Privatrechtswissenschaft (ZfPW)*, 66–93; Blanchard and Johnson, *Macroeconomics* (6th Edition, Pearson, 2012); Bindseil, 'Tiered CBDC and the financial system', (January 2020), available at: https://www.ecb.europa.eu/pub/pdf/scpwps/ecb.wp2351~c8c18bbd60.en.pdf (last accessed 10.4.2021); Blemus and Guégan, 'Initial Crypto-Asset Offerings (ICOs), Tokenization and Corporate Governance' (April 2019), available at https://papers.ssrn.com/sol3/papers.cfm?abstract_id=3350771 (last accessed 21.1.2021); Bofinger, *Grundzüge der Volkswirtschaftslehre, Eine Einführung in die Wissenschaft* (Pearson, 2013); Bonneau, Miller, Clark, Narayanan, Kroll and Felten, 'SoK: Research Perspectives and Challenges for Bitcoin and Cryptocurrencies', 2015 *IEEE Symposium on Security and Privacy*, 104–121; Bouri, Molnár, Azzi, Roubaud and Hagfors, 'On the hedge and safe haven properties of Bitcoin: Is it really more than a diversifier?', (2017) 20 *Finance Research Letters*, 192–198; Bouri, Shahzad, Roubaud, Kristoufek and Lucey, 'Bitcoin, gold, and commodities as safe havens for stocks: New insight through wavelet analysis' (2020) 77 *The Quarterly Review of Economics and Finance*, 156–164; Brodeur, Gray, Islam, Bhuiyan and Suraiya, 'A Literature Review of the Economics of COVID-19' (2020), available at: http://hdl.handle.net/10419/222316 (last accessed 10.4.2021); Brunnermeier, James and Landau, 'The Digitalization of Money' (2019), available at: https://scholar.princeton.edu/sites/default/files/markus/files/02c_digitalmoney.pdf (last accessed 10.4.2021); Cermak, 'Can Bitcoin Become a Viable Alternative to Fiat Currencies? An Empirical Analysis of Bitcoin's Volatility Based on a GARCH Model' (May 2017), available at: https://papers.ssrn.com/sol3/papers.cfm?abstract_id=2961405 (last accessed 21.1.2021); Cheah and Fry, 'Speculative bubbles in Bitcoin markets? An empirical investigation into the fundamental value of Bitcoin', (2015) 130 *Economics Letters*, 32–36; Cheung, Roca and Su, 'Crypto-currency bubbles: An application of the Phillips–Shi–Yu (2013) methodology on Mt. Gox bitcoin prices', (2015) 47 (23) *Applied Economics*, 2348–2358; Ciaian, Rajcaniova and d'Artis Kancs, 'The economics of BitCoin price formation', (2015) 48 (19) *Applied Economics*, 1799–1815; Cohney, Hoffman, Sklaroff and Wishnick, 'Coin-Operated Capitalism', (2019) 119(3) *Columbia Law Review*, 591–676; Dachevsky and Kornblihtt, 'The reproduction and crisis of capitalism in Venezuela under Chavismo', (2017) 44(1) *Latin American Perspectives*, 78–93; Dwork and Noar, 'Pricing via Processing or Combatting Junk-Mail', (1992) *Annual International Cryptology Conference-CRYPTO*, 139–147; ECB Crypto-Assets Task Force, 'Crypto-Assets: Implications for financial stability, monetary policy, and payments and market infrastructure', (2019) 223 *ECB Occasional Paper Series*, 1–38; Eichengreen, *Globalizing Capital: A History of the International Monetary System*, (Princeton University Press, 2019); Finan, Lasaosa and Sunderland, 'Tiering in CHAPS', (2013) 53(4) *Bank of England Quarterly Bulletin*, 371–378; Fisch, 'Initial coin offerings (ICOs) to finance new ventures', (2019) 34 *Journal of Business Venturing*, 1–22; Foley, Karlsen and Putniņš, 'Sex, Drugs, and Bitcoin: How Much Illegal Activity Is Financed through Cryptocurrencies?', (2019) 32(5) *The Review of Financial Studies*, 1798–1853; Fry and Cheah, 'Negative bubbles and shocks in cryptocurrency markets', (2016) 47 *International Review of Financial Analysis*, 343–352; Galloway, *The Four: The hidden DNA of Amazon, Apple, Facebook and Google*, (Random House Large Print, 2017); Garber, *Famous First Bubbles, The Fundamentals of Early Manias*, (The MIT Press,

Part A. Introduction

2001); Haber and Stornetta, 'How to time-stamp a digital document', (1991) 3(2) *Journal of Cryptology*, 99–111; Habersack, Mülbert and Schlitt, *Unternehmensfinanzierung am Kapitalmarkt*, (Otto Schmidt, 2019); Haffke and Fromberger, 'ICO Market Report 2017. Performance Analysis of Initial Coin Offerings' (December 2018), available at: https://ssrn.com/abstract=3309271 (last accessed 21.1.2021); Fromberger and Haffke, 'ICO Market Report 2018/2019 – Performance Analysis of 2018's Initial Coin Offerings' (December 2019), available at: https://ssrn.com/abstract=3512125 (last accessed 21.1.2021); Halaburda and Sarvary, *Beyond Bitcoin, The Economics of Digital Currencies*, (Palgrave, 2016); Harari, *Money*, (Vintage Publishing, 2018); Hayek, *The Denationalisation of Money: The Argument Refined*, (3rd Edition, The Institute of Economic Affairs, 1978); Houser and Stratmann, 'Gordon Tullock and experimental economics', (2012) 152 *Public Choice*, 211–222; Katsiampa, 'Volatility estimation for Bitcoin: A comparison of GARCH models', (2017) 158 *Economics Letters*, 3–6; Katz and Shapiro, 'Technology adoption in the presence of network externalities', (1986) 94(4) *Journal of Political Economy*, 822–841; Kindleberger, 'Bubbles', in Eatwell, Milgate and Newman, *The World of Economics* (Palgrave, 1991), 20–22; Kindleberger and Aliber, *Manias, panics and crashes: a history of financial crises*, (5th Edition, Wiley, 2005); Klein, Pham, Thu and Walther, 'Bitcoin is not the New Gold – A comparison of volatility, correlation, and portfolio performance', (2018) 59 *International Review of Financial Analysis*, 105–116; Klöhn, Parhofer and Resas, 'Initial Coin Offerings (ICOs)', (2018) *Zeitschrift für Bankrecht und Bankwirtschaft (ZBB)*, 89–106; Konrad, *Strategy and Dynamics in Contests*, (Oxford University Press, U.S.A, 2009); Krause and Tolaymat, 'Quantification of energy and carbon costs for mining cryptocurrencies', (2018) 1 *Nature Sustainability*, 711–718; Langenbucher, 'European Securities Law – Are we in need of a new definition? A thought inspired by initial coin offerings', (2018) 2/3 *Revue trimestrielle de droit financier (RTDF)*, 40–48; Leshno and Strack, 'Bitcoin: An Axiomatic Approach and an Impossibility Theorem' (October 2019), available at: https://papers.ssrn.com/sol3/papers.cfm?abstract_id=3487355 (last accessed 23.1.2021); Lim, Matros and Turocy, 'Bounded rationality and group size in Tullock contests: Experimental evidence', (2014) 99 *Journal of Economic Behavior & Organization*, 155–167; Makin and Layton, 'The global fiscal response to COVID-19: Risks and repercussions', (2021) 69(7) *Economic Analysis and Policy*, 340–349; Mankiw, *Macroeconomics*, (7th Edition, Worth Publishers, 2010); March and Sahm, 'Asymmetric discouragement in asymmetric contests', (2017) 151 *Economics Letters*, 23–27; Martin, *Drugs on the dark net: How cryptomarkets are transforming the global trade in illicit drugs*, (Palgrave Macmillan, London, 2014); Mas-Colell, Whinston and Green, *Microeconomic Theory*, (Oxford University Press, 1995); MCKee and Stuckler, 'If the world fails to protect the economy, COVID-19 will damage health not just now but also in the future.' (2020) 26 *Nature Medicine*, 640–642; McKinnon, *The Rules of the Game, International Money and Exchange Rates*, (The MIT Press, 1996); Merkle, 'Protocols for public key cryptosystems, Proceedings Symposium on Security and Privacy', (1980) *IEEE Computer Society*, 122–133; Mises, *Theorie des Geldes und der Umlaufmittel* (Duncker & Humblot, Munich and Leipzig, 1912); Nakamoto, 'Bitcoin: A Peer-to-Peer Electronic Cash System' (2008), available at: https://perma.cc/MU7N-AWPD (last accessed 21.1.2021); Narayanan, Bonneau, Felten, Miller and Goldfeder, *Bitcoin and cryptocurrency technologies: A comprehensive introduction*, (Princeton University Press, 2016); Niepelt, 'Reserves for All? Central Bank Digital Currency, Deposits, and their (Non)-Equivalence', (2020) 16 (3) *International Journal of Central Banking*, 211–238; Ong, Lee, Li and Lee, 'Evaluating the Potential of Alternative Cryptocurrencies', in Lee and Chuen, *Handbook of Digital Currency, Bitcoin, Innovation, Financial Instruments, and Big Data* (Acedemic Press, 2015), 81–135; Radford, 'The Economic Organisation of a P.O.W. Camp', (1945) 12(48) *Economica*, 189–201; Richter, *Geldtheorie, Vorlesung auf der Grundlage der Allgemeinen Gleichgewichtstheorie und der Institutionenökonomik* (Springer Berlin Heidelberg, 1987); Rohr and Wright, 'Blockchain-Based Token Sales, Initial Coin Offerings and the Democratization of Public Capital Markets', (2019) 70(2) *Hastings Law Journal*, 463–524; Romer, *Advanced Macroeconomics*, (4th Edition, McGraw-Hill Irwin, 2012); Schumpeter, *Capitalism, Socialism, and Democracy* (Herper & Brothers,1942); Selmi, Mensi, Hammoudeh and Bouoiyour , 'Is Bitcoin a hedge, a safe haven or a diversifier for oil price movements? A comparison with gold', (2018) 74 *Energy Economics*, 787–801; Senner and Sornette, 'The Holy Grail of Crypto Currencies: Ready to Replace Fiat Money?', (2019) 53(4) *Journal of Economic Issues*, 966–1000; Sheremeta, Overbidding and heterogeneous behavior in contest experiments, (2013) 27(3) *Journal of Economic Surveys*, 491–514; Shiller, *Irrational Exuberance*, (3rd Edition, Princeton University Press, 2000). Shy, *The Economics of Network Industries*, (Cambridge University Press, 2001); Stoll, Klaassen and Gallersdörfer, 'The Carbon Footprint of Bitcoin', (2019) 3(7) *Joule*, 1647–1661; Süßmuth, 'Bitcoin and Web Search Query Dynamics: Is the price driving the hype or is the hype driving the price?' (2019), available at: https://papers.ssrn.com/sol3/papers.cfm?abstract_id=3422258 (last accessed 21.1.2021); Takaishi and Adachi, 'Taylor effect in Bitcoin time series', (2018) 172 *Economics Letters*, 5–7; Thum, 'Die ökonomischen Kosten des Bitcoin-Mining', (2018) 71(2) *ifo Schnelldienst*, 18–20; Tullock, 'Efficient Rent Seeking', in Buchanan, Tollison and Tullock, *Toward a Theory of the Rent-Seeking Society* (Texas A & M University Press, 1980), 97–112; van Aubel, 'Initial Coin Offerings (ICOs)', in Habersack, Mülbert and Schlitt, *Unternehmensfinanzierung am Kapitalmarkt* (Otto Schmidt 2019), 697–747; Vigna and Casey, *The Age of Cryptocurrency: How Bitcoin and the Blockchain*

Are Challenging the Global Economic Order, (MacMillan, 2016); White, 'The Market for Cryptocurrencies', (2015) 35(2) *Cato Journal*, 383–402; Yermack, 'Is Bitcoin a Real Currency? An Economic Appraisal', in Lee and Chuen, *Handbook of Digital Currency, Bitcoin, Innovation, Financial Instruments, and Big Data*, (Academic Press, 2015), 31–43; Yli-Huumo, Ko, Choi, Park and Smolander, 'Where Is Current Research on Blockchain Technology? A Systematic Review', (2016) 11(10) *PLOS ONE*, 1–27; Zetzsche, Buckley, Arner and Föhr, 'The ICO Gold Rush: It's a Scam, It's a Bubble, It's a Super Challenge for Regulators', (2019) 60(2) *Harvard International Law Journal*, 267–315; Zetzsche, Buckley, Arner and Föhr, 'The ICO Gold Rush: It's a Scam, It's a Bubble, It's a Super Challenge for Regulators' (August 2018), available at: https://papers.ssrn.com/sol3/papers.cfm?abstract_id=3072298 (last accessed 21.1.2021). Zickgraf, 'Initial Coin Offerings – Ein Fall für das Kapitalmarktrecht?', (2018) 9 *Die Aktiengesellschaft (AG)*, 293–308.

Outline

	para.
A. Introduction	1
B. Present Economic Importance	4
I. Current (Market) Developments	6
1. Quantitative Analysis	6
2. Speculative Bubble on the Market for Crypto Assets	12
II. Bitcoin	17
1. Market Share and Capitalisation	17
2. Number of Transactions, Transaction Duration, Volume, and Amount	19
3. Transaction Fees	21
4. Token Volume Growth	27
5. Acceptance as Means of Payment	32
III. Initial Coin Offerings (ICOs)	35
1. Issue Object, Issue Volume, Number of Issues, and Market Capitalisation	37
2. Geographic Distribution	41
3. Risks of Abuse	42
C. Crypto Assets as a Complementary Currency	44
I. Characteristics of a Currency	46
1. Primary Monetary Functions	46
2. Secondary Monetary Functions	49
II. Currency Characteristics of Crypto Assets	58
1. Currency Properties of Bitcoin	61
2. Payment Transaction System	69
3. Further Tokens, Stable Coins	74
D. Crypto Assets Beyond the Currency Issue	78
I. Resource Allocation and Negative Externalities	79
1. Resource Consumption	81
2. Energy Consumption	85
E. Conclusion and Outlook	90

A. Introduction

In this chapter, the **basic economic aspects** of crypto assets are examined in more detail. From an economic perspective, the use of crypto assets for the implementation of digital currencies is, at present, still the main focus of attention. Consequently, a large part of the chapter will elaborate on this facet of crypto assets. Yet, further relevant economic aspects of crypto assets as well as their economic implications will also be discussed. 1

First, based on an extensive quantitative analysis, current developments of the most important crypto assets and of the market for Initial Coin Offerings (ICOs) will be described (→ para. 6 et seqq.). Together with a general introduction to the economic 2

Part A. Introduction

requirements for a currency (→ para. 46 et seqq.), this will serve as a basis to evaluate the potential of decentralised, peer-to-peer crypto assets, such as Bitcoin, to serve as a counter-model to and possible substitute for traditional government currencies and payment systems (→ para. 58 et seqq.). In this context, other types of tokens, in particular so-called stable coins, will also be briefly touched on, as they represent an interesting alternative to the actual crypto assets from a **monetary theory** point of view (→ para. 74 et seqq.).

3   Besides the monetary-theoretical view, there are many other aspects of crypto assets that are of keen interest to economists. To some extent, these will also be considered in this chapter. For example, the high resource and energy consumption necessary to mine crypto assets is critically analysed (→ para. 78 et seqq.). Finally, the central points are summarized and an outlook describing possible **future developments** of crypto assets is provided (→ para. 90 et seqq.).

B. Present Economic Importance

4   Although the economic principles and cryptographic concepts underlying crypto assets were already published more than a decade ago in the now famous article by Satoshi Nakamoto[1] and are mainly based on even older developments in the field of cryptography,[2] it is only in recent years that scientists from a wide range of fields, including economics, as well as the general public, have increasingly shown interest in crypto assets and the associated blockchain technology. The widespread fascination can indeed be mainly attributed to the exponential increase in the price of crypto assets, such as Bitcoin, Ether (Ethereum), and XRP (Ripple),[3] in early 2017[4] and the recent price jumps at the end of 2020 and the beginning of 2021 amidst the continuing Covid-19 pandemic.

5   Thus, an understanding of the current economic conditions and developments of crypto assets is not only informative in itself, but also allows to draw conclusions about their prevailing state of significance. For this reason, **current developments** of important crypto assets are examined in detail hereafter.[5] These are particularly important as they serve as a basis for the argumentation in the remaining part of this chapter. At the same time, it should be noted that the analysis, in several respects, can only represent a snapshot in time.[6] However, many of the observations described below as well as the statements derived from these observations are of a fundamental nature and should not lose their validity in the foreseeable future.

---

[1] Nakamoto, 'Bitcoin: A Peer-to-Peer Electronic Cash System' (2008), available at: https://perma.cc/MU7N-AWPD (last accessed 21.1.2021).

[2] Haber and Stornetta, 'How to time-stamp a digital document', (1991) 3(2) *Journal of Cryptology*, 99 (101 et seqq., 105 Merkle, 'Protocols for public key cryptosystems, Proceedings Symposium on Security and Privacy', (1980) *IEEE Computer Society*, 122 (124 et seqq.); Dwork and Noar, 'Pricing via Processing or Combatting Junk-Mail', (1992) *Annual International Cryptology Conference-CRYPTO*, 139 (143 et seq., 145 et seq.); Back, 'A partial hash collision based postage scheme' (1997), available at: https://perma.cc/2B8F-8ZQN (last accessed 23.1.2021).

[3] Unlike Bitcoin and Ether, however, XRP is not based on blockchain technology, but on its own ledger system and the associated consensus algorithm (XRP LCP).

[4] Süßmuth, 'Bitcoin and Web Search Query Dynamics: Is the price driving the hype or is the hype driving the price?' (2019), available at: https://papers.ssrn.com/sol3/papers.cfm?abstract_id=3422258 (last accessed 21.1.2021).

[5] In addition, the developments of other major asset classes are also presented. These primarily serve the purpose of being able to place the observations for the crypto assets into context.

[6] In addition to price developments, which are difficult to predict due to the high volatility, these include in particular the possible uses and relative importance of the various crypto assets.

§ 2. Economics of Crypto Assets

No.	Name	Code	Price	Volume	Market Capitalisation	Tokens in Circulation	Max. Number of Tokens	Consensus Algorithm
1	Bitcoin	BTC	$ 56,701.60	$ 68,490,007,500	$ 1,062,945,604,328	18,687,212	21,000,000	Proof-of-Work
2	Ether (Ethereum)	ETH	$ 2,336.86	$ 39,567,972,794	$ 270,915,048,487	115,551,757	-	Proof-of-Work / Proof-of-Stake *
3	Binance Coin	BNB	$ 568.03	$ 8,922,843,492	$ 87,450,235,791	153,432,897	200,000,000	Proof-of-Work / Proof-of-Stake °
4	XRP (Ripple)	XRP	$ 1.38	$ 15,834,825,400	$ 63,443,625,819	45,404,028,640	100,000,000,000	XRP LCP °
5	Tether	USDT	$ 1.00	$ 171,698,830,693	$ 48,688,231,239	48,689,996,565	-	Proof-of-Work / Proof-of-Stake °
6	Cardano	ADA	$ 1.27	$ 4,817,060,170	$ 40,544,669,205	31,948,309,441	45,000,000,000	Proof-of-Stake
7	Dogecoin	DOGE	$ 0.33	$ 27,743,410,740	$ 40,883,892,981	129,265,966,024	-	Proof-of-Work
8	Polkadot	DOT	$ 34.92	$ 3,307,987,925	$ 32,606,277,441	931,543,323	-	Proof-of-Stake
9	Litecoin	LTC	$ 267.43	$ 9,635,690,426	$ 17,891,506,609	66,752,415	84,000,000	Proof-of-Work
10	Bitcoin Cash	BCH	$ 955.85	$ 8,073,363,195	$ 17,742,061,365	18,714,144	21,000,000	Proof-of-Work

* The Ethereum-Network changes, as part of the Casper implementation, the consensus algorithms from Proof-of-Work to Proof-of-Stake.
° The XRP Ledger Consensus Protocol (XRP LCP) is a low-latency byzantine agreement Protocol. It is a decentralized system which is not based on the blockchain technology.
° Tether is based, depending on the used protocoll, either on the Bitcoin (Proof-of-Work) or on the Ethereum (Proof-of-Work / Proof-of-Stake) blockchain.
° Binance Coin is based on the Ethereum blockchain.

Table 1: Overview of the ten (crypto) tokens with the highest market capitalisation (as of 20.4.2021)[7]

I. Current (Market) Developments

1. Quantitative Analysis

To obtain an overview of the prevailing conditions on the market for crypto assets, Figure 1 shows the **market developments** (prices, price changes, distribution of price changes, volatilities) of three of the currently most important crypto assets (in terms of market capitalization as of April 20, 2021, → Table 1) Bitcoin, Ether, and XRP[8] since 2013 (or in the case of Ether, since August 7, 2015[9]).[10] On the one hand, this allows for a classification of the current situation in the historical context of crypto assets. On the other hand, this analysis sets out the quantitative basis for a comparison of the dynamics of crypto assets with the simultaneously occurring developments of selected **conventional asset classes** (→ para. 8 et seqq.). 6

Figure 1, first and foremost, depicts the historical price trend of the selected crypto assets. The daily percentage price changes, their distributions, and the volatilities calculated on the basis of the changes (monthly rolling average) are also shown. In an identical manner, the market developments of conventional asset classes are shown in Figure 2. 7

In addition to the **exponential price increase**, which peaked at the end of 2017 and the beginning of 2018 as well as again at the end of 2020 and the beginning of 2021, the sometimes unusually high price swings and the consistently **high volatility** of the three crypto assets are particularly noteworthy. This becomes quite clear when comparing the 8

---

[7] See CoinMarketCap, ECB, own calculations.
[8] As can be seen in Table 1, XRP has, as of 20.4.2021, only the fourth highest market capitalization of all crypto currencies. Yet, the high volatility of prices and, as a direct consequence, the high fluctuations in the overall valuations result in a constantly changing order of the crypto assets with respect to their market capitalization. In light of these continued changes and considering its historical importance (→ Figure 4), XRP – instead of Binance Coin – is examined in more detail in the following analysis.
[9] For Ether, whose market launch took place on 30.7.2015, CoinMarketCap has provided price data since 7.8.2015.
[10] For the quantitative analysis of the crypto asset price developments, mainly price data from the website CoinMarketCap, cf. *CoinMarketCap*, available at: https://coinmarketcap.com (last accessed 21.1.2021), are used. Besides CoinMarketCap, there are numerous other providers of historical (price) data on crypto assets. These include for example: Brave New Coin, CoinDesk, BitcoinAverage, Bitcoincharts, Blockchain.com, Quandl, CoinGecko. In addition, (historical) Bitcoin prices can also be obtained directly from file sharing services such as Bitstamp, Gemini, Kraken or Gdax. It is important to note that the prices for crypto assets can vary significantly from one exchange platform to another due to demand and supply effects.

Part A. Introduction

diagrams for crypto assets with those in Figure 2 for established currencies (here: EUR/USD), conventional asset classes such as gold (here: 3 pm fixing), or for security indices that are usually regarded as volatile (here: German Stock Index, DAX → Figure 2).

9   Regarding the price development of crypto assets, a comparison with conventional asset classes is also worthwhile. As Figure 3 illustrates, the **relative performance** (reference point January 3, 2017) of crypto assets – especially Bitcoin – corresponds to a multiple of the performance of the Euro, gold, or the German Stock Index (DAX). However, the enormous price increase of Bitcoin is accompanied by considerable interim losses in value, ultimately leading to the observed high price volatility.

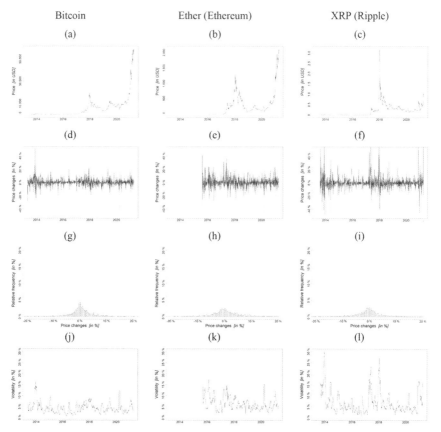

Figure 1: (a)–(c): Price developments (in USD), (d)–(f): percentage price changes (daily), (g)–(i): frequency distributions of percentage (daily) price changes, (j)–(l): volatilities (monthly, moving average) of price changes[11]

10   The high fluctuation in prices of crypto assets is also reflected in their frequency distributions. These show a much greater dispersion than is the case for conventional currencies, gold, or the German Stock Index.[12] Table 2 also shows the higher (central) moments (skewness and kurtosis) of the distributions of the price changes. The high values clearly indicate that the price changes of crypto assets are far from normally

---

[11] Ibid.
[12] Cf. also the volatilities or variances in Table 2.

distributed. These findings are supported both by corresponding statistical tests[13] as well as by other relevant publications.[14]

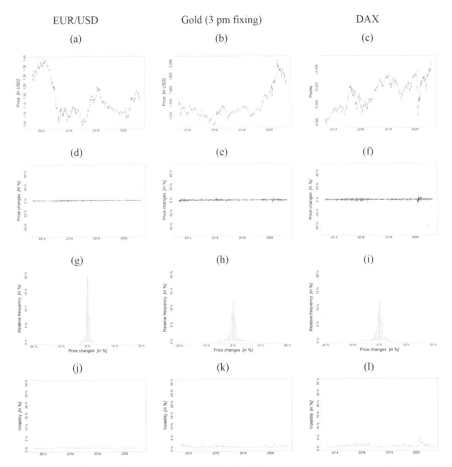

Figure 2: (a)–(c): Price developments (in USD), (d)–(f): percentage price changes (daily), (g)–(i): frequency distributions of percentage (daily) price changes, (j)–(l): volatilities (monthly, moving average) of price changes[15]

For further, more detailed statistical studies and econometric analyses that contribute to a deeper understanding of the price dynamics of crypto assets, the interested reader is referred to the numerous publications in the respective journals.[16]

---

[13] Cf. the test statistics (Jaque-Bera and Shapiro-Wilk) in Table 2.

[14] Klein, Pham, Thu and Walther, 'Bitcoin is not the New Gold – A comparison of volatility, correlation, and portfolio performance', (2018) 59 *International Review of Financial Analysis*, 105 (107 et seqq.); Katsiampa, 'Volatility estimation for Bitcoin: A comparison of GARCH models', (2017) 158 *Economics Letters*, 3 (3 et seqq.).

[15] Source: St. Louis Fed (FRED), own calculations.

[16] Cf. Klein, Pham, Thu and Walther, 'Bitcoin is not the New Gold – A comparison of volatility, correlation, and portfolio performance', (2018) 59 *International Review of Financial Analysis*, 105 (107 et seqq.); Takaishi and Adachi, 'Taylor effect in Bitcoin time series', (2018) 172 *Economics Letters*, 5 (5 et seqq.); Bariviera, Basgall, Hasperué and Naiouf, 'Some stylized facts of the Bitcoin market', (2017) 484 *Physica A: Statistical Mechanics and its Applications*, 82 (84 et seqq.).

Part A. Introduction

No.	Name	Mean	Median	Volatility	Variance	Skewness	Kurtosis	Minimum	Maximum	Jaque Bera test °	Shapiro Wilk test °
1	Bitcoin	0.40%	0.30%	5.11%	0.26%	-0.7120	12.1847	-46.47%	22.51%	3,679*** (0.00)	0.9129*** (0.00)
2	Ether (Ethereum)	0.54%	0.08%	6.98%	0.49%	0.1620	10.7831	-55.07%	39.14%	2,584*** (0.00)	0.9029*** (0.00)
3	XRP (Ripple)	0.50%	-0.17%	8.97%	0.80%	1.8743	20.3715	-55.04%	75.08%	13,449*** (0.00)	0.7768*** (0.00)
4	EUR/USD	0.01%	0.00%	0.42%	0.00%	0.0431	4.0535	-1.78%	1.74%	48*** (0.00)	0.9919*** (0.00)
5	Gold	0.04%	0.03%	0.89%	0.01%	-0.2665	8.1706	-5.26%	5.13%	1,151*** (0.00)	0.9425*** (0.00)
6	DAX	0.03%	0.07%	1.29%	0.02%	-1.0073	20.4202	-13.05%	10.41%	13,095*** (0.00)	0.8561*** (0.00)

° Both, the Jaque Bera test and the Shapiro Wilk test are statistically testing for normally distributed (null hypothesis) data.
*** p < 0,01; ** p < 0,05; * p < 0,1

Table 2: Distributional characteristics of the most important (crypto-)assets[17] and other asset classes (time period: 2.1.2009–9.4.2021)[18]

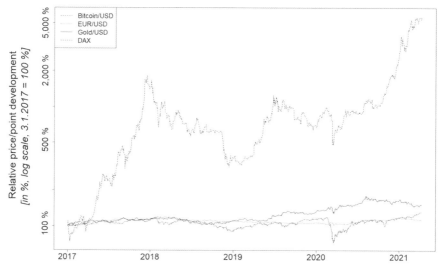

Figure 3: Relative price developments (3.1.2017 = 100 %) for Bitcoin, EUR, gold (all in USD) and the DAX[19]

2. Speculative Bubble on the Market for Crypto Assets

12   When discussing crypto assets, usually the economic phenomenon of a **financial or speculative bubble** is brought forward at some point.[20] In light of the extreme price dynamics (→ para. 8 et seqq.), both in 2017/2018 and in 2020/2021, this is not surprising at all. Indeed, the common definition of a speculative bubble[21] as a strong price increase

---

[17] As argued before (→ para. 6), despite a lower market capitalization, XRP instead of Binance Coin is listed in Table 2 due to its historical importance.
[18] See CoinMarketCap, EZB, own calculations.
[19] See CoinMarketCap, St. Louis Fed (FRED), own calculations.
[20] Cf. Cheah and Fry, 'Speculative bubbles in Bitcoin markets? An empirical investigation into the fundamental value of Bitcoin', (2015) 130 *Economics Letters*, 32 (32 et seqq.).
[21] Besides the rational of Kindleberger/Aliber that is used here, there exists a large number of definitions in the economic literature that attempt to capture the 'fuzzy' concept of a speculative

followed by an equally strong price decline[22] suggests that the already several times observed extreme price increases and subsequent price declines of crypto assets constitute the **archetype of a financial bubble**.

Besides, it can also be argued that the repeatedly observed developments of crypto assets fulfil the classic characteristics of a speculative bubble: An initial rise in price attracts additional interested parties, especially speculators, in the hope of being able to make a profit by buying and selling crypto assets. The price increase and/or the high price level is – instead of realistically assessing the fundamental value – maintained by the **enthusiasm of the investors** until a general reversal of expectations leads to a collapse of prices.[23]

In light of the above, it is difficult to deny that the exponential price increases of all major crypto assets at the end of 2017 and the beginning of 2018 – and presumably also at the end of 2020, beginning of 2021 – were nothing more than a speculative bubble.[24] However, in the wake of the speculative bubble that occurred in the entire crypto token market in 2017/2018, prices have levelled off at a relatively high level in relative terms and have not converged towards zero. In contrast, at the end of 2020 and during the first months of 2021 the prices have hit again new record heights that were more than double the previous record prices in 2017/2018. This is astonishing in so far as a crypto token (or more precise: a currency token) in its original form is a digital token which is neither a financial claim or liability nor a property right towards an entity.[25] The question therefore remains as to whether crypto assets are forming a speculative bubble that now exists already for over a decade.

The clearly non-zero, positive price of crypto assets is first of all an indication that there is a fundamental demand for them. The question now is whether the demand is based to a large degree or even solely on the expectation of possible future price increases (speculation), or whether crypto assets fulfil benefits that approximately justify such (high) positive prices. From an economic point of view, this can be formulated as the question of the **intrinsic value** or **fundamental value** of crypto assets. If, as it is argued,[26] crypto assets do not have an intrinsic value or have an intrinsic value that is however significantly lower than the current price level, there is inevitably a speculative bubble on the market for crypto assets, which is the result of (long-term) **irrational behaviour**.[27]

That this is indeed the case, is supported by various studies. For example, the price of Bitcoin is not significantly influenced by **macroeconomic factors**.[28] This is

---

bubble, a large number of definitions exist which attempt to precisely capture the 'fuzzy' concept of a speculative bubble. See also Garber, *Famous First Bubbles, The Fundamentals of Early Manias*, (2001), 4 et seq.

[22] Kindleberger and Aliber, *Manias, panics and crashes: a history of financial crises*, (2005), 21 et seq.

[23] Kindleberger, 'Bubbles', in Eatwell, Milgate and Newman, *The World of Economics* (1991), 20 et seqq.; Shiller, *Irrational Exuberance*, (2000), 57, 59 et seq.

[24] The price rise and subsequent price fall in 2017/2018 were more extreme than in the dot-com bubble, *See* ECB Crypto-Assets Task Force, 'Crypto-Assets: Implications for financial stability, monetary policy, and payments and market infrastructure', (2019) 223 *ECB Occasional Paper Series*, 1 (14, Chart 5).

[25] This is not to be understood in the legal sense, but as a narrow or original definition of a crypto asset. *See* also ibid, 7.

[26] Cheah and Fry, 'Speculative bubbles in Bitcoin markets? An empirical investigation into the fundamental value of Bitcoin', (2015) 130 *Economics Letters*, 32 (32, 34).

[27] Long-term backward induction by rational market participants would bring the current Bitcoin price to zero. However, in the short term, and due to expected irrational behavior of other market participants, the purchase of Bitcoins can be very rational, as a lot of money can be made from it. *See* also Shiller, *Irrational Exuberance*, (2000), 66 et seqq.

[28] Ciaian, Rajcaniova and d'Artis Kancs, 'The economics of BitCoin price formation', (2015) 48 (19) *Applied Economics*, 1799 (1800, 1811, 1813).

Part A. Introduction

an indication that short-term, **speculative motives** play a role. Further analyses even completely deny Bitcoin an intrinsic or fundamental value.[29] If there exists no fundamental value, this is the optimal breeding ground for speculative bubbles that arise or continue to exist solely as a result of expected future price increases.[30] In the case of Bitcoin, this even appears to be a self-reinforcing process: the price increases, which were most likely initially caused by Bitcoin enthusiasts, triggered the hype about crypto assets in the first place, which has now set off another **cascade effect**.[31]

II. Bitcoin

1. Market Share and Capitalisation

17 Among the numerous crypto assets,[32] Bitcoin, Ether (Ethereum) and XRP (Ripple) stand out due to their persisting very **high market capitalisation** as compared to other crypto assets. The market capitalisation of a crypto token is calculated by multiplying the number of tokens in circulation by its current market price. In April 2021, the crypto assets Bitcoin, Ether (Ethereum) and XRP (Ripple) accounted for more than 70 % of total market capitalisation,[33] i.e. the combined market capitalisation of all traded tokens.[34] As Figure 4 shows, Bitcoin remains by far the most important crypto token in terms of market capitalisation. Even though the incumbent's market share became significantly less in the course of the crypto token hype starting in mid-2017, it recovered to around 65 % in late-2019 and oscillates around 60 % at the time of writing this chapter (April, 2021). Thus, more than 12 years after being first mentioned in a cryptography mailing list,[35] Bitcoin continues to defend its dominant position in the market for crypto assets.

18 Besides its predominant role as a **market leader**, Bitcoin has various other economic characteristics. These will be discussed in the following and, in combination with the market price data (→ para. 6 et seqq.), will form the basis for the subsequent argumentation in the remaining part of the chapter. It should be noted that the following analysis relates specifically to Bitcoin. This is mainly due to the fact that Bitcoin, as the most established crypto token, has a high availability of data. However, at the same time most conclusions drawn can also be applied to many other crypto assets and are thus general in nature.

---

[29] Fry and Cheah, 'Negative bubbles and shocks in cryptocurrency markets', (2016) 47 *International Review of Financial Analysis*, 343 (349 et seqq.); Cheah and Fry, 'Speculative bubbles in Bitcoin markets? An empirical investigation into the fundamental value of Bitcoin', (2015) 130 *Economics Letters*, 32 (32, 34); Cheung, Roca and Su, 'Crypto-currency bubbles: An application of the Phillips–Shi–Yu (2013) methodology on Mt. Gox bitcoin prices', (2015) 47 (23) *Applied Economics*, 2348 (2348, 2356 et seq.).

[30] Athey, Parashkevov, Sarukkai and Xia, 'Bitcoin Pricing, Adoption, and Usage: Theory and Evidence' (August 2016), available at: https://siepr.stanford.edu/sites/default/files/publications/17-033_1.pdf (last accessed 21.1.2021).

[31] Süßmuth, 'Bitcoin and Web Search Query Dynamics: Is the price driving the hype or is the hype driving the price?' (2019), 30 et seq. available at: https://papers.ssrn.com/sol3/papers.cfm?abstract_id=3422258 (last accessed 21.1.2021).

[32] The website *CoinMarketCap* lists 9,420 tokens (as of 21.4.2021) with a total market capitalisation of USD 2.04 trillion (equivalent to EUR 1.7 trillion).

[33] The combined share of market capitalization that can be allotted to the top ten crypto assets amounts to USD 1.55 trillion (EUR 1.3 trillion) or to 82.4 % of total market capitalization; see *CoinMarketCap*.

[34] See *CoinMarketCap*.

[35] Cf. *Bitcoin P2P e-cash paper*, available at: https://www.metzdowd.com/pipermail/cryptography/2008-October/014810.html (last accessed 20.4.2021).

§ 2. Economics of Crypto Assets

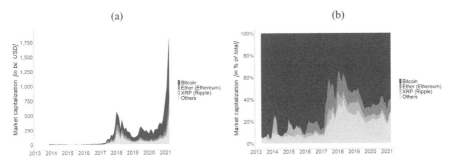

Figure 4: Market capitalisation of the most important crypto assets over time: (a) absolute market capitalisation, (b) proportional market capitalisation[36]

2. Number of Transactions, Transaction Duration, Volume, and Amount

In addition to the **number of transactions**, Figure 5 shows the daily **transaction volume**, the average amount transferred per transaction, and the median duration until a transaction that was placed in the **mempool**[37] is confirmed in the Bitcoin blockchain. From an economic point of view, this data is of particular interest when assessing Bitcoin's economic importance, its circulation, and possible use cases. 19

The **processing time** until a Bitcoin transaction is confirmed by a miner is, with on average between 7 and 15 minutes, relatively short (Figure 5). This would enable Bitcoin to be used as an everyday means of payment. There has also been a steady increase in the number of transactions. Yet, with even at peak times a maximum of 500,000 transactions per day, this is a negligible figure compared to conventional payment systems.[38] With a maximum of USD 12 billion, the transaction volume processed via the Bitcoin blockchain also plays no role in **international payment transactions**.[39] At the same time, the average **transaction amount** – depending on the respective current Bitcoin price, ranging between USD 1,000 and USD 40,000 – indicates that the Bitcoin blockchain is mainly used to transfer comparatively large sums of value. 20

3. Transaction Fees

The high transaction amounts can be attributed, among others, to the **transaction fees** (→ § 1 para. 36), which are in absolute terms, far from negligible (see also Figure 6). Admittedly, these are lower compared to the fees charged by conventional **payment service providers** such as WesternUnion, Visa, or PayPal, especially for international payments. However, disregarding the current (2020/2021) and the previous crypto hype (2017/2018) with transaction fees between USD 20 and USD 50, one usually must pay on average between USD 3 and USD 5 per transaction in order to get it confirmed by a Bitcoin miner. Thus, for transactions with smaller amounts, known as **micropayments**, the Bitcoin blockchain does not satisfy the efficiency criterion. 21

---

[36] See *CoinMarketCap*, own calculations.
[37] The mempool, short for memory pool, contains all pending transactions that have been commissioned but have not yet been included in a block by miners.
[38] In 2018, comprising card payments, credit transfers, and direct debits, there were 90.7 billion cashless payment transactions in the euro area alone. *See* ECB, 'Payments and Settlement Systems Statistics', available at: https://sdw.ecb.europa.eu/browseExplanation.do?node=9689709 (last accessed 21.1.2021).
[39] Bank for International Settlements, 'Triennial Central Bank Survey, Foreign exchange turnover in April 2019' (April 2019), available at: https://www.bis.org/statistics/rpfx19_fx.pdf (last accessed 21.1.2021).

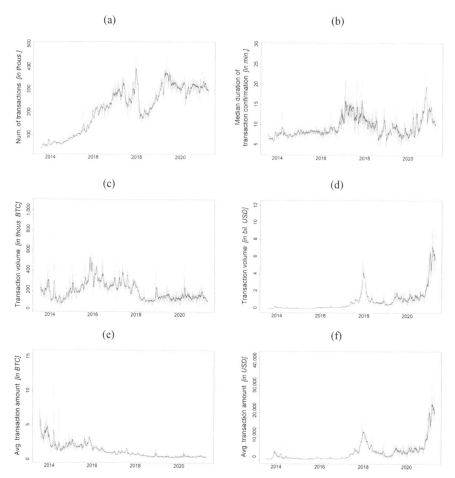

Figure 5: Bitcoin blockchain (grey: daily, black: moving monthly average): (a) number of transactions, (b) average transaction confirmation time, (c) transaction volume (in Bitcoin), (d) transaction volume (in USD), (e) average transaction amount (in Bitcoin), (f) average transaction amount (in USD)[40]

22   It should be noted that the transaction fees are purely voluntary fees paid as an incentive to the miners for confirming the transaction as soon as possible (→ § 1 para. 36). The actual total cost incurred during a transaction (i.e. the total remuneration or compensation for the successful miner) also includes the **block reward** (§ 1 para. 35 et seq.). At first glance, the block reward, as the much larger share of the mining compensation, does not have to be borne by either party directly involved in a transaction. The Bitcoin blockchain is therefore (at least currently) a highly **subsidized payment system**.

23   The subsidy is, however, not as usually provided by an external institution but is generated during the mining of new tokens, i.e. via the creation of new Bitcoins. These are paid out to the successful miners in the form of the above mentioned block

---

[40] See *Blockchain*, available at: blockchain.com, St. Louis Fed (FRED), own calculations.

§ 2. Economics of Crypto Assets

rewards – a process that is comparable to the principle of **seigniorage**[41] in conventional money creation.

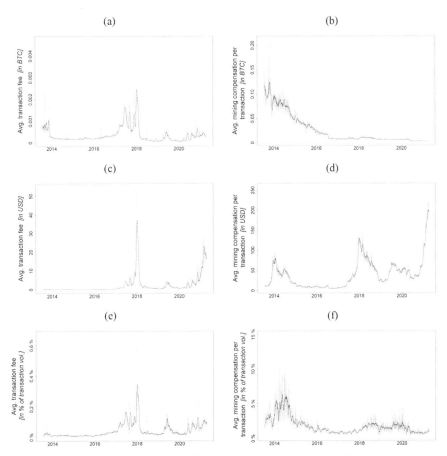

Figure 6: Bitcoin blockchain (grey: daily, black: moving monthly average): (a) Average transaction fee (in Bitcoin), (b) Average mining compensation per transaction (in Bitcoin), (c) Average transaction fee (in USD), (d) Average mining compensation per transaction (in USD), (e) Average transaction fee (in % of transaction volume), (f) Average mining compensation per transaction (in % of transaction volume)[42]

Since the creation of new tokens contributes to an increase in the number of Bitcoins in circulation, it also leads, at least theoretically, to a devaluation of existing Bitcoins. Thus, as long as new tokens are generated,[43] the Bitcoin shows **inflationary tendencies**.[44] The subsidization of the fees that arise in the process of confirming transactions

---

[41] Seigniorage is the turnover generated by printing money. See Romer, *Advanced Macroeconomics* (2012), 513.
[42] Ibid.
[43] The last Bitcoins will be generated by about the year 2140; *see* Ammous, *The Bitcoin Standard: The Decentralized Alternative to Central Banking* (2018), 178, Figure 14.
[44] On the importance of inflation and monetary growth, *see* Romer, *Advanced Macroeconomics* (2012), 513 et seqq.

Part A. Introduction

via the Bitcoin blockchain is ultimately borne by the owners of existing Bitcoin tokens in the form of **inflation costs**.

25   Against this background, the fees which, averaging 0.1 % of the transaction amount, appear at first glance very low, must be viewed in a differentiated manner. If, in addition to the transaction fees, the block reward, also known as **Coinbase**, is included in the calculations, it can be observed that it indeed accounts for the majority of the actual total transaction costs. As Figure 6 shows, taking the block reward into account, i.e. considering the mining compensation rather than the transaction fee, the costs of one transaction increase to USD 30 to USD 50 with up to USD 250 during the ongoing crypto hype in 2021.

26   Yet, even if the actual costs were to be paid by the parties involved, the total transaction costs for a payment over the Bitcoin blockchain only amount to around 2 % of the transaction sum and thus, are in many cases still lower than those charged by traditional payment system providers.[45] Nevertheless, due to the block reward the total costs (mining reward) theoretically incurred during a Bitcoin transaction correspond to up to 10 times the subsidized and currently payable transaction fee.

4. Token Volume Growth

27   The main reason for the low transaction fees constitutes itself in the generation of new tokens as block rewards for the successful full nodes in the proof-of-work verification process (→ § 1 para. 38). However, the creation of new Bitcoin tokens is not unlimited and follows a fixed path defined in the underlying source code, the Bitcoin Core. It explicitly specifies the size of the block reward (in terms of Bitcoins) for each already successfully verified block as well as the block reward for any block that will be verified in the future (→ § 1 para. 2, 35). Furthermore, since the time for verifying a block – on average 10 minutes – is also pre-defined in the source code, the design of the Bitcoin blockchain implies a deterministic growth path for the **token volume**.

28   Initially, 50 Bitcoin tokens were issued as a block reward for each successful block verification. After 210,000 confirmed blocks, the block reward was halved to 25 Bitcoins per block for the first time on November 28, 2012.[46] As Figure 7 illustrates , the halving was accompanied by a reduction in annualized token volume growth from an average of 30 % to less than 15 %. The last **halving** of the block reward so far from 12.5 to 6.25 Bitcoins took place on May 11, 2020 (compare also Figure 7), and is expected to be repeated next on May 6, 2024.[47] The deterministic growth path also allows for precise predictions about the number of Bitcoin tokens in circulation at any (future) point in time as well as about the maximum number of Bitcoins that will ever be issued.[48]

29   However, it should be noted that, contrary to what is often implied, token volume growth does affect the underlying inflation of the Bitcoin but is not equal to it. In economic theory, inflation is understood to be the average increase in the price level over a certain period of time.[49] The determining factor of inflation is thus the **purchasing**

---

[45] In the case of the online payment provider PayPal 2.49%, *see PayPal*, available at: https://www.paypal.com/de/webapps/mpp/ua/useragreement-full#r17 (last accessed 21.1.2021), and for WesternUnion at least 2 %, *see* WesternUnion Gebuehren, available at: https://www.westernunion.com/de/de/gebuehren.html (last accessed 21.1.2021), of the payment amount must be paid.

[46] See Bitcoinblockhalf, available at: https://www.bitcoinblockhalf.com/ (last accessed 22.4.2021).

[47] Ibid.

[48] The number of Bitcoins is limited to 21 million tokens; *see* among others Bitcoinblockhalf, available at: https://www.bitcoinblockhalf.com/ (last accessed 21.1.2021).

[49] See e.g. Blanchard and Johnson, *Macroeconomics* (2012), 7.

§ 2. Economics of Crypto Assets

power of Bitcoin, which is determined by what and how many goods one receives in exchange for a Bitcoin. Although in some cases it is indeed possible, at least theoretically,[50] to pay for goods and services using Bitcoins, the amount of Bitcoins to be paid is based almost always on the value of the good or service in terms of the respective national or supra-national currency (→ para. 65). Hence, inflation in the Bitcoin ecosystem is mainly driven by changes in the market value of Bitcoin.

Additionally, taking into account the highly volatile Bitcoin price (see Figure 1 and → para. 8), it becomes instantly apparent that the change in purchasing power (measured here in USD) and thus the inflation deviates significantly from the deterministic token volume growth. For example, the actual change in the purchasing power of Bitcoin on a quarterly basis from 2013 to 2019 fluctuated between -50 % (corresponding to an inflationary trend) and +100 % (deflationary trend),[51] while the token volume growth in the same period ranges from 1 % to 4 %.[52]   30

From an economic point of view, it can therefore be concluded that the block reward generates a positive (and deterministic) token volume growth and thus, ceteris paribus, inflationary tendencies in the Bitcoin ecosystem. Yet, this only holds if one assumes a constant demand for Bitcoins.   31

5. Acceptance as Means of Payment

An approximately constant demand for Bitcoins would be generated if Bitcoins were, among other things, used as a general means of payment. Yet, in addition to low transaction fees, a necessary prerequisite would be the widespread acceptance of Bitcoin. The more contact points, especially online merchants, offer Bitcoin as a means of payment, the more people will use Bitcoin, which in turn will lead to an even further increase of widespread acceptance.[53]   32

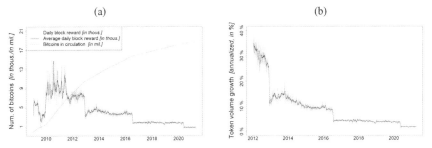

Figure 7: Growth of the Bitcoin token volume (grey: daily, black: moving monthly average): (a) absolute number of new and circulating Bitcoins, (b) percentage change in Bitcoin token volume[54]

---

[50] See the subsequent comments on the acceptance of Bitcoin as a means of payment.
[51] See *CoinMarketCap*, *Blockchain*, available at: blockchain.com, St. Louis Fed (FRED), own calculations.
[52] For example, if one considers the period from June 2013 to June 2019, the average token volume growth is 0.64 % per month and the average actual inflation rate is -2.37 % per month, i.e. on average, Bitcoin shows deflationary tendencies despite positive token volume growth. This compares to an average monthly inflation rate of 0.13 % for the USA; see *CoinMarketCap*, *Blockchain*, available at: blockchain.com, U.S. Bureau of Labor Statistics, own calculations.
[53] This is a classic example of network economics: The utility of a good grows with the number of its users; see Shy, *The Economics of Network Industries* (2001), 3.
[54] See *Blockchain*, available at: blockchain.com, own calculations.

Part A. Introduction

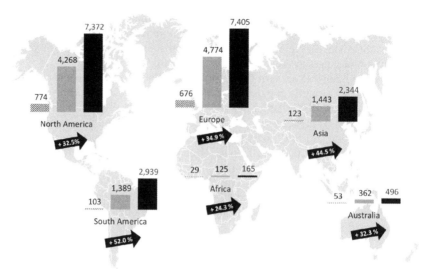

Figure 8: Development of the number of venues accepting Bitcoin as a means of payment from 2013 to 2021, growth rates depict annualized yearly averages (as of April 2021)[55]

33   The fact that Bitcoin is (at least theoretically) accepted as a means of payment by merchants is shown by the Coinmap website[56] and Figure 8, which lists companies (20,721 companies, as of April 19, 2021)[57] that indicate Bitcoin as a possible means of payment. Nevertheless, in Europe and also in the USA there seems to be very little willingness on the part of consumers to use this payment method.[58]

34   Figure 8 also shows, broken down by continent, the absolute and percentage changes in the number of companies that claim to accept Bitcoin. Here it can be observed that the number of acceptance points has grown significantly since 2013 across all continents. However, the average annual growth rates are particularly pronounced in South America (+52.0 %) and Asia (+44.5 %).[59] This is likely due to **macroeconomic and political developments** on these continents. While in South America, especially in Argentina and Venezuela, people want to hedge against the threat of hyperinflation – a result of the continuing difficult financial situations in their countries – and thus, exchange their local currencies for Bitcoins. The increase in Bitcoin acceptance points in Asia, on the other hand, is probably a result of the sharply rising number of Asian Bitcoin mining facilities and the locally high number of Bitcoin transactions.[60]

---

[55] *Coinmap*, own calculations.
[56] See *Coinmap*, available at: https://coinmap.org/ (last accessed 20.4.2021).
[57] Ibid.
[58] A non-representative survey conducted in June 2019 by the author with the help of Saskia Hutschenreiter and Elisa Rodepeter among the listed companies that are based in Munich, Berlin, and at the West Coast of the USA showed that none of the approximately 25 companies inquired has received a payment in form of Bitcoin within the last 12 months.
[59] The growth rates for the entire period from 2013 to 2021 are 2,753.4 % for South America and 1,805.7 % for Asia. In comparison, the total growth rates for Europe (995.4 %) and North America (852.5 %) are more moderate (*Coinmap*, own calculations).
[60] Süßmuth, 'Bitcoin and Web Search Query Dynamics: Is the price driving the hype or is the hype driving the price?' (2019), 4 f, available at: https://papers.ssrn.com/sol3/papers.cfm?abstract_id=3422258 (last accessed 21.1.2021).

III. Initial Coin Offerings (ICOs)

Prompted by the global increasing awareness of Bitcoin and its widespread acceptance (→ para. 33), several other (crypto) tokens have been developed since the Bitcoin block chain was first initiated.[61] Alongside the hype about crypto assets at the end of 2017 and the beginning of 2018, this development was also promoted by the Ethereum network enabling the creation of crypto tokens in a comparatively simple manner (→ § 1 para. 83 and Figure 9).[62] The main aim of many of these token initiatives is to raise capital for a wide variety of projects.[63] In line with initial public offerings (IPOs) of companies, the sales of newly created tokens (token sales) are therefore also referred to as **initial coin offerings (ICOs)** (→ § 1 para. 81 et seqq.). 35

From an economic point of view, ICOs are particularly interesting in two respects: On the one hand, they represent a further vehicle for **raising capital** (→ § 1 para. 81). Particularly for newly founded but also for established companies, ICOs might be considered as an alternative to conventional methods for collecting capital from investors. On the other hand, a detailed analysis of ICOs provides an indication of the extent to which a **tokenisation** of the financial and economic system has already taken place. Henceforth, with a focus on scope and geographical distribution, in the following a brief overview of the still young history as well as current developments of ICOs is provided (→ para. 37 et seqq.). In addition, the not inconsiderable risks of abuse associated with ICOs are also considered (→ para. 42 et seq.). 36

1. Issue Object, Issue Volume, Number of Issues, and Market Capitalisation

The empirical findings on the type of tokens issued are ambiguous: A broad-based study concludes that utility tokens (45 %) and currency tokens (34 %) were offered by the majority, while only a small proportion of ICOs issued investment tokens (13 %).[64] In contrast, another study found that the share of currency tokens (20.9 %) was significantly lower, while that of utility tokens (68 %) was much higher; however, this empirical study also rates investment tokens (26.1 %) as the least issued token category.[65] This noticeable difference can be attributed, on the one hand, to financial regulatory incentives for the issuers to categorise their tokens as utility tokens and, on the other hand, to a certain extent also to the methodological differences of the studies.[66] 37

---

[61] *CoinMarketCap*, for example, currently lists 9,420 tokens (as of 21.4.2021).

[62] See also Haffke and Fromberger, 'ICO Market Report 2017. Performance Analysis of Initial Coin Offerings' (December 2018), 12, available at: https://ssrn.com/abstract=3309271 (last accessed 21.1.2021); Fromberger and Haffke, 'ICO Market Report 2018/2019 – Performance Analysis of 2018's Initial Coin Offerings' (December 2019), 13, available at: https://ssrn.com/abstract=3512125 (last accessed 21.1.2021).

[63] Fisch, 'Initial coin offerings (ICOs) to finance new ventures', (2019) 34 *Journal of Business Venturing*, 1 (2); Blemus and Guégan, 'Initial Crypto-Asset Offerings (ICOs), Tokenization and Corporate Governance' (April 2019), 8, available at https://papers.ssrn.com/sol3/papers.cfm?abstract_id=3350771 (last accessed 21.1.2021).

[64] Zetzsche, Buckley, Arner and Föhr, 'The ICO Gold Rush: It's a Scam, It's a Bubble, It's a Super Challenge for Regulators', (2019) 60(2) *Harvard International Law Journal*, 267 (277, Figure 3).

[65] Adhami, Giudici and Martinazzi, 'Why do businesses go crypto? An empirical analysis of Initial Coin Offerings', (2018) 100 *Journal of Economics and Business*, 64 (5 et seq., Table 3).

[66] Zetzsche, Buckley, Arner and Föhr, 'The ICO Gold Rush: It's a Scam, It's a Bubble, It's a Super Challenge for Regulators', (2019) 60(2) *Harvard International Law Journal*, 267 (277 et seq.).

Part A. Introduction

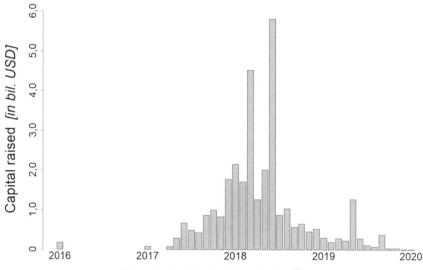

Figure 9: Capital raised through ICOs[67]

38 All in all, the market has grown enormously since mid-2017. While in 2016 a combined USD 250 million were raised, the **issuing volume** in 2017 was already around USD 6.5 billion[68] and rose to over USD 21.5 billion in 2018.[69] More than 95 % of the issue proceeds to date have been generated since June 2017.[70] The total volume issued during the period from January, 2016 to March, 2020 amounts to an estimated USD 32 billion (see also Figure 9);[71] an empirical study from 2019 even assumes that a total of more than USD 75 billion was raised by ICOs.[72]

39 The distribution of the (targeted) emission volumes provides a clear picture: While smaller ICOs (USD 1 million – 10 million) are quite common (18.1 %), the majority of issuances (41 %) are in the mid-size segment (USD 10 million – 100 million). Even large-volume issues (USD 100 million – USD 1 billion) are not uncommon (9.7 %), although 'mega-ICOs' (USD 1billion – USD 10 billion) have so far remained the absolute exception (0.9 %).[73] With regard to the number of

---

[67] CoinSchedule, own calculations.
[68] Haffke and Fromberger, 'ICO Market Report 2017. Performance Analysis of Initial Coin Offerings' (December 2018), 8, available at: https://ssrn.com/abstract=3309271 (last accessed 21.1.2021).
[69] CoinSchedule, 'Total Funds Raised per Month 2016, 2017, 2018' (December 2018), available at https://www.coinschedule.com/stats/Jan+01%2C+2018+to+Dec+31%2C+2018 (last accessed 21.1.2021).
[70] Similarly Zetzsche, Buckley, Arner and Föhr, 'The ICO Gold Rush: It's a Scam, It's a Bubble, It's a Super Challenge for Regulators', (2019) 60(2) *Harvard International Law Journal*, 267 (268 Fn. 3).
[71] CoinSchedule, 'Crypto Token Sales Market Statistics: All time' (March 2016), available at https://www.coinschedule.com/stats/Jan+01%2C+2016+to+Mar+27%2C+2019 (last accessed 15.5.2019); for the period 01/2017 – 03/2019, the block-chain analysis company Smith + Crown reports a similarly high total issue volume (USD 21.5 billion), see Smith + Crown, TOKEN SALE ACTIVITY TRACKER, available at https://www.smithandcrown.com/ico-tracker/ (last accessed 27.3.2018).
[72] Zetzsche, Buckley, Arner and Föhr, 'The ICO Gold Rush: It's a Scam, It's a Bubble, It's a Super Challenge for Regulators', (2019) 60(2) *Harvard International Law Journal*, 267 (268, 290 et seq.).
[73] Zetzsche, Buckley, Arner and Föhr, 'The ICO Gold Rush: It's a Scam, It's a Bubble, It's a Super Challenge for Regulators' (August 2018), available at: https://papers.ssrn.com/sol3/papers.cfm?abstract_id=3072298 (last accessed 21.1.2021). Note 1: In the empirical study by Zetzsche/Buckley/Arner/Föhr the (target) emission volume could not be determined for 28.2 % of the ICOs investigated. If one assumes a

§ 2. Economics of Crypto Assets

ICOs conducted, estimates range from approximately 1,250 to 3,000 and up to 5,320 emissions.[74]

The large number of ICOs and the impressive growth of the **primary market** in 2017 and 2018 contrasts with a disillusioning development of the **secondary market**:[75] While the market capitalisation of the issued tokens was still around USD 30 billion in March/April 2018,[76] it was only around USD 14 billion in March 2019.[77] Yet, the concrete values must be considered with caution given considerable price fluctuations (→ para. 8) within short time intervals. In light of the strong interim increase in total volume issued (spring 2018: < USD 10 billion;[78] March 2019: > USD 28 billion), the decline in market capitalisation is a clear indication that ICOs have not yet created long-lasting value in economic terms. Nevertheless, the considerable total volume of issues proves that the economic importance of the market for ICOs is not to be underestimated.[79]

40

2. Geographic Distribution

Approximately a third (34.6 %) of the ICOs were initiated from Europe (EU: 22.2 %) which is well ahead of Asia (17 %) and North America (14 %).[80] This is in

41

---

normal distribution for these cases, the dominance of medium-sized emissions (USD 10 million – 100 million) becomes even clearer. If only the ICOs with determinable emission volumes are considered (=71.8 % of the ICOs examined), the distribution is as follows: USD 1 million – 10 million: 25.2 %; USD 10 million – 100 million: 57.1 %; USD 100 million – 1 billion: 13.5 %; USD 1 billion – 10 billion: 1.2 %. Note 2: Issuing volumes of more than USD 1 billion have so far only been achieved by EOS (USD 4.198 billion) and Telegram (USD 1.7 billion), see CoinSchedule 'Top 10 Token Sales by Funds Raised', available at https://www.coinschedule.com/stats (last accessed 21.1.2021).

[74] Smith & Crown, 'Token Sale Activity Tracker, available at https://www.smithandcrown.com/ico-tracker/#methodology: 1249 (01/2017 – 03/2019) (last accessed 21.1.2021); Zetzsche, Buckley, Arner and Föhr, 'The ICO Gold Rush: It's a Scam, It's a Bubble, It's a Super Challenge for Regulators' (August 2018), available at: https://papers.ssrn.com/sol3/papers.cfm?abstract_id=3072298 (last accessed 21.1.2021); Zetzsche, Buckley, Arner and Föhr, 'The ICO Gold Rush: It's a Scam, It's a Bubble, It's a Super Challenge for Regulators', (2019) 60(2) *Harvard International Law Journal*, 267 (272).

[75] For a detailed analysis of the market price developments of crypto assets issued in the context of ICOs, see Haffke and Fromberger, 'ICO Market Report 2017. Performance Analysis of Initial Coin Offerings' (December 2018), 14 et seqq. available at: https://ssrn.com/abstract=3309271 (last accessed 21.1.2021); Fromberger and Haffke, 'ICO Market Report 2018/2019 – Performance Analysis of 2018's Initial Coin Offerings' (December 2019), 15 et seqq., available at: https://ssrn.com/abstract=3512125 (last accessed 21.1.2021).

[76] Zickgraf, 'Initial Coin Offerings – Ein Fall für das Kapitalmarktrecht? ', (2018) 9 *Die Aktiengesellschaft (AG)*, 293; Klöhn, Parhofer and Resas, 'Initial Coin Offerings (ICOs)', (2018) *Zeitschrift für Bankrecht und Bankwirtschaft (ZBB)*, 89, in each case with reference to figures from CoinMarketCap at the time.

[77] See for the so-called 'Circulating Supply': CoinMarketCap, 'Cryptocurrency Market Capitalizations', available at https://coinmarketcap.com/Token/views/all/ (last accessed 13.3.2019). In terms of 'Total Supply', this results in a significantly higher market capitalisation of over USD 84 billion, see *CoinMarketCap*, available at: https://coinmarketcap.com/Token/views/market-cap-by-total-supply/ (last accessed 13.3.2019). However, there is also a significant decline in 'Total Supply', as Rohr and Wright, 'Blockchain-Based Token Sales, Initial Coin Offerings and the Democratization of Public Capital Markets', (2019) 70(2) *Hastings Law Journal*, 463 (480 et seq.), in their study for January 2018, still report a market capitalization of USD 365 billion.

[78] See again: Klöhn, Parhofer and Resas, 'Initial Coin Offerings (ICOs)', (2018) *Zeitschrift für Bankrecht und Bankwirtschaft (ZBB)*, 89: approx. USD 8 billion by February 2018; Zickgraf, 'Initial Coin Offerings – Ein Fall für das Kapitalmarktrecht? ', (2018) 9 *Die Aktiengesellschaft (AG)*, 293: over USD 7 bn by the end of March 2018, both with further references.

[79] Similarly van Aubel, 'Initial Coin Offerings (ICOs)', in Habersack, Mülbert and Schlitt, *Unternehmensfinanzierung am Kapitalmarkt* (2019), 697, § 20 para. 1.

[80] Zetzsche, Buckley, Arner and Föhr, 'The ICO Gold Rush: It's a Scam, It's a Bubble, It's a Super Challenge for Regulators' (August 2018), available at: https://papers.ssrn.com/sol3/papers.cfm?abstract_

line with the global distribution of venues accepting crypto assets as a means of payment (→ para. 33 et seq.). However, when looking at the market capitalisation, the USA (1st place), as **country of origin** of the issuers, is clearly ahead of Singapore (2nd place), and China (3rd place). In June 2018, the combined market capitalisation of ICOs originating from the UK (4th place), Switzerland (5th place), and Germany (7th place) was not even half (approx. USD 7.6 bn) the market capitalisation of ICOs initiated from Singapore, China, and Hong Kong (approx. USD 16.3 bn), or of ICOs initiated from the USA (approx. USD 17.8 bn).[81]

3. Risks of Abuse

42 As a result of the rapid growth of Initial Coin Offerings, also their vulnerability to **abuse** has increased.[82] On the one hand, this is due to insufficient and sometimes incorrect information provided to investors in the **white papers**: In about two thirds (67.1 %) of the issues, the white papers did not contain a valid business address, and in a good fifth (20.47 %) of the ICOs examined, not even the company acting as issuer was named. In addition, just under a third (31.04 %) of the white papers did not make any statements about the initiators of the ICO and over two thirds (67.3 %) of the documents did not disclose the law applicable to the specific ICO.[83] In addition, central **investment information** (e.g. (maximum) number of tokens issued, vesting commitments, commitments to (un)modifiability of the Smart Contract) described in the white papers often deviate from the actual mechanisms implemented in the **Smart Contracts** (→ § 1 para. 62 et seqq.) associated to the respective ICO.[84]

43 Whether the missing and/or incorrect information is (aimed to be) deliberately used to the detriment of investors remains an open question. Estimates suspect that approximately 10 % of ICOs are to be classified as fraud (→ § 1 para. 82). In any case, an insufficient information base opens up numerous opportunities for the initiators to overreach investors. In addition, the current circumstances make it considerably more difficult for investors to enforce the law. The same scepticism is also warranted with regard to **pre-ICOs** (→ § 1 para. 84) that open up the opportunity for so-called 'pump and dump-schemes". Pre-ICOs were carried out for approximately 20 % of the ICOs prior to their public offering.[85] Overall, it can only be hoped that maturing market mechanisms and upcoming **monitoring practices** by supervisory authorities will lead to improvements and thus, decrease the vulnerability to abuse in the future.

---

id=3072298 (last accessed 21.1.2021). Note: The study was prepared in 2018, i.e. including the United Kingdom as a member of the European Union.

[81] Ibid.

[82] Similarly Klöhn, Parhofer and Resas, 'Initial Coin Offerings (ICOs)', (2018) *Zeitschrift für Bankrecht und Bankwirtschaft (ZBB)*, 89, which point to a blurring of 'innovation and hot air' in numerous offers; *see* also Langenbucher, 'European Securities Law – Are we in need of a new definition? A thought inspired by initial coin offerings', (2018) 2/3 *Revue trimestrielle de droit financier (RTDF)*, 40 (41).

[83] Zetzsche, Buckley, Arner and Föhr, 'The ICO Gold Rush: It's a Scam, It's a Bubble, It's a Super Challenge for Regulators' (August 2018), available at: https://papers.ssrn.com/sol3/papers.cfm?abstract_id=3072298 (last accessed 21.1.2021); *see* already here Behme and Zickgraf, 'Zivil- und gesellschaftsrechtliche Aspekte von Initial Coin Offerings (ICOs)', (2019) *Zeitschrift für die gesamte Privatrechtswissenschaft (ZfPW)*, 66 (72 Fn. 37).

[84] See, inter alia, Cohney, Hoffman, Sklaroff and Wishnick, 'Coin-Operated Capitalism', (2019) 119(3) *Columbia Law Review*, 591 (595, 610 et seqq., 635 et seqq., 640 et seqq.); Behme and Zickgraf, 'Zivil- und gesellschaftsrechtliche Aspekte von Initial Coin Offerings (ICOs)', (2019) *Zeitschrift für die gesamte Privatrechtswissenschaft (ZfPW)*, 66 (72 Fn. 37).

[85] Zetzsche, Buckley, Arner and Föhr, 'The ICO Gold Rush: It's a Scam, It's a Bubble, It's a Super Challenge for Regulators' (August 2018), available at: https://papers.ssrn.com/sol3/papers.cfm?abstract_id=3072298 (last accessed 21.1.2021).

C. Crypto Assets as a Complementary Currency

The central subject of the current economic discussion on crypto and especially currency tokens is the question of whether they are, in the classical sense, money or even a currency. Although the economic importance and implications of crypto assets are many times more diverse and go far beyond the **currency aspect**, this question is still the focus of scientific debate in this field.[86] This is mainly attributable to the predominant position of Bitcoin and to its associated intention of establishing a payment and currency system independent of any intermediary.[87]

To reflect the ongoing debate, the currency aspect of crypto assets will be discussed in detail in this section. In particular, it will be examined whether these tokens – commonly categorised as **currency tokens** (→ § 1 para. 70) – actually fulfil the **requirements for a currency** that are classically regarded as necessary from an economic perspective. To this end, first, the theoretical **monetary functions** are presented (→ para. 46 et seqq.), followed by an examination of the most important currency token Bitcoin in light of the outlined currency characteristics (→ para. 58 et seqq.). Based on this, further types of crypto or currency tokens, which are often summarised under the term Altcoins (→ § 1 para. 68), are discussed (→ para. 74 et seqq.). These usually attempt in different ways to implement the various characteristics of money and/or of currencies, which, as will be demonstrated below, are indeed not necessarily fulfilled by Bitcoin.

I. Characteristics of a Currency

1. Primary Monetary Functions

In monetary theory, a currency traditionally fulfils or should fulfil three basic functions, the so-called **primary monetary functions** (→ § 9 para. 6, 10 et seqq.):[88]
1. **Medium of exchange function**: A currency serves as a medium of exchange and enables or simplifies the exchange of goods and services.
2. **Store of value function**: A currency serves as a store of value and thus offers the possibility to retain a value over an indefinite period of time.
3. **Unit of account function**: A currency serves as a unit of account by which the value of a good or service can be expressed.

Many of the commonly used currencies today, such as the Euro, the US-Dollar, or even less common ones like the Danish Krone, meet each of these three monetary theoretical requirements. In most cases, the fulfilment of the primary monetary functions are limited on a regional level (for example in the case of the Danish Krone). However, in certain cases, such as the Euro or the US-Dollar, it is indeed possible to speak of a supra-regional

---

[86] Yermack, 'Is Bitcoin a Real Currency? An Economic Appraisal', in Lee and Chuen, *Handbook of Digital Currency, Bitcoin, Innovation, Financial Instruments, and Big Data*, (Academic Press, 2015), 32; Ammous, *The Bitcoin Standard: The Decentralized Alternative to Central Banking*, (2018), 167 et seq.

[87] See, inter alia, Nakamoto, 'Bitcoin: A Peer-to-Peer Electronic Cash System' (2008), available at: https://perma.cc/MU7N-AWPD (last accessed 21.1.2021).

[88] Bofinger, *Grundzüge der Volkswirtschaftslehre, Eine Einführung in die Wissenschaft*, (2013), 279 et seqq.; Ali, Barrdear, Clews and Southgate, 'Innovations in payment technologies and the emergence of digital currencies', (2014) 54(3) *Bank of England Quarterly Bulletin*, 276 (278); Richter, *Geldtheorie, Vorlesung auf der Grundlage der Allgemeinen Gleichgewichtstheorie und der Institutionenökonomik*, (1987), 103 et seqq.

or even **global acceptance** as a currency and of the corresponding primary monetary functions. Examples include the transaction settlements in global trade or the international investment and asset management.[89]

48 Besides well-known and currently used currencies, there are many other (historical) examples in which objects of various forms have fulfilled the outlined monetary functions over a limited period of time or to a certain extent and can therefore be classified as currency in a narrow, economic sense. Examples include cigarettes in prisoner-of-war camps during World War II or shells in Africa 4,000 years ago.[90]

2. Secondary Monetary Functions

49 Based on the three primary monetary functions (→ para. 46), it is possible to derive further properties of currencies, which are referred to as **secondary monetary functions**. On the one hand, these specify the characteristics of a currency in more detail, but are also in part necessary prerequisites for the fulfilment of the primary monetary functions. In addition, the secondary monetary functions allow for a even more precise evaluation of crypto assets with regard to the currency issue.

50 In order for a currency to be used as a means of payment, it is advantageous in the short term and indispensable in the long term to be easy to handle and highly transportable. This is particularly evident for transactions involving the exchange of large amounts or a large quantity of the currency. For transactions that take place over long distances, ease of handling and transportability are also crucial.

51 Another necessary precondition – at least at a local or regional level – is a widespread acceptance of the currency in commerce and, more generally, among the population. Only if the currency is accepted at a sufficient number of locations in exchange for goods, services, or for the settlement of debts, it can ultimately fulfil its function as a means of payment. This is a phenomenon that is classically described in economics as a (positive) network externality or **network effect**:[91] The larger the (currency) network, the greater the benefit for all network participants. Only when there is a sufficient number of network participants[92] – in the case of a currency, the number of persons and companies that accept it – does the currency satisfy the prerequisite to act as a means of exchange and payment as described above.

52 In addition to physical or digital requirements for storage and durability, a currency must also show a certain degree of price stability to fulfil the store of value function. The value of the currency should therefore fluctuate only to a certain extent over time and should only exhibit slight inflationary (fall in value and thus decrease in the purchasing power of the currency) or deflationary (rise in value and thus increase in the purchasing power of the currency) tendencies. At the core of the store of value function is the confidence of the population that the future purchasing power of a currency will be largely the same as today's. If the store of value function is not fulfilled, as is the case, for example, in periods of **hyperinflation**, confidence in a currency can quickly erode. This will inevitably have the consequence that the other

---

[89] See Bank for International Settlements, 'Triennial Central Bank Survey, Foreign exchange turnover in April 2019' (April 2019), 4 (5 et seqq.), available at: https://www.bis.org/statistics/rpfx19_fx.pdf (last accessed 21.1.2021).

[90] Radford, 'The Economic Organisation of a P.O.W. Camp', (1945) 12(48) *Economica*, 189 (191); Harari, *Money*, (2018), 7.

[91] Shy, *The Economics of Network Industries*, (2001), 3, (187 et seqq.); Katz and Shapiro, 'Technology adoption in the presence of network externalities', (1986) 94(4) *Journal of Political Economy*, 822 (823 et seqq.).

[92] The critical network size for this can be considerable; see Shy, *The Economics of Network Industries* (2001), 104, 113.

two monetary functions – medium of exchange and unit of account – will also only be fulfilled to a limited extent.

However, price stability is not only important for the store of value function. It also plays an important role in the fulfilment of the unit of account function. Indeed, if a price instability of the currency makes it necessary to make frequent adjustments to displayed prices in order to ensure an accurate representation of value, it makes only limited sense to display the prices of products and services in units of this currency. The usefulness of displaying prices in this very currency is also questionable if the currency is not widely used and enjoys only limited acceptance. 53

In addition to the factors of high acceptance and price stability, the **fungibility** of a currency is also a necessary prerequisite for fulfilling the value measurement function. In this context fungibility means the property that any physical or digital unit of a currency corresponds to any other unit of the same currency that is equal in nominal value. This particularly implies that differences in the nature of specific currency units, such as age or previous owners, have no effect on their value.[93] In other words, a fungible currency is **memoryless**. If a currency is not fungible, its use as a unit of account involves considerable additional effort. For example, to determine the value of a given set of currency units, one would not only have to count the amount of the given currency units, but one would also have to identify the additional value-determining dimensions and take them into account accordingly. Since this involves considerable **search and transaction costs**, a currency whose fungibility cannot be guaranteed is only to a very limited extent suitable for use as a unit of account or for measuring the value of other objects.[94] 54

Besides the secondary monetary functions there are further characteristics which must be regarded as, at least partly necessary prerequisites for the (simultaneous) fulfilment of several monetary functions. For example, a **double or multiple spending** of a currency unit should not be possible. It must therefore be ensured that the same monetary unit can only be used in a single transaction and not simultaneously for several transactions with possibly different parties. In addition, the **counterfeit protection** of a currency must also be guaranteed. If both of these requirements were not met to a large extent, a currency could in the long run fulfil neither its store of value nor its medium of exchange function. 55

As of today, in many cases[95] a currency has no or only a very low underlying (material) value, which is far from its nominal value. Most currencies are thus **fiat money**.[96] The value of a fiat currency is derived purely from the benefits created by the monetary functions described above. Conversely, this means that a currency does not necessarily have to have an **intrinsic value** in order to fulfil the monetary functions. 56

---

[93] Boldly speaking, the fungibility of a currency means that, for example in the case of the euro, every euro coin has the same purchasing power, regardless of age, condition (at least to the extent that it is still recognisable), or former owners of the coin.

[94] Moreover, a currency that is not fungible would also have very limited use as a means of payment or exchange.

[95] Historically, this was not always the case: Items used as currency, had a material value equal to that of the currency; see Harari, *Money* (2018), 13 et seq.
The gold standard, which was used inter alia before World War I and during the Bretton Woods currency regime, is also an example of a period in which currencies had an inherent value; see Eichengreen, *Globalizing Capital: A History of the International Monetary System* (2019), 53 et seqq., 79 et seqq.

[96] Fiat money, or fiat currency, is money which, unlike commodity money such as gold or silver, has no intrinsic value but still fulfils the three monetary functions. Moreover, unlike it is the case for monetary regimes such as the gold standard, fiat money does not involve a claim on gold or on other metals; see Mankiw, *Macroeconomics* (2010), 81 et seqq.

57 With this in mind, it is at first sight all the more surprising that societies worldwide are able to coordinate on a regional or even on a supra-national level to use common currencies. However, this can be attributed to state intervention and, in particular, to the official designation of a currency that fulfils the necessary criteria mentioned above as (un)restricted **legal tender**. The determination as legal tender[97] requires that, unless otherwise agreed, each creditor of a monetary claim[98] must accept from the debtor – as fulfillment of the claim – the equivalent in the respective currency that corresponds to the amount of the claim (see → § 13 para. 7).[99] At least to a certain extent, these legal measures induce a widespread acceptance of the currency among the population. Only this very acceptance makes the de facto adaptation of a currency as a medium of exchange and a means of payment possible (→ para. 46).

II. Currency Characteristics of Crypto Assets

58 Mainly based on the previously gained insights into the current state of crypto assets (→ para. 6 et seqq.), the following section examines, from an economic perspective, the extent to which crypto assets fulfil the three basic monetary functions (→ para. 46) and its downstream characteristics, i.e. the secondary monetary functions (→ para. 49 et seqq.). Special focus is again placed on Bitcoin. Bitcoin is not only still the most important crypto token in terms of market value (→ Table 1), but due to its pioneering role it is also the most widely known and widely accepted crypto token, especially among currency tokens (→ Figure 4). In view of these facts, it can be argued without further ado that from a verification of the monetary theoretical requirements for the special case of Bitcoin, generally valid statements regarding the monetary functions of most other crypto assets can be derived. To a certain extent, Bitcoin thus takes on the role of the supremum, i.e. the smallest upper bound, of the set of crypto assets.

59 Following the analysis of the monetary functions for Bitcoin, further (crypto) tokens will also be examined in more detail (→ para. 74 et seqq.). These usually try to address, in different ways, the problems that Bitcoin exhibits with respect to the monetary functions by offering different approaches to overcome the very same.

60 Bitcoin and other crypto assets do not embody the first attempt to create a – in the sense of Friedrich A. Hayek[100] – **private currency**, which is exclusively digital in nature and exists parallel to respective state currency system.[101] However, Bitcoin differs from previous attempts to establish a digital currency in that there is no central counterparty that is responsible for the currency or can significantly influence it. As

---

[97] See e.g., § 14 para. 1 S. 2 of the law for the German Federal Bank (BbankG) and § 5103, Chapter 51, Title 31 of the law for the Bank of the United States of America.

[98] This also applies to a state which, in the role as a creditor, itself accepts the currency, in particular to settle tax debts. It is precisely this fact that leads economists like Paul Krugman to say '[…] fiat currencies have underlying value because men with guns say they do."; see Krugman, 'Transaction Costs and Tethers: Why I'm a Crypto Skeptic' (July 2018), available at https://www.nytimes.com/2018/07/31/opinion/transaction-costs-and-tethers-why-im-a-crypto-skeptic.html (last accessed 27.4.2019).

[99] See Deutsche Bundesbank, 'Geld und Geldpolitik', available at https://www.bundesbank.de/de/publikationen/schule-und-bildung/geld-und-geldpolitik-606038 (last accessed 20.1.2020).

[100] Cf. Hayek, *The Denationalisation of Money: The Argument Refined* (1978), 46 et seqq.; White, 'The Market for Cryptocurrencies', (2015) 35(2) *Cato Journal*, 383 (383, 386 et seq.).

[101] Examples of private digital currency systems are the Linden Dollar, available at https://secondlife.com/currency/ (last accessed 3.2.2019) or the World of Warcraft (WoW) gold, available at https://us.shop.battle.net/en-us/product/world-of-warcraft-token (last accessed 3.2.2019); Examples of private currency systems that are not (exclusively) digital include local currencies such as the Chiemgauer, available at https://www.chiemgauer.info (last accessed 13.5.2019) or the Calgary dollar, available at http://www.calgarydollars.ca/ (last accessed 13.5.2019).

already described before (→ § 1 para. 1), it is a **decentralized system**. This ultimately distinguishes Bitcoin not only from all previous digital currencies of private origin, but also from national currencies for which the central banks and/or the states themselves are responsible. Ultimately, however, this is precisely the basic idea and, from an economic perspective, the attraction of Bitcoin and the Bitcoin blockchain: A (monetary) system without a central counterparty or institution – neither state nor private – which, at least theoretically, can easily change the underlying rules (here: source code) of the system.

1. Currency Properties of Bitcoin

In order to fulfil its function as a medium of exchange and thus as a means of payment, widespread acceptance of Bitcoin is necessary. Henceforth, Bitcoin should not only be offered by (online) stores and companies as a possible means of payment, but should also accordingly be used by the population for paying their purchases. There are various companies scattered over the globe that (theoretically) accept Bitcoin as an additional means of payment (→ para. 32 et seq.).[102] However, at the same time it must be noted that this payment option is only used to a very limited extent by customers.[103] The reasons for this are manifold and include, among others, the generally complex manageability of Bitcoin transactions,[104] the relatively high transaction costs for micropayments and medium-sized transaction amounts (→ para. 21), as well as the – compared to other payment methods – lengthy duration for a transaction to be confirmed on the blockchain.[105] All these aspects significantly impede the use of Bitcoin for everyday payment transactions. 61

Although it generally seems that Bitcoin fails to serve as a medium of exchange and a means of payment, there are some noteworthy exceptions of markets where Bitcoin prevails indeed as a means of payment. Particularly, participants on the (global) online **black market**, also known as **Darknet**,[106] use, or at least used, Bitcoin in its function as an unregulated and pseudonymous payment system for settling illegal activities.[107] In 2017, approximately 30 % of all Bitcoin transactions could be associated with illegal activities.[108] On average, the parties involved in these illicit transactions usually transfer significantly more often, yet significantly less Bitcoins to a conspicuously larger number of counterparties.[109] Hence, due to its characteristics, Bitcoin is one of the payment methods of choice, especially on the black market (→ § 12 para. 2 et seqq.). 62

---

[102] Interestingly, among these companies that accept Bitcoin as payment for their products and services, none of the so-called 'Four Horsemen' Amazon, Apple, Facebook, and Google (cf. Galloway The Four 2) can be found; see *Amazon*, available at: https://www.amazon.com/gp/help/customer/display.html?nodeId=201132710; *Apple*, available at: https://www.apple.com/shop/help/payments; *Facebook*, available at: https://www.facebook.com/business/help/212763688755026, *Google*, available at: https://support.google.com/google-ads/answer/2375433 (last accessed 21.1.2021).

[103] Athey, Parashkevov, Sarukkai and Xia, 'Bitcoin Pricing, Adoption, and Usage: Theory and Evidence' (August 2016), 30, available at: https://siepr.stanford.edu/sites/default/files/publications/17-033_1.pdf (last accessed 21.1.2021).

[104] To be able to pay with Bitcoin, a wallet must first be opened.

[105] As described before (→ para. 20), the median time until a transaction is confirmed in the blockchain lies between 10 and 15 minutes.

[106] E.g. Martin, *Drugs on the dark net: How cryptomarkets are transforming the global trade in illicit drugs*, (2014), 1 et seqq.

[107] Foley, Karlsen and Putniņš, 'Sex, Drugs, and Bitcoin: How Much Illegal Activity Is Financed through Cryptocurrencies?', (2019) 32(5) *The Review of Financial Studies*, 1798 (1798 et seqq., 1847 et seq.).

[108] From 2009 to 2017, an average of more than 46 % of transactions (peak in 2012/13 with more than 80 % of transactions) can be attributed to illegal activities, see ibid, 1800.

[109] Ibid, 1833.

63 The blockchain technology on which Bitcoin and many other crypto assets are based is by definition a **digital memory** (→ § 1 para. 1), whose storage function is particularly pronounced due to its decentralized nature. Thus, crypto tokens in general and Bitcoin in particular fulfil the necessary requirements regarding **storage** and **durability**. In contrast or parallel to conventional (fiat) currencies, the decisive question remains whether crypto assets can retain their value over longer periods of time. Various examples, including also more recent ones, impressively illustrate that in general even government legitimated (fiat) currencies not necessarily fulfil the storage of value function. Examples include the cases of the Zimbabwe Dollar, the Venezuelan Bolívar, or the Argentine Peso. Due to high rates of inflation and in some cases even showing hyperinflationary tendencies, these state currencies only fulfil the function of value-preservation to a very limited extent.[110] This has led to a high capital flight for all mentioned currencies and, despite their state designation as legal tender, to a very limited use of the currency as means of exchange and payment

64 A similar situation can also be observed for crypto assets like Bitcoin. Although Bitcoin has experienced an exponential increase in value since its introduction, it is however also associated with strong temporary losses in value (→ Figure 1). As a result, the price volatility of Bitcoin is very high (→ Figure 1) and hence, the storage of value function is only satisfied at a very limited scope.[111] The very same conclusion can be reached when analysing Bitcoin in the light of the literature on speculative bubbles (→ para. 12 et seqq.). Nevertheless, Bitcoin and other crypto assets are increasingly being viewed as an **investment** opportunity or even as a separate asset class.[112] This generally suggests that the store of value function and the associated possible shift in consumption and purchasing power to future points in time is temporarily and to a certain extent fulfilled or, at least, by the respective investors presumed to be fulfilled.

65 The high price volatility of Bitcoin serves also as a strong argument against its use as a **numéraire**, as this would require frequent price adjustments for merchants and companies. This also explains that even companies that accept Bitcoin as a possible means of payment continue to quote prices (exclusively) in their respective local currency or in more common currencies such as the US-Dollar or the Euro.[113] The existence of payment processors for transactions with Bitcoin, such as Bitpay,[114] alone shows that under normal circumstances Bitcoin is not used as a unit of account. However, there are certain exceptions: On the former Darknet trading site **Silk Road**, Bitcoin has acted both as a means of payment and as a unit of account.[115] In addition,

---

[110] The exact reasons for the emergence of the respective currency crises differ considerably. For a more detailed analysis, *see* Dachevsky and Kornblihtt, 'The reproduction and crisis of capitalism in Venezuela under Chavismo', (2017) 44(1) *Latin American Perspectives*, 78 (78 et seqq., 88 et seqq.).

[111] This applies even more to many of the other crypto assets due to their significantly higher volatilities.

[112] Bouri, Molnár, Azzi, Roubaud and Hagfors, 'On the hedge and safe haven properties of Bitcoin: Is it really more than a diversifier?', (2017) 20 *Finance Research Letters*, 192 (193, 196 et seqq.); Yermack, 'Is Bitcoin a Real Currency? An Economic Appraisal', in Lee and Chuen, *Handbook of Digital Currency, Bitcoin, Innovation, Financial Instruments, and Big Data*, (Academic Press, 2015), 35 Fn. 2.

[113] An unrepresentative, international analysis of companies listed on coinmap.org by the author has shown that none of the companies considered uses Bitcoin as a unit of account or unit of value. *See* also Ali, Barrdear, Clews and Southgate, 'Innovations in payment technologies and the emergence of digital currencies', (2014) 54(3) *Bank of England Quarterly Bulletin*, 276 (280).

[114] See White, 'The Market for Cryptocurrencies', (2015) 35(2) *Cato Journal*, 383 (385); Bitpay, available at: https://bitpay.com/, (last accessed 21.1.2021).

[115] See inter alia Foley, Karlsen and Putniņš, 'Sex, Drugs, and Bitcoin: How Much Illegal Activity Is Financed through Cryptocurrencies?', (2019) 32(5) *The Review of Financial Studies*, 1798 (1799).

on the market for crypto assets and especially on **crypto exchanges**, a large proportion of other tokens are also traded and/or quoted with Bitcoin as numéraire.[116]

In contrast, the fungibility of Bitcoin is, due to the technical characteristics of the blockchain, not given. In theory, different Bitcoins do have the same value. However, the information stored on the blockchain allows the entire history of a Bitcoin to be traced back (→ § 1 para. 4 et seqq., 102 et seqq.). Hence, Bitcoins that are, for example, associated to **illegal activities** can be identified and, at least theoretically, be confiscated by appropriate governmental authorities, even if the current owners of the Bitcoins have no connection with the alleged offence. Alternatively, crypto exchanges may attempt or even be forced to ban these **'dirty' Bitcoins** from being traded at the exchange (→ § 1 para. 104).[117] Since the association with illegal activities is much more likely for older Bitcoins,[118] the market will price these accordingly and the value of a Bitcoin will decline as the frequency of transactions and age of the Bitcoin increases. This violates the condition of fungibility which, due to the above-mentioned interrelationships, would ultimately result in high efficiency losses when using Bitcoin as a unit of account.[119] 66

At the same time, both double spending and counterfeiting of Bitcoins can virtually be excluded due to the technical design of the underlying blockchain technology and the employed proof-of-work consensus mechanism. This precisely constitutes the technological innovation of Bitcoin. Indeed, it was, ceteris paribus, the proof-of-work consensus mechanism which made it possible in the first place to establish some form of a digital currency in a decentralized system, without the necessity of a reputable central institution or of a trustworthy third party. 67

Overall, Bitcoin and cryptographic tokens feature in general the basic technical prerequisites of a (digital) currency in terms of counterfeit protection and the provision of a solution to the **double spending problem**. However, the further necessary and sufficient economic requirements for a currency are only met to a certain extent.[120] In particular, the medium of exchange and the unit of account functions prove to be challenges that are difficult to overcome at present. 68

2. Payment Transaction System

Even if crypto assets are currently not fully eligible as money from an economic point of view, they as well as the underlying blockchain technology form the basis for a fully, decentrally organized, international **payment system**[121] that operates completely independently of a trustworthy central third party or institution, e.g. a central bank, and 69

---

[116] Ammous, *The Bitcoin Standard: The Decentralized Alternative to Central Banking* (2018), 212 et seq.

[117] Cermak, 'Can Bitcoin Become a Viable Alternative to Fiat Currencies? An Empirical Analysis of Bitcoin's Volatility Based on a GARCH Model' (May 2017), available at: https://papers.ssrn.com/sol3/papers.cfm?abstract_id=2961405 (last accessed 21.1.2021).

[118] It is not only the age of a Bitcoin and thus the purely statistically higher probability of the existence of illegal transactions that plays a role here, but also the fact that Bitcoins were initially used especially for transactions in the darknet etc. See Foley, Karlsen and Putniņš, 'Sex, Drugs, and Bitcoin: How Much Illegal Activity Is Financed through Cryptocurrencies?', (2019) 32(5) *The Review of Financial Studies*, 1798 (1799, 1805).

[119] Cermak, 'Can Bitcoin Become a Viable Alternative to Fiat Currencies? An Empirical Analysis of Bitcoin's Volatility Based on a GARCH Model' (May 2017), 25–28, available at: https://papers.ssrn.com/sol3/papers.cfm?abstract_id=2961405 (last accessed 21.1.2021).

[120] This represents a purely economic evaluation of crypto assets and especially of Bitcoin against the background of the monetary functions. For a legal assessment refer to (→ § 9 paras. 7 et seqq., 13 et seqq., 34 et seq.).

[121] The tasks of a payment transaction system comprise the clearing and settlement of payment orders. See Gabler Wirtschaftslexikon Zahlungsverkehrssystem, available at https://wirtschaftslexikon.gabler.de/definition/zahlungsverkehrssystem-51166/version-274368 (last accessed 20.12.2019).

Part A. Introduction

without additional intermediaries such as commercial banks.[122] Instead, the blockchain technology solves the above mentioned double-spending problem – a crucial premise for a functioning payment system – by means of **cryptographic consensus mechanisms** (→ § 1 para. 28 et seqq.).[123]

70 Unlike existing payment systems, such as TARGET2 and Fedwire, or the payment and money transfer systems of private providers, such as paydirekt, PayPal, and Western Union, a payment system based on cryptographic tokens, such as Bitcoin, and on the blockchain technology is independent of any central provider, either public or private. This means that users do not need to trust **intermediaries** or a **central counterparty**. In conventional payment systems this is indispensable.

71 In addition, a payment system based on the blockchain technology is not exposed to the **credit and liquidity risks** normally inherent in existing systems.[124] The decentralised organisation of the system also spreads the operational risk over a large number of nodes (→ § 1 para. 7 et seqq.), which makes a system failure virtually impossible.[125] In terms of financial stability, this is certainly to be welcomed. In return, however, the risk of system-wide fraud increases, for example in the form of a 51 %-attack.[126]

72 Another difference between conventional payment systems and the Bitcoin blockchain or other crypto token systems is that the latter requires only an access to the internet to be used for carrying out payments. Thus, it is a location-independent payment system (compared to Western Union) for which the possession of a bank account is not mandatory (compared to TARGET2 or PayPal). Particularly for the population in developing countries where access to (standard) financial services remains difficult, crypto token based payment systems can provide the opportunity to (intern-)nationally transfer money. It is therefore not surprising that the Bitcoin system is used, for example, by migrants, to transfer **remittances** to their families and friends in their respective countries of origin.[127] This is also facilitated by the significantly lower transaction fees of the Bitcoin system compared to the fees charged by the usual payment providers (→ para. 25 et seq.).

73 In summary, it can be concluded that crypto assets do not fulfil the classical monetary functions (→ paras. 46, 58 et seqq.). Yet, the blockchain technology enables the creation of a decentralised payment and transaction system which has several advantages over existing systems, including but not being limited to the independence from central (third-party) providers or to more favourable transaction fees (→ para. 21 et seqq.).[128] It can thus be argued that the originary benefit of Bitcoin is to be derived from the provision of an international payment system that is independent of a central third party. From a theoretical economic point of view, it is only this very benefit that justifies a positive valuation of and the observed (high) market prices of Bitcoin and other crypto assets.[129]

---

[122] Ali, Barrdear, Clews and Southgate, 'Innovations in payment technologies and the emergence of digital currencies', (2014) 54(3) *Bank of England Quarterly Bulletin*, 262 (267 et seqq.).

[123] Ibid, 267, 270.

[124] Ibid, 270 et seq.; Finan, Lasaosa and Sunderland, 'Tiering in CHAPS', (2013) 53(4) *Bank of England Quarterly Bulletin*, 371 (373).

[125] Ali, Barrdear, Clews and Southgate, 'Innovations in payment technologies and the emergence of digital currencies', (2014) 54(3) *Bank of England Quarterly Bulletin*, 262 (271).

[126] In a 51 % attack, an attempt is made to raise more than half of the hash rate, which enables the cancellation of already confirmed transactions and thus, double spending.

[127] Vigna and Casey, *The Age of Cryptocurrency: How Bitcoin and the Blockchain Are Challenging the Global Economic Order* (2016), 210 et seqq.

[128] Ali, Barrdear, Clews and Southgate, 'Innovations in payment technologies and the emergence of digital currencies', (2014) 54(3) *Bank of England Quarterly Bulletin*, 262 (272) come to a similar conclusion.

[129] Mises, *Theorie des Geldes und der Umlaufmittel* (1912), 93 et seqq.

3. Further Tokens, Stable Coins

In addition to Bitcoin, there are many other tokens,[130] some of which have been initiated as direct competitors to Bitcoin, others for different reasons and with a wide variety of objectives. These (crypto) tokens[131] are based either on their own or on an already existing blockchain (→ § 1 para. 83).[132] For monetary policy purposes, the tokens that attempt to solve the above-mentioned economic problems of Bitcoin with regard to the monetary functions (→ para. 61 et seqq.) are of primary interest. 74

This applies in particular to so-called **stable coins** (→ § 1 para. 76 and § 9 para. 36).[133] The intended goal of stable coins is to reduce the high price volatility observed for Bitcoin and other crypto assets, as this high volatility is considered the main obstacle to a widespread application and use as means of payment (→ paras. 8, 64). Similar to the gold standard or the dollar standard adopted as part of the Bretton Woods Agreement,[134] a **fixed exchange rate** is tried to be established between the stable coin and a specific anchor currency,[135] in most cases the US dollar.[136] The most prominent representative of stable coins is the US Dollar Tether (USDT). 75

Stable coins largely eliminate price volatility by agreeing on and enforcing a fixed exchange rate. However, this requires a central, trustworthy third party to ensure that the fixed exchange rate is maintained[137] or, comparable to a central bank, to restore it, if necessary, using suitable **market interventions**.[138] In most cases, this role is reserved for the initiator of the stable coin. However, this obviously contradicts the very idea of a decentralised currency independent of a trustworthy counterparty. Moreover, by fixing the stable coin to a national currency as well as fully backing it by the same currency (e.g. as it is presumably the case for the US Dollar Tether), the monetary policy of the responsible central bank is imported one-to-one into the stable coin system. Again, this clearly contradicts the basic idea behind Bitcoin.[139] In fact, since the providers of currency backed stable coins are usually private companies, there is also a **counterparty default risk** that should at no circumstances be underestimated.[140] 76

---

[130] *CoinMarketCap*, for example, lists, as of April 21, 2021, 9,420 different tokens with a total market capitalization of USD 2.04 trillion; cf. *CoinMarketCap*, available at https://coinmarketcap.com/all/views/all/ (last accessed 21.4.2020).

[131] Not every token is automatically a crypto asset based on cryptographic approaches and technologies.

[132] For an overview of other token types *see* Bonneau, Miller, Clark, Narayanan, Kroll and Felten, 'SoK: Research Perspectives and Challenges for Bitcoin and Cryptocurrencies', 2015 *IEEE Symposium on Security and Privacy*, 113 et seqq.; Ong, Lee, Li and Lee, 'Evaluating the Potential of Alternative Cryptocurrencies', in Lee and Chuen, *Handbook of Digital Currency, Bitcoin, Innovation, Financial Instruments, and Big Data* (Acedemic Press, 2015), 83 et seqq.

[133] A categorisation of stable coins can be found in Senner and Sornette, 'The Holy Grail of Crypto Currencies: Ready to Replace Fiat Money? ', (2019) 53(4) *Journal of Economic Issues*, 966 (976 et seqq.).

[134] The US-Dollar was again tied to gold at a fixed exchange rate; *see* McKinnon, *The Rules of the Game, International Money and Exchange Rates*, (1996), 53.

[135] However, it does not necessarily have to be an already existing national currency. Alternatively, other crypto assets as well as securities (also indices), or commodities are also conceivable.

[136] Eichengreen, *Globalizing Capital: A History of the International Monetary System* (2019), 53 et seqq., 79 et seqq.; Richter, *Geldtheorie, Vorlesung auf der Grundlage der Allgemeinen Gleichgewichtstheorie und der Institutionenökonomik* (1987), 181, 282.

[137] This is achieved by hedging the issued quantity of stable coins with an identical quantity of the anchor currency.

[138] Senner and Sornette, 'The Holy Grail of Crypto Currencies: Ready to Replace Fiat Money? ', (2019) 53(4) *Journal of Economic Issues*, 966 (978).

[139] *See* p2pfoundation, available at: p2pfoundation.ning.com/forum/topics/bitcoin-open-source (last accessed 21.1.2021).

[140] Senner and Sornette, 'The Holy Grail of Crypto Currencies: Ready to Replace Fiat Money? ', (2019) 53(4) *Journal of Economic Issues*, 966 (979).

77 Although there are many further tokens that show very promising approaches to fulfilling the monetary functions – for example tokens with an **algorithmic money supply** control.[141] Yet, these are all only of minor or even of no importance for the overall crypto asset market. Interested readers may nonetheless be referred to the corresponding literature.[142]

D. Crypto Assets Beyond the Currency Issue

78 Even if the economic debate on crypto assets is mainly dominated by the currency aspect, it is, from an economic perspective, still helpful to analyse the facets of crypto assets that go beyond this topic. For this reason, the remaining remarks will focus on the implications and consequences of the proof-of-work consensus mechanism that lies at the heart of the blockchain technology: the **overinvestment** on the part of the miners (→ para. 83 et seq.) and the high **energy consumption** that results from the process of mining (→ para. 85 et seqq.).

I. Resource Allocation and Negative Externalities

79 Since the creation of Bitcoin in 2008, the number of Full Nodes in the Bitcoin blockchain has changed quite dramatically: temporarily to over 210,000 Full Nodes, of which were around 18,000 so-called Listening/Super Nodes[143] (January 2018), to 55,000 Full Nodes and 6,000 Listening/Super Nodes in October 2019, back up to 85,000 Full Nodes and 7,000 Listening/Super Nodes in April 2021.[144] Especially due to the enormous price increases (→ para. 8) in recent years, mining of Bitcoin and other crypto assets has become a worthwhile global industry, with estimated revenues in 2019 of EUR 4.70 billion (revenues in 2018: EUR 4.74 billion).[145]

80 As a direct consequence, the demand for high performance (special) hardware, such as ASIC miners,[146] which are indispensable for successful mining, as well as the energy consumption required to run this hardware have increased exponentially.[147] Based on such developments, two economically relevant questions instantly arise:

---

[141] For example, for Basis (formerly Basecoin) an algorithm for controlling the money supply was planned before the project was discontinued due to the threat of regulation. Cf. Al-Naji, Chen and Diao, 'Basis: A Price-Stable Cryptocurrency with an Algorithmic Central Bank' (June 2018), 10 et seqq., available at: https://www.basis.io/basis_whitepaper_en.pdf (last accessed 22.1.2021).

[142] See for example Bonneau, Miller, Clark, Narayanan, Kroll and Felten, 'SoK: Research Perspectives and Challenges for Bitcoin and Cryptocurrencies', 2015 *IEEE Symposium on Security and Privacy*, 114 et seqq.; Ong, Lee, Li and Lee, 'Evaluating the Potential of Alternative Cryptocurrencies', in Lee and Chuen, *Handbook of Digital Currency, Bitcoin, Innovation, Financial Instruments, and Big Data* (Acedemic Press, 2015), 83 et seqq.; Senner and Sornette, 'The Holy Grail of Crypto Currencies: Ready to Replace Fiat Money? ', (2019) 53(4) *Journal of Economic Issues*, 966 (973 et seqq.).

[143] For the difference between a Full Node and a Listening/Super Node *see Hackernoon*, available at https://hackernoon.com/lets-talk-about-bitcoin-nodes-e9502193198c (last accessed 21.1.2021).

[144] *Dashjr*, available at: http://luke.dashjr.org/programs/bitcoin/files/charts/historical-dygraph.html (last accessed 13.4.2021); *Coin Dance*, available at: https://coin.dance/nodes/core (last accessed 13.4.2021).

[145] Own calculations based on data from the St. Louis Fed (FRED) and Bendiksen and Gibbons, 'The Bitcoin Mining Network – Trends, Composition, Average Creation Cost, Electricity Consumption & Sources' (December 2019), available at: https://coinsharesgroup.com/research/bitcoin-mining-network-december-2019 (last accessed 21.1.2021).

[146] ASICs stands for Application-Specific Integrated Circuits, *see also* Narayanan, Bonneau, Felten, Miller and Goldfeder, *Bitcoin and cryptocurrency technologies: A comprehensive introduction* (2016), 248 et seq.

[147] Depending on the studies used, energy consumption in 2018 is estimated at 2,550 to 12,080 MW (2017: 100–1,727 MW); see on this Stoll, Klaassen and Gallersdörfer, 'The Carbon Footprint of Bitcoin', (2019) 3(7) *Joule*, 1647 (1649 Figure 1).

§ 2. Economics of Crypto Assets

1. Does the mining of crypto assets constitute an **efficient allocation** of resources?
2. Does the mining of crypto assets generate **negative externalities**?[148]

1. Resource Consumption

To answer the question of efficient resource allocation in a non-trivial manner, it must first be assumed that Bitcoin and other blockchain based crypto assets are, in some way or another, useful systems. Since in particular the Bitcoin blockchain has established a decentralized payment and transaction system that shows certain advantages (→ para. 69 et seqq.) over existing systems and may be put to use accordingly (→ para. 72 et seq.), in the following it is assumed that these systems do make sense and thus, their existence is desirable.[149]

In essence, Bitcoins mining is a **contest** in which miners (contest participants) try to solve an essentially simple and meaningless cryptographic problem (lottery) as quickly as possible (→§ 1 para. 38 et seq.). Whoever solves the problem first will be rewarded with the right to add the next block to the existing blockchain, which is accompanied by the receipt of a certain amount of Bitcoins[150] (contest prize) that is known beforehand. However, all other miners who also participated in the contest for this specific block will be left empty-handed.[151] The probability of solving the cryptographic problem can be increased by investing in appropriate hardware (costly investment to increase the probability of winning). In standard economic literature this type of competition is referred to as **Tullock contest**[152] or lottery contest.[153]

However, the Tullock contest has a fundamental economic problem: Assuming common knowledge among participants, in theory a **Nash equilibrium** exists, i.e. there is a situation in which the contest participants have no (monetary) incentive to unilaterally deviate from their chosen strategies (Nash strategies) that determine the outcome of the contest.[154] However, experimental studies show that participants, to supposedly increase their winning probability, consistently tend to invest amounts that are far too high, i.e. that exceed the size of investments as specified by the Nash strategy.[155] This overinvestment is not only inefficient in terms of overall welfare, but

81

82

83

---

[148] Or to put it another way: Does the mining of Bitcoins and other crypto assets result in social costs that do not have to be borne by the Miners?
[149] It is indeed questionable whether it is necessary and reasonable to build hardware worldwide and operate it with the corresponding energy expenditure in order to solve redundant cryptographic problems. However, this is difficult to answer, as this question can ultimately be traced back to the fundamental question of the sense and necessity of the Bitcoin system. For this reason, it is pointed to the general market mechanism (cf. Bofinger Grundzüge der Volkswirtschaftslehre 64, 258) which ensures – at least if it is assumed that there is no inherent market failure – that it must be economically viable, at least in the long run, for companies and private individuals involved in the mining of Bitcoins and other crypto assets to exert the necessary effort.
[150] The number of Bitcoins received by the miner consists of the coinbase and transaction costs (→ para. 22).
[151] Thum, 'Die ökonomischen Kosten des Bitcoin-Mining', (2018) 71(2) *ifo Schnelldienst*, 18 (18).
[152] Tullock, 'Efficient Rent Seeking', in Buchanan, Tollison and Tullock, *Toward a Theory of the Rent-Seeking Society* (1980), 98 et seq.
[153] For a detailed introduction see Konrad, *Strategy and Dynamics in Contests* (2009), 42 et seq.; March and Sahm, 'Asymmetric discouragement in asymmetric contests', (2017) 151 *Economics Letters*, 23 (23 et seq.).
[154] Konrad, *Strategy and Dynamics in Contests* (2009), 42 et seq.
[155] See inter alia March and Sahm, 'Asymmetric discouragement in asymmetric contests', (2017) 151 *Economics Letters*, 23 (24 et seqq.); Lim, Matros and Turocy, 'Bounded rationality and group size in Tullock contests: Experimental evidence', (2014) 99 *Journal of Economic Behavior & Organization*, 155 (161 et seq.); Sheremeta, Overbidding and heterogeneous behavior in contest experiments, (2013) 27(3) *Journal of Economic Surveys*, 491 (495 et seqq.).

also illustrates irrational behaviour on the individual level. Precisely this irrational behaviour can also be observed to a certain extent among Bitcoin miners ultimately leading to an **inefficient allocation** of resources with regard to the usage of computer hardware and the raw material required to build them.[156]

84 However, experimental studies also show that a possible strategy for contest participants to avoid the problem of overinvestment is to join forces and cooperate.[157] In fact, this is also the result, which can not only be shown in theory assuming risk-averse miners,[158] but which is also found as a positive result in reality: Bitcoin and other crypto token miners join together in large **mining pools** with the purpose of an increase in the winning probability and, as a result, of income smoothing (→ § 1 para. 40 et seqq.). In this way, the additional negative externalities resulting from the overinvestment,[159] such as the high consumption of energy required to operate the mining hardware (→ para. 85), as well as the associated **carbon dioxide emissions** (→ para. 87 et seq.) can also be reduced. However, at the same time the formation of mining pools increases the centralization of the respective blockchain, which again fundamentally contradicts the original idea of a decentralized system.

2. Energy Consumption

85 Closely related to the use of specific mining hardware (→ para. 80) is the high consumption of energy that arises while operating the hardware. Current studies estimate the worldwide annual energy consumption for Bitcoin alone at up to 73 TWh per year (as of November 2019; in comparison, as of November 2018: 35–72 TWh).[160] This puts Bitcoin, regarding its annual energy consumption, at the level of countries such as Austria and Venezuela.[161] If the energy consumption of other crypto assets such as Ethereum or Bitcoin Cash is also taken into account, the value is even higher.[162]

86 Since the energy consumption leads to costs that must directly be borne by the Bitcoin miners and which, assuming rational behaviour, (should) be accounted for before deciding on a market entry or exit or before making investment decisions regarding the mining hardware, this seems at first not to pose any economic problem. Once more, the concept of the **market mechanism** can be applied, which ensures profitability of the market participants in the long run.[163]

---

[156] Halaburda and Sarvary, *Beyond Bitcoin, The Economics of Digital Currencies* (2016), 116.

[157] Houser and Stratmann, 'Gordon Tullock and experimental economics', (2012) 152 *Public Choice*, 211 (212).

[158] Leshno and Strack, 'Bitcoin: An Axiomatic Approach and an Impossibility Theorem' (October 2019), 9, available at: https://papers.ssrn.com/sol3/papers.cfm?abstract_id=3487355 (last accessed 23.1.2021).

[159] Halaburda and Sarvary, *Beyond Bitcoin, The Economics of Digital Currencies* (2016), 116.

[160] Stoll, Klaassen and Gallersdörfer, 'The Carbon Footprint of Bitcoin', (2019) 3(7) *Joule*, 1647 (1649, 1657); Krause and Tolaymat, 'Quantification of energy and carbon costs for mining cryptocurrencies', (2018) 1 *Nature Sustainability*, 711 (711); Digiconomist Bitcoin Energy Consumption Index, available at: https://digiconomist.net/bitcoin-energy-consumption (last accessed 21.1.2021).

[161] For this comparison, the estimated upper limit of energy consumption is used, see Digiconomist Bitcoin Energy Consumption Index, available at: https://digiconomist.net/bitcoin-energy-consumption (last accessed 21.1.2021).

[162] Stoll, Klaassen and Gallersdörfer, 'The Carbon Footprint of Bitcoin', (2019) 3(7) *Joule*, 1647 (1656); Digiconomist Bitcoin Energy Consumption Index, available at: https://digiconomist.net/bitcoin-energy-consumption (last accessed 21.1.2021).

[163] Thum, 'Die ökonomischen Kosten des Bitcoin-Mining', (2018) 71(2) *ifo Schnelldienst*, 18 (19); generally for the market mechanism Bofinger, *Grundzüge der Volkswirtschaftslehre, Eine Einführung in die Wissenschaft* (2013), 64, 258.

§ 2. Economics of Crypto Assets

However, energy consumption is also associated with implicit costs that are not relevant to the profitability when mining crypto assets. Depending on the energy source used to generate the electricity necessary for running the mining hardware, carbon dioxide (CO2) may originate as a by-product. The environmental damage caused by such emissions is however not internalised by the miners during their production decisions, but instead is passed on to the general public. Hence, in the economic sense it constitutes an exemplary negative externality.[164] Given the high energy consumption, it is not surprising that the carbon dioxide emissions caused by Bitcoin mining are also considerable. With emissions ranging from 22 to 54 megatons (as of November 2018)[165] and 35 megatons (as of November 2019),[166] the carbon dioxide emissions of Bitcoin correspond to those of countries like Portugal (2018) or Denmark (2019).[167] 87

Of course, the emissions resulting from the mining of crypto assets are strongly dependent on the energy sources used for power generation. According to a recent report, 73 % of the electricity required for Bitcoin mining is actually generated from renewable energy sources, whereas only 27 % of the electricity used is based on conventional energy production.[168] By consciously choosing a location, it is therefore quite possible for miners to reduce their CO2 emissions. 88

Another way to reduce the power consumption required to maintain a blockchain system is to adjust the consensus mechanism. While the proof-of-work consensus mechanism, currently used by Bitcoin, Ethereum, and many other crypto assets, is very energy-intensive,[169] other mechanisms, such as the **proof-of-stake** approach (→ § 1 para. 58 et seq.) which is based solely on game-theoretic and economic incentives, allow consensus to be reached in a much more efficient way.[170] 89

E. Conclusion and Outlook

The focus of economic analyses is still primarily on the (possible) effects of crypto assets on conventional currencies and, associated with this, on possible changes in the (international) payment systems.[171] However, crypto assets and the underlying blockchain technology are repeatedly described as – in the sense of Schumpeter's '**creative destruction**'[172] – a disruptive innovation that has the potential not only to alter currency markets but also to have a lasting impact on various industries and the public sector. 90

---

[164] Mas-Colell, Whinston and Green, *Microeconomic Theory* (1995), 350 et seqq.

[165] Stoll, Klaassen and Gallersdörfer, 'The Carbon Footprint of Bitcoin', (2019) 3(7) *Joule*, 1647 (1654), Digiconomist Bitcoin Energy Consumption Index, available at: https://digiconomist.net/bitcoin-energy-consumption (last accessed 21.1.2021).

[166] See Digiconomist Bitcoin Energy Consumption Index, available at: https://digiconomist.net/bitcoin-energy-consumption (last accessed 21.1.2021).

[167] See Global Carbon Atlas CO2 Emissions, available at: http://www.globalcarbonatlas.org/en/CO2-emissions (last accessed 21.1.2021).

[168] Bendiksen and Gibbons, 'The Bitcoin Mining Network – Trends, Composition, Average Creation Cost, Electricity Consumption & Sources' (December 2019), 9, available at: https://coinsharesgroup.com/research/bitcoin-mining-network-december-2019 (last accessed 21.1.2021).

[169] Vigna and Casey, *The Age of Cryptocurrency: How Bitcoin and the Blockchain Are Challenging the Global Economic Order*, (2016), 145 et seqq.

[170] For the description of the modus operandi of PoW and PoS (→ § 1 para. 38 et seq., 58 et seq.).

[171] This is due to Bitcoin's predominant position, not only in terms of market capitalisation (Table 1), but also in research; *see* Yli-Huumo, Ko, Choi, Park and Smolander, 'Where Is Current Research on Blockchain Technology? -A Systematic Review', (2016) 11(10) *PLOS ONE*, 1 (19 et seqq.).

[172] Schumpeter, *Capitalism, Socialism, and Democracy* (1942), 81 et seqq.

91 Yet, there is still a long way to go until this will materialize. For now, it must be noted that crypto assets such as Bitcoin neither fully satisfy the functions normally associated with a currency, nor do they have a profound impact on the **monetary policy** of central banks or on the **financial stability**. Against this background, the question arises whether the genuine intention underlying crypto assets and especially Bitcoin – namely the establishment of a functioning alternative monetary and payment system that is independent of central institutions[173] – will become generally accepted.[174]

92 Beyond the original idea of an independently issued currency, a noticeable influence of crypto assets on the real economy cannot be determined at present. The exponential rise in prices observed on the market for crypto assets at the end of 2017 and at the beginning of 2018 which is associated with an increase in the number of as well as with an increase in the amount of capital raised with ICOs has led to a certain 'tokenisation' of the real economy. Yet, many of these projects ultimately turned out to be cases of fraud. Moreover, almost simultaneously with the significant drop in prices on the market for crypto assets the hype around ICOs also collapsed. Despite such significant market movements there were no effects observed for conventional capital markets nor for the economy in general. This clearly indicates the extremely limited or almost non-existent connection between the world of crypto assets and the real economy.

93 The reasons for the more recent crypto hype at the end of 2020 and the beginning of 2021 which seems to only slowly abate at the time of writing this chapter (April 2021) might be different, the conclusions that must be inferred are of a similar pattern. The Covid-19 pandemic, still raging in April 2021, ultimately prompted central banks around the world to decrease interest rates and increase money supply.[175] The low level of interest rates and a widespread fear of a steep rise in the general price level, both direct implications of the current monetary policy, urges both private and institutional investors to search for investment opportunities that yield acceptable interest rates and/or that are counterfeit against inflationary trends. As a result, prices on capital markets in general and crypto markets in particular are reaching new record heights (→ para. 7 et seqq.). Yet, it is not clear at all if crypto assets or, more specific, currency tokens suffice to fulfil, as often claimed,[176] the function of an inflation hedge in the digital age – similar to the (historical) role of gold – that would justify price multiplications of the magnitude described above (→ para. 8). Once more, crypto assets seem to become or

---

[173] Nakamoto, 'Bitcoin: A Peer-to-Peer Electronic Cash System' (2008), available at: https://perma.cc/MU7N-AWPD (last accessed 21.1.2021).

[174] It should be noted that this does not necessarily apply to (crypto) tokens issued by companies, centralized institutions, or the state, such as Libra (now referred to as Diem, → § 9 para. 7, 40) or Central Bank Digital Currencies (CBDC).

[175] The reasons for the extensive market interventions by central banks around the globe are manifold, the main causes being the stabilization of financial markets and the (in-)direct financing of newly issued public debt. The latter increased during the Covid-19 pandemic to levels unseen before, as governments implemented Keynesian-style politics to strengthen the market demand while at the same time providing voluminous subsidies to firms, predominantly in the private sector. The support of both, the demand side and the supply side of the economy, was and still is necessary as the Covid-19 pandemic corresponds, unlike most global crises before, to a simultaneous aggregate supply and aggregate demand shock; *see* Makin and Layton, 'The global fiscal response to COVID-19: Risks and repercussions', (2021) 69(7) *Economic Analysis and Policy*, 340 (343 et seqq.); McKee and Stuckler, 'If the world fails to protect the economy, COVID-19 will damage health not just now but also in the future.' (2020) 26 *Nature Medicine*, 641; for a current overview of the literature on the economic consequences of the COVID-19 crisis: *see* Brodeur, Gray, Islam, Bhuiyan and Suraiya, 'A Literature Review of the Economics of COVID-19' (2020), available at: http://hdl.handle.net/10419/222316 (last accessed 10.4.2021).

[176] Cf. *Deutsche Welle*, available at: https://p.dw.com/p/3neSN (last accessed 10.4.2021); *ventureburn*, available at: https://ventureburn.com/2021/01/is-bitcoin-the-new-gold/ (last accessed 10.4.2021); *FAZ*, available at: https://www.faz.net/aktuell/wirtschaft/digitec/bitcoin-ist-der-erste-digitale-rohstoff-17139107.html

already are detached from the developments observed on conventional capital markets and in the real economy.[177]

However, this is not to say that crypto assets have no inherent benefit. First of all, it can be argued that they possibly represent another building block in the digitisation of the economy. Also with regard to an international payment system, crypto assets may well play a major role in the (near) future. Especially in countries with untrustworthy (financial) institutions, the use of crypto assets offers a way to avoid interactions with such intermediaries. Moreover, the announcement of Facebook and the Libra Association to launch the presumably blockchain based currency token Libra (now referred to as Diem[178]) lead all major international central banks to seriously explore the opportunities and risks of the blockchain technology and crypto based tokens[179] as a possible way to launch Central Bank Digital Currencies (CBDC), i.e. a digital form of legal tender issued by a central bank.[180] After all, the above arguments and the rather pessimistic outlook may only present a current **snapshot** that can shift quite rapidly given the ever faster changing dynamics that are nowadays encountered almost everywhere. **94**

---

[177] Cf. Klein, Pham, Thu and Walther, 'Bitcoin is not the New Gold – A comparison of volatility, correlation, and portfolio performance', (2018) 59 *International Review of Financial Analysis*, 105 (107 et seqq.); Selmi, Mensi, Hammoudeh and Bouoiyour, 'Is Bitcoin a hedge, a safe haven or a diversifier for oil price movements? A comparison with gold', (2018) 74 *Energy Economics*, 787 (788 et seqq.); Bouri, Shahzad, Roubaud, Kristoufek and Lucey, 'Bitcoin, gold, and commodities as safe havens for stocks: New insight through wavelet analysis' (2020) 77 *The Quarterly Review of Economics and Finance*, 163.

[178] Cf. *Handelsblatt*, available at: https://www.handelsblatt.com/finanzen/maerkte/devisen-rohstoffe/aus-libra-wird-diem-zweiter-anlauf-fuer-facebooks-kryptowaehrung/26696068.html?ticket=ST-4863258-mGh6qCQyWdaic4bzUVgf-ap4 (last accessed 10.4.2021).

[179] Blockchain or, more generally speaking, distributed ledger technology is one among different possibilities considered by central authorities to issue a digital currency or CBDC; *see* Bank for International Settlements, 'Central bank digital currencies', (March 2018), 1, available at: https://www.bis.org/cpmi/publ/d174.pdf (last accessed 10.4.2021); Bindseil, 'Tiered CBDC and the financial system', (January 2020), 4, available at: https://www.ecb.europa.eu/pub/pdf/scpwps/ecb.wp2351~c8c18bbd60.en.pdf (last accessed 10.4.2021).

[180] For more in-depth information on Central Bank Digital Currencies (CBDC): Bank for International Settlements, 'Central bank digital currencies', (March 2018), 1 (2 et seqq.), available at: https://www.bis.org/cpmi/publ/d174.pdf (last accessed 10.4.2021); Bindseil, 'Tiered CBDC and the financial system', (January 2020), 4 (5 et seqq.), available at: https://www.ecb.europa.eu/pub/pdf/scpwps/ecb.wp2351~c8c18bbd60.en.pdf (last accessed 10.4.2021), Niepelt, 'Reserves for All? Central Bank Digital Currency, Deposits, and their (Non)-Equivalence', (2020) 16 (3) *International Journal of Central Banking*, 211 (212 et seqq.); Brunnermeier, James and Landau, 'The Digitalization of Money', (2019), 1, (2 et seqq.), available at: https://scholar.princeton.edu/sites/default/files/markus/files/02c_digitalmoney.pdf (last accessed 10.4.2021).

PART B
EU REGULATION

§ 3
International Jurisdiction and Applicable Law

Literature: Arons, 'All roads lead to Rome' (2008) 26 *Nederlands Internationaal Privaatrecht*, 481; Bachmann, 'Die internationale Zuständigkeit für Klagen wegen fehlerhafter Kapitalmarktinformation' (2007) 27 *Praxis des Internationalen Privat- und Verfahrensrechts*, 77–86; von Bar and Mankowski, *Internationales Privatrecht I* (2nd edn, C.H. Beck, Munich, 2003); Barsan, 'Legal Challenges of Initial Coin Offerings (ICO)' (2017) 12 *Revue Trimestrielle de Droit Financier*, 54–65; Benicke, 'Prospektpflicht und Prospekthaftung bei grenzüberschreitenden Emissionen', in Mansel, Pfeiffer, Kronke, Kohler and Hausmann (eds), *Festschrift für Erik Jayme, Band I* (Munich, 2004), 25–37; Boehm and Pesch, Bitcoins: Rechtliche Herausforderungen einer virtuellen Währung – Eine erste juristische Einordung (2014) 17 *Zeitschrift für IT-Recht und Digitalisierung*, 75–79; de Vauplane, 'Blockchain and Intermediated Securities' (2018) 36 *Nederlands Internationaal Privaatrecht*, 94–103; Dickinson, 'Cryptocurrencies and the Conflict of Laws', in Fox and Green (eds), *Cryptocurrencies in Public and Private Law* (Oxford, 2019); Dombalagian, 'Choice of Law and Capital Markets Regulation' (2008) 82 *Tulane Law Review*, 1903–1947; Dutta, 'Die neuen Haftungsregeln für Ratingagenturen in der Europäischen Union: Zwischen Sachrechtsvereinheitlichung und europäischem Entscheidungseinklang' (2013) 67 *Zeitschrift für Wirtschafts- und Bankrecht*, 1729–1736; Einsele, 'Internationales Prospekthaftungsrecht – Kollisionsrechtlicher Anlegerschutz nach der Rom II-Verordnung' (2012) 20 *Zeitschrift für Europäisches Privatrecht*, 23–46; Einsele, 'Kapitalmarktrechtliche Eingriffsnormen – Bedarf die Rom I-Verordnung einer Sonderregel für harmonisiertes europäisches Recht?' (2012) 32 *Praxis des Internationalen Privat- und Verfahrensrechts*, 481–491; Einsele, 'Kapitalmarktrecht und Internationales Privatrecht' (2017) 81 *Rabels Zeitschrift für ausländisches und internationales Privatrecht*, 781–814; Floer, *Internationale Reichweite der Prospekthaftung. Zum Kollisionsrecht der Haftung für fehlerhafte Verkaufs- und Börsenzulassungsprospekte*, Studien zum Bank- und Börsenrecht (Nomos, Baden-Baden, 2002); Fox, 'Cryptocurrencies in the Common Law of Property' (2018), available at https://ssrn.com/abstract=3232501 (accessed 1.9.2020); Garcimartín Alférez, 'The Rome I Regulation: Exceptions to the Rule on Consumer Contracts and Financial Instruments' (2009), 5 *Journal of Private International Law*, 85–103; Garcimartín Alférez, 'The law applicable to prospectus liability in the European Union' (2011) 5 *Law and Financial Markets Review*, 449–457; Gsell, Krüger, Lorenz and Reymann (eds), *beck-online.GROSSKOMMENTAR zum Zivilrecht* (BeckOGK) (München, as of 1.10.2020); Guillaume, 'Aspects of private international law related to blockchain transactions', in Kraus, Obrist and Hari (eds), *Blockchains, Smart Contracts, Decentralised Autonomous Organisations and the Law* (Cheltenham, 2019), 49–82; Hacker and Thomale, 'Crypto-Securities Regulation: ICOs, Token Sales and Cryptocurrencies under EU Financial Law' (2017), https://ssrn.com/abstract=3075820 (accessed 1.9.2020); Hamburg Group for Private International Law, 'Comments on the European Commission's Draft Proposal for a Council Regulation on the Law Applicable to Non-Contractual Obligations' (2003) 67 *Rabels Zeitschrift für ausländisches und internationales Privatrecht*, 1–56; von Hein, 'Deliktischer Kapitalanlegerschutz im europäischen Zuständigkeitsrecht (EuGH, S. 32)' (2005) 25 *Praxis des Internationalen Privat- und Verfahrensrechts*, 17–23; von Hein, 'Die Internationale Prospekthaftung im Lichte der Rom II-Verordnung', in Baum, Fleckner, Hellgardt, Roth, et al. (eds), *Perspektiven des Wirtschaftsrechts* (Berlin, 2008), 371; Heinze and Steinrötter, 'Wann fällt ein Vertrag in den Bereich der ausgerichteten Tätigkeit des Unternehmers i.S.d. Art. 17 Abs. 1 lit. c EuGVVO?' (2016) 36 *Praxis des Internationalen Privat- und Verfahrensrechts*, 545–549; Hellgardt and Ringe, 'Internationale Kapitalmarkthaftung als Corporate Governance' (2009) 173 *Zeitschrift für das gesamte Handels- und Wirtschaftsrecht*, 802–839; Junker, 'Der Reformbedarf im Internationalen Deliktsrecht der Rom II-Verordnung drei Jahre nach ihrer Verabschiedung' (2010) 56 *Recht der internationalen Wirtschaft*, 257–269; Kiel, *Internationales Kapitalanlegerschutzrecht*, Recht des internationalen Wirtschaftsverkehrs (De Gruyter, Berlin, 1994); Kment, *Grenzüberschreitendes Verwaltungshandeln*, Jus Publicum (Mohr Siebeck, Tübingen, 2010); Kreuzer, Wagner and Reder, 'Internationale Zuständigkeit', in Dauses and Ludwigs (eds), *Handbuch des EU-Wirtschaftsrechts* (Munich, 2019), Q. II.; Kumpan, 'Börsen und außerbörsliche Handelssysteme. Die kollisionsrechtliche Behandlung von grenzüberschreitenden Wertpapierhandelsdienstleistungen', in Zetzsche and Lehmann (eds), *Grenzüberschreitende Finanzdienstleistungen* (Tübingen, 2018), § 9; Kuntz, 'Internationale Prospekthaftung nach Inkrafttreten des Wertpapierprospektgesetzes' (2007) 61 *Zeitschrift für Wirtschafts- und Bankrecht*, 432–440; Langenbucher, 'Digitales Finanzwesen – Vom Bargeld zu virtuellen Währungen' (2018) 218 *Archiv für die civilistische Praxis*, 385–429; Lehmann, 'Das Finanzmarktrecht im Internationalen Privatrecht', in Zetzsche and Lehmann (eds), *Grenzüberschreitende Finanzdienstleistungen* (Tübingen, 2018), § 1; Lehmann, 'Financial Instruments', in Ferrari and Leible (eds), *Rome I Regulation* (Munich, 2009), 85; Lehmann, 'Proposition d'une règle spéciale dans le Règlement Rome II pour les délits financiers, Revue critique' (2012) 101 *Revue critique de droit international privé*, 485–519; Lehmann, 'Vorschlag für eine Reform der Rom II-Verordnung im Bereich der Finanzmarktdelikte' (2012) 32 *Praxis des Internationalen Privat- und Verfahrensrechts*, 399–405; Lehmann, 'Where does Economic Loss Occur?' (2011) 7 *Journal of Private International Law*, 527–550; Lehmann, 'Who Owns Bitcoin? Private Law Facing the Blockchain' (2019) 21 *Minnesota Journal of Law, Science & Technology*, 93–136; Lehmann and Krysa, 'Blockchain, Smart Contracts und Token aus der Sicht des (Internationalen) Privatrechts' (2019), 12 *Bonner Rechtsjournal*, 90–96; MacLean, 'Governing the blockchain: how to determine applicable law' [2017] *Butterworths Journal of International Banking and Financial Law*, 359; Mankowski, 'Enge Verbindung zu früher geschlossenem Verbrauchervertrag – Gerichtsstand' (2016) 69 *Neue Juristische Wochenschrift*, 699–700; Mankowski, 'EuGH: Zuständigkeit für Prospekthaftungsklagen' [2019] *Lindenmaier-Möhring Kommentierte BGH-Rechtsprechung*, 413748; Martiny, 'Virtuelle Währungen, insbesondere Bitcoins, im Internationalen Privat- und Zivilverfahrensrecht' (2018) 38 *Praxis des Internationalen Privat- und Verfahrensrechts*, 553–565; Maume, 'Initial Coin Offerings and EU Prospectus Disclosure' (2020) 31 *European Business Law Review*, 185–209; Moloney, 'Reform or revolution? The financial crisis, EU financial markets law, and the European securities and markets authority' (2011) 60 *International & Comparative Law Quarterly*, 521–533; Möslein, 'Conflicts of Laws and Codes', in Lianos, Hacker, Eich and Dimitropoulos (eds), *Regulating Blockchain: Techno-Social and Legal Challenges* (Oxford, 2019), Chapter 15; Müller, 'EuGVVO: Gerichtsstand für Schadensersatzklage eines Verbrauchers wegen Wertverlust einer Finanzinvestition' (2015) 26 *Europäische Zeitschrift für Wirtschaftsrecht*, 218–226; Müller, *Finanzinstrumente in der Rom I-VO*, Studien zum Internationalen Privat- und Verfahrensrecht (JWV, Jena, 2011); *Münchener Kommentar zum Bürgerlichen Gesetzbuch: BGB, Internationales Privatrecht I, Europäisches Kollisionsrecht, Einführungsgesetz zum Bürgerlichen Gesetzbuche (Art. 1–26)*, Vol. 12 (MüKoBGB) (8th edn, München, 2020); *Münchener Kommentar zum Bürgerlichen Gesetzbuch: BGB, Internationales Privatrecht II, Internationales Wirtschaftsrecht, Einführungsgesetz zum Bürgerlichen Gesetzbuche (Art. 25–253)*, Vol. 12 (MüKoBGB) (7th edn, München, 2017); *Münchener Kommentar zur Zivilprozessordnung: ZPO (§§ 946–1120), EGZPO, GVG, EGGVG, UKlaG, Internationales und Europäisches Zivilprozessrecht*, Vol. 3 (MüKoZPO) (5th edn, München, 2017); Omlor, 'Blockchain-basierte Zahlungsmittel' (2018) 51 *Zeitschrift für Rechtspolitik*, 85–89; Poelzig, 'Grenzüberschreitende Markmanipulation', in Zetzsche and Lehmann (eds), *Grenzüberschreitende Finanzdienstleistungen* (Tübingen, 2018), § 14; Raskin, 'Realm of the Coin: Bitcoin and Civil Procedure' (2015) 20 *Fordham Journal of Corporate & Financial Law*, 969–1011; Rühl, 'Smart Contracts und anwendbares Recht', in Braegelmann and Kaulartz (eds), *Rechtshandbuch Smart Contracts* (Munich, 2019), § 12; Savelyev, 'Contract law 2.0: 'Smart' contracts as the beginning of the end of classic contract law' (2017) 26 *Information & Communications Technology Law*, 116–134; Savigny, *System des heutigen römischen Rechts*, Vol. 8 (Berlin, 1849); Schmitt, 'Die kollisionsrechtliche Anknüpfung der Prospekthaftung im System der Rom II-Verordnung' (2010) 10 *Zeitschrift für Bank und Kapitalmarktrecht*, 366–371; Schmitt, Bhatti and Storck, 'Die neue europäische Prospekt-Verordnung – ein großer Wurf?' (2019) 27 *Zeitschrift für Europäisches Privatrecht*, 287–314; Schroeter, 'Grenzüberschreitende Verhaltenspflichten und Haftung von Ratingagenturen', in Zetzsche and Lehmann (eds), *Grenzüberschreitende Finanzdienstleistungen* (Tübingen, 2018), § 11; Schulze and others, *Bürgerliches Gesetzbuch, Handkommentar* (HK-BGB) (10th edn, Baden-Baden, 2019); Seiler and Seiler, 'Sind Kryptowährungen wie Bitcoin (BTC), Ethereum (ETH) und Ripple (XRP) als Sachen im Sinne des ZGB zu behandeln?' (2018) 5 *sui-generis*, 150–163; Seitz, 'Distributed Ledger Technology & Bitcoin – Zur rechtlichen Stellung eines Bitcoin-"Inhabers"' (2017) 20 *Kommunikation und Recht*, 763–769; Spindler and Biller, 'Rechtsprobleme von Bitcoins als virtuelle Währung' (2014) 68 *Zeitschrift für Wirtschafts- und Bankrecht*, 1357–1369; Staudinger and Steinrötter, 'Das neue Zuständigkeitsregime bei zivilrechtlichen Auslandssachverhalten: die Brüssel Ia-VO' (2015) 55 *Juristische Schulung*, 1–8; Staudinger and Steinrötter, 'Kausalität des Ausrichtens auf Wohnort der Verbrauchergerichtsstand bei Vertragsschluss (Urteilsanmerkung)' (2013) 66 *Neue Juristische Wochenschrift*, 3505–3506; Staudinger and Steinrötter, 'Verfahrens- sowie kollisionsrechtlicher Verbraucherschutz bei Online-Geschäften' (2011) 21 *Europäisches Wirtschafts- und Steuerrecht*, 70–75; Steinrötter, *Beschränkte Rechtswahl im Internationalen Kapitalmarktprivatrecht und akzessorische Anknüpfung an das Kapitalmarktordnungsstatut. Modell für eine einheitliche kapitalmarktprivatrechtliche Qualifikation am Beispiel des Prospekthaftungs- und Übernahmeprivatrechts de lege lata und ferenda*, Studien zum Internationalen Privat- und Verfahrensrecht (JWV, Jena, 2014); Steinrötter, 'Der notorische Problemfall der grenzüberschreitenden Prospekthaftung' (2015) 61 *Recht der internationalen Wirtschaft*, 407–414; Steinrötter, 'Vermeintliche Ausschließlichkeitsrechte an binären Codes' (2017)

§ 3. International Jurisdiction and Applicable Law

20 *Zeitschrift für IT-Recht und Digitalisierung*, 731–736; Steinrötter, 'Zuständigkeits- und kollisionsrechtliche Implikationen des europäischen Haftungstatbestands für fehlerhaftes Rating' (2015) 36 *Zeitschrift für Wirtschaftsrecht*, 110–115; Steinrötter and Bohlsen, 'Erfolgsort bei grenzüberschreitender Kapitalmarkt-Prospekthaftung im internationalen Zuständigkeitsrecht ('Löber')' [2/2019] *juris PraxisReport Internationales Wirtschaftsrecht*, Anm. 1; Teubner, '"Verbund', 'Verband' oder 'Verkehr'?' (1990) 54 *Zeitschrift für das gesamte Handels- und Wirtschaftsrecht*, 295–324; Thiede and Lorscheider, 'Die internationale Zuständigkeit für Ansprüche von Anlegern aus Prospekthaftung' (2019) 30 *Europäische Zeitschrift für Wirtschaftsrecht*, 274–280; Verse, 'Zur Reform der Kapitalmarktinformationshaftung im Vereinigten Königreich' (2012) 76 *Rabels Zeitschrift für ausländisches und internationales Privatrecht*, 893–920; Wagner, R., 'Anmerkung zu 'Verbrauchergerichtsstand bei enger Verbindung zu früher geschlossenem Verbrauchervertrag'' (2016) 27 *Europäische Zeitschrift für Wirtschaftsrecht*, 269–270; Weber, 'Internationale Prospekthaftung nach der Rom II-Verordnung' (2008) 62 *Zeitschrift für Wirtschafts- und Bankrecht*, 1581–1588; Wendelstein, 'Die Behandlung der Prospekthaftung des Emittenten im europäischen Zuständigkeitsrecht' (2016) 9 *Zeitschrift für das Privatrecht der Europäischen Union*, 140–148; Wright and de Filippi, 'Decentralized Blockchain Technology and the Rise of Lex Cryptographia' (2015), available at https://ssrn.com/abstract=2580664 (accessed 1.9.2020); Zech, 'Building a European Data Economy – The European Commission's Proposal for a Data Producer's Right' (2017) 9 *Zeitschrift für geistiges Eigentum*, 317–330; Zech, 'Information as Property' (2015) 6 *Journal of Intellectual Property, Information Technology and Electronic Commerce Law*, 192–197; Zickgraf, 'Initial Coin Offerings – Ein Fall für das Kapitalmarktrecht?' (2018) 63 *Die Aktiengesellschaft*, 293–308; Zimmer, *Internationales Gesellschaftsrecht. Das Kollisionsrecht der Gesellschaften und sein Verhältnis zum Internationalen Kapitalmarkt und Unternehmensrecht*, Recht der Internationalen Wirtschaft (Verlag Recht und Wirtschaft, Heidelberg, 1996); Zimmermann, 'Blockchain-Netzwerke und Internationales Privatrecht – oder: der Sitz dezentraler Rechtsverhältnisse' (2018) 38 *Praxis des Internationalen Privat- und Verfahrensrechts*, 566–573.

Outline

	para.
A. Introduction	1
B. General considerations	4
C. 'Ownership' or 'property' issues	6
D. Contractual Relationships in Initial Coin Offerings	8
I. International Jurisdiction	9
II. Applicable law	15
1. Choice of Law	16
2. Applicable law in the Absence of a Choice of Law	20
E. Contractual Relationships in the Secondary Market	24
I. International Jurisdiction	24
II. Applicable Law	25
F. Contracts with Intermediaries	27
I. International Jurisdiction	28
1. Platform Contract	28
2. Follow-up Contracts	31
II. Applicable Law	33
1. Platform Contract	33
2. Follow-up Contracts	34
G. E-Commerce and Distance Contracts	35
H. Prospectus Liability	36
I. International Jurisdiction	39
II. Applicable Law	43
1. Prospectus Requirements and the 'European Passport'	43
2. Prospectus Liability	45
3. Prospectus Disclosure Requirements and Prospectus Liability	51
4. Other Capital Market Tort Law Cases	52
I. (Other) Liability Law	53
I. International Jurisdiction	54
II. Applicable Law	55

Part B. EU Regulation

J. Mining and Mining Pools 56
    I. International Jurisdiction 57
        1. Mining 57
        2. Mining Pools 58
    II. Applicable Law 59
        1. Mining 59
        2. Mining Pools 60

A. Introduction

1   Transactions of crypto tokens (for the terms → § 1 para. 68 et seqq.) are **typically cross-border operations**.[1] This requires (at the latest in the case of dispute) the determination of the place of (international) jurisdiction (via the respective law of jurisdiction as part of International Procedural Law (IPL)). Based on this[2] the applicable substantive law must be ascertained (via Private International Law (PIL) respectively Conflict of Laws)[3].

2   In the field of crypto tokens, **previous practice has neglected** questions of international jurisdiction or applicable private and regulatory law. This may have been done under the misconception that this was a priori an area not accessible to the law[4] or that some kind of 'lex cryptographia'[5] replaced traditional law.[6] However, clauses on jurisdiction, arbitration[7] and choice of law are also regularly found (namely in the 'white papers' when crypto assets are first issued; → § 1 para. 85).[8] Although the questions of the competent court and the applicable law are the first step in every legal analysis,[9] academia has focused on problems of substantive law, while the **analysis of the IPL and PIL aspects is still in its infancy**.[10] However, the relevance of these questions has already been recognised.[11]

---

[1] Guillaume, 'Aspects of private international law related to blockchain transactions', in Kraus, Obrist and Hari (eds), *Blockchains, Smart Contracts, Decentralised Autonomous Organisations and the Law* (2019), 49 (59 et seq.).

[2] Each EU judge applies the Private International Law of the respective lex fori, which does, of course, include relevant EU provisions.

[3] PIL and Conflict of Laws are used synonymously here.

[4] See, for example, Savelyev, 'Contract law 2.0: 'Smart' contracts as the beginning of the end of classic contract law' (2017) 26 *Information & Communications Technology Law*, 116 (132): '[…] smart contracts […] may operate without any overarching legal framework'.

[5] Note Wright and de Filippi, 'Decentralized Blockchain Technology and the Rise of Lex Cryptographia' (2015) available at https://ssrn.com/abstract=2580664 or http://dx.doi.org/10.2139/ssrn.2580664 (accessed 1.9.2020); lately Guillaume, 'Aspects of private international law related to blockchain transactions', in Kraus, Obrist and Hari (eds), *Blockchains, Smart Contracts, Decentralised Autonomous Organisations and the Law* (2019), 49 (71 et seqq.).

[6] In this sense also the valid assumption of Möslein, 'Conflicts of Laws and Codes: Defining the Boundaries of Digital Jurisdictions', in Lianos, Hacker, Eich and Dimitropoulos (eds), *Regulating Blockchain* (2019), 275; Rühl, 'Smart Contracts und anwendbares Recht', in Braegelmann and Kaulartz (eds), *Smart Contracts* (2019), § 12, para. 1 et seq.; cf. the proposal of Lehmann, 'Who Owns Bitcoin? Private Law Facing the Blockchain' (2019) 21 *Minnesota Journal of Law, Science & Technology*, 93 (166 et seqq.) aiming at a harmonious interaction of the distributed ledger technology (as a fact) and the law.

[7] Cf. Ageyev, 'Cryptonomica: ex aequo et bono and new lex mercatoria' (2019), available at https://beck-link.de/ttr5v (accessed 1.9.2020).

[8] Martiny, 'Virtuelle Währungen, insbesondere Bitcoins, im Internationalen Privat- und Zivilverfahrensrecht' (2018) 38 *Praxis des Internationalen Privat- und Verfahrensrechts*, 553 (557).

[9] Questions of this kind in connection with smart contracts are considered irrelevant: Savelyev, 'Contract law 2.0: 'Smart' contracts as the beginning of the end of classic contract law' (2017) 26 *Information & Communications Technology Law*, 116 (132 et seq.).

[10] Martiny, 'Virtuelle Währungen, insbesondere Bitcoins, im Internationalen Privat- und Zivilverfahrensrecht' (2018) 38 *Praxis des Internationalen Privat- und Verfahrensrechts*, 553 (565).

[11] European Securities and Markets Authority (ESMA), Report: 'The Distributed Ledger Technology Applied to Securities Markets', 18: 'Another important legal issue […] would be to determine the applicable

§ 3. International Jurisdiction and Applicable Law

This chapter offers a **first guide to** international jurisdiction and applicable law. The focus is on investment, utility, and currency tokens (for the terms → § 1 para. 70 et seqq.), while hybrid forms are excluded. However, as a general rule, the focus of the respective hybrid token may be taken as a guideline for the assessment. If its priority tends more in the direction of an investment token, it is most likely to be treated as such regarding IPL and PIL.

This chapter also covers questions of 'ownership' respectively 'property' of crypto tokens (→ para. 6 et seq.), contractual relationships in the Initial Coin Offering (ICO) (→ para. 8 et seqq.) and transactions on the secondary market (→ para. 24 et seqq.), with respect to intermediaries (→ para. 27 et seqq.) and e-commerce and distance contracts (→ para. 35). Finally, this chapter deals with prospectus liability under capital markets law (→ para. 36 et seqq.), further elements of capital market tort law (→ para. 52) and other liability law (→ para. 53 et seqq.) and mining and mining pools (→ para. 56 et seqq.).

Regarding the issue of international jurisdiction, from the perspective of EU lawyers[12] the most relevant source of law is Regulation (EU) No. 1215/2012 (**Brussels Ibis Regulation**)[13]. In order to determine the applicable law, primarily recourse to Regulation (EC) No. 593/2008 (**Rome I**)[14] and Regulation (EC) No. 864/2007 (**Rome II**)[15], each of which is designed as a 'loi uniforme',[16] is necessary. The respective national IPL/PIL rules apply subsidiarily.

B. General considerations

With new technologies, no matter how disruptive they may appear, there is **no application problem** regarding IPL and PIL in principle.[17] They relate first and foremost to the **function of the phenomenon** to be assessed and the system concept of the connecting factor contains several abstract legal questions. In this respect, one can even speak of **legal matters that are genuinely open to technology**.[18] Problems arise

---

law'; Financial Markets Law Committee (FMLC), 'Distributed Ledger Technology and Governing Law: Issues of Legal Uncertainty', March 2018, para. 1.3.: 'an international conflict of law framework for financial transactions and systems using DLT needs to be developed as a matter of priority'.

[12] Note the Swiss perspective described by Guillaume, 'Aspects of private international law related to blockchain transactions', in Kraus, Obrist and Hari (eds), *Blockchains, Smart Contracts, Decentralised Autonomous Organisations and the Law* (2019), 49 (61 et seqq.).

[13] Regulation (EU) No. 1215/2012 of the European Parliament and of the Council on jurisdiction and the recognition and enforcement of judgments in civil and commercial matters, OJ L 351, 20.12.2012 p. 1–32. The predecessor legal act was the Brussels I Regulation, Regulation (EC) No. 44/2001 on jurisdiction and the recognition and enforcement of judgments in civil and commercial matters, OJ L 12, 16.1.2001 p.1–23. Other relevant sources of law are the Parallel Agreement with Denmark (OJ 2013 L 79, 4) and the revised Lugano Convention between the EU, Norway, Denmark, Switzerland and Iceland (OJ 2009 L 147, 5; corrected by OJ 2009 L 147, 44; extended by OJ 2011 L 138, 1).

[14] Regulation (EC) No. 593/2008 of the European Parliament and of the Council on the law applicable to contractual obligations (Rome I), OJ L 177, 4.7.2009 p. 6–16.

[15] Regulation (EC) No. 864/2007 of 11.7.2007 on the law applicable to non-contractual obligations (Rome II), OJ L 199, 31.7.2007 p. 40–49.

[16] This means that Member States apply the Rome II Regulation not only in cases involving third countries; it is also possible to refer to third states substantive law, Art. 2 Rome I Regulation and Art. 3 Rome II Regulation.

[17] Dickinson, 'Cryptocurrencies and the Conflict of Laws', in Fox and Green (eds), *Cryptocurrencies in Public and Private Law* (2019), § 5 para. 5.07 et seqq., 5.121: 'no need to panic and throw the existing toolbox away'; Rühl, 'Smart Contracts und anwendbares Recht', in Braegelmann and Kaulartz (eds), *Smart Contracts* (2019), § 12, para. 41.

[18] Rühl, 'Smart Contracts und anwendbares Recht', in Braegelmann and Kaulartz (eds), *Smart Contracts* (2019), § 12 para. 41.

where ubiquitous phenomena occur precisely in the connecting factor, i.e. the criterion which establishes the connection to the relevant legal system,[19] which is exemplarily true for the connection to the place of success in the case of financial losses in the context of token.[20] Because of its 'neutrality of connection', the decentralised approach of the blockchain seems to pose even greater problems for the right of referral a prima vista,[21] for the traditional PIL is (next to the possibility to choose the applicable law) characterised by the **principle of the closest connection** (between the legal phenomenon in question and a legal system).[22] The same applies to the IPL, even if it is based on different interests in detail. With the endeavour to find out this closest (in particular 'geographical') connection, taking into account Conflict of Laws interests, everything decentralised becomes a natural antagonist[23]. However, this chapter does not deal with the international legal treatment of blockchain technology or the distributed ledger network 'as such' (there is no need to search for the competent court or the applicable law insofar),[24] but rather with various specific scenarios in connection with crypto tokens, namely contracts and torts. The fact that these are based on the blockchain technology is largely irrelevant for their (international) legal evaluation.[25] Rather, the traditional legal points of reference (sometimes with some modifications) can be brought into position.[26] The fact that the respective parties (namely the defendant) often cannot be identified may pose problems in practice. However, this is not a matter of IPL/PIL in the first place. Nevertheless, there is still room de lege ferenda in various places for the **creation of new special IPL/PIL provisions** which could lead to an improvement in legal certainty (→ para. 21, 25, 42).

---

[19] Cf. Martiny, 'Virtuelle Währungen, insbesondere Bitcoins, im Internationalen Privat- und Zivilverfahrensrecht' (2018) 38 *Praxis des Internationalen Privat- und Verfahrensrechts*, 553 (557).

[20] Lehmann, 'Where does Economic Loss Occur?' (2011) 7 *Journal of Private International Law*, 527.

[21] In this direction Barsan, 'Legal Challenges of Initial Coin Offerings (ICO)' (2017) 12 *Revue Trimestrielle de Droit Financier*, 54 (63); Guillaume, 'Aspects of private international law related to blockchain transactions', in Kraus, Obrist and Hari (eds), *Blockchains, Smart Contracts, Decentralised Autonomous Organisations and the Law* (2019), 49 (69 et seq.); Zimmermann, 'Blockchain-Netzwerke und Internationales Privatrecht – oder: der Sitz dezentraler Rechtsverhältnisse' (2018) 38 *Praxis des Internationalen Privat- und Verfahrensrechts*, 566.

[22] Cf. Savigny, *System des heutigen römischen Rechts*, Vol. VIII (1849), 108; Guillaume, 'Aspects of private international law related to blockchain transactions', in Kraus, Obrist and Hari (eds), *Blockchains, Smart Contracts, Decentralised Autonomous Organisations and the Law* (2019), 49 (61 et seq.); Lehmann, 'Who Owns Bitcoin? Private Law Facing the Blockchain' (2019) 21 *Minnesota Journal of Law, Science & Technology*, 93 (94, 111).

[23] Zimmermann, 'Blockchain-Netzwerke und Internationales Privatrecht – oder: der Sitz dezentraler Rechtsverhältnisse' (2018) 38 *Praxis des Internationalen Privat- und Verfahrensrechts*, 566; cf. also Guillaume, 'Aspects of private international law related to blockchain transactions', in Kraus, Obrist and Hari (eds), *Blockchains, Smart Contracts, Decentralised Autonomous Organisations and the Law* (2019), 49 (71): 'the traditional approach of private international law is antithetical to the essence of the blockchain'; Lehmann, 'Who Owns Bitcoin? Private Law Facing the Blockchain' (2019) 21 *Minnesota Journal of Law, Science & Technology*, 93 (112): 'completely de-nationalized and not connected to any particular country, which makes it impossible to determine the state with the closest connection'.

[24] Lehmann, 'Who Owns Bitcoin? Private Law Facing the Blockchain' (2019) 21 *Minnesota Journal of Law, Science & Technology*, 93 (125); Lehmann and Krysa, 'Blockchain, Smart Contracts und Token aus der Sicht des (Internationalen) Privatrechts' (2019) 12 *Bonner Rechtsjournal*, 90 (94); see, however, in detail concerning the applicable law with regard to the blockchain: Zimmermann, 'Blockchain-Netzwerke und Internationales Privatrecht – oder: der Sitz dezentraler Rechtsverhältnisse' (2018) 38 *Praxis des Internationalen Privat- und Verfahrensrechts*, 566 (568 et seqq.).

[25] Rühl, 'Smart Contracts und anwendbares Recht', in Braegelmann and Kaulartz (eds), *Smart Contracts* (2019), § 12 para. 5.

[26] See also Zimmermann, 'Blockchain-Netzwerke und Internationales Privatrecht – oder: der Sitz dezentraler Rechtsverhältnisse' (2018) 38 *Praxis des Internationalen Privat- und Verfahrensrechts*, 566 (568).

§ 3. *International Jurisdiction and Applicable Law*

Finally, in order to avoid misunderstandings, it should be noted that **smart** 5
contracts are not contracts in the legal sense, but only specific if-then conditions
that can be used particularly in the conclusion or execution of the contract
(→ § 1 para. 62 et seqq.). Smart contracts do therefore not represent a legal category,
rather a matter of **factual elements which** are to be **subsumed under law (including
IPL/PIL provisions)**.[27]

C. 'Ownership' or 'property' issues

The initiation of a blockchain, Initial Coin Offerings (ICOs) and mining can be 6
considered as **original acts of creation of tokens**, while the **derivative transfer** takes
place by means of a secondary market transaction (→ § 1 para. 78).[28] However, it is
unclear what exactly the **object of this transfer** is.[29] Crypto tokens are fungible and
valuable[30] digital goods, but there are no a priori rights to them, in particular **no
exclusive rights**.[31] They are neither physical objects[32] nor (in the absence of a
corresponding will to be legally bound within the peer-to-peer network) claims,[33]
but rather intangible property without intellectual property protection.[34] The fact
that relative (contractual) rights to tokens can, of course, be established has no effect
on the determination of the legal nature of the token in a sense of 'ownership' or
'property'. Due to the lack of such positions, IPL and PIL struggle to address such
issues. For example, the lex rei sitae concept (the law of the state where the object of
the property right is located applies) does not fit here.[35] The same is true regarding

---

[27] Cf. Lehmann, 'Who Owns Bitcoin? Private Law Facing the Blockchain' (2019) 21 *Minnesota Journal of Law, Science & Technology*, 93 (124). Cf. Rome I Regulation, Art. 12; Rühl, 'Smart Contracts und anwendbares Recht', in Braegelmann and Kaulartz (eds), *Smart Contracts* (2019), § 12 para. 11.

[28] Similarly, Omlor, 'Blockchain-basierte Zahlungsmittel' (2018) 51 *Zeitschrift für Rechtspolitik*, 85 (86).

[29] Lehmann, 'Who Owns Bitcoin? Private Law Facing the Blockchain' (2019) 21 *Minnesota Journal of Law, Science & Technology*, 93: '[…] it is far from clear how virtual currencies and other crypto assets are transferred and acquired'.

[30] Seitz, 'Distributed Ledger Technology & Bitcoin – Zur rechtlichen Stellung eines Bitcoin-'Inhabers'' (2017) 20 *Kommunikation und Recht*, 763 (765).

[31] Martiny, 'Virtuelle Währungen, insbesondere Bitcoins, im Internationalen Privat- und Zivilverfahrensrecht' (2018) 38 *Praxis des Internationalen Privat- und Verfahrensrechts*, 553 (556 et seq.).

[32] From a Swiss perspective: Seiler and Seiler, 'Sind Kryptowährungen wie Bitcoin (BTC), Ethereum (ETH) und Ripple (XRP) als Sachen im Sinne des ZGB zu behandeln?' (2018) 5 *sui-generis*, 150; Guillaume, 'Aspects of private international law related to blockchain transactions', in Kraus, Obrist and Hari (eds), *Blockchains, Smart Contracts, Decentralised Autonomous Organisations and the Law* (2019), 49 (62 et seq.); from a Common Law perspective: Fox, 'Cryptocurrencies in the Common Law of Property' (2018), available at https://ssrn.com/abstract=3232501 (accessed 1.9.2020).

[33] For German substantive law: Spindler and Biller, 'Rechtsprobleme von Bitcoins als virtuelle Währung' (2014) 68 *Zeitschrift für Wirtschafts- und Bankrecht*, 1357 (1359 et seq.); different view from a Swiss perspective: Guillaume, 'Aspects of private international law related to blockchain transactions', in Kraus, Obrist and Hari (eds), *Blockchains, Smart Contracts, Decentralised Autonomous Organisations and the Law* (2019), 49 (62 et seq.).

[34] Martiny, 'Virtuelle Währungen, insbesondere Bitcoins, im Internationalen Privat- und Zivilverfahrensrecht' (2018) 38 *Praxis des Internationalen Privat- und Verfahrensrechts*, 553 (556).

[35] Guillaume, 'Aspects of private international law related to blockchain transactions', in Kraus, Obrist and Hari (eds), *Blockchains, Smart Contracts, Decentralised Autonomous Organisations and the Law* (2019), 49 (61 et seqq.); Lehmann, 'Who Owns Bitcoin? Private Law Facing the Blockchain' (2019) 21 *Minnesota Journal of Law, Science & Technology*, 93 (114); Lehmann and Krysa, 'Blockchain, Smart Contracts und Token aus der Sicht des (Internationalen) Privatrechts' (2019) 12 *Bonner Rechtsjournal*, 90 (95 et seq.); cf. however, Financial Markets Law Committee (FMLC), 'Distributed Ledger Technology and Governing Law: Issues of Legal Uncertainty' (March 2018), para. 7.1. et seqq., available at https://beck-link.de/5fsy6 (accessed 11.12.2020) and Raskin, 'Realm of the Coin: Bitcoin

assignments of claims (cf. Art. 14 Rome I Regulation).[36] As a point of reference for a legal classification, the private key appears as a kind of 'digital cheque' which gives the de facto power of the transfer.[37] If the respective token is understood as a concrete date in the form of the private key, one may assume a kind of '**data ownership**',[38] which could be more or less convincing depending on the property concepts of the respective legal state system.[39] As the legal concept of 'data ownership' has not gained acceptance in most states and there is no EU IPL/PIL provision dealing with this issue, a meta level analysis does not (yet) seem effective here. In this case, the respective contractual relationship (para. 8 et seqq.) becomes even more important. Here, it must be taken into account that the transfer of the crypto token is not a contract itself but the performance of a contract.[40] Finally, having identified a contractual focus on the level of IPL/PIL, this does not consequently mean that contractual obligations between the participants in a crypto asset system exist on the substantive law level. This is in fact a question of the respective applicable substantive law (cf. Art. 10(1) Rome I Regulation).[41]

7 However, some states, e.g., Germany, recently started to work on legislative proposals, which could grant a kind of property-like status. One may speak of a specific '**token property**'.[42] Pursuant to § 2 subpara. 3 of the draft on the law regarding the introduction of electronic securities (Gesetz über elektronische Wertpapiere, 'eWpG') of the German Federal Ministry of Justice and Consumer Protection and the German Federal Ministry of Finance 'an electronic security [which includes crypto securities] is deemed to be a moveable [thing] within the meaning of section 90 of the [German] Civil Code.' This results, in principle, in the application of the corresponding German property law provisions. Pursuant to the Conflict of Laws rule, § 32 of the draft, 'rights to and dispositions of an electronic security are subject to the law of the state whose supervision the registrar, who maintains electronic securities register in which security is registered, is subject to.'

---

and Civil Procedure' (2015) 20 *Fordham Journal of Corporate & Financial Law*, 969 (988 et seqq., 1011): 'courts should treat bitcoins just as they treat other forms of tangible [!] property. Innovative technology does not have to mean innovative jurisprudence'.

[36] See Dickinson, 'Cryptocurrencies and the Conflict of Laws', in Fox and Green (eds), *Cryptocurrencies in Public and Private Law* (2019), § 5, para. 5.103 et seqq.

[37] Seitz, 'Distributed Ledger Technology & Bitcoin – Zur rechtlichen Stellung eines Bitcoin-'Inhabers'' (2017) 20 *Kommunikation und Recht*, 763 (765).

[38] For a discussion of 'data ownership' see, for example: Zech, 'Information as Property' (2015) 6 *Journal of Intellectual Property, Information Technology and Electronic Commerce Law*, 192; Zech, 'Building a European Data Economy – The European Commission's Proposal for a Data Producer's Right' (2017) 9 *Zeitschrift für geistiges Eigentum*, 317.

[39] In Germany, for example, such a 'data ownership' is not convincing: Steinrötter, 'Vermeintliche Ausschließlichkeitsrechte an binären Codes' (2017) 20 *Zeitschrift für IT-Recht und Digitalisierung*, 731.

[40] Lehmann, 'Who Owns Bitcoin? Private Law Facing the Blockchain' (2019) 21 *Minnesota Journal of Law, Science & Technology*, 93 (124).

[41] Dickinson, 'Cryptocurrencies and the Conflict of Laws', in Fox and Green (eds), *Cryptocurrencies in Public and Private Law* (2019), § 5, para. 5.31.

[42] Lehmann, 'Who Owns Bitcoin? Private Law Facing the Blockchain' (2019) 21 *Minnesota Journal of Law, Science & Technology*, 93 (112): 'a property law analysis may also seem apposite because the coins or other assets encrypted on the blockchain often have market value and can be assimilated to goods which are the object of property law' and (123): 'As has been shown above, it is impossible to identify such a law [regarding the 'property transfer'] for completely distributed ledgers. […] It is thus not only impossible, but also useless to search for the law that 'governs' a transfer on the blockchain'; Dickinson, 'Cryptocurrencies and the Conflict of Laws', in Fox and Green (eds), *Cryptocurrencies in Public and Private Law* (2019), § 5, para. 5.99: 'In many cases, questions of property in a cryptocurrency may, at best, be of secondary or consequential importance'.

D. Contractual Relationships in Initial Coin Offerings

The issuance of crypto tokens for the purpose of raising capital on a primary market in exchange for (other) crypto or fiat currency is called an Initial Coin Offering (→ § 1 para. 81 et seqq.). Contractual claims arise from the subscription agreement between issuer and purchaser (including 'Terms & Conditions'). Issuers often make use of formal agreements on international jurisdiction and applicable law.[43] The subscription agreement must be distinguished from the 'white paper', which is (at least to some extent) similar to a prospectus under capital markets law (→ para. 36 et seqq.).

I. International Jurisdiction

From the perspective of EU lawyers, it is possible to bring an action at the **defendant's domicile** by means of the actor sequitur forum rei (Art. 4 Brussels Ibis Regulation). In principle, an **agreement** on the place of jurisdiction (Art. 25 Brussels Ibis Regulation), or a situation in which the defendant **enters an appearance** (Art. 26 Brussels Ibis Regulation) are also possible.

In a typical Initial Public Offering (IPO), the subscription agreement is concluded between an issuer and a financial intermediary (in particular, banks or institutional investors). Accordingly, IPO primary market contracts are consumer contracts only in very exceptional cases.[44] In the context of ICOs, the subscription contract is typically concluded directly between the issuer and the token purchaser. In this respect, **the consumer jurisdiction rules** pursuant to Art. 17 et seq. Brussels Ibis Regulation apply. The ECJ classified prospectus liability as a tort in the 'Kolassa'[45] case. However, this does not preclude the 'normal' contractual qualification. On the contrary, 'Kolassa' could be interpreted that in the case of certain contractual issues, for example in the context of bond conditions and in particular in the case of the issuance of the bonds themselves, a (consumer) contract qualification is still possible. In contrast to the special consumer PIL provision (Rome I Regulation), there is no respective exclusion in EU jurisdiction law. Art. 17(3) Brussels Ibis Regulation does not provide for a corresponding counterpart.

First, it is necessary that the proceedings relate to **contracts or contractual claims between a consumer and an entrepreneur**. The classification as a consumer must be established specifically in relation to the act in question: whoever acts in the exercise of his professional or commercial activity is a professional, whoever acts 'as a private individual' is a consumer.[46] If there is no contract for the sale of goods on instalment credit terms or a contract for a loan repayable by instalments, or for any other form of credit made to finance the sale of goods (Art. 17(1)(a) or (b) Brussels Ibis Regulation), Art. 17(1)(c) Brussels Ibis Regulation applies. This means that the material scope of application of the consumer protection rule is relevant if the contract has been concluded with a person who **pursues commercial or professional**

---

[43] Martiny, 'Virtuelle Währungen, insbesondere Bitcoins, im Internationalen Privat- und Zivilverfahrensrecht' (2018) 38 *Praxis des Internationalen Privat- und Verfahrensrechts*, 553 (562).

[44] Cf. Steinrötter, *Beschränkte Rechtswahl im Internationalen Kapitalmarktprivatrecht und akzessorische Anknüpfung an das Kapitalmarktordnungsstatut* (2014), 424 on the PIL capital market agreement.

[45] ECJ, Judgment of 28 January 2015, *Kolassa*, C-375/13, ECLI:EU:C:2015:37.

[46] Opinion of AG Cruz Villalón, Judgment of 23 December 2015, *Hobohm*, C-297/14, ECLI:EU:C:2015:556, para. 26; cf. on the concept of consumer recently Judgment of 3 October 2019, *Petruchová*, C-208/18, ECLI:EU:C:2019:825.

activities in the Member State of the consumer's domicile or, by any means, directs such activities to that Member State or to several States including that Member State, and the contract falls within the scope of such activities. According to the criteria formulated by the ECJ in the 'Pammer' case, such a 'direction' requires that 'the trader must have manifested its intention to establish commercial relations with consumers from one or more other Member States, including that of the consumer's domicile'.[47] For conventional advertising media such as advertising via the press, radio, television or cinema in the consumer's country of residence or offers directly to the consumer (e.g. by mail or representatives), such an intention can be assumed.[48] However, **advertising via the Internet** can be accessed worldwide. This is also the case for ICOs. Thus, it must be determined on the basis of indications whether the trader was prepared to conclude a contract with the respective consumers.[49] Among the 'strong' criteria, the ECJ counts, for example, 'mention that it is offering its services or its goods in one or more Member States designated by name. The same is true of the disbursement of expenditure on an internet referencing service to the operator of a search engine in order to facilitate access to the trader's site by consumers domiciled in various Member States, which likewise demonstrates the existence of such an intention'.[50] 'Weaker' indicators are those caused by 'the international nature of the activity at issue,[51] such as certain tourist activities; mention of telephone numbers with the international code; use of a top-level domain name other than that of the Member State in which the trader is established, for example '.de', or use of neutral top-level domain names such as '.com' or '.eu'; the description of itineraries from one or more other Member States to the place where the service is provided; and mention of an international clientele composed of customers domiciled in various Member States, in particular by presentation of accounts written by such customers'[52]. If language and currency may be specified on Internet sites, this can also be considered.[53] Information regarding the electronic respectively geographical address or a telephone number without an international prefix are irrelevant.[54]

11   According to the ECJ judgment 'Mühlleitner',[55] it is not absolutely necessary that the legal transaction resulting from the 'directing' is then also **concluded at a distance**.[56] In the controversial 'Emrek'[57] decision, the ECJ finally stated that **no causal connection**

---

[47] ECJ, Judgment of 7 December 2010, *Pammer*, C-144/09, ECLI:EU:C:2010:740, para. 75.

[48] Ibid, para. 65.

[49] Ibid, para. 76: 'evidence demonstrating that the trader was envisaging doing business with consumers domiciled in other Member States, including the Member State of that consumer's domicile, in the sense that it was minded to conclude a contract with those consumers'.

[50] Ibid, para. 81.

[51] Sceptical Staudinger and Steinrötter, 'Verfahrens- sowie kollisionsrechtlicher Verbraucherschutz bei Online-Geschäften' (2011) 21 *Europäisches Wirtschafts- und Steuerrecht*, 70 (72), para. 39.

[52] ECJ, Judgment of 7 December 2010, *Pammer*, C-144/09, ECLI:EU:C:2010:740, para. 83.

[53] Ibid, para. 84; affirmative Staudinger and Steinrötter, 'Verfahrens- sowie kollisionsrechtlicher Verbraucherschutz bei Online-Geschäften' (2011) 21 *Europäisches Wirtschafts- und Steuerrecht*, 70 (73).

[54] ECJ, Judgment of 7 December 2010, *Pammer*, C-144/09, ECLI:EU:C:2010:740, para. 77 et seq.

[55] ECJ, Judgment of 6 September 2012, *Mühlleitner*, C-190/11, ECLI:EU:C:2012:542, para. 45.

[56] This was previously unclear, as a joint statement by the Commission and the Council (published in: 21 *Praxis des Internationalen Privat- und Verfahrensrechts* (2001), 259 (261)) stipulated that the website must offer to conclude a distance contract and that the agreement must actually have been concluded in this way for the protection rule to apply. The joint declaration was adopted in Rome I Regulation, recital 24 sentence 1.

[57] ECJ, Judgment of 17 October 2013, *Emrek*, C-218/12, ECLI:EU:C:2013:666, para. 32; different opinion previously German Federal Court (BGH) 17.9.2008 – III ZR 71/08 – *Neue Juristische Wochenschrift* (NJW) 2009, 298.

between the 'direction' and the conclusion of the contract was required.[58] However, the causality remains significant as a further objective indication in the sense of the 'Pammer' catalogue, which is intended to allow a conclusion to be drawn on the will to 'direct'.[59]

Occasionally, the publication of an ICO **white paper** on a website may provide an **indication of such a 'direction'** towards a particular state. However, the information contained in the white paper (language used in the white paper or on the website itself; currency to purchase tokens) may only be useful in **exceptional cases to determine the country of destination**. This is because the white paper is regularly written in English as the lingua franca of the Internet. The website extensions are often '.com', '.io' or '.net', and sometimes the tokens to be issued are to be acquired with other crypto tokens, not with fiat currencies (→ § 1 para. 84).[60] Issuers wishing to avoid 'directing' to a certain state, i.e. to exclude a certain jurisdiction, should try to do so **by means of a disclaimer**,[61] according to which the token issue is not directed at that very state.

According to Art. 17(1)(c) var. 2 Brussels Ibis Regulation, the contract at issue in the specific proceedings must be **'within the scope'** of this 'directed' activity. This can be of particular relevance for **follow-up contracts with intermediaries** (→ para. 31 et seq.). Even before the ECJ case 'Hobohm' (→ para. 31), it was generally accepted that consumer courts also apply to 'follow-up contracts of the same type' and to amendments, extensions and additions to the original contract.[62] The above could be relevant in this context, for example, in the case of the **subsequent resale of securities** pursuant to Art. 5 Regulation (EU) No. 1129/2017 (Prospectus Regulation)[63]. 12

Furthermore, in 'Maletic', the ECJ extended the scope of the consumer jurisdiction to the effect that the term 'other party to a contract' in Art. 18(1) Brussels Ibis Regulation also designates the party to the contract of the trader with whom the consumer has concluded the contract in question, who is domiciled in the consumer's Member State of residence, even if the contractual relationships are formally separate.[64] This may have to be taken into account in the case of certain distribution arrangements, such as the **use of (financial) intermediaries** (→ para. 27 et seqq.), and perhaps even rating agencies. 13

Example:
The A company based in Estonia would like to issue crypto tokens. The subscription is possible online. All information, including the white paper, is available via the website with the ending '.com'. The website advertises, among other things, another ICO that has already taken place, including an overview of the countries in which this issue was particularly successful. This includes Germany with 37 %. The website also offers the option of switching to the German

---

[58] Critically to this Staudinger and Steinrötter, 'Kausalität des Ausrichtens auf Wohnort für Vertragsschluss – Verbrauchergerichtsstand (Urteilsanmerkung)' (2013) 66 *Neue Juristische Wochenschrift*, 3505.
[59] ECJ, Judgment of 17 October 2013, *Emrek*, C-218/12, ECLI:EU:C:2013:666, para. 29.
[60] Barsan, 'Legal Challenges of Initial Coin Offerings (ICO)' (2017) 12 *Revue Trimestrielle de Droit Financier*, 54 (64).
[61] In practice, it is still unclear whether one can really 'escape' from 'direction' with it; see Staudinger and Steinrötter, 'Verfahrens- sowie kollisionsrechtlicher Verbraucherschutz bei Online-Geschäften' (2011) 21 *Europäisches Wirtschafts- und Steuerrecht*, 70 (72).
[62] For contract amendments and contract extensions see German Federal Court (BGH) 5.10.2010 – VI ZR 159/09 – 64 *Neue Juristische Wochenschrift* (NJW) 2011, 532 (533 et seq.), para. 18 et seq.; for general information on supplements, extensions and amendments as well as on similar follow-up contracts see Mankowski, 'Enge Verbindung zu früher geschlossenem Verbrauchervertrag – Gerichtsstand' (2016) 69 *Neue Juristische Wochenschrift*, 699.
[63] Regulation (EU) No. 1129/2017 of the European Parliament and of the Council on the prospectus to be published when securities are offered to the public or admitted to trading on a regulated market, and repealing Directive 2003/71/EC, OJ L 168, 30.6.2017 p. 12–82.
[64] ECJ, Judgment of 14 November 2013, *Maletic*, C-478/12, ECLI:EU:C:2013:735, para. 28 et seq.

language. The 'Terms & Conditions', which can also only be viewed online, stipulate a place of jurisdiction in Estonia. B from Germany subscribes a certain number of tokens for his private investment and receives a confirmation. However, he only receives half of the desired tokens, even though he has already transferred the entire amount. He demands the allocation of the remaining tokens and files a lawsuit in Germany. A claims that Estonia alone is the state of jurisdiction. In the present case, however, the protective jurisdiction for consumers applies, which leads to the exclusion of jurisdiction agreements pursuant to Art. 19 Brussels Ibis Regulation. The consumer can sue at his place of residence according to Art. 18(1) var. 2 Brussels Ibis Regulation because the conditions of Art. 17(1) Brussels Ibis Regulation are met: A 'direction' towards Germany is indicated by the advertising with the previous issue of tokens (including the reference to the strong participation from Germany) as well as the possibility to switch to the German language, and finally from the concrete causality between the website appearance and conclusion of the contract.

14   If the outlined requirements of Art. 17 et seq. Brussels Ibis Regulation are not met, a **contractual qualification** in accordance with Art. 7 No. 1 Brussels Ibis Regulation **is** nevertheless possible – this may even be the case if the requirements of the consumer court jurisdiction regarding the term 'contract' were not met,[65] because the requirements for the concept of contract are arguably lower in this respect. For the question of whether a contractual qualification appears appropriate,[66] it depends, in contrast to Art. 7 No. 2 Brussels Ibis Regulation on whether the issuer **'voluntarily' created the obligation in question**[67] or whether a contractual interpretation appears **'indispensable' for the determination of the breach of duty** in question ('Brogsitter').[68] This may be the case for ICOs if the **interpretation of the subscription agreement or the associated form agreements** is 'indispensable' in order to answer whether there has been a breach of duty. If this is the case and if the person domiciled in the EU is to be sued in another Member State, this is possible in the court of the place where the obligation has been or would have been performed.[69] This place of performance can be determined by agreement.[70] In the absence of such an agreement, the place of performance is to be assessed according to the 'Tessili' Doctrine of the ECJ, i.e. (unfortunately) not autonomously in terms of Union law, but according to the law that is applied to the obligation in question[71] under the Conflict of Laws rules of the court dealing with the dispute.[72]

II. Applicable law

15   The law applicable to primary market agreements[73] is determined by the Conflict of Laws provisions of the **Rome I Regulation** (cf. Art. 10, Art. 12 Rome I Regula-

---

[65] Kreuzer, Wagner and Reder, 'Internationale Zuständigkeit', in Dauses and Ludwigs (eds), *Handbuch des EU-Wirtschaftsrechts* (January 2019), Q. II., para. 124 et seq. with further references.
[66] See Barsan, 'Legal Challenges of Initial Coin Offerings (ICO)' (2017) 12 *Revue Trimestrielle de Droit Financier*, 54 (63).
[67] For example: ECJ, Judgment of 17 September 2002, *Tacconi*, C-334/00, ECLI:EU:C:2002:499.
[68] ECJ, Judgment of 13 March 2014, *Brogsitter*, C-548/12, ECLI:EU:C:2014:148, para. 25.
[69] See also ECJ, Judgment of 20 April 2016, *Profit Investment SIM*, C-366/13, ECLI:EU:C:2016:282.
[70] Critical Staudinger and Steinrötter, 'Das neue Zuständigkeitsregime bei zivilrechtlichen Auslandssachverhalten: die Brüssel Ia-VO' (2015) 55 *Juristische Schulung*, 1 (7): formal requirements of Art. 25 Brussels Ibis Regulation need to be applied.
[71] ECJ, Judgment of 6 October 1976, *de Bloos/Buyer*, C- 14/76, ECLI:EU:C:1976:134.
[72] ECJ, Judgment of 6 October 1976, *Tessili*, C-12/76, ECLI:EU:C:1976:133; critical Staudinger and Steinrötter, 'Das neue Zuständigkeitsregime bei zivilrechtlichen Auslandssachverhalten: die Brüssel Ia-VO' (2015) 55 *Juristische Schulung*, 1 (7).
[73] Only if no contract has been concluded despite close contact between the issuer and the potential acquirer can the Union law 'culpa in contrahendo' be considered (overemphasis of 'cic' in this respect by Barsan, 'Legal Challenges of Initial Coin Offerings (ICO)' (2017) 12 *Revue Trimestrielle de Droit*

tion).⁷⁴ The 'voluntarily criterion' (→ para. 14) applies mutatis mutandis to the delimitation of non-contractual obligations and thus to the Rome II Regulation (as does the 'Brogsitter' Doctrine in principle; see also → para. 14). The exception in Art. 1(2)(d) Rome I Regulation, does not apply, since – if and to the extent that one affirms the security character of the respective tokens – the obligation does not arise precisely from the fungibility of the security.⁷⁵ It has to be noted that an ICO regarding investment tokens or utility tokens with an investment focus means that – contrary to the typical IPO, where intermediaries are involved – issuer and subscriber or acquirer have **a direct contractual relationship**.

1. Choice of Law

Firstly, the issuer of the ICO can choose the applicable law with the subscriber in accordance with Art. 3 Rome I Regulation thus exercising party autonomy.⁷⁶ Here, some **limitations** regarding the choice of law need to be taken into account. This applies in particular to the 'domestic clause' of Art. 3(3) Rome I Regulation and the 'internal market demarcation clause' of Art. 3(4) Rome I Regulation (both are based on 'simple' ius cogens) as well as to the intervention of overriding mandatory provisions under Art. 9 Rome I Regulation ('qualified' ius cogens). Which provisions are to be qualified as overriding mandatory provisions within the meaning of Art. 9 Rome I Regulation is a matter of interpretation; (unfortunately) there can be no universal answer here.⁷⁷ It is conceivable that certain **supervisory market regulation provisions** could be applied as overriding mandatory provisions,⁷⁸ i.e. provisions which always need to be applied independently of the otherwise applicable private law. In any case, these must be provisions that are intended to serve (at least also and predominantly) macro-interests (note the definition in Art. 9(1) Rome I Regulation). Non-governmental legal regimes, namely 'self-made' rules, such as those of a blockchain system, are a priori ineligible under EU Conflict of Laws.⁷⁹

16

The **special consumer protection** PIL rule of Art. 6 Rome I Regulation is ultimately not applicable at least for investment and for utility tokens⁸⁰ with investment focus.

17

Financier, 54 (64)). However, the then relevant Art. 12(1) Rome II Regulation refers in any case to the hypothetical contract statute in accordance with Rome I Regulation.

⁷⁴ Steinrötter, *Beschränkte Rechtswahl im Internationalen Kapitalmarktprivatrecht und akzessorische Anknüpfung an das Kapitalmarktordnungsstatut* (2014), 425.

⁷⁵ Martiny, 'Virtuelle Währungen, insbesondere Bitcoins, im Internationalen Privat- und Zivilverfahrensrecht' (2018) 38 *Praxis des Internationalen Privat- und Verfahrensrechts*, 553 (560); see already Müller, *Finanzinstrumente* (2011), 157 et seqq.; Steinrötter, *Beschränkte Rechtswahl im Internationalen Kapitalmarktprivatrecht und akzessorische Anknüpfung an das Kapitalmarktordnungsstatut* (2014), 425.

⁷⁶ See also Lehmann, 'Who Owns Bitcoin? Private Law Facing the Blockchain' (2019) 21 *Minnesota Journal of Law, Science & Technology*, 93 (112 et seqq.); Martiny, 'Virtuelle Währungen, insbesondere Bitcoins, im Internationalen Privat- und Zivilverfahrensrecht' (2018) 38 *Praxis des Internationalen Privat- und Verfahrensrechts*, 553 (558).

⁷⁷ Too wide interpretation by Barsan, 'Legal Challenges of Initial Coin Offerings (ICO)' (2017) 12 *Revue Trimestrielle de Droit Financier*, 54 (65): 'It finally appears that with regards to conflict of laws […], national investor protection rules will always be applicable because of their mandatory nature'.

⁷⁸ Martiny, 'Virtuelle Währungen, insbesondere Bitcoins, im Internationalen Privat- und Zivilverfahrensrecht' (2018) 38 *Praxis des Internationalen Privat- und Verfahrensrechts*, 553 (563); see also Einsele, 'Kapitalmarktrecht und Internationales Privatrecht' (2017) 81 *Rabels Zeitschrift für ausländisches und internationales Privatrecht*, 781 (793 et seqq.); Einsele, 'Kapitalmarktrechtliche Eingriffsnormen – Bedarf die Rom I-Verordnung einer Sonderregel für harmonisiertes europäisches Recht?' (2012) 32 *Praxis des Internationalen Privat- und Verfahrensrechts*, 481.

⁷⁹ Dickinson, 'Cryptocurrencies and the Conflict of Laws', in Fox and Green (eds), *Cryptocurrencies in Public and Private Law* (2019), § 5, para. 5.37.

⁸⁰ This also applies to Barsan, 'Legal Challenges of Initial Coin Offerings (ICO)' (2017) 12 *Revue Trimestrielle de Droit Financier*, 54 (65). But see also de Vauplane, 'Blockchain and Intermediated Securities' (2018) 36 *Nederlands Internationaal Privaatrecht*, 94 (102).

According to its paragraph 4, subpara. d, it does not apply to 'rights and obligations which constitute a financial instrument and rights and obligations constituting the terms and conditions governing the issuance or offer to the public [...] of transferable securities'. This makes perfect sense if the choice of law on the basis of a concrete comparison pursuant to Art. 6(2)(2) Rome I Regulation would otherwise entail the risk of an inconsistent contract statute ('law mix'). This is what the EU legislator rightly seeks to avoid in capital markets law (Rome I Regulation, recital 29), because the IPO or ICO is likely to become considerably more difficult and more expensive if investors did not invest under the same law, i.e. under different and possibly even contradictory conditions.[81] The **general rules** of Art. 3 et. seq. Rome I Regulation apply here.

Example:
With regard to the example of → para. 13 – the issue is for **investment tokens** in this variation – the 'Terms & Conditions', which can also only be viewed online, specify the choice of Estonian law. B from Germany subscribes a certain number of tokens for his private investment and receives a confirmation. However, he only receives half of the desired tokens, even though he has already transferred the entire amount. He demands the transfer of the remaining tokens and refers to German law. A replies that Estonian law is applicable. The special Conflict of Laws rule for consumer contracts, Art. 6 Rome I Regulation, is not relevant because of its paragraph 4 subpara. d. The choice of Estonian law is thus possible in principle pursuant to Art. 3(1)(1) Rome I Regulation.

18   In the case of **currency tokens**, on the other hand, the consumer protection Conflict of Laws rule does apply. In this respect, in the light of Rome I Regulation, recitals 7, 24 p. 2, the remarks on Art. 17 et seq., Brussels Ibis Regulation in particular on 'direction', apply accordingly (→ para. 10 et seqq.). In terms of legal consequences, the abovementioned 'law mix' between the chosen statute and the ius cogens of the consumer's country of habitual residence, which in the specific case appears more favourable to the consumer than the counterpart of the chosen law, occurs pursuant to Art. 6(2) Rome I Regulation (→ para. 17). The form of the choice of law is governed by the law of the consumer's habitual residence pursuant to Art. 11(4) Rome I Regulation. In addition, the provisions of the Directive 93/13/EEC (Directive on Unfair Contract Terms)[82] shall be observed in the case of choice of law provisions in Terms and Conditions.[83]

Example:
With regard to the example of → para. 13, 17 – the issue is for **currency tokens** in this variation. Since the exclusion of Art. 6(4)(d) Rome I Regulation is not relevant in this respect due to the lack of securities status of utility tokens, the chosen Estonian law applies in accordance with Art. 6(2)(1) Rome I Regulation in conjunction with Art. 3. However, German mandatory contract law, which in the specific case appears more favourable to B than its Estonian functional counterpart, would be applicable within the Estonian contract statute. I.e. there could be a 'law mix', consisting of Estonian and German law.

19   De lege ferenda (at least as far as capital markets law is concerned, i.e., for investment and partly for utility tokens), further restrictions of party autonomy are conceivable for reasons of predictability of the applicable law,[84] for example by restricting the choice of law to the legal systems of the countries in which the issue is to be made (deselection e.g. of US law and geo-blocking at the technical level).

---

[81] See Garcimartín Alférez, 'The Rome I Regulation: Exceptions to the Rule on Consumer Contracts and Financial Instruments' (2009) 5 *Journal of Private International Law*, 85 (92); Lehmann, 'Financial Instruments', in Ferrari and Leible (eds), *Rome I Regulation* (2009), 85 (95).
[82] Directive 93/13/EEC on unfair terms in consumer contracts, OJ L 95, 21.4.1993 p. 29–34.
[83] ECJ, Judgment of 28 July 2016, *VKI/Amazon*, C-191/15, ECLI:EU:C:2016:612.
[84] See Steinrötter, *Beschränkte Rechtswahl im Internationalen Kapitalmarktprivatrecht und akzessorische Anknüpfung an das Kapitalmarktordnungsstatut* (2014), 425.

2. Applicable law in the Absence of a Choice of Law

In the absence of a choice of law, the connection to a national legal system is to be **20** determined objectively. As already explained (→ para 17), the special Conflict of Laws rule of Art. 6 Rome I Regulation (consumer protection) is not applicable to investment tokens and those utility tokens in which the investment character predominates (Art. 6(4)(d) Rome I Regulation). In this respect, the basic rule of Art. 4 Rome I Regulation applies. Whether the ICO subscription contract is regularly a contract of sale[85] pursuant to Art. 4(1)(d) Rome I Regulation appears doubtful, since this PIL provision only refers to movable property. However, it is possible to assess the 'purchase' of a token simply on the basis of Art. 4(2) Rome I Regulation and thus on the principle of **'characteristic performance of the contract'**. Thus, the legal system of the issuer's habitual residence would be applicable since it provides the power of transfer over the respective token.[86] In this way, a desirable result is also achieved insofar as only one legal system dominates the facts of the case (detached from the individual acquirer).[87] Nevertheless, one may be sceptical whether it is at all possible to determine the characteristic performance of an ICO contract (money against tokens to be issued or – a fortiori – tokens already available on the market against tokens to be issued).[88]

It also seems worth considering using the **escape clause** of Art. 4(3) Rome I Regula- **21** tion to link to the regulatory law governing the issue. This appears convincing from a legal policy perspective, because in this way two closely related matters would be subject to the same national law. For the 'normal cases', i.e. exchange 'tokens for money', this 'accessoriness solution' via paragraph 3 seems to be quite feasible; the same result could be achieved for the 'exchange-like cases' ('tokens for tokens') via paragraph 4. However, linking such a regulatory statute with a state is not (any longer) easy due to the direct validity of the Prospectus Regulation (since 21.7.2019).[89] An alternative could be seen in the link to the **administrative** procedure (i.e. to the [first] authority responsibility for the ICO)[90]. Incidentally, this is ultimately an approach that is in line with the basic ideas of the German Federal Government's recently published legislative proposal.[91]

Example:
The A company with its registered office in Estonia would like to issue **investment tokens** via a website which is directed towards Germany (→ para. 10 et seqq.). A choice of law does not exist. The Estonian supervisory authority is competent. B from Germany subscribes a certain number of tokens for his private investment and receives a confirmation. However, he only receives half of the desired tokens, even though he has already transferred the entire amount. He demands the transfer of the remaining tokens and refers to German law. Due to Art. 6(4)(d) Rome I Regulation the recourse to the consumer protection standard is excluded.

---

[85] This is what Martiny, 'Virtuelle Währungen, insbesondere Bitcoins, im Internationalen Privat- und Zivilverfahrensrecht' (2018) 38 *Praxis des Internationalen Privat- und Verfahrensrechts*, 553 (562) finds.

[86] Martiny, 'Virtuelle Währungen, insbesondere Bitcoins, im Internationalen Privat- und Zivilverfahrensrecht' (2018) 38 *Praxis des Internationalen Privat- und Verfahrensrechts*, 553 (559) seeks to achieve this result, which is linked to the issuer's residence, by applying Rome I Regulation, Art. 4, para. 3 or 4.

[87] In this direction already: Steinrötter, *Beschränkte Rechtswahl im Internationalen Kapitalmarktprivatrecht und akzessorische Anknüpfung an das Kapitalmarktordnungsstatut* (2014), 427.

[88] Barsan, 'Legal Challenges of Initial Coin Offerings (ICO)' (2017) 12 *Revue Trimestrielle de Droit Financier*, 54 (63 et seqq.).

[89] Art. 4(2) Prospectus Regulation.

[90] The competence of the supervisory authority, such as German BaFin (not to be confused with the relevant court of jurisdiction) is based on the applicable regulatory law (strict principle of parallelism; Kment, *Grenzüberschreitendes Verwaltungshandeln* (2010), 154 et seq.).

[91] BMF/BMJV (German Ministry of Finance with Ministry of Justice and Consumer Protection), 'Eckpunkte für die regulatorische Behandlung von elektronischen Wertpapieren und Krypto-Token' (7.3.2019), 4.

It seems convincing to take up the administrative procedure as relevant connecting factor that is taking place here in Estonia under Art. 4(3) Rome I Regulation. Accordingly, Estonian contract law applies.

22   In the case of **currency tokens**, on the other hand, the consumer protection Conflict of Laws rule does apply. In this respect, reference is made to the remarks on Art. 17 et seq. Brussels Ibis Regulation whose interpretation results apply accordingly here. In terms of legal consequences, the legal system of the consumer's **habitual residence** is to be taken as a minimum standard. However, doubts remain: If one uses the escape clause above (→ para. 21) to orientate oneself to the regulatory statute, the question arises whether the different assessment can really be justified objectively by the classification as a currency token alone. In principle, the actual differences for the acquirer of currency, investment and utility tokens only justify the differentiated Conflict of Laws treatment to a limited extent.

> **Example:**
> The A company based in Estonia would like to issue **currency tokens** via a website that is directed towards Germany (→ para. 10 et seqq.). A choice of law does not exist. The Estonian supervisory authority is competent. Private individual B from Germany subscribes a certain number of tokens and receives a confirmation. However, he only receives half of the desired tokens, even though he has already transferred the entire amount. He demands the transfer of the remaining tokens and refers to German law. Because of Art. 6(1) Rome I Regulation the legal system of the consumer's country of residence, i.e. German law, applies here.

23   If the requirements of the consumer protection Conflict of Laws rule are not met, Art. 4 Rome I Regulation, also applies here. Due to their de facto payment function, currency tokens are only weakly defined in terms of PIL with regard to the principle of contractual performance (Art. 4(2) Rome I Regulation); here too, it is convincing to take the place of the **issuer's registered office** into account. To link to the habitual residence of the respective token acquirer would be problematic in view of the typically pseudonymous structure of the blockchain and thus the predictability postulate (→ para. 41). Moreover, this would contradict the principle of contractual performance and ultimately lead to a fragmentation of law which is not desirable for (capital) markets.[92] In addition, Art. 4(1)(h) Rome I Regulation deals with certain capital market contracts, but not with the primary market agreement.[93] Finally, it should be noted that mandatory rules within the meaning of Art. 9(1) Rome I Regulation may 'perforate' the statute of the contract. Another question, and therefore only mentioned in passing, is that the **cooperation of several companies in order to implement an ICO** can **probably** be qualified under **the Conflict of Laws rule regarding corporate law**, which is why the scope of application of the Rome I Regulation would remain closed in this respect (see Art. 1(2)(d) Rome I Regulation, thereof).

E. Contractual Relationships in the Secondary Market

I. International Jurisdiction

24   Disputes concerning secondary market contracts can always be brought before the courts at the **defendant's (Member State) domicile** (Art. 4 Brussels Ibis Regulation). In

---

[92] Cf. MacLean, 'Governing the blockchain: how to determine applicable law' [2017] *Butterworths Journal of International Banking and Financial Law*, 359.
[93] Cf. Garcimartín Alférez, 'The Rome I Regulation: Exceptions to the Rule on Consumer Contracts and Financial Instruments' (2009) 5 *Journal of Private International Law*, 85 (95).

principle, an **agreement on the place of jurisdiction** (Art. 25 Brussels Ibis Regulation)[94], is also conceivable. The same applies to the defendants **entering an appearance** (Art. 26 Brussels Ibis Regulation). Finally, the **place of performance** of Art. 7(1) Brussels Ibis Regulation may be relevant (→ para. 14).

II. Applicable Law

It is obvious that secondary market contracts between the individual participants in the blockchain network (nodes; → § 1 para. 7 et seqq.) are also contractually qualifiable from the perspective of the EU PIL and must therefore be assessed in accordance with the Rome I Regulation.[95] The choice of the relevant Conflict of Laws rule is more difficult.[96] For **investment tokens** and utility tokens with an investment focus, Art. 6(4)(e) Rome I Regulation and Art. 4(1)(h) Rome I Regulation could be applicable at first glance. This would initially have the consequence that the special PIL rule for consumer protection in Art. 6 Rome I Regulation would not be relevant in this respect. Furthermore, Art. 4(1)(h) Rome I Regulation, would lead to the application of that capital market regulation law, which already governs the 'multilateral system'[97] in regulatory terms. This is an **accessory connection** of contract law to the **mandatory 'law of the system'**, i.e. to the law of the state which has the supervision of the respective trading system.[98] In the present case, therefore, it is a question of the stock exchange law that also applies to trading platforms (→ § 1 para. 90 et seqq.), which is, however, still partly lacking. In the absence of such supervisory law (and thus of the relevant connecting factor), Art. 4(1)(h) Rome I Regulation does not yield any results.[99] The reference to Art. 4(1)(17) Directive 2004/39/EC (MiFID I Directive),[100] with regard to the concept of 'financial instruments' now refers to Art. 4(1)(15) (Annex I (C)) Directive 2014/65/EU (MiFID II Directive)[101]. This means that transferable securities are covered by the term 'financial instruments'. This applies to investment tokens, and in some cases also to utility tokens, but to currency tokens it is to be denied (see → 20). Indeed, the above Conflict of Laws rules – Art. 6(4)(e) Rome I Regulation and Art. 4(1)(h) Rome I Regulation– are aimed at secondary

25

---

[94] Subject to Art. 19 Brussels Ibis Regulation if the consumer's place of jurisdiction is determined in accordance with Art. 17 et seq. Brussels Ibis Regulation.
[95] Martiny, 'Virtuelle Währungen, insbesondere Bitcoins, im Internationalen Privat- und Zivilverfahrensrecht' (2018) 38 *Praxis des Internationalen Privat- und Verfahrensrechts*, 553 (565).
[96] Cf. Guillaume, 'Aspects of private international law related to blockchain transactions', in Kraus, Obrist and Hari (eds), *Blockchains, Smart Contracts, Decentralised Autonomous Organisations and the Law* (2019), 49 (79): 'the only option is to provide […] for the application of the lex fori'. This is not convincing as this supports forum shopping; Lehmann and Krysa, 'Blockchain, Smart Contracts und Token aus der Sicht des (Internationalen) Privatrechts' (2019) 12 *Bonner Rechtsjournal*, 90 (95).
[97] Art. 4(1)(17) MiFID I Directive corresponds to Art. 4(1)(22) MiFiD2 Directive.
[98] Kumpan, 'Börsen und außerbörsliche Handelssysteme. Die kollisionsrechtliche Behandlung von grenzüberschreitenden Wertpapierhandelsdienstleistungen', in Zetzsche and Lehmann (eds), *Grenzüberschreitende Finanzdienstleistungen* (2018), § 9, para. 6, fn. 11, para. 19 et seq., para. 34.
[99] Correctly worked out by Kumpan, 'Börsen und außerbörsliche Handelssysteme. Die kollisionsrechtliche Behandlung von grenzüberschreitenden Wertpapierhandelsdienstleistungen', in Zetzsche and Lehmann (eds), *Grenzüberschreitende Finanzdienstleistungen* (2018), § 9, para. 50.
[100] Directive 2004/39/EC of the European Parliament and of the Council on markets in financial instruments amending Council Directives 85/611/EEC and 93/6/EEC and Directive 2000/12/EC of the European Parliament and of the Council and repealing Council Directive 93/22/EEC, OJ L 145, 30.4.2004 p. 1–44.
[101] Directive 2014/65/EU of the European Parliament and of the Council of 15 May 2014 on markets in financial instruments and amending Directives 2002/92/EC and 2011/61/EU, OJ L 173, 12.6.2016, 349–496.

(capital) market contracts. Nevertheless, in the end they do not apply.[102] This is because they focus on securities admitted to regulated markets and thus make the accessory connection of this type of secondary market contract to the applicable law of the trading venue.[103] It is questionable whether crypto trading platforms are currently subject to a corresponding regulatory framework. As far as they would fall under the regulatory definition of the **multilateral system**, the regulatory law applicable to these trading venues would also be relevant for them, which in turn would provide a suitable starting point for the accessory contractual connection. However, it is not perfectly clear, whether they could be defined as 'multilateral systems'. To the extent that and as long as an accessory link to a regulatory statute is currently still missing, such an alignment de lege ferenda would certainly be worth considering.

26 However, it would be more convincing to apply Art. 6(4)(e) Rome I Regulation **by analogy** (at least for investment tokens and utility tokens with securities elements) in order to at least avoid the otherwise occurring 'law mix' in the event of a choice of law (Art. 6(2) Rome I Regulation; → para. 17 et seq.). Assuming that no exclusion under Art. 6(4)(e) Rome I Regulation applies to all types of tokens (and in any case to currency tokens), the special Conflict of Laws rule for **consumer contracts** can in principle be applied.[104] Its specific requirements would have to be met; in addition to the 'direction' criterion, this applies in particular to the b2c component (→ para. 10 et seqq.). In the event of an 'objective connection', i.e. the absence of a choice of law, the law of the consumer's country of habitual residence applies (Art. 6(1) Rome I Regulation); if there is a choice of law, a **comparison of favourability** must be made in the application of substantive law, which could result in a 'law mix' (→ para. 17 et seq.). If the requirements of Art. 6(1) Rome I Regulation are not met in concreto (e.g. because two private parties are contracting) or if the aforementioned analogy is assumed, the general rules of Art. 3 Rome I Regulation (choice of law; on the limits of the choice of law → para. 16) and Art. 4 ('objective connection') must be applied. This is probably often the case.

If the subject matter of the contract is the exchange of **fiat money for tokens**, it should first be noted that the UN Convention on Contracts for the International Sale of Goods (CISG) does not apply because of Art. 1(1) CISG ('contracts for the sale of goods', understood as physical, movable objects[105]), even if standard software is considered to be covered by this provision and the extension to 'digital content' is increasingly being affirmed.[106] In view of the fact that within the 'objective connection' Art. 4(1)(a) Rome I Regulation requires, according to the clear wording, the physical nature of the object of sale for the contract of sale, pursuant to Art. 4(2) Rome I Regulation the law regime of the habitual residence of the party providing the contractual characteristic performance is decisive.[107] The obligation to transfer the

---

[102] Likewise, Martiny, 'Virtuelle Währungen, insbesondere Bitcoins, im Internationalen Privat- und Zivilverfahrensrecht' (2018) 38 *Praxis des Internationalen Privat- und Verfahrensrechts*, 553 (561), regarding Bitcoin and Ripple: Dickinson, 'Cryptocurrencies and the Conflict of Laws', in Fox and Green (eds), *Cryptocurrencies in Public and Private Law* (2019), § 5, para. 5.51.

[103] Steinrötter, *Beschränkte Rechtswahl im Internationalen Kapitalmarktprivatrecht und akzessorische Anknüpfung an das Kapitalmarktordnungsstatut* (2014), 428.

[104] Dickinson, 'Cryptocurrencies and the Conflict of Laws', in Fox and Green (eds), *Cryptocurrencies in Public and Private Law* (2019), § 5, para. 5.70.

[105] Wagner, in BeckOGK, CISG, Art. 1, para. 9.

[106] Magnus, in Staudinger BGB, Vol. 2, CISG, Art. 1, para. 44.

[107] For example, Zimmermann, 'Blockchain-Netzwerke und Internationales Privatrecht – oder: der Sitz dezentraler Rechtsverhältnisse' (2018) 38 *Praxis des Internationalen Privat- und Verfahrensrechts*, 566 (569); see also Rühl, 'Smart Contracts und anwendbares Recht', in Braegelmann and Kaulartz (eds), *Smart Contracts* (2019), § 12, para. 27.

§ 3. International Jurisdiction and Applicable Law

crypto tokens would then be characteristic for the contract.[108] This means that the legal system of the **habitual residence of the token seller** applies, which does not appear to be unproblematic in view of the pseudonymity of the seller due to the lack of predictability of the applicable law by the token buyer.[109] If the object of the legal transaction is the exchange of tokens for goods or services, the applicability of the legal system of the place of habitual **residence of the contracting party** transferring the contractual goods or providing the contractual service shall be decisive according to Art. 4(2) Rome I Regulation.[110] However, it also seems possible that an autonomous interpretation of EU law could be used to classify the contract under Art. 4(1)(a) Rome I Regulation (goods in exchange for tokens)[111] or Art. 4(1)(b) Rome I Regulation (services in exchange for tokens)[112];[113] all of this would lead to the same result. However, it is not necessary to accept the rather uncertain approach of qualifying tokens for goods as an exchange contract under Conflict of Laws rules and thus taking Art. 4(4) Rome I Regulation as a basis.[114] If tokens are used as a means of payment within the meaning of Art. 53 et seqq. CISG (which is to be denied at the end of the day)[115], the CISG would be applicable to the purchase of goods against crypto tokens.[116]

If the exchange of **tokens for tokens** is the subject of the agreement, the principle of the closest connection simply applies under Art. 4(4) Rome I Regulation which is not highly problematic here. It would not contribute to legal certainty to have such individual case considerations for lightning-fast, automated legal transactions.

Example:
A (habitual residence in Spain and working there as a hairdresser) acquires cryptotokens from B (habitual residence in Poland). In return, B receives a) a sum of money, b) a new haircut, c) another type of cryptotoken (e.g. Bitcoin vs. Ether), in the latter case they have come together through a trading platform based in Malta.
a) Polish contract law applies pursuant to Art. 4(2) Rome I Regulation.
b) Spanish contract law applies (either under Art. 4(2) Rome I Regulation or under Art. 4(1)(a), (b) Rome I Regulation).
c) There is a strong case for applying Maltese law via Art. 4(4) Rome I Regulation.

---

[108] Martiny, 'Virtuelle Währungen, insbesondere Bitcoins, im Internationalen Privat- und Zivilverfahrensrecht' (2018) 38 *Praxis des Internationalen Privat- und Verfahrensrechts*, 553 (561); Zimmermann, 'Blockchain-Netzwerke und Internationales Privatrecht – oder: der Sitz dezentraler Rechtsverhältnisse' (2018) 38 *Praxis des Internationalen Privat- und Verfahrensrechts*, 566 (569).

[109] Lehmann, 'Who Owns Bitcoin? Private Law Facing the Blockchain' (2019) 21 *Minnesota Journal of Law, Science & Technology*, 93 (114).

[110] Zimmermann, 'Blockchain-Netzwerke und Internationales Privatrecht – oder: der Sitz dezentraler Rechtsverhältnisse' (2018) 38 *Praxis des Internationalen Privat- und Verfahrensrechts*, 566 (569).

[111] Dickinson, 'Cryptocurrencies and the Conflict of Laws', in Fox and Green (eds), *Cryptocurrencies in Public and Private Law* (2019), § 5, para. 5.10.

[112] Ibid, para. 5.52 et seqq.

[113] At least lit. b is interpreted extensively anyway, as is acknowledged; Staudinger in HK-BGB Rome I-VO Art. 4 para. 4; cf. also Rühl, 'Smart Contracts und anwendbares Recht' in Braegelmann and Kaulartz (eds), *Smart Contracts* (2019), § 12, para. 27, fn. 92.

[114] That is what Martiny, 'Virtuelle Währungen, insbesondere Bitcoins, im Internationalen Privat- und Zivilverfahrensrecht' (2018) 38 *Praxis des Internationalen Privat- und Verfahrensrechts*, 553 (561) suggests.

[115] The 'purchase price' in the sense of Art. 53 CISG means a 'sum of money'; Fountoulakis, in BeckOGK, CISG, Art. 53, para. 7.

[116] Martiny, 'Virtuelle Währungen, insbesondere Bitcoins, im Internationalen Privat- und Zivilverfahrensrecht' (2018) 38 *Praxis des Internationalen Privat- und Verfahrensrechts*, 553 (561); cf. also Rühl, 'Smart Contracts und anwendbares Recht', in Braegelmann and Kaulartz (eds), *Smart Contracts* (2019), § 12 marginal no. 8.

F. Contracts with Intermediaries

27 Although blockchain-based crypto tokens are designed so that they could do without the typical (financial) intermediaries, various commercial providers have 'interposed' themselves as third parties in practice. This sometimes appears to be necessary in order to bring potential counterparties together by means of 'matchmaking' (→ § 5 para. 2). In particular, the derivative acquisition of tokens is usually carried out via so-called 'crypto-to-crypto exchanges' (exchange of tokens for tokens; → § 5 para. 37 et seqq.) or 'fiat-to-crypto exchanges' (exchange of fiat currency for tokens; → § 5 para. 33 et seqq.), in which the acquirers can participate directly. Here, there are arrangements in which the users contract with the platforms and in which users are brought together directly and conclude contracts with one another (→ § 5 para. 4 et seqq.).

I. International Jurisdiction

1. Platform Contract

28 A platform contract between provider and user can be structured differently in detail, but always has the character of a **continuing obligation** as well as a **framework contract** and is aimed at bringing users together. The (central) platform often safekeeps the private key (→ § 5 para. 21 et seqq.). In terms of substantive law, this is regularly a **mixed type of contract** with elements of service or agency, possibly also work and services contracts law (→ § 5 para. 24 et seqq.). The custody of the private key also involves fiduciary components (→ § 5 para. 22).

29 Disputes arising from the platform contract may always be brought before the courts of the Member State where the defendant is domiciled (Art. 4 Brussels Ibis Regulation). The defendant can, of course, accept the jurisdiction of the respective court (Art. 26 Brussels Ibis Regulation). Conceivable is also a **jurisdiction agreement**, which must take into account the formal requirements of Art. 25 Brussels Ibis Regulation and is subject to Art. 19 Brussels Ibis Regulation which is only 'activated' if the **consumer protection jurisdiction** is given under Art. 17 et seq. Brussels Ibis Regulation. This is entirely conceivable but must be examined in each individual case (on the – in particular – situational conditions → para. 11). Here, the extensions by the ECJ in the Cases 'Hobohm' and 'Maletic' deserve special attention (→ para. 13, 31).

30 Otherwise, **the 'contractual jurisdiction'** pursuant to Art. 7(1)(b) second indent Brussels Ibis Regulation remains. In an autonomous interpretation, the platform contract is to be classified as a **contract for provision of services**. This term is to be understood extensively.[117] This means that a person domiciled in a Member State can be sued in another Member State if the place of performance is in the latter state, understood as the place where 'the services were provided or should have been provided' under the contract. First and foremost, it depends on where the service is actually to be provided under the contract.[118] However, the determination is not easy for online contracts[119] and the use of blockchain technology potentially makes the identification process even more difficult. If it is not possible to determine the place of

---

[117] Dörner, in Saenger, ZPO EuGVVO, Art. 7, para. 20.
[118] Ibid, para. 21.
[119] Gottwald, in MüKoZPO, Brussels Ia-VO, Vol. 3, Art. 7, para. 30.

performance one must (also in the light of recital 7, Art. 4(1)(b) Rome I Regulation) in case of doubt refer to the registered office of the service provider.[120] If the platform contract is (primarily) **free of charge**, the contractual jurisdiction follows from Art. 7(1) (c), (a) Brussels Ibis Regulation. Here, the (critical) formulas of the ECJ in the cases 'Tessili' and 'de Bloos' apply (→ para. 14).

Example:
Trading Platform X, based in Bulgaria, is a recently founded start-up that (still) has a purely Bulgarian Internet presence. A from Germany is fluent in Bulgarian and meets X by chance. He concludes a framework agreement (against payment) online and enters into trading with crypto tokens via X. Due to a lack of 'direction' towards the German market, the provisions on consumer jurisdiction do not apply. Art. 7(1)(b) second indent Brussels Ibis Regulation does not help in the case of an action brought by A under the framework contract, since no actual place of performance can be determined (at least not one that is outside the State of residence of X). There is strong evidence that Bulgaria is the state of the competent court.

2. Follow-up Contracts

In addition to the contract between the users (= secondary market contract, → para. 24 et seqq.), one may recognise a legal transaction with a **'brokerage' component** (such as an [atypical] agency agreement) **between the users and the platform** (decentralised fiat-to-crypto exchanges; decentralised crypto-to-crypto exchanges) (→ § 5 para. 7 et seqq.). Since the content of these supplementary agreements is strongly influenced by the framework agreement, in the area of international jurisdiction an equal assessment of framework contract (→ para. 27 et seqq.) and follow up contract seems appropriate. This is in line with the ECJ decision 'Hobohm'.[121] Here, the ECJ dealt with the second prerequisite of Art. 17(1)(c) var. 2 Brussels Ibis Regulation namely that the contract at issue in the specific proceedings must fall 'within the scope' of the 'directed' activity. The ECJ examined under what conditions a 'connection' between several contracts can include a – viewed in isolation, not 'directed' – subsequent contract in the area of a 'directed' activity and thus in the jurisdiction of Art. 17(1)(c) Brussels Ibis Regulation.[122] The court affirmed this in the event that a 'close link'[123] existed between the two contracts.[124] In addition to the economic (not necessarily legal) connection between the two contracts which the ECJ identifies[125] as a precondition for that 'close link', the ECJ cites other factors which may justify a 'close link' between two contracts in an overall assessment by the national courts, namely 'in particular whether the parties to both of those contracts are identical in law and in fact, whether the economic objective of those contracts concerning the same specific subject-matter is identical and whether the [isolated not directed] contract complements the [directed] contract, in that it seeks to make it possible for the economic objective of the [last one] to be achieved'[126].

---

[120] Ibid.
[121] ECJ, Judgment of 23 December 2015, *Hobohm*, C-297/14, ECLI:EU:C:2015:8445; for further details Heinze and Steinrötter, 'Wann fällt ein Vertrag in den Bereich der ausgerichteten Tätigkeit des Unternehmers i. S. d. Art. 17 Abs. 1 lit. c EuGVVO?' (2016) 36 *Praxis des Internationalen Privat- und Verfahrensrechts*, 545.
[122] ECJ, Judgment of 23 December 2015, *Hobohm*, C-297/14, ECLI:EU:C:2015:844, para. 29.
[123] Wagner, R., 'Anmerkung zu 'Verbrauchergerichtsstand bei enger Verbindung zu früher geschlossenem Verbrauchervertrag" (2016) 27 *Europäische Zeitschrift für Wirtschaftsrecht*, 269 (270): legal concept detrimental to predictability.
[124] ECJ, Judgment of 23 December 2015, *Hobohm*, C-297/14, ECLI:EU:C:2015:844, para. 33.
[125] Ibid, para. 36.
[126] Ibid, para. 37.

32 In the case of centrally operating fiat-to-crypto exchanges and crypto-to-crypto exchanges (trading platforms), no contract is concluded between the users from the outset. From the point of view of an informed third party, the central trading platform itself is therefore the contracting party to the secondary market contract (for the international legal handling of this contract, → para. 24 et seqq.). Whether the settlement of account balances in the case of pure off-chain intermediaries is already covered by the framework agreement or whether it constitutes an additional agreement (→ para. 28), which in substantive law are to be regarded, e.g., as a mandate with a custody component, may be left open from an IPL perspective. Either way, in terms of international jurisdiction, a **parallel assessment with regard to the framework agreement** (→ para. 28 et seqq.) seems appropriate.

II. Applicable Law

1. Platform Contract

33 Subject to its para. 4, subpara. a[127], the **consumer protection PIL rule** of Art. 6 Rome I Regulation applies to both paid and unpaid platform contracts, provided that the (in particular situational) requirements are met (→ para. 10 et seqq. regarding the IPL pendant). This means that agreements and clauses on the **choice of law** are possible, but in addition to the general limits of party autonomy, particular attention must be paid to Art. 6(2) Rome I Regulation ('favourability test' of the chosen law with the ius cogens of the consumer's country of habitual residence, → para. 17). In the **absence of a choice of law**, the law of the country in which the consumer has his **habitual residence** must be applied (Art. 6(1) Rome I Regulation). Both in the case of Art. 6(4)(a) Rome I Regulation and when the (situational) requirements of the special Conflict of Laws provision are not met, the **general rules** apply. A choice of law is then possible under the conditions of Art. 3 Rome I Regulation. Otherwise, the law of the provider's habitual residence constitutes the contractual statute – either pursuant to Art. 4(1)(b) Rome I Regulation (in the case of a platform contract for remuneration) or Art. 4(2) Rome I Regulation (in the case of a platform contract for no remuneration).

> **Example:**
> Trading platform X, based in Japan, is a recently founded start-up with a (still) purely Japanese Internet presence. A from Germany is fluent in Japanese and meets X by chance. He concludes a framework agreement (against payment) online and enters into trading with cryptotokens via X. There is no agreement on the choice of law. Since Art. 6 Rome I Regulation is not applicable because it lacks the situational requirements, the law of the State of residence of X is to be applied in accordance with Art. 4(1)(b), Art. 19(1) Rome I Regulation, i.e. Japanese law.

2. Follow-up Contracts

34 For the follow-up contracts (subject to Art. 6(4)(a) Rome I Regulation), Art. 6(1), 2 Rome I Regulation applies regularly. If this is not the case and there is no choice of law (Art. 3 Rome I Regulation), an 'objective connection' of the subsequent contracts to the framework agreement (see → para. 27 et seqq.) pursuant to Art. 4(3) Rome I Regulation seems conceivable.

---

[127] This paragraph excludes 'a contract for the supply of services where the services are to be supplied to the consumer exclusively in a country other than that in which he has his habitual residence'.

G. E-Commerce and Distance Contracts

The fact that crypto tokens are regularly purchased online for a fee finally activates general consumer protection rules.[128] **Distance contract law** is to be qualified in terms of IPL/PIL as consumer contract law (→ § 4 para. 15 et seqq.).[129] In principle, Art. 17 et seq. Brussels Ibis Regulation apply to the place of jurisdiction (→ para. 10 et seqq.) and Art. 6 Rome I Regulation to the applicable law of the contract (→ para. 17 et seqq.). However, particular attention should be paid to Art. 6(4)(a) Rome I Regulation. In order to avoid misunderstandings, it should be emphasised that consumer-protective substantive law falls under the **contractual qualification** – irrespective of whether Art. 6 Rome I Regulation or Art. 3 et seq. Rome I Regulation is relevant in concreto. A distinction must be made for **e-commerce** issues which do not necessarily require a consumer contract. They fall in principle under 'normal' contract law.[130]

35

Example:
Private individual A from Germany purchases crypto tokens via a central crypto trading platform based in Hong Kong, which is aimed at a worldwide audience and explicitly advertises with a large European clientele. A choice of law clause provides for the choice of Indonesian law. Art. 6 Rome I Regulation is excluded due to Art. 6(4)(a) Rome I Regulation. Since those consumer protection rules are not internationally mandatory in the sense of Art. 9(1) Rome I Regulation, Indonesian contract law applies. If it turns out that the choice of law agreement is invalid, Hong Kong contract law comes into effect pursuant to Art. 4(1)(b) Rome I Regulation.

H. Prospectus Liability

If a company issues tokens through the ICO and these are also securities as defined by EU (or also national) law, various questions of capital markets law arise, in particular those relating to the obligation to publish a prospectus and regarding the corresponding liability (→ § 7 para. 30 et seqq.).[131] Especially in the early phase of the ICOs, however, there were simply no officially approved securities prospectuses (→ § 7 para. 2). One may, at most, think of the ICO white papers being classified as (regularly inadequate) prospectuses (as defined in the Prospectus Regulation).[132] An overarching practical problem (also) in liability law is, of course, the **difficult**

36

---

[128] Namely the respective national implementation of: Directive 2011/83/EU of the European Parliament and of the Council on consumer rights, amending Council Directive 93/13/EEC and Directive 1999/44/EC of the European Parliament and of the Council and repealing Council Directive 85/577/EEC and Directive 97/7/EC of the European Parliament and of the Council, OJ L 304, 22.11.2011 p. 64–88; Directive 2000/31/EC of the European Parliament and of the Council on certain legal aspects of information society services, in particular electronic commerce, in the Internal Market (Directive on electronic commerce), OJ L 178, 17.7.2000 p. 1–16.

[129] Rühl, 'Smart Contracts und anwendbares Recht', in Braegelmann and Kaulartz (eds), *Smart Contracts* (2019), § 12, para. 33.

[130] Different view by Rühl, 'Smart Contracts und anwendbares Recht', in Braegelmann and Kaulartz (eds), *Smart Contracts* (2019), § 12, para. 33: qualification as consumer contracts.

[131] See also Maume, 'Initial Coin Offerings and EU Prospectus Disclosure' (2020) 31 *European Business Law Review*, 185.

[132] Barsan, 'Legal Challenges of Initial Coin Offerings (ICO)' (2017) 12 *Revue Trimestrielle de Droit Financier*, 54: 'Every ICO starts with a white paper, very similar to a prospectus, that describes the project and the rights given to the investors'.

37 For the question of whether the EU securities prospectus regime or primary market publicity applies to crypto tokens (prospectus requirement pursuant to Art. 3(1) Prospectus Regulation), the first question is whether the ICO involves **'securities' as defined by capital markets law.** This is initially not a question of Conflict of Laws but rather of substantive law (→ § 7 para. 33 et seqq.). Here, the type of token to be evaluated, more precisely the rights associated with it, provide the answer.[134] **Investment tokens**, which grant investors rights to profits (or regular interest), sometimes even shareholder-like participation rights such as voting rights, are very similar to conventional securities and are regularly securities in the legal sense.[135] In the case of **utility tokens**, although the issuer grants the holders access to products or services and not financial entitlements, capital gains are nevertheless conceivable through the trading of utility tokens on secondary markets. Such a token can therefore be characterized as a hybrid between consumption and investment. A classification as a security[136] is appropriate if, from a functional point of view, the acquisition of a utility token **objectively represents an investment** and is at least also carried out as an act of **corporate financing**, i.e. the use of the good/service is not the main focus.[137] Finally, **currency tokens** (e.g. Bitcoins) have a value retention and payment function. They are typically used to pay for goods or services that are not offered by the issuer itself (otherwise known as utility tokens). They are therefore **not securities**,[138] which is why there is insofar no need for a prospectus under capital markets law.

38 Both **international procedural and private international law interests** call for an interpretation in the area of international capital markets law which takes into account, first and foremost, the **predictability of the relevant jurisdiction or applicable law**.[139] This means that the number of courts of jurisdiction and the number of legal systems governing the facts of the case should be kept to a minimum.[140] That the EU legislator

---

[133] Martiny, 'Virtuelle Währungen, insbesondere Bitcoins, im Internationalen Privat- und Zivilverfahrensrecht' (2018) 38 *Praxis des Internationalen Privat- und Verfahrensrechts*, 553 (564); Rühl, 'Smart Contracts und anwendbares Recht', in Braegelmann and Kaulartz (eds), *Smart Contracts* (2019), § 12, para. 41; cf. also Möslein, 'Conflicts of Laws and Codes: Defining the Boundaries of Digital Jurisdictions', in Lianos, Hacker, Eich and Dimitropoulos (eds,) *Regulating Blockchain* (2019), 275.

[134] The presentation and classification in the following paragraph is based first and foremost on the instructive remarks of Zickgraf, 'Initial Coin Offerings – Ein Fall für das Kapitalmarktrecht?' (2018) 63 *Die Aktiengesellschaft*, 293 (295 et seq.); see also Hacker and Thomale, Crypto-Securities Regulation, 26 et seq.; for the regulatory classification, see: ESMA, 13.11.2017, ESMA50-157-828 and BaFin, 20.2.2018, GZ: WA 11-QB 4100-2017/0010.

[135] Classification as a security either via MiFiD2, Art. 4, para. 1, no. 44, subpara. a or MiFiD2, Art. 4, para. 1, no. 44, subpara. B.

[136] Probably in accordance with MiFiD2, Art. 4, para. 1, no. 44, subpara. B.

[137] Zickgraf, 'Initial Coin Offerings – Ein Fall für das Kapitalmarktrecht?' (2018) 63 *Die Aktiengesellschaft*, 293 (305); in contrast, referring to the (profit) intentions of market participants: Hacker and Thomale, Crypto-Securities Regulation, 34 et seq., which is arguably in line with the approach of the US Securities and Exchange Commission (SEC) using the so-called Howey Test (SEC v. W.J. Howey Co., 328 U.S. 293 [1946] ['Howey']): most recently Framework for 'Investment Contract' Analysis of Digital Assets, available at: http://tinyurl.com/y6evto9w (accessed 1.9.2020).

[138] Different view Hacker and Thomale, Crypto-Securities Regulation, 35 et seq.

[139] Steinrötter, 'Der notorische Problemfall der grenzüberschreitenden Prospekthaftung' (2015) 61 *Recht der internationalen Wirtschaft*, 407 et seq.; also with regard to international jurisdiction: Thiede and Lorscheider, 'Die internationale Zuständigkeit für Ansprüche von Anlegern aus Prospekthaftung' (2019) 30 *Europäische Zeitschrift für Wirtschaftsrecht*, 274 (277 et seq.); on the complex relationship of financial market law to PIL: Lehmann, 'Das Finanzmarktrecht im Internationalen Privatrecht', in Zetzsche and Lehmann (eds), *Grenzüberschreitende Finanzdienstleistungen* (2018), § 1, para. 5 et seqq.

[140] Steinrötter, 'Der notorische Problemfall der grenzüberschreitenden Prospekthaftung' (2015) 61 *Recht der internationalen Wirtschaft*, 407 (408).

has a similar view can be derived from Art. 4(1)(h) Rome I Regulation and Art. 6(4)(e) Rome I Regulation according to which in the case of certain capital market agreements of the secondary market only one legal system should govern the facts of the case. Specifically, the provision provides for an accessory connection to the regulatory statute – an approach that is generally to be favoured for large parts of international capital market private law.[141]

I. International Jurisdiction

The **Brussels Ibis Regulation** does not provide for any special provision for capital market information liability in general or prospectus liability in particular. While the exclusive jurisdictions pursuant to Art. 24 Brussels Ibis Regulation can never be relevant to the respective case, **jurisdiction agreements**[142] (Art. 25 Brussels Ibis Regulation) and **situations where the defendant enters an appearance** (Art. 26 Brussels Ibis Regulation) as well as the **general jurisdiction** of the actor sequitur forum rei (Art. 4 Brussels Ibis Regulation) remain conceivable as a forum. A **contractual qualification** which does not only include the special jurisdiction of Art. 7(1) Brussels Ibis Regulation but even the consumer jurisdiction according to Art. 17 et seq. Brussels Ibis Regulation is not relevant,[143] for it makes no difference to the functional evaluation of the legal concept of prospectus liability to a connecting factor (bundling of legal issues in a system concept) whether a contract exists between the parties or not.[144] 39

The main issue for prospectus liability is rather the **optional jurisdiction of the tort under Art. 7(2) Brussels Ibis Regulation**. In the 'Kolassa'[145] case, the ECJ dealt for the first time with international jurisdiction for claims (inter alia) arising from prospectus liability. The ECJ qualified prospectus liability at the meta level of IPL as tortious. According to general opinion, the special place of jurisdiction conveys the possibility of bringing an action at the plaintiff's choice both at the **place of success and the place of action** (ubiquity theory).[146] However, according to its introductory sentence, it only applies if the defendant domiciled in the EU is to be sued 'in another Member State' than in the Member State in which the defendant is domiciled.[147] The place of action within the meaning of Art. 7(2) Brussels Ibis Regulation is arguably **the relevant place of establishment of the token issuer**.[148] This is where the information (prospectus; white paper) is produced and from where a possible decision to upload it to a website is 40

---

[141] Steinrötter, *Beschränkte Rechtswahl im Internationalen Kapitalmarktprivatrecht und akzessorische Anknüpfung an das Kapitalmarktordnungsstatut* (2014), passim. Recently published Legislative Papers of the German Federal Government seem to share this point of view also for cryptotokens in the starting point: BMF/BMJV, 'Eckpunkte für die regulatorische Behandlung von elektronischen Wertpapieren und Krypto-Token' (7.3.2019), 4.

[142] Bachmann, 'Die internationale Zuständigkeit für Klagen wegen fehlerhafter Kapitalmarktinformation' (2007) 27 *Praxis des Internationalen Privat- und Verfahrensrechts*, 77 (81), however, is sceptical about jurisdiction clauses.

[143] Open to such a qualification, however, Winner and Schmidt, 'Recht des Primärmarkts: Grenzüberschreitende Haftung für fehlerhafte Prospekte und Anlegerinformationen', in Zetzsche and Lehmann (eds), *Grenzüberschreitende Finanzdienstleistungen* (2018), § 12, para. 19 et seqq.

[144] Admittedly, this legal relationship as such may also result in contractually qualifying claims at the meta-level (e.g. in the event of a breach of bond conditions etc.).

[145] ECJ, Judgment of 28 January 2015, *Kolassa*, C-375/13ECLI:EU:C:2015:37.

[146] Gottwald, in MüKoZPO, Brussels Ia-VO, Vol. 3, Art. 7, para. 54 with further references.

[147] Otherwise, recourse remains in particular to Brussels Ibis Regulation, Art. 4.

[148] Also Barsan, 'Legal Challenges of Initial Coin Offerings (ICO)' (2017) 12 *Revue Trimestrielle de Droit Financier*, 54 (63); Winner and Schmidt, 'Recht des Primärmarkts: Grenzüberschreitende Haftung

made.[149] The previous ECJ case law does not contradict this. It is certainly convincing to start with that 'decisional centre' in order to counteract the potential multiplication of jurisdictions, which would be the consequence if one would have a recourse to, for example, the place of notification.[150] Otherwise, there is a risk that the law of jurisdiction for capital market offences will be impaired, especially since the legal practitioner already has to cope with the fragmentation of international jurisdiction at the place of success in the context of scattered torts. Namely, the **specification of the place of success** has always been problematic in the case of pure financial loss,[151] which is the subject of prospectus liability in the context of crypto tokens. After the 'Kronhofer' judgment,[152] which is, at best, only partially helpful in this respect the residence of the injured party alone cannot justify the place of success. However, based on 'Kolassa' it is clear that the place of success regularly corresponds to the location of the account which suffered the loss (main branch[153] of the credit institution) – at least if the injured party is also domiciled there.[154] This was recently confirmed by the ECJ in the 'Löber' case,[155] after the court seemed to have taken a different direction in the case of 'Universal Music'[156]. In addition to the **location of the account and the residence of the investor**, the ECJ mentioned **further criteria** for the individual case analysis, such as the domicile of the participating banks, the affiliation of the secondary market or the notifying bank to a Member State and the place of the investment decision.[157] The bank account thus remains a central, albeit not the sole factor. So far (unfortunately) **no coherent system** has been developed for these cases.[158] It must be conceded, however, that this concretisation of the

---

für fehlerhafte Prospekte und Anlegerinformationen', in Zetzsche and Lehmann (eds), *Grenzüberschreitende Finanzdienstleistungen* (2018), § 12, para. 28.

[149] See Barsan, 'Legal Challenges of Initial Coin Offerings (ICO)' (2017) 12 *Revue Trimestrielle de Droit Financier*, 54 (63); Thiede and Lorscheider, 'Die internationale Zuständigkeit für Ansprüche von Anlegern aus Prospekthaftung' (2019) 30 *Europäische Zeitschrift für Wirtschaftsrecht*, 274 (277).

[150] Müller, 'EuGVVO: Gerichtsstand für Schadensersatzklage eines Verbrauchers wegen Wertverlust einer Finanzinvestition' (2015) 26 *Europäische Zeitschrift für Wirtschaftsrecht*, 218 (223); Steinrötter, 'Der notorische Problemfall der grenzüberschreitenden Prospekthaftung' (2015) 61 *Recht der internationalen Wirtschaft*, 407 (410 et seq.).

[151] Lehmann, 'Where does Economic Loss Occur?' (2011) 7 *Journal of Private International Law*, 527. Legal Literature has so far mostly been recourse on the place of the disposition or location of the assets: Steinrötter, *Beschränkte Rechtswahl im Internationalen Kapitalmarktprivatrecht und akzessorische Anknüpfung an das Kapitalmarktordnungsstatut* (2014), 181 et seqq. with numerous references.

[152] ECJ, Judgment of 10 June 2004, *Kronhofer*, C-168/02, ECLI:EU:C:2004:364.

[153] Müller, 'EuGVVO: Gerichtsstand für Schadensersatzklage eines Verbrauchers wegen Wertverlust einer Finanzinvestition' (2015) 26 *Europäische Zeitschrift für Wirtschaftsrecht*, 218 (224).

[154] Winner and Schmidt, 'Recht des Primärmarkts: Grenzüberschreitende Haftung für fehlerhafte Prospekte und Anlegerinformationen', in Zetzsche and Lehmann (eds), *Grenzüberschreitende Finanzdienstleistungen* (2018), § 12, para. 33 et seq.; other view by Thiede and Lorscheider, 'Die internationale Zuständigkeit für Ansprüche von Anlegern aus Prospekthaftung' (2019) 30 *Europäische Zeitschrift für Wirtschaftsrecht*, 274 (278), who refer to the place of distribution of the prospectus. Since approved prospectuses are regularly published in electronic form (Prospectus Regulation, recital 62 p. 1), this criterion hardly seems suitable for invoking a specific legal system.

[155] ECJ, Judgment of 12 September 2018, *Löber*, C-304/17, ECLI:EU:C:2018:701.

[156] ECJ, Judgment of 16 June 2016, *Universal Music*, C-12/15, ECLI:EU:C:2016:449; against a relativization by the case 'Universal Music' see Winner and Schmidt, 'Recht des Primärmarkts: Grenzüberschreitende Haftung für fehlerhafte Prospekte und Anlegerinformationen', in Zetzsche and Lehmann (eds), *Grenzüberschreitende Finanzdienstleistungen* (2018), § 12, para. 45 et seq., 49.

[157] ECJ, Judgment of 12 September 2018, *Löber*, C-304/17, ECLI:EU:C:2018:701, para. 32 et seqq.

[158] Mankowski, 'EuGH: Zuständigkeit für Prospekthaftungsklagen' [2019] *Lindenmaier-Möhring Kommentierte BGH-Rechtsprechung*, 413748; Steinrötter and Bohlsen, 'Erfolgsort bei grenzüberschreitender Kapitalmarkt-Prospekthaftung im internationalen Zuständigkeitsrecht ('Löber')' [2/2019] *juris PraxisReport Internationales Wirtschaftsrecht*, Anm. 1; the latest ruling of the ECJ complicates the legal situation even further: ECJ, Judgment of 12 May 2021, *Vereinigung von Effectenbeziffers*, C-709/19, ECLI:EU:C:2021:377.

place of success in each individual case, despite its inadequacies,[159] sets certain standards for the legal practitioner and already covers a large part of the cases in practice.

What remains unclear is the weighting of the (non-exhaustive)[160] criteria in individual cases. For example, it is not clear whether the bank account in question is sufficient even if the investor is domiciled in another Member State. However, this typically is the case, especially if other factors are involved.[161] In particular, it is hardly detrimental to the criterion of proximity of evidence and predictability from the plaintiff's point of view that he cannot sue in his place of residence in such cases. This is because anyone who invests assets abroad must also expect that his asset jurisdiction is established there. Furthermore, the foreign court is then undoubtedly 'close to the evidence'.[162]

The ratio decidendi of the ECJ case law may now be applied to prospectus liability **41** at the ICO in such a way that the place where the damage occurs is seen in the **investor's wallet**; or at least this is regarded as the central criterion.[163] However, this is not convincing. The link to the investor's wallet is not the same as that to the bank account. This is because the wallet never contains cryptographic units of value as a counterpart to fiat money in bank accounts, but rather accommodates the private key (→ § 1 para. 25).[164] Furthermore, the investor can store the wallet via apps (e.g. in clouds), on external storage media or on the hard disk of his computer.[165] In contrast to the branch of the bank which manages the bank account, the link to the wallet would therefore be highly dynamic, dependent on coincidences and therefore sometimes inadequate. How can the counterpart be expected to know where the respective user keeps his paper wallet or hardware wallet? Such connecting factors are the opposite of what the interests of the capital market IPL and PIL require, namely the highest possible predictability of the competent court and the applicable law.[166] At best, the concrete entry in the distributed ledger is comparable with the book credit balance at the bank (→ § 1 para. 20).[167] However, this – in any case decentralized – book position is not practicable here.

In the case of different investors, but even in the case of scattered financial losses of **42** only one investor, all EU jurisdictions can theoretically be taken into account in

---

[159] No deficits identified by Thiede and Lorscheider, 'Die internationale Zuständigkeit für Ansprüche von Anlegern aus Prospekthaftung' (2019) 30 *Europäische Zeitschrift für Wirtschaftsrecht*, 274 (279 et seq.).

[160] Also presumed by Thiede and Lorscheider, 'Die internationale Zuständigkeit für Ansprüche von Anlegern aus Prospekthaftung' (2019) 30 *Europäische Zeitschrift für Wirtschaftsrecht*, 274 (280).

[161] Previously already Lehmann, 'Vorschlag für eine Reform der Rom II-Verordnung im Bereich der Finanzmarktdelikte' (2012) 32 *Praxis des Internationalen Privat- und Verfahrensrechts*, 399 (400); for the place of disposal, however, v. Hein, 'Deliktischer Kapitalanlegerschutz im europäischen Zuständigkeitsrecht (EuGH, S. 32)' (2005) 25 *Praxis des Internationalen Privat- und Verfahrensrechts*, 17 (21 et seq.); for the market place Bachmann, 'Die internationale Zuständigkeit für Klagen wegen fehlerhafter Kapitalmarktinformation' (2007) 27 *Praxis des Internationalen Privat- und Verfahrensrechts*, 77 (82).

[162] By justifying the foreseeability for the defendant by the fact that the defendant submitted a notification in a particular Member State, the ECJ in 'Kolassa' fails to recognize that the bank account of the applicant must by no means be in the State of the respective issuance (or public offer); Müller, 'EuGVVO: Gerichtsstand für Schadensersatzklage eines Verbrauchers wegen Wertverlust einer Finanzinvestition' (2015) 26 *Europäische Zeitschrift für Wirtschaftsrecht*, 218 (224).

[163] Also considered by Barsan, 'Legal Challenges of Initial Coin Offerings (ICO)' (2017) 12 *Revue Trimestrielle de Droit Financier*, 54 (63).

[164] See Seitz, 'Distributed Ledger Technology & Bitcoin – Zur rechtlichen Stellung eines Bitcoin-"Inhabers"' (2017) 20 *Kommunikation und Recht*, 763 et seq.

[165] Martiny, 'Virtuelle Währungen, insbesondere Bitcoins, im Internationalen Privat- und Zivilverfahrensrecht' (2018) 38 *Praxis des Internationalen Privat- und Verfahrensrechts*, 553 (555).

[166] For the interests see Steinrötter, 'Der notorische Problemfall der grenzüberschreitenden Prospekthaftung' (2015) 61 *Recht der internationalen Wirtschaft*, 407 (407 et seq.).

[167] Seitz, 'Distributed Ledger Technology & Bitcoin – Zur rechtlichen Stellung eines Bitcoin-"Inhabers"' (2017) 20 *Kommunikation und Recht*, 763 (765).

relation to a single defective prospectus by **way of individual case examination** – in the style of a mosaic approach broken down according to the respective asset location[168] – wherever this location is to be found. It is obvious that this leads to considerable inconvenience for the parties involved as well as for the courts and that the private enforcement intended by capital market tort law is on the one hand potentially inhibiting and on the other hand **incalculable** for issuers. A methodically justifiable correction of the special jurisdiction rule (such as via the escape clause within para. 49 PIL) is not possible under current IPL. However, the number of possible jurisdictions is currently too large, which is why de lege ferenda a special rule should be considered (namely as exclusive jurisdiction), which establishes, for example, a parallelism with the applicable law (→ para. 43 et seqq.).[169]

Example:
The Y Company, which is domiciled in Austria, issues investment tokens and a corresponding prospectus that proves to be incorrect. A from Germany claims, after losses, that he had relied on the erroneous prospectus statement and that his investment decision was also based on it. He had indicated clearing accounts in Italy and in Germany with the Y Company for the settlement of the issue. He is now asserting prospectus liability claims before a German court. According to Art. 7(2) Brussels Ibis Regulation this is possible – but only for the damage that occurred via the German clearing account. For an action for compensation for the remaining damage in Italy, a place of success would also be required there. However, if only A's account is to be located in Italy, this is probably not enough. Of course, A is at liberty to sue Y for the total damage before Austrian courts (Art. 4(1) Brussels Ibis Regulation).

II. Applicable Law

1. Prospectus Requirements and the 'European Passport'

43 Since 21.7.2019,[170] the legislative starting point for the obligation to publish a prospectus within the EU has been the Prospectus Regulation, previously national provisions (in implementation of the Prospectus Directive 2003/71/EC[171]). According to Art. 3(1) Prospectus Regulation the issuer of a security, in this case an investment token or a utility token with investment character, must generally issue a prospectus. According to Art. 20(1) Prospectus Regulation the prospectus may only be published after it has been reviewed and approved by the competent authority. This **disclosure obligation** is an **'administrative matter'** within the meaning of Art. 1(1)(2) Rome I and Rome II Regulation.[172] In this way, the material scope of application of the 'Rome regime' is not relevant.

44 However, the concretisation of the territorial scope of the EU prospectus regime is a Conflict of Laws issue. This applies in particular to Art. 3(1)(3) Prospectus Regulation, according to which 'securities shall only be offered to the public in the Union after prior publication of a prospectus in accordance with this Regulation' or 'shall only be admitted to trading on a regulated market situated or operating within the Union after prior publication of a prospectus in accordance with this Regulation'. Once the territorial scope of application has been opened up, the provisions implying an

---

[168] Cf. also ECJ, Judgment of 7 March 1995, *Shevill*, C-68/93, ECLI:EU:C:1995:61.
[169] See Steinrötter, 'Der notorische Problemfall der grenzüberschreitenden Prospekthaftung' (2015) 61 *Recht der internationalen Wirtschaft*, 407 (413 et seq.).
[170] Prospectus Regulation, Art. 49, para. 2.
[171] Directive 2003/71/EC of the European Parliament and of the Council on the prospectus to be published when securities are offered to the public or admitted to trading and amending Directive 2001/34/EC, OJ L 345, 31.12.2003, p. 64–89.
[172] v. Hein, 'Die Internationale Prospekthaftung im Lichte der Rom II-Verordnung', in Baum, Fleckner, Hellgardt, Roth, et al. (eds), *Perspektiven des Wirtschaftsrechts* (2008), 371 (387).

obligation to publish a prospectus have **regulatory dimensions**, which is reflected at the Conflict of Laws level in their **mandatory character**; such regulations are thus basically 'unilaterally' established as capital market regulation law,[173] i.e. they (only) refer to themselves. The same applies to the provisions on the form of the prospectus.[174] It must be found out by interpretation to what extent the prospectus requirements here 'want' to be applicable in the case of cross-border issues, which – as seen – requires a qualified internal market reference.[175] In order to ensure that investors active in several Member States only have to use a single prospectus to fulfil their prospectus obligations, the EU legislator has established the **'European passport'**[176] (Art. 24 Prospectus Regulation; → ***). This instrument also has implications under Conflict of Laws.[177] It ensures that market supervision law abandons its typically 'unilateral' form (reference only to 'itself' from an PIL perspective) in favour of the 'country of origin principle' within the internal market.[178] The 'overlap'[179] leading to a 'multilateralisation' at the Conflict of Laws level relates solely to the question of compliance with the disclosure obligation (and the corresponding responsibility of the authorities)[180], while the obligation as such continues to be 'unilaterally' attached.[181] In other words: For legal practitioners from other **EU/EEA countries**, the European passport gives way to a partial, country-of-origin 'overlapping effect' with regard to the disclosure requirements, which seems quite appropriate in view of the harmonised obligations in the internal market.[182] However, the situation is different in **non-EU states**, i.e. issues that were subject to a prospectus requirement in such a state for the first time (issuer established in a non-EU state), have not yet been recognised by any Member State authority and will only be approved in accordance with Art. 29 Prospectus Regulation under the conditions stated therein (equivalence assessment). In this respect, there is no 'overlap' in the previous way.[183] The 'unilateral' linking of the respective prospectus regulation law, i.e. the mere examination of its respective territorial scope, is maintained here.

2. Prospectus Liability

If an existing obligation to publish a (correct) prospectus is violated, the question arises as to liability and – above all – its connection to PIL. This is all the more urgent since the core of prospectus liability[184] is still left to the legislation of the Member

---

[173] See Einsele, 'Internationales Prospekthaftungsrecht – Kollisionsrechtlicher Anlegerschutz nach der Rom II-Verordnung' (2012) 20 *Zeitschrift für Europäisches Privatrecht*, 23 (25).
[174] Steinrötter, *Beschränkte Rechtswahl im Internationalen Kapitalmarktprivatrecht und akzessorische Anknüpfung an das Kapitalmarktordnungsstatut* (2014), 115.
[175] Ibid,, 115 et seq.
[176] Prospectus Regulation, recital 3 sentence 2: 'Harmonising such disclosure allows for the establishment of a cross-border passport mechanism which facilitates the effective functioning of the internal market in a wide variety of securities.'.
[177] In detail Steinrötter, *Beschränkte Rechtswahl im Internationalen Kapitalmarktprivatrecht und akzessorische Anknüpfung an das Kapitalmarktordnungsstatut* (2014), 116 et seqq.
[178] v. Bar and Mankowski, *IPR*, Vol. 1 (2nd edn, 2003), § 4, para. 73.
[179] Benicke, 'Prospektpflicht und Prospekthaftung bei grenzüberschreitenden Emissionen', in Mansel, Kronke and Pfeiffer (eds), *FS Jayme* (2004), 25 (31 et seq.).
[180] Prospectus Regulation, Art. 2, subpara. o, subpara. m; Kuntz, 'Internationale Prospekthaftung nach Inkrafttreten des Wertpapierprospektgesetzes' (2007) 61 *Zeitschrift für Wirtschafts- und Bankrecht*, 432 (436).
[181] Steinrötter, *Beschränkte Rechtswahl im Internationalen Kapitalmarktprivatrecht und akzessorische Anknüpfung an das Kapitalmarktordnungsstatut* (2014), 126 et seqq.
[182] Ibid, 132.
[183] For the legal situation under the Prospectus Directive 2003/71/EC: ibid, 134 et seq.
[184] Cf. Prospectus Regulation, Art. 11.

States[185] and there are in part **significant differences in the respective legal systems**.[186] It is therefore not surprising that the Conflict of Laws treatment of prospectus liability has repeatedly been the subject of legal controversies.[187] In the meantime, it has been clarified that prospectus liability is to be qualified as **tortious** and is subject to Rome II Regulation.[188] In particular, the exemptions in Art. 1(2)(c) Rome II Regulation do not apply.[189] Recent ECJ rulings on the IPL had further underlined the tortious qualification, which had already been assumed to be the predominant one before (→ para. 40). In this respect, according to recital 7 Rome I and II Regulation a 'harmony requirement' applies with regard to the interpretation of the Brussels Ibis Regulation as well as the Rome I and Rome II Regulation. This is at least the case if the interpretation of the connecting factor in the Brussels Ibis Regulation is not due to any specific procedural consideration,[190] which is not evident in the case of prospectus liability.[191] Unlike in the area of ratings,[192] there is no priority (substantive) EU law (see also Art. 27 Rome II Regulation).[193] Furthermore, prospectus liability does – despite implying market regulation policy elements with regard to its purpose of private enforcement – not have an overriding mandatory character (see Art. 16 Rome I Regulation).[194]

46   In the absence of a special Conflict of Laws rule,[195] the **general rules** apply. This means, first of all, that in principle a **choice of law** is possible. This choice, if effective, takes precedence over 'objective' PIL rules. After the occurrence of the event giving rise to the damage (cf. Art. 14(1)(a) Rome II Regulation), the exercise of party autonomy is limited primarily by the domestic and internal market clause[196] of Art. 14(2), (3) Rome II Regulation. This subsequent choice of law will de facto fail often due to the

---

[185] Cf. at that time the optimism of Moloney, 'Reform or revolution? The financial crisis, EU financial markets law, and the European securities and markets authority' (2011) 60 *International & Comparative Law Quarterly*, 521 (525): '[…] harmonization of liability regimes […] also seems to be in train'; sceptically, however, already at that time Verse, 'Zur Reform der Kapitalmarktinformationshaftung im Vereinigten Königreich' (2012) 76 *Rabels Zeitschrift für ausländisches und internationales Privatrecht*, 893 (896).

[186] See for example Dombalagian, 'Choice of Law and Capital Markets Regulation' (2008) 82 *Tulane Law Review*, 1903 (1916 et seqq.); Weber, 'Internationale Prospekthaftung nach der Rom II-Verordnung' (2008) 62 *Zeitschrift für Wirtschafts- und Bankrecht*, 1581 each with further references.

[187] Inter alia: Arons, 'All roads lead to Rome' (2008) 26 *Nederlands Internationaal Privaatrecht*, 481; Garcimartín Alférez, 'The law applicable to prospectus liability in the European Union' (2011) 5 *Law and Financial Markets Review*, 449.

[188] In detail Steinrötter, *Beschränkte Rechtswahl im Internationalen Kapitalmarktprivatrecht und akzessorische Anknüpfung an das Kapitalmarktordnungsstatut* (2014), 135 et seqq.; most recently Schmitt, Bhatti and Storck, 'Die neue europäische Prospekt-Verordnung – ein großer Wurf?' (2019) 27 *Zeitschrift für Europäisches Privatrecht*, 287 (309).

[189] In detail v. Hein, 'Die Internationale Prospekthaftung im Lichte der Rom II-Verordnung', in Baum, Fleckner, Hellgardt, Roth, et al. (eds), *Perspektiven des Wirtschaftsrechts* (2008), 371 (379 et seqq).

[190] v. Hein, in Kropholler and v. Hein, EUGVVO, Art. 5, para. 72; Wagner, G., in Stein and Jonas (eds), EuGVVO, Art. 5, para. 120 et seq.

[191] Vice versa from PIL to jurisdiction: Bachmann, 'Die internationale Zuständigkeit für Klagen wegen fehlerhafter Kapitalmarktinformation' (2007) 27 *Praxis des Internationalen Privat- und Verfahrensrechts*, 77 (81 et seq.).

[192] Rating Regulation, Art. 35 a.

[193] Steinrötter, *Beschränkte Rechtswahl im Internationalen Kapitalmarktprivatrecht und akzessorische Anknüpfung an das Kapitalmarktordnungsstatut* (2014), 148 et seqq.

[194] Ibid, 164 et seq.; different view by Kiel, *Internationales Kapitalanlegerschutzrecht* (1994), 173, 245 et seq.

[195] However, note the proposal of the German Council for PIL, published in IPRax 2012, 470; in addition Lehmann, 'Proposition d'une règle spéciale dans le Règlement Rome II pour les délits financiers, Revue critique' (2012) 101 *Revue critique de droit international privé*, 485.

[196] Rome II Regulation, Art. 14, para. 3 is not likely to apply to the liability level, as the EU legislator has not regulated prospectus liability claims.

§ 3. International Jurisdiction and Applicable Law

fact that the token investor, already sensitised at this stage, will probably no longer readily accept choice of law suggestions of the issuer.[197] On the other hand, a **choice of law that was agreed on in advance** is, according to Art. 14(1)(b) Rome II Regulation only possible if 'all the parties are pursuing a commercial activity' and the choice of law has been 'freely' negotiated. For private purchasers of tokens, such a possibility is therefore out of the question.[198] But even for commercial respectively institutional investors, the issuer's choice of law clause would have to be at least seriously open to question in order to be able to speak of 'free negotiation' – which is possible for general terms and conditions, but is certainly the exception.[199] Further barriers to the choice of law may exist if the forum has its own overriding mandatory rules under Art. 16 Rome II Regulation. Here, too (→ para. 16), the classification of a provision as an overriding mandatory provision is a matter of interpretation in the individual case.

After all, an effective choice of law is in practice rather the **exception**, especially since de lege lata further restrictions on the choice of law can already be considered. Because of the market regulation law element of prospectus liability (albeit below the threshold of the overriding mandatory provision), it would appear justifiable, by way of a **teleological reduction,** to regard only Member State law that has a substantial connection to the facts of the case as available.[200] Under the previous law, these were, in the preferred view, those legal systems in which the issuer was subject to the obligation to publish a prospectus in the specific case.[201] The fact that only Member State law should be selectable arose from the fact that prospectus liability provisions serve to enforce EU regulatory concepts by private parties and that outside the internal market it is by no means certain that the legal systems there provide for efficiently structured (or any) prospectus claims at all.[202] Under current law, one might consider restricting the choice of law to Member States' legal systems in general. 47

Example:
The commercial investor A, with its head office in Germany, acquires investment tokens when issued by the Dutch company Y. The prospectus of Y is faulty. A choice of law clause provides for the application of Georgian law. A would like to compensate for the losses and is considering filing prospectus liability claims. According to Art. 14(1)(b) Rome II Regulation the prior choice of law is in principle possible, as A is engaged in a 'commercial activity'. However, it would appear preferable to reduce Art. 14 Rome II Regulation teleologically to the extent that only Member State law can be chosen because of the market-controlling function of prospectus liability law. The choice of Georgian law would therefore be inadmissible. One would fall back on the 'objective connecting rules' of Art. 4 Rome II Regulation (→ para. 48).

---

[197] See Schmitt, 'Die kollisionsrechtliche Anknüpfung der Prospekthaftung im System der Rom II-Verordnung' (2010) 10 *Zeitschrift für Bank und Kapitalmarktrecht*, 366 (369).
[198] Cf. Steinrötter, *Beschränkte Rechtswahl im Internationalen Kapitalmarktprivatrecht und akzessorische Anknüpfung an das Kapitalmarktordnungsstatut* (2014), 168.
[199] Ibid; for different view (general terms and conditions always inadmissible here), see Leible, 'Rechtswahl im IPR der außervertraglichen Schuldverhältnisse nach der Rom II-Verordnung' (2008) 54 *Recht der internationalen Wirtschaft*, 257 (260).
[200] In detail Steinrötter, *Beschränkte Rechtswahl im Internationalen Kapitalmarktprivatrecht und akzessorische Anknüpfung an das Kapitalmarktordnungsstatut* (2014), 172 et seq.; Steinrötter, 'Der notorische Problemfall der grenzüberschreitenden Prospekthaftung' (2015) 61 *Recht der internationalen Wirtschaft*, 407 (412); note also the proposal of Einsele, 'Internationales Prospekthaftungsrecht – Kollisionsrechtlicher Anlegerschutz nach der Rom II-Verordnung' (2012) 20 *Zeitschrift für Europäisches Privatrecht*, 23 (42 et seq.). Even for an exclusion of the choice of law in toto: v. Hein, 'Die Internationale Prospekthaftung im Lichte der Rom II-Verordnung', in Baum, Fleckner, Hellgardt, Roth, et al. (eds), *Perspektiven des Wirtschaftsrechts* (2008), 371, 395.
[201] Steinrötter, 'Der notorische Problemfall der grenzüberschreitenden Prospekthaftung' (2015) 61 *Recht der internationalen Wirtschaft*, 407 (412).
[202] Ibid. Prospectus Regulation, Art. 11, para. 1 stipulates that the Member States must provide for effective prospectus liability rules.

48 In the absence of an effective choice of law, the **'objective connecting rules'** apply in this context. However, the embedding in the Rome II system leads to difficulties here. While there is widespread agreement that the Conflict of Laws rules of the Rome II Regulation should not be applied without modification because of the special features of prospectus liability, the proposed solutions in the legal literature diverge considerably. In the absence of a relevant special PIL provision, recourse to Art. 4 Rome II Regulation, needs to be made. However, with its focus on individually injured parties, the provision **does not** appear **appropriate from the** perspective of capital markets tort law, which also wants to regulate the conduct of market participants (as a whole) and the capital market.[203] In this respect (despite recital 7 Rome II Regulation), the ECJ's jurisprudence on the Brussels Ibis Regulation provides only limited assistance. In particular, the ratio decidendi of the 'Kolassa' case (para. 40) cannot be applied in such a way that Art. 4(1) Rome II Regulation, i.e. the link to the place of success (in contrast to its IPL counterpart, the provision does not include the place of action as well), is always relevant and thus Art. 4(2), (3) Rome II Regulation would be negligible.[204] Thus, the more specific provision of Art. 4(2) Rome II Regulation in conjunction with Art. 19 Rome II Regulation, would take precedence over the basic rule of para. 1.[205]

However, the common habitual residence as a connecting factor for prospectus liability seems inappropriate in the light of, for example, the capital markets law principle of equal treatment of investors, a possible divergence of the common habitual residence from the placement of the tokens and the place of approval of the prospectus.[206] Determining the place of success in accordance with Art. 4(1) Rome I Regulation is notoriously difficult in the case of pure financial losses,[207] especially since scattered torts result in a mosaic view that is hardly manageable;[208] this applies in particular to capital market liability.[209] Particularly bearing in mind that it is possible to make dispositions of assets via online accounts from anywhere in the world, finding the closest physical connection seems almost impossible. The location of the asset or the private key cannot always be reliably

---

[203] Einsele, 'Kapitalmarktrecht und Internationales Privatrecht' (2017) 81 *Rabels Zeitschrift für ausländisches und internationales Privatrecht*, 781 (787 et seq.); sceptical, however: Wendelstein, 'Die Behandlung der Prospekthaftung des Emittenten im europäischen Zuständigkeitsrecht' (2016) 9 *Zeitschrift für das Privatrecht der Europäischen Union*, 140 (141).

[204] Steinrötter, 'Der notorische Problemfall der grenzüberschreitenden Prospekthaftung' (2015) 61 *Recht der internationalen Wirtschaft*, 407 (412 et seq.); cf. also Lehmann, in MüKoBGB, Vol. 12 (2017), IntFinMarktR, para. 550 et seq.

[205] recital 18 sentence 2 Rome II Regulation.

[206] In detail also Einsele, 'Internationales Prospekthaftungsrecht – Kollisionsrechtlicher Anlegerschutz nach der Rom II-Verordnung' (2012) 20 *Zeitschrift für Europäisches Privatrecht*, 23 (30); Lehmann, 'Vorschlag für eine Reform der Rom II-Verordnung im Bereich der Finanzmarktdelikte' (2012) 32 *Praxis des Internationalen Privat- und Verfahrensrechts*, 399 (401); Lehmann, 'Das Finanzmarktrecht im Internationalen Privatrecht', in Zetzsche and Lehmann (eds), *Grenzüberschreitende Finanzdienstleistungen* (2018), § 1, para. 64; Weber, 'Internationale Prospekthaftung nach der Rom II-Verordnung' (2008) 62 *Zeitschrift für Wirtschafts- und Bankrecht*, 1581 (1586); other view, admittedly before the Rome II Regulation came into force: Zimmer, *Internationales Gesellschaftsrecht* (1996), 64.

[207] Lehmann, 'Where does Economic Loss Occur?' (2011) 7 *Journal of Private International Law*, 527; critical of the link to the place of performance in the case of financial losses as a whole: Hamburg Group for Private International Law, 'Comments on the European Commission's Draft Proposal for a Council Regulation on the Law Applicable to Non-Contractual Obligations' (2003) 67 *Rabels Zeitschrift für ausländisches und internationales Privatrecht*, 1 (11).

[208] Dörner, in HK-BGB, Rome II Regulation, Art. 4, para. 7.

[209] Lehmann, 'Das Finanzmarktrecht im Internationalen Privatrecht', in Zetzsche and Lehmann (eds), *Grenzüberschreitende Finanzdienstleistungen* (2018), § 1, para. 63; in detail Steinrötter, *Beschränkte Rechtswahl im Internationalen Kapitalmarktprivatrecht und akzessorische Anknüpfung an das Kapitalmarktordnungsstatut* (2014), 182 et seqq.

§ 3. International Jurisdiction and Applicable Law

determined due to its digital nature, nor is it necessarily convincing.[210] The link to the wallet is also flawed as it does not consistently show a substantial connection to a certain state and its legal system. From the point of view of those responsible for the prospectus, all legal systems of the world potentially had to be observed in all conceivable forms of the place of success[211] (Art. 3 Rome II Regulation),[212] which placed an equally heavy strain on both the capital markets law and the international private law requirement of predictability of the applicable law. This also placed an excessive burden on token issuers and would have a potentially transaction-inhibiting effect.[213] It is no coincidence that the EU legislator has explicitly advocated the application of only one legal system per transaction under private capital markets law elsewhere (Art. 4(1)(h) Rome I Regulation, Art. 6, (4) (c), (d) Rome I Regulation, recitals 28 et seq. and 7 Rome I Regulation[214]; cf. also recital 4 Prospectus Regulation. The recourse to Art. 4(2), (1) Rome II Regulation is therefore not convincing for a harmonized internal capital market[215] – there is initially no reason to assess this differently for crypto tokens (to be qualified as securities) than for other transactions under capital markets law.

On the other hand, the desired certainty, in particular sufficient predictability, would be achieved by a PIL command which would ideally lead to one applicable law for all investors or at least to a very limited number of jurisdictions.[216] Dogmatically, this path de lege lata only leads via the **escape clause of Art. 4(3)(1) Rome II Regulation**.[217] This PIL provision is breaking through the general rules of para. 1, 2 in the case 'where it is clear from all the circumstances of the case that the tort/delict is manifestly more closely connected with a country other than that indicated in paragraphs 1 or 2'. The wording alone makes it clear that a restrictive application of the escape clause appears to be induced. Although this is primarily intended to correct individual cases, one is not prevented from the outset from including a whole group of cases – namely that of prospectus liability – under this.[218] It is questionable

49

---

[210] Martiny, 'Virtuelle Währungen, insbesondere Bitcoins, im Internationalen Privat- und Zivilverfahrensrecht' (2018) 38 *Praxis des Internationalen Privat- und Verfahrensrechts*, 553 (559).
[211] Location of the damaged property, place of disposition of property, location of the main property, centre of assets, centre of interest of the aggrieved party (regularly: habitual residence), market place; see Steinrötter, *Beschränkte Rechtswahl im Internationalen Kapitalmarktprivatrecht und akzessorische Anknüpfung an das Kapitalmarktordnungsstatut* (2014), 182 et seqq.
[212] In detail also Lehmann, 'Vorschlag für eine Reform der Rom II-Verordnung im Bereich der Finanzmarktdelikte' (2012) 32 *Praxis des Internationalen Privat- und Verfahrensrechts*, 399 (400); other approach by Einsele, 'Kapitalmarktrecht und Internationales Privatrecht' (2017) 81 *Rabels Zeitschrift für ausländisches und internationales Privatrecht*, 781 (788 et seqq.), who (primarily) links to the placement market via Rome II Regulation, Art. 4, para. 1.
[213] This is the finding on IPOs: Steinrötter, *Beschränkte Rechtswahl im Internationalen Kapitalmarktprivatrecht und akzessorische Anknüpfung an das Kapitalmarktordnungsstatut* (2014), 190 et seq.
[214] Steinrötter, 'Der notorische Problemfall der grenzüberschreitenden Prospekthaftung' (2015) 61 *Recht der internationalen Wirtschaft*, 407 (413).
[215] See Hellgardt and Ringe, 'Internationale Kapitalmarkthaftung als Corporate Governance' (2009) 173 *Zeitschrift für das gesamte Handels- und Wirtschaftsrecht*, 802 (825).
[216] Steinrötter, *Beschränkte Rechtswahl im Internationalen Kapitalmarktprivatrecht und akzessorische Anknüpfung an das Kapitalmarktordnungsstatut* (2014), 191.
[217] On the question why Rome II Regulation, Art. 4, para. 3 sentence 2 does not apply: Steinrötter, *Beschränkte Rechtswahl im Internationalen Kapitalmarktprivatrecht und akzessorische Anknüpfung an das Kapitalmarktordnungsstatut* (2014), 192 et seqq.
[218] In detail ibid, 195 et seqq.; see also Winner and Schmidt, 'Recht des Primärmarkts: Grenzüberschreitende Haftung für fehlerhafte Prospekte und Anlegerinformationen', in Zetzsche and Lehmann (eds), *Grenzüberschreitende Finanzdienstleistungen* (2018), § 12, para. 71: 'The formation of case groups [via the escape clause] will probably not be avoidable in the end'; different view, e.g., Lehmann, 'Das Finanzmarktrecht im Internationalen Privatrecht', in Zetzsche and Lehmann (eds), *Grenzüberschreitende Finanzdienstleistungen* (2018), § 1, para. 67.

how the escape clause should now be specified. The connection to a 'market place'[219] is itself in need of concretization; the approaches of the legal literature partly diverge quite clearly.[220] In the end, the 'market place' link suffers from a precise definition of the relevant trading venue that is capable of consensus.[221] Under the regime of the Prospectus Directive 2003/71/EC, an accessory link to the law of the Member State approving the prospectus was therefore preferable,[222] for this led to the fact that in the case of securities as defined by Art. 2(1)(a) Prospectus Directive 2003/71/EC only one legal system, namely that of the home Member State pursuant to Art. 2(1)(m) Prospectus Directive 2003/71/EC answered questions of liability with regard to the entire issue (because of the European passport). Under the Prospectus Regulation, this possibility of orientation to the relevant prospectus approval statute for the question of the accessory connection of prospectus liability seems to be dropped. This is because the EU Regulation is directly applicable (Art. 288 (2) of the Treaty on the Functioning of the European Union) without any reference to directive transformations which in turn 'point' to a specific Member State. However, it is also conceivable under the new law to link to the **legal system of the Member State whose authority has approved the prospectus**, for it is still a Member State authority, not a supranational one,[223] which approves the prospectus.[224] This is the authority of the 'home Member State' and thus regularly that of the issuer's registered office (Art. 20 Prospectus Regulation in conjunction with Art. 2(r), (m) Prospectus Regulation).

Example:
The commercial investor A, with its head office in Germany, acquires investment tokens when issued by the Dutch company Y. The prospectus of Y approved in the Netherlands is incorrect. A choice of law clause provides for the application of Georgian law. A wishes to compensate for the losses and is considering filing prospectus liability claims. Since the choice of law fails (see → para. 46 et seq.), the applicable law must be determined by Art. 4 Rome II Regulation. It seems preferable here to link to the legal system of the Member State whose authorities have approved the prospectus in accordance with Art. 4(3) Rome II Regulation. Thus, Dutch prospectus liability law applies in this case.

50 In the case of **non-securitised investments or third-country issuers of tokens** without a European passport, the liability law of the country in which the prospectus

---

[219] Garcimartín Alférez, 'The law applicable to prospectus liability in the European Union' (2011) 5 *Law and Financial Markets Review*, 449 (453); Weber, 'Internationale Prospekthaftung nach der Rom II-Verordnung' (2008) 62 *Zeitschrift für Wirtschafts- und Bankrecht*, 1581 (1586); Floer, *Prospekthaftung* (2002), 141 et seq. (before the Rome II Regulation came into force).

[220] Place of acquisition, place of placement, place of effect, place of issue of the prospectus, place of orientation, multi-level (rather complex) proposals for concretisation; for all this: Steinrötter, *Beschränkte Rechtswahl im Internationalen Kapitalmarktprivatrecht und akzessorische Anknüpfung an das Kapitalmarktordnungsstatut* (2014), 201 et seqq. with further references.

[221] See also Junker, 'Der Reformbedarf im Internationalen Deliktsrecht der Rom II-Verordnung drei Jahre nach ihrer Verabschiedung' (2010) 56 *Recht der internationalen Wirtschaft*, 257 (264).

[222] In detail Steinrötter, *Beschränkte Rechtswahl im Internationalen Kapitalmarktprivatrecht und akzessorische Anknüpfung an das Kapitalmarktordnungsstatut* (2014), 216 et seqq.; accessory to the 'prospectus obligation' (which is not always consistent with the approach here), e.g., Benicke, 'Prospektpflicht und Prospekthaftung bei grenzüberschreitenden Emissionen', in Mansel, Kronke and Pfeiffer (eds), *FS Jayme* (2004), 25 (36 et seq.); different view by Einsele, 'Kapitalmarktrecht und Internationales Privatrecht' (2017) 81 *Rabels Zeitschrift für ausländisches und internationales Privatrecht*, 781 (809 et seqq.).

[223] Although ESMA does exist, it does not render the national authorities obsolete, but cooperates with the national supervisory authorities (cf. Art. 34 Prospectus Regulation).

[224] Art. 31(1), Art. 32, recitals 8, 11, 69 Prospectus Regulation.

was approved had to be applied in an accessory manner.[225] In this way, a very limited (and predictable) number of legal systems was at least achieved. This approach can also be maintained in principle.[226]

3. Prospectus Disclosure Requirements and Prospectus Liability

The need to clarify the relationship between the statutes of prospectus publicity and liability – which in principle have to be assessed separately[227] under Conflict of Laws – follows from the fact that the existence, content and fulfilment or breach of the corresponding publicity requirements are important for the question if and to what extent prospectus liability can be considered. Correctly, the existence, content and **(non-)fulfilment of the prospectus obligation** from the perspective of liability is a **'preliminary question'** in terms of Conflict of Laws,[228] which must be answered according to the PIL rules of the respective forum.[229]

51

4. Other Capital Market Tort Law Cases

For other cases of liability under capital market tort law or capital market information law (namely: regular and ad hoc disclosure as well as insider trading law),[230] the statements on prospectus liability (→ para. 45 et seqq.) for investment tokens as well as utility tokens with investment focus shall apply accordingly if the tokens meet the definition of 'transferable securities'.[231] For **ratings of crypto tokens**, the directly applicable liability provision of Art. 35a Regulation (EU) No. 462/2013 (Rating Regulation)[232] needs to be taken into account. In material terms, however, it is largely a mere 'norm shell', because unfortunately central terms used in this provision (e.g. 'damage', 'gross negligence') are not open to the actually preferable autonomous interpretation under EU law. Rather, the terms mentioned 'shall be interpreted and applied in accordance with the applicable national law as determined by the relevant rules of private international law' (Art. 35a(4)(1) Rating Regulation).[233] The relevant tort statute

52

---

[225] Steinrötter, *Beschränkte Rechtswahl im Internationalen Kapitalmarktprivatrecht und akzessorische Anknüpfung an das Kapitalmarktordnungsstatut* (2014), 240 et seq.
[226] See recitals 70, 79 Prospectus Regulation. The German Federal Government has recently considered an accessoriness approach very similar to the one proposed here, BMF/BMJV Eckpunkte für die regulatorische Behandlung von elektronischen Wertpapieren und Krypto-Token vom 7.3.2019, 4.
[227] Lehmann, 'Vorschlag für eine Reform der Rom II-Verordnung im Bereich der Finanzmarktdelikte' (2012) 32 *Praxis des Internationalen Privat- und Verfahrensrechts*, 399 (405).
[228] At the same time, according to the approach advocated here, the 'publicity statute' is the connecting factor for liability.
[229] In detail Steinrötter, *Beschränkte Rechtswahl im Internationalen Kapitalmarktprivatrecht und akzessorische Anknüpfung an das Kapitalmarktordnungsstatut* (2014), 261 et seq.; Winner and Schmidt, 'Recht des Primärmarkts: Grenzüberschreitende Haftung für fehlerhafte Prospekte und Anlegerinformationen', in Zetzsche and Lehmann (eds), *Grenzüberschreitende Finanzdienstleistungen* (2018), § 12, para. 12 et seq.; see on international market manipulation Poelzig, 'Grenzüberschreitende Markmanipulation', in Zetzsche and Lehmann (eds), *Grenzüberschreitende Finanzdienstleistungen* (2018), § 14, para. 52 et seq.
[230] See Art. 14 and 17 Regulation (EU) No. 596/2014 of the European Parliament and of the Council on market abuse (Market Abuse Regulation) and repealing Directive 2003/6/EC of the European Parliament and of the Council and Commission Directives 2003/124/EC, 2003/125/EC and 2004/72/EC, OJ L 173, 12.6.2014 p. 1–61.
[231] Cf. in detail Steinrötter, *Beschränkte Rechtswahl im Internationalen Kapitalmarktprivatrecht und akzessorische Anknüpfung an das Kapitalmarktordnungsstatut* (2014), 418 et seq.
[232] Regulation (EU) No. 462/2013 of the European Parliament and of the Council amending Regulation (EC) No 1060/2009 on credit rating agencies, OJ L 146, 31.5.2013 p. 1–33.
[233] In detail, e.g. Schroeter, 'Grenzüberschreitende Verhaltenspflichten und Haftung von Ratingagenturen', in Zetzsche and Lehmann (eds), *Grenzüberschreitende Finanzdienstleistungen* (2018), § 11.

is to be determined via Art. 14 Rome II Regulation (limitation to Member State law, para. 49) or Art. 4(3)(1) Rome II Regulation (place of the use of the rating).[234]

I. (Other) Liability Law

53 Apart from capital market tort law (→ para. 45 et seqq.), a different treatment of liability under IPL/PIL seems appropriate. Here, the **classical function of liability law**, protection of the individually injured party, is so strongly in the foreground that marketplace solutions or the adaptation of the private statute to regulatory law are not feasible. In the context of crypto tokens, various forms of data crimes can be considered, such as the use of botnets to generate new tokens or the infiltration of computers[235], compromised user accounts[236] and secret mining.[237] In addition, there is also the spying out of the private key and its subsequent unauthorized use; this has already occurred via so-called 'SIM swapping'[238]. The manipulation of a data record by a blockchain participant would also be (theoretically) conceivable.[239] One can leave it to the **applicable tort law** (para. 55), in what way crypto tokens are tortuously protected and whether to call the protected legal status 'property' (para. 6 et seq.) or something else.[240]

I. International Jurisdiction

54 Legal action may be brought at the **defendant's Member State domicile** (Art. 4 Brussels Ibis Regulation) and, where appropriate, at the Member States **place where the action took place and where it was successful** (Art. 7(2) Brussels Ibis Regulation). **Agreements on the place of jurisdiction** (Art. 25 Brussels Ibis Regulation) are also conceivable. Finally, it is possible that the defendant **enters an appearance** (Art. 26 Brussels Ibis Regulation).

II. Applicable Law

55 The relevant legal act for the determination of the substantive liability law is the **Rome II Regulation**, whose exception of the scope of application pursuant to its Art. 1 (2)(c) does not apply, since the obligation does not result from the tradability of the tokens.[241] Modifications as in the case of capital market tort law are not necessary,

---

[234] Steinrötter, 'Zuständigkeits- und kollisionsrechtliche Implikationen des europäischen Haftungstatbestands für fehlerhaftes Rating' (2015) 36 *Zeitschrift für Wirtschaftsrecht*, 110 (115); different view by Dutta, 'Die neuen Haftungsregeln für Ratingagenturen in der Europäischen Union: Zwischen Sachrechtsvereinheitlichung und europäischem Entscheidungseinklang' (2013) 67 *Zeitschrift für Wirtschafts- und Bankrecht*, 1729.
[235] There have already been successful hacker attacks: BTC-ECHO, available at https://beck-link.de/m8sby (accessed 1.9.2020).
[236] Heise, available at https://beck-link.de/ndf83 (accessed 1.9.2020).
[237] Boehm and Pesch, Bitcoins: Rechtliche Herausforderungen einer virtuellen Währung – Eine erste juristische Einordung (2014) 17 *Zeitschrift für IT-Recht und Digitalisierung*, 75 (77).
[238] Cf. t3n – digital pioneers, available at https://beck-link.de/84s7e (accessed 1.9.2020).
[239] Zimmermann, 'Blockchain-Netzwerke und Internationales Privatrecht – oder: der Sitz dezentraler Rechtsverhältnisse' (2018) 38 *Praxis des Internationalen Privat- und Verfahrensrechts*, 566 (570), according to whom damage is rarely conceivable in view of the technical architecture of the blockchain.
[240] Lehmann, 'Who Owns Bitcoin? Private Law Facing the Blockchain' (2019) 21 *Minnesota Journal of Law, Science & Technology*, 93 (128).
[241] Martiny, 'Virtuelle Währungen, insbesondere Bitcoins, im Internationalen Privat- und Zivilverfahrensrecht' (2018) 38 *Praxis des Internationalen Privat- und Verfahrensrechts*, 553 (564).

which is why the legal practitioner must 'work through' the 'traditional' sequence of checks, i.e. Art. 4(2), (1), (3) Rome II Regulation.[242] That practical problems may arise (inter alia) due to the ubiquity of the internet is a separate issue. Furthermore, claims based on **unjust enrichment** are possible if the **private key is stolen** and this results in an unauthorised transmission of crypto tokens.[243] Here Art. 10 Rome II Regulation is to be referred to.[244]

J. Mining and Mining Pools

Of the legal relationships on the primary and secondary market described above, a distinction must be made between those in mining (this also includes other forms of generating new tokens, e.g. by means of 'forging'; on the concept of mining → § 1 para. 80) and those within a mining pool (→ § 1 para. 40 et seqq.). Miners sometimes join together in mining pools (staking pools) in order to jointly exercise the proof of work (proof of stake) and to 'mine' new tokens (§ 1 para. 58 et seqq.). While it may still be possible to construct a legally binding will of the miners to each other,[245] the precise **contractual classification of the pool** is **already completely unclear at the substantive law level**. Thus, the application of company law (namely partnership law) may also be considered.[246] Sometimes the legal concept of a 'contract network' is also used.[247]

56

I. International Jurisdiction

1. Mining

In addition to the possibility for the defendant to **enter an appearance** (Art. 26 Brussels Ibis Regulation), **agreements on the place of jurisdiction** (Art. 25 Brussels Ibis Regulation) and the general **actor sequitur jurisdiction** (Art. 4 Brussels Ibis Regulation), mining can be translated at the meta level of IPL by contract. Here, the **consumer protection provisions** of Art. 17 et seqq. Brussels Ibis Regulation can apply in principle just as much as (subsidiarily) the **optional jurisdiction** rule of Art. 7(1) Brussels Ibis Regulation. The concept of contract is understood extensively[248] and in principle also

57

---

[242] Sceptical Guillaume, 'Aspects of private international law related to blockchain transactions', in Kraus, Obrist and Hari (eds), *Blockchains, Smart Contracts, Decentralised Autonomous Organisations and the Law* (2019), 49 (64).
[243] See also Langenbucher, 'Digitales Finanzwesen – Vom Bargeld zu virtuellen Währungen' (2018) 218 *Archiv für die civilistische Praxis*, 385 (407 et seq.).
[244] Martiny, 'Virtuelle Währungen, insbesondere Bitcoins, im Internationalen Privat- und Zivilverfahrensrecht' (2018) 38 *Praxis des Internationalen Privat- und Verfahrensrechts*, 553 (564).
[245] For example, Seitz, 'Distributed Ledger Technology & Bitcoin – Zur rechtlichen Stellung eines Bitcoin-'Inhabers'' (2017) 20 *Kommunikation und Recht*, 763 (764); sceptical Langenbucher, 'Digitales Finanzwesen – Vom Bargeld zu virtuellen Währungen' (2018) 218 *Archiv für die civilistische Praxis*, 385 (406); Omlor, 'Blockchain-basierte Zahlungsmittel' (2018) 51 *Zeitschrift für Rechtspolitik*, 85 (86).
[246] Martiny, 'Virtuelle Währungen, insbesondere Bitcoins, im Internationalen Privat- und Zivilverfahrensrecht' (2018) 38 *Praxis des Internationalen Privat- und Verfahrensrechts*, 553 (559); Seitz, 'Distributed Ledger Technology & Bitcoin – Zur rechtlichen Stellung eines Bitcoin-'Inhabers'' (2017) 20 *Kommunikation und Recht*, 763 (764) each with further references.
[247] Omlor, 'Blockchain-basierte Zahlungsmittel' (2018) 51 *Zeitschrift für Rechtspolitik*, 85 (86); cf. already Teubner, '"Verbund", "Verband" oder "Verkehr"?' (1990) 54 *Zeitschrift für das gesamte Handels- und Wirtschaftsrecht*, 295.
[248] Gottwald, in MüKoZPO, Brussels Ia-VO, Vol. 3, Art. 7, para. 6.

includes unilateral legal transactions.²⁴⁹ In this context, the subsumptions under the concept of 'direction' in Art. 17(1) Brussels Ibis Regulation and the 'place of performance' in the sense of Art. 7(1) Brussels Ibis Regulation are likely to be problematic. In the light of the relevant ECJ jurisprudence, Art. 17(1) Brussels Ibis Regulation requires the consideration of the catalogue of indications (→ para. 10 et seqq.). The place of performance in the sense of Art. 7(1) Brussels Ibis must be identified according to the substantive law designated by the forum's Conflict of Laws rules (→ para. 14).

2. Mining Pools

58 Exclusive jurisdiction does not apply to disputes within a mining pool. In particular, Art. 24(2) Brussels Ibis Regulation, which concerns specific questions in the internal relationship of companies, is not relevant here. Conceivable, however, are – ranked according to priority – court competences based on **the entering of an appearance** (Art. 26 Brussels Ibis Regulation) as well as **agreements on jurisdiction** (Art. 25 Brussels Ibis Regulation), actions in the **contractual jurisdiction** (Art. 7(1) Brussels Ibis Regulation) and finally on the **general actor sequitur jurisdiction** (Art. 4 Brussels Ibis Regulation). The protective provisions of Art. 17 et seqq. Brussels Ibis Regulation are generally irrelevant, since in most cases there is no consumer contract (→ para. 10).

II. Applicable Law

1. Mining

59 The legal transaction of mining is **contractual**²⁵⁰ on the level of Conflict of Laws and – unless there is a choice of law (Art. 3 Rome I Regulation) – falls under Art. 4(2) Rome I Regulation. The contractual concept of the Rome I Regulation must be interpreted correspondingly broadly and, in the preferred view, also covers unilateral legal transactions; an analogous application of the Rome I Regulation is therefore not necessary.²⁵¹ The **characteristic element** of such a contract is provided by the party issuing the '**reward**'²⁵² (the initiator of the blockchain or the issuer of the token), so that the law of the state of residence applies (at least until the protocol is changed by the majority of nodes). However, Art. 6 Rome I Regulation may also be relevant²⁵³ if its requirements are met (→ para. 10 et seqq. Regarding the IPL pendant). In this case, the **chosen law is** applicable, if necessary, in conjunction with the specifically more favourable mandatory law of the country of residence of the consumer (Art. 6(2) Rome I Regulation) **or** – in the absence of a choice of law – the law of the country in which the consumer has established **his habitual residence** is applicable.

2. Mining Pools

60 Conflict of Laws rules to be applied to mining pools do not arise from a qualification under corporate law. The function of a mining pool is to bundle resources (especially computer capacity) in order to be able to mine new crypto tokens and then

---

²⁴⁹ Geimer, in Geimer and Schütze, EuGVVO, Art. 5, para. 53; v. Hein, in Kropholler and v. Hein, EuGVVO, Art. 5, para. 10.
²⁵⁰ Martiny, in MüKoBGB, Rome I-VO, Vol. 12, Art. 4, para. 283.
²⁵¹ On the dispute in this regard: Martiny, in MüKoBGB, Rome I-VO, Vol. 12, Art. 1, para. 20 with further references.
²⁵² Ferrari, in IntVertragsR, Art. 4 Rom I-VO para. 112; Köhler, in BeckOGK, Rome I-VO, Art. 4, para. 407.
²⁵³ Köhler, in BeckOGK, Rome I-VO, Art. 4 para. 407.

§ 3. International Jurisdiction and Applicable Law

distribute the reward according to the resource involved. In this respect, a **contractual** (no consumer law → para. 58) **qualification** seems preferable.[254] It is rather improbable that a user would like to commit himself towards unknown persons (possibly in a number unknown to him) to establish an association (participating in legal relations with third parties) and then to promote a common corporate purpose. An external company, for which, in principle, the Conflict of Laws principle would then be relevant,[255] which would immediately bring the exception of the scope of application of Art. 1(2)(f) Rome I Regulation concerning the Rome I Regulation in toto into play, is therefore not given here. Consequently, **at least typically, the Rome I Regulation applies**. In the case of a purely internal company, it should allegedly be possible to loosen up the Conflict of Laws rules at the centre of management in accordance with Art. 4(3) Rome I Regulation.[256] However, this fails to recognise (irrespective of the question of whether the stage of an internal company in the case of a mining pool has already been reached and whether it would then be contractually qualified[257] at all) that the escape clause can only be activated in accordance with its wording if a statute pursuant to paras. 1 and 2 has already been found. This is typically not the case here. This is because there is neither a type of contract in the catalogue of Art. 4(1) Rome I Regulation nor can a contractual performance by individual participants be identified as being characteristic of a contract within the meaning of Art. 4(2) Rome I Regulation. On the contrary, in the case of the personal connection that can be found without a sufficient organisational structure,[258] the application of the **catch-all** provision of Art. 4(4) Rome I Regulation is dogmatically preferable.[259] However, the **'closest connection'** in this sense requires contouring. The previous proposals, the 'place of the [main] pursuit of the purpose of the company'[260] or the 'focus of this cooperation'[261], appear to be practicable to a limited extent at best. In the latter case, it is also being considered whether the **'management of the network'**, i.e. in particular the one who controls the access, carried out by an external party (probably meaning the 'pool operator' in a 'managed mining pool'; → § 1 para. 54), could be decisive. That means that the **habitual place of residence** of this operator would constitute the main focus, which would also result from the service contract between the individual nodes and the manager (in this respect, Art. 4(1)(b) Rome I Regulation applies). All this would be an accessory connection to this service contract by way of Art. 4(4) Rome I Regulation[262].[263] This would appear to be practicable and dogmatically justifiable, at least to some extent, but would be limited in its area of application to

---

[254] Martiny, 'Virtuelle Währungen, insbesondere Bitcoins, im Internationalen Privat- und Zivilverfahrensrecht' (2018) 38 *Praxis des Internationalen Privat- und Verfahrensrechts*, 553 (559).

[255] Zimmermann, 'Blockchain-Netzwerke und Internationales Privatrecht – oder: der Sitz dezentraler Rechtsverhältnisse' (2018) 38 *Praxis des Internationalen Privat- und Verfahrensrechts*, 566 (569).

[256] Ibid.

[257] Martiny, in MüKoBGB, Rome I-VO, Vol. 12, Art. 1, para. 72.

[258] Köhler, in BeckOGK, Rome I-VO, Art. 4, para. 564; Martiny, in MüKoBGB, Rome I-VO, Vol. 12, Art. 1, para. 71.

[259] Martiny, 'Virtuelle Währungen, insbesondere Bitcoins, im Internationalen Privat- und Zivilverfahrensrecht' (2018) 38 *Praxis des Internationalen Privat- und Verfahrensrechts*, 553 (559).

[260] Ibid.

[261] Zimmermann, 'Blockchain-Netzwerke und Internationales Privatrecht – oder: der Sitz dezentraler Rechtsverhältnisse' (2018) 38 *Praxis des Internationalen Privat- und Verfahrensrechts*, 566 (569).

[262] Arg.: Since neither a standard case pursuant to Art. 4(1) Rome I Regulation nor a contractual performance characteristic of a contract pursuant to Art. 4(2) Rome I Regulation can be identified, the default clause of Art. 4(4) and not the escape clause of Art. 4(3) must be applied.

[263] See in this sense for centrally managed blockchain networks: Zimmermann, 'Blockchain-Netzwerke und Internationales Privatrecht – oder: der Sitz dezentraler Rechtsverhältnisse' (2018) 38 *Praxis des Internationalen Privat- und Verfahrensrechts*, 566 (569).

'managed mining pools'. Ultimately, the 'closest link' will have to be determined on a **case-by-case basis**. Since the legal situation is still unclear in this respect and awaits preparation by legal academia and the courts, it is **urgently recommended that a choice of law,** which is in principle possible under Art. 3 Rome I Regulation is made – even though it is clear that this also encounters difficulties in practice.

§ 4
Consumer Protection

Literature: European Commission, 'Proposal for a Regulation of the European Parliament and the Council on Markets in Crypto-Assets, and amending Directive (EU) 2019/1937' COM(2020) 593 final, available at https://beck-link.de/zy2x5; Ferrari, in: *J. von Staudingers Kommentar zum Bürgerlichen Gesetzbuch: Internationales Vertragsrecht 1* (Sellier/de Gruyter, 2016); Föhlisch and Löwer, 'Das Widerrufsrecht bei Gutscheinen im Fernabsatz', (2015) 17 *Kommunikation & Recht* 298; Henning-Bodewig, 'Distance Sales of Heating Oil and the Consumer's Right of Withdrawal – A Fair Balance?' (2016) 5 *Journal of European Consumer and Market Law* 87; Kainer, 'Der Verbrauchergerichtsstand bei Kapitalanlagegeschäften', (2018) 29 *Zeitschrift für Bankrecht und Bankwirtschaft/Journal of Banking Law and Banking* 368; Maume and Fromberger, 'Regulation of Initial Coin Offerings: Reconciling US and EU Securities Laws' (2019) 19 *Chicago Journal of International Law* 548; Moles and Terry, *The Handbook of International Financial Terms* (Oxford, Oxford University Press, 1997); Wendehorst, 'Platform Intermediary Services and Duties under the E-Commerce Directive and the Consumer Rights Directive', (2016) 5 *Journal of European Consumer and Market Law* 30.

Outline

	para.
A. Overview	1
I. Applicable Legislation	1
II. Token Categories and Type of Acquisition	5
B. Key Definitions	8
I. Consumer	8
II. Seller	11
1. Under the Consumer Rights Directive	11
2. Under the MiCAR Draft	14
C. The Right of Withdrawal	15
I. Under the CRD	15
1. General	15
2. Distance Contract	16
3. Purpose of the Right of Withdrawal in Distance Contracts	17
4. Exceptions	20
a) Price Depending on Fluctuations in Financial Markets	20
aa) Financial Markets	21
bb) Dependent on Fluctuations	22
cc) Different Token Categories	25
b) No Digital Content	30
5. Consequences	33
II. Under the MiCAR Draft	36
D. Information Obligations	40

A. Overview

I. Applicable Legislation

Many token acquisitions are carried out for private purposes. This raises the question of the application of EU consumer protection rules. The most important issue is whether the acquirer of the token has a **right of withdrawal** – which is at the heart of EU consumer protection. This will be the central topic of this chapter. **1**

2   The key piece of EU legislation is the Directive 2011/83/EC on consumer rights (**Consumer Rights Directive, CRD**).¹ Other relevant EU legislation is the Directive 2000/31/EC on E-Commerce² and Directive 93/13/EEC on unfair terms in consumer contracts.³ As they do not concern the right of withdrawal directly, they are of lower relevance for this chapter.

An important preliminary question is applicable law and jurisdiction in relation to consumer contracts, which is set out in Regulation (EU) 1215/2012 (Brussels Ibis),⁴ Regulation (EC) 593/2008 (Rome I)⁵ and Regulation (EC) 864/2007 (Rome II).⁶ These will be discussed in detail in chapter 3 of this book (→ § 3 para. 9 et seqq.).

3   Not relevant for this chapter is Directive 2002/65/EC on financial services and direct marketing (**Financial Services Directive, FSD**).⁷ It applies to the provision of financial services online. The Directive mentions typical financial services as examples: bank accounts, credit cards, portfolio management, etc (Rec. 19 FSD). It focuses on long-term agreements (separating between the initial service agreement and successive transactions (Rec. 19 FSD). The non-crypto equivalent of a token acquisition (which would be the acquisition of a share, bond, or fund) is not mentioned. That is straightforward because selling something to someone is not the same thing as providing a service for someone. Token sales are more comparable to the sale of goods, which generally falls within the scope of Directive 97/7/EC on distance contracts (Rec. 10 FSD)⁸ and its successor, the CRD. Thus, issuing tokens is not a financial service within the scope of the FSD.

4   In September 2020, the European Commission published its draft for the Regulation of Markets in Crypto-assets (**MiCAR Draft**).⁹ In this, it also puts emphasis on consumer protection. Most significantly, in simplified terms, the Commission sets out a right of withdrawal for consumers who buy crypto-assets from an issuer or a crypto-asset service provider (→ para. 14). It is obvious that the MiCAR regime was drafted with the CRD in mind because many elements are copied from the Directive. Although MiCAR will provide a specific regime for crypto assets, the CRD (in particular, the right of withdrawal) will remain applicable. This is clarified by Rec. 16 MiCAR Draft.

---

¹ Directive 2011/83/EC of the European Parliament and of the Council on consumer rights, amending Council Directive 93/13/EEC and Directive 1999/44/EC of the European Parliament and of the Council and repealing Council Directive 85/577/EEC and Directive 97/7/EC of the European Parliament and of the Council, OJ L 304, 22.11.2011 p. 64–88.

² Directive 2000/31/EC of the European Parliament and of the Council on certain legal aspects of information society services, in particular electronic commerce, in the Internal Market (Directive on electronic commerce), OJ L 178, 17.7.2000 p. 1–16.

³ Council Directive 93/13/EEC on unfair terms in consumer contracts, OJ L 95, 21.4.1993 p. 29–34.

⁴ Regulation (EU) No. 1215/2012 of the European Parliament and of the Council on jurisdiction and the recognition and enforcement of judgments in civil and commercial matters, OJ L 351, 20.12.2012 p. 1–32.

⁵ Regulation (EC) No. 593/2008 of the European Parliament and of the Council on the law applicable to contractual obligations (Rome I), OJ L 177, 4.7.2009 p. 6–16.

⁶ Regulation (EC) No. 864/2007 of 11.7.2007 on the law applicable to non-contractual obligations (Rome II), OJ L 199, 31.7.2007 p. 40–49.

⁷ Directive 2002/65/EC of the European Parliament and of the Council concerning the distance marketing of consumer financial services and amending Council Directive 90/619/EEC and Directives 97/7/EC and 98/27/EC, OJ L 271, 9.10.2002 p. 16–24.

⁸ Directive 97/7/EC of the European Parliament and of the Council on the protection of consumers in respect of distance contracts, OJ L 144, 4.6.1997 p. 19–27.

⁹ European Commission, 'Proposal for a Regulation of the European Parliament and the Council on Markets in Crypto-Assets, and amending Directive (EU) 2019/1937' (24 September 2020, COM(2020) 593 final).

II. Token Categories and Type of Acquisition

In legal literature and practice, a distinction is usually made between **currency tokens**, **utility tokens** and **investment tokens** (the so-called token archetypes, → § 1 para. 168). For the purposes of this chapter, it is assumed that (only) investment tokens are transferable securities under Art. 4(1)(44) of Directive 2014/65/EU on markets in financial instruments (MiFiD2, → § 7 para. 133)[10], and thus financial instruments under Art. 4(1)(15) MiFID2. **Derivatives** on any token are also transferable securities under MiFID2,[11] and thus financial instruments for the purposes of the chapter.

The central definition in the MiCAR Draft is **crypto-asset**, which means a digital representation of value or rights which may be transferred and stored electronically, using distributed ledger or similar technology (Art. 3(1)(2) MiCAR Draft). This applies to, for example, currency tokens. Subcategories of crypto-assets under the MiCAR Draft with additional features are **asset-referenced tokens**, **e-money tokens** and **utility tokens** (Art. 3(1)(3)-(5) MiCAR Draft). Importantly, the MiCAR regime does not apply to crypto-assets that classify as financial instruments under MiFID2 (Art. 2(2)(a) MiCAR Draft).

Another distinction needs to be made between two different types of token purchases. The **initial acquisition** refers to the 'sale' of tokens directly from the issuer to the acquirer (initial coin offering, ICO). The **second acquisition**, on the other hand, refers to a subsequent transaction between non-issuers, comparable to trading in securities on a stock exchange. In the case of **utility tokens**, a distinction must also be made between the purchase of the token and the **redemption** of the token (→ para. 134).

B. Key Definitions

I. Consumer

The application of EU consumer law requires that the acquiring party is a consumer. Under the CRD, the consumer is defined in Art. 2(1) as **any natural person who is acting for purposes which are outside his trade, business, craft or profession**. The definition in Art. 3(1)(28) MiCAR Draft is identical.

In practice, this simple definition can be difficult to apply. The problem is that the other party (the trader, → para. 11) often does not know if the transaction is carried out as a part of the buyer's profession. Sometimes the purposes are mixed, i.e. if the goods are used both for private and for business purposes.[12] In **case of doubt**, the transaction must be regarded as a consumer contract. Only if the issuer can **clearly identify the customer as a trader** (e.g. by the legal form or the business and shipping address) it can be assumed with sufficient certainty that the transaction is of commercial nature.[13]

Many tokens are bought with a **view for profit**. Even tokens that do not have a focus on investment (that means, all tokens that are not investment tokens) are often traded at crypto exchanges. They are bought and sold with the expectation of increases in price,

---

[10] Directive 2014/65/EU of the European Parliament and of the Council of 15 May 2014 on markets in financial instruments and amending Directives 2002/92/EC and 2011/61/EU, OJ L 173, 12.6.2016 p. 349–496.
[11] Maume and Fromberger, 'Regulation of Initial Coin Offerings: Reconciling US and EU Securities Laws' (2019) 19 *Chicago Journal of International Law*, 548 (583) with further references.
[12] An example would be a car that is used for the buyer's business as well as for private trips.
[13] ECJ, Judgment of 20 January 2005, *Gruber/Baywa AG*, C-464/01, para. 51 et seq.

and thus profits. This is at odds with the basic idea of consumer law, which is literally focusing on goods/services and their **consumption**. However, even investments do not necessarily have a business purpose and are thus carried out for private purposes – provided that the scope or frequency of investments is not big enough to constitute some kind of business.[14] For example, the European Court of Justice (ECJ) has ruled in a non-crypto case that a private purpose exists if the transaction in question is carried out to cover own needs.[15] Thus, an intention to make a profit does not rule out the classification as a consumer.[16]

10 Token subscribers often have to **confirm** in a dialogue box that they are **not consumers** before concluding the legal transaction. The general terms and conditions of many issuers and crypto exchanges contain clauses with similar objectives. However, such an exemption from consumer protection is not possible. As stated above (→ para. 8), the seller/issuer has to assume that the other party is a consumer. It is not possible for the trader/business to get rid of their obligations under consumer law by having the other party tick boxes. Rather, the status of the buyer/subscriber (=consumer or not) must be ascertained by **further measures** taken by the entrepreneur.[17] This could be requiring a scan of the business registration, an excerpt from the business register, or a corporate letterhead.

II. Seller

1. Under the Consumer Rights Directive

11 The seller/issuer of the tokens needs to be a trader under Art. 2(2) CRD. This is defined as **any natural person or any legal person**, irrespective of whether privately or publicly owned, who is **acting,** including through any other person acting in his name or on his behalf, **for purposes relating to his trade, business, craft or profession**. In other words, the trader is the opposite of the consumer.[18]

A typical situation for the application of the CRD is a (private) buyer acquiring or disposing of a token on a centralised crypto trading platform. In this situation, the contract is concluded between the platform operator and the consumer.

12 The classification as a trader is about the exercise of **commercial activity**. This requires that the respective person/entity enters a market for goods/services and submits to the relevant rules of business.[19] The trader needs to act independently and compete with other participants for a certain period.[20] This includes **start-ups**. Developing a product or a service is commercial activity, even if there is no revenue yet. This is often the case for utility tokens or investment tokens that are issued to fund the development

---

[14] For example, a professional investment fund manager.

[15] ECJ, Judgment of 3 July 1997, *Benincasa*, C-269/95, para. 32. The German Federal Court of Justice has taken a similar view, see German Federal Court of Justice (Bundesgerichtshof), judgment of 30 September 2009, VIII ZR 7/09, para. 11.

[16] See, e.g., Ferrari, in: *J. von Staudingers Kommentar zum Bürgerlichen Gesetzbuch: Internationales Vertragsrecht 1* (Sellier/de Gruyter, 2016), Art. 6 Rome I, para. 14 with further references. Quite similarly, the German Federal Court of Justice ruled that the management of assets by purchasing and holding shares in a limited company is by itself not a commercial activity, see German Federal Court of Justice (Bundesgerichtshof), judgment of 9 February 2017, VIII ZR 7/09, para. 18 et seqq.

[17] Higher Regional Court of Hamm (Oberlandesgericht Hamm), judgment of 16 November 2016, I-12 U 52/17, para. 35 (on the German equivalent of Art. 2(1) CRD).

[18] There is hardly any situation where a party to the contract is neither consumer nor trader. This could be a registered association (=a legal person) that is not carrying on a business.

[19] Kainer, 'Der Verbrauchergerichtsstand bei Kapitalanlagegeschäften' (2018) 29 *Zeitschrift für Bankrecht und Bankwirtschaft/Journal of Banking Law and Banking* 368 (370), with further references.

[20] Ibid.

of a product or service. Even if the party does not have a fully functioning product yet, this is still a commercial activity. This also applies to transactions that are carried out as preparation for starting a business in the future.[21]

Issuing a token for **fundraising** purposes (usually investment tokens, but also utility 13 tokens) is also commercial activity. Admittedly, a fundraising via an ICO is not strictly speaking part of a business such as selling a product. However, fundraising is a direct prerequisite for the exercise of commercial activity. 'In exercise' must therefore be interpreted broadly in accordance with the meaning and purpose of the provision. This is in line with the idea that preparatory work for the business is already the pursuit of a business. The fact that fundraising involves uncertainties is addresses by Art. 16(b) CRD (→ para. 12).

2. Under the MiCAR Draft

Unlike the CRD, the MiCAR framework does not apply to traders. Instead, Art. 12(1) 14 MiCAR Draft refers to issuers and to crypto-asset service providers.

An **issuer of crypto-assets** is a legal person who offers to the public any type of crypto-assets (→ para. 6) or seeks admission of such crypto-assets to a trading platform (Art. 3(1)(6) MiCAR Draft). In contrast to traders under the CRD, there is no need for a distinct commercial activity (→ para. 12). It appears that the MiCAR Draft rests on the assumption that issuing tokens is by nature carried out commercially.

A **crypto-asset service provider** means any person whose occupation or business is the provision of crypto-asset services to third parties on a professional basis (Art. 3(1)(8) MiCAR Draft). Under Art. 12(1) MiCAR Draft, the right of withdrawal also applies if tokens are offered by the crypto-asset service provider on behalf of the issuer, and not by the issuer itself (→ para. 38).

C. The Right of Withdrawal

I. Under the CRD

1. General

The key element of consumer protection is the right of revocation according to Art. 9(1) 15 CRD. This requires a contract between consumer and trader (→ para. 8 et seqq.), concluded by means of distance contract (→ para. 16), while none of the exceptions set out in Art. 16 CRD apply (→ para. 20 et seqq.).

2. Distance Contract

The right of withdrawal requires that the contract in question is a **distance contract**. 16 This is defined in Art. 2(7) CRD as any contract concluded between the trader and the consumer under an organised distance sales or service-provision scheme without the simultaneous physical presence of the trader and the consumer, with the exclusive use of one or more means of distance communication up to and including the time at which the contract is concluded.

'Organised' within the meaning of Art. 2(7) CRD means that the sale is organised by the trader (for example, on the trader's website). The contract is concluded 'with the

---

[21] ECJ, Judgment of 3 July 1997, *Benincasa*, C-269/95, para. 19 (no consumer at the time of conclusion of the contract for the purpose of exercising a future commercial activity).

exclusive use of means of **distance communication**' if the parties are not present. Again, a website is a typical example. Token sales (via ICO or later on a secondary market) are conducted through websites or apps, so there is little doubt that they are distance contracts under the CRD. Direct (non-distance) contract is the absolute exception.

Art. 2(7) CRD does not set out the different types of contracts covered by the definition. This is straightforward because the legal classification (sale of goods, sale of rights, swap, gift, etc.) depends on the Member States' contract laws. This means that every type of token transaction, provided that there is some kind of contractual basis, can be subject to Art. 2(7) CRD.

3. Purpose of the Right of Withdrawal in Distance Contracts

17   The EU lawmakers implemented a right of withdrawal in distance contracts because the consumer is put at a **structural disadvantage** in comparison to 'regular' contracts (with both parties present). According to Rec. 37 CRD, the purpose of the right of withdrawal is that the consumer is not able to see the goods before concluding the contract. This means that consumers are not able to investigate the goods and get a good feeling for what they are buying. In addition, Rec. 36 refers to the limitations of the provision of information in online situations. Thus, another main reason for the right of withdrawal is that the consumer is not able to ask the seller questions.[22] The predecessor of the CRD (the Directive 97/7 EC on the protection of consumer contracts in distance contracts) similarly explains in Rec. 14 that the buyer is not able to ascertain the nature of the service (which also relates to the possibility to ask questions).

18   The question is if this purpose is in line with token sales. For these, online transactions are the normal situation and not (as suggested by the CRD) an untypical situation. It is hardly possible to acquire them in a physical form with both parties present. It is not possible (or even: necessary!) to physically investigate the tokens or to have a chat with the salesperson about characteristics or alternatives. In other words, for token sales, a buying consumer is not put at a structural disadvantage in comparison to a (physical) sale of the equivalent goods. Thus, it is highly questionable whether the rights of withdrawal under the CRD should be applied to crypto assets. So, the purpose of Art. 9 CRD suggests that there should be no right of withdrawal.

19   However, the situation is different for **utility tokens**. They offer access to an underlying service or access to infrastructure. Sometimes the utility token can be redeemed later for a specified good or service. Thus, utility tokens are often compared to vouchers (→ § 1 para. 73). In these cases, the purpose of the right of withdrawal applies. If consumers acquire utility tokens, they typically do not have the opportunity to try the underlying good/service in advance. For comparison: if the consumer had not acquired a utility token, but the underlying good or service instead, there would be no doubts about the application of the right of withdrawal. For example, a consumer ordering a book online would have a right of withdrawal according to Art. 9 CRD. The same applies if the consumer orders a book voucher.[23] It would be incoherent if the result was any different if the voucher was embodied in a utility token and not in a piece of paper. Thus, it would be coherent to apply the right of withdrawal as set out in Art. 9(1) CRD to utility tokens.

---

[22] See, e.g., the German Federal Court of Justice (Bundesgerichtshof), judgment of 21 October 2004, III ZR 380/03 (lack of contact as one of the main reasons for the right of withdrawal).

[23] Regarding the German implementation of the CRD: Föhlisch and Löwer, 'Das Widerrufsrecht bei Gutscheinen im Fernabsatz', (2015) 17 *Kommunikation & Recht* 298.

§ 4. Consumer Protection

4. Exceptions

a) Price Depending on Fluctuations in Financial Markets. According to Art. 16(b) 20
CRD, the right of withdrawal does not apply to the supply of goods or services for which the price is dependent on fluctuations in the financial markets which cannot be controlled by the trader and which may occur within the withdrawal period. Tokens are typically traded on licensed or non-licensed trading platforms (for details, → § 5), and these platforms are subject to typical market price fluctuations. In fact, due to lower market capitalisation the fluctuations are often even higher than on 'normal' markets. So, the question is if and to what extent the right of withdrawal can be applied to these tokens.

aa) Financial Markets. The term **financial markets** is not defined under EU law. 21
There is no internationally accepted definition either. Generally speaking, the financial markets are a part of the financial system. A financial market is a market in which financial assets are traded.[24] A typical example for such a market is a securities exchange. However, financial markets do not necessarily have a physical location because supply and demand can also meet online. In the context of crypto assets, a market could also be a network of servers around the globe (so-called decentralised trading platforms, → § 1 para. 97 et seqq.).

Financial markets bring together investors and offerors of financial products. The typical product traded would be securities such as shares, bonds or derivatives. However, the term 'financial markets' commonly includes the markets where **commodities, currencies and other products** are traded.[25] It also comprises **capital markets, foreign exchange markets, money markets, futures markets, cash markets**, etc. In other words, more or less everything could be classified as 'financial markets' if there is supply/demand and a market price, and this market somehow relates to financing businesses.

A financial market does not need to be a regulated market under EU legislation (for example, MiFID2) or other national laws. Over-the-counter markets (**OTC markets**) are also part of the financial markets. This would, for example, apply to non-regulated crypto trading platforms.

bb) Dependent on Fluctuations. The more important part of the definition under 22
Art. 16(b) CRD is that the price is dependent on fluctuations in a market which cannot be controlled by the trader. The price in this context is the volatile market price in the (financial) markets, not the purchase price demanded by the issuer or seller. The term 'controlled' refers to the idea that the price is primarily subject to market mechanism and not determined by the seller.[26]

The idea of Art. 16(b) CRD is that assets traded in financial markets are by their very 23
nature volatile in price. The investor bears the risk of price developments. Granting a right of withdrawal would move this risk to the seller of the asset – which is not the purpose of consumer regulation.

This purpose in combination and the wording ('fluctuations') of Art. 16(b) CRD thus requires that the respective token types are actually **traded**. Otherwise, there would be no

---

[24] Moles and Terry, *The Handbook of International Financial Terms* (Oxford, Oxford University Press, 1997), 220.

[25] In a decision regarding § 312g of the German Civil Code (which is based on Art. 16 CRD), the German Federal Court of Justice also took this view, explicitly mentioning markets for metals, commodities and futures, see Federal Court of Justice (Bundesgerichtshof), judgment of 17 June 2015, VIII ZR 249/14.

[26] Higher Regional Court of Karlsruhe (Oberlandesgericht Karlsruhe), Judgment of 13 September 2011, 17 U 104/10.

discernible market volatility and no 'fluctuations' as required by Art. 16(b) CRD. Mere tradability of the token is not sufficient. It is not necessary that the respective market is licensed and/or subject to regulation. This means this includes OTC crypto markets.

24   However, it is not necessary that the **respective token that is transferred is actually traded** at a crypto exchange.[27] This flows from the wording of Art. 16(b) CRD, which only requires that the price of the token 'depends' on fluctuations on the financial market. The price of an asset can depend on the current price at a marketplace even if the asset in question is not listed there. A good (non-crypto) example is the exchange rate for currencies. If a customer exchanges one fiat currency for another using a bank, the money in question is not traded at an exchange, but the respective exchange rate as set in the foreign exchange markets applies. A similar example is the purchase/sale of gold at a jewelry store.

25   cc) **Different Token Categories.** Art. 16(b) CRD will typically apply to **investment tokens** that are listed at a crypto trading platform. Investment tokens are tradeable securities within the meaning of MiFID2 ($\rightarrow$ § 7 para. 33 et seqq.), and thus part of the financial markets.

26   The same applies to **currency tokens**. As discussed above ($\rightarrow$ para. 21), the term 'financial market' is to be interpreted broadly and includes foreign exchange and money market instruments. Currency tokens might not be a legal equivalent to fiat currency. However, they are used for the purposes of payment and are commonly traded. Payment systems are also part of the financial markets. Thus, there is sufficient similarity between currency tokens and foreign exchange markets.

27   **Utility tokens** are arguably the only of the three token archetypes whose primary function has little to do with the financial markets. The primary purpose of a utility token is to grant access to a good, service or platform. However, it cannot be denied that many utility tokens are also traded at trading platforms, some of them with considerable market capitalisation. This presents a problem. On the one hand, a utility token builds on the idea of consumption. On the other hand, users have established utility token as a tradeable asset class in practice. The consequence is a mixture of consumption and investment.

28   The focus should be on the **primary purpose** of tokens. Investment tokens and currency tokens clearly fall within the concept of financial markets – thus, it is straightforward that the right of withdrawal does not apply. In contrast, the primary purpose of the utility token is the underlying right (or: the voucher). The fact that the utility token is actually traded does not change this. However, this only applies if the token was not acquired at a trading platform. In this case it would be clear that the volatility is a defining aspect of the asset acquired.

The German Federal Court of Justice took a similar view regarding the supply of heating oil.[28] In the respective case the buyer had bought heating oil from a supplier and withdrew from the contract later, complying with all formalities. The Court held that the primary purpose of the acquisition of oil was consumption and the fact that oil is traded on commodities markets was irrelevant. Thus, the Court affirmed the existence of a right of withdrawal. Although the situation has little to do with utility tokens at first glance, it is highly comparable: in both cases a product that is supposed to be consumed was also traded in the financial markets.

---

[27] Not to be confused with the question as to whether token is generally being traded at a trading platform.

[28] Federal Court of Justice (Bundesgerichtshof), judgment of 17 June 2015, VIII ZR 249/14; for discussion and criticism, see Henning-Bodewig, 'Distance Sales of Heating Oil and the Consumer's Right of Withdrawal – A Fair Balance?' (2016) 5 *Journal of European Consumer and Market Law* 87.

§ 4. Consumer Protection

However, the situation is different if the utility token was acquired at a crypto trading platform. Here the speculative/investment aspect of the transaction is dominant – and obvious for the acquirer. In this case there is a parallel to the financial markets and to the other token archetypes. If, on the other hand, the utility token is acquired outside these markets (for example, directly from the issuer in an ICO), the consumption character is dominant. **29**

b) No Digital Content. According to Art. 16(m) CRD, the right of withdrawal does not apply to 'digital content which is not supplied on a tangible medium if the performance has begun with the consumer's prior express consent and his acknowledgment that he thereby loses his right of withdrawal'. **30**

EU Directives usually distinguish between goods and services. The CRD includes digital content as a third category. Digital content is also subject to the right of withdrawal. This is clarified by Rec. 19 CRD, stating that '(f)or such contracts, the consumer should have a right of withdrawal'. However, as stated above, traders could rid themselves of the right of withdrawal if they obtain the consumer's consent for the contract to be executed immediately. This would result in a significant reduction of consumer protection.

The issue is if this exception from the right of withdrawal applies to tokens. Art. 2(11) CRD defines **digital content** as 'data which are produced and supplied in digital form'. This wording suggests that this definition applies to all types of tokens. Art. 16(m) CRD also requires that the data is not supplied on a tangible medium. Rec. 19 CRD clarifies that tangible mediums are, for example, CDs or DVDs. The data needs to be 'supplied' to the other party on this medium, so there needs to be a physical data carrier that is physically transferred between the parties. At first glance, this exception set out in Art. 16(m) CRD applies to the transfer of tokens because they are transferred without such a physical medium. Tokens are transaction histories stored digitally in the blockchain (→ § 1 para. 16 et seq). Their transfer takes place without any physical carrier or storage medium being handed over between the parties. **31**

However, the **regulatory purpose** of Art. 16(m) CRD suggests that the provision does not apply to token sales. Rec. 19 CRD mentions 'computer programs, applications (apps), games, music, videos and texts' as examples of digital content. If these are stored on a tangible medium, they should be treated like goods (see also Rec. 19 CRD). If not, Art. 16(m) CRD applies as a special rule. The background is that music, videos etc. are **consumed** (watched, read, etc.) by the buyer. The 'non-tangible medium' describes technologies such as streaming or downloading. In these cases, the consumer often wants to listen to the music or watch the video straightaway. Here, it makes sense to allow him to waive the right of withdrawal. Otherwise, the video could be streamed and then 'returned' (i.e., the right of withdrawal could be exercised). This would put the consumer at a serious advantage and jeopardise the business cases of streaming or downloading portals. **32**

This idea is not comparable to token sales. A token does not convey any 'content'. The token conveys certain rights (for example, to use a service or to receive certain payments). This has little to do with a book that is stored electronically. The fact that tokens are stored electronically does not make them 'content'. Besides, tokens are not streamed or downloaded. Every token is unique and exits only once. In this regard, tokens are more like physical goods, which also only exist once and cannot be duplicated. In contrast, digital content can be duplicated in non-limited numbers when offered for download or streaming. Thus, the technical setup of tokens is also different from 'digital content' as envisaged under the CRD. In sum, it is much more convincing to treat tokens as goods and not as digital content.

5. Consequences

33 As a consequence, consumers have a right of withdrawal of 14 days subject to Art. 9(1) CRD. The 14-day period starts with the conclusion of the contract. The applicable procedure is set out in Art. 11–13 CRD. In short, the goods and payments received have to be returned. As a general rule, this shall not result in additional costs for the consumer.

34 For **utility tokens** the situation is more complicated. Generally, two types of utility tokens can be distinguished. First, utility tokens that give access to a network or a platform. They grant the token holder a permanent (or at least: continuous) right. This is comparable to a continuous service contract. In this case, Art. 9(2)(a) CRD applies, stating that the withdrawal period commences with the conclusion of the contract. Second, utility tokens can also grant a one-off right comparable to a voucher. If the token is **redeemed**, the token holder has the right to the underlying asset against the token issuer. If this underlying asset is a good within the meaning of CRD (for example, the product that was developed by the issuer), Art. 9(2)(b) CRD applies. In this case, the withdrawal period does not start before the consumer has received the goods. Thus, the right of withdrawal could, in theory, commence and end months after the contract was concluded – depending on when the voucher is redeemed.

35 According to Art. 6(1)(h) CRD, the trader needs to **inform** the consumer about the right of withdrawal. If this is not the case, the withdrawal period extends to 12 months, starting with the conclusion of the contract (Art. 10(1) CRD). This is a problem for issuers, because to the knowledge of the author this information is hardly ever given in utility token sales. As a result, this mechanism could allow acquirers of utility tokens to get rid of utility tokens that did not perform well.[29]

II. Under the MiCAR Draft

36 According to Art. 12(1) MiCAR Draft, consumers have a right of withdrawal. This does not apply to asset-referenced tokens and e-money tokens. The MiCAR Draft does not provide any explanation for this exception. Given that investment tokens (= financial instruments under MiFID2) are not covered by MiCAR (→ para. 6), this essentially narrows down the application of Art. 12(1) MiCAR Draft to utility tokens and (non-backed) currency tokens.

37 The right of withdrawal does not apply to tokens that are admitted to trading on a crypto trading platform (Art. 12(4) MiCAR Draft).

38 Art. 12 MiCAR Draft covers direct token sales by the issuer as well as indirect sales that are carried out through a crypto-asset service provider, placing the tokens on behalf of the issuer. An **issuer of crypto-assets** is a legal person who offers to the public any type of crypto-assets or seeks admission for these crypto-assets to a crypto-asset trading platform (Art. 3(1)(6) MiCAR Draft, → para. 14). This means that a right of withdrawal only exists for trading in the primary market, nor for subsequent trading – even if the crypto assets are not traded on a crypto trading platform.

The **crypto-asset service provider** (→ para. 14) needs to be placing the tokens on behalf of the issuer. Placing is defined in Art. 3(1)(15) MiCAR Draft as the marketing of newly-issued crypto-assets or of crypto-assets that are already issued but that are not admitted to a crypto trading platform yet. This also makes it clear that the secondary market (on trading platforms) is not covered by the right of withdrawal in this situation

---

[29] At the time of writing this chapter, there were several cases in German courts with litigants arguing that they have a right of withdrawal under the CRD.

§ 4. Consumer Protection

It needs to be noted that the consumer's right of withdrawal in these cases is not against the service provider, but also against the issuer. This is straightforward because the service provider is acting on behalf of the issuer.

Like under the CRD, the right of withdrawal lasts for **14 days**. It starts with the day that the purchase contract was entered into (Art. 12(1)(2) MiCAR Draft). The issuer needs to inform the customer about the right of withdrawal in the crypto-asset white paper according to Art. 5 MiCAR Draft (Art. 12(3) MiCAR Draft). However, the MiCAR Draft does not specify any consequences if this is not the case. In particular, there is no extension to twelve months (→ para. 35).

39

If the issuer has set a time limit on the offer to the public, the right of withdrawal ends with the **end of the subscription period** (Art. 12(5) MiCAR Draft).

D. Information Obligations

Art. 6 CRD sets out extensive information obligations for the trader. He needs to inform the customer, for example, of the **characteristics of the products, the trader's name, the trader's address, the total price, arrangements for payment and delivery**, etc. At first glance, this seems to be a substantial problem for the trader (=token seller). Token trading takes place online only. The setting is mostly anonymous, in particular at decentralised trading venues. A seller will hardly ever know who the other party is, let alone if the party is a consumer. In addition, most trading venues do not offer the possibility to convey the information.[30]

40

However, in practice the problem is probably not as big as it first appears. On **decentralised crypto trading platforms** (→ § 1 para. 97 et seqq.) the sellers will only rarely be traders (→ para. 11). It is much more common that transactions are carried out by private persons trying to make profits. On **centralised crypto trading platforms** (§ 1 para. 97 et seqq.), the platform operator is the seller of the tokens. These operators have all the information necessary to meet their information obligations: if such operators provide investment services under MiFID2 (§ 8 para. 14 et seqq.), they need to identify their clients under anti-money laundering (AML) regulation (for details, § 10). Operators of centralised trading platforms typically also provide wallet custody services under MiCAR. As such, they have to identify the other party (Art. 67(1)(a) MiCAR Draft). In short, operators of centralised trading platform that are compliant with the applicable regulation should have all the information they need. The necessary information will typically be contained in the **whitepaper** that every issuer of crypto assets must publish (Art. 4 MiCAR Draft). The seller can make reference to the whitepaper during the transaction process.

41

---

[30] This is also a problem for non-crypto platforms, see Wendehorst, 'Platform Intermediary Services and Duties under the E-Commerce Directive and the Consumer Rights Directive', (2016) 5 *Journal of European Consumer and Markets Law* 30.

§ 5
Intermediaries of Secondary Crypto Trade – Contractual Issues and International Contract Law

Literature: Akman, 'Online Platforms, Agency, and Competition Law: Mind the Gap' (2019) 43 *Fordham International Law Journal*, 209; Anagnostopoulou, 'The EU Digital Single Market and the Platform Economy', in Nikas (ed), *Economic Growth in the European Union: Analyzing SME and Investment Policies* (Springer, Cham, 2020), 43; Aravindakshan, 'Cyberattacks: a look at evidentiary thresholds in International Law' (2020) *Indian Journal of International Law*, available at https://doi.org/10.1007/s40901-020-00113-0; Berlee, 'Digital Inheritance in the Netherlands' [2017] *Journal of European Consumer and Market Law*, 256; Biallaß, 'Aspekte des Vertragsschlusses bei Internet-Auktionen' in Borges (ed), *Rechtsfragen der Internet-Auktion* (2nd edn, Baden-Baden, 2014), 13; Biallaß, 'Das Vertragsverhältnis zwischen Plattformbetreiber und Nutzer' in Borges (ed), *Rechtsfragen der Internet-Auktion* (2nd edn, Baden-Baden, 2014), 61; Binding, 'Consumer protection law in the People's Republic of China' [2014] *China-EU Law Journal*, 223; Bräutigam and Rücker (eds), *E-Commerce, Rechtshandbuch* (C.H. Beck, München, 2017); Bunte and Zahrte (eds), *AGB-Banken, AGB-Sparkassen, Sonderbedingungen* (5th edn, München, 2019); Burgard, 'Online-Marktordnung und Inhaltskontrolle' [2001] *Zeitschrift für Wirtschafts- und Bankrecht*, 2102; Busch, Dannemann, Schulte-Nölke, Wiewiórowska-Domagalska and Zoll, 'The ELI Model Rules on Online Platforms' [2020] *Journal of European Consumer and Market Law*, 61; Busch, Schulte-Nölke, Wiewiórowska-Domagalska and Zoll, 'The Rise of the Platform Economy: A New Challenge for EU Consumer Law?' [2016] *Journal of European Consumer and Market Law*, 3; Busch, 'Towards Fairness and Transparency in the Platform Economy? A First Look at the P2B Regulation', in De Franceschi and Schulze (eds), *Digital Revolution – New Challenges for Law* (2019), 57; Chrobak, 'Proprietary Rights in Digital Data? Normative Perspectives and Principles of Civil Law', in Bakhoum, Conde Gallego, Mackenrodt and Surblytė-Namavičienė (eds), *Personal Data in Competition, Consumer Protection and Intellectual Property Law* (Berlin, 2018), 253; Dannemann and Schulze (eds), *German Civil Code: Bürgerliches Gesetzbuch (BGB)* (Baden-Baden, 2020); Drăgan, 'Illegal Access to a Computer System from the Standpoint of the Current Criminal Code' (2019) 23 *Journal of Legal Studies*, 33; Dreyer and Haskamp, 'Die Vermittlungstätigkeit von Plattformen' [2017] *Zeitschrift für Vertriebsrecht*, 359; Edisherashvili, 'Legal Regalments of E-Signature' (2020) 25 *Journal of Legal Studies*, 98; Engert, 'Digitale Plattformen' (2018) *Archiv für die civilistische Praxis* 218, 304; Erman, *Handkommentar mit AGG, EGBGB, ErbbauRG, LPartG, ProdhaftG, VBVG, VersAusglG, WEG und ausgewählten Rechtsquellen des IPR*, Vol. 1 (Erman BGB) (16th edn, Köln, 2020); Falkhofen, 'Car Data Platforms and the EU Acquis for Digital Services – How the digital transformation of the car interacts with EU data protection, cybersecurity and competition law' [2018] *Computer Law Review International*, 165; Fenwick, McCahery and Vermeulen, 'The End of "Corporate" Governance: Hello "Platform" Governance!' (2019) 20 *European Business Organization Law Review*, 171; Frei and Jung, 'Revised Control of Unfair Terms in Swiss Law – Consumer Protection by Competition Law?' [2015] *Journal of European Consumer and Market Law*, 165; Grundmann and Hacker, 'Digital Technology as a Challenge to European Contract Law' (2017) 13 *European Review of Contract Law*, 255; Grušić, 'Long-Term Business Relationships and Implicit Contracts in European Private Law' (2016) 12 *European Review of Contract Law*, 395; Gsell, Krüger, Lorenz and Reymann (eds), beck-online.GROSSKOMMENTAR zum Zivilrecht (BeckOGK BGB) (München, as of 1.7.2020); Harbinja, 'Digital Inheritance in the United Kingdom' [2017] *Journal of European Consumer and Market Law*, 253; Hau and Poseck (eds), *Beck'scher Online-Kommentar zum Zivilrecht* (BeckOK BGB) (München, as of 1.8.2020); Härting, *Internetrecht* (6th edn, Köln, 2017); Canaris and Grigoleit, 'Interpretation of Contracts', in Hartkamp, Hesselink, Hondius, Mak and du Perron (eds), *Towards a European Civil Code* (4th edn, The Hague, 2011); Hellgardt, 'Privatautonome Modifikation der Regeln zu Abschluss, Zustandekommen und Wirksamkeit des Vertrags – Möglichkeit und Grenzen der Abdingbarkeit der §§ 116 ff., 145 ff. BGB innerhalb von Geschäftsbeziehungen und auf privaten Marktplätzen' (2013) *Archiv für die civilistische Praxis* 213, 760; Hellwege, 'It is necessary to strictly distinguish two forms of fairness control!' [2015] *Journal of European Consumer and Market Law*, 129; Henke, Singbartl and Zintl, 'Mietwohnungsüberlassung an Touristen: Wimdu, Airbnb & Co. aus zivilrechtlicher Perspektive – Neues von der "kollaborativen Wirtschaft"' [2018] *Neue Zeitschrift für Miet- und Wohnungsrecht*, 1; Hoch, *Die Besteuerungssystematik von Kapitalanlagen – Geltendes Recht und Reformvorschlag für eine kohärente Kapitalanlagenbesteuerung* (Mohr Siebeck, Tübingen, 2019); Hoch, 'Crowdfunding, Bitcoins,

§ 5. Intermediaries of Secondary Crypto Trade

Initial Coin Offerings – Rechtliche Herausforderungen für den Gesetzgeber im Zeitalter der Digitalisierung', in Husemann and others (eds), *Strukturwandel und Privatrecht, Jahrbuch Junge Zivilrechtswissenschaft* (Baden-Baden, 2019), 215; Hoeren, Sieber der Holznagel, *Handbuch Multimedia-Recht* (47th edn, C.H. Beck, München, 2018); Hornuf, Klöhn and Schilling, 'Financial Contracting in Crowdinvesting: Lessons from the German Market' (2018) 19 *German Law Journal*, 509; Huang, Yang and Yang Loo, 'The Development and Regulation of Cryptoassets: Hong Kong Experiences and a Comparative Analysis' (2020) 21 *European Business Organization Law Review*, 319; Janal, 'Die Flugbuchung für 'Mr. noch unbekannt' und andere widersprüchliche Erklärungen im elektronischen Geschäftsverkehr' (2015) *Archiv für die civilistische Praxis* 215, 830; Kartikaningtyas, 'The Role of Central Counterparty as a Risk Mitigator in Capital Market Transaction in Indonesian Law Perspective' (2007) 20th Australasian Finance & Banking Conference 2007 Paper; Kaulartz and Matzke, 'Die Tokenisierung des Rechts' [2018] *Neue Juristische Wochenschrift*, 3278; Kull, 'The Adequacy of Existing Estonian Laws for the Platform Economy' [2016] *Journal of European Consumer and Market Law*, 52; Langhanke and Schmidt-Kessel, 'Consumer Data as Consideration' [2015] *Journal of European Consumer and Market Law*, 218; Loos, 'Standard terms for the use of the Apple App Store and the Google Play Store' [2016] *Journal of European Consumer and Market Law*, 10; Loritz, 'Die Realität des Aktientransfers in Zeiten der Dauerglobalurkunde – Sachgerechtes Verständnis des Zivilrechts als Grundlage zur Vermeidung steuerlicher Irrwege – Teil I' [2017] *Betriebs-Berater*, 2327; Luzak, 'You too will be judged: erga omnes effect of registered unfair contract terms in Poland' [2017] *Journal of European Consumer and Market Law*, 120; Mackenrodt, 'Digital Inheritance in Germany' [2018] *Journal of European Consumer and Market Law*, 41; Maeschaelck, 'Digital Inheritance in Belgium' [2018] *Journal of European Consumer and Market Law*, 37; Mak, 'Private Law Perspectives on Platform Services' [2016] *Journal of European Consumer and Market Law*, 19; Maultzsch, 'Contractual Liability of Online Platform Operators: European Proposals and established Principles' [2018] *European Review of Contract Law*, 209; Maultzsch, 'Verantwortlichkeit der Plattformbetreiber', in Blaurock, Schmidt-Kessel and Erler (eds), *Plattformen, Geschäftsmodell und Verträge* (Baden-Baden, 2018), 223; Mehar and others, 'Understanding a Revolutionary and Flawed Grand Experiment in Blockchain: The DAO Attack' (2017) 21 *Journal of Cases on Information Technology*, 19; Meschkowski and Wilhelmi, 'Investorenschutz im Crowdfunding' [2013] *Betriebs-Berater*, 1411; Meyer, 'Einbeziehung und Geltungsbereich von AGB', in Borges (ed), *Rechtsfragen der Internet-Auktion* (2nd edn, Baden-Baden, 2014), 36; Meyer, 'Stopping the Unstoppable: Termination and Unwinding of Smart Contracts' [2020] *Journal of European Consumer and Market Law*, 17; Mikk and Sein, 'Digital Inheritance: Heirs' Right to Claim Access to Online Accounts under Estonian Law' (2018) 27 *Juridica International*, 117; Možina, 'Retail business, platform services and information duties' [2016] *Journal of European Consumer and Market Law*, 25; *Münchener Kommentar zum Bürgerlichen Gesetzbuch: BGB, Erbrecht (§§ 1922–2385), §§ 27–35 BeurkG*, Vol. 11 (MüKoBGB) (8th edn, München, 2020); *Münchener Kommentar zum Bürgerlichen Gesetzbuch: BGB, Schuldrecht Allgemeiner Teil I (§§ 241–310)*, Vol. 2 (MüKoBGB) (8th edn, München, 2019); *Münchener Kommentar zum Bürgerlichen Gesetzbuch: BGB, Schuldrecht Allgemeiner Teil II (§§ 311–432)*, Vol. 3 (MüKoBGB) (8th edn, München, 2019); *Münchener Kommentar zum Bürgerlichen Gesetzbuch: BGB, Schuldrecht Besonderer Teil III (§§ 631–704)*, Vol. 6 (MüKoBGB) (8th edn, München, 2020); Nabilou and Asimakopoulos, 'In CCP we trust … or do we? Assessing the regulation of central clearing counterparties in Europe' (2020) 15 *Capital Markets Law Journal*, 70; Nemeth and Morais Carvalho, 'Digital Inheritance in the European Union' [2017] *Journal of European Consumer and Market Law*, 253; Pavillon, 'Private Standards of Fairness in European Contract Law' (2014) 10 *European Review of Contract Law*, 85; Pisuliński, 'Internet platforms under Polish law' [2016] *Journal of European Consumer and Market Law*, 62; Pittl and Gottardis, 'Smart Contracts – An Analysis from the Perspective of Austrian Law' [2019] *Journal of European Consumer and Market Law*, 205; Podszun and Kreifels, 'Digital Platforms and Competition Law' [2016] *Journal of European Consumer and Market Law*, 33; Preuß, 'Digitaler Nachlass – Vererbbarkeit eines Kontos bei einem sozialen Netzwerk' [2018] *Neue Juristische Wochenschrift*, 3146; Redeker, *IT-Recht* (7th edn, C.H. Beck, München, 2020); Resta, 'Digital Inheritance', in De Franceschi and Schulze (eds), *Digital Revolution – New Challenges for Law* (München, 2019), 88; Sattler, 'From Personality to Property? Revisiting the Fundamentals of the Protection of Personal Data', in Bakhoum, Conde Gallego, Mackenrodt and Surblytė-Namavičienė (eds), *Personal Data in Competition, Consumer Protection and Intellectual Property Law* (Berlin, 2018); Sénéchal, 'The Diversity of the Services provided by Online Platforms and the Specificity of the Counter-performance of these Services — A double Challenge for European and National Contract Law' [2016] *Journal of European Consumer and Market Law*, 39; Schammo, 'Undisruption' in the SME Funding Market: Information Sharing, Finance Platforms and the UK Bank Referral Scheme' (2019) 20 *European Business Organization Law Review*, 29; Schimansky, Bunte and Lwowski, *Bankrechts-Handbuch*, Vol. I (5th edn, C.H. Beck, München, 2017); Schweitzer, 'Digitale Plattformen als private Gesetzgeber: Ein Perspektivenwechsel für die europäische 'Plattform-Regulierung'' [2019] *Zeitschrift für Europäisches Privatrecht*, 1; Sein, 'Legal problems of electronic platform economy – Estonian perspective', in Blaurock, Schmidt-Kessel and Erler (eds), *Plattformen, Geschäftsmodell und Verträge* (Baden-Baden, 2018), 79; Söbbing, 'Platform as a service – Grundlagen, Plattformverträge, AGB, Impressumspflicht' [2016] *Der IT-Rechts-Berater*, 140; Söbbing and Jakob, 'Online-Plattformen – Die Hotspots der Digitalwirtschaft rechtlich betrachtet' [2016] *Zeitschrift zum Innovations- und Technikrecht*, 149; Sørensen, 'Private Law Perspectives on Platform Services' [2016] *Journal of European Consumer and Market Law*, 15; Spindler, 'Crowdfunding und Crowdinvesting – Sach- und kollisionsrechtliche Einordnung sowie Überlagerung durch die E-Commerce-Richtlinie' [2017] *Zeitschrift für Bankrecht und Bankwirtschaft*, 129; Spindler, 'Deliktische Haftung der Plattformbetreiber', in Spindler and Wiebe (eds), *Internet-Auktionen und Elektronische Marktplätze* (2nd edn, Köln, 2005), 211; Staudinger, J. von Staudingers Kommentar zum Bürgerlichen Gesetzbuch mit Einführungsgesetz und Nebengesetzen: Buch 2, Recht der Schuldverhältnisse: Einleitung zum Schuldrecht: §§ 241–243: Treu und Glauben (Staudinger BGB) (Berlin, 2019); Twigg-Flesner, 'Legal and Policy Responses to Online Platforms – A UK Perspective', in Blaurock, Schmidt-Kessel and Erler (eds), *Plattformen, Geschäftsmodell und Verträge* (Baden-Baden, 2018), 139; Tereszkiewicz, 'Digital Platforms: Regulation and Liability in the EU Law' (2018) 26 *European Review of Private Law*, 903; Weber, 'Central Counterparties in the OTC Derivatives Market from the Perspective of the Legal Theory of Finance, Financial Market Stability and the Public Good' (2016) 17 *European Business Organization Law Review*, 71; Weber, 'Liability in the Internet of Things' [2017] *Journal of European Consumer and Market Law*, 207; Wendehorst, 'Platform Intermediary Services and Duties under the E-Commerce Directive and the Consumer Rights Directive' [2016] *Journal of European Consumer and Market Law*, 30; Wójtowicz, 'Law applicable to Distribution Contracts and Contracts of Sale–Relationship between Framework Agreement and Application Contracts' (2018) 14 *European Review of Contract Law*, 138; Wüsthof, 'Germany's Supreme Court Rules in Favour of 'Digital Inheritance''' [2018] *Journal of European Consumer and Market Law*, 205; Zumbansen, 'Contracting in the Internet: German Contract Law and Internet Auctions' (2001) 2 *German Law Journal*, E1.

Outline

	para.
A. Intermediaries and Their Functions	1
B. General Structures of Underlying Contracts	4
I. Contract between Users and Trading Platforms	7
II. Categorisation of the Platform's Activity	24
III. On-Chain Intermediaries	32
1. Fiat-to-Crypto Exchange	33
2. Crypto-to-Crypto Exchange	37
a) Central Crypto-to-Crypto Exchange	38
b) Decentralised Crypto-to-Crypto Exchange	41
IV. Off-Chain Intermediaries	43
1. General Contractual Relations between User and Platform	44
2. Contractual Relations during a Transaction	46
C. Further Obligations of Trading Platforms	48
D. Defaults and Breach of Contractual Obligations	58
I. On-Chain-Intermediary	59
1. Trading Platform	59
2. Users	61
II. Off-Chain Intermediary	65
E. General Terms and Conditions	67
I. Frequently Used General Terms and Conditions within Platform Agreements	71
II. General Terms and Conditions with Implication for User Contracts	73

A. Intermediaries and Their Functions

1   The main and widely emphasized advantage of the blockchain and its applications, i.e. crypto-currencies and especially initial coin offerings, is the complete renunciation of intermediaries of any kind. This basically means all transactions and the issuance of

§ 5. Intermediaries of Secondary Crypto Trade

tokens can be carried out via the blockchain itself. In general, the involvement of third parties to assist with transactions is unnecessary, resulting in lower transactional costs.[1] However, this intermediary-free processing mostly fails if the user desires to trade his or her tokens. Such a trade of previously acquired tokens and the corresponding legal transactions is generally referred to as the **secondary market**. But the main difficulty for secondary transactions lies in the search for a suitable contractual partner who is interested in concluding the inverse transaction. For instance, if a user sells tokens for fiat currency, another user must be willing to purchase the offered tokens for the desired amount of fiat currency. However, finding and matching two counterparties willing to enter the inverse crypto transaction can prove difficult. This problem cannot be solved by simply using the blockchain. After all, the blockchain does not mediate secondary trading partners, it only provides the infrastructure for primary transactions. Therefore, secondary trading without intermediaries is hardly feasible, leading to a deterioration of token tradability and diminishing the overall economic value of crypto tokens. To improve the efficiency of finding contractual partners, the secondary market still requires intermediaries to match the parties. Hence, secondary transactions are usually conducted via specialised trading platforms appropriately designed to meet individual needs. Thus, secondary crypto trade constitutes a significant exception of the blockchain's fundamental **rule of freedom from intermediaries**.

In the digital world, those intermediaries consist of online platforms.[2] According to the European approach, an online platform 'refers to an undertaking operating in two (or multi)-sided markets, which uses the Internet to enable interactions between two or more distinct but interdependent groups of users so as to generate value for at least one of the groups'.[3] As for the token trade, the exact procedure of transactions on such specialised trading platforms varies depending on their design and objective. Registered users can generally publish their wish to buy or sell tokens on the platform's 'marketplace'. These 'offers' can be reviewed and perceived by interested parties and are, therefore, available to the broad public. Thus, the main purpose of such platforms is **matching** various interested parties and **brokering** transactions. In summary, these trading platforms can be classified as **transaction-related matching platforms,** offering a form of digital intermediation.[4]

2

---

[1] Huang, Yang and Yang Loo, 'The Development and Regulation of Cryptoassets: Hong Kong Experiences and a Comparative Analysis' (2020) 21 *European Business Organization Law Review*, 319 (326).

[2] The term 'online platform' has no specific definition and can be used interchangeably with the terms 'electronic platform' or 'digital platform'.

[3] European Commission, 'Public consultation on the regulatory environment for platforms, online intermediaries, data and cloud computing and the collaborative economy' (European Commission, 24 September 2015), available at https://ec.europa.eu/digital-agenda/en/news/public-consultation-regulatory-environment-platforms-online-intermediaries-data-and-cloud (accessed 30.3.2021); see for more details Sénéchal, 'The Diversity of the Services provided by Online Platforms and the Specificity of the Counter-performance of these Services — A double Challenge for European and National Contract Law' [2016] *Journal of European Consumer and Market Law*, 39 (40).

[4] In this context, the German Federal Cartel Office (Bundeskartellamt) distinguishes two main types of platforms: The so-called matchmaking platforms and the so-called attention platforms. The former category is subdivided into those with and without a transactional orientation, BKartA B6-113/15, 'Arbeitspapier – Marktmacht von Plattformen und Netzwerken', 19 et seq.; similar Fenwick, McCahery and Vermeulen, 'The End of 'Corporate' Governance: Hello 'Platform' Governance!' (2019) 20 *European Business Organization Law Review*, 171 (172); for a similar definition Busch, Schulte-Nölke, Wiewiórowska-Domagalska and Zoll, 'The Rise of the Platform Economy: A New Challenge for EU Consumer Law?' [2016] *Journal of European Consumer and Market Law*, 3 (3); in more detail concerning matchmaking of finance platforms Schammo, 'Undisruption' in the SME Funding Market: Information Sharing, Finance Platforms and the UK Bank Referral Scheme' (2019) 20 *European Business Organization*

3   Token transactions mediated by and processed through such trading platforms can be further divided into two major sub-categories. The first type of transaction includes the trade of fiat currencies for tokens. The platforms dedicated to this type of transaction are generally referred to as fiat-to-crypto exchanges. The second platform category enables the exchange of one type of token for another type, for instance Bitcoin for Litecoin. Intermediaries specialised in such transactions are referred to as crypto-to-crypto exchanges (→ § 1 para. 90 et seqq.).

B. General Structures of Underlying Contracts

4   Underlying the transaction of secondary crypto trades, users and platforms conclude a broad variety of legal relationships. Due to Art. 9 para. 1 of the E-Commerce Directive[5], every Member State of the EU allows contracts to be concluded by electronic means and has ascertained equality to offline agreements. From a European perspective, however, in the absence of general principles or definitions, the formation of a digital contract is solely influenced by national law of the individual Member States.[6]

5   Token trading platforms use a **considerable variety of contractual agreements** and structures and are influenced by the platform's main purpose. Therefore, the actual provisions used in the agreement depend on the classification of the platform as a crypto-to-crypto or a fiat-to-crypto exchange. From a legal point of view, however, a precise allocation of existing trading platforms to a specific sub-category is often virtually impossible. A closer review of existing trading platforms and their structures reveals that often both transaction categories, e.g., both token exchange transactions ('token for token') and token sales ('token for fiat currency') are offered by the same intermediary. Thus, the actual platform design and the individual implementation of user transactions determine the legal classification. As such, a more detailed **distinction** between the possible transactions is required. The various transactions can be carried out either **on-chain**, e.g., using blockchain transactions for implementation of contract, or **off-chain**, e.g., on the intermediary's digital infrastructure, adjusting solely the user's token 'account balances' in their individual platform account (→ § 1 para. 94 et seqq.).

6   As a result, the respective circumstances of **each individual case** must always be considered to correctly classify the existing legal relationships. The assessment of contractual relationships either exclusively between users or between the users and the trading platform must therefore be evaluated by general principles of the respective national civil laws and their general legal doctrine.[7] Nevertheless, the relevant legal aspects of these contracts are mostly identical, regardless of the intermediary's jurisdiction, allowing some general statements.

Law Review, 29 (31, 32 et seq.); for an overview of competition law regarding digital platforms Podszun and Kreifels, 'Digital Platforms and Competition Law' [2016] *Journal of European Consumer and Market Law*, 33; Tereszkiewicz, 'Digital Platforms: Regulation and Liability in the EU Law' (2018) 26 *European Review of Private Law*, 903 (907).

[5] Directive 2000/31/EC.

[6] Grušić, 'Long-Term Business Relationships and Implicit Contracts in European Private Law' (2016) 12 *European Review of Contract Law*, 395 (400), with additional references.

[7] Also stating the absence of legislative acts about (digital) remote contracts Edisherashvili, 'Legal Regalements of E-Signature' (2020) 25 *Journal of Legal Studies*, 98 (100); Maultzsch, 'Contractual Liability of Online Platform Operators: European Proposals and established Principles' [2018] *European Review of Contract Law*, 209 (210 et seq.).

§ 5. Intermediaries of Secondary Crypto Trade

I. Contract between Users and Trading Platforms

Regardless of the specific design and purpose of the trading platform, one common aspect exists on almost every online platform: Before users can benefit from the full service offered by the platform, a registration on the platform's website is mandatory. For this purpose, the prospective user first enters into a so-called **platform agreement** with the platform (operator). The main features of these agreements are identical and are not influenced by the platform category or the specific form of transactions processed by the intermediary. The contents of most platform agreements exhibit numerous resemblances and do not differ substantively. Only after concluding such a contractual relationship, does the user gain access to the full range of services offered by the trading platform. This fundamental and basic contract is generally referred to as a so-called **platform (usage) agreement**. The user's will to be legally bound is manifested in the registration and creation of a user account.[8] The intermediary itself 'enforces' this contractual basis and its deriving rules through the obligation to register.[9] In this respect, similar provisions apply as for other online contracts.[10] The platform agreement shows significant parallels in general contractual structures to other well-known intermediary platforms.[11] As such, the legal approaches developed for these platforms can be used as a general indication for the characterisation of contractual relationships within the secondary crypto trade. Mostly, they contain and combine elements of agency contracts[12], service contracts but sometimes also elements of brokerage contracts.[13]

7

The precise **legal classification** of these platform agreements can only be based on the provisions agreed upon by the parties, i.e. the trading platform and the user. Therefore, the actual rights, obligations and general legal framework require evaluation on a case-by-case basis. The crucial reference points for this evaluation are the comprehensive general **terms and conditions** provided by the platform. The terms and conditions must be accepted by the user during the registration process to gain full

8

---

[8] Možina, 'Retail business, platform services and information duties' [2016] *Journal of European Consumer and Market Law*, 25 (25 et seq.); Wendehorst, 'Platform Intermediary Services and Duties under the E-Commerce Directive and the Consumer Rights Directive' [2016] *Journal of European Consumer and Market Law*, 30 (31).

[9] Maultzsch, 'Contractual Liability of Online Platform Operators: European Proposals and established Principles' [2018] *European Review of Contract Law*, 209 (211).

[10] Cf. BGH 14 June 2006 – I ZR 75/03 – (2006) *Neue Juristische Wochenschrift*, 2976; Edisherashvili, 'Legal Regalments of E-Signature' (2020) 25 *Journal of Legal Studies*, 98 (100); Meyer, 'Einbeziehung und Geltungsbereich von AGB', in Borges (ed), *Rechtsfragen der Internet-Auktion* (2014), 36 (38 et seq.); Söbbing and Jakob, 'Online-Plattformen – Die Hotspots der Digitalwirtschaft rechtlich betrachtet' [2016] *Zeitschrift zum Innovations- und Technikrecht*, 149 (151); Pisuliński, 'Internet platforms under Polish law' [2016] *Journal of European Consumer and Market Law*, 62 (63).

[11] Comparable platforms are for example online shopping platforms like eBay, amazonMarketplace or idealo.

[12] An agency contract is typically defined as a (fiduciary) relationship existing between two persons, where the agent acts on behalf of a principal in return for payment, which is normally called 'commission.', see Akman, 'Online Platforms, Agency, and Competition Law: Mind the Gap' (2019) 43 *Fordham International Law Journal*, 209 (227).

[13] Maultzsch, 'Contractual Liability of Online Platform Operators: European Proposals and established Principles' [2018] *European Review of Contract Law*, 209 (211); Pisuliński, 'Internet platforms under Polish law' [2016] *Journal of European Consumer and Market Law*, 62 (62 et seq.); Sénéchal, 'The Diversity of the Services provided by Online Platforms and the Specificity of the Counter-performance of these Services — A double Challenge for European and National Contract Law' [2016] *Journal of European Consumer and Market Law*, 39 (40).

access to the trading platform. Thus, they are a crucial part of the platform agreement. These terms are generally unilaterally determined by the trading platform and the user is mostly unable to influence them. Therefore, these provisions mostly classify as contractual not individually negotiated terms according to Art. 3 para. 1 and 2 of the EU Councils Directive on Unfair Terms in Consumer Contracts (GTC-Directive).[14]

9   The **general terms and conditions** have a significant impact on the contractual relationship between the trading platform and its user and define further details. They typically describe the rights and obligations of the contracting parties and mostly represent the interests of the provider, in this case the trading platform.[15] However, the intermediary cannot fully dictate contractual terms in its sole discretion. The provisions of the GTC-Directive limit the freedom of contract on account of professional parties if the other party is a so-called consumer. According to Art. 2 b) GTC-Directive, a consumer is any natural person who is acting for purposes which are outside his trade, business, or profession. In this case, the GTC-Directive prohibits the use of 'unfair terms'. A pre-formulated term qualifies as 'unfair' if, contrary to the requirement of good faith, it causes a significant imbalance in the parties' rights and obligations arising under the contract, to the detriment of the consumer, Art. 3 para. 1 GTC-Directive. If a term is classified 'unfair', it is non-binding for the consumer.[16] Further legal consequences are provided by national law of the respective Member State. Additionally, the exact interpretation of deriving national legal provisions is entrusted to the national courts.[17]

10 For instance, the **German legislator** has implemented such provisions in §§ 305 et seq. German Civil Code (BGB). These provisions specify legal consequences for unfair terms. If the requirements of § 305 para. 2 BGB are met and the general terms and conditions have been effectively included in the platform agreement, they become part of the contract.[18] Subsequently, they are subject of a fairness control. §§ 307 to 309 BGB state various catalogues of forbidden clauses. If a clause fulfils these criteria, it is deemed unfair as of Art. 3 para. 1 GTC-Directive. As a result, the clause is deemed invalid according to § 306 para. 1 BGB. Nevertheless, the rest of the contract generally remains valid without the unfair term.

11 Similar provisions exist in **Austrian law**, if general terms and conditions grossly disadvantage one party, § 879 Austrian General Civil Code (ABGB). § 6 Consumer Protection Act (KSchG) describes disadvantageous terms in more detail, which are non-binding for the consumer.[19]

12 Same considerations apply in the **Dutch Burgerlijk Wetboek** (Dutch Civil Code). Book 6 Art. 233 (a) states the voidance of standard terms and conditions, if e.g., the provision is unreasonably burdensome for the counterparty. During the incorporation process of the Directive, the **French legislator** changed the definition of an unfair term,

---

[14] Directive 93/13/EEC, amended by Directive 2011/83/EU.

[15] Maultzsch, 'Contractual Liability of Online Platform Operators: European Proposals and established Principles' [2018] *European Review of Contract Law*, 209 (212).

[16] For a general approach on fairness control see Hellwege, 'It is necessary to strictly distinguish two forms of fairness control!' [2015] *Journal of European Consumer and Market Law*, 129 et seq.

[17] An overview over French, Dutch and English provisions Pavillon, 'Private Standards of Fairness in European Contract Law' (2014) 10 *European Review of Contract Law*, 85 (90 et seq.).

[18] Härting, *Internetrecht* (6th edn, 2017), para. 1054 et seq.; Söbbing and Jakob, 'Online-Plattformen – Die Hotspots der Digitalwirtschaft rechtlich betrachtet' [2016] *Zeitschrift zum Innovations- und Technikrecht*, 149 (151); Söbbing, 'Platform as a Service: Grundlagen, Plattformverträge, AGB, Impressumspflicht' [2016] *Der IT-Rechts-Berater*, 140 (142); Billing, in Bräutigam and Rücker (eds), *E-Commerce*, 4th part B, para. 10; Müller-Riemenschneider, in Bräutigam and Rücker (eds), *E-Commerce*, 7th part B, para. 19.

[19] For an overview of these provisions see Pittl and Gottardis, 'Smart Contracts – An Analysis from the Perspective of Austrian Law' [2019] *Journal of European Consumer and Market Law*, 205 (207).

which was based on a 'good faith' criterion. Nowadays, any term causing a significant imbalance in the contracting parties rights and obligations is deemed unfair.[20]

On the contrary, **UK law** had no prior provisions similar to the European Directive and therefore implemented a new one, copying the exact wording of Art. 3.[21] In Poland, the consequences of the use of an unfair term are part of the general prohibition of practices harmful to consumers' collective interests.[22]

In **Switzerland**, the law on control of unfair terms is in competition law rather than contract law. Art. 8 of the **Swiss Unfair Competition Act** (UCA) was mostly inspired by the European GTC-Directive and shall provide effective protection of the weaker party against a user of a standard term, including a 'good faith'-criterion. According to Art. 8 UCA, a term is deemed unfair if it establishes a both significant and unjustified disproportion between contractual rights and obligations to the detriment of the consumer in contradiction to the principle of good faith. However, the provision does not provide any further definitions of the notion of 'standard terms' or 'consumer' and is subject to broad interpretation.[23]

Similar to these European regulations, **China** has implemented the **Law of the People's Republic of China on Protecting Consumers' Rights and Interests** (CPL) in 1993. Additionally, there are further miscellaneous laws to protect consumers, leading to a highly fragmented and inconsistent legal landscape.[24] According to the CPL, the consumer has, for instance, the right to obtain truthful information and the right to a fair contract, whereas a businessperson has basic obligations such as an obligation to disclose their true identity, provide truthful information and to ascertain receptivity to consumers' proposals.[25] Similar to EU regulation, a businessperson is obliged not to use unfair conditions in the general terms and conditions according to Art. 24 para. 1 CPL. Any unfair term is rendered void according to Art. 24 para. 2 CPL. Only individual agreements are granted precedence according to the supplementary provision of Art. 42 Contract Law of the PR China.[26]

Occasionally, contractual rights and obligations are not explicitly specified in the trading platform's terms and conditions or in the platform agreement. In these cases, they need to be determined according to general **legal interpretation** rules.[27] A key factor is the **will of the parties.** As a first essential aspect, the user must be able to comprehensively use the platform's infrastructure. After successful registration, the user gains full access to the website. Moreover, the user obtains comprehensive information about the transaction options available on the trading platform and is allowed to place orders for token transactions himself. Furthermore, the trading platform frequently offers further information, such as a display of the current price of the tokens tradable on the platform or general knowledge sections, such as explanations of technical requirements for token purchases.[28]

---

[20] Pavillon, 'Private Standards of Fairness in European Contract Law' (2014) 10 *European Review of Contract Law*, 85 (89).

[21] Ibid.

[22] Luzak, 'You too will be judged: erga omnes effect of registered unfair contract terms in Poland' [2017] *Journal of European Consumer and Market Law*, 120 (120).

[23] Frei and Jung, 'Revised Control of Unfair Terms in Swiss Law – Consumer Protection by Competition Law?' [2015] *Journal of European Consumer and Market Law*, 165, passim.

[24] Binding, 'Consumer protection law in the People's Republic of China' [2014] *China-EU Law Journal*, 223 (228).

[25] Ibid., 229 et seq.

[26] Ibid., 235.

[27] For a general overview on interpretation rules from a comparative point of view Canaris and Grigoleit, 'Interpretation of Contracts' in Hartkamp, Hesselink, Hondius, Mak and du Perron (eds), *Towards a European Civil Code* (2011), 587.

[28] For example, the Questions and Answers of Bitcoin Deutschland AG, available at https://www.bitcoin.de/en/faq (accessed 30.3.2021).

17   By creating a user account, a continuing obligation between user and trading platform is established.[29] Subsequently, the platform operator is obligated to keep the offered services available as agreed, and is liable for the non-performance of its obligations.[30] This aspect can also include the obligation to provide the user with permanent access to the digital infrastructure of the website and to enable token trades. From a user's perspective, uninterrupted access to his or her account balance might be of paramount importance to efficiently manage tokens and take advantage of favourable buying or selling opportunities. Nevertheless, the terms and conditions are a key reference point for legal interpretation. An obligation for permanent access to the platform's website might not always be in the interest of the platform provider. Most matching platforms generally stipulate clauses which regularly exclude permanent access to the website, restricting the obligations of the platform provider[31] and **reducing risks of liability**. If the terms and conditions of the platform agreement do not include any specific statements, the necessity of unlimited access needs to be interpreted considering the parties' interest. Since the parties' interests run contrary to each other, a case-by-case-decision is required.

18   The ability to access the platform's services without limitation or interruption can be of enormous importance for users. But given the general susceptibility of technical equipment to failure, trading platforms mostly will not be willing to take on such liability risks without restriction. In this regard, comparable difficulties occur in **online banking systems** regarding customers' access to their accounts. Credit institutions and banks must generally ensure the availability to online banking systems to customers. Accordingly, accessibility is a main obligation[32] and cannot be excluded.

19   For example, the German Federal Court of Justice has ruled that general terms and conditions of credit institutions, which limit the institution's liability for temporary restrictions and interruptions of access to online services for technical reasons are invalid due to the enormous importance of unrestricted access for the customer.[33] Same rules apply even in cases of gross negligence.

20   Given the similar mechanisms of online banking and token trading, said legal considerations should be transferable. Nevertheless, unforeseeable temporary restrictions of access due to technical interruptions or previously announced maintenance work outside of usual business hours ought to be permissible.[34] Such activities do not constitute a breach of contract and therefore do not cause liability of the platform. Nevertheless, trading platforms should implement availability clauses in their service description within the permissible legal limits.[35]

---

[29] For a general definition of continuing obligations see Schulze, in Dannemann and Schulze (eds), *German Civil Code (BGB)*, §§ 311–360, para. 17.

[30] Engert, 'Digitale Plattformen' (2018) *Archiv für die civilistische Praxis* 218, 304 (321); Pisuliński, 'Internet platforms under Polish law' [2016] *Journal of European Consumer and Market Law*, 62 (64); similar Martens, in BeckOGK BGB, § 314, para. 22; on the prerequisites of a continuing obligation in general see Gaier, in *MüKoBGB*, § 314, para. 7 et seq.

[31] Henke, Singbartl and Zintl, 'Mietwohnungsüberlassung an Touristen: Wimdu, Airbnb & Co. aus zivilrechtlicher Perspektive' [2018] *Neue Zeitschrift für Miet- und Wohnungsrecht*, 1 (3 et seq.) with reference to the Wimdu platform; with reference to liability risks Biallaß, 'Aspekte des Vertragsschlusses bei Internet-Auktionen' in Borges (ed), *Rechtsfragen der Internet-Auktion* (2014), 13 (19); Kull, 'The Adequacy of Existing Estonian Laws for the Platform Economy' [2016] *Journal of European Consumer and Market Law*, 52 (55).

[32] Maihold, in Schimansky, Bunte and Lwowski (eds), *Bankrechts-Handbuch*, § 55, para. 52; Becker, in BeckOK BGB, § 309 No. 7, para. 27.

[33] BGH 12 December 2000 – XI ZR 138/00 – (2001) *Neue Juristische Wochenschrift*, 751.

[34] Zahrte, in Bunte and Zahrte (eds), *AGB-Banken, AGB-Sparkassen, Sonderbedingungen*, 4. part VI. B., para. 38.

[35] In detail Redeker, *IT-Recht* (7th edn, 2020), para. 1003 et seq.

§ 5. Intermediaries of Secondary Crypto Trade

If the intermediary is an **on-chain platform**, additional peculiarities need to be considered. After the user completes his or her registration, an on-chain platform creates a **wallet** for the user and simultaneously **manages** the corresponding private key. The user, however, does not receive any direct access to his or her private key and only has knowledge of the public key (→ § 1 para. 97). In these cases, the platform agreement contains additional **administrative obligations**. These additional administrative services are provided by the on-chain intermediary – mostly free of charge.[36] Furthermore, the wallet itself does not involve any additional costs.[37]

21

Given the heterogeneity of the underlying catalogue of terms and conditions, the platform contract cannot be clearly assigned to any specific type of contract. Anyway, the mere registration does not obligate the user to pay if he or she does not carry out further transactions. If the trading platform manages the user's private key, it acts as a trustee. Furthermore, the platform is obligated to publish their user's order on their website. The availability of offers published by other users is part of the platform agreement as well. Therefore, the actual legal rights and obligations deriving from the platform agreement need to be evaluated on a **case-by-case basis**.

22

However, the legal impact of the platform agreement is not limited to the platform-user relationship. Additionally, the platform agreement also contains co-determining elements for future token transactions between users concluded on the platform. The platform's rules particularly **apply to the modalities of conclusion of the users' transaction contracts**, but frequently regulate their execution and handling as well. The legally binding effect of the platform's terms and conditions on contracts between the users is an often discussed topic and predominantly[38] declined.[39] Nevertheless, users are virtually almost always **forced to comply** as the terms and conditions are implemented into the platform's digital structure.[40] At the

23

---

[36] The provision of personal data by platform users could be considered a fee; in detail Langhanke and Schmidt-Kessel, 'Consumer Data as Consideration' [2015] *Journal of European Consumer and Market Law*, 218; Twigg-Flesner, 'Legal and Policy Responses to Online Platforms – A UK Perspective', in Blaurock, Schmidt-Kessel and Erler (eds), *Plattformen* (2018), 139 (152 et seq.) with additional references; for the possibility of personal data as property Sattler, 'From Personality to Property? Revisiting the Fundamentals of the Protection of Personal Data', in Bakhoum, Conde Gallego, Mackenrodt and Surblytė-Namavičienė (eds), *Personal Data in Competition, Consumer Protection and Intellectual Property Law* (2018), V, 27 (39 et seq.); Chrobak, 'Proprietary Rights in Digital Data? Normative Perspectives and Principles of Civil Law', in Bakhoum, Conde Gallego, Mackenrodt and Surblytė-Namavičienė (eds), *Personal Data in Competition, Consumer Protection and Intellectual Property Law* (2018), 253 (254 et seq.).

[37] The general terms and conditions of online platforms regularly state that the administration of wallets does not generate additional costs but can be terminated at any time.

[38] Some scholars express the opinion, that accepting the terms and conditions leads to a binding effect for the parties. Thus, the platform's terms and conditions should prevail in any case. From a practical perspective, the discussion seems to be redundant, because users are mostly not able to deviate from the platform's structure, which is based on and reflects its terms and conditions, Pisuliński, 'Internet platforms under Polish law' [2016] *Journal of European Consumer and Market Law*, 62 (63).

[39] Burgard, 'Online-Marktordnung und Inhaltskontrolle' [2001] *Zeitschrift für Wirtschafts- und Bankrecht*, 2102 (2107); Schweitzer, 'Digitale Plattformen als private Gesetzgeber: Ein Perspektivwechsel für die europäische 'Plattform-Regulierung'' [2019] *Zeitschrift für Europäisches Privatrecht* , 1 (5 et seq.); Janal, 'Erklärungen im elektronischen Geschäftsverkehr' (2015) *Archiv für die civilistische Praxis* 215, 830 (844); in a certain way, platforms appear to be 'drafters of contract', see Hornuf, Klöhn and Schilling, 'Financial Contracting in Crowdinvesting: Lessons from the German Market' (2018) 19 *German Law Journal*, 509 (518 et seq.); Loos, 'Standard terms for the use of the Apple App Store and the Google Play Store' [2016] *Journal of European Consumer and Market Law*, 10 (12), using the example of terms and conditions of app stores.

[40] Schweitzer, 'Digitale Plattformen als private Gesetzgeber: Ein Perspektivwechsel für die europäische 'Plattform-Regulierung' [2019] *Zeitschrift für Europäisches Privatrecht*, 1 (3 et seq.); Hellgardt, 'Privatautonome Modifikation der Regeln zu Abschluss, Zustandekommen und Wirksamkeit des Vertrags' (2013)

same time, the platform agreement stipulates a **fee** payable to the intermediary for every transaction concluded on the platform.[41]

II. Categorisation of the Platform's Activity

24   As trading platforms offer a broad range of different services, general legal categorisations of platforms appear rather ambitious. Building on the classification as matching platforms, an essential aspect of their services concerns matching the interest of two different users. In this respect, trading platforms are often referred to as **brokers**. Generally, a broker agreement sets forth the terms, rights, and obligations upon which the broker ought to match two different parties with inverse legal intentions. It may suffice to merely introduce suitable parties, but it may also be necessary to assist with the contract's negotiation or implementation. The specific content is therefore subject to prior individual agreement between broker and client.

25   From a **German** perspective, this contract can be qualified as a (atypical) broker agreement according to § 652 para. 1 sent. 1 BGB. In this respect, same discussions exist for archetypal matching platforms such as eBay, amazonMarketplace or Airbnb.[42]

26   Same considerations apply from an Estonian perspective. The services offered by the platform are not brokerage in the strict meaning of the law but may be interpreted as modified brokerage services. In this case, the platform might be treated as an intermediary.[43] In other cases, the contract may combine different elements, for instance elements of a service or use contract, depending on the individual situation.[44] In any event, it is not a contract sui generis.[45]

27   As for **Polish Law**, no specific provisions exist for contracts with digital platforms either. According to the general rules, if the platform provides assistance in administrating and performing such contracts, it may be seen as a broker.[46] In **Denmark** the qualification of an online platform as an intermediary might have an additional impact. According to **Danish consumer law**, any contract concluded using platform services will be regarded as a contract between a consumer and a business entity by force of law, even if the seller himself is a consumer.[47]

28   From a **UK perspective**, the platform would generally not be regarded as an agent. The legal relationships might either be a set of three two-party contracts or a more

---

Archiv für die civilistische Praxis 213, 760 (774); Engert, 'Digitale Plattformen' (2018) *Archiv für die civilistische Praxis* 218, 304 (320).

[41] For this purpose, → para. 30 et seqq.

[42] On the classification of intermediary platforms as brokers in detail Engert, 'Digitale Plattformen' (2018) *Archiv für die civilistische Praxis* 218, 304 (323 et seq.); Dreyer and Haskamp, 'Die Vermittlungstätigkeit von Plattformen' (2017) *Zeitschrift für Vertriebsrecht*, 359; on crowdfunding Meschkowski and Wilhelmi, 'Investorenschutz im Crowdinvesting' [2013] *Betriebs-Berater*, 1411 (1413); in contrast Henke, Singbartl and Zintl, 'Mietwohnungsüberlassung an Touristen: Wimdu, Airbnb & Co. aus zivilrechtlicher Perspektive' [2018] *Neue Zeitschrift für Miet- und Wohnungsrecht*, 1 (3).

[43] Kull, 'The Adequacy of Existing Estonian Laws for the Platform Economy' [2016] *Journal of European Consumer and Market Law*, 52 (56); with reference to AirBnB: Sein, 'Legal problems of electronic platform economy – Estonian perspective', in Blaurock, Schmidt-Kessel and Erler (eds), *Plattformen* (2018), 79 (89 et seq.).

[44] Sein, 'Legal problems of electronic platform economy – Estonian perspective', in Blaurock, Schmidt-Kessel and Erler (eds), *Plattformen* (2018), 79 (89 et seq.).

[45] Ibid.

[46] Focusing on insurance platforms: Pisuliński, 'Internet platforms under Polish law' [2016] *Journal of European Consumer and Market Law*, 62 (62).

[47] Sørensen, 'Private Law Perspectives on Platform Services' [2016] *Journal of European Consumer and Market Law*, 15 (17 et seq.).

complex three-party contract.[48] For further determination, the substantive rights and obligations between the parties qualify the legal relationship. The main problematic aspect constitutes the necessity of 'consideration' (the offer of something of economic value by each party) in **English contract law**.[49]

Nevertheless, the activity of trading platforms cannot always be categorised as a classic broker service. The prerequisite would be an **(in)direct influence** on the user's decision to conclude a contract, which consciously and purposefully causes or promotes the willingness to conclude a contract.[50] In this respect, the mere possibility to review offers for token transactions is mostly considered insufficient.[51] As most platforms do not actively pursue such specific matching activities, but only publish offers for token sales, their activity is comparable to a billboard or the marketplace section of a newspaper. The mere registration on a platform does not create specific possibilities to form a contract. The platform agreement instead provides **services beyond mere brokerage**. It obliges the platform to provide the technical and digital infrastructure to enter contracts. This virtual space needs to simultaneously offer evaluation, payment, and a communication system for efficiently placing transaction offers.[52] Thus, the platform agreement only regulates the terms of service of this virtual space.

Therefore, the token trading platform mostly does **not actually broker** token transactions between users. Regarding archetypical matching platforms such as eBay or amazonMarketplace, the actual transaction process and services provided by token trading platforms are very different. On said classic matching platforms, the user initiates searches for specific products or a general product group via the platform's search engine. The search algorithm finds and displays a variety of products matching the search criteria. Usually, different sellers, who offer the specific product, are listed at the same time. The user has a choice with whom to conclude the desired contract. However, users of a crypto trading platform mostly do not conduct comparable search processes. Unlike classic matching platforms, crypto trading platforms only offer their users the possibility of acquiring a single specific 'product': the tradable tokens. Users accessing the platform's website already know which product they would like to purchase and do not require any further research. Logically, the website only lists offers for the corresponding token types previously placed and uploaded by other users. The user can now search this list for a suitable offer. As a result, there are no actual brokerage activities performed by the platform at any time, neither by direct action nor through the provision of any further assistance such as advanced search algorithms. Instead, the trading platform only offers a virtual space to publish trading offers like a billboard. This way, the platform remains inactive and merely functions as a **distribution medium**. Although it is possible to sort offers according to some further criteria, for instance such as the tradable volume, this feature merely provides a simplification for the user to display results. Otherwise, the platform has no sufficient or active

---

[48] Twigg-Flesner, 'Legal and Policy Responses to Online Platforms – A UK Perspective', in Blaurock, Schmidt-Kessel and Erler (eds), *Plattformen* (2018), 139 (148 et seq.).

[49] Ibid.

[50] Roth, in *MüKoBGB*, § 652, para. 106; Fervers, in Dannemann and Schulze (eds), *German Civil Code (BGB)*, § 652, para. 4 et seq.

[51] BGH 4 June 2009 – III ZR 82/08 – (2009) *Neue Juristische Wochenschrift Rechtsprechungs-Report*, 1282 (1283).

[52] Henke, Singbartl and Zintl, 'Mietwohnungsüberlassung an Touristen: Wimdu, Airbnb & Co. aus zivilrechtlicher Perspektive' [2018] *Neue Zeitschrift für Miet- und Wohnungsrecht*, 1 (3); Wendehorst, 'Platform Intermediary Services and Duties under the E-Commerce Directive and the Consumer Rights Directive' [2016] *Journal of European Consumer and Market Law*, 30 (30); also Dreyer and Haskamp, 'Die Vermittlungstätigkeit von Plattformen' (2017) *Zeitschrift für Vertriebsrecht*, 359 (361); Neubauer and Steinmetz, in Hoeren, Sieber and Holznagel (eds), *Handbuch Multimedia-Recht*, Part 14, para. 8.

influence on the user's willingness to conclude a contract. As a consequence, neither crypto-to-crypto exchanges nor fiat-to-crypto exchanges can be qualified as brokers. Therefore, payments made by users are not considered commissions, but rather transaction fees for general services provided during the execution and processing of the contract.

31 The trading platform, however, qualifies as a **broker** if it offers **actual matchmaking** and actively introduces two users with opposing interests or promises such activities in its service description. Intermediaries which only display an exchange rate on their website, without any specific offers published by their users, are actively matching buyers and sellers. This process of matching their users is conducted by the intermediary or its matching algorithm. In these cases, the platform's active brokerage is a necessity to facilitate the conclusion of contracts. The platform actively participates with a direct influence on their users. As a result, such trading platforms are comparable to the aforementioned online shopping platforms (→ para. 30). Hence, the same legal considerations apply. To determine if a trading platform qualifies as a broker or simply offers a virtual 'billboard', the contractual documents and specific design of the individual platform must be reviewed. Consequently, the classification requires an individual examination of the facts on a case-by-case basis.

III. On-Chain Intermediaries

32 On-chain intermediaries process token transactions directly via a blockchain transaction. Hence, the direct use of the blockchain is the key feature of this type of trading platform. The contract is implemented on the blockchain in form of a **smart contract**. To process blockchain transactions, each user must have his or her own wallet. To ensure the uninterrupted implementation of transactions, on-chain intermediaries usually set up those wallets for their users and mostly manage their private keys. The direct access to the private keys gives the on-chain intermediaries the opportunity to fully manage the wallets and exert full control over the user's funds. This management component is, in addition to trust, part of the platform agreement between the user and the on-chain trading platform.

1. Fiat-to-Crypto Exchange

33 Fiat-to-crypto exchanges allow the trade of fiat currency for tokens (→ § 1 para. 90 et seqq.). If two users of an on-chain fiat-to-crypto exchange conclude such a contract, further rights and obligations are established between the users and the on-chain platform. These further contractual obligations are largely determined by the terms and conditions of the platform agreement. To characterise the rights and obligations of the involved parties in greater detail, it is imperative to distinguish between centralised and decentralised fiat-to-crypto exchanges. Centralised fiat-to-crypto exchanges are very similar to centralised crypto-to-crypto exchanges and provide equal features. Consequently, **legal considerations** are **mostly identical** (→ para. 37). However, **decentralised** fiat-to-crypto exchanges **differ**.

34 Before a user is given the opportunity to conclude contracts on the platform's infrastructure, i.e. to publish offers to sell or buy tokens for fiat currency, on-chain trading platforms typically require the user to transfer tokens to a public key to create a certain '**minimum account margin**'. Same rules apply to fiat currency, which can be used to purchase tokens. The public key is usually given to the user by the fiat-to-crypto exchange and is the counterpart to the private key the fiat-to-crypto exchange holds for

the user. This creates a further contractual obligation between the fiat-to-crypto exchange and the user, which grants the fiat-to-crypto exchange sole access to the wallet. On the other hand, the fiat-to-crypto exchange is obliged to manage the wallet. Thereby, it acts as a trustee.[53] This obligation is created by transferring tokens to the public key.

On-chain intermediaries who manage wallets for their users are also obligated to take precautions to adequately secure and protect the private keys and the user's tokens against **cyberattacks**. The actual design of these **security systems** is subject to their sole discretion. However, they should be designed according to the current state of the art, which should render a run-of-the-mill cyberattack unsuccessful. 35

The on-chain intermediary's **fee** for the contract implementation and the transaction's execution is usually split between both parties involved in the transaction. The terms and conditions of on-chain fiat-to-crypto exchanges regularly state that, in the case of a two-party-transaction, each user is obliged to pay an independent fee. Alternatively, one total fee occurs for the transaction, but only half must be paid by each individual user.[54] In the latter case, users mostly do **not bear joint liability**, as the terms and conditions of the platform agreement regularly state that each user is only liable for his or her part of the transaction fee. 36

2. Crypto-to-Crypto Exchange

Crypto-to-crypto exchanges provide a direct exchange (→ § 1 para. 92) of different types of tokens, without a need for an intermediary use of fiat currency. In legal terms, crypto-to-crypto exchanges can be divided into two different categories: A centralised type, in which the crypto-to-token exchange is directly involved in the transaction process, and a decentralised type, in which the crypto-to-crypto exchange has a status similar to a fiat-to-crypto exchange. 37

a) Central Crypto-to-Crypto Exchange. A central crypto-to-crypto exchange processes the transaction itself. Both types of tokens exchanged by the users are sent to a public key of the crypto-to-crypto exchange (→ § 1 para. 97). First, the user transfers the tokens of type A he or she wishes to trade to a public key of the crypto-to-crypto exchange. In return, the platform transfers the desired tokens of type B to its user. To calculate the worth of the two different types, the central crypto-to-crypto exchange publishes '**exchange rates**', which determine how much each tradable token is worth in respect to the other kind. However, the user does not receive the full number of tokens according to the exchange rate. Instead, the number of tokens is reduced by the platform's **transaction fee**. Due to this direct involvement of the on-chain crypto-to-crypto exchange, it can prove difficult to **determine the user's contractual partner**. Two possibilities arise and need to be reviewed on a case-by-case basis. Either the crypto-to-crypto exchange itself or a third party, which owns the desired tokens of type B, can be the actual contractual partner.[55] 38

---

[53] Expressly stipulated by § 12 para. 3 of the general terms and conditions of Bitcoin Deutschland AG, Terms and Conditions, available at https://www.bitcoin.de/de/agb#agb-4 (accessed 30.3.2021).

[54] Cf. for example § 19 No. 2 of the general terms and conditions of Bitcoin Deutschland AG, available at https://www.bitcoin.de/de/agb#agb-4 (accessed 30.3.2021); Wendehorst, 'Platform Intermediary Services and Duties under the E-Commerce Directive and the Consumer Rights Directive' [2016] *Journal of European Consumer and Market Law*, 30 (30); for different fee models see Možina, 'Retail business, platform services and information duties' [2016] *Journal of European Consumer and Market Law*, 25 (25).

[55] For platform constellations in general, Sein, 'Legal problems of electronic platform economy – Estonian perspective', in Blaurock, Schmidt-Kessel and Erler (eds), *Plattformen* (2018), 79 (83 et seq.) and

39 The activity of a central crypto-to-crypto exchange can be compared to the settlement in **stock trading** and **stock exchange transactions**. In these cases, a so-called 'central counterparty' is involved in every transaction for stabilising effects. Therefore, sellers and buyers do not directly conclude stock purchase agreements. Instead, a **central counterparty** is involved in every purchase agreement and becomes the contractual partner of both seller and buyer to ensure proper contract execution.[56] Thus, contracting parties do not directly settle a purchase contract. Instead, two separate contracts are concluded with the central counterparty. In general, the central counterparty collects all orders and settles and matches the orders (so-called **netting**) by transferring shares.[57] This procedure is comparable to the concept of a central on-chain crypto-to-crypto exchange. Direct legal contact only exists between the crypto-to-crypto exchange and the individual user, granting the platform full control over every transaction. Generally, the actual counterparty, i.e. exchange partner, from whom the desired tokens of type B were acquired, is never identified. Hence, attributable to its central position within the transaction processing, the crypto-to-crypto exchange is **comparable** to the central counterparty in stock trading.

40 This **strong** position is a decisive factor in determining the user's contractual partner. Additionally, the actual behaviour of the crypto-to-crypto exchange on the one hand, and its general terms and conditions on the other must be considered. Because of the lack of any contact between buyer and seller, the other token holder cannot be the counterparty. According to the jurisprudence of the CJEU, a person or entity who seems to be acting as the counterparty, but is not actually stating its actual role in its terms of service and therefore is **creating confusion and misleading a consumer can be liable**.[58] This ruling creates the opportunity to base the interpretation of legally relevant behaviour on the perspective of an objective party.[59] Considering the **point of view of an informed and objective third party**, the behaviour of such a trading platform and the circumstances of the conclusion of contract will regularly suggest an exchange contract between user and platform.[60] Therefore, the crypto-to-crypto exchange becomes the **contractual partner** of its

---

Maultzsch, 'Verantwortlichkeit der Plattformbetreiber', in Blaurock, Schmidt-Kessel and Erler (eds), *Plattformen* (2018), 223 (228 et seq.); from a GTC legal perspective Engert, 'Digitale Plattformen' (2018) *Archiv für die civilistische Praxis* 218, 304 (313).

[56] Hoch, *Die Besteuerungssystematik von Kapitalanlagen* (2019), 470; see also Nabilou and Asimakopoulos, 'In CCP we trust … or do we? Assessing the regulation of central clearing counterparties in Europe' (2020) 15 *Capital Markets Law Journal*, 70 (70 et seq.); Kartikaningtyas, 'The Role of Central Counterparty as a Risk Mitigator in Capital Market Transaction in Indonesian Law Perspective' (2007), 20th Australasian Finance & Banking Conference 2007 Paper, 19 et seq., available at https://ssrn.com/abstract=1008727 (accessed 30.3.2021).

[57] Weber, 'Central Counterparties in the OTC Derivatives Market from the Perspective of the Legal Theory of Finance, Financial Market Stability and the Public Good' (2016) 17 *European Business Organization Law Review*, 71; Loritz, 'Die Realität des Aktientransfers in Zeiten der Dauerglobalurkunde – Sachgerechtes Verständnis des Zivilrechts als Grundlage zur Vermeidung steuerlicher Irrwege – Teil I' [2017] *Betriebs-Berater*, 2327 (2330).

[58] EuGH, Judgment of 9 November 2016, *Wathelet*, C-149/15, ECLI:EU:C:2016:840.

[59] In detail with reference to the 'Wathelet'-case Tereszkiewicz, 'Digital Platforms: Regulation and Liability in the EU Law' (2018) 26 *European Review of Private Law*, 903 (910 et seq.); as well from an Estonian perspective with references to the 'Wathelet'-case Sein, 'Legal problems of electronic platform economy – Estonian perspective', in Blaurock, Schmidt-Kessel and Erler (eds), *Plattformen* (2018), 79 (83 et seq., 86 et seq.).

[60] On resulting problems if a platform does not reveal its actual position and function Kull, 'The Adequacy of Existing Estonian Laws for the Platform Economy' [2016] *Journal of European Consumer and Market Law*, 52 (54); Wendehorst, 'Platform Intermediary Services and Duties under the E-Commerce Directive and the Consumer Rights Directive' [2016] *Journal of European Consumer and Market Law*, 30 (32).

user.[61] The crypto-to-crypto exchange thereby acquires a right to a **transaction fee**. This can either be a so-called **flat** fee or a **percentage fee**. It is usually directly deducted from the tokens exchanged with the user, i.e. the user receives less tokens than the exchange rate would suggest. In this aspect, the business model of crypto-to-crypto exchanges is comparable to fiat-crypto exchanges.[62]

b) Decentralised Crypto-to-Crypto Exchange. In contrast to the central type, a decentralised on-chain crypto-to-crypto exchange is not directly involved in the transaction (→ § 1 para. 97, 99 et seqq.). Instead, the exchange contract is concluded between users themselves. Nevertheless, the platform is (indirectly) involved on two levels. On the one hand, it provides a **virtual trading opportunity/marketplace** and enables users to find contractual partners. On the other hand, the platform accompanies the performance of contract. Also, the decentralised crypto-to-crypto exchange partly calculates and suggests a **token price**. If a user wants to buy or sell tokens at this price, he or she includes the platform's suggested price in his or her offer. 41

Regarding the contractual structures and content, the user agreements are structured according to the terms and conditions stated by the platform agreement. The intermediary receives a **transaction fee conditional upon successful conclusion** of a contract. In addition, contractual elements regarding the publication of offers on the platform's website as well as contractual elements, which represent the support of the user in the execution and handling of the contract, are suggested by the platform agreement. 42

IV. Off-Chain Intermediaries

Both crypto-to-crypto exchanges and fiat-to-crypto exchanges may process token transactions outside the blockchain. In this case, they use the so-called **off-chain method** which shifts the execution solely to the platform's infrastructure. Transactions exclusively occur on a **record level** within the user's platform accounts (→ § 1 para. 96). Therefore, off-chain trading platforms **exclusively provide contractual relationships** between the participants, i.e. the off-chain intermediary and the users, without the transfer of any actual tokens. Since the off-chain intermediary acts as a middleman for every transaction comparable to a '**bookkeeper**', these platforms are mostly structured as central platforms. For legal classification of the resulting contractual relationships, it is irrelevant whether the tokens are exchanged for other tokens or for fiat currency. In both cases, users only have a **virtual account balance** on the intermediary's website. There is no 'actual' transfer of tokens between the users. Therefore, the platform does not need to create wallets for their users. As a result, the users only have (legal) claims against the platform to transfer/pay the respective tokens or fiat currency. This results in an exclusively **contractual construct**. 43

1. General Contractual Relations between User and Platform

As with on-chain intermediaries, users need to sign a mandatory **platform agreement** with the intermediary by registering on the platform. Thus far, no differences 44

---

[61] For example, the crypto exchange Changelly. The user 'transfers' the number of token A that he/she intends to trade to Changelly. Changelly determines the 'best' exchange rate and 'transfers' the exchanged tokens B to the user's public key in the corresponding blockchain, see *Changelly*, How it works, available at https://changelly.com/how-it-works (accessed 30.3.2021).

[62] Transaction fees can also be paid using platform-specific utility tokens. Binance, for example, offers such a system. The main advantage of using these utility tokens is a reduction of the transaction fee and therefore cutting costs.

exist. However, before the user can actively use and conclude transactions via the platform, he or she must first generate an '**account balance**' on the platform. The user could either **transfer tokens** to a public key provided by the platform or, in case of fiat-to-crypto exchanges, by **transferring fiat currency** to the intermediary's bank account. After creating a positive account balance, the user can employ the services of the platform and start trading.

45 This transfer creates an **additional contractual relationship** with the off-chain intermediary regarding the tokens or fiat currency credited to the account balance. The platform is hereby obliged to hold the received tokens or fiat currency as a **trustee** for the benefit of the user and to manage the account balances. Additionally, the user has a contractual repayment claim he or she can raise at any given moment. Therefore, he or she can force the platform to **retransfer** the tokens or fiat currency. The **repayment claim** can be fulfilled by transferring the tokens to a public key or the fiat currency to a bank account previously specified by the user. The platform typically provides these services **free of charge**.

2. Contractual Relations during a Transaction

46 Only registered users can enter a transaction on an off-chain platform. By implementing a transaction, the platform merely adjusts the respective user's **virtual account balance**. The users involved in the transaction do not receive any further information about their respective counterparties. Because of the off-chain character, no information about public keys needs to be exchanged. However, since users do not have direct access to their tokens/fiat currency deposited in their accounts, a direct transfer is impossible. The platform needs to **assist in every transaction**. Therefore, users do not transfer any actual token/fiat currency, but trade their respective **repayment claims against the off-chain intermediary**. The users relinquish their claims, irrespective of the character of the underlying contract.

47 For the actual execution of this exchange agreement, the platform's **participation** is **mandatory**. Due to its fiduciary relationships with both users, the platform is obligated to adjust the users' account balances according to the exchange agreements. The conclusion of contract between users also **implies the instruction** to the platform to adjust the respective account balances (→ para. 44). In return, the platform receives a **transaction fee**, which shall regularly be borne equally by both users. The entitlement to this transaction fee is based on the respective contractual relationships with the platform.

C. Further Obligations of Trading Platforms

48 The contractual relationships between the intermediaries and their users may result in **additional contractual obligations**. However, the platform operator usually does not want to assume any further obligations regarding the proper performance of user contracts.[63] Nevertheless, additional obligations of the intermediary towards its users can be derived from any of the contracts concluded between the parties. For example, obligations may arise from the platform contract which the trading platforms first

---

[63] Pisuliński, 'Internet platforms under Polish law' [2016] *Journal of European Consumer and Market Law*, 62 (63); Maultzsch, 'Contractual Liability of Online Platform Operators: European Proposals and established Principles' [2018] *European Review of Contract Law*, 209 (211); Kull, 'The Adequacy of Existing Estonian Laws for the Platform Economy' [2016] *Journal of European Consumer and Market Law*, 52 (55).

§ 5. Intermediaries of Secondary Crypto Trade

conclude with their users or from pre-contractual negations and corresponding claims.[64] Alternatively, depending on the legal situation, further individual contracts entered into between user and the intermediary could be considered as a basis for additional contractual obligations. Such obligations may be of various shapes.

As an example, users may have **a right to information** against the platforms. These rights to information mostly entitle the user to specific information and are a special form of the obligation to cooperate.[65] In this case, two different categories of information can be distinguished: On the one hand, the user's request for his or her **own information** and, on the other, information requests concerning the **information about third parties**. In practice, the request for information on the **identity** of the respective contractual partner is quite frequent. Particularly in case of default or breach of contract, it is crucial to not only know anonymised usernames, but to obtain more detailed personal information for further legal actions. Such information can regularly be provided by the platforms without further ado. Platforms based in the European Union are obliged to collect their users' personal data, such as names and addresses, according to Art. 13, 14 of the Directive on the Prevention of the Use of the Financial System for the Purposes of Money Laundering or Financing of Terrorism (→ § 10 para. 105, 108 et seqq.).[66] 49

However, the extent of such a right to information is unclear. As a result, every request needs to be considered on **a case-by-case-basis**. At first glance, this seems to be comparable to requests made in cases of social media or rating platforms, e.g., in the health sector. For instance, some platforms grant patients the opportunity to rate their health care professionals such as doctors. Potential patients' decision which doctor to choose might, therefore, be influenced by those ratings. If a health care professional receives a negative and/or untruthful rating, he or she might not only be interested to have it deleted, but also to know who gave the negative review and why. However, a general right to information is mostly denied.[67] 50

Nevertheless, these cases differ immensely from the situation in question. After all, there is **no contractual relationship** between the third-party requesting information and the rating platform. In contrast, the user and the trading platform have concluded at least a platform agreement, which may generate corresponding contractual obligations. 51

If a user requests (personal) information about another user, no general right to information exists at this point. Instead, an **individual case-by-case decision** needs to be made, in which the requesting party's interest must be balanced against the counterparty's **interest in protecting their data**. The platform has a fundamental duty to protect the personal data of its users from unauthorized access by third parties. In this respect, the **GDPR** is applicable. Therefore, the third party needs a legitimate reason for their request. Otherwise, the platform is prohibited from disclosing any information 52

---

[64] Maultzsch, 'Verantwortlichkeit der Plattformbetreiber', in Blaurock, Schmidt-Kessel and Erler (eds), *Plattformen* (2018), 223 (250); Kull, 'The Adequacy of Existing Estonian Laws for the Platform Economy' [2016] *Journal of European Consumer and Market Law*, 52 (55 et seq.); Maultzsch, 'Contractual Liability of Online Platform Operators: European Proposals and established Principles' [2018] *European Review of Contract Law*, 209 (235).

[65] Bachmann, in *MüKoBGB*, § 241, para. 125; Schulze, in Dannemann and Schulze (eds), *German Civil Code (BGB)*, § 242 para. 17; Olzen, in *Staudinger BGB*, Vol. 2, § 241, para. 168 et seq., 439.

[66] Directive 2015/849/EU, amending Regulation (EU) No. 648/2012, and repealing Directive 2005/60/EC and Directive 2006/70/EC.

[67] BGH 1 July 2014 – VI ZR 345/13 – (2014) *Neue Juristische Wochenschrift*, 2651; Müller-Riemenschneider, in Bräutigam and Rücker (eds), *E-Commerce*, 7th part E, para. 14 et seq.; Spindler, 'Deliktische Haftung der Plattformbetreiber', in Spindler and Wiebe (eds), *Internet-Auktionen und Elektronische Marktplätze* (2005), 211, para. 55; for the prerequisites of a duty of information see Schulze, in Dannemann and Schulze (eds), *German Civil Code (BGB)*, § 242 para. 17.

about its users (→ § 6 para. 55 et seqq.). Such third-party requests might be permissible according to Art. 6 (1)(f) GDPR. This requires a legitimate interest of the requesting user or third party (→ § 6 para. 67 et seq.). Ultimately, the decision in each individual case must be the result of a fair **balance between the interests** of the other user and the requesting user. A crucial fact in this consideration is the inherent **pseudonymity** in blockchain and associated transactions. The lack of knowledge of the counterparty's real-life identity is not only accepted by the contracting users but is usually an explicitly desired and mutually agreed-upon feature. Thus, it does not seem disproportionate that users face consequences and need to accept the disadvantages of this pseudonymity as well. Nevertheless, the requesting user's interest in information will often outweigh the interest in pseudonymity. Additional key factors can be lack of experience in business practices or other factors requiring additional protection of the requesting party. Additionally, dishonest conduct or discrimination against a minor can be a factor for a legitimate request. However, every request must be decided upon after careful consideration.

53   If a third party who is not a registered user requests information, legal considerations may differ. In these cases, **no contractual relationship** between the requesting party and the platform exists. Such requests for information regularly occur in the event **of death** of a user. In this case, the heirs desire access to the deceased's account and seek knowledge of the public/private keys or the user's data (such as username and password). But if the heirs do not have any knowledge of the passwords, it is imperative that the intermediary assists in accessing the inherited funds. In this respect, similarities arise with the so-called '**digital inheritance**'[68] regarding user accounts on social media platforms.

54   Generally speaking, most countries do not have specific laws dealing adequately with this issue at the moment. Depending on the specific jurisdiction, different consequences occur. From a **German** perspective, the Federal Court of Justice has recently ruled that in the event of death of a user, the ownership of the account passes on to his or her heirs due to **universal succession**, § 1922 para. 1 BGB. In general, the inherited funds not only include legal property, but also legal relationships and derivative rights and obligations,[69] including rights and obligations deriving from the platform contract. The Court did not see a violation of data protection regulations, the personal rights of the deceased or the rights of people who were communicating with the deceased through the network's services.[70]

Same considerations apply in **Estonia**: Similar to German law, the heir replaces the deceased as a universal successor. Therefore, **digital accounts are transferred to the heir by force of law**, giving the heir the right to request information to existing contracts, access the e-accounts, request information on passwords, and (alternatively) terminate the contract.[71] However, the heir might need legal

---

[68] The digital inheritance is mostly defined as a body of assets and data left behind by a deceased person as well as the corresponding legislation in this matter, Nemeth and Morais Carvalho, 'Digital Inheritance in the European Union' [2017] *Journal of European Consumer and Market Law*, 253.

[69] Müller-Christmann, in *BeckOK BGB*, § 1922, para. 24; Preuß, in *BeckOGK BGB*, § 1922, para. 175; Preuß, 'Digitaler Nachlass – Vererbbarkeit eines Kontos bei einem sozialen Netzwerk' [2018] *Neue Juristische Wochenschrift*, 3146 (3148); Leipold, in *MüKoBGB*, § 1922, para. 19; Lieder, in *Erman BGB*, § 1922, para. 8 et seq.

[70] BGH 12 July 2018 – III ZR 183/17 – (2006) *Neue Juristische Wochenschrift*, 3178; see also Wüsthof, 'Germany's Supreme Court Rules in Favour of 'Digital Inheritance'' [2018] *Journal of European Consumer and Market Law*, 205; Mackenrodt, 'Digital Inheritance in Germany' [2018] *Journal of European Consumer and Market Law*, 41; Resta, 'Digital Inheritance', in De Franceschi and Schulze (eds), *Digital Revolution – New Challenges for Law* (2019), 88, para. 22 et seq.

[71] Mikk and Sein, 'Digital Inheritance: Heirs' Right to Claim Access to Online Accounts under Estonian Law' (2018) 27 *Juridica International*, 117 (119 et seq., 127).

§ 5. Intermediaries of Secondary Crypto Trade

certificates stipulating his or her position as the legally rightful heir and the actual death of the deceased.[72]

In the **United Kingdom**, it is recommended to include **lists of digital accounts and passwords to assert the deceased's will**, even though this might create conflicts with existing terms of service.[73] From a **Belgian** perspective, legal relationships with providers of digital services constitute contracts. According to Art. 1122 of the Belgian Civil Code, the deceased's **legal successor inherits every contract** the deceased formerly concluded, unless the contract's wording or nature prevents it. Thus, it is argued that digital service contracts and therefore digital assets can be part of the estate.[74] An accompanying right to information would only be consequent. In the end, in every jurisdiction with inheritance laws based on the principle of universal succession, these considerations should be transferable.

Since contracts with a token trading platform primarily grant property rights positions with almost no personal content, these **considerations can be transferred accordingly**. Since the heir obtains the contractual rights and obligations of the deceased and takes his or her place, he/she has a right of access to the account and consequently also a corresponding right to information.

The platform agreement might also state an obligation to **maintain permanent accessibility of the platform's website** for users. In many cases, however, intermediaries try to exclude the permanent accessibility in their general terms and conditions in order to avoid claims, e.g., for compensation, by users in the event of technical issues.[75] This includes access to the platform's structure and, particularly with off-chain intermediaries, the retrieval of account balances.

Additionally, the platform and especially off-chain intermediaries have extensive **obligations to cooperate**. Due to the fiduciary elements of the underlying contracts, the platform is obligated to manage its users' account balances. To ensure the actual execution of user contracts, it is imperative that the off-chain intermediary adjusts the account balances according to the contract concluded between users.

However, not only the platform, but also the **user** may be subject to additional contractual obligations. In this respect, the user must comply with the **restrictions and trading conditions** set forth by the trading platform in (permissible) general terms and conditions to enable correct transaction processing. But, as the website interface, i.e. the design of the homepage and its inherent restrictions, is usually adapted to the platform's general terms and conditions, users are mostly not able to diverge.[76] Additionally, the user must keep **his or her password secret** and is obligated to **provide correct data** upon registration on the intermediary's website.[77]

---

[72] From a Dutch perspective Berlee, 'Digital Inheritance in the Netherlands' [2017] *Journal of European Consumer and Market Law*, 256 (260).

[73] Harbinja, 'Digital Inheritance in the United Kingdom' [2017] *Journal of European Consumer and Market Law*, 253 (254 et seq.).

[74] Maeschaelck, 'Digital Inheritance in Belgium' [2018] *Journal of European Consumer and Market Law*, 37 (40).

[75] Thus Biallaß, 'Aspekte des Vertragsschlusses bei Internet-Auktionen', in Borges (ed), *Rechtsfragen der Internet-Auktion* (2014), 13 (19).

[76] Možina, 'Retail business, platform services and information duties' [2016] *Journal of European Consumer and Market Law*, 25 (26); Grundmann and Hacker, 'Digital Technology as a Challenge to European Contract Law' (2017) 13 *European Review of Contract Law*, 255 (274).

[77] Biallaß, 'Das Vertragsverhältnis zwischen Plattformbetreiber und Nutzer', in Borges (ed), *Rechtsfragen der Internet-Auktion* (2014), 61 (67 et seq.); for formal requirements upon registration from an Estonian perspective see Kull, 'The Adequacy of Existing Estonian Laws for the Platform Economy' [2016] *Journal of European Consumer and Market Law*, 52 (53).

D. Defaults and Breach of Contractual Obligations

58   As in any other legal relationship, the parties of a contract might not be able or willing to fulfil their obligations. Hence, defaults or other kinds of breach of contract may occur. Within the crypto-trade business, a variety of different legal contracts between different parties exist and, thus, may be breached. However, only those infringements resulting from the contractual relationships between the intermediaries and their users are of further interest in this chapter. As for contracts between users, claims against the platform operator can only be raised if the terms and conditions of the platform agreement contain any specific provisions such as **warranties or guarantees**.[78] Therefore, the trading platform generally is **not liable** for any **defaults in user to user relationships**.[79] Since users and platforms conclude at least one legal relationship, i.e. the platform agreement, an underlying contractual basis always exists. However, a distinction must be made between platform categories.

I. On-Chain-Intermediary

1. Trading Platform

59   As for centralised crypto-to-crypto and crypto-to-fiat-exchanges, there are no specific characteristics which need to be considered. In those cases, the platform is the contractual partner in user transactions. Therefore, general rules apply, and the platform is **liable for any contractual interruptions, defaults or a breach of contract**.[80] However, the situation differs for decentralised platforms. If users conclude contracts and transactions via the platform, the decentralised exchange gains the right to a **transaction fee**. In this case, it might be relevant to state the exact time upon which the intermediary is entitled to its fee. This is particularly relevant if a user contract concluded via the platform is **not executed**. Therefore, it is necessary to determine which service provided by the intermediary constitutes its right to the fee. If the transaction fee is granted just for any kind of matchmaking between users, the platform would be entitled with the conclusion of the user contract. If, on the other hand, the fee is paid for a successful transaction and, thus, as a fee for the platform's assistance in the process, the digital infrastructure or confirmations, it can only be demanded if these services are provided in a successful transaction. If the users fail to execute, the platform did not provide billable services.

60   This question needs to be resolved by **interpreting** the contracts concluded between the intermediary and the user. Generally, the platform will desire a claim for the transaction fee upon **effective conclusion of contract** between the users. The platform will regularly not be willing to accept the risk of the contract's execution, which depends

---

[78] Maultzsch, 'Contractual Liability of Online Platform Operators: European Proposals and established Principles' [2018] *European Review of Contract Law*, 209 (211); Možina, 'Retail business, platform services and information duties' [2016] *Journal of European Consumer and Market Law*, 25 (29) see also Busch, Schulte-Nölke, Wiewiórowska-Domagalska and Zoll, 'The Rise of the Platform Economy: A New Challenge for EU Consumer Law?' [2016] *Journal of European Consumer and Market Law*, 3 (8 et seq.), discussing additional criteria for a liability of the platform.

[79] Kull, 'The Adequacy of Existing Estonian Laws for the Platform Economy' [2016] *Journal of European Consumer and Market Law*, 52 (56); Twigg-Flesner, 'Legal and Policy Responses to Online Platforms – A UK Perspective', in Blaurock, Schmidt-Kessel and Erler (eds), *Plattformen* (2018), 139 (158).

[80] See in detail Tereszkiewicz, 'Digital Platforms: Regulation and Liability in the EU Law' (2018) 26 *European Review of Private Law*, 903 (908 et seq.).

2. Users

From a user's point of view, claims against the intermediary may arise in the event of **contractual infringements**. However, the user can only obtain claims against the platform if the claim itself arises from an actual legal contract with the intermediary. Therefore, the user only has additional claims against the intermediary if the default occurs in this contractual relationship, i.e. the platform agreement. In the case of default or breach of contract within any user (token exchange) contract, the user must adhere to his or her respective contractual partner. General claims against the intermediary are mostly unfeasible, unless additional contractual agreements, for example in the form of guarantees, have been made.[81]

If the user frequents an on-chain-intermediary, who records the users' account balances with a public key on the blockchain, there is a risk that stored tokens might get lost due to a **cyberattack**. In this respect, the user might want to **claim damages** from the on-chain intermediary. But the user can only substantiate claims for damages if the intermediary did not take sufficient precautions against such cyberattacks. This might be the case if the platform had unsuitable or insufficient security measures.

These cases show similarities to the (in-)famous cyberattack on a blockchain platform called '**The DAO**'. 'The DAO' was one of the most successful crowdfunding projects of all time. It was launched via the Ethereum blockchain and quickly raised funds in the amount of about 60 million EUR. However, 'The DAO' was hacked due to a breach in the programming and the investors' funds could only be secured with a so-called **hard fork**.[82] As a further example, the cryptocurrency exchange **Binance** shows that secondary crypto-trading platforms are not spared by hackers. Binance became the target of a cyberattack in early May 2019. In the process, the crypto exchange suffered a loss of 7,000 Bitcoins which equalled about 40 million USD at the time. The stolen Bitcoins had been stored in a so-called hot wallet, which is connected to the Internet.[83]

Currently, no national jurisdiction stipulates special liability for damages caused by cyberattacks on blockchain networks.[84] Therefore, a solution must be found via the general

---

[81] Regarding the discussion on extended liability of platforms Maultzsch, 'Verantwortlichkeit der Plattformbetreiber', in Blaurock, Schmidt-Kessel and Erler (eds), *Plattformen* (2018), 223 (224 et seq.); Maultzsch, 'Contractual Liability of Online Platform Operators: European Proposals and established Principles' [2018] *European Review of Contract Law*, 209 (211); Možina, 'Retail business, platform services and information duties' [2016] *Journal of European Consumer and Market Law*, 25 (29) see also Busch, Schulte-Nölke, Wiewiórowska-Domagalska and Zoll, 'The Rise of the Platform Economy: A New Challenge for EU Consumer Law?' [2016] *Journal of European Consumer and Market Law*, 3 (8 et seq.), discussing additional criteria for a liability of the platform.

[82] For more information about 'The DAO' and the respective cyberattack see Mehar and others, 'Understanding a Revolutionary and Flawed Grand Experiment in Blockchain: The DAO Attack' (2017) 21 *Journal of Cases on Information Technology*, 19 et seq.

[83] Cf. Böhm, 'Binance loses Bitcoin worth 40 million dollars', available at https://www.spiegel.de/netzwelt/web/binance-populaere-kryptoboerse-verliert-bitcoin-im-wert-von-40-millionen-dollar-a-1266307.html (accessed 30.3.2021); Bernegg, 'Crypto exchange hacked!', available at https://www.deraktionaer.de/artikel/aktien/krypto-boerse-binance-gehackt-die-wichtigsten-fragen-und-antworten-477580.html (accessed 30.3.2021).

[84] Weber, 'Liability in the Internet of Things' [2017] *Journal of European Consumer and Market Law*, 207 (209); for a legal criminal point of view Drăgan, 'Illegal Access to a Computer System from the Standpoint of the Current Criminal Code' (2019) 23 *Journal of Legal Studies*, 33–43.

provisions of the respective national law of obligations, contract or in some cases tort law.[85] In any event, the intermediary would be liable for user tokens lost through such attacks. Insufficient security measures generally lead to **breach of duty** and **liability for damages.** In practical terms, users' losses are usually replaced at least by the larger, reputable intermediaries. To hedge risks, explicitly of cyberattacks, Binance launched a so-called **Secure Asset Fund for Users** (SAFU) in July 2018, in which 10 % of its transaction fees are collected in a separate 'cold', i.e. offline, wallet. Those funds are deemed a **contingency reserve** to compensate losses explicitly caused by unforeseeable cyberattacks.[86]

II. Off-Chain Intermediary

65   In general, there are no substantial legal differences between on-chain and off-chain intermediaries with respect to further obligations. In these cases, **general legal rules for breach of contract** apply as well. Since the transactions are not tracked via blockchain, but only through bookkeeping of the intermediary, off-chain intermediaries do not have similar problems of unwinding contracts as on-chain intermediaries. If a user wants to withdraw from or terminate the contract, the tokens can be **refunded** without further ado. The off-chain intermediary is also contractually obliged to do so. In advance of a refund, the off-chain intermediary can demand proof of the (legitimate) withdrawal. But since the users interact exclusively via the platform, this will not be an obstacle: Either the platform's infrastructure provides a corresponding mechanism or communication between users can serve as proof.

66   From a user's perspective, claims against the platform may primarily arise as **claims for damages** due to the loss of user tokens. Although tokens only exist on a book-keeping level and are only stored as a booking status on the off-chain intermediary's website, the equivalent of the tokens allocated to the users is often actually held by the off-chain intermediary. Depending on the type of wallet chosen for these 'safety' tokens, involuntary losses are possible as well. For example, cold wallets can simply be stolen or lost. Additionally, hot wallets can be hacked. Depending on the specific contractual obligations of the platform agreement, the user could have claims for damages or an unlimited contractual redemption claim against the intermediary.

E. General Terms and Conditions

67   By registering on the platform, the user is forced to accept a comprehensive catalogue of **general terms and conditions.** These terms are pre-formulated and unilaterally provided by the platform operator. The user has no influence on their substance. Therefore, they qualify as contractual terms which have not been individually negotiated according to Art. 3 para. 1 and 2 of the GTC-Directive. They become part of the platform contract between user and intermediary and define the rights and obligations of the parties in more detail.

68   Lately, the EU released the Regulation on promoting fairness and transparency for business users of online intermediation services (**P2B-Regulation**).[87] The Regulation

---

[85] For an Indian perspective on cyberattacks Aravindakshan, 'Cyberattacks: a look at evidentiary thresholds in International Law' [2020] *Indian Journal of International Law*, available at https://doi.org/10.1007/s40901-020-00113-0 (accessed 30.3.2021).

[86] Cf. the description of SAFU, Binance-Academy Secure Asset Funds for Users (SAFU), available at https://www.binance.vision/glossary/secure-asset-fund-for-users (accessed 30.3.2021).

[87] Regulation (EU) No. 2019/1150.

not only reaffirms the need for terms and conditions drafted in **plain and intelligible language**. It also redefines additional obligations considering availability of said terms and conditions as well as the availability of information regarding any respective changes. Any non-compliant provisions are deemed null and void according to Art. 3 para. 3 P2B-Regulation.[88] However, the Regulation is **limited to platform-to-business relations**. Thus, the Regulation will not have a deep impact on secondary crypto trade. Nevertheless, the extension of a fairness control of standard terms to business to business relationships is a remarkable new step.[89]

The provisions of the general terms and conditions do not simply state the rights and obligations of the user or the intermediary. Rather, they set an additional framework for any future transaction concluded and implemented via the platform's infrastructure. These so-called framework agreements contain binding obligations which may result in the formation of further contracts, usually between the same parties, whose provisions are determined by the (firstly formed) framework agreement.[90] Therefore, the legal implications for any subsequent agreements between user and platform are determined by the platform's terms and conditions. This **'legal framework'** enables the intermediary to set all terms for any future contracts carried out and concluded in its ongoing business relationship with its user.[91] **69**

Additionally, further provisions stated by the general terms and conditions **have direct impact** on user contracts. Although the platform's general terms and conditions accepted within the platform agreement are set between intermediary and user, they directly affect user's legal transactions (→ para. 57, 73). If user contracts or legally relevant behaviour of users' need to be interpreted, the platform's framework can be an indication and need to be considered when interpreting the behaviour of and contractual relationships between users.[92] Thus, the platform's provisions are indirectly included into these contracts, unless the users explicitly deviate from these regulations.[93] **70**

---

[88] In more detail Busch, 'Towards Fairness and Transparency in the Platform Economy? A First Look at the P2B Regulation', in De Franceschi and Schulze (eds), *Digital Revolution – New Challenges for Law* (2019), 57 et seq.; Anagnostopoulou, 'The EU Digital Single Market and the Platform Economy', in Nikas (ed), *Economic Growth in the European Union: Analyzing SME and Investment Policies* (2020), 43 (48 et seq.); Busch, Dannemann, Schulte-Nölke, Wiewiórowska-Domagalska and Zoll, 'The ELI Model Rules on Online Platforms' [2020] *Journal of European Consumer and Market Law*, 61 (64 et seq.).

[89] Falkhofen, 'Car Data Platforms and the EU Acquis for Digital Services – How the digital transformation of the car interacts with EU data protection, cybersecurity and competition law' [2018] *Computer Law Review International*, 165 (169 et seq.).

[90] Wójtowicz, 'Law applicable to Distribution Contracts and Contracts of Sale–Relationship between Framework Agreement and Application Contracts' (2018) 14 *European Review of Contract Law*, 138 (143) with further references.

[91] Maultzsch, 'Contractual Liability of Online Platform Operators: European Proposals and established Principles' [2018] *European Review of Contract Law*, 209 (211); Grundmann and Hacker, 'Digital Technology as a Challenge to European Contract Law' (2017) 13 *European Review of Contract Law*, 255 (273 et seq.); from a UK perspective Twigg-Flesner, 'Legal and Policy Responses to Online Platforms – A UK Perspective', in Blaurock, Schmidt-Kessel and Erler (eds), *Plattformen* (2018), 139 (147 et seq.); Možina, 'Retail business, platform services and information duties' [2016] *Journal of European Consumer and Market Law*, 25 (26).

[92] Similar Zumbansen, 'Contracting in the Internet: German Contract Law and Internet Auctions' (2001) 2 *German Law Journal*, E1, marg. 6 et. seq.; for German rulings see BGH 15 February 2017 – VIII ZR 59/16 – (2017) *Neue Juristische Wochenschrift*, 1660 (1661); 10 December 2014 – VIII ZR 90/14 – (2015) *Neue Juristische Wochenschrift*, 1009 (1010); 24 August 2016 – VIII ZR 100/15 – (2017) *Neue Juristische Wochenschrift*, 468 (468 et seq.).

[93] For a detailed discussion on the effects of the general terms and conditions of a platform operator/intermediary in the user relationship Meyer, 'Einbeziehung und Geltungsbereich von AGB', in Borges (ed), *Rechtsfragen der Internet-Auktion* (2014), 36 (46 et seq.); see also Grundmann and Hacker, 'Digital Technology as a Challenge to European Contract Law' (2017) 13 *European Review of Contract Law*, 255 (274) and Engert, 'Digitale Plattformen' (2018) *Archiv für die civilistische Praxis* 218, 304 (344 et seq.).

I. Frequently Used General Terms and Conditions within Platform Agreements

71 Platform agreements between intermediary and user often introduce clauses which (should) lead to **limitations or exclusions of liability** for the benefit of the platform. These clauses might be regarded as unfair according to Art. 3 para. 1 GTC-Directive and its Annex I, para. 1 (a) and (b). Therefore, these terms are subject to legal considerations for general terms and conditions,[94] without any particularities. In this context, general terms and conditions may be used to limit or describe the intermediary's obligations in greater detail. Terms stating that the intermediary does not provide any advisory services were already popular and frequently used within crowdfunding schemes and are likewise implemented by token trading platforms.[95] Such terms are used to limit the platform's liability: If it is not obligated to provide a specific service, it cannot be held liable in case of 'breach of duty'. Whether these clauses can effectively limit the platform's obligations has not yet been conclusively determined by the courts. However, scholars doubt the lawfulness of this practice, especially if the platform creates expectations about a specific obligation.[96]

72 The intermediary's general terms and conditions will also often contain agreements on jurisdiction or the right to choose a jurisdiction. The validity of such clauses must be assessed in each individual case (→ § 3 para. 17 et seqq, 46).

II. General Terms and Conditions with Implication for User Contracts

73 As mentioned above, the general terms and conditions often contain provisions with **implications for the contracts** concluded exclusively **between users**. For instance, most platforms regularly determine which behaviour constitutes a binding offer. In practical terms, users will mostly not be able to deviate from these provisions. The interface of the intermediary's website is regularly programmed accordingly. Therefore, an arbitrary deviation from the intermediary's specifications is hardly feasible.[97]

---

[94] For the general admissibility of liability exclusions from a European perspective Loos, 'Standard terms for the use of the Apple App Store and the Google Play Store' [2016] *Journal of European Consumer and Market Law*, 10 (13); from a German perspective Grundmann, in *MüKoBGB*, § 276, para. 183 et seq. with additional references; see Schulze, in Dannemann and Schulze (eds), *German Civil Code (BGB)*, §§ 276 para. 12.

[95] Kull, 'The Adequacy of Existing Estonian Laws for the Platform Economy' [2016] *Journal of European Consumer and Market Law*, 52 (55); similar considerations apply to Airbnb, see Mak, 'Private Law Perspectives on Platform Services' [2016] *Journal of European Consumer and Market Law*, 19 (20 et seq.).

[96] Cf. on this problem in the context of crowdfunding Hoch, 'Crowdfunding, Bitcoins, Initial Coin Offerings – Rechtliche Herausforderungen für den Gesetzgeber im Zeitalter der Digitalisierung', in Husemann and others (eds), *Strukturwandel und Privatrecht* (2018), 215 (221 et seq.) with additional references; Spindler, 'Crowdfunding und Crowdinvesting – Sach- und kollisionsrechtliche Einordnung sowie Überlagerung durch die E-Commerce-Richtlinie' [2017] *Zeitschrift für Bankrecht und Bankwirtschaft*, 129 (135) with additional references; similar Meschkowski and Wilhelmi, 'Investorenschutz im Crowdinvesting' [2013] *Betriebs-Berater*, 1411 (1414); Sørensen, 'Private Law Perspectives on Platform Services' [2016] *Journal of European Consumer and Market Law*, 15 (18) for Uber, but transferable to this specific topic.

[97] Schweitzer, 'Digitale Plattformen als private Gesetzgeber: Ein Perspektivwechsel für die europäische 'Plattform-Regulierung'' [2019] *Zeitschrift für Europäisches Privatrecht*, 1 (3 et seq.); Možina, 'Retail business, platform services and information duties' [2016] *Journal of European Consumer and Market Law*, 25 (26); Hellgardt, 'Privatautonome Modifikation der Regeln zu Abschluss, Zustandekommen und Wirksamkeit des Vertrags' (2013) *Archiv für die civilistische Praxis* 213, 760 (774); Engert, 'Digitale Plattformen' (2018) *Archiv für die civilistische Praxis* 218, 304 (320).

§ 5. *Intermediaries of Secondary Crypto Trade*

Many general terms and conditions **prohibit the user to withdraw from or unwind** exchange/purchase agreements. This is common practice in blockchain-related platforms and transactions. The technical reason for this frequently used term is the fundamental immutability of the blockchain: Once a transaction has been included in a block, it is no longer possible to retroactively delete it. The inclusion of a transaction on the blockchain is therefore permanent. Instead, a reversal (→ § 1 para. 14) can only be achieved by means of a second, opposing transaction, which in turn incurs transaction costs.[98]

To avoid these practical difficulties and additional costs, especially on-chain intermediaries include provisions that **exclude the users' right of withdrawal**. However, such clauses can be problematic under the GTC-Directive if the user qualifies as a consumer. As a result, such terms can be deemed unfair according to Art. 3 para. 1 GTC-Directive. More specifically, a term shall be regarded as unfair if, contrary to the requirement of good faith, it causes a significant imbalance in the parties' rights and obligations arising under the contract, to the detriment of the consumer. The Annex of the GTC-Directive lists examples for unfair terms. For instance, a clause which enables the supplier of services to increase his or her price without giving the consumer the corresponding right to cancel the contract, is deemed void. The actual evaluation is subject to a case-by-case decision and deeply influenced by national law. Therefore, depending on individual circumstances, single terms might be non-binding for the user according to Art. 6 para. 1 GTC-Directive.

74

75

---

[98] In more detail to unwinding blockchain-based contracts Meyer, 'Stopping the Unstoppable: Termination and Unwinding of Smart Contracts' [2020] *Journal of European Consumer and Market Law*, 17 (20 et seq.).

§ 6
Data Protection

Literature: Article 29 Data Protection Working Party, 'Opinion 4/2007 on the concept of personal data' (20.7.2007), WP 136, 01248/07/EN, available at https://ec.europa.eu/justice/article-29/documentation/opinion-recommendation/files/2007/wp136_en.pdf (accessed 26.8.2021); Article 29 Data Protection Working Party, 'Opinion 1/2010 on the concepts of 'controller' and 'processor'' (16.2.2010), WP 169, 00264/10/EN, available at https://ec.europa.eu/justice/article-29/documentation/opinion-recommendation/files/2010/wp169_en.pdf (accessed 26.8.2021); Bechtolf and Vogt, 'Datenschutz in der Blockchain – Eine Frage der Technik – Technologische Hürden und konzeptionelle Chancen' (2018) 8 *Zeitschrift für Datenschutz*, 66; Berger, 'Blockchain – Mythos oder Technologie für die öffentliche Verwaltung?' (2017) 132 *Deutsches Verwaltungsblatt*, 1271; Blockchain Bundesverband, 'Blockchain, data protection, and the GDPR' (25.5.2018), available at https://www.bundesblock.de/wp-content/uploads/2019/01/GDPR_Position_Paper_v1.0.pdf (accessed 26.8.2021); Böhme and Pesch, 'Technische Grundlagen und datenschutzrechtliche Fragen der Blockchain-Technologie' (2017) 41 *Datenschutz und Datensicherheit*, 473; Commission Nationale Informatique & Libertés (CNIL), 'Blockchain – Solutions for a responsible use of the blockchain in the context of personal data' (2018), available at https://www.cnil.fr/sites/default/files/atoms/files/blockchain_en.pdf (accessed 26.8.2021); Drescher, *Blockchain Basics – A Non-Technical Introduction in 25 Steps* (Springer Science+Business Media, New York, 2017); Ehmann and Selmayr (eds), *Kommentar zur Datenschutz-Grundverordnung (DS-GVO)* (2nd edn, Munich, 2018); Erbguth, 'Datenschutz auf öffentlichen Blockchains' (2018), available at https://erbguth.ch/Erbguth_DatenschutzBlockchains.pdf (accessed 26.8.2021); Erbguth and Fasching, 'Wer ist Verantwortlicher einer Bitcoin-Transaktion? – Anwendbarkeit der DS-GVO auf die Bitcoin-Blockchain' (2017) 7 *Zeitschrift für Datenschutz*, 560; European Economic Area Joint Committee, 'Decision No 154/2018' (6.7.2018), available at https://www.efta.int/sites/default/files/documents/legal-texts/eea/other-legal-documents/adopted-joint-committee-decisions/2018%20-%20English/154-2018.pdf (accessed 26.8.2021); European Union Blockchain Observatory and Forum, 'Blockchain and the GDPR' (18.10.2018), available at https://www.eublockchainforum.eu/sites/default/files/reports/20181016_report_gdpr.pdf (accessed 26.8.2021); Feiler, Forgó and Weigl, *The EU General Data Protection Regulation (GDPR): A Commentary* (Globe Law and Business Ltd, UK, 2018); Finck, 'Blockchain and the General Data Protection Regulation' (2019), available at https://www.europarl.europa.eu/RegData/etudes/STUD/2019/634445/EPRS_STU(2019)634445_EN.pdf (accessed 26.8.2021); Finck, 'Blockchains and Data Protection in the European Union' (2018) 4 European Data Protection Law Review, 17; Gassner, 'Blockchain in EU E-Health – Blocked by the barrier of data protection?' (2018) 2 *Compliance Elliance Journal*, 3; Gola (ed), *Kommentar zur Datenschutzgrundverordnung (DS-GVO)* (2nd edn, Munich, 2018); Haffke, Fromberger and Zimmermann, 'Cryptocurrencies and anti-money laundering: the shortcomings of the fifth AML Directive (EU) and how to address them' (2019) 21 *Journal of Business Research*, 125, available at https://doi.org/10.1057/s41261-019-00101-4 (accessed 26.8.2021); Hofert, 'Blockchain-Profiling – Verarbeitung von Blockchain-Daten innerhalb und außerhalb der Netzwerke' (2017) 7 *Zeitschrift für Datenschutz*, 161; Janicki and Saive, 'Privacy by Design in Blockchain-Netzwerken – Verantwortlichkeit und datenschutzkonforme Ausgestaltung von Blockchains' (2019) 9 *Zeitschrift für Datenschutz*, 251; Krupar and Strassemeyer, 'Datenschutz auf der Blockchain – die Innovationsfeindlichkeit der DS-GVO' (2018) *Deutsche Stiftung für Recht und Informatik Tagungsband*, 343; Kühling and Buchner (eds), *Kommentar zur Datenschutzgrundverordnung (DS-GVO) und zum Bundesdatenschutzgesetz (BDSG)* (3rd edn, Munich, 2020); Kühling, Klar and Sackmann, *Datenschutzrecht* (5th edn, C.F. Müller, Heidelberg, 2021); Kuner, Bygrave and Docksey (eds), *The EU General Data Protection Regulation (GDPR) – A Commentary* (UK, 2020); Martini and Weinzierl, 'Die Blockchain-Technologie und das Recht auf Vergessenwerden – Zum Dilemma zwischen Nicht-Vergessen-Können und Vergessen-Müssen' (2017) 36 *Neue Zeitschrift für Verwaltungsrecht*, 1251; Pesch and Böhme, 'Datenschutz trotz öffentlicher Blockchain? – Chancen und Risiken bei der Verfolgung und Prävention Bitcoin-bezogener Straftaten' (2017) 41 *Datenschutz und Datensicherheit*, 93; Peters, 'Strafbarkeitsrisiken beim Betrieb einer Blockchain – Als Transaktionen verkleidete strafrechtlich relevante Daten' (2018) 21 *Multimedia und Recht*, 644; Quiel, 'Blockchain-Technologie im Fokus von Art. 8 GRC und DS-GVO – Ein Zwiespalt zwischen Innovation und unionalem Datenschutzrecht?' (2018) 42 *Datenschutz und Datensicherheit*, 566; Schmid, *Die Nutzung von Cloud-Diensten durch kleine und mittelständische Unternehmen – Eine datenschutzrechtliche Betrachtung der Auslagerung von Kunden-, Personal- und Mandantendaten* (Duncker & Humblot, Berlin, 2017); Schrey and Thalhofer, 'Rechtliche Aspekte der Blockchain' (2017) 70 *Neue Juristische Wochenschrift*, 1431; The Washington Post, 'Venezuela launches the 'petro', its cryptocurrency' (2018), available at https://www.washingtonpost.com/news/worldviews/wp/2018/02/20/venezuela-launches-the-petro-its-cryptocurrency/

§ 6. Data Protection

(accessed 26.8.2021); World Food Programme, 'What is 'blockchain' and how is it connected to fighting hunger?' (2017), available at https://insight.wfp.org/what-is-blockchain-and-how-is-it-connected-to-fighting-hunger-7f1b42da9fe (accessed 26.8.2021).

Outline

	para.
A. Data Protection Challenges in a Blockchain	1
B. Data Processing Operations	10
I. Management of User Data	10
II. Initiation of Transactions	14
III. Assignment of the Transaction by the Recipient	16
C. Applicability of the GDPR	17
I. Material Scope	17
II. Territorial Scope	27
D. The Roles of the Participants under the GDPR	33
I. Participants under the GDPR	34
II. Central Blockchain	38
III. Trading Platforms	41
IV. Decentralized Blockchain	44
V. Assignment of the Transaction by the Recipient	54
E. Lawfulness of Processing	55
I. Consent	58
II. Necessity for the Performance of a Contract	61
III. Necessity for the Purposes of the Legitimate Interests	67
IV. Processing on Behalf	69
V. Transfers of Personal Data to Third Countries	74
F. Data Subjects' Rights	79
I. Data Subjects' Rights and the Blockchain Technology	79
II. Right of Access	83
III. Right to Rectification	84
IV. Right to Erasure and Right to Be Forgotten	86
G. Data Protection Supervision and Consequences of Violations under the GDPR	89
I. Data Protection Supervision	89
II. Remedies, Liability and Penalties	91
H. Possibility of Designing a Data Protection Compliant Blockchain	93
I. Exclusion of the Applicability of the GDPR	94
II. Enabling the Enforcement of Data Subjects' Rights	99
I. Conclusion	103

A. Data Protection Challenges in a Blockchain

Blockchain technology poses major challenges for data protection law in the European Union[1]. The reason for this is the **decentralized structure** of the blockchain technology and its characteristic feature that the blocks stored in a blockchain can basically neither be changed nor deleted retroactively (→ § 1, para. 1, 5). In May 2018, data protection law in the European Union underwent the most far-reaching change in recent decades with the application of the Regulation (EU) 2016/679 of the European Parliament and of the Council of 27 April 2016 on the protection of

---

[1] Whenever data protection law in the European Union or the Member States of the European Union is mentioned in this article, this also refers to data protection law and the Member States of the European Economic Area, as the GDPR was incorporated into the EEA Agreement by Decision of 6 July 2018, European Economic Area Joint Committee, 'Decision No 154/2018' (6.7.2018), available at https://beck-link.de/65r4r (accessed 26.8.2021).

natural persons with regard to the processing of personal data and on the free movement of such data and repealing Directive 95/46/EC, the so-called **EU General Data Protection Regulation (GDPR)**. The GDPR is primarily designed for data processing operations in central systems. Although data processing operations in decentralized systems are also regulated by the GDPR, provisions specifically designed to address the processing of data in decentralized systems cannot be found in the GDPR.[2]

2   The change of the legal instrument from the Data Protection Directive to a regulation directly applicable in the Member States was supposed to lead to a **full harmonization** of data protection law in the European Union.[3] The 'patchwork'[4] of the divergent data protection standards previously existing in the individual Member States is to be dissolved by the GDPR. Therefore, since 25 May 2018, uniform data protection provisions have been applicable in principle to all Member States.[5] However, it is to be expected that the patchwork of divergent data protection standards cannot be completely dissolved, as the GDPR provides for a large number of **opening clauses**. Where the GDPR provides for opening clauses, national legislators may adopt their own provisions or specify provisions of the GDPR as long as they do not violate the basic principles of the GDPR.[6]

3   The GDPR lays down rules relating to the protection of natural persons with regard to the processing of personal data and rules relating to the free movement of personal data, Art. 1(1) GDPR. These two objectives of the GDPR are of equal importance.[7] The **term 'data protection'** is easily misunderstood, because 'data protection' is not the protection of data, but rather the protection of natural persons, the so-called 'data subjects', against unlawful processing of their data.[8] In addition, the GDPR aims to create a uniform level of protection to ensure the functioning of the European internal market through the free movement of data.[9] The provisions of the GDPR are based on principles which are laid down in Art. 5 GDPR. These principles include the lawfulness, fairness and transparency of processing, purpose limitation of data, data minimisation, accuracy of data, storage limitation, integrity, confidentiality, and accountability.

4   Although blockchain technology has existed for several years and has become widely known, particularly in the context of the Bitcoin[10] blockchain, the European Union's institutions have failed in the legislative process of the GDPR to create provisions that specifically address data processing operations in decentralized systems. Since the provisions of the GDPR are basically designed for central data processing systems, it is a challenge to subsume data processing operations in a decentralized blockchain under the applicable provisions of the GDPR (→ para. 93 et seqq.).

5   The automatic processing of data naturally takes place in a blockchain. A distinction must be made between several constellations[11], which must be evaluated

---

[2] Finck, 'Blockchains and Data Protection in the European Union' (2018) 4 *European Data Protection Law Review*, 17; Gassner, 'Blockchain in EU E-Health – Blocked by the barrier of data protection?' (2018) 2 *Compliance Elliance Journal*, 3 (15).
[3] Kuner, Bygrave and Docksey, in Kuner, Bygrave and Docksey (eds), *GDPR*, 10 et seq.
[4] Kühling/Raab, in Kühling and Buchner (eds), *DS-GVO*, Introduction para. 41.
[5] Selmayr and Ehmann, in Ehmann and Selmayr (eds), *DS-GVO*, Introduction para. 1.
[6] Kuner, Bygrave and Docksey, in Kuner, Bygrave and Docksey (eds), *GDPR*, 10 et seq.; Feiler, Forgó and Weigl, *The EU General Data Protection Regulation (GDPR): A Commentary* (2018), 17.
[7] Selmayr and Ehmann, in Ehmann and Selmayr (eds), *DS-GVO*, Art. 1, para. 1.
[8] Pötters, in Gola (ed), *DS-GVO*, Art. 1, para. 8.
[9] Ibid, para. 16.
[10] Bitcoin, available at https://bitcoin.org/en/ (accessed 26.8.2021).
[11] Drescher, *Blockchain Basics – A Non-Technical Introduction in 25 Steps* (2017), 213 et seqq.

§ 6. Data Protection

differently when considering data processing operations in a blockchain from the perspective of data protection law. However, there are practically endless possibilities for designing or programming a blockchain within these individual constellations. For this reason, the following explanations can only provide an indication for the assessment of data protection law in a blockchain. Ultimately, it will often be necessary to consider the respective design of a blockchain in each individual case.

A **public permissioned blockchain** as well as a **private permissionless blockchain** and a **private permissioned blockchain** (→ § 1, para. 10 et seqq.) – hereinafter referred to as **central blockchain** – have a central entity. This **central entity** is usually the initiator of the blockchain and grants access authorization for a private blockchain and/or write authorization for a permissioned blockchain. The concept of a blockchain with a central entity actually contradicts the idea underlying the blockchain technology that there should be no central actor. Examples for the use of a central blockchain for the transfer of tokens are the World Food Programme of the United Nations[12], the crypto currency 'Petro' in Venezuela[13] and the interbank trading[14].

In contrast, in a **public permissionless blockchain** (→ § 1, para. 10 et seqq.) – hereinafter referred to as a **decentralized blockchain** – there is no central entity which assumes an organizational or monitoring function. All data processing operations only take place between users, i.e. peer-to-peer (→ § 1, para. 1). The decentralized blockchain is mainly used as a concept for the transfer of tokens, since it corresponds to the ideal image that no central actor should be able to exert an influence on the blockchain and the transactions within the blockchain. Examples of decentralized blockchains are the Bitcoin[15] and the Ethereum[16] blockchain.

Another constellation of a data processing operation in a blockchain is the use of **trading platforms** (cryptocurrency exchanges: fiat-to-crypto exchanges and crypto-to-crypto exchanges, → § 1, para. 90 et seqq.). In the case of transactions carried out by these providers, a distinction must be made as to whether they are only carried out internally within the provider of a trading platform (off-chain, → § 1, para. 96) or actually on a blockchain (on-chain, → § 1, para. 95).

In the following, the data processing operations that take place when using a blockchain to transfer tokens are described first (→ para. 10 et seqq.). This is followed by explanations on the applicability of the GDPR (→ para. 17 et seqq.) and the roles of the participants in a blockchain under the GDPR (→ para. 33 et seqq.). It is then clarified whether the data processing operations in a blockchain are permissible under data protection law (→ para. 55 et seqq.). After that, it is shown what rights the data subjects have and what problems exist regarding the enforcement of these rights when using a blockchain to transfer tokens (→ para. 79 et seqq.). A brief overview of data protection supervision and the legal consequences of data protection violations follows (→ para. 89 et seqq.). Subsequently, it is discussed whether there are possibilities to implement a blockchain in accordance with data protection law (→ para. 93 et seqq.). Finally, a short conclusion follows (→ para. 103).

---

[12] World Food Programme, 'What is 'blockchain' and how is it connected to fighting hunger?' (6.3.2017) available at https://beck-link.de/ey24h (accessed 26.8.2021).
[13] The Washington Post, 'Venezuela launches the 'petro', its cryptocurrency' (21.2.2018), available at https://beck-link.de/3k43z (accessed 26.8.2021).
[14] R3, available at https://www.r3.com/about/ (accessed 26.8.2021).
[15] Bitcoin, available at https://bitcoin.org/en/ (accessed 26.8.2021).
[16] Ethereum, available at https://www.ethereum.org/ (accessed 26.8.2021).

B. Data Processing Operations

I. Management of User Data

10   When using blockchain technology to transfer tokens, data is not only processed during the execution of transactions. Rather, a distinction must be made between various data processing operations in a blockchain. The first processing step takes place when a wallet (→ § 1, para. 25 et seqq.) is created, more precisely when the user's public key and private key (→ § 1, para. 16 et seqq.) are generated. The data processing operations that take place at this time can be summarized under the keyword '**management of user data**'.

11   In the case of a **central blockchain**, the user must regularly register with the central entity with her or his data, for example name and e-mail address, to be able to use the blockchain. During registration, the user's personal data are collected by the central entity, i.e. the user's personal data are processed by the central entity. The truthfulness of the data provided is irrelevant for data protection considerations. The GDPR expressly contains provisions on the treatment of incorrect data.[17]

12   If a user wants to carry out transactions by herself or himself within a **decentralized blockchain**, she or he first needs a wallet. If the user installs the protocol software of a blockchain, this software generates public key and private key via an algorithm. Public key and private key are assigned to the user. Since the software automatically generates public key and private key from the program code of the blockchain and no central entity is involved in the key generation, no processing of user data takes place during this process. If, on the other hand, the user makes use of the services of a **wallet or interface provider** (→ § 1, para. 25 et seqq.), data processing takes place if the respective provider requires the user to register in advance.

13   If the user wants to use a trading platform, a differentiated view must be taken. Only in the case of a **central trading platform** (→ § 1, para. 97 et seq), the user has to register with the provider first. Most of these providers currently already collect personal data from the user during registration. In the case of a **decentralized trading platform** (→ § 1, para. 99 et seq.), no prior registration is necessary. However, the user must link her or his wallet with the trading platform. It is therefore necessary, among other things, to enter the public key, which represents a user's personal data (→ para. 22). Consequently, the provider of a decentralized trading platform also collects data from the user. In the meantime, the providers of fiat-to-crypto exchanges are always legally **obliged to** collect and store their users' personal data; in the case of providers of crypto-to-crypto exchanges, only those that also manage the user's private key are legally obliged to collect and store their users' personal data (→ para. 23).

II. Initiation of Transactions

14   After a blockchain user has downloaded the protocol software, the database of the respective blockchain, in which all transactions that have been carried out so far are stored, is transmitted to her or him by other full nodes (→ § 1, para. 7 et seq.) via peer-to-peer procedure. This database is updated regularly by each full node so that all full nodes have an up-to-date version of the database and can provide it. Each full node

---

[17] Herbst, in Kühling and Buchner (eds), *DS-GVO*, Art. 16, para. 14.

requires the database in order to be able to verify new blocks which should be attached to the blockchain. The transmission of the current version of the blockchain database is a prerequisite for the execution and verification of transactions in the following step.

Further data processing operations take place when **transactions are initiated** within a blockchain. If a transaction is initiated by a blockchain user, the transaction is first announced to all full nodes (→ § 1, para. 19). When the transaction is announced, the transaction data are transmitted as a minimum content. **Transaction data**[18] are the public keys of sender and recipient of a transaction, the transaction ID (→ § 1, para. 24) and the number of tokens being transferred. However, additional content can also be attached to a transaction. These data are called **content data**. Depending on the programming of a blockchain, content data can be, for example, texts, images, programs, etc.[19] If the content data contain personal data of third parties, the processing of the personal data of the third parties also takes place.

III. Assignment of the Transaction by the Recipient

If a transaction takes place within a blockchain to **settle a liability**, the transaction recipient will assign the completed transaction to the transaction sender. However, the **assignment** of transaction data to existing customer data does not take place for every transaction of tokens. An example of such an assignment process is when the transaction recipient runs an online store for goods or services and she or he offers 'payment' with tokens. To be precise, this processing operation takes place outside the blockchain. However, this process is so closely linked to the transaction data within a blockchain that this processing operation will also be considered in this article. Either the transaction sender names a reference number, for example, within the content data of the transaction which is then used by the transaction recipient to assign the transaction to an order that has been placed in the online store, or the transaction sender gives the transaction recipient her or his public key or the transaction ID directly.

C. Applicability of the GDPR

I. Material Scope

In the case of a central blockchain (→ para. 20) and the use of trading platforms (→ para. 23), the **material scope** of the GDPR, Art. 2 GDPR, is generally opened. In contrast, in the case of a decentralized blockchain (→ para. 21 et seqq.), it must be decided on a case-by-case basis whether the GDPR is applicable, although the scope is likely to be opened in the vast majority of cases.

The material scope of the GDPR is opened when **personal data** are **processed** wholly or partly by automated means, Art. 2(1) GDPR. 'Processing' means any operation or set of operations which is performed on personal data or on sets of personal data, including the collection of the personal data, intermediate steps such as transmission or use, and the erasure or destruction of the personal data, Art. 4(2) GDPR. 'Personal data' means any information relating to an **identified or identifiable** natural person, the so-called

---

[18] Finck, 'Blockchains and Data Protection in the European Union' (2018) 4 *European Data Protection Law Review*, 17 (22 et seqq.) differentiates between transaction data stored within the blocks of a blockchain and the public keys of transaction sender and recipient.
[19] Peters, 'Strafbarkeitsrisiken beim Betrieb einer Blockchain – Als Transaktionen verkleidete strafrechtlich relevante Daten' (2018) 21 *Multimedia und Recht*, 644 (645).

'**data subject**', Art. 4(1) GDPR. Data relating to an identified person specifically name that person.[20] If the person is not specifically named, a personal reference may still exist if the person is identifiable. An identifiable natural person is one who can be identified, directly or indirectly, in particular by reference to an identifier such as a name, an identification number, location data, an online identifier or to one or more factors specific to the physical, physiological, genetic, mental, economic, cultural or social identity of that natural person, Art. 4(1) GDPR. A person is therefore identifiable if it is possible to determine the identity of the person, possibly via several intermediate steps.[21] To determine whether a natural person is identifiable, account should be taken of all the **means** reasonably likely to be used either by the controller or by another person to identify the natural person directly or indirectly.[22]

19   However, there has long been disagreement as to when the possibility of identification exists, or whether the possibility of identification available to anybody results in the data controller also being able to assign the data to the data subject.[23] The longstanding controversy[24] as to whether the possibility of identifying a person should be based on objective criteria or only on the subjective knowledge and possibilities of the data processor was not resolved by the GDPR, as many had hoped. In the Breyer ruling on the personal reference of dynamic IP addresses, the CJEU commented on this data protection issue.[25] The CJEU takes a **mediating view**[26] and combines both subjective and objective components. The question of identifiability should not only consider the knowledge and possibilities of the processor herself or himself, but also additional knowledge of third parties that the processor can easily access. In addition, third party information must be included if the processor has legal means to access this data.[27] Based on the CJEU's judgment, the German Federal Court of Justice (Bundesgerichtshof, BGH), ruled[28] that the dynamic IP address constituted personal data because the processor had legal means that could reasonably be used, with the help of third parties, to identify the data subject on the basis of the stored IP address.[29] The question of the identifiability of blockchain users must therefore be based on the CJEU's principles of personal reference.

20   The central entity in a **central blockchain** is comparable to an internet service provider (ISP). Just as every ISP can trace an IP address assigned by it to a user of the ISP, the central entity can establish a connection between the public key and the personal data of the blockchain user, which the user left when registering with the central entity, and thus to the user.[30] The **public key**, which in the case of a blockchain

---

[20] Gola, in Gola (ed), *DS-GVO*, Art. 4, para. 4.
[21] Ibid, para. 5.
[22] Recital 26 GDPR; Article 29 Data Protection Working Party, 'Opinion 4/2007 on the concept of personal data' (20.7.2007), WP 136, 01248/07/EN, available at https://beck-link.de/b8c4y (accessed 26.8.2021).
[23] Gola, in Gola (ed), *DS-GVO*, Art. 4, para. 17.
[24] In detail: Schmid, *Die Nutzung von Cloud-Diensten durch kleine und mittelständische Unternehmen – Eine datenschutzrechtliche Betrachtung der Auslagerung von Kunden-, Personal- und Mandantendaten* (2017), 82 et seqq. with further annotations.
[25] ECJ, Judgment of 19 October 2016, *Breyer*, C-582/14, EU:C:2016:779.
[26] Ibid, para. 39 et seqq.
[27] Ibid, para. 49.
[28] Judgment of the German Federal Court of Justice (BGH) 16.5.2017 – VI ZR 135/13.
[29] Ibid, para. 25 et seq.
[30] Martini and Weinzierl, 'Die Blockchain-Technologie und das Recht auf Vergessenwerden – Zum Dilemma zwischen Nicht-Vergessen-Können und Vergessen-Müssen' (2017) 36 *Neue Zeitschrift für Verwaltungsrecht*, 1251 (1253); Schrey and Thalhofer, 'Rechtliche Aspekte der Blockchain' (2017) 70 *Neue Juristische Wochenschrift*, 1431 (1433).

for the transfer of tokens is an expression of the user's economic identity according to Art. 4(1) GDPR, therefore constitutes **personal data**. With the public key, the central entity can attribute further transaction data and content data to the respective users. Since the central entity can attribute the various data in the central blockchain to the user, these data are personal to the central entity and the material scope of the GDPR is opened.[31]

Any person can participate in a **decentralized blockchain**. There is no central entity that manages the users participating in a blockchain. However, due to CJEU's mediating view, even in the case of a decentralized blockchain, in case of doubt, the data within the blockchain will mainly be **personal** and thus the material scope of the GDPR will be opened.[32]

The transaction and content data of a decentralized blockchain can be viewed by any person. Since, according to the CJEU's mediating view, the identifiability of a person is also given if the processor is able to attribute the data to a person with **additional knowledge** obtained through reasonable effort, there is a certain probability that third parties can establish a link between a public key and other data making the person identifiable by using Big Data applications with reasonable effort.[33] The user can avoid this association by generating a new public and private key for each transaction. But even then, Big Data applications can recognize certain patterns and may be able to establish a link between transactions and the people involved.[34] If there is even the slightest chance that third parties will be able to establish the connection between the public key and a user, the data processing operations within the blockchain are within the scope of the GDPR because of the high degree of protection of the user's **informational self-determination**.

If the blockchain user uses **trading platforms**, these providers can also connect the public key with other data of the user, which the user has to provide, for example, when registering with central trading platforms, and thus establish the **personal reference**.[35] With the adoption of the **Fifth Anti-Money Laundering Directive**[36], which came into force on 9 July 2018 and had to be implemented in national law by 10 January 2020, all providers of fiat-to-crypto exchanges and providers of crypto-to-crypto exchanges that also manage the user's private key are now subject to the Anti-Money Laundering Directive.[37] Whereas it was previously left to the providers of such services to determine

---

[31] For the same result, see Janicki and Saive, 'Privacy by Design in Blockchain-Netzwerken – Verantwortlichkeit und datenschutzkonforme Ausgestaltung von Blockchains' (2019) 9 *Zeitschrift für Datenschutz*, 251 (252); Schrey and Thalhofer, 'Rechtliche Aspekte der Blockchain' (2017) 70 *Neue Juristische Wochenschrift*, 1431 (1433).

[32] See also German Federal Court of Justice (BGH) 16.5.2017 – VI ZR 135/13 – with notes from Bierekoven, 'Anmerkung zu einer Entscheidung des BGH (Urteil vom 16.5.2017 – VI ZR 135/13, NJW 2017, 2416) zu einer dynamischen IP-Adresse als personenbezogenes Datum' (2017) 70 *Neue Juristische Wochenschrift*, 2419 (2420).

[33] Martini and Weinzierl, 'Die Blockchain-Technologie und das Recht auf Vergessenwerden – Zum Dilemma zwischen Nicht-Vergessen-Können und Vergessen-Müssen' (2017) 36 *Neue Zeitschrift für Verwaltungsrecht*, 1251 (1253).

[34] Pesch and Böhme, 'Datenschutz trotz öffentlicher Blockchain? – Chancen und Risiken bei der Verfolgung und Prävention Bitcoin-bezogener Straftaten' (2017) 41 *Datenschutz und Datensicherheit*, 93 (95).

[35] See also Hofert, 'Blockchain-Profiling – Verarbeitung von Blockchain-Daten innerhalb und außerhalb der Netzwerke' (2017) 7 *Zeitschrift für Datenschutz*, 161 (164).

[36] Directive 2018/843/EU.

[37] Haffke, Fromberger and Zimmermann, 'Cryptocurrencies and anti-money laundering: the shortcomings of the fifth AML Directive (EU) and how to address them' (2019) 21 *Journal of Banking Regulation*, 134 et seq., available at https://beck-link.de/5barx (accessed 26.8.2021).

Part B. EU Regulation

and store the true identity of their users, now it is their duty to do so (for details see → § 10, para. 42 et seqq.).

24 If a blockchain is used to transfer tokens to 'pay' for goods or services, the assignment of a person to a transaction is necessary to fulfil the respective liabilities. If the blockchain user 'pays' in an online store with tokens, it is possible for the transaction recipient to assign the blockchain user's public key to a customer account and thus to a person.[38] The transaction recipient can then also track further transactions of the transaction sender as long as the sender carries out the transactions with the same public key.[39]

25 Since the users in a blockchain do not usually appear with their name but with their public key, the use of a blockchain is often referred to as anonymous.[40] **Anonymity** in the sense of data protection law only exists, however, if the data controller or processor cannot attribute the data to a data subject (on the role of the participants under the GDPR → para. 33 et seqq.). The GDPR is not applicable to anonymous data.[41] If, on the other hand, the user does not appear under her or his name but under her or his public key within a blockchain, there is no anonymity if a data controller or processor can attribute the data to the person. As seen above, the central entity in a central blockchain and trading platforms can basically attribute the public key of a blockchain user to her or his person. It is also possible to regularly attribute the public key to a person in a decentralized blockchain. Since there is an attribution between the public key and the person, one speaks of **pseudonymity** (→ § 1, para. 17). Pursuant to Art. 4(5) GDPR, data are pseudonymised if personal data are processed in such a manner that the personal data can no longer be attributed to a specific data subject without the use of additional information. Thus, when data are pseudonymised, the data are still personal data, so that the GDPR is applicable.

26 The material scope of the GDPR to processing operations within a blockchain for the transfer of tokens would only be excluded if the processing of personal data is carried out by a natural person in the course of a purely **personal or household activity**, Art. 2 (2)(c) GDPR. Although the French Data Protection Authority, Commission Nationale Informatique & Libertés (CNIL), announced that the exception is applicable when for example a natural person buys or sells Bitcoins on her or his own behalf,[42] the exception does not apply even in the case of processing by private individuals in the context of the blockchain, since these processing operations have an economic link and therefore no longer belong to the sphere of personal or household activities.[43] The CJEU has also emphasized the view time and time again that the household exemption has to be interpreted narrowly.[44]

---

[38] See also Pesch and Böhme, 'Datenschutz trotz öffentlicher Blockchain? – Chancen und Risiken bei der Verfolgung und Prävention Bitcoin-bezogener Straftaten' (2017) 41 *Datenschutz und Datensicherheit*, 93 (95).

[39] Haffke, Fromberger and Zimmermann, 'Cryptocurrencies and anti-money laundering: the shortcomings of the fifth AML Directive (EU) and how to address them' (2019) 21 *Journal of Banking Regulation*, 129, available at https://beck-link.de/5barx (accessed 26.8.2021).

[40] Schrey and Thalhofer, 'Rechtliche Aspekte der Blockchain' (2017) 70 *Neue Juristische Wochenschrift*, 1431 (1434).

[41] Recital 26 GDPR.

[42] Commission Nationale Informatique & Libertés (CNIL), 'Blockchain – Solutions for a responsible use of the blockchain in the context of personal data' (2018), available at https://beck-link.de/b782w (accessed 26.8.2021).

[43] Recital 18 GDPR.

[44] Finck, 'Blockchain and the General Data Protection Regulation' (2019), 11 et seqq., available at https://beck-link.de/3ds3b (accessed 26.8.2021).

§ 6. Data Protection

II. Territorial Scope

Given the global distribution of blockchain participants, a blockchain is usually cross- 27 border in nature.[45] The **territorial scope** of the GDPR for personal data in a central blockchain is therefore opened if the central entity or a miner/forger (→ § 1, para. 38, 58) or a full node (→ § 1, para. 7 et seq.) involved in a transaction has an **establishment** within the EU or the use of the blockchain is offered to data subjects within the EU (→ para. 32). The GDPR applies to a decentralized blockchain if the transaction sender or a miner/forger or a full node[46] involved in a transaction has an establishment within the EU (→ para. 32).

If providers of trading platforms are involved in the data processing operations, the 28 territorial scope is opened if these providers have an establishment within the EU or if the use of their services is offered to data subjects within the EU (→ para. 32).

If the data from a blockchain is assigned to the transaction sender by the transaction 29 recipient in a further processing step, the GDPR applies to this processing step if the transaction recipient has an establishment in the EU or the recipient offers goods or services to data subjects within the EU (→ para. 32).

The territorial scope of the GDPR is always opened if personal data are processed in 30 the context of the activities of an establishment within the EU, Art. 3(1) GDPR, or when a controller or processor not established in the EU offers its goods or services to data subjects in the EU or monitors the behaviour of these data subjects, Art. 3(2) GDPR.

Art. 3(1) GDPR does not require that the data processing itself takes place within the 31 EU. Rather, the territorial scope of the GDPR is independent of the physical location of the processing, i.e. independent of the location of the servers or the IT infrastructure, for example.[47] Art. 3(2) GDPR also applies to processing operations carried out in the context of the offering of goods and services for which the data subjects do not have to make payments. It is not necessary to conclude a contract.[48] However, an offer is only made if the controller or the processor has also intended such an offer to the data subject. The mere accessibility of a website, for example, is not sufficient to be able to speak of offering.[49]

The territorial scope of the GDPR is linked to the **roles of the participants under the** 32 **GDPR** (→ para. 33 et seqq.). Thus, the territorial scope depends on who is **the controller or the processor** for the processing operations in a blockchain. If the data processing operations are carried out as part of the activities of an establishment of the controller or processor or if they offer their goods or services to data subjects in the EU, the territorial scope of the GDPR is opened.

D. The Roles of the Participants under the GDPR

In a central blockchain, the central entity, i.e. the initiator of the blockchain, is the 33 controller (→ para. 38). The sender and recipient of a transaction and third parties whose personal data are processed within the content data of a transaction are data

---

[45] Finck, 'Blockchains and Data Protection in the European Union' (2018) 4 *European Data Protection Law Review*, 17 (27).
[46] This includes wallet and interface providers.
[47] Recital 22 GDPR.
[48] Svantesson, in Kuner, Bygrave and Docksey (eds), *GDPR*, 89.
[49] Recital 23 GDPR.

subjects (→ para. 40). In a decentralized blockchain, each transaction sender is the controller of the transaction initiated by her or him (→ para. 50). At the same time, the transaction sender is also the data subject of this transaction (→ para. 53). Other data subjects are the transaction recipient and third parties whose data are processed within the content data of a transaction (→ para. 53). When trading platforms are used, these providers are controllers (→ para. 41 et seqq.).[50] In all the above-mentioned constellations, the full nodes, which also include the miners/forgers, are processors of the transactions in which they are involved (→ para. 39, 52). For the further processing step of assigning the data from the blockchain by the transaction recipient, the recipient is the controller and the transaction sender is the data subject (→ para. 54).

I. Participants under the GDPR

34   The GDPR defines in Art. 4 the data subject, the controller, the processor and the third party. **Data subject** is the identified or identifiable natural person whose data are being processed, Art. 4(1) GDPR. This group of persons may also include non-EU citizens if the data subject's data are processed by controllers or processors within the territorial scope of the GDPR.[51]

> **Example:**
> If company C, which itself operates an online store, stores the address data of its customers, the customers are the data subjects, as the address data are personal data processed by company C.

35   **Controller** is the natural or legal person, public authority, agency or other body which, alone or jointly with others, determines the **purposes and means of the processing** of personal data, Art. 4(7) GDPR. The controller is therefore the person who has the actual power to determine the purposes and means.[52] The purpose of the processing is the expected result which is intended or which guides the planned actions, i.e. the 'why'. The means of processing is the way in which a result or objective is achieved, i.e. the 'how'.[53] The decision on the purposes of the processing in principle implies a classification as a controller, whereas a decision on the means implies the classification as a controller only if essential aspects of the means are decided upon. It is therefore possible that the processor decides on the technical and organisational means.[54] If two or more controllers jointly determine the purposes and means of the processing, they are **joint controllers**, Art. 26 GDPR.

> **Example:**
> If company C, which itself operates an online store, stores the address data of its customers, company C is the controller, as it determines the purposes and means of processing the customer data.

36   **Processor** is a natural or legal person, public authority, agency or other body which processes personal data on behalf of the controller, Art. 4(8) GDPR. Like data con-

---

[50] In the case of a central blockchain in addition to the initiator of the blockchain.
[51] Klar and Kühling, in Kühling and Buchner (eds), *DS-GVO*, Art. 4(1), para. 3.
[52] Article 29 Data Protection Working Party, 'Opinion 1/2010 on the concepts of 'controller' and 'processor'' (16.2.2010), WP 169, 00264/10/EN, 1 and 8 et seqq., available at https://beck-link.de/c2n6m (accessed 26.8.2021).
[53] Bygrave and Tosoni, in Kuner, Bygrave and Docksey (eds), *GDPR*, 150 et seq.
[54] Article 29 Data Protection Working Party, 'Opinion 1/2010 on the concepts of 'controller' and 'processor'' (16.2.2010), WP 169, 00264/10/EN, available at https://beck-link.de/c2n6m (accessed 26.8.2021).

trollers, processors process personal data. The difference between processor and controller is that processors cannot determine the purposes and only to a limited extent the means of processing. Furthermore, processors are subject to the **instructions** of the controller (on processing on behalf → para. 69 et seqq.).[55]

> **Example:**
> If company C does not operate an online store itself, but commissions company P to do so, while retaining the authority to issue instructions as to how the online store should look like and what data should be collected from customers, company P is the processor for the controller, namely company C.

Third party is a natural or legal person, public authority, agency or body other than the data subject, controller, processor and persons who, under the direct authority of the controller or processor are authorised to process personal data, Art. 4(10) GDPR. If personal data is transferred to third parties and processed by them, these third parties are then also data controllers within the meaning of the GDPR.[56] 37

> **Example:**
> Company C, which operates an online store, sells the personal data of its customers to a marketing company T, which wants to use the data to send advertising. At the beginning, marketing company T is an uninvolved third party, as it is not the data subject, controller or processor. However, if it receives the personal data of its customers from company C, marketing company T itself becomes the data controller.

II. Central Blockchain

The **central entity**, i.e. the initiator of a central blockchain, determines the **purposes and means** of the data processing operations that are carried out within the blockchain. In addition to the processing operations for transactions, this also includes the management of user data. In a central blockchain, the respective transaction sender initiates the transfer of tokens and determines to whom she or he wants to transfer how many tokens. Ultimately, however, the transaction sender is not free to choose the means of transferring tokens; instead, the central entity provides the means to the transaction sender. The central entity can also change the programming of the blockchain at any time or withdraw the user's right to access the blockchain or add new blocks to the blockchain. Therefore, the central entity is to be regarded as the **controller**.[57] In the case of a central blockchain, this is also most closely in line with the aim of the GDPR to protect the data subjects as extensively as possible, since the data subjects can contact the central entity known to them by name in order to assert their rights. 38

Neither **miners/forgers** nor **full nodes** are controllers, as they do not determine the purposes or means of the data processing operations within the central blockchain (for details on the responsibility of miners/forgers and full nodes within a decentralized blockchain → para. 47 et seq.). However, since they process personal data, they can only be given the **classification as processor** under the GDPR.[58] For the purposes 39

---

[55] Ibid, 24 et seq.
[56] Klabunde, in Ehmann and Selmayr (eds), *DS-GVO*, Art. 4, para. 45.
[57] See also Finck, 'Blockchain and the General Data Protection Regulation' (2019), 43 et seq., available at https://beck-link.de/3ds3b (accessed 26.8.2021); Blockchain Bundesverband, 'Blockchain, data protection, and the GDPR' (25.5.2018), 7, available at https://beck-link.de/zt7en (accessed 26.8.2021); Finck, 'Blockchains and Data Protection in the European Union' (2018) 4 *European Data Protection Law Review*, 17 (26).
[58] Blockchain Bundesverband, 'Blockchain, data protection, and the GDPR' (25.5.2018), 7, available at https://beck-link.de/zt7en (accessed 26.8.2021); Finck, 'Blockchains and Data Protection in the European Union' (2018) 4 *European Data Protection Law Review*, 17 (27).

of considering the role of the participants under data protection law, it is irrelevant whether a data processing agreement has actually been concluded between the data controller and the processors or whether all the requirements of the GDPR for data processing on behalf have been complied with. This is only relevant regarding the consequences for the participants if no data processing agreement has been concluded or if the requirements of the GDPR for processing on behalf have not been complied with (on processing on behalf → para. 69 et seqq.).

40   Since the transaction sender uses her or his public key for transactions, which the central entity can attribute to the blockchain user, the **transaction sender** is the **data subject**. The **transaction recipient** is also the **data subject**, since her or his public key is also contained in the transaction data. If personal data of a third party is processed within the content data of a transaction, this third party is also the data subject.

III. Trading Platforms

41   If the blockchain user uses trading platforms, these providers carry out the transactions – and thus the data processing – on behalf of the transaction sender. In the case of **off-chain transactions**, these providers determine both the means and the purposes of the processing, as they provide the platform and have control over all transactions carried out on it. In the case of off-chain transactions, these providers are therefore controllers and the actual transaction sender is, together with the transaction recipient, the data subject.

42   A distinction must be made in the case of **on-chain transactions**: In a central blockchain, the trading platforms take the place of the transaction sender. The trading platforms then do not determine the purposes and means of data processing. This is still done by the central entity. However, the trading platforms are not data subjects either, since it is not their own data that is processed, but the data of the transaction sender and recipient. Rather, trading platforms in this constellation are processors.

43   Also, in the case of a decentralized blockchain, the trading platforms take the place of the transaction sender for **on-chain transactions**. Since the transaction sender is the controller for a decentralized blockchain (→ para. 50), these providers take the place of the transaction sender as the controller and are therefore controllers themselves.

IV. Decentralized Blockchain

44   The GDPR is basically designed for processing operations in central data processing systems.[59] This can be seen, for example, from the fact that under the provisions of the GDPR there is either one controller or several joint controllers. In the case of a central blockchain or when using central trading platforms, the allocation of responsibility for processing transactions is unproblematic, as there is a 'large' entity to which responsibility for these transactions can be attributed. With a decentralized blockchain, on the other hand, there is no central entity to whom responsibility for the processing transactions in a blockchain can be attributed. It is a challenge to extend the requirements of the GDPR for controllers or joint controllers to a decentralized blockchain.[60]

---

[59] Ibid, 17; Krupar and Strassemeyer, 'Datenschutz auf der Blockchain – die Innovationsfeindlichkeit der DS-GVO' (2018) *Deutsche Stiftung für Recht und Informatik Tagungsband*, 343 (348 et seq.).

[60] See also Finck, 'Blockchains and Data Protection in the European Union' (2018) 4 *European Data Protection Law Review*, 17 (26); Krupar and Strassemeyer, 'Datenschutz auf der Blockchain – die

§ 6. Data Protection

In the absence of a central controller, there are a few participants that could be classified as controller under the GDPR.

Since the provisions of the GDPR are basically designed for central processing operations, determining responsibility in a decentralized blockchain is not without problems. If the transaction sender initiates a transaction within a decentralized blockchain, this must first be verified by the full nodes and then be attached to a block by a miner/forger (→ § 1, para. 38 et seq., 58 et seq.). The newly created block must then be verified again by the full nodes (→ § 1, para. 19). This raises the question of the role of the participants under the GDPR. 45

The view[61] that applying the standards of the GDPR on responsibility is generally problematic and that this would lead to the consequence that there could be **no controller** within a decentralized blockchain must be rejected.[62] The participants in a decentralized blockchain use this type of blockchain so that they are not dependent on a central entity. This view would, however, lead to a situation in which the data subjects could in fact not exercise their rights (→ para. 79 et seqq.). Just because the user of a decentralized blockchain wants to use a decentralized system for the transmission of tokens, does not mean she or he wants to be left defenceless. 46

Similarly, the view[63] must be rejected that **each full node** of a decentralized blockchain is the **controller** or that **all full nodes** are **joint controllers** within the meaning of Art. 26 GDPR.[64] For each full node to be the controller, she or he would have to be able to define the purposes and means of the data processing operations in the decentralized blockchain. However, each individual full node is interchangeable. Due to the peer-to-peer structure of a blockchain, transactions take place even if a particular full node no longer participates in the blockchain network. Switching individual full nodes on and off has no effect on the transactions within a blockchain for a widely used blockchain with a large number of full nodes.[65] It would therefore be wrong to consider all individual full nodes as controllers. All currently active full nodes together are also no joint controllers within the meaning of Art. 26 GDPR. This is because Art. 26 GDPR requires that the joint controllers determine the purposes and means of processing together. An agreement between the data controllers is therefore necessary. Such an agreement does not normally take place among the full nodes of a blockchain.[66] 47

Just like the full nodes, the **miners/forgers** are **not to be** regarded either **individually as controllers or together as joint controllers** within the meaning of Art. 26 48

Innovationsfeindlichkeit der DS-GVO' (2018) *Deutsche Stiftung für Recht und Informatik Tagungsband*, 343 (348 et seq.).

[61] Finck, 'Blockchains and Data Protection in the European Union' (2018) 4 *European Data Protection Law Review*, 17 (24); Böhme and Pesch, 'Technische Grundlagen und datenschutzrechtliche Fragen der Blockchain-Technologie' (2017) 41 *Datenschutz und Datensicherheit*, 473 (478 et seq.).

[62] See also Janicki and Saive, 'Privacy by Design in Blockchain-Netzwerken – Verantwortlichkeit und datenschutzkonforme Ausgestaltung von Blockchains' (2019) 9 *Zeitschrift für Datenschutz* 251 (253).

[63] Finck, 'Blockchains and Data Protection in the European Union' (2018) 4 *European Data Protection Law Review*, 17 (26 et seq.); Schrey and Thalhofer, 'Rechtliche Aspekte der Blockchain' (2017) 70 *Neue Juristische Wochenschrift*, 1431 (1433 et seq.).

[64] Krupar and Strassemeyer, 'Datenschutz auf der Blockchain – die Innovationsfeindlichkeit der DS-GVO' (2018) *Deutsche Stiftung für Recht und Informatik Tagungsband*, 343 (346 et seq.); Berger, 'Blockchain – Mythos oder Technologie für die öffentliche Verwaltung?' (2017) 132 *Deutsches Verwaltungsblatt*, 1271 (1273).

[65] See also Erbguth and Fasching, 'Wer ist Verantwortlicher einer Bitcoin-Transaktion? – Anwendbarkeit der DS-GVO auf die Bitcoin-Blockchain' (2017) 7 *Zeitschrift für Datenschutz*, 560 (563).

[66] See also Böhme and Pesch, 'Technische Grundlagen und datenschutzrechtliche Fragen der Blockchain-Technologie' (2017) 41 *Datenschutz und Datensicherheit*, 473 (479); Martini and Weinzierl, 'Die Blockchain-Technologie und das Recht auf Vergessenwerden – Zum Dilemma zwischen Nicht-Vergessen-Können und Vergessen-Müssen' (2017) 36 *Neue Zeitschrift für Verwaltungsrecht*, 1251 (1254).

GDPR.[67] The miners/forgers do have an economic interest in the formation of new blocks on the basis of the rewards to which they are entitled and the sum of the transaction fees (→ § 1, para. 33 et seqq.). However, the miners/forgers depend on the blockchain users carrying out transactions. The miners/forgers are generally not able to design the blockchain themselves, but add the transactions initiated by the transaction senders to the blocks.[68] For this reason, the miners/forgers cannot be considered individually as controllers. Only the majority of the miners/forgers could design the blockchain themselves and thus decide on the purposes of the processing.[69] An agreement among the majority of the miners/forgers is usually not made.[70] Therefore, the miners/forgers are also no joint controllers together within the meaning of Art. 26 GDPR.[71]

49 The original **programmers or the initiators** of a decentralized blockchain determine the means and purposes of processing through the program code at first. However, it does not seem appropriate to make them responsible for the transactions that later take place in the blockchain. Rather, the programmers or initiators of a decentralized blockchain relinquish control over the purposes and means when the program code or protocol software is published. They are no longer involved in the individual processing operations within the framework of the transactions carried out.[72]

50 In contrast, the **sender of the respective transaction** within a decentralized blockchain is the **controller**.[73] Each transaction sender defines the purpose of the transaction she or he initiated. Strictly speaking, the transaction sender does not determine the available means herself or himself, since she or he uses the existing structures of the decentralized blockchain.[74] However, the transaction sender adopts the means made available by the programmers or initiators of the blockchain. Since there is no central entity – as is the case with the central blockchain – in the decentralized blockchain that specifies the means, but it is necessary to determine a data controller within a decentralized blockchain, the **combination** of the **purposes** set by the transaction sender and the **means** adopted by her or him is sufficient to justify the responsibility of the transaction sender. This is also supported by the fact that there is no entity within

---

[67] See also Krupar and Strassemeyer, 'Datenschutz auf der Blockchain – die Innovationsfeindlichkeit der DS-GVO' (2018) *Deutsche Stiftung für Recht und Informatik Tagungsband*, 343 (347); Commission Nationale Informatique & Libertés (CNIL), 'Blockchain – Solutions for a responsible use of the blockchain in the context of personal data' (2018), 2, available at https://beck-link.de/b782w (accessed 26.8.2021).

[68] Martini and Weinzierl, 'Die Blockchain-Technologie und das Recht auf Vergessenwerden – Zum Dilemma zwischen Nicht-Vergessen-Können und Vergessen-Müssen' (2017) 36 *Neue Zeitschrift für Verwaltungsrecht*, 1251 (1253), compare the role of miners with telecommunications service providers.

[69] Krupar and Strassemeyer, 'Datenschutz auf der Blockchain – die Innovationsfeindlichkeit der DS-GVO' (2018) *Deutsche Stiftung für Recht und Informatik Tagungsband*, 343 (347 et seq.).

[70] Agreements between miners are conceivable within the framework of mining pools (→ § 1, para. 40). Despite the agreements, the mining pools do not regularly represent the majority of all miners.

[71] Krupar and Strassemeyer, 'Datenschutz auf der Blockchain – die Innovationsfeindlichkeit der DS-GVO' (2018) *Deutsche Stiftung für Recht und Informatik Tagungsband*, 343 (347 et seq.).

[72] See also Finck, 'Blockchain and the General Data Protection Regulation' (2019), 45 et seq., available at https://beck-link.de/3ds3b (accessed 26.8.2021); Blockchain Bundesverband, 'Blockchain, data protection, and the GDPR' (25.5.2018), 6, available at https://beck-link.de/zt7en (accessed 26.8.2021).

[73] See also Krupar and Strassemeyer, 'Datenschutz auf der Blockchain – die Innovationsfeindlichkeit der DS-GVO' (2018) *Deutsche Stiftung für Recht und Informatik Tagungsband*, 343 (347); Martini and Weinzierl, 'Die Blockchain-Technologie und das Recht auf Vergessenwerden – Zum Dilemma zwischen Nicht-Vergessen-Können und Vergessen-Müssen' (2017) 36 *Neue Zeitschrift für Verwaltungsrecht*, 1251 (1253 et seq.); different view: European Union Blockchain Observatory and Forum, 'Blockchain and the GDPR' (18.10.2018), 18, available at https://beck-link.de/xvw5b (accessed 26.8.2021).

[74] Quiel, 'Blockchain-Technologie im Fokus von Art. 8 GRC und DS-GVO – Ein Zwiespalt zwischen Innovation und unionalem Datenschutzrecht?' (2018) 42 *Datenschutz und Datensicherheit*, 566 (569).

a decentralized blockchain that can evaluate the content of a transaction or who could eliminate it. As long as the transaction sender is the owner of the token to be transferred and has authenticated the transaction with her or his private key, the transaction can be added to a block by a miner/forger and be verified by the full nodes.[75] A joint responsibility of all transaction senders within the meaning of Art. 26 GDPR is out of the question, as there are usually no agreements between the various transaction senders.[76]

Admittedly, this result may be unsatisfactory in terms of the exercise of data subjects' rights. However, there is hardly any constellation in a decentralized blockchain in which the exercise of the data subjects' rights is unproblematic. If one considers the individual transaction sender to be the data controller, there is at least the possibility of being able to identify her or him and thus enable the possibility that contact can be established. Whether the data subjects can actually enforce their rights against the data controller is another question (→ para. 81). 51

As with the central blockchain (→ para. 39), the **miners/forgers** and the **full nodes** are also **processors** in the decentralized blockchain, as they process the personal data in the context of the transactions but are not themselves data controllers. Here, too, it is irrelevant regarding the role of the participants under the GDPR whether a data processing agreement has actually been concluded between the controller and the processors or whether the requirements of the GDPR for processing on behalf have been complied with (on processing on behalf → para. 69 et seqq.). 52

In a decentralized blockchain, however, the **sender of a transaction** is not only the controller for the respective transaction, but also the **data subject**, since her or his own data are also processed within the transaction.[77] The data subject is also the **transaction recipient**, since her or his public key is processed, and possibly third parties whose personal data are processed within the content data. 53

V. Assignment of the Transaction by the Recipient

If the transaction recipient processes the transaction data from a blockchain, for example, in order to **assign** a transaction from the transaction sender to a customer of her or his online store, the **transaction recipient** is the **controller** for the processing operation by which the transaction is attributed to the purchase and the customer in the online store.[78] 54

E. Lawfulness of Processing

The principle of '**lawfulness of processing**' (Art. 5(1)(a) GDPR) means that, in principle, any processing of personal data relating to a natural person requires a legal basis, otherwise the processing is prohibited. The GDPR specifies finally and exhaus- 55

---

[75] Erbguth and Fasching, 'Wer ist Verantwortlicher einer Bitcoin-Transaktion? – Anwendbarkeit der DS-GVO auf die Bitcoin-Blockchain' (2017) 7 *Zeitschrift für Datenschutz*, 560 (564).

[76] Martini and Weinzierl, 'Die Blockchain-Technologie und das Recht auf Vergessenwerden – Zum Dilemma zwischen Nicht-Vergessen-Können und Vergessen-Müssen' (2017) 36 *Neue Zeitschrift für Verwaltungsrecht*, 1251 (1254).

[77] See also Finck, 'Blockchains and Data Protection in the European Union' (2018) 4 *European Data Protection Law Review*, 17 (27); different view: Bygrave and Tosoni, in Kuner, Bygrave and Docksey (eds), *GDPR*, 154.

[78] See also Krupar and Strassemeyer, 'Datenschutz auf der Blockchain – die Innovationsfeindlichkeit der DS-GVO' (2018) *Deutsche Stiftung für Recht und Informatik Tagungsband*, 343 (347).

tively in Art. 6 GDPR **provisions that permit** the processing of personal data.[79] When processing personal data within a blockchain, Art. 6(1)(a), (b) and (f) GDPR are generally considered to be possible permissions.

56 As a permission for data processing in a blockchain, **consent** (→ para. 58 et seqq.) is only possible for a central blockchain and for the use of trading platforms due to the requirement of an informed decision. But even in these cases, consent is **not practicable**, as the user can withdraw it at any time. However, data processing operations in a central blockchain and with providers of trading platforms can in principle be based on **Art. 6 (1)(b) GDPR** (→ para. 62).

57 In a decentralized blockchain, data processing can be justified by **Art. 6(1)(b) GDPR** (→ para. 63 et seqq.). This is the case both when there is a contract between the transaction sender and the transaction recipient, for example, when the transaction sender is a customer of the transaction recipient in an online store, and when there is no contract between the transaction sender and the transaction recipient. The transaction recipient can justify the processing step of attributing the transmission of the tokens to the transaction recipient on the basis of the existing contract with the transaction sender in accordance with Art. 6(1)(b) GDPR. If personal data of third parties are processed within the **content data** of transactions, **only Art. 6(1)(f) GDPR** (→ para. 67 et seq.) can be considered as a permission, but in most cases, this will not be possible.

I. Consent

58 Art. 6(1)(a) GDPR regulates **consent**. If the data subject gives her or his consent to the processing of her or his personal data, the processing is lawful. Art. 7 GDPR contains more detailed requirements for a valid consent. The controller must be able to prove that the data subject has consented to the processing of her or his data, Art. 7(1) GDPR. The data subject must be able to make an **informed decision**, i.e. she or he requires information from the controller as to who will process her or his personal data and for what purpose.[80] Moreover, consent must be given **voluntarily**, i.e. it is not possible to link consent to access to services.[81] The data subject may **withdraw** consent at any time, which will make future processing unlawful, unless otherwise permitted. The lawfulness of data processing operations carried out up to the time of withdrawal is not affected by the withdrawal.[82]

59 In the case of a central blockchain and trading platforms, the central entity or the service providers can in principle provide the data subject with the information necessary for consent. However, it is problematic that the consent is withdrawable and thus the lawfulness of future processing operations would no longer be given after exercising the right of withdrawal if there is no other legal basis for the processing. Despite the possibility of consent in principle, a different legal basis for permission would therefore be preferable.

60 In the case of a decentralized blockchain, in which the respective transaction sender is the controller for the transaction initiated by her or him, there is on the one hand the problem that the data subject would have to give her or his consent to the transaction

---

[79] Kotschy, in Kuner, Bygrave and Docksey (eds), *GDPR*, 325 and 329; Feiler, Forgó and Weigl, *The EU General Data Protection Regulation (GDPR): A Commentary* (2018), 19 et seq., 74, 84.
[80] Buchner and Kühling, in Kühling and Buchner (eds), *DS-GVO*, Art. 7, para. 59 et seq.
[81] Ibid, para. 41; Kosta, in Kuner, Bygrave and Docksey (eds), *GDPR*, 352 et seq.
[82] Buchner and Kühling, in Kühling and Buchner (eds), *DS-GVO*, Art. 7, para. 33 et seqq.; Kosta, in Kuner, Bygrave and Docksey (eds), *GDPR*, 351.

sender as the controller, who can change with every transaction and will often not be known to the transaction recipient due to the existing pseudonymity within a decentralized blockchain.[83] On the other hand, a decentralized blockchain will lack the information that is needed for an informed decision of the data subject, since the purposes and means of processing are determined by the changing group of persons of the transaction sender.[84]

II. Necessity for the Performance of a Contract

According to **Art. 6(1)(b) GPDR**, the processing of personal data is also lawful if the processing is necessary for the **performance of a contract** to which the data subject is party or in order to take steps at the request of the data subject prior to entering into a contract.

Both in the case of a central blockchain and the use of trading platforms, a **contractual relationship** exists between the providers and the users (→ § 7, para. 4 et seqq.). In the case of a central blockchain, the central entity requires the user data for the management of the access and/or write authorization. If this entity were not allowed to collect data from the users, it would not be able to fulfil its task of user management. When using trading platforms, Art. 6(1)(b) GDPR also offers a legal basis of permission for the provider when it comes to user management and transactions. In the case of on-chain transactions, Art. 6(1)(b) GDPR can be used to justify data processing if the personal data of the transaction sender are processed.

In the case of a decentralized blockchain, Art. 6(1)(b) GDPR can generally be considered as justification if a **contractual obligation** exists between the transaction sender and the transaction recipient in which the transaction sender has undertaken to transmit tokens to the transaction recipient.

If, on the other hand, there is **no contractual obligation** between the transaction sender and the transaction recipient, or if the personal data of the transaction recipient who is not a contractual partner of the respective trading platforms are processed by trading platforms in the context of on-chain transactions, the wording of Art. 6(1)(b) GDPR does not allow this, since it refers to a **contract or a pre-contractual measure**. Paragraph 28(1) first sentence No. 3 of the German Federal Data Protection Act (BDSG) in the version before May 2018, which, like Art. 6(1)(b) GDPR, could justify the processing of personal data within existing obligations, referred not only to the contract as an obligation between the controller and the data subject, but also to obligations similar to legal transactions. These **contractual obligations similar to legal transactions** also included the so-called '**contract-like relationship of trust**'. This included, for example, membership in associations, contracts of courtesy, invalid contracts or even management without a mandate.[85] Even if the contractual obligations are no longer mentioned in Art. 6(1)(b) GDPR, it is nevertheless obvious to classify such contract-like relationships of trust under the 'contract' in Art. 6(1)(b) GDPR if the contract-like relationship of trust is

---

[83] See also Schrey and Thalhofer, 'Rechtliche Aspekte der Blockchain' (2017) 70 *Neue Juristische Wochenschrift*, 1431 (1434).

[84] See also Quiel, 'Blockchain-Technologie im Fokus von Art. 8 GRC und DS-GVO – Ein Zwiespalt zwischen Innovation und unionalem Datenschutzrecht?' (2018) 42 *Datenschutz und Datensicherheit*, 566 (571).

[85] Buchner and Petri, in Kühling and Buchner (eds), *DS-GVO*, Art. 6, para. 29; Hofert, 'Blockchain-Profiling – Verarbeitung von Blockchain-Daten innerhalb und außerhalb der Netzwerke' (2017) 7 *Zeitschrift für Datenschutz*, 161 (165).

based on an autonomous decision by the data subject, as is the case when a contractual obligations is concluded.[86]

65 The users of a decentralized blockchain are not members of an organisation. However, the blockchain users consciously submit to a decentralized register management by a decentralized blockchain based on an **autonomous decision**. The users thus face a de-facto organisation, the decentralized blockchain, whose rules are derived from the protocol software of the blockchain. This relationship is to be subsumed under a contract-like relationship of trust similar to a contract and thus also falls under the concept of contract in Art. 6(1)(b) GDPR.[87] The processing of personal data of blockchain users in a decentralized blockchain is therefore justified under Art. 6(1)(b) GDPR.[88]

66 If, on the other hand, personal data are processed within the **content data** that are attributed to a third party who is not in any contractual relationship with the controller or is not a user of the blockchain, such processing cannot be justified under Art. 6(1)(b) GDPR. **Only Art. 6(1)(f) GDPR** can then be considered a possible permission. Such a constellation can occur, for example, if a blockchain user transfers personal data of persons who are not users of the same blockchain within the content data of the blockchain.

III. Necessity for the Purposes of the Legitimate Interests

67 Pursuant to **Art. 6(1)(f) GDPR**, the processing of the data subject's personal data is also lawful if the processing is **necessary for the purposes of the legitimate interests** pursued by the controller or by a third party, except where such interests are overridden by the interests or fundamental rights and freedoms of the data subject which require protection of personal data, in particular, where the data subject is a child. Art. 6(1)(f) GDPR may be the legal basis for a permission of the processing if there is **no contractual relationship** between the data controller and the data subject. To check if the processing can be lawful under Art. 6(1)(f) GDPR, a balance must be struck between the legitimate interests of the controller and the interests of the data subject.[89]

68 If personal data of third parties are processed in the blockchain – for example within the content data – the **various interests** of the participants must be **balanced**. In the case of 'uninvolved' third parties, the balancing of interests is generally at the expense of the data controller, since the interest of the third party in her or his right to informational self-determination outweighs the interest of the data controller in processing the data of the third party.[90]

IV. Processing on Behalf

69 In both central and decentralized blockchains, the data subjects' personal data are processed not only by the data controllers but also by **processors**. In all

---

[86] Buchner and Petri, in Kühling and Buchner (eds), *DS-GVO*, Art. 6, para. 29 et seq.; different view: Schulz, in Gola (ed), *DS-GVO*, Art. 6, para. 31.

[87] Hofert, 'Blockchain-Profiling – Verarbeitung von Blockchain-Daten innerhalb und außerhalb der Netzwerke' (2017) 7 *Zeitschrift für Datenschutz*, 161 (164).

[88] Schulz, in Gola (ed), *DS-GVO*, Art. 6, para. 35: whether data processing in a blockchain can be justified under Art. 6(1)(b) DS-GVO depends largely on the classification of the relationship between the data subject and the blockchain network and the 'smart contracts' executed within the blockchain as contractual relationships.

[89] Buchner and Petri, in Kühling and Buchner (eds), *DS-GVO*, Art. 6, para. 148 et seqq.; Kotschy, in Kuner, Bygrave and Docksey (eds), *GDPR*, 338 et seq.

[90] See also Schrey and Thalhofer, 'Rechtliche Aspekte der Blockchain' (2017) 70 *Neue Juristische Wochenschrift*, 1431 (1434).

§ 6. Data Protection

types of blockchain, all **full nodes** and **miners/forgers** involved in a transaction are processors (→ para. 39, 52).

Art. 28 GDPR lays down the **conditions** for the implementation of valid data processing on behalf. Among other things, the controller has the duty to use only a processor who provides sufficient guarantees that the processing will meet the requirements of the GDPR and ensures the protection of the data subject's rights, Art. 28(1) GDPR. The basis of the processing on behalf is a **contract or other legal act (called 'data processing agreement' or 'DPA')** concluded between the controller and the processor, which sets out the subject-matter and duration of the processing, the nature and purpose of the processing, the type of personal data, the categories of data subjects and the obligations and rights of the controller, Art. 28(3) GDPR. The data processing agreement shall be in writing. However, it may also be in an electronic form, Art. 28(9) GDPR. The 'electronic form' does not require a qualified electronic signature; exchanging the data protection agreement with a sufficient signature also satisfies the formal requirement.[91] The processor and any person acting under the authority of the controller or the processor, who has access to personal data, shall not process those data except on **instructions** from the controller, unless required to do so by Union or Member State law, Art. 29 GDPR. 70

In a central blockchain, a **data processing agreement is generally possible** between the central entity and all full nodes or miners/forgers, since the central entity assigns the access and/or write authorization to the full nodes or miners/forgers and could conclude a data processing agreement with the full nodes or miners/forgers as part of the registration for the central blockchain. As the controller who determines the purposes and means of processing, the central entity can also issue instructions to the miners/forgers or full nodes and can also enforce them on the basis of its position as the entity issuing the access and/or write authorization. 71

In the case of a decentralized blockchain, there is **no possibility of a data processing agreement explicitly concluded** between the transaction sender as the controller and the miners/forgers or full nodes as processors. Each controller, i.e. each transaction sender, would have to conclude a data processing agreement with the miners/forgers and full nodes involved in creating the blocks and verifying the transactions. It is obvious that the conclusion of an explicit data processing agreement between the transaction sender and the participating miners/forgers and full nodes in a decentralized blockchain is not possible due to the pseudonymity of the participants. However, it would be quite possible to **integrate** a data processing agreement **into the protocol software** of the blockchain. Art. 26(9) GDPR also allows a sufficient signature for the conclusion of the data processing agreement. If data are processed on behalf without concluding a data processing agreement, the **payment of fines** pursuant to Art. 83 GDPR is the consequence (→ para. 92). 72

The **authority** of the respective transaction sender to issue **instructions** to the miners/forgers or the full nodes is also problematic. The transaction sender cannot issue instructions to these blockchain users. On the other hand, however, the miners/forgers or full nodes cannot act on their own authority either, since their task is defined by the blockchain programming. However, since the GDPR is not directly designed for decentralized data processing operations, it is sufficient for the requirement of the GDPR to have the authority to issue instructions if the miners/forgers or full nodes are **bound by the programming of the blockchain** within the blockchain architecture **in order to comply**. 73

---

[91] Hartung, in Kühling and Buchner (eds), *DS-GVO*, Art. 28, para. 94 et seqq.

Part B. EU Regulation

V. Transfers of Personal Data to Third Countries

74 The data processing operations in a blockchain are regularly cross-border in nature, mostly also across the borders of the EU. If personal data are transferred to third countries in the process, special requirements must be placed on these **third country transfers**. When checking the lawfulness of data transfers to third countries, a **two-stage check** must be carried out. At the first stage, there must be a legal basis for the permission to transfer the personal data (→ para. 55 et seqq.). At the second stage, however, the conditions of Art. 44-Art. 50 GDPR must also be fulfilled. If these conditions for the first and/or second stage are not met, data transfers to third countries are not justified.[92]

75 Data transfers to third countries can only be lawful if the EU Commission has decided that an **adequate level of data protection** exists in the third country (Art. 45 GDPR), if **guarantees** have been given by the controller or the processor (Art. 46 GDPR), if **binding corporate rules** (Art. 47 GDPR) exist or if an **exception** (Art. 49 GDPR) is applicable.

76 The EU Commission has so far determined an **appropriate level of data protection** for the **following countries**: Andorra, Argentina, the Faroe Islands, Guernsey, the Isle of Man, Israel, Jersey, Canada, New Zealand, Switzerland, Uruguay and the UK.[93] No such determination has been made for the USA. The **EU-US Privacy Shield Agreement**, which, as the successor to the Safe Harbor Agreement, permitted lawful data transfers to the USA, has now been declared null and void by the CJEU.[94]

77 According to Art. 49(1)(a) GDPR, a data transfer or a set of transfers of personal data to a third country can also take place if the data subject has **explicitly consented** to the proposed transfer, after having been informed of the possible risks of such transfers for the data subject due to the absence of an adequacy decision and appropriate safeguards. Just as at the first stage (→ para. 58 et seqq.), consent as legal basis is basically possible in the case of a central blockchain or trading platforms, although this is **not practicable** due to the withdrawability of the consent. In contrast, consent is out of the question for a decentralized blockchain.

78 If, on the other hand, the conditions of Art. 44-Art. 50 GDPR for data transfers to third countries are not met, these data transfers are **not justified** and violate the GDPR. In the case of a central blockchain, this problem can be circumvented by only admitting participants from third countries that fulfil the conditions of Art. 44-Art. 50 GDPR. However, where – as in the case of any decentralized blockchain – any person can participate in the blockchain, this problem can only be eliminated if the **GDPR is not applicable in the first place** because no personal data are being processed within the blockchain (→ para. 94 et seqq.).

F. Data Subjects' Rights

I. Data Subjects' Rights and the Blockchain Technology

79 The data subjects whose personal data are processed within a blockchain are entitled to extensive rights against the data controllers. These data subjects' rights include a

---

[92] Kuner, in Kuner, Bygrave and Docksey (eds), *GDPR*, 762; Finck, 'Blockchains and Data Protection in the European Union' (2018) 4 *European Data Protection Law Review*, 17 (28).

[93] Schröder, in Kühling and Buchner (eds), *DS-GVO*, Art. 45, para. 34; Feiler, Forgó and Weigl, *The EU General Data Protection Regulation (GDPR): A Commentary* (2018), 35.

[94] ECJ, Judgment of 16 July 2020, C-311/18, EU:C:2020:559.

§ 6. Data Protection

right of access, Art. 15 GDPR (→ para. 83), a **right to rectification**, Art. 16 GDPR (→ para. 84 et seq.), a **right to erasure**, Art. 17(1) GDPR and a **right to be forgotten**, Art. 17(2) GDPR (→ para. 86 et seqq.). The protection of the data subjects' rights is generally problematic, if not impossible, within all types of blockchain due to the immutability of the data stored in a blockchain.[95] Data subjects are not able to waive their rights because those rights are not disposable.[96]

In principle, data subjects can exercise their rights against the data controllers. However, this is not possible if the data subject processes her or his own personal data. For example, if a transaction sender processes her or his own personal data in a decentralized blockchain, she or he is not only the data subject but also the data controller (for her or his own data and those of the transaction recipient). The data subject/controller cannot exercise the rights of the data subject against herself or himself due to the direction of protection of the GDPR.

All types of blockchain have in common that **enforcement difficulties** exist with regard to the data subjects' rights. In the case of a central blockchain, the controller to whom the rights are to be addressed is known. To enforce the rights, however, the central entity must be able to influence the miners/forgers and the full nodes.[97] If a data processing agreement exists between the central entity and the miners/forgers and full nodes (→ para. 69 et seqq.), the central entity can use its authority to persuade the miners/forgers or full nodes to cooperate.

In a decentralized blockchain, the main difficulty is to find the controller, against whom the rights can then be enforced.[98] If this is successful, there arises the problem in case of a decentralized blockchain that the transaction sender would have to get the miners/forgers and the full nodes to cooperate. Since the transaction senders cannot give instructions to the miners/forgers or the full nodes, the enforcement of the data subjects' rights will not succeed. A data subject whose personal data are processed within the content data will also find it very difficult – if not impossible – to demand the data subject's rights from the transaction sender.

II. Right of Access

According to Art. 15 GDPR the data subject may request confirmation from the controller as to whether or not personal data concerning her or him are being processed. The right of access is enforceable for all types of blockchain.[99] In the case of a central blockchain, the central entity, as the controller, can provide information to the data subject. In the case of a decentralized blockchain, the right of access is more problematic, as there is no central entity acting as the data controller that could provide information. In the case of a decentralized blockchain, however, all

---

[95] Berger, 'Blockchain – Mythos oder Technologie für die öffentliche Verwaltung?' (2017) 132 *Deutsches Verwaltungsblatt*, 1271 (1273); Schrey and Thalhofer, 'Rechtliche Aspekte der Blockchain' (2017) 70 *Neue Juristische Wochenschrift*, 1431 (1434).

[96] Berger, 'Blockchain – Mythos oder Technologie für die öffentliche Verwaltung?' (2017) 132 *Deutsches Verwaltungsblatt*, 1271 (1273); Schrey and Thalhofer, 'Rechtliche Aspekte der Blockchain' (2017) 70 *Neue Juristische Wochenschrift*, 1431 (1435).

[97] Martini and Weinzierl, 'Die Blockchain-Technologie und das Recht auf Vergessenwerden – Zum Dilemma zwischen Nicht-Vergessen-Können und Vergessen-Müssen' (2017) 36 *Neue Zeitschrift für Verwaltungsrecht*, 1251 (1255).

[98] Comparable: Martini and Weinzierl, 'Die Blockchain-Technologie und das Recht auf Vergessenwerden – Zum Dilemma zwischen Nicht-Vergessen-Können und Vergessen-Müssen' (2017) 36 *Neue Zeitschrift für Verwaltungsrecht*, 1251 (1255).

[99] Critical to this: Finck, 'Blockchains and Data Protection in the European Union' (2018) 4 *European Data Protection Law Review*, 17 (29).

Part B. EU Regulation

data can be viewed by all blockchain users.[100] This means that the data subjects can view the processed data themselves and thus provide the information themselves.[101] If the blockchain user uses a trading platform, the data subject can enforce the right of access against this provider. When the transaction recipient assigns transactions, the transaction sender can enforce the right of access against the transaction recipient.

III. Right to Rectification

84   Art. 16 GDPR regulates the right to rectification. According to this provision, the data subject may immediately request the controller to rectify inaccurate personal data concerning her or him or to complete incomplete personal data, including by means of providing a supplementary statement. A distinction must be made between the two alternatives in Art. 16 GDPR. In the case of a rectification, data must be erased and replaced by the correct data, whereas in the case of a completion, data is only added.[102] Due to the basic structure of a blockchain, which is designed in such a way that no modification of data stored in the blocks is intended, because otherwise all subsequent blocks would have to be recreated, the right to rectification is in principle problematic for all types of blockchain. It is therefore also argued that the blockchain architecture is not compatible with the right to rectification.[103]

85   The question arises as to the meaning and purpose of the right to rectification. The right to rectification enables the data subject to ensure that the correct data are ultimately processed.[104] So the focus is not on deleting the incorrect data, but on correcting the incorrect data. **Correcting the incorrect data** can be achieved in a blockchain by adding the correct data in a block following the incorrect data, which then serves as a starting point for further processing operations. Although this procedure does not correspond to the wording of the rectification in Art. 16 GDPR, a **teleological reduction** of the provision can achieve the result that the rectification of incorrect data by adding the correct data to a block meets the requirements of Art. 16 GDPR.[105]

IV. Right to Erasure and Right to Be Forgotten

86   The right to erasure of data is regulated in Art. 17(1) GDPR. Accordingly, under the reasons set out in Art. 17(1)(a)-(f) GDPR, the data subject may request the immediate erasure of personal data from the data controller. In addition, the data subject can

---

[100] Example of a publicly viewable blockchain: Blockchain.com, available at https://www.blockchain.com/explorer (accessed 26.8.2021).
[101] Schrey and Thalhofer, 'Rechtliche Aspekte der Blockchain' (2017) 70 *Neue Juristische Wochenschrift*, 1431 (1434); critical to this: Finck, 'Blockchains and Data Protection in the European Union' (2018) 4 *European Data Protection Law Review*, 17 (30): the right of access is designed to ensure that the controller takes active steps and passes the information on to the data subject.
[102] Krupar and Strassemeyer, 'Datenschutz auf der Blockchain – die Innovationsfeindlichkeit der DS-GVO' (2018) *Deutsche Stiftung für Recht und Informatik Tagungsband*, 343 (353).
[103] Schrey and Thalhofer, 'Rechtliche Aspekte der Blockchain' (2017) 70 *Neue Juristische Wochenschrift*, 1431 (1435).
[104] Herbst, in Kühling and Buchner (eds), *DS-GVO*, Art. 16, para. 1 et seqq.
[105] Krupar and Strassemeyer, 'Datenschutz auf der Blockchain – die Innovationsfeindlichkeit der DS-GVO' (2018) Deutsche Stiftung für Recht und Informatik Tagungsband; critical to this: Finck, 'Blockchains and Data Protection in the European Union' (2018) 4 *European Data Protection Law Review*, 17 (29).

enforce the right to be forgotten according to Art. 17(2) GDPR. The data subject may demand that the data controller, taking account of the available technology and the cost of implementation, informs other data controllers which are processing the personal data that the data subject has requested the erasure by such controllers of any links to, or copy or replication of those personal data.

87 Due to the typical blockchain architecture, the right to erasure in a blockchain is not enforceable.[106] According to Art. 17(1) GDPR, the controller must erase the data in such a way that access is no longer possible or only possible with disproportionately high effort. A cancellation or reversal of transactions does not meet the requirements of Art. 17(1) GDPR, because a cancellation or reversal means that the original data remain accessible within the blockchain.[107] In contrast to the right to rectification, there is also no possibility here of achieving compatibility by means of a teleological reduction of Art. 17(1) GDPR (on other approaches → para. 93 et seqq.). If the data controller does not comply with a person's right to erasure, the data subject may lodge a complaint with a supervisory authority under Art. 77 GDPR. In addition, fines may be imposed pursuant to Art. 83(5)(b) GDPR (→ para. 91 et seq.).

88 The right to be forgotten according to Art. 17(2) GDPR is again only problematic with regard to the decentralized blockchain, since the controller as a 'simple' blockchain user has the obligation to inform other controllers who have taken the data from the blockchain that they must also delete it but lacks any possibility of influence.

G. Data Protection Supervision and Consequences of Violations under the GDPR

I. Data Protection Supervision

89 Art. 51 et seqq. GDPR contains provisions on data protection supervision. Since the material provisions of data protection law do not need to be implemented, but apply without any further administrative or other enforcement steps, the authorities responsible for data protection only exercise supervision over data controllers and processors and are therefore called '**supervisory authorities**' or more generally '**Data Protection Authorities**' ('**DPAs**').[108] The supervisory authorities monitor compliance with data protection provisions in accordance with public law principles and sanction violations. The **independence** of the supervisory authorities should facilitate their task.[109]

90 The **cooperation** of the supervisory authorities was a major concern in the revision of the European data protection provisions of the GDPR. In the 'predecessor' of the GDPR, Directive 95/46/EC of the European Parliament and of the Council of 24 October 1995 on the protection of individuals with regard to the processing of personal data and on the free movement of such data, or DPD for short, 'forum shopping' was still possible, i.e. companies chose to establish themselves in the Member State in which the level of data protection was relatively low or where the human resources available for data protection

---

[106] Schrey and Thalhofer, 'Rechtliche Aspekte der Blockchain' (2017) 70 *Neue Juristische Wochenschrift*, 1431 (1435).
[107] Martini and Weinzierl, 'Die Blockchain-Technologie und das Recht auf Vergessenwerden – Zum Dilemma zwischen Nicht-Vergessen-Können und Vergessen-Müssen' (2017) 36 *Neue Zeitschrift für Verwaltungsrecht*, 1251 (1254).
[108] Bygrave, in Kuner, Bygrave and Docksey (eds), *GDPR*, 266; Kühling, Klar and Sackmann, *Datenschutzrecht* (5th Edition, 2021), para. 712.
[109] Kühling, Klar and Sackmann, *Datenschutzrecht* (5th Edition, 2021), para. 714.

supervision were very limited.¹¹⁰ The GDPR now applies the so-called **'one-stop shop principle'**. The supervisory authority in the country of the establishment is the lead supervisory authority, which is also responsible for any cross-border processing by the controller or the processor. However, the data subject should be able to contact the supervisory authority at her or his place of residence. Cooperation between supervisory authorities within Member States is therefore necessary. If a data subject lodges a complaint with the supervisory authority at her or his place of residence, the latter will refer the case to the lead supervisory authority, i.e. the supervisory authority of the Member State where the company has its (main) establishment. The lead supervisory authority deals with the case and involves the other supervisory authority as the supervisory authority concerned in the proceedings.¹¹¹

II. Remedies, Liability and Penalties

91 Remedies, liability and penalties are regulated in Art. 77 et seqq. GDPR. According to Art. 77 GDPR, for example, every data subject has the right to lodge a **complaint** with a supervisory authority. The data subject may also assert civil law claims against the controller and the processor in accordance with Art. 82 GDPR. In this sense, the data subject may claim compensation for data protection violations if the data subject has suffered damage as a result. In this context, non-material damage can also be compensated.

92 Data controllers and processors are also threatened with **heavy fines** from the supervisory authorities if data protection violations are discovered. The fines are so high because it is difficult for the supervisory authorities to detect data protection violations in the internal data processing operations of the controllers or processors.¹¹² The conditions for the imposition of fines are regulated in Art. 83 GDPR. According to Art. 83 GDPR, the **fines** can in principle be up to 20 million euros, or in the case of an undertaking, up to four percent of the total worldwide annual turnover of the preceding financial year, whichever is higher. Even in the case of less serious infringements, the fines can still be up to 10 million euros, or in the case of an undertaking, up to two percent of the total worldwide annual turnover of the preceding financial year, whichever is higher. The amount of the fine is determined according to the assessment criteria in Art. 83(1) and (2) GDPR.

H. Possibility of Designing a Data Protection Compliant Blockchain

93 Blockchain technology sometimes reaches its limits when it comes to compliance with data protection law. The question arises as to how a blockchain can be designed in such a way that it **complies with data protection law**. One possibility would be to design a blockchain in such a way that it does not fall within the scope of the GDPR at all (→ para. 94 et seqq.). Since the greatest incompatibility of blockchain technology with the GDPR is the enforcement of the data subjects' rights, a possible implementation could also be to design a blockchain in such a way that data can be subsequently altered or erased within the blockchain, or to store personal data from the blockchain at a place outside the blockchain where subsequent alterations and erasure of the data can

---

¹¹⁰ Hijmans, in Kuner, Bygrave and Docksey (eds), *GDPR*, 921; Kuner, Bygrave and Docksey, in Kuner, Bygrave and Docksey (eds), *GDPR*, 39 et seq.; Kühling, Klar and Sackmann, *Datenschutzrecht* (5th Edition, 2021), para. 716.

¹¹¹ Kuner, Bygrave and Docksey, in Kuner, Bygrave and Docksey (eds), *GDPR*, 36 et seq.; Kühling, Klar and Sackmann, *Datenschutzrecht* (5th Edition, 2021), para. 733 et seqq.

¹¹² Kühling, Klar and Sackmann, *Datenschutzrecht* (5th Edition, 2021), para. 715.

be carried out (→ para. 99 et seqq.). However, many of the options mentioned are **criticised** for nullifying the advantages of blockchain technology.[113]

I. Exclusion of the Applicability of the GDPR

The GDPR applies only to the processing of personal data (→ para. 17 et seqq.). If no personal data are stored within the blockchain or if the personal data within a blockchain can be modified in such a way that the data no longer contain any personal reference and cannot be restored with a reasonable amount of time and expense, the scope of the GDPR would no longer apply. 94

It would be possible to **outsource the personal data from the blockchain** and to refer only within the blockchain to the data stored outside the blockchain. This idea may work in various use cases, for example if ownership or similar data are being stored in the blockchain. However, this solution is useless for a blockchain for transferring tokens, since the public keys must at least still be stored within the blockchain. However, the public keys can themselves be personal data, which is why the GDPR would still be applicable to the blockchain despite the outsourcing of the other data.[114] 95

Another way of implementing a blockchain that complies with data protection law is the **anonymization** of personal data in a blockchain. The GDPR is not applicable to anonymous data.[115] Anonymization of data can be achieved through **encryption**.[116] If the personal data were to be encrypted in a blockchain so that no controller or processor could assign it to a person, the scope of the GDPR would no longer apply. However, for the personal data to be anonymous, the encryption must either be carried out by the blockchain user herself or himself or the controller or processor must not have access to the key. If the controller or processor has the key, it is possible to decrypt the data; the data are then no longer anonymous but merely pseudonymous, which does not remove the applicability of the GDPR.[117] 96

Approaches for such encryption are the so-called **'homomorphic' encryption** and the so-called **'zero knowledge proofs'**.[118] Research on homomorphic encryption has been going on for several years. Data that are encrypted in this way can be processed in an encrypted state despite the encryption. However, homomorphic encryption is still in its infancy. It is not expected to be used for blockchain encryption in the near future.[119] 97

---

[113] Martini and Weinzierl, 'Die Blockchain-Technologie und das Recht auf Vergessenwerden – Zum Dilemma zwischen Nicht-Vergessen-Können und Vergessen-Müssen' (2017) 36 *Neue Zeitschrift für Verwaltungsrecht*, 1251 (1257).
[114] Finck, 'Blockchains and Data Protection in the European Union' (2018) 4 *European Data Protection Law Review*, 17 (23, 25); Erbguth, 'Datenschutz auf öffentlichen Blockchains' (2018), 2.3. and 3.1.2, available at https://beck-link.de/v2847 (accessed 26.8.2021).
[115] Recital 26 GDPR.
[116] Erbguth, 'Datenschutz auf öffentlichen Blockchains' (2018), 3.1, available at https://beck-link.de/v2847 (accessed 26.8.2021); different view: Finck, 'Blockchains and Data Protection in the European Union' (2018) 4 *European Data Protection Law Review*, 17 (22): encryption is not sufficient to remove the scope of the GDPR.
[117] Schmid, *Die Nutzung von Cloud-Diensten durch kleine und mittelständische Unternehmen – Eine datenschutzrechtliche Betrachtung der Auslagerung von Kunden-, Personal- und Mandantendaten* (2017), 90 et seq. with further annotations.
[118] European Union Blockchain Observatory and Forum, 'Blockchain and the GDPR' (18.10.2018), 23, available at https://beck-link.de/xvw5b (accessed 26.8.2021).
[119] Schmid, *Die Nutzung von Cloud-Diensten durch kleine und mittelständische Unternehmen – Eine datenschutzrechtliche Betrachtung der Auslagerung von Kunden-, Personal- und Mandantendaten* (2017), 92 with further annotations; Böhme and Pesch, 'Technische Grundlagen und datenschutzrechtliche Fragen der Blockchain-Technologie' (2017) 41 *Datenschutz und Datensicherheit*, 473 (480 et seq.); Finck,

98 At present, however, the use of zero-knowledge proofs is already possible. Zero-knowledge proofs make it possible to verify transactions in which only the arithmetic correctness is checked, but the content of the transaction cannot be read. The blockchain then only shows that a transaction has taken place, but not which public keys were used.[120] Examples of encrypted blockchains are Zcash[121] and Monero[122].

99 However, anonymization can also be achieved through the use of tumblers (→ § 1, para. 106 et seq.). Using a tumbler, for example, eliminates the reference to a person in a decentralized blockchain, because it is no longer possible to attribute the public key to a person even through Big Data applications without disproportionately high effort.

II. Enabling the Enforcement of Data Subjects' Rights

99 In principle, the data in a blockchain cannot be changed. This would require changing all blocks, starting from the block in which the change was made.[123] Exceptionally, data in a blockchain can also be changed if the majority of the full nodes agree to split off the blockchain, so-called **forking** (→ § 1, para. 30). However, forking is not the means of choice to carry out 'simple' and frequently occurring changes, such as altering or erasing personal data in the blockchain.[124]

100 One way to remove outdated or incorrect data from a blockchain without destroying the chain is the so-called **pruning**. This involves erasing transactions from older blocks whose result has already become the starting point for new transactions. However, the method of pruning is sometimes viewed critically.[125]

101 One possible way of implementing a blockchain that conforms to data protection law is to design the blockchain in a special way. One could develop a blockchain in which subsequent changes are possible. **Chameleon hash functions** turn a blockchain into a so-called **redactable blockchain**. In a redactable blockchain, there is a second hash function that is a back door to the data stored in a blockchain. Using the chameleon hash function, data already stored in a blockchain can be changed without changing the actual first hash of the changed block. Therefore, the following blocks do not have to be recalculated. In a central blockchain, the central entity could be the guardian of the chameleon hash function. In the case of a decentralized blockchain, the only possibility would be to make the key pair for the chameleon hash function available to all full nodes or only to certain trusted full nodes, which would then be allowed to make changes to the

---

'Blockchain and the General Data Protection Regulation' (2019), 33 et seq., available at https://beck-link.de/3ds3b (accessed 26.8.2021).

[120] Finck, 'Blockchains and Data Protection in the European Union' (2018) 4 *European Data Protection Law Review*, 17 (25); Martini and Weinzierl, 'Die Blockchain-Technologie und das Recht auf Vergessenwerden – Zum Dilemma zwischen Nicht-Vergessen-Können und Vergessen-Müssen' (2017) 36 *Neue Zeitschrift für Verwaltungsrecht*, 1251 (1256); a detailed explanation can be found at Erbguth, 'Datenschutz auf öffentlichen Blockchains' (2018), 2.4., available at https://beck-link.de/v2847 (accessed 26.8.2021).

[121] Zcash, available at https://z.cash (accessed 26.8.2021).

[122] Monero, available at https://www.getmonero.org (accessed 26.8.2021).

[123] Bechtolf and Vogt, 'Datenschutz in der Blockchain – Eine Frage der Technik – Technologische Hürden und konzeptionelle Chancen' (2018) 8 *Zeitschrift für Datenschutz*, 66 (70).

[124] Bechtolf and Vogt, 'Datenschutz in der Blockchain – Eine Frage der Technik – Technologische Hürden und konzeptionelle Chancen' (2018) 8 *Zeitschrift für Datenschutz*, 66 (70); Finck, 'Blockchains and Data Protection in the European Union' (2018) 4 *European Data Protection Law Review*, 17 (31).

[125] Finck, 'Blockchains and Data Protection in the European Union' (2018) 4 *European Data Protection Law Review*, 17 (30); Martini and Weinzierl, 'Die Blockchain-Technologie und das Recht auf Vergessenwerden – Zum Dilemma zwischen Nicht-Vergessen-Können und Vergessen-Müssen' (2017) 36 *Neue Zeitschrift für Verwaltungsrecht*, 1251 (1254 et seq.).

blockchain.¹²⁶ Changing data within a blockchain may work well with a central blockchain where the central entity has decision-making power, but with a decentralized blockchain this solution reaches its limits due to a lack of consensus among the full nodes.

The outsourcing of data (→ para. 95) does not remove the personal reference and **102** thus the applicability of the GDPR. However, this implementation of a blockchain offers the possibility of subsequently modifying or erasing data stored outside the blockchain, thus enabling the data subjects' rights to be enforced and therefore comply with data protection law.

I. Conclusion

As a rule, the scope of the GDPR is opened to data processing operations within a **103** blockchain. Since the GDPR is designed for central data processing operations, there are problems in determining the controller in a decentralized blockchain. In the case of a central blockchain and the use of trading platforms, data processing operations within a blockchain can theoretically be justified on the basis of consent pursuant to Art. 6(1)(a) GDPR, but this is not practicable because of the possibility of withdrawal of the consent. In the overwhelming majority of cases, however, data processing operations can be justified by the permission regulated in Art. 6(1)(b) GDPR, either if there is a contract between the participants or if a contract-like relationship of trust can be assumed. The conclusion of a data processing agreement is particularly problematic in a decentralized blockchain. Depending on the non-EU countries to which the data are transferred within a blockchain, transfers to these third countries can be problematic and often even lead to the unlawfulness of the data processing operations carried out. Due to the blockchain architecture, the enforcement of data subjects' rights is difficult, in some cases even impossible. Possible solutions for a blockchain that conforms to data protection law could be the encryption of personal data in the blockchain, a blockchain that can also be changed afterwards (so-called redactable blockchain) or the outsourcing of personal data to a place outside the blockchain.

---

[126] Finck, 'Blockchains and Data Protection in the European Union' (2018) 4 *European Data Protection Law Review*, 17 (31); Martini and Weinzierl, 'Die Blockchain-Technologie und das Recht auf Vergessenwerden – Zum Dilemma zwischen Nicht-Vergessen-Können und Vergessen-Müssen' (2017) 36 *Neue Zeitschrift für Verwaltungsrecht*, 1251 (1256 et seq.); Erbguth, 'Datenschutz auf öffentlichen Blockchains' (2018), 2.1., available at https://beck-link.de/v2847 (accessed 26.8.2021).

§ 7
Initial Coin Offerings (ICOs)

Literature[*]: Akerlof, 'The Market for 'Lemons': Quality Uncertainty and the Market Mechanism' (1970) 84 *Quarterly Journal of Economics*, 488; Arlen and Carney, 'Vicarious Liability for Fraud on Securities Markets: Theory and Evidence' [1992] *University of Illinois Law Review*, 691; Armour and others, *Principles of Financial Regulation* (Oxford University Press, Oxford, 2016); Assmann, Schlitt and von Kopp-Colomb (eds), *Wertpapierprospektgesetz* (WpPG) (3rd edn, Otto Schmidt, Köln, 2017); Assmann, Schneider and Mülbert (eds), *Wertpapierhandelsrecht* (7th edn, Otto Schmidt, Köln, 2019); Autorité des Marchés Financiers, 'Discussion Paper on Initial Coin Offerings', available at https://beck-link.de/3smxv (accessed 11.4.2021); BaFin, 'Initial Coin Offerings: Hinweisschreiben zur Einordnung als Finanzinstrumente, GZ: WA 11-QB 4100- 2017/0010 2' (20.2.2018), available at https://beck-link.de/2na3t (accessed 11.4.2021); BaFin, 'Merkblatt: Zweites Hinweisschreiben zu Prospekt- und Erlaubnispflichten im Zusammenhang mit der Ausgabe sogenannter Krypto-Token, GZ: WA 51-Wp 7100-2019/0011 und IF 1-AZB 1505-2019/0003' (16.8.2019), available at https://beck-link.de/tz6vv (accessed 11.4.2021); Barsan, 'Legal Challenges of Initial Coin Offerings (ICO)' [2017] *Revue Trimestrielle de Droit Financier*, 54; Bebchuk and Ferrell, 'Rethinking Basic' (2014) 69 *Business Lawyer*, 671; Behme and Zickgraf, 'Zivil- und gesellschaftsrechtliche Aspekte von Initial Coin Offerings (ICOs)' (2019) 5 *Zeitschrift für die gesamte Privatrechtswissenschaft*, 66; Bialluch-von Allwörden und von Allwörden, 'Initial Coin Offerings: Kryptowährungen als Wertpapier oder Vermögensanlage?' (2018) 72 *Zeitschrift für Wirtschafts- und Bankrecht*, 2118; Bitbond, 'Wertpapierprospekt', available at https://beck-link.de/65wpm (accessed 11.4.2021); Black, 'The Legal and Institutional Preconditions for Strong Securities Markets' (2001) 48 *UCLA Law Review*, 781; Brandeis, *Other People's Money and How the Bankers Use It* (F.A. Stokes, New York, 1914); Canadian Securities Administrators, 'CSA Staff Notice 46-307, Cryptocurrency Offerings' (24.8.2017), available at https://beck-link.de/6npac (accessed 11.4.2021); Canadian Securities Administrators, 'CSA Staff Notice 46-308, Securities Law Implications for Offerings of Tokens' (11.6.2018), available at https://beck-link.de/65wd2 (accessed 11.4.2021); Catalini and Gans, 'Some Simple Economics of the Blockchain' (27.11.2016), available at https://beck-link.de/w5c3x (accessed 11.4.2021); Chatard and Mann, 'Initial Coin Offerings und Token-Handel im funktionalen Rechtsvergleich – Entwicklung deutscher Leitlinien auf Grundlage des Diskussionsstands in der Schweiz, Frankreich und Deutschland' (2019) 22 *Neue Zeitschrift für Gesellschaftsrecht*, 567; Clayton, 'Chairman's Testimony on Virtual Currencies: The Roles of the SEC and CFTC, Before the Committee on Banking, Housing, and Urban Affairs, United States Senate' (6.2.2018), available at https://beck-link.de/prp6v (accessed 11.4.2021); Coffee, Sale and Henderson, *Securities Regulation* (Foundation Press, New York, 2015); Commission, 'Proposal for a Regulation of the European Parliament and of the Council on Markets in Crypto-assets, and amending Directive (EU) 2019/1937' COM (2020), 593 final; Darby and Karni, 'Free Competition and the Optimal Amount of Fraud' (1973) 16 *Journal of Law & Economics*, 67; D'Onfro, 'Facebook is reversing its ban on cryptocurrency ads' (CNBC, 26.6.2018), available at https://beck-link.de/fx2z2 (accessed 11.4.2021); ESMA, 'Advice on Initial Coin Offerings and Crypto-Assets' (9.1.2019), available at https://beck-link.de/dm5hb (accessed 11.4.2021); ESMA, 'Statement: ESMA alerts firms involved in Initial Coin Offerings (ICOs) to the need to meet relevant regulatory requirements' (13.11.2017), available at https://beck-link.de/srv7w (accessed 11.4.2021); Fama, 'Efficient Capital Markets: Review of Theory and Empirical Work' (1970) 25 *Journal of Finance*, 383; Ferrell and Roper, 'Price Impact, Materiality, and Halliburton II' (2015) 93 *Washington University Law Review*, 553; FINMA, 'Wegleitung für Unterstellungsanfragen betreffend Initial Coin Offerings (ICOs)' (16.2.2018), available at https://beck-link.de/f5fad (accessed 11.4.2021); Fischel, 'Use of Modern Finance Theory in Securities Fraud Cases Involving Actively Traded Securities' (1982) 38 *Business Lawyer*, 1; Fleischer, *Gutachten F für den 64. Deutschen Juristentag* (C. H. Beck, München, 2002); Fuchs (ed), *Wertpapierhandelsgesetz* (WpHG) (2nd edn, C. H. Beck, München, 2016); Fußwinkel and Kreiterling, 'Blockchain-Technologie – Gedanken zur Regulierung' (1/2018) BaFin Perspektiven, available at https://beck-link.de/a7mkv (accessed 11.4.2021); Goshen and Parchomovsky, 'The Essential Role of Securities Regulation' (2006) 55 *Duke Law Journal*, 711; Hacker and Thomale, 'Crypto-Securities Regulation: ICOs, Token Sales and Cryptocurrencies under EU Financial Law' [2018] *European Company and Financial Law Review*, 645; Haffke and Fromberger, 'ICO Market Report 2017.

---

[*] See for further references on the German literature: Zickgraf, '§ 11 – Initial Coin Offerings (ICOs)', in Maume and Maute (eds), *Rechtshandbuch Kryptowerte* (2020), § 11.

§ 7. Initial Coin Offerings (ICOs)

Performance Analysis of Initial Coin Offerings' (2019), available at https://beck-link.de/wx3dp (accessed 11.4.2021); Hahn and Wilkens, 'ICO vs. IPO – Prospektrechtliche Anforderungen bei Equity Token Offerings' (2019) 31 *Zeitschrift für Bankrecht und Bankwirtschaft*, 10; Hildner, 'Bitcoins auf dem Vormarsch: Schaffung eines regulatorischen Level Playing Fields?' (2016) 16 *Zeitschrift für Bank- und Kapitalmarktrecht*, 485; Hinman, 'Digital Asset Transactions: When Howey Met Gary (Plastic), Remarks at the Yahoo Finance All Markets Summit: Crypto' (14.6.2018), available at https://beck-link.de/y3p8b (accessed 11.4.2021); HM Treasury, Financial Conduct Authority and the Bank of England, 'Cryptoassets Taskforce: Final Report' (October 2018), available at https://beck-link.de/w3xv5 (accessed 4.11.2021); Holmström, 'Moral Hazard and Observability' (1979) 10 *Bell Journal of Economics*, 74; Irwin, 'Stated expectations as functions of probability and desirability of outcomes' (1953) 21 *Journal of Personality*, 329; Jensen and Meckling, 'Theory of the firm: Managerial behavior, agency costs and ownership structure' (1976) 3 *Journal of Financial Economics*, 305; Jentzsch, 'Decentralized Autonomous Organization To Automate Governance' (2016), available at https://beck-link.de/7anas (accessed 11.4.2021); Just, Voß, Ritz and Zeising (eds), *Wertpapierprosektgesetz* (1st edn, C. H. Beck, München, 2009); Kaulartz and Matzke, 'Die Tokenisierung des Rechts' (2018) 71 *Neue Juristische Wochenschrift*, 3278; Kirsch, von Wieding und Höbener, 'Bilanzierungsfähigkeit von Krypto-Token aus einem Hard Fork und Airdrop nach IFRS' (2020) 15 *Zeitschrift für Internationale Rechnungslegung*, 495; Klöhn, 'Die Ausweitung der bürgerlich-rechtlichen Prospekthaftung durch das 'Rupert Scholz'-Urteil des BGH' (2012) 66 *Zeitschrift für Wirtschafts- und Bankrecht*, 97; Klöhn, 'Die neue Prospektfreiheit 'kleiner' Wertpapieremissionen unter 8 Mio. €' (2018) 40 *Zeitschrift für Wirtschaftsrecht*, 1713; Klöhn, '§ 6 – Kapitalmarktrecht', in Langenbucher (ed), *Europäisches Privat- und Wirtschaftsrecht* (4th edn, Nomos, Baden-Baden, 2017); Klöhn, 'Marktbetrug (Fraud on the Market)' (2014) 178 *Zeitschrift für das gesamte Handels- und Wirtschaftsrecht*, 671; Klöhn (ed), *Marktmissbrauchsverordnung* (München, 2018); Klöhn and Parhofer, 'Bitcoins sind keine Rechnungseinheiten – ein Paukenschlag und seine Folgen' (2018) 40 *Zeitschrift für Wirtschaftsrecht*, 2093; Klöhn, Parhofer and Resas, 'Initial Coin Offerings (ICOs)' (2018) 30 *Zeitschrift für Bankrecht und Bankwirtschaft*, 89; *Kölner Kommentar zum Wertpapierhandelsgesetz* (Kölner-KommWpHG) (2nd edn, Carl Heymanns, München, 2014); Krüger and Lampert, 'Augen auf bei der Token-Wahl – privatrechtliche und steuerrechtliche Herausforderungen im Rahmen eines Initial Coin Offerings' [2018] *Betriebs-Berater*, 1154; Kunda, 'Motivated inference: self-serving generation and evaluation of causal theories' (1987) 53 *Journal of Personality & Social Psychology*, 636; Langenbucher, *Aktien- und Kapitalmarktrecht* (4th edn, C.H. Beck, München, 2019); Langenbucher, 'Digitales Finanzwesen – Vom Bargeld zu virtuellen Währungen' (2018) 218 *Archiv für die civilistische Praxis*, 385; Langenbucher, 'European Securities Law – Are we in need of a new definition? A thought inspired by initial coin offerings' [2018] *Revue Trimestrielle de Droit Financier*, 40; Langevoort, 'Basic at Twenty: Rethinking Fraud on the Market' [2009] *Wisconsin Law Review*, 151; Loss, Seligman and Paredes, *Fundamentals of Securities Regulation* (7th edn, Wolters Kluwer, New York, 2018); Maume, 'Initial Coin Offerings and EU Prospectus Disclosure' (2020) 31 *European Business Law Review*, 185; Maume and Fromberger, 'Regulation of Initial Coin Offerings: Reconciling U.S. and E.U. Securities Laws' (2019) 19 *Chicago Journal of International Law*, 548; Molla, 'Twitter, Google and Facebook have banned cryptocurrency ads – but these networks still haven't' (recode, 26.3.2018), available at https://beck-link.de/cy4fr (accessed 11.4.2021); Moloney, *EU Securities and Financial Markets Regulation* (3rd edn, Oxford University Press, Oxford, 2014); Monetary Authority of Singapore, 'A Guide To Digital Token Offerings' (2018), available at https://beck-link.de/4nzy7 (accessed 11.4.2021); People's Bank of China, 'Public Notice of the PBC, CAC, MIIT, SAIC, CBRC, CSRC and CIRC on Preventing Risks of Fundraising through Coin Offering' (8.9.2017), available at https://beck-link.de/hm4n3 (accessed 11.4.2021); Pilarowski and Yue, 'China Bans Initial Coin Offerings and Cryptocurrency Trading Platforms, China Regulation Watch' (21.9.2017), available at https://beck-link.de/st6ry (accessed 11.4.2021); Pitchford, 'How Liable Should a Lender Be? The Case of Judgment-Proof Firms and Environmental Risk' (1995) 85 *American Economic Review*, 1171; Richter and Furubotn, *Neue Institutionenökonomik* (4th edn, Mohr Siebeck, Tübingen, 2010); Rohr and Wright, 'Blockchain-Based Token Sales, Initial Coin Offerings, and the Democratization of Public Capital Markets' (2018) *Cardozo Legal Studies Research Paper* No. 527, available at https://beck-link.de/peh4b (accessed 11.4.2021); Rohr and Wright, 'Blockchain-Based Token Sales, Initial Coin Offerings, and the Democratization of Public Capital Markets' (2019) 70 *Hastings Law Journal*, 463; Samuelson, 'Proof That Properly Anticipated Prices Fluctuate Randomly' (1965) 6 *Industrial Management Review*, 41; Schwark and Zimmer (eds), *Kapitalmarktrechts-Kommentar* (5th edn, C. H. Beck, München, 2020); Securities and Exchange Commission, 'In the Matter of Munchee Inc.: Securities Act of 1933 Release No. 10445' (11.12.2017), available at https://beck-link.de/yd3ne (accessed 11.4.2021); Securities and Exchange Commission, 'Report of Investigation Pursuant to Section 21(a) of the Securities Exchange Act of 1934: The DAO' (25.7.2017) Release No. 81207, available at https://beck-link.de/5pfa8 (accessed 11.4.2021); Securities and Markets Stakeholder Group, 'Advice to ESMA: Own Initiative Report on Initial Coin Offerings and Crypto-Assets' (19.10.2018), available at https://beck-link.de/y47xy (accessed 11.4.2021); Sester, 'Fallen Anteile an Geschlossenen Fonds unter den Wertpapierbegriff der MiFID bzw. des FRUG?'

Part B. EU Regulation

(2008) 20 *Zeitschrift für Bankrecht und Bankwirtschaft*, 369; Shavell, *Economic Analysis of Accident Law* (Harvard University Press, Cambridge, 1987); Shavell, 'The judgment proof problem' (1986) 6 *International Review of Law & Economics*, 45; Spence, 'Job Market Signaling' (1973) 87 *Quarterly Journal of Economics*, 355; Spindler, 'Initial Coin Offerings und Prospektpflicht und -haftung' (2018) 72 *Zeitschrift für Wirtschafts- und Bankrecht*, 2109; Summers, 'The Case of the Disappearing Defendant: An Economic Analysis' (1983) 132 *University of Pennsylvania Law Review*, 145; Thaler, 'From Homo Economicus to Homo Sapiens' (2000) 14 *Journal of Economic Perspectives*, 133; Thompson, 'Federal Corporate Law: Torts and Fiduciary Duty' (2006) 31 *Journal of Corporation Law*, 877; van Aubel, '§ 20 – Initial Coin Offerings (ICOs)', in Habersack, Mülbert and Schlitt (eds), *Unternehmensfinanzierung am Kapitalmarkt* (4th edn, Otto Schmidt, Köln, 2019); Veil, *European Capital Markets Law* (2nd edn, Hart Publishing, Oxford, 2017); Veil, 'Token-Emissionen im europäischen Kapitalmarktrecht' (2019) 183 *Zeitschrift für das gesamte Handels- und Wirtschaftsrecht*, 346; Voß, 'Geschlossene Fonds unter dem Rechtsregime der Finanzmarkt-Richtlinie (MiFID)?' (2007) 7 *Zeitschrift für Bank- und Kapitalmarktrecht*, 45; Weinstein, 'Unrealistic optimism about future life events' (1980) 39 *Journal of Personality and Social Psychology*, 806; Weinstein and Klein, 'Unrealistic Optimism: Present and Future' (1996) 15 *Journal of Social & Clinical Psychology*, 1; Weitnauer, 'Initial Coin Offerings (ICOs): Rechtliche Rahmenbedingungen und regulatorische Grenzen' (2018) 18 *Zeitschrift für Bank- und Kapitalmarktrecht*, 231; Zetzsche, Buckley, Arner and Föhr, 'The ICO Gold Rush: It's a Scam, It's a Bubble, It's a Super Challenge for Regulators' (19.11.2017), available at https://beck-link.de/k23ak (accessed 11.4.2021); Zickgraf, '§ 11 – Initial Coin Offerings (ICOs)', in Maume and Maute (eds), *Rechtshandbuch Kryptowerte* (C.H. Beck, München, 2020); Zickgraf, 'Initial Coin Offerings – Ein Fall für das Kapitalmarktrecht?' (2018) 63 *Die Aktiengesellschaft*, 293; Zickgraf, 'Primärmarktpublizität in der Verordnung über Märkte für Kryptowerte (MiCAR) – Teil 1' (2021) 21 *Zeitschrift für Bank- und Kapitalmarktrecht*, 196; Zickgraf, 'Primärmarktpublizität in der Verordnung über Märkte für Kryptowerte (MiCAR) – Teil 2' (2021) 21 *Zeitschrift für Bank- und Kapitalmarktrecht*, 362; Zynis, 'A Brief History Of Mastercoin' (2013), available at https://beck-link.de/xx5an (accessed 11.4.2021).

Outline

	para.
A. Historical Development	1
B. Economic Background	4
I. Economic Foundations of the Primary Market	4
II. Economic Foundations of the Primary Market for Tokens	7
III. Corporate Fundraising via ICOs	8
1. Opportunities	8
2. Risks	10
C. Comparative Legal Overview	13
I. North America	14
1. USA	14
2. Canada	15
II. Asia	16
1. China	16
2. Hong Kong	17
3. Singapore	18
III. Europe	19
1. EU	19
2. United Kingdom	22
3. France	23
4. Germany	24
5. Austria	27
6. Switzerland	28
IV. Summary	29
D. Initial Coin Offerings in EU Capital Markets Law	30
I. Prospectus Obligation under EU Prospectus Regulation	31
1. Formal Requirements of 'Transferable Security'	33
a) Transferability	34
b) Standardisation	38
aa) General Requirements	38
bb) Issuer Level or Asset Class	39

c) Negotiability in the Narrow Sense.. 44
     aa) General Requirements.. 44
     bb) Possibility of bona fide acquisition as a prerequisite of
         negotiability?... 45
  2. Substantial Requirement of 'Transferable Security': Functional
     Comparability with the non-exhaustive List of Examples of
     Art. 4(1)(44) MiFID2 47
     a) Investment Tokens... 48
     b) Utility Tokens.. 52
        aa) General Remarks 53
        bb) Legal Analysis of Utility Tokens... 56
            (1) First View: Utility Tokens are not Transferable
                Securities.. 56
            (2) Second View: Utility Tokens are Transferable
                Securities.. 58
            (3) Preferable View: A Differentiating Approach to Utility
                Tokens.. 61
     c) Currency Tokens 65
     d) Hybrid Tokens 69
     e) Token Derivatives... 70
     f) Tokens not Conveying Any Rights 71
  3. Exemptions from the Prospectus Obligation.............................. 72
     a) Investor-Related Exemptions 73
     b) Exemptions related to Transaction Volume......................... 76
  4. Content of the Prospectus... 78
  5. Approval and Publication of the Prospectus.............................. 81
  6. Advertisements 86
  7. Prospectus Liability.. 88
E. Regulation on Markets in Crypto-Assets.. 89
  I. Background and Overview... 89
  II. Scope.. 91
  III. Obligation to Publish a Crypto-Asset White Paper................... 96
  IV. Content and Form of the Crypto-Asset White Paper................ 98
  V. Marketing Communications.. 101
  VI. Regulatory Procedure... 103
  VII. Right of Withdrawal.. 108
  VIII. General Obligations of Issuers of Crypto-Assets..................... 110
  IX. Liability of Issuers of Crypto-Assets.. 111

A. Historical Development

Starting with the **Initial Coin Offering** (ICO) of Mastercoin in July 2013,[1] ICOs have emerged in recent years as a popular means of early-stage financing for start-up companies via the capital market. Since mid-2017, there was initially a strong increase in the number and volume of ICOs (2016: > USD 250 million; 2017: > USD 6.5 billion; 2018: > USD 21.5 billion[2]; 2019: > USD 3 billion),[3] so that corporate financing via **token**

1

---

[1] Cf. Zynis, 'A Brief History Of Mastercoin' (2013), available at https://beck-link.de/xx5an (accessed 11.4.2021); see for further milestones Zickgraf, '§ 11 – Initial Coin Offerings (ICOs)', in Maume and Maute (eds), *Rechtshandbuch Kryptorecht* (2020), § 11, para. 1.

[2] See for further references on the empirical data for the years 2016 – 2018: Zickgraf, '§ 11 – Initial Coin Offerings (ICOs)', in Maume and Maute (eds), *Rechtshandbuch Kryptowerte* (2020), § 11, para. 1.

[3] Likewise Haffke and Fromberger, 'ICO Market Report 2017. Performance Analysis of Initial Coin Offerings' (2019), 8, 11 (2017: > USD 6.5 billion), available at https://beck-link.de/wx3dp (accessed 11.4.2021); Haffke and Fromberger, 'ICO Market Report 2018/2019. Performance Analysis of 2018's Initial Coin Offerings' (2019), 3, 9 (2018: > USD 14 billion), available at https://papers.ssrn.com/sol3/

sales[4] was – at least for blockchain-oriented companies – no longer a mere alternative to traditional venture capital financing, but appeared to be replacing it as the main source of financing.[5] However, the rapid growth of the ICO market reached its (preliminary) peak in 2018:[6] At this point in time, the first cases of fraud (Bitconnect) and hacking attacks on issuers (The DAO) as well as crypto exchanges (Mt. Gox) had become public.[7] These events had led numerous Internet platforms and various social networks to the decision to no longer present advertisements for ICOs on their websites.[8]

2   The early phase of the ICOs was characterised by initiators who largely ignored the (uncertain) **regulatory requirements**; as a result, the issuers did not publish **securities prospectuses** approved by regulatory authorities.[9] However, in July 2017 the Securities and Exchange Commission (SEC) put an abrupt end to the widespread misconception in the blockchain scene that ICOs were not subject to securities regulation when it classified the tokens offered by The DAO as securities.[10] Numerous other supervisory authorities followed the SEC's example and subsequently commented on the regulatory classification of ICOs under existing capital markets laws (→ para. 13 et seqq.). In the aftermath of these events, a lively scholarly debate on the legal assessment of ICOs under capital market law has developed.[11]

---

papers.cfm?abstract_id=3512125 (accessed 11.4.2021); Haffke and Fromberger, 'ICO Market Report 2019/2020. Performance Analysis of 2019's Initial Coin Offerings' (2019), 3, 9 (2019: > USD 3 billion), available at https://papers.ssrn.com/sol3/papers.cfm?abstract_id=3770793 (accessed 11.4.2021); see for further empirical data Veil, 'Token-Emissionen im europäischen Kapitalmarktrecht' (2019) 183 *Zeitschrift für das gesamte Handels- und Wirtschaftsrecht*, 346 (347).

[4] In the legal literature, the terms 'Initial Coin Offering (ICO)' and 'Token Sale' are both common, without any difference regarding substance, cf. Hacker and Thomale, 'Crypto-Securities Regulation: ICOs, Token Sales and Cryptocurrencies under EU Financial Law' [2018] *European Company and Financial Law Review*, 645; Klöhn, Parhofer and Resas, 'Initial Coin Offerings (ICOs)' (2018) 30 *Zeitschrift für Bankrecht und Bankwirtschaft*, 89 (90); Zickgraf, 'Initial Coin Offerings – Ein Fall für das Kapitalmarktrecht?' (2018) 63 *Die Aktiengesellschaft*, 293. The term Security Token Offering (STO) or Equity Token Offering (ETO), on the other hand, is associated with the legal statement that the offered tokens constitute securities, cf. Hahn and Wilkens, 'ICO vs. IPO – Prospektrechtliche Anforderungen bei Equity Token Offerings' (2019) 31 *Zeitschrift für Bankrecht und Bankwirtschaft*, 10 (14).

[5] Klöhn, Parhofer and Resas, 'Initial Coin Offerings (ICOs)' (2018) 30 *Zeitschrift für Bankrecht und Bankwirtschaft*, 89 (90) with further references.

[6] See the declining overall emission volume from 2018 to 2019; cf. Haffke and Fromberger, 'ICO Market Report 2019/2020. Performance Analysis of 2019's Initial Coin Offerings' (2019), 9, 12 et seq., available at https://papers.ssrn.com/sol3/papers.cfm?abstract_id=3770793 (accessed 11.4.2021).

[7] See Klöhn, Parhofer and Resas, 'Initial Coin Offerings (ICOs)' (2018) 30 *Zeitschrift für Bankrecht und Bankwirtschaft*, 89 (90).

[8] The platforms and social networks include Baidu, Google, Tencent and Twitter, cf. Molla, 'Twitter, Google and Facebook have banned cryptocurrency ads – but these networks still haven't' (recode, 26.3.2018), available at https://beck-link.de/cy4fr (accessed 11.4.2021). Facebook had not presented any advertisements for a while, but now allows advertising from verified providers again, cf. D'Onfro, 'Facebook is reversing its ban on cryptocurrency ads' (CNBC, 26.6.2018), available at https://beck-link.de/fx2z2 (accessed 11.4.2021).

[9] Cf. Zickgraf, 'Initial Coin Offerings – Ein Fall für das Kapitalmarktrecht?' (2018) 63 *Die Aktiengesellschaft*, 293.

[10] Securities and Exchange Commission, 'Report of Investigation Pursuant to Section 21(a) of the Securities Exchange Act of 1934: The DAO' (25.7.2017) Release No. 81207, available at https://beck-link.de/5pfa8 (accessed 11.4.2021).

[11] Cf. from the international literature: Rohr and Wright, 'Blockchain-Based Token Sales, Initial Coin Offerings, and the Democratization of Public Capital Markets' (2018) *Cardozo Legal Studies Research Paper* No. 527, available at https://beck-link.de/peh4b (accessed 11.4.2021); Barsan, 'Legal Challenges of Initial Coin Offerings (ICO)' [2017] *Revue Trimestrielle de Droit Financier*, 54; Hacker and Thomale, 'Crypto-Securities Regulation: ICOs, Token Sales and Cryptocurrencies under EU Financial Law' [2018] *European Company and Financial Law Review*, 645; Langenbucher, 'European Securities Law – Are we in need of a new definition? A thought inspired by initial coin offerings' [2018] *Revue Trimestrielle de Droit Financier*, 40; Maume and Fromberger, 'Regulation of Initial Coin Offerings: Reconciling U.S. and E.U.

§ 7. Initial Coin Offerings (ICOs)

Currently, the market for ICOs is in a phase of consolidation and maturation: 3 Emission volumes have declined since their peak in 2018 and the secondary market performance is weak.[12] However, given the total emission volume (overall > USD 25 billion, see → para. 2), the economic importance of the ICO market should not be underestimated.[13] Intermediaries and specialised consultants have emerged, contributing to the professionalisation of the market.[14] The (ongoing) evolution of the ICO market and the establishment of supervisory practices is reflected by ICOs in which issuers have published securities prospectuses approved by the competent regulatory authorities. The first such ICO in Europe was conducted in November 2018 via a securities prospectus approved by the Austrian Financial Market Authority (FMA)).[15] In 2019, another ICO was undertaken using a securities prospectus approved by the German Bundesanstalt für Finanzdienstleistungsaufsicht (BaFin).[16]

B. Economic Background

I. Economic Foundations of the Primary Market

From a Law & Economics perspective, primary market regulation aims at increasing 4 the **allocational efficiency** of the market and **reducing the issuers' cost of capital**.[17] These policy goals are heavily affected by the quality of information which is available to investors when making their investment decisions: After all, securities represent **credence goods**[18], whose future value depends on the performance of the issuer.[19] Thus, considerable information asymmetries exist between the issuer (including managers/ board members and existing investors) and potential investors, which lead to **principal-agent conflicts**.[20] For instance, there are often insufficient incentives for the issuer and

---

Securities Laws' (2019) 19 *Chicago Journal of International Law*, 548; see for an overview of the German literature: Zickgraf, '§ 11 – Initial Coin Offerings (ICOs)', in Maume and Maute (eds), *Rechtshandbuch Kryptowerte* (2020), § 11, para. 2.

[12] Haffke and Fromberger, 'ICO Market Report 2019/2020. Performance Analysis of 2019's Initial Coin Offerings' (2019), 9, 12 et seq., 17 et seqq., available at https://papers.ssrn.com/sol3/papers.cfm?abstract_id=3770793 (accessed 11.4.2021).

[13] Similar van Aubel, '§ 20 – Initial Coin Offerings (ICOs)', in Habersack, Mülbert and Schlitt (eds), *Unternehmensfinanzierung am Kapitalmarkt* (2019), § 20, para. 1.

[14] See for example the Blockchain analyst firm Smith + Crown.

[15] The prospectus was drawn up by Hydrominer IT-Services GmbH and was approved by the Austrian Finanzmarktaufsicht (FMA) on November 26, 2018, cf. SVLaw, available at https://beck-link.de/6cthv (accessed 11.4.2021); with regard to the first ICO where an officially approved securities prospectus was used, it is sometimes referred to the transaction of Neon Exchange AG, whose prospectus was approved by the Liechtenstein FMA. In any case, both ICOs took place in short intervals, cf. Veil, 'Token-Emissionen im europäischen Kapitalmarktrecht' (2019) 183 *Zeitschrift für das gesamte Handels- und Wirtschaftsrecht*, 346 (352, 353).

[16] Bitbond, 'Wertpapierprospekt', available at https://beck-link.de/65wpm (accessed 11.4.2021); see also Veil, 'Token-Emissionen im europäischen Kapitalmarktrecht' (2019) 183 *Zeitschrift für das gesamte Handels- und Wirtschaftsrecht*, 346 (353) and → § 17 para. 7 et seqq.

[17] Moloney, *EU Securities and Financial Markets Regulation* (3rd edn, 2014), 38; see generally for the regulatory goals of capital markets regulation: Coffee, Sale and Henderson, *Securities Regulation* (2015), 3 et seqq.

[18] Cf. the seminal article on credence goods by Darby and Karni, 'Free Competition and the Optimal Amount of Fraud' (1973) 16 *Journal of Law & Economics*, 67.

[19] Moloney, *EU Securities and Financial Markets Regulation* (3rd edn, 2014), 55; similar Armour and others, *Principles of Financial Regulation* (2016), 101; Coffee, Sale and Henderson, *Securities Regulation* (2015), 7.

[20] Cf. Jensen and Meckling, 'Theory of the firm: Managerial behavior, agency costs and ownership structure' (1976) 3 *Journal of Financial Economics*, 305.

its managers to disclose detrimental information, while there is at the same time a potential risk of sugar coating the issuer's current situation and future prospects.[21] To the extent that investors are unable to assess the quality and intrinsic value of the securities offered because of information asymmetries, capital will be misallocated and even the entire market may collapse.[22]

5   Capital markets law addresses these problems with **disclosure obligations** (in particular, the obligation to publish a securities prospectus, → para. 30 et seqq.), which it imposes on issuers of securities and which are intended to reduce the prevailing informational asymmetries.[23] First of all, this obligation protects the investors, who can subsequently make an **informed investment decision**. Simultaneously, the disclosure obligations increase the allocational efficiency of the market, because the information provided enables investors to identify the most promising business ventures and avoid investing in less promising projects.[24] Moreover, the disclosure obligations prevent the potential collapse of the overall market: If investors were unable to assess the quality of the securities on offer due to a lack of sufficient information and there were qualitatively different securities offers on the market, rational investors would protect themselves from the risk of acquiring low quality-securities by reducing their willingness to pay (risk discount).[25] As a result, issuers of high-quality securities would no longer receive adequate returns, potentially making them leave the market. Then, only those issuers of low-quality securities would remain on the market (**adverse selection**), to which rational investors would react by further reducing their willingness to pay. In the end, this adverse selection would lead to the collapse of the entire primary market (**market for lemons**).[26]

6   Disclosure requirements reduce **information asymmetries** between issuers and investors and thus prevent the collapse of the market due to adverse selection. In addition to protecting the market, the obligation to publish a securities prospectus also serves to protect issuers, who are thereby supported in giving credible signals (**signalling**[27]) with respect to the quality of the securities offered.[28] The provision of (financial) information on the securities offered in a standardised form via

---

[21] Coffee, Sale and Henderson, *Securities Regulation* (2015), 7, 8; Moloney, *EU Securities and Financial Markets Regulation* (3rd edn, 2014), 56; Black, 'The Legal and Institutional Preconditions for Strong Securities Markets' (2001) 48 *UCLA Law Review*, 781 (786); Fleischer, *Gutachten F für den 64. Deutschen Juristentag* (2002), F41 et seq.

[22] Klöhn, '§ 6 – Kapitalmarktrecht', in Langenbucher (ed), *Europäisches Privat- und Wirtschaftsrecht* (4th edn, 2017), 363; Klöhn, 'Die Ausweitung der bürgerlich-rechtlichen Prospekthaftung durch das 'Rupert Scholz'-Urteil des BGH' (2012) 66 *Zeitschrift für Wirtschafts- und Bankrecht*, 97 (98); more details regarding the market for lemons → para. 5.

[23] Fleischer, *Gutachten F für den 64. Deutschen Juristentag* (2002), F41; Klöhn, 'Die Ausweitung der bürgerlich-rechtlichen Prospekthaftung durch das 'Rupert Scholz'-Urteil des BGH' (2012) 66 *Zeitschrift für Wirtschafts- und Bankrecht*, 97 (98). In this context, reference is often made to the well-known quote by former Supreme Court judge Louis Brandeis: 'Sunlight is said to be the best of disinfectants (...)', cf. Brandeis, *Other People's Money and How the Bankers Use It* (1914), 92; cf. Loss, Seligman and Paredes, *Fundamentals of Securities Regulation* (7th edn, 2018), 11: 'Then, too, there is the recurrent theme throughout these statutes of disclosure, again disclosure, and still more disclosure.'.

[24] Klöhn, '§ 6 – Kapitalmarktrecht', in Langenbucher (ed), *Europäisches Privat- und Wirtschaftsrecht* (4th edn, 2017), 363.

[25] See generally for this notion within the context of capital market disclosure obligations: Coffee, Sale and Henderson, *Securities Regulation* (2015), 7.

[26] Cf. Black, 'The Legal and Institutional Preconditions for Strong Securities Markets' (2001) 48 *UCLA Law Review*, 781 (786); see also the seminal article on adverse selection and the so-called market for lemons: Akerlof, 'The Market for 'Lemons': Quality Uncertainty and the Market Mechanism' (1970) 84 *Quarterly Journal of Economics*, 488.

[27] Cf. Spence, 'Job Market Signaling' (1973) 87 *Quarterly Journal of Economics*, 355.

[28] Moloney, *EU Securities and Financial Markets Regulation* (3rd edn, 2014), 54, 56.

a prospectus also reduces the risk of unconsciously acquiring a low-value investment asset, thus reducing the need for investors to take this risk into account and at the same time increasing investors' willingness to pay, which in turn reduces the cost of capital for issuers. Nevertheless, the **disclosure obligations** cause **(transaction) costs** for issuers. This means that a **balance** must be struck between the declining **cost of capital** resulting from improved market and investor protection and the **(transaction) costs** arising from the disclosure obligations.[29] In comparison to alternative policy approaches, such as information gathering by investors, requiring the **issuer** to disclose material information via a securities prospectus clearly seems to be preferable because the issuer can provide the relevant information **more cheaply**.[30] Furthermore, the publication of a securities prospectus also reduces the multiple search costs of investors, thereby promoting operational efficiency of the capital market.[31]

II. Economic Foundations of the Primary Market for Tokens

From a Law & Economics perspective, ICOs should be regulated by capital markets law if the **tokens** offered represent **credence goods** (→ para. 4), so that information asymmetries exist between investors and initiators, which can lead to **agency conflicts** because of the (apparent) correlation between the value of the tokens and the current situation as well as the future performance of the issuer.[32] If such information asymmetries exist in a particular case, they are at least as pronounced in ICOs as in the primary market for 'conventional' securities (IPOs) due to the highly innovative and technically complex business models of the issuers.[33] Against this background, the existing disclosure requirements of capital markets law must be applied in order to avoid misallocations of capital. In such cases, the application of the capital market legal framework to ICOs is by no means contrary to the interests of issuers, but rather prevents an otherwise imminent market failure and at the same time reduces issuers' cost of capital (→ para. 4 et seqq.). 7

III. Corporate Fundraising via ICOs

1. Opportunities

With regard to the possible advantages of corporate funding through ICOs[34], a distinction must be made between the **financing method** and the **business models** of the issuers (→ para. 9). Raising capital using an ICO mainly offers the advantage of (potentially) **reducing transaction costs**: Because of the direct sale of the tokens via the Internet, the issuer does not need traditional intermediaries (e.g. investment banks); instead, the allocation of the tokens is handled by smart contracts (→ § 1 para. 62 8

---

[29] Coffee, Sale and Henderson, *Securities Regulation* (2015), 7 et seq., 11; Moloney, *EU Securities and Financial Markets Regulation* (3rd edn, 2014), 56 with further references.
[30] Fleischer, *Gutachten F für den 64. Deutschen Juristentag* (2002), F41 with further references on the debate about public vs. private ordering of disclosure of relevant information.
[31] Klöhn, '§ 6 – Kapitalmarktrecht', in Langenbucher (ed) *Europäisches Privat- und Wirtschaftsrecht* (4th edn, 2017), 363 et seq.
[32] Similar Klöhn, Parhofer and Resas, 'Initial Coin Offerings (ICOs)' (2018) 30 *Zeitschrift für Bankrecht und Bankwirtschaft*, 89 (101).
[33] Ibid, 95.
[34] Cf. HM Treasury, Financial Conduct Authority and the Bank of England, 'Cryptoassets Taskforce: Final Report' (October 2018), 31 et seq., available at https://beck-link.de/w3xv5 (accessed 4.11.2021).

et seqq., 86), which reduces the overall cost of raising capital.[35] In addition, offering tokens via the Internet enables issuers to address a global investor audience.[36] For investors, ICOs provide **direct access to early-stage investments** in start-up companies, while allowing financial instruments to be traded on reasonably liquid secondary markets. Until recently, such investments were usually only available to professional venture capital funds, and the respective investment assets[37] could usually not be traded on secondary markets, making them illiquid investments.[38] Furthermore, the blockchain technology, on which ICOs are based, enables the cost-effective and fast (cross-border) transfer of the tokens.[39] In terms of technical implementation, the blockchain thus opens up **innovation potential** for financing practices of companies via the capital market.[40]

9 Not directly related to the ICO as a method of financing are the **business models** which shall be financed by the proceeds of the emissions. The issuers' innovative, mostly blockchain-based business models are often characterised by a reduction of transaction costs, which is supposed to be achieved by the **elimination of intermediaries** (disintermediation) and the **use of smart contracts**.[41] Enterprises that are financed through the issuance of **utility tokens** are also characterised by the attempt to monetise **network effects**: In simple terms, this goal can be achieved by rewarding contributions of one group of users to the respective network with tokens that a second group of users needs to utilise the services of the network, whereby the demand for tokens of the second group of users establishes a connection between the value of the utility tokens and the value of the network, which can be monetised by the first group of users through a sale of the tokens.[42] As a result, the investors, the contributing users and the initiators can profit from the (decentralised) networks' increase in value.[43] Compared to a conventional financial investment in a network operator (e.g. Facebook, Twitter etc), such an operational design comes with the advantage that a **direct connection** is established between the value of the network and the value of the utility token.[44]

---

[35] Similar: Veil, 'Token-Emissionen im europäischen Kapitalmarktrecht' (2019) 183 *Zeitschrift für das gesamte Handels- und Wirtschaftsrecht*, 346 (347 et seq., 353); cf. Maume, 'Initial Coin Offerings and EU Prospectus Disclosure' (2020) 31 *European Business Law Review*, 185 (189).

[36] Rohr and Wright, 'Blockchain-Based Token Sales, Initial Coin Offerings, and the Democratization of Public Capital Markets' (2018) *Cardozo Legal Studies Research Paper* No. 527, 28, available at https://beck-link.de/peh4b (accessed 11.4.2021); Zickgraf, 'Initial Coin Offerings – Ein Fall für das Kapitalmarktrecht?' (2018) 63 *Die Aktiengesellschaft*, 293 (294).

[37] In contrast to classical venture capital financing, however, ICO investors regularly do not receive shares in the company but profit participation rights or vouchers; see in detail: Behme and Zickgraf, 'Zivil- und gesellschaftsrechtliche Aspekte von Initial Coin Offerings (ICOs)' (2019) 5 *Zeitschrift für die gesamte Privatrechtswissenschaft*, 66 (76 et seqq.).

[38] Klöhn, Parhofer and Resas, 'Initial Coin Offerings (ICOs)' (2018) 30 *Zeitschrift für Bankrecht und Bankwirtschaft*, 89 (94).

[39] Catalini and Gans, 'Some Simple Economics of the Blockchain' (27.11.2016), 11 et seq., available at https://beck-link.de/w5c3x (accessed 11.4.2021).

[40] Zickgraf, 'Initial Coin Offerings – Ein Fall für das Kapitalmarktrecht?' (2018) 63 *Die Aktiengesellschaft*, 293 (307, 308).

[41] See in detail: Klöhn, Parhofer and Resas, 'Initial Coin Offerings (ICOs)' (2018) 30 *Zeitschrift für Bankrecht und Bankwirtschaft*, 89 (93 et seqq.).

[42] Cf. Behme and Zickgraf, 'Zivil- und gesellschaftsrechtliche Aspekte von Initial Coin Offerings (ICOs)' (2019) 5 *Zeitschrift für die gesamte Privatrechtswissenschaft*, 66 (71) with examples and further references.

[43] This also provides considerable incentives for early participation in the network, cf. Klöhn, Parhofer and Resas, 'Initial Coin Offerings (ICOs)' (2018) 30 *Zeitschrift für Bankrecht und Bankwirtschaft*, 89 (94); Chatard and Mann, 'Initial Coin Offerings und Token-Handel im funktionalen Rechtsvergleich – Entwicklung deutscher Leitlinien auf Grundlage des Diskussionsstands in der Schweiz, Frankreich und Deutschland' (2019) 22 *Neue Zeitschrift für Gesellschaftsrecht*, 567.

[44] Klöhn, Parhofer and Resas, 'Initial Coin Offerings (ICOs)' (2018) 30 *Zeitschrift für Bankrecht und Bankwirtschaft*, 89 (94 et seq.).

2. Risks

However, the opportunities of corporate funding through ICOs (→ para. 8 et seq.) are contrasted by specific risks of the ICO market:[45] First, **information asymmetries** between investors and initiators are particularly high. Distinguishing between promising and worthless ventures is very difficult for investors because the **business models** are either in a very **early stage** and consist of a **mere business idea**[46] or the existing (sophisticated) business model is hard to grasp for many investors due to its **technical complexity**. Further, the **information** provided to investors in the white papers is often **insufficient**.[47] The **lack of intermediaries** (e.g. investment banks), which typically operate in markets with high levels of information asymmetry and contribute to the functioning of these markets as gatekeepers, is therefore particularly detrimental to the ICO market.[48] Against this background, it seems questionable whether the absence of classical intermediaries[49], which at first glance leads to a reduction of transaction costs, is really enhancing efficiency.

The fact that the vast majority of ICOs are designed for a **single round of financing** – i.e. the prospect of poorer future financing conditions does not affect issuers' current behaviour – , makes the informational asymmetries and the lack of intermediaries even more dangerous for investors as this situation favours shady issuers.[50] Moreover, the offerings are structured in a way that can be disadvantageous for investors:[51] In most cases, instead of going through a standardised bookbuilding procedure, the price is set unilaterally by the initiators. Subsequently, the tokens are offered on a take it or leave it-basis and early subscriber discounts are frequently granted (→ § 1 para. 84), maximum limits with regard to the number of tokens offered (so-called hard caps[52]) are waived and the offer period can be extended as desired by the issuer. In combination, these elements can lead to a herd behaviour of investors.[53] Due to the lack of officially approved securities prospectuses in the past, investors can also not rely on an intervention by capital market supervisory authorities.[54]

---

[45] See also HM Treasury, Financial Conduct Authority and the Bank of England, 'Cryptoassets Taskforce: Final Report' (October 2018), 33 et seqq., available at https://beck-link.de/w3xv5 (accessed 4.11.2021).
[46] Klöhn, Parhofer and Resas, 'Initial Coin Offerings (ICOs)' (2018) 30 *Zeitschrift für Bankrecht und Bankwirtschaft*, 89 (95); Langenbucher, 'European Securities Law – Are we in need of a new definition? A thought inspired by initial coin offerings' [2018] *Revue Trimestrielle de Droit Financier*, 40 (41).
[47] Same finding: Chatard and Mann, 'Initial Coin Offerings und Token-Handel im funktionalen Rechtsvergleich – Entwicklung deutscher Leitlinien auf Grundlage des Diskussionsstands in der Schweiz, Frankreich und Deutschland' (2019) 22 *Neue Zeitschrift für Gesellschaftsrecht*, 567 (568); Spindler, 'Initial Coin Offerings und Prospektpflicht und -haftung' (2018) 72 *Zeitschrift für Wirtschafts- und Bankrecht*, 2109 (2110).
[48] Klöhn, Parhofer and Resas, 'Initial Coin Offerings (ICOs)' (2018) 30 *Zeitschrift für Bankrecht und Bankwirtschaft*, 89 (96).
[49] See for the 'new' intermediaries Veil, 'Token-Emissionen im europäischen Kapitalmarktrecht' (2019) 183 *Zeitschrift für das gesamte Handels- und Wirtschaftsrecht*, 346 (353 et seq.).
[50] Klöhn, Parhofer and Resas, 'Initial Coin Offerings (ICOs)' (2018) 30 *Zeitschrift für Bankrecht und Bankwirtschaft*, 89 (95 et seq.); Behme and Zickgraf, 'Zivil- und gesellschaftsrechtliche Aspekte von Initial Coin Offerings (ICOs)' (2019) 5 *Zeitschrift für die gesamte Privatrechtswissenschaft*, 66 (71 et seq.).
[51] Cf. in detail on the following: Klöhn, Parhofer and Resas, 'Initial Coin Offerings (ICOs)' (2018) 30 *Zeitschrift für Bankrecht und Bankwirtschaft*, 89 (95 et seq.); cf. Langenbucher, 'European Securities Law – Are we in need of a new definition? A thought inspired by initial coin offerings' [2018] *Revue Trimestrielle de Droit Financier*, 40 (41).
[52] See on this in detail: Zickgraf, 'Initial Coin Offerings – Ein Fall für das Kapitalmarktrecht?' (2018) 63 *Die Aktiengesellschaft*, 293 (294).
[53] For a comprehensive overview of the characteristics of the offer procedure and the consequences, see Klöhn, Parhofer and Resas, 'Initial Coin Offerings (ICOs)' (2018) 30 *Zeitschrift für Bankrecht und Bankwirtschaft*, 89 (95 et seq.).
[54] Behme and Zickgraf, 'Zivil- und gesellschaftsrechtliche Aspekte von Initial Coin Offerings (ICOs)' (2019) 5 *Zeitschrift für die gesamte Privatrechtswissenschaft*, 66 (72).

12   In contrast, the main risk for the issuers is of a regulatory nature. After all, the **legal assessment** of the various token categories by the **supervisory authorities**, which has not yet been definitively clarified (→ para. 14 et seqq.), as well as the uncertain assessment of ICOs by the **courts**, create considerable legal uncertainty for issuers. Furthermore, the cross-border character of an ICO means that an issuer may have to comply with the capital market laws of many different jurisdictions.[55]

C. Comparative Legal Overview

13   ICOs have been conducted in numerous jurisdictions in recent years, so that a comparative legal analysis as well as a presentation of the **capital market supervisory authorities'** positions might be instructive.[56] The following overview is limited to the most important **North American**, **Asian** and **European** jurisdictions.

I. North America

1. USA

14   In July 2017, the **Securities and Exchange Commission** (SEC) became the first regulatory agency to address the legal assessment of ICOs under existing securities regulation.[57] The SEC assessed the tokens offered by The DAO, which provided investors with both profit and voting rights and thus could be clearly classified as investment tokens from a typological point of view.[58] In its investigative report, the SEC came to the conclusion that the offered tokens were **investment contracts** and therefore securities as defined in Section 2(a)(1) of the Securities Act (= 15 U.S.C. Section 77b (a) (1)) and Section 3(a)(10) of the Securities Exchange Act (= 15 U.S.C. Section 78c (a) (10)).[59] This legal opinion was derived by applying the **Howey test** developed by the U.S. Supreme Court, according to which an investment contract is a 'contract, transaction, or scheme whereby a person invests his money in a common enterprise and is led to expect profits solely from the efforts of the promoter or a third party'.[60] The crucial

---

[55] Weitnauer, 'Initial Coin Offerings (ICOs): Rechtliche Rahmenbedingungen und regulatorische Grenzen' (2018) 18 *Zeitschrift für Bank- und Kapitalmarktrecht*, 231 (232); see for the applicable law → § 3, para. 36 et seqq., 43 et seqq.

[56] See extensively on the following: Zickgraf, 'Initial Coin Offerings – Ein Fall für das Kapitalmarktrecht?' (2018) 63 *Die Aktiengesellschaft*, 293 (297 et seq.); Chatard and Mann, 'Initial Coin Offerings und Token-Handel im funktionalen Rechtsvergleich – Entwicklung deutscher Leitlinien auf Grundlage des Diskussionsstands in der Schweiz, Frankreich und Deutschland' (2019) 22 *Neue Zeitschrift für Gesellschaftsrecht*, 567 (568 et seqq.); Maume and Fromberger, 'Regulation of Initial Coin Offerings: Reconciling U.S. and E.U. Securities Laws' (2019) 19 *Chicago Journal of International Law*, 548 (563 et seqq.).

[57] For comprehensive analysis of the legal situation in the US, → § 22.

[58] See on the characteristics of the tokens offered by The DAO: Jentzsch, 'Decentralized Autonomous Organization To Automate Governance' (2016), 1 et seqq., available at https://beck-link.de/7anas (accessed 11.4.2021).

[59] Securities and Exchange Commission, 'Report of Investigation Pursuant to Section 21(a) of the Securities Exchange Act of 1934: The DAO' (25.7.2017) Release No. 81207, available at https://beck-link.de/5pfa8 (accessed 11.4.2021); cf. Klöhn, Parhofer and Resas, 'Initial Coin Offerings (ICOs)' (2018) 30 *Zeitschrift für Bankrecht und Bankwirtschaft*, 89 (97).

[60] U.S. Supreme Court 27 May 1946 – SEC v. Howey Co., 328 U.S. 293 (298 et seq.); the Howey test consists of four requirements: 1.) an investment of money, 2.) in a common enterprise, 3.) reasonable expectation of profits, 4.) from the efforts of others; extensively on the requirements: Rohr and Wright, 'Blockchain-Based Token Sales, Initial Coin Offerings, and the Democratization of Public Capital Markets' (2018) *Cardozo Legal Studies Research Paper* No. 527, 44 et seqq., available at https://beck-link.

§ 7. Initial Coin Offerings (ICOs)

point is that the qualification of a security under US securities regulation is not assessed on the basis of the respective instrument's legal form, but the economic realities of the individual transaction (**substance over form**).[61] Consequently, the SEC also classified the utility tokens offered by Munchee Inc. as securities.[62] In the opinion of the SEC's former chairman, almost all ICOs offered securities as defined in US securities regulation.[63] However, the SEC is sceptical about the classification of currency tokens as securities, according to a statement of a senior official.[64] As a legal consequence the qualification of a token as a security leads to registration and disclosure obligations according to § 5 Securities Act (= 15 U.S.C. § 77e; in particular to the obligation to publish a securities prospectus).[65]

2. Canada

The legal assessment of ICOs with respect to Canadian securities regulation corresponds to the legal situation in the US, as the criteria of the **Howey test** are also used in Canada to define the term **investment contract** (e.g. Section 1 (1) Ontario Securities Act, Section 1 (1) British Columbia Securities Act, Section 1 lit. (ggg)(xiv) Alberta Securities Act, Section 1 (7) Québec Securities Act).[66] In their report on ICOs, the **Canadian Securities Administrators** (CAS) also point out to the obligation to publish a securities prospectus (e.g. Section 53 (1) Ontario Securities Act, Section 61 (1) British Columbia Securities Act, Section 110 (1) Alberta Securities Act, Section 11 (1) Québec Securities Act) if a token is classified as a security.[67]

15

---

de/peh4b (accessed 11.4.2021); see also Langenbucher, 'European Securities Law – Are we in need of a new definition? A thought inspired by initial coin offerings' [2018] *Revue Trimestrielle de Droit Financier*, 40 (45 et seqq.); see also → § 22 para. 7 et seqq.

[61] U.S. Supreme Court 16 June 1975 – United Housing Foundation, Inc. v. Forman, 421 U.S. 837 (848); U.S. Supreme Court 18 December 1967 – Tcherepnin v. Knight, 389 U.S. 332 (336); U.S. Supreme Court 27 May 1946 – SEC v. Howey Co., 328 U.S. 293 (298).

[62] Securities and Exchange Commission, 'In the Matter of Munchee Inc.: Securities Act of 1933 Release No. 10445' (11.12.2017), available at https://beck-link.de/yd3ne (accessed 11.4.2021); see extensively on the case: Zickgraf, 'Initial Coin Offerings – Ein Fall für das Kapitalmarktrecht?' (2018) 63 *Die Aktiengesellschaft*, 293 (305); cf. Zetzsche, Buckley, Arner and Föhr, 'The ICO Gold Rush: It's a Scam, It's a Bubble, It's a Super Challenge for Regulators' (19.11.2017), 24, available at https://beck-link.de/k23ak (accessed 11.4.2021).

[63] Clayton, 'Chairman's Testimony on Virtual Currencies: The Roles of the SEC and CFTC, Before the Committee on Banking, Housing, and Urban Affairs, United States Senate' (6.2.2018), available at https://beck-link.de/prp6v (accessed 11.4.2021):'(…) there are cryptocurrencies that, at least as currently designed, promoted and used, do not appear to be securities (…) But by and large, the structures of ICOs that I have seen involve the offer and sale of securities (…)'.

[64] Hinman, 'Digital Asset Transactions: When Howey Met Gary (Plastic), Remarks at the Yahoo Finance All Markets Summit: Crypto' (14.6.2018), available at https://beck-link.de/y3p8b (accessed 11.4.2021): 'But this also points the way to when a digital asset transaction may no longer represent a security offering. If the network on which the token or coin is to function is sufficiently decentralised – where purchasers would no longer reasonably expect a person or group to carry out essential managerial or entrepreneurial efforts – the assets may not represent an investment contract. Moreover, when the efforts of the third party are no longer a key factor for determining the enterprise's success, material information asymmetries recede. (…) And so, when I look at Bitcoin today, I do not see a central third party whose efforts are a key determining factor in the enterprise. (…) Applying the disclosure regime of the federal securities laws to the offer and resale of Bitcoin would seem to add little value. (…) And (…) current offers and sales of Ether are not securities transactions.'.

[65] Cf. Coffee, Sale and Henderson, *Securities Regulation* (2015), Chapter 2.

[66] Supreme Court of Canada 16.11.1977 – Pacific Coast Coin Exchange v. Ontario Securities Commission, 2 S.C.R. 112 (126 et seqq.).

[67] Canadian Securities Administrators, 'CSA Staff Notice 46-307, Cryptocurrency Offerings' (24.8.2017), 3 et seqq., available at https://beck-link.de/6npac (accessed 11.4.2021); cf. Canadian Securities Administrators, 'CSA Staff Notice 46-308, Securities Law Implications for Offerings of Tokens' (11.6.2018), available at https://beck-link.de/65wd2 (accessed 11.4.2021).

Part B. EU Regulation

II. Asia

1. China

16 The policy approach to the regulation of ICOs by the Chinese supervisory authorities[68] is the most restrictive in international comparison. After all, as early as September 2017, the performance of ICOs was completely banned and the repayment of previously invested funds to the investors was ordered.[69]

2. Hong Kong

17 The **Securities and Futures Commission** (**SFC**) has pointed out that the existing capital market regulations are in principle applicable to ICOs.[70] The SFC also stated that it considers at least investment tokens to be **securities** as defined in § 2(1) in conjunction with Schedule 1 – Part 1, § 1 Securities and Futures Ordinance.[71] Whether utility tokens are qualified as securities by the SFC is not clear from the published statements, but the statements can be interpreted to mean that utility tokens are not subject to Hong Kong's capital market laws.[72] If securities are offered in an ICO in Hong Kong, special registration and approval requirements apply (sections 38D, 342 Companies (Winding Up and Miscellaneous Provisions) Ordinance).[73]

3. Singapore

18 The **Monetary Authority of Singapore** (**MAS**) classifies investment tokens as **capital markets products** or **securities** as defined in Section 2(1) of the Securities and Futures Act.[74] Utility tokens, however, explicitly do not qualify as securities.[75] Section 240 of the Securities and Futures Act mandates the publication of a securities prospectus for public offerings of securities in Singapore.

III. Europe

1. EU

19 In a first brief statement in 2017 the **European Securities and Markets Authority** (**ESMA**) pointed out that various provisions of European capital markets law may apply

---

[68] For comprehensive analysis of the legal situation in the People's Republic of China, → § 27.

[69] People's Bank of China, 'Public Notice of the PBC, CAC, MIIT, SAIC, CBRC, CSRC and CIRC on Preventing Risks of Fundraising through Coin Offering' (8.9.2017), available at https://beck-link.de/hm4n3 (accessed 11.4.2021); see on this Pilarowski and Yue, 'China Bans Initial Coin Offerings and Cryptocurrency Trading Platforms, China Regulation Watch' (21.9.2017), available at https://beck-link.de/st6ry (accessed 11.4.2021); cf. Choudhury, 'China bans companies from raising money through ICOs, asks local regulators to inspect 60 major platforms' (4.9.2017), available at https://beck-link.de/3xx7d (accessed 11.4.2021).

[70] For comprehensive analysis of the legal situation in Hong Kong, → § 26.

[71] Securities and Futures Commission, 'Statement on initial coin offerings' (5.9.2017), available at https://beck-link.de/8hypp (accessed 5.7.2019).

[72] Securities and Futures Commission, 'SFC warns of cryptocurrency risks' (9.2.2018), available at https://beck-link.de/4f8h7 (accessed 11.4.2021): 'ICO issuers are typically assisted by market professionals such as lawyers, accountants and consultants for advice to structure the offering as utility Token to fall outside the purview of the SFO and to circumvent the scrutiny of the SFC.'.

[73] Securities and Futures Commission, 'Statement on initial coin offerings' (5.9.2017), available at https://beck-link.de/8hypp (accessed 11.4.2021).

[74] For comprehensive analysis of the legal situation in Singapore, → § 23.

[75] Monetary Authority of Singapore, 'A Guide To Digital Token Offerings' (2018), available at https://beck-link.de/4nzy7 (accessed 11.4.2021).

§ 7. Initial Coin Offerings (ICOs)

to ICOs.[76] In 2018 a survey of the National Competent Authorities (NCAs) was carried out, the results of which have since been presented in a consultation paper by ESMA for the European Commission:[77] In the course of the study, several case studies were presented, although the exact typology is not clear from the paper. According to the report, the majority of the NCAs are of the opinion that **investment tokens** are **transferable securities** within the meaning of Art. 4(1)(44) of Directive 2014/65/EU (MiFID2); the existence of profit rights is considered to be sufficient for a token to be classified as a transferable security.[78] Pure **utility tokens** ('pure utility-type crypto-assets'), on the other hand, are not classified as transferable securities by any NCA.[79] However, certain **hybrid tokens** are qualified as transferable securities by the national supervisory authorities, although the exact characteristics of these hybrid tokens are not disclosed in the report.[80] Yet, it can be concluded from the fact that the consultation paper speaks of 'pure utility-type crypto-assets' when excluding utility tokens from the definition of transferable securities in Art. 4(1)(44) MiFID2 that at least certain hybrid utility tokens are considered transferable securities by the NCAs. Pure **currency tokens** were excluded from the case studies at the outset, as ESMA considers their qualification as transferable securities to be unlikely.[81] Regarding the legal consequences, ESMA refers in its report to a large body of capital markets regulation (including the Prospectus Regulation, MiFID2, MAR, AIFMD), which may be applicable as a result of the qualification of a token as a financial instrument within the meaning of Art. 4(1)(15) MiFID2, highlighting in particular the requirement to publish a prospectus under Art. 3(1) Regulation (EU) 2017/1129 of the European Parliament and of the Council of 14 June 2017 on the prospectus to be published when securities are offered to the public or admitted to trading on a regulated market and repealing Directive 2003/71/EC (EU Prospectus Regulation).[82]

In its recommendation to ESMA, the **Securities and Markets Stakeholder Group (SMSG)** took the view that neither currency tokens nor utility tokens are covered by MiFID2. Nevertheless, regulating specific aspects was suggested. The SMSG considers investment tokens to be financial instruments as defined in Art. 4(1)(15) MiFID2 and transferable securities as defined in Art. 4(1)(44) MiFID2, because and to the extent that the tokens are transferable, if either (1) a financial claim is conveyed by the token or (2) a claim in kind as well as voting rights are granted with respect to the project.[83] 20

In September 2020, the European Commission has published a proposal for a Regulation on Markets in Crypto-Assets (MiCAR).[84] In essence, Art. 4 – 14 MiCAR will regulate offers of utility tokens to the public and create a special set of (disclosure) obligations for issuers of crypto-assets (→ para. 89 et seqq.). 21

---

[76] ESMA, 'Statement: ESMA alerts firms involved in Initial Coin Offerings (ICOs) to the need to meet relevant regulatory requirements' (13.11.2017), available at https://beck-link.de/srv7w (accessed 11.4.2021).

[77] ESMA, 'Advice on Initial Coin Offerings and Crypto-Assets' (9.1.2019), 19 et seqq., para. 80 et seqq., available at https://beck-link.de/dm5hb (accessed 11.4.2021).

[78] Ibid, 19 et seq., paras. 82, 85.

[79] Ibid, 20, para. 86.

[80] Ibid, 19 et seq., para. 82.

[81] Ibid, 19, para. 80: 'Pure payment-type crypto-assets were not included in the sample set on purpose as they are unlikely to qualify as financial instruments.'.

[82] Ibid, 21, para. 91 et seqq.

[83] Securities and Markets Stakeholder Group, 'Advice to ESMA: Own Initiative Report on Initial Coin Offerings and Crypto-Assets' (19.10.2018), para. 46 et seqq., 48 et seqq., available at https://beck-link.de/y47xy (accessed 11.4.2021), see also there for the qualification of some investment tokens as derivatives.

[84] Commission, 'Proposal for a Regulation of the European Parliament and of the Council on Markets in Crypto-assets, and amending Directive (EU) 2019/1937' COM (2020), 593 final.

2. United Kingdom

22　The legal assessment of ICOs by the **Financial Conduct Authority (FCA)** is largely unclear, as the FCA referred in its statement to the necessity of 'case by case' assessment without providing clear guidelines.[85] In this context, the FCA confined itself to the statement that numerous ICOs (probably) did not fall under the existing regulatory regime, although some tokens could be classified as **transferable securities** (as defined by Section102A(3) Financial Services and Markets Act 2000, Art. 4(1)(44) MiFID2) and could therefore be subject to the requirement to publish a prospectus (Section 85(1) Financial Services and Markets Act 2000).[86] The **Cryptoassets Taskforce**, which is composed of the Treasury, the FCA and the Bank of England, has expressed itself somewhat more precisely: It qualifies investment tokens ('security tokens') as transferable securities within the meaning of Art. 4(1)(44) MiFID2, but rejects this qualification for utility tokens and currency tokens.[87]

3. France

23　The **Autorité des Marchés Financiers (AMF)** addressed the legal assessment of ICOs in a discussion paper in a timely manner:[88] According to the AMF, the legal assessment of ICOs under capital markets law should depend on a case-by-case approach. If the (investment) tokens convey dividend rights and participation rights, the AMF qualifies the tokens as titres de capital émis par les sociétés par actions in the sense of Art. L 211-1(2)(1) Code monétaire et financier because of the comparable legal features of the instruments.[89] Besides, a special, **optional approval procedure** has been created for issuers of **utility tokens** by Articles L. 552-1 – 552-7 Code monétaire et financier[90] in conjunction with Articles 711-1 – 715-2 Règlement général de l'Autorité des Marchés Financiers.[91]

4. Germany

24　In its first guidance letter on ICOs, the **Bundesanstalt für Finanzdienstleistungsaufsicht (BaFin)** gave insight to its regulatory assessment of ICOs.[92] BaFin refrained from trying to qualify the various token categories as **financial instruments** within the meaning of Art. 4(1)(15) MiFID2 or as **transferable securities** within the meaning of Art. 4(1)(44) MiFID2 (see → para. 33 et seqq.), since in its opinion the rights conveyed by a token need to be examined on a **case-by-case basis** (substance over form).

---

[85] For comprehensive analysis of the legal situation in the UK, → § 18.

[86] Financial Conduct Authority, 'Initial Coin Offerings' (9.12.2017), available at https://beck-link.de/73nez (accessed 11.4.2021). Note: The regulatory situation in the UK – especially the references in the Financial Services and Markets Act 2000 to EU legal acts such as MiFID2 – might change in the future given the conclusion of the EU-UK Withdrawal Agreement.

[87] HM Treasury, Financial Conduct Authority and the Bank of England, 'Cryptoassets Taskforce: Final Report' (October 2018), 11, 18, 20, 43, available at https://beck-link.de/w3xv5 (accessed 4.11.2021); cf. on 'security tokens' Financial Conduct Authority, 'Cryptoassets' (3.7.2019), available at https://beck-link.de/p686v (accessed 11.4.2021).

[88] For comprehensive analysis of the legal situation in France, → § 16.

[89] Autorité des Marchés Financiers, 'Discussion Paper on Initial Coin Offerings', 5, 7 et seq., available at https://beck-link.de/3smxv (accessed 11.4.2021).

[90] Loi 'Pacte' n°2019-486 du 22 mai 2019 – Art. 85.

[91] Autorité des Marchés Financiers, 'Règlement général en vigueur au 23/5/2021', available at https://beck-link.de/cw73v (accessed 11.4.2021); cf. Chatard and Mann, 'Initial Coin Offerings und Token-Handel im funktionalen Rechtsvergleich – Entwicklung deutscher Leitlinien auf Grundlage des Diskussionsstands in der Schweiz, Frankreich und Deutschland' (2019) 22 *Neue Zeitschrift für Gesellschaftsrecht*, 567 (570 et seqq.) with further references.

[92] For comprehensive analysis of the legal situation in Germany, → § 17.

§ 7. Initial Coin Offerings (ICOs)

Nonetheless, BaFin presented its legal assessment of some uncertainties regarding the legal concept of securities (→ para. 33 et seqq.) in the context of crypto assets:[93]

1. In the opinion of BaFin, the **trading platforms** on which the secondary market trading with the tokens takes place after the closing of an ICO are to be regarded as **capital markets** as defined by European capital markets law (this conclusion becomes relevant in the context of the tradability of tokens: it clarifies the legal term 'capital market' which is used in Art. 4(1)(44) MiFID2, see → para. 44).
2. The **securitisation** of a token in a certificate does **not** constitute a **mandatory requirement** of a transferable security within the meaning of European capital markets law. In the view of BaFin, it is rather sufficient that the owner of a token can be documented in each case by means of the blockchain technology or a comparable technology (this assessment becomes relevant in the context of the tradability of tokens: there is no need for securitisation or the possibility of a bona fide purchase, → para. 45 et seq.).
3. Regarding the rights which are necessary for a token to be classified as a transferable security, the **conveyance of shareholder rights** or **contractual claims under the law of obligations** or **claims comparable to such claims** through a token is found to be sufficient by BaFin (this finding becomes relevant in terms of the functional comparability and resemblance of a token with the exemplary list of transferable securities in Art. 4(1)(44) MiFID2, → para. 47 et seqq.).

In its second guidance letter, BaFin explained in more detail the formal and material criteria of the term 'transferable security' regarding crypto assets. In the opinion of BaFin, the issued tokens are regularly **transferable** (→ para. 34 et seqq.), because and to the extent that they can be transferred to other users. In addition, BaFin reiterates that crypto trading platforms can be regarded as capital markets; provided that the tokens also convey **identical rights**, i.e. if they are comparable in terms of type of rights conveyed and are thus **standardised** (→ para. 38 et seqq.), BaFin takes the view that they are **negotiable on the capital market**. In continuation of its first guidance letter, BaFin again rejected a securitisation requirement for an instrument to qualify as a transferable security. In addition, BaFin specified which rights must be associated with a token in order for it to be functionally comparable to classic securities in substantial respects (→ para. 47 et seqq.): A token must convey **financial rights** or **membership rights**. Financial rights are presumed to be present by BaFin if the repayment of the invested capital at the end of the maturity of the token or regular payments are provided for, which are linked to the ownership of the token. BaFin defines relevant membership rights as dividend rights or dividend-like payment rights (e.g. the distribution of additional tokens) as well as participation rights conveyed by the token with regard to 'enterprises related to the ICO'. A security-like right that is sufficient for the definition of a transferable securities is certainly present if 'the token conveys to its holder an equity interest similar to that of a shareholder or a debt interest comparable to that of a debt security creditor'.[94]

On the basis of the more precise remarks regarding the substantive criteria of the concept of a 'transferable security', BaFin was able to present its regulatory assessment

---

[93] BaFin, 'Initial Coin Offerings: Hinweisschreiben zur Einordnung als Finanzinstrumente, GZ: WA 11-QB 4100- 2017/0010' (20.2.2018), 2, available at https://beck-link.de/2na3t (accessed 11.4.2021); cf. Fußwinkel and Kreiterling, 'Blockchain-Technologie – Gedanken zur Regulierung' (1/2018) BaFin Perspektiven, 54 et seqq., available at https://beck-link.de/a7mkv (accessed 11.4.2021).

[94] See in detail: BaFin, 'Merkblatt: Zweites Hinweisschreiben zu Prospekt- und Erlaubnispflichten im Zusammenhang mit der Ausgabe sogenannter Krypto-Token, GZ: WA 51-Wp 7100-2019/0011 und IF 1-AZB 1505-2019/0003' (16.8.2019), 8, available at https://beck-link.de/tz6vv (accessed 11.4.2021).

of the various token categories in more detail in its second guidance letter: BaFin qualified **investment tokens** as **transferable securities** in terms of the Wertpapierprospektgesetz (WpPG), the Wertpapierhandelsgesetz (WpHG) and the Prospectus Regulation, whereas **utility tokens** and **currency tokens** were generally **not** classified as **transferable securities**. In the case of **hybrid tokens**, BaFin stated that the **main or primary functions** of a particular token are decisive for its regulatory classification (→ para. 69). Once again, BaFin also emphasised that the typological denomination of a token provides only a first indication for its legal assessment. After all, solely the rights attached to a token in the **individual case** determine its legal qualification (substance over form).[95]

5. Austria

27   In its statement on ICOs,[96] the **Financial Market Authority** (**FMA**) clearly expressed the view that '**security token[s]**' (= investment tokens) are to be regarded as **transferable securities** within the meaning of § 1(1)(4) Kapitalmarktgesetz (KMG) and § 1(5) Wertpapieraufsichtsgesetz (WAG). In particular, a securitisation in a certificate is not required. Instead, **documentation** of the token owner using **blockchain technology** or **DLT** is deemed sufficient. In FMA's view, the other formal requirements of the legal concept of a 'transferable security' (in particular, **negotiability on the capital market**) are fulfilled in the case of security tokens, as is the substantive requirement of **functional comparability** with the non-exhaustive list of transferable securities in Art. 4(1)(44) MiFID2. With regard to **utility tokens**, FMA indicated that the classification as a transferable security pursuant to section § 1(1)(4) KMG and § 1(5) WAG depends on whether the token in question has a significant **investment component**; however, the FMA left open the precise criteria for the assumption of such an investment component or investment function – beyond the conveyance of financial claims. The FMA did not qualify '**payment token[s]**' (= currency tokens) as transferable securities, though.[97]

6. Switzerland

28   For its regulatory assessment, the **Eidgenössische Finanzmarktaufsicht** (**FINMA**) referred to the various token categories ('Zahlungs-Token' (= curency tokens), 'Nutzungs-Token' (= utility tokens) and 'Anlage-Token' (= investment tokens)), which it defined based on their economic function.[98] Because of their function as a means of payment and the resulting **lack of comparability** with traditional securities, FINMA rejected the classification of **currency tokens** as securities within the meaning of Art. 2(b) Finanzmarktinfrastrukturgesetz (FinfraG). In the case of **utility tokens**, FINMA differentiated according to the **economic function** of the particular token: If the focus is on the **right to receive a service** or **access to a** '**digital usage**' and the token can already be deployed for this purpose, the required connection to the capital market is lacking, so that the utility token cannot be considered an 'Effekte' (= security). However, if an utility token has an **investment function** in economic respect, FINMA classifies it as a security within the meaning of Art. 2(b) FinfraG. The same applies to

---

[95] BaFin, 'Merkblatt: Zweites Hinweisschreiben zu Prospekt- und Erlaubnispflichten im Zusammenhang mit der Ausgabe sogenannter Krypto-Token, GZ: WA 51-Wp 7100-2019/0011 und IF 1-AZB 1505-2019/0003' (16.8.2019), 5 et seq., available at https://beck-link.de/tz6vv (accessed 11.4.2021).
[96] Finanzmarktaufsicht, ICO, available at https://www.fma.gv.at/kontaktstelle-fintech-sandbox/fintech-navigator/initial-coin-offering/ (accessed 11.4.2021).
[97] Ibid.
[98] For comprehensive analysis of the legal situation in Switzerland, → § 19.

investment tokens, which FINMA always qualifies as securities because and to the extent that these tokens convey financial entitlements, are standardised and are suitable for mass trading.[99]

IV. Summary

From the comparative legal overview, it can be concluded that **investment tokens** qualify as **(transferable) securities** in all jurisdictions and are therefore subject to the respective capital market regulation. A uniform legal assessment can also be observed with regard to **currency tokens**, which are **not** classified as (transferable) securities by any supervisory authority. In contrast, the comparative legal overview has revealed **considerable differences** in the legal qualification of **utility tokens** under securities regulation: While some Asian supervisory authorities (Hong Kong (SFC), Singapore (MAS)) tend not to classify utility tokens as securities, a **differentiating regulatory approach** is evident in **North America** (especially in the US (SEC)) and **Europe**. In this context, the SEC's approach based on the Howey test, which is taking into account the economic realities of the individual transaction (substance over form, → para. 14) comes very close to the approaches of FMA (→ para. 27) and FINMA (→ para. 28), both of which focus on the investment function of the respective utility token (→ para. 61 et seqq.). In **Europe**, however, there is also a **strong tendency** in that pure utility tokens are not classified as transferable securities. This applies in particular to the supervisory practice of BaFin (→ para. 26) and is further supported by the consultation paper of ESMA (→ para. 19). The creation of an optional, special regime for utility tokens by the French legislator (→ para. 23) and the European Commission's proposal of **Art. 4 – 14 MiCAR** (→ para. 89 et seqq,) point in a similar direction.

D. Initial Coin Offerings in EU Capital Markets Law

Many and diverse capital markets law issues arise in connection with ICOs (also → § 8 and → § 11). This chapter is devoted solely to the regulatory requirements of the **primary market**, focussing in particular on a potential **prospectus obligation** for ICOs.

I. Prospectus Obligation under EU Prospectus Regulation

The obligation to publish a prospectus under EU Prospectus Regulation depends largely on whether the tokens offered constitute **transferable securities** as defined by Art. 4(1)(44) MiFID2, which simultaneously represent **financial instruments** within the meaning of Art. 4(1)(15) in conjunction with Annex I Section C (1) MiFID2. Due to the reference in Art. 4(1)(15), Annex I Section C (1) MiFID2, the definition of transferable securities is crucial for the applicability of secondary market regulation, in particular for the application of the Market Abuse Regulation (Art. 2(1) MAR, Art. 3(1)(1) MAR; for details → § 11 para. 7). Therefore, the legal concept of 'transferable securities' affects the

---

[99] FINMA, 'Wegleitung für Unterstellungsanfragen betreffend Initial Coin Offerings (ICOs)' (16.2.2018), 2 et seqq., available at https://beck-link.de/f5fad (accessed 11.4.2021); see extensively on the Swiss regulatory situation Chatard and Mann, 'Initial Coin Offerings und Token-Handel im funktionalen Rechtsvergleich – Entwicklung deutscher Leitlinien auf Grundlage des Diskussionsstands in der Schweiz, Frankreich und Deutschland' (2019) 22 *Neue Zeitschrift für Gesellschaftsrecht*, 567 (568 et seqq.) with further references.

scope of application of other areas of capital markets law, so that the remarks contained in this chapter are also of considerable importance beyond EU Prospectus Regulation.

32 Pursuant to Art. 3(1) EU Prospectus Regulation (see for the international scope of application → § 3 para. 44), the obligation to publish a prospectus arises when securities are offered to the public.[100] Art. 2(a) EU Prospectus Regulation defines the term 'security' by referring to the definition of transferable security contained in Art. 4(1)(44) MiFID2 with the exception of money market instruments as defined in Art. 4(1)(17) MiFID2 with a maturity of less than 12 months. In the case of ICOs, the obligation to publish a prospectus depends essentially on the question of whether the tokens offered constitute securities. For a particular instrument to qualify as a security, it must meet the formal (→ para. 33 et seqq.) and substantive requirements (→ para. 47 et seqq.) of the definition of transferable securities in Art. 4(1)(44) MiFID2.

1. Formal Requirements of 'Transferable Security'

33 Art. 4(1)(44) MiFID2 defines transferable securities as 'those classes of securities which are negotiable on the capital market'. The decisive criterion therefore turns out to be **negotiability on the capital market**, which requires the transferability, standardisation and tradability of the instruments (negotiability in the narrow sense).[101]

34 a) **Transferability.** In order for a token to qualify as a security, it must be transferable, since negotiability necessarily requires the instrument to be transferable.[102] Transferability requires that neither legal nor factual obstacles impair the free saleability by the owner.[103] In the case of tokens, there are no legal impediments, as neither formal requirements nor other restrictions (→ para. 36 et seq., for restrictions on sale) are usually stipulated for their transfer.[104] Rather, investment and utility tokens that grant the respective holder rights against the issuer can be transferred at least via a contractual agreement (for example, transfer under German civil law according to §§ 398(1), 413 of the Civil Code (BGB).[105] Also, factual obstacles to the free sale are typically not present with respect to tokens (for factual obstacles to sale → para. 37)[106], as these can be traded

---

[100] See in detail on the following: Zickgraf, 'Initial Coin Offerings – Ein Fall für das Kapitalmarktrecht?' (2018) 63 *Die Aktiengesellschaft*, 293 (298 et seqq.); see on the requirements of an offer to the public: Meyer, in Habersack, Mülbert and Schlitt (eds), *Unternehmensfinanzierung am Kapitalmarkt* (2019), § 36, para. 4.

[101] Klöhn, in Klöhn (ed), *Marktmissbrauchsverordnung*, Art. 2, para. 11.

[102] Hacker and Thomale, 'Crypto-Securities Regulation: ICOs, Token Sales and Cryptocurrencies under EU Financial Law' [2018] *European Company and Financial Law Review*, 645 (663 et seqq.); Zickgraf, 'Initial Coin Offerings – Ein Fall für das Kapitalmarktrecht?' (2018) 63 *Die Aktiengesellschaft*, 293 (299); for this reason other authors support a merging of the criterion of 'transferability' in the criterion of 'negotiability': Klöhn, Parhofer and Resas, 'Initial Coin Offerings (ICOs)' (2018) 30 *Zeitschrift für Bankrecht und Bankwirtschaft*, 89 (100); Kumpan, in Schwark and Zimmer (eds), *Kapitalmarktrechts-Kommentar*, § 2, para. 11.

[103] Ritz and Zeising, in Just, Voß, Ritz and Zeising (eds), *Wertpapierprosektgesetz*, § 2, para. 33.

[104] Rohr and Wright, 'Blockchain-Based Token Sales, Initial Coin Offerings, and the Democratization of Public Capital Markets' (2018) *Cardozo Legal Studies Research Paper* No. 527, 35, available at https://beck-link.de/peh4b (accessed 11.4.2021); Hacker and Thomale, 'Crypto-Securities Regulation: ICOs, Token Sales and Cryptocurrencies under EU Financial Law' [2018] *European Company and Financial Law Review*, 645 (663 et seq.); Zickgraf, 'Initial Coin Offerings – Ein Fall für das Kapitalmarktrecht?' (2018) 63 *Die Aktiengesellschaft*, 293 (299).

[105] Zickgraf, 'Initial Coin Offerings – Ein Fall für das Kapitalmarktrecht?' (2018) 63 *Die Aktiengesellschaft*, 293 (299); Behme and Zickgraf, 'Zivil- und gesellschaftsrechtliche Aspekte von Initial Coin Offerings (ICOs)' (2019) 5 *Zeitschrift für die gesamte Privatrechtswissenschaft*, 66 (88).

[106] See on the exceptional ICO of EOS, Hacker and Thomale, 'Crypto-Securities Regulation: ICOs, Token Sales and Cryptocurrencies under EU Financial Law' [2018] *European Company and Financial Law Review*, 645 (664).

on crypto exchanges with sufficient liquidity.[107] Therefore, it can be assumed in principle that the tokens issued in the course of an ICO are transferable.

The fact that the transfer of tokens via the blockchain can be initiated unilaterally in technical terms by authorizing the transaction using the private key is no argument against the assumption of a contractual agreement on the transfer.[108] Although it is true that the token transaction is a merely factual process, according to the will of the parties, the actual technical transfer of the (investment or utility) token simultaneously transfers the right represented by the token. Therefore, from the perspective of the other party, there is an offer for the conclusion of a contract, which is implicitly accepted by the other party without the declaration of acceptance having to be sent to the applicant, since such a declaration is not to be expected according to general custom.[109]

35

There are usually no legal obstacles to the transfer of currency tokens. Even if there are legal restrictions on the sale in a particular case (e.g. lock-ups), the transferability of the tokens is not removed as can be seen e contrario from Art. 51 (1) subpara. 2 MiFID2 and the **free negotiability** mentioned there, which is **not a prerequisite** for the legal concept of 'transferable securities' as defined in Art. 4(1)(44) MiFID2.[110] With regard to the regulation of the primary market in particular, this view is also supported by the fact that pursuant to Art. 7(7)(a)(v) Prospectus Regulation, information on 'any restrictions on the free transferability of the securities' must be included in the prospectus.[111]

36

Whether exceptionally occurring factual obstacles to sale eliminate the transferability or tradability and thus bar a token from being qualified as a transferable security, appears to be largely unclear so far. One example is the ICO of EOS, where the tokens could technically no longer be transferred via the blockchain after the end of the token sale, but were rather permanently assigned to a specific public key (permanent technical lock-up).[112] In initial statements in the legal literature, it is considered possible that such technical transfer barriers eliminate the (legal) transferability of the tokens (for the future).[113] Since ESMA has indicated in another context that the assessment of the

37

---

[107] Rohr and Wright, 'Blockchain-Based Token Sales, Initial Coin Offerings, and the Democratization of Public Capital Markets' (2018) *Cardozo Legal Studies Research Paper* No. 527, 29, available at https://beck-link.de/peh4b (accessed 11.4.2021); Hacker and Thomale, 'Crypto-Securities Regulation: ICOs, Token Sales and Cryptocurrencies under EU Financial Law' [2018] *European Company and Financial Law Review*, 645 (663) with further references.

[108] Opposing opinion van Aubel, '§ 20 – Initial Coin Offerings (ICOs)', in Habersack, Mülbert and Schlitt (eds), *Unternehmensfinanzierung am Kapitalmarkt* (2019), § 20, para. 46.

[109] Cf. Kaulartz and Matzke, 'Die Tokenisierung des Rechts' (2018) 71 *Neue Juristische Wochenschrift*, 3278 (3280).

[110] Roth, in *KölnerKommWpHG*, § 2, para. 32; Assmann, in Assmann, Schneider and Mülbert (eds), *Wertpapierhandelsrecht*, § 2, para. 13; Kumpan, in Schwark and Zimmer (eds), *Kapitalmarktrechts-Kommentar*, § 2, para. 10.

[111] For this reason, ESMA also concludes that, as a rule, contractual restrictions on the transferability (lock-ups) do not affect the status of an instrument as a transferable security, cf. ESMA, 'Questions and Answers on the Prospectus Regulation', ESMA/2019/ESMA31-62-1258, Version 8 (May 2021), Question 14.12, 61 et seq., available at https://www.esma.europa.eu/sites/default/files/library/esma31-62-1258_prospectus_regulation_qas.pdf (accessed 18.6.2021); see also Hacker and Thomale, 'Crypto-Securities Regulation: ICOs, Token Sales and Cryptocurrencies under EU Financial Law' [2018] *European Company and Financial Law Review*, 645 (663 et seq.).

[112] See for a technical lock-up Krüger and Lampert, 'Augen auf bei der Token-Wahl – privatrechtliche und steuerrechtliche Herausforderungen im Rahmen eines Initial Coin Offerings' [2018] *Betriebs-Berater*, 1154 (1156).

[113] In this direction: Hacker and Thomale, 'Crypto-Securities Regulation: ICOs, Token Sales and Cryptocurrencies under EU Financial Law' [2018] *European Company and Financial Law Review*, 645 (664).

transferability of an instrument also depends on the intensity of the restrictions in the individual case[114] and the permanent assignment of a token to a certain public key appears to be a particularly intense factual impediment to the transfer, an exclusion of the transferability of a token on the basis of technical precautions seems to be conceivable at least in the case of **permanent technical restrictions**. However, it should be noted that this does not legally preclude the transfer of a token and the rights conveyed by it. To provide the buyer with the factual power of disposal over the rights associated with the token, the seller would have to give the buyer access to the corresponding public key after the legal transfer, though. Without assigning the token to another public key, this would be possible for the seller by communicating the corresponding private key that belongs to the public key to which the token is permanently assigned. Therefore, the transfer would take place completely beyond the blockchain. However, such a procedure is virtually impossible if the token transaction is or shall be processed – as it is regularly the case – via crypto exchanges by way of anonymous mass transactions. After all, under these circumstances the factual tradability of the tokens via crypto exchanges and thus the **negotiability on the capital market** (for this purpose → para. 33 et seqq.) is considerably more difficult, if not even de facto largely impossible. Therefore, **transferability** and **negotiability in the narrow sense** (**tradability**) (→ para. 44 et seqq.) do not appear to be given, at least not in the case of permanent factual obstacles to the token transfer.[115] Overall, however, the requirements of transferability and tradability should not be interpreted too strictly to give appropriate weight to teleological considerations of the various capital market rules referring to the definition of (transferable) securities.[116]

38   **b) Standardisation. aa) General Requirements.** The wording of Art. 4(1)(44) MiFID2 ('classes of securities') implies the requirement of standardisation of instruments.[117] The teleological background of this prerequisite is rooted in the creation of **institutional** and **operational efficiency** of the capital market, because efficient trading in securities at low transaction costs is only ensured if instruments are standardised.[118] The requirement of standardisation is satisfied if the instruments are **mutually exchangeable**, i.e. if they can be identified solely by the type and number of units.[119] On the other hand, there is a lack of sufficient standardisation in the case of instruments that have been individually structured according to the wishes of individual investors.[120]

---

[114] ESMA, 'Questions and Answers on the Prospectus Regulation', ESMA/2019/ESMA31-62-1258, Version 8 (May 2021), Question 14.12, 61 et seq., available at https://www.esma.europa.eu/sites/default/files/library/esma31-62-1258_prospectus_regulation_qas.pdf (accessed 18.6.2021).
[115] Likewise also Maume and Fromberger, 'Regulation of Initial Coin Offerings: Reconciling U.S. and E.U. Securities Laws' (2019) 19 *Chicago Journal of International Law*, 548 (574 et seq.).
[116] Cf. Kumpan, in Schwark and Zimmer (eds), *Kapitalmarktrechts-Kommentar*, § 2, para. 10.
[117] Klöhn, in Klöhn (ed), *Marktmissbrauchsverordnung*, Art. 2, para. 19; Veil, 'Token-Emissionen im europäischen Kapitalmarktrecht' (2019) 183 *Zeitschrift für das gesamte Handels- und Wirtschaftsrecht*, 346 (356).
[118] Roth, in *KölnerKommWpHG*, § 2, para. 24; see for the functions of the capital market Fuchs, in Fuchs (ed), *WpHG*, Introduction, para. 16.
[119] Von Kopp-Colomb and Schneider, in Assmann, Schlitt and von Kopp-Colomb (eds), *WpPG*, § 2, para. 14; Ritz and Zeising, in Just, Voß, Ritz and Zeising (eds), *Wertpapierprosektgesetz*, § 2, paras. 35, 40; Voß, 'Geschlossene Fonds unter dem Rechtsregime der Finanzmarkt-Richtlinie (MiFID)?' (2007) 7 *Zeitschrift für Bank- und Kapitalmarktrecht*, 45 (50).
[120] Begr. RegE, BT-Drs. 16/4028, 54 (no individual design by taking into account special investor wishes, e.g. with regard to term, volume and base price; 'keine individuelle Ausgestaltung durch Berücksichtigung spezieller Kundenwünsche zB hinsichtlich Laufzeit, Volumen und Basispreis'); Klöhn, in Klöhn (ed), *Marktmissbrauchsverordnung*, Art. 2, para. 19; Fuchs, in Fuchs (ed), *WpHG*, § 2, para. 14; Assmann, in Assmann, Schneider and Mülbert (eds), *Wertpapierhandelsrecht*, § 2, para. 11.

§ 7. Initial Coin Offerings (ICOs)

bb) Issuer Level or Asset Class. Whether standardisation of instruments at the issuer level (concrete or issuer-specific determination) is sufficient[121] or uniformity of the **entire asset class** (abstract or cross-issuer determination) is necessary,[122] is disputed in the legal literature. In view of the diversity of the rights associated with a token on a case-by-case basis, i.e. the lack of uniformity as an asset class, this controversial question is particularly crucial in the context of ICOs.[123] 39

The wording of Art. 4(1)(44) MiFID2, which refers to 'classes' of securities, is used as an argument for the requirement of an **abstract** or **cross-issuer determination** of standardisation. However, if one considers that, according to the predominant view, the feature is only intended to express the need for a generic structure of the rights,[124] the wording loses its persuasive power, since a generic structure can also be assumed if the rights are merely uniform at issuer level. Thus, the **wording** is **open to both interpretations**.[125] 40

Neither can the **alleged lack of legal certainty** of a concrete or issuer-related determination of standardisation provide an argument for the necessity of an abstract or cross-issuer determination.[126] After all, there is no reason why the individual determination of standardisation for each issuer should result in legal uncertainties; after all, all that is required in order to answer the question of standardisation is a schematic comparison of the legal rights conveyed by the instruments at the issuer level, which is easily feasible.[127] In any case, an abstract determination of the standardisation on a cross issuer-basis would not be subject to less legal uncertainty, because 'asset classes' would have to be distinguished which is an even more complex subject matter (comparison of a large number of issuers and financial instruments). 41

The sufficiency of an **issuer-related determination** of standardisation is further supported by the criterion's **purpose**, which is to ensure efficient trading at low transaction costs. After all, in the case of standardisation at the individual issuer level, the instruments/tokens can be identified by type and number of units and can be traded under the name of the issuer or the instrument/token. Thus, issuer-related standardisation of instruments enables efficient and transaction cost-saving trading in 42

---

[121] Zickgraf, 'Initial Coin Offerings – Ein Fall für das Kapitalmarktrecht?' (2018) 63 *Die Aktiengesellschaft*, 293 (300) with further references; Hacker and Thomale, 'Crypto-Securities Regulation: ICOs, Token Sales and Cryptocurrencies under EU Financial Law' [2018] *European Company and Financial Law Review*, 645 (667 et seq.); Langenbucher, 'European Securities Law – Are we in need of a new definition? A thought inspired by initial coin offerings' [2018] *Revue Trimestrielle de Droit Financier*, 40 (45); Maume and Fromberger, 'Regulation of Initial Coin Offerings: Reconciling U.S. and E.U. Securities Laws' (2019) 19 *Chicago Journal of International Law*, 548 (580 et seq.).

[122] Sester, 'Fallen Anteile an Geschlossenen Fonds unter den Wertpapierbegriff der MiFID bzw. des FRUG?' (2008) 20 *Zeitschrift für Bankrecht und Bankwirtschaft*, 369 (375, 378, 379); Voß, 'Geschlossene Fonds unter dem Rechtsregime der Finanzmarkt-Richtlinie (MiFID)?' (2007) 7 *Zeitschrift für Bank- und Kapitalmarktrecht*, 45 (51 et seqq., 53), each with further references.

[123] Hacker and Thomale, 'Crypto-Securities Regulation: ICOs, Token Sales and Cryptocurrencies under EU Financial Law' [2018] *European Company and Financial Law Review*, 645 (667); Veil, 'Token-Emissionen im europäischen Kapitalmarktrecht' (2019) 183 *Zeitschrift für das gesamte Handels- und Wirtschaftsrecht*, 346 (356).

[124] Cf. Assmann, in Assmann, Schneider and Mülbert (eds), *Wertpapierhandelsrecht*, § 2, para. 11; Roth, in *KölnerKommWpHG*, § 2, para. 24.

[125] Hacker and Thomale, 'Crypto-Securities Regulation: ICOs, Token Sales and Cryptocurrencies under EU Financial Law' [2018] *European Company and Financial Law Review*, 645 (667); Zickgraf, 'Initial Coin Offerings – Ein Fall für das Kapitalmarktrecht?' (2018) 63 *Die Aktiengesellschaft*, 293 (300).

[126] Opposing opinion Ritz and Zeising, in Just, Voß, Ritz and Zeising (eds), *Wertpapierprosektgesetz*, § 2, para. 40.

[127] Zickgraf, 'Initial Coin Offerings – Ein Fall für das Kapitalmarktrecht?' (2018) 63 *Die Aktiengesellschaft*, 293 (300).

these instruments.[128] In light of the **manifold relevance of the legal concept of 'transferable securities'** for the applicability of **primary** and **secondary capital markets law** (cf. only Art. 2(1) MAR, Art. 3(1)(1) MAR in conjunction with Art. 4 (1)(15), Annex I Section C (1) MiFID2), further teleological arguments can be put forward in favour of an issuer-related determination of standardisation: In primary market law, the prospectus requirement (Art. 3(1) Prospectus Regulation) aims at reducing information asymmetries between the issuer and the investors in order to increase the allocational efficiency of the market, reduce the cost of capital to issuers and prevent the collapse of the market (→ para. 4 et seqq.). However, corresponding **information asymmetries** do not only exist in the case of standardisation of the asset class to which a certain instrument belongs, but even more so in the case of a difference in the rights associated with the instruments of individual issuers, which is added to the diversity of the different issuers' business models. Moreover, the intended conveyance of information to investors regarding all securities offered is provided through the prospectus and the envisaged **cost advantages** of this approach are realised if the instruments are standardised on the issuer level.[129] Taking into account the purpose of the disclosure obligations on the secondary market (in particular, **Art. 17 MAR**, but also **periodic disclosure obligations** as set forth in Art. 4, 5 Directives 2004/109/EC, 2013/50/EU), an issuer-related standardisation of instruments also seems sufficient, since the regulatory goal is, once again, the **reduction of informational asymmetries between investors and a particular issuer**. Furthermore, the consideration that bonds, which indisputably qualify as transferable securities (Art. 4(1)(44)(b) MiFID2), are typically structured individually with regard to interest, maturity, collateral and possible subordination also argues for an issuer-related determination of standardisation.[130]

43 If this issuer-related benchmark of standardisation is taken as a basis, the **tokens** sold in ICOs can regularly be regarded as **standardised**, since the rights which the tokens embody in practice are largely uniformly structured at the **issuer level**.[131] This also applies if the tokens are issued as fragmented/partial tokens.[132]

44 **c) Negotiability in the Narrow Sense. aa) General Requirements.** The concept of transferable securities as defined in Art. 4(1)(44) MiFID2 also requires that the instruments are negotiable on the '**capital market**'. With regard to the wording ('negotiable'; German: 'gehandelt werden *können*'), the **abstract possibility** of negotiability is considered sufficient whereas the actual existence of a (capital) market for the instrument is not required.[133] Nevertheless, the actual **tradability** of an instrument on an organised market as defined in Art. 4(1)(21) MiFID2 or a multilateral trading facility as defined in Art. 4(1)(22) MiFID2 shall be an **indication** that it qualifies as a 'transferable secur-

---

[128] Hacker and Thomale, 'Crypto-Securities Regulation: ICOs, Token Sales and Cryptocurrencies under EU Financial Law' [2018] *European Company and Financial Law Review*, 645 (667 et seq.); Veil, 'Token-Emissionen im europäischen Kapitalmarktrecht' (2019) 183 *Zeitschrift für das gesamte Handels- und Wirtschaftsrecht*, 346 (356).

[129] Zickgraf, 'Initial Coin Offerings – Ein Fall für das Kapitalmarktrecht?' (2018) 63 *Die Aktiengesellschaft*, 293 (300).

[130] Veil, 'Token-Emissionen im europäischen Kapitalmarktrecht' (2019) 183 *Zeitschrift für das gesamte Handels- und Wirtschaftsrecht*, 346 (356).

[131] Hacker and Thomale, 'Crypto-Securities Regulation: ICOs, Token Sales and Cryptocurrencies under EU Financial Law' [2018] *European Company and Financial Law Review*, 645 (668 et seq.).

[132] Maume and Fromberger, 'Regulation of Initial Coin Offerings: Reconciling U.S. and E.U. Securities Laws' (2019) 19 *Chicago Journal of International Law*, 548 (581).

[133] Assmann, in Assmann, Schneider and Mülbert (eds), *Wertpapierhandelsrecht*, § 2, para. 12; Fuchs, in Fuchs (ed), *WpHG*, § 2, para. 17; Roth, in *KölnerKommWpHG*, § 2, para. 35.

§ 7. Initial Coin Offerings (ICOs)

ity'.¹³⁴ Whether **crypto exchanges** constitute multilateral trading facilities is uncertain,¹³⁵ although such a classification seems convincing.¹³⁶ If crypto exchanges should be classified as **multilateral trading facilities**, the negotiability of the tokens on the capital market would already be indicated by this fact. However, this point is not even decisive for the legal concept of transferable securities as defined in Art. 4(1)(44) MiFID2, because the definition only contains the requirement of negotiability 'on the capital market' and thus does not refer to the trading venues of Art. 4(1)(21)-(24) MiFID2.¹³⁷ For the legal concept of 'transferable securities' it is therefore only relevant whether crypto exchanges fulfil the requirements that must be met by a '**capital market**' in the sense of Art. 4(1)(44) MiFID2. The existence of a capital market is generally assumed if there is a central institution that is intended to lead to a meeting of supply and demand for certain trading objects and is accessible to a large number of possible participants.¹³⁸ Since crypto exchanges are generally publicly accessible and match supply and demand for tokens, they regularly fulfil the aforementioned requirements so that the actual trading of tokens on crypto exchanges indicates the negotiability of the tokens on the capital market.¹³⁹

bb) **Possibility of bona fide acquisition as a prerequisite of negotiability?** It is a 45 disputed issue whether the negotiability of instruments requires the possibility of acquisition in good faith.¹⁴⁰ Since tokens are **not physical objects** (Sachen) in the sense of § 90 German Civil Code, their bona fide acquisition is not possible under German property law (§§ 932 et. seqq. German Civil Code).¹⁴¹ Therefore, the tradability of the

---

¹³⁴ Roth, in *KölnerKommWpHG*, § 2, para. 28; Fuchs, in Fuchs (ed), *WpHG*, § 2, para. 16.
¹³⁵ This depends on the exchange's setup and structure, → § 8, para. 18 et seqq.
¹³⁶ Hacker and Thomale, 'Crypto-Securities Regulation: ICOs, Token Sales and Cryptocurrencies under EU Financial Law' [2018] *European Company and Financial Law Review*, 645 (665); Zickgraf, 'Initial Coin Offerings – Ein Fall für das Kapitalmarktrecht?' (2018) 63 *Die Aktiengesellschaft*, 293 (301).
¹³⁷ Zickgraf, 'Initial Coin Offerings – Ein Fall für das Kapitalmarktrecht?' (2018) 63 *Die Aktiengesellschaft*, 293 (301); opposing opinion Klöhn, in Klöhn (ed), *Marktmissbrauchsverordnung*, Art. 2, para. 11, 18, who interprets the term 'capital market' (Art. 4(1)(44) MiFID2) as 'trading venue' (Art. 4(1) No. 24 MiFID2).
¹³⁸ Roth, in *KölnerKommWpHG*, § 2, para. 28 et seqq.; similar on MiFID I: European Commission, Your Questions on MiFID (31.10.2008) Question No. 2, 45 ('The notion of 'capital market' is not explicitly defined in MiFID. It is a broad one and is meant to include all contexts where buying and selling interest in securities meet.'); more restrictive: Maume and Fromberger, 'Regulation of Initial Coin Offerings: Reconciling U.S. and E.U. Securities Laws' (2019) 19 *Chicago Journal of International Law*, 548 (576 et seqq.).
¹³⁹ BaFin, 'Initial Coin Offerings: Hinweisschreiben zur Einordnung als Finanzinstrumente, GZ: WA 11-QB 4100- 2017/0010' (20.2.2018), 2, available at https://beck-link.de/2na3t (accessed 11.4.2021); Hacker and Thomale, 'Crypto-Securities Regulation: ICOs, Token Sales and Cryptocurrencies under EU Financial Law' [2018] *European Company and Financial Law Review*, 645 (665); Zickgraf, 'Initial Coin Offerings – Ein Fall für das Kapitalmarktrecht?' (2018) 63 *Die Aktiengesellschaft*, 293 (301); opposing opinion Klöhn, in Klöhn (ed), *Marktmissbrauchsverordnung*, Art. 2, para. 18.
¹⁴⁰ Against the requirement: Hacker and Thomale, 'Crypto-Securities Regulation: ICOs, Token Sales and Cryptocurrencies under EU Financial Law' [2018] *European Company and Financial Law Review*, 645 (666); Klöhn, Parhofer and Resas, 'Initial Coin Offerings (ICOs)' (2018) 30 *Zeitschrift für Bankrecht und Bankwirtschaft*, 89 (100, 101); Spindler, 'Initial Coin Offerings und Prospektpflicht und -haftung' (2018) 72 *Zeitschrift für Wirtschafts- und Bankrecht*, 2109 (2112); Zickgraf, 'Initial Coin Offerings – Ein Fall für das Kapitalmarktrecht?' (2018) 63 *Die Aktiengesellschaft*, 293 (301 et seq.); in favor of this requirement: Bialluch-von Allwörden and von Allwörden, 'Initial Coin Offerings: Kryptowährungen als Wertpapier oder Vermögensanlage?' (2018) 72 *Zeitschrift für Wirtschafts- und Bankrecht*, 2118 (2120 et seq.); Roth, in *KölnerKommWpHG*, § 2, para. 34; Fuchs, in Fuchs (ed), *WpHG*, § 2, para. 18.
¹⁴¹ Hacker and Thomale, 'Crypto-Securities Regulation: ICOs, Token Sales and Cryptocurrencies under EU Financial Law' [2018] *European Company and Financial Law Review*, 645 (666); Zickgraf, 'Initial Coin Offerings – Ein Fall für das Kapitalmarktrecht?' (2018) 63 *Die Aktiengesellschaft*, 293 (301) with further references.

tokens as defined in Art. 4(1)(44) MiFID2 depends decisively on the aforementioned issue of bona fide acquisition.

46   In the end, the negotiability of financial instruments should not hinge upon the possibility of a bona fide acquisition. First, the **EU legal background** of Art. 4(1)(44) MiFID2 argues against this requirement, because it would have the consequence that the legal concept of transferable securities would be determined, inter alia, by the national rules on the bona fide acquisition of property, which would lead to an **unintended national division of the legal situation**.[142] Second, such a requirement is **not reflected in the wording** of Art. 4(1)(44) MiFID2 at all.[143] Third, it can also **not be justified by teleological considerations** either: One should keep in mind that capital markets law is intended to regulate financial market processes and the behaviour of market participants, but not the transfer or assertion of rights from securities.[144] However, the need for market and investor protection exists irrespective of the legal nature of the transfer of financial instruments, as soon as trading actually takes place on the market and the applicability of the manifold market and investor protecting rules (examples: prohibition of insider trading and market manipulation according to Art. 14, 15 MAR) depends on the interpretation of Art. 4 (1)(44) MiFID2 (see Art. 2(1) MAR, Art. 3(1)(1) MAR in conjunction with Art. 4(1)(15), Annex I Section C (1) MiFID2). Therefore, an instrument should qualify as a 'transferable security' irrespective of the possibility of a bone fide acquisition to ensure that those rules can be applied in line with their regulatory purpose (i.e. market and investor protection).[145]

2. Substantial Requirement of 'Transferable Security': Functional Comparability with the non-exhaustive List of Examples of Art. 4(1)(44) MiFID2

47   The transferability, standardisation and negotiability of an instrument are not sufficient to establish its status as transferable securities within the meaning of Art. 4(1)(44) MiFID2. Rather, an instrument's structure must give rise to regulatory issues which capital markets law addresses. This teleological link, which is also reflected in the wording of Art. 4(1)(44) MiFID2 ('on the **capital market**'), can be realised by an **abstract**, **typological definition** of the concept of securities and a more **precise elaboration** of these abstract features, taking into account the **non-exhaustive list of examples** in Art. 4(1)(44)(a)-(c) MiFID2. The **functional comparability** of an instrument with the non-exhaustive list of examples ensures that suitable criteria for differentiation are also available for innovative instruments and hard cases.[146] As a preliminary result, it can therefore be stated that there is a **large degree**

---

[142] Klöhn, in Klöhn (ed), *Marktmissbrauchsverordnung*, Art. 2, para. 17.
[143] Zickgraf, 'Initial Coin Offerings – Ein Fall für das Kapitalmarktrecht?' (2018) 63 *Die Aktiengesellschaft*, 293 (302).
[144] Kumpan, in Schwark and Zimmer (eds), *Kapitalmarktrechts-Kommentar*, § 2, para. 4; Zickgraf, 'Initial Coin Offerings – Ein Fall für das Kapitalmarktrecht?' (2018) 63 *Die Aktiengesellschaft*, 293 (301 et seq.).
[145] Zickgraf, 'Initial Coin Offerings – Ein Fall für das Kapitalmarktrecht?' (2018) 63 *Die Aktiengesellschaft*, 293 (302); also → para. 31, → § 14 para. 7, 19 et seqq., 42 et seqq.
[146] Zickgraf, 'Initial Coin Offerings – Ein Fall für das Kapitalmarktrecht?' (2018) 63 *Die Aktiengesellschaft*, 293 (302) with further references; Hacker and Thomale, 'Crypto-Securities Regulation: ICOs, Token Sales and Cryptocurrencies under EU Financial Law' [2018] *European Company and Financial Law Review*, 645 (669 et seq.); Klöhn, Parhofer and Resas, 'Initial Coin Offerings (ICOs)' (2018) 30 *Zeitschrift für Bankrecht und Bankwirtschaft*, 89 (100); skeptical, using a phenomenological definition of transferable securities under Art. 4(1)(44) MiFID2: Langenbucher, 'European Securities Law – Are we in need of a new definition? A thought inspired by initial coin offerings' [2018] *Revue Trimestrielle de Droit Financier*, 40 (44 et seqq., 47 et seq.).

of convergence between European and the US securities regulation, as in the US, too, the comparability of certain instruments with conventional financial instruments was taken into account in some cases when determining their status as a security (family resemblance).[147] In the following, it is thus necessary to examine the functional comparability of investment, utility, currency and hybrid tokens with the non-exhaustive list of examples in Art. 4(1)(44)(a)-(c) MiFID2. For the sake of clarification, it is important to stress that a particular token's legal qualification under European capital markets law is solely determined by the rights which it conveys whereas the mere titling of a token (i.e. as an investment, utility or currency token) is irrelevant. Therefore, the value of the subsequent categorisation solely consists in systemizing the typical cases.

a) **Investment Tokens.** Investment Tokens are characterised (in particular) by the fact that they convey **profit rights** or other **monetary claims** against an issuer (→ § 1 para. 71). Hence, there is every reason to consider such tokens to be functionally comparable to the non-exhaustive list of examples in Art. 4(1)(44) MiFID2 and to qualify them as transferable securities.[148] After all, these tokens 'give rise to regulatory issues comparable to traditional financial instruments', so that, in line with **recital 8 MiFID2**, their qualification as securities seems appropriate.[149] The recital expresses the legislator's idea that the legal concept 'transferable security'[150] is intended to cope with all arrangements and situations that are characterised by regulatory issues specific to the capital market, such as the existence of **information asymmetries** and **agency conflicts** between issuers and investors.[151] In the case of investment tokens, such information asymmetries are present to the extent that the value of the tokens depends on the (future) profitability of the issuer. Therefore, both the application of primary market regulation (e.g. the obligation to publish a prospectus) and of secondary market regulation (e.g. Art. 17 MAR) seem reasonable to reduce information asymmetries.[152] This applies to investment tokens at least (see for the exception → para. 49), if they are

48

---

[147] Klöhn, Parhofer and Resas, 'Initial Coin Offerings (ICOs)' (2018) 30 *Zeitschrift für Bankrecht und Bankwirtschaft*, 89 (100); cf. U.S. Supreme Court 21 February 1990 – Reves vs. Ernst & Young, 494 U.S. 56; U.S. Court of Appeals (5th Circuit) 20 May 1981 – Williamson vs. Tucker, 645 F.2d 404; U.S. Supreme Court 28 May 1985 – Landreth Timber Co. vs. Landreth, 471 U.S. 681; opposing opinion Langenbucher, 'European Securities Law – Are we in need of a new definition? A thought inspired by initial coin offerings' [2018] *Revue Trimestrielle de Droit Financier*, 40 (44 et seqq., 47 et seqq.).
[148] Predominant opinion, cf. Klöhn, Parhofer and Resas, 'Initial Coin Offerings (ICOs)' (2018) 30 *Zeitschrift für Bankrecht und Bankwirtschaft*, 89 (102); Hacker and Thomale, 'Crypto-Securities Regulation: ICOs, Token Sales and Cryptocurrencies under EU Financial Law' [2018] *European Company and Financial Law Review*, 645 (671 et seqq.); Zickgraf, 'Initial Coin Offerings – Ein Fall für das Kapitalmarktrecht?' (2018) 63 *Die Aktiengesellschaft*, 293 (302 et seq.); Spindler, 'Initial Coin Offerings und Prospektpflicht und -haftung' (2018) 72 *Zeitschrift für Wirtschafts- und Bankrecht*, 2109 (2112 et seq.); Veil, 'Token-Emissionen im europäischen Kapitalmarktrecht' (2019) 183 *Zeitschrift für das gesamte Handels- und Wirtschaftsrecht*, 346 (360); Maume, 'Initial Coin Offerings and EU Prospectus Disclosure' (2020) 31 *European Business Law Review*, 185 (192 et seq.). See on the comparative legal analysis, → para. 29.
[149] Hacker and Thomale, 'Crypto-Securities Regulation: ICOs, Token Sales and Cryptocurrencies under EU Financial Law' [2018] *European Company and Financial Law Review*, 645 (673); Zickgraf, 'Initial Coin Offerings – Ein Fall für das Kapitalmarktrecht?' (2018) 63 *Die Aktiengesellschaft*, 293 (302); also referring to recital 8 MiFID2: Klöhn, Parhofer and Resas, 'Initial Coin Offerings (ICOs)' (2018) 30 *Zeitschrift für Bankrecht und Bankwirtschaft*, 89 (101).
[150] Although recital 8 refers to 'financial instruments', this represents no obstacle, since Art. 4 (1) No. 15 MiFID2 also includes 'transferable securities' listed in Annex I Section C (1) MIFID2.
[151] Klöhn, Parhofer and Resas, 'Initial Coin Offerings (ICOs)' (2018) 30 *Zeitschrift für Bankrecht und Bankwirtschaft*, 89 (101); Veil, 'Token-Emissionen im europäischen Kapitalmarktrecht' (2019) 183 *Zeitschrift für das gesamte Handels- und Wirtschaftsrecht*, 346 (360).
[152] See in detail on this: Zickgraf, 'Initial Coin Offerings – Ein Fall für das Kapitalmarktrecht?' (2018) 63 *Die Aktiengesellschaft*, 293 (302 et seq.).

acquired in order to achieve a financial return, because capital markets law addresses precisely risks associated with financial investments.¹⁵³

49 An **exception** should be made for those 'investment tokens' which only grant (shareholder-like) **rights of participation in the intra-corporate affairs** (→ § 1 para. 71), but do not grant any flow of monies.¹⁵⁴ Since there is no connection between the value of the token and the business activity of the issuer in the case of such tokens, capital market-specific information asymmetries and agency conflicts between the investors and the issuer are absent. Although it is true that the instruments mentioned in Art. 4(1)(44)(a) MiFID2 regularly **also** grant participation rights, it must be kept in mind that these rights are essentially a mere means to the end of securing the investors' financial rights – i.e. the profit rights – by way of internal corporate governance. Therefore, in the case of the transferable securities listed in Art. 4(1)(44)(a) MiFID2, participation rights prove to be a **mere annex** to the residual claims of shareholders. The view that investment tokens must necessarily convey profit rights or other financial entitlements in order to be classified as transferable securities within the meaning of Art. 4(1)(44) MiFID2 is also supported by a **systematic interpretation:** a financial return on the capital market can be achieved through all types of transferable securities listed in Art. 4(1)(44) MiFID2 on the basis of direct (lit. a) and b)) or indirect (lit. c)) financial claims against an issuer. Investment tokens, which only convey participation rights, also do not give rise to regulatory issues comparable to traditional financial instruments which is, however, crucial in light of recital 8 of MiFID2.¹⁵⁵

50 To the extent that a particular investment token conveys pecuniary rights or claims for payment against an issuer and thus qualifies as a transferable security (above → para. 48), it needs to be clarified whether such an investment token is more comparable with the instruments listed in Art. 4(1)(44)(a) MiFID2 or the instruments listed in Art. 4(1)(44)(b) MiFID2. The distinction should be made according to **economic criteria**: In order to fall under lit. a), an investment token needs to convey an **equity interest** in a legal entity.¹⁵⁶ If, in contrast, the investment conveys a mere **debt**

---

[153] Hacker and Thomale, 'Crypto-Securities Regulation: ICOs, Token Sales and Cryptocurrencies under EU Financial Law' [2018] *European Company and Financial Law Review*, 645 (673); Klöhn, Parhofer and Resas, 'Initial Coin Offerings (ICOs)' (2018) 30 *Zeitschrift für Bankrecht und Bankwirtschaft*, 89 (101); Zickgraf, 'Initial Coin Offerings – Ein Fall für das Kapitalmarktrecht?' (2018) 63 *Die Aktiengesellschaft*, 293 (302 et seq.).

[154] In my opinion, it would be more convincing not to speak of investment tokens in such cases in the first place. In accordance with this view, the conveyance of financial rights or payment claims is often regarded as a mandatory feature of an investment token, cf. FINMA, 'Wegleitung für Unterstellungsanfragen betreffend Initial Coin Offerings (ICOs)' (16.2.2018), 2 et seqq., available at https://beck-link.de/f5fad (accessed 11.4.2021); Rohr and Wright, 'Blockchain-Based Token Sales, Initial Coin Offerings, and the Democratization of Public Capital Markets' (2018) *Cardozo Legal Studies Research Paper* No. 527, 24, available at https://beck-link.de/peh4b (accessed 11.4.2021); Zickgraf, 'Initial Coin Offerings – Ein Fall für das Kapitalmarktrecht?' (2018) 63 *Die Aktiengesellschaft*, 293 (295). However, tokens that only grant participation rights are sometimes also referred to as investment tokens, cf. BaFin, 'Merkblatt: Zweites Hinweisschreiben zu Prospekt- und Erlaubnispflichten im Zusammenhang mit der Ausgabe sogenannter Krypto-Token, GZ: WA 51-Wp 7100-2019/0011 und IF 1-AZB 1505-2019/0003' (16.8.2019), 8, available at https://beck-link.de/tz6vv (accessed 11.4.2021); → § 1, para. 71.

[155] Different Maume and Fromberger, 'Regulation of Initial Coin Offerings: Reconciling U.S. and E.U. Securities Laws' (2019) 19 *Chicago Journal of International Law*, 548 (577); probably also BaFin, 'Merkblatt: Zweites Hinweisschreiben zu Prospekt- und Erlaubnispflichten im Zusammenhang mit der Ausgabe sogenannter Krypto-Token, GZ: WA 51-Wp 7100-2019/0011 und IF 1-AZB 1505-2019/0003' (16.8.2019), 8, available at https://beck-link.de/tz6vv (accessed 11.4.2021); Veil, 'Token-Emissionen im europäischen Kapitalmarktrecht' (2019) 183 *Zeitschrift für das gesamte Handels- und Wirtschaftsrecht*, 346 (349, 360 et seq.).

[156] Klöhn, Parhofer and Resas, 'Initial Coin Offerings (ICOs)' (2018) 30 *Zeitschrift für Bankrecht und Bankwirtschaft*, 89 (101 et seq.).

§ 7. Initial Coin Offerings (ICOs)

interest, it falls under lit. b).[157] This approach is supported by systematic considerations, since the examples mentioned in 4(1)(44)(a) MiFID2 represent typical equity investments, whereas a bond, the prime example of an instrument falling under Art. 4(1)(44)(b) MiFID2,[158] is a typical debt investment. This approach also proves to be consistent with regard to the (few) legal consequences resulting from this differentiation: For example, it becomes relevant in terms of the information to be included in the prospectus (Art. 2(b) and (c) EU Prospectus Regulation in conjunction with Art. 13(1)(1)(a) EU Prospectus Regulation).[159] Art. 13(1)(1)(a) EU Prospectus Regulation indirectly indicates that an economic approach is decisive by stating that 'a consistent approach shall be taken with regard to information required in a prospectus for securities which have a similar economic rationale, notably derivative securities'. If a clear classification is feasible based on this economic distinction, no further considerations need to be made. In **unclear cases**, however, it must also be taken into account whether the instrument conveys **rights similar to those of shareholders**, and only if this additional condition is fulfilled should the instrument be classified under lit. a).[160] Therefore, the following applies to the classification of investment tokens: If the token conveys **financial rights** in the form of an **equity interest** (e.g. profit rights), it falls under Art. 4(1)(44)(a) MiFID2; this applies all the more if shareholder-like participation rights (e.g. voting rights) are also granted.[161] If, on the other hand, an investment token merely conveys **financial claims** in the form of a **debt interest**, the investment token is comparable to the bonds mentioned in lit. b).

51 Generally speaking,[162] investment tokens are to be classified as transferable securities which are either comparable to the instruments mentioned in lit. a) or the instruments mentioned in lit. b).[163] For this purpose, it is merely, but strictly, necessary that the tokens convey financial claims against the issuer; the mere granting of participation rights (e.g. voting rights) through an investment token does not make it a transferable security.

52 **b) Utility Tokens.** The qualification and handling of utility tokens under capital markets law has proven to be the most controversial and complex issue in connection with ICOs. In the legal literature and among the supervisory authorities, two opposing positions are essentially at odds with each other (see also → para. 56 et seqq.): While some assume that utility tokens are to be classified as transferable securities at least under specific conditions, others generally reject the qualification of utility tokens as transferable securities.[164]

---

[157] See for further distinguishing criteria Veil, 'Token-Emissionen im europäischen Kapitalmarktrecht' (2019) 183 *Zeitschrift für das gesamte Handels- und Wirtschaftsrecht*, 346 (358 et seqq.); see also Kumpan, in Schwark and Zimmer (eds), *Kapitalmarktrechts-Kommentar*, § 2, para. 84.

[158] Assmann, in Assmann, Schneider and Mülbert (eds), *Wertpapierhandelsrecht*, § 2, para. 31.

[159] Klöhn, Parhofer and Resas, 'Initial Coin Offerings (ICOs)' (2018) 30 *Zeitschrift für Bankrecht und Bankwirtschaft*, 89 (102, fn. 120).

[160] Similar Klöhn, Parhofer and Resas, 'Initial Coin Offerings (ICOs)' (2018) 30 *Zeitschrift für Bankrecht und Bankwirtschaft*, 89 (102).

[161] Hacker and Thomale, 'Crypto-Securities Regulation: ICOs, Token Sales and Cryptocurrencies under EU Financial Law' [2018] *European Company and Financial Law Review*, 645 (671 et seqq.).

[162] If one considers the conveyance of payment claims/financial rights as a constitutive feature of an investment token, all investment tokens would classify as transferable securities, cf. Zickgraf, 'Initial Coin Offerings – Ein Fall für das Kapitalmarktrecht?' (2018) 63 *Die Aktiengesellschaft*, 293 (302 et seq., 307). In other words, every token that conveys such rights fulfils the substantial requirements of the concept of transferable securities as defined in Art. 4(1)(44) MiFID2.

[163] Zickgraf, 'Initial Coin Offerings – Ein Fall für das Kapitalmarktrecht?' (2018) 63 *Die Aktiengesellschaft*, 293 (303); Barsan, 'Legal Challenges of Initial Coin Offerings (ICO)' [2017] *Revue Trimestrielle de Droit Financier*, 54 (62).

[164] BaFin (Germany), MAS (Singapore) and (probably also) SFC (Hong Kong) assume, that utility tokens do not constitute securities, → 17 et seq., 26. See from the legal literature: Veil, 'Token-Emissionen im europäischen Kapitalmarktrecht' (2019) 183 *Zeitschrift für das gesamte Handels- und Wirtschaftsrecht*,

53 **aa) General Remarks.** A characteristic feature of utility tokens is that they grant their holder a right to use a product, use a service or access a platform against a particular issuer (→ § 1 para. 73).[165] Therefore, it is in principle possible to classify utility tokens as negotiable financial claims under the law of obligations falling under the definition of a **bond** pursuant to Art. 4(1)(44)(b) MiFID2.[166] From a systematic perspective, however, utility tokens do not easily fit into the list of instruments referred to in Art. 4(1)(44)(b) MiFID2 since monetary claims are regularly attached to those instruments, as is evident from the prominent position of the 'bond' as the prime example of those instruments.[167] But at least with respect to primary market regulation, this is not essential; rather, the **granting of rights of use** may be sufficient for the assumption of a transferable security: In the context of the EU Prospectus Regulation, this can be justified by means of an argumentum e contrario from Art. 1(2)(f) EU Prospectus Regulation, which excludes from its scope of application 'non-fungible shares of capital whose main purpose is to provide the holder with a right to occupy an apartment, or other form of immovable property or a part thereof and where the shares cannot be sold on without that right being given up'. After all, Art. 1(2) EU Prospectus Regulation demonstrates that the instruments listed are regarded as transferable securities and that the legislator has recognised the situation where rights of use are granted by a security. From the merely singular exception of the rights of use mentioned in Art. 1(2)(f) EU Prospectus Regulation, it can be inferred e contrario that instruments which solely convey rights of use can also be regarded as transferable securities.[168] The legal assessment of utility tokens under capital markets law thus proves to be an open question and must ultimately be dealt with by means of **teleological considerations**.

54 However, a **determination** of the status as a transferable security **based on the subjective intentions of investors**, which primarily focuses on whether the prospect of profits resulting from the issuer's efforts is subjectively 'a significant motive of the typical token investor', proves to be rather **inadequate**.[169] If one bases the qualification (in the absence of objective evidence) on the aspect whether, from an empirical point of view, the majority of investors acquire the tokens with the intention of making a profit and the issuer knew or should have known this, one will usually conclude that the utility token proves to be a transferable security because the intention of making a profit is present with most investors.[170] Such an approach decouples the classification of an

---

346 (363 et seq.); Hacker and Thomale, 'Crypto-Securities Regulation: ICOs, Token Sales and Cryptocurrencies under EU Financial Law' [2018] *European Company and Financial Law Review*, 645 (673 et seqq., 681 et seqq.).

[165] See on the characteristic features of utility tokens Zickgraf, 'Initial Coin Offerings – Ein Fall für das Kapitalmarktrecht?' (2018) 63 *Die Aktiengesellschaft*, 293 (296) with further references.

[166] Hacker and Thomale, 'Crypto-Securities Regulation: ICOs, Token Sales and Cryptocurrencies under EU Financial Law' [2018] *European Company and Financial Law Review*, 645 (674); cf. Zickgraf, 'Initial Coin Offerings – Ein Fall für das Kapitalmarktrecht?' (2018) 63 *Die Aktiengesellschaft*, 293 (303 et seq.) with further references on the relevant criteria of the legal concept.

[167] Hacker and Thomale, 'Crypto-Securities Regulation: ICOs, Token Sales and Cryptocurrencies under EU Financial Law' [2018] *European Company and Financial Law Review*, 645 (675).

[168] Zickgraf, 'Initial Coin Offerings – Ein Fall für das Kapitalmarktrecht?' (2018) 63 *Die Aktiengesellschaft*, 293 (304).

[169] In favour of this view: *Hacker* and *Thomale*, 'Crypto-Securities Regulation: ICOs, Token Sales and Cryptocurrencies under EU Financial Law' (2017) Social Science Research Network 1 (34, 36 et seqq.); against this view: Zickgraf, 'Initial Coin Offerings – Ein Fall für das Kapitalmarktrecht?' (2018) 63 *Die Aktiengesellschaft*, 293 (306); same result as here: Langenbucher, 'European Securities Law – Are we in need of a new definition? A thought inspired by initial coin offerings' [2018] *Revue Trimestrielle de Droit Financier*, 40 (46, 48).

[170] *Hacker* and *Thomale*, 'Crypto-Securities Regulation: ICOs, Token Sales and Cryptocurrencies under EU Financial Law' (2017) Social Science Research Network 1, (34 et seq.).

instrument as a transferable security from the (functional) comparability of the respective instrument with the non-exhaustive list of examples in Art. 4(1)(44)(a) – (c) MiFID2.[171] Another argument against this approach is presented by the fact that the need for market and investor protection through disclosure obligations under capital markets law is completely independent of the subjective intentions of investors and must therefore be determined on the basis of objective criteria. After all, the disclosure obligations under capital markets law primarily provide information concerning the issuer, so that this regulatory regime proves to be inappropriate if there is no objective need by market participants to receive information on a particular issuer. If there is an (objective) information asymmetry with regard to the contractual performance agreed upon, capital markets law would thus not provide market participants with the desired information despite their intention to make a profit.[172]

From a teleological point of view, it is therefore of crucial importance for the legal assessment of utility tokens whether there is an **objective need for information** on the part of the investors which is **related to the issuer** (→ para. 61 et seqq,). Insofar, it is relevant whether the envisaged profits are to be achieved through 'decisive efforts of the issuer'.[173] After all, in cases where the financial return depends on the efforts of others, a typical principal-agent relationship[174] arises between the investors and the management, whereby the information asymmetries pose the risk of ex post opportunistic behaviour (moral hazard)[175] by the managers, from which investors should be protected by capital markets law.[176] Accordingly, **issuer-related information asymmetries**, which lead to agency conflicts in the context of a long-term relationship between the investors and the issuer, prove to be essential for the qualification of a utility token as a transferable security. In contrast, a pure utility token (synonymous: utility token without investment function, → para. 61, 63), which should not be classified as a transferable security, is present if the **information asymmetries** are merely **product-** or **goods-related** (related to the object of the contractual agreement) and/or the **relationship** between the investors and the issuer is **not long-term**, so that despite existing information asymmetries no principal-agent relationship, in which the risk of moral hazard is present, arises. As a consequence, the legal assessment of utility tokens under capital markets law primarily rests upon the quality of the information asymmetries, which in turn are significantly influenced by the development stage of the project underlying the utility token (→ para. 62). 55

bb) Legal Analysis of Utility Tokens. *(1) First View: Utility Tokens are not Transferable Securities.* Some scholars generally reject the classification of utility tokens as transferable securities.[177] The first argument put forward for this view is that utility 56

---

[171] See Zickgraf, 'Initial Coin Offerings – Ein Fall für das Kapitalmarktrecht?' (2018) 63 *Die Aktiengesellschaft*, 293 (306) with further remarks on the consequences of the 'subjective approach'.
[172] For details, see ibid, 306.
[173] Convincing in this respect: *Hacker* and *Thomale*, 'Crypto-Securities Regulation: ICOs, Token Sales and Cryptocurrencies under EU Financial Law' (2017) Social Science Research Network 1 (34: 'decisive efforts of the issuer'); see also Zickgraf, 'Initial Coin Offerings – Ein Fall für das Kapitalmarktrecht?' (2018) 63 *Die Aktiengesellschaft*, 293 (306).
[174] See on the principal-agent-theory: Jensen and Meckling, 'Theory of the firm: Managerial behavior, agency costs and ownership structure' (1976) 3 *Journal of Financial Economics*, 305.
[175] See for a definition: Holmström, 'Moral Hazard and Observability' (1979) 10 *Bell Journal of Economics*, 74; Richter and Furubotn, *Neue Institutionenökonomik* (4th edn, 2010), 218.
[176] Klöhn, Parhofer and Resas, 'Initial Coin Offerings (ICOs)' (2018) 30 *Zeitschrift für Bankrecht und Bankwirtschaft*, 89 (101).
[177] Veil, 'Token-Emissionen im europäischen Kapitalmarktrecht' (2019) 183 *Zeitschrift für das gesamte Handels- und Wirtschaftsrecht*, 346 (363 et seq.); Weitnauer, 'Initial Coin Offerings (ICOs): Rechtliche Rahmenbedingungen und regulatorische Grenzen' (2018) 18 *Zeitschrift für Bank- und Kapitalmarktrecht*,

tokens lack the monetary claims characteristic of the instruments covered by Art. 4(1) (44)(a) and (b) MiFID2.[178] For this reason, the purpose of the obligation to publish a prospectus shall not be affected: The information asymmetries that arise are said to be product-related; to this extent, there is no capital market-specific information asymmetry.[179] This view is convincing in the case of pure utility tokens without an investment component.[180] As far as the utility tokens have an **investment component**, however, capital market-specific information asymmetries and agency conflicts can occur (→ para. 61 et seqq.). This fact is also recognised by the supporters of the more restrictive view when they point out that, if the tokens are tradable, substantial capital gains can be realised by investors and that these prospective gains are significantly influenced by the efforts of the issuer and the initiators.[181] However, this point shall be irrelevant since information asymmetries are said to be primarily product-related in the case of utility tokens. As a consequence, so the argument goes, addressing these informational asymmetries via securities regulation would blur the boundaries between capital markets law and consumer protection law. After all, possible losses in value for token holders shall usually be the result of the missing benefit of the product or service to which the utility token provides access, and this is said to be a problem that is typically addressed by the mechanisms of consumer protection law.[182]

57 However, this view ignores the fact that in the case of a utility token with an investment component, there is a **long-term (legal) relationship** (risk of ex post opportunism, moral hazard) between the investors and the issuer with pronounced agency conflicts. This reprents a significant distinction from the usual situation of consumer protection law (ex ante information asymmetries at the time of conclusion of the contract, adverse selection). Addressing such problems is a traditional objective of capital markets law,[183] which therefore proves to be a suitable regulatory regime for utility tokens with an investment function. Apart from this aspect, the accurate observation that holders of utility tokens do not have a residual interest and that the tokens are therefore not comparable with 'shares in companies' referred to in Art. 4(1)(44)(a) MiFID2 is

---

231 (233); Hacker and Thomale, 'Crypto-Securities Regulation: ICOs, Token Sales and Cryptocurrencies under EU Financial Law' [2018] *European Company and Financial Law Review*, 645 (673 et seqq., 681 et seqq.).

[178] See in detail: Hacker and Thomale, 'Crypto-Securities Regulation: ICOs, Token Sales and Cryptocurrencies under EU Financial Law' [2018] *European Company and Financial Law Review*, 645 (674 et seq.); similar Veil, 'Token-Emissionen im europäischen Kapitalmarktrecht' (2019) 183 *Zeitschrift für das gesamte Handels- und Wirtschaftsrecht*, 346 (363): No supply of capital on a temporary basis, but rather the purchase of a product or the possibility of using services.

[179] Hacker and Thomale, 'Crypto-Securities Regulation: ICOs, Token Sales and Cryptocurrencies under EU Financial Law' [2018] *European Company and Financial Law Review*, 645 (675); Veil, 'Token-Emissionen im europäischen Kapitalmarktrecht' (2019) 183 *Zeitschrift für das gesamte Handels- und Wirtschaftsrecht*, 346 (363 et seq.): 'Securities regulation (…) not the suitable regime.' ('Wertpapierregulierung (…) nicht das passende Regime.').

[180] Cf. Zickgraf, 'Initial Coin Offerings – Ein Fall für das Kapitalmarktrecht?' (2018) 63 *Die Aktiengesellschaft*, 293 (304).

[181] Hacker and Thomale, 'Crypto-Securities Regulation: ICOs, Token Sales and Cryptocurrencies under EU Financial Law' [2018] *European Company and Financial Law Review*, 645 (681).

[182] Ibid, 682 et seq.; similar Veil, 'Token-Emissionen im europäischen Kapitalmarktrecht' (2019) 183 *Zeitschrift für das gesamte Handels- und Wirtschaftsrecht*, 346 (363 et seq.), who refers to structural and functional differences between shares and bonds on the one hand and utility tokens on the other hand; unlike a shareholder or bondholder, the holder of a utility token does not provide capital (for a limited period of time), which he is to receive back at a later date (at least in the case of bonds), which is why a functional comparability with the non-exhaustive list of examples mentioned in Art. 4(1)(44)(a) – (c) MiFID2 is not given in the case of utility tokens.

[183] Klöhn, Parhofer and Resas, 'Initial Coin Offerings (ICOs)' (2018) 30 *Zeitschrift für Bankrecht und Bankwirtschaft*, 89 (101 et seqq.). See on the economic foundations, → para. 4 et seqq.

irrelevant.[184] After all, the functional comparability of utility tokens with the instruments mentioned in Art. 4(1)(44)(b) MiFID2 is the main issue. Compared to utility tokens, these instruments differ in that they regularly convey monetary claims.[185] However, this aspect is not decisive as the exemption in Art. 1(2)(f) Prospectus Regulation shows e contrario; rather, the possibility of realising a financial return (by way of sale via the secondary market) seems sufficient.[186] Thus, a general rejection of the qualification of utility tokens as transferable securities is not convincing.

(2) Second View: Utility Tokens are Transferable Securities. Other scholars support the idea of generally classifying utility tokens as transferable securities.[187] It is argued that **futures contracts** and **options** on contracts that result in a claim to delivery of a commodity are also classified as securities (within the meaning of Art. 4(1)(44)(c) MiFID2).[188] It is true that options can be classified as transferable securities within the meaning of Art. 4(1)(44)(c) MiFID2.[189] However, Art. 4(1)(44)(c) MiFID2 requires that the instruments give 'the right to acquire or sell any such transferable securities or give rise to a cash settlement determined by reference to transferable securities, currencies, interest rates or yields, commodities or other indices or measures'. Utility tokens do neither convey a right to acquire or sell a security, nor do they result in a cash settlement that is dependent on these underlyings. Utility tokens grant a right to use a product or service or access a platform.

Nevertheless, it is correct that utility tokens are often comparable to futures contracts (e.g., the delivery of oil or grain) as they embody similar claims of future performance.[190] At first glance, it therefore appears possible to classify the rights conveyed by utility tokens as derivative contracts relating to commodities that can be physically settled within the meaning of Annex I Section C (6) MiFID2.[191] But even if one were to make such a classification, one would not be able to qualify utility tokens as transferable securities by way of this reasoning. Instead, utility tokens could only be classified as derivatives as defined in Art. 4(1)(49) MiFID2, which are defined in Art. 2(1)(29) MiFIR as those financial instruments contained in Art. 4(1)(44)(c) MiFID2 and Annex I Section C (4–10) MiFID2. It follows from the systematic interpretation of Art. 2 (1) No. 29 MiFIR that the instruments listed in Annex I Section C (4–10) MiFID2 are not always to be regarded simultaneously as transferable securities within the meaning of

---

[184] Cf. Hacker and Thomale, 'Crypto-Securities Regulation: ICOs, Token Sales and Cryptocurrencies under EU Financial Law' [2018] *European Company and Financial Law Review*, 645 (682).

[185] Hacker and Thomale, 'Crypto-Securities Regulation: ICOs, Token Sales and Cryptocurrencies under EU Financial Law' [2018] *European Company and Financial Law Review*, 645 (675); Weitnauer, 'Initial Coin Offerings (ICOs): Rechtliche Rahmenbedingungen und regulatorische Grenzen' (2018) 18 *Zeitschrift für Bank- und Kapitalmarktrecht*, 231 (233).

[186] Klöhn, Parhofer and Resas, 'Initial Coin Offerings (ICOs)' (2018) 30 *Zeitschrift für Bankrecht und Bankwirtschaft*, 89 (102).

[187] Spindler, 'Initial Coin Offerings und Prospektpflicht und -haftung' (2018) 72 *Zeitschrift für Wirtschafts- und Bankrecht*, 2109 (2113).

[188] Ibid, with further references.

[189] See for § 2(1)(3)(b) WpHG (German Securities Act) which has an identical wording: Assmann, in Assmann, Schneider and Mülbert (eds), *Wertpapierhandelsrecht*, § 2, para. 36.

[190] Spindler, 'Initial Coin Offerings und Prospektpflicht und -haftung' (2018) 72 *Zeitschrift für Wirtschafts- und Bankrecht*, 2109 (2113).

[191] See on the requirements (especially tradability on a regulated market, a MTF or an OTF and the existence of a commodity within the meaning of Art. 2, No. 6 Delegated Regulation (EU) 2017/565): Klöhn, in Klöhn (ed), *Marktmissbrauchsverordnung*, Art. 2, para. 74 et seqq. Whether utility tokens are to be classified as physically settled commodity derivative contracts is beyond the scope of this study and shall therefore not be decided at this point. For the present context, it is a sufficient finding that such a qualification would not lead to the status of a transferable security within the meaning of Art. 4(1)(44) MiFID2.

Art. 4(1)(44)(c) MiFID2.[192] However, a (plausible) classification of utility tokens under Annex I Section C (6) MiFID2 would lead to their qualification as financial instruments pursuant to Art. 4(1)(15) MiFID2.

60   Hence, it is crucial for the functional comparability of utility tokens with the non-exhaustive list of examples given in Art. 4(1)(44) MiFID2 whether capital market-specific information asymmetries and agency conflicts exist between issuers and investors.[193] Yet, such dangers are by no means always present in utility tokens; at least they do not necessarily arise due to the mere embodiment of rights in a blockchain-based and tradable token.[194] While the **derivative financial instruments** of Art. 4(1)(44) (c) MiFID2 mostly obtain their capital market-specific complexity through the **connection to an underlying**,[195] a **utility token** embodies the **underlying itself**. This does not result in any capital market-specific information asymmetries, as is illustrated by the occasionally cited example of the sale of a tulip bulb via the blockchain. This example does not differ from the sale of a tulip bulb in a flower shop to an extent which would justify the application of capital markets law.[196] If there is no need of market participants for issuer-related information (as in the example), capital markets law is not the appropriate regulatory regime.[197] Against this background, utility tokens cannot generally be qualified as transferable securities within the meaning of Art. 4(1)(44) MiFID2.

61   *(3) Preferable View: A Differentiating Approach to Utility Tokens.* The classification of a utility token under capital markets law should be determined on a case-by-case basis taking into account its economic structure.[198] In this context, the important question is whether **capital market-specific information asymmetries** exist between the issuer and the investors and whether **agency conflicts** may arise because of these; in particular, it is highly relevant to what extent the realisation of a financial profit depends on the efforts of the issuer, because utility tokens would be functionally comparable to traditional financial instruments under these circumstances (see recital 8 MiFID2).[199] If, on the other hand, **product-related information asymmetries** prevail, the token is to be considered a 'pure utility token' without an investment function, which cannot be qualified as a transferable security.[200]

62   Two aspects are of primary importance when determining the functional comparability of utility tokens with traditional transferable securities: First, the classification depends on the question whether the products, services or platforms, which can be used by a token holder, still need to be **developed** or significantly **enhanced**. If this is

---

[192] Similar: Klöhn, in Klöhn (ed), *Marktmissbrauchsverordnung*, Art. 2, para. 58 ('in part'; 'Zum Teil').
[193] Similar starting point: Spindler, 'Initial Coin Offerings und Prospektpflicht und -haftung' (2018) 72 *Zeitschrift für Wirtschafts- und Bankrecht*, 2109 (2113).
[194] Against this argument: Spindler, ibid.
[195] See generally: Klöhn, in Klöhn (ed), *Marktmissbrauchsverordnung*, Art. 2, para. 43 et seqq., 58 et seqq.
[196] See for this example: Zetzsche, Buckley, Arner and Föhr, 'The ICO Gold Rush: It's a Scam, It's a Bubble, It's a Super Challenge for Regulators' (19.11.2017), 37, available at https://beck-link.de/k23ak (accessed 11.4.2021).
[197] Zickgraf, 'Initial Coin Offerings – Ein Fall für das Kapitalmarktrecht?' (2018) 63 *Die Aktiengesellschaft*, 293 (304).
[198] Zickgraf, 'Initial Coin Offerings – Ein Fall für das Kapitalmarktrecht?' (2018) 63 *Die Aktiengesellschaft*, 293 (304 et seqq.); Klöhn, Parhofer and Resas, 'Initial Coin Offerings (ICOs)' (2018) 30 *Zeitschrift für Bankrecht und Bankwirtschaft*, 89 (102 et seq.); Hacker and Thomale, 'Crypto-Securities Regulation: ICOs, Token Sales and Cryptocurrencies under EU Financial Law' [2018] *European Company and Financial Law Review*, 645 (681 et seqq., 684).
[199] See also → para. 48 with further references.
[200] Zickgraf, 'Initial Coin Offerings – Ein Fall für das Kapitalmarktrecht?' (2018) 63 *Die Aktiengesellschaft*, 293 (304).

the case, the value of the rights conveyed by the utility token depend largely on the efforts of the issuer, which means that there is an objective need for information on the issuer, capital market-specific information asymmetries are present and agency conflicts may thus arise.[201] The second relevant aspect is closely related: To the extent that the services conveyed by the token are to be provided in the future, the token also functions as a **corporate financing tool** for the issuer. This latter aspect is crucial because under these circumstances the token is comparable with the financial instruments mentioned in Art. 4(1)(44)(a) and (b) MiFID2 (recital 8 MiFID2) and capital market-specific risks in the form of (issuer-related) information asymmetries and agency conflicts exist.[202]

In order to determine whether the **investment and corporate financing function** 63 (= qualification as transferable security, utility token with investment function) or the **utility function** (= no qualification as transferable security, utility token without investment function) of a particular token predominates, one should take into account the following indicators:[203]

Some aspects suggest the qualification of a utility token as a transferable security under EU law:

– the inability to use the product/service/platform at the time the token is offered
– the sole option to use the goods by acquiring the token (especially, if the token is limited in quantity), if it can only be purchased on the primary or the secondary (capital) markets and/or
– the highlighting of the token's tradability and profit opportunities in the issuer's promotional materials.

Other factors indicate that the utility token should not be qualified as a transferable security:

– the ability to use the product/service/platform at the time the token is offered,
– the existence of alternative distribution channels (e.g., direct purchase of the service from the respective company or the option to use the goods by purchasing a token which is not limited in quantity) and/or
– the absence of advertising statements by the issuer indicating an investment function of the utility token.

---

[201] Zickgraf, 'Initial Coin Offerings – Ein Fall für das Kapitalmarktrecht?' (2018) 63 *Die Aktiengesellschaft*, 293 (304 et seq.); Klöhn, Parhofer and Resas, 'Initial Coin Offerings (ICOs)' (2018) 30 *Zeitschrift für Bankrecht und Bankwirtschaft*, 89 (102 et seq.); Langenbucher, 'European Securities Law – Are we in need of a new definition? A thought inspired by initial coin offerings' [2018] *Revue Trimestrielle de Droit Financier*, 40 (41); critical on this: Spindler, 'Initial Coin Offerings und Prospektpflicht und -haftung' (2018) 72 *Zeitschrift für Wirtschafts- und Bankrecht*, 2109 (2113 et seq.).

[202] Klöhn, Parhofer and Resas, 'Initial Coin Offerings (ICOs)' (2018) 30 *Zeitschrift für Bankrecht und Bankwirtschaft*, 89 (103); Zickgraf, 'Initial Coin Offerings – Ein Fall für das Kapitalmarktrecht?' (2018) 63 *Die Aktiengesellschaft*, 293 (304 et seq.); critical van Aubel, '§ 20 – Initial Coin Offerings (ICOs)', in Habersack, Mülbert and Schlitt (eds), *Unternehmensfinanzierung am Kapitalmarkt* (2019), § 20, para. 111 et seq.

[203] Cf. Securities and Exchange Commission, 'In the Matter of Munchee Inc.: Securities Act of 1933 Release No. 10445' (11.12.2017), available at https://beck-link.de/yd3ne (accessed 11.4.2021); see also FINMA, 'Wegleitung für Unterstellungsanfragen betreffend Initial Coin Offerings (ICOs)' (16.2.2018), 2 et seqq., available at https://beck-link.de/f5fad (accessed 11.4.2021); Rohr and Wright, 'Blockchain-Based Token Sales, Initial Coin Offerings, and the Democratization of Public Capital Markets' (2018) *Cardozo Legal Studies Research Paper* No. 527, 56 et seq., 69 et seqq., 99 et seqq., available at https://beck-link.de/peh4b (accessed 11.4.2021); Zickgraf, 'Initial Coin Offerings – Ein Fall für das Kapitalmarktrecht?' (2018) 63 *Die Aktiengesellschaft*, 293 (305); Klöhn, Parhofer and Resas, 'Initial Coin Offerings (ICOs)' (2018) 30 *Zeitschrift für Bankrecht und Bankwirtschaft*, 89 (102 et seq.); Hacker and Thomale, 'Crypto-Securities Regulation: ICOs, Token Sales and Cryptocurrencies under EU Financial Law' (2017) Social Science Research Network 1 (34 et seq.).

64 However, when examining individual cases it is important to keep in mind that the non-exhaustive criteria listed above are neither a necessary nor a sufficient condition to classify an utility token as a transferable security. The determining factor must always be an individual case-by-case analysis of the economic structure of the respective token, which must lead to a functional comparability with traditional transferable securities due to the existence of capital market-specific risks.[204] The differentiating legal assessment of utility tokens supported in this chapter largely corresponds to the approach of the SEC (→ para. 14), the FMA (→ para. 27) and the FINMA (→ para. 28), both in terms of the result and regarding the relevant criteria. While BaFin could be understood in its first publications to also take a differentiating position in the legal assessment of utility tokens based on the criteria mentioned here,[205] it has meanwhile made clear that, in general, it does not consider utility tokens to be transferable securities.[206]

65 **c) Currency Tokens.** Pure currency tokens are not transferable securities within the meaning of Art. 4(1)(44) MiFID2.[207] This result follows from the explicit 'exception of instruments of payment' from the legal concept of transferable securities.[208] The legal term 'instruments of payments' includes cash, cheques and other liquid funds, provided that they are commonly used as a means of payment.[209] The **payment function** of a currency token represents its **main characteristic** (→ § 1 para. 70), which is why it is similar to conventional instruments of payments in terms of its purpose, although it is not such an instrument in the legal sense.[210] The classification as legal tender is ruled out from the outset (cf. Art. 128 (1) sentence 3 TFEU, Art. 10 sentence 2 of Regulation (EC) 974/98, Art. 11 sentence 2 of Regulation (EC) 974/98), and there is also no claim against an issuer which would be necessary for a classification as e-money (cf. Art. 2 No. 2 of Directive 2009/110/EC, → § 9 para. 10 et seqq., 34 et seq.).[211] Although currency tokens do not fit into the existing categories of instruments of payment because of these differences, currency tokens are much closer to these instruments

---

[204] Klöhn, Parhofer and Resas, 'Initial Coin Offerings (ICOs)' (2018) 30 *Zeitschrift für Bankrecht und Bankwirtschaft*, 89 (102).

[205] Fußwinkel and Kreiterling, 'Blockchain-Technologie – Gedanken zur Regulierung' (1/2018) BaFin Perspektiven, 61, available at https://beck-link.de/a7mkv (accessed 11.4.2021).

[206] BaFin, 'Merkblatt: Zweites Hinweisschreiben zu Prospekt- und Erlaubnispflichten im Zusammenhang mit der Ausgabe sogenannter Krypto-Token, GZ: WA 51-Wp 7100-2019/0011 und IF 1-AZB 1505-2019/0003' (16.8.2019), 5, available at https://beck-link.de/tz6vv (accessed 11.4.2021).

[207] Predominant opinion: Hacker and Thomale, 'Crypto-Securities Regulation: ICOs, Token Sales and Cryptocurrencies under EU Financial Law' [2018] *European Company and Financial Law Review*, 645 (676 et seqq.); Zickgraf, 'Initial Coin Offerings – Ein Fall für das Kapitalmarktrecht?' (2018) 63 *Die Aktiengesellschaft*, 293 (306 et seq.); Spindler, 'Initial Coin Offerings und Prospektpflicht und -haftung' (2018) 72 *Zeitschrift für Wirtschafts- und Bankrecht*, 2109 (2118); Maume and Fromberger, 'Regulation of Initial Coin Offerings: Reconciling U.S. and E.U. Securities Laws' (2019) 19 *Chicago Journal of International Law*, 548 (581); for comparative analysis → para. 29.

[208] Zickgraf, 'Initial Coin Offerings – Ein Fall für das Kapitalmarktrecht?' (2018) 63 *Die Aktiengesellschaft*, 293 (306 et seq.); Maume and Fromberger, 'Regulation of Initial Coin Offerings: Reconciling U.S. and E.U. Securities Laws' (2019) 19 *Chicago Journal of International Law*, 548 (581).

[209] Assmann, in Assmann, Schneider and Mülbert (eds), *Wertpapierhandelsrecht*, § 2, para. 16; Roth, in *KölnerKommWpHG*, § 2, para. 41; Kumpan, in Schwark and Zimmer (eds), *Kapitalmarktrechts-Kommentar*, § 2, para. 12.

[210] Klöhn, in Klöhn (ed), *Marktmissbrauchsverordnung*, Art. 2, para. 85; Zickgraf, 'Initial Coin Offerings – Ein Fall für das Kapitalmarktrecht?' (2018) 63 *Die Aktiengesellschaft*, 293 (307); Spindler, 'Initial Coin Offerings und Prospektpflicht und -haftung' (2018) 72 *Zeitschrift für Wirtschafts- und Bankrecht*, 2109 (2114).

[211] Hacker and Thomale, 'Crypto-Securities Regulation: ICOs, Token Sales and Cryptocurrencies under EU Financial Law' [2018] *European Company and Financial Law Review*, 645 (678); Hildner, 'Bitcoins auf dem Vormarsch: Schaffung eines regulatorischen Level Playing Fields?' (2016) 16 *Zeitschrift für Bank- und Kapitalmarktrecht*, 485 (489); Klöhn, in Klöhn (ed), *Marktmissbrauchsverordnung*, Art. 2, para. 85.

than to transferable securities, which argues against their status as transferable securities.[212] The fact that the exemption of currency tokens from the definition of transferable securities can be based on a mere comparability with instruments of payment follows inversely from the fact that, in order to establish the status of a transferable security, the functional comparability with the instruments listed in Art. 4 (1)(44) MiFID2 was also taken into account and considered to be sufficient. The function of currency tokens, which is comparable to conventional means of payment, has also been recognised by the ECJ for the purposes of the VAT Directive and, in the specific case, Bitcoins have not been classified as securities but as contractual and direct means of payment between the operators that accept them (→ § 13 para. 9 et seqq.).[213]

Moreover, in the case of currency tokens, there is a **lack of functional comparability** with the instruments listed in Art. 4(1)(44) MiFID2: In contrast to these, **currency tokens do not grant any claims against an issuer**, so that their (secondary market) performance does not depend on the business performance of an issuer, but on general market developments.[214] The same is implied when the lack of 'connection to tangible assets'[215] is referred to and the comparability with commodities or precious metals (especially gold) is emphasised.[216] This characteristic in itself distinguishes currency tokens systematically from the examples in Art. 4(1)(44) MiFID2 and clearly distinguishes them from utility tokens, which at least convey claims against an issuer.[217] From a teleological point of view, this situation ultimately leads to a lack of capital market-specific information asymmetries and agency conflicts that could be addressed by disclosure obligations under capital markets law; the purpose of capital markets regulation in general and the obligation to publish a prospectus in particular are not affected by currency tokens and there is also no comparability with conventional financial instruments (cf. recital 8 MiFID2).[218] In this respect, the risks inherent in currency tokens (e.g. exchange rate and liquidity risks) should be better managed by means of **banking supervision** and **payment services law**.[219]

66

No other legal assessment seems to be necessary if the platform required for the currency token is not yet available but is to be developed with the proceeds of the emission.[220] After all, in such cases the investors' claim against an issuer for access to a

67

---

[212] See extensively on this aspect: Hacker and Thomale, 'Crypto-Securities Regulation: ICOs, Token Sales and Cryptocurrencies under EU Financial Law' [2018] *European Company and Financial Law Review*, 645 (676 et seqq.) with further references; see also Zickgraf, 'Initial Coin Offerings – Ein Fall für das Kapitalmarktrecht?' (2018) 63 *Die Aktiengesellschaft*, 293 (307).
[213] ECJ, Judgment of 22 October 2015, *Hedqvist*, C-264/14, EU:C:2015:718, para. 42, 55.
[214] Zickgraf, 'Initial Coin Offerings – Ein Fall für das Kapitalmarktrecht?' (2018) 63 *Die Aktiengesellschaft*, 293 (307).
[215] Klöhn, in Klöhn (ed), *Marktmissbrauchsverordnung*, Art. 2, para. 88.
[216] Cf. Langenbucher, 'Digitales Finanzwesen – Vom Bargeld zu virtuellen Währungen' (2018) 218 *Archiv für die civilistische Praxis*, 385 (390); Hacker and Thomale, 'Crypto-Securities Regulation: ICOs, Token Sales and Cryptocurrencies under EU Financial Law' [2018] *European Company and Financial Law Review*, 645 (678); Zickgraf, 'Initial Coin Offerings – Ein Fall für das Kapitalmarktrecht?' (2018) 63 *Die Aktiengesellschaft*, 293 (296 et seq., 307); similar Klöhn, in Klöhn (ed), *Marktmissbrauchsverordnung*, Art. 2, para. 87 with further references.
[217] Cf. Zickgraf, 'Initial Coin Offerings – Ein Fall für das Kapitalmarktrecht?' (2018) 63 *Die Aktiengesellschaft*, 293 (307).
[218] Zickgraf, 'Initial Coin Offerings – Ein Fall für das Kapitalmarktrecht?' (2018) 63 *Die Aktiengesellschaft*, 293 (307).
[219] Hacker and Thomale, 'Crypto-Securities Regulation: ICOs, Token Sales and Cryptocurrencies under EU Financial Law' [2018] *European Company and Financial Law Review*, 645 (679 et seq.); Spindler, 'Initial Coin Offerings und Prospektpflicht und -haftung' (2018) 72 *Zeitschrift für Wirtschafts- und Bankrecht*, 2109 (2114).
[220] Opposing opinion van Aubel, '§ 20 – Initial Coin Offerings (ICOs)', in Habersack, Mülbert and Schlitt (eds), *Unternehmensfinanzierung am Kapitalmarkt* (2019), § 20, para. 121 et seq.

platform is of primary importance, so the particular token should be classified as a utility token, which would have to be qualified as a transferable security on the basis of the above-mentioned criteria (→ para. 61 et seqq.).[221] The economic comparability with a utility token with an investment function[222] means that in the cases just described there is not a mere currency token offered, but a (hybrid) utility token with a potential investment function. However, pure currency tokens still cannot be qualified as transferable securities.

68   In the case of currency tokens, it is also **irrelevant** for the qualification as a transferable security (see also → para. 54) whether the **intention to make a profit** is the decisive motive for the majority of market participants.[223] This analysis is once again based on the idea that capital markets law, in the absence of an objective issuer-related asymmetry of information between the issuer and investors, does not provide market participants with the necessary information even if they act with the intention of making a profit (→ para. 54).

69   **d) Hybrid Tokens.** In many instances tokens are of a hybrid nature and combine the elements of several types of tokens, so that they cannot be clearly assigned to one of the abovementioned token categories.[224] The legal assessment of a hybrid token depends on whether certain rights conveyed by it would justify its qualification as a transferable security **when considered in isolation**.[225] Thus, hybrid tokens that solely grant the rights of pure utility tokens (without an investment function) are just as little subject to the legal concept of Art. 4(1)(44) MiFID2 as are hybrid tokens conveying rights of pure currency tokens.[226]

70   **e) Token Derivatives.** In principle, derivative financial instruments based on a **token as an underlying** can be classified as transferable securities as defined by Art. 4(1)(44)(c) MiFID2.[227] For such instruments, the scope of application of numerous capital markets legal provisions is given (→ § 11 para. 9, 19 et seqq.).

---

[221] Same finding: van Aubel, '§ 20 – Initial Coin Offerings (ICOs)', in Habersack, Mülbert and Schlitt (eds), *Unternehmensfinanzierung am Kapitalmarkt* (2019), § 20, para. 121, et seq, 122.

[222] Van Aubel, '§ 20 – Initial Coin Offerings (ICOs)', in Habersack, Mülbert and Schlitt (eds), *Unternehmensfinanzierung am Kapitalmarkt* (2019), § 20, para. 122.

[223] Zickgraf, 'Initial Coin Offerings – Ein Fall für das Kapitalmarktrecht?' (2018) 63 *Die Aktiengesellschaft*, 293 (307); opposing opinion: Hacker and Thomale, 'Crypto-Securities Regulation: ICOs, Token Sales and Cryptocurrencies under EU Financial Law' (2017) Social Science Research Network 1 (35 et seq.).

[224] Weitnauer, 'Initial Coin Offerings (ICOs): Rechtliche Rahmenbedingungen und regulatorische Grenzen' (2018) 18 *Zeitschrift für Bank- und Kapitalmarktrecht*, 231 (232); Veil, 'Token-Emissionen im europäischen Kapitalmarktrecht' (2019) 183 *Zeitschrift für das gesamte Handels- und Wirtschaftsrecht*, 346 (349).

[225] Zickgraf, 'Initial Coin Offerings – Ein Fall für das Kapitalmarktrecht?' (2018) 63 *Die Aktiengesellschaft*, 293 (307); more cautious: Hacker and Thomale, 'Crypto-Securities Regulation: ICOs, Token Sales and Cryptocurrencies under EU Financial Law' [2018] *European Company and Financial Law Review*, 645 (681 et seqq.); slightly different also: BaFin, 'Merkblatt: Zweites Hinweisschreiben zu Prospekt- und Erlaubnispflichten im Zusammenhang mit der Ausgabe sogenannter Krypto-Token, GZ: WA 51-Wp 7100-2019/0011 und IF 1-AZB 1505-2019/0003' (16.8.2019), 6, available at https://beck-link.de/tz6vv (accessed 11.4.2021), which refers to the main function of the token.

[226] Cf. Zickgraf, 'Initial Coin Offerings – Ein Fall für das Kapitalmarktrecht?' (2018) 63 *Die Aktiengesellschaft*, 293 (307).

[227] Maume and Fromberger, 'Regulation of Initial Coin Offerings: Reconciling U.S. and E.U. Securities Laws' (2019) 19 *Chicago Journal of International Law*, 548 (583 et seq.); Kumpan, in Schwark and Zimmer (eds), *Kapitalmarktrechts-Kommentar*, § 2, para. 85; at least for Bitcoin-derivatives (= currency tokens as an underlying) also Klöhn and Parhofer, 'Bitcoins sind keine Rechnungseinheiten – ein Paukenschlag und seine Folgen' (2018) 40 *Zeitschrift für Wirtschaftsrecht*, 2093 (2099 et seq.).

f) Tokens not Conveying Any Rights. If a token does not confer any rights, it cannot be classified as a transferable security within the meaning of Art. 4(1)(44) MiFID2. The reasons for this result are the same as those considerations that argue against the transferable security-status of pure currency tokens (→ para. 65 et seqq.). 71

3. Exemptions from the Prospectus Obligation

When offering securities to the public under Art. 3(1) EU Prospectus Regulation the initiators of an ICO can only avoid the obligation to publish a prospectus by structuring the offer in such a way that it falls under one of the exemptions of Art. 1(4) EU Prospectus Regulation or Art. 3(2) EU Prospectus Regulation. 72

a) Investor-Related Exemptions. Pursuant to Art. 1(4)(a) EU Prospectus Regulation, the obligation to publish a prospectus (see Art. 3(1) EU Prospectus Regulation) does not apply to an offer of securities addressed solely to '**qualified investors**'. Art. 2(e) Prospectus Regulation defines 'qualified investors' by referring, inter alia, to the persons and entities listed in Section I points 1 to 4 of Annex II and Section II of Annex II of Directive 2014/65/EU (AIFM Directive). Accordingly, the list of qualified investors includes institutional investors (e.g., credit institutions, investment firms, insurance companies, pension funds, large undertakings/companies, governments, etc.) and (private) investors with sufficient expertise, experience and knowledge. 73

If the investors are not qualified investors within the meaning of Art. 2(e) EU Prospectus Regulation, there is nevertheless no obligation to publish a prospectus pursuant to Art. 1(4)(b) EU Prospectus Regulation if the offer of securities is addressed to **fewer than 150 natural or legal persons per Member State**. 74

However, these two exemptions are of **limited use for ICOs**: This is due to the fact that the prevailing **pseudonymity**, which is inherent in an archetypal Blockchain (→ § 1 para. 17, 102 et seqq.), complicates the identification and verification of the qualified investors (Art. 1(4)(a) EU Prospectus Regulation) as well as the adherence to the upper limit of fewer than 150 not qualified investors per Member State (Art. 1(4)(b) EU Prospectus Regulation).[228] Thus, the qualification of the investors and their domicile would have to be determined by traditional means; in contrast, the determination by means of a smart contract does not seem to be feasible.[229] Besides, transactions which were structured in a way that would fall under one of these exemptions would abandon the basic idea of direct access of private investors to primary market emissions, which is characteristic of ICOs.[230] If utility tokens (with an investment function) are issued, there is the additional disadvantage that such a structuring makes it much more difficult to realise the network effects which are envisaged through the sale of the tokens.[231] Thus, the above-mentioned exemptions will primarily be considered by issuers who wish to 75

---

[228] Hacker and Thomale, 'Crypto-Securities Regulation: ICOs, Token Sales and Cryptocurrencies under EU Financial Law' [2018] *European Company and Financial Law Review*, 645 (687 et seq.); Maume, 'Initial Coin Offerings and EU Prospectus Disclosure' (2020) 31 *European Business Law Review*, 185 (201).

[229] Van Aubel, '§ 20 – Initial Coin Offerings (ICOs)', in Habersack, Mülbert and Schlitt (eds), *Unternehmensfinanzierung am Kapitalmarkt* (2019), § 20, para. 124 et seq.

[230] Hacker and Thomale, 'Crypto-Securities Regulation: ICOs, Token Sales and Cryptocurrencies under EU Financial Law' [2018] *European Company and Financial Law Review*, 645 (688); Maume, 'Initial Coin Offerings and EU Prospectus Disclosure' (2020) 31 *European Business Law Review*, 185 (201).

[231] See generally for this purpose of utility tokens: Klöhn, Parhofer and Resas, 'Initial Coin Offerings (ICOs)' (2018) 30 *Zeitschrift für Bankrecht und Bankwirtschaft*, 89 (93 et seq.); see also Behme and Zickgraf, 'Zivil- und gesellschaftsrechtliche Aspekte von Initial Coin Offerings (ICOs)' (2019) 5 *Zeitschrift für die gesamte Privatrechtswissenschaft*, 66 (70 et seq.).

finance the costs of an ICO with the help of prior token sales (→ § 1 para. 84; sometimes also referred to as a pre-ICO).[232]

76 **b) Exemptions related to Transaction Volume.** According to Art. 1(4)(c) EU Prospectus Regulation, there is no obligation to publish a prospectus for offers of securities with a minimum denomination per unit of EUR 100,000. Pursuant to Art. 1 (4)(d) EU Prospectus Regulation, the same applies to an offer of securities addressed to investors who acquire securities for a total consideration of at least EUR 100,000 per investor, for each separate offer. Apart from the abondance of the basic idea of access for private investors to primary market emissions, the use of this exemption is further complicated by the fact that oftentimes cryptocurrencies (i.e. currency tokens) are used as consideration in ICOs and the conversion (rate) required to comply with the thresholds is subject to great uncertainty due to the high volatility of the tokens.[233]

77 The Member States' right of choice provided for in Art. 3(2) EU Prospectus Regulation proves to be an exception which could theoretically be practicable for issuers. According to this provision, the Member States have the option to exempt a public offer of securities from the obligation to publish a prospectus if it is not subject to a notification pursuant to Art. 25 EU Prospectus Regulation (→ para. 85) regarding the passport procedure) and the total consideration of the offer over a period of 12 months does not exceed EUR 8,000,000.[234] Apart from the difficulties already mentioned with regard to the correct calculation of the thresholds when currency tokens are used as consideration[235], the use of this exemption is subject to the least practical difficulties. However, the German regulation in § 3(2) WpPG, which was enacted to implement the option granted by Art. 3(2) EU Prospectus Regulation, cannot be taken advantage of in order to conduct an ICO without a prospectus, given the currently existing transaction structures, due to the mediatisation requirement provided for in § 6 WpPG (i.e., exclusive brokerage of the securities by way of investment advice or investment brokerage via an investment services company that also monitors compliance with the subscription limits provided for in § 6 WpPG).[236] Irrespective of this, an issuer also has the option to conduct an offer with a total consideration of less than EUR 1,000,000, calculated over a period of 12 months, without the obligation to publish a prospectus, cf. Art. 1(3) EU Prospectus Regulation.[237] For ICOs, the use of this exemption is probably the most suitable. This applies in particular to transactions, in which a future ICO shall be financed by a simplified private sale or Pre-ICO (→ § 1 para. 84).

---

[232] Van Aubel, '§ 20 – Initial Coin Offerings (ICOs)', in Habersack, Mülbert and Schlitt (eds), *Unternehmensfinanzierung am Kapitalmarkt* (2019), § 20, para. 128.

[233] Hacker and Thomale, 'Crypto-Securities Regulation: ICOs, Token Sales and Cryptocurrencies under EU Financial Law' [2018] *European Company and Financial Law Review*, 645 (688); see in detail: Maume, 'Initial Coin Offerings and EU Prospectus Disclosure' (2020) 31 *European Business Law Review*, 185 (196 et seqq.).

[234] Germany has already made use of this option in § 3 Nr. 2 Wertpapierprospektgesetz (WpPG).

[235] Cf. Hacker and Thomale, 'Crypto-Securities Regulation: ICOs, Token Sales and Cryptocurrencies under EU Financial Law' [2018] *European Company and Financial Law Review*, 645 (688); van Aubel, '§ 20 – Initial Coin Offerings (ICOs)', in Habersack, Mülbert and Schlitt (eds), *Unternehmensfinanzierung am Kapitalmarkt* (2019), § 20, para. 126.

[236] Klöhn, 'Die neue Prospektfreiheit 'kleiner' Wertpapieremissionen unter 8 Mio. €' (2018) 40 *Zeitschrift für Wirtschaftsrecht*, 1713 (1716, 1721).

[237] However, if the offer exceeds 100,000 EUR, the offeror must prepare a securities information sheet (Wertpapier-Informationsblatt, WIB) in accordance with § 3a Wertpapierprospektgesetz (WpPG), cf. Klöhn, 'Die neue Prospektfreiheit 'kleiner' Wertpapieremissionen unter 8 Mio. €' (2018) 40 *Zeitschrift für Wirtschaftsrecht*, 1713 (1717 et seq.).

4. Content of the Prospectus

A securities prospectus shall contain the **necessary information** which is **material to an investor** for making an **informed assessment** of the financial situation of the issuer, the rights attaching to the securities and the reasons for the issuance and its effects on the issuer, Art. 6(1) EU Prospectus Regulation. Pursuant to Art. 6(2) EU Prospectus Regulation, the information in a prospectus shall be written and presented in an easily analysable, concise and comprehensible form.

Except for the financial information pursuant to Art. 6(1)(a) EU Prospectus Regulation, the provision of which is likely to prove quite demanding due to the short business history of the issuers and the valuation difficulties caused by the new business models,[238] there are no special features for issuers of investment tokens. From a practical point of view, a feasible way to comply with this requirement of the prospectus could be to follow the recommendations of ESMA with regard to **start-up companies**.[239] Art. 6(1)(b) EU Prospectus Regulation requires that the rights attaching to the securities are described in detail, which is of particular importance in the case of utility tokens (with an investment function). In addition to the naming of the specific rights conveyed by the token, the value-determining factors (e.g., the (non-)existence of alternative distribution channels to obtain the service, application of a so-called burning mechanism[240], etc.) should also be disclosed to comply with Art. 6(1)(b) EU Prospectus Regulation. In any case, the prospectus should reflect the particularities of the individual token issuance.[241]

Detailed provisions on the content of the prospectus can be found in Art. 7, 13 et seq. EU Prospectus Regulation and in the Commission Delegated Regulation (EU) 2019/980.[242]

5. Approval and Publication of the Prospectus

According to Art. 20(1) EU Prospectus Regulation, a prospectus shall only be published after it has been approved by the competent authority. In this context, Art. 20(2) subp. 1 EU Prospectus Regulation provides that the competent authority shall notify the issuer or the offeror of its decision regarding the approval of the

---

[238] Klöhn, Parhofer and Resas, 'Initial Coin Offerings (ICOs)' (2018) 30 *Zeitschrift für Bankrecht und Bankwirtschaft*, 89 (95 et seq.); Behme and Zickgraf, 'Zivil- und gesellschaftsrechtliche Aspekte von Initial Coin Offerings (ICOs)' (2019) 5 *Zeitschrift für die gesamte Privatrechtswissenschaft*, 66 (71 et seq.).

[239] ESMA, 'ESMA update of the CESR recommendations (ESMA/2011/81)' (23.3.2011), para. 135 et seqq., available at https://beck-link.de/h285y (accessed 11.4.2021); van Aubel, '§ 20 – Initial Coin Offerings (ICOs)', in Habersack, Mülbert and Schlitt (eds), *Unternehmensfinanzierung am Kapitalmarkt* (2019), § 20, para. 131.

[240] The term 'burning' is commonly used to describe the redemption of the token after the service has been used without a resale by the issuer. This leads to a shortage of the existing supply of tokens and theoretically to an increase in the market value of the remaining tokens. Such a mechanism was also envisaged in the case of Munchee Inc., cf. Securities and Exchange Commission, 'In the Matter of Munchee Inc.: Securities Act of 1933 Release No. 10445' (11.12.2017), 5, available at https://beck-link.de/yd3ne (accessed 11.4.2021).

[241] Spindler, 'Initial Coin Offerings und Prospektpflicht und -haftung' (2018) 72 *Zeitschrift für Wirtschafts- und Bankrecht*, 2109 (2115); cf. Hahn and Wilkens, 'ICO vs. IPO – Prospektrechtliche Anforderungen bei Equity Token Offerings' (2019) 31 *Zeitschrift für Bankrecht und Bankwirtschaft*, 10 (19 et seqq.).

[242] Commission Delegated Regulation (EU) 2019/980 of 14 March 2019 supplementing Regulation (EU) 2017/1129 of the European Parliament and of the Council as regards the format, content, scrutiny and approval of the prospectus to be published when securities are offered to the public or admitted to trading on a regulated market, and repealing Commission Regulation (EC) No. 809/2004, Official Journal of the European Union L 166/26.

prospectus within 10 working days (Art. 2(t) EU Prospectus Regulation) of the submission of the draft prospectus, though a failure of the competent authority to take a decision on the prospectus within these time limits shall not be deemed to constitute an approval of the application pursuant to Art. 20(2) subp. 2 EU Prospectus Regulation. In the case of ICOs, the 20-working-day period of Art. 20(3) EU Prospectus Regulation will be relevant in most cases because offerors will regularly be issuers whose securities have not yet been admitted to trading on a regulated market and who have not previously offered securities to the public.

82   In terms of contents, the competent authority does not examine the prospectus for accuracy but only for **completeness**, **comprehensibility** and **consistency** of the information contained therein, Art. 20 (4) EU Prospectus Regulation. If the competent authority finds that the prospectus does not meet these standards and therefore changes or supplementary information are needed, it shall notify the issuer or the offeror promptly (at the latest within the time limits of Art. 20(2) subp. 1, (3) EU Prospectus Regulation), clearly specify the changes and the supplementary information that are needed, Art. 20 (4) subpar. 1 EU Prospectus Regulation; in this case, according to Art. 20(4) subpar. 2 EU Prospectus Regulation a new limit (as set out in Art. 20(2) subp. 1 EU Prospectus Regulation) shall then apply from the date on which a revised draft prospectus or the supplementary information requested are submitted to the competent authority. To avoid time delays, issuers should thus contact the competent authority at an early stage and coordinate the entire process with the authority if a transaction shall be conducted.[243]

83   The **competent authority** (cf. Art. 2(o) EU Prospectus Regulation) is the authority designated by the respective Member State in accordance with Art. 31 EU Prospectus Regulation. As the provisions on cross-border offerings in Art. 24, 25 EU Prospectus Regulation indicate, the competent authority is generally the competent authority of the **home Member State** (Art. 2(m) EU Prospectus Regulation).[244] For issuers established in the Union, the home Member State and thus also the competence of the administrative authority depends on the location of the registered office, Art. 2(m)(i) EU Prospectus Regulation.[245]

84   After approval, the issuer or the offeror shall make the prospectus available to the public at a reasonable time in advance of, and at the latest at the beginning of the offer to the public, Art. 21(1) subp. 1 EU Prospectus Regulation. According to Art. 21(2) EU Prospectus Regulation, the prospectus shall be deemed available to the public if it is published in electronic form on the website of the issuer or the offeror (lit. a), the financial intermediaries placing or selling the securities (lit. b) or the operator of the regulated market or multilateral trading facility (MTF) (lit. c). More detailed provisions

---

[243] See for the established practice of BaFin: Meyer, in Habersack, Mülbert and Schlitt (eds), *Unternehmensfinanzierung am Kapitalmarkt* (2019), § 36, para. 81.

[244] The fact that Art. 20 (1) EU Prospectus Regulation, in contrast to Art. 13(1) Directive 2003/71/EC, no longer expressly refers to the 'competent authority of the home Member State' but only to the 'competent authority' does not change the legal situation. This view is further supported against the background of recital 14 of Directive 2003/71/EC, which has been adopted unchanged in content and is now reflected in recital 11 of the EU Prospectus Regulation, which continues to refer to the 'home Member State'. Art. 20 (8), (10) EU Prospectus Regulation also imply that the 'competent authority' in the meaning of Art. 20 (1) EU Prospectus Regulation refers to the 'competent authority of the home Member State', because in this respect no reasons are apparent which would indicate that different authorities should be addressed in the different paragraphs; same result: Maume, 'Initial Coin Offerings and EU Prospectus Disclosure' (2020) 31 *European Business Law Review*, 185 (202).

[245] See for the competence in cases of third country issuers and decentralised networks as issuers: Maume, 'Initial Coin Offerings and EU Prospectus Disclosure' (2020) 31 *European Business Law Review*, 185 (202 et seqq.).

on the accessibility and design of the prospectus available on the website are contained in Art. 21(3) and (4) EU Prospectus Regulation. In terms of time, the prospectuses that are also published on the website of the competent authority of the home Member State (Art. 21(5) EU Prospectus Regulation) and of ESMA (Art. 21(6) EU Prospectus Regulation) must remain publicly available in electronic form for at least ten years after their publication on the websites, Art. 21(7) EU Prospectus Regulation.

In view of the fact that ICOs are mostly marketed via the Internet and often address a global investor audience,[246] the so-called **European passport** is of particular importance for issuers of ICOs: The passport (Art. 24 EU Prospectus Regulation) allows the issuer to offer the securities to the public in one or more Member States, or in a Member State other than the home Member State using the prospectus approved by the home Member State, which remains valid for such offers; the EU Prospectus Regulation only requires that ESMA and the competent authority of the host Member State (Art. 2(n) Prospectus Regulation) be informed in accordance with the procedure laid down in Art. 25 EU Prospectus Regulation (see also → § 3 para. 44). 85

6. Advertisements

Art. 22 EU Prospectus Regulation lays down special requirements with regard to advertising that relates to a public offer of securities.[247] Advertising is defined in Art. 2(k) EU Prospectus Regulation as a communication relating to a specific offer of securities to the public and at the same time aiming to specifically promote the potential subscription or acquisition of securities. In the case of ICOs, such advertising via **social media platforms** is one of the central aspects[248], so that the following principles will be highly relevant in practice for the vast majority of ICOs. The requirements of Art. 22(2)–(5) EU Prospectus Regulation shall apply only to cases where the issuer or the offeror is subject to the obligation to draw up a prospectus (Art. 22(1) subp. 2 EU Prospectus Regulation) and, with the exception of Art. 22(5) EU Prospectus Regulation, are not limited to issuers and offerors of securities. In view of the frequent mandating of advertising companies and specialised consultants, this seems sensible. 86

First, advertisements shall state that a prospectus has been or will be published and indicate where investors are or will be able to obtain it, Art. 22(2) EU Prospectus Regulation. Moreover, according to Art. 22 (3) EU Prospectus Regulation, the advertising shall be **clearly recognizable** as such and the information contained in it shall **not** be **inaccurate** or **misleading**; furthermore, it shall be **consistent with the information contained in the prospectus**. Pursuant to Art. 22(4) EU Prospectus Regulation, the latter also applies to information disclosed orally or in written form, even if it is not for advertising purposes and therefore does not constitute advertising within the meaning of Art. 2(k) EU Prospectus Regulation. Finally, the equal treatment of investors (in terms of obtainable information) is the aim of the obligations of conduct applicable to issuers and offerors of securities under Art. 22(5) EU Prospectus Regulation: If material information is disclosed by an issuer or an offeror and 87

---

[246] Rohr and Wright, 'Blockchain-Based Token Sales, Initial Coin Offerings, and the Democratization of Public Capital Markets' (2018) *Cardozo Legal Studies Research Paper* No. 527, 28, available at https://beck-link.de/peh4b (accessed 11.4.2021).

[247] See on the need for regulation and the risks of advertisement on the capital market: Klöhn, 'Die Ausweitung der bürgerlich-rechtlichen Prospekthaftung durch das 'Rupert Scholz'-Urteil des BGH' (2012) 66 *Zeitschrift für Wirtschafts- und Bankrecht*, 97 (98 et seq.) with further references.

[248] Zickgraf, 'Initial Coin Offerings – Ein Fall für das Kapitalmarktrecht?' (2018) 63 *Die Aktiengesellschaft*, 293 (294); Rohr and Wright, 'Blockchain-Based Token Sales, Initial Coin Offerings, and the Democratization of Public Capital Markets' (2018) *Cardozo Legal Studies Research Paper* No. 527, 27 et seq., available at https://beck-link.de/peh4b (accessed 11.4.2021).

addressed to one or more selected investors in oral or written form, such information shall be disclosed to all other investors to whom the offer is addressed, in the event that a prospectus is not required to be published in accordance with Art. 1(4) or (5) EU Prospectus Regulation (lit. a); be included in the prospectus or in a supplement to the prospectus in accordance with Art. 23(1) EU Prospectus Regulation, in the event that a prospectus is required to be published (lit. b). Through these obligations, the legislator seeks to effectively **prevent preferential treatment** of individual investors. This regulatory goal shall be achieved through the competent authorities' powers to exercise control over the compliance of advertising activity, relating to an offer of securities to the public (Art. 22(6) EU Prospectus Regulation, Art. 32(1)(e) EU Prospectus Regulation). With regard to the legal consequences of a violation of these obligations under private law, the Regulation does not contain precise provisions. However, Art. 22(11) EU Prospectus Regulation in conjunction with recital 64 s. 4 indicate that at least the EU provisions on consumer protection and unfair commercial practices may apply in the case of violations. Since in both areas of regulation there are only directives that are (at least generally) not directly applicable, the reference of the legislator remains unclear. In any case, neither from Art. 22(11) EU Prospectus Regulation nor from recital 64 s. 4 Prospectus Regulation can be inferred, which provisions of those directives the legislators had in mind and wanted to be applied in the event of a violation of Art. 22 EU Prospectus Regulation. The most appropriate rules that could be applied in cases of violation of Art. 22 EU Prospectus Regulation would probably be Art. 6, 7 Directive 2005/29/EC (Unfair Commercial Practices Directive, possibly in conjunction with Annex II).

7. Prospectus Liability

88 Pursuant to Art. 11 EU Prospectus Regulation the Member States shall ensure that responsibility for the information given in a prospectus attaches at least to the **issuer** or its **administrative, management** or **supervisory bodies**, the **offeror**, the **person asking for the admission to trading on a regulated market** or the **guarantor**, as the case may be. As a result of Art. 11 EU Prospectus Regulation, civil liability for deficiencies of the prospectus is governed by the **law of the Member States** (→ § 3 para. 45 et seqq.)[249]:
- Germany: §§ 9 et seq. Wertpapierprospektgesetz (WpPG), as well as 'civil law prospectus liability' (*bürgerlich-rechtliche Prospekthaftung*)[250]
- United Kingdom: Section 90 Financial Services and Markets Act (FSMA)
- Italy: Art. 94(8) Testo Unico della Finanza (TUF)
- Austria: § 22 Kapitalmarktgesetz (KMG)
- Spain: Art. 38 Ley del Mercado de Valores (LMV)
- France: Art. 1240 Code Civil

E. Regulation on Markets in Crypto-Assets

I. Background and Overview

89 On the 24th of September 2020 the European Commission released its Proposal for a Regulation of the European Parliament and of the Council on Markets in Crypto-assets,

---

[249] Veil, *European Capital Markets Law* (2nd edn, 2017), § 17, para. 60 et seqq.
[250] See extensively on this: Zickgraf, '§ 11 – Initial Coin Offerings (ICOs)', in Maume and (eds), *Rechtshandbuch Kryptorecht* (2020), § 11, para. 91 et seqq.

and amending Directive (EU) 2019/1937 (henceforth: **MiCAR**).[251] The Commission's proposal is part of the Digital Finance Package and pursues four regulatory objectives: the establishment of legal certainty, the support of innovation, guaranteeing appropriate levels of consumer and investor protection and market integrity and ensuring financial stability.[252]

The proposal consists of nine titles covering different subject matters: 90

Title	Subject Matter	Relevant Articles
Title I	Subject Matter, Scope and Definitions	Art. 1 – 3
Title II	Crypto-Assets, other than asset-referenced tokens or e-money tokens	Art. 4 – 14
Title III	Asset-referenced tokens	Art. 15 – 42
Title IV	Electronic money tokens	Art. 43 – 52
Title V	Authorisation and operating conditions for Crypto-Asset Service providers	Art. 53 – 75
Title VI	Prevention of Market Abuse involving Crypto-Assets	Art. 76 – 80
Title VII	Competent Authorities, the EBA and ESMA	Art. 81 – 120
Title VIII	Delegated acts and implementing acts	Art. 121
Title IX	Transitional and final provisions	Art. 122 – 126

This chapter will focus on Title II of the Regulation (see for an overview of Titles III and IV → § 9).

II. Scope

According to Art. 2(1) MiCAR the Regulation applies to **persons that are engaged** 91 **in the issuance of crypto-assets** or **provide services related to crypto-assets in the Union**. Thus, the legal concept 'crypto-asset' becomes central to the scope of the Regulation. Art. 3(1)(2) MiCAR defines a crypto-asset as a digital representation of value or rights which may be transferred and stored electronically, using distributed ledger technology or similar technology. This legal concept is defined in such a **broad way** that, as a starting point, all token categories (investment, utility and currency tokens) fall under the scope of MiCAR (provided that they are based on DLT or similar technology).[253]

However, the Regulation does not apply to **financial instruments** as defined in Art. 4 92 (1)(15) MiFID2 (see Art. 2(2)(a) MiCAR). As a consequence, investment tokens are not regulated by MiCAR since they qualify as transferable securities within the meaning of Art. 4(1)(44) MiFID2 (→ para. 48 et seqq.) and thus represent financial instruments as defined in Art. 4(1)(15) in conjunction with Annex II MiFID2.

Although utility tokens with an investment component were qualified as transferable 93 securities within the meaning of Art. 4(1)(44) MiFID2 (→ para. 61 et seqq.), once Mi-

---

[251] Commission, 'Proposal for a Regulation of the European Parliament and of the Council on Markets in Crypto-assets, and amending Directive (EU) 2019/1937' COM (2020), 593 final.
[252] Ibid, 1 (2 et seq.).
[253] See recital 8 MiCAR.

CAR enters into force and becomes applicable, **all types of utility tokens** will be covered by MiCAR. After all, Art. 4 – 14 MiCAR contain specific disclosure obligations for issuers of crypto assets (see Art. 3(6) MiCAR). Therefore, the arguments (such as ensuring market and investor protection) that have so far suggested a classification of utility tokens with an investment function as transferable securities, no longer argue for such an interpretation, since **Art. 4 – 14 MiCAR** contain a **special and tailor-fit regime** which adequately covers the need for regulation of these crypto-assets. In view of this change in the overall regulatory situation, utility tokens with an investment function should no longer be qualified as transferable securities within the meaning of Art. 4(1)(44) MiFID2, as soon as MiCAR becomes applicable. As a consequence, even utility tokens with an investment function will not be subject to Art. 2 (2) lit. a) MiCAR and all types of utility tokens will be regulated by MiCAR.[254]

94 Finally, MiCAR also deals with **asset-referenced tokens** (see Art. 3(1)(3) MICAR) and **electronic money tokens** (Art. 3(1)(4) MICAR), which represent special types of currency tokens and are commonly known as '**stable coins**'. Those crypto-assets are regulated in Titles III, IV MiCAR and will not be the subject of this chapter.

95 As regards Art. 4 et seqq. MiCAR, the Regulation constantly refers to 'issuer(s) of) crypto-assets, other than asset-referenced tokens or e-money tokens'. Taken together with the general exclusion of financial instruments by Art. 2(2)(a) MiCAR, **Art. 4 – 14 MiCAR** contain a **special (disclosure) regime** for issuers of **utility tokens** in connection with offers to the public and applications for an admission of such crypto-assets to trading on a trading platform for crypto-assets.[255] In the course of the following remarks, the utility tokens covered by Art. 4 – 14 MiCAR will be called **crypto-assets** without explicitly mentioning the **exclusion of asset-referenced tokens and e-money tokens** in every instance.

III. Obligation to Publish a Crypto-Asset White Paper

96 Art. 4(1) MiCAR sets out the crucial requirement for ICOs, requiring issuers of crypto-assets in particular to draft (Art. 4(1)(a), Art. 5 MiCAR), notify (Art. 4(1)(b), Art. 7 MiCAR) and publish (Art. 4(1)(c), Art. 8 MiCAR) a **crypto-asset white paper**. Only after the publication of such a white paper may issuers offer their crypto-assets throughout the Union and seek admission to trading of such crypto-assets on a trading platform for crypto-assets (see Art. 10(1) MiCAR).

97 Important **exemptions** from this general obligation can be found in Art. 4(2) MiCAR. First, in the case of so-called **airdrops**, i.e., ICOs in which crypto assets are offered for free[256], there is no obligation to draft, notify and publish a crypto-asset white paper (Art. 4(2)(a) MiCAR). This seems sensible, because airdrops are closer to marketing campaigns[257] and lack the central feature of an ICO (= a consideration paid by investors), which leads to a decreased need for investor and market

---

[254] Zickgraf, 'Primärmarktpublizität in der Verordnung über Märkte für Kryptowerte (MiCAR) – Teil 1' (2021) 21 *Zeitschrift für Bank- und Kapitalmarktrecht*, 196 (198 et seq.).

[255] Zickgraf, 'Primärmarktpublizität in der Verordnung über Märkte für Kryptowerte (MiCAR) – Teil 1' (2021) 21 *Zeitschrift für Bank- und Kapitalmarktrecht*, 196 (199).

[256] Kirsch, von Wieding and Höbener, 'Bilanzierungsfähigkeit von Krypto-Token aus einem Hard Fork und Airdrop nach IFRS' (2020) 15 *Zeitschrift für Internationale Rechnungslegung*, 495 (495 et seq., 499 et seq.); Zickgraf, 'Primärmarktpublizität in der Verordnung über Märkte für Kryptowerte (MiCAR) – Teil 1' (2021) 21 *Zeitschrift für Bank- und Kapitalmarktrecht*, 196 (200); different understanding of airdrops: → § 1 para. 84).

[257] Kirsch, von Wieding and Höbener, 'Bilanzierungsfähigkeit von Krypto-Token aus einem Hard Fork und Airdrop nach IFRS' (2020) 15 *Zeitschrift für Internationale Rechnungslegung*, 495 (500).

protection.²⁵⁸ However, the exemption does not apply, if personal data is to be provided by potential purchasers or if the issuer receives from the prospective holders of those crypto-assets any third party fees, commissions, monetary benefits or non-monetary benefits in exchange for those crypto-assets (Art. 4(2) subp. 2 MiCAR).²⁵⁹ Second, the same applies for crypto-assets which are automatically created through **mining** as a reward for the maintenance of the DLT or the validation of transactions (Art. 4(2)(b) MiCAR). As a consequence, typical cryptocurrencies such as Bitcoin are exempted from the above-mentioned requirements. After all, in the case of currency tokens there is a lack of capital market-specific information asymmetries and agency conflicts that could be addressed by disclosure obligations under capital markets law (→ para. 65 et seqq.).²⁶⁰ Third, if crypto-assets are **unique and not fungible** with other crypto-assets (Art. 4(2)(c) MiCAR), they are also exempt from the requirements of Art. 4(1)(b)–d) MiCAR. From an economic perspective, disclosure obligations addressed to the issuer serve to lower overall information costs, since it can generally be assumed that the issuer's costs of gathering and publishing relevant information in a publication document are lower than the investors' combined costs of acquiring such information on the issuer (→ para. 6). However, if a unique or customised crypto-asset is concerned, a publication document cannot fulfil the above-mentioned task of informing a great number of investors; a cost-benefit-analysis therefore suggests that no (costly) information document should be published in such a case.²⁶¹ The **remaining exemptions** contained in Art. 4(2)(d)–(f) MiCAR are modelled on the Prospectus Regulation (→ para. 73 et seq., 76).

IV. Content and Form of the Crypto-Asset White Paper

According to Art. 5(1) the crypto-asset white paper shall contain the following information: 98
- a detailed description of the issuer and a presentation of the main participants involved in the project's design and development (lit. a);
- a detailed description of the characteristics of the offer to the public, in particular the number of crypto-assets that will be issued or for which admission to trading is sought, the issue price of the crypto-assets and the subscription terms and conditions (lit. b);
- a detailed description of the characteristics of the offer to the public, in particular the number of crypto-assets that will be issued or for which admission to trading is sought, the issue price of the crypto-assets and the subscription terms and conditions (lit. c);
- a detailed description of the rights and obligations attached to the crypto-assets and the procedures and conditions for exercising those rights (lit. d);
- information on the underlying technology and standards applied by the issuer of the crypto-assets allowing for the holding, storing and transfer of those crypto-assets (lit. e);

---

[258] Zickgraf, 'Primärmarktpublizität in der Verordnung über Märkte für Kryptowerte (MiCAR) – Teil 1' (2021) 21 *Zeitschrift für Bank- und Kapitalmarktrecht*, 196 (200).

[259] Ibid.

[260] Although the wording is ambiguous, cryptocurrencies using proof-of-work and proof-of-stake should fall under Art. 4(2)(b) MiCAR likewise, as these to mechanism represent functionally (not: technically → § 1 para. 58 et seq.) equivalent procedures, see Zickgraf, ibid.

[261] Zickgraf, 'Primärmarktpublizität in der Verordnung über Märkte für Kryptowerte (MiCAR) – Teil 1' (2021) 21 *Zeitschrift für Bank- und Kapitalmarktrecht*, 196 (200 et seq.).

- a detailed description of the risks relating to the issuer of the crypto-assets, the crypto-assets, the offer to the public of the crypto-asset and the implementation of the project (lit. f);
- the disclosure items specified in Annex I MiCAR (lit. g) – which mainly clarify the information duties set out in Art. 5(1)(a)–(f) MiCAR.

99 The information referred to in Art. 5(1) MiCAR shall be **fair, clear** and **not misleading**; furthermore, the crypto-asset white paper shall **not** contain **material omissions** and shall be presented in a **concise and comprehensible form** (Art. 5 (2) MiCAR). A particularly important requirement is given by Art. 5(4) MiCAR: the crypto-asset white paper shall **not** contain any **assertions on the future value** of the crypto-assets, other than the statement referred to in Art. 5(5) MiCAR, unless the issuer of those crypto-assets can guarantee such future value. This is due to the fact that numerous ICOs had been structured in a way which could lead to a herd behaviour among investors (→ para. 11). Moreover, the buyers of crypto-assets were by a huge part comprised of retail investors who tend to be over-optimistic and wishful in their thinking.[262] If statements about the future value of a crypto asset, which in fact cannot be guaranteed by the issuer, were permissible, this would further promote the aforementioned biases, which is why the explicit prohibition of such statements in the crypto-asset white paper seems highly appropriate in view of the findings from **behavioural finance** research. Excessive euphoria shall also be prevented by the **mandatory warnings** of Art. 5(5) MiCAR: the crypto-asset white paper shall contain a clear and unambiguous statement that (a) the crypto-assets may lose their value in part or in full; (b) the crypto-assets may not always be transferable; (c) the crypto-assets may not be liquid; (d) where the offer to the public concerns utility tokens, that such utility tokens may not be exchangeable against the good or service promised in the crypto-asset white paper, especially in case of failure or discontinuation of the project.[263]

100 The **issuer** of the crypto-assets and the **management body** (see Art. 3(1)(18) MiCAR) each have to take **responsibility for the crypto-asset white paper** (Art. 5(3), (6) MiCAR). In particular, the issuer's statement needs to include the notice that the white paper has not been reviewed or approved by any competent authority in any Member State of the European Union, which is obviously connected to the elimination of an ex-ante approval procedure (see Art. 7 MiCAR) of the publication document.[264] Additionally, the crypto-asset white paper needs to contain a summary (Art. 5(7) MiCAR), it shall be dated (Art. 5(8) MiCAR), drawn up in at least one of the official languages of the home Member State or in a language customary in the sphere of international finance (Art. 5(9) MiCAR) and shall be made available in machine readable formats (Art. 5(10) MiCAR).

---

[262] See generally: Thaler, 'From Homo Economicus to Homo Sapiens' (2000) 14 *Journal of Economic Perspectives*, 133; Weinstein and Klein, 'Unrealistic Optimism: Present and Future' (1996) 15 *Journal of Social & Clinical Psychology*, 1; Kunda, 'Motivated inference: self-serving generation and evaluation of causal theories' (1987) 53 *Journal of Personality & Social Psychology*, 636; Weinstein, 'Unrealistic optimism about future life events' (1980) 39 *Journal of Personality and Social Psychology*, 806; Irwin, 'Stated expectations as functions of probability and desirability of outcomes' (1953) 21 *Journal of Personality*, 329; in the context of ICOs: Klöhn, Parhofer and Resas, 'Initial Coin Offerings (ICOs)' (2018) 30 *Zeitschrift für Bankrecht und Bankwirtschaft*, 89 (95).
[263] Zickgraf, 'Primärmarktpublizität in der Verordnung über Märkte für Kryptowerte (MiCAR) – Teil 1' (2021) 21 *Zeitschrift für Bank- und Kapitalmarktrecht*, 196 (202 et seq.).
[264] Zickgraf, 'Primärmarktpublizität in der Verordnung über Märkte für Kryptowerte (MiCAR) – Teil 1' (2021) 21 *Zeitschrift für Bank- und Kapitalmarktrecht*, 196 (203).

V. Marketing Communications

Art. 6 MiCAR addresses marketing communications which constitute an integral part of a typical ICO.[265] Therefore, Art. 6 MiCAR mandates that all marketing communications relating to an offer to the public of crypto-assets or to the admission of such crypto-assets to trading on a trading platform for such crypto-assets shall be **clearly identifiable** as such (lit. a), the information in the marketing communications shall be **fair**, **clear** and **not misleading** (lit. b), the information in the marketing communications shall be **consistent with the information in the crypto-asset white paper**, where such a crypto-asset white paper is required in accordance with Art. 4(c) and the marketing communications shall **clearly state that a crypto-asset white paper has been published** and **indicate the address of the website of the issuer** of the crypto-assets concerned (lit. d.). 101

Art. 6(a) MiCAR seems to be of particular importance for the investors of ICOs. After all, the investors' judgement of an ICO's prospects will differ greatly if a statement of a supposed expert is not a neutral recommendation but turns out to be a paid advertisement. Equally important are the obligations of Art. 6(c) an (d) MiCAR, since most (retail) investors do not read the white papers.[266] As a consequence, one can assume that most investors base their investment decision on the marketing communications. Thus, the obligation of Art. 6(c) MiCAR is a key provision to ensure the practical efficacy of the entire disclosure regime and to effectively reduce the existing information asymmetries between the issuers and investors. The reference to the white paper required by Art. 6(d) MiCAR also tries to cope with this factual problem and aims to promote the white paper as the primary source of investors' information.[267] 102

VI. Regulatory Procedure

In clear deviation from the system of Art. 20 EU Prospectus Regulation there is **no requirement of an ex ante approval of the crypto-asset white paper** (nor of marketing communications) by competent authorities prior to the publication within MiCAR (see Art. 7(1) MiCAR). Rather, the issuers shall notify their crypto-asset white paper, and, in case of marketing communications as referred to in Art. 6, such marketing communications, to the competent authority of their home Member State (see Art. 3 (1) No. 22 MiCAR) at least 20 working days before publication of the crypto-asset white paper (Art. 7 (2) MiCAR). In line with this change of the procedural system MiCAR implicitly requires the issuers to self-evaluate if they are subject to another regulatory regime. After all, according to Art. 7 (3) MiCAR the crypto-asset white paper shall explain why the crypto-asset described in the crypto-asset white paper is not to be considered a financial instrument as defined in Art. 4(1)(15) MiFiD2 (lit. a), electronic money as defined in in Art. 2(2), of Directive 2009/110/EC (lit. b), a deposit as defined 103

---

[265] Rohr and Wright, 'Blockchain-Based Token Sales, Initial Coin Offerings, and the Democratization of Public Capital Markets' (2019) 70 *Hastings Law Journal*, 463 (478); Zickgraf, 'Initial Coin Offerings – Ein Fall für das Kapitalmarktrecht?' (2018) 63 *Die Aktiengesellschaft*, 293 (294).

[266] See generally on this with regard to the primary market: Langenbucher, *Aktien- und Kapitalmarktrecht* (4th edn, 2019), 310, 311; with regard to the secondary market: Thompson, 'Federal Corporate Law: Torts and Fiduciary Duty' (2006) 31 *Journal of Corporation Law*, 877 (880); Klöhn, 'Marktbetrug (Fraud on the Market)' (2014) 178 *Zeitschrift für das gesamte Handels- und Wirtschaftsrecht*, 671 (674).

[267] Zickgraf, 'Primärmarktpublizität in der Verordnung über Märkte für Kryptowerte (MiCAR) – Teil 1' (2021) 21 *Zeitschrift für Bank- und Kapitalmarktrecht*, 196 (203 et seq.).

in Art. 2(1) (3), of Directive 2014/49/EU (lit. c) or a structured deposit as defined in Art. 4(1)(43) MiFiD2 (lit. d). The procedure between the NCAs and ESMA is regulated in Art. 7 (4) and (5) MiCAR.

104 In view of the large number of relatively small emissions of crypto-assets[268], the elimination of an official approval procedure promises considerable savings in administrative costs. Nevertheless, it must be kept in mind that the reduction of ex-ante regulation potentially increases the risk violations against the disclosure obligations ex-post. **Deregulation at the procedural level** (ex-ante) is therefore supplemented by a **more rigorous liability system** (ex-post, see Art. 14 MiCAR) in order to ensure an adequate level of overall market and investor protection.[269]

105 Art. 8 (1) MiCAR requires issuers of crypto-assets to publish their crypto-asset white paper, and, where applicable, their marketing communications, on their website, which shall be publicly accessible, by no later than the starting date of the offer to the public of those crypto-assets or the admission of those crypto-assets to trading on a trading platform for crypto-assets; these shall remain available on the issuer's website for as long as the crypto-assets are held by the public. Furthermore, Art. 7 (2) MiCAR states that the published crypto-asset white paper, and, where applicable, the marketing communications, shall be identical to the version notified to the relevant competent authority.

106 Issuers of crypto-assets that set a time limit on their offer to the public of those crypto-assets have to publish on their website the result of the offer within 16 working days from the end of the subscription period (Art. 9 (1) MiCAR). Additionally, such issuers shall have effective arrangements in place to monitor and safeguard the funds, or other crypto-assets, raised during such offer (Art. 9 (2) MiCAR). In particular, the issuers shall ensure that the funds or other crypto-assets collected during the offer to the public are either kept in by a credit institution, where the funds raised during the offer to the public takes the form of fiat currency (lit. a) or a crypto-asset service provider authorised for the custody and administration of crypto-assets on behalf of third parties (lit. b). This provision obviously intends to prevent incidents such as the ICO of The DAO, where a hacker attack initially resulted in the loss of a large part of the proceeds of the issuance.[270]

107 Should there be any change or new fact that is likely to have a significant influence on the purchase decision of any potential purchaser of such crypto-assets, or on the decision of holders of such crypto-assets to sell or exchange such crypto-assets, then the issuers of crypto-assets have to modify their white paper (Art. 11(1) MiCAR). In that instance, the issuer shall immediately inform the public on its website of the notification of a modified crypto-asset white paper with the competent authority of its home Member State and shall provide a summary of the reasons for which it has notified a modified crypto-asset white paper (Art. 11(2) MiCAR). To facilitate the location of the changes for investors the order of the information in a modified crypto-asset white paper and in modified marketing communications shall be consistent with that of the original document (Art. 11(3) MiCAR). The following regulatory

---

[268] Zetzsche, Buckley, Arner and Föhr, 'The ICO Gold Rush: It's a Scam, It's a Bubble, It's a Super Challenge for Regulators' (19.11.2017), 10, available at https://beck-link.de/k23ak (accessed 11.4.2021); → § 2 para. 39.

[269] See generally on the relationship between ex-ante regulation and ex-post liability from a Law & Economics perspective: Shavell, *Economic Analysis of Accident Law* (1987), 279 et seqq.; see also Zickgraf, 'Primärmarktpublizität in der Verordnung über Märkte für Kryptowerte (MiCAR) – Teil 2' (2021) 21 *Zeitschrift für Bank- und Kapitalmarktrecht*, 362 (362 et seq.).

[270] Securities and Exchange Commission, 'Report of Investigation Pursuant to Section 21(a) of the Securities Exchange Act of 1934: The DAO' (25.7.2017) Release No. 81207, available at https://beck-link.de/5pfa8 (accessed 11.4.2021).

procedure is structured in accordance with the general procedure of Art. 7, 8 MiCAR and can be found in Art. 11(4) – (6) MiCAR. In any case, the modified document(s) shall be time stamped, be marked as the applicable version and remain available for as long as the crypto-assets are held by the public (Art. 11(7) MiCAR).[271]

VII. Right of Withdrawal

Art. 12(1) subp. 1 MiCAR provides for a right of withdrawal for consumers who buy such crypto-assets directly from the issuer or from a crypto-asset service provider placing crypto-assets on behalf of that issuer. This right takes into account the fact that the **regulatory issues** arising in the vast majority of utility tokens (whose primary market regulation Art. 4 – 14 MiCAR essentially aim at, → para. 95) are very close to those of **consumer protection law**. After all, the emphasis is often on **product-specific information asymmetries** between buyers and sellers of a particular good or service.[272] Pursuant to Art. 12(1) subp. 2 MiCAR consumers shall have 14 calendar days to withdraw their agreement to purchase those crypto-assets without incurring any cost and without giving reasons; this period of withdrawal shall begin from the day of the consumers' agreement to purchase those crypto-assets. The procedure of reimbursement is regulated in detail by Art. 12(2) MiCAR. To secure the practical efficacy and use of the withdrawal right, Art. 12(3) MiCAR requires issuers of crypto-assets to provide information on the right of withdrawal in their crypto-asset white paper.

108

It should be noted that there is no right of withdrawal where the crypto-assets are admitted to trading on a trading platform for crypto-assets according to Art. 12(4) MiCAR. This seems to be a fair rule, because the admission to trading is independent of the consumer's investment decision, which has taken place when the consumer bought the crypto-asset and has led to the right of withdrawal mentioned in Art. 12(1) at that time. Considering these circumstances, the granting of another right of withdrawal in the case of the subsequent admission of those crypto-assets to trading on a trading platform for crypto-assets would relieve the consumer from the general risk of market fluctuations without any justification. In order to ensure reliability for the issuers of crypto-assets with regard to the proceeds of the emission, Art. 12(5) MiCAR stipulates that the right of withdrawal shall not be exercised after the end of the subscription period, if issuers of crypto-assets have set a time limit on their offer to the public of such crypto-assets in accordance with Art. 9 MiCAR.[273]

109

VIII. General Obligations of Issuers of Crypto-Assets

Since the ICO-market was in part home to dubious participants, Art. 13 MiCAR provides for general obligations of the issuers of crypto-assets, which actually just describe sincere and honest behaviour in legal relations. In particular, pursuant to Art. 13(1) MiCAR issuers of crypto-assets shall act honestly, fairly and professionally (lit. a); communicate with the holders of crypto-assets in a fair, clear and not misleading

110

---

[271] Zickgraf, 'Primärmarktpublizität in der Verordnung über Märkte für Kryptowerte (MiCAR) – Teil 2' (2021) 21 *Zeitschrift für Bank- und Kapitalmarktrecht*, 362 (363 et seq.).
[272] → para. 56, 61.
[273] Zickgraf, 'Primärmarktpublizität in der Verordnung über Märkte für Kryptowerte (MiCAR) – Teil 2' (2021) 21 *Zeitschrift für Bank- und Kapitalmarktrecht*, 362 (364).

manner (lit. b); prevent, identify, manage and disclose any conflicts of interest that may arise and maintain all of their systems and security access protocols to appropriate Union standards (lit. d). According to Art. 13(2) MiCAR, issuers shall also act in the best interests of the holders of such crypto-assets and shall treat them equally, unless any preferential treatment is disclosed in the crypto-asset white paper, and, where applicable, the marketing communications. In view of the common early-subscriber discounts, Art. 13(2) MiCAR represents a very important rule which allows potential investors to better understand the chances of the project's success[274] and their economic stake in the undertaking.[275] Where an offer to the public of crypto-assets is cancelled for any reason, issuers of such crypto-assets shall ensure that any funds collected from purchasers or potential purchasers are duly returned to them as soon as possible pursuant to Art. 13(3) MiCAR.

IX. Liability of Issuers of Crypto-Assets

111   Art. 14 MiCAR provides for a minimum harmonisation (see Art. 14(4) MiCAR) as regards the civil liability of issuers. Investors can derive their claims directly from Art. 14 MiCAR, which represents a sharp deviation from Art. 11 EU Prospectus Regulation. According to Art. 14(1) MiCAR a 'holder of crypto assets' is entitled to claim damages. Unfortunately, the wording is imprecise, as it seems unclear whether buyers of crypto-assets, which do not hold those crypto-assets any more, are also entitled to claim damages. From a teleological point of view, those investors should be able to claim the difference between the subscription price and the fundamental value of the crypto-asset at the time of the purchase (Kursdifferenzschaden) in order to give the defendants an incetive to comply with the disclosure obligations.

112   **Defendants** of the claim are – individually – the **issuer of crypto-assets** and its **management body** (see Art. 3(1)(18) MiCAR). The reason for the extension of liability to the management body is that the majority of issuers have been young start-up companies with very little capital. Therefore, the issuer's behavioural incentives created by (civil) liability to fulfil the disclosure obligations of MiCAR may be inadequately low, since the issuer's shareholders have much to gain in the transaction, but hardly anything to lose through the potential liability in view of the issuer's low capitalisation (judgment proof problem).[276] To solve this **problem of underdeterrence**, the legislator can make other parties liable for potential breaches[277], as has been done in the case of Art. 14(1) MiCAR.[278]

113   In order to be entitled to claim damages, investors need to prove (see Art. 14(2) MiCAR) that the issuer or the management body has **infringed Art. 5 MiCAR**, by

---

[274] In particular, such a disclosure allows potential investors to assess whether the high demand for crypto-assets in the course of an ICO is due to the prospects of the undertaking's economic success or merely because of early-subscriber discounts.

[275] Zickgraf, 'Primärmarktpublizität in der Verordnung über Märkte für Kryptowerte (MiCAR) – Teil 2' (2021) 21 *Zeitschrift für Bank- und Kapitalmarktrecht*, 362 (364 et seq.).

[276] See generally on the judgment-proof-problem: Summers, 'The Case of the Disappearing Defendant: An Economic Analysis' (1983) 132 *University of Pennsylvania Law Review*, 145; Shavell, 'The judgment proof problem' (1986) 6 *International Review of Law & Economics*, 45; see also Pitchford, 'How Liable Should a Lender Be? The Case of Judgment-Proof Firms and Environmental Risk' (1995) 85 *American Economic Review*, 1171; in the context of capital markets law: Arlen and Carney, 'Vicarious Liability for Fraud on Securities Markets: Theory and Evidence' [1992] *University of Illinois Law Review*, 691 (707).

[277] Shavell, 'The judgment proof problem' (1986) 6 *International Review of Law & Economics*, 45 (54).

[278] See for further discussion: Zickgraf, 'Primärmarktpublizität in der Verordnung über Märkte für Kryptowerte (MiCAR) – Teil 2' (2021) 21 *Zeitschrift für Bank- und Kapitalmarktrecht*, 362 (365 et seq.).

providing in its crypto-asset white paper or in a modified crypto-asset white paper information which is not complete, fair or clear or by providing information which is misleading. However, pursuant to Art. 14(3) MiCAR, a holder of crypto-assets shall not be able to claim damages for the information provided in a summary as referred to in Art. 5(7) MiCAR, including the translation thereof, except where the summary is misleading, inaccurate or inconsistent when read together with the other parts of the crypto-asset white paper (lit. a) or the summary does not provide, when read together with the other parts of the crypto-asset white paper, key information in order to aid consumers and investors when considering whether to purchase such crypto-assets (lit. b).

According to Art. 14(2) MiCAR investors also need to prove that the infringement had an **impact on his or her decision to buy,** sell or **exchange** the said crypto-assets. However, in capital markets law the burden to proof such a causation of the misinformation is typically dispensed (**fraud-on-the-market-theory**).[279] After all, according to the semi-strong Efficient Capital Market Hypothesis (ECMH), all publicly known information is reflected in the market price.[280] Consequently, there is a causal relationship between the misinformation and the market price (price causality).[281] If the difference between the subscription price and the fundamental value of the crypto-asset at the time of the purchase is claimed by the investor, there should be no requirement to prove that the infringement had an impact on the investment decision. Rather, it should be assumed that the infringement had such a causal impact (on the purchase for the specific price).[282] However, if the investor claims for rescission of the whole transaction, there should be a burden of proof that the infringement had an impact on the investment decision, because the reasoning of the fraud-on-the-market theory does not apply in this case, as it solely assumes price-causality but not transaction-causality of the infringement.[283]

Pursuant to Art. 14(1) MiCAR, holders of crypto-assets may claim damages. This wording indicates that the **difference between the subscription price and the fundamental value** of the crypto-asset at the time of the purchase (so-called Kursdifferenzschaden) can be claimed by the investor (although Art. 14(1) MiCAR's wording is ambiguous about buyers' claims that do not currently hold the crypto-assets anymore (→ para. 111). Furthermore, investors are also entitled to claim for **repayment of the**

---

[279] U.S. Supreme Court 23 June 2014 – *Halliburton Co. v. Erica P. John Fund Inc.*, 573 U.S. 258; U.S. Supreme Court 7 March 1988 – *Basic v. Levinson*, 485 U.S. 224, 241 et seqq.; Fischel, 'Use of Modern Finance Theory in Securities Fraud Cases Involving Actively Traded Securities' (1982) 38 *Business Lawyer*, 1 (3 et seqq., 9 et seqq.); Ferrell and Roper, 'Price Impact, Materiality, and Halliburton II' (2015) 93 *Washington University Law Review*, 553; Bebchuk and Ferrell, 'Rethinking Basic' (2014) 69 *Business Lawyer*, 671; Langevoort, 'Basic at Twenty: Rethinking Fraud on the Market' [2009] *Wisconsin Law Review*, 151; Goshen and Parchomovsky, 'The Essential Role of Securities Regulation' (2006) 55 *Duke Law Journal*, 711 (766 et seqq.); Klöhn, 'Marktbetrug (Fraud on the Market)' (2014) 178 *Zeitschrift für das gesamte Handels- und Wirtschaftsrecht*, 671.

[280] Fama, 'Efficient Capital Markets: Review of Theory and Empirical Work' (1970) 25 *Journal of Finance*, 383; Samuelson, 'Proof That Properly Anticipated Prices Fluctuate Randomly' (1965) 6 *Industrial Management Review*, 41.

[281] Fischel, 'Use of Modern Finance Theory in Securities Fraud Cases Involving Actively Traded Securities' (1982) 38 *Business Lawyer*, 1 (3 et seqq., 9 et seqq.); Goshen and Parchomovsky, 'The Essential Role of Securities Regulation' (2006) 55 *Duke Law Journal*, 711 (766 et seqq.); Klöhn, 'Marktbetrug (Fraud on the Market)' (2014) 178 *Zeitschrift für das gesamte Handels- und Wirtschaftsrecht*, 671 (674 et seq., 697 et seqq.).

[282] Zickgraf, 'Primärmarktpublizität in der Verordnung über Märkte für Kryptowerte (MiCAR) – Teil 2' (2021) 21 *Zeitschrift für Bank- und Kapitalmarktrecht*, 362 (366 et seqq.).

[283] Klöhn, 'Marktbetrug (Fraud on the Market)' (2014) 178 *Zeitschrift für das gesamte Handels- und Wirtschaftsrecht*, 671 (695).

purchase price against the redemption of the crypto-asset (so-called Vertragsabschlussschaden or Rückabwicklungsschaden), as the wording of Art. 14 (1) MiCAR ('holder of crypto-assets') indicates.[284]

---

[284] Zickgraf, 'Primärmarktpublizität in der Verordnung über Märkte für Kryptowerte (MiCAR) – Teil 2' (2021) 21 *Zeitschrift für Bank- und Kapitalmarktrecht*, 362 (369).

§ 8
Financial Services Regulation

Literature: Bundesanstalt für Finanzdienstleistungsaufsicht (BaFin), 'Guidance Notice on management board members pursuant to the German Banking Act (Kreditwesengesetz – KWG), the German Payment Services Supervision Act (Zahlungsdiensteaufsichtsgesetz – ZAG) and the German Capital Investment Code (Kapitalanlagegesetzbuch – KAGB)' (4 January 2016, last amended 31 January 2017), 20, available at https://beck-link.de/a5tfb; Cherednychenko, 'European Securities Regulation, Private Law and the Investment Firm-Client Relationship', (2009) 17 *European Review of Private Law* 925; Deutsche Bundesbank (German Federal Reserve Bank), 'Notice on the granting of authorisation to provide financial services pursuant to section 32(1) of the German Banking Act' (18 November 2016), available at https://beck-link.de/sbkp2; European Commission, 'Proposal for a Regulation of the European Parliament and the Council on Markets in Crypto-Assets, and amending Directive (EU) 2019/1937' COM (2020) 593 final, available at https://beck-link.de/zy2x5; Geva, 'Banking in the Digital Age – Who is Afraid of Payment Disintermediation?' (EBI Institute Working Paper 2018/23), https://papers.ssrn.com/abstract_id=3153760; Gortsos, 'The Commission's 2020 Proposal for a Markets in Crypto-assets Regulation ('MiCAR')' (May 2021), available at https://papers.ssrn.com/abstract_id=3842824; International Organization of Securities Commissions, 'Fit and Proper Assessment – Final Report' (December 2009), 4, available at https://beck-link.de/w6bwx; Kaja et al, 'FinTech And The Law & Economics of Disintermediation', ECGI Working Paper 540/2020, available at https://papers.ssrn.com/abstract_id=3683427; Maume, 'In Uncharted Territory – Banking Supervision meets Fintech', *Corporate Finance* 2017, 373–378; Maume, 'Reducing Legal Uncertainty and Regulatory Arbitrage for Robo-Advice', (2019) 16 *European Company and Financial Law Review*, 622; Maume and Fromberger, 'Regulation of Initial Coin Offerings: Reconciling U.S. and E.U. Securities Laws' (2019) 19 *Chicago Journal of International Law*, 548; Maume, 'Initial Coin Offerings and EU Prospectus Disclosure', (2020) 31 *European Business Law Review*, 185; Schwark and Zimmer (eds.), *Kapitalmarktrechts-Kommentar* (C.H. Beck, 5th ed. 2020); Schwennicke and Auerbach (eds.), *Kreditwesengesetz* (C.H. Beck, 4th ed. 2021); Veil, 'Sources of Law and Principles of Interpretation', in: Veil (ed.), *European Capital Markets Law* (2nd ed., 2017); Tison, 'The Civil Law Effects of MiFID in a Comparative Law Perspective', Financial Law Institute Working Paper WP 2010-05 (April 2010), available at https://ssrn.com/abstract=1596782; Zetzsche et al, 'The Markets in Crypto-Assets Regulation (MICA) and the EU Digital Finance Strategy', EBI Working Paper Series No. 2020/77 (December 2020), available at https://papers.ssrn.com/abstract_id=3725395.

Outline

	para.
A. Overview	1
I. Types of Intermediaries	1
II. Applicable Regulation	2
III. Key Elements of MiFID2 and MiCAR	6
B. Geographical Scope of Application	8
I. Background	8
II. Cross-Border Provision of Services	9
III. EU/EEA Passporting	11
IV. MiCAR	13
C. Regulated Activities	14
I. Background	14
II. Crypto Exchanges	15
1. Distinction Between Regulated Activities	15
2. Commercial Activity	17
3. Multilateral Trading Facility	18
a) Under MiFID2	18
b) Under MiCAR	24
4. Organised Trading Facility	26

5. Dealing on Own Account	29
6. Execution of Orders	30
III. Crypto Exchange Services	31
IV. Crypto.ATMs	32
V. Wallet Custody	34
D. Authorisation	37
I. Overview	37
II. Initial Capital Endowment	39
III. Requirements for Management Body	40
IV. Provision of Investment Services without Authorisation	44
V. Crypto-Asset Services under MiCAR	46

A. Overview

I. Types of Intermediaries

1   A major advantage of crypto assets is disintermediation.[1] In short, this term refers to the idea that crypto assets can be transferred without or with a smaller number of intermediaries between market participants. For example, the transfer of a currency token can be a peer-to-peer transaction without the involvement of banks or other financial services. Similarly, and unlike listed shares, security tokens do not require elaborate chains of intermediaries. However, even the use of crypto assets often requires the activity of specific intermediaries, especially when trading reaches a certain level of organisation (for example, on crypto trading platforms). Otherwise, these markets will find it difficult to provide sufficient levels of liquidity.

In this context, two types of intermediaries need to be distinguished. First, crypto-specific financial intermediaries offer services that relate to crypto assets only. These are crypto-to-crypto or fiat-to-crypto exchanges (decentralised or centralised), crypto-ATMs, or wallet providers. Secondly, 'regular' financial intermediaries might also provide financial services that relate to crypto assets. This could be a portfolio management service also investing in crypto assets for the clients. This chapter focuses on the crypto-specific provision of financial services.

II. Applicable Regulation

2   The main legal source for financial services in the EU is Directive 2014/65/EU on markets in financial instruments (**MiFID2**)[2]. This is complemented by Directive 2013/36/EU on the prudential supervision of credit institutions and investment firms (CRD IV)[3]. For financial services, this has been mostly replaced by Directive (EU) 2019/2034 (Investment Firms Directive, **IFD**)[4]. MiFID2 is complemented by the Commission

---

[1] See on disintermediation generally Geva, 'Banking in the Digital Age – Who is Afraid of Payment Disintermediation?' (EBI Institute Working Paper 2018/23); available at https://papers.ssrn.com/abstract_id=3153760; Kaja et al, 'FinTech and The Law & Economics of Disintermediation' (ECGI Working Paper 540/2020); available at https://papers.ssrn.com/abstract_id=3683427.

[2] Directive 2014/65/EU of the European Parliament and of the Council on markets in financial instruments and amending Directives 2002/92/EC and 2011/61/EU, OJ L 173, 12.6.2016 p. 349–496.

[3] Directive 2013/36/EU of the European Parliament and of the Council on access to the activity of credit institutions and the prudential supervision of credit institutions and investment firms, amending Directive 2002/87/EC and repealing Directives 2006/48/EC and 2006/49/EC, OJ L 17, 27.6.2013 p. 338–436.

[4] Directive (EU) 2019/2034 of the European Parliament and of the Council on the prudential supervision of investment firms and amending Directives 2002/87/EC, 2009/65/EC, 2011/61/EU, 2013/36/EU, 2014/59/EU and 2014/65/EU, OJ L 314, 5.12.2019 p. 64–114.

§ 8. *Financial Services Regulation*

Delegated Regulation (EU) 2017/565 (**MiFID2-DelReg**).[5] It contains more details about the interpretation of various MiFID2 rules. The European Securities Markets Authority (ESMA) has also issued guidance and Q&A on various issues under MiFID2.

The key requirement for the application of MiFID2 and IFD is that the financial service in question relates to **financial instruments** as set out in Art. 4(1)(15) MiFID2. The MiFID2 rules are relevant for financial services regarding investment tokens because these tokens typically classify as 'transferable securities', and thus financial instruments under MiFID2 (for details, → § 7 para. 33).

MiFID2 is based on the idea of **full harmonisation**.[6] This means that Member States are typically not able to impose stricter rules than prescribed by MiFID2. However, this principle only applies to areas that are subject to the Directive. In other words, if a certain financial asset does not meet the definition of a financial instrument under Art. 4(1)(15) MiFID2, Member States can decide to impose **additional national regulation**. This is particularly relevant for utility tokens and currency tokens as they are not financial instruments. An infamous example is the German financial markets regulator BaFin's established view that Bitcoin and other currency tokens are 'units of account' under German banking laws.[7] As a consequence, providing Bitcoin-related financial services in Germany is subject to German banking laws. This is a particular hassle for non-German financial service providers because the MiFID2 passporting rules (→ para. 11) do not apply. The consequence is that these service providers might require authorisation in Germany.

In September 2020, the European Commission published its draft for the Regulation of Markets in Crypto Assets (**MiCAR Draft**).[8] Although the MiCAR framework for **crypto-asset services** has been clearly modelled after the MiFID2 framework, the wording can deviate significantly. The simple reason is that MiCAR (an EU Regulation) will be directly applicable in the Member States. This requires some modifications of the wording that is used in MiFID2. In addition, MiCAR is crypto-specific whilst MiFID2 is technology neutral (which means it applies to all kinds of conduct, whether crypto-based or not). However, the underlying regulatory ideas are similar to those of MiFID2.

The proposed MiCAR regime contains specific rules for certain (but not all) types of crypto assets and the respective financial services.[9] Importantly, MiCAR will not apply to financial instruments under MiFID2. In other words, MiCAR will regulate most other crypto assets (currency tokens, utility tokens, e-money tokens, etc.). The result is a clear division between the financial services regulation of investment tokens and all other tokens. Although changes to the MICAR Draft during the further parliamentary process are likely, this chapter will also discuss the proposed framework briefly.

An area closely related to financial services laws is EU **anti-money-laundering (AML) regulation**. This is because, in short, investment firms under MiFID2 are also subject to

3

4

5

---

[5] Commission Delegated Regulation (EU) 2017/565 supplementing Directive 2014/65/EU of the European Parliament and of the Council as regards organisational requirements and operating conditions for investment firms and defined terms for the purposes of that Directive, OJ L 87, 31.3.2017 p. 1–83.

[6] See for the different concepts and their application in EU financial markets regulation Veil, in: Veil (ed.), *European Capital Markets Law* (2nd ed., 2017), 65–66.

[7] For details, → § 17 para. 30.

[8] European Commission, 'Proposal for a Regulation of the European Parliament and the Council on Markets in Crypto-Assets, and amending Directive (EU) 2019/1937', 24 September 2020, COM(2020) 593 final, available at https://beck-link.de/zy2x5.

[9] For an overview of MiCAR, see Gortsos, 'The Commission's 2020 Proposal for a Markets in Crypto-assets Regulation ('MiCAR')' (May 2021), available at https://papers.ssrn.com/abstract_id=3842824; Zetzsche et al, 'The Markets in Crypto-Assets Regulation (MICA) and the EU Digital Finance Strategy', EBI Working Paper Series No. 2020/77 (December 2020), available at https://papers.ssrn.com/abstract_id=3725395.

EU-based AML laws. For crypto assets, the link between these two areas is particularly relevant due to the alleged suitability of certain crypto assets for money-laundering. However, these issues will be discussed in another chapter of this book (→ § 10).

III. Key Elements of MiFID2 and MiCAR

6   Like all EU Directives, MiFID2 needs to be transposed into national laws. Supervision and enforcement are carried out by national regulators, the so-called **competent authorities** (Art. 4(1)(26) MiFID2). This means that there is a possibility for regulatory arbitrage because national regulators differ in their approaches, their resources and funding, the quality of staff, etc.

As an EU Regulation, MiCAR applies directly in the Member States and does not require transposition. However, it also applies the idea of a (national) competent authority (Art. 3(1)(24) MiCAR Draft). This leaves room for arbitrage, although arguably to a lesser extent.

Importantly, MiFID2 and MiCAR merely prescribe a **public supervision regime**. It does not extend to civil law (contracts, litigation, etc.).[10] As a consequence, the contractual framework for financial services regarding crypto assets might differ significantly between the Member States. This includes civil litigation in case of a breach of contract.

7   Broadly speaking, **four key elements** of the MiFID2 framework can be identified. First, financial service providers require authorisation by the national authorities (Art. 5 MiFID2, → para. 37). Secondly, it sets out organisational and personal requirements for authorisation (for example, Art. 9 and Art. 16 MiFID2, → para. 40). Thirdly, financial service providers are subject to prudential requirements (in particular, initial capital endowments under Art. 15 MiFID2 and Art. 9 IFD, → para. 39), depending on the type of service they are providing. Fourthly, the provision of services is subject to some governance requirements, in particular the duty to act in the client's best interest (Art. 24 MiFID2).

MiCAR is based on the same elements: governance requirements (Art. 59 MiCAR Draft), prudential requirements (Art. 60 MiCAR Draft), organisational requirements (Art. 61 MiCAR Draft) and the authorisation requirement (Art. 53 MiCAR Draft). Supervision also lies with the competent authority (Art. 81 and Art. 53 MiCAR Draft).

B. Geographical Scope of Application

I. Background

8   As the MiFID2 framework is carried out by the national competent authorities, the question is which rules apply in cross-border settings (so if a financial services provider from Member State A provides services in Member State B). The main issue is which regulator is responsible for authorisation. This is closely related to the EU passporting regime.

---

[10] For discussion MiFID2 and the public/private dichotomy, see Tison, 'The Civil Law Effects of MiFID in a Comparative Law Perspective', Financial Law Institute Working Paper WP 2010-05 (April 2010), available at https://ssrn.com/abstract=1596782; Maume, 'Reducing Legal Uncertainty and Regulatory Arbitrage for Robo-Advice', (2019) 16 *European Company and Financial Law Review*, 622 (640 et seqq); Cherednychenko, 'European Securities Regulation, Private Law and the Investment Firm-Client Relationship', (2009) 17 *European Review of Private Law* 925.

II. Cross-Border Provision of Services

In EU financial markets law, it is a general principle that the applicability of regulation is based on the provision of a service in a certain country, and not on its origin (the so-called **market** or **destination principle**). For example, Art. 3(1) of Regulation (EU) 2017/1129 (Prospectus Regulation)[11] requires all securities offered in the EU to include a prospectus, regardless of their origin (for details, see § 7 para. 31). This approach is also a known principle in international private law (→ § 3). It is convincing because it makes the regulator with the closest ties to the service (not to the service provider!) the responsible authority.

Crypto-related services are typically offered over the internet and thus available around the globe. Technically speaking, this means that they are offered in all countries, making all national regulators potentially responsible for authorisation. This would be highly inefficient. Thus, the question is not only if a certain financial service is available in the particular Member State. It is also necessary that potential customers in this Member State are **targeted** by the financial service providers marketing efforts.

Whether or not a particular Member State is targeted needs to be determined based on an **overall assessment**.[12] A potential **disclaimer** that the service is not aimed at customers from certain countries is only one of several indicators. Other indicators might be a (non-generic) top-level domain, language, product description, financial or other country-specific customer information, price information and payment modalities as well as the naming of contact persons in that state.[13] The placement of advertisements in certain Member States is also an important criterion.

However, these criteria were developed for standard internet sales. They are only of limited use for crypto-related services.[14] In many cases, English is the only available language and payment with currency tokens is common. Thus, language and currency are no conclusive indicators for the 'targeted market'. Offers in crypto-related products and services are literally global and are therefore aimed at customers in many countries. Therefore, for crypto-related services (as well as for ICOs), it is correct to ask whether there are indications that **effectively exclude** offerings in a particular state. If this is not the case, providers must take actual measures to prevent customers resident in a particular country from using their crypto-related services[15] (so-called geo-blocking). It would be possible to combine a query of the IP address with an online verification of the user's identity. A simple question of the customer's country of origin using an input mask without a reliable check is not sufficient due to the potential for abuse.

III. EU/EEA Passporting

Pursuant to Art. 34 MiFID2, an authorisation under Art. 5 MiFID2 is not required if a financial service provider from another Member State has received a correspond-

---

[11] Regulation (EU) No. 1129/2017 of the European Parliament and of the Council on the prospectus to be published when securities are offered to the public or admitted to trading on a regulated market, and repealing Directive 2003/71/EC, OJ L 168, 30.6.2017 p. 12–82.

[12] See, for example, BaFin, 'Notes regarding the licensing for conducting cross-border banking business and/or providing cross-border financial services' (1 April 2005, only the German version is binding), available at https://beck-link.de/c8fa3.

[13] Ibid.

[14] On the parallel problem regarding ICOs and prospectus requirements, see Maume, 'Initial Coin Offerings and EU Prospectus Disclosure', (2020) 31 *European Business Law Review*, 185 (198 et seqq).

[15] The typical example would be the exclusion of investors from the US, trying to avoid the keen eye of the US Securities and Exchange Commission.

ing licence from the competent supervisory authority in that Member State. This idea flows from the freedom to provide services (Art. 56 TFEU) and the freedom of establishment (Art. 49 TFEU). This is commonly known as 'passporting'. In this case, a mere **notification** of the resident national regulator is required subject to Art. 34(2) MiFID2.

12 However, there is a hidden problem here. The passporting presupposes that a licence is available in the home Member State and that the services offered in the other market are covered by the licence. This is unproblematic within the scope of application of MiFID2 because the definitions of relevant financial services and financial instruments are identical. However, beyond the MiFID2 framework (→ para. 3) it is possible that one Member State prescribes an authorisation requirement for a specific service whereas another Member State might not. In this case, a financial service provider offering services in the Member States with **stricter requirements** cannot rely on passporting because it did not (and: could not) receive prior authorisation in relation to the service in question. The popular example are service providers from other Member States offering services relating to Bitcoin in Germany. The German BaFin holds the view that currency tokens are units of account under German banking laws (→ para. 3). Thus, if a financial service provider from another Member State has not been authorised by its home regulator to provide Bitcoin related services (because it is not regulated in that Member State), it would need to get authorised from BaFin. This is time-consuming and presents liability risks.

IV. MiCAR

13 As the MiCAR framework is set out in the form of an EU Regulation, its transnational application is less complicated than for MiFID2. MiCAR applies to all persons that are engaged in the issuance of crypto-assets or provide services related to crypto-assets in the European Union (Art. 2(1) MiCAR Draft). Crypto-asset services shall only be provided by legal persons that have a registered office in an EU Member State and have received authorisation by the national competent authorities (Art. 53(1) MiCAR Draft).

An authorisation as a crypto-asset service is valid **for the whole European Union** (Art. 53(3) MiCAR Draft). If the service is provided across borders, the provider of crypto-asset services is not required to have a physical presence in the territory of a host Member State (which is the Member State where the provider offers its services, Art. 3 (1)(23) MiCAR Draft).

C. Regulated Activities

I. Background

14 The key term for regulated entities under MiFID2 is **investment firm**. According to Art. 4(1)(1) MiFID2, these are all legal persons whose regular occupation or business is the provision of investment services to third parties. These investment services are listed in Section C of Annex I to MiFID2. They include, inter alia, the reception and transmission of orders; the execution of orders on behalf of clients; dealing on own account; portfolio management; investment advice; the operation of a multilateral trading facility. All these services need to be provided in relation to financial instruments (→ para. 2). This means that any of these services, if provided in relation to

investment tokens, is an investment service. As a consequence, the investment firm offering the service requires authorisation under Art. 5 MiFID2 (→ para. 37). If the services are only offered in relation to currency tokens or utility tokens, they are not regulated under MiFiD2 (but potentially MiCAR).

However, although these services can be provided in relation to crypto assets, they are not crypto-specific. In contrast, activities such as the operation of a crypto trading platform (→ para. 15 et seqq.), the provision of crypto exchange services (→ para. 31), or the operation of crypto-ATMs (→ para. 32). These will be discussed in this part of the chapter.

The most prominent topic with regards to the regulation of crypto assets over the last years has been the **initial coin offering (ICO)**.[16] Issuing securities is not a financial service under MiFID2, and neither is issuing crypto assets.[17] **Wallet custody services** are not subject to MiFID2 either, even if they relate to investment tokens (and thus, transferable securities). The same applies to the **mining/minting** of coins (→ § 1 para. 38). Accordingly, these activities will not be discussed in this chapter.

The MiCAR Draft sets out a list of specific **crypto-asset services** in Art. 3(1)(9), such as the operation of trading platforms or the exchange of crypto-assets for fiat currency – which of course do not apply to financial instruments regulated under MiFID2. Interestingly, Art. 2(6) MiCAR Draft sets out a comparative list of crypto-asset services (under MiCAR) and the equivalent investment services (under MiFID2, → para. 47).

II. Crypto Exchanges

1. Distinction Between Regulated Activities

The most important crypto intermediaries are trading platforms, i.e. crypto exchanges. They can be organised in different ways. The underlying structure could be a multilateral trading facility (MTF, → para. 18), an organised trading facility (OTF, → para. 26), an investment firm dealing on own account (→ para. 29), or the execution of orders on behalf of clients (→ para. 30). The distinction between these different investment services is important because they are subject to different organisational requirements (in particular, MTF and OTF) and have different initial capital endowments. This can make a huge difference for younger fintechs considering starting a crypto trading platform.

Under MiCAR, the situation is comparable. Art. 3(1)(11) MiCAR Draft defines the 'trading platform for crypto-assets' (→ para. 24). This definition is a near exact copy of the MTF under MiFID2. It is also possible that trading platforms for non-securities under MiCAR are structured in different ways, similar to MiFID2.

Due to the variety of possible manifestations of crypto trading platforms, a generalised assessment of their legal structure is not possible. However, it is virtually not conceivable that such a platform could function without carrying out at least one of the activities regulated under MiFID2 or MiCAR. Therefore, if a crypto trading platform offers transactions in investment tokens, it is nearly almost certain that it will be regulated. In principle, this is to be welcomed, as this is the only way to create lasting confidence in the new crypto market structures.

---

[16] See, generally, Maume and Fromberger, 'Regulation of Initial Coin Offerings: Reconciling U.S. and E.U. Securities Laws' (2019) 19 *Chicago Journal of International Law*, 548.

[17] However, please note the authorisation requirement for offering asset-referenced tokens to the public (Art. 15(1) MiCAR Draft).

2. Commercial Activity

17   Only the provision of investment services as a **regular occupation or business** requires authorisation under Art. 5 MiFID2. Neither MiFID2 nor the Delegated Acts contain any further definition of the size or complexity required to qualify as a business. This is problematic because it leads to legal uncertainty and different interpretations across the EU Member States. The wording ('business or occupation') suggests that the platform must be operated with some **view for profit**, or at least require clients to pay consideration to cover the operator's expenses. In addition, it suggests some **continuity** of the operation. The bar for these requirements should not be set too high because the aim of MiFID2 is to protect investors – and for investor protection it cannot be relevant how big the service providers business operation is. For example, the German BaFin has taken the view that the operation of an MTF will typically meet the definition of a business because of its complexity.[18]

For non-security tokens under **MiCAR**, the respective requirement is set out in the definition of 'crypto-asset service provider' in Art. 3(1)(8) MiCAR Draft. The wording is ('occupation or business') is similar but does not include 'regular'. However, there is no reason to assume that the requirements are not congruent with Art. 5 MiFID2.

3. Multilateral Trading Facility

18   **a) Under MiFID2.** The multilateral trading facility (MTF) is probably the most complex and most professional way to run a crypto trading platform. Operating an MTF does not only require authorisation under Art. 5 MiFID. Art. 19 MiFID2 also provides **specific requirements for the operation** of an MTF. Operators of an MTF also need to have in place certain procedures for the **trading process and the finalisation of transactions** under Art. 18 MiFID2. They must establish and maintain **compliance** with all legal obligations under Art. 31 MiFID2. In short, in terms of regulation, running an MTF is not so different from running a fully-fledged stock exchange. In practice, only well-established market participants will be able to deal with the regulatory requirements. At the time of writing this chapter, only very few crypto-MTF have been authorised in the (pre-Brexit) EU, for example the *Börse Stuttgart Digital Exchange* (BSDEX), which is operated by Stuttgart Stock Exchange, and the British *LMAX Exchange*, and *Crypto Facilities*. As at now, most trading in crypto assets continues to take place on platforms located in countries outside the EU.

As for all investment services under MiFID2, the service must relate to financial instruments (→ para. 2). This means that an MTF needs to offer (inter alia, but not exclusively) the purchase/sale of investment tokens.

19   Importantly, authorisation as an MTF or as a trading platform for crypto assets triggers the application of the **market conduct rules** as set out in Regulation (EU) 596/2014[19] (for details, → § 11). If a financial instrument is traded on an MTF within the EU, for example, the prohibition of market manipulation and insider dealing as well as the obligation to make ad-hoc disclosures apply. The classification of a crypto exchange as an MTF is therefore not only important for its operator, but also for issuers and traders.

---

[18] BaFin, 'Tatbestand des Betriebs eines multilateralen Handelssystems gemäß § 1 Abs. 1a Satz 2 Nr. 1b KWG' (7 December 2009, last updated 12 May 2021), available at https://beck-link.de/d6hmd.

[19] Regulation (EU) No. 596/2014 of the European Parliament and of the Council on market abuse (Market Abuse Regulation) and repealing Directive 2003/6/EC of the European Parliament and of the Council and Commission Directives 2003/124/EC, 2003/125/EC and 2004/72/EC, OJ L 173, 12.6.2014 p. 1–61.

According to Art. 4(1)(22) MiFID2, MTF means a multilateral system, operated by an investment firm of a market operator, which brings together multiple third-party buying and selling interests in financial instruments – in the system and in accordance with non-discretionary rules – in a way that results in a contract.

The first prerequisite for a **system** is the existence of a set of rules as the basis for trading. There should be at least rules on membership, admission to trading, trading between members, reporting of completed transactions and transparency obligations. However, operators of a trading venue cannot avoid the classification as an MTF by simply not setting up or publishing official rules. This is relevant in the crypto sector, as access to many trading venues requires only a simple registration, often without even a reference to general terms and conditions. It is also usually not possible for customers to see which rules apply to trading. Sufficient in the sense of the regulation are therefore conditions of participation – of whatever kind – as well as the factual existence of trading rules. This includes rules in the form of protocols and/or computer code.

Multilateral requires that the system is essentially a market, which means that supply and demand meet. Bilateral systems, in which customers always conclude contracts with the operator of the system, are not covered.[20] The focus is here on the economic effects of the transaction.[21] If these affect the participants in the trading system and not its operator, the trading system is multilateral. If the economic consequences of a centrally structured trading platform are solely borne by the operator, then, due to the lack of a marketplace function, the trading system is merely a bilateral system and not an MTF.

The **interest in buying or selling** financial instruments is to be interpreted widely. It includes orders, quotes, and expressions of interest.[22] The classification under contract law is irrelevant. The combination of the interests of the participants must be carried out according to **defined rules within the system**. This means that the so-called "matching" takes place automatically and neither the parties nor the platform operator has any possibility to intervene in the matching of the parties' interests. In contrast to forum-like trading platforms, it is therefore not possible to decide on an MTF whether the transaction is to be concluded with a specific contracting party.[23] For trading platforms, the requirements for MTF-classification are usually met they match offers and demand automatically.

b) Under MiCAR. MiCAR does not refer to an MTF but to a 'trading platform for crypto-assets'. It is defined in Art. 3(1)(11) MiCAR Draft as a trading platform 'within which multiple third-party buying and selling interests for crypto-assets can interact in a manner that results in a contract, either by exchanging one crypto-asset for another or a crypto-asset for fiat currency that is legal tender'. This definition is similar, but not identical to the MTF-definition under MiFID2 (→ para. 20). Most significantly, it does not require non-discretionary rules. However, the phrase 'within which multiple third-party buying and selling interests … can interact' strongly suggests a market function that is comparable to an MTF. However, the wording does not require non-discretionary rules, which means that the operator has discretion when bringing together the parties (like the operator of an OTF, → para. 26).

Similar to MiFID2, Art. 68 MiCAR Draft sets out obligations for the operation of a trading platform for crypto-assets. Although there are many similarities, these are

---

[20] From the German literature: Schwennicke, in: Schwennicke and Auerbach (eds.), *Kreditwesengesetz*, § 1 para. 100; Kumpan, in: Schwark/Zimmer (eds.), *Kapitalmarktrechts-Kommentar*, § 2 WpHG para. 90.
[21] Kumpan, in: Schwark and Zimmer (eds.), *Kapitalmarktrechts-Kommentar*, § 2 WpHG para. 90.
[22] BaFin, 'Tatbestand des Betriebs eines multilateralen Handelssystems gemäß § 1 Abs. 1a Satz 2 Nr. 1b KWG' (7 December 2009, last updated 12 May 2021), available at https://beck-link.de/d6hmd.
[23] Ibid.

more crypto-specific than their counterparts in Art. 18/19 MiFID2. For example, under Art. 68(1)(3) MiCAR Draft, the '**quality of the crypto-asset**' needs to be assessed. This does not refer to the underlying asset (if any), but to the technical implementation. For this purpose, the trading platform shall take into account 'the experience, track record and reputation of the issuer and its development team'. In other words, the operator of a trading platform needs to undertake a technical assessment of the crypto asset.

In addition, only tokens are to be admitted that do not have an **inbuilt anonymisation function** (Art. 68(1)(4) MiCAR Draft). Art. 68(3) MiCAR Draft requires the operating rules to be drafted in one of the **official languages** of the European Union, or in another language 'that is customary in the sphere of finance'.

Authorisation as a trading platform for crypto assets also triggers market conduct rules. These are not housed in Regulation (EU) 596/2014, but in Art. 76 et seqq. MiCAR (→ § 11).

4. Organised Trading Facility

26 A crypto trading platform might also classify as an organised trading facility (OTF) pursuant to Art. 4(1)(23) MiFID2. An OTF is a multilateral system (which is not a regulated market or an MTF) in which multiple third-party buying and selling interests in bonds, structured finance products, emission allowances or derivatives are able to interact in the system in a way that results in a contract. Again, the key prerequisite is that the facility offers (inter alia, but not exclusively) the sale or purchase of investment tokens.

27 The definition of the OTF shares two core elements with that of the MTF, namely multilateralism (→ para. 22) and the system (→ para. 21). However, there are two important differences. First, **shares** cannot be traded on an OTF. This distinction is not relevant for the crypto sector as at now. Crypto assets (including investment tokens) are not real shares, but bonds.[24] Secondly, trading on an OTF does not have to be carried out according to non-discretionary rules. The operator of the OTF therefore has **discretion** in the matching of orders and in deciding whether to place or withdraw them.

28 Similar to an MTF, the OTF also needs to have in place certain procedures for the trading process and the finalisation of transactions under Art. 18 MiFID2. In addition, Art. 20 MiFID2 sets out specific rules for OTF.

5. Dealing on Own Account

29 Dealing on own account means trading against proprietary capital resulting in the conclusion of transactions in financial instruments (Art. 4(1)(6) MiFID2). In other words, the investment firm buys the financial instruments from the clients and/or sells them to the clients. This would be a typical setup for centralised trading platforms (→ § 1 para. 97), but also for a crypto exchange services (→ para. 31, not to be confused with a crypto exchange!).

The MiCAR equivalent of 'dealing on own account' is 'the exchange of crypto-assets for fiat currency' (Art. 3(1)(12) MiCAR Draft) or/and 'the exchange of crypto-assets for other crypto-assets' (Art. 3(1)(13) MiCAR Draft). In both cases, the purchase or sale must be carried out using proprietary capital.

---

[24] A typical investment token grants its holder the right to participate in the issuer's profits, or a fixed payment. This makes them comparable to bonds. However, holding such a token does not convey the status of a shareholder. It can be expected that 'real' share tokens will be issued in the near future.

6. Execution of Orders

According to Art. 4(1)(5) MiFID2, the execution of orders on behalf of others means 30 acting to conclude agreements to buy or sell financial instruments on behalf of clients. In other words, in contrast to dealing on own account (→ para. 29), the financial service provider is **acting for the client and not for themself**. The contract is concluded between the market participants and not between the market operator and the buyer/seller. This will typically be the case for **decentralised platforms** (→ § 1 para. 97) where the operator is limited to providing a market infrastructure and then leaves everything else to the parties. The MiCAR equivalent is 'execution of order for crypto-assets on behalf of third parties' (Art. 3(1)(14) MiCAR Draft).

III. Crypto Exchange Services

A crypto exchange service is the **exchange of crypto assets for fiat currency or for** 31 **other crypto assets** (not to be confused with operating a crypto exchange/a crypto trading platform). However, as stated above, a centralised crypto trading platform could be organised like an exchange service – if the operator is always contracting with the client (→ para. 22).

If a crypto exchange service is offered regarding investment tokens (and thus, financial instruments under MiFID2), it is typically regulated as 'dealing on own account' according to Art. 4(1)(6) MiFID2, which is defined as 'trading against proprietary capital resulting in the conclusion of transactions in one or more financial instruments'.

If the crypto exchange service relates to crypto assets under MiCAR, it is regulated as 'the exchange of crypto-assets for fiat currency' (Art. 3(1)(12) MiCAR Draft) or as 'the exchange of crypto-assets for other crypto-assets' (Art. 3(1)(13) MiCAR Draft). In both cases, the purchase or sale must be carried out using proprietary capital.

IV. Crypto-ATMs

Over the last years, crypto-ATMs have become more and more popular. These are 32 automated teller machines (ATM) that transfer crypto assets from and to wallets. The traded crypto assets are typically Bitcoins, and occasionally also Ether or Monero. These so-called crypto-ATMs function similarly to normal ATMs. In the course of the transaction, the customer uses a smartphone and a QR code to link his wallet to the ATM, enabling it to transfer the crypto assets to/from the wallet.

Structurally, a crypto-ATM is nothing but a **stationary form of crypto exchange** 33 **point**. Depending on its design, the operator could act as a contractual partner to the customer. This would then be a case of dealing on own account (MiFID2) or the exchange of crypto-assets for fiat currency or other crypto-assets (→ para. 29). The German BaFin recently took the view that this is typically the case.[25]

If the ATM operator is not party to the contract but carrying out the transaction on behalf of both parties, the service could also be an execution of orders as set out in Art. 4(1)(5) MiFID2. The MiCAR equivalent is Art. 3(1)(14), the 'execution of orders for crypto-assets on behalf of third parties' (→ para. 30).

---

[25] BaFin, 'Aufstellen von Krypto-ATM: Erlaubnis der BaFin erforderlich' (8 September 2020), available at https://beck-link.de/d33da.

V. Wallet Custody

34   Wallet custody services are only regulated under MiCAR, but not under MiFID2. The cumbersome legal term under MiCAR is 'the custody and administration of crypto-assets on behalf of third parties'. It is defined under Art. 3(1)(10) MiCAR Draft as 'safekeeping or controlling, on behalf of third parties, crypto-assets or the means of access to such crypto-assets, where applicable in the form of private cryptographic keys'.[26]

35   The fact that wallet custody is not subject to MiFID2 might, in theory, result in a **regulatory gap**. If a wallet custody provider only offers its services for investment token, neither MiFID2 nor MiCAR would apply. However, this is not a realistic scenario. Most tokens are either currency tokens or utility tokens. Restricting oneself to investment tokens in order to avoid regulation seems an odd business case. In addition, Member States might opt to introduce a national authorisation requirement for investment tokens. For example, Germany has introduced the wallet custody service in 2020 as a distinct financial service, including an authorisation requirement.[27]

36   Art. 67 MiCAR Draft sets out **specific obligations** for wallet custody services.[28] For example, the service provider needs to identify the client (Art. 67(1)(a) MiCAR Draft). This closes an essential gap in the regulation because the EU AML rules do not apply to crypto-asset services (in contrast to financial services under MiFID2). Most significantly, Art. 67(8) MiCAR Draft stipulates that the service provider is **liable to the clients for the loss of crypto-assets** resulting from a malfunction or hacks. This presents a huge risk for the provision of wallet custody services.

D. Authorisation

I. Overview

37   As discussed above, the provision of crypto-related investment services (in particular, for operating a crypto trading platform, → para. 15, an exchange service → para. 31, or a crypto ATM, → para. 32) requires authorisation under MiFID2 if they are rendered as a business or an occupation (→ para. 17) and involve investment tokens. Amongst other requirements, the application for authorisation must demonstrate a sufficient initial capital endowment (→ para. 39) and a qualified management (→ para. 40); for authorisation under MiCAR, → para. 46.

38   Small companies and start-ups will often struggle to meet these requirements, in particular the capital endowment and the requirements for the management. For this reason, it might be worthwhile to enter into a cooperation agreement with an existing financial service provider or bank and thus 'hide' under an existing licence.[29] This is by

---

[26] This differs slightly from the definition of wallet custody under AML law, namely Art. 1(2)(d)(19) of Directive (EU) 2018/843 (AMLD5). For details, → § 10 para. 49).

[27] See § 17, para. 32. This took place in the wake of the implementation of AMLD5 – although the Directive did not prescribe an authorisation requirement for wallet custody services, but merely the application of AML regulation).

[28] For more details, see Zetzsche et al, 'The Markets in Crypto-Assets Regulation (MICA) and the EU Digital Finance Strategy', EBI Working Paper Series No. 2020/77 (December 2020), 20, available at https://papers.ssrn.com/abstract_id=3725395.

[29] On this topic, see generally Maume, 'In Unchartered Territory – Banking Supervision meets Fintech', (2017) *Corporate Finance*, 373.

no means unusual. According to market participants, this symbiosis has developed into a serious business area for banks in times of low interest rates.

II. Initial Capital Endowment

The amount of the initial capital is set out in Art. 15 MiFID2 in conjunction with the new Directive (EU) 2019/2034 (Investment Firms Directive, IFD). The IFD provides for a prudential supervision regime for investment firms, applying the same definitions as MiFID2. 39

For dealing on own account (→ para. 29) (Art. 9(1) IFD) the initial capital is EUR 750,000. For the operation of an MTF the initial capital is EUR 150,000 (Art. 9(3) IFD), and for execution-only services EUR 75,000 (Art. 9(2) IFD).

The initial capital for OTF (→ para. 26) depends on whether the operator engages in dealing on own account. If this is the case, the initial capital is EUR 750,000 (Art. 9(1) IFD); if not, the initial capital is EUR 150,000 (Art. 9(3) IFD).

III. Requirements for Management Body

According to Art. 9(4) MiFID2, the national competent authority shall refuse authorisation if it is not satisfied that the members of the firm's management body are not of sufficient good repute, possess knowledge, skills and experience and commit sufficient time to perform their functions in the investment firm. This is commonly referred to as a fit-and-proper test.[30] 40

The applicant needs to be of **sufficient good repute**. This needs to be assessed in the context of a case-by-case assessment. Offering financial services and running an investment firm is protected by the freedom of occupation under Art. 15 of the Charter of Fundamental Rights of the European Union. Thus, although the wording of Art. 9(4) MiFID2 might suggest otherwise, the authorisation can only be refused if there are facts that indicate that the member of the management body is not of good repute. In other words, there needs to be the assumption that a candidate is of good repute unless there are strong indicators against it. Reasons for a lack of good repute include, in particular, **criminal offences** related to business activities. Particularly relevant are property- and tax-related crimes, or money laundering.[31] Minor infringements can also be relevant if they suggest a tendency to disregard legal rules in general. 41

The assessment of **knowledge, skills and experience** is more complex. To demonstrate the problem, the criteria applied by the German BaFin are explained in brief.[32] First, the candidate needs to have some level of **theoretical knowledge**. This could be vocational training and courses of study (bank apprenticeship, business studies) in the relevant area, but also additional certificates and specialised courses while being on the job. The second requirement is **practical experience** in the relevant field. This includes experience in the field of financial services as well as knowledge of core business elements such as risk management and compliance. This can be demonstrated by 42

---

[30] A 'fit and proper person' means a person who is financially sound, competent, reputable and reliable, see International Organization of Securities Commissions, 'Fit and Proper Assessment – Final Report' (December 2009), 4, available at https://beck-link.de/w6bwx.

[31] BaFin, 'Guidance Notice on management board members pursuant to the German Banking Act (Kreditwesengesetz – KWG), the German Payment Services Supervision Act (Zahlungsdiensteaufsichtsgesetz – ZAG) and the German Capital Investment Code (Kapitalanlagegesetzbuch – KAGB)' (4 January 2016, last amended 31 January 2017), 20, available at https://beck-link.de/a5tfb.

[32] For details, see ibid, 18 et seqq.

business experience in a position that is of sufficient importance in the hierarchy in a comparable firm. The third prerequisite is **management experience**. This may have been acquired through the management of a company or through the management of organisational units within a company. The expectation here is that the candidate will have decision-making and administrative powers of his or her own as well as staff management. § 25c(1) of the German Banking Act (KWG) stipulates the assumption that a managing director who has held a management position at an institution for at least **three years** is professionally qualified to manage an institution of comparable size and type of business. The same applies if the person in question was hierarchically active directly below the management.

43   The application of these established tests to small crypto start-ups could be problematic. For example, it will probably be difficult to find suitable institutes for comparison due to the novelty of the industry. Thus, it will often be impossible to make use of the three-year-assumption. Entrepreneurs in the field of crypto are often young and have never worked for a bank or similar financial service providers – and most certainly not in a leading position. Thus, the outlined requirements can hardly be met. Founders have little choice but to either appoint an external specialist as managing director or to use the license of an established company.

IV. Provision of Investment Services without Authorisation

44   Art. 70(1) MiFID2 provides that the Member States need to implement sanctions for breaches of the MiFID2 framework that are effective, proportionate and dissuasive. Providing investment services without the required authorisation is specifically referred to as a punishable infringement (Art. 70(4) MiFID2).

45   The consequences for providing investment services without authorisation are set out in Art. 71(6) MiFID2). The **maximum fine** needs to be higher than EUR 5 million. If the perpetrator is a legal entity, the maximum fine can alternatively be up to 10 % of the total annual turnover of the legal person in the last year. Member States are expressly allowed to foresee criminal sanctions in these cases.[33] In addition, the business operation can be shut down and an operated market suspended. The competent authority can also issue a temporary or (in serious cases) a permanent ban against members of the management body to exercise management functions in investment firms in the future.

V. Crypto-Asset Services under MiCAR

46   Crypto-asset services may only be provided in the European Union if they have been authorised (Art. 53(1) MiCAR Draft). Similar to the MiFID2 regime, authorisation is granted by the national competent authority. It seems likely that the Member States will assign this function (Art. 81 MiCAR Draft) to the national financial markets regulator. However, it would also be possible to establish new, specialised national bodies for the digital markets. A popular example is Malta, which created the Malta Digital Innovation Authority in 2019.

47   The separation between investment tokens (which are financial instruments under MiFID2) and non-investment tokens (which are regulated under MiCAR) might be sensible through the lens of regulation. However, it may appear superficial in practice. A financial service will most likely offer investment services for **all kinds of tokens**,

---

[33] For example, in Germany, providing investment services without permission is a criminal offence punishable with imprisonment of not more than five years, § 54(1) KWG.

notwithstanding what the regulatory framework would be. Investment tokens, currency tokens and utility tokens are all considered as possible vehicles for investment purposes.

For this reason, Art. 2(6) MiCAR stipulates that an investment firm that is authorised under Art. 5 MiFID2 **does not need authorisation under MiCAR** where they only provide one or several crypto-asset services **equivalent to investment services under MiFID2**. For this purpose, the following services are considered as equivalent:[34]

- trading platform for crypto-assets (Art. 3(1)(11) MiCAR Draft) → multilateral trading facility (MTF, Art. 4(1)(22) MiFID2)/organised trading facility (OTF, Art. 4(1)(23) MiFID2),
- crypto-asset exchange services (crypto-to-crypto and crypto-to-fiat, Art. 3(1)(12) and (13) MiCAR) if using proprietary capital → dealing on own account (Art. 4(1)(6) MiFID2),
- the execution of orders for crypto-assets on behalf of third parties (Art. 3(1)(14) MiCAR Draft) → the exchange of crypto-assets for fiat currency (Art. 3(1)(12) MiCAR Draft) or the exchange of crypto-assets for other crypto-assets (Art. 3(1)(13) MiCAR Draft), depending on the consideration rendered.

In other words, if an established investment firm has either already started to offer services regarding investment tokens and plans to **expand the service to crypto-assets under MiCAR**, no new authorisation is required. Although not addressed specifically, the same would apply if a financial service provider decides to introduce a new service comprising all token types. In this case, only registration under MiFID2 would be required.

If the provision of a crypto-asset service is not covered by Art. 2(6) MiCAR and authorisation is required under Art. 53 MiCAR Draft, Art. 54(2) sets out a **comprehensive list of documents** that need to be produced. However, according to Art. 54(3) MiCAR Draft, if prior authorisation as an investment firm has been granted, the competent authority shall not require the applicant to file the respective information again (provided that the competent authority has access to this information).

Art. 60(1) MiCAR Draft also sets out **initial capital endowments** for providers of crypto-asset services. Similar to MiFID2, the capital required depends on the nature of the service offered. Annex IV to the MiCAR Draft sets the minimum requirements as follows: for the execution of orders (Art. 3(1)(14)) EUR 50,000, for wallet custody services (Art. 3(1)(10)) EUR 125,000, and for exchange services (Art. 3(1)(12) and (13)) or the operation of a trading platform (Art. 3(1)(11)) EUR 150,000.

---

[34] Only the services with relevance to this chapter are listed. Other services include, inter alia, investment advice, portfolio management or the placing of securities.

§ 9
E-Money Tokens, Stablecoins, and Token Payment Services

Literature: Al-Naji, Chen and Diao, 'Basis: A Price-Stable Cryptocurrency with an Algorithmic Central Bank' (2018), available at https://beck-link.de/b8256 (accessed 3.10.2020); Auffenberg, 'E-Geld auf Blockchain-Basis' (2019) 19 *Zeitschrift für Bank- und Kapitalmarktrecht*, 341; BaFin, 'Merkblatt – Hinweise zum Zahlungsdiensteaufsichtsgesetz (ZAG)' (29.11.2017) available at https://beck-link.de/5venp (accessed 20.08.2021); Bank for International Settlements, 'G7 Working Group on Stablecoins, Investigating the impact of global stablecoins' (October 2019), available at https://beck-link.de/czeb3 (accessed 6.8.2020); Barrier, 'The Payment with Bitcoins and other Virtual Currencies – Risks, liabilities and regulatory responses', in De Franceschi and Schulze (eds), *Digital Revolution – New Challenges for Law* (Baden-Baden, 2019), 327; beck.online-GROSSKOMMENTAR zum BGB (BeckOGK) (München, 2021); Bindseil, 'Tiered CBDC and the financial system' (January 2020), ECB Working Paper No. 2351, available at https://beck-link.de/yen3s (accessed 4.3.2021); Casper and Terlau (eds), *Zahlungsdiensteaufsichtsgesetz (ZAG)* (2nd edn, München, 2020); De Filippi, 'Bitcoin: a regulatory nightmare to a libertarian dream' (2014) 3 Internet Policy Review, available at https://beck-link.de/8hexm (accessed 5.1.2021); Deutsche Bundesbank, 'Monthly Report July 2019' (July 2019), available at https://beck-link.de/p7vmk (accessed 20.08.2021); Diem Association, 'Whitepaper v2.0, Cover letter' (April 2020), available at https://beck-link.de/6nnnk (accessed 10.1.2021); European Central Bank (ECB), 'Report on digital euro' (October 2020), available at https://beck-link.de/tc4mx (accessed 3.10.2020); EBA, 'Report with advice for the European Commission on crypto assets' (January 2019), available at https://beck-link.de/e8dmh (accessed 16.12.2019); Financial Conduct Authority, 'Guidance on Cryptoassets, Feedback and Final Guidance to CP 19/3, PS19/22' (July 2019), available at https://beck-link.de/86rff (accessed 20.08.2021); Financial Conduct Authority, 'Payment Services and Electronic Money – Our Approach, The FCA's role under the Payment Services Regulations 2017 and the Electronic Money Regulations 2011' (June 2019), available at https://beck-link.de/3kmn3 (accessed 20.08.2021); Financial Conduct Authority, The Perimeter Guidance Manual – Guidance on the Scope of the Electronic Money Regulations (2011); Friedman, 'Currency Competition: A Skeptical View.', in Salin (ed), *Currency Competition and Monetary Union* (The Hague, 1984), 42; Gikay, 'Regulating decentralized cryptocurrencies under payment services law: Lessons from European Union Law.' (2019) 10 *Journal of Law, Technology & the Internet*, 1; Grigo, Hansen, Patz and Wachter, 'Decentralized Finance (DeFi) – A new Fintech Revolution? The Blockchain Trend explained' (2020), available at https://beck-link.de/xa2xn (accessed 3.10.2020); Hayek, *Denationalisation of Money – The Argument Refined: An Analysis of the Theory and Practice of Concurrent Currencies* (3rd edn, Institute of Economic Affairs, London, 1990); HM Treasury, Financial Conduct Authority, Bank of England, 'Cryptoassets Taskforce: final report' (October 2018) available at https://beck-link.de/y3syp (accessed 20.08.2021); Kubát, 'Virtual Currency Bitcoin in the Scope of Money Definition and Store of Value' (2015), 30 *Procedia Economics and Finance*, 409; Leonard, 'Bitcoin ATM Explained – The Pros and Cons of Buying Cryptocurrency through an ATM' (coincodex.com, 2020), available at https://beck-link.de/c7c2b (accessed 30.8.2020); MakerDAO, 'The Maker Protocol: MakerDAO's Multi-Collateral Dai (MCD) System', available at https://beck-link.de/6p5ps (accessed 6.8.2020); Möslein and Omlor, 'Die europäische Agenda für innovative Finanztechnologien (FinTech)' (2018) 18 *Zeitschrift für Bank- und Kapitalmarktrecht*, 236; Nakamoto, 'Bitcoin: A Peer-to-Peer Electronic Checkout System' (2008), available at https://beck-link.de/66dce (accessed 19.1.2019); Nabilou and Prüm, 'Ignorance, Debt and Cryptocurrencies: The Old and the New in the Law and Economics of Concurrent Currencies' (2018) 4 *Journal of Financial Regulation*, 5(1), 29, available at https://beck-link.de/zw826 (accessed 5.8.2020); Omlor, 'Blockchain-basierte Zahlungsmittel – Ein Arbeitsprogramm für Gesetzgeber und Rechtswissenschaft' (2018) 51 *Zeitschrift für Rechtspolitik*, 85; Omlor, 'E-Geld im reformierten Zahlungsdiensterecht' (2017) 35 *Zeitschrift für Wirtschaftsrecht*, 1836; Sandner, Gross, Grale and Schulden, 'The Digital Programmable Euro, Libra and CBDC: Implications for European Banks' (2020), available at https://beck-link.de/m5ehw (accessed 5.8.2020); Shmatenko and Möllenkamp, 'Digitale Zahlungsmittel in einer analog geprägten Rechtsordnung – A bit(coin) out of control – Rechtsnatur und schuldrechtliche Behandlung von Kryptowährungen' (2018) 21 *Zeitschrift für IT-Recht und Recht der Digitalisierung*, 495; Terlau, '§ 55a – Elektronisches Geld, virtuelle Währungen (Bitcoins, Ether Coins)', in Schimansky, Bunte and Lwowski (eds), *Bankrechts-Handbuch, Vol. I* (5th edn, C.H.Beck, München, 2017); Vardi, 'Bit by Bit: Assessing the Legal Nature of Virtual Currencies', in Gimigliano (ed), *Bitcoin and Mobile Payments. Constructing a European Union Framework* (Palgrave Macmillan, London, 2016), 55; Von der Groeben, Schwarze and Hatje (eds), *Europäisches Unionsrecht, Vol. 3* (7th edn, Baden-Baden, 2015); Wharton Blockchain and

§ 9. E-Money Tokens, Stablecoins, and Token Payment Services

Digital Asset Project in collaboration with the World Economic Forum, 'DeFi Beyond the Hype – The Emerging World of Decentralized Finance' (May 2021), 9, available at https://beck-link.de/mkzd8 (accessed 31.5.2021); Wilusz, 'Legal determinants of electronic money systems development in European Union', in Dubiński (ed), *Prawny i ekonomiczny przegląd prawa gospodarczego* (2nd edn, Wydawnictwo Naukowe UAM, 2011), 125; Yermack, 'Is Bitcoin a Real Currency?', in Lee (ed), *Handbook of Digital Currency* (Elsevier, 2015), 31.

Outline

	para.
A. Introduction	1
B. Funds under EU Payment Services Law	5
C. Tokens as Electronic Money	8
I. Definition of Electronic Money	10
1. Monetary Value	11
2. Electronically Stored	13
3. Represented by a Claim on the Issuer	15
4. Receipt of Funds	20
5. Issuance	24
6. Purpose of Making Payment Transactions	27
7. Acceptance by a Third Party	29
8. Exemptions for Certain Instruments and Payment Transactions	30
a) Storage on instruments pursuant to Art. 3(k) PSD2	31
b) Use for Payment Transactions pursuant to Art. 3(l) PSD2	33
II. Classification of Currency Tokens	34
III. Classification of Stablecoins	36
IV. Classification of Investment Tokens	41
V. Classification of Utility Tokens	43
VI. Hybrid Tokens	46
D. Stablecoins, E-Money Tokens and Utility Tokens under MiCAR	50
I. Scope of the Markets in Crypto-Assets Regulation	51
II. Currency Tokens as Crypto-Assets under MiCAR	54
III. Stablecoins under MiCAR	55
1. (Significant) Asset-Referenced Tokens	56
2. (Significant) E-Money Tokens	58
3. Algorithmic Stablecoins	62
IV. Utility Tokens under MiCAR	64
E. Payment Services in connection with Token Business Models	65
I. Basic Objectives of the Regulation of Payment Services	65
II. General Conditions for Payment Services	68
1. Three-Party Relationship	68
2. Funds	70
III. Different Token Business Models	73
1. Installation and Operation of Token-ATMs	75
a) Purchase and Sale of Currency Tokens via Token ATMs	75
b) Service enabling Cash to be placed on/withdrawals from a Payment Account	77
2. Crypto Bank Account	78
3. No Execution of Payment Transactions by Wallet Providers	79
4. Operation of Crypto Exchanges	81
a) Money Remittance	82
b) Acquiring of Payment Transactions	90
5. Money Remittance within the Framework of ICOs	94
F. Authorisation Requirements and Ongoing Obligations for E-Money Business and Payment Services	95
I. Authorisation for Electronic Money Institutions	95
II. Authorisation for Payment Service Providers	97
III. Supervisory and Follow-Up Obligations of Institutions	98

    G. Requirements for Issuers of Crypto Assets under MiCAR 101
        I. Issuers of Crypto Assets 101
       II. Authorisation Requirements 105
          1. Issuers of Utility Tokens and Crypto Assets 105
          2. Issuers of Asset-referenced Tokens 106
          3. Issuers of E-Money Tokens 107
      III. Ongoing Obligations of Issuers of Crypto Assets 109
          1. Issuers of Utility Tokens and Crypto Assets 109
          2. Issuers of Asset-Referenced Tokens 111
          3. Issuers of E-Money Tokens 115

A. Introduction

1   The creation of the first 50 **Bitcoins** and the '**Block 0**' on 3 January 2009 may be referred to – with a little pathos – as 'zero hour' for blockchain-based cryptographic tokens. Bitcoins are supposed to be an alternative to existing payment systems – without a central bank that issues and controls 'its' money and without any intermediary banks and other payment service providers.[1]

2   With that in mind, this chapter addresses the question of how Bitcoins and other currency tokens as well as stablecoins and utility tokens are to be classified under current EU payment services and e-money laws. Furthermore, in this chapter some token business models are assessed which might entail payment services regulated under European payment services law.

3   Currently, the relevant rules are set out in the Directive (EU) 2015/2366 (Second Payment Services Directive, PSD2), replacing the Directive 2007/64/EC (First Payment Services Directive, PSD1), and the Directive 2009/110/EC (Second Electronic Money Directive, EMD2). PSD2 and EMD2 have led to full harmonisation of the regulation of payment services and the electronic money business in the European Union and the European Economic Area. A key regulatory objective of PSD2 is to promote innovation in payment transactions.

4   Based on the concepts of EU payment services law, the various tokens cannot be deemed **money**, i.e. banknotes, coins or scriptural money (→ para. 5 et seqq.). However, tokens may qualify as **electronic money** due to their specific design and intended application (→ para. 8 et seqq.). Irrespective of the qualification of certain tokens as electronic money under EMD2, **business models based on tokens**, such as the operation of crypto exchanges, may require authorisation as payment services (→ para. 73 et seqq.). Subsequently, an overview of the legal consequences of the qualification of tokens under EMD2 or token business models under **EU payment services law** is given (→ para. 95 et seqq.). Additionally, this chapter gives a general outlook to the upcoming changes the **Proposal for a Regulation on Markets in Crypto-assets** (COM(2020) 593 final of 24.9.2020, 'MiCAR Draft') might entail for crypto assets (→ para. 101 et seqq.).

B. Funds under EU Payment Services Law

5   For their applicability, the central provisions of EU payment services law require that a **transfer of funds** of some kind takes place (→ para. 20 et seqq.). The term 'funds' is

---

[1] 'A purely peer-to-peer version of electronic cash would allow online payments to be sent directly from one party to another without going through a financial institution', Nakamoto, 'Bitcoin: A Peer-to-Peer Electronic Checkout System' (2008), available at https://beck-link.de/66dce (accessed 19.1.2019).

§ 9. E-Money Tokens, Stablecoins, and Token Payment Services

therefore relevant for the question of whether token transactions are to be regarded as payment services within the meaning of Art. 4(3) PSD2. Pursuant to Art. 4(25) PSD2, 'funds' are 'banknotes and coins, scriptural money or electronic money as defined in Art. 2(2) EMD2'. The law governing payment services and electronic money business as part of the established banking and payment services system is based on an understanding of '**banknotes and coins**' and '**scriptural money**' that are each denominated in legal currency. 'Banknotes and coins' – and derived from them the 'scriptural money' – are the established forms of money. The question therefore arises: Are Bitcoins and other cryptocurrencies also to be included here as the 'new money'?

From an economic perspective, money is characterised by its function as a **medium of exchange**, a means of payment, a store of value and a unit of account.[2] Based on this definition, it seems at first glance reasonable to assume that at least currency tokens such as Bitcoin or Ether are to be qualified as money, because they are intended precisely to serve as a means of payment or exchange. However, the classification of currency tokens as money is regularly denied due to their lack of a value retention function because of their high volatility and their lack of actual value stability (→ § 2 para. 58 et seqq.).[3]

6

From a legal perspective, the decisive factor is whether or not it is a **legal means of payment** or currency issued and put into circulation by the state for which there is a statutory obligation to accept it. According to a European understanding of legal currency, the classification of a means of payment as legal currency presupposes that a debtor can free himself from his monetary debt by paying cash with the creditor not being allowed to refuse such payment.[4] So far, there is no general statutory legal obligation to accept currency tokens or other tokens. Currency tokens, thus, generally (currently still) lack the issuance and recognition by government that would legally qualify them as money or government currency.[5] That this might change in the future is illustrated by the ongoing discussions on European level regarding the issuance of **Central Bank Digital Currencies** (CBDC) on the basis of distributed ledger technology (DLT).[6] Accordingly, the European Banking Authority (EBA) ascertains that tokens are neither banknotes nor coins nor scriptural money and that tokens, therefore, only

7

---

[2] Yermack, 'Is Bitcoin a Real Currency?', in Lee (ed), *Handbook of Digital Currency* (2015), 31 et seqq. (sec. III); Nabilou and Prüm, 'Ignorance, Debt and Cryptocurrencies: The Old and the New in the Law and Economics of Concurrent Currencies' (2018) 4 *Journal of Financial Regulation*, 5(1), 29, available at https://beck-link.de/zw826 (accessed 5.8.2020).

[3] For Bitcoin see Yermack, 'Is Bitcoin a Real Currency?', in Lee (ed), *Handbook of Digital Currency* (2015), 31 et seqq. (sec. III.C.); On the discussion of the pros and cons of privatization of money in general: Hayek, *Denationalisation of Money – The Argument Refined: An Analysis of the Theory and Practice of Concurrent Currencies* (3rd edn., 1990), 38; Friedman, 'Currency Competition: A Skeptical View.', in Salin (ed.), *Currency Competition and Monetary Union* (1984), 42. However, the validity of this argument is limited because there are numerous examples of national currencies for which value stability does not exist due to their extreme volatility and whose qualification as money in the legal context is nevertheless undisputed.

[4] Bank of England, 'What is legal tender?', available at https://beck-link.de/k7epx (accessed 5.8.2020); Omlor, 'Blockchain-basierte Zahlungsmittel – Ein Arbeitsprogramm für Gesetzgeber und Rechtswissenschaft' (2018) 51 *Zeitschrift für Rechtspolitik*, 85 (87) deepens the understanding of a legal currency in the sense of EU currency law, which according to it must have three characteristics: the obligation to accept, acceptance at full nominal value and the effect of exemption for payment obligations. Cf. also Commission Recommendation of 22 March 2010 (2010/191/EU) on the scope and effects of legal tender of euro banknotes and coins, 1.

[5] The government of El Salvador has announced in 2021 to accept Bitcoin as legal tender. Barrier, 'The Payment with Bitcoins and other Virtual Currencies – Risks, liabilities and regulatory responses', in De Franceschi and Schulze (eds.), *Digital Revolution – New Challenges for Law*, 327.

[6] ECB, 'Report on digital euro' (October 2020), available at https://beck-link.de/tc4mx (accessed 3.10.2020); Bindseil, 'Tiered CBDC and the financial system' (January 2020) ECB Working Paper No. 2351, available at https://beck-link.de/yen3s (accessed 4.3.2021); Sandner, Gross, Grale and Schulden,

constitute 'funds' in the sense of European payment services law where they qualify as electronic money (→ para. 8 et seqq.).[7]

C. Tokens as Electronic Money

8   EMD2 regulates the issuance of electronic money. Hence, if tokens were to qualify as electronic money, their issuance would be subject to the supervision of the **national competent authorities**.

9   In its report of 9 January 2019, the EBA took the view that tokens may not generally fulfil the criteria of electronic money in terms of the EMD2 but that certain tokens can be designed in such a way that all criteria of electronic money are fulfilled.[8] At this point of time, national authorities had already reported to the EBA five instances where they considered the respective business model to meet all criteria of electronic money. In particular, the **UK Cryptoassets Taskforce** highlighted in its final report in October 2018 that certain utility tokens can fall under the definition of electronic money.[9] However, as far as can be ascertained, there are no court decisions on this subject yet.

I. Definition of Electronic Money

10   According to Art. 2(2) EMD2, electronic money 'means electronically, including magnetically, stored monetary value as represented by a claim on the issuer which is issued on receipt of funds for the purpose of making payment transactions (…), and which is accepted by a natural or legal person other than the electronic money issuer.'

1. Monetary Value

11   The term 'monetary value' is the linguistic reference point for the other features of the definition. Therefore, the term does not place a restriction on the definition of electronic money. This is reflected by Rec. 5 and 6 EMD2 which describe various forms of monetary values that are not considered to be electronic money.

12   National authorities seem to support this understanding as they assign only very limited meaning to the term 'monetary value'.[10] Legal literature does not set out requirements for 'monetary value' when defining electronic money either.[11] Sometimes, it is assumed that the term 'monetary value' presupposes a **value retention** function of

---

'The Digital Programmable Euro, Libra and CBDC: Implications for European Banks' (2020), available at https://beck-link.de/m5ehw (accessed 5.8.2020).
[7] EBA, 'Report with advice for the European Commission on crypto assets' (January 2019), 14, available at https://beck-link.de/e8dmh (accessed 16.12.2019).
[8] Ibid.
[9] HM Treasury, Financial Conduct Authority, Bank of England, 'Cryptoassets Taskforce: final report' (October 2018), 17, available at https://beck-link.de/y3syp (accessed 20.08.2021).
[10] BaFin, 'Merkblatt – Hinweise zum Zahlungsdiensteaufsichtsgesetz (ZAG)' (29.11.2017), section 4 lit. a) aa), available at https://beck-link.de/5venp (accessed 20.08.2021). According to the BaFin the term 'monetary value' encompasses any type of medium of exchange which is generally accepted as payment for certain goods and services or even only in a certain socio-cultural environment or only by the parties to a multilateral framework agreement; Financial Conduct Authority, 'Payment Services and Electronic Money – Our Approach, The FCA's role under the Payment Services Regulations 2017 and the Electronic Money Regulations 2011' (June 2019), para. 2.33, available at https://beck-link.de/3kmn3 (accessed 20.08.2021): The FCA does not display 'monetary value' as an own criterion for electronic money.
[11] Terlau, '§ 55a – Elektronisches Geld, virtuelle Währungen (Bitcoins, Ether Coins)', in Schimansky, Bunte and Lwowski (eds), *Bankrechts-Handbuch*, Vol. I (2017), § 55a, para. 11; Kubát, 'Virtual Currency Bitcoin in the Scope of Money Definition and Store of Value' (2015) 30 *Procedia Economics and Finance*,

2. Electronically Stored

According to Rec. 8 EMD2, the definition of electronic money should be '**technically neutral**'. Thus, it can be concluded that the criteria of 'electronically (…) stored' can be understood in a broad sense. Accordingly, any electronic payment scheme can be shaped as electronic money irrespective of the type and location of the storage device as long as the other criteria are met.[13]

Consequently, tokens cannot be excluded from the definition of electronic money simply because they are based on the **blockchain technology**. Transactions or tokens might not be stored on a single data carrier but rather on the servers of each full node participating in the respective blockchain (→ § 1 para. 7 et seqq.). However, even if the storage is decentral it is nonetheless 'electronic'. It is also irrelevant that each token might not be assigned to a specific person by name or by company name but 'only' by the respective public key.[14]

3. Represented by a Claim on the Issuer

In order to qualify as electronic money, the monetary value must represent a claim on the issuer. In Germany, legal scholars have argued that means of payment based on the blockchain technology can never be qualified as electronic money due to the constitutive lack of a central issuer.[15]

There is indeed no central issuer, when tokens are created by means of so-called **mining/forging** (→ § 1 para. 38) such as Bitcoins (→ § 2 para. 17 et seqq.). However, the matter is different when all tokens are already present at the initiation of the blockchain or when the tokens are 'defined' on an already existing blockchain by a **smart contract** (→ § 1 para. 62 et seqq.). Here, the initiator of the blockchain or the smart contract can be deemed 'issuer' in the sense of EMD2. In these cases, it is necessary to deal with the question whether requirements for the concrete content of the claim against the issuer can be inferred from the EMD2 and if so, what these requirements are.

According to Art. 11(2) EMD2, electronic money issuers must, upon request by the electronic money holder, redeem at any moment and at par value the monetary value

---

409 (411); De Filippi, 'Bitcoin: a regulatory nightmare to a libertarian dream' (2014) 3 *Internet Policy Review*, available at https://beck-link.de/8hexm (accessed 5.1.2021).

[12] Casper, in Casper and Terlau (eds.), ZAG, § 1, para. 16; Foerster, in *BeckOGK*, § 675c, para. 270.

[13] BaFin, 'Merkblatt – Hinweise zum Zahlungsdiensteaufsichtsgesetz (ZAG)' (29.11.2017), para. 4 lit. a) aa), available at https://beck-link.de/5venp (accessed 20.08.2021); Financial Conduct Authority, The Perimeter Guidance Manual – Guidance on the Scope of the Electronic Money Regulations (2011), Chapter 3, Question 9; Terlau, in Casper and Terlau (eds.), ZAG, § 1a, para. 44 et seqq.; Terlau, '§ 55a – Elektronisches Geld, virtuelle Währungen (Bitcoins, Ether Coins)', in Schimansky, Bunte and Lwowski (eds), *Bankrechts-Handbuch*, Vol. I (2017), § 55a, para. 15 et seqq.; Foerster, in *BeckOGK*, § 675c, para. 271; Wilusz, 'Legal determinants of electronic money systems development in European Union', in Dubiński (ed), *Prawny i ekonomiczny przegląd prawa gospodarczego* (2011), 125.

[14] According to BaFin, 'Merkblatt – Hinweise zum Zahlungsdiensteaufsichtsgesetz (ZAG)' (29.11.2017), para. 4 lit. a) aa), available at https://beck-link.de/5venp (accessed 20.08.2021), it is irrelevant whether the name of the customer is recorded.

[15] Omlor, 'E-Geld im reformierten Zahlungsdiensterecht' (2017) 35 *Zeitschrift für Wirtschaftsrecht*, 1836 (1838); Möslein and Omlor, 'Die europäische Agenda für innovative Finanztechnologien (FinTech)' (2018) 18 *Zeitschrift für Bank- und Kapitalmarktrecht*, 236 (243); Omlor, 'Blockchain-basierte Zahlungsmittel – Ein Arbeitsprogramm für Gesetzgeber und Rechtswissenschaft' (2018) 51 *Zeitschrift für Rechtspolitik*, 85 et seqq.

of the electronic money held. German scholars have therefore argued that tokens are not electronic money if the issuer does not stipulate that the tokens be exchanged back into legal currency at a **fixed rate**.[16] This view is to be countered by the fact that Art. 11(2) EMD2 does not establish the criteria of electronic money but rather the legal consequences if a monetary value constitutes electronic money. The issuer of tokens cannot escape their qualification as electronic money by contractually excluding the right of redemption – provided that all other criteria are met.

18 If the qualification of a token as electronic money is to be made conditional on the content of the claim against which it is issued, such must be determined according to the regulatory purpose of Art. 11 EMD2. According to Rec. 18 EMD2, electronic money must be redeemable in order to 'preserve the confidence of the electronic money holder'. The object of this confidence results from the criteria 'execution of payment transactions' (→ para. 27 et seqq.) and **third-party acceptance** (→ para. 29). The issuer of electronic money 'promises' that such electronic money can be used as an effective means of payment not only with himself but also with third parties. People will only use electronic money if they have confidence in this promise.

19 Hence, tokens can only be qualified as electronic money if they are intended to be used as a means of payment with third parties as a replacement for cash or scriptural money on the basis of the legal relationship between the token holder and the issuer (i.e. the **claim embodied in the monetary value**). In these cases, the contractual exclusion of the right of redemption – for example in general terms and conditions – does not prevent the monetary value from qualifying as electronic money.

4. Receipt of Funds

20 The claim must have been issued on a receipt of funds, i.e. an amount in cash, scriptural money or electronic money. Hence, the term 'funds' covers not only legal currency, but also any privately issued means of payment which in turn qualify as electronic money under EMD2.

21 Legal currency in this sense is not only the Euro but are also foreign currencies of countries outside the Euro area and the European Union. Payments in **foreign currencies**, such as the US dollar, constitute a receipt of funds. It is true that Art. 128 (1)(3) TFEU stipulates that only banknotes issued by the European Central Bank and the national central banks are legal currency in the EU. However, this is only to emphasise that, due to the transfer of monetary sovereignty to the European Union, the member states whose currency is the Euro have lost the competence to define their legal currency independently.[17] The purpose of Art. 128 TFEU is to extend the competences of the European Union and not to restrict the scope of application of the European payment services law.

---

[16] Shmatenko and Möllenkamp, 'Digitale Zahlungsmittel in einer analog geprägten Rechtsordnung – A bit(coin) out of control – Legal nature and contractual treatment of crypto-currencies' (2018) 21 *Zeitschrift für IT-Recht und Recht der Digitalisierung*, 495 et seq.; Köndgen, in *BeckOGK*, § 675c, para. 135; Auffenberg, 'E-Geld auf Blockchain-Basis' (2019) 19 *Zeitschrift für Bank- und Kapitalmarktrecht*, 341 et seqq.; similar to Omlor, 'Electronic Money in the Reformed Payment Services Law' (2017) 35 *Zeitschrift für Wirtschaftsrecht*, 1836 (1838), who therefore considers electronic money to be scriptural money with electronic storage. In contrast to the German provision Section 33 (1) of the Payment Services Supervision Act ('Zahlungsdiensteaufsichtsgesetz – ZAG'), Art. 11(2) EMD2 does not explicitly state that the redemption must be made in legal currency. However, it can be assumed that EMD2 must also be understood in this way. Cf. also Rec. 45 MiCAR Draft which explicitly addresses the redemption in fiat currency.

[17] Papaschalis, in von der Groeben, Schwarze and Hatje (eds.), *Europäisches Unionsrecht*, Art. 128, para. 45.

§ 9. E-Money Tokens, Stablecoins, and Token Payment Services

For an **ICO** (→ § 1 para. 81) tokens may be issued against payment of **currency tokens** such as Bitcoin or Ether. These currency tokens are not 'funds' in the terms of EMD2 as they neither qualify as legal currency nor fulfil all the requirements of electronic money (→ para. 34 et seqq.). Consequently, tokens issued solely against payment of currency tokens cannot be electronic money. However, tokens can still constitute electronic money if one part of the tokens is paid in legal currency – it is therefore: all or none. Even if part of the tokens were not issued on the receipt of funds, this does not alter the fact that the issuer is subject to the prudential supervision according to Title II of EMD2 (provided that the other criteria of electronic money are fulfilled). Furthermore, treating only some part of tokens from the same ICO as electronic money would result in legal uncertainty. This is all the truer since – depending on the technical design of the ICO – not every single token is necessarily individually identifiable (cf. the serial number on the banknote). Often only a certain amount of a defined total number of tokens is allocated to an individual public key (cf. the balance of a bank account). 22

Finally, it makes sense that the issuer cannot avoid the qualification as electronic money by only accepting currency tokens, but at the same time instigating the 'buyer' to make use of a third-party service provider with whom he pays the corresponding amount in euros and the provider delivers the corresponding amount directly to the issuer in currency tokens. This is because EMD2 does not stipulate that the payment of the amount of money must be made directly to the issuer.[18] 23

5. Issuance

In order to be considered electronic money, monetary values must be issued on the receipt of funds. The German BaFin denies the qualification of Bitcoin as electronic money, inter alia, arguing that Bitcoin is not 'issued' on the receipt of funds, but rather 'created in computer networks without **consideration**'.[19] 24

Such a narrow understanding of the term to the effect that the act of creation itself must take place in return for the payment of a sum of money would mean that most tokens would not qualify as electronic money just for this reason. The 'creation' of any type of tokens takes place without consideration (i.e. an amount of money). This applies not only to tokens that – like Bitcoins – are created by **mining** but usually also to tokens that are defined by a **smart contract** and then assigned (either by the issuer or another smart contract) to a specific address or public key on the respective blockchain. 25

However, it is doubtful that BaFin intended to imply such a far-reaching exclusion of all other tokens from the electronic money concept with its statement on Bitcoin. This is because not only the 'creation' of Bitcoins but also their attribution to a certain public key is without consideration when mining Bitcoin. To exclude tokens in general from the definition of electronic money on the basis of a mere technicality would also contradict the openness to technological development called for in Rec. 8 EMD2. 26

6. Purpose of Making Payment Transactions

In order to qualify as electronic money, the monetary values must be issued for the 'purpose of making payment transactions'. According to Art. 4(5) PSD2, 'payment 27

---

[18] Cf. Terlau, '§ 55a – Elektronisches Geld, virtuelle Währungen (Bitcoins, Ether Coins)', in Schimansky, Bunte and Lwowski (eds.), *Bankrechts-Handbuch*, Vol. I (2017), § 55a, para. 28.
[19] BaFin, 'Merkblatt – Hinweise zum Zahlungsdiensteaufsichtsgesetz (ZAG)' (29.11.2017), para. 4 lit. a) aa), available at https://beck-link.de/5venp (accessed 20.08.2021).

transaction' means an act (...) of placing, transferring, or withdrawing funds'.[20] Pursuant to Art. 4(25) PSD2, 'funds' are banknotes and coins, scriptural money or electronic money (→ para. 5). Therefore, the criteria 'payment transaction' refers to the very same concept that it is actually intended to define (in both cases: electronic money). It is therefore appropriate to refer only to the act of **transaction** (i.e. provision, transmission or withdrawal) rather than its object (i.e. the funds) when defining electronic money.[21]

28   According to literature, it should also be irrelevant whether the unit of **value is negotiable**, i.e. can be used countless times, or whether the unit of value, once issued, can only be used for a single payment transaction.[22] This is relevant for tokens since, consequently, a so-called 'burning' (→ § 1 para. 6; § 7) cannot prevent the qualification as electronic money provided the other criteria are fulfilled.

7. Acceptance by a Third Party

29   The definition of electronic money furthermore presupposes that the monetary value is 'accepted by a natural or legal person other than the electronic money issuer'. According to BaFin, also parent companies, their subsidiaries or a franchise head office and its franchisees can be deemed **third parties**. Also, several persons jointly issuing a monetary value can at the same time act as acceptors.[23] The reason that two-person relationships are excluded from the scope of EMD2 is the comparatively lower risk for payment transactions in the event of issuer default.[24]

8. Exemptions for Certain Instruments and Payment Transactions

30   According to Art. 1(4) and (5) EMD2, the regulation of electronic money does not apply to monetary values stored on instruments exempted as specified in Art. 3(k) PSD2 and to monetary value that is used to make payment transactions as specified in Art. 3(l) PSD2.

31   **a) Storage on instruments pursuant to Art. 3(k) PSD2.** The exemption in Art. 3(k) PSD2 refers to 'instruments allowing the holder to acquire goods or services only in the premises of the issuer or within a limited network of service providers under direct commercial agreement with a professional issuer'. Examples for such instruments in the context of 'normal' payment transactions are **debit and credit cards** and the entire transaction process in online banking.[25]

32   It can be assumed that the exemption may also apply to tokens. This is because the blockchain, on which the tokens are stored, enables payment orders to be issued via the key pair of a private and a public key. The pair of a private and a public key (where applicable in conjunction with one or more smart contracts) also serves

---

[20] The EMD2 refers to the predecessor provision in PSD1, which is however identical in wording to the current provision in PSD2.
[21] Accordingly, the BaFin defines the payment transaction in the context of the definition of electronic money as any transfer of monetary assets from the customer to the acceptor. BaFin, 'Merkblatt - Hinweise zum Zahlungsdiensteaufsichtsgesetz (ZAG)' (29.11.2017), para. 4 lit. a) aa), fn. 108, available at https://beck-link.de/5venp (accessed 20.08.2021).
[22] Terlau, '§ 55a - Elektronisches Geld, virtuelle Währungen (Bitcoins, Ether Coins)', in Schimansky, Bunte and Lwowski (eds), *Bankrechts-Handbuch*, Vol. I (2017), § 55a, para. 30.
[23] BaFin, 'Merkblatt - Hinweise zum Zahlungsdiensteaufsichtsgesetz (ZAG)' (29.11.2017), section 4 lit. a) aa), available at https://beck-link.de/5venp (accessed 20.08.2021); also: Terlau, '§ 55a - Elektronisches Geld, virtuelle Währungen (Bitcoins, Ether Coins)', in Schimansky, Bunte and Lwowski (eds), *Bankrechts-Handbuch*, Vol. I (2017), § 55a, para. 32 et seq.
[24] Terlau, '§ 55a - Elektronisches Geld, virtuelle Währungen (Bitcoins, Ether Coins)', in Schimansky, Bunte and Lwowski (eds.), *Bankrechts-Handbuch*, Vol. I (2017), § 55a, para. 32.
[25] Casper, in Casper and Terlau (eds.), *ZAG*, § 1, para. 41 et seq.

as **identification and verification** of the person who is entitled to initiate the transaction and is therefore quite comparable to a payment instrument such as a credit card.

b) Use for Payment Transactions pursuant to Art. 3(l) PSD2. The exemption in Art. 3(l) PSD2 refers to 'payment transactions by a provider of electronic communications networks or services provided in addition to electronic communications services for a subscriber to the network or service (i) for purchase of digital content and voice-based services, regardless of the device used for the purchase or consumption of the digital content and charged to the related bill; or (ii) performed from or via an electronic device and charged to the related bill within the framework of a charitable activity or for the purchase of tickets'. As the exemption is limited to a very specific group of products and services, it is not likely to become relevant for many business models using tokens. Furthermore, the exception is subject to low maximum amounts (EUR 50 per transaction and EUR 500 per month and customer). 33

II. Classification of Currency Tokens

Even if the term currency token is understood as tokens whose main function is the 'use as a means of payment' (→ para. 7), tokens such as **Bitcoin**, **Ether** or **Ripple** do not qualify as electronic money or funds. While currency tokens can regularly be deemed a monetary value stored electronically and are accepted by third parties in terms of the definition of electronic money, currency tokens usually lack a central issuer because they are created by so-called forging/mining (→ § 1 para. 80). Hence, currency token are not 'issued' but 'created' in computer networks. Furthermore, the 'value' of currency tokens is not based on a claim (i.e., casually spoken, a monetary promise from whomever) but on the factual circumstance[26] that the other participants of the respective blockchain assign a certain value to the token (→ § 1 para. 70). 34

Currently, European law does not regulate currency tokens but they will qualify as **crypto assets** under the upcoming European framework for markets in crypto assets which will be based on the MiCAR (→ para. 51 et seqq.). 35

III. Classification of Stablecoins

Stablecoins[27] (→ § 1 para. 76; § 2 para. 74 et seqq.) are digital tokens whose values are pegged to an existing currency or basket of currencies, commodities or other crypto assets in order to maintain a stable value.[28] Although still and constantly evolving, there are in general three different categories of stablecoins: asset-backed stablecoins, 36

---

[26] Cf. also Gikay, 'Regulating decentralized cryptocurrencies under payment services law: Lessons from European Union Law.' (2019) 10 *Journal of Law, Technology & the Internet*, 1 (21); Vardi, 'Bit by Bit: Assessing the Legal Nature of Virtual Currencies', in Gimigliano (ed.), *Bitcoin and Mobile Payments. Constructing a European Union Framework* (2016), 55 et seqq.

[27] Deutsche Bundesbank, 'Monthly Report July 2019' (July 2019), 43 et seq., available at https://beck-link.de/p7vmk (accessed 20.08.2021); Bank for International Settlements, 'G7 Working Group on Stablecoins, Investigating the impact of global stablecoins' (October 2019), available at https://beck-link.de/czeb3 (accessed 6.8.2020); Financial Conduct Authority, 'Guidance on Cryptoassets, Feedback and Final Guidance to CP 19/3, PS19/22' (July 2019), para. 3.12, 18, available at https://beck-link.de/86rff (accessed 20.08.2021); StableCoin Index, available at https://beck-link.de/7r56p (accessed 6.8.2020).

[28] Wharton Blockchain and Digital Asset Project, DeFi Beyond the Hype – The Emerging World of Decentralized Finance (May 2021), 3, available at https://beck-link.de/mkzd8 (accessed 31.5.2021).

algorithmic stablecoins and custodial or centralized stablecoins.[29] "**Algorithmic stablecoins** attempt to maintain the peg through dynamic expansion and contraction of token supply."[30] "**Asset-backed stablecoins** use smart contracts to assemble and liquidate collateral in the form of cryptocurrencies or other assets."[31] Whereby, also custodial stablecoins are often referred to as asset-backed stablecoins. **Custodial stablecoins** may as well be issued as asset-backed tokens being covered by a certain amount of collateral or reserve in fiat currencies such as the US Dollar or the Euro or other high-quality assets such as gold as the underlying (→ § 1 para. 75 et seqq.). These custodial stablecoins are mostly used for payments. The commitment to a legal currency as the equivalent value is achieved by the issuer's promise to exchange the respective tokens back at the nominal value into a legal currency. This fulfils the requirement for electronic money being 'represented by a claim on the issuer'. Provided that such stablecoins also meet the other parts of the definition (in particular that of third-party acceptance), they would qualify as electronic money (→ para. 10).[32]

37 However, in many instances the issuer does not guarantee for the conversion of the stablecoins into legal currency.[33] This circumstance does not necessarily preclude their qualification as electronic money (→ para. 17). The plans of the **Libra Association**, which was renamed on December 1, 2020 to **Diem Association**, have stimulated a lively discussion and attracted most of the regulators' attention on the topic of stablecoins and the regulatory frameworks around them.[34] The mission of Libra (renamed to 'Diem') is 'a simple global payment system and financial infrastructure that empowers billions of people'.[35] The Diem Association is a consortium consisting of Facebook and other companies such as the major platform providers Spotify and Uber. Together they want to issue the **stablecoin 'Diem'** (formerly known as '**Libra**') which is to be used for payment processing in digital networks or e.g. also in messenger services.[36] For each

---

[29] Wharton Blockchain and Digital Asset Project, DeFi Beyond the Hype – The Emerging World of Decentralized Finance (May 2021), 9, available at https://beck-link.de/mkzd8 (accessed 31.5.2021).

[30] Wharton Blockchain and Digital Asset Project, DeFi Beyond the Hype – The Emerging World of Decentralized Finance (May 2021), 9, available at https://beck-link.de/mkzd8 (accessed 31.5.2021).

[31] Wharton Blockchain and Digital Asset Project, DeFi Beyond the Hype – The Emerging World of Decentralized Finance (May 2021), 9, available at https://beck-link.de/mkzd8 (accessed 31.5.2021).
One popular example of a crypto-collateralized stablecoin is Dai, which is built on the Ethereum blockchain and issued by MakerDAO, an open-source project on the Ethereum blockchain and a Decentralized Autonomous Organization created in 2014. The project is managed by people around the world who hold MakerDAO governance token, so called MKR. 'Through a system of scientific governance involving Executive Voting and Governance Polling, MKR holders manage the Maker Protocol and the financial risks of Dai to ensure its stability, transparency, and efficiency'. 'The Dai stablecoin is a decentralized, unbiased, collateral-backed cryptocurrency soft-pegged to the US Dollar. Users generate Dai by depositing collateral assets into Maker Vaults within the Maker Protocol. Every Dai in circulation is directly backed by excess collateral, meaning that the value of the collateral is higher than the value of the Dai debt, and all Dai transactions are publicly viewable on the Ethereum blockchain'. 'To generate Dai, the Maker Protocol accepts as collateral any Ethereum-based asset that has been approved by MKR holders', such as Ether – MakerDAO, 'The Dai Stablecoin', MakerDAO, 'The Maker Protocol: MakerDAO's Multi-Collateral Dai (MCD) System', available at https://beck-link.de/tk5bf (accessed 6.8.2020).

[32] Financial Conduct Authority, 'Guidance on Cryptoassets, Feedback and Final Guidance to CP 19/3, PS19/22' (July 2019), Chapter 3.12, Appendix 1 No. 71, available at https://beck-link.de/86rff (accessed 20.08.2021).

[33] Deutsche Bundesbank, 'Monthly Report July 2019' (July 2019), 44, available at https://beck-link.de/p7vmk (accessed 20.08.2021).

[34] Sandner, Gross, Grale and Schulden, 'The Digital Programmable Euro, Libra and CBDC: Implications for European Banks' (2020), available at https://beck-link.de/m5ehw (accessed 5.8.2020).

[35] Diem Association, The Diem mission, available at https://beck-link.de/4nabf (accessed 10.1.2021).

[36] Diem Association, 'Whitepaper v2.0, Cover letter' (April 2020), available at https://beck-link.de/6nnnk (accessed 10.1.2021); Deutsche Bundesbank, 'Monthly Report July 2019' (July 2019), 44, available at https://beck-link.de/p7vmk (accessed 20.08.2021).

newly created Libra Coin,[37] a basket consisting of bank deposits and short-term government bonds will be used as security or rather as a reserve of real assets – the 'Libra Reserve' – to build confidence in the intrinsic value.[38] The Diem Association (now the Diem Networks SARL) had filed an application for a payment system license in Switzerland with the Swiss FINMA in April 2020. The Diem Networks SARL has withdrawn the application in the meantime in May 2021. The Diem Group plans to launch the payment system from the USA in a first phase and for the time being will focus on US participants.[39]

In the public discussions several stakeholders had raised their concerns with regard to the initial Libra project, a multi-currency Coin (LBR) having the potential to interfere with the monetary sovereignty and monetary policy of a country. The Diem Association reacted and envisioned not only a multi-currency Diem Coin, but also single-currency stablecoins (e.g. USD, EUR, GBP, etc.). According to the Diem Association, 'each single-currency stablecoin will be supported by a Reserve of cash or cash-equivalents and very short-term government securities denominated in that currency and issued by the home country of that currency. Single-currency stablecoins will only be minted and burned in response to market demand for that coin. Because of the 1:1 backing of each coin, this approach would not result in new net money creation'. The different Diem Coins are supposed to be accepted in many places by multiple third parties and are easy to access for their users.[40] The Diem Association stressed that a Diem Coin cannot always be exchanged for the same amount of a particular local currency. 'The Libra network would not itself provide for, record, or settle conversions between Libra Coins and fiat currency or other digital assets; instead, any such exchange functionality would be conducted by third-party financial service providers.'[41] Except the element of 'claim against the issuer', Libra or Diem fulfils the requirements of electronic money (→ para. 10). It represents a digital currency which can also be acquired against payment of an amount of money in order to carry out payment transactions which are used not only against the Diem Association but also against as many third parties as possible. The non-guaranteed conversion into a legal currency does not automatically exclude Diem's qualification as electronic money (→ para. 17). **38**

Given the variety of asset-backed tokens covered under the term 'stablecoin', the EU legislators have envisioned a **bespoke regime for crypto assets** in order to establish harmonised requirements at EU level which will be implemented by **MiCAR**. The MiCAR also contains requirements on stablecoin issuers that do not (yet) qualify as electronic money issuers. **39**

Apart from privately issued stablecoins, central banks also assess the introduction of digital currencies issued by a central bank, so-called **Central Bank Digital Currencies** (CBDC). For example, the European Central Bank (ECB) assesses the introduction and possible scope of Euro CBDC, including 'the possible issuance of a retail CBDC available to the general public (households and businesses) while safeguarding the legal currency of euro cash'.[42] As expressed in the Digital Finance Strategy, the European Commission **40**

---

[37] As the Whitepaper v2.0 of the Diem Association still refers to Libra after the renaming to Diem, the following statements hereinafter accordingly contain references to Libra until an update of the Whitepaper will be available.
[38] Diem Association, 'Whitepaper v2.0, Cover letter' (April 2020), section 4, available at https://beck-link.de/6nnnk (accessed 10.1.2021).
[39] FINMA, Diem withdraws licence application in Switzerland (12.5.2021), available at https://beck-link.de/mb74n (accessed 24.5.2021).
[40] Ibid.
[41] Ibid.
[42] Bindseil, 'Tiered CBDC and the financial system' (January 2020), ECB Working Paper No. 2351, available at https://beck-link.de/yen3s (accessed 4.3.2021); Sandner, Gross, Grale and Schulden, 'The

supports the work by central banks (in particular the ECB),[43] which complements the Commission's proposed regulatory framework on asset-referenced tokens used for payment purposes.[44] However, the 'potential impacts of CBDC on monetary policy, financial stability and competition, and to avoid undue disintermediation'[45] will need to be further assessed in order to provide a sound framework for CBDC.

IV. Classification of Investment Tokens

41 The ownership of **investment tokens** usually results in **participation rights in future profits** of the issuer, in claims to fixed payments or in co-determination rights (→ § 1 para. 71). An investment token presupposes the existence of an issuer who issues the token in return for a claim against himself. Investment tokens might, therefore, be considered **financial instruments** under MiFID2.

42 However, investment tokens in general have no payment function. Therefore, investment tokens usually do not represent a 'monetary value', i.e. any kind of means of payment. In any case, they are not intended to be used in a payment transaction.

V. Classification of Utility Tokens

43 Most **utility tokens** that have been issued so far have represented a 'claim' for a certain **good or service** against the issuer. The holder can redeem the token at the issuing company for the goods or services associated with the token. In this regard, the utility token is often used as a **means of payment** between the token holder and the issuer to pay for certain goods or services within a specific business model. The monetary value embodied in the utility token is to be transferred from one person to another. For the classification of the respective utility token as electronic money, the characteristics of third-party acceptance and representation by a claim on the issuer are decisive.

44 Utility tokens that are supposed to serve as a 'means of payment' only between the issuer and the token holder do not qualify as electronic money. Utility token will usually be used towards and accepted by a third party in business models that are not limited to the development and provision of services, but also entail the creation of a marketplace or platform for these services.

45 Consequently, the majority of utility tokens does not qualify as electronic money. The European Commission considers this a lack of regulation and wants to include utility tokens in the MiCAR to ensure consumer protection.[46] Whereby the council suggested to exclude utility tokens.[47]

VI. Hybrid Tokens

46 The term '**hybrid token**' is not clearly defined. It may be used for the digital representation of rights that combine one or more core functions of an investment

---

Digital Programmable Euro, Libra and CBDC: Implications for European Banks' (2020), available at https://beck-link.de/m5ehw (accessed 5.8.2020).

[43] European Commission, 'Digital Finance Strategy' (Communication) COM(2020) 591 final, 10.
[44] European Commission, 'Retail Payments Strategy for the EU' (Communication) COM(2020) 592 final, 14.
[45] Ibid.
[46] Cf. European Commission, 'Digital Finance Strategy' (Communication) COM(2020) 591 final, 9.
[47] Council of the European Union, Working Paper MiCA: Revised Presidency compromise proposal 19.5.2021 (WK 6646/2021 INIT, 2020/0265 (COD)), recital 8b.

token with a payment or utility function. These could be, for instance, tokens that **finance a business model** by participating the investor economically and being a payment for certain services of the issuer or a third party at the same time.

In regard to the regulatory classification of such hybrid tokens, it must be detected on a case-by-case basis which function predominantly shapes them or on which functions the focus of the respective hybrid token lies. 47

According to Art. 4(44) MiFID2, 'instruments of payment' are expressly excluded from the definition of 'transferable securities' (→ § 7 para. 69). Hybrid tokens with a predominant payment function, even though not necessarily qualifying as an instrument of payment in the sense of MiFID2, would in principle not be considered securities, provided that the investment component is only linked to the performance of the token, e.g. due to increasing market penetration and recognition as a private means of payment. Such hybrid tokens with an emphasis on a function as currency token (→ para. 34) will be regulated by MiCAR (→ para. 54 et seqq.). 48

Transferable hybrid tokens with a **predominant investment component** (i.e. the token holder is provided with membership rights or contractual claims to assets comparable to those of a shareholder or holder of a debt instrument, → § 1 para. 71) qualify as transferable securities in terms of MiFID2. Such hybrid tokens would be outside the scope of MiCAR according to Art. 2(2)(a) MiCAR Draft (→ para. 52). At the same time, they will regularly not be classified as electronic money. This is because the value of the token derives precisely from the holder's participation in the loss and profit of a company and not its usability as a means of payment or exchange. Hybrid tokens with a predominant investment component represent a company value and not a monetary value such as electronic money (→ para. 10). So, from a regulatory perspective, there will be no room for hybrid tokens, as they would be deemed securities under MiFID2, if they fulfil the requirements of a transferable security, even though they might in addition provide a payment or utility functionality. 49

D. Stablecoins, E-Money Tokens and Utility Tokens under MiCAR

As outlined above some **crypto assets** might already qualify as e-money (→ para. 10 et seqq.), whereas the majority of crypto assets, such as crypto currencies, stablecoins and utility tokens, fall – beyond EU legislation aimed at combating money laundering and terrorism financing (→ § 10 para. 9 et seqq.) – outside the scope of EU legislation for payments or financial services (Rec. 3 MiCAR Draft). In order to provide legal clarity and certainty to promote the safe development of crypto assets and the use of distributed ledger technology (DLT) not only for financial services but also for alternative payment instruments based on DLT, the EU Commission introduced a **harmonised framework for crypto assets** based primarily on the **Regulation on Markets in Crypto-Assets** (Rec. 4 MiCAR Draft). The MiCAR framework intends to 'support innovation and fair competition, while ensuring a high level of consumer protection and market integrity in crypto asset markets' (Rec. 5 MiCAR Draft). With this framework, the EU legislators further intend to 'ensure financial stability and address monetary policy risks that could arise from crypto assets that aim at stabilising their price by referencing a currency, an asset or a basket of such' (Rec. 5 MiCAR Draft). There is no definite timeline for the final MiCAR yet. The final version will be issued after the trilog procedures between Commission, EP and Council.[48] 50

---

[48] Berichterstatter Report Council 2 paper.

I. Scope of the Markets in Crypto-Assets Regulation

51   Art. 2(1) MiCAR Draft applies to persons that are engaged in the **issuance of crypto assets** or provide **services related to crypto assets** (crypto asset service providers → § 8 para. 56) in the EU. The term '**crypto asset**' is defined in Art. (3)(1)(2) MiCAR Draft as 'a digital representation of value or rights which may be transferred and stored electronically, using distributed ledger technology or similar technology'. In order to keep pace with the technological developments and the constantly evolving innovations in the DLT and crypto assets space, this definition is as broad as possible to capture all types of crypto assets that were falling outside the scope of European financial services law (Rec. 8 MiCAR Draft). For three sub-categories of crypto assets the MiCAR Draft contains more specific requirements, namely for **utility tokens** (→ para. 64), **asset-referenced tokens** (→ para. 56 et seqq.) and **e-money tokens** (→ para. 58 et seqq.).

52   Pursuant to Art. 2(2)(a) MiCAR Draft, the Regulation would not apply to crypto assets that qualify as **financial instruments** under MiFID2 (→ § 7 para. 92). Thus, investment tokens lie outside the scope of MiCAR as they are already covered by EU financial services laws. Further, e-money already regulated under EMD2 lies outside the scope of MiCAR unless such electronic money qualifies as e-money token as per Art. 2 (2)(b) MiCAR Draft. Crypto assets that qualify as deposits and structured deposits or securitisation would also not be covered by the proposal, according to Art. 2(2)(c)-(e) MiCAR Draft, as specific EU regulation already exists.

53   Art. 2(3)(a) MiCAR Draft will neither apply to central banks and their **central bank digital currencies** nor to services related to such CBDC provided by such central banks (Rec. 7 MiCAR Draft, → para. 7). Whereas services provided by other market participants related to CBDC would qualify them as crypto asset service providers.

II. Currency Tokens as Crypto-Assets under MiCAR

54   Currency Tokens such as Bitcoin or Ether would qualify as crypto assets according to Art. 3(1)(2) MiCAR Draft.

III. Stablecoins under MiCAR

55   MiCAR distinguishes between three different types of crypto assets that are commonly discussed under the term '**stablecoins**'. However, the term 'stablecoin' itself is not mentioned in the MiCAR except for 'algorithmic stablecoins'. In light of this, MiCAR introduces the new terms of (**significant**) **asset-referenced token** (→ para. 56) and (**significant**) **e-money token** (→ para. 58) as well as **algorithmic stablecoins**. Depending on the qualification of the respective crypto asset as asset-referenced token, e-money token or algorithmic stablecoin different regulatory requirements will apply.

1. (Significant) Asset-Referenced Tokens

56   An **asset-referenced token** is defined as 'a type of crypto asset that purports to maintain a stable value by referring to the value of several fiat currencies that are legal currency, one or several commodities or one or several crypto assets, or a combination of such assets', Art. 3(1)(3) MiCAR Draft. The term 'referring' shall indicate that an asset-referenced token is actually 'backed' by the respective kind of reference assets

(Rec. 37 MiCAR Draft). An example for an asset-referenced token would be the Maker stablecoin **Dai**[49] (→ para. 36). Although Dai is soft-pegged to the US Dollar (1 Dai = 1 USD) and might be considered as 'referring' to the value of only one fiat currency and not several, Dai would not qualify as e-money token as per Art. 3(1)(4) MiCAR Draft (→ para. 58 et seqq.) as they are not issued on receipt of funds (→ para. 20 et seqq.). As Dai are generated or issued by depositing Ethereum-based assets (e.g. Ether) as collateral that have been approved by MKR holders, they would qualify as asset-referenced tokens under MiCAR.

Some asset-referenced tokens have the potential to become widely adopted by users as a means of exchange. Depending on the criteria set out in Art. 39(1) MiCAR such as the size of the customer base of the promoters of asset-referenced tokens or the shareholders of the issuer, a potential high market capitalization, high payment transaction volumes, the size of the reserve of assets (→ para. 112), the significance of cross-border activities or the interconnectedness to the financial system, some asset-referenced tokens might raise challenges regarding monetary sovereignty or financial stability (Rec. 51 MiCAR Draft). Such asset-referenced tokens might then be classified as **significant asset-referenced tokens** with additional and more stringent regulatory requirements than for asset-referenced tokens. A prominent example for such a significant asset-referenced token would be the Diem Coin (→ para. 37 et seqq.). 57

2. (Significant) E-Money Tokens

According to Art. 3(1)(4) MiCAR '**electronic money token**' or '**e-money token**' is a type of crypto asset the main purpose of which is to be used as a means of exchange and that purports to maintain a stable value by referring to the value of a fiat currency that is legal tender. Apparently, the definition of e-money tokens in the MiCAR contains fewer criteria than the definition of electronic money in the EMD2. Therefore, Art. 44 MiCAR Draft, by derogation of Art. 11 EMD2, regulates which requirements regarding the issuance and redeemability of e-money tokens shall apply to their issuers. 58

The criterion 'to be used as a **means of exchange**' in MiCAR is basically comparable to the criterion 'purpose of making payment transactions' in the EMD2. The scope of 'means of exchange' is considerably broader, however, because unlike a 'payment transaction' it does not presuppose the use of funds, i.e. money in the traditional sense (→ para. 5 et seqq.), for the transaction. However, the compelling link of e-money tokens to money in the traditional sense results from the prerequisite that they must refer to the value of a fiat currency that is legal tender in order to purport to maintain a stable value. It is questionable to what extent a restriction of the term results from the presupposed purpose of **value stability**. For a token to be used as an effective medium of exchange, it must typically also be stable in value. 59

In comparison to EMD2, e-money tokens encompass exclusively **crypto assets**, i.e. tokens using 'distributed ledger technology or similar technology' as per Art. 3(1)(4) MiCAR Draft for storage. As a result, it can be assumed that the term e-money token under the MiCAR includes all tokens that currently qualify as electronic money tokens under the EMD2. This is in line with the purpose of the Regulation. According to Rec. 10 MiCAR any definition of e-money tokens 'should be as wide as possible to capture all the types of crypto assets referencing one single fiat currency that is **legal tender**' in order to 'avoid circumvention of the rules laid down in the EMD2'. 60

---

[49] MakerDAO, 'The Maker Protocol: MakerDAO's Multi-Collateral Dai (MCD) System', 'The Dai StableCoin', available at https://beck-link.de/b64b6 (accessed 6.8.2020); Grigo, Hansen, Patz and Wachter, 'Decentralized Finance (DeFi) – A new Fintech Revolution? The Blockchain Trend explained' (2020), 11, available at https://beck-link.de/xa2xn (accessed 3.10.2020).

61   E-money tokens with a particularly large distribution can be classified as 'significant' by the EBA according to Art. 50 et. seq. MiCAR Draft, with the consequence that additional supervisory requirements apply (→ para. 116). The requirements for the classification of e-money tokens as 'significant' correspond to those for the corresponding classification of asset-referenced tokens (→ para. 113).

3. Algorithmic Stablecoins

62   In general, **algorithmic stablecoins** which may be pegged to a fiat currency achieve their pegging by **algorithms** and **smart contracts** (→ para. 36) that manage the increase or decrease of the supply of the tokens issued, without being backed by a fiat currency or cryptocurrency.[50] If the price of an algorithmic stablecoin would fall below the price of the fiat currency it tracks, the smart contract and the implemented algorithm would reduce the token supply. Vice versa, if the price of the algorithmic stablecoin would be higher than the price of the fiat currency it is pegged, new algorithmic stablecoins would be issued in order to reduce the value of the stablecoin.[51]

63   MiCAR refers to algorithmic stablecoins as 'stablecoins that aim at maintaining a stable value, via protocols, that provide for the increase or decrease of the supply of such crypto assets in response to changes in demand' (Rec. 26 MiCAR Draft). Such algorithmic stablecoins should not be considered as asset-referenced tokens (→ para. 56 et seqq.), provided that they do not aim at stabilising their value by referencing one or several other assets (Rec. 26 MiCAR Draft). In this regard, the term 'referencing' would as well indicate, as the term 'referring' (→ para. 56) does, that a stablecoin would need to be actually backed by other assets. Instead, algorithmic stablecoins which achieve their pegging only by algorithms and smart contracts would qualify as crypto assets (→ para. 51) and not as asset-referenced tokens or e-money tokens.

IV. Utility Tokens under MiCAR

64   The proposal of a EU framework for markets in crypto assets MiCAR also contains a legal definition for **utility tokens** (→ para. 43 et seqq.). According to Art. 3(1)(5) MiCAR Draft, a utility token is defined as 'a type of crypto asset which is intended to provide digital access to a good or service, available on DLT, and is only accepted by the issuer of that token'.

E. Payment Services in connection with Token Business Models

I. Basic Objectives of the Services Directive

65   Annex I PSD2, as referred to in Art. 4(3) PSD2, lists the **payment services** regulated under PSD2, such as services enabling cash to be placed on a payment account (No. 1) or enabling cash withdrawals (No. 2) as well as all the operations required for operating

---

[50] Some examples of algorithmic stablecoin projects, which are no longer operating, with stablecoins pegged to the US Dollar 1:1, were Carbon and Basis: Al-Naji, Chen and Diao, 'Basis: A Price-Stable Cryptocurrency with an Algorithmic Central Bank' (2018), available at https://beck-link.de/b8256 (accessed 3.10.2020); Binance Academy, 'What Are Stablecoins?', available at https://beck-link.de/y2srt (accessed 3.10.2020).

[51] Binance Academy, 'What Are Stablecoins?', available at https://beck-link.de/y2srt (accessed 3.10.2020).

a payment account; the execution of payment transactions (No. 3 and 4), the acquiring of payment transactions (No. 5) or money remittance (No. 6).

In principle, a payment service takes place in a three-party relationship between the payer, the payee and the payment service provider whereby a payment service provider normally acquires possession of customer funds. The only exceptions are the payment initiation service pursuant to Art. 4(15) PSD2 and the account information service pursuant to Art. 4(16) PSD2 where the payment service provider never comes into possession of customer funds.

One main objective of the PSD2 is the supervision of payment service providers to ensure the proper execution of payment services in order to foster an integrated internal market for safe electronic payments since a payment service provider moves third-party funds or funds entrusted to him by his payment service users (Rec. 5–7 MiCAR Draft). Institutional supervision of payment service providers therefore aims to ensure the functioning of electronic payment transactions and to strengthen the confidence of payment service users in the proper functioning of those transactions (Rec. 6 MiCAR Draft).

II. General Conditions for Payment Services

1. Three-Party Relationship

Art. 1(2)(b) PSD2 only regulates the respective rights and obligations of payment service users and payment service providers in relation to the provision of payment services. This means that only the relationship between the **payer** and their **payment service provider** and the relationship between the **payee** and their payment service provider is regulated by the PSD2 and not the respective legal relationship between the payer and the payee.

If one assumes the basic idea of a Bitcoin transaction (→ para. 1), a transaction can take place regularly without the intervention of an intermediary between sender and recipient. If, for example, two parties have agreed on accepting Bitcoins as a means of payment and the corresponding Bitcoin transaction takes place directly from the one Bitcoin address of the 'payer' to the Bitcoin address of the recipient, there is no payment intermediary or payment service provider and, thus, no three-party relationship which is a prerequisite for the payment services regulated by the PSD2. Full Nodes (→ § 1 para. 8) do not perform any function as intermediary third party and are therefore not to be equated with payment intermediaries or payment service providers.

2. Funds

In addition to a three-party relationship, the term '**funds**' as set out in Art. 4(25) PSD2 (→ para. 20 et seqq.) is relevant for the existence of payment services. If the business model stipulates that the responsible party does not come into contact with customer funds at any time, the requirements of a payment service are usually not met.[52] The term customer funds only refers to legally recognised currencies or means of payment in the form of banknotes and coins, scriptural money or electronic money.

Tokens designed and issued as electronic money would be considered customer funds. Thus, if a company issues cryptographic tokens by using DLT or blockchain technology which are classified as electronic money (→ para. 10) in order to provide one of the payment services listed in Art. 4(3) (Annex I) PSD2, the respective national law

---

[52] Excluding payment initiation and account information services.

transforming PSD2 would apply.[53] For example, if a company offers the execution of payment transactions on the basis of electronic money tokens by issuing payment instruments as defined in Art. 4(14) PSD2, and/or by acquiring payment transactions and money remittance, such activity would fall within the scope of the PSD2 as those tokens qualifying as electronic money would be funds by virtue.[54] According to Art. 63 (4) MiCAR Draft, crypto asset service providers (→ § 8 para. 56) may themselves, or through a third party, provide payment services related to the crypto asset service they offer, provided that the crypto asset service provider itself, or the third-party, is a licensed payment institution according to PSD2 (→ para. 97).

72 **Currency tokens** such as Bitcoin and Ether, on the other hand, do not fall under the term 'funds' and are, therefore, not protected as customer funds even if they are used and recognised between the parties as complementary currency issued under private law and thus as a means of payment. If the payment transaction for the purchase of tokens is exclusively in currency tokens such as Bitcoin, Ether or other tokens, this does not constitute a payment service under PSD2. The mere holding and transfer of currency tokens as a blockchain-based means of payment does not constitute a payment service.

III. Different Token Business Models

73 Depending on the design of the specific token business model, the respective operator or service provider may also provide **payment services under the PSD2**. The qualification as a payment service does not lapse if they are provided together with other services such as financial or investment services. Whether or not a payment service subject to authorisation exists depends on the respective business model and the specific contractual arrangements between the parties involved.

74 There are several business models where different token types can be purchased or exchanged for funds or so-called fiat money (→ § 8 para. 1) or vice versa, e.g. currency tokens can be exchanged for funds. Currency tokens can be acquired against cash or card payments via Token Automated Teller Machines ('**Token ATM**') such as Bitcoin ATMs. There are also Token ATM devices that can be used to exchange currency tokens for cash. In addition, there are various online platforms that are operated as **crypto exchanges** (→ § 8 para. 15 et seqq.), some of which act as intermediaries between token purchasers and token sellers in payment processing.

1. Installation and Operation of Token-ATMs

75 **a) Purchase and Sale of Currency Tokens via Token ATMs.** In various countries around the world, **Token ATMs** are set up where currency tokens such as Bitcoin or Ether can be bought or sold.[55] These Token ATMs work and look similar to a normal ATM or cash machine,[56] but are actually more like a stationary exchange for currency tokens. Basically, the person wishing to purchase tokens (e.g. Bitcoins) enters the respective amount of Bitcoin they wish to receive in the Token ATM's user interface.[57]

---

[53] In Germany, the provisions of the PSD2 are transposed into the Payment Services Act (Zahlungsdiensteaufsichtsgesetz – ZAG).
[54] EBA, 'Report with advice for the European Commission on crypto assets' (January 2019), 14, 2.1.2, available at https://beck-link.de/e8dmh (accessed 16.12.2019).
[55] An overview of the individual locations of Currency Token ATMs can be found at: Coin ATM Radar, available at https://beck-link.de/k3hv2 (accessed 30.8.2020).
[56] Bitcoin ATMs: bitcoin.com, available at https://beck-link.de/3zxpn (accessed 30.8.2020).
[57] Leonard, 'Bitcoin ATM Explained – The Pros and Cons of Buying Cryptocurrency through an ATM' (coincodex.com, 2020), available at https://beck-link.de/c7c2b (accessed 30.8.2020).

§ 9. E-Money Tokens, Stablecoins, and Token Payment Services

The wallet address of the purchaser to which the Bitcoin transaction is to be sent is scanned by a QR code displayed on the Token ATM via the purchaser's mobile phone. A corresponding amount of cash is then inserted into the Token ATM, similar to a cash deposit at an ATM. Some Token ATMs also accept debit or credit card payments. Once the cash has been collected, the Bitcoin transaction is triggered at the purchaser's specified public key and the number of Bitcoins purchased can be verified by the purchaser, e.g. by means of a blockchain scan.

If Bitcoins are sold via a Token ATM, the Token ATM in general provides the customer with a QR code displayed on screen or printed on paper.[58] This QR code must be scanned with the seller's smartphone to transfer Bitcoin to the operator of the Bitcoin ATM. Depending on the device type, the customer may also receive a PIN sent to their smartphone. The seller enters this PIN at the Token ATM and gets paid out the desired amount in a fiat currency in the form of cash. 76

b) Service enabling Cash to be placed on/withdrawals from a Payment Account. However, the establishment and operation of Token ATMs do not normally constitute a payment service in the sense of **incoming or outgoing payment transactions** pursuant to Annex I No. 1 and 2 PSD2. According to the legal definition, these payment services are services **enabling cash to be placed on** or **cash withdrawals from a payment account**, as well as all transactions required for the operation of a payment account. According to the definition in Art. 4(12) PSD2, a payment account means an 'account held in the name of one or more payment service users which is used for the execution of payment transactions'. A payment service provider who carries out incoming or outgoing payment transactions serves as an **interface between cash and scriptural money**. The payment of cash into a currency Token ATM, on the other hand, does not result in the issuer converting the paid in amount of money into scriptural money on a payment account of the token ATM user. The wallet or the specified public key of the user does not constitute a payment account in the sense of PSD2. Additionally, the currency tokens bought or exchanged are not scriptural money either. 77

2. Crypto Bank Account

Where a payment service provider links a payment account to a **wallet**[59] through which trading with currency tokens can be paid directly through the payment account, the maintenance of a payment account shall fulfil the payment services of enabling cash to be placed on and the withdrawal from payment accounts as in Annex I PSD2, No. 1 and 2. Furthermore, the respective execution of payment transactions through it shall also fulfil the requirements of the payment service of execution of payment transaction as in Annex I PSD2, No. 3 or 4. However, the linking of the payment account with a wallet of the customer does not mean that the provision of a wallet for currency token would constitute a payment service, provided that electronic money tokens are not settled via the wallet. 78

3. No Execution of Payment Transactions by Wallet Providers

Under Art. 4(5) PSD2, a payment transaction 'means an act, initiated by the payer or on his behalf or by the payee, of placing, transferring or withdrawing funds, irrespective 79

---

[58] Ibid.
[59] The German company Nuri (formerly known as Bitwala), for example, offers its customers such a crypto bank account. As a white label solution, the German Solarisbank offers bank accounts and the issuing of debit cards to such businesses by way of outsourcing, so that the companies can link their existing products such as trading of currency tokens and wallets with actual bank accounts and cards.

of any underlying obligations between the payer and the payee'. The payment service of the execution of payment transaction within the meaning of Annex I PSD2, shall be operated by anyone who provides 'the execution of payment transactions, including the transfer of funds to a payment account with the user's payment service provider or with another payment service provider' without granting credit. Basically, the payment transaction involves the transfer of scriptural money in any form by means of direct debit, credit transfer or payment cards. For the payment service provider, this means that the payment transaction must be executed by the payment service provider itself and not merely initiated.

80 A **custodial wallet provider** whose business model provides for the safekeeping of private keys of its customers is able to execute transactions of tokens (→ § 8 para. 34 et seqq.). If in such case the customer knows their public key but has no direct access to their private key, the customer cannot execute the transaction itself, but can at most initiate it. If the tokens, which are the subject of a transaction, do not fulfil the requirements of 'funds', a payment transaction is out of question as defined in Art. 4 (5) PSD2. Whereas the transfer of tokens, which qualify as electronic money, by the wallet provider would at least be comparable to a payment transaction for protective purposes. In such a case, the account that a user maintains with their custodial wallet provider would usually be considered a payment account. Considering e-money tokens according to MiCAR, the provision of a custodial wallet might instead qualify as a crypto asset service in the form of 'the custody and administration of crypto assets on behalf of third parties' as defined in Art. 3(9)(a) MiCAR Draft and not as the provision of a payment account, as e-money tokens are considered crypto assets (Art. 3(2) MiCAR Draft).

4. Operation of Crypto Exchanges

81 Depending on the respective business model and the specific contractual agreements of the parties involved, the operator of a **crypto exchange** might provide, among other things, payment services. For example, the operator of a crypto exchange, through which tokens can be exchanged for legal currency, or legal currency can be exchanged for tokens, may provide the payment services of **money remittance** or **acquiring of payment transactions** in the case of payment processing in a three-party relationship, provided that the operator of the crypto exchange comes into contact with customer funds.

82 **a) Money Remittance.** Pursuant to Art. 4(22) PSD2, **money remittance** 'means a payment service where funds are received from a payer, without any payment accounts being created in the name of the payer or the payee, for the sole purpose of transferring a corresponding amount to a payee or to another payment service provider acting on behalf of the payee, and/or where such funds are received on behalf of and made available to the payee'.

83 A money remittance service provider can operate on the side of the payer (1st alternative), the payee (2nd alternative) or both. However, to be considered a money remittance service provider, it is not necessary for the service provider to act on behalf of several payees or payers. Money remittance under the first alternative covers situations where, for example, a payer hands over cash to a money remittance service provider so that the latter passes on the corresponding amount to the payee or his payment service provider. The transfer can be carried out by physically transporting cash, possibly in a different denomination or currency, and transferring it to the payee in cash. However, it also includes the forwarding of information, whereby someone else,

§ 9. E-Money Tokens, Stablecoins, and Token Payment Services

in conjunction with the payment service provider at the payee's location, is induced to hand over a corresponding amount of cash to the payee or his payment service provider. In this way, service providers such as Western Union or MoneyGram which offer their own branch and agency network operate using their own communication, transfer and clearing networks.

It is irrelevant in case of money remittance how the payment service user ultimately brings in the funds whether in cash or by transfer, cheque, electronic cash, direct debit and the like, or whether there is a set-off. The same way, the money remittance service is provided by the person who receives a transfer of funds from a payer for transmission and thereby receives scriptural money on his account, and subsequently transfers the corresponding amount of money through his payment account to a payment account of the payee. 84

A money remittance transaction requires that funds are transferred without there being a payment account-based relationship between the payment service provider and the payment service user and that a money remittance service provider does not link its service to a payment account held by a customer with another payment service provider. Money remittance is merely a fall-back from payment services linked to payment accounts and is subsidiary to them. 85

The operator of a **crypto exchange** provides the payment service of money remittance in such cases, in which the operator forwards the equivalent value of the tokens as funds on behalf of the token buyer via the operator's payment account to the recipient of the payment in exchange for the tokens sold by the latter. The operator of a crypto exchange acts on the one hand as a payment service provider on the side of the token buyer, e.g. by accepting the amount of money by means of a transfer to his payment account for transmission to the payee. On the other hand, the operator of the crypto exchange acts as a payment service provider on the payee's side by accepting the corresponding amount of money and making it available to the payee, as a rule by transferring it to the payee's payment account, which is managed by a payment service provider other than the remittance service provider. 86

A prerequisite is that the platform operator does not maintain a payment account for the token buyer as payer or the exchange recipient or token seller as payee.[60] A user account that the token buyer or seller creates when registering on the website of the crypto exchange typically does not meet the requirements of such a payment account, as it is not used for the execution of payment transactions per se. It is also far from being the case that the wallet set up for the user by the operator of an on-chain crypto exchange is to be regarded as such a payment account in the sense of PSD2. For a wallet to be considered as a payment account it would have to be possible to provide, transmit or withdraw funds via such a wallet. 87

If the equivalent value in fiat money for a token purchase is transferred directly between the payer and the payee, e.g. by means of a transfer from the payment account of the token buyer to that of the token seller, there is no transfer of funds by the crypto exchange operator. 88

In cases where the crypto exchange itself is the counterparty to a token sell or buy order with a user, the exchange might not provide money remittance services as it receives the payments from a user as consideration for the sale of tokens to the user. A party who executes the underlying transaction in its entirety as a contracting party and purchases tokens itself and then resells them to a token buyer, assuming all rights 89

---

[60] BT-Drs. 18/11495, 107; BaFin, 'Merkblatt – Hinweise zum Zahlungsdiensteaufsichtsgesetz (ZAG)' (29.11.2017), section 2 lit. e), available at https://beck-link.de/ra76f (accessed 20.08.2021).

and obligations, is not acting as a party to the contract in the sense of a money remittance service. In the case of two sales transactions that are processed independently of each other – even if they concern the same tokens – no remittance of funds and therefore no money remittance transaction takes place. Payments of funds received from a token buyer are received by the crypto exchange operator in return as the seller of the token. Payments made by the operator to a token seller are made as genuine consideration for the purchase of the tokens by the crypto exchange operator. This does not constitute a transfer of payments as part of a money remittance transaction, as there is no three-party payment processing that would be a prerequisite for money remittance.

90   b) **Acquiring of Payment Transactions.** Pursuant to Art. 4(44) PSD2, **acquiring of payment transactions** 'means a payment service provided by a payment service provider contracting with a payee to accept and process payment transactions, which results in a transfer of funds to the payee'.

91   Since the acquiring of payment transactions only refers to the relationship between the payee and the payment service provider, the acquiring business is the more specific case compared to money remittance.

92   If the operator of a crypto exchange accepts payments in the form of funds from the token buyer on behalf of the token seller and transfers these payments to the token seller as the payee, this process constitutes acquiring of payment transactions, provided that a corresponding contractual agreement exists between the payee and the operator of a crypto exchange.

93   In addition, it is possible that an operator of a crypto exchange provides both the money remittance services and the acquiring of payment transactions in combination, if the operator acts on behalf of both sides, i.e. token seller and buyer, and receives and transfers money. The extent to which a payment service subject to authorisation exists is to be assessed according to the specific contractual agreements between the parties involved.

5. Money Remittance within the Framework of ICOs

94   If several companies are involved in an ICO and investors can also buy tokens in fiat currencies, it should be ensured in the structuring of the collection of investor funds and the respective payment flows that no money remittance business requiring a licence is involved, unless the respective service provider has a licence from its national competent authority. If a company, which would be regarded as the issuer of the tokens, commissions another company to receive the funds of the token purchasers, and only then forwards these funds to the accounts of the issuer, the requirements of money remittance would generally be fulfilled.

F. Authorisation Requirements and Ongoing Obligations for E-Money Business and Payment Services

I. Authorisation for Electronic Money Institutions

95   In general, any legal person wishing to issue electronic money in a member state of the EU, requires authorisation of its respective **national competent authority** as an electronic money institution in line with the requirements laid out under Title II EMD2. Depending on the transposition of EMD2 into the respective national laws of a member

state, some electronic money issuers such as the European **Central Bank** might not require an additional authorisation to issue electronic money.

Art. 6 EMD2 entitles electronic money institutions additionally to provide payment services, grant credit related to payment services, provide operational services and closely related ancillary services related to the issuance of electronic money or the provision of payment services and operate payment systems as defined in Art. 4(7) PSD2. The content of the application for authorisation as an electronic money institution derives from Title II EMD2 and the respective transpositions into the laws of the member states.

II. Authorisation for Payment Service Providers

According to Art. 5 and 11 PSD2, any legal person who wishes to provide payment services in a member state of the European Union needs to apply for **authorisation** to the national competent authority of the home member state unless it is subject to an exemption in Art. 11(1) PSD2. For instance, payment service providers already licensed to operate as an electronic money institution do not require any additional licence under PSD2. The requirements and documentations that the application for authorisation as a payment service institution must contain are set out in Art. 5 and its subsequent articles of PSD2. They are further specified in the respective national laws transposing PSD2.

III. Supervisory and Follow-Up Obligations of Institutions

As a **payment institution** and as an **electronic money institution**, there are follow-up obligations under supervisory law in addition to the obligation to obtain a licence. These institutions must have sufficient initial capital and must meet the capital adequacy requirements at all times. If a company wishes to engage exclusively in money remittance services, an initial capital equivalent to at least EUR 20,000.00 must be available when applying for a licence according to Art. 7(a) PSD2. Payment institutions that wish to carry out the cash placing or withdrawal business, payment transactions with or without the granting of credit or the acquisition business must be able to provide an initial capital equivalent to at least EUR 125,000.00 at the free disposal of the company when the application is submitted pursuant to Art. 7(c) PSD2. For Electronic money institutions, on the other hand, Art. 4 EMD2 states that a minimum initial capital of the equivalent of EUR 350,000.00 must be freely available to the company.

In addition, according to Art. 10 PSD2, **safeguarding requirements** must be considered when accepting funds. When funds are accepted for the issuance of electronic money, the safeguarding requirements in Art. 7 EMD2 must also be taken into account. The focus is on the asset-based separation of the customer funds being safeguarded from the funds of the payment institution, which means that the funds of the customers of a payment service provider are left in the economic ownership of the customers, thus, reducing the insolvency risk of the payment institution for the customer. An institution must also have a proper business organisation as well as appropriate risk management and control mechanisms. A proper business organisation also must ensure effective anti-money laundering and anti-terrorist financing measures (Rec. 37 MiCAR Draft). Appropriate measures and processes for the prevention of money laundering will be a key priority in the supervision of crypto exchanges.

100 In determining whether a service provider should be classified as a payment institution, the respective nature of the tokens associated with a payment service is not decisive. Decisive will be whether there is a three-party relationship between the payer, the payee and the payment service provider whereby a payment service provider normally comes into possession of customer funds. With regard to the supervisory approval and follow-up obligations, there are therefore no differences between the various token business models and 'classic' payment services. The same applies to electronic money issuers provided their token fulfils the functions of electronic money (→ para. 10 et seqq.). There are currently no supervisory exceptions or special provisions for blockchain-based electronic money.

G. Requirements for Issuers of Crypto Assets under MiCAR

I. Issuers of Crypto Assets

101 Issuers of tokens, that qualify as **crypto assets** (→ para. 51) pursuant to the MiCAR, have to observe the regulatory requirements according to MiCAR regarding in particular their authorisation, operation, organisation and governance. Depending on the respective type of crypto asset they are issuing, MiCAR contains some more specific requirements, especially for issuers of (significant) asset-referenced tokens and (significant) e-money tokens.

102 According to Art. 3(1)(6) MiCAR Draft, an '**issuer of crypto assets**' is defined as a 'legal person who offers to the public any type of crypto asset or seeks the admission of such crypto assets to a trading platform for crypto assets'. An '**offer to the public**' is defined in Art. 3(1)(7) MiCAR Draft as 'an offer to third parties to acquire a crypto asset in exchange for fiat currency or other crypto assets'.

103 Regardless of the token type issued, an issuer of crypto assets, according to Art. 4(1)(a) MiCAR Draft, shall be established as a legal entity if it wants to offer crypto assets to the public in the EU or seek an admission for trading such crypto assets on a trading platform for crypto assets (→ § 8 para. 24).

104 An issuer of utility tokens and crypto assets, which do not qualify as asset-referenced tokens or e-money tokens, can as well be a **legal entity** established in a third country, whereas issuers of asset-referenced tokens need to be established within the European Union, as do issuers of e-money tokens. According to Art. 43(1)(a) MiCAR Draft, e-money token issuers need to be authorised as credit institution within the meaning of Art. 4(1) of Regulation (EU) 575/2013 or as an electronic money institution within the meaning of EMD2.

II. Authorisation Requirements

1. Issuers of Utility Tokens and Crypto Assets

105 Issuers of utility tokens and crypto assets which do not qualify as asset-referenced tokens or e-money tokens, shall not require authorisation as issuers to offer such crypto assets to the public or seek their admission to trading on a trading platform for crypto assets.

2. Issuers of Asset-referenced Tokens

106 Art. 15(1) MiCAR Draft states that **issuers of asset-referenced tokens** need to be authorised by the competent authority of their home Member State to offer asset-

referenced tokens to the public in the European Union or to seek their admission to trading on a trading platform for crypto assets. Only credit institutions which are authorised in accordance with Art. 8 of Directive 2013/36/EU will not need to apply for an additional authorisation under Art. 15(4) MiCAR Draft as an issuer of asset-referenced tokens. Further, an authorisation is not required if the requirements of Art. 15(3) MiCAR Draft are fulfilled, namely the average outstanding amount of asset-referenced tokens does not exceed EUR 5,000,000, or the equivalent amount in another currency, over the period of 12 months, calculated at the end of each calendar day, or if the asset-referenced tokens are solely addressed to qualified investors and can only be held by them and not by retail investors.

3. Issuers of E-Money Tokens

Issuers of e-money tokens need to be authorized as credit institution or as an electronic money institution pursuant to EMD2. Due to the comprehensive reference in Art. (1)(b) MiCAR Draft, the regulations of EMD2 widely apply to e-money tokens. It can be assumed that in the scope of application of the MiCAR, its provisions take precedence over those of EMD2 as **lex specialis** (Rec. 10 MiCAR Draft). 107

Art. 43(2)(a) MiCAR Draft exempts such e-money tokens from the authorization requirement that are exclusively marketed, distributed and held by **qualified investors**. Furthermore, Art. 43(2)(b) MiCAR Draft exempts e-money tokens where a specified amount is not exceeded – the limits are the same as for asset-referenced tokens (→ para. 106). Lower thresholds set by Member States in accordance with Art. 9(1)(a) EMD2 will, however, also apply to the MiCAR. Exempted e-money issuers must produce a crypto asset white paper and notify the competent authority. 108

III. Ongoing Obligations of Issuers of Crypto Assets

1. Issuers of Utility Tokens and Crypto Assets

For issuers of **utility tokens** and **crypto assets** which do **not qualify as asset-referenced tokens or e-money tokens**, Art. 13 MiCAR Draft contains some obligations regarding the conduct of their business such as the obligation to act honestly, fairly and professionally but no further requirements regarding organisational or governance arrangements. 109

Furthermore, respective issuers need to observe the MiCAR requirements regarding the draft and notification of a crypto assets white paper and their marketing communications (→ § 4 para. 39). 110

2. Issuers of Asset-Referenced Tokens

Chapter 2 of the MiCAR Draft contains stricter obligations for issuers of asset-referenced tokens such as information obligations towards their token holders (Art. 26 MiCAR Draft) and to competent authorities (Art. 29 MiCAR Draft), the establishment of a complaints handling procedure (Art. 27 MiCAR Draft), the implementation and maintenance of policy procedures to prevent, identify, manage and disclose conflict of interests (Art. 28 MiCAR Draft) as well as to implement certain governance arrangements (Art. 30 MiCAR Draft) and to have own funds in place (Art. 31 MiCAR Draft). 111

Further, MiCAR will contain legal requirements for the reserve of assets an issuer of asset-referenced tokens has to maintain, in particular, regarding the composition of the 112

reserve of assets and their management (Art. 32 MiCAR Draft), as well as, regarding the custody of the reserve assets (Art. 33 MiCAR Draft) and their investment (Art. 34 MiCAR Draft). Apart from that, MiCAR requires issuers of asset-referenced tokens to have policies and procedures in place with regard to the rights granted to token holders (Art. 35 MiCAR Draft).

113 For issuers of significant asset-referenced tokens (→ para. 56 et seqq.) Art. 41 MiCAR Draft contains specific **additional obligations** with regard to their remuneration policy in light of an effective risk management, a liquidity management procedure in light of redemption requests from token holders. Furthermore, pursuant to Art. 41(4), 31(1) MiCAR Draft the capital requirements of own funds might be higher than for non-significant asset-referenced tokens – 3 % and not 2 % of the average amount of reserve assets, in case 3 % of the average amount of reserve assets would be higher than EUR 350,000.

114 Art. 42 MiCAR Draft further requires issuers of asset-referenced tokens to have in place a plan to support an orderly wind-down of their activities which shall be reviewed and updated regularly.

3. Issuers of E-Money Tokens

115 As an additional instrument to achieve transparency and accountability, Art. 43(1)(c), 46, 47 MiCAR Draft introduce the obligation to publish a white paper when issuing e-money tokens. In addition, Art. 48 MiCAR Draft contains specific requirements for the marketing communication relating to an offer of e-money tokens.

116 Furthermore, Art. 44 MiCAR Draft contains special requirements with regards to the issuance and redemption of e-money tokens. Under EMD2 not only the issuance of e-money tokens must be at **par value**, but also holders of e-money tokens must be provided with a redemption claim at par value. According to Art. 44(7) MiCAR Draft, where the issuer of e-money tokens does not fulfil legitimate redemption requests within a specified time period, such claim can be asserted against entities ensuring the safeguarding of funds received by issuers of e-money tokens or against any natural or legal person in charge of distribution of e-money tokens on behalf of issuers of e-money tokens. Art. 49 MiCAR Draft stipulates that e-money token issuers must invest funds received in exchange for e-money tokens not only in secure, low-risk assets as defined by EMD2, but such assets must also be denominated in the same currency as the ones referenced by the e-money tokens. Specific additional obligations apply for issuers of significant e-money tokens according to Art. 52 MiCAR Draft, which refers to the respective provisions on significant asset-references tokens (→ para. 113).

§ 10
Anti-Money Laundering

Literature: Berger and Rübsamen (eds), *Bundesbankgesetz* (BBankG) (2nd edn, Berlin, 2014); Brian, Frey and Krais, 'Umsetzung der Fünften Geldwäsche-Richtlinie in Deutschland' (2019) 12 *Corporate Compliance Zeitschrift*, 245; Busemann, 'Dunkelfeldstudie über den Umfang der Geldwäsche in Deutschland und über Geldwäscherisiken in einzelnen Wirtschaftssektoren' (August 2015), available at https://beck-link.de/vc3vk (accessed 29.4.2021); Claassen, *Grundlagen der Geldtheorie* (2nd edn, Springer, Berlin, 1980); CipherTrace, 'Cryptocurrency Anti-Money Laundering Report' (January 2019), available at https://beck-link.de/w4awh (accessed 29.4.2021); Diergarten, ' § 34 – Geldwäsche', in Hauschka, Moosmayer and Lösler (eds), *Corporate Compliance* (3rd edn, Munich, 2016), 1063; Erbs and Kohlhaas (eds), *Strafrechtliche Nebengesetze (GWG)*, (January 2019, incl. 223rd suppl., Munich, 2019); European Banking Authority, 'Report with advice for the European Commission on crypto-assets' (January 2019), available at https://beck-link.de/kc78a (accessed 29.4.2021); Frey and Pelz (eds), *Beck'scher Online-Kommentar GWG* (BeckOK GwG, 2019); Foley, Karlsen and Putniņš 'Sex, Drugs, and Bitcoin: How Much Illegal Activity Is Financed Through Cryptocurrencies?', *Review of Financial Studies* (forthcoming); Fromberger and Haffke, 'ICO Market Report 2018/2019 – Performance Analysis of 2018's Initial Coin Offerings' (2019), available at https://ssrn.com/abstract=3512125, (accessed 29.4.2021); Fromberger, Haffke and Zimmermann, 'Kryptowerte und Geldwäsche – Eine Analyse der 5. Geldwäscherichtlinie sowie des Gesetzesentwurfs der Bundesregierung' (2019) 19 *Zeitschrift für Bank- und Kapitalmarktrecht*, 377; Grzywotz, *Virtual Currencies and Money Laundering, Internetrecht und Digitale Gesellschaft* (Duncker & Humblot, Berlin, 2019); Haffke, Fromberger and Zimmermann, 'Cryptocurrencies and anti-money laundering: the shortcomings of the fifth AML Directive (EU) and how to address them' (2020) 21 *Journal of Banking Regulation*, 125; Hauschka, Moosmayer and Lösler, ' § 1 – Einführung', in Hauschka, Moosmayer and Lösler, *Corporate Compliance*, (3rd edn, Munich, 2016), 1; Helmrich, 'Handelsunternehmen und Geldwäsche' (2009) 62 *Neue Juristische Wochenzeitschrift*, 3686; Herzog (ed), *Geldwäschegesetz* (GWG) (4th edn, Munich, 2020); HM Treasury, FCA and Bank of England, 'Final report' (October 2018) available at https://beck-link.de/w3xv5 (accessed 29.4.2021); Holtenmöller, *Geldtheorie und Geldpolitik* (Mohr Siebeck, Heidelberg, 2008); Keding, 'Die aufsichtsrechtliche Behandlung von Machine-to-Machine-Zahlungen unter Rückgriff auf Peer-to-Peer-Netzwerke' (2018) 72 *Zeitschrift für Wirtschafts- und Bankrecht*, 64; Krais, *Geldwäsche und Compliance* (C. H. Beck, Munich, 2018); Maume and Haffke, ' § 15 – Geldwäsche-Compliance' in Maume, Maute and Fromberger (eds), *Rechtshandbuch Kryptowerte* (Munich, 2020), 417; Maume, ' § 12 – Finanzdienstleistungsaufsichtsrecht', in Maume, Maute and Fromberger (eds), *Rechtshandbuch Kryptowerte*, (Munich, 2020), 332; Maume, Haffke and Zimmermann, 'Bitcoin versus Bargeld – Die geldwäscherechtliche Verpflichtung von Güterhändlern bei Zahlungen mit Kryptowährungen' (2019) 12 *Corporate Compliance Zeitschrift*, 149; Mishkin, *The Economics of Money, Banking and Financial Markets* (2nd edn, Pearson, Boston, 2009); Moritz, *Geldtheorie und Geldpolitik* (3rd edn, Vahlen, Munich, 2012); *Münchener Kommentar zum Strafgesetzbuch* (MünchKommStGB) (3rd edn, Munich, 2017); Palandt (ed), *Bürgerliches Gesetzbuch* (BGB) (79th edn, Munich, 2020); Rabin, *Monetary Theory* (Edward Elgar Publishing, 2004); Terlau, 'Blockchain-basiertes Geld im Währungs-, Aufsichts-, Geldwäsche-, Wertpapier-,Steuerrecht', in Möslein and Omlor (eds), *Fintech-Handbuch* (Munich, 2019), 476; United Nations Office on Drugs and Crime (UNODC), 'Estimating Illicit Financial Flows Resulting from Drug Trafficking and Other Transnational Organized Crimes – Research Report' (October 2011), available at https://beck-link.de/f56h4 (accessed 29.4.2021); Vandezande, 'Virtual currencies under EU anti-money laundering law' (2017) 33 *Computer Law and Security Review*, 341; Vandezande, *Virtual Currencies: A Legal Framework* (Intersentia Ltd, 2018).

Outline

	para.
A. Introduction	1
B. Crypto Assets and Money Laundering Compliance	4
I. Introduction	4
II. Crypto Assets and the Money Laundering Phenomenon	6
III. Comparison with Cash and Fiat Money	8
C. Regulatory System of Anti-Money Laundering in the EU	9

Part B. EU Regulation

I. Overview – Structure and Level of Harmonisation	9
II. Tokens in the EU AML System	12
1. Tokens as Virtual Currencies	13
2. Tokens as Securities	25
3. Tokens as Electronic Money	26
4. Transactions	27
5. Tokens and the Concept of Cash within AML Law	29
III. Competent Authority, Territorial Scope and Financial Intelligence Units	30
1. Competent Authorities	30
2. Territorial Scope	32
3. Financial Intelligence Units (FIUs)	36
IV. Licensing or Registration Regime	39
D. Crypto Intermediaries as Obliged Entities	42
I. Fiat-to-Crypto Exchanges	43
II. Crypto-to-Crypto Exchanges	45
III. Wallet Providers	49
IV. Tumblers	53
V. Issuers of Tokens	54
VI. Miners	60
VII. Other Obliged Entities	61
1. Persons Trading in Goods	61
2. Art Market Participants	62
3. Intermediaries with Regards to Electronic Money	64
4. Banks and Other Obliged Entites	66
E. AML Obligations for Crypto Intermediaries	67
I. Overview	67
II. Risk Assessment and Risk Management (Art. 6–8 AMLD4)	70
1. General Principles	70
2. Fiat-to-Crypto Exchanges and Custodian Wallet Providers	77
3. Issuers of Tokens	78
4. Art Market Participants	79
III. Customer Due Diligence (Art. 10–20 AMLD4)	81
1. Prohibition of Anonymous Accounts	81
2. When to Apply CDD Measures (Art. 11 AMLD4)	82
a) Overview	82
b) Calculation of the Thresholds	84
c) Establishment of a Business Relationship and Occasional Transactions	90
(aa) Fiat-to-Crypto Exchanges	90
(1) Establishment of a Business Relationship	90
(2) Occasional Transactions	95
(bb) Custodian Wallet Provider	96
(cc) Art Market Participants (and Other Persons Trading in Goods)	98
(dd) Electronic Money Institutions, Electronic Money Agents and Electronic Money Distributors	102
d) Suspicion of Money Laundering or Terrorist Financing	103
3. Content of CDD Measures	105
a) Overview	105
b) The Customer's Identity (Art. 13(1)(a) AMLD4)	108
(aa) General information	108
(bb) Identification – Information to be Collected	110
(cc) Verification of the Customer's Identity	113
c) Identification of the Beneficial Owner (lit. b)	116
d) Purpose and Intended Nature of the Business Relationship (lit. c)	120

- e) Monitoring the Ongoing Business Relationship (lit. d) 121
- f) Politically Exposed Persons (PEP, Art. 20(a) AMLD4) 122
- 4. Simplified or Enhanced CDD Measures (Art. 15–24 AMLD4). 123
  - a) General information 123
    - (aa) Simplified CDD Measures (AMLD4, Art. 15–17) 125
    - (bb) Enhanced CDD Measures (Art. 18–24 AMLD4) 127
  - b) Fiat-to-Crypto Exchanges and Custodian Wallet Providers 132
  - c) Issuers of Tokens 135
  - d) Credit Institutions 136
  - f) Electronic Money Institutions, Electronic Money Agents, Electronic Money Distributors 139
    - (aa) Simplified Due Diligence Obligations 139
    - (bb) Refrain from Applying Certain General CDD Measures (Art. 12 AMLD4) 141
- 5. Performance of General CDD Measures by Third Parties (Art. 25–29 AMLD4) 144
- 6. Unability to Comply with CDD Obligations 145
- IV. Suspicious Transaction Reporting (Art. 33–35 AMLD4) 146
  - 1. Filing a Suspicious Transaction Report (Art. 33–34 AMLD4) 146
  - 2. Transactions in Case of Filing a Suspicious Transaction Report (Art. 35 AMLD4) 148
- V. Transparency Registers on Beneficial Ownership 154
- VI. Central Database for Public Keys 158
- F. Sanctions 159
  - I. Administrative Sanctions and Measures 159
    - 1. General 159
    - 2. Norm Addressees and Responsibility 160
    - 3. Provisions Subject to Sanctions 161
    - 4. Measures and Sanctions 162
  - II. Criminal Sanctions 164
- G. Other EU AML Policies and Further Developments 165
  - I. Directive (EU) 2018/1673 – Definition of Money Laundering 165
  - II. The AML Action Plan and Further AML Developments 168

A. Introduction

Recent scandals in various sectors of the economy show that compliances failures can have significant legal and financial consequences. This also applies to money laundering. In this area alone, supervisory authorities have recently imposed fines in the high three-digit million range on individual financial institutions.[1] Especially for younger companies in the FinTech sector, the implementation of money laundering regulations is associated with major personnel and organisational difficulties.[2] However, companies outside the banking and financial services sector which trade in goods are also affected.[3]

---

[1] For example, the German authorities have imposed fines on the Deutsche Bank, Freifeld and Schuetze, 'Deutsche fined $ 630 million for failures over Russian money-laundering' (Reuters, 31.1.2017), available at https://beck-link.de/3wsdf (accessed 29.4.2021), or the ING, Sterling and Meijer, 'Dutch bank ING fined $ 900 million for failing to spot money laundering' (Reuters, 4.9.2018), available at https://beck-link.de/xps67 (accessed 29.4.2021).

[2] For example, the German financial markets regulator (Bundesanstalt für Finanzdienstleistungsaufsicht, BaFin) ordered the fintech bank N26 to improve its AML controls, see Megaw, 'Regulator orders N26 to improve anti-money laundering controls, (Financial Times, 22.5.2019), available at https://beck-link.de/cfs46 (accessed 29.4.2021).

[3] See Maume, Haffke and Zimmermann, 'Bitcoin versus Bargeld – Die geldwäscherechtliche Verpflichtung von Güterhändlern bei Zahlungen mit Kryptowährungen' (2019) 12 *Corporate Compliance Zeitschrift*, 149.

2   The tension between the apparent anonymity conveyed by cryptocurrencies and their worldwide circulation on the one hand and money laundering regulation on the other hand is obvious. In some cases, there are even calls for a general ban on 'cryptocurrencies' (i.e. currency tokens) with reference to money laundering and terrorist financing.[4] This may seem exaggerated and unrealistic. However, it illustrates the serious concerns about the potential use of Bitcoin and other currency tokens.

3   Part B of this chapter (→ para. 4 et seqq.) introduces the concept of Anti-Money Laundering (AML) and Terrorist Financing (CFT) compliance. Part C (→ para. 9 et seqq.) discusses the regulatory system on the EU level in the context of the three token archetypes (currency/investment/utility). Part D (→ para. 42 et seqq.) deals with the possible obligations of typical crypto intermediaries. Part E (→ para. 67 et seqq.) provides an overview over the types of obligations of these companies. Part F (→ para. 159 et seqq.) discusses the possible sanctions for AML violations.

B. Crypto Assets and Money Laundering Compliance

I. Introduction

4   In simple terms, compliance means 'respecting'[5] or following applicable law.[6] Originally from Anglo-Saxon legal terminology, there is no uniform definition in EU Law. A compliance violation can be based on a breach of **internal** or **external** obligations or **rules**. Anti-Money Laundering legislation imposes various duties on particular market participants and is thus part of external compliance.

5   A company can violate many external regulations in the course of its business operations.[7] Some, such as antitrust law, do not (yet) raise issues specific for tokens. However, token-specific compliance risks currently exist in the areas of money laundering and terrorism financing, tax compliance, in particular the tax treatment of token transactions (→ § 13 para. 8 et seqq.), financial market compliance, in particular the obligation to obtain a licence (→ § 8 para. 37 et seqq.) and issue a prospectus (→ § 7 para. 31 et seqq.), and data protection compliance (→ § 6).

II. Crypto Assets and the Money Laundering Phenomenon

6   The global scale of money laundering and terrorist financing cannot be accurately determined. According to a study by the United Nations Office on Drugs and Crime (UNODC), money laundering in 2009 accounted for 2.7 % of global GDP, or a total of USD 1.6 trillion.[8] In the EU alone, figures of money laundered in 2014 may be as high as hundreds of billions of Euros, amounting to approx. 1.3 % of the EU's GDP per

---

[4] For example, represented by Nobel Prize winner *Joseph Stieglitz*, see Davis, 'Joseph Stiglitz: 'We should shut down the cryptocurrencies'' (CNBC, 6.5.2019), available at https://beck-link.de/d8wkk (accessed 29.4.2021).

[5] European Commission, 'Compliance with competition rules: what's in it for business?' (February 2013), available at https://beck-link.de/rd648 (accessed 29.4.2021).

[6] Hauschka, Moosmayer and Lösler, '§ 1 – Einführung', in Hauschka, Moosmayer and Lösler (eds) *Corporate Compliance*, § 1, para. 2.

[7] For an overview of a company's main compliance risks, see Hauschka, Moosmayer and Lösler (eds), *Corporate Compliance*, §§ 17–35.

[8] United Nations Office on Drugs and Crime (UNODC), 'Estimating Illicit Financial Flows Resulting from Drug Trafficking and Other Transnational Organized Crimes – Research Report' (October 2011), 5, available at https://beck-link.de/f56h4 (accessed 29.4.2021).

year.[9] Accordingly, the corruption that is sometimes associated with money laundering causes immense damage to national economies. In an international comparison, the EU's position is, overall, below average in terms of money laundering risk.[10] However, the situation is still not satisfactory: for example, Belgium, Cyprus, Malta, the Netherlands and Spain have been listed as 'major money laundering destinations.'[11] Germany is often referred to as a 'paradise' for money launderers.[12] The reasons for this are the high acceptance of cash, especially in the retail sector,[13] and the lack of supervision.[14]

The share of tokens in these money laundering activities cannot be reliably determined either. However, tokens have several characteristics that make them particularly suitable for money laundering.[15]

First, money launderers benefit from the **decentralised nature** of the blockchain technology (→ § 1 para. 1 et seqq.). Its architecture usually does not have a central authority for the authorisation and control of payments. There are no banks that assume these roles as they do in the circulation of fiat money. Suspicious transactions in a decentralised blockchain are therefore not recognised or reported centrally.

Secondly, since the blockchain is at least **pseudonymous** (→ § 1 para. 102 et seqq.), the use of tokens for the purpose of money laundering is obvious: The correlation between a public key and a real name is not apparent to blockchain participants or to third parties.[16] Furthermore, a person can create any number of such pseudonyms. By using tumblers (→ § 1 para. 106 et seq.) or privacy tokens (→ § 1 para. 108 et seqq.), even (almost) complete anonymity can be achieved.

Thirdly, concealing the origin of assets is made easier by the fact that tokens can be transferred **across national borders** without any additional effort. Assets can be transferred in the form of tokens without having to pass through border controls. There is no need for a physical meeting between money launderers, middlemen and money recipients (cf. cash). This is why tokens are (allegedly) used increasingly in terrorism financing campaigns.[17]

---

[9] Europol, 'From Suspicion to Action – Converting Financial Intelligence into Greater Operational Impact' (September 2017), 26, available at https://beck-link.de/tnwy7 (accessed 29.4.2021).
[10] Basel Institute on Governance, 'Ranking money laundering and terrorist financing risks around the world' (Basel AML Index, 9th Public edn, 2020), 7 et seq., available at https://beck-link.de/prf46 (accessed 29.4.2021).
[11] Basel Institute on Governance, 'Ranking money laundering and terrorist financing risks around the world' (Basel AML Index, 9th Public edn, 2020), 8, available at https://beck-link.de/prf46 (accessed 29.4.2021).
[12] Iwersen, Hildebrand, Keuchel and Drost, 'Deutschland ist nach wie vor ein Paradies für Geldwäscher' (Handelsblatt, 19.11.2019), available at https://beck-link.de/ap7mm (accessed 29.4.2021).
[13] Kabisch, Klimm, Strozyk and Willmroth, 'Wie Kokain-Millionen in Deutschland gewaschen werden' (Süddeutsche Zeitung, 14.11.2018), available at https://beck-link.de/28msx (accessed 29.4.2021).
[14] Maume, Haffke and Zimmermann, 'Bitcoin versus Bargeld – Die geldwäscherechtliche Verpflichtung von Güterhändlern bei Zahlungen mit Kryptowährungen' (2019) 12 *Corporate Compliance Zeitschrift*, 149 (156 et seq.).
[15] Cf. Grzywotz, *Virtuelle Kryptowährungen und Geldwäsche* (2019), 98 et seqq; see also the supranational risk assessment of the European Commission, → para. 73.
[16] Maume, Haffke and Zimmermann, 'Bitcoin versus Bargeld – Die geldwäscherechtliche Verpflichtung von Güterhändlern bei Zahlungen mit Kryptowährungen' (2019) 12 *Corporate Compliance Zeitschrift*, 149 (151 et seq.).
[17] In August 2020, the largest ever seizure of terrorist organizations cryptocurrency accounts has taken place in the US, see US Department of Justice, 'Global Disruption of Three Terror Finance Cyber-Enabled Campaigns' (August 2020), available at https://beck-link.de/3dbk8 (accessed 29.4.2021); see also Foley, Karlsen and Putniņš, 'Sex, Drugs, and Bitcoin: How Much Illegal Activity Is Financed Through Cryptocurrencies?', *Review of Financial Studies* (forthcoming).

III. Comparison with Cash and Fiat Money

8   Modern payment transactions and their regulation are based on cash and book money. From an anti-money laundering perspective, both forms of money come with certain risks.[18] The use of **cash** is **anonymous**. The risk of being used for money laundering purposes is high as it is not possible to trace the use of cash without identity checks having been carried out. On the other hand, its physical form and border controls set **de facto limits** to international cash transfers. Due to their technical design (→ para. 7), crypto assets (in particular, cryptocurrencies) are even more dangerous than cash under anti-money laundering law in terms of international circulation.

Book money, on the other hand, is much less dangerous under the existing regulatory system. It is true that it is **highly fit for circulation** – especially in an international context. However, it is not transferred anonymously, but via real names (of the payer and the payee).[19] When accounts are opened and large amounts of cash are deposited or withdrawn, the bank checks the identity of the customer in order to fulfil its AML obligations. Therefore, cashless transactions constitute, at least on paper, a **closed system** that allows for the identification of payment flows. The effectiveness of this system depends to a large extent on the diligence of the banks as gatekeepers. In contrast to crypto assets, it is not possible to switch to a direct peer-to-peer transfer; the involvement of a bank or a related financial service as an intermediary is mandatory. This makes crypto assets **more dangerous** from a money laundering point of view than book money **in terms of anonymity**. So, it is fair to say that in the light of AML, crypto assets combine the specific risks of both cash and book money.

C. Regulatory System of Anti-Money Laundering in the EU

I. Overview – Structure and Level of Harmonisation

9   Since 1991, EU Member States have been obliged by Directives to transpose certain AML requirements for private entities into national law. On an EU level, the first requirements were introduced by Council Directive 91/308/EEC on the 10th of June 1991 (this is what is referred to as the 'First Anti-Money Laundering Directive', in short 'AMLD1'). As the topic has become more and more relevant over the past decades, the rules have been altered and expanded several times. Currently in force is Directive (EU) 2015/849 (Fourth Anti-Money Laundering Directive, AMLD4). Some rules in AMLD4 have been amended and/or expanded by Directive (EU) 2018/843 (Fifth Anti-Money Laundering Directive, AMLD5) which alters the text of the AMLD4. AMLD5 had to be implemented by Member States by 10 January 2020 (see Art. 4(1) AMLD5).[20] Many countries have implemented changes shortly after this deadline. Still, at the time of writing this chapter (August 2020), three countries have not implemented AMLD5 on a

---

[18] Maume, Haffke and Zimmermann, 'Bitcoin versus Bargeld – Die geldwäscherechtliche Verpflichtung von Güterhändlern bei Zahlungen mit Kryptowährungen' (2019) 12 *Corporate Compliance Zeitschrift*, 149 (151 et seq.).

[19] See Regulation (EU) No. 2015/847 on information accompanying transfers of funds and repealing Regulation (EC) No. 1781/2006, OJ L 141, 5.6.2015 p. 1–18.

[20] Wherever reference is made to AMLD4 in this chapter, it shall be understood as referring to the consolidated version of AMLD4 and AMLD5. Wherever reference is made to a change in legislation originating in AMLD5, the exact provision of AMLD5 is also stated.

national level (Cyprus, Portugal and Spain). Provisions on the criminal offence of money laundering have been harmonised across the EU in a sixth AML Directive (→ para. 165 et seqq.). Currently, the European Commission is also drafting a proposal on an AML Regulation to harmonise AML efforts (→ para. 171).

EU AML legislation follows a **two-tiered structure**: Only those companies that are defined as so-called **obliged entities** in Art. (2)(1) AMLD4 are subject to AML laws ('who?'). In a second step, these obliged entities have to fulfil certain **obligations under anti-money laundering law** ('what?').

Member states may, by following a risk-based approach, **extend the scope of obliged entities** to other professions and undertakings if these engage in activities 'which are particularly likely to be used for the purposes of money laundering or terrorist financing' (Art. (4)(1) AMLD4). If they choose to do so, they need to notify the European Commission (Art. (4)(2) AMLD4). This is particularly relevant in the context of crypto intermediaries that are not within the scope of EU AML policies. According to Art. 5 AMLD4, Member states may also adopt or retain in force **stricter AML requirements** that obliged entities have to meet. This means that both with regards to obliged entities and their requirements, EU anti-money laundering law is **only partially harmonised**.

This chapter will focus on AML regulation on the EU level. Where appropriate, reference to specific national rules will be made.

II. Tokens in the EU AML System

The status of crypto intermediaries as obliged entities in EU AML law (→ para. 42 et seqq.) is defined by reference to certain behaviours and kinds of goods on the market. The terms 'virtual currencies' (→ para. 13 et seqq.), 'transferable security' (→ para. 25) and 'electronic money' (→ para. 26) are particularly relevant in this context.

1. Tokens as Virtual Currencies

With AMLD5, a definition of so-called **virtual currencies** is introduced for the first time in EU law. This was necessitated by the fact that several crypto intermediaries were not covered under the existing regime of AMLD4.[21] By introducing AMLD5, European Union legislators wanted to make sure that competent authorities of Member States are 'able, through obliged entities, to monitor the use of virtual currencies' (Rec. 8 AMLD5). The approach is to gather as much information for national authorities as possible in order to achieve this goal.

The **definition** of a virtual currency is according to Art. 1(2)(d) AMLD5 (Art. 3(18) AMLD4):

> 'a digital representation of value that is not issued or guaranteed by a central bank or a public authority, is not necessarily attached to a legally established currency and does not possess a legal status of currency or money, but is accepted by natural or legal persons as a means of exchange and which can be transferred, stored and traded electronically.'

The term is technologically neutral. The representation of value can be made digitally on any medium or technology. Virtual currencies thus include tokens issued on a blockchain but are not limited thereto. All technically possible forms of tokens are covered by this aspect of the definition.

---

[21] See European Commission, 'Strengthened EU rules to prevent money laundering and terrorism financing—Fact Sheet' (July 2018), available at https://beck-link.de/ksh88 (accessed 29.4.2021).

15   In order to assess which tokens are covered by the definition, one needs to assess the term's five conditions separately.

16   First, any digital representation issued or guaranteed by a **central bank or a public authority** is excluded. This means that any future so-called 'central bank digital currencies (CBDC)', even if issued or guaranteed by a central bank from outside the European Union, would be excluded from virtual currencies within the meaning of AMLD5.

17   Second, virtual currencies would **not need to be attached** to a legally established currency. This 'requirement' is rather to be understood as a clarification: Both tokens attached to a legally established currency and those that are not fall under the term virtual currency. As a consequence, stable coins (→ § 1 para. 76 and → § 9 para. 36 et seqq.) can also be virtual currencies.

18   Third, any digital representation of value that holds the **legal status of currency or money cannot** be classified as a virtual currency. This is meant to exclude electronic money within the meaning of Art. 2 Directive 2009/100/EC (→ § 9 para. 34 et seq.). However, tokens can still be classified as electronic money.

19   Fourth, a token must be able to be '**transferred, stored and traded electronically**.' The technical possibility that it is done so is sufficient – there is no need for the token to be actually transferred, stored and traded.[22] This is usually the case for all types of tokens issued on a blockchain: They can all be transferred via the blockchain, stored in some type of wallet (→ § 1 para. 25 et seqq.) and traded (on cryptocurrency exchanges – although possible for almost all tokens, most tokens issued are not actually traded there[23]). While this does not exclude any of the token categories as such, tokens that have been equipped with a so-called technical **lock-up** (→ § 1 para. 84) are **not virtual currencies**. Their technical specifications prohibit them from being transferred to a different wallet.

20   Fifth, and most importantly, virtual currencies 'must be **accepted by natural or legal persons as a means of exchange**.' This requirement addresses the actual use of a token. The use given in the definition – 'means of exchange' – is not defined in AMLD5. Rec. 10 AMLD5 lists potential uses: While virtual currencies 'can be used as a means of payment, they could also be used for other purposes [...] such as means of exchange, investment, store-of-value products or use in online casinos.' The Directive's aim is to cover 'all the potential uses of virtual currencies.'[24]

It must therefore be determined what is meant by the term 'as a means of exchange'. There are **two different interpretations** – a broader and a more restrictive one.

21   The term 'means of exchange' could be interpreted as '**accepted as a medium in an exchange**'. In theory, all types of tokens can be 'exchanged'. Under this broad interpretation, all possible uses of virtual currencies mentioned in the recital would be covered the definition in the legal text: currency tokens are exchanged for goods and services; investment tokens are traded on exchanges; and utility tokens can be

---

[22] See Haffke, Fromberger and Zimmermann, 'Cryptocurrencies and anti-money laundering: the shortcomings of the fifth AML Directive (EU) and how to address them' (2020) 21 *Journal of Banking Regulation*, 125 (131).

[23] See Fromberger and Haffke 'ICO Market Report 2018/2019 – Performance Analysis of 2018's Initial Coin Offerings' (2019), available at https://ssrn.com/abstract=3512125 (accessed 29.4.2021). To be technically precise, only the private key is or can be stored. Tokens are part of the blockchain – they cannot be stored elsewhere.

[24] Vandezande, 'Virtual currencies under EU anti-money laundering law' (2017) 33 *Computer Law and Security Review*, 341 (351).

'redeemed' in exchange for goods and services. This view seems to have been taken by the ECB upon the proposal of AMLD5.[25]

However, this interpretation is not to be preferred.[26] Rather, the term should be construed in a narrower sense.[27] This is for three main reasons. First, if it were to be interpreted widely, it would have **no limiting function** at all. Nearly every item could be exchanged in the way construed above (e.g. stones, pumpkins). This would expand AML regulation to unwarranted territories.[28] Second, Rec. 10 AMLD5 conflicts with the **wording of Art. 1(2)(d) AMLD5,** which only lists one possible use (means of exchange). The recital shows that the legislator was well aware that it is not the only and overarching use: Other uses are *listed together with* means of exchange in the *same list* of examples. This is also shown by the fact that the list in the recitals is not meant to be understood as exclusive ('such as'). Third, and most importantly, the term 'meant of exchange' must be given its **economically correct interpretation**.[29] It is well known in economics and used to describe a function of money.[30] In short, means of exchange are not used for consumption or production, but facilitate trade between people that are not interested in consuming or trading each other's goods directly. The terms 'means of payment' and 'means of exchange – which are expressly used separately in Rec. 10 – are usually used interchangeably by scholars.[31] Even though there might be minor differences, the term 'means of exchange' already covers all means of payment.[32]

The correct interpretation thus limits the term 'virtual currency' to those tokens used as an intermediary asset in trade without the traders having an interest in their consumption. This means that while **currency tokens are virtual currencies, investment tokens and utility tokens are not**.[33] Hybrid tokens are virtual currencies in case their main use is similar to those of currency tokens.

As AMLD4 and AMLD5 only harmonise national laws at a minimum level and Member States may enact stricter and more far-reaching AML provisions (→ para. 11),

---

[25] See European Central Bank, 'Opinion on a proposal for a directive of the European Parliament and of the Council amending Directive (EU) 2015/849 on the prevention of the use of the financial system for the purposes of money laundering or terrorist financing and amending Directive 2009/101/EC, OJ C 459/3, 9.12.2016, p. 3–6.
[26] See Haffke, Fromberger and Zimmermann, 'Cryptocurrencies and anti-money laundering: the shortcomings of the fifth AML Directive (EU) and how to address them' (2020) 21 *Journal of Banking Regulation*, 125 (132, 133).
[27] The UK Cryptoassets Taskforce also took this view, see HM Treasury, FCA and Bank of England, 'Final report' (October 2018), 3, available at https://beck-link.de/w3xv5 (accessed 29.4.2021).
[28] See Haffke, Fromberger and Zimmermann, 'Cryptocurrencies and anti-money laundering: the shortcomings of the fifth AML Directive (EU) and how to address them' (2020) 21 *Journal of Banking Regulation*, 125 (132).
[29] For the discussion on this and for further references, see Haffke, Fromberger and Zimmermann, 'Cryptocurrencies and anti-money laundering: the shortcomings of the fifth AML Directive (EU) and how to address them' (2020) 21 *Journal of Banking Regulation*, 125 (132 et seq.).
[30] Rabin, *Monetary Theory* (2004), 22 et seqq.; Mishkin, *The Economics of Money, Banking and Financial Markets* (2nd edn, 2009), 54 et seq.; Moritz, *Geldtheorie und Geldpolitik* (3rd edn, 2012), 6 et seq.; Holtenmöller, *Geldtheorie und Geldpolitik* (2008), 25 et seq.
[31] See with further references: Haffke, Fromberger and Zimmermann, 'Cryptocurrencies and anti-money laundering: the shortcomings of the fifth AML Directive (EU) and how to address them' (2020) 21 *Journal of Banking Regulation*, 125 (133); also Claassen, *Grundlagen der Geldtheorie* (2nd edn, 1980), 37 et seqq., who uses the German term 'Zahlungsmittel' (means of payment) to describe the phenomenon of a 'Tauschmittel' (means of exchange).
[32] See Haffke, Fromberger and Zimmermann, 'Cryptocurrencies and anti-money laundering: the shortcomings of the fifth AML Directive (EU) and how to address them' (2020) 21 *Journal of Banking Regulation*, 125 (133).
[33] Ibid.

this conclusion only applies to the EU level. National definitions of the term 'virtual currency' (or their national translations) may thus be wider and may also cover forms of investment and/or utility tokens. Germany, for example, expanded the term to investment tokens, but not to utility tokens.[34] The UK, which – despite Brexit – has implemented AMLD5, chose to cover all forms of tokens. However, the UK limited the definition to 'cryptographically secured digital representations of value or contractual rights that uses a form of distributed ledger technology…'.[35] This deviates from the technologically neutral definition of AMLD5 and thus constitutes a implementation deficit. Other countries like Austria or Ireland implemented the literal definition as provided by AMLD5.[36]

2. Tokens as Securities

25   AMLD5 refers to the term 'securities' in Art. 2(1)(3)(b)(ii) and (iii) without giving a definition. As the term is used multiple times in EU law, it must be interpreted uniformly throughout the different legal instruments. The only viable interpretation is that it refers to the term of 'transferable securities' within the meaning of Art. 4(1)(44) of Directive 2014/65/EU (MiFID2). This term applies to investment tokens and some kinds of utility tokens, but not to currency tokens (→ § 7 para. 47 et seq.).

3. Tokens as Electronic Money

26   As a general rule, currency tokens are not electronic money according to Art. 2 Directive 2009/100/EC (→ § 9 para. 34 et seq.). In the special case of **stable coins** (→ § 1 para. 76), however, this should be the case. While investment tokens are not electronic money, this may be the case for certain **utility tokens** (→ § 9 para. 43 et seqq.). Companies whose business model involves tokens that qualify as electronic money may therefore be classified as obliged entities (→ para. 64 et seqq.).

4. Transactions

27   The transaction is an important starting point for obligations under AML law. The term is not defined in AMLD4 or AMLD5. Therefore, Member States have some leeway when implementing it into national law. Still, the term is part of EU law and must therefore be given a uniform interpretation on the EU level.[37]

---

[34] On this, see Maume and Haffke, '§ 15 – Geldwäsche-Compliance' in Maume, Maute and Fromberger (eds), *Rechtshandbuch Kryptowerte* (2020), § 15, para. 14.

[35] See Section 14A(3)(a) of The Money Laundering, Terrorist Financing and Transfer of Funds (Information on the Payer) Regulations 2017, as amended by The Money Laundering Terrorist Financing (Amendment) Regulations 2019.

[36] For Austria, see § 2, No. 21 of the Austrian Anti-Money Laundering Act (Finanzmarkt-Geldwäschegesetz – FM-GwG); for Ireland, see Section 24(1) of the Criminal Justice (Money Laundering and Terrorist Financing) Act 2010 as amended by Criminal Justice (Money Laundering and Terrorist Financing) (Amendment) Act 2020.

[37] Terms of a provision of EU Law which makes no express reference to the law of the Member States for the purpose of determining its meaning and scope must, according to settled case law of the CJEU, be given an autonomous and uniform interpretation throughout the European Union, while having regard to the context of the provision and the objective pursued by the legislation in question, see for example ECJ, Judgment of 3 September 2014, *Deckmyn and Vrijheidsfonds*, C-201-13, EU:C:2014:2132, para. 14; ECJ, Judgment of 21 October 2010, *Padawan SL v Sociedad general de Autores y Editores de Espana (SGAE)*, C-467-08, EU:C:2010:620, para. 32; ECJ, Judgment of 2 April 2009, *Proceedings brought by A*, C-523-07, EU:C:2009:225, para. 34; ECJ, Judgment of 19 September 2000, *Grand Duchy of Luxemburg v Berthe Linster, Aloyse Linster and Yvonne Linster*, C-287-98, EU:C:2000:468, para. 43; ECJ, Judgment of 18 January 1984, *Ekro BV Vee-en Vleeshandel v Produktschap voor Vee en Vlees*, C-327-82, EU:C:1984:11, para. 11.

§ 10. Anti-Money Laundering

One can thus take a look at national definitions of the tern. For example, § 1(5)(1) of the German Anti-Money Laundering Act (GwG) defines the term (translated by the authors) as: act or, insofar as there is a connection between them, several acts which have as their object or effect or cause or effect a movement of money or another transfer of assets. The UK AML Act, on the other hand, does not define the term specifically.

However, AMLD4 itself gives an indication for the minimum requirement for a 'transaction'. Art. 3(3) AMLD4 defines the term **property**. This is, among other things, 'assets of any kind, whether corporeal or incorporeal, movable or immovable, tangible or intangible (...).' This definition is broad and includes money and all other kinds of assets. Since the overarching purpose of AML regulation is to prevent the circulation of money and other assets that have been obtained illegally,[38] the pivotal term 'transaction' should apply at least to all transfers of ownership of, or possession of, 'property' within the meaning of Art. 3(3) AMLD4. In the case of intermediary activities, the legal transaction mediated is to be considered the respective transaction. 28

With regards to tokens, their owner has **exclusive (factual) access** to them via his private key. Tokens are also transferrable. The owners are therefore granted an **asset** by buyers and sellers on trading platforms or within the framework of initial coin offerings (→ § 1 para. 81 et seqq.). Thus, the transfer of any token is a transfer of assets and a transaction within the meaning of AMLD4.[39] This interpretation is also warranted as virtual currencies present new risks and challenges for money laundering which should be addressed appropriately (Directive 2018/1673/EU, Rec. 6; on this Directive → para. 166). These risks could not be addressed appropriately if despite virtual currencies being covered AMLD5, a transfer of tokens would not be.

5. Tokens and the Concept of Cash within AML Law

AMLD5 uses the terms 'cash' and 'payments in cash'. Cash is not legally defined in primary EU law[40] or in AMLD4 or AMLD5. It is typically equated with **banknotes and coins** and thus with legal tender.[41] This coincides with Regulation (EC) No. 974/98 on the introduction of the euro, which repeatedly refers to banknotes and coins. As the term cash has been incorporated in AMLD4 before specifics like virtual currencies were introduced by AMLD5, any extension of the term 'cash' to these forms of currencies would have to be expressly stated. This has not been done. Virtual currencies have even been specifically distinguished from money with legal status (→ para. 13 et seqq.). Therefore, tokens cannot be included in the definition of cash within the meaning of EU AML law. 29

---

[38] Contrary to the general understanding of the language, the object of money laundering is not just money; see in particular Art. 2 et seqq. of Directive 2018/1673/EU on combating money laundering by criminal law, OJ L 284, 12.11.2018 p. 22–30; Figura, in Herzog, *GwG*, § 1, para. 42 et seq.

[39] Expressly stated for the interpretation of German AML law: Neuheuser, in *MünchKommStGB*, § 261, para. 31 and for tokens in general Keding, 'Die aufsichtsrechtliche Behandlung von Machine-to-Machine-Zahlungen unter Rückgriff auf Peer-to-Peer-Netzwerke', (2018) 72 *Zeitschrift für Wirtschafts- und Bankrecht*, 64 (68).

[40] This should not be confused with the status of the euro as the EU's currency, as defined by Art. 3(4) of the Treaty on the European Union.

[41] See e.g. https://dictionary.cambridge.org/dictionary/english/cash, which clearly defined cash as 'money in the form of notes and coins rather than cheques or credit cards'; for Germany ('Bargeld') see Berger and Rübsamen, in Berger and Rübsamen (eds), *BbankG*, § 14, para. 6: 'The Bundesbank provides the commercial banks with demand-driven cash via its branches' (see § 10, para. 8 et seqq.); (...) As a rule, the banknotes and coins are transported by private security service providers."; also the German Duden defines defines cash or cash money as money in bank notes or coins.

III. Competent Authority, Territorial Scope and Financial Intelligence Units

1. Competent Authorities

30　There is no central authority on an EU level that is responsible for supervising obliged entities throughout the Union (for future plans, → para. 172). AMLD4 assigns the responsibility for supervising AML regulation to the so called 'competent authorities' of the Member States. The competent authority of the home Member State shall ensure compliance for group-wide policies and procedures, while those of the host Member State shall supervise branches and subsidiaries (Art. 28 AMLD4, Recs. 52 and 53).

31　AMLD4 and AMLD5 do not make any special provisions on the national organisation of competent authorities. Therefore, Member States are free to decide and organise their competent authorities within their relevant territories as they see fit. While financial institutions are usually centrally supervised by one authority, for other professions such as lawyers and tax consultants, the competent authority might be the national or regional professional body.[42] Supervision might thus be highly fragmented. In Germany, for example, the supervision regime is split up into more than 200 different authorities, depending on the type of obliged entity and their seat.[43] The national and regional fragmentation can cause problems in the consistent application of laws and may increase the costs authorities and businesses face in their tasks under AML law. It is also for these reasons that the EU is currently planning on establishing an EU level supervisor, at least for some obliged entities (→ para. 172).

2. Territorial Scope

32　Pursuant to Art. 3(1) and Art. 3(2)(f) AMLD4, States must ensure that their AML law applies to those credit and financial services institutions of the home Member State as well as to branches of these types of institutions, irrespective of whether their head office is situated within the EU or in a third country. This means that EU AML law requires Member States to apply their AML laws to those credit and financial institutions which have their **registered office** in that state, as well as to branches that are located within the Union, irrespective of whether the head office of that institution is situated in a Member State or in a third country.

33　EU AML law does not require Member States to also apply their AML laws to registered offices of those institutions abroad. This is not mandatory, even if the undertaking specifically targets a market within the Union. Even after the implementation of AMLD5 this remains unchanged. However, it may be necessary to consider that countries may require such undertakings to be licensed under their financial services supervision regime.

34　For **persons trading in goods and persons storing, trading or acting as intermediaries in the works of art,** territorial applicability of EU AML law is not specifically set

---

[42] See, for example, § 50 GwG or Section 7(1) of the UKs The Money Laundering, Terrorist Financing and Transfer of Funds (Information on the Payer) Regulations 2017.

[43] For example, for traders in goods alone, in Germany, 107 different supervisory authorities exist, depending on the region, see Maume, Haffke and Zimmermann, 'Bitcoin versus Bargeld – Die geldwäscherechtliche Verpflichtung von Güterhändlern bei Zahlungen mit Kryptowährungen' (2019) 12 *Corporate Compliance Zeitschrift*, 149 (156); for other professions, the district court (Landgericht) or the professional body might be the supervisory authority, see § 50 GwG.

out. As the competent authority in case of international undertakings is defined by Art. 28 AMLD4 via branches and subsidiaries, this must mean that Member States are at least required to supervise those persons trading in goods and those persons storing, trading or acting as intermediaries in the works of art that have a physical branch or subsidiary in their territory, regardless of the country of the head office. This view is also supported by Rec. 52 AMLD4 which relates supervisory responsibility to the operation of 'establishments', i.e. physical presences in a Member State.

The question remains if national AML laws apply if there is no physical presence of an obliged entity in a Member State. This problem arises, inter alia, for **persons trading in goods solely or predominantly online (online traders)**. Persons trading in goods are defined, by their wording, in relation to their activities (also → para. 61). It is therefore logical to also assess the territorial application based on to their activities. 35

If the activities are carried out from a head office, branch, subsidiary or other physical presence **in another Member State,** AMLD4 does not require other Member States to also supervise these companies, even if the markets of these other Member States are specifically targeted. This is for two reasons: First, authorities of that Member State could regularly not carry out their supervisory duties effectively if they would need access to documents and sites located in another Member State.[44] And secondly, this would lead to double supervision of the same entity by authorities of two Member States. However, it should also be noted that AMLD4 does not prohibit Member States from extending their AML laws to these entities. In the light of effective supervision, such expansion should only be enacted by Member States after careful consideration.

This leads to a different conclusion if the activities are carried out from a head office, branch, subsidiary or other physical presence situated **in a third country**. In such case, this entity would not be supervised by a competent authority within the Union. This result cannot have been envisaged by AMLD4 as potential money laundering can 'damage the integrity, stability and reputation of the financial sector, and threaten the internal market of the Union as well as international development' (Rec. 1 AMLD4). If these problems are to be addressed on a European level, as stipulated by Rec. 1(2) AMLD4, such activities should be supervised by a competent authority located within the Union. While AMLD4 and AMLD5 do not make it mandatory to supervise these activities with regards to AML policies, Member States are highly encouraged to do so to ensure effective protection of the stability of the Union's internal market.

3. Financial Intelligence Units (FIUs)

Each Member State is required to establish **a Financial Intelligence Unit (FIU)** to prevent, detect and effectively combat money laundering and terrorist financing (Art. 32(1) AMLD4). This has to be a separate institution from the competent authority. 36

In contrast to supervision, the FIU is responsible for **receiving and analysing suspicious transaction reports** (→ para. 146 et seq.) and any other related information. It shall analyse these reports and disseminate their results to the relevant authorities (e.g., the prosecution) where there are grounds to suspect money laundering, other predicate offences or terrorist financing (Art. 32(3) AMLD4). 37

To fulfil these tasks, it must be given effective access to all relevant information. While operating, the FIU shall be independent and autonomous. This means that the 38

---

[44] On this, see Rec. 53 AMLD4, which states that the supervisory authority of the host Member State (where there is a physical presence) shall retain responsibility for enforcing the establishment's compliance and carry out onsite inspections and offsite monitoring.

FIU is autonomous in their decisions to analyse suspicious transaction reports, whether to forward them and in which way, as well as which additional information to gather in the process.

IV. Licensing or Registration Regime

39   There is **no central registration or licensing regime** for AML intermediaries on an EU level. Rather, Art. 47(1) AMLD4 requires Member states to ensure that providers of exchange services between virtual currencies and fiat currencies (fiat-to-crypto exchanges, → para. 43 et seq.) as well as custodian wallet providers (→ para. 50) are registered. Unlike currency exchange offices or providers of gambling services, crypto intermediaries **do not require licensing** or authorisation under AMLD5.[45]

40   However, as the EU AML regime is **only partially harmonised** (→ para. 11), Member states **may adopt stricter measures**. For example, in Germany, crypto intermediaries are classified as financial institutions ('Finanzdienstleistungsinstitute') under German banking law and thus require authorisation by the German BaFin (for the German regime, → § 17).

41   Unlike Art. 32, 33 MiFID2, EU AML law **does not provide for a passporting regime** (→ § 8 para. 11 et seq.). However, Member States could accept the AML registration in another Member State as satisfying the requirement of registration in their own Member State by enacting respective legislation. Nevertheless, such legislation is highly unlikely as Member States would want to ensure that crypto intermediaries are at least known if they operate within their Member State, especially as they need to be supervised effectively.

D. Crypto Intermediaries as Obliged Entities

42   Before AMLD5 came into force, there were no specific standards or definitions for companies or intermediaries providing services relating to crypto assets. It was the prevailing opinion that fiat-to-crypto and crypto-to-crypto exchanges, wallet providers and tumbler services were not obliged entities under AMLD4.[46] The question is, therefore, how AMLD5 has changed the **status of crypto intermediaries as obliged entities**.

For this, it is important to note that the following definitions often relate to the terms 'virtual currency'; as stated above, this term only covers currency tokens and not investment or utility tokens (→ para. 23), but Member States may have enacted more comprehensive legislation in this regard (→ para. 11, 24).

I. Fiat-to-Crypto Exchanges

43   Art. 1(1)(1)(c) AMLD5 introduced a new obliged entity, referred to as **'providers engaged in exchange services between virtual currencies and fiat currencies.'** This

---

[45] However, authorisation might be required under EU financial services law (in particular, MiFID2, → § 8 para. 37 et seqq.).
[46] Houben and Snyers, 'Cryptocurrencies and Blockchain' Brussels, (July 2018), 62, available at https://beck-link.de/8pt8x (accessed 29.4.2021); Vandezande, *Virtual Currencies: A Legal Framework* (2018), 286, 298–303 and 309 et seq., also citing the view of the European Commission, see European Commission, 'Strengthened EU rules to prevent money laundering and terrorism financing—Fact Sheet' (July 2018), available at https://beck-link.de/ksh88 (accessed 29.4.2021).

definition covers all fiat-to-crypto exchanges (→ § 1 para. 91) if they trade at least one virtual currency within the meaning of AMLD5 (→ para. 13 et seqq.) against a fiat currency. This definition only covers currency tokens and does not include investment or utility tokens. **Exchanges are covered** by the definition even if they exchange fiat and virtual currencies in one direction only – a reciprocal exchange is not required (on this, → para. 56).

The definition also covers **both centralised and decentralised forms** of fiat-to-crypto exchanges (for the distinction, → § 1 para. 97 et seqq.). Centralised forms clearly engage in exchange services as they buy and sell tokens directly from their users. Decentralised exchanges do not do so but are still to be classified as 'providers engaged in exchange services' because Art. 1(1)(c) AMLD5 does not state any requirements on how this service is rendered. Providers of exchange services that provide a platform to conduct the exchange – even without being a contracting party in the transaction – also 'engage' in the exchange. Their service is an indispensable part for the users to be able to conduct the transaction.[47] Thus, Member States are required to make both centralised and decentralised fiat-to-crypto exchanges obliged entities under their national AML laws.

II. Crypto-to-Crypto Exchanges

The obliged entity introduced by Art. 1(1)(c) AMLD5 (→ para. 43) **does not include providers of exchange services that only exchange one virtual currency into other virtual currencies** (crypto-to-crypto exchange, → § 1 para. 92). Thus, if a provider of a crypto-to-crypto exchange does not fulfil the definition of any other obliged entity, they are not covered by EU AML law.

This decision by EU lawmakers seems odd. AMLD5 itself states that criminals can 'transfer money into the Union financial system or *within virtual currency networks*.' The origin of tokens used can also be disguised by exchanging them between different blockchains.[48] To address this fact, the **transfer of money into the** EU within the network of virtual currencies would also **need to be monitored**. This could be done best by having crypto-to-crypto exchanges to identify customers and report suspicious transactions (→ para. 146 et seqq.) – in other words, **by making them obliged entities** as well. This was also envisaged by the European Securities and Markets Authority (ESMA) and the European Banking Authority (EBA).[49] In addition, it would also synchronise the AML laws for fiat currencies and virtual currencies: The provider of exchange services of one fiat currency into another fiat currency (bureaux de change) is already an obliged entity (see Art. 2(1)(2) and Art. 3 (2)(a) AMLD4).

However, despite AMLD5 not covering crypto-to-crypto exchanges specifically, **Member States may opt to make them obliged entities** under their national laws as this is specifically allowed for by Art. 4(2) AMLD4 (→ para. 11). For example,

---

[47] Haffke, Fromberger and Zimmermann, 'Cryptocurrencies and anti-money laundering: the shortcomings of the fifth AML Directive (EU) and how to address them' (2020) 21 *Journal of Banking Regulation*, 125 (134).

[48] Ibid, 135.

[49] See European Securities and Markets Authority, 'Advice – Initial Coin Offerings and Crypto-Assets' (January 2019) 36, available at https://beck-link.de/7caf4 (accessed 29.4.2021); see European Banking Authority, 'Report with advice for the European Commission on crypto-assets' (January 2019), 20 et seq., available at https://beck-link.de/kc78a (accessed 29.4.2021); See also the recommendations of the FATF, 'Regulation of virtual assets' (October 2018), available at https://beck-link.de/3hznn (accessed 29.4.2021).

Germany,[50] the United Kingdom,[51] Austria[52] and Malta[53] have done so when implementing AMLD5 into their national laws, while Ireland has not done so.[54]

48   However, providers of crypto-to-crypto exchanges are covered by EU AML law if they meet the definition of **other obliged entities** listed in AMLD4 or AMLD5, for example if the exchange also acts as a fiat-to-crypto exchange (→ para. 43 et seq.) or as a custodian wallet provider (→ para. 50).

III. Wallet Providers

49   AMLD5 introduces a second new obliged entity with regards to crypto assets – so called **'custodian wallet providers'** (Art. 1(1)(c) AMLD5). These are now defined in Art. 3(1) AMLD4 as 'an entity that provides services to safeguard private cryptographic keys on behalf of its customers, to hold, store and transfer virtual currencies.' The question is which types of wallet providers (→ § 1 para. 27) are covered by this definition. The main issue is whether the service provided 'safeguards private cryptographic keys on behalf of its customers.'

50   **Custodian wallet providers** (→ § 1 para. 27) offer their customers wallets in which their **private keys are stored**. As not to remember and manually enter the private key for every transaction makes the service more convenient for the user, many wallet providers operate in this manner. They clearly safeguard private cryptographic keys and **fall under the definition**.[55]

51   **Non-custodian wallet providers** (→ § 1 para. 27), on the other hand, are **not an obliged entity** under EU AML law. If they only provide means for users to store their private keys themselves, they are not covered by AMLD5. Neither are interface providers (→ § 1 para. 27) as they do also not safeguard (i.e. store) the customer's private key.[56]

52   Thus, Member States are only required to make custodian wallet providers subject to their national AML laws. Member States may make non-custodian wallet providers obliged entities under their national laws as this is allowed for by Art. 4(2) AMLD4. While most countries like Germany have not done so, Austria's law on this remains open to some interpretation.[57]

IV. Tumblers

53   **Tumbler operators** (→ § 1 para. 106 et seq.) are currently **not covered** by Art. 2 AMLD4 and thus not subject obligations under EU AML law. This has remained

---

[50] § 2(2) GWG and § 1(1a) of the Kreditwesengesetz (German Banking Act, 'KWG').

[51] Section 14A(1)(b) of The Money Laundering, Terrorist Financing and Transfer of Funds (Information on the Payer) Regulations 2017, as amended by The Money Laundering Terrorist Financing (Amendment) Regulations 2019.

[52] § 1(1) and § 2(22)(c) FM-GwG.

[53] Art. 2(1) of the Prevention of Money Laundering and Funding of Terrorism Regulations 373.01 (Subsidiary Legislation).

[54] Section 25(1) of the Criminal Justice (Money Laundering and Terrorist Financing) Act 2010 as amended by Criminal Justice (Money Laundering and Terrorist Financing) (Amendment) Act 2020.

[55] Haffke, Fromberger and Zimmermann, 'Cryptocurrencies and anti-money laundering: the shortcomings of the fifth AML Directive (EU) and how to address them' (2020) 21 *Journal of Banking Regulation*, 125 (134 et seq.).

[56] Ibid.

[57] See § 2(22)(d) FM-GwG and for the interpretation problems see Völkel, 'Begutachtungsentwurf eines Bundesgesetzes, mit dem das FM-GwG, das WiEReG, das KontRegG und das GSpG geändert werden' (April 2019), available at https://beck-link.de/ekw5t (accessed 29.4.2021).

unchanged after the implementation of AMLD5.⁵⁸ However, Member States may opt to make tumbler services obliged entities under their national laws as this is allowed for by Art. 4(2) AMLD4 (→ para. 11).⁵⁹ There might be some legitimate use cases for tumbler services.⁶⁰ The core aim of AML law is still based on identifying customers of certain industries and suspicious transactions within them. However, **making tumbler services subject to AML law is thus highly warranted**. While Germany, for example, has not done so, Austria has.⁶¹

V. Issuers of Tokens

Provided that a certain token does not constitute electronic money and its issuer is therefore not an electronic money issuer (→ para. 64), **token issuers** are **not expressly listed** as obliged entities under AMLD4. However, they might fall within the scope of Art. 2(1)(3)(g) AMLD4 as 'providers engaged in exchange services between virtual currencies and fiat currencies.' Even if this provision was intended to apply to fiat-to-crypto exchanges, if correctly interpreted, it is to be understood as to also cover issuers of virtual currencies. 54

If virtual currencies are issued, the goal is to raise capital. Therefore, the token is not issued for free, but usually either **in exchange for other virtual currencies or fiat currency** (→ § 1 para. 81 et seqq.).⁶² If fiat currency is accepted by the issuer, this essentially means that fiat currency is exchanged for virtual currency in the ICO. 55

This is not changed by the fact that issuers then only offer a one-way exchange from fiat into the issued virtual currency. A **reciprocal exchange is not required** to be classified as a 'provider engaged in exchange services'. A unilateral exchange is sufficient. The term *'services'* is not to be understood to require an exchange in both directions, but rather that the exchange is to be offered repeatedly, meaning multiple times.⁶³ This excludes private and non-recurring exchanges, but not the repeated issuing over a longer period in an ICO. 56

Issuing tokens is a service in this context. The concept of a service is to be interpreted autonomously under EU law, the **national contractual classification** is **irrelevant**.⁶⁴ In the absence of a definition of the term service in AMLD4 or AMLD5, 57

---

⁵⁸ Haffke, Fromberger and Zimmermann, 'Cryptocurrencies and anti-money laundering: the shortcomings of the fifth AML Directive (EU) and how to address them' (2020) 21 *Journal of Banking Regulation*, 125 (136).
⁵⁹ An example is Austria; see § 2(22)(c) nFM-GwG which specifically covers the case exchanging one virtual currency into the same virtual currency.
⁶⁰ Such legitimate use cases might be based on privacy or political reasons, e.g. to keep payments to health providers fully private; see CipherTrace, 'Cryptocurrency Anti-Money Laundering Report' (January 2019), 11, available at https://beck-link.de/w4awh (accessed 29.4.2021).
⁶¹ Haffke, Fromberger and Zimmermann, 'Cryptocurrencies and anti-money laundering: the shortcomings of the fifth AML Directive (EU) and how to address them' (2020) 21 *Journal of Banking Regulation*, 125 (136).
⁶² An exception is the so-called 'airdrop' in which tokens are handed out for free as a marketing tool. However, these airdrops typically complement 'regular' token sales that involve consideration on the subscriber's side.
⁶³ Haffke, Fromberger and Zimmermann, 'Cryptocurrencies and anti-money laundering: the shortcomings of the fifth AML Directive (EU) and how to address them' (2020) 21 *Journal of Banking Regulation*, 125 (137).
⁶⁴ Terms of Union law which do not refer to the law of the Member States for the purpose of determining their meaning and significance must, according to the settled case-law of the ECJ, be interpreted autonomously and uniformly throughout the territory of the Union, taking into account the context of the provision and the objective associated with the provision, see e.g. ECJ, Judgment of 3 September 2014, *Deckmyn and Vrijheidsfonds*, C-201-13, EU:C:2014:2132, para. 14; ECJ, Judgment of

the concept of service in Art. 56, 57 TFEU needs to be taken into account.[65] This term is interpreted broadly.[66] Services are all activities that are usually provided **for remuneration** and are not subject to any other fundamental freedom under EU law. Commercial activities are only listed as examples. The service in the sense of EU law therefore does not necessarily require the service to be offered on a continuing basis. The **issue of virtual currencies** against fiat money can be such a service since participation in the ICO is also to be understood as a **service**. Furthermore, although it is not required under the definition as outlined above, an ICO usually runs over a longer period of time anyway.[67]

58   This interpretation is also supported by the **purpose of the provision**. While making issuers obliged under AML laws may not have been initially intended by EU lawmakers, this consequence is reasonable as issuing tokens is a way to get hold of pseudonymous assets.[68] As AMLD5 only covers currency tokens (→ para. 23), their use for payment makes them highly suitable for abuse.[69] The large volume of some ICOs also makes them particularly suitable for money laundering.[70] We also need to keep in mind that issuers in 'regular' IPOs cooperate with service providers such as banks and other financial service providers when placing shares at a stock exchange. These institutions are subject to Art. 2(1) AMLD4 as financial institutions and credit institutions, making them subject to AML obligations. This is not the case for ICOs, which are typically marketed directly to the subscribers without the involvement of intermediaries. Thus, making ICO issuers subject to AML laws would close a gaping hole in the regulatory quilt.

59   As a result, Art. 2(1)(3)(g) AMLD4 should be **interpreted in a way that issuers of virtual currencies are also obliged entities.** Member States are therefore obliged to make them subject to their national AML laws. Not doing so could possibly make them subject to legal proceedings in front of the CJEU brought by the European Commission.

VI. Miners

60   **Miners** (→ § 1 para. 38 et seqq.) **and mining pools** (→ § 1 para. 40 et seqq.) of crypto assets are **not covered** by AMLD4. They could be subject to EU AML law if their activities fulfil the definition of another (non-blockchain related) obliged entity. Even if this is theoretically possible, it will be the exception rather than the norm. Member

---

21 October 2010, *Padawan SL v Sociedad general de Autores y Editores de Espana (SGAE)*, C-467-08, EU:C:2010:620, para. 32; ECJ, Judgment of 2 April 2009, *Proceedings brought by A*, C-523-07, EU:C:2009:225, para. 34; ECJ, Judgment of 19 September 2000, *Grand Duchy of Luxemburg v Berthe Linster, aloyse Linster and Yvonne Linster*, C-287-98, EU:C:2000:468, para. 43; ECJ, Judgment of 18 January 1984, *Ekro BV Vee-en Vleeshandel v Produktschap voor Vee en Vlees*, C-327-82, EU:C:1984:11, para. 11.

[65] EU law also refers to this in relation to services, see e.g. Art. 4 (1) to (3) of Directive 2006/123/EC on services in the internal market, OJ L 376, 27.12.2006, pp. 36–68, see Fromberger, Haffke and Zimmermann, 'Kryptowerte und Geldwäsche – Eine Analyse der 5. Geldwäscherichtlinie sowie des Gesetzesentwurfs der Bundesregierung' (2019) 19 *Zeitschrift für Bank- und Kapitalmarktrecht*, 377 (383).

[66] See Grüneberg, in Palandt, *BGB*, § 312, subpara. 3 mwN.

[67] Haffke, Fromberger and Zimmermann, 'Cryptocurrencies and anti-money laundering: the shortcomings of the fifth AML Directive (EU) and how to address them' (2020) 21 *Journal of Banking Regulation*, 125 (137).

[68] Ibid.

[69] Ibid.

[70] For the distribution of the volume of ICOs see Fromberger and Haffke, 'ICO Market Report 2018/2019 – Performance Analysis of 2018's Initial Coin Offerings' (2019), available at https://ssrn.com/abstract=3512125 (accessed 29.4.2021).

VII. Other Obliged Entities

1. Persons Trading in Goods

A highly relevant example of obliged entities are **persons trading in goods**. According to Art. 2(1)(3)(e) AMLD4, a person trading in goods must be made an obliged entity to the extent that payments are made or received in cash in an amount of EUR 10.000 or more. The form of the trading 'person' is irrelevant – it can be both natural and legal persons trading in goods. Businesses only providing services (e.g. repairs, cafes, delivery services) are not persons trading in goods.[71]

Persons trading in goods can come into contact with crypto assets when they sell goods commercially and accept currency tokens as a means of payment. However, Member States do not need to make every person trading in goods an obliged entity under EU AML law, but only those which make or receive cash in amount of EUR 10,000 or more. It is irrelevant how many such transactions are made, but only that it is generally done or, in case of early businesses, that such transactions are likely as part of their business model. The term 'cash' does not cover crypto assets (→ para. 29). It should be noted, however, that Member States may (→ para. 11) choose to include more persons trading in goods in their list of obliged entities; Germany, for example, has done so.[72]

2. Art Market Participants

Art. 1(1)(c) AMLD5 introduced two new (usually non-blockchain related) obliged entities, which are now set out in Art. 2(1)(3)(i) and (j) AMLD4, namely persons trading or acting as intermediaries in the trade of works of art and persons storing, trading or acting as intermediaries in the trade of works of art when this is carried out by free ports. These intermediaries shall be jointly referred to as **'art market participants'**[73] and are only to be made subject to AML law where the value of the transaction or a series of linked transactions amounts to EUR 10,000 or more. The threshold is defined in relation to the *value of (a) transction(s)* instead of the method of payment which also covers payments in crypto token; on the calculation of the value of a transaction in EUR that is made in currency tokens (→ para. 84 et seqq.).

The arts and crafts sector is particularly susceptible to money laundering, as it is usually concerned with individual transactions of high volume. In practice, these transactions are occasionally carried out via currency tokens. An art intermediary is for example someone who commercially arranges the conclusion of purchase contracts

---

[71] Häberle, in Erbs and Kohlhaas (eds), *GWG*, § 1, para. 10; Brian, Frey and Krais, 'Umsetzung der Fünften Geldwäsche-Richtlinie in Deutschland' (2019) 12 *Corporate Compliance Zeitschrift*, 245 (247); Krais, *Geldwäsche und Compliance* (2018), 89; Helmrich, 'Handelsunternehmen und Geldwäsche' (2009) 62 *Neue Juristische Wochenzeitschrift*, 3686.

[72] On the German specifics for persons trading in goods, see Maume, Haffke and Zimmermann, 'Bitcoin versus Bargeld – Die geldwäscherechtliche Verpflichtung von Güterhändlern bei Zahlungen mit Kryptowährungen' (2019) 12 *Corporate Compliance Zeitschrift*, 149; Maume and Haffke, '§ 15 – Geldwäsche-Compliance' in Maume, Maute and Fromberger (eds), *Rechtshandbuch Kryptowerte* (2020), § 15, paras. 53–56 and 80.

[73] This is also the term used in the UK's AML Act, see Section 14(1)(d) of The Money Laundering, Terrorist Financing and Transfer of Funds (Information on the Payer) Regulations 2017, as amended by The Money Laundering Terrorist Financing (Amendment) Regulations 2019.

for works of art; this also includes auctioneers and gallery owners. Warehouse keepers of art warehouses are also subject to this provision.[74]

3. Intermediaries with Regards to Electronic Money

64 If crypto assets are electronic money in the sense of Art. 2(2) Directive 2009/110/EC (→ § 9 para. 34 et seqq., and → para. 26), intermediaries with regards to this electronic money may be an obliged entity under EU AML law. This covers in particular **issuers of electronic money** within the meaning of Art. 2(3) Directive 2009/110/EC. These have been granted authorisation to issue electronic money under the laws of a Member State.

65 These issuers may distribute and redeem electronic money through natural or legal persons which act on their behalf ('**agents' or 'distributors'**). According to Art. 19(1)(b) AMLD4 these are **not themselves obliged entities** under EU AML law, but issuers need to have documentation in place that the agent or distributor will comply with AML obligations.

4. Banks and Other Obliged Entites

66 Even obliged entities whose business models are not designed specifically for tokens and who are subject to the AML regime, can come into contact with crypto assets. This can in turn trigger certain AML obligations (→ para. 67 et seqq.).

Of course, this is the case for **banks (credit institutions)** to which the EU AMLDs apply according to Art. 2(1)(1) AMLD4. Other obliged entities who come into contact with crypto assets are, for example, legal professionals (Art. 2(1)(3)(b) AMLD4)[75] or auditors, external accountants and tax advisors (Art. 2(1)(3)(a) AMLD4) or **providers of gambling services** (Art. 2(1)(3)(f) AMLD4).[76] However, this does not necessarily result in token-specific problems when applying the obligations under AML law.

E. AML Obligations for Crypto Intermediaries

I. Overview

67 The obligations under AML law can be divided into three topics; (1) obligations relating to risk assessment, Art. 6–8 AMLD4 (→ para. 70 et seqq.); (2) customer due diligence obligations, Art. 10–29 (→ para. 81 et seqq.); (3) suspicious transaction reporting obligations, Art. 33–39 AMLD4, (→ para. 146 et seqq.).

68 EU AML law basically follows a **risk-based approach**. Companies, business relationships and transactions within the meaning of the AMLD4 may vary depending on their risk for money laundering and terrorist financing. There may be considerable differences in the risk between obliged entities and their business models. It would, therefore,

---

[74] On this, see Brian, Frey and Krais, 'Umsetzung der Fünften Geldwäsche-Richtlinie in Deutschland' (2019) 12 *Corporate Compliance Zeitschrift*, 245 (248 et seq.).

[75] It is interesting to note that on an EU level, Member States are not obligated to make all legal professionals obliged entities, but only those that are concerned with/participating in/assisting in planning or carrying out of certain activities listed in AMLD4; these activities are largely financial or real estate related. Member States may, however, chose to make more or all legal professionals obliged entities.

[76] It should be noted that Member States may decide to exempt providers of certain gambling services from some or all of the national laws transposing EU AML laws 'on the basis of the proven low risk posed by the nature and, where appropriate, scale of operations of such services', Art. 2(2) AMLD4.

be neither logical nor purposeful to treat all companies the same when it comes to AML obligations. Each company must be assessed on a **case-by-case basis**.

Generally, if an obliged entity is head of a **corporate group**, group-wide policies and procedures need to be implemented, at least at the level of branches or majority-owned subsidiaries, irrespective of their location, Art. 45(1) AMLD4. The establishments usually have to adhere to the national AML laws of the country in which they operate, Art. 45(2) AMLD4, unless this is a third country with less strict AML/CFT standards than those of the home Member State of the group, in case of which that home Member State law shall be adhered to if possible, Art. 45(3) AMLD4.

II. Risk Assessment and Risk Management (Art. 6–8 AMLD4)

1. General Principles

The first category of requirements for obliged entities relate to **AML risk management**. On the level of the obliged entity, it comprises the entity's AML risk assessment as well as policies, controls and procedures to mitigate and manage the identified risks.

Member States must ensure that **obliged entities** conduct an appropriate **risk assessment** to identify and assess their risks of money laundering and terrorist financing (Art. 8(1)(1) AMLD4). Said Article lists risk factors that these obliged entities minimally need to consider, namely customer-based risks, country or geographic risks, product or service risks, transaction risks as well as risks related to delivery channels. Concrete steps of these risk assessments are left to the Member States to decide. These should be proportionate in relation to nature and size of the obliged entity in question (Art. 8(1)(2) AMLD4). In other words: the more complex and riskier the business, the more extensive the risk assessment should be.[77]

According to Art. 8(2) AMLD4, the risk assessment is to be **documented** and kept up-to-date. EU AML law does not prescribe the form of documentation or the frequency of necessary updates. Member States are allowed to have their own policies in this regard. In general, though, a risk assessment should be documented in permanent form, either in writing or in a corresponding electronic format.

The risk assessments shall further be made available to the relevant competent authorities or self-regulatory bodies (→ para. 30 et seq.). However, the concrete form of this requirement is left to the Member States, allowing them to enforce this rule only leniently. In sectors in which the AML risks are 'clear and understood', competent authorities may decide not to require individual risk assessments of obliged entities at all, if not otherwise stipulated by their national laws (Art. 8(2) AMLD4).

Based on these individual risk assessments, obliged entities need to set up **policies, controls and procedures** in order to effectively mitigate and manage AML and CFT risks. These measures are therefore the direct consequence of the individual risk assessments. In designing policies, controls and procedures, the obliged entities shall also take into account risk assessments made by Member States on a national level ('national risk assessment') as well as those published on an EU level every two-years ('supranational risk assessment').[78]

---

[77] For Germany, see Herzog, in Herzog, *GwG*, § 5, para. 14.
[78] The two previously published supranational risk assessment are European Commission, 'Report from the Commission to the European Parliament and the Council on the assessment of the risks of money laundering and terrorist financing affecting the internal market and relation to cross-border activities' COM (2019) 370 final, as well as European Commission, 'Report from the Commission to the European Parliament and the Council on the assessment of the risks of money laundering and terrorist financing affecting the internal market and relation to cross-border activities' COM (2017) 240 final.

74 The policies, controls and procedures need to include at least those specified in Art. 8(4) AMLD4. The list of measures therein is not exhaustive (*'shall include'*) which means Member States are free to expand the list. The measures prescribed by Member States must also be proportionate, i.e. they must correspond to the risk situation of the individual obliged entity and its nature and size (Art. 8(3) AMLD4).

The **minimum internal policies**, controls and procedures are, for example, model risk management practices, reporting structures, record-keeping, customer due diligence (→ para. 81 et seqq.), employee screening and compliance management. The latter shall include, where appropriate with regards to size and nature of the business, the appointment of a compliance officer at management level (which is usually referred to as a money laundering reporting officer (MLRO) if only carrying out AML-related tasks). Thus, Member States are not required to make it mandatory for all obliged entities to appoint a compliance officer with regards to AML but can rather do so on a risk-based approach. Whether this is mandatory for crypto intermediaries thus depends on the respective national laws.

75 Related to their internal policies, controls and procedures, Art. 46(1) AMLD4 requires obliged entities to take measures, proportionate to their nature, size and risks, to make employees aware of national AML provisions implementing EU AML law. Essentially, this requires ongoing risk-based **employee trainings**, which can be done **web-based**. Usually, such employee web-based trainings can be done every year or every other year.

76 Additionally, where according to the nature and size of the business it seems appropriate, Member State shall ensure that obliged entities establish an independent audit function to test these policies, controls and procedures. However, this will most likely only be appropriate for rather larger undertakings.

The obliged entity must be also required to obtain approval from an employee in its senior management for the measures taken; it must ensure to monitor and enhance the measures, where appropriate (Art. 8(5) AMLD4).

2. Fiat-to-Crypto Exchanges and Custodian Wallet Providers

77 The risk assessments by fiat-to-crypto exchanges and custodian wallet providers will have to regularly come to the conclusion that the suitability of crypto assets for money laundering (→ para. 7) leads to the **money laundering risk** of their business model being relatively **'high'**. This is already envisaged by the supranational risk assessment (→ para. 73).

The internal policies, controls and procedures (→ para. 73 et seqq.) must therefore be particularly detailed and carefully designed. Their exact scope is not determined by EU law and cannot be stated exhaustively here; national law is to be studied carefully in this regard. For example, for obliged entities whose risk assessment reveals a higher risk of money laundering, it would be plausible to repeat the necessary internal controls in shorter cycles or to increase the frequency of employee training. In addition, the handling of money laundering risks should be reviewed more regularly, or the risk assessment should be updated more frequently. Moreover, attention should be paid to technical developments in the market in order to be able to respond adequately and promptly to current trends or patterns in money laundering and terrorist financing with respective internal measures. Appropriate **market observation** therefore appears to be necessary. Furthermore, it could be worthwhile for fiat-to-crypto exchanges to subject their risk-appropriate money laundering prevention programme to an external, independent audit.

3. Issuers of Tokens

Issuers of tokens will most likely have a lower AML risk than fiat-to-crypto exchanges or custodian wallet providers. This is because their offer is limited in time and it is not at all known at the time of an ICO whether the buyer will be able to sell it for a similar price or at a crypto exchange at all.[79] The internal policies, controls and procedures taken by token issuers can therefore be less rigid and be repeated in longer cycles. 78

4. Art Market Participants

Art market participants (→ para. 62) are required to conduct individual risk assessments and put in place internal policies, controls and procedures if they are made subject to national AML laws. They have to at least do so when the value of a transaction or a series of linked transactions amounts to EUR 10,000 or more, irrespective or the measure of payment (→ para. 62) as they are then a to be made obliged entity. Payments via tokens are therefore to be treated the same as other payments in this regard (for the calculation of the threshold in case of payment via tokens, → para. 84 et seqq.). 79

The risk assessments and measures taken by art market participants depend on the individual business model of the entity. If these persons accept payment via currency tokens (even if only relatively sparsely), this fact needs to be considered carefully when assessing the entity's risk for money laundering. Such pseudonymous ways of payment can pose serious risks and need to be followed up by respective measures, e.g. by raising the level of awareness among employees or by an increased carefulness in executing customer due diligence. 80

III. Customer Due Diligence (Art. 10–20 AMLD4)

1. Prohibition of Anonymous Accounts

Financial and credit institutions must be prohibited from keeping or opening anonymous accounts, passbooks or safe-deposit boxes (Art. 10(1) AMLD4). Customer due diligence (CDD) measures must be applied to these accounts. However, fiat-to-crypto exchanges (→ para. 43 et seq.) and custodian wallet providers (→ para. 50) are not obliged as financial institutions within the meaning of AMLD4, unless otherwise falling under this definition. They are therefore not covered by this prohibition. Electronic money institutions, on the other hand, are covered (→ para. 64); as are, of course, banks as credit institutions. 81

2. When to Apply CDD Measures (Art. 11 AMLD4)

a) **Overview.** The general CDD measures (→ para. 105 et seqq.) shall be performed by the obliged entities – subject to the provisions for reduced and enhanced CDD measures (→ para. 123 et seqq.) – in the circumstances as prescribed by Art. 11 AMLD4: 82
- when **establishing a business relationship** within the meaning of Art. 3(13)(a) AMLD4,
- for occasional transactions (carried out outside a business relationship), if they
  a) amount to **15,000 EUR** or more, irrespective of whether the transaction is carried out in a single operation or in several operations which appear to be linked (lit. b), or

---

[79] See Fromberger and Haffke 'ICO Market Report 2018/2019 – Performance Analysis of 2018's Initial Coin Offerings' (2019), available at https://ssrn.com/abstract=3512125 (accessed 29.4.2021).

b) constitute a **transfer of funds** as defined in Art. 3(9) of Regulation (EU) 2015/847[80] and **which exceeds 1,000 EUR** (lit. b)
- regardless of any derogation, exemption or threshold, where there is a suspicion of money laundering or terrorist financing (→ para. 103, 146 et seq.) (lit. e),
- when there are doubts about the veracity or adequacy of previously obtained customer identification data (lit. f).

There are special rules and problems concerning other persons trading in goods and, art market participants (→ para. 98 et seqq.).

83   The CDD measures must be applied to all new customers; they must also be applied to existing customers at appropriate times on a risk-based approach, when relevant circumstances of a customer change or when the obliged entity has the duty to contact the customer for the purpose of reviewing any information relation to the beneficial owner (Art. 14(5) AMLD4).

84   **b) Calculation of the Thresholds.** To calculate the thresholds that trigger CDD measures (→ para. 82), several transactions may be cumulatively relevant instead of only single transactions. If a contracting party **simultaneously** carries out **several transactions** which taken individually are below the threshold value, the individual values must be added together to calculate the threshold value.

85   Normally, the conversion of the transaction value into EUR for securities transactions, metals and foreign currencies is based on the current market value.[81] Fees and commissions charged by obligors in connection with the transaction should not be taken into account for the calculation of the threshold value. The **calculation of the value** of a transaction (in EUR) **related to crypto assets** is unclear. A distinction must be made between three cases.

86   If a **price in a fiat currency** (e.g. EUR or USD) for a transaction in connection with crypto assets is already known in advance through a conversion rate, this price must be used. This is the case, for example, if tokens are to be bought or sold on a crypto exchange at a fixed price (in a fiat currency). Prices in foreign currencies may have to be converted according to the usual procedure (use of the current exchange rate, → para. 85).

87   More often the transaction value is not known in advance. This is the case, for example, when tokens are transferred by a (custodian) wallet provider or are exchanged for other crypto assets (e.g., by a crypto-to-crypto exchange). For the calculation of the threshold values, the question is whether the token is traded or not (or no longer traded).

88   If the token is **traded**, obligors should follow the normal procedure for foreign currencies (→ para. 85). In contrast to securities, foreign currencies and metals, there is not a (universally) agreed price that is known internationally. Therefore, prices of larger, well-known crypto exchanges (with sufficient trading volume) should be used. The website *CoinMarketCap*[82], for example, lists prices of individual tokens at various fiat-to-crypto or crypto-to-crypto exchanges. In case of doubt, an average value of three exchanges with sufficient trading volume listed on CoinMarketCap should be used to determine the price. If no price is available in EUR or USD, but the price is only known in Bitcoin or Ethereum, for example, the conversion can also be carried out using these larger currency tokens for which (almost) uniform prices are known.

---

[80] Regulation (EU) 2015/847 of 20 May 2015 on information accompanying transfers of funds.

[81] Cf. Figura, in Herzog, *GwG*, § 10, para. 76; Häberle, in Erbs and Kohlhaas, *GwG*, § 10, para. 14; as well as constant previous administrative practice of the BaFin, see the statement of the former Bundesaufsichtsamt für das Kreditwesen (Federal Banking Office), on measures by credit institutions to combat and prevent money laundering of 30 March 1998, Z 5 - E 100, No. 13 para. 3.

[82] See https://coinmarketcap.com/ (accessed 29.4.2021).

However, the calculation of threshold values for transactions with tokens that are **not** **89** **(or no longer) listed** is problematic. In the absence of an available, current market value, the last known market value, if available, should be used. If the token has not yet been traded, the ICO price should be used. If this is also not known, obliged entities should estimate the value of a transaction according to general principles and empirical values and document their assessment.

c) Establishment of a Business Relationship and Occasional Transactions. (aa) **90**
Fiat-to-Crypto Exchanges. *(1) Establishment of a Business Relationship.* The central term for obligations relating to CDD is the **business relationship**. According to Art. 3 (13) AMLD4, this means 'a business, professional or commercial relationship which is connected with the professional activities of an obliged entity and which is expected, at the time when the contract is established, to have an element of duration.' If the service of a fiat-to-crypto exchange is used, the relationship arising from this is undoubtedly connected with the (commercial or professional) activities of these companies. Whether such a contact by a user is expected to have 'an element of duration' within the meaning of Art. 3(13) AMLD4 is usually unclear at that point in time. An *ex-ante* consideration of the probable development of the business relationship is necessary.[83] It does not matter whether the relationship subsequently turns out to be of more long-lasting nature.

A business relationship usually includes only those contacts that are part of the **91** **typical business tasks or services**[84] of the obliged entity. It does not include relationships which serve purely to maintain operations (e.g., maintenance or supply contracts). Accordingly, a business relationship generally comprises the **services/products used by the customer** or which are available to the customer.[85]

A typical example of a business relationship with a rather clear element of duration is **92** an **agreement to open a current account.** However, a transaction that is envisaged to only take place once is not sufficient to establish a business relationship. In cases of doubt, it should be assessed whether any future obligations arise out of the relationship or agreement in question for the parties concerned. If this is the case, an element of duration is more likely to be established than not.

On **central fiat-to-crypto exchanges,** users must generally create an account in order **93** to process a transaction via the platform (→ § 1 para. 90 et seqq.). The central crypto exchange or exchange cannot normally assume *ex ante* that the registration of a user represents a one-time business contact. Rather, it enables the user to use the relevant platform beyond a one-off transaction and thus to carry out a (possibly) large number of exchange transactions. In addition, usually some form of agreement is concluded upon opening the account which entails follow-up obligations for the fiat-to-crypto exchange. There is no individual contact.[86]

The opening of user accounts also serves not only to maintain the operation of the platform (→ para. 91) but is rather a **service available to the user**. The central fiat-to-crypto exchange may also perform the function of a custodian (or non-custodian) wallet provider for the user (→ § 1 para. 97).

---

[83] See Figura, in Herzog, *GwG*, § 1, para. 29.
[84] Ibid, para. 27.
[85] Deutsche Kreditwirtschaft (The German Banking Industry Committee), 'Auslegungs- und Anwendungshinweise der DK zur Verhinderung von Geldwäsche, Terrorismusfinanzierung und 'sonstigen strafbaren Handlungen''' (February 2014), 8, available at https://beck-link.de/t7c52 (accessed 29.4.2021).
[86] Other view Terlau, 'Blockchain-basiertes Geld im Währungs-, Aufsichts-, Geldwäsche-, Wertpapier-, Steuerrecht', in Möslein and Omlor (eds), *Fintech-Handbuch*, § 20, para. 168.

As a result, this means that the user's registration generally establishes a business relationship with the fiat-to-crypto exchange which can be assumed to have an element of duration. In this case, the user must therefore be identified in accordance with CDD obligations upon registration and generally before the first transaction is carried out (→ para. 109).

94　For **decentralised fiat-to-crypto exchanges,** an individual case by case assessment is necessary. If registration is required or if an agreement with follow-up obligations is concluded with the user, a business relationship must be assumed, as in the case of centralised exchanges (→ para. 93). If a business relationship is not to be assumed, for example because the user does not register and no agreement with follow-up obligations is concluded, identification is generally not necessary.

95　*(2) Occasional Transactions.* However, if a transfer of funds as defined in Art. 3(9) of Regulation (EU) 2015/847 on information accompanying transfers of funds (Funds Transfer Regulation, hereinafter: FTR) takes place outside a business relationship as an occasional transaction, the situation is different. This requires the transfer of 'funds' as defined in Art. 3(8) FTR via a payment service provider as defined in Art. 3(5) FTR. Fiat-to-crypto exchanges may be **payment service providers** (→ § 9 para. 81 et seqq.). However, according to Art. 4(25) PSD2,[87] monetary amounts are only banknotes, coins, scriptural money and electronic money.[88] Therefore, if fiat money or tokens qualifying as electronic money (→ § 9 para. 34 et seqq.) with a value of EUR 1,000 or more are forwarded by the payer to the payee via the fiat-to-crypto exchange as payment service provider in the context of a transaction via a fiat-to-crypto exchange, the customer must also be identified.[89] If this is not the case, the customer must be identified outside of a business relationship if the value of the transaction to be executed amounts to EUR 15,000 or more.

96　**(bb) Custodian Wallet Provider.** Custodian wallet providers (→ § 1 para. 27) require their users to register on their platforms. This establishes a business relationship with the users within the meaning of Art. 3(13) AMLD4. This is because, as with fiat-to-crypto exchanges, it can be assumed that the relationship will have an element duration at the point when it is established (→ para. 93). CDD obligations must therefore be carried out before the user's registration is accepted.

97　If no business relationship is established, the circumstances for triggering CDD obligations for occasional transactions (→ para. 82) may apply in the same fashion. These are, in particular, occasional transactions outside the business relationship in the amount of at least EUR 1,000 or EUR 15,000 (Art. 4(1) AMLD4, → para. 90) as well as in the case of a suspicion of money laundering or terrorist financing (Art. 11(e) AMLD4, → para. 103).

98　**(cc) Art Market Participants (and Other Persons Trading in Goods).** Like for providers of gambling services, Art. 11(c) AMLD4 provides for a **special rule** for when '**persons trading in goods**' need to apply the CDD measures: this is 'when carrying out carrying out occasional transactions in cash amounting to EUR 10.000 or more, whether the transaction is carried out in a single operation or in several operations which appear to be linked.'

---

[87] Directive (EU) 2015/2366 of 25 November 2015 on payment services in the internal market (PSD2).
[88] Art. 3(8) FTR still refers to the PSD1 (Directive 2007/64/EC of 13 November 2007 on payment services in the internal market); the reference is to be construed as to refer to PSD2 as the updated version.
[89] Other view Terlau, 'Blockchain-basiertes Geld im Währungs-, Aufsichts-, Geldwäsche-, Wertpapier-, Steuerrecht', in Möslein and Omlor (eds), *Fintech-Handbuch,* § 20, para. 169.

§ 10. Anti-Money Laundering

99 It has to be determined whether this is a special rule superseding Art. 11(a) and (b) AMLD4 (see → para. 82). This is unclear. There even seem to be differences between Member States in this regard. While Germany's national implementation of the clause does supersede its implementations of Art. 11(a) and (b) AMLD4,[90] in the UK it applies additionally.[91] Both ways of interpretation of this part of the Directive are at least arguable. Rec. 6 AMLD4 states that persons trading in goods should be covered 'to the extent' that they make or receive payments of EUR 10.000 or more. This wording supports the interpretation that Art. 11(c) AMLD4 is a lex specialis. This would mean that the UK's national implementation is going beyond what is required by AMLD4.

100 It is also **unclear to whom this rule shall apply**. Originally incorporated in AMLD4, the term 'persons trading in goods' is used – instead of 'other persons trading in goods' as in Art. 2(1)(3)(e) AMLD4. Other persons trading in goods are clearly also persons trading in goods. Since the introduction of art market participants as obliged entities (→ para. 62 et seq.), the scope of the provision got unclear. Art market participants that trade in works of art might also be 'a person trading in goods' (while not being an 'other person trading in goods').

101 It is most likely that EU lawmakers simply forgot to include a similar rule for art market participants as for 'other persons trading goods' (without the reference to cash payments). This is supported by the fact that art market participants were not included in the Commissions original proposal of the Directive[92], but was added later in the discussions (without any reference to why in the recitals). It would also not make much sense to apply the threshold of 15.000 EUR to art market participants – otherwise, this would be in conflict with the aim of the threshold of 10.000 EUR in their definition as obliged entities.

Thus, by way of analogy to other persons trading in goods, the provision should be read so that Member States need to ensure that art market participants must fulfil CDD obligations when they receive or make payments that amount to 10.000 EUR or more, irrespective of the way of payment, which thus includes currency tokens. This is supported by the fact that Germany and the UK have adopted such rules in a similar way as their national laws had done so for other persons trading in goods already.

102 **(dd) Electronic Money Institutions, Electronic Money Agents and Electronic Money Distributors. Issuers of electronic money (electronic money institutions)** must comply with the general CDD obligations if they establish a business relationship within the meaning of Art. 3(13) AMLD4 when issuing electronic money (→ para. 26, 90). This will regularly be the case in non-token-specific circumstances, e.g. when issuing a prepaid card, because it can be assumed that the connection to the card user will have a certain element of duration. In the case of virtual prepaid cards for individual transactions (e.g. token-based virtual prepaid cards) or the issuance of

---

[90] See § 10, paras. 3 and 6a GwG; that § 10, para. 6a GwG applies instead of § 10, para. 3, nos. 1 and 2 GwG, see Figura, in Herzog, *GwG*, § 10, para. 115 as well as Krais, in Frey and Pelz (eds), *BeckOK GwG*, § 10, para. 66; on proposed alterations to this norm with regards to crypto assets, see Maume, Haffke and Zimmermann, 'Bitcoin versus Bargeld – Die geldwäscherechtliche Verpflichtung von Güterhändlern bei Zahlungen mit Kryptowährungen' (2019) 12 *Corporate Compliance Zeitschrift*, 149 (154 et seqq.).

[91] See Section 27(1), (2) and (3) of The Money Laundering, Terrorist Financing and Transfer of Funds (Information on the Payer) Regulations 2017, as amended by The Money Laundering Terrorist Financing (Amendment) Regulations 2019.

[92] European Commission, 'Proposal for a Directive of the European Parliament and of the Council amending Directive (EU) 2015/849 on the prevention of the use of the financial system for the purposes of money laundering or terrorist financing and amending Directive 2009/101/EC' COM (2016) 450 final.

server-based electronic money,[93] a case-by-case assessment is necessary.[94] If several transactions are to be expected over a certain period of time, a business relationship within the meaning of Art. 3(13) AMLD4 is usually established here. Past transactions may also be relevant indicators for such assessments.

For the scope of these due diligence obligations for obliged entities with respect to electronic money, Member States can choose to derogate from the usual rules, see → para. 139 et seqq. This exception is important for electronic money institutions and agents.

103 **d) Suspicion of Money Laundering or Terrorist Financing.** According to Art. 11(f) AMLD4, CDD obligations shall apply to all obliged entities, irrespective of any derogation, exemption or threshold (within the obligations), when there is a suspicion of money laundering or terrorist financing (→ para. 146 et seq.).

104 Even if the suspicion of money laundering within the meaning of Art. 33(1) AMLD4 only requires the existence of facts **giving reasonable to a suspicion of money laundering** (→ para. 147), transactions with crypto assets **cannot give** rise to a **general suspicion of money laundering** as they can be (and usually are) used in legitimate ways.[95] However, if there are other anomalies (e.g., unfounded changes in normal payment behaviour), this may lead to a suspicion of money laundering and thus make it necessary to identify the customer. For such scenarios, an assessment is necessary in each individual case.

3. Content of CDD Measures

105 **a) Overview.** CDD measures can be divided into general, reduced and enhanced due diligence measures. In principle, Member States must ensure that obliged entities comply with the general due diligence measures (Art. 13 and Art. 14 AMLD4). According to Art. 13(1), these shall compromise:

– **identifying the customer and verifying the customer's identity** and, if applicable, the persons acting on its behalf (lit. a) (→ para. 108 et seqq.)
– **identifying the beneficial owner** and taking reasonable measures to verify that person's identity (lit. b) (→ para. 116 et seqq.)
– assessing and, as appropriate, obtaining information on the **purpose and intended nature of the business relationship** (lit. c) (→ para. 120)
– **ongoing** monitoring of the business relationship, including scrutiny of transactions (lit. d) (→ para. 121).

106 The extent of such measures may be determined by obliged entities on a risk-based approach (Art. 13(2) AMLD4), taking into account, inter alia, the purpose of the relationship, the level of assets used or the size of the transaction as well as the regularity or duration of the business relationship (Art. 13(3) and Annex 1 AMLD4). Nevertheless, obliged entities must still be able to demonstrate that the measures taken were appropriate in comparison to the risks identified (Art. 13(4) AMLD4). It is generally insufficient to exclusively rely on information taken from the national transparency registers (→ para. 154 et seqq.) when fulfilling CDD requirements (Art. 30(8) AMLD4).

107 Member States must also ensure that for transactions or business relationships with politically exposed persons, obliged entities additionally have in place risk management

---

[93] Server-based electronic money is electronic money that is stored in the issuer's system and accessed by the user via an electronic money account.
[94] See also Terlau, 'Blockchain-basiertes Geld im Währungs-, Aufsichts-, Geldwäsche-, Wertpapier-, Steuerrecht', in Möslein and Omlor (eds), *Fintech-Handbuch*, § 20, para. 147.
[95] There are legitimate uses of crypto assets. For details see Haffke, Fromberger and Zimmermann, 'Cryptocurrencies and anti-money laundering: the shortcomings of the fifth AML Directive (EU) and how to address them' (2020) 21 *Journal of Banking Regulation*, 125 (136).

systems to determine whether the customer or beneficial owner is a politically exposed person (e.g., a head of state or minister) (Art. 20(a) AMLD4); on this and possible consequences (→ para. 122, 128).

b) The Customer's Identity (Art. 13(1)(a) AMLD4). (aa) General information. Obliged 108 entities must identify each customer and verify the customer's identity in the circumstances prescribed in Art. 11 AMLD4 (→ para. 82). This is what is commonly referred to as the **Know-Your-Customer check ('KYC check')**. According to Art. 13(1)(a) AMLD4, verification of the customer's identify shall be done based on documents, data or information retained from a reliable or independent source. This is particularly relevant in the context of crypto assets as respective transactions take place online, complicating the KYC check.

Verification of the identity of the customer must be carried out **before the business** 109 **relationship is established** or before a transaction is carried out (Art. 14(1) AMLD4). By way of derogation, Member States may allow identification to be carried out during the establishment of the business relationship if this is necessary to prevent an interruption of the normal conduct of business and if there is little risk of money laundering (Art. 14(2) AMLD4). Similarly, such derogation is also permitted for the opening of an account by credit or financial institutions if transactions cannot be carried out before the customer and its ultimate beneficial owner(s) have been identified and their identities verified (Art. 14(3) AMLD4).

(bb) Identification – Information to be Collected. AMLD4 does not contain speci- 110 fications as to which data the obliged entity must request from the customer (as a natural person) to verify its identity. However, Art. 30(5) AMLD4 subpara. 2 can serve as guidance as it specifies which information must be publicly accessible for everyone in the transparency register on beneficial ownership (→ para. 155). This compromises at least the name, the month and year of birth, the country of residence and the nationality. As this information is the minimum information for the public to identify beneficial owners of a company, it is advisable for obliged entities to use it to identify the customer. However, obliged entities should not solely rely on entries in the national transparency registers. Especially in case doubts arise, obliged entities are forced to make further inquiries.

Thus, it is argued here that customers should be identified with their name (first and last name, and, if possible, middle names), their date of birth, their address and their nationality. Any further information, like place of birth, should be included where possible. Further specifications are up for the Member States to clarify.

In the case of a legal person or partnership, AMLD4 does not prescribe which type of 111 information to collect. Member States may thus specify in their national laws which information is to be collected. Nevertheless, it seems reasonable to identify the legal persons at least by the following information: **name** or denomination, **legal form**, **registration number** (if any), **address** of the registered office or principal place of business and the members and names of the **representative body** (e.g., management board) or the names of the legal representatives, if applicable. If members of the representative body or legal representatives of the legal person are themselves legal entities, obliged entities are also encouraged to record the above information about these entities (excluding members of the representative body).

When entering into a new business relationship with a trust or a corporate or other 112 legal entity which is subject to the registration of beneficial ownership information in the corresponding register (→ para. 154 et seqq.), obliged entities shall collect proof of registration or an excerpt from that register (Art. 14(1) AMLD4).

(cc) Verification of the Customer's Identity. The obliged entity must **verify** the 113 customer's identity based on documents, data or information obtained from a reliable and independent source (Art. 13(1)(a) AMLD4). Further details on the type of documents, data or information are not provided by AMLD4 and are, therefore, left to the Member States. The normal case for verification, however, is usually via some form of **official identity document**; the types of documents may depend on national particularities. An **extract from a commercial or company register** (if applicable), founding documents or equivalent documents could be used for legal persons or partnerships. When proof of registration in or an excerpt from the register on beneficial ownership information is obtained (→ para. 112, 154 et seqq.), this information should also be taken into account.

114   In normal business practice, it might not always be possible to first record and then verify the information provided by the contracting party; it should therefore be just as feasible in practice to take the information provided by the customer directly from the appropriate documents.[96]

115   Due to the **physical absence of both parties** to the contract, it is most often not possible to verify the identity 'on site' for transactions involving crypto assets. Therefore, alternative procedures with an appropriate level of security must be used. Sending a scan of the identity card by e-mail or website without verification of the identity is generally not sufficient.

Art. 13(1) AMLD4 allows other means by which the identity of customers may be verified: electronic identification means, relevant trust services or another secure, remote and electronic identification process regulated, recognised or accepted by the relevant national authorities. **Electronic identification means and trust services** are defined by the eIDAS Regulation.[97] Electronic identification means are material or immaterial units containing person identification data and which are used for authentication for an online service (Art. 3(2) eIDAS); trust services are electronic services used to create, verify and validate electronic signatures, seals, time stamps or certificates (Art. 3(16) eIDAS). Other electronic identification processes may be laid out by the national legislatures.

This allows crypto intermediaries to identify the customer via their online interfaces and to verify the identity by making use of electronic identification processes as laid out by the relevant Member State. Amongst others, this may for example be some form of video identification process.[98]

116   **c) Identification of the Beneficial Owner (lit. b).** The obliged entity must identify the (different) beneficial owner(s) of his/her customer. The term 'beneficial owner' is defined in Art. 3(6) AMLD4 as the natural **person(s) who ultimately owns or controls the customer** and/or the natural person(s) on whose behalf a transaction or activity is being conducted. It is thus to be noted that legal persons cannot be beneficial owners, but only natural persons.[99]

117   As a rule, the customer can be asked for the respective information first. For intermediaries in relation to crypto assets, this can be done during the **registration process** by obtaining a confirmation that the customer, in case of him/her being natural person, is not acting on someone else's behalf (e.g., by ticking the appropriate box). In this way, the user/customer confirms that he is not acting on behalf of other beneficial owners that would otherwise need to be identified. If suspicions arise that such

---

[96] Cf. Diergarten, '§ 34 – Geldwäsche', in Hauschka, Moosmayer and Lösler (eds), *Corporate Compliance*, § 34, para. 47 et seq.

[97] Regulation No. 910/2014 of 23 July 2014 on electronic identification and trust services for electronic transactions in the internal market (eIDAS).

[98] For example, in Germany, verification of the identity of the customer is allowed via a so called 'Video-Ident' process, see BaFin, 'Videoidentifizierungsverfahren' (April 2017), available at https://beck-link.de/b3r42 (accessed 29.4.2021).

[99] Häberle, in Erbs and Kohlhaas (eds), *GwG*, § 3, paras. 1 and 5.

beneficial owners do exist, such confirmation without any other actions by the obliged entity would not suffice.

Art. 3(6)(a) AMLD4 contains a non-exhaustive list of **examples** for corporate entities as to who is to be at least included among their beneficial owners. The beneficial owner is the natural person(s) who ultimately owns or controls a legal entity, by directly or indirectly owning a 'sufficient percentage' of the shares, voting rights or ownership interest (Art. 3(6)(a)(i) AMLD4). A percentage of 25 % plus one share or ownership interest is to be regarded as an indication of direct or indirect ownership; however, it is left up to the Member States to adopt other criteria or lower thresholds (Art. 3(6)(a)(ii) AMLD4). 118

If beneficial owners cannot be determined for corporate entities in this way, the natural person(s) who hold position of senior management official(s) are to be taken fictitiously as the beneficial owner(s) (Art. 3(6)(a)(ii) AMLD4). Their identities then have to be verified with reasonable measures (Art. 13(1)(b) AMLD4; for rules on trusts and other legal entities, see Art. 3(6)(b)-(c) AMLD4).

Additionally, Art. 13(1)(b) AMLD4 requires the obliged entity to take reasonable measures to verify that person's identity so that the obliged entity is satisfied that it knows who the beneficial owner is. For legal entities or similar arrangements, this requires understanding the ownership and control structure of the other party. Such measures thus need to be taken in a risk-sensitive approach. Obtaining information from the customer is obviously not a reasonable measure to verify the identity, even if the customer itself appears to be credible. 119

d) Purpose and Intended Nature of the Business Relationship (lit. c). Obliged entities must always obtain information about the purpose and nature of the intended business relationship. This is often obvious given the circumstances. If, for example, the desired product indicates a certain purpose, the purpose is already apparent from this choice. This is often the case for mass products. Similarly, the opening of a current account by natural persons indicates its use as an account for the execution of payment transactions or the opening of a securities account indicates its use for the administration and safekeeping of securities. However, in order to determine the purpose and nature of the business relationship, it may be useful, particularly in the case of business models relating to crypto assets, to require the contracting party to **state** whether it wishes to use the intended business relationship (e.g., a Bitcoin wallet or a user account at a fiat-to-crypto exchange) for purely **private or business purposes**. If there are indications that contradict this statement (e.g., observing deviating transaction patterns during the ongoing monitoring of the business relationship, → para. 121), further checks are necessary. 120

e) Monitoring the Ongoing Business Relationship (lit. d). Obliged entities must monitor the business relationship, which includes scrutiny of transactions carried out in its course. This is intended to detect discrepancies with existing knowledge about the customer and its risk profile. For this purpose, it is important – especially for companies dealing in crypto assets such as crypto exchanges or wallet providers – to set up **technical systems** which enable the business relationship and transactions to be monitored (→ para. 134), i.e. (partially automated) **transaction monitoring**. Only in this way can anomalies be identified, transactions and their patterns checked and, if necessary, risk classifications changed. In particular, it must be checked whether the transactions within the scope of the business relationship correspond to the documents and information available at the obliged entity and to the customer profile and, if necessary, whether this can be reconciled with information on the source of the customer's funds. Additionally, on a risk-based approach, documents, data and information held by the obliged entity about the customer are kept up to date. 121

122 **f) Politically Exposed Persons (PEP, Art. 20(a) AMLD4).** Within the framework of the CDD obligations, it is also necessary (Art. 20(a) AMLD4) that customers and, if any, beneficial owners are checked on a risk-based approach for their **status as a politically exposed person (PEP)**. These are persons that are or have been entrusted with prominent public functions, including those listed in Art. 3(9) AMLD4. According to Art. 23 AMLD4, the check shall also include whether they are family members or close associates of PEPs within the meaning of Art. 3(10) and (11) AMLD4.

This is necessary to be able to assess whether enhanced CDD measures (→ para. 128) can or must be applied. In practice, such a check is usually carried out using software-based solutions that access (fee-based) databases that list PEPs.[100]

4. Simplified or Enhanced CDD Measures (Art. 15–24 AMLD4).

123 **a) General information.** As a direct consequence of the **risk-based approach** (→ para. 68), Member States may allow obliged entities to apply simplified CDD measures (Art. 15–17 AMLD4) or must make them subject to enhanced CDD obligations (Art. 18–24), under the conditions laid down in the respective provisions and as described below.

124 Generally, both Member States and obliged entities have to pay attention to the list of risk factors in Annex II and Annex III to AMLD4 when assessing whether to (allow to) apply simplified or enhanced CDD measures respectively (Art. 16 and Art. 18(3) AMLD4). These are **customer risk factors**, the **product, service, transaction or delivery risk factors** and **geographical risk factors**. According to Art. 40(1)(a) AMLD4, if required to be carried out by obliged entities, such risk assessment should be documented and kept in case FIU or competent authorities seek to inspect it.

125 **(aa) Simplified CDD Measures (AMLD4, Art. 15–17).** If allowed for by Member States, obliged entity entities may apply simplified CDD measures where there is a **lower degree of risk of money laundering** or terrorist financing inherent in the business relationship or transaction. This risk assessment shall be required before applying the **simplified measures** (Art. 15(2) AMLD4). It should be documented in case requested for by the relevant authorities (Art. 40(1)(a) AMLD4). It shall at least take into account the risk factors mentioned in Annex II to AMLD4 (→ para. 124), as required by Art. 16 AMLD4.

126 It is left to the **Member States** to **decide the exact scope of simplified CDD measures**, if any. However, the Joint Guidelines of the Joint Committee of European Supervisory Authorities (ESAs) on simplified and enhanced due diligence give some examples. If allowed, obliged entities may appropriately reduce the extent of the measures taken to fulfil the general CDD obligations (→ para. 105 et seqq.). This may include, for example, adjusting the quantity and/or quality of information obtained for identification, verification or monitoring, e.g., by verifying the identity of the customer by one source only.[101] Likewise, the frequency and/or intensity of monitoring or update requirements might be adjusted.[102]

---

[100] Such a database is, e.g., the World Compliance database of the provider LexisNexis, which also contains PEP lists; access can be subject to considerable costs.

[101] Joint Committee of the European Supervisory Authorities (ESAs), 'Joint Guidelines under Articles 17 and 18(4) of Directive (EU) 2015/849 on simplified and enhanced customer due diligence and the factors credit and financial institutions should consider when assessing the money laundering and terrorist financing risk associated with individual business relationships and occasional transactions' (April 2018), 45, available at https://beck-link.de/hy2fy (accessed 29.4.2021).

[102] Ibid.

However, Art. 15(3) AMLD4 requires Member States to **keep in place** the requirement of **sufficiently monitoring transactions and business relationships** (→ para. 121), even in case of simplified CDD measures applying. This is to keep at least a basic level of monitoring the customer for changes in his behaviour or for unusual and suspicious transactions.

(bb) Enhanced CDD Measures (Art. 18–24 AMLD4). If, on the other hand, there is 127 a **higher risk of money laundering** or terrorist financing or in the specific cases referred to in Art. 18a-24 AMLD4, enhanced due diligence measures must be taken. The basis for a higher degree of risk can be information taken from the individual risk assessment (→ paras. 70 et seqq.) and, for individual customers or transactions, the risk factors mentioned in Annex III to AMLD4 (→ para. 124). Enhanced CDD measures **apply additionally to the general measures** (→ para. 105 et seqq.).

AMLD4 provides a non-exhaustive list of cases in which enhanced CDD measures must be applied. Four cases can be distinguished.

If a contracting party is a **PEP** (Art. 20 AMLD4) **or a family member or a close** 128 **associate** of a PEP (Art. 23 AMLD4, → para. 122), then the measures set out in Art. 20 (b) AMLD4 must also be carried out in case of business relationships with the aforementioned persons. These include obtaining **senior management approval** for establishing/continuing the business relationship; conducting **enhanced, ongoing monitoring** of the business relationship; and taking adequate measures to establish the source of wealth/funds that are involved in the transaction or business relationship.

If a business relationship or a transaction involves so called '**high-risk third** 129 **countries**', the measures set out in Art. 18a AMLD4 in particular must be taken. A 'high-risk country' is identified by the European Commission by way of a Delegated Regulation (Art. 9(2) AMLD4). The list was most recently changed in May 2020.[103] The measures additionally needed to be taken are, amongst others, obtaining additional information on the customer, beneficial owner and the intended nature of the business relationship; obtaining senior management approval for establishing/continuing the business relationship as well as obtaining additional information on the source of funds/wealth of the customer or beneficial owner.

For **cross-border correspondent relationships** involving execution of payments with 130 a third-country institution, credit and financial institutions shall be required to take a least the measures of Art. 19 AMLD4. These include assessing the institution's AML/ CFT controls and to gather information about their business as well as the reputation and quality of their supervision. This is less relevant for crypto intermediaries.

Generally, when a **transaction is complex, unusually large, conducted in an** 131 **unusual pattern** or does not have an apparent economic or lawful purpose (in the following commonly referred to as 'suspicious transactions'), obliged entities are required to examine the background and purpose of each such transaction, see Art. 18 (2) AMLD4. This applies to both transactions carried out as part of a business relationship or outside it.

Suspicious transactions cannot (and should not) be categorised.[104] Any **assessments in this regard must be made on a case-by-case basis.** Customer- and product-specific facts must always be taken into account; for example, a large transaction may be

---

[103] The latest change was made by Commission Delegated Regulation (EU) No. 2020/855 of 7 May 2020 amending the original Delegated Regulation (EU) No. 2016/1675.

[104] One should be cautious when schematising any transaction patterns which appear to be suspicious as otherwise the persons concerned can easily adapt their behaviour and switch to alternative transaction patterns. This is one of the reasons why national competent authorities are reluctant to provide such rigid guidance.

suspicious for one customer while it appears normal in relation to the transaction behaviour of another.

As a result of classifying a transaction as suspicious, the **background and purpose of the transaction** must be investigated as far as reasonably possible. AMLD4 does not itself define what measures need to be taken. In line with Art. 18(4) AMLD4, the ESAs have issued the aforementioned joint guidelines on the risk factors and measures concerning simplified and enhanced due diligence measures (→ para. 126). In case of suspicious transactions, obliged entities should for example 'establish(.) the source and destination of funds or find (…) out more about the customer's business to ascertain the likelihood of the customer making such transactions.'[105]

Additionally, the underlying business relationship, if any, must be subjected to **increased continuous monitoring** in order to be able to determine whether the activities or transactions of the customer also appear suspicious (Art. 18(2) subpara. 2 AMLD4). Depending on the result of this increased monitoring, further measures might be advisable.

132 **b) Fiat-to-Crypto Exchanges and Custodian Wallet Providers.** Pursuant Art. 13(2) and (3) and Art. 15–18 AMLD4, fiat-to-crypto intermediaries and custodian wallet providers shall take CDD measures which are appropriate to the risks of each individual case.

Various factors must be taken into account when determining whether general, simplified or enhanced CDD measures are appropriate in a particular case. National competent authorities may issue guidelines for crypto intermediaries;[106] these shall be considered by the respective obliged entities in order to comply with national AML provisions. Therefore, **no EU wide schematisation** of cases is possible.

133 Relevant information provided by the seller may be where the funds to be exchanged (i.e., tokens) were purchased or otherwise obtained. Such information may be available on a blockchain itself if the latter is public. In cases of doubt or where appropriate, further information on the origin of the funds may be demanded from the customer.

For the question of whether enhanced due diligence measures need to be applied, the possible **use of tumblers** is of particular importance. There are providers who can **estimate the probability** for a use of tumblers for a token within a transaction, at least for some blockchains. However, such services can also be manipulated.[107] If such services can be used by (central) fiat-to-crypto exchanges and custodian wallet providers and it they are not associated with disproportionate costs, they should be included in day-to-day operations. For this purpose, it is necessary to **observe the market** for such service providers (at least until a market standard has been established).

Further risk factors might be whether a previous exchange of the tokens was carried out via a regulated fiat- or crypto-to-crypto exchange, as well as which means of

---

[105] Joint Committee of the European Supervisory Authorities (ESAs), 'Joint Guidelines under Articles 17 and 18(4) of Directive (EU) 2015/849 on simplified and enhanced customer due diligence and the factors credit and financial institutions should consider when assessing the money laundering and terrorist financing risk associated with individual business relationships and occasional transactions' (April 2018), 51, available at https://beck-link.de/hy2fy (accessed 29.4.2021).

[106] For example, for Germany, see BaFin, 'Sorgfaltspflichten im Zusammenhang mit virtuellen Währungen – Hinweise für ein angemessenes risikoorientiertes Vorgehen' (October 2018), available at https://beck-link.de/7yfms (accessed 29.4.2021).

[107] For example, by so-called 'dusting', a tumbler can transfer a minimal amount to the public keys of many users of a blockchain and thus 'contaminate' them. The analysis software may then be disturbed, see CipherTrace, 'Cryptocurrency Anti-Money Laundering Report' (January 2019), 11 available at https://beck-link.de/w4awh (accessed 29.4.2021).

payment (bank transfer, payment by anonymous means etc.) were used to purchase the virtual currencies.

To be able to assess whether a transaction is unusually complex, unusually large or carried out in an unusual pattern within the meaning of Art. 18(2) AMLD4 (→ para. 131) and thus whether enhanced CDD measures are to be fulfilled, fiat-to-crypto exchanges and custodian wallet providers should ensure by means of **technical measures** that such transactions can be detected and, if necessary, assessed. This could be done, for example, by means of appropriate systems, comparable to **transaction screening systems** for credit institutions.[108]

c) Issuers of Tokens. Depending on the business model, issuers of tokens may be able to assume a **lower money laundering risk**. In these cases, the simplified due diligence obligations apply (this is assuming that issuers are obliged entities, → para. 54 et seqq.). This may be because issuers of tokens are usually only providing their service for a short period of time and it is not clear whether the tokens' value will be stable at all. They also usually do not have prior transaction experience from or with their customers. However, issuers of tokens still need to pay attention to any elements of suspicion in a transaction.

d) Credit Institutions. The question arises for banks as to how outgoing and incoming payments from or for customers in connection with transactions involving crypto assets are treated under AML law. Due to uncertainty, some banks **completely forgo customers** who conduct business with crypto assets. Irrespective of any CDD obligations, a suspicious transaction report must be filed in the event of a suspicion of money laundering or terrorist financing (→ para. 146 et seq.). Such a cautious approach may be advisable from a compliance point of view. In most cases, though, it does not make economic sense and is certainly not required by EU AML provisions.

Like for fiat-to-crypto exchanges and custodian wallet providers, **various factors** must be taken into account when determining whether general, simplified or enhanced CDD measures are appropriate in a particular case (→ para. 124). No generally applicable European guidance exists on this point with regards to crypto assets. Thus, a case-by-case assessment is necessary.

Credit institutions should consider, for example, volume and frequency of crypto transactions. When compared with the customer's usual transaction behaviour, banks might get an indication on whether a transaction is unusual in this regard. In cases where there is a new or change in transaction behaviour, the customer could be asked for information on where the tokens were obtained from.

The bank could – in theory – also take into account the risk factors which crypto exchanges or wallet providers take into account (→ para. 133 et seq.), namely the use of **tumblers** or whether the tokens sold/bought were exchanged via **(un)regulated exchanges**. However, credit institutions usually do not have access to such information as this requires information on the tokens traded as well as a connection to the blockchain itself. This is only accessible to the crypto exchange or wallet provider itself. In case of doubt, information on the exchange platform(s) and the means used to purchase the virtual currencies can only be obtained by questioning the customer. However, if the crypto exchange used is part of a larger group of companies, e.g., as a subsidiary of a bank, the (possibly automated) query of such information may nevertheless be possible.

---

[108] Credit institutions usually use the 'FICO TONBELLER Siron AML' system, available at www.fico.com/de/products/fico-tonbeller-siron-aml (accessed 29.4.2021). Corresponding solutions for crypto assets are conceivable or under development, see e.g. 'immutableinsight' – Blockchain Data Analytics solutions from Immutable Insight GmbH, available at www.immutableinsight.com (accessed 29.4.2021).

139 **f) Electronic Money Institutions, Electronic Money Agents, Electronic Money Distributors. (aa) Simplified Due Diligence Obligations.** Electronic money issuers, agents and distributors (→ paras. 64 et seq.) may also make use of the general provisions for simplified or enhanced CDD measures. Annex II to AMLD4 contains examples of factors for a **potentially lower risk** as referred to in Art. 16 AMLD4 (→ para. 124). These enable the obliged entities with respect to electronic money to assume a lower money laundering risk in individual cases. In doing so, obliged entities may refer in particular to factors no. 2, lit. d and lit. e of Annex II. According to these factors, the risk of money laundering is reduced if a product or service that is appropriately defined and limited is offered to certain customers with the aim of increasing access for financial inclusion (factor no. 2, lit. d). Products where the risks of money laundering are managed by other factors, such as purse limits or transparency of 'ownership'[109] (e.g., certain types of electronic money (factor no. 2, lit. e)), also indicate a lower risk. The latter could be the case if the allocation of electronic money is accessible via a transparent register.

140 However, an overall assessment of factors and risk parameters must always be carried out on a case-by-case basis in order to assign a risk to a product/transaction. Reference should also be made here to possible factors according to Annex III to AMLD4, which indicate an increased risk for money laundering. The adequacy of the assessment should be **documented** so that it can be **submitted** to the supervisory authority if necessary (→ para. 124). For the simplified due diligence measures that can be taken in case of a lower risk (→ in particular, para. 125 et seq.). In practice, obliged entities should contact the competent supervisory authority to coordinate appropriate steps, if necessary.

141 **(bb) Refrain from Applying Certain General CDD Measures (Art. 12 AMLD4).** Under the rules set out in Art. 12 AMLD4, Member States may allow obliged entities (→ para. 42 et seqq., 64) to **refrain entirely** from applying the general CDD obligations of Art. 13(1)(a)-(c) and Art. 14 AMLD4 (→ para. 105 et seqq.) regarding electronic money. Ongoing monitoring of the business relationship and transactions pursuant Art. 13(1)(d) AMLD4 (→ para. 121) must still be complied with. Likewise, enhanced due diligence measures might still need to be applied if necessary, e.g., if the customer is a politically exposed person, family member or close associate of a PEP (→ para. 122, 128).

142 The requirements of Art. 12 AMLD4 must be met **cumulatively** in order for Member States being allowed to exempt obliged entities from applying the general CDD measures with regards to electronic money. After the implementation of AMLD5, the **six conditions** laid out in Art. 12 AMLD4 were made even more restrictive.

For the exception to apply, the payment instrument must not be reloadable or have a maximum monthly payment transaction limit of 150 EUR which can only be used in one Member State; must not be able to store more than 150 EUR electronically; is used exclusively for the purchase of goods or services; cannot be funded with anonymous electronic money; and transactions or business relationships attached to it must be sufficiently monitored by the issuer for suspicious transactions.

Additionally, Art. 12(2) AMLD4 requires that the exemption shall not apply in case of 'remote payment transactions' as defined in Art. 14(6) PSD2 (i.e., online payments) of more than 50 EUR per transaction. Member States may also enact stricter provisions and decide to lower this threshold even further. The exception thus becomes de facto irrelevant in the context of crypto assets, as online payments with crypto assets will

---

[109] 'Ownership' within the meaning of Annex II is not to be understood in a civil law sense but is rather a question of the actual allocation (e.g., of tokens).

generally exceed a value of 50 EUR.¹¹⁰ The exception may also not apply in case of redemption in cash or cash withdrawals of the monetary value of the electronic money where the amount is higher than 50 EUR.

In addition, Art. 12(3) AMLD4 requires credit and financial institutions acting as acquirers to accept payments with anonymous prepaid cards issued in third countries only if these cards meet the requirements of Art. 12(1) and 2 AMLD4 as set out above. Member States may also choose not to accept any such payments carried out by using anonymous prepaid cards (Art. 12(3) subpara. 2 AMLD4). 143

5. Performance of General CDD Measures by Third Parties (Art. 25–29 AMLD4)

According to Art. 25(1) AMLD4, Member States may permit obliged entities to **rely on third parties** to meet the general CDD obligations pursuant to Art. 13(1)(a)-(c) AMLD4 (→ para. 105 et seqq.). However, the responsibility for meeting CDD requirements remains with obliged entity (Art. 25(2) AMLD4). 144

Third parties can be other obliged entities, member organisations or federations of obliged entities, as well as other institutions or persons that are not situated in a high-risk third country (→ para. 129), apply the CDD requirements consistently with EU AML law and are supervised in a manner equivalent to that prescribed by AMLD4 (Art. 26 AMLD4). Also possible are outsourcing or agency relationships where the service provider is to be regarded as part of the entity (Art. 29 AMLD4).

6. Unability to Comply with CDD Obligations

If an obliged entity is not able to meet the CDD obligations set out in Art. 13(1)(a)-(c) AMLD4 (→ para. 105 et seqq.), Member States must ensure that it terminates existing business relationships, does not establish a new business relationship and does not carry out the transaction (through a bank account or by other means) (Art. 14(4) AMLD4). Obliged entities are then at least also required to 'consider making a suspicious transaction report to the FIU' (→ para. 146 et seq.). For both obligations, Member States shall include an exception for certain professions (lawyers, tax advisors, etc.) when they ascertain the legal position of their client or represent the client in judicial proceedings, including advice on such proceedings (Art. 14(4) subpara. 2). 145

IV. Suspicious Transaction Reporting (Art. 33–35 AMLD4)

1. Filing a Suspicious Transaction Report (Art. 33–34 AMLD4)

If an obliged entity knows, suspects, or has reasonable grounds to suspect that funds are the proceeds of criminal activity or are related to terrorist financing, it shall file a report to the national FIU, Art. 33(1)(a) AMLD4, including attempted transactions. Such suspicious transaction report shall at least be considered when an obliged entity is not able to fulfil the general CDD obligations as laid out in Art. 13(1)(a)-(c) AMLD4 (→ para. 105 et seqq.). This could be the case if the customer is not willing to deliver the necessary documents or information to disclose the beneficial owner. 146

the requirement shall be **interpreted broadly**.¹¹¹ Obliged entities are not required to make a legal assessment of the facts that make them suspicious. It is sufficient if facts 147

---

¹¹⁰ See also Terlau, 'Blockchain-basiertes Geld im Währungs-, Aufsichts-, Geldwäsche-, Wertpapier-Steuerrecht' in Möslein and Omlor (eds), *Fintech-Handbuch,* § 20, para. 159.

¹¹¹ Deutscher Bundestag (German Bundestag), 'Entwurf eines Gesetzes über das Aufspüren von Gewinnen aus schweren Straftaten (Gewinnaufspürungsgesetz GewAufspG)' (May 1992), 15, available at

only indicate a money laundering offence, for example if the origin of the funds from a preceding offence or their use for terrorist financing **appear possible**.[112]

2. Transactions in Case of Filing a Suspicious Transaction Report (Art. 35 AMLD4)

148 When a transaction appears suspicious and for which a suspicious transaction report thus would need to be filed (→ para. 146 et seq.), a transaction may be carried out **only after such report has been filed and** only after the obliged entity has complied with any **further specific instructions** by the FIU or competent authorities in accordance with the law of the individual Member State, Art. 35(1) AMLD4. Such additional requirement may, for example, be a certain period which needs to pass and in which the relevant authority can prohibit carrying out the transaction, if necessary.

If it is impossible to postpone the transaction until filing a suspicious transaction report or if postponement is likely to frustrate efforts to pursue the beneficiaries of a suspected operation, the transaction may be carried out and a suspicious transaction report shall be filed to the FIU immediately thereafter (Art. 35(2) AMLD4), subject to other provisions (e.g., Art. 14(4) AMLD4, → para. 145). In practice, this is the case for money exchange transactions, deposits or withdrawals at bank counters or when changing chips in casinos.[113] A postponement may also not be possible if 'the customer expressly wishes the immediate execution of the financial transaction.'[114]

However, a suspicious transaction can also be rejected (as a precautionary measure) by the obliged entity.

149 Irrespective of the time limit or urgency of the case, transactions should always be rejected where the suspicion of **money laundering or terrorist financing is almost certainly true**.[115] In cash transactions, this could be the case for an unusual cash deposit by suitcase, for which no explanation or only a completely inadequate, implausible explanation can be provided upon request. Where such a high probability of money laundering exists, obligors are advised to refuse carrying out the transaction in order to avoid administrative or criminal sanctions. In cases of doubt, obliged entities can also contact competent authorities or the FIU.

150 For crypto intermediaries, no such groups of cases have yet emerged. Supervisory authorities or other EU institutions have not issued any explanations or advice in this respect for crypto intermediaries. However, the principles described above should be followed, so that a distinction can be made between the **following situations.**

151 For a suspicion of money laundering to become almost inevitable, **several clear suspicions** must accumulate without a plausible explanation for a transaction being apparent. In the case of crypto intermediaries, this could be, for example, when a transaction with a conspicuously high amount of an anonymous payment token (e.g., Monero) coincides with an abnormal transaction behaviour by the customer. If the suspicion is detected in advance, the transaction must be stopped. If the clear suspicion cannot be disproven, e.g., even after carrying out enhanced customer due diligence

---

http://beck-link.de/w7er5 (accessed 29.4.2021); Häberle, in Erbs and Kohlhaas (eds), *GwG*, § 10, para. 19; Figura, in Herzog, *GwG* § 10, para. 94.

[112] Häberle in Erbs and Kohlhaas (eds), GwG, § 10, para. 19.

[113] Barreto da Rosa, in Herzog, *GwG*, § 46, para. 15; Deutscher Bundestag (German Bundestag), 'Entwurf eines Gesetzes über das Aufspüren von Gewinnen aus schweren Straftaten (Gewinnaufspürungsgesetz GewAufspG)' (May 1992), 18, available at http://beck-link.de/w7er5 (accessed 29.4.2021).

[114] Deutscher Bundestag (German Bundestag), 'Entwurf eines Gesetzes über das Aufspüren von Gewinnen aus schweren Straftaten (Gewinnaufspürungsgesetz GewAufspG)' (May 1992), 18, available at http://beck-link.de/w7er5 (accessed 29.4.2021).

[115] Barreto da Rosa, in Herzog, *GwG*, § 46, para. 15 et seq.

measures (→ para. 127 et seqq.), the transaction must be rejected, and a suspicious transaction report must be filed.

If there is a suspicion of money laundering or terrorist financing, for which a suspicious transaction report would need to be filed according to Art. 33(1)(a) AMLD4, but without certainty about the existence of money laundering, the transaction should be postponed if possible. 152

In the case of **on-chain transactions** (→ § 1 para. 95), a postponement does not normally appear possible. The essence of such a transaction is its inclusion in a blockchain. It is carried out promptly. Thus, an 'incoming transaction' (i.e., the 'receipt' of incoming crypto assets) in a 'wallet' cannot be rejected by a wallet provider, as it is already entered in the blockchain. In the case of crypto exchanges, a postponement would also run counter to the basic idea of a multilateral trading system: Trading with a time delay of possibly a couple of days is not appropriate and is not compatible with the nature of such a system. In such cases, the intermediary must therefore proceed in accordance with Art. 35(2) AMLD4, even in cases of suspicion for money laundering.

However, for **off-chain transactions** (→ § 1 para. 96), a postponement is technically possible. For example, an internal crediting of tokens could be finalised after filing a suspicious transaction report and after complying with any further national requirements (→ para. 148). An integration of the transaction into the blockchain does not take place yet. However, whether a postponement is possible must be determined on the basis of a case-by-case examination by the obliged entity. The type and purpose of the transaction, its urgency as well as the customer and his/her transaction behaviour must be taken into account.

Rejected transactions, whether with or without a suspicious transaction report, **do not result in an automatic 'freezing'** of tokens. If the blockchain itself does not provide a 'freezing' option for tokens, suspicious tokens can be transferred like normal tokens. However, it is not unlikely that the execution of a suspicious, rejected transaction would also be rejected (as a precaution) by other intermediaries. 153

V. Transparency Registers on Beneficial Ownership

Since the adoption of AMLD5, Member States need to ensure that 'corporate and other legal entities incorporated within their territory' are required to obtain and hold information on their beneficial ownership, including details of the beneficial interests held (Art. 30(1) AMLD4) in its revised form. This applies not only to obliged entities, but to **all corporate and legal entities** incorporated in a member state. Such information on beneficial ownership is to be provided to obliged entities when they carry out CDD obligations, Art. 30(1) AMLD4. 154

All such information on beneficial ownership of corporate or legal entities is to be held in a **central register in each Member State** (Art. 30(3) AMLD4). This register may, for example, be the commercial register, companies register, or another public register. For example, in Germany, a separate register has been set up, while in France information can be gathered from the commercial register.[116] National registers shall be connected in accordance with the requirements laid out in Art. 30(10) AMLD4. 155

Crypto intermediaries are thus part of this obligation and must enter information on their beneficial ownership in these national transparency registers as well. The information held in the register must at least include name, date of birth, country of residence

---

[116] All national transparency registers can be found at EU Transparency Registers, Dentons, available at www.transparencyregisterlaws.com (accessed 29.4.2021).

and nationality (cf. Art. 30 (5) AMLD4). Exact details on which information is stored in the database is not regulated by EU AML law. However, it must always clearly identify beneficial owners.

156 Obliged entities are required to report any discrepancies between information on the beneficial ownership of entities as held in the registers and known to them. In this way, the information held in the register shall be kept up to date, adequate and accurate (Art. 30(4) AMLD4).

157 After the implementation of AMLD5, the scope of persons being permitted access to the national registers has been expanded. It must be made available to competent authorities, FIUs, obliged entities when carrying out CDD obligations and **to any member of the general public**. It is not necessary anymore to prove a legitimate interest in accessing the register.

However, Member States are (still) able to make their national register available on the condition of online registration and on the payment of a fee (Art. 30(5a) AMLD4). Such fee may not exceed the administrative costs of making the information available and may include costs for developing and maintaining the register. Only public authorities and FIUs may not be made subject to such restrictions (Art. 30(5a) AMLD4). Such fees can spark criticism as it discourages searches without initial suspicions. Larger, broadly diversified data searches, e.g. by journalists, can lead to considerable costs.

VI. Central Database for Public Keys

158 Even after AMLD5 came into force, there is no obligation for the Member States to introduce a register, accessible to the FIUs, from which 'wallet addresses' (i.e., public keys) can be associated with the users' identities. Such a register would enable investigating and prosecuting authorities to access users' identities behind the **public key** as quickly and easily as possible in suspicious cases.[117] This would thus partially 'de-pseudonymise' the blockchain. According to the amended Art. 65(1) subpara. 3 AMLD4, the European Commission is obliged to examine the necessity of such a register as well as of self-declaration forms for the use of virtual currency users by 11 January 2022 and, if necessary, to submit a corresponding legislative proposal by then.

F. Sanctions

I. Administrative Sanctions and Measures

1. General

159 AMLD4 does **not contain** a **harmonised sanction administrative sanctions regime** that would be applicable across the Union. Rather, it sets out the **framework** and establishes **minimum rules** concerning sanctions for breaches of national transpositions of EU AML law. According to Art. 58(4) AMLD4, administrative sanctions and measures shall generally be imposed by the respective competent authorities (→ para. 30 et seq.). Any sanction or measure in national laws shall in any way be effective, proportionate and dissuasive (Art. 58(1) AMLD4). Criminal sanctions are left to the Member States (→ para. 164).

---

[117] Directive 2018/843/EU (AMLD5) – with the full reference in footnote 23.

2. Norm Addressees and Responsibility

AMLD4 does not specify which persons are to be held responsible for the breaches of **160** AML law. Obviously, the obliged entity itself, which can be either a natural or a legal person, is liable. For the latter, Art. 58(3) AMLD4 requires Member States to ensure that sanctions and measures can be applied to members of the management board and to other natural persons responsible for the breach. This could in particular be the Compliance/Money Laundering Reporting Officer (→ para. 74). It is also left to the Member States which degree of responsibility (slight, normal, gross negligence or intention) they want to require for the respective sanctions to apply. This is of particular importance if employees other than the members of the management board should be held accountable.

3. Provisions Subject to Sanctions

Art. 59(1) AMLD4 specifies that serious, systematic or repeated breaches at least **161** against the requirements laid down in the following Articles of AMLD4 shall be subject to the minimum sanctions set out below (→ para. 162 et seq.):
– Arts. 10–24 (customer due diligence, → para. 81 et seqq.)
– Arts. 33–35 (suspicious transaction reporting, → para. 146 et seq.)
– Art. 40 (record keeping, → para. 124 et seq.)
– Arts. 45–46 (group-wide controls and employee training, → para. 69, 75)

This catalogue notably does not include breaches of obligations relating to individual risk assessments and individual internal controls, policies and procedures (→ para. 70 et seqq.).

4. Measures and Sanctions

For breaches of the provisions listed in Art. 59(1) ALD4 (→ para. 161), Art. 59(2) **162** AMLD4 sets out a catalogue of measures and administrative sanctions that must be available to the competent authorities. These can (but do not have to) be applied cumulatively. Details are up to the national implementations. These measures include a public statement identifying the person responsible for the breach, an order to cease conduct and to desist from repetition, withdrawal or suspension of authorisation of the obliged entity as well as a temporary ban against persons responsible for the breach from exercising managerial functions. Member States are free to empower competent authorities with further sanctions, Art. 59(4) AMLD4.

In addition, **administrative pecuniary sanctions** may be issued. For these, AMLD4 **163** sets out the minimal levels that competent authorities must at least be able to impose. Member States may thus also have in place provisions which only allow lower sanctions to be imposed in certain cases. However, Art. 59(4) AMLD4 also allows Member States to impose pecuniary sanctions exceeding the minimal levels as laid out below.

Fines in AMLD4 are structured in a **two-step system**. Generally, competent authorities must at least be able to impose sanctions of **up to twice the amount of the benefit derived from the breach or at least 1,000,000 EUR**, Art. 59(2)(e)AMLD4. The benefit derived, for example, includes profits from a transaction carried out or a business relationship established or maintained, even though these were prohibited. However, such a benefit is likely to be generated only in exceptional cases.

In addition, at a second stage, a **higher fine** could be imposed where the obliged entity is a **credit institution or a financial institution**. Financial service providers that require authorisation as an investment firm under Art. 5 MiFID2 (→ § 8 para. 37 et seqq.) are financial institutions within the meaning of Art. 3(2) AMLD4. So if a service provider dealing in crypto assets falls within the scope of application of MiFID2, it would be subject to this higher level of fines. This could be the case for operators of crypto exchanges, which might be covered by Art. 2 (1)(g) or (h) (crypto exchange services or custodian wallet providers), but also by Art. 4(1)(22) MiFID2 as a multilateral trading facility (→ § 8 para. 18 et seqq.).

Member States are free to expand this second stage to other obliged entities and some have done so.[118] For the entities covered by the second stage, **maximum fines must be at minimum 5,000,000 EUR** in the case of natural persons, and at least 5,000,000 EUR or 10 % of the total annual turnover in the case of legal persons (Art. 59(3) AMLD4). In case an obliged entity is part of a group, the annual turnover is taken to be that of the ultimate parent undertaking.

II. Criminal Sanctions

164   AMLD4 does **not contain minimal rules on criminal sanctions** against breaches of their national implementations. However, Art. 58(2) AMLD4 specifically provides for the possibility of Member States to do so. The minimum rules on administrative sanctions do not prejudice the Member States' right to impose criminal sanctions additionally. It is even permitted for Member States to deviate from the minimum administrative sanctions (and not lay down any such administrative measures) for breaches which are subject to criminal sanctions (Art. 58(2) subpara. 2 AMLD4). In this case, the European Commission needs to be notified about the implementation of such rules. If Member States impose criminal sanctions, Art. 58(2) subpara. 3 AMLD4 provides that enforcement authorities shall be informed by the competent authority in a timely manner of possible breaches.

G. Other EU AML Policies and Further Developments

I. Directive (EU) 2018/1673 – Definition of Money Laundering

165   AMLD4 does not define the criminal offence of money laundering or terrorist financing – the exact definition was left to the Member States. Thus, the predicate offences and types of property or funds used therein were not harmonised throughout the Union. With regards to crypto assets, this could lead to situations in which proceeds of crime involving tokens were not or could not be treated in the same way as other, 'traditional' offences.

The Financial Action Taskforce (FATF), which sets out international recommendations and guidelines for AML/CFT regimes for its members (of which the European Commission is one), thus recommends **extending money laundering** and terrorist financing offences **to any type of property**, funds or assets, whether digital or not.[119]

---

[118] For example, Germany has included fiat-to-crypto, crypto-to-crypto exchanges and custodian wallet providers in the definition of financial institutions, making them subject to the second stage regime for administrative pecuniary sanctions, see § 1(2) GwG and § 1(1a) KWG.

[119] Financial Action Task Force (FATF), 'Virtual Assets and Virtual Asset Service Providers – Guidance for a Risk-Based-Approach' (June 2019), 21, available at https://beck-link.de/3ewrm (accessed 29.4.2021), which interprets the general FATF recommendations in relation to virtual asset service providers; for the general recommendations see FATF, 'International Standards on Combating Money Laundering and The Financing of Terrorism & Proliferation – The FATF Recommendations' (October 2020), Note to Recommendation 3, Para. 3, available at https://beck-link.de/trf53 (accessed 29.4.2021).

As a consequence, the EU enacted Directive 2018/1673/EU, also referred to as the **sixth AML Directive (AMLD6)**. It aims to set out minimum rules concerning the **definition of criminal offences** and sanctions in the area of money laundering (Art. 1(1) AMLD6). It states criminal offences in relation to money laundering that are to be made punishable under the Member States' national laws (Art. 3 AMLD6). Therefore, it defines – as a minimum harmonisation – the respective predicate criminal offences for money laundering (Art. 2(1) AMLD6) and types of property (Art. 2(2) AMLD6). It also sets out minimum rules for sanctions for money laundering, confiscation and jurisdiction.

166

With regards to crypto assets and virtual currencies, Rec. 6 of AMLD6 acknowledges the risks and challenges posed by this technological advancement and states that Member States should address these risks appropriately. Therefore, Art. 2(2) AMLD6 ensures that Member States must extend the criminal offences covered by money laundering to assets of any kind, whether corporeal or incorporeal, movable or immovable, tangible or intangible. This includes crimes related to virtual assets, such as crypto assets. In this regard, the above mentioned FATF guidance is thus followed.

167

II. The AML Action Plan and Further AML Developments

However, the above mentioned **FATF guidance on virtual assets** (→ para. 165) is not followed by the European Commission and its current AML policies in all regards. For example, the FATF guidelines recommend to expand the scope of AML law to virtual assets which do not include only tokens used for payment but also for investment purposes.[120] The current definition of virtual currencies (→ para. 13 et seqq.) would thus have to be expanded to other uses of virtual currencies, like investment tokens (→ § 1 para. 71 et seq.) and possibly some forms of utility tokens (→ § 1 para. 73).

168

Likewise, the current scope of obliged entities would also need an overhaul if the EU AML regime were to fully comply with the FATF recommendations. These recommend making all so called **'virtual asset service providers'** subject to its Member States' AML legal instruments.[121] These are notably non-custodian wallet providers, crypto-to-crypto exchanges as well as the provision of financial services related to an issuer's offer and/or sale of a virtual asset and thus also providers of ICOs.[122] Likewise, this **expansion** is recommended to providers of tumblers.

169

The FATF recommendations regarding virtual assets were issued in 2019 and thus after AMLD5 (and AMLD6) were accepted and signed into law on an EU level (but before the deadline for transposing AMLD5 into national laws). Thus, the aforementioned **changes and expansions** with regards to crypto intermediaries and the definition of virtual assets in AML Law are to be expected **on the EU level** as well. The European Commission has in the meantime adopted an Action Plan for a comprehensive Union policy on preventing money laundering and terrorist financing.[123] Therein, the European Commission refers to exactly these FATF recommendations and states that the 'scope of EU legislation needs to be expanded' to address the challenges by new technological innovations.[124] While the

170

---

[120] Financial Action Task Force (FATF), 'Virtual Assets and Virtual Asset Service Providers – Guidance for a Risk-Based-Approach' (June 2019), 13 et seq., available at https://beck-link.de/3ewrm (accessed 29.4.2021).
[121] Ibid.
[122] Although it needs to be noted that in some circumstances these might qualify as 'investment firms' under MiFID2 (→ § 8 para. 14) and are thus subject to AMLD4 as 'financial institutions'.
[123] European Commission, 'Communication from the Commission on an Action Plan for a comprehensive Union policy on preventing money laundering and terrorist financing' C (2020) 2800 final.
[124] Ibid.

European Commission does not state exactly which new obliged entities are to be expected under EU AML law, one can expect these changes to happen soon. The Council 'urges' the European Commission to put these expansions within their **next legislative proposal to be expected in Q3 2021** (→ Para. 171).[125]

171 In addition, the EU is planning to **harmonise national AML/CFT legislations** to a stronger degree. To do so, an EU rulebook on the AML framework might be published.[126] However, even more importantly, certain parts the AMLDs might be put into a **directly applicable EU AML Regulation**; these would, inter alia, include obliged entities, CDD requirements, internal controls, reporting as well as beneficial ownership obligations.[127] A legislative proposal in this regard is to be **expected in Q3 2021**. It is to be seen whether these changes are to include crypto intermediaries or whether these parts of the AML framework will remain in a Directive.

172 A more harmonised EU AML framework also brings with it the need for an effective, **EU wide supervision**. The Commission is planning to put in place an integrated AML/CFT supervisory system.[128] The exact nature of such supervisor is yet to be seen in the legislative proposal. The Council requests the Commission to keep in mind the subsidiarity principle when defining the supervisor's responsibilities.[129] It calls for a risk-based approach on the competencies of the new supervisor. However, it recommends focusing the supervisor's responsibilities to credit institutions, payment institutions, bureaux de change, electronic money institutions and virtual assets service providers according to the FATF recommendations.[130] The scope might be expanded in the future. Such EU supervisor is likely to have certain direct supervisory powers with regards to these entities, like inspections as well as the right to instruct national supervisors.[131] It is to be seen whether a single EU level supervisor will enhance the effectiveness of AML supervision, especially with regards to new technological developments.

---

[125] Council of the European Union, 'Council Conclusions on anti-money laundering and countering the financing of terrorism' (November 2020), 17, available at https://beck-link.de/54w5z (accessed 29.4.2021); the proposal has been delayed until Q3 2021.

[126] European Commission, 'Communication from the Commission on an Action Plan for a comprehensive Union policy on preventing money laundering and terrorist financing' C (2020) 2800 final.

[127] Ibid.

[128] Ibid.

[129] Council of the European Union, 'Council Conclusions on anti-money laundering and countering the financing of terrorism' (November 2020), 25, available at https://beck-link.de/54w5z (accessed 29.4.2021).

[130] Ibid.

[131] Ibid.

§ 11
Market Abuse

Literature: Bhattacharya and Daouk, 'The World Price of Insider Trading' (2002) 57 *Journal of Finance*, 75; Black, 'The Legal and Institutional Preconditions for Strong Securities Markets' (2001) 48 *UCLA Law Review*, 781; Börner, 'Kryptowährungen und strafbarer Marktmissbrauch' (2018) *Neue Zeitschrift für Wirtschafts-, Steuer- und Unternehmensstrafrecht*, 48–54; Brealy, Mayers and Allen, *Principles of Corporate Finance* (12. edn, McGraw-Hill Education, Oxford 2017); Coleman, 'Bitcoin Price Manipulated by Cryptocurrency Trading Bots', (2018) WSJ, CCN, available at https://perma.cc/8652-9G3Y (accessed 10.4.2019); ESMA, 'Final Report – ESMA's Technical Advice on Delegated Acts Concerning the Market Abuse Regulation' (ESMA/2015/224, 3.2.2015); ESMA, 'MAR Guidelines – Deferral of Disclosure of Inside Information' (ESMA/2016/1478 EN), 20.10.2016; ESMA, 'Questions and Answers on the Market Abuse Regulation' (ESMA70-145-111, last updated 29 March 2019); Hamrick, Rouhi, Mukherjee, Feder, Gandal, Moore and Vasek, 'The Economics of Cryptocurrency Pump and Dump Schemes', (2019) SSRN, available at https://perma.cc/G85K-U7K2 (accessed 10.4.2019); Haffke and Fromberger, 'ICO Market Report 2017. Performance Analysis of Initial Coin Offerings (Presentation Slides)', (2019), available at https://perma.cc/7HH5-ET7F (accessed 27.12.2018); Haffke, Fromberger and Zimmermann, 'Virtual Currencies and Anti-Money Laundering – The Shortcomings of the 5th AML Directive (EU) and How to Address Them', 2019 SSRN, available at https://perma.cc/Q66Z-SW6X (accessed 3.2.2019); International Organization of Securities Commissions, 'Investigating and Prosecuting Market Manipulation, Report of the Technical Committee of IOSCO' (May 2000), available at http://www.iosco.org (accessed 31.8.2021); International Organization of Securities Commissions, 'Objectives and Principles of Securities Regulation' (June 2010), available at https://perma.cc/BTR8-FRS3 (accessed 12.4.2018); Klöhn (ed), *Marktmissbrauchsverordnung: MAR* (C.H. Beck, Munich 2018); Krause and Brellochs, 'Insider trading and the disclosure of inside information after Geltl v Daimler-A comparative analysis of the ECJ decision in the Geltl v Daimler case with a view to the future European Market Abuse Regulation' [2013] 8(3) *Capital Markets Law Journal*, 283–299.; Lehmann and Kumpan, *European Financial Services Law* (Baden-Baden 2019); Manne, *Insider Trading and the Stock Market* (New York 1966); Maume, 'Initial Coin Offerings and EU Prospectus Disclosure' (2020) 31 *European Business Law Journal*, 185-208; Maume and Fromberger, 'Regulation of Initial Coin Offerings: Reconciling U.S. and E.U. Securities Laws' (2019) 19 *Chicago Journal of International Law*, 548–585; Maume and Kellner, 'Paradigmenwechsel oder Placebo? Directors' Dealings unter der Marktmissbrauchsverordnung' (2017) 46 *Zeitschrift für Unternehmens- und Gesellschaftsrecht*, 273–311; Meyer, Veil and Rönnau, *Handbuch zum Marktmissbrauchsrecht* (C.H Beck, Munich 2017); Rooney, 'Much of bitcoin's 2017 boom was market manipulation, research says', (2018) CNBC: available at https://perma.cc/AZ8E-KYUS (accessed 10.4.2019); Veil (ed), *European Capital Markets Law* (2nd edn, Hart Publishing, Oxford 2017); Ventoruzzo and Mock (eds), *Market Abuse Regulation – Commentary and Annotated Guide* (Oxford University Press, Oxford 2017).

Outline

	para.
A. Overview	1
B. Definitions	6
I. Financial Instruments and Transferable Securities	7
1. Definition	7
2. Token Categories	8
3. Derivatives	9
II. MAR-Regulated Markets	10
III. Territorial Scope of Application	11
IV. The Competent Authority	13
V. The Proposed MiCA-Regime	16

C. Prohibited Conduct 19
  I. Market Manipulation, Art. 15 MAR 19
    1. Purpose 19
    2. Prohibited Conduct 21
      a) Definitions and Statutory Examples 21
      b) Problems of the Effects-based Approach 22
      c) Regulatory Gap for Currency and Utility Tokens 23
    3. Criminal and Administrative Sanctions 25
  II. Insider Dealing, Art. 14 MAR 28
    1. Purpose 28
    2. Prohibited Conduct 30
      a) Structure 30
      b) Inside information 31
      c) Forms of Insider Dealing 36
    3. Criminal and Administrative Sanctions 39
  III. Market Conduct and the Proposed MiCA-Regime 40
D. Disclosure and Transparency Obligations 42
  I. Public Disclosure of Inside Information, Art. 17 MAR 42
    1. Purpose 42
    2. Disclosure Obligation 45
    3. Exemptions 50
    4. Criminal and Administrative Sanctions 52
  II. Managers' Transactions, Art. 19 MAR 53
    1. Purpose 53
    2. Disclosure Obligation 55
    3. Trading Ban 60
    4. Criminal and Administrative Sanctions 62
  III. Disclosure Rules under the Proposed MiCA-Regime 63

A. Overview

1   Some crypto assets are 'transferable securities' according to Art. 4(1)(44) Directive 2014/65/EU (MiFiD2)[1]. This is the first and most important requirement for the application of EU capital markets law. For example, initial coin offerings of investment tokens (=transferable securities) to the public are generally subject to the obligation to publish a prospectus pursuant to Art. 3(1) Regulation (EU) No. 1129/2017 (Prospectus Regulation, → § 7 para. 31)[2]. Financial services regarding transferable securities often require authorisation pursuant to Art. 5 MiFiD2 (→ § 8 para. 37). The related question, which is discussed in this chapter, is to what extent the rules of the secondary financial markets (i.e. the rules governing securities trading) apply to tokens that are listed at a crypto exchange.

2   In the EU, the secondary market is primarily regulated by **Regulation (EU) No. 596/2014 on Market Abuse** (MAR)[3], which came into force in 2016.[4] It replaced Directive

---

[1] Directive 2014/65/EU of the European Parliament and of the Council on markets in financial instruments and amending Directives 2002/92/EC and 2011/61/EU, OJ L 173, 12.6.2016, 349–496.

[2] Regulation (EU) No. 1129/2017 of the European Parliament and of the Council on the prospectus to be published when securities are offered to the public or admitted to trading on a regulated market, and repealing Directive 2003/71/EC, OJ L 168, 30.6.2017 p. 12–82.

[3] Regulation (EU) No. 596/2014 of the European Parliament and of the Council on market abuse (Market Abuse Regulation) and repealing Directive 2003/6/EC of the European Parliament and of the Council and Commission Directives 2003/124/EC, 2003/125/EC and 2004/72/EC, OJ L 173, 12.6.2014 p. 1–61.

[4] For an overview of the legislative history, see Gerner-Beuerle, in Lehmann and Kumpan (eds), *European Financial Services Law* (2019), 647–649; Veil in Veil (ed), *European Capital Markets Law* (2017), para. 1.

2003/6/EC.[5] The European Commission has adopted more than a dozen downstream acts that further specify individual MAR rules. The European Securities and Markets Authority (ESMA) has also issued several guidelines on individual issues and a fairly comprehensive "Q&A".[6]

The core areas of the securities trading law regulated in the MAR are
- The prohibition of insider dealing (Art. 14 MAR) (→ para. 28)
- The prohibition of market manipulation (Art. 15 MAR) (→ para. 19)
- The obligation to publish inside information (Art. 17 MAR) (→ para. 42)
- The obligation to publish own dealings by managers (so-called "directors' dealings", Art. 19 MAR) (→ para. 53)

The administrative sanctions are set out in Art. 30 MAR. As the EU does not have the power to directly regulate criminal law, Directive 2014/57/EU (CRIM-MAD)[7] sets out the Member States' obligation to make breaches of certain MAR provisions criminal offences.

This chapter will not discuss in detail all single questions of these regulatory topics. Instead, the basic mechanisms are explained, with a special focus on questions that are particularly relevant for crypto assets. For more general questions on the laws of securities trading, reference is made to the literature covering the application of the MAR.

3 The MAR is built on the general objectives of capital markets regulation.[8] Art. 1 MAR explicitly mentions the **protection of investors** and the protection of **financial market integrity**.[9] These aims are promoted through two mechanisms: firstly, the prohibition of certain conduct (insider dealing, market manipulation) and secondly, transparency obligations (publication of proprietary trading and price-sensitive inside information). The third purpose of capital markets regulation, the preservation of systemic stability, is of lesser importance in this regard.

Another purpose of the MAR is the harmonisation of capital markets regulation in the EU Member States. The idea is to prevent trade barriers and distortion of competition[10] that might arise through regulatory and supervisory arbitrage. For this reason, the MAR applies the idea of **full harmonisation**.[11] This means that the MAR rules directly apply in all Member States, overriding contradicting national rules, unless the MAR specifically allows for deviation. Outside the MAR's scope of application, e.g. with regard to currencies and means of payment, deviations are permitted. This is relevant for currency tokens and utility tokens, which are not "tradeable securities" under MiFiD2 (§ 7 para. 33 et seqq).

4 The MAR is **technology neutral**, which means that it does not address specific technologies but instead certain conduct in the financial markets. Whether and to what extent this conduct involves new technologies is not relevant. Thus, the MAR is applicable to crypto assets in principle (subject to certain requirements discussed in

---

[5] Directive 2203/6/EC of the European Parliament and of the Council on insider dealing and market manipulation (market abuse), OJ L 96, 12.4.2013, 16–25.
[6] ESMA, Questions and Answers on the Market Abuse Regulation (ESMA70-145-111, last updated 29 March 2019).
[7] Directive 2014/57/EU of the European Parliament and of the Council on criminal sanctions for market abuse (market abuse directive), OJ L 173, 12.6.2014, 179–189.
[8] International Organization of Securities Commissions, *'Objectives and Principles of Securities Regulation'* (June 2010), 3: 'protecting investors; ensuring that markets are fair, efficient and transparent; reducing systemic risk'.
[9] Recital 8.
[10] Recitals 4, 5.
[11] For more details, see Walla, in Veil (ed), *European Capital Markets Law* (2017), § 4, para. 54–57.

this chapter). The MAR rests on the idea of securities that are traded at well-established markets. At a certain point in their life cycle, established companies turn to the capital markets to cover their financing needs beyond the banks. This takes place at one of the known stock exchanges or a comparable marketplace. However, investment tokens are often issued by start-ups. They are traded at trading platforms (crypto-to-crypto and fiat-to-crypto exchanges; see → § 1 para. 90) whose legal status is sometimes unclear and that are not run by incumbent market operators. This raises the question of whether the MAR framework is sensible in the light of token trading and where there is a need for amendments to the current legislation.

5   In September 2020, the European Commission published its draft for the Regulation of Markets in Crypto Assets (**MiCA Draft**). This proposed new regime contains specific rules for certain (but not all) types of crypto assets. Although changes during the parliamentary process are likely, this chapter will also discuss the proposed rules on crypto assets.

B. Definitions

6   According to Art. 2(1), the MAR applies to financial instruments (→ para. 7) admitted to trading on a regulated market or a multilateral trading facility or for which an application for admission to trading on a regulated market or a multilateral trading facility has been made (→ para. 10).[12] Further, the respective conduct (for example, insider dealing) needs to have an impact on a market within the EU (→ para. 11).

I. Financial Instruments and Transferable Securities

1. Definition

7   The MAR applies to **financial instruments**.[13] This term has the same meaning as in Art. 4(1)(15) MiFiD2. The different financial instruments are listed in Section C of the MiFiD2 Annex. In addition to various forms of derivative contracts and emission certificates, these are primarily transferable securities as set out in Art. 4(1)(44) MiFiD2. **Transferable securities** is the pivotal definition for the application of EU capital markets laws. Transferable securities are those classes of securities which are negotiable on the capital market, with the exception of instruments of payment. Art. 4(1)(44) MiFiD2 lists shares, bonds and respective derivatives as examples of transferable securities.

2. Token Categories

8   There is wide consensus among commentators that **investment tokens** are transferable securities (for details, → § 7 para. 33). In contrast, **utility tokens** are not covered by Art. 4(1)(44) MiFiD2 because they do not have security-like properties. Thus, the MAR does not apply to utility tokens. **Currency tokens** are no transferable securities either as they are subject to the exception for payment instruments (→ § 7 para. 65).

---

[12] Other covered trading schemes such as auction platforms for greenhouse gas emission allowances are not relevant here.

[13] See, generally Veil, in Veil (ed), *European Capital Markets Law* (2017), § 8.

3. Derivatives

Art. 4(1)(44) MiFiD2 lists **derivatives** as transferable securities. They are defined here as all securities 'which give the right to buy or sell such securities or which result in a cash payment determined by reference to transferable securities, currencies, interest rates or yields, commodities or other indices or measures'. This means that the scope of assets underlying the derivative is wide. As a result, derivatives on **all underlying instruments** (and thus, currency tokens such as the Bitcoin!) are transferable securities under Art. 4(1)(44) MiFiD2.[14] The consequence is that trading currency tokens such as Bitcoin is not subject to the MAR rules whereas trading a currency token derivative (for example, a Bitcoin futures contract) is.

II. MAR-Regulated Markets

As a second requirement for the application of the MAR, the financial instruments (→ para. 7) need to be traded on a market within the MAR's scope of application. This includes **regulated markets** (Art. 3(1)(6) MAR; Art. 4(1)(21) MiFiD2), **multilateral trading facilities** (MTF, Art. 3(1)(7) MAR; Art. 4(1)(22) MiFiD2) and **organised trading facilities** (OTF, Art. 3(1)(8) MAR; Art. 4(1)(23) MiFiD2). If investment tokens that meet the requirements of Art. 4(1)(44) MiFiD2 are traded on one of these markets,[15] the MAR framework applies.[16]

All these markets require authorisation by the national regulator under Art. 5 MiFiD2 (for more details, → § 8 para. 37). However, for the application of the MAR it is irrelevant whether or not the necessary authorisation has been granted. The only requirement is that the statutory requirements are met. Thus, a market operator cannot avoid the onerous application of MAR rules by not obtaining the necessary regulatory approval.

III. Territorial Scope of Application

Pursuant to Art. 2(4), the MAR applies to activities within the EU and in third countries outside the EU.[17] However, third-country activities must have an effect on a market within the meaning of Art. 2(1) and (2) MAR (so-called **'impact principle'**).[18] This requirement is not expressly stated in the MAR. However, Art. 2(1) uses terms of EU regulation such as 'MTF' or 'regulated market'. This implies an application limited to markets within the EU because markets in third countries would not be considered an MTF within the meaning of MiFiD2.

Crypto trading platforms are accessible via the internet from all around the world. That means that insider dealing within the meaning of the MAR can be carried out from any country within or outside the EU, on the condition that it influences transferable securities on a regulated trading platform in the EU. However, it can be difficult to ascertain if a trading platform is located 'in' the EU. The problem is that, in contrast to traditional stock exchanges, crypto markets do not necessarily have an

---

[14] Maume and Fromberger, 'Regulation of Initial Coin Offerings: Reconciling U.S. and E.U. Securities Laws' [2019] 19 *Chicago Journal of International Law,* 548 (583 f.).
[15] Crypto exchanges will typically be structured as an MTF, → § 8 para. 15.
[16] But note the territorial scope of application, → para. 11.
[17] See also Gerner-Beuerle, in Lehmann and Kumpan (eds), *European Financial Services Law* (2019), 654.
[18] Veil, in Meyer/Veil/Rönnau (eds), *Handbuch zum Marktmissbrauchsrecht,* (2017), 118.

established physical location. They are new virtual constructs. In principle, the operator of a trading platform may domicile in country A, while the servers required for operation are in country B and services are offered to investors in country C. The creators of the MAR were obviously not aware of this possibility. The result is a regulatory gap.

If the operator **domiciles in an EU Member State**, the country-of-origin principle should be applied.[19] The idea behind country-of-origin is that goods or services are able to circulate freely in the EU if lawfully introduced in any Member State. The most common example in the financial market context is Art. 5(1) MiFiD2, requiring a financial service provider to obtain authorisation from the national regulator in its home EU Member State. It would be coherent to make crypto exchanges without a physical market location but with an operator domiciled in the EU subject to the MAR, too. The national regulator of that Member State (the competent authority, → para. 13) would then be responsible for oversight of the trading platform operator (under MiFiD2) as well as for trading on this platform (under the MAR).

The situation is more difficult if the exchange operator **domiciles outside the EU**. It would be effective to extend the scope of MAR application to these trading platforms (if they are available for investors in the EU). The main argument is that if available via the internet, this 'market' is not limited to certain regions, countries or continents. This would include the EU. Such an interpretation would be in line with the impact principle (→ para. 11). However, it is doubtful that courts would accept such a wide interpretation of Art. 2 MAR as it would de facto make EU market conduct rules applicable to all internet-based financial markets. Besides, most of these markets would not be authorised in the EU anyway. In this case, the MAR would not apply as it only covers EU-regulated markets (→ para. 10).

IV. The Competent Authority

13   Another issue is how to determine the responsible national regulator. Each EU Member State designates a 'competent authority' for the implementation of the MAR. In accordance with Art. 22 MAR, it is responsible for actions relating to financial instruments admitted to trading on a regulated market, an MTF or an OTF on its territory or for which a corresponding admission has been applied for. This is an example of *lex mercatus* (i.e. the law of the market). Art. 22 MAR is intended to ensure that trading venue and supervisory authority are geographically synchronised. It can be applied without problems to well-established trading venues with a fixed location. The necessary powers of the competent authority are set out in Art. 23 MAR.

14   However, this approach falls short **if the market operator does not domicile** in the EU but offers services in the EU via the internet (which means there is no regulated market in a Member State and thus no competent authority). This is essentially the same issue as the MAR's territorial scope of application (→ para. 11) and particularly relevant for trading platforms that operate on a global scale. Neither Art. 22 MAR ('Competent Authorities') nor Art. 3 MAR ('Definitions') address this setting, which means that the MAR does not grant any investigation or enforcement powers regarding conduct on markets in third countries. However, this would not be an issue as conduct on these markets would most likely not be subject to the MAR anyway (→ para. 11).

---

[19] See also Maume, 'Initial Coin Offerings and EU Prospectus Disclosure' (2020) 31 *European Business Law Journal*, 185 (202).

The competent authorities are responsible for **conduct outside the EU that has impact on regulated markets in the EU** ('impact principle', → para. 11). The obvious problem is that a Member State cannot grant its regulatory powers outside its territory. In these cases, the respective competent authority must rely on support from and cooperation with regulators in the third country. For conduct in other EU Member States, Art. 25 MAR puts an obligation on competent authorities to cooperate with each other.

V. The Proposed MiCA Regime

The proposed MiCA regime (→ para. 5) will introduce a distinct set of rules for crypto assets. In short, the MiCA Draft covers currency tokens, utility tokens, e-money tokens and asset-referenced tokens (for more details, → § 8 para. 4). However, MiCA will not apply to financial instruments within the meaning of MiFiD2, so investment tokens will still be regulated under the MAR.

According to Art. 76 MiCA Draft, the specific MiCA rules on market abuse will apply to crypto-assets admitted to trading on a **trading platform for crypto-assets**. The MiCA Draft does not give a definition for this kind of platform. It would make sense to harmonise this definition with 'DLT multilateral trading facility' within the meaning of Art. 2(3) of the 'Proposal for a Regulation on a pilot regime for market infrastructures based on distributed ledger technology'.[20]

Similar to the MAR, the Member States will have to designate competent authorities according to Art. 3(1)(24). The powers of these competent authorities are set out in Art. 82 MiCA Draft. They resemble the powers set out in Art. 23 MAR.

C. Prohibited Conduct

I. Market Manipulation, Art. 15 MAR

1. Purpose

Art. 15 MAR prohibits market manipulation and the attempt thereof.[21] This prohibition protects the free and undistorted **formation of market prices**. The criminalisation of market manipulation is one of the two cornerstones of market conduct rules, along with the prohibition of insider dealing.

The wording of Art. 15 MAR is vague. The problem is that market manipulation does not necessarily require misleading or false statements. Instead, market conduct itself can be manipulative (effects-based approach, → para. 22), for example sending false signals to the markets by following certain transaction patterns. However, financial markets transactions always have some influence on supply and demand. Especially transactions of larger volumes can have an impact on market prices. The question is how to distinguish between 'normal' behaviour that impacts on market prices and prohibited conduct, and how to detect the latter.[22]

---

[20] European Commission, '*Proposal for a Regulation of the European Parliament and of the Council on a pilot regime for market infrastructures based on distributed ledger technology*' (Undated, COM (2020) 594/3).

[21] For general overview, see Mock, in Ventoruzzo and Mock (eds), *Market Abuse Regulation* (2017), 311–313.

[22] IOSCO, 'Investigating and Prosecuting Market Manipulation, Report of the Technical Committee of IOSCO' (May 2000), 13, available at http://www.iosco.org (accessed 31.08.2021).

To make matters worse, the definitions and examples of rules contained in Art. 12 and Art. 15 MAR are not based on a stringent regulatory idea. Instead, they focus on a set of examples of conduct that has been observed in the past.[23] The result is a high level of uncertainty, both for market participants and regulators.

20 Market manipulation is **particularly relevant** in the crypto asset context. For example, the media reported extensive manipulation of the Bitcoin price by 'bots'.[24] Allegedly, the high flight of Bitcoin in 2017 was largely fuelled by manipulation.[25] 'Pump & Dump' attacks[26] are common for tokens with a low market capitalization.[27] Special caution is required when trading investment tokens on OTFs. Since, unlike on MTFs, operators are also allowed to conduct proprietary trading, the temptation to manipulate prices is particularly strong.

As discussed in this chapter, the application of Art. 15 MAR to crypto asset trading is an issue. For example, the effects-based approach is particularly problematic in this context (→ para. 22). There is also a massive regulatory gap because Art. 15 MAR can only be applied to investment tokens (→ para. 8).

2. Prohibited Conduct

21 **a) Definitions and Statutory Examples.** Art. 15 MAR bans market manipulation and the attempt thereof. Further specifics are given in Art. 12(1) MAR. Accordingly, the term market manipulation covers (simplified)

a. entering into a transaction, placing an order to trade or any other behaviour which gives **false or misleading signals** as to the supply of, demand for, or price of, a financial instrument,
b. entering into a transaction, placing an order to trade or any other activity or behaviour which affects or is likely to affect the price of one or several financial instruments, which employs **any form of deception or contrivance**;
c. **disseminating information** through the media, including the internet, which gives false or misleading signals as to the supply of, demand for, or price of, a financial instrument,
d. **transmitting false or misleading information** or providing false or misleading inputs **in relation to a benchmark** where the person who made the transmission or provided the input knew or ought to have known that it was false or misleading.

In addition, Art. 12(2) MAR lists specific examples of conduct that constitutes market manipulation (e.g. the targeted placement and cancellation of trading orders). Annex I MAR also contains a list of indicators for the determination of manipulative acts, which are supposed to simplify the handling of Art. 12 MAR in practice.

22 **b) Problems of the Effects-based Approach.** Art. 12(1)(a) and (b) MAR (→ para. 21) follow an effects-based definition approach. This means that the crucial issue is not the action carried out by the alleged perpetrator, but the effect achieved in the respective market. In other words, it is the effect (carried by the perpetrator's intention) that

---

[23] For an overview of different forms of conduct, see Teigelack in Veil (ed), *European Capital Markets Law* (2017), 236–237.
[24] Coleman, 'Bitcoin Price Manipulated by Cryptocurrency Trading Bots', WSJ, available at https://perma.cc/8652-9G3Y (accessed 10.4.2019).
[25] Rooney, 'Much of bitcoin's 2017 boom was market manipulation, research says', available at https://perma.cc/AZ8E-KYUS (accessed 10.4.2019).
[26] The term describes the artificial 'inflation' of a market with the aim of selling one's own tokens at a profit when other investors enter the market.
[27] See Hamrick, Rouhi, Mukherjee, Feder, Gandal, Moore and Vasek, 'The Economics of Cryptocurrency Pump and Dump Schemes', available at https://perma.cc/G85K-U7K2 (accessed 10.4.2019).

counts for breaches of Art. 15 MAR. Commentators have criticised that this approach is not very predictable. A reliable distinction between legitimate and prohibited market behaviour is hardly possible.[28]

This can be problematic for crypto asset trading. Crypto markets are **highly volatile**.[29] Price fluctuations of over 20 per cent or more per day are common.[30] In crypto markets with low liquidity, even small market movements can have a major impact on prices. Unusual (but legitimate!) trades can easily be interpreted as the generation of an abnormal or artificial price level within the meaning of Art. 12(1)(a) MAR. This is particularly true for derivative markets, where the swings are usually even stronger.

However, it is clear that not every action that triggers strong price movements in such an environment is market manipulation. Therefore, high emphasis needs to be placed on the statutory requirement of 'giving misleading signals' (→ para. 21) and the subjective elements (in particular, intention). Simply causing strong price movements is insufficient, even under an effects-based approach. Otherwise, it would be impossible to draw a reliable distinction between admissible market practice and the market manipulation. In this regard, guidance provided by national regulators and the ESMA would be most welcome.

c) **Regulatory Gap for Currency and Utility Tokens.** Currency tokens and utility tokens are not subject to the prohibition of market manipulation (→ para. 8). This might be convincing through the lens of regulatory theory because the information asymmetries regarding these tokens are significantly smaller than for investment tokens. However, the result is a considerable gap in investor protection. Currency tokens are traded on the same systems and on the same markets as investment tokens. Thus, the **risk of manipulation** is identical for both token types. For utility tokens, the problem is highly comparable.

The MiCA Draft includes currrency and utility tokens in its scope of application, so it is likely that this regulatory gap will be closed when the regime comes into force. Until then, the Member States can address the issue regarding their domestic financial market. This is because these tokens are no financial instruments within the meaning of the MAR. Therefore, the principle of full harmonisation (→ para. 3) does not apply. In such a case, Member States can enact additional rules on issues not covered by the MAR,[31] for example regarding currency tokens and utility tokens.

3. Criminal and Administrative Sanctions

Art. 30 MAR sets out the consequences of breaches of MAR provisions. Art. 30 MAR does not apply directly but obligates Member States to ensure that the national competent authorities can impose certain administrative actions. This is complemented by a list of supervisory powers available to national competent authorities in Art. 31 MAR. Pursuant to Art. 5 MAR-CRIM Member States must take all necessary steps to ensure that market manipulation constitutes a criminal offence.[32]

---

[28] Schmolke, in Klöhn (ed), *Marktmissbrauchsverordnung* (2018), Art. 12 para. 10.

[29] See e.g. the studies by Haffke and Fromberger, 'ICO Market Report 2019/2020. Performance Analysis of 2019's Initial Coin Offerings', (2020), available at https://ssrn.com/abstract=3770793 (accessed 26.5.2021).

[30] Börner, 'Kryptowährungen und strafbarer Marktmissbrauch' (2018) *Neue Zeitschrift für Wirtschafts-, Steuer- und Unternehmensstrafrecht*, (48) 53.

[31] For example, German law extends to scope of application of the MAR to currencies and commodities, see § 25 of the German Securities Trading Act (Wertpapierhandelsgesetz, WpHG).

[32] For more details, see Mock, in Ventoruzzo and Mock (eds), *Market Abuse Regulation* (2017), 334–336; Gerner-Beuerle, in Lehmann and Kumpan (eds), *European Financial Services Law* (2019), 767.

26 For **natural persons**, the national maximum administrative pecuniary sanction for breaches of Art. 15 is at least EUR 5 million (or in Member States whose currency is not the Euro, the corresponding value in national currency on 2 July 2014). For **legal persons** the maximum penalty is at least EUR 15 million or 15 per cent of the total annual turnover based on the last available accounts as approved by the management body. Art. 30(3) MAR allows the Member States to establish higher sanctions.

According to Art. 5 CRIM-MAD, Member States need to make sure that serious and intentional cases of market manipulation are criminal offences. Criminal liability includes inciting, aiding and abetting, Art. 6 CRIM-MAD. Art. 7 CRIM-MAD sets out that the maximum term of imprisonment is at least four years.

27 **Private law remedies** such as compensation or injunction are not set out in the MAR. They are subject to Member State laws.

II. Insider Dealing, Art. 14 MAR

1. Purpose

28 The second pillar of the securities trading framework is the prohibition of insider dealing as set out in Art. 14 MAR. The aim of this prohibition is to protect market integrity. Equal opportunities in terms of information are a prerequisite for investor confidence in the markets. Issuers, their affiliates (including intermediaries) and current shareholders are in a favoured position in respect of information. They might make use of internal information to maximise their profits.[33] Such conduct, or even rumours of such conduct, undermines investor confidence in the integrity of the financial markets and poses a threat to markets' efficiency; in particular, the cost of equity.

29 The prohibition of insider dealing is linked to the disclosure obligation under Art. 17 MAR (→ para. 42). The MAR assumes a seamless transition between Art. 14 and Art. 17. Inside information – insofar as it directly affects the issuer – must be published as soon as possible in accordance with Art. 17 MAR unless the company can postpone publication. Until then, the ban of insider dealing regarding this specific information applies.

2. Prohibited Conduct

30 a) **Structure.** According to Art. 14 MAR, insider dealing is prohibited. Art. 14 distinguishes between three alternatives:[34]
a) engaging in and attempting to engage in insider dealing,
b) recommend that another person engage in insider dealing or induce another person to engage in insider dealing, or
c) unlawfully disclose inside information.

Insider dealing is defined in Art. 8 MAR. Art. 9 MAR provides for exceptions for legitimate behaviour and Art. 10 MAR regulates unlawful disclosure. For issuers of tokens that are subject to the ban on insider dealing (i.e. investment tokens), there is nothing different about the application of these rules.

---

[33] Bernard Black, 'The Legal and Institutional Preconditions for Strong Securities Markets' (2001) 48 *UCLA Law Review* 781 (796–799); Bhattacharya and Daouk, 'The World Price of Insider Trading' (2002) 57 *Journal of Finance* 75 (76–77).

[34] For an overview, see Hansen, in Ventoruzzo and Mock (eds), *Market Abuse Regulation* (2017), 326–331; Gerner-Beuerle, in Lehmann and Kumpan (eds), *European Financial Services Law* (2019), 768–770.

b) Inside information. The basis of the facts is the **inside information** regulated in 31 Art. 7 MAR. According to Art. 7(1)(a), an inside information is an information that is 'of a precise nature, which has not been made public, relating, directly or indirectly, to one or more issuers or to one or more financial instruments, and which, if it were made public, would be likely to have a significant effect on the prices of those financial instruments'. **Typical examples** of inside information are information on forthcoming company takeovers, delistings, squeeze-outs, dividend reductions, profit warnings and crisis reports, changes in the corporate structure and capital measures, but also changes in the composition of the company's management.

Art. 7 MAR refers to financial instruments. The ban on insider dealing therefore 32 covers **investment tokens** that meet the requirements of "transferable securities" pursuant to Art. 4(1)(44) MiFiD2 (→ para. 7).

The ban on insider dealing does not apply to **currency tokens**. Unlike for the framework for market manipulation (→ para. 23), this is coherent from a regulatory perspective. The insider dealing ban is based on the idea that a market participant who has superior knowledge about a listed company must not exploit this advantage.[35] However, currency tokens are typically based on a decentralised blockchain. They lack the connection to an issuing company and thus also the potential information advantage.

For **utility tokens**, the argument of the decentralized structure does not apply because they are linked to an issuer. Nevertheless, it is consistent that they are not covered by the insider dealing ban in its current form. The reason is that they lack the investment character which is the main reason for the creation of value in the markets. For a share it is an objective price-determining factor whether the company will be better or worse off in the future.[36] This determines the return of investment. For utility tokens (which are more comparable to vouchers than to investments) it is objectively important whether the service can be provided and what quality the service has. However, this is not an objective factor that determines the value of a company and thus the value of an investment. If investors use utility tokens – contrary to the issuing institution's intention – for speculation purposes, this does not change the underlying setup.

According to Art. 7(2) MAR, the information is sufficiently **precise** if circumstances 33 either already exist or can reasonably be expected to exist in the future.[37] This can be verifiable facts, but also subjective evaluations such as value judgements, expressions of opinion or a prognosis. Even rumours can be precise information.[38]

Future-related information must have a sufficient probability of happening. This can be either the final result of a longer development or any intermediate step on the way there, see Art. 7(3) MAR. Recital 16 explains that, on the basis of an overall assessment, there must be a **realistic probability that** the event will occur. This corresponds to the ECJ-ruling *Geltl*.[39] A probability of at least over 50 per cent is therefore necessary, but

---

[35] See the list of potential offenders under Art. 8(4) MAR.
[36] The so-called 'fundamental value', see in more details Brealy, Mayers and Allen, *Principles of Corporate Finance* (2017), 19 ff.
[37] For more details, see Ventoruzzo and Picciau, in Ventoruzzo and Mock (eds), *Market Abuse Regulation* (2017), 189–192.
[38] Gerner-Beuerle, in Lehmann and Kumpan (eds), *European Financial Services Law* (2019), 677; Veil, in Veil (ed), *European Capital Markets Law* (2017), 202–203.
[39] The Court of Justice of European Union, Judgment of 28 June 2012, *Geltl v Daimler AG*, C-19/11, ECLI:EU:C:2012:397, para. 49. See also Krause and Brellochs, '*Insider trading and the disclosure of inside information after Geltl v Daimler-A comparative analysis of the ECJ decision in the Geltl v Daimler case with a view to the future European Market Abuse Regulation*' [2013] 8(3) *Capital Markets Law Journal*, 283–299.

not an extremely high probability. The probability of occurrence must be assessed from the perspective of the prudent investor. Information becomes precise when, according to the expected causal process and general life experience, nothing will go wrong, and the given situation will occur. These formulas are particularly relevant for **protracted processes and events**.[40] These drag on for weeks, months or even years (for example, company takeovers). In this context, general prospects or trends will, over time, result in increasingly reliable information which, at a certain point in time, will become precise information in accordance with Art. 7(2) MAR.

34 The information must **not be public knowledge**. This means that the information is not disseminated among direct market participants. Conversely, the information is known if an unspecified number of people could take note of it and it could be assumed that the information was factored into the price of the financial instrument. However, this is not only the case when the general investing public has taken note, but when the information is known to (specialised) market participants.[41]

The **relevant public** is for classical exchanges that of the Member State in which the exchange or the trading venue is located. It is not necessary that the information has been made available to investors throughout the EU. This needs to be modified for trading platforms. Since the public is not spatially closed off, the basic principle here is that the information must be known throughout the EU. This corresponds to the result for securities that are admitted to several stock exchanges in the EU area. In these cases, it is required that the public in all the Member States concerned must have access to the information. The availability in English, which is the language commonly used in both financial and Internet circles, should be considered. Here it can be assumed that every user can process the relevant information. If, on the other hand, trading on a trading platform should only take place in a language that is not universally understood (and thus in any language other than English), then the level of familiarity depends on the availability of the information in those EU member states in which this language is an official language. Thus, if a trading platform is to operate exclusively in Polish, it depends on whether the general investing public in Poland has the opportunity to learn about it.

35 The information must have **significant influence** on the price of the financial instrument.[42] This so-called 'materiality' is intended to exclude minor cases. The basis for this price relevance is an objective prognosis ex-ante, which is based on the time at which insider dealing was carried out and considers the circumstances of the individual case. Art. 7(4) MAR specifies that information has significant influence if a knowledgeable investor would probably use it as part of the basis for his investment decision. So instead of giving a percentage limit (for example, price movement of 5 per cent), a subjective test about the incentive for the investor and whether the transaction is worthwhile for him is required.[43]

36 c) **Forms of Insider Dealing.** Art. 8 MAR complements Art. 14, providing further details on the prohibited conduct. According to Art. 8(1) MAR, 'insider dealing arises where a person possesses inside information and uses that information by **acquiring or disposing** of, for its own account or for the account of a third party, directly or indirectly, financial instruments to which that information relates.' According to Art. 8 (1)(2) MAR, this includes cancelling or amending an order. Recital 24 explains that if a

---

[40] Ventoruzzo/Picciau, in Ventoruzzo and Mock (eds), *Market Abuse Regulation* (2017), 195–196.
[41] Ventoruzzo/Picciau, in Ventoruzzo and Mock (eds), *Market Abuse Regulation* (2017), 198.
[42] For detailed discussion, see Veil, in Veil (ed), *European Capital Markets Law* (2017), 204–209.
[43] Krause, in Meyer, Veil and Rönnau, *Handbuch zum Marktmissbrauchsrecht* (2017), § 6 para. 121–124.

person is in possession of inside information and then carries out the transaction, 'it should be implied that that person has used that information'. In other words, Art. 8(1) MAR stipulates the refutable assumption that all orders carried out by an insider (who naturally has access to inside information) are prohibited insider dealing. Art. 9 MAR regulates some exceptions to this presumption. Of particular relevance are sufficient organizational factual and legal precautions within the company (so-called *Chinese Walls*) in accordance with Art. 9(1) MAR.

According to Art. 8(2) MAR, **recommending** or **inducing** within the meaning of Art. 14(b) MAR arises if a person possesses inside information and, on the basis of this information, recommends to third parties to acquire or dispose of the corresponding financial instruments or to cancel or modify orders, or induces third parties to do so. An inducement is an action with the aim of influencing the will of another person and persuading him to buy or sell. It is irrelevant whether or not the induced person carries out the transaction. A recommendation, on the other hand, is a statement in which the insider describes the transaction as advantageous for the addressee in order to persuade him or her to carry it out. Although 'inducing' is the broader term, 'recommending' is more relevant in practice. 37

Both alternatives require the perpetrator to be in possession of the inside information. However, unlike Art. 14(c) MAR (→ para. 30), the inside information does not have to be passed on to the other person.

Art. 10 MAR provides further details on **unlawful disclosure** under Art. 14(c) MAR. This prohibition is intended to counteract the increased risks caused by the dissemination of inside information. In contrast to Art. 14(b) MAR, no targeted influence on third parties is required. However, the inside information itself must be passed on to the third party. It is not necessary that third parties take note of the information or act after having received it.[44] 38

3. Criminal and Administrative Sanctions

The criminal liability of insider dealing follows the same pattern as that of market manipulation (→ para. 25). The maximum term of imprisonment is at least four years for breaches of Art. 14(a) and (b) MAR and at least two years for breaches of Art. 14(c) (see Art. 7 CRIM-MAD). 39

III. Market Conduct and the Proposed MiCA-Regime

Under the proposed MiCA regime, Art. 78 MiCA Draft prescribes the ban of **insider dealing**. The wording is identical with the rules contained in Art. 14 MAR and Art. 8 MAR. The definition of inside information (Art. 78(1) MiCA) duplicates the definition in Art. 7(1) MAR. The only difference is that Art. 78(1) MiCA does not cover derivatives on crypto-assets. However, this is straightforward as derivatives on any underlying assets are financial instruments within the meaning of MiFiD2 (→ para. 9). 40

Similarly, Art. 80 MiCA Draft contains the prohibition of **market manipulation**. The proposed wording slightly deviates from Art. 12 MAR (for example, 'secures' instead of 'sets'), but carries the same meaning. However, Art. 80 MiCA Draft omits some specific bans that are addressed in the MAR, such as benchmark manipulation or 'marking the close'. It also does not allow for established market practices (cf. Art. 13 MAR). 41

---

[44] Meyer, in Meyer, Veil and Rönnau (eds), *Handbuch zum Marktmissbrauchsrecht* (Munich 2017), § 8 para. 6.

D. Disclosure and Transparency Obligations

I. Public Disclosure of Inside Information, Art. 17 MAR

1. Purpose

42   The most important obligation of a listed issuer is public disclosure of inside information subject to Art. 17 MAR.[45] This is commonly referred to as 'ad-hoc disclosure'. According to Art. 17 MAR, the issuer shall disclose inside information that concerns him directly **as soon as possible** to the markets. This reduces information asymmetries and the possibility of insider dealings.[46] For issuers, being subject to this disclosure regime is a radical change in the company's structure. This is because potential inside information must be identified throughout the whole company. In a second step, it needs to be assessed and then finally reported to company management. This causes additional costs and creates a high liability risk in the event of non-compliance. Meeting these obligations without a structured compliance system hardly seems possible.

43   Ad-hoc disclosure is linked to the prohibition of insider dealing (Art. 14 MAR). The MAR assumes a seamless transition. In principle, inside information must be published immediately in accordance with Art. 17 MAR, unless the information does not directly concern the issuer (→ para. 46) or the company can postpone publication (→ para. 50).

44   Art. 17(8) MAR regulates the special case of lawfully **disclosing inside information to third parties**. Accordingly, inside information disclosed to third parties by the issuer or by a person acting on its behalf or for its account needs to be disclosed to the markets. This does not apply if the person receiving the information is obliged to maintain secrecy. Thus, Art. 17(8) MAR emphasizes equal access to information as a basic principle of capital market regulation.

2. Disclosure Obligation

45   According to Art. 17 MAR, issuers must immediately disclose to the public **inside information** that directly concerns them. As for insider dealing, the term 'inside information' is defined in Art. 7 MAR.

46   The inside information must concern the **issuer directly**. This excludes general market events of which participants should be informed anyway from the disclosure obligation. The same applies to events in other companies. However, an event that does not directly concern the issuer may as well trigger an ad-hoc disclosure obligation if its results directly affect the issuer and are relevant to the share price. A classic example is the volcanic eruption that causes an airline to issue a profit warning due to flight cancellations. In the field of crypto assets, general announcements by supervisory authorities that have a direct impact on the issuer and its business model would be a conceivable example.

47   The MAR assumes that financial instruments are issued by an existing company. According to Art. 3(1)(21) MAR, an issuer is a legal entity under private or public law which issues financial instruments or proposes to issue them. This can be problematic in the case of investment tokens, because they can be issued **without**

---

[45] For detailed overview of the regulatory background and history, see Pietrancosta, in Ventoruzzo and Mock (eds), *Market Abuse Regulation* (2017), 347–353.

[46] Koch, in Veil (ed), *European Capital Markets Law* (2017), 348–349.

an issuer. A well-known example is the DAO token, which attracted worldwide attention.[47] Another example would be an ICO campaign initiated by a start-up that is not incorporated. In these cases, the addressee of the norm is missing.

This problem is specific to tokens and does not arise in classical capital market law. It would be conceivable that the duty laid down in Art. 17 MAR would simply run dry and the investment tokens could be traded without the corresponding disclosure requirements. However, this is to be rejected because of the **purpose** of Art. 17 MAR. The provision promotes a 'level playing field' for investors and reduces information asymmetries. This facilitates investor confidence in the respective markets and trading platforms. If investment tokens with an issuer and investment tokens without an issuer were traded in the same market segment at the same time, this would result in information arbitrage between these two tokens. This is in stark contrast to the idea of a level playing field. Therefore, investment tokens with a decentralised structure should not be listed/traded at a trading platform. A listing would be a breach of the MAR. Operators of trading platforms (if organised as an MTF, → § 8 para. 18) have to monitor their platforms (Art. 32(1) MiFiD2) and report possible breaches (Art. 32(2) MiFiD2, expressly referring to breaches of the MAR). Failure to do so may result in revocation of the operating licence subject to Art. 8 MiFiD2.

The ad-hoc disclosure obligation only applies to issuers who have either **applied for admission to trading** themselves or have approved this admission. This is clarified by Recital 49. 48

Disclosure needs to be made **as soon as possible**. This does not mean 'at once', but without undue delay. So issuers have time to a detailed assessment of the situation (for example, veracity of the information, reliability of a source, calculations, etc.). 49

The further modalities of publication are set out in Art. 17(1)(2) MAR, in Art. 2, 3 of the Implementing Regulation (EU) No. 1055/2016[48] and in complementing Member State laws.

3. Exemptions

Of particular relevance is the possibility of a temporary **deferment of publication** under Art. 17(4) MAR. This protects the legitimate interests of the issuer, as early disclosure can have significant disadvantages. ESMA has published guidance on this deferral option.[49] 50

The conditions for deferment are:
- suitability of prompt disclosure to prejudice the legitimate interests of the issuer,
- postponement is not likely to mislead the public; and
- the issuer can ensure continued confidentiality.

ESMA has identified different examples in its guidelines.[50] Appropriate cases for postponement could be, among others:
- the possible threat to ongoing negotiations, e.g. in the case of takeovers and mergers, but also in cases where the financial viability of the issuer depends on the outcome of the negotiations;

---

[47] See for the DAO token in detail: Hacker and Thomale, 'Crypto-Securities Regulation: ICOs, Token Sales and Cryptocurrencies under EU Financial Law', (2017) SSRN, 10, available at papers.ssrn.com/sol3/papers.cfm?abstract_id=3075820&download=yes (accessed 31.08.2021).

[48] Commission Implementing Regulation (EU) 1055/2016 laying down implementing technical standards with regard to the technical means for appropriate public disclosure of inside information and for delaying the public disclosure of inside information in accordance with Regulation (EU) No 596/2014 of the European Parliament and of the Council, OJ L 173, 30.6.2016 p. 47–51.

[49] ESMA, *'MAR Guidelines – Deferral of disclosure of inside information'* (ESMA/2016/1478 EN).

[50] ESMA, *'MAR Guidelines – Deferral of disclosure of inside information'* (ESMA/2016/1478 EN) 4–5.

- the need for pending approval of a decision by internal mechanisms of the company or by a governmental authority;
- the development of a product or an invention, the prompt disclosure of which would jeopardise the issuer's intellectual property rights.

The supervisory authorities must be informed of the deferral under Art. 17(4) MAR. In its notification the issuer needs to lay out to the authorities to what extent the above conditions are met.

51   Exemption is granted **by decision of** the issuer and on its own responsibility. This means that issuers cannot argue in hindsight that the material conditions for a deferral would have been met if the issuer had taken a decision earlier.

4. Criminal and Administrative Sanctions

52   Like for insider dealings and market manipulation (→ para. 25), Art. 30 MAR provides an administrative sanction regime for breaches of Art. 17 MAR. For **natural persons**, the national maximum administrative pecuniary sanction is at least EUR 1 million (or in Member States whose currency is not the Euro, the corresponding value in national currency on 2 July 2014). For **legal persons** the maximum penalty is at least EUR 2.5 million or 2 per cent of the total annual turnover based on the last available accounts as approved by the management body. Art. 30(3) MAR allows the Member States to establish higher sanctions.

The CRIM-MAD does not require Member States to provide criminal sanctions for breaches of Art. 17 MAR.

II. Managers' Transactions, Art. 19 MAR

1. Purpose

53   Unless prohibited by Art. 14 MAR, directors and managers are of course allowed to buy or sell financial products that were issued by their employer. However, these so-called 'directors' dealings' are also subject to restrictions and obligations.[51] First, all proprietary trading must be disclosed to the markets in accordance with Art. 19(1) MAR and reported to the national regulator (→ para. 55). Secondly, Art. 19(11) MAR provides for a trading ban thirty days before mandatory periodic company reports (→ para. 60). Art. 19 MAR is supplemented by the Delegated Regulation (EU) No. 522/2016[52], setting out further details.

54   Art. 19(1) MAR has three purposes. The **disclosure obligation** (→ para. 55) simplifies the **prosecution of (negligent) insider dealing**. Second, and much more important, disclosure of proprietary transactions has an **indicator effect** on the markets. It is assumed that managers have a good overview of the 'health' of the issuer and that this knowledge influences their transactions. For example, if a company director has the feeling that the company is overall decline and this will show in the next years, this is a big incentive for getting rid of shares. Thirdly, the disclosure requirement is intended to promote **market fairness**. Assuming that

---

[51] For general overview, see Dell'Erba, in Ventoruzzo and Mock (eds), *Market Abuse Regulation* (2017), 311–313.

[52] Commission Delegated Regulation (EU) 2016/522 supplementing Regulation (EU) No 596/2014 of the European Parliament and of the Council as regards an exemption for certain third countries public bodies and central banks, the indicators of market manipulation, the disclosure thresholds, the competent authority for notifications of delays, the permission for trading during closed periods and types of notifiable managers' transactions, OJ L 88, 5.4.2016 p. 1–18.

proprietary trading actually has an indicator effect, investors can benefit from the knowledge advantage of the managers (idea of the 'level playing field').

The **trading ban** (→ para. 60) under Art. 19(11) MAR focuses on fairness. The idea is that immediately before annual, half-yearly or quarterly reports, there is a particularly high probability that managers will exploit their information advantage.

2. Disclosure Obligation

Art. 19(1) MAR applies to persons who perform **management tasks**. According to Art. 3(1)(25)(a) MAR, these are all members of the executive bodies, members of the management board, their deputies and members of the supervisory board. Pursuant to Art. 3(1)(25)(b) MAR, persons with executive functions are also senior executives who have regular access to inside information about the issuer and who are authorized to make business decisions about future developments of the issuer. 55

Art. 19(1) MAR also applies to **persons closely associated** with these managers. According to Art. 3(1)(26) MAR, these are spouses, dependent children or relatives who have lived in the same household for at least one year. The obligation also applies to companies in which these closely related persons perform management functions.

According to Art. 19(5) MAR, issuers are obliged to **instruct** their managers in writing about their reporting obligations. These in turn have to inform the persons closely related to them in writing and keep a copy of the document. In addition, issuers must maintain lists of all managers and persons closely associated with them. 56

Pursuant to Art. 19(1)(a) MAR, the reporting obligation concerns trades 'relating to the shares or debt instruments of that issuer or to derivatives or other financial instruments linked thereto'. This is a contrast to other MAR provisions, which typically refer to financial instruments only. Since investment tokens are financial instruments (→ para. 8) linked to an issuer, the disclosure obligation applies. 57

According to Art. 19(8) MAR, the reporting obligation only arises if the transactions reach a **total volume of EUR 5,000** within a calendar year. There is no netting, which means that the sales cannot be offset against purchases. For derivatives with physical settlement, the reference price is the transaction amount, whereas in the case of derivatives with cash settlements (e.g. swaps), the reference price is the nominal value multiplied by the reference price.[53] 58

It is the view of ESMA that, the transactions of all addressees of Art. 19 MAR (so management and persons close to them) must be considered individually and cannot be aggregated.[54] This means that for the purpose of calculating the EUR 5,000 threshold, transactions by persons closely associated with the manager are not attributed to the manager.

Managers referred to in Art. 19(1) MAR need to report the transaction pursuant to Art. 19(1)(2) MAR to the issuer and to the national regulator at the latest within **three business days**. The period begins with the conclusion of the transaction under the applicable national contract law.[55] Pursuant to Art. 19(3) MAR the issuer is under an obligation to make the transaction publicly available (i.e., on their website) no later than three business days after the transaction. 59

---

[53] ESMA, 'Final Report – ESMA's Technical Advice on Delegated Acts Concerning the Market Abuse Regulation' (ESMA/2015/224, 03.02.2015), 45.
[54] ESMA, 'Questions and Answers on the Market Abuse Regulation' (ESMA70-145-111, last updated 29.3.2019) Q7.3.
[55] Semrau, in Klöhn (ed), *Marktmissbrauchsverordnung* (2018), Art. 19 para. 60.

3. Trading Ban

60 According to Art. 19(11) MAR, executives may not, directly or indirectly, engage in proprietary trading for 30 calendar days before the announcement of an interim financial report or a year-end report which the issuer is obliged to make public (so-called '**closed period**'). The issuer's reporting obligation may arise from stock exchange regulations as well as national law. However, there is no trading ban before ad hoc announcements.[56]

The trading ban is particularly relevant in the case of start-ups, since the founders regularly hold large parts of the share capital and must often sell it with short notice for financing reasons. For these issuers, Art. 19(11) MAR might become relevant if they issued investment tokens.

61 According to Art. 19(12) MAR, the issuer may exempt the manager from the trading ban. The prerequisites are regulated by Art. 19(12) MAR in conjunction with Art. 7 of Regulation (EU) No. 522/2016. In companies without a supervisory board and with only one managing director, the effect is that managing directors can exempt themselves from the trading ban. This would most likely be the case for many start-ups that issued investment tokens.

4. Criminal and Administrative Sanctions

62 Like for insider dealings and market manipulation (→ para. 25), Art. 30 MAR provides an administrative sanction regime for breaches of Art. 19 MAR. For **natural persons**, the national maximum administrative pecuniary sanction is at least EUR 500,000 (or in Member States whose currency is not the Euro, the corresponding value in national currency on 2 July 2014). For **legal persons**, the maximum penalty is at least EUR 1 million. Art. 30(3) MAR allows the Member States to establish higher sanctions.

The CRIM-MAD does not require Member States to provide criminal sanctions for breaches of Art. 19 MAR.

III. Disclosure Rules under the Proposed MiCA-Regime

63 Art. 77(1) Draft MiCA obligates crypto-asset issuers to **disclose inside information** as soon as possible. The wording is nearly identical to Art. 17(1) MAR. It is also possible to delay disclosure subject to specific requirements (cf. Art. 17(4) MAR).

64 However, the Draft MiCA does not contain any rules on **managers' transactions** (cf. Art. 19 MAR, → para. 53). This is inconsistent as Art. 19 MAR is linked to the ban of insider trading under Art. 14 MAR. Mirroring only one of these two rules in the MiCA does not seem straightforward.

---

[56] Maume and Kellner, 'Paradigmenwechsel oder Placebo? Directors' Dealings unter der Marktmissbrauchsverordnung' (2017) 46 *Zeitschrift für Unternehmens- und Gesellschaftsrecht*, 273 (293).

§ 12
Confiscation

Literature: Al Jawaheri, Al Sabah, Boshmaf and Erbad, 'Deanonymizing Tor hidden service users through Bitcoin transactions analysis', arXiv:1801.07501v3 [cs.CR], 10.7.2019; Antonopoulos, *Mastering Bitcoin: Programming the open blockchain* (2nd edn, O'Reilly, Sebastopol, 2017); Antonopoulos and Wood, *Mastering Ethereum: Building Smart Contracts and DApps* (O'Reilly, Sebastopol, 2019); Bacarese and Sellar, 'Civil Asset Forfeiture in Practice' in Rui and Sieber (eds), *Non-Conviction-Based Confiscation in Europe* (Berlin, 2015), 211; Béres, Seres, Benczúr and Quintyne-Collins, 'Blockchain is Watching You: Profiling and Deanonymizing Ethereum Users', arXiv:2005.14051v2 [cs.CR], 13.10.2020; Biryukov, Khovratovich and Pustogarov, 'Deanonymisation of clients in Bitcoin P2P network', arXiv:1405.7418v3 [cs.CR], 5.7.2014; Blanco Cordero, 'Modern Forms of Confiscation and Protection of Third Parties', in Ligeti and Simonato (eds), *Chasing Criminal Money. Challenges and Perspectives on Asset Recovery in the EU* (Oxford, 2017), 139; Boucht, 'Asset confiscation in Europe – past, present, and future challenges' (2019) 26 *Journal of Financial Crime*, 526; Boucht, 'Civil Asset Forfeiture and the presumption of innocence under article 6 (2) ECHR' (2014) 5 *New Journal of European Criminal Law*, 221; Boucht, 'Extended criminal confiscation: Criminal Assets or Criminal Owners?' in Ligeti and Simonato (eds), *Chasing Criminal Money. Challenges and Perspectives on Asset Recovery in the EU* (Oxford, 2017), 117; Boucht, *The Limits of Asset Confiscation: On the Legitimacy of Extended Appropriation of Criminal Proceeds* (Hart Publishing, Oxford, 2017); Brown, 'Cryptocurrency and criminality: The Bitcoin Opportunity' (2016) 89 *The Police Journal: Theory, Practice and Principles*, 327; Campbell, 'Criminal Labels, the European Convention on Human Rights and the Presumption of Innocence' (2013) 76 *Modern Law Review*, 681; Campbell, *Organised Crime and the Law: A Comparative Analysis* (Hart Publishing, Oxford, 2013); Cassella, 'Civil Asset Recovery – The American Experience', in Rui and Sieber, (eds), *Non-Conviction-Based Confiscation in Europe* (Berlin, 2015), 13; Engelhardt and Klein, 'Bitcoins – Geschäfte mit Geld, das keines ist: Technische Grundlagen und zivilrechtliche Betrachtung' (2014) 17 *Zeitschrift für IT-Recht und Recht der Digitalisierung*, 355; Esser, 'A Civil Asset Recovery Model – The German Perspective and European Human Rights' in Rui and Sieber (eds), *Non-Conviction-Based Confiscation in Europe* (Berlin, 2015), 69; Eurojust, 'Report on non-conviction-based confiscation' (General Case 751/NMSK – 2012, 2.4.2013), 9 et seq. available at https://beck-link.de/s5bap (accessed 1.6.2021); Fernandez-Bertier, 'The confiscation and recovery of criminal property: a European Union state of the art' [2016] *ERA Forum*, 323; Fröwis, Gottschalk, Haslhofer, Rückert and Pesch, 'Safeguarding the evidential value of forensic cryptocurrency investigations' (2020) 33 *Forensic Science International: Digital Investigation*, Article 200902, DOI: 10.1016/j.fsidi.2019.200902; Goger, 'Bitcoins im Strafverfahren: Virtuelle Währung und reale Strafverfolgung' (2016) 19 *Zeitschrift für IT-Recht und Recht der Digitalisierung*, 431; Grzywotz, *Virtuelle Kryptowährungen und Geldwäsche* (Duncker & Humblot, Berlin, 2019); Heine, 'Bitcoins und Botnetze – Strafbarkeit und Vermögensabschöpfung bei illegalem Bitcoin-Mining' (2016) 36 *Neue Zeitschrift für Strafrecht*, 441; Hüttemann, 'Grundlagen und Bedeutung der grenzüberschreitenden Vermögensabschöpfung unter besonderer Berücksichtigung der Verordnung (EU) 2018/1805 – Teil 2' (2019) 8 *Neue Zeitschrift für Wirtschafts-, Steuer- und Unternehmensstrafrecht*, 248; John, 'Zur Sachqualität und Eigentumsfähigkeit von Kryptotoken – eine dogmatische (Neu)Betrachtung' (2020) 20 *Zeitschrift für Bank und Kapitalmarktrecht*, 76; Kappos, Yousaf, Maller and Meiklejohn, 'An Empirical Analysis of Anonymity in Zcash', (27th USENIX Security Symposium, 2018) available at https://beck-link.de/vdvz6 (accessed 14.6.2021); Kaulartz and Matzke, 'Die Tokenisierung des Rechts' (2018) 71 *Neue Juristische Wochenschrift*, 3278; Kert, 'Verfall und Abschöpfung in Österreich' (2016) 5 *Neue Zeitschrift für Wirtschafts-, Steuer- und Unternehmensstrafrecht*, 203; Klusman and Dijkhuizen, 'Deanonymisation in Ethereum Using Existing Methods for Bitcoin', (7.2.2018), available at https://beck-link.de/pp24mzim (accessed 14.6.2021); Kütük and Sorge, 'Bitcoin im deutschen Vollstreckungsrecht – Von der "Tulpenmanie" zur "Bitcoinmanie"' (2014) 17 *Zeitschrift für IT-Recht und Recht der Digitalisierung*, 643; Ligeti and Simonato, 'Asset Recovery in the EU: Towards a Comprehensive Enforcement Model beyond Confiscation? An Introduction', in Ligeti and Simonato (eds), *Chasing Criminal Money. Challenges and Perspectives on Asset Recovery in the EU* (Oxford, 2017), 1; Linoy, Stakhanova and Matyukhina, 'Exploring Ethereum's Blockchain Anonymity Using Smart Contract Code Attribution' (15th International Conference on Network and Service Management, 2019) available at https://beck-link.de/38p43 (accessed 14.6.2021); Marstaller and Zimmermann, *Non-conviction-based confiscation in Deutschland?* (Nomos, Baden-Baden, 2018); Mazzacuva, 'The Problematic Nature of Asset Recovery Measures: Recent Developments of the Italian Preventive Confiscation' in Ligeti and Simonato (eds), *Chasing Criminal Money. Challenges and Perspectives on Asset Recovery in the EU* (Oxford, 2017), 101; Meyer, 'Recognizing the Unknown – the New Confiscation Regulation' (2020) 10 *European Criminal Law Review*, 140; Milone, 'On the borders of criminal law. A tentative assessment of italian 'non-conviction based extended confiscation'' (2017) 8 *New Journal of European Criminal Law*, 150; Nelen, 'Hit them where it hurts most? The proceeds-of-crime approach in the Netherlands' (2004) 41 *Crime, Law & Social Change*, 517; Nikolov, 'General characteristics of civil forfeiture' (2011) 14 *Journal of Money Laundering Control*, 16; Ochnio, 'The problematic scope of extended confiscation in comparative perspective' (2019) 52 Nowa Kodyfikacja Prawa Karnego, 119; Panzavolta and Flor, 'A Necessary Evil? The Italian 'Non-Criminal System' of Asset Forfeiture' in Rui and Sieber (eds), *Non-Conviction-Based Confiscation in Europe* (Berlin, 2015), 111; Panzavolta, 'Confiscation and the Concept of Punishment: Can There be a Confiscation Without a Conviction' Ligeti and Simonato (eds), *Chasing Criminal Money. Challenges and Perspectives on Asset Recovery in the EU* (Oxford, 2017), 25; Pieth, 'Recovering stolen assets – a new issue' in Pieth (ed), *Recovering stolen assets* (Bern, 2008), 3; Quesnelle, 'On the linkability of Zcash transactions', arXiv: 1712.01210v1 [cs.CR], 4.12.2017; Rückert, 'Cryptocurrencies and fundamental rights' [2019] *Journal of Cybersecurity*, 1; Rückert, 'Token im Strafverfahren', in Maume, Maute and Fromberger (eds), *Rechtshandbuch Kryptowerte* (München, 2020), 585; Rückert, 'Vermögensabschöpfung und Sicherstellung bei Bitcoins – Neue juristische Herausforderungen durch die ungeklärte Rechtsnatur von virtuellen Währungseinheiten' (2016) 19 *Zeitschrift für IT-Recht und Recht der Digitalisierung*, 295; Rui, 'Non-conviction based confiscation in the European Union — an assessment of Art. 5 of the proposal for a directive of the European Parliament and of the Council on the freezing and confiscation of proceeds of crime in the European Union' [2012] *ERA Forum*, 349; Rui, 'Introduction' in Rui and Sieber (eds), *Non-Conviction-Based Confiscation in Europe* (Berlin, 2015), 1; Rui and Sieber, 'Non-Conviction-Based Confiscation in Europe – Bringing the Picture Together' in Rui and Sieber (eds), *Non-Conviction-Based Confiscation in Europe* (Berlin, 2015), 245; Simonato, 'Directive 2014/42/ EU and Non-Conviction Based Confiscation: A Step Forward on Asset Recovery?' (2015) 6 *New Journal of European Criminal Law*, 213; SerHack and the Monero Community, *Mastering Monero: The future of private transactions* (Independently Published, 2018); Silfversten, Favaro, Slapakova, Ishikawa, Liu and Salas, 'Exploring the use of Zcash cryptocurrency for illicit or criminal purposes', (RAND Corporation research report, 2020), 5, available at https://beck-link.de/tx8r2 (accessed 14.6.2021); Simonato, 'Extended confiscation of criminal assets: limits and pitfalls of minimum harmonisation in the EU' (2016) 41 *European Law Review*, 727; Simser, 'Perspectives on Civil Forfeiture' in Young (ed), *Civil Forfeiture of Criminal Property: Legal Measures for Targeting the Proceeds of Crime* (Edward Elgar, Cheltenham, 2009), 13; Smith, 'Civil Asset Recovery: The English Experience' in Rui and Sieber (eds), *Non-Conviction-Based Confiscation in Europe* (Berlin, 2015), 31; Strauch and Handke, 'Kryptotoken in Zwangsvollstreckung und Insolvenz', in Maume, Maute and Fromberger (eds), *Rechtshandbuch Kryptowerte* (München, 2020), 265; UNODC, 'Estimating illicit financial flows resulting from drug trafficking and other transnational organized crimes' (Research Report, 31.8.2011), 7, available at https://beck-link.de/86vk6 (accessed 14.6.2021); Walter, 'Bitcoin, Libra und sonstige Kryptowährungen aus zivilrechtlicher Sicht' (2019) 72 *Neue Juristische Wochenschrift*, 3609; Weigend, 'Assuming that the Defendant Is Not Guilty: The Presumption of Innocence in the German System of Criminal Justice' (2014) 8 *Criminal Law and Philosophy*, 285.

Outline

	para.
A. Introduction	1
B. Forensic Methods	9
C. Object of Confiscation	11
I. Confiscation of Crypto Assets	11
II. Legal Nature of Crypto Assets	15
III. Confiscation Order	19
1. Confiscation of the Crypto Assets themselves	19
2. Value Confiscation	21
3. Confiscation of Contractual Claims against Token Service Providers	22
D. Types of Confiscation	23
I. Criminal Confiscation	23
II. Third Party Confiscation	25
III. Extended Confiscation	26
1. Definition	26
2. Scope of Application	28
3. Standard of Proof	30
IV. Non-Conviction Based Confiscation	32
E. Freezing Orders	37

§ 12. Confiscation

F. Fundamental Rights and Procedural Safeguards	42
I. Criminal Sanction	43
II. Fundamental Rights	45
1. Inevitably Affected Rights	46
2. Right against Self-Incrimination	48
3. Ne Bis In Idem	50
4. Proportionality	51
III. Procedural Safeguards	53
G. Cross-Border Confiscation of Crypto Assets	55
I. Mutual Legal Assistance	58
II. Principle of Mutual Recognition	60

A. Introduction

Crypto assets are becoming more and more popular. Even if the total amount of Bitcoin, Ether, Monero and other so-called cryptocurrencies spent daily is still low compared to fiat currency, the relevance of cryptocurrencies in connection with **criminal activity** cannot be overestimated.[1] The high degree of anonymity (even if, technically speaking, it is rather a 'pseudonymity' in the most relevant blockchain systems, → § 1 para. 17; → § 6 para. 25) is highly attractive to criminals. 1

Cryptocurrencies are frequently used for facilitating money laundering, terrorist financing, tax evasion, and they are a widely accepted – if not the main – **payment method** for the purchase of illegal goods **on the dark web** as well as in connection with extortion, blackmail and ransomware attacks.[2] Crypto assets themselves may become the object of crime if they are acquired by illegal mining, fraud, theft or by a hacker attack on crypto exchanges.[3] An attack on high-profile Twitter account holders like Joe Biden, Barack Obama, Bill Gates and Elon Musk in 2020 posted fake texts on their behalf on Twitter, offering to pay back double anyone who transferred Bitcoin to a particular public address.[4] After only a few hours, almost 400 transactions were recorded, amounting to as much as BTC 12.87 (≈ EUR 100,000).[5] 2

---

[1] Brown, 'Cryptocurrency and criminality: The Bitcoin Opportunity' (2016) 89 *The Police Journal: Theory, Practice and Principles*, 327 et seq.

[2] Silfversten, Favaro, Slapakova, Ishikawa, Liu and Salas, 'Exploring the use of Zcash cryptocurrency for illicit or criminal purposes' (RAND Corporation research report, 2020), 5, available at https://beck-link.de/tx8r2 (accessed 14.6.2021).

[3] Brown, 'Cryptocurrency and criminality: The Bitcoin Opportunity' (2016) 89 *The Police Journal: Theory, Practice and Principles*, 327 et seq.; Goger, 'Bitcoins im Strafverfahren: Virtuelle Währung und reale Strafverfolgung' (2016) 19 *Zeitschrift für IT-Recht und Recht der Digitalisierung*, 431 (432); Europol, '6 arrested in the UK and Netherlands in € 24 Million Cryptocurrency Theft' (Press Release, 25.6.2019) available at https://beck-link.de/rtbd7 (accessed 14.6.2021); Edmondson and James, 'Beware of These Top Bitcoin Scams' (The Balance, 30.9.2020), available at https://beck-link.de/4x5zt (accessed 14.6.2021); Silfversten, Favaro, Slapakova, Ishikawa, Liu and Salas, 'Exploring the use of Zcash cryptocurrency for illicit or criminal purposes', (RAND Corporation research report, 2020), 5 et seq., available at https://beck-link.de/tx8r2 (accessed 14.6.2021).

[4] "Public address" and "public key" are used synonymously throughout this book. References regarding the attack: Lerman, Zakrzewski and Marks, 'Biden, billionaires and corporate accounts targeted in Twitter hack' (Washington Post, 16.7.2020), available at https://beck-link.de/6fsac (accessed 14.6.2021); BBC, 'Major US Twitter accounts hacked in Bitcoin scam' (BBC News, 16.7.2020), available at https://www.bbc.com/news/technology-53425822 (accessed 19.4.2021); Carrie Wong and Paul, 'Twitter hack: accounts of prominent figures, including Biden, Musk, Obama, Gates and Kanye compromised' (The Guardian, 16.7.2020), available at https://beck-link.de/7yebe (accessed 14.6.2021); Miranda, 'Avoiding a cryptocurrency scam' (United States Federal Trade Commission, 16.7.2020), available at https://beck-link.de/k6fw2 (accessed 14.6.2021).

[5] See the Blockchain record of the public address "bc1qxy2kgdygjrsqtzq2n0yrf2493p83kkfjhx0wlh" mentioned in the Tweets, available at https://beck-link.de/arwe5 (accessed 14.6.2021).

Part B. EU Regulation

3   A general principle says that **crime should not pay**. This is considered a moral imperative.[6] Therefore, the fight against crime needs to tackle one of the most important motivations of criminals by taking away financial profits obtained by criminal activities. Severe legal consequences for committing crime, including the freezing and confiscation of the instrumentalities and proceeds of crime, are among the most effective **means of combating organised crime**.[7] A popular view even expects confiscation of proceeds of crime to be a stronger deterrent for criminals than long-term imprisonment.[8] Confiscation of proceeds of crime usually serves several purposes. It may be a form of punishment, deter and prevent crime, disrupt criminal organisations, restore the status quo ante and compensate the victims of the crime.[9]

4   Most national criminal procedure law regimes already provide for the confiscation of the proceeds of crimes. However, law enforcement agencies get hold of only a very small amount of criminal assets. According to Europol estimations, between 0.7 and 1.28 % of the annual EU gross domestic product (GDP) is involved in suspicious financial activity.[10] The United Nations Office on Drugs and Crime (UNODC) assumes that criminal proceeds reached up to 3.6 % of the global GDP in 2009.[11] However, only an estimated 1.1 % of criminal profits are being confiscated at EU level.[12] Confiscation of proceeds of crime therefore still remains underdeveloped and underutilised.[13]

5   The financial turnover of **dark web marketplaces** is in the millions if not billions, mainly in cryptocurrencies.[14] Law enforcement agencies have taken down several illegal online marketplaces with enormous turnover. Each time, platform operators and

---

[6] Boucht, *The Limits of Asset Confiscation: On the Legitimacy of Extended Appropriation of Criminal Proceeds* (2017), 7, 13; Boucht, 'Asset confiscation in Europe – past, present, and future challenges' (2019) 26 *Journal of Financial Crime*, 526; Commission, 'Asset Recovery and Confiscation: Ensuring that Crime Does Not Pay', COM (2020) 217 final; Ligeti and Simonato, 'Asset Recovery in the EU: Towards a Comprehensive Enforcement Model beyond Confiscation? An Introduction' in Ligeti and Simonato (eds), *Chasing Criminal Money. Challenges and Perspectives on Asset Recovery in the EU* (2017), 1 et seq.

[7] Directive 2014/42/EU of the European Parliament and of the Council on the freezing and confiscation of instrumentalities and proceeds of crime in the European Union, OJ L 127, 29.4.2014 p. 39–50, recital 3; Regulation (EU) No. 1805/2018 of the European Parliament and of the Council on the mutual recognition of freezing orders and confiscation orders, recital 3.

[8] Cassella, 'Civil Asset Recovery – The American Experience', in Rui and Sieber (eds), *Non-Conviction-Based Confiscation in Europe* (2015), 13 (15); DBB Law 'Comparative Law Study of the Implementation of Mutual Recognition of Orders to Freeze and Confiscate Criminal Assets in the European Union' (Final Findings Report, JUST/2011/JPEN/PR/0153/A4), 442 available at https://beck-link.de/h4k6s (accessed 14.6.2021); Fernandez-Bertier, 'The confiscation and recovery of criminal property: a European Union state of the art' (2016) 17 *ERA Forum*, 323 (325); Ligeti and Simonato, 'Asset Recovery in the EU: Towards a Comprehensive Enforcement Model beyond Confiscation? An Introduction' in Ligeti and Simonato (eds), *Chasing Criminal Money. Challenges and Perspectives on Asset Recovery in the EU* (2017), 1; criticizing this assumption: Nelen, 'Hit them where it hurts most? The proceeds-of-crime approach in the Netherlands' (2004) 41 *Crime, Law & Social Change*, 517 (524 et seq.).

[9] Cassella, 'Civil Asset Recovery – The American Experience' in Rui and Sieber (eds), *Non-Conviction-Based Confiscation in Europe* (2015), 13 (14 et seq.); Boucht, *The Limits of Asset Confiscation: On the Legitimacy of Extended Appropriation of Criminal Proceeds* (2017), 10.

[10] Europol, 'From Suspicion to Action: Converting Financial Intelligence Into Greater Operational Impact' (2017), 26, available at https://beck-link.de/k5x8f (accessed 14.6.2021).

[11] UNODC, 'Estimating illicit financial flows resulting from drug trafficking and other transnational organized crimes' (Research Report, 31.8.2011), 7, available at https://beck-link.de/86vk6 (accessed 14.6.2021).

[12] Europol, 'Does crime still pay? Criminal Asset Recovery in the EU' (2016), 4, 10 et seq., available at https://beck-link.de/rp74y (accessed 19.4.2021).

[13] Commission, 'Proposal for a directive of the European Parliament and of the Council on the freezing and confiscation of proceeds of crime in the European Union', COM (2012) 85 final, 2 et seq.

[14] Crystal, 'Darknet Use and Bitcoin — A Crypto Activity Report by Crystal Blockchain' (Crystal Blockchain analytics, 19.5.2020), available at https://beck-link.de/2m48x (accessed 14.6.2021).

§ 12. Confiscation

vendors have been arrested and huge amounts in profit from illegal sales both in cash and in cryptocurrencies have been confiscated.[15] These facts lead to the assumption that law enforcement agencies currently collect only a small fraction of illegal assets, both in fiat currencies and in cryptocurrencies.

However, there is a huge gap between the issuance of court orders and the execution thereof. With the increased use of crypto assets, the **difficulties associated with confiscation** of proceeds of crime pile up. There are multiple problems related to confiscation of crypto assets. The first is finding the person owning a public address in a blockchain system (→ § 1 para. 102 et seq.). While there is considerable research on tracing transactions and on the deanonymisation of blockchain users,[16] even against shielding and mixing techniques (→ § 1 para. 106 et seq.),[17] the confiscation of crypto assets remains a challenge. In contrast to the confiscation of cash or money in a bank account, the confiscation of crypto assets **requires the cooperation** of the holder of the respective **private key** because no transaction is possible without it (→ § 1 para. 16 et seq.).[18] 6

An additional problem is that it is often not clear which rules apply to the confiscation of crypto assets. First, many jurisdictions do not have any special rules regulating crypto assets. Second, in order to apply existing general rules, the legal nature of crypto assets in some jurisdictions needs to be determined which is not easy and subject to ongoing discussions. Third, in cross-border cases, different sets of general rules may apply and lead to difficulties in finding the right norm. 7

This chapter aims to provide an overview of the legal framework of confiscation in the European Union as well as different issues law enforcement agencies and courts face when confiscating crypto assets. Section B (→ para. 9 et seq.) introduces forensic methods used for freezing and confiscation of crypto assets. Section C (→ para. 11 et seq.) focuses on the object of confiscation, be it the crypto assets themselves by means of *in specie* confiscation or the confiscation of a corresponding amount of money by means of value confiscation instead. Section D (→ para. 22 et seq.) gives an overview of different types of confiscation provided in the European Union legal framework and its transposition into 8

---

[15] Takedown of Silk Road marketplace: USD 48 million worth in bitcoin seized, US Department of Justice, (Press Release, 29.9.2017), available at https://beck-link.de/z6zkk (accessed 14.6.2021); takedown of Wall Street Market and Valhalla Marketplace: 6-digit-amounts in bitcoin and Monero seized, see Europol, 'Double Blow To Dark Web Marketplaces' (Press Release, 3.5.2019), available at https://beck-link.de/xc64d (accessed 14.6.2021); Operation "DisrupTor": USD 6.5 million confiscated in cash and cryptocurrencies, see Europol, 'International Sting Against Dark Web Vendors Leads To 179 Arrests' (Press Release, 22.9.2020), available at https://beck-link.de/7r2ac (accessed 14.6.2021).

[16] Al Jawaheri, Al Sabah, Boshmaf and Erbad, 'Deanonymizing Tor hidden service users through Bitcoin transactions analysis', arXiv:1801.07501v3 [cs.CR], 10.7.2019; Béres, Seres, Benczúr and Quintyne-Collins, 'Blockchain is Watching You: Profiling and Deanonymizing Ethereum Users', arXiv:2005.14051v2 [cs.CR], 13.10.2020; Biryukov, Khovratovich and Pustogarov, 'Deanonymisation of clients in Bitcoin P2P network', arXiv:1405.7418v3 [cs.CR], 5.7.2014; Fröwis, Gottschalk, Haslhofer, Rückert and Pesch, 'Safeguarding the evidential value of forensic cryptocurrency investigations' (2020) 33 *Forensic Science International: Digital Investigation*, 1; Klusman and Dijkhuizen, 'Deanonymisation in Ethereum Using Existing Methods for Bitcoin', (7.2.2018), available at https://beck-link.de/pp24mzim (accessed 14.6.2021); Linoy, Stakhanova and Matyukhina, 'Exploring Ethereum's Blockchain Anonymity Using Smart Contract Code Attribution' (15th International Conference on Network and Service Management, 2019), available at https://beck-link.de/38p43 (accessed 14.6.2021).

[17] Quesnelle, 'On the linkability of Zcash transactions', arXiv: 1712.01210v1 [cs.CR], 4.12.2017; Kappos, Yousaf, Maller and Meiklejohn, 'An Empirical Analysis of Anonymity in Zcash', (27th USENIX Security Symposium, 2018), available at https://beck-link.de/vdvz6 (accessed 14.6.2021).

[18] Antonopoulos, *Mastering Bitcoin: Programming the open blockchain* (2nd edn, 2017), 57 et seq.; Antonopoulos and Wood, *Mastering Ethereum: Building smart contracts and dapps* (2019), 15 et seq., 62 et seq.; SerHack and the Monero Community, *Mastering Monero: The future of private transactions* (2018), 56 et seq.; Matthews, 'Why The FBI Can't Get Its Hands on Silk Road Kingpin's $80 Million Hoard' (TIME Magazine, 11.10.2013), available at https://beck-link.de/t6ct8 (accessed 14.6.2021).

national law in the Member States. Section E (→ para. 37 et seq.) presents peculiarities of freezing orders with respect to crypto assets. Section F (→ para. 42 et seq.) deals with fundamental rights which might be violated in the course of confiscation. Section G (→ para. 55 et seq.) introduces mutual legal assistance instruments in EU law.

B. Forensic Methods

9 Tracking and **tracing crypto assets** is significantly more difficult than searching for stolen paintings. However, law enforcement agencies have developed different strategies to tackle this issue. The easiest case is a cooperating suspect who confesses his crimes and hands over the private key to their tainted crypto wallet. Sometimes, virtual assets are not encrypted, sometimes the private key is stored in a way that law enforcement agencies get hold of it, e.g. by way of searching the suspect's premises. If, on the other hand, the suspect does not cooperate, many jurisdictions have ways to force a convicted person – if need be, by way of coercive penalty payment or even coercive punitive detention[19] – to either transfer the confiscated crypto assets to a public address of the state or disclose the necessary private key.

10 If law enforcement believes that a suspect owns crypto assets which may be subject to confiscation, a first step is to track the payment flows by analysing the publicly available blockchain in order to obtain all the necessary information for the confiscation order. The **blockchain analysis** is supported by different service providers and analysis tools, for example Chainalysis, CipherTrace, Elliptic, BlockSci, GraphSense etc.[20] These and other tools use address **clustering heuristics** and attribution tags in order to follow the monetary flows to an exit point, usually a crypto exchange, at which crypto assets are converted into fiat currency.[21] The monetary transactions to and from a suspect public address may also be followed backwards to a point at which the suspected person opened an account at a crypto exchange, although this is not always the case. Law enforcement agencies can contact crypto exchanges and request the disclosure of relevant account data. If the private key to a suspect public address is stored at a crypto custodian, cooperation requests directed to these can also deliver the required information. This way, pseudonymous users of blockchain-based cryptocurrencies can be deanonymised and suspects may be identified.[22] The use of mixing services (also known as tumblers, → § 1 para. 106 et seq.) can make deanonymisation of suspects more difficult and results less reliable. However, reverse engineering can sometimes help overcome these difficulties.

C. Object of Confiscation

I. Confiscation of Crypto Assets

11 To date, there are **no specific rules** regulating the confiscation of crypto assets which is why the general rules apply. In order to recover proceeds of crime and thus

---

[19] In Germany, for example, pursuant to the Civil Procedure Code, section 888; see Heine, 'Bitcoins und Botnetze – Strafbarkeit und Vermögensabschöpfung bei illegalem Bitcoin-Mining' (2016) 36 *Neue Zeitschrift für Strafrecht*, 441 (445).
[20] For an overview see Fröwis, Gottschalk, Haslhofer, Rückert and Pesch, 'Safeguarding the evidential value of forensic cryptocurrency investigations' (2020) 33 *Forensic Science International: Digital Investigation*, 1.
[21] Address clustering heuristics group addresses found in blockchain transactions that are likely to belong to the same owner. See Fröwis et al, ibid, 2.
[22] For detailed information see Fröwis et al, ibid, 2, 4.

§ 12. Confiscation

make financially motivated crime less attractive, the EU has established minimum rules on the freezing and confiscation of property in criminal matters by means of **Directive 2014/42/EU** which has been adopted by all EU Member States except Denmark.[23] These minimum rules apply at least to the crimes mentioned in Art. 3 Directive 2014/42/EU such as for example corruption, counterfeiting of means of payment, money laundering, terrorism, illicit drug trafficking, organised crime, human trafficking, sexual abuse of children, child pornography and attacks against information systems. The Member States are free to implement the minimum rules without limitation to certain criminal offences. Framework Decisions 2001/500/JHA[24] and 2005/212/JHA,[25] in contrast, are applicable to other offences and require Member States to enable confiscation following a final conviction in a criminal proceeding. Many Member States have transposed these confiscation rules into their national law without restricting them to certain crimes. Therefore, the confiscation of crypto assets usually follows the rules set out in the framework decisions and the directive as transposed into national law. This contribution will focus on the rules in the directive as common ground.

The first problem courts and law enforcement authorities face when confiscating crypto assets is the question if and how crypto assets themselves can be subject to confiscation. Directive 2014/42/EU requires the transposition of certain minimum standards of confiscation into the Member States' national law regimes. The basis is set out in Art. 4(1) which provides for the confiscation of instrumentalities and proceeds of crime or property of a corresponding value. All EU Member States have implemented the confiscation of proceeds of crime subject to a final conviction for a criminal offence.[26] The scope of application of the directive is supposed to cover a very broad range of assets.[27] **'Proceeds'** in the sense of Art. 2(1) includes 'any economic advantage derived directly or indirectly from a criminal offence' and 'may consist of any form of property and includes any subsequent reinvestment or transformation of direct proceeds and any valuable benefits'. 12

In addition to the *in specie* **confiscation** of an identified asset, the law in most EU Member States provides for **value confiscation** based on Art. 4(1) Directive 2014/42/EU, i.e. the confiscation of property of value corresponding to the proceeds of crime, be it the confiscation of different assets[28] or the conviction to pay a corresponding amount of money.[29] 13

As Directive 2014/42/EU suggests, the object of confiscation can be any economic advantage and any form of property, irrespective of its legal nature. However, in some 14

---

[23] Directive 2014/42/EU, recital 44; Ireland opted to take part in the adoption and application of the directive, see recital 42; Commission, 'Asset recovery and confiscation: Ensuring that crime does not pay', COM (2020) 217, 3.
[24] Council Framework Decision 2001/500/JHA on money laundering, the identification, tracing, freezing, seizing and confiscation of instrumentalities and the proceeds of crime, OJ L 182, 5.7.2001 p. 1–2.
[25] Council Framework Decision 2005/212/JHA on confiscation of crime-related proceeds, instrumentalities and property, OJ L 68, 15.3.2005 p. 49–51.
[26] Commission, 'Asset recovery and confiscation: Ensuring that crime does not pay' COM (2020) 217, 7 final.
[27] Directive 2014/42/EU, recital 12.
[28] These Member States are (as of June 2020): Austria, Belgium, Bulgaria, Cyprus, Czech Republic, Finland, France, Greece, Hungary, Italy, Latvia, Luxembourg, Malta, Poland, Portugal, Slovakia, Slovenia, Spain, and Sweden. For reference see Commission, 'Asset recovery and confiscation: Ensuring that crime does not pay' COM (2020) 217, 7 final.
[29] As is the case in Croatia, Estonia, Germany, Ireland, Lithuania and the Netherlands. For reference see Commission, 'Asset recovery and confiscation: Ensuring that crime does not pay' COM (2020) 217, 7 final.

jurisdictions, the legal framework sparks discussions regarding the confiscation of crypto assets themselves compared to the confiscation of a corresponding value.

II. Legal Nature of Crypto Assets

15 The legal nature of crypto assets is unclear and the subject of lively discussions. Crypto assets, be it Bitcoin, Ether, Monero, Litecoin or any other virtual currency, are surely no physical objects. Neither are they a right of an absolute or relative nature.[30] Nevertheless, law enforcement authorities and courts in many jurisdictions claim that **crypto assets themselves may be subject to confiscation** and that recourse to value confiscation is not necessary.[31]

16 In Germany, for example, within the rules on legal consequences of confiscation § 75 of the Strafgesetzbuch (German Criminal Code, 'StGB') mentions that the state obtains the property of confiscated 'things and rights' under certain conditions. This is why the legal nature of crypto assets was deemed relevant for the question if crypto assets could be confiscated as such at all.[32] Some authors argued that the specific wording of said rules also applied to the confiscation order, narrowing the scope of the general rules for confiscation which do not contain any restriction in that regard. The German legal framework did therefore not allow for the confiscation of the crypto assets themselves which left only the property of a corresponding value as object of confiscation.[33] However, the German Federal Court of Justice ruled in the meantime that the wording of the entire legal framework needed to be interpreted in a wider sense, denying any restriction by § 75 StGB and that therefore German confiscation rules did not discriminate with regard to the legal nature of confiscated assets.[34]

17 Crypto assets have a specific **market value** and can be exchanged for fiat currency or other kinds of property at any point in time. The owner of crypto assets has the de facto power of disposal.[35] Blockchain-based crypto assets are sufficiently **delimitable** regarding the storage in the blockchain and the combination of public and private

---

[30] Goger, 'Bitcoins im Strafverfahren: Virtuelle Währung und reale Strafverfolgung' (2016) 19 *Zeitschrift für IT-Recht und Recht der Digitalisierung*, 431 (432); Kütük and Sorge, 'Bitcoin im deutschen Vollstreckungsrecht – Von der "Tulpenmanie" zur "Bitcoinmanie"' (2014) 17 *Zeitschrift für IT-Recht und Recht der Digitalisierung*, 643 (644).

[31] See for example German Federal Court of Justice (Bundesgerichtshof) 27.7.2017 – 1 StR 412/16 – *Neue Zeitschrift für Strafrecht* 2018, 401 (404 et seq.); in this sense also Goger, 'Bitcoins im Strafverfahren: Virtuelle Währung und reale Strafverfolgung' (2016) 19 *Zeitschrift für IT-Recht und Recht der Digitalisierung*, 431 (433).

[32] Grzywotz, *Virtuelle Kryptowährungen und Geldwäsche* (2019), 216; Rückert, 'Vermögensabschöpfung und Sicherstellung bei Bitcoins – Neue juristische Herausforderungen durch die ungeklärte Rechtsnatur von virtuellen Währungseinheiten' (2016) 19 *Zeitschrift für IT-Recht und Recht der Digitalisierung*, 295 (296 et seq.).

[33] Grzywotz, *Virtuelle Kryptowährungen und Geldwäsche* (2019), 216; Rückert, 'Vermögensabschöpfung und Sicherstellung bei Bitcoins – Neue juristische Herausforderungen durch die ungeklärte Rechtsnatur von virtuellen Währungseinheiten' (2016) 19 *Zeitschrift für IT-Recht und Recht der Digitalisierung*, 295 (296 et seq.).

[34] German Federal Court of Justice (Bundesgerichtshof) 27.7.2017 – 1 StR 412/16 – *Neue Zeitschrift für Strafrecht*, 2018, 401 (405); in this sense also Goger, 'Bitcoins im Strafverfahren: Virtuelle Währung und reale Strafverfolgung' (2016) 19 *Zeitschrift für IT-Recht und Recht der Digitalisierung*, 431 (433).

[35] German Federal Court of Justice (Bundesgerichtshof) 27.7.2017 – 1 StR 412/16 – *Neue Zeitschrift für Strafrecht* 2018, 401 (405); If the holder of crypto assets is also a material beneficiary, is subject to ongoing discussions, see for example German Federal Court of Justice (Bundesgerichtshof) 27.7.2017 – 1 StR 412/16 with notes from Safferling, 'Illegales Bitcoinschürfen' (2018) 38 *Neue Zeitschrift für Strafrecht*, 405 (406).

§ 12. Confiscation

keys of the wallet known to the owner.³⁶ Therefore, **crypto assets** fulfil all necessary requirements to be **subject to confiscation**. However, in Member States with provisions for value confiscation, crypto assets might not themselves be subject to confiscation but the affected person may be ordered to pay an amount of money corresponding to the value of the crypto assets or the confiscation of other assets of an equivalent value may be ordered.³⁷ The rules for differentiation between *in specie* confiscation, i.e. the confiscation of the original crypto asset, and value confiscation vary across the Member States and may even vary depending on the kind of crypto asset.

In jurisdictions in which *in specie* confiscation of crypto assets is possible there may even be additional value confiscation in case the crypto assets depreciated in value since the criminal activity.³⁸ **18**

III. Confiscation Order

1. Confiscation of the Crypto Assets themselves

In specie confiscation of crypto assets is only possible if a **sufficient link** of individualised crypto assets to the criminal activity can be established. This may be the case if the entire amount of crypto assets in a determined public address derives from the criminal activity in question or the tainted crypto assets are not intermingled with crypto assets from a legitimate source.³⁹ **19**

It is not sufficient to confiscate only the (hardware) wallet or the relevant private key as the owner might have a copy and could still dispose of the crypto assets assigned to the public address in question.⁴⁰ Law enforcement authorities rather need to **transfer** the confiscated crypto assets to a public address owned by the state in order to obtain full custody of the crypto assets.⁴¹ **20**

2. Value Confiscation

As subsidiary or alternative to the *in specie* confiscation, Directive 2014/42/EU requires the Member States to introduce rules for the confiscation of different property of a value corresponding to the value of the crypto assets. In case of value confiscation, the **point in time for the determination of the value** plays a very important role, as crypto assets are usually highly volatile. Directive 2014/42/EU does not give guidance in this respect. At least in cases in which *in specie* confiscation is impossible from the beginning, the moment of acquisition of the proceeds of crime in the course of the **21**

---

[36] Relating to Bitcoins: German Federal Court of Justice (Bundesgerichtshof) 27.7.2017 – 1 StR 412/16, *Neue Zeitschrift für Strafrecht* 2018, 401 (405).

[37] Austria, Belgium, Bulgaria, Cyprus, Czech Republic, Finland, France, Greece, Hungary, Italy, Latvia, Luxembourg, Malta, Poland, Portugal, Slovakia, Slovenia, Spain and Sweden foresee the confiscation of other assets, whereas the confiscation of a corresponding amount of money is possible in Croatia, Germany, Estonia, Ireland, Lithuania and the Netherlands, see Commission, 'Asset recovery and confiscation: Ensuring that crime does not pay', COM (2020) 217, 7 final.

[38] See for example the German Criminal Code, section 73c, para. 2 and the Spanish Criminal Code, Art. 127, para. 3, subpara. 2.

[39] See for example German Federal Court of Justice (Bundesgerichtshof) 10.4.2018 – 2 StR 24/18.

[40] Goger, 'Bitcoins im Strafverfahren: Virtuelle Währung und reale Strafverfolgung' (2016) 19 *Zeitschrift für IT-Recht und Recht der Digitalisierung*, 431 (433); Rückert, 'Token im Strafverfahren', in Maume, Maute and Fromberger (eds), *Rechtshandbuch Kryptowerte*, § 23, para. 43.

[41] Rückert, 'Vermögensabschöpfung und Sicherstellung bei Bitcoins – Neue juristische Herausforderungen durch die ungeklärte Rechtsnatur von virtuellen Währungseinheiten' (2016) 19 *Zeitschrift für IT-Recht und Recht der Digitalisierung*, 295 (298 et seq.).

criminal activity should be the decisive point in time for the determination of the value if the affected person is to be deprived of any unjustified enrichment deriving from the criminal activity.[42]

3. Confiscation of Contractual Claims against Token Service Providers

22   In certain cases, the object of confiscation may not be crypto assets themselves but a contractual claim instead. This covers situations where the suspect or a third person does not dispose of the private keys but deposits them with token service providers such as crypto exchanges, crypto custodians or wallet service providers. If the affected person does not even dispose of crypto assets but only has a contractual claim for profit participation, the contractual claims against said providers may be the object of confiscation. Contractual claims are economic advantages and may be hence considered as property in the sense of Art. 4(1) Directive 2014/42/EU.

D. Types of Confiscation

I. Criminal Confiscation

23   EU Member States have a great variety of confiscation regimes.[43] The EU is in the process of harmonisation in order to increase efficiency of asset recovery. The standard case of confiscation which is common to all EU jurisdictions is (regular) criminal confiscation. It is the kind of confiscation on which Directive 2014/42/EU is built. Art. 4(1) defines it as confiscation **subject to a final conviction for a criminal offence**. The conviction may also result from proceedings in absentia.

> **Example:**
> Smith is convicted of selling illegal drugs and weapons on the dark web. In the final judgment, the court orders the confiscation of all Zcash Smith received as payment, amounting to EUR 500,000 in total.

24   Directive 2014/42/EU does not limit itself to criminal confiscation after conviction but mentions different other kinds which will be addressed in the following sections.

II. Third Party Confiscation

25   The suspected or accused person may wish to secure the profit obtained in the course of the criminal activity and therefore transfer the proceeds of crime to a third party, be it a spouse, relative or friend. For these cases, Art. 6 Directive 2014/42/EU makes an exception to the rule that, generally, confiscation is only ordered against a person who has committed a crime. Art. 6(1) requires the Member States to provide for *in specie* or value confiscation against a person who is **not responsible for the crime in question**. However, the third party retains their **bona fide rights** pursuant to national law if they

---

[42] Deutscher Bundestag (German Bundestag), 'Entwurf eines Gesetzes zur Reform der strafrechtlichen Vermögensabschöpfung' (September 2016), 67 available at https://beck-link.de/ysb82 (accessed 14.6.2021).

[43] Ligeti and Simonato, 'Asset Recovery in the EU: Towards a Comprehensive Enforcement Model beyond Confiscation? An Introduction' in Ligeti and Simonato (eds), *Chasing Criminal Money. Challenges and Perspectives on Asset Recovery in the EU* (2017), 1 (5); DBB Law 'Comparative Law Study of the Implementation of Mutual Recognition of Orders to Freeze and Confiscate Criminal Assets in the European Union' (Final Findings Report, JUST/2011/JPEN/PR/0153/A4), 442 available at https://beck-link.de/h4k6s (accessed 14.6.2021).

obtained the property without reason to believe that the property was subject to confiscation.[44] The question if the national bona fide rules apply to crypto assets at all, is subject to lively discussions in the Member States.[45]

> Example:
> Smith buys a new house. As payment, he transfers EUR 500,000 in Zcash (see example above) to Miller's public address, which previously did not hold any other Zcash. The court orders the confiscation of the Zcash in Miller's public address by way of third party confiscation. Miller opposes the confiscation stating that he acquired the Zcash in good faith.

III. Extended Confiscation

1. Definition

Sometimes, a convicted person is suspected to be involved in further criminal activities and possesses property to an extent which does not correspond to their lawful income and the value of their assets, their financial situation and lifestyle. These assets cannot be confiscated by way of regular criminal confiscation but require an additional instrument. The so-called extended confiscation is supposed to fill this gap. It **requires a conviction for a criminal offence**, usually but not necessarily an offence that aims at generating economic profit, and addresses situations in which assets cannot clearly and causally be linked to prior offences but the assets nevertheless are assumed to be illicit.[46]

26

> Example:
> During criminal proceedings for illegal mining of Bitcoins amounting to a value of EUR 50,000, the public prosecutor finds out that the accused person, Jones, owns a very expensive new car, and detects additional Bitcoins at Jones' public address, amounting to a value of EUR 100,000. Jones is unemployed and does not have any legitimate source of income beyond social assistance. The car and the additional Bitcoins can be subject to extended confiscation if Jones is finally convicted of a criminal offence for illegal mining even if the conviction only covers the illegal mining of Bitcoins amounting to EUR 50,000.

Following some jurisdictions which have known this instrument for some time, extended confiscation was introduced at EU level by Art. 3 Framework Decision 2005/212/JHA.[47] However, the framework decision was not a big success as the transposition into national law was deficient and authorities were reluctant to execute foreign extended confiscation orders due to the differences in the national regimes.[48] Art. 5

27

---

[44] For more detail regarding the conditions required to admit a confiscation from a third party refer to Blanco Cordero, 'Modern Forms of Confiscation and Protection of Third Parties' in Ligeti and Simonato (eds), *Chasing Criminal Money. Challenges and Perspectives on Asset Recovery in the EU* (2017), 139 (144 et seq.).

[45] See from a German perspective Engelhardt and Klein, 'Bitcoins – Geschäfte mit Geld, das keines ist: Technische Grundlagen und zivilrechtliche Betrachtung' (2014) 17 *Zeitschrift für IT-Recht und Recht der Digitalisierung*, 355 (357); John, 'Zur Sachqualität und Eigentumsfähigkeit von Kryptotoken – eine dogmatische (Neu)Betrachtung' (2020) 20 *Zeitschrift für Bank und Kapitalmarktrecht*, 76; Kaulartz and Matzke, 'Die Tokenisierung des Rechts' (2018) 71 *Neue Juristische Wochenschrift*, 3278 (3283); Walter, 'Bitcoin, Libra und sonstige Kryptowährungen aus zivilrechtlicher Sicht' (2019) 72 *Neue Juristische Wochenschrift*, 3609 (3613 et seq.).

[46] Boucht, 'Extended criminal confiscation: Criminal Assets or Criminal Owners?' in Ligeti and Simonato (eds), *Chasing Criminal Money. Challenges and Perspectives on Asset Recovery in the EU* (2017), 117 (119).

[47] For more detail on the minimum standards set out in the framework decision refer to Boucht, *The Limits of Asset Confiscation: On the Legitimacy of Extended Appropriation of Criminal Proceeds* (2017), 33 et seq.

[48] Directive 2014/42/EU, recitals 8, 19; Commission, 'Proposal for a directive of the European Parliament and of the Council on the freezing and confiscation of proceeds of crime in the European Union', COM (2012) 85, 10 et seq. final; Boucht, *The Limits of Asset Confiscation: On the Legitimacy of Extended Appropriation of Criminal Proceeds* (2017), 36; Simonato, 'Extended confiscation of criminal

Directive 2014/42/EU takes over from there and **aims at harmonising extended confiscation** at least for the offences listed in para. 2. It requires the Member States to enable extended confiscation by implementing one single standard as opposed to different standards in the framework decision.

2. Scope of Application

28 Extended confiscation may be limited to certain criminal offences as mentioned in Art. 3(1) Framework Decision 2005/212/JHA and Art. 5(2) Directive 2014/42/EU. This has been **implemented differently** across the Member States. While some jurisdictions[49] apply extended confiscation to a list of offences, sometimes in addition to other offences punishable by a specified minimum custodial sentence[50] or limited to criminal offences which generate a financial gain,[51] other jurisdictions[52] do not limit the scope of application of extended confiscation, but apply it to all offences regardless of the type or punishment.[53] The very broad scope of application and even a tendency towards application to all kinds of criminal offences has been criticised severely in literature.[54] In Germany, doubts have been expressed that the transposition of Directive 2014/42/EU is in compliance with the constitution.[55]

29 Extended confiscation in the sense of the directive means the confiscation of property belonging to a convicted person when the committed criminal offence is liable to give rise to economic benefit and the court is satisfied, on the basis of the circumstances of the case, that the **property in question is derived from (any prior) criminal conduct**. The determination of the property which is subject to extended confiscation is not easy. The directive offers some guidance by mentioning that the disproportionality of the value of the property in question to the lawful income of the convicted person may be an indication for the criminal origin of the property. Some Member States have added a specific threshold for the value of property subject to extended confiscation or even specific figures for the **minimum disproportion**.[56] Other Member States have set up **time limits** with reference to the commission of the offence; if the acquisition of the property in question was outside the specified time frame, the property may not be considered as originating from criminal conduct.[57]

3. Standard of Proof

30 While Art. 3(2) Framework Decision 2005/212/JHA sets the minimum standard of proof at the court being 'fully convinced based on specific facts', Art. 5(1)

---

assets: limits and pitfalls of minimum harmonisation in the EU' (2016) 41 *European Law Review* 727 (729 et seq.).

[49] These Member States are Austria, Belgium, Bulgaria, Croatia, Czech Republic, Estonia, Greece, Ireland, Spain, Hungary, Portugal, Slovenia, Finland and Sweden.

[50] Austria, Czech Republic, Finland, France, Ireland, Luxembourg, Malta, Romania and Sweden.

[51] Finland, France, Latvia, Luxembourg, Netherlands, Poland and Romania.

[52] Cyprus, Germany, Italy and Lithuania.

[53] Commission, 'Asset recovery and confiscation: Ensuring that crime does not pay' COM (2020) 217, 9 final.

[54] Boucht, *The Limits of Asset Confiscation: On the Legitimacy of Extended Appropriation of Criminal Proceeds* (2017), 29, 39 et seq.; Ochnio, 'The problematic scope of extended confiscation in comparative perspective' (2019) 52 Nowa Kodyfikacja Prawa Karnego, 119 (131).

[55] Bundesrechtsanwaltskammer (German Federal Bar Association), 'Stellungnahme 15/2016 zum Referentenentwurf zur Reform der strafrechtlichen Vermögensabschöpfung' (June 2016), available at https://beck-link.de/x8x77 (accessed 14.6.2021).

[56] Commission, 'Asset recovery and confiscation: Ensuring that crime does not pay' COM (2020) 217, 8 final.

[57] Ibid.

Directive 2014/42/EU only requires the court to be **'satisfied on the basis of the circumstances of the case'** that the property in question is derived from criminal conduct. The standard of proof applicable to extended confiscation varies in the Member States. It ranges from a 'reasonable assumption' (e.g. in Austria) or a 'reasonable belief' that the property is derived from illicit activity (e.g. in Finland) via a qualified balance of probabilities ('clearly more probable than not') that the property in question is the proceeds of criminal activities (e.g. in Sweden) to the requirement of being fully convinced that the property derives from criminal conduct (e.g. in Germany).[58]

A high standard of proof reduces the risk of confiscating legitimate property but also renders extended confiscation less efficient and may even defeat the purpose of extended confiscation.[59] Therefore, in most Member States the otherwise strict standards for the rules of evidence are lowered considerably when it comes to extended confiscation.[60]

IV. Non-Conviction Based Confiscation

Non-conviction based confiscation goes one step further than extended confiscation. It **does not require a criminal conviction** at all nor any causal link of the property subject to confiscation to a specified criminal offence.[61] It is sufficient to establish – to a certain standard of proof – that the **property in question derives from criminal conduct**. In some Member States, non-conviction based confiscation may be ordered in separate civil or administrative proceedings.[62]

Example:
Brown is a member of an organisation which imports illegal drugs into the European Union. On 7 March 2021, German police detect a huge amount of cocaine in the trunk of a car on the way from the Netherlands to Austria. Whereas the driver of the car, who is connected to the criminal organisation, faces criminal charges some time later, the identities of the buyer and seller of the drugs remain unknown. There is no evidence for Brown's personal participation in the business. However, on 7 March 2021, Brown receives a transaction of 4.85 Bitcoins which equals the exact price for the cocaine sold on the same day. Brown previously held only 0.2 Bitcoins at a different public address. Because of the temporal link between the drug sale and the Bitcoin transaction, and in absence of any legitimate source for these funds, the court is convinced that the 4.85 Bitcoins received by Brown on 7 March 2021 constitute payment for the drug sale. The court orders the confiscation of these Bitcoins from Brown's public address.

---

[58] For an overview and further jurisdictions see ibid; legislation: Austrian Criminal Code, Section 20b, para. 2; Finnish Criminal Code, Chapter 10, Section 3, para. 1; German Criminal Code, Section 73a, para. 1, in the interpretation of the German Federal Court of Justice (Bundesgerichtshof) 16.7.2020 – 4 StR 91/20, para. 7; Swedish Criminal Code, Chapter 36, Section 1 b.

[59] Boucht, 'Extended Confiscation: Criminal Assets or Criminal Owners?', in Ligeti and Simonato (eds), *Chasing Criminal Money. Challenges and Perspectives on Asset Recovery in the EU* (2017), 117 (132).

[60] Boucht, *The Limits of Asset Confiscation: On the Legitimacy of Extended Appropriation of Criminal Proceeds* (2017), 28.

[61] Boucht, *The Limits of Asset Confiscation: On the Legitimacy of Extended Appropriation of Criminal Proceeds* (2017), 67 et seq.; see also Cassella, 'Civil Asset Recovery – The American Experience' in Rui and Sieber (eds), *Non-Conviction-Based Confiscation in Europe* (2015), 13 (17); Rui, 'Introduction' in Rui and Sieber (eds), *Non-Conviction-Based Confiscation in Europe* (2015), 1 et seq.; Milone, 'On the borders of criminal law. A tentative assessment of italian "non-conviction based extended confiscation"' (2017) 8 *New Journal of European Criminal Law*, 150 et seq.

[62] Commission, 'Analysis of non-conviction based confiscation measures in the European Union', SWD (2019) 1050, 2 final.

33   The instrument of non-conviction based confiscation has a long tradition in the **United States** which dates back to the confiscation of pirate ships in the 18th century.[63] As the owners of pirate ships were hard to find, the United States introduced so-called proceedings *in rem*. In such proceedings, the object of confiscation is the defendant of a case, leading to unusual case names such as *United States v. The Brig Ann, United States v. $ 65,000 in U.S. Currency* or *United States v. 2005 Mercedes Benz E500*, whereas any person seeking to claim a right in the object of confiscation needs to intervene in order to prevent the confiscation.[64] In modern times, non-conviction based confiscation is a big success in the United States. It accounts for 83 % of confiscated assets across the US, with drug trafficking cases playing an important role since the 1980s.[65]

34   In the **European Union**, however, this action against the property without prosecution of the perpetrator is **fairly new**. The first EU Member States to introduce non-conviction based confiscation in their national confiscation regime were Italy, and much later Ireland, the United Kingdom, Bulgaria and Slovenia.[66] The proposal for a directive on the freezing and confiscation of proceeds of crime in the European Union contained a set of rules for what was considered similar to non-conviction based confiscation in Art. 5. However, the rules faced severe criticism and did not make it into the final version of Directive 2014/42/EU.[67] What was finally enacted in Art. 4(2) is a substitute for criminal confiscation in cases in which criminal proceedings are initiated but criminal confiscation is not possible due to illness or absconding of the suspected person. Due to its **close link to criminal proceedings**, it is not considered a classic non-conviction based confiscation.[68]

35   Most Member States have gone beyond these minimum requirements and have introduced a more far-reaching version of non-conviction based confiscation.[69] These legislative changes have been harshly criticised[70] but are nevertheless deemed very

---

[63] Cassella, 'Civil Asset Recovery – The American Experience' in Rui and Sieber (eds), *Non-Conviction-Based Confiscation in Europe* (2015), 13 (19); Rui, 'Non-conviction based confiscation in the European Union — an assessment of Art. 5 of the proposal for a directive of the European Parliament and of the Council on the freezing and confiscation of proceeds of crime in the European Union' [2012] *ERA Forum* 349 (350 with further reference).

[64] Cassella, 'Civil Asset Recovery – The American Experience' in Rui and Sieber (eds), *Non-Conviction-Based Confiscation in Europe* (2015), 13 (17, 20).

[65] Ibid, 20 et seq. (figures from 2011).

[66] Rui, 'Non-conviction based confiscation in the European Union — an assessment of Art. 5 of the proposal for a directive of the European Parliament and of the Council on the freezing and confiscation of proceeds of crime in the European Union' [2012] 13 *ERA Forum*, 349 (350); Rui, 'Introduction' in Rui and Sieber (eds), *Non-Conviction-Based Confiscation in Europe* (2015), 1 (3); Nikolov, 'General characteristics of civil forfeiture' (2011) 14 *Journal of Money Laundering Control*, 16 (23).

[67] Commission, 'Proposal for a directive of the European Parliament and of the Council on the freezing and confiscation of proceeds of crime in the European Union', COM (2012) 85 final, Art. 5; Commission, 'Analysis of non-conviction based confiscation measures in the European Union', SWD (2019) 1050, 4; Rui and Sieber, 'Non-Conviction-Based Confiscation in Europe – Bringing the Picture Together' in Rui and Sieber (eds), *Non-Conviction-Based Confiscation in Europe* (2015), 245 (276 et seq.); Rui, 'Non-conviction based confiscation in the European Union — an assessment of Art. 5 of the proposal for a directive of the European Parliament and of the Council on the freezing and confiscation of proceeds of crime in the European Union' [2012] *ERA Forum*, 349 (353 et seq.).

[68] Rui, 'Non-conviction based confiscation in the European Union — an assessment of Art. 5 of the proposal for a directive of the European Parliament and of the Council on the freezing and confiscation of proceeds of crime in the European Union' [2012] *ERA Forum*, 349 (355 et seq.).

[69] Commission, 'Asset recovery and confiscation: Ensuring that crime does not pay' COM (2020) 217, 7, 14 final; Commission, 'Analysis of non-conviction based confiscation measures in the European Union', SWD (2019) 1050, 2 et seq. final.

[70] Boucht, *The Limits of Asset Confiscation: On the Legitimacy of Extended Appropriation of Criminal Proceeds* (2017), 69 et seq.; especially with regard to the standard of proof: Marstaller and Zimmermann, *Non-conviction-based confiscation in Deutschland?* (2018), 53 et seq.

§ 12. Confiscation

effective and useful in situations in which criminal confiscation is not possible, be it an acquittal due to statute of limitations or that the suspect is a fugitive or has died.[71]

In the EU, **four different models of non-conviction based confiscation** can be distinguished.[72] Some Member States use a hybrid system of more than one of the following models or a cross between several models.[73] The **first model** is a very basic form of non-conviction based confiscation. It is a proceeding against a person who cannot be convicted in an already initiated criminal proceeding for technical reasons. These reasons include death, illness, absconding, immunity or young age of the suspected or accused person.[74] 25 EU Member States (all except Bulgaria and Ireland) primarily use classic non-conviction based confiscation.[75] The **second model** is based on extended confiscation as explained above (→ para. 26 et seq.). Pursuant to this model, the court may extend the criminal confiscation of certain assets following a conviction in a criminal proceeding to further assets belonging to the convicted person which derive from (similar) criminal conduct. While the first two models require a specific criminal proceeding against a person, this restriction does not hold for the following two models. The **third model** comprises different kinds of *in rem* proceedings. These procedures can be conducted against the assets themselves instead of the persons. The assets need to be identified as proceeds of crime.[76] In the **fourth model**, the 'unexplained wealth model', the assets do not even need to be identified as deriving from criminal conduct. The proceedings in this model can simply be based on the disproportion between the assets acquired by a person and their declared lawful income.[77]

36

E. Freezing Orders

As crypto assets can be transferred from one public address to another within minutes and thus escape the law enforcement authorities' grip, it is very important to have an **efficient mechanism for freezing** assets in order to preserve the assets for possible subsequent confiscation. Freezing and confiscating assets largely depends on the authorities' capacity to trace and identify them.[78] In order to ensure fast EU-wide tracing of illicit assets, Art. 1(1) Council Decision 2007/845/JHA[79] obliges Member States to set up national asset recovery offices.

37

---

[71] Simser, 'Perspectives on Civil Forfeiture' in Young (ed), *Civil Forfeiture of Criminal Property: Legal Measures for Targeting the Proceeds of Crime* (2009), 13 (19 et seq.); Boucht, *The Limits of Asset Confiscation: On the Legitimacy of Extended Appropriation of Criminal Proceeds* (2017), 70 et seq.; Cassella, 'Civil Asset Recovery – The American Experience' in Rui and Sieber (eds), *Non-Conviction-Based Confiscation in Europe* (2015), 13 (14 et seq.).

[72] Commission, 'Analysis of non-conviction based confiscation measures in the European Union', SWD (2019) 1050, 2 et seq.; Eurojust, 'Report on non-conviction-based confiscation' (General Case 751/NMSK – 2012, 2.4.2013), 9 et seq. available https://beck-link.de/s5bap (accessed 1.6.2021).

[73] Camden Asset Recovery Inter-Agency Network (CARIN), Manual (5th Edition, 2015), 22 et seq., available at https://www.carin.network/documents (19.4.2021).

[74] Commission, 'Analysis of non-conviction based confiscation measures in the European Union', SWD (2019) 1050, 3.

[75] Ibid, 6.

[76] Ibid, 2.

[77] Ibid, 2.

[78] Commission, 'Proceeds of Organised Crime: Ensuring that Crime Does Not Pay', COM (2020) 217, 15 final.

[79] Council Decision 2007/845/JHA concerning cooperation between Asset Recovery Offices of the Member States in the field of tracing and identification of proceeds from, or other property related to, crime, OJ L 332, 18.12.2007 p. 103–105.

38 Due to the unclear legal nature of crypto assets and the lack of special rules for freezing crypto assets, there is no consensus on how to freeze crypto assets.[80] Art. 7 Directive 2014/42/EU provides for the freezing of property as the temporary prohibition of transfer, destruction, conversion, disposal or movement of property or temporarily assuming custody or control of property, Art. 2(5).

39 If the **private key** is not stored in the suspected person's wallet but is **deposited at a service provider** such as a crypto exchange or crypto custodian, the subject of confiscation is the suspected person's contractual claim against the service provider. This claim may be frozen according to the respective national rules of freezing and confiscating contractual claims. No special rules are required for the freezing of an amount of fiat money in case national law only provides for value confiscation with regard to cryptocurrencies.

40 The situation is different, however, if the **crypto assets as such** are the object of the freezing order and the suspected person retains the private key. In order to preserve the crypto assets for future confiscation, law enforcement authorities must obtain the private key, e.g. by seizing a hardware wallet, and transfer the relevant crypto assets to a public address held by the state. Law enforcement authorities need to be very careful to transfer the assets to the correct address because the crypto assets are irreversibly lost otherwise. The authorities also need to wait for the transaction to be validated and monitor the risk of complications such as hard forks or other protocol changes which could render the transaction invalid (→ § 1 para. 30).

41 Art. 10(2) Directive 2014/42/EU provides for the sale of frozen or confiscated property. As the value of crypto assets tends to be very volatile, it is usually advisable to **sell the crypto assets** immediately in order to prevent any loss of value.[81]

F. Fundamental Rights and Procedural Safeguards

42 Confiscation is possible in a wide range of cases, even if the property subject to confiscation belongs to a third party or does not derive from criminal conduct which has been proven at trial. Therefore, a number of fundamental rights issues arise.

I. Criminal Sanction

43 One of the most vividly discussed questions in this context and the basis for any further discussion of the applicability of certain fundamental and procedural rights is whether confiscation can be characterised as a criminal sanction or not. The answer depends on the national confiscation regime, and needs to be determined by the **classification of the measure in national law** and the nature of the offence or the severity of the sanction, pursuant to the European Court of Human Rights.[82] Most jurisdictions agree that the confiscation of proceeds of crime is not

---

[80] Rückert, 'Token im Strafverfahren' in Maume, Maute and Fromberger (eds), *Rechtshandbuch Kryptowerte*, § 23, para. 41 et seq.

[81] Goger, 'Bitcoins im Strafverfahren: Virtuelle Währung und reale Strafverfolgung' (2016) 19 *Zeitschrift für IT-Recht und Recht der Digitalisierung*, 431 (434); Rückert, 'Vermögensabschöpfung und Sicherstellung bei Bitcoins – Neue juristische Herausforderungen durch die ungeklärte Rechtsnatur von virtuellen Währungseinheiten', (2016) 19 *Zeitschrift für IT-Recht und Recht der Digitalisierung*, 295 (299); Strauch and Handke, 'Kryptotoken in Zwangsvollstreckung und Insolvenz' in Maume, Maute and Fromberger (eds), *Rechtshandbuch Kryptowerte*, § 10, para. 31, with further reference.

[82] The European Court of Human Rights has established the so-called 'Engel criteria' for the determination of the character as criminal sanction. For further information see Boucht, 'Civil Asset

§ 12. Confiscation

regarded as a criminal sanction because it does not establish the criminal liability of a person but the criminal nature of property.[83] It is rather a measure *sui generis*[84] and non-conviction based confiscation is sometimes even considered more preventive than punitive in nature.[85] Some authors argue that confiscation of proceeds of crime does not fall within the scope of the principle of culpability, which has been approved by the European Court of Human Rights with regard to non-conviction based confiscation as long as the confiscation measure is predominantly preventive.[86] This view grants only a minimum level of fundamental rights protection and may well be disputed. The non-conviction based confiscation regime as formulated in Art. 4(2) Directive 2014/42/EU is connected to criminal proceedings which do not lead to a conviction for mere factual reasons of the absence of the accused person. It can therefore pose a threat to the **presumption of innocence**.[87]

Forfeiture and the presumption of innocence under article 6 (2) ECHR' (2014) 5 *New Journal of European Criminal Law*, 221 (237); Meyer, 'Recognizing the Unknown – the New Confiscation Regulation' (2020) 10 *European Criminal Law Review*, 140; Rui and Sieber, 'Non-Conviction-Based Confiscation in Europe – Bringing the Picture Together' in Rui and Sieber (eds), *Non-Conviction-Based Confiscation in Europe* (2015), 245 (247); Simonato, 'Directive 2014/42/EU and Non-Conviction Based Confiscation: A Step Forward on Asset Recovery?' (2015) 6 *New Journal of European Criminal Law*, 213 (218).

[83] Bacarese and Sellar, 'Civil Asset Forfeiture in Practice' in Rui and Sieber (eds), *Non-Conviction-Based Confiscation in Europe* (2015), 211 (213 et seq., 216); Esser, 'A Civil Asset Recovery Model – The German Perspective and European Human Rights' in Rui and Sieber (eds), *Non-Conviction-Based Confiscation in Europe* (2015), 69 (73, 78 et seq.); Rui and Sieber, 'Non-Conviction-Based Confiscation in Europe – Bringing the Picture Together' in Rui and Sieber (eds), *Non-Conviction-Based Confiscation in Europe* (2015), 245 (247); Simonato, 'Directive 2014/42/EU and Non-Conviction Based Confiscation: A Step Forward on Asset Recovery?' (2015) 6 *New Journal of European Criminal Law*, 213 (218); with respect to the United Kingdom: Smith, 'Civil Asset Recovery: The English Experience' in Rui and Sieber (eds), *Non-Conviction-Based Confiscation in Europe* (2015), 31 (33 et seq.); see also Marstaller and Zimmermann, *Non-conviction-based confiscation in Deutschland?* (2018), 61 et seq., 79; Panzavolta, 'Confiscation and the Concept of Punishment: Can There be a Confiscation Without a Conviction' in Ligeti and Simonato (eds), *Chasing Criminal Money. Challenges and Perspectives on Asset Recovery in the EU* (2017), 25 (33 et seq.).

[84] Kert, 'Verfall und Abschöpfung in Österreich' (2016) 5 *Neue Zeitschrift für Wirtschafts-, Steuer- und Unternehmensstrafrecht*, 203 (206); Esser, 'A Civil Asset Recovery Model – The German Perspective and European Human Rights' in Rui and Sieber (eds), *Non-Conviction-Based Confiscation in Europe* (2015), 69 (73, 78 et seq.).

[85] Boucht, 'Civil Asset Forfeiture and the presumption of innocence under article 6 (2) ECHR' (2014) 5 *New Journal of European Criminal Law*, 221 (223); Rui and Sieber, 'Non-Conviction-Based Confiscation in Europe – Bringing the Picture Together' in Rui and Sieber (eds), *Non-Conviction-Based Confiscation in Europe* (2015), 245 (246); for further information on the Italian concept of preventive confiscation see Mazzacuva, 'The Problematic Nature of Asset Recovery Measures: Recent Developments of the Italian Preventive Confiscation' in Ligeti and Simonato (eds), *Chasing Criminal Money. Challenges and Perspectives on Asset Recovery in the EU* (2017), 101; Milone, 'On the borders of criminal law. A tentative assessment of italian "non-conviction based extended confiscation"' (2017) 8 *New Journal of European Criminal Law*, 150; Panzavolta and Flor, 'A Necessary Evil? The Italian "Non-Criminal System" of Asset Forfeiture' in Rui and Sieber (eds), *Non-Conviction-Based Confiscation in Europe* (2015), 111 (118 et seq.).

[86] Esser, 'A Civil Asset Recovery Model – The German Perspective and European Human Rights' in Rui and Sieber (eds), *Non-Conviction-Based Confiscation in Europe* (2015), 69 (74); Boucht, 'Civil Asset Forfeiture and the presumption of innocence under article 6 (2) ECHR' (2014) 5 *New Journal of European Criminal Law*, 221 (239 with further reference).

[87] Simonato, 'Directive 2014/42/EU and Non-Conviction Based Confiscation: A Step Forward on Asset Recovery?' (2015) 6 *New Journal of European Criminal Law*, 213 (228); in the context of extended confiscation see Boucht, *The Limits of Asset Confiscation: On the Legitimacy of Extended Appropriation of Criminal Proceeds* (2017), 28 et seq.; see also Weigend, 'Assuming that the Defendant Is Not Guilty: The Presumption of Innocence in the German System of Criminal Justice' (2014) 8 *Criminal Law and Philosophy*, 285 (298).

44 The **stigmatising effect** of confiscation measures – especially with regard to third party, extended and non-conviction based confiscation – which assume that the affected person's property derives from criminal conduct, therefore cannot be overrated.[88]

II. Fundamental Rights

45 Several fundamental rights and procedural guarantees may be affected in the course of investigating, freezing and confiscating crypto assets.

1. Inevitably Affected Rights

46 It goes without saying that the right to private property is affected most by confiscation measures. The **right to private property** is laid down in Art. 17 of the Charter of Fundamental Rights (CFR), in Art. 1 of the European Convention on Human Rights (ECHR) and in the Member States' constitutions. It is far from clear if crypto assets are protected by this right but there are good reasons to argue in favour of protection as they are delimitable, convey de facto exclusive power of disposal and have a market value.[89]

47 When tracing illicit crypto assets successfully, law enforcement authorities most likely obtain personal data of the affected person among others. By searching the blockchain and combining the information with data sets from other sources such as investigation records, the affected person may become identifiable.[90] Hence, investigation measures in the course of freezing and confiscating crypto assets fall under the scope of the right to data protection as set out in Art. 8 CFR and Art. 8 ECHR.[91]

2. Right against Self-Incrimination

48 Especially in the context of crypto assets, the right against self-incrimination (*nemo tenetur se ipsum accusare*) plays an important role. For the freezing and confiscation of crypto assets, law enforcement authorities heavily rely on the affected person. If the authorities do not find a hardware wallet or a paper wallet which enables them to seize the relevant private key(s) and transfer the crypto assets to a state-held public address, there is no way to freeze or confiscate the crypto assets without the help of the affected person. Whereas the right to silence may cease to apply in criminal confiscation proceedings after a final conviction, it needs to be respected in the time before final conviction. Freezing of crypto assets as well as extended, non-conviction based and third-party confiscation orders may hence be extremely difficult, if not impossible, to execute if the affected person does not cooperate.

49 Even if national law provides for coercive measures in a non-conviction based confiscation scheme, obtained information may not be used in subsequent criminal proceedings.[92]

---

[88] Campbell, 'Criminal Labels, the European Convention on Human Rights and the Presumption of Innocence' (2013) 76 *Modern Law Review*, 681 (705); Campbell, *Organised Crime and the Law: A Comparative Analysis* (2013), 219 et seq.

[89] For more details see Rückert, 'Cryptocurrencies and fundamental rights' [2019] *Journal of Cybersecurity*, 1 (7).

[90] Ibid.

[91] Ibid.

[92] See for example the defendant's duty to file an affidavit listing their entire property or income following an order of discovery during civil forfeiture in the Irish Proceeds of Crime Act 1996, section 9, para. 1. The courts prohibit the use of the information in any criminal proceedings against the affected person or their family members, see High Court of Ireland 26.6.1997 – 3 IR 185, Gilligan v. Criminal Assets Bureau [1998], paras. 115 et seq.

3. Ne Bis In Idem

The principle of *ne bis in idem* may be affected – depending on the character of confiscation measures as a **criminal sanction** in national law – if for example crypto assets are confiscated by means of extended or non-conviction based confiscation and the assumption is that they derive from criminal conduct for which the affected person has previously been acquitted.[93]

4. Proportionality

Extended and non-conviction based confiscation could deprive a person of their entire possessions. The European framework does not prevent the Member States from taking away a **person's livelihood** as it does not set any limits. Recital 18 of Directive 2014/42/EU only mentions that the Member States are allowed to restrict confiscation if it would otherwise be difficult for the affected person to survive. Hence, national law can set limits according to national and EU constitutional standards. And it should do so, as resocialisation is difficult without sufficient means.[94]

Even if not all of the affected person's possessions are subject to confiscation, the measure needs to be proportionate, especially when taking into account the ubiquitous risk of judicial error.[95] The national confiscation regimes of several EU Member States provide for **additional safeguards**. An important safeguard is the limitation of confiscation to cases in which the value of the property subject to confiscation exceeds a certain minimum threshold[96] or in which the disproportion between the lawful income of the accused person and their property is bigger than a determined minimum amount.[97] Time limits within which the acquired assets may be considered as originating from criminal conduct can exclude previous acquisitions and thus set further limits to confiscation of assets, especially with regard to extended and non-conviction based confiscation.[98]

III. Procedural Safeguards

Effective judicial remedies need to be in place in order to challenge confiscation of legitimate property or double confiscation, for example in cases of judicial cooperation if several Member States confiscate both the assets themselves by *in specie* confiscation and the assets' value by value confiscation.

---

[93] Simonato, 'Directive 2014/42/EU and Non-Conviction Based Confiscation: A Step Forward on Asset Recovery?' (2015) 6 *New Journal of European Criminal Law*, 213 (224); Panzavolta, 'Confiscation and the Concept of Punishment: Can There be a Confiscation Without a Conviction' Ligeti and Simonato (eds), *Chasing Criminal Money. Challenges and Perspectives on Asset Recovery in the EU* (2017), 25 (31).

[94] Boucht, *The Limits of Asset Confiscation: On the Legitimacy of Extended Appropriation of Criminal Proceeds* (2017), 9.

[95] Ochnio, 'The problematic scope of extended confiscation in comparative perspective' (2019) 52 Nowa Kodyfikacja Prawa Karnego, 119 (122).

[96] The threshold in Lithuania, for example, is EUR 12,5000, and in Poland PLN 200,000; see Commission, 'Proceeds of Organised Crime: Ensuring that Crime Does Not Pay', COM (2020) 217, 8 final.

[97] Examples can be found in Bulgaria (minimum amount BGN 150,000) and Slovenia (EUR 50,000); see Commission, 'Proceeds of Organised Crime: Ensuring that Crime Does Not Pay', COM (2020) 217, 8 final.

[98] Some Member States exclude acquisitions which date back more than 5 (Belgium, Hungary, Poland and Romania), 6 (Cyprus and Ireland) or 10 years (Bulgaria) before indictment; others set the time limit at 5 (Czech Republic, Lithuania and Poland) or 6 years (Netherlands) before committing the offence; see Commission, 'Proceeds of Organised Crime: Ensuring that Crime Does Not Pay', COM (2020) 217, 8 final.

54   All persons affected by measures according to Directive 2014/42/EU, including third parties who are not being prosecuted but who claim to be the owner of the confiscated property or to have other property rights such as the right of usufruct, have the **right to an effective remedy** and to a **fair trial** to uphold their rights, pursuant to Art. 8. Hence, any freezing or confiscation order and its reasoning should be communicated to the affected person as soon as possible after the order's execution. The affected person may then challenge the order before a court, Art. 8(6).

G. Cross-Border Confiscation of Crypto Assets

55   In a globalised world, criminal offences often cross borders and so do instrumentalities and proceeds of crime. With cybercrimes and the use of crypto assets as currency tokens, it is even easier to act in the territory of different states without physically crossing a border. The competence of national prosecution, however, ends at national borders. Due to the **principle of territoriality**, the prosecuting state is not competent to confiscate assets located in another state. It therefore needs legal assistance from another state in whose territory the assets in question are located.

56   Decentralised crypto assets do not have a fixed location. They are stored in the blockchain which runs on the computers of several full node participants in the respective blockchain system (→ § 1 para. 8) around the world. In order to freeze and/or confiscate crypto assets, it is necessary to both seize the private key and transfer the crypto assets to a public address held by the state. The storage place of the private key, for example a paper or hardware wallet, is relevant for determining the competent state. In case the contractual claims of the suspected, accused or convicted person against a crypto exchange, wallet service provider or crypto custodian are subject to confiscation instead of the crypto assets themselves, the statutory seat of the respective crypto exchange, wallet service provider or crypto custodian may be the decisive factor.

57   In order to increase effectivity and efficiency of confiscation measures, **effective cross-border cooperation** of law enforcement authorities is essential. There are several judicial cooperation tools in force but so far, the EU Member States have only rarely used them to freeze and confiscate assets located outside their own territory.[99] The EU has therefore passed a regulation in order to facilitate mutual legal assistance in the field of freezing and confiscation of assets.[100]

I. Mutual Legal Assistance

58   The legal basis for mutual legal assistance is usually found in **bilateral** or **multilateral agreements** on mutual legal assistance. General rules on mutual legal assistance in criminal matters exist on European level in the European Convention on Mutual Assistance in Criminal Matters of 1959 and in the Convention on Mutual Assistance in Criminal Matters between the Member States of the European Union of 2000.

59   Several UN Conventions contain rules for mutual legal assistance in confiscation: the UN Convention against Illicit Traffic in Narcotic and Psychotropic Substances of 1988 (the Vienna Convention), for the Suppression of the Financing of Terrorism 1999,

---

[99] Commission, 'Proposal for a Regulation of the European Parliament and of the Council on the mutual recognition of freezing and confiscation orders' COM (2016) 819 final.
[100] Regulation (EU) 2018/1805 of the European Parliament and of the Council of 14 November 2018 on the mutual recognition of freezing orders and confiscation orders, OJ L303, 28.11.2018, 1.

against Transnational Organized Crime 2000 (Palermo Convention) and the UN Convention against Corruption 2003. The Council of Europe Conventions on Laundering, Search, Seizure and Confiscation of the Proceeds of Crime (and on the financing of terrorism) of 1990 and 2005 are an additional instrument for mutual legal assistance between the Member States of the Council of Europe.

II. Principle of Mutual Recognition

The European Council of Tampere in 1999 introduced the principle of **mutual recognition** of judicial decisions as a cornerstone of judicial cooperation in the European Union.[101] Framework Decisions 2003/577/JHA[102] and 2006/783/JHA[103] are already based on this principle. However, both framework decisions were considered to hinder judicial cooperation rather than facilitate it, as their transposition was far from conductive for harmonisation.[104] This is why the European Parliament and the Council chose a different approach by adopting **Regulation (EU) No. 1805/2018** on 14 November 2018,[105] the first regulation in the field of mutual recognition.

Regulation (EU) No. 1805/2018 applies to all freezing and confiscation orders issued within the framework of proceedings in criminal matters, and does therefore not cover any such orders issued in administrative or civil matters.[106] It replaces the Framework Decisions 2003/577/JHA and 2006/783/JHA, see Art. 39 Regulation (EU) No. 1805/2018 for all EU Member States except Ireland and Denmark.[107] The scope of Regulation (EU) No. 1805/2018 is broader than the scope of Directive 2014/42/EU as its application is not limited to specific criminal offences. It also covers other types of freezing and confiscation orders outside the scope of Directive 2014/42/EU. So, if the issuing Member State has a very far-reaching concept of non-conviction based confiscation (e.g. unexplained wealth proceedings), the executing Member State has to execute the confiscation order even if its national law does not provide for this kind of confiscation.[108]

For proceedings in relation to an extensive list of criminal offences punishable by a custodial sentence of a maximum of at least three years in the issuing state, the executing state is supposed to execute any freezing or confiscation order without verification of the double criminality of the offences giving rise to the freezing or confiscation order. In relation to all other offences, the executing state may make the execution of the freezing or confiscation order subject to the condition of double criminality, Art. 3(2) Regulation (EU) No. 1805/2018.

---

[101] European Parliament, 'Tampere European Council 15 and 16.10.1999 – Presidency Conclusions' para. 33, available at https://www.europarl.europa.eu/summits/tam_en.htm (accessed 19.4.2021).
[102] Council Framework Decision 2003/577/JHA on the execution in the European Union of orders freezing property or evidence, OJ L 196, 2.8.2003 p. 45–55.
[103] Council Framework Decision 2006/783/JHA on the application of the principle of mutual recognition to confiscation orders, OJ L 328, 24.11.2006, 59–78.
[104] Ligeti and Simonato, 'Asset Recovery in the EU: Towards a Comprehensive Enforcement Model beyond Confiscation? An Introduction' in Ligeti and Simonato (eds), *Chasing Criminal Money. Challenges and Perspectives on Asset Recovery in the EU* (2017), 1 (6).
[105] Regulation (EU) 1805/2018 on the mutual recognition of freezing orders and confiscation orders, OJ L303, 28.11.2018 p. 1–38. Ireland and Denmark do not take part in the adoption of the regulation and are not bound by it, see recitals 56 et seq. of the regulation. For criticism of the regulation, especially with regard to human rights, see Meyer, 'Recognizing the Unknown – the New Confiscation Regulation' (2020) 10 *European Criminal Law Review*, 140.
[106] Art. 1(1) and (4) Regulation (EU) No. 1805/2018.
[107] The framework decisions continue to apply for mutual legal assistance between any Member State and Ireland or Denmark as well as between Ireland and Denmark.
[108] Regulation (EU) No. 1805/2018, recital 13.

Part B. EU Regulation

63   Freezing orders and confiscation orders are transmitted directly from the competent authority in the issuing state – if need be, after validation by a judge, court or public prosecutor[109] – to the competent authority or a central authority in the executing state. The executing authority has to recognise and carry out the orders **without delay** and with the same speed and priority as for similar domestic cases, Art. 7(1), Art. 9(1), Art. 18(1), Art. 20(3) Regulation (EU) No. 1805/2018. In cases in which immediate freezing is necessary to prevent the removal or destruction of the instrumentalities and proceeds of crime, the regulation provides for an **urgent execution** of a freezing order within maximum 96 hours, Art. 9(3) Regulation (EU) No. 1805/2018. This may still be too long, as one can argue that assets which are detected and not frozen within 24 hours might as well be gone.[110]

64   There is no general consensus among the Member States whether crypto assets should be confiscated *in specie* or whether a value-based approach is preferred, i.e. confiscating a determined amount of money instead of the crypto assets. Regulation (EU) No. 1805/2018 does not give any guidance on this issue, but rules that the execution of a freezing or confiscation order is governed by the law of the executing state.[111] If the execution is legally impossible pursuant to the law of the executing state, the executing state is supposed to consult with the issuing state on how to proceed.[112] It can be concluded that the executing state is not forced to confiscate crypto assets as such if its national law only provides for value confiscation of crypto assets.

65   Only if one of the **grounds for non-recognition** and non-execution in Art. 8 or Art. 19 Regulation (EU) No. 1805/2018 applies, the executing authority may deny recognition and execution of a freezing or confiscation order.[113] Among these grounds are the principle of *ne bis in idem*, privileges or immunities, the freedom of the press, the freedom of expression in other media, double criminality requirements and – in extreme cases – fundamental rights as set out in the Charter, in particular the right to an effective remedy, the right to a fair trial and the right of defence.

---

[109] Regulation (EU) No. 1805/2018, recital 22.
[110] Pieth, 'Recovering stolen assets – a new issue', in Pieth (ed), Recovering stolen assets (2008), 3 (11).
[111] Regulation (EU) No. 1805/2018, recital 43.
[112] Regulation (EU) No. 1805/2018, recital 41.
[113] For detailed information and criticism of the grounds for non-recognition see Hüttemann, 'Grundlagen und Bedeutung der grenzüberschreitenden Vermögensabschöpfung unter besonderer Berücksichtigung der Verordnung (EU) 2018/1805 – Teil 2' (2019) 8 *Neue Zeitschrift für Wirtschafts-, Steuer- und Unternehmensstrafrecht*, 248 (253 et seq.).

§ 13
Value Added Tax

Literature: Bal, 'Taxing Virtual Currency: Challenges and Solutions' (2015) 43 *Intertax*, 380 (386 et seq.); Bal, 'VAT Treatment of Initial Coin Offerings', (2018) 29 *International VAT Monitor*, 125; Bunjes (ed), *Umsatzsteuergesetz: UStG* (17th edn, München, 2018); Capaccioli, 'VAT & Bitcoin' (2014) 23 *EC Tax Review*, 361; Dietsch, 'Umsatzsteuerliche Behandlung von Bitcoin-Mining' (2018) 11 *Mehrwertsteuerrecht*, 250; Ehrke-Rabel and Zechner, 'VAT Treatment of Cryptocurrency Intermediation Services' (2020) 48 *Intertax*, 498; Hanych, *VAT on Cryptocurrencies* (Simple Tax, Czech Republic, 2018); Kollmann, *Taxable Supplies and Their Consideration in European VAT: With Selected Examples of the Digital Economy* (International Bureau of Fiscal Documentation, 2019); Maume, Maute and Fromberger (eds), *Rechtshandbuch Kryptowerte* (München, 2020); Pfeiffer, 'Zur umsatzsteuerlichen Behandlung von Bitcoins' (2014) 29 *Österreichische Steuerzeitung*, 434; Pielke, 'Besteuerung digitaler Währungen – Steuerliche Aspekte von Bitcoin und anderen blockchainbasierten Zahlungsmitteln' (2018) 64 *Internationales Steuer- und Wirtschaftsrecht*, 234; Pielke, 'Umsatzsteuerliche Behandlung von Bitcoins nach dem Urteil des EuGH' (2016) 9 *Mehrwertsteuerrecht*, 150; Schlund and Pongratz, 'Distributed-Ledger-Technologie und Kryptowährungen – eine rechtliche Betrachtung' (2018) 56 *Deutsches Steuerrecht*, 598; Terra, Kajus and Henkov (eds), *Commentary on European VAT* (Online version, International Bureau of Fiscal Documentation, Amsterdam, 2019); Tipke and Lang (eds), *Steuerrecht* (23rd edn, Köln, 2018); Wolf, 'Bitcoin and EU VAT' (2014) 25 *International VAT Monitor*, 254.

Outline

	para.
A. Overview	1
B. Basic Features of the European VAT System	5
C. Exchange of Currency Tokens	9
I. Exchange of Fiat Currencies into Currency Tokens	10
II. Wallets and Platforms	15
D. Exchange of Other Token Types	19
I. Utility Token	20
II. Investment Token	23
1. Equity Token	25
2. Debt Token	28
III. Hybrid Tokens	30
E. Mining and Forging	31
I. Taxable Transaction	32
II. Place of Supply	41
III. Tax Exemption	43
F. Outlook	48

A. Overview

1 This chapter serves as a contribution to the international discussion on the treatment of crypto tokens for purposes of European value added tax (VAT). Due to the nature of VAT as a tax levied on transactions, only acquiring tokens and selling tokens are relevant transactions. This contribution will therefore not examine whether any capital gains which arise from tokens are subject to VAT. This question can only be answered when examining national income tax legislation, thus there can be no standardized European answer.[1]

---
[1] Kollmann, in Maume, Maute and Fromberger (eds), *Rechtshandbuch Kryptowerte*, § 17.

2   This chapter analyses whether exchanging currency tokens into legal tender and using currency tokens as a means of payment are subject to VAT in the European Union (→ para. 9 et seq.). Furthermore, this chapter analyses, whether exchanging other types of tokens for legal tender gives rise to VAT at all, and if so, whether it can be exempt from VAT (→ para. 19 et seq.). Finally, mining and forging of tokens are examined (→ para. 31 et seq.). In particular, it is examined whether the already existing legal opinions on currency tokens can also be transferred to other token types.

3   The growing popularity of crypto tokens has drawn the attention of tax authorities, which see the potential tax revenue from taxing this novel type of transaction. Quite generally speaking, the variance of tokens available on the market is constantly increasing, i.e. that different tokens have different functionalities (→ § 1 para. 70), which can lead to differences in their tax treatment. Tax authorities and tax courts are aware of these differences, so scholars and taxpayers should be aware that the judgments issued by the Court of Justice of the European Union (ECJ) so far are only applicable to individual specific cases. So far, the ECJ has only decided on the VAT treatment of Bitcoin.[2] Following the Hedqvist judgment, national tax authorities issued initial statements on the taxation of cryptocurrencies with a pure payment function (= currency tokens).[3] On the other hand, there is considerable legal uncertainty regarding the treatment of other types of crypto tokens as well as issuing of crypto tokens for corporate financing in initial coin offerings (ICOs).

4   In contrast to income taxes, exchange rate gains and losses are irrelevant for the purposes of value added tax. VAT taxes the consumption of goods and services, being designed as a **tax on transactions**[4]: VAT applies to transactions between the service provider and the service recipient. Without the provision of supply from a business to a consumer (final consumer or other business), there is generally no taxation with VAT. Thus, a brief overview of the basic functioning of VAT is given in order to explain important basics for further analysis (→ para. 5 et seq.).

B. Basic Features of the European VAT System

5   In the European Union, VAT legislation is based on EU law. According to Art. 113 TFEU, legislation on turnover taxes is to be harmonised within the EU to the extent necessary to ensure the functioning of the internal market and to avoid distortions of competition. Several directives have already been issued in implementation of Art. 113 TFEU. When interpreting European countries' VAT laws, therefore, reference always needs to be made to the VAT Directive and the relevant case law of the European Court of Justice.

6   Pursuant to Art. 2 VAT Directive,[5] supplies of goods and services for consideration which are provided by an **entrepreneur** within the scope of his business (= taxable person) are subject to VAT. Such an **exchange of services presupposes** that (i) there is a supplier and a recipient (= two different parties); that (ii) the supply rendered is matched by a consideration; and that (iii) there is a reciprocal legal relationship in

---

[2] ECJ, Judgment of 22 October 2015, *Hedqvist*, C-264/14, EU:C:2015:498.
[3] Bundesministerium der Finanzen (German Federal Ministry of Finance) 27.2.2018 – III C 3 – S 7160-b/13/10001 – Bundessteuerblatt Teil I (BStBl I) 2018, 316; for an overview of other countries' guidances see Wolters Kluwer Global Daily Tax News, Analysis & Commentary: Virtually Taxed, (29.3.2019).
[4] Englisch, '§ 17 – Umsatzsteuer', in Tipke and Lang (eds), *Steuerrecht*, § 17, para. 10–22.
[5] Art. 2 Directive 2006/112/EC (VAT Directive) on the common system of value added tax, OJ L 347, 11.12.2006 p. 1–118.

whatsoever form between the supply and the consideration. The place of supply and the applicable tax exemptions can only be determined once the existence of a supply has been confirmed.

A **supply** can basically consist of doing, tolerating or refraining from doing something. A supply is therefore everything that can be the subject to legal transactions. However, in order to be subject to VAT, only services in the economic sense come into consideration, i.e. services in which the company's own economic interest is pursued beyond the mere payment of remuneration.[6] In the words of the ECJ, 'a consumable benefit must be provided to an identifiable consumer'.[7] A mere payment such as a transfer or money is not a supply in the economic sense.

Pursuant to Art. 73 VAT Directive, **consideration** can be paid either by the recipient of the service or by a third party. This payment can be made in cash or in kind.

For a transaction to constitute a taxable supply, the supply of goods or services and the consideration must be mutually related. Services are rendered against payment if there is a legal relationship between the service provider and the service recipient in which mutual services are exchanged, whereby the remuneration received by the supplier constitutes the actual equivalent of the service rendered to the service recipient. The consideration must therefore be provided for the sake of the supply.[8] In the case of a contractual basis in the sense of a mutual contract, there is usually an exchange of services.

C. Exchange of Currency Tokens

This section first deals with the VAT treatment of exchanging conventional currencies to virtual currency tokens. The VAT implications of exchanging utility tokens, investment tokens, and hybrid tokens are described in the following sections below (→ para. 19 et seq.).

I. Exchange of Fiat Currencies into Currency Tokens

The VAT discussion on the exchange of conventional currencies (legal tender) into virtual currencies began on the European Union level with the judgment of the ECJ in the Hedqvist case in 2015.[9] The case is as follows: Mr. David Hedqvist intended to offer services in the form of the exchange of conventional currencies into the virtual currency Bitcoin and vice versa. The Swedish Administrative Court was not certain on how this issue had to be treated under European VAT and therefore referred the question to the ECJ as to whether buying and selling Bitcoin against Swedish Krones for an exchange fee is exempt from VAT.

The European Court of Justice ruled that the exchange of conventional currencies into the virtual currency Bitcoin and vice versa is a supply of a service against payment within the meaning of Art. 2(1)(c) VAT Directive. This presupposes that i) a taxable person (ii) provides a consumable benefit to an identifiable beneficiary. The service

---

[6] Terra and Kajus, 'Chapter 1.3.4. Extensions and limitations of the scope' in Terra and Kajus (eds), *Commentary on European VAT*, Chapter 1.3.4; see also German Federal Fiscal Court (Bundesfinanzhof) 31.7.1969 – V 94/65 – Bundessteuerblatt Teil II, (BStBl II) 1969, 637.
[7] ECJ, Judgment of 29 February 1996, *Mohr/Finanzamt Bad Segeberg*, C-215/94, EU:C:1996:72; ECJ, Judgment of 18 December 1997, *Landboden-Agrardienste/Finanzamt Calau*, C-384/95, EU:C:1997:627.
[8] ECJ, Judgment of 3 March 1994, *Tolsma/Inspecteur der Omzetbelasting*, C-16/93, EU:C:1994:80.
[9] ECJ, Judgment of 22 October 2015, *Hedqvist*, C-264/14, EU:C:2015:498.

must also be provided (iii) in return for a consideration and (iv) there must be a direct connection between the service provided and the consideration received. The ECJ affirmed these characteristics in its judgement.[10]

11   The more controversial question, namely whether the relevant exchange transactions are covered by the **tax exemption** under Art. 135(1)(e) VAT Directive, was also answered in the affirmative by the ECJ.[11] The issue was whether transactions involving Bitcoin could be subsumed under the wording of the exemption in Art. 135(1)(e) VAT Directive, since according to the wording only transactions 'concerning currency, bank notes and coins used as legal tender' are exempt from tax. The ECJ justified its decision by stating that, due to the different language versions of Art. 135(1)(e) VAT Directive, the wording cannot be used to clearly determine whether only conventional currencies are actually exempt from VAT.[12] Because of the differences between the various language versions of the VAT Directive, it is necessary to interpret the provision in its context and according to its meaning and purpose. In the case of Art. 135(1)(e) VAT Directive, the purpose of this provision is to eliminate the difficulties encountered in the taxation of financial transactions in determining the basis of assessment and the amount of deductible VAT. Since such difficulties can also arise when exchanging conventional currencies into crypto currencies which are not legal tender, a restriction of the tax exemption would not be justified.[13]

12   This leads to the conclusion that although the exchange of Bitcoins into conventional currencies is in principle a taxable service, it is exempt from VAT. In addition, the grounds of the judgment also contain general comments on the VAT treatment of virtual currencies. Accordingly, other currency tokens that are accepted as a contractual direct means of payment between economic operators and that do not serve any purpose other than their use as means of payment are to be treated in the same way as Bitcoin; they are therefore exempt from VAT.

13   It is unclear whether the exchange of one virtual currency to another virtual currency is also covered by the same tax exemption. According to the wording of Art. 135(1)(e) VAT Directive, the exemption should not be applicable, as there is no legal tender involved at all.[14] However, as it is possible that different language versions use different wording, the interpretation of the wording must not be too strict.[15] As mentioned by the ECJ in the Hedqvist case, in such cases, the interpretation should be based on the context and on the aim and purpose of the provision.[16]

Similar to the exchange of legal tender, the difficulty of determining the taxable amount and the amount of deductible VAT also applies when exchanging two types of cryptocurrencies. The purpose of the tax exemption under Art. 135(1)(e) VAT Directive therefore suggests that it is applicable to the exchange of two types of virtual currencies which serve no purpose other than the use as a means of payment. Furthermore, the ECJ gives a hint in the *Hedqvist* judgment that the exchange of other 'virtual currencies with bi-directional flow, which – without being legal tender – are a means of payment accepted by the parties to a transaction' into legal tender should be treated similar to the

---

[10] ECJ, Judgment of 22 October 2015, *Hedqvist*, C-264/14, EU:C:2015:498; see also already ECJ, Judgment of 14 July 1998, *Commissioners of Customs & Excise v First National Bank of Chicago*, C-172/96, EU:C:1998:354.

[11] ECJ, Judgment of 22 October 2015, *Hedqvist*, C-264/14, EU:C:2015:498, para. 57.

[12] ECJ, Judgment of 22 October 2015, *Hedqvist*, C-264/14, EU:C:2015:498, para. 46 et seq.

[13] ECJ, Judgment of 22 October 2015, *Hedqvist*, C-264/14, EU:C:2015:498, para. 50 et seq.

[14] Dietsch, 'Umsatzsteuerliche Behandlung von Bitcoin-Mining' (2018) 11 *Mehrwertsteuerrecht*, 250 (254).

[15] ECJ, Judgment of 22 October 2015, *Hedqvist*, C-264/14, EU:C:2015:498, para. 46.

[16] ECJ, Judgment of 22 October 2015, *Hedqvist*, C-264/14, EU:C:2015:498, para. 47.

exchange of Bitcoin into legal tender.[17] This could suggest the applicability of the tax exemption to exchange transactions involving two types of cryptocurrencies.

In summary, the exchange from one cryptocurrency to another cryptocurrency is not covered by the wording of Art. 135(1)(e) VAT Directive. However, due to the meaning and purpose of the provision, it also seems convincing to apply Art. 135(1)(e) VAT Directive to the exchange of two types of cryptocurrencies.

As a consequence of the tax exemption, the question is whether the use of cryptocurrencies as a means of payment should be treated equal to the use of legal tender or whether the transaction should be treated as a barter transaction. Taking into account the principle of equal treatment, this should not be regarded as a barter transaction, since currency tokens are to be treated in the same way as legal tender. This means that using a cryptocurrency as a mere remuneration is therefore not a taxable transaction, and, accordingly, paying with bitcoin for a good or a service is no barter transaction.[18]

Following the idea that paying for a supply with a currency token should be treated in the same way as paying with legal tender, the following issue arises: When paying with currency tokens, it is unclear how to calculate the taxable amount. The solution could be to apply Art. 91(2) VAT Directive, according to which 'the exchange rate applicable shall be the latest selling rate recorded, at the time VAT becomes chargeable, on the most representative exchange market'. This could be the last published exchange rate on currency exchange platforms on the internet (e.g. CoinMarketCap)[19].

II. Wallets and Platforms

Even though the supply of currency tokens is tax exempt, VAT may be incurred for transactions regarding so-called **wallets**. These are a kind of electronic purse and are used for storing private keys (→ § 1 para. 25). If a wallet provider charges a fee for the provision of the wallet, it is quite evident that this is an electronically supplied service pursuant to Art. 58(1)(c) VAT Directive and Art. 7(1) of VAT implementing regulation.[20] This is because currency tokens are issued and distributed over the internet, so they do not constitute goods within the meaning of Art. 14 VAT Directive. Rather, they meet the definition of electronically supplied services being 'delivered over the Internet or an electronic network and, the nature of which renders their supply essentially automated and involving minimal human intervention, and impossible to ensure in the absence of information technology'.[21]

The **place of supply** for an electronically supplied service provided to a business is the recipient's place of business in accordance with the general place of supply rule for businesses in Art. 44 VAT Directive. For consumers, the special place of supply rule for electronically supplied services of Art. 58(1)(c) VAT Directive is applicable. This is the place where the customer is established, has his permanent address or usually resides, regardless of whether the customer is a business or consumer and regardless of whether the supplier is based in the EU or outside the EU.[22] For the determination of where the

---

[17] ECJ, Judgment of 22 October 2015, *Hedqvist*, C-264/14, EU:C:2015:498, para. 50.
[18] See also Bundesministerium der Finanzen (German Federal Ministry of Finance) 27.2.2018 – III C 3 – S 7160-b/13/10001 – Bundessteuerblatt Teil I (BStBl I) 2018, 316.
[19] https://coinmarketcap.com.
[20] Art. 58(1)(c) VAT Directive, Art. 7(1) Regulation (EU) No. 282/2011 (VAT Implementing Regulation) laying down implementing measures for Directive 2006/112/EC, on the common system of value added tax, OJ L 77, 23.3.2011 p. 1–22.
[21] Art. 1(1) VAT Implementing Regulation.
[22] Art. 24 VAT Implementing Regulation, amended by Regulation (EU) No. 1042/2013 as regards the place of supply of services, OJ L 284, 26.10.2013 p. 1–9.

customer is established, has his permanent address or usually resides – should this not be obvious from the circumstances – there exists a list of assumptions in the VAT implementing regulation.[23] If services are supplied through his fixed land line, it shall be presumed that the location of the customer is at the place of installation of the fixed land line; if services are supplied through mobile networks, it shall be presumed that the location of the customer is the country identified by the mobile country code of the SIM card. Further evidence includes, among other things, the billing address of the customer; the IP address of the device used by the customer or any geolocation procedure; bank details; or also the mobile country code (SIM card).[24] Accordingly, the place of the supply for offering a wallet will be in the European Union for both business and final consumer recipients, if the customer is established in one of the EU Member States.

17   However, it is not clear whether a **tax exemption** could be applicable in these cases,[25] especially considering that Art. 135(1)(d) VAT Directive exempts transactions concerning deposit and current accounts, payments, transfers, debts, cheques and other negotiable instruments. It can be expected that the different national tax authorities will take different points of view on this aspect. If considered as taxable, the place of supply will – regardless whether the service is supplied to a business or to a consumer – be at the place of the customer, thus making it necessary for the supplier to fulfil its VAT obligations in each country where users of the wallet are located.[26]

18   On European Union level, there is also no official statement on whether any of the tax exemptions of Art. 135(1) VAT Directive regarding banking and financial services is applicable to **currency token exchange platforms**.[27] The same exemption as for wallets, Art. 135(1)(d) VAT Directive, could be applicable. Another possibility would be to apply Art. 135(1)(e) VAT Directive, as applied by the ECJ in the *Hedqvist* case.[28]

Nonetheless, if considered taxable by the national tax legislator or tax authorities, similar to wallet providers, exchange platform operators provide an electronically supplied service pursuant to Art. 58(1)(c) VAT Directive and Art. 7(1) VAT implementing regulation, with the place of supply being the location of the consumer.

D. Exchange of Other Token Types

19   This section deals with the VAT classification of supplies of other types of tokens. This can take place, for example, in the context of **initial coin offerings (ICOs)**. This is the first acquisition of tokens after they were issued. It is useful to differentiate between the different token types. In general, ICOs issue utility tokens, investment tokens, or hybrid tokens.[29] The following section therefore deals with the VAT classification of the issue of utility tokens, investment tokens, and hybrid tokens.[30] In case the VAT

---

[23] Art. 24b Amended VAT Implementing Regulation.
[24] Art. 24f Amended VAT Implementing Regulation.
[25] For the analysis of Art. 135(1)(d) VAT Directive see in detail below, para. 44 et seq.
[26] For more information on how to fulfil VAT obligations for electronically supplied services see Commission, 'Guide to the VAT mini One Stop Shop (MOSS)', available at https://beck-link.de/m7eka (accessed 20.2.2021).
[27] Ehrke-Rabel and Zechner, 'VAT Treatment of Cryptocurrency Intermediation Services' (2020) 48 *Intertax*, 498 (507 et seq.).
[28] ECJ, Judgment of 22 October 2015, *Hedqvist*, C-264/14, EU:C:2015:498; see also above para. 10 et seq.
[29] If currency tokens are issued at an ICO, the principles for exchanging currency tokens apply.
[30] The purchase of 'other' tokens is also possible (→ § 1 para. 71). These are tokens that have other functionalities but are not accepted for payment. If 'other' tokens are acquired for payment, the general VAT rules for other services must be applied.

treatment differs for an initial acquisition (e.g. an ICO) from a second, derivative acquisition (e.g. acquiring tokens on a secondary market), different rules apply and will be described separately. The form of consideration, that is, whether the consideration is fiat money or another type of token, is irrelevant for the assessment of VAT liability and the subsequent analysis. There is as yet no legal basis, case law or administrative opinion on the VAT treatment of ICOs and the secondary purchase of utility tokens, investment tokens and hybrid tokens.

I. Utility Token

Utility tokens are similar to digital vouchers (→ § 1 para. 73). From a VAT point of view, according to Art. 30a(1) VAT Directive, a **voucher** is 'an instrument carrying a right to receive a supply of goods or services, or to receive a price discount or rebate with regard to a supply of goods or services and where there is a corresponding obligation to fulfil this right'. The issuer of a utility token promises to provide a supply in consideration for the token in the future. A utility token will therefore be regarded as a voucher from a VAT perspective. Depending on the specific design of the token, one can either purchase a specific, predefined type of supply or one of several possible supplies. It is therefore necessary to consider the circumstances of the individual case to determine whether the voucher is a single-purpose voucher or a multi-purpose voucher.[31] 20

Regarding utility tokens, it could be also argued that tokens are solely used as a means of collecting funds for the development of the issuing company. Accordingly, neither the supply nor the corresponding price could be clearly identified. If the issuing company is not successful, the investors might get nothing in return. Therefore, it may be argued that at the time of an ICO, there is no direct link between the tokens issued and the services rendered by the issuing company in the future. Thus, there would be no taxable event. In other words, at the time of issuing the tokens, the ICO itself may not be regarded as a taxable event for VAT purposes. However, the latter view does not seem convincing, since in many cases the taxable supply consists of the possibility to use and enjoy a good or a service.[32] In fact, whether it is actually used or enjoyed is not important. Thus, a description of the treatment of utility tokens as single- or multi-purpose vouchers will follow in the following paragraph.

A **single-purpose voucher is** a voucher for which the place of supply of the service to which the voucher relates and the VAT due in respect thereof is already known at the time of issuance of the voucher.[33] A single-purpose voucher can be redeemed for a predefined type of good or service. For example, if a shop only sells T-shirts, it is already certain that the standard VAT rate will apply and where the place of supply will be. Thus, any voucher issued will be regarded as a single-purpose voucher. In accordance with Art. 65 VAT Directive, in the case of a single-purpose voucher, a supply between the business and the recipient is assumed at the time of issuance of the voucher. Issuing the voucher is therefore subject to VAT. The actual supply of the good or service obtained with the single-purpose voucher is not subject to VAT. The place of supply, the tax rate and whether a tax exemption is applicable depend on the type of service to which the voucher relates. If a utility token is similar to a single-purpose voucher, i.e. if 21

---

[31] Hanych, *VAT on Cryptocurrencies* (2018), 54 et seq.; Bal, 'VAT Treatment of Initial Coin Offerings' (2018) 29 *International VAT Monitor*, 125.
[32] Kollmann, *Taxable Supplies and Their Consideration in European VAT* (2019), 127 et seq.
[33] Art. 30a(2) VAT Directive.

it can only be exchanged for a specific supply, the issuance of the utility token is subject to VAT, but not the later actual performance.

22 If the criteria for a single-purpose voucher are not met, the utility token will qualify as a **multi-purpose voucher**.[34] For example, if the T-shirt shop also sells books, any voucher issued would be a multi-purpose voucher, since it is not clear whether the voucher will be redeemed for a T-shirt, subject to standard VAT rate, or a book, subject to reduced VAT rate. According to Art. 193 VAT Directive the actual supply of the good or the service obtained with the multi-purpose voucher is subject to VAT. A transfer of the multi-purpose voucher preceding this supply of goods or services is thus not subject to VAT. Therefore, if at the time of purchase of the utility token it is still unclear which specific goods or services will be received for the token, treatment of the Utility Token as a multipurpose voucher is convincing. In such cases, the actual delivery or other services are subject to VAT, not issuing the token.

II. Investment Token

23 From a VAT perspective, investment tokens are similar to equity or debt capital. Equity tokens are comparable to a share in a company that can convey voting rights and secure a share in the future profits of the company. Debt tokens are comparable to bonds, which convey a claim to fixed payments or is similar to a credit claim in favour of the purchaser (→ § 1, para. 71). A case-by-case examination of how the investment token is actually structured is essential for the assessment of the VAT situation.

24 ECJ case law, which states that currency tokens are neither a security giving rise to a right of ownership in legal entities nor a comparable security,[35] does not apply to investment tokens. Investment tokens differ from currency tokens, so that investment tokens cannot be classified as a means of payment.

1. Equity Token

25 Since equity tokens are similar to equity shares in a company, it makes sense to apply the provisions applicable to company shares and the corresponding ECJ case law to equity tokens. In concrete terms, this means that the **first issue of** equity tokens by means of an ICO will likely not qualify as a taxable transaction for purposes of VAT.

According to the ECJ case law, holding shares in a company is not an economic activity, because there is no exploitation of property for obtaining income therefrom on a continuing basis.[36] Any dividend yielded by acquiring and holding shares is only the result of ownership of these shares.[37] The entry of a new shareholder against payment of a contribution is therefore not a supply for purposes of VAT.[38] Due to the similarity of equity tokens with company shares, this ECJ case law should also be applicable to ICOs with equity tokens and their issue should therefore not be a taxable transaction.

26 A subsequent **resale** of the equity token acquired in an ICO is not covered by this case law. Nevertheless, the subsequent purchase and sale of securities is not a taxable

---

[34] Art. 30a(3) VAT Directive.

[35] ECJ, Judgment of 22 October 2015, *Hedqvist*, C-264/14, EU:C:2015:498, para. 55.

[36] ECJ, Judgment of 20 June 1991, *Polysar Investments Netherlands/Inspecteur der Invoerrechten en Accijnzen*, C-60/90, EU:C:1991:268, para. 12; EJC, Judgment of 26 June 2003, *KapHag*, C-442/01, EU: C:2003:381, para. 37 et seq.

[37] ECJ, Judgment of 6 February 1997, *Harnas & Helm v Staatssecretaris van Financiën*, C-80/95, EU: C:1997:56, para. 15.

[38] Cf. on partnerships ECJ, Judgment of 26 June 2003, *KapHag*, C-442/01, EU:C:2003:381; on corporations ECJ, Judgment of 26 May 2005, *Kretztechnik*, C-465/03, EU:C:2005:320.

activity per se, because it is not an economic activity within the meaning of Art. 9(1) VAT Directive[39]. From the company's point of view, a change in the shareholder structure is therefore not subject to VAT. However, if the previous owner of the equity token has held it as part of his existing business assets and if the sale of the token is made against payment as part of a taxable supply of services, the sale is subject to VAT.[40]

The **tax exemption** under Art.135(1)(f) VAT Directive covers 'transactions, including   27
negotiation but not management or safekeeping, in shares, interests in companies or associations, debentures and other securities'. This tax exemption is applicable to the 'brokerage' of sales of shares and other securities. The VAT Directive does not further explain what is meant by 'other securities'. Regarding this question, the ECJ pointed out that an instrument would only qualify as a security, if the transfer of the instrument implied the acquisition of a right of ownership over the issuer or claim against the issuer and the instrument could be exchanged for money or goods.[41] This means that the term 'other securities' would cover instruments similar to those mentioned in Art. 135(1)(f) VAT Directive. An example could be an intermediary generating turnover as a broker for equity tokens, regardless whether the tokens constitute an interest in a partnership or a share in a corporation.[42] Accordingly, it seems likely that the tax exemption of Art. 135(1)(f) VAT Directive will also apply to the resale of equity tokens.

2. Debt Token

Issuing **debt tokens** might qualify as a taxable service for purposes of VAT. Due to   28
the similarity to bonds, the rules and case law on bonds may be applied to debt tokens.

The issue of bonds (debt capital) by a company is not a benefit and therefore not taxable. By issuing bonds, the issuing company aims at the acquisition of capital and does not wish to perform regarding some existing obligation. The investor therefore does not receive any supply but invests in a capital investment. ICOs with debt tokens should therefore also not fulfil the concept of a taxable supply for purposes of VAT.

As with shares in companies, the **resale** of securities of a bond-like nature is not   29
subject to VAT because it is not an economic activity.[43] This is because bonds, just like company shares, are not 'used' to generate sustainable income, as any payments are only made on the basis of ownership.[44] Consequently, the resale of debt tokens purchased from an ICO will not be considered a VAT-able transaction unless they are held as business assets. Professional trading in debt tokens-if taxable-could also fall under the **tax exemption** of Art. 135(1)(f) VAT Directive for professional securities trading.[45]

III. Hybrid Tokens

Hybrid tokens have several properties and functions of other token types. For VAT   30
purposes, they are usually a supply of services that is made up of several parts. In

---

[39] ECJ, Judgement of 29 April 2004, *EDM*, C-77/01, EU:C:2004:243.
[40] ECJ, Judgment of 29 October 2009, *SKF*, C-29/08, EU:C:2009:665.
[41] ECJ, Judgment of 12 June 2014, *Granton Advertising*, C-461/12, EU:C:2014:1745.
[42] German Federal Fiscal Court (Bundesfinanzhof) 18.12.1975 – V R 131/73 – Bundessteuerblatt Teil II (BStBl II) 1976, 265; German Federal Fiscal Court (Bundesfinanzhof) 12.01.1989 – V R 43/84 – Bundessteuerblatt Teil II (BStBl II) 1989, 339; Section 4.8.10 of the Umsatzsteuer-Anwendungserlass (German VAT Application Guideline, 'UStAE').
[43] ECJ, Judgment of 29 April 2004, *EDM*, C-77/01, EU:C:2004:243.
[44] ECJ, Judgment of 22 June 1993, *Sofitam/Ministre chargé du Budget*, C-333/91, EU:C:1993:261.
[45] Terra, Kajus and Henkov, 'Chapter 9.3.2.6 Shares and securities (Art. 135(1)(f))', in Terra and Kajus (eds), *Commentary on European VAT*, Chapter 9.3.2.6.

Part B. EU Regulation

principle the ECJ considers each supply to be separate and independent.[46] Nonetheless, if the individual parts of the supply cannot reasonably be provided independently of each other a single service is to be assumed.[47] For example, when paying a price for a good including shipment, the delivery part can be regarded as a means to better enjoy the principal supply of the good, thus there exists one single composite supply.

With hybrid tokens, one element can often be considered the main component and the other elements as secondary components. To determine whether this is the case, the view of an average consumer must be taken into account.[48] For example, if the token mainly resembles a utility token with additional minor elements of an investment token, it will be quite likely that the VAT treatment is based on the main component, i.e. the utility token component.[49]

E. Mining and Forging

31   Mining and forging are the common procedures for creating new tokens on an existing block chain. A detailed analysis will be given for mining of currency tokens. However, the considerations made apply analogously to the forging of currency tokens, since it is not relevant for VAT purposes whether the reward for generating a new block and the associated remuneration is awarded on the basis of the computing power used or on the basis of the tokens used (→ § 1 para. 33).

I. Taxable Transaction

32   In contrast to the exchange of currency tokens, there is neither European case law nor any EU commission statement dealing with the tax treatment of **mining and forging**. Nevertheless, there is a range of literature and statements of national tax authorities on this issue.[50] Most commentators and national tax authorities are of the opinion that mining of cryptocurrencies is not a taxable transaction.[51] It is argued that

---

[46] ECJ, Judgment of 25 February 1999, *CCP*, C-349/96, EU:C:1999:93, para. 29.
[47] ECJ, Judgment of 25 February 1999, *CCP*, C-349/96, EU:C:1999:93, para. 29.
[48] ECJ, Judgment of 25 February 1999, *CCP*, C-349/96, EU:C:1999:93, para. 29.
[49] ECJ, Judgment of 22 October 1998, *Madgett and Baldwin*, C-308/96, EU:C:1998:496.
[50] Bundesministerium der Finanzen (German Federal Ministry of Finance) 27.2.2018 – III C 3 – S 7160-b/13/10001 – Bundessteuerblatt Teil I (BStBl I) 2018, 316; Deutscher Bundestag (German Bundestag), 'Schriftliche Fragen mit den in der Woche vom 2. Januar 2018 eingegangenen Antworten der Bundesregierung' (BT-Drs. 19/370, 5.1.2018), Question 25, available at https://dserver.bundestag.de/btd/19/003/1900370.pdf (accessed 22 Aug 2021); Bundesfinanzministerium (Austrian Ministry of Finance), 'Steuerliche Behandlung von Krypto-Assets' (January 2020), available at https://beck-link.de/e2byp (accessed 19.11.2020); Irish Revenue, 'Tax and Duty Manual: Taxation of Cryptocurrency Transactions Part 02-01-03' (April 2020), available at https://beck-link.de/d33bf (accessed 22 Aug 2021); Danish Skat, 'Bitcoin mining og tilrådighedsstillelse af datakapacitet – moms og godtgørelse af elafgifter' (SKM2017.453.SR, June 2017), available at https://beck-link.de/e78vf (accessed 22 Aug 2021); Wolf, 'Bitcoin and EU VAT' (2014) 25, *International VAT Monitor* 2014, 254 (257); Kontozis, 'VAT treatment of cryptocurrencies' (PwC Cyprus, 17.4.2019), available at https://beck-link.de/vwes5 (accessed 21.03.2021) regarding the Cypriote view; Dietsch, 'Umsatzsteuerliche Behandlung von Bitcoin-Mining' (2018) 11 *Mehrwertsteuerrecht*, 250 (253).
[51] Bundesministerium der Finanzen (German Federal Ministry of Finance) 27.2.2018 – III C 3 – S 7160-b/13/10001 – Bundessteuerblatt Teil I (BStBl I) 2018, 316; Deutscher Bundestag (German Bundestag), 'Schriftliche Fragen mit den in der Woche vom 2. Januar 2018 eingegangenen Antworten der Bundesregierung' (BT-Drs. 19/370, 5.1.2018), Question 25, available at https://dserver.bundestag.de/btd/19/003/1900370.pdf (accessed 22 Aug 2021); Bundesfinanzministerium (Austrian Ministry of Finance), 'Steuerliche Behandlung von Krypto-Assets' (January 2020), available at https://beck-link.de/

the transaction fee, which miners can receive from other users, is paid voluntarily and that it is not directly related to the services rendered by the miner.[52] Also, the remuneration in the form of the receipt of new tokens automatically paid by the system is not consideration for the miner's services, since they are not provided in the context of a supply for consideration.[53] Moreover, it is argued that there is no identifiable consumer for the mining services.[54]

As described (→ para. 5 et seqq.), in order for a transaction to fall within the scope of VAT, a (i) taxable person must (ii) provide a consumable benefit to an identifiable consumer (= supply), (iii) a consideration needs to be given and (iv) there has to exist a legal relationship between supply and consideration. In principle, it can be assumed that the miner will regularly act as a taxable person in accordance with Art. 9(1) VAT Directive, because he or she most likely performs the mining services on a continuing basis to generate revenue through the intensive use of resources. 33

Most authors[55] as well as national tax authorities[56] seem to assume that even though the miner provides a consumable benefit, there is no identifiable consumer for the mining service. In addition, it is argued that even though the newly mined tokens would constitute a suitable consideration the mined tokens are not given as a consideration for the mining service. Accordingly, there would be a lack of the reciprocity character of the received tokens, as well as a mutual relationship between the service and the consideration. 34

However, a different interpretation seems possible.[57] It is arguable that the miner provides a **service**. As described in (→ § 1 para. 28), transaction data is stored in the block chain. Each block therefore contains the data of numerous transactions. The 35

---

e2byp (accessed 19.11.2020); Kontozis, 'VAT treatment of cryptocurrencies' (PwC Cyprus, 17.4.2019), available at https://beck-link.de/vwes5 (accessed 21.03.2021) regarding the Cypriote view; Wolf, 'Bitcoin and EU VAT' (2014) 25 *International VAT Monitor* 2014, 254 (257).

[52] Bundesministerium der Finanzen (German Federal Ministry of Finance) 27.2.2018 – III C 3 – S 7160-b/13/10001 – Bundessteuerblatt Teil I (BStBl I) 2018, 316; Deutscher Bundestag (German Bundestag), 'Schriftliche Fragen mit den in der Woche vom 2. Januar 2018 eingegangenen Antworten der Bundesregierung' (BT-Drs. 19/370, 5.1.2018), Question 25, available at https://dserver.bundestag.de/btd/19/003/1900370.pdf (accessed 22 Aug 2021).

[53] Bundesministerium der Finanzen (German Federal Ministry of Finance) 27.2.2018 – III C 3 – S 7160-b/13/10001 – Bundessteuerblatt Teil I (BStBl I) 2018, 316; Deutscher Bundestag (German Bundestag), 'Schriftliche Fragen mit den in der Woche vom 2. Januar 2018 eingegangenen Antworten der Bundesregierung' (BT-Drs. 19/370, 5.1.2018), Question 25, available at https://dserver.bundestag.de/btd/19/003/1900370.pdf (accessed 22 Aug 2021); Kontozis, 'VAT treatment of cryptocurrencies' (PwC Cyprus, 17.4.2019), available at https://beck-link.de/vwes5 (accessed 21.03.2021) regarding the Cypriote view; Wolf, 'Bitcoin and EU VAT' (2014) 25 *International VAT Monitor* 2014, 254 (257).

[54] Bundesministerium der Finanzen (German Federal Ministry of Finance) 27.2.2018 – III C 3 – S 7160-b/13/10001 – Bundessteuerblatt Teil I (BStBl I) 2018, 316; Deutscher Bundestag (German Bundestag), 'Schriftliche Fragen mit den in der Woche vom 2. Januar 2018 eingegangenen Antworten der Bundesregierung' (BT-Drs. 19/370, 5.1.2018), Question 25, available at https://dserver.bundestag.de/btd/19/003/1900370.pdf (accessed 22 Aug 2021); Bundesfinanzministerium (Austrian Ministry of Finance), 'Steuerliche Behandlung von Krypto-Assets' (January 2020), available at https://beck-link.de/e2byp (accessed 19.11.2020); Wolf, 'Bitcoin and EU VAT' (2014) 25 *International VAT Monitor* 2014, 254 (257).

[55] Pielke, 'Umsatzsteuerliche Behandlung von Bitcoins nach dem Urteil des EuGH' (2016) 9 *Mehrwertsteuerrecht*, 150 (152); Pfeiffer, 'Zur umsatzsteuerlichen Behandlung von Bitcoins' (2014) 17 *Österreichische Steuerzeitung*, 434; Wolf, 'Bitcoin and EU VAT' (2014) 25 *International VAT Monitor* 2014, 254 (257); Capaccioli, 'VAT & Bitcoin' (2014) 23 *EC Tax Review*, 361; Bal, 'Taxing Virtual Currency: Challenges and Solutions' (2015) 43 *Intertax*, 380 (386 et seq.).

[56] Bundesministerium der Finanzen (German Federal Ministry of Finance) 27.2.2018 – III C 3 – S 7160-b/13/10001 – Bundessteuerblatt Teil I (BStBl I) 2018, 316; Bundesfinanzministerium (Austrian Ministry of Finance), 'Steuerliche Behandlung von Krypto-Assets' (January 2020), available at https://beck-link.de/e2byp (accessed 2.8.2020).

[57] See also Dietsch, 'Umsatzsteuerliche Behandlung von Bitcoin-Mining' (2018) 11 *Mehrwertsteuerrecht*, 250 (253).

verification of a transaction and the merging of several transactions into a new block is carried out by the miner. The miner who manages to generate a new block by solving a mathematical task receives a reward in the form of newly issued tokens (→ § 1 para. 33). The inclusion of a transaction in a new block results in the transaction being considered valid by the block chain participants as soon as further blocks have been added to the chain strand (→ § 1 para. 28). In other words, the miner confirms a transaction with tokens by checking that a token has only been used once, writing the transaction into a block and thus encoding it. The miner therefore provides a consumable benefit to both parties of the verified transaction. The mining service is thus not only provided to an anonymous network of participants, but to both parties of a transaction. These recipients of the mining service are identifiable consumers, since the public keys of the parties involved and the transaction ID are publicly accessible. Thus, it is clearly defined and traceable to which public key a certain token is assigned (→ § 1 para. 17). The view that mining provides a consumable benefit to an identifiable service recipient is therefore also justifiable.

36 The remuneration for the successful mining of a new block consists of newly mined tokens and the transaction fees provided by the parties (→ § 1 para. 35). Based on the wording of the VAT Directive, one can see that the newly mined tokens are suitable consideration for a supply: According to Art. 73 VAT Directive, the taxable amount includes '… everything which constitutes consideration obtained or to be obtained by the supplier, in return for the supply, from the customer or a third party…'. Therefore, the consideration does not necessarily have to be money in the sense of conventional currencies, even a consideration in kind would be possible. Furthermore, the consideration can even be given by a third party.

37 In order to be able to affirm a taxable supply of goods and services subject to VAT, there must still be a reciprocal relationship between the goods or services and the consideration. Whether or not a private law obligation exists between the miner and the two parties to the transaction to be verified is not relevant for VAT purposes.[58] A sufficient link may also exist in cases where the legal transaction is void or invalid under private law, but where de facto a supply is performed for consideration.

38 The prevailing opinion in the literature as well as the tax authorities assume that the remuneration received by the miner is not sufficiently linked to the mining service.[59] This is based on the idea that the mined currency tokens are automatically allocated to the miner and that the transaction fee generally incurred is paid 'voluntarily' to the miner. Furthermore, based on ECJ's line of reasoning it is argued that the amount of the consideration depends on external circumstances and not on the mining service.[60]

39 Contrary to the view taken by the tax authorities, it can be assumed that the transaction fees are not paid on a voluntary basis. Transaction fees are paid primarily in order to prioritise one's own transaction.[61] Since bundling transactions into a new

---

[58] ECJ, Judgment of 17 September 2002, *Town and County Factors*, C-498/99, EU:C:2002:494.

[59] Cf. inter alia Wolf, 'Bitcoin and EU VAT' (2014) 25 *International VAT Monitor* 2014, 254 (257); Schlund and Pongratz, 'Distributed-Ledger-Technologie und Kryptowährungen – eine rechtliche Betrachtung' (2018) 56 *Deutsches Steuerrecht*, 598 (603); Pielke, 'Besteuerung digitaler Währungen – Steuerliche Aspekte von Bitcoin und anderen blockchainbasierten Zahlungsmitteln' (2018) 64 *Internationales Steuer- und Wirtschaftsrecht*, 234 (236); and also Bundesministerium der Finanzen (German Federal Ministry of Finance) 27.2.2018 – III C 3 – S 7160-b/13/10001 – Bundessteuerblatt Teil I (BStBl I) 2018, 316, but without further explanation.

[60] Cf. also ECJ, Judgment of 3 March 1994, *Tolsma/Inspecteur der Omzetbelasting*, C-16/93, EU:C:1994:80, para. 17, on this argument.

[61] Cf. e.g. Die Redaktion von Coin-Hero, 'Bitcoin Transaktionskosten sinken weiter: So günstig wie lang nicht mehr' (Coin Hero, 26.2.2018), available at https://beck-link.de/n2ybf (accessed 27.1.2019).

block in the blockchain is a very demanding and intensive process regarding computing power, the transaction fees also serve as compensation for the electricity and hardware costs incurred by the mining.[62] A miner will therefore first add the transaction with the highest fees to the transaction bundle of a new block. The view that the transaction fees are paid on a voluntary basis is therefore not convincing. On the contrary, the transaction fees paid by the parties are sufficiently linked to the mining service and thus fulfil the definition of consideration for purposes of VAT. The taxable amount of the mining service in this case is the transaction fee received.

Most likely for the newly created currency token, the majorities' view, i.e. that new tokens do not constitute consideration, could be followed. However, this is not because of the lack of an identifiable consumer, since the consumer can be determined by means of the public key. The problem rather lies in the predefined amount of the remuneration made available by the blockchain system.[63] In such cases, the ECJ generally denies that a direct link between the supply and the consideration exists, since the consideration is not dependent on the content of the supply, but solely on other circumstances unrelated to the supply.[64] A similar argument can also be put forward for the mining process. As a rule, the number of newly mined currency tokens does not directly depend on the computing power that the miner had to provide, but only on how many tokens the code of the blockchain provides as block reward at the time of block creation (→ § 1 para. 35). In fact, with higher computing power it is more likely to receive the block reward, but ultimately, it is randomly determined who will generate the new token. However, the amount of the block reward is predefined and independent of the computing power used. Therefore, for newly mined currency tokens, the author is of the opinion that the requirement of consideration is not met. **40**

II. Place of Supply

If a miner supplies a service for consideration, then the question arises where the **place of supply** is. Since many miners are not resident in the European Union, the question is whether VAT could be levied at all. However, mining services constitute electronically supplied services within the meaning of Art. 58(1)(c) VAT Directive and Art. 7(1) VAT implementing regulation, as these are automatically provided by computers and no human intervention is necessary. For business to business supplies, the electronically supplied service is taxed in accordance with the general rule of Art. 44 VAT Directive at the customer's place of establishment. As regards consumers as recipients of the supply, electronically supplied services are taxed in the country where the customer is established, has his permanent address or usually resides, regardless of whether the customer is a business or consumer and regardless of whether the supplier is based in the EU or outside the EU.[65] Thus, if a mining service is supplied to a recipient resident in the EU, the place of supply always is the place of the customer. **41**

Since mining verifies a payment transaction between two users of a token system, it is questionable where exactly the **recipient** is located, because it is not clear who exactly the recipient is. In fact, both parties to the crypto-payment transaction benefit from miner's actions. The transferor and the recipient of the token are both dependent on **42**

---

[62] 'Die Bitcoin Gebühren', available at https://beck-link.de/522hf (accessed 27.1.2019).
[63] Kollmann, *Taxable Supplies and Their Consideration in European VAT* (2019), 177 et seq.
[64] ECJ, Judgment of 29 October 2009, *Commission/Finland*, C-246/08, EU:C:2009:671.
[65] Art. 20 to 24 VAT Implementing Regulation, Art. 1(2)(c)(d) Amended VAT Implementing Regulation (place of supply of services).

the mining services, as this is the only way to make the transfer of a token valid. If the transaction is made through a platform, one possibility would be to refer to the location of the platform through which the payment transaction is executed. However, this makes it easy to avoid VAT by using a platform in a non-EU country. Another possibility would be to focus on the party that pays the transaction fees. From a technical perspective, this will be the transferor of the token. Nonetheless, for VAT it is decisive who economically will pay the transaction fee. As this can be either the transferor or the recipient of the token, the party who bears the cost would be considered the recipient of the mining service.

III. Tax Exemption

43   If the conclusion is reached that the supply of a mining service is taxable within the EU, it must also be examined whether a tax exemption is applicable.

As regards currency tokens, the much-cited ECJ ruling C-264/14, *Hedqvist*, does not apply for the mining-process, as it solely deals with the question of whether the exchange of fiat currencies into currency tokens is exempt from VAT. Pursuant to the ECJ's interpretation of Art. 135(1)(e) VAT Directive, the exchange of conventional currencies into currency tokens is exempt from VAT (→ para. 11). This rule mainly covers the money exchange business but does not include the mining of new currency tokens, as mining is not an exchange of (neither virtual nor conventional) currencies. The VAT treatment of the mining process has not yet been analysed by the ECJ.

44   Another possibility would be to apply the tax exemption of Art. 135(1)(d) VAT Directive. This rule exempts 'transactions, including negotiation, concerning deposit and current accounts, payments, transfers, debts, cheques and other negotiable instruments, but excluding debt collection'. It is apparent from the wording of Art. 135(1)(d) VAT Directive that the transactions covered by that provision concern services related to a transfer of funds. These are typical banking transactions, but they do not necessarily have to be carried out by banks or financial institutions.[66]

45   As regards the interpretation in accordance with the wording of the provision, one might argue that mining services are beyond the scope of the exemption of Art. 135(1)(d) VAT Directive. It is true that it is consistent with settled ECJ case law that tax exemptions should generally be interpreted narrowly, as these exemptions are exceptions to the general principle that generally all supplies are subject to VAT.[67] However, the wording may not be interpreted this narrowly as to deprive the tax exemption of its scope.[68]

The transactions covered by Art. 135(1)(d) concern services or instruments whose operation involves a transfer of money.[69] By definition, mining involves combining transactions that take place within a blockchain network into new blocks. The miner thus provides a virtual payment service.

According to the ECJ, a virtual currency is a 'direct means of payment between the operators that accept it' and does not fall under the concept of debt, cheques and other

---

[66] ECJ, Judgment of 22 October 2015, *Hedqvist*, C-264/14, EU:C:2015:498, para. 37; Heidner, in Bunjes, *UStG*, § 4, para. 26.
[67] ECJ, Judgment of 22 October 2015, *Hedqvist*, C-264/14, EU:C:2015:498, para. 34.
[68] ECJ, Judgment of 22 October 2015, *Hedqvist*, C-264/14, EU:C:2015:498, para. 35.
[69] See also ECJ, Judgment of 12 June 2014, *Granton Advertising*, C-461/12, EU:C:2014:1745, with notes from Grube, 'Verkauf von Rabattkarten nicht umsatzsteuerbefreit – Granton Advertising' (2014) 7 *Mehrwertsteuerrecht*, 434 (437), on the interpretation of the draft of Art. 135(1)(d) VAT Directive under EU law.

negotiable instruments referred to in Art. 135(1)(d) VAT Directive.[70] Accordingly, mining could be a service in accordance with a transfer of funds, so that even the wording of Art. 135(1)(d) VAT Directive could be met.

The aim and purpose of Art. 135(1)(d) VAT Directive, like Art. 135(1)(e) VAT Directive, is to eliminate difficulties in determining the taxable amount and the amount of deductible VAT.[71] Since such difficulties may also arise in connection with payment transactions with currency tokens, a restriction of this tax exemption to the payment and the transfer of legal tender would not be justified. This interpretation also complies with the EU law principle of fiscal neutrality. It states that goods or services which are similar and therefore in competition with each other may not be treated differently with regard to VAT.[72] In this context, it must be considered from the consumer's point of view as to whether the verification of crypto-payment transactions is similar to verification of traditional payments and remittance verification. It must therefore be assessed from the consumer's perspective whether the same needs of the consumer are satisfied.

The main differences between currency tokens and conventional currencies are the absence of a central control authority and the fact that the mining process can only be performed by computer algorithms. Whether a consumer is interested in such a central control authority with possible human involvement for a single payment flow is questionable anyway, especially in times of PayPal, Google Pay and Apple Pay. After all, the miners are also carrying out the tasks of the supervisory authority, but in a decentralised form. There are therefore good reasons to apply the tax exemption of Art. 135(1)(d) VAT Directive to the mining of currency tokens.

It should be noted that the tax exemption of Art. 135(1)(d) VAT Directive is only applicable to currency tokens. If investment tokens are mined, the tax exemption of Art. 135(1)(f) VAT Directive may be applicable (→ para. 27 et 29.).

F. Outlook

The increased practical relevance of tokens draws the attention of the national tax authorities. This contribution has shown that despite some tax authorities' guidance on specific currency token cases, there is still considerable legal uncertainty. In addition to the outlined problems, the importance of blockchain technology will increase.

Blockchain technology enables much more than just trading tokens. It can also be used in the context of **tax administration**, e.g. for VAT reporting. Blockchain technology can be used to automatically create contracts and the corresponding invoices. One invoice thus contains the digital fingerprint of the entire supply chain. This results in an unalterable record of all transactions made. Automated data exchange would enable the tax authorities to obtain forgery-proof reporting of a company's transactions and thus charge VAT and refund input VAT in real time. Companies would thus no longer suffer from cash flow disadvantages.

The verification of special documents and the recording of the corresponding product shipments are also easier to carry out using blockchain technology. Until now, docu-

---

[70] ECJ, Judgment of 22 October 2015, *Hedqvist*, C-264/14, EU:C:2015:498, with notes from Grube, 'Umtausch der virtuellen Währung "Bitcoin" in konventionelle Währungen nicht mehrwertsteuerpflichtig – David Hedqvist' (2015) 8 *Mehrwertsteuerrecht*, 930 (933).
[71] ECJ, Judgment of 22 October 2015, *Hedqvist*, C-264/14, EU:C:2015:498, para. 36; Heidner, in Bunjes, *UStG*, § 4, para. 26.
[72] ECJ, Judgment of 11 September 2014, *K Oy*, C-219/13-K, EU:C:2014:2207, para. 24.

ments have had to be created, sent, viewed and checked at different locations, and thus an administrative process often delays the products' shipments. With a blockchain accessible to all market participants, all transactions can be recorded in real time and all documents would be retrievable without delay.

51 In addition, the networking between the tax authorities of different countries can be facilitated in this way, thus putting a stop to cross-border VAT fraud. Blockchain technology can therefore lead to more legal certainty for tax administrations and companies and herald a new era of cooperative tax compliance.

§ 14
Accounting

Literature: Accounting Research and Development Foundation (ARDF), 'Tentative Agenda Decision – Holdings of Cryptocurrencies' (2019), available at https://beck-link.de/8pe3a (accessed 28.9.2020); Accounting Standards Committee of Germany (ASCG), 'The IFRS IC's tentative agenda decisions in its March 2019 meeting' (2019), available at https://beck-link.de/8k367 (accessed 28.9.2020); Alibhai and others, *Wiley Interpretation and Application of IFRS Standards* (John Wiley & Sons, Newark, 2019); Australian Accounting Standards Board (AASB), 'Digital currency – A case for standard setting activity' (2016), available at https://beck-link.de/x33tr (accessed 28.9.2020); BDO, 'IFRS 15 in the spotlight: Accounting for vouchers' (13.3.2017), available at https://beck-link.de/7wbr4 (accessed 28.9.2020); Brüggemann/Hitz/Sellhorn, 'Intended and Unintended Consequences of Mandatory IFRS Adoption: A Review of Extant Evidence and Suggestions for Future Research' (2013) 22 *European Accounting Review*, 1; Canadian Accounting Standards Board (AcSB), 'Tentative Agenda Decision – Holdings of Cryptocurrencies' (2019), available at https://beck-link.de/yvm7f (accessed 28.9.2020); Canadian Securities Administrators, 'Tentative Agenda Decision – Holdings of Cryptocurrencies' (2019), available at https://beck-link.de/khp8m (accessed 28.9.2020); Chartered Professional Accountants Canada (CPAC), 'An Introduction to Accounting for Cryptocurrencies' (2018), available at https://beck-link.de/xhsk7 (accessed 26.10.2020); Christensen/Hail/Leuz, 'Mandatory IFRS reporting and changes in enforcement'(2013) 56 *Journal of Accounting and Economics*, 147; Deloitte, 'Thinking Allowed – Cryptocurrency: Financial reporting implications' (16.7.2018), available at https://beck-link.de/p4a4k (accessed 28.9.2020); Dixon/Lo/O'Donovan/Ruddenklau, 'Cryptoassets – What's the impact on your financial statements?' (April 2019), available at https://beck-link.de/e4hxf (accessed 28.9.2020); European Financial Reporting Advisory Group (EFRAG), 'Accounting for Cryptoassets: Holder and Issuer Perspective' (5.3.2020), available at https://tinyurl.com/ewdbdksr (accessed 28.9.2020); Ernstberger/Hitz/Stich, 'Enforcement of Accounting Standards in Europe: Capital-Market-Based Evidence for the Two-Tier Mechanism in Germany' (2012) 21 *European Accounting Review*, 253; European Commission, 'Overview of the use of options provided in the IAS Regulation (1606/2002) in the EU as at December 2018', available at https://beck-link.de/ydz4r (accessed 28.9.2020); EY, 'Applying IFRS – Accounting by holders of crypto assets' (2019), available at https://beck-link.de/z57bm (accessed 28.9.2020); IFRIC, 'Staff Paper – Holdings of Cryptocurrencies' (2019), available at https://beck-link.de/xar47 (accessed 28.9.2020); IFRSbox, 'How to account for gift cards?', available at https://beck-link.de/p3c7v (accessed 28.9.2020); Kadlecová, 'Cryptocurrencies under IFRSs' (23.5.2019), available at https://www.dreport.cz/en/blog/cryptocurrencies-under-ifrss/ (accessed 28.9.2020); Keiling/Romeike, 'Die Bilanzierung von Kryptowährungen – Wie Coins und Tokens im IFRS-Abschluss zu erfassen sind' (2018) 18 *Zeitschrift für internationale und kapitalmarktorientierte Rechnungslegung*, 268; Korea Accounting Standards Board (KASB), 'Comments on the Tentative Agenda Decision Relating to Holdings of Cryptocurrencies' (14.5.2019), available at https://beck-link.de/re8n4 (accessed 28.9.2020); Lloyd, 'Feature: Agenda decisions – time is of the essence' (20.3.2019), available at https://beck-link.de/3zpc8 (accessed 28.9.2020); Leopold/Vollmann, 'In depth – A look at current financial reporting issues: Cryptographic assets and related transactions: accounting considerations under IFRS' (December 2019), available at https://beck-link.de/682ef (accessed 28.9.2020).

Outline

	para.
A. Basics of IFRS	1
B. Accounting for Crypto Assets	5
I. Currency Token	5
1. Recognition	5
2. Measurement	7
a) Initial Measurement	8
aa) Case 1: Acquisition at a Trading Platform	9
bb) Case 2: Acquisition as Customer Payment	10
cc) Case 3: Acquisition during an ICO	11
b) Subsequent Measurement	12

II. Investment Token	14
1. Recognition	14
a) Intangible Assets	15
b) Tangible Assets	16
c) Cash and Cash Equivalents	17
d) Inventories	18
e) Financial Instruments	19
2. Measurement	20
a) Initial measurement	21
aa) Case 1: Acquisition at a Trading Platform	22
bb) Case 2: Acquisition as Customer Payment	23
cc) Case 3: Acquisition during an ICO	24
b) Subsequent Measurement	25
III. Utility Tokens	26
1. Recognition	26
a) Intangible Assets	27
b) Tangible Assets	28
c) Cash and Cash Equivalents	29
d) Inventories	30
e) Financial Instruments	31
2. Measurement	32
a) Initial Measurement	33
aa) Case 1: Acquisition at a Trading Platform	34
bb) Case 2: Acquisition as Customer Payment	35
cc) Case 3: Acquisition during an ICO	36
b) Subsequent Measurement	37
IV. Hybrid Tokens	38
V. Further Aspects of Accounting for Crypto Assets	39
C. Summary	44

A. Basics of IFRS

1   '**International Financial Reporting Standards**' (IFRS) or previously labelled as 'International Accounting Standards' (IAS) are a set of international applicable accounting rules developed and issued by the International Accounting Standards Board (IASB), formerly known as International Accounting Standards Committee (IASC).[1] In 2002, the European Union (EU) adopted the so-called IAS Regulation (Regulation No. 1606/2002 of the European Parliament[2]). This Regulation became effective for **fiscal years beginning on or after the 1st January 2005** and requires IAS/IFRS Standards as the financial reporting standards for consolidated financial statements of all European companies whose debt or equity securities trade on a regulated market in Europe. Member states, however, are permitted to extend the scope of application for IFRS. Currently, all EU member states allow IFRS, at least for some unlisted firms. For example, Germany requires IFRS for companies that have applied for listing and permitted IFRS for individual financial statements of large corporations to be published in the federal gazette. Spain requires IFRS for non-listed groups in which there is a listed undertaking and permits IFRS for non-listed companies' consolidated financial statements. Portugal permits IFRS for annual financial statements for non-financial listed companies and requires IFRS for annual financial statements for banks and for all other listed companies if no IFRS consoli-

---

[1] Alibhai et al, *Wiley Interpretation and Application of IFRS Standards* (2019), 4 et seqq.
[2] For more details see IFRS, available at https://beck-link.de/azs3a (accessed 9.1.2021).

dated financial statement is published.[3] In order to become binding law in the EU, new IFRS must be 'endorsed'[4] by the EU (Regulation No. 1606/2002). The application of IFRS accounting standards is strictly enforced.[5]

The goal of the IASB is to develop IFRS that bring **transparency, accountability and efficiency** to financial markets around the world.[6] The objective of financial reporting under IFRS is stated in the Conceptual Framework (CF): 'to provide financial information about the reporting entity that is useful to current and potential investors, lenders and other creditors in making decisions relating to providing resources to the entity' (CF 1.2). These decisions involve buying, selling or holding equity and debt instruments (CF 1.2a), providing or settling loans and other forms of credit (CF 1.2b), and exercising rights or otherwise influence management actions (CF 1.2c). IFRS are not primarily designed for tax purposes or measurement of dividend payments like other GAAPs.[7]

To achieve these goals, **useful information** is defined as being relevant and faithfully presented (CF 2.5). Comparability, verifiability, timeliness and understandability are enhancing qualitative characteristics for the usefulness of information (CF 2.23).

The elements of IFRS are **assets, liabilities**, and **equity** relating to firms' financial position and **income** and **expenses** relating to firms' financial performance (CF 4.1). A complete set of financial statements comprises (a) a statement of financial position as at the end of the period (balance sheet), (b) a statement of profit or loss and other comprehensive income[8], (c) a statement of changes in equity, (d) a statement of cash flows for the period and (e) notes, comprising significant accounting policies and other explanatory information (IAS 1.10).

The statement of financial position comprises **assets, indicating the use of funds, as well as liabilities and equity, indicating the source of financing.** Under IFRS, equity is the residual interest in the assets of the entity after deducting all its liabilities. IFRS do not prescribe the order in which items are presented in the statement of financial position (IAS 1.57). Instead, sorting is based on shared characteristics for presentation and disclosure purposes (CF 7.7). IFRS proposes that line items are presented separately for current and non-current assets (liabilities), except when an order based on liquidity is more relevant (IAS 1.60). An item is defined as 'current' if it is part of the normal operating activities or if it is expected to be realized/settled within a year.[9]

To recognize an item, it must (1) meet the definition of an asset, liability, equity, income or expense (CF 5.6) and (2) provide users of financial statements information that is useful (CF 5.7). For measurement purposes, IFRS relies on either **historical cost**

---

[3] European Commission, 'Overview of the use of options provided in the IAS Regulation (1606/2002) in the EU as at December 2018', available at https://beck-link.de/ydz4r (accessed 28.9.2020). In addition, the IASB offers dedicated standards for small and medium-sized entities. The *IFRS for SMEs* focus on the information needs of lenders, creditors and other users of SME financial statements who are interested in information about cash flows, liquidity and solvency.

[4] Alibhai et al, *Wiley Interpretation and Application of IFRS Standards* (2019), 12.

[5] Christensen/Hail/Leuz, 'Mandatory IFRS reporting and changes in enforcement' (2013) 56 *Journal of Accounting and Economics*, 147 et seqq.; Ernstberger/Hitz/Stich, 'Enforcement of Accounting Standards in Europe: Capital-Market-Based Evidence for the Two-Tier Mechanism in Germany' (2012) 21 *European Accounting Review*, 253 et seqq.

[6] Alibhai et al, *Wiley Interpretation and Application of IFRS Standards* (2019), 1.

[7] Ernstberger/Hitz/Stich, 'Enforcement of Accounting Standards in Europe: Capital-Market-Based Evidence for the Two-Tier Mechanism in Germany' (2012) 21 *European Accounting Review*, 253 et seqq.

[8] The statement of profit or loss is within the IFRS the primary source of information about an entity's financial performance for the reporting period. However, income and expenses may also be temporarily included in other comprehensive income (OCI) in one period being reclassified back to the statement of profit and loss in a future period. This approach ensures a more faithful presentation of firms' financial performance and a provision more relevant information. (CF 7.19).

[9] Alibhai et al, *Wiley Interpretation and Application of IFRS Standards* (2019), 7.

or current values for initial and subsequent measurement (CF 6.1) depending on the qualitative characteristics of usefulness (CF 6.2).[10]

B. Accounting for Crypto Assets

I. Currency Token

1. Recognition

5   A currency token can only be **recognised** on the balance sheet if it meets the **definition of an asset** (CF 5.6) and if the recognition **provides** users of financial statements **useful information**, i.e. the information is relevant and faithfully represented (CF 5.7).

6   IFRS defines an asset as a (1) present economic resource (2) controlled by the entity as (3) a result of past events (CF 4.3).

An economic resource is a right that has the potential to produce economic benefits (CF 4.4). Rights either correspond to an obligation of another party to receive cash, goods or services, or to exchange economic resources (CF 4.6 (a)), or the right to use physical objects or intellectual property (CF 4.6 (b)). A company that holds a currency token has the right to use or sell this currency token, so holding a currency token must be considered as a right. The meaning of 'economic benefits' is broad, too. According to CF 4.16 (d) an economic benefit is, among others, the possibility to receive cash or other economic resources by selling the economic resource.[11] However, many currency tokens do not provide a contractual right to economic benefits. Instead, economic benefits are likely to result from a future sale to a willing buyer, or by exchanging the currency token for goods or services.[12] This requirement is usually fulfilled given the high trading volume of some currency tokens like Bitcoin.[13]

Next, **control** links an economic resource to an entity (CF 4.19). Control is given if an entity is able to control the use of an economic resource and to obtain economic benefits that may flow from it (CF 4.20). In other terms, when a company directly holds currency tokens via its own wallet the company has legal ownership and control over the token.[14]

A **past event** is not formally defined. In general, it refers to a historical point in time when a company bought or received an asset. Because currency tokens are usually bought, this criterion is fulfilled, too. Taken together, a currency token fulfils all requirements of an asset. Whether the recognition of an asset provides useful information is usually irrelevant.

2. Measurement

7   In June 2019, the **International Financial Reporting Interpretations Committee (IFRIC) clarified that IAS 38 should be applied for cryptocurrencies**[15] and, thus, also

---

[10] Ibid, 80.

[11] Other attributes of economic benefits comprise the receipt of contractual cash flows or economic resources (CF 4.16a), the exchange of economic resources (CF 4.16b), the production of cash inflows or avoidance of cash outflows (CF 4.16c), or the extinction of liabilities (CF 4.16e).

[12] EY, 'Applying IFRS – Accounting by holders of crypto assets' (2019), 17, available at https://beck-link.de/z57bm (accessed 28.9.2020).

[13] See CoinMarketCap, available at https://coinmarketcap.com/ (accessed 9.1.2021) for an overview of trading volume for different token.

[14] EY, 'Applying IFRS – Accounting by holders of crypto assets' (2019), 4, available at https://beck-link.de/z57bm (accessed 28.9.2020).

[15] IFRIC defines cryptocurrencies as (1) a digital or virtual currency recorded on a distributed ledger that uses cryptography for security, (2) not issued by a jurisdictional authority or other party and (3) do

for currency tokens.[16] An intangible asset is an (1) identifiable (2) non-monetary asset (3) without physical substance (IAS 38.8). An asset is identifiable if it is separable, i.e. it is capable of being separated or divided from the entity and sold or transferred (IAS 38.12 (a)). The Committee observed that a holding of currency tokens (when they are not held for sale in the ordinary course of business)[17] meets the definition of an intangible asset in IAS 38 employing the definition of 'non-monetary' items in IAS 21 that (a) it is capable of being separated from the holder and sold or transferred individually, and (b) it does not give the holder a right to receive a fixed or determinable number of units of currency.[18] A company that uses a different approach, i.e. a different accounting standard, than proposed by the IFRIC decision, does not make an accounting error. However, after an IFRIC decision, companies are expected to implement an accounting policy change that mirrors the IFRIC decision.[19]

For measurement purposes, it is necessary to distinguish between initial measurement (measurement at recognition) and subsequent measurement (measurement after recognition).

a) Initial Measurement. Because the **measurement method depends on the way a company acquires a currency token**, we consider the following cases: (1) Acquisition at a trading platform, (2) Acquisition as customer payment and (3) Acquisition during an Initial Coin Offering (ICO) (→ § 1 para. 81 et seqq.). 8

aa) Case 1: Acquisition at a Trading Platform. The **cost** of an acquired currency token comprises its **purchase price, including any directly attributable costs**, e.g. transaction fees (IAS 38.27). 9

Example:
Company X buys 10 currency tokens on Binance (Crypto-Exchange) for 1,000 EUR each via bank account. Transaction fees amount to 10 EUR for each currency token. The total costs for this transaction are 10,100 EUR.

---

not give rise to a contract between the holder and another party. Currency Tokens fulfil all these requirements.

[16] IFRIC, 'Staff Paper – Holdings of Cryptocurrencies' (2019), 1, available at https://beck-link.de/xar47 (accessed 28.9.2020).

[17] In the case that tokens are held for sale in the ordinary course of business, IAS 2 applies.

[18] IFRIC, 'Staff Paper – Holdings of Cryptocurrencies' (2019), 8, available at https://beck-link.de/xar47 (accessed 28.9.2020). As of May 2020, there is an ongoing debate whether the decision made by the IFRIC are applicable for cryptocurrencies. Most critique is drawn that IAS 38 was not developed for intangible assets such as cryptocurrencies because cryptocurrencies inherently differ in nature from the types of intangible assets discussed in IAS 38, see AcSB, 'Tentative Agenda Decision – Holdings of Cryptocurrencies' (2019), available at https://beck-link.de/yvm7f (accessed 28.9.2020); ARDF, 'Tentative Agenda Decision – Holdings of Cryptocurrencies' (2019), available at https://beck-link.de/8pe3a (accessed 28.9.2020); KASB, 'Comments on the Tentative Agenda Decision Relating to Holdings of Cryptocurrencies' (14.5.2019), available at https://beck-link.de/re8n4 (accessed 28.9.2020); ASCG, 'The IFRS IC's tentative agenda decisions in its March 2019 meeting' (2019), available at https://beck-link.de/8k367 (accessed 28.9.2020). In July 2020, the EFRAG issued a discussion paper acknowledging concerns regarding accounting for crypto assets. Until end of July 2021 the IASB requests comments on three potential avenues to address potential issues: (1) no amendments to IFRS standards, (2) amend and/or clarify existing IFRS standards, (3) new standard on crypto assets (liabilities) or digital assets (liabilities). While IFRS IC agenda decision only focuses on cryptocurrencies where there is no claim on the issuing Party, the EFRAG focuses on a broad set of cryptographic assets: EFRAG, 'Accounting for Cryptoassets: Holder and Issuer Perspective' (5.3.2020), 14 et seqq., available at https://beck-link.de/n58na (accessed 28.9.2020).

[19] Lloyd, 'Feature: Agenda decisions – time is of the essence' (20.3.2019), available at https://beck-link.de/3zpc6 (accessed 28.9.2020).

Account company X	Debit	Credit
Intangible Assets (currency tokens)	10,100 EUR	
Bank Account		10,100 EUR

10   **bb) Case 2: Acquisition as Customer Payment.** A company sells goods or services to a customer and, thus, recognises a trade receivable. The customer pays the bill using currency tokens. Because this contract fulfils all requirements of IFRS 15.9 and does not meet the exception criteria of IFRS 15.5, the measurement rules of IFRS 15 instead of IAS 38 must be applied (IAS 38.3 (i)). Because a payment using **currency tokens** is a non-cash consideration, it must be **measured at fair value (IFRS 15.66)**.

Example 2: Company X sells units of computing power. Customer Y purchases 100 Gigabyte of computing power for 1 week on account for 1,000 EUR.

Account company X	Debit	Credit
Sales Revenue		1,000 EUR
Trade receivable	1,000 EUR	

Y pays the temporary computing power after usage using two currency tokens worth 500 EUR each.

Account company X	Debit	Credit
Trade receivable		1,000 EUR
Intangible Assets (currency tokens)	1,000 EUR	

11   **cc) Case 3: Acquisition during an ICO.** During an ICO, the investing company usually gives a specific number of crypto assets (mostly high liquid currency tokens) to the issuing company. As a reward, the investing company receives a specific amount of the issued crypto assets (here: currency tokens, → § 1 para. 70 et seqq.). **IFRS 15 cannot be applied because, during an ICO,** there exists no contract with a customer (IFRS 15.6). Instead, the investing company exchanges high liquid currency tokens (=intangible asset) for issued currency tokens (=intangible asset). Therefore, the rules of **IAS 38.45** according to the exchange of intangible assets **must be applied**, and the cost of the received currency tokens must be measured at its fair value unless the transaction lacks commercial substance or the fair values of the received and given up assets cannot be measured reliably.

Example 3: The start-up Y issues its own-created currency token called 'Y-token'. Each token can be purchased for 500 EUR. Company X purchases 10 'Y-token'. The transaction amount is settled with a transfer of 5 currency tokens, each worth 1.000 EUR.

Account company X	Debit	Credit
Intangible Assets (currency token)		5,000 EUR
Intangible Assets (currency token)	5,000 EUR	

b) Subsequent Measurement. For subsequent measurement, an entity has the choice between the cost model and the revaluation model. Because the cost model reflects the pattern of consumption, which is irrelevant for items like currency tokens, it does not provide useful information.[20] The application of the revaluation model requires the existence of an active market.[21] Because currency tokens are homogenous goods and usually frequently traded, requirements for an active market are fulfilled.[22] Thus, **we suggest applying the revaluation model**. The revaluation model requires that an intangible asset shall be carried at its revalued amount. The revalued amount of an asset is defined as fair value at the date of the revaluation less any subsequent accumulated depreciation and subsequent accumulated impairment losses (IAS 38.75). The frequency of revaluations depends on the volatility of the asset's fair value.[23] Because currency tokens often face a high price volatility, annual revaluation is mostly necessary (IAS 38.79).

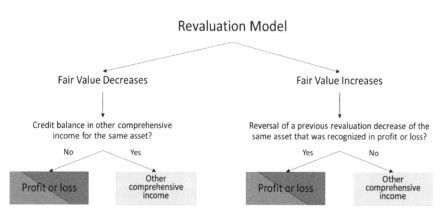

Figure 1: Revaluation method (IAS 38)

In general, a **revaluation increase** shall be recognised in **other comprehensive income** (as part of the equity) (IAS 38.85) and a **revaluation loss** shall be recognised in **profit or loss** (IAS 38.86). Depending on whether the asset already had been revaluated before, a revaluation increase might also be recognised in the profit or loss and a revaluation decrease in the other comprehensive income (see Figure 1; IAS 38.85–86).

II. Investment Token

1. Recognition

By analogy with **currency tokens** (→ para. 5 et seqq.) investment tokens also **fulfil the definition and recognition requirements of an asset.**

---

[20] AASB, 'Digital currency – A case for standard setting activity' (2016), 16, available at https://beck-link.de/x33tr (accessed 28.9.2020); Canadian Securities Administrators, 'Tentative Agenda Decision – Holdings of Cryptocurrencies' (2019), 2, available at https://beck-link.de/khp8m (accessed 28.9.2020).
[21] Dixon/Lo/O'Donovan/Ruddenklau, 'Cryptoassets – What's the impact on your financial statements?' (April 2019), 2, available at https://beck-link.de/e4hxf (accessed 28.9.2020).
[22] An active market is defined as a market in which transactions for the asset or liability take place with sufficient frequency and volume to provide pricing information on an ongoing basis (IFRS 13 Appendix).
[23] Alibhai et al, *Wiley Interpretation and Application of IFRS Standards* (2019), 183.

Because IFRIC clarified accounting rules only for currency tokens but not for investment and utility tokens, it is necessary to clarify which type of asset an investment token is and, thus, which measurement rules have to be applied. IAS 1.54 gives an orientation for potential classifications: property plant and equipment (IAS 1.54 (a)), investment property (IAS 1.54 (b)), intangible assets (IAS 1.54 (c)), financial assets (IAS 1.54 (d)), inventories (IAS 1.54 (g)) or cash and cash equivalents (IAS 1.54 (i)).

15   a) **Intangible Assets.** Building on the definition of an intangible asset (→ para. 7), investment tokens can be sold separately from the entity and are by nature without physical substance. To clarify whether investment tokens are monetary assets, we distinguish between **investment tokens that grant the right to participate in future profits of the issuer or the right to claim fixed payments**[24] and **investment tokens that grant voting rights** (→ § 1 para. 71 et seq.). Following the argumentation of the IFRIC that monetary items have the right to receive a fixed or determinable number of units of currency, investment tokens granting payment rights are considered to be monetary and, thus, do not meet the definition criteria of an intangible asset (IAS 38.8). In addition, **investment tokens granting payment rights** fulfil the requirements of a financial instrument and thus, **IAS 38 cannot be applied** (IAS 38.2). By contrast, investment **tokens granting voting rights** are non-monetary and fulfil the requirements of an **intangible asset**.

16   b) **Tangible Assets.** It is not possible to apply IAS 16 or IAS 40 for investment tokens, because property, plant and equipment and investment property are tangible assets (IAS 16.6; IAS 40.5), whereas investment tokens are intangible by nature.[25]

17   c) **Cash and Cash Equivalents.** Cash comprises cash on hand and demand deposits (IAS 7.6). Because of the digital nature of investment tokens, it is not possible to consider investment tokens as cash on hand. It might be possible to argue that investment tokens are a kind of demand deposit.[26] However, IAS 32.A3 characterises cash as a medium of exchange. That means, as long as there is no financial institution involved, they cannot be considered as cash. Investment tokens are not used as an exchange medium and are not designed as an exchange medium thus investment tokens cannot be considered as cash.

IAS 7.7 characterises cash equivalents to be held for the purpose of meeting short-term cash commitments rather than for investment or other purposes. Because **investment tokens** are held for investment purposes, it is **not possible to recognise investment tokens as cash equivalents**.[27]

18   d) **Inventories.** IAS 2.6 defines inventories as assets that (1) are held for sale in the ordinary course of business, (2) are in the process of production for such sale or (3) are consumed in the production process or in the rendering of services as to materials or supplies. Usually, only token traders hold tokens in the ordinary course of

---

[24] For simplicity, we use for the rest of the chapter the term "investment tokens granting payment rights" to refer to investment tokens that grant the right to participate in future profits of the issuer or the right to claim fixed payments.
[25] Leopold/Vollmann, 'In depth – A look at current financial reporting issues: Cryptographic assets and related transactions: accounting considerations under IFRS' (December 2019), 5, available at https://beck-link.de/682ef (accessed 28.9.2020).
[26] Deloitte, 'Thinking Allowed – Cryptocurrency: Financial reporting implications' (16.7.2018), 12, available at https://beck-link.de/p4a4k (accessed 28.9.2020).
[27] CPAC, 'An Introduction to Accounting for Cryptocurrencies' (2018), 6, available at https://beck-link.de/xhsk7 (accessed 26.10.2020).

business[28] and usually, only miners could have investment tokens in the process of production. Furthermore, investment tokens cannot be considered as a kind of material or supply. Therefore, **most companies cannot recognise investment tokens as inventories**.

e) **Financial Instruments.** IAS 32.11 defines a financial instrument as any contract that gives rise to a financial asset of one entity and a financial liability or equity instrument of another entity. IAS 32.13 defines a contract as an agreement between two or more parties that has clear economic consequences that the parties have little if any, discretion to avoid. **The requirements of a contract should be given in any case a company acquires an investment token**. A financial asset is, among others, a contractual right to receive cash or another financial asset (IAS 32.11). A financial liability is, among others, the contractual obligation to deliver cash or another financial asset (IAS 32.11). Investment tokens granting **payment rights fulfil the requirements of a financial instrument**, because it is a contract between two parties that gives rise to a financial asset (fixed or variable payments) for one entity (holder) and a financial liability (fixed or variable payments; debt tokens (→ § 1 para. 72) or equity tokens (→ § 1 para. 72)) of another entity (issuer). **Investment tokens that grant voting rights** do not give rise to financial asset/liability and, thus, **cannot be recognised as financial instruments**.

2. Measurement

For measurement purposes, it is necessary to distinguish between **initial measurement** (measurement at recognition) and **subsequent measurement** (measurement after recognition).

a) **Initial Measurement.** Because the **measurement** method **depends on the way a company acquires an investment token**, we consider the following cases:

aa) **Case 1: Acquisition at a Trading Platform.** The cost of an investment token granting voting rights comprise the purchase price, including any directly attributable costs, e.g. transaction fees (IAS 38.27) (→ para. 9).

Investment tokens with payment rights are measured at fair value (IFRS 9.5.1.1), which is usually equal to the **transaction price**, i.e. the **fair value of the consideration given or received** (IFRS 9.B5.1.1). It is necessary to consider any transaction costs that are directly attributable to the acquisition (IFRS 9.5.1.1). Investment tokens with payment rights usually do not give rise to cash flows that are solely payments of principal and interest on the principal amount outstanding and, thus, are classified as financial instruments measured at fair value through profit or loss (IFRS 9.4.1.4). Because of this classification, **transaction costs are recognised as expenses** in the period they occur (IFRS 9.5.1.1).

Example 4: Company X purchases 5 investment tokens on Binance that will pay fixed yearly dividends of 20 EUR via bank account. Each investment token costs 100 EUR. Transaction costs for all investment tokens are 50 EUR. The fair value of the tokens equals the purchase price.

---

[28] Leopold/Vollmann, 'In depth – A look at current financial reporting issues: Cryptographic assets and related transactions: accounting considerations under IFRS' (December 2019), 5, available at https://beck-link.de/682ef (accessed 28.9.2020).

Account company X	Debit	Credit
Financial assets at fair value through profit or loss (investment tokens)	500 EUR	
Other expenses (profit or loss)	50 EUR	
Bank Account		550 EUR

23 **bb) Case 2: Acquisition as Customer Payment.** A company sells goods or services to a customer and, thus, recognises a receivable. The **customer pays the bill using investment tokens**. Because this contract fulfils all requirements of IFRS 15.9 and does not meet the exception of IFRS 15.5, the measurement rules of IFRS 15, instead of IAS 38 (IAS 38.3 (i)) and instead of IFRS 9 (IFRS 9.2.1 (j)), must be applied. Therefore, **investment tokens must be measured at its fair value** (IFRS 15.66) (→ para. 10).

24 **cc) Case 3: Acquisition during an ICO.** During an ICO, the investing company usually gives a specific amount of crypto assets (mostly high liquid currency tokens) to the issuing company. As a reward, the **investing company receives a specific amount of the issued crypto assets** (here: investment tokens, → § 1 para. 71 et seq.). IFRS 15 cannot be applied because, during an ICO, there exists no contract with a customer (IFRS 15.6). Instead, the investing company exchanges high liquid currency tokens (=intangible asset) for issued investment tokens (=asset). For issued **investment tokens granting voting rights**, the rules of **IAS 38.45**, according to the exchange of assets, must be applied, and the cost of the received investment tokens must be measured at its fair value. Investment tokens granting **payment rights** also must be **measured at its fair value** (IFRS 9.5.1.1).

25 **b) Subsequent Measurement.** For **investment tokens granting voting rights**, an entity has the **choice between the cost model and the revaluation model**. Because the cost model reflects the pattern of consumption, which is irrelevant for items like investment tokens, it does not provide useful information.[29] Thus, we suggest applying the revaluation model (→ para. 12).

Investment tokens granting payment rights usually do not give rise to cash flows that are solely payments of principal and interest on the principal amount outstanding and, thus, are classified as financial instruments that are **measured at fair value** through profit or loss (IFRS 9.4.1.4).

III. Utility Tokens

1. Recognition

26 By analogy with currency tokens (→ para. 5 et seqq.) and investment tokens (→ para. 14 et seqq.) **utility tokens** also **fulfil the definition and recognition requirements of an asset**.[30]

---

[29] AASB, 'Digital currency – A case for standard setting activity' (2016), 16, available at https://beck-link.de/x33tr (accessed 28.9.2020). If the investment token grants *voting rights* for a fixed time, the cost model would better reflect patterns of consumption and be more applicable.

[30] EFRAG, 'Accounting for Cryptoassets: Holder and Issuer Perspective' (5.3.2020), 3 et seq., available at https://beck-link.de/n58na (accessed 28.9.2020). The EFRAG notes that prior scams may cast doubt on the enforceability of the rights and, thus, if utility token may qualify as assets. In general, the risky nature of utility tokens does hinder recognition.

Because IFRIC clarified accounting rules only for currency tokens but not for investment and utility tokens, it is necessary to clarify which type of asset (e.g. inventory, financial instrument or intangible asset) a utility token is and, thus, which measurement rules have to be applied. By analogy with investment tokens (→ para. 14 et seqq.) we follow IAS 1.54 as an orientation (→ para. 14).

a) **Intangible Assets.** By analogy with investment tokens granting voting rights (→ para. 15), **utility tokens** are identifiable non-monetary assets without physical substance and, thus, **fulfil the requirements of an intangible asset** (IAS 38.8). 27

b) **Tangible Assets.** By analogy with investment tokens (→ para. 16) **it is not possible for utility tokens to apply IAS 16 or IAS 40**, because property, plant and equipment and investment property are tangible assets (IAS 16.6; IAS 40.5) whereas utility tokens are intangible by nature. 28

c) **Cash and Cash Equivalents.** By analogy with investment tokens (→ para. 17) utility tokens can neither be considered as cash nor held for the purpose of meeting short-term cash commitments. Therefore, **it is not possible to recognise utility tokens as cash or cash equivalents**. 29

d) **Inventories.** By analogy with investment tokens (→ para. 18), utility tokens can only be recognised as inventories for token traders (held in the ordinary course of business) and miners (in the process of production for sale). Therefore, **most companies cannot recognise utility tokens as inventories**. 30

e) **Financial Instruments.** IAS 32.11 defines a financial instrument as any contract that gives rise to a financial asset of one entity and a financial liability or equity instrument of another entity. **Utility tokens are similar to a digital voucher**, i.e. they embody a 'claim' for a certain performance by the issuer (→ § 1 para. 73). Therefore, utility tokens do not give rise to a financial asset, financial liability or equity instrument and, thus, **cannot be recognised as financial instruments**. 31

2. Measurement

For measurement purposes, it is necessary to distinguish between **initial measurement** (measurement at recognition) and **subsequent measurement** (measurement after recognition). 32

a) **Initial measurement.** Because the measurement method depends on the way a company acquires utility tokens, we consider the following cases: 33

aa) **Case 1: Acquisition at a Trading Platform.** The **cost** of a utility token comprises the **purchase price, including any directly attributable costs**, e.g. transaction fees (IAS 38.27) (→ para. 9). 34

bb) **Case 2: Acquisition as Customer Payment.** A company sells goods or services to a customer and, thus, recognises a receivable. **The customer pays the bill using utility tokens**. Because this contract fulfils all requirements of IFRS 15.9 and does not meet one the scope out criteria of IFRS 15.5, the measurement rules of IFRS 15 instead of IAS 38 (IAS 38.3 (i)) must be applied. Therefore, **utility tokens must be measured at fair value** (IFRS 15.66) (→ para. 10). 35

cc) **Case 3: Acquisition during an ICO. During an ICO,** the investing company usually gives a specific amount of crypto assets (mostly high liquid currency tokens) to the issuing company. As a reward, the investing company receives a specific amount of 36 the issued crypto assets (here: utility tokens, → § 1 para. 73). IFRS 15 cannot be applied, because during an ICO exists no contract with a customer (IFRS 15.6). Instead, the investing company exchanges high liquid currency tokens (=intangible asset) for issued utility tokens (=intangible asset). Therefore, the **rules of IAS 38.45**, according to the exchange of assets, **must be applied**, and the cost of the received utility tokens must be measured at its fair value (→ para. 11).

37 **b) Subsequent Measurement.** For subsequent measurement, the entity has a choice between the cost model and the revaluation model. Because the cost model reflects the pattern of consumption, which is irrelevant for items like utility tokens, it does not provide useful information.[31] Thus, **we suggest applying the revaluation model** (→ para. 12).

IV. Hybrid Tokens

38 **Accounting of hybrid tokens depends on the composition of these tokens**. For example, if a hybrid token combines a variable payment right based on the issuers' profit and voting rights, this token could be recognised and measured similar to equity instruments.[32] In more complex cases like the combination of a utility token and fixed payment rights, it could be useful to follow the split accounting rules of compound financial instruments (IAS 32.28). In this case, the cost of the hybrid token needs to be split.[33] In the case of non-uniformity with existing token categories, companies need to refer to IAS 8.12 ff. and develop an accounting approach based on the requirements in IFRSs dealing with similar and related issues and the conceptual framework.

V. Further Aspects of Accounting for Crypto Assets

39 Next to the above-discussed holder perspective of crypto assets accounting, we will now briefly discuss the issuance of different crypto assets, i.e. the issuer perspective. There are **two steps** to analyse. The **consideration received and consequences of the token issuance**. Both aspects depend on the characteristics of the transaction and are, therefore, subject to a case-by-case assessment. The nature of the tokens could result in these being recognised as equity, liabilities or revenues.[34] Thus, we offer some general application guidance for basic scenarios.

40 The consideration received may be paid in cash or other crypto assets. If the consideration is not paid in cash, e.g., using a token, **journal entries depend on the characteristics of received consideration**.[35]

---

[31] AASB, 'Digital currency – A case for standard setting activity' (2016), 16, available at https://beck-link.de/x33tr (accessed 28.9.2020). In the case of a utility token, we need to distinguish between the token and the token right. Until redemption, a token has an indefinite life. If the token right is exercised, the right usually expires after a fixed time period. Thus, after redemption, the token right is subject to scheduled depreciations under the cost model.

[32] Keiling/Romeike, 'Die Bilanzierung von Kryptowährungen – Wie Coins und Tokens im IFRS-Abschluss zu erfassen sind' (2018) 18 *Zeitschrift für internationale und kapitalmarktorientierte Rechnungslegung*, 274.

[33] See for more information: Keiling/Romeike, 'Die Bilanzierung von Kryptowährungen – Wie Coins und Tokens im IFRS-Abschluss zu erfassen sind' (2018) 18 *Zeitschrift für internationale und kapitalmarktorientierte Rechnungslegung*, 274.

[34] Kadlecová, 'Cryptocurrencies under IFRSs' (23.5.2019), available at https://www.dreport.cz/en/blog/cryptocurrencies-under-ifrss/ (accessed 28.9.2020).

[35] Leopold/Vollmann, 'In depth – A look at current financial reporting issues: Cryptographic assets and related transactions: accounting considerations under IFRS' (December 2019), 12, available at https://

Accounting for the consequences of token issuances depends on the characteristics of the issued token.[36] **In case of a currency token**, the issuer does not enter into agreement to provide any payments, goods or services. The holder realizes an economic benefit by selling the currency token. Thus, **there are no future obligations** the token issuer needs **to account for**. 41

If a firm **issues** an **investment token granting payment rights**, the issuer enters into an agreement to deliver cash in future periods. This term structure meets the definition of a financial instrument, in detail a financial liability (IAS 32.11). Thus, the **issuer must apply IFRS 9** to account for future payments. 42

In case of a utility token, the issuer enters into an agreement to provide a service after redemption of the token. A utility token is similar to a voucher that embodies a 'claim' for a certain performance by the issuer (→ § 1 para. 73). In case of a voucher, IFRS 15 IG B44 requires recognition of a contract liability to account for the unused right, i.e. the voucher.[37] By analogy, **issuer of a token need to recognize a contract liability**, too. 43

C. Summary

Generally, **currency tokens, investment tokens and utility tokens must be recognized in the balance sheet of a company**. Currency tokens, investment tokens granting voting rights and utility tokens must be recognised as intangible assets following IAS 38. Investment tokens granting payment rights, however, must be recognised as financial assets following IAS 32 and IFRS 9. Initial **measurement for each token depends on the specific case**, i.e. whether the token is purchased, received as payment for sold goods or received as payment for an issued token as part of an ICO. Purchased currency tokens, investment tokens granting voting rights and utility tokens on a crypto asset platform are initially measured with their purchase price, including all directly attributable costs (IAS 38.27). The initial measurement of investment tokens granting payment rights deviates, as they must be measured at fair value (IFRS 9.5.1.1). If crypto assets are received as payment for selling goods, all tokens need to be measured at fair value (IFRS 15.66). Last, all crypto asset which are received as payment during an ICO, must be measured at fair value (IAS 38.45 respectively IFRS 9.5.1.1). For subsequent measurement, we suggest applying the revaluation model (IAS 38.75) for currency tokens, investment tokens granting voting rights and utility tokens. Investment tokens granting payment rights have to be measured at fair value through profit or loss (IFRS 9.4.1.4). 44

Hybrid tokens as a mixture of multiple token attributes cannot be generalised. These tokens need to be analysed on an individual case. A summary of the recognition, presentation and measurement for currency, investment and utility token can be found in: 45

---

beck-link.de/682ef (accessed 28.9.2020); EFRAG, 'Accounting for Cryptoassets: Holder and Issuer Perspective' (5.3.2020), 65, available at https://beck-link.de/n58na (accessed 28.9.2020).
[36] Dixon/Lo/O'Donovan/Ruddenklau, 'Cryptoassets – What's the impact on your financial statements?' (April 2019), 2, available at https://beck-link.de/e4hxf (accessed 28.9.2020).
[37] BDO, 'IFRS 15 in the spotlight: Accounting for vouchers' (13.3.2017), available at https://beck-link.de/7wbr4 (accessed 28.9.2020); IFRSbox, 'How to account for gift cards?', available at https://beck-link.de/p3c7v (accessed 28.9.2020).

| | | Currency Tokens | Investment Tokens | | Utility Tokens |
			granting payment rights	granting voting rights	
Recognition		Obligation (→ para. 5 et seqq.)	Obligation (→ para. 14)	Obligation (→ para. 14)	Obligation (→ para. 26)
Presentation		Intangible asset (IAS 38) (→ para. 7)	Financial asset at fair value through profit or loss (IFRS 9) (→ para. 19)	Intangible asset (IAS 38) (→ para. 15)	Intangible asset (IAS 38) (→ para. 27)
Measurement	Initial — Case 1	Purchase price including attributable costs (IAS 38.27) (→ para. 9)	Fair Value (IFRS 9.5.1.1) (→ para. 22)	Purchase price including attributable costs (IAS 38.27) (→ para. 22)	Purchase price including attributable costs (IAS 38.27) (→ para. 34)
	Initial — Case 2	Fair value (IFRS 15.66) (→ para. 10)	Fair value (IFRS 15.66) (→ para. 23)	Fair value (IFRS 15.66) (→ para. 23)	Fair value (IFRS 15.66) (→ para. 35)
	Initial — Case 3	Fair value (IAS 38.45) (→ para. 11)	Fair Value (IFRS 9.5.1.1) (→ para. 24)	Fair value (IAS 38.45) (→ para. 24)	Fair value (IAS 38.45) (→ para. 36)
	Subsequent	Revaluation Model (IAS 38.75) (→ para. 12)	Financial asset at fair value through profit or loss (IFRS 9.4.1.4) (→ para. 25)	Revaluation Model (IAS 38.75) (→ para. 25)	Revaluation Model (IAS 38.75) (→ para. 37)

§ 15
Crypto Assets & Funds

Literature: AMF, Questions & Answers on the Digital Asset Service Providers Regime, (AMF Position DOC-2020-07, 22.9.2020), 16, available at https://beck-link.de/38e6a (accessed 26.08.2021); Easterbrook and Fischel, 'Voting in Corporate Law' (1983) 26 *Journal of Law and Economics*, 395; Easterbrook and Fischel, *The Economic Structure of Corporate Law* (Harvard University Press, 1991; Groffen and Spoor, 'The Netherlands', in Van Setten and Busch (eds), *Alternative Investment Funds in Europe – Theory and Practice*, (Oxford University Press, 2014); Hooghiemstra, 'FCP-RAIFs & Management Companies – Does the Omnibus Law Really End All Controversy?' (November 2019), available at https://ssrn.com/abstract=3489022 (accessed 26.08.2021); Hooghiemstra, 'The Pan-European Pension Product Regulation – Europe's Solution to the 'Pensions Gap' (August 2020), available at http://dx.doi.org/10.2139/ssrn.3676918 (accessed 26.08.2021); Hooghiemstra, 'Towards Modernization of the Luxembourg Legal Form 'Toolbox' for Funds' (December 2019), available at https://ssrn.com/abstract=3509731 (accessed 26.08.2021); Hooghiemstra, *Depositaries in European Investment Law – Towards Harmonization in Europe* (Eleven International Publishing, Utrecht, 2018), 223; Kamptner, 'Auswirkungen der AIFM-Richtlinie auf Spezialfonds' [2013] *Österreichische Bankwissenschaftliche Gesellschaft*, 127; Klebeck & Eckner, 'Interplay between AIFMD and the UCITSD', in Zetzsche (ed) *The Alternative Investment Fund Managers Directive – European Regulation of Alternative Investment Funds* (2nd edn, Kluwer Law International B.V., Alphen aan den Rijn, 2020), 64; Kremer and Lebbe, 'Collective Investment Schemes in Luxembourg – Law and Practice' (2nd edn, Oxford University Press, Luxembourg 2014), 314; Morley and Curtis, 'Taking Exit Rights Seriously: Why Governance and Fee Litigation Don't Work in Mutual Funds' (2010) 120 *Yale Law Journal*, 84; Morley, The Separation of Funds and Managers: A Theory of Investment Fund Structure and Regulation, (2014) 124 *Yale Law Journal*, 1228; Müller, *Die Rechtsstellung der Depotbank im Investmentgeschäft nach deutschem und schweizerischem Recht* (Neckar-Druck- und Verlagsgesellschaft, Benningen, 1969); Nenova, 'The Value of Corporate Voting Rights and Control: A Cross-Country Analysis' (2003) 68 *Journal of Financial Economics*, 325; Ohl, *Die Rechtsbeziehungen innerhalb des Investment-Dreiecks* (Duncker & Humblot, Berlin, 1989); Partsch and Boyer, 'La Société en Commandite Simple – Constitution et Gouvernance', in Boyer, Coribisier, Dusemon, Mischo, Panichi, Partsch, Pogorzelski, Schleimer, Schummer and Steichen (eds), *Les Commandites en Droit Luxembourgeois* (edition, Groupe Larcier s.a., ORT, 2013); Riassetto, 'L'obligation de restitution du dépositaire d'OPC en droit Luxembourgeois' (2013) 94 *Journal des Tribunaux Luxembourg*, 167; Riassetto, 'Responsabilité de la société de gestion et du dépositaire d'un OPC envers les actionnaires d'une société cible, note sous Cass. com. fr. 27 mai 2015', (2015) 16 *Revue de Droit Bancaire et Financier*, 65; Seegebarth, *Stellung und Haftung der Depotbank im Investment-Dreieck* (Peter Lang, Frankfurt am Main, 2004); Sitkoff, 'An Agency Costs Theory of Trust Law' (2004) 89 *Cornell Law Review*, 621; Thompson and Edelman, 'Corporate Voting' (2009) 62 *Vanderbilt Law Review*, 127; Van der Velden, 'Civielrechtelijke aspecten van fondsen voor gemene rekening' [2011] *Vastgoed Fiscaal en Civiel*, 6; Van Meerten and Hooghiemstra, 'PEPP – Towards a Harmonized European Legislative Framework for Personal Pensions' (June 2017), available at https://papers.ssrn.com/sol3/papers.cfm?abstract_id=2993991 (accessed 26.08.2021); Von Savigny, *System des heutigen Römischen Rechts Vol. I* (1st edn, Veit, Berlin); Wegman, *Investor Protection: towards additional EU Regulation of Investment Funds?* (Kluwer Law International, Leiden University, 2016); Zetzsche and Hanke, 'Risk Management', in Zetzsche (ed), *The Alternative Investment Fund Managers Directive – European Regulation of Alternative Investment Funds* (2nd edn, Kluwer Law International B.V., Alphen aan den Rijn, 2020), 315; Zetzsche and Eckner, 'Appointment, Authorization and Organisation of the AIFM', in Zetzsche (ed), *The Alternative Investment Fund Managers Directive – European Regulation of Alternative Investment Funds* (2nd edn, Kluwer Law International B. V., Alphen aan den Rijn, 2020), 221; Zetzsche and Hooghiemstra, 'Securitizations and SPVs under the STSR and AIFMD', in Zetzsche (ed), *The Alternative Investment Fund Managers Directive – European Regulation of Alternative Investment Funds* (2nd edn, Kluwer Law International B. V., Alphen aan den Rijn, 2020), 375; Zetzsche and Veidt, 'The AIFMD's Third-Country Rules and the Equivalence Concept', in Zetzsche (ed) *The Alternative Investment Fund Managers Directive – European Regulation of Alternative Investment Funds* (2nd edn, Kluwer Law International B. V., Alphen aan den Rijn, 2020), 795; Zetzsche and Preiner, 'Das liechtensteinische AIFM-Gesetz: Die erste Umsetzung der europäischen AIFM-Richtlinie, (2013) 59 *Recht der internationalen Wirtschaft*, 265; Zetzsche and Preiner, 'Scope of the AIFMD', in Zetzsche (ed) *The Alternative Investment Fund Managers Directive – European Regulation of Alternative Investment Funds* (2nd edn, Kluwer Law International B. V., Alphen aan den Rijn, 2015), 61; Zetzsche, 'Aktivlegitimation gemäß §§ 78, 89 KAGB im Investment-Drei- und -Viereck', in Casper, Klöhn, Roth and Schmies (eds), *Festschrift für Johannes Köndgen* (RWS Verlag, Köln 2016), 677; Zetzsche, 'Investment Law as Financial Law: From Fund Governance over Market Governance to Stakeholder Governance?', in Birkmose, Neville and Sørensen (eds), *The European Financial Market in Transition* (Kluwer, Alphen aan den Rijn, 2012), 341; Zetzsche, 'Prime Brokerage under AIFMD', in Zetzsche (ed), *The Alternative Investment Fund Managers Directive – European Regulation of Alternative Investment Funds* (2nd edn, Kluwer Law International B. V., Alphen aan den Rijn, 2020), 545; Zetzsche, 'Die allgemeine Kontrollpflicht der Verwahrstelle im Investmentdreieck – Teil 1' [2017] *Zeitschrift für Finanzmarktrecht*, 107-127; Zetzsche, 'Die allgemeine Kontrollpflicht der Verwahrstelle im Investmentdreieck – Teil 2' [2017] *Zeitschrift für Finanzmarktrecht*, 222; Zetzsche, 'Die Irrelevanz und Konvergenz des Organisationsstatuts von Investmentfonds' (2012) 111 *Zeitschrift für vergleichende Rechtswissenschaften*, 382; Zetzsche, Buckely, Arner and Föhr, 'The ICO Gold Rush: It's a Scam, It's a Bubble, It's a Super Challenge for Regulators' (2019) 63 *Harvard International Law Journal*, 2; Zetzsche, *Prinzipien der kollektiven Vermögensanlage* (Mohr Siebeck, Tübingen, 2015); Zetzsche,' Fondsregulierung im Umbruch – ein rechtsvergleichender Rundblick zur Umsetzung der AIFM-Richtlinie' (2014) 26 *Zeitschrift für Bankrecht und Bankwirtschaft*, 22.

Outline

	para.
A. Introduction	1
B. EU Investment Fund Law – A Law & Economics Explanation	4
I. Overview	4
II. Fund Governance	12
1. The 'Investment Triangle' and 'Investment Quadrangle'	13
a) The Investment Triangle	13
b) The 'Investment Quadrangle'	19
2. The Structural Separation between 'Investments' & 'Management'	22
a) 'Investments' and 'Management'	23
b) Exit as a Substitute for Control	24
III. The Role of the AIFMD & UCITSD in Fund Governance	26
C. The Impact on Fund Managers (AIFMs & UCITS ManCos)	38
I. 'Full AIFMs' versus 'Small AIFMs' – De-minimis Exemption	39
1. De-minimis Exemption	39
2. Implications DLT for Small AIFMs	41
II. Duties of Fund Managers under the AIFMD & UCITSD	42
1. Overview	42
2. 'Core Services': Investment Management, Administration & Marketing	45
a) Investment Management Function	45
b) Administration Services	51
c) Marketing	53
3. 'Non-Core Services': MiFID II Portfolio Management Services	56
III. Investment Management	61
1. AIFMD – Limit on Types of Investment Strategy	61
2. UCITSD – Limits by Product Regulation	64
IV. Fund administration: The Impact of DLT & Smart Contracts	65
1. Overview: The Current EU Fund Distribution Process	66
2. The Impact of DLT on Distribution – Example: Funds DLT	70
3. Conclusion: Impact on Account Management & Order Processing	72
V. Marketing: The Distribution of Tokenised Fund Units/Shares	76
1. The Tokenisation of Fund Units/Shares & Distribution	76
a) The Benefits of Tokenisation of Fund Units/Shares	76
b) Legal Form Neutrality under the AIFMD and UCITSD	80
c) 'Units' (and 'Shares') under the AIFMD and UCITSD	83
aa) 'Units' (and 'Shares') under the AIFMD	84
bb) 'Units' (and 'Shares') under the UCITSD	89

d) The Issuance of Crypto Assets by AIFs/UCITS under the
AIFMD and UCITSD 93
   aa) The Issuance of 'Crypto-Units' and 'Crypto-Shares' by
   AIFs & UCITS 93
   bb) The Issuance of Crypto Assets other than 'Units' and
   'Shares' by AIFs/UCITS? 97
e) Tokenised Fund 'Units' & 'Shares' under the Member State Laws 99
f) Forms of Units/Shares 102
   aa) Materialised Securities or Bearer Securities 104
   bb) Dematerialised Securities 106
   cc) Registered Securities 108
g) Exclusion from the Scope of the (Draft) MiCAR 123
    2. Impact on Distribution – From a B2B2C to D2C Model 134
    VI. 'Non-Core Services': (MiFID II &) MiCAR Portfolio Management
    Services? 139
D. Product regulation: Investing in Tokenised Assets 148
   I. The Benefits of Investing in Tokenised Assets for Funds 148
   II. AIFs 153
   III. UCITS 158
E. Depositary Regulation 167
   I. The Depositary under the AIFMD & UCITSD 167
      1. Eligible Entities 170
         a) UCITSD 170
         b) AIFMD 171
         c) The Impact of DLT on Eligible Entities 175
      2. Safekeeping 176
         a) Financial Instruments that 'Can be Held in Custody' 177
         b) 'Other Assets' 182
         c) The 'Custody' of Crypto Assets 185
            aa) ESMA's Position 185
            bb) Definition -'Crypto Assets that can be Held in Custody'... 187
      3. Control 203
      4. Delegation under the AIFMD/UCITSD 205
         a) Delegation for AIF/UCITS Depositaries 205
         b) The Impact of DLT on Delegation 209
      5. Depositary Liability under the AIFMD & UCITSD 212
         a) Liability under the AIFMD & UCITSD 212
         b) The Impact of DLT on the Depositary's liability 214
   II. 'Crypto asset Custodians' under the EC's 'Digital Finance Package'.. 218
      1. DLT Market Infrastructure Regulation 219
         a) DLT MTFs 223
         b) DLT Securities Settlement System – 'Investor CSDs' 227
      2. MiFID2 – (Financial Instruments) Crypto Asset Custodians 230
      3. MiCAR – (Non-Financial Instrument) Crypto asset Custodians... 235
   III. Frictional Boundaries of 'Crypto asset Custody' under EU Financial
   Law 247
F. DLT and its Future Impact on Funds 248
G. Conclusion 249

A. Introduction

The emergence of blockchain, other distributed ledger technologies ('**DLT**') and the 1
potential of asset tokenisation has led to a lot of attention in the past three years.
Despite 'ICO scams'[1] in 2017–2020, the use of DLT-based tokens in financial markets

---

[1] Initial coin offering ('ICO'); see also Zetzsche, Buckley, Arner and Föhr, 'The ICO Gold Rush: It's a Scam, It's a Bubble, It's a Super Challenge for Regulators' (2019) 63 *Harvard International Law Journal*, 2.

has nevertheless kept growing, and asset tokenisation has become one of the most prominent use-cases of DLTs in the financial markets. Tokenised assets include securities (e.g. stocks and bonds), but also commodities (e.g. gold) and other non-financial assets (e.g. real estate). Asset tokenisation has potential cross-cutting implications for financial market practices and participants, market infrastructures and regulators across a large range of financial instruments and asset classes.[2]

2   Given the above, a discussion on the potential implications of asset tokenisation and DLT in general for European investment funds is warranted. Increased use of DLT and asset tokenisation could have widespread potential benefits in terms of cost and speed efficiencies, increased transparency and liquidity. Although the use of DLT and tokenisation in (EU) investment funds is currently limited, its potential is significant. Careful consideration of the possible impact of DLT and the use of asset tokenisation in the field of (EU) investment funds will allow policy makers to anticipate potential perils linked to the wider use of DLT by (EU) investment funds.

3   This contribution provides an overview of the use of DLT and asset tokenisation for (EU) investment funds. It starts by giving a concise overview of EU investment fund law in general. In particular, Section B explains the law and economics of EU fund governance consisting of a tripartite relationship between fund managers, depositaries and investors. Section C touches upon the to be expected impact of DLT and asset tokenisation on fund managers. It analyses in detail the impact of DLT on the tasks of fund managers under the Directive 2011/61/EU on Alternative Investment Fund Managers (AIFMD)[3] and Directive 2009/65/EC on the coordination of laws, regulations and administrative provisions relating to undertakings for collective investment in transferable securities (UCITSD)[4] consisting of investment management, administration and marketing. Section D discusses the restrictions of EU investment fund investing in tokenised assets set by EU and national eligible asset requirements (i.e. 'product regulation'). Section E discusses the impact of DLT and tokenised assets on AIFMD and UCITSD depositaries, Section F discusses the to be expected impacts of DLT on (EU) investment funds on the short, medium and long-term and Section G concludes.

B. EU Investment Fund Law – A Law & Economics Explanation

I. Overview

4   All EU investment funds are characterised by a fiduciary relationship between investors, fund managers and depositaries in a collective investment setting. The governance of EU investment funds, i.e. *fund governance*, under the AIFMD and UCITSD is fundamentally different from the governance of ordinary companies and partnerships under corporate and commercial law.[5] This section seeks to explain the

---

[2] OECD, 'The Tokenisation of Assets and Potential Implications for Financial Markets' (OECD Blockchain Policy Series, 17.1.2020), available at https://beck-link.de/7cfw3 (accessed 11.04.2020).
[3] Directive 2011/61/EU on Alternative Investment Fund Managers and amending Directives 2003/41/EC and 2009/65/EC and Regulations (EC) No. 1060/2009 and (EU) No. 1095/2010, OJ L 174, 1.7.2011 p. 1–73, as amended ('AIFMD').
[4] Directive 2009/65/EC on the coordination of laws, regulations and administrative provisions relating to undertakings for collective investment in transferable securities (UCITS), OJ L 302, 17.11.2009 p. 32–96, as amended ('UCITSD').
[5] Hooghiemstra, 'Towards Modernization of the Luxembourg Legal Form 'Toolbox' for Funds' (2019) available at https://ssrn.com/abstract=3509731 (accessed 26.08.2021).

governance of EU investment funds from a law and economics perspective. By doing so, this section forms the background in which the DLT developments and their impact on EU investment funds and its corresponding EU legal framework should be read.

II. Fund Governance

Both commercial and corporate law are not designed to resolve the agency/fiduciary relationship between investors and fund managers. For this reason, the EU legislator has with the AIFMD and UCITSD over the past 30 years laid down a specific framework regulatory framework for investment funds. Furthermore, many Member States, such as Luxembourg, have developed in the past few decades 'lex specialis' legal forms for funds (i.e. **Fund Forms**') in regulatory law that are better suited to *fund governance*.[6] Under the AIFMD and UCITSD, intermediary, product and sales regulation form the three pillars of EU investment law. Prior to discussing this, however, first the fiduciary relationship between fund managers, investors and depositaries under the AIFMD and UCITSD will be addressed from a law and economics viewpoint.

1. The 'Investment Triangle' and 'Investment Quadrangle'

a) **The Investment Triangle.** Irrespective of the type of AIF or UCITS, all governance relationships of AIFs and UCITS under the AIFMD and UCITSD involve a **tripartite relationship** between an AIFM[7]/UCITS ManCo[8], a depositary and a number of investors.[9]

In Germany, this tripartite governance structure has been for a couple of decades in the literature being referred to as '*das Anlagedreieck*' or in English: the 'investment triangle'.[10] The investment triangle is to be observed under both the AIFMD and UCITSD. Both directives impose the 'investment triangle' mandatory for investor protection reasons.[11] In the mandatory tripartite governance relationship the AIFMD and the UCITSD impose requirements on the two involved intermediaries: the AIFM/UCITS ManCo and the depositary. Both the relationship between the investors and the AIFM/UCITS ManCo, at the one, and the relationship between the investors and depositary are of a fiduciary nature. Investors, apart from exiting a fund, do not have any means to perform (residual) control towards these intermediaries.

The 'core' duties of both AIFMs and UCITS ManCos under the AIFMD and UCITSD is to perform (discretionary) portfolio and risk management on behalf of their investors.[12] Contrary to discretionary mandates with portfolio managers under MiFID II[13], investors may only exit the fund under the conditions that are being imposed upon them under the constitutional documents of the AIF/UCITS. They are thus not

---

[6] Ibid.

[7] Alternative investment fund manager.

[8] UCITS Management Company authorised under the UCITSD ('UCITS ManCo'; and together with AIFMs refered to as 'ManCo').

[9] Zetzsche, Prinzipien der kollektiven Vermögensanlage (2015), para. 21.

[10] Seegebarth, Stellung und Haftung der Depotbank im Investment-Dreieck (2004); Ohl, Die Rechtsbeziehungen innerhalb des Investment-Dreiecks (1989).

[11] Zetzsche, 'Investment Law as Financial Law: From Fund Governance over Market Governance to Stakeholder Governance?', in: Birkmose, Neville and Sørensen (eds), The European Financial Market in Transition, 341 .

[12] Van der Velden, 'Civielrechtelijke aspecten van fondsen voor gemene rekening', [2011] *Vastgoed Fiscaal en Civiel*, 6.

[13] Directive 2014/65/EU on markets in financial instruments and amending Directive 2002/92/EC and Directive 2011/61/EU, OJ L 173, 12.6.2014 p. 349–496, as amended ('MiFID2').

able to give investment directions to the fund manager regarding the investment policy, as is the case with discretionary mandates. Instead, upon subscription they commit themselves towards the investment policy of an AIF/UCITS that is being described in the fund's private placement memorandum ('**PPM**')/prospectus.

9   For this reason, the mandatory '**investment triangle**' under both the AIFMD, as well as, the UCITSD require the appointment of a depositary that is safekeeping the fund's assets and performs additional oversight/controlling duties towards the AIFM/UCITSD ManCo. The safekeeping of the fund's assets ensures so-called asset segregation, *i.e.* the fund's assets are being segregated from the (operational) assets of the AIFM/UCITS ManCo, the depositary and the assets of the other investors that invest in the fund.[14] This has two objectives. First, the AIFM/UCITS ManCo is not able to dispose of the assets of the fund without the consent of the depositary. The mandatory involvement of two intermediaries in disposing over the fund's property minimises the risk that fund managers misappropriate the assets of the fund. Second, the asset segregation function deriving from the depositary's safekeeping task ensures that the creditors of the AIFM/UCITS ManCo, the depositary, or of any of the investors in a fund may claim the fund's assets.

10   Furthermore, the depositary is exercising a number of oversight duties towards the AIFM/UCITS ManCo. In particular, the depositary ensures that the AIFM/UCITS ManCo is investing the fund's assets in conformity with the investment policy as laid down in the fund's constitutive documents. The depositary will take measures towards the AIFM/UCITS ManCo in case of non-compliance.[15]

11   The depositary's oversight task relates to the collective investment nature of investment funds. In individual investment relationships, such as discretionary mandates concluded with portfolio managers, only a 'custodian' is appointed that merely safekeeps assets. The reason for this is that individual investors are able to exercise a larger degree of control towards both portfolio managers and custodians. In case something displeases them, they are able to terminate their portfolio management and custodian contract.[16] The collective investment nature of *fund governance* leads to 'collective action problems'. It is, therefore, cheaper to entrust a single intermediary, i.e. a 'custodian' being referred to under the AIFMD and UCITSD as 'depositary', with additional oversight/controlling duties towards the AIFM/UCITS ManCo. All investors in a fund bear the costs related to the performance of oversight/controlling duties towards investors equally. The 'checks and balances' (mutual control) being performed by both the depositary and AIFM/UCITS ManCo towards each other compensate for the passiveness of most investors that results from the collective investment nature of investment funds and the fiduciary relationship between AIFMs/UCITS ManCos, at the one, and investors, at the other hand.

12   **b) The 'Investment Quadrangle'.** Both the AIFMD and UCITSD are '**legal form neutral**'. Both directives impose, regardless of the legal in which an AIF or UCITS is established, the same requirements on AIFMs/UCITS ManCos and depositaries. Depending upon the legal form being employed and the AIFMD/UCITSD implementation laws of individual Member States, there is a fourth (relatively inactive) actor involved in

---

[14] Morley, 'The Separation of Funds and Managers: A Theory of Investment Fund Structure and Regulation' (2014) 124 *Yale Law Journal*, 1228 et seq.
[15] Zetzsche, 'Die allgemeine Kontrollpflicht der Verwahrstelle im Investmentdreieck – Teil 1' [2017] *Zeitschrift für Finanzmarktrecht*, 107–127; Zetzsche, 'Die allgemeine Kontrollpflicht der Verwahrstelle im Investmentdreieck – Teil 2' [2017] *Zeitschrift für Finanzmarktrecht*, 222.
[16] Hooghiemstra, Depositaries in European Investment Law – Towards Harmonization in Europe (2018), 223 et seq.

fund governance.[17] In some Member States, such as Luxembourg, there is (predominantly) a fourth actor involved in fund governance. These 'fourth actors' are mainly 'general partners' of limited partnerships, '(supervisory) boards' of investment companies and 'management companies', i.e. legal entities appointed for 'common funds' other than the AIFM or UCITS ManCo, as is the case in Luxembourg.[18] In this contribution, fund governance that includes such a 'fourth actor' is in this contribution being referred to as the '**investment quadrangle**'.

The 'fourth actor' only can take upon a supervisory role, within a private (corporate) law meaning, of the work carried out by the AIFM/UCITS ManCo in relation to the AIF/UCITS it is responsible for without being allowed to take binding decisions as to fulfil its private (corporate) law duties. Irrespective of whether a 'fourth actor' is involved in *fund governance*, its role is, however, limited, as both the AIFMD and UCITSD assign the core duties of portfolio and risk management to AIFMs and UCITS ManCos that are being appointed on behalf of the fund.

2. The Structural Separation between 'Investments' & 'Management'

The 'investment triangle' as mandatory tripartite governance structure under the AIFMD and UCITSD is being required for any type of AIF or UCITS, irrespective of the legal form of the AIF and UCITS employed. The reason for this is that the underlying law and economics theory of the structural separation between 'investments' and 'management' is applicable to all types of AIFs and UCITS.

a) 'Investments' and 'Management'. All AIFs and UCITS are characterised by a **structural separation of 'investments' and 'management'** in which the investment assets of investors, *i.e.* the fund's assets, and the operational assets of AIFMs/UCITS ManCos are segregated into two separate sets of asset patrimonies.[19] Under the structural separation between 'investments' and 'management', the fund's assets remain to be legally/beneficiary owned by the investors in a fund, whereas the 'operational assets' of the AIFM/UCITS ManCo remain to be legally owned by the shareholders of the AIFM/UCITS ManCo and depositary respectively.

The AIFMD and UCITSD mandatory impose this structural separation by means of the 'investment triangle' as a tripartite governance structure that includes the AIFM/UCITS ManCo, the investors and the depositary. The 'investment triangle' is being governed by both the AIFMD and UCITSD (regulatory law), as well as, the legal form employed and regulates the fiduciary governance relationship between the three parties and asset partitioning.

b) Exit as a Substitute for Control. The structural separation of 'investments' and 'management' limit the 'residual control' and 'residual earnings' of investors with regard to the operational assets of both the AIFM/UCITS ManCo and depositary. This is the case for both UCITS and AIFs, as the investors are not shareholders of these two intermediaries, but their exposure is limited to the residual (control and) earnings (the profits and losses) of the AIF's/UCITS' assets, *i.e.* the fund's asset patrimony that is being managed by the AIFM/UCITS ManCo. The reason for this is that discretionary (collective) portfolio management as 'core service' performed by AIFMs/UCITS ManCos is, by definition, not compatible, with granting investors voting rights as a control

---

[17] Zetzsche, 'Aktivlegitimation gemäß §§ 78, 89 KAGB im Investment-Drei-und –Viereck', in: Casper, Klöhn, Roth and Schmies (eds), *Festschrift für Johannes Köndgen*, 677.
[18] See Hooghiemstra, 'FCP-RAIFs & Management Companies – Does the Omnibus Law Really End All Controversy?' (2019), available at https://ssrn.com/abstract=3489022 (accessed 26.08.2021).
[19] See Art. 21(11)(d)(iii) AIFMD; Art. 22a(3) UCITSD.

mechanism.[20] Should voting rights be granted to investors without any restrictions, the investor having the largest stake in an AIF/UCITS would be able to unilaterally decide the investment policy to be executed by the AIFM/UCITS ManCo to the detriment of other investors. Investors do not want to worry about changes in terms of the investment policy to which they are contractually being bound to.[21] Instead, the principle of 'equal treatment' in relation to investors applies and investors are being granted an **'exit right'** under the conditions being posed under the fund's constitutional documents. The strength of the 'exit right' as a governance tool depends upon the type of fund involved. Investors have in a UCITS, for example, at least, bi-monthly a redemption right. The exit rights granted to investors in open-end funds are stronger compared to closed-end funds, such as venture capital and real estate funds.

18   The structural separation of 'investments' and 'management' has important benefits for both AIFMs/UCITS ManCos and investors.[22] At the one hand, the structural separation between 'investments' and 'management' ensures that both intermediaries involved in fund governance are able to exploit economies of scope and scale by being able to offer their services to multiple clients. This ensures that both intermediaries are not being limited to the 'duration' of a single fund but can act as professional 'repeat players' and earn fees from multiple clients at the same time. Investors, therefore, can benefit of a high degree of specialisation of these intermediaries. At the other hand, the role of AIFMs/UCITS ManCos as 'repeat players' acting for multiple clients in parallel ensures that the fixed costs involved in their operational activities are being borne by multiple clients, resulting in lower fees for the services performed by AIFMs/UCITS Mancos and depositaries for fund investors.

III. The Role of the AIFMD & UCITSD in Fund Governance

19   The limitation of residual earnings and control of investors in relation to AIFM/UCITS ManCos resulting from the separation of 'investments' and 'management' leads to agency costs.[23] These are not completely being resolved by the 'exit rights' that investors have under the AIF's/UCITS' constitutional documents. The 'investment triangle' under the AIFMD and UCITSD resolve agency costs within the **tripartite fiduciary relationship** by means of intermediary, product and sales regulation that are 'communicating vessels'.[24] The AIFMD and UCITSD impose conduct of business rules and prudential regulation to AIFMs/UCITS ManCos and depositaries. This so-called 'intermediary regulation' has investor and market protection as its object.

20   Conduct of business rules are specifying the general duty of loyalty/care that AIFMs/UCITS ManCos (i.e. 'manager regulation') and depositaries (i.e. 'depositary regulation') have towards investors and are intended to curb fraud and conflicts of interest that result from the structural separation between 'investments' and 'manage-

---

[20] Easterbrook and Fischel, 'Voting in Corporate Law' (1983) 26 Journal of Law and Economics, 395 ; Nenova, 'The Value of Corporate Voting Rights and Control: A Cross-Country Analysis'(2003) 68 *Journal of Financial Economics*, 325; Thompson and Edelman, 'Corporate Voting' (2009) 62 *Vanderbilt Law Review*, 127.

[21] Morley and Curtis, 'Taking Exit Rights Seriously: Why Governance and Fee Litigation Don't Work in Mutual Funds' (2010) 120 *Yale Law Journal*, 84.

[22] In this respect, 'control' relates to the voting rights in the company in which the AIFM/UCITS ManCo is established.

[23] Sitkoff, 'An Agency Costs Theory of Trust Law' (2004) 89 *Cornell Law Review*, 621.

[24] See Van Meerten and Hooghiemstra, 'PEPP – Towards a Harmonized European Legislative Framework for Personal Pensions' (2017), 94 et seq., available at https://papers.ssrn.com/sol3/papers.cfm?abstract_id=2993991 (accessed 26.08.2021).

ment'.²⁵ These are organisational requirements targeting the intermediaries, such as 'fit & properness' requirements²⁶, an adequate risk organisation²⁷, internal audit²⁸ and requirements in relation to delegation.²⁹ Additionally, prudential requirements include certain initial and on-going capital requirements that ensure that investors are availed from the negative consequences of potential insolvencies of intermediaries and systemic risk.³⁰

Furthermore, AIFs and UCITS are subject to 'product regulation'. These are the 'national product laws', at the one, and the EU product laws, including the UCITSD, MMFR³¹, EuVECAR³²/EuSEFR³³ and ELTIFR³⁴, at the other hand. These are specific rules that regulate the investment portfolios of AIFs and UCITS, such as the eligible investments³⁵, diversification³⁶ and concentration rules³⁷. Product regulation requirements have to be implemented in the constitutive documents of AIFs/UCITS and are complementary to 'intermediary regulation'. 'Intermediary regulation' has as its object to curb agency costs arising from the delegation of discretionary management of the portfolios of AIFs/UCITS to AIFMs/UCITS ManCos. In practice, 'product regulation' is primarily required for AIFs and UCITS that may market to non-professional investors, such as retail³⁸ and high-net worth individuals ('**HNWIs**'), such as 'well-informed investors' in Luxembourg law.³⁹ 'Product regulation' thus limits the discretion in managing investment portfolios performed by AIFMs/UCITS ManCos and is not only complementary to, but also (partly) substitutes 'intermediary regulation'.⁴⁰

Intermediary and product regulation are under the AIFMD and UCITSD supplemented by 'sales regulation' that intends to inform investors not only in the pre-

---

²⁵ Art. 12 et seq. AIFMD; Art. 14 et seq. UCITSD; See Zetzsche and Eckner, 'Appointment, Authorization and Organisation of the AIFM', in: Zetzsche (ed.), The Alternative Investment Fund Managers Directive – European Regulation of Alternative Investment Funds, 221.
²⁶ Art. 8(1)(c) AIFMD; Art. 7(1)(b) UCITSD.
²⁷ Art. 15 AIFMD, Art. 51 UCITSD.
²⁸ Art. 14(1)(d) en (e) UCITSD; Art. 12(1)(f) AIFMD.
²⁹ Art. 20 AIFMD; Art. 13 UCITSD; Klebeck & Eckner, 'Interplay between AIFMD and the UCITSD', in: Zetzsche (ed.), The Alternative Investment Fund Managers Directive – European Regulation of Alternative Investment Funds.
³⁰ Zetzsche, 'Die Irrelevanz und Konvergenz des Organisationsstatuts von Investmentfonds' (2012) 111 Zeitschrift für vergleichende Rechtswissenschaften, 382.
³¹ Regulation (EU) 2017/1131 on money market funds, OJ L 169, 30.6.2017 p. 8–45, as amended ('MMFR').
³² Regulation (EU) No 345/2013 on European venture capital funds, OJ L 115, 25.4.2013 p. 1–17, as amended ('EuVECAR').
³³ Regulation (EU) No 346/2013 on European social entrepreneurship funds, OJ L 115, 25.4.2014 p. 18–38, as amended ('EuSEFR').
³⁴ Regulation (EU) 2015/760 on European long-term investment funds, OJ L 123, 19.5.2015 p. 98–121, as amended ('ELTIFR').
³⁵ See Art. 50 UCITSD; Art. 2(11), (12), (14) MMFR, Art. 3 EuVECAR/EuSEFR and Art. 10 ELTIFR; see for the 'product regulation' that has been introduced under the AIFMD for retail-AIFs in Germany, France, Ireland and Luxembourg: Zetzsche 'Die Irrelevanz und Konvergenz des Organisationsstatuts von Investmentfonds' (2012) 111 Zeitschrift für vergleichende Rechtswissenschaften, 382 (566).
³⁶ Art. 52(1) UCITSD; Art. 17(1) en (2) MMFR; Art. 3(b) en (e) EuVECAR/EuSEFR and Art. 13(1) ELTIFR.
³⁷ Art. 52(2) UCITSD; Art. 17(1) en (2) MMFR; Art. 3(b) en (e) EuVECAR/EuSEFR and Arts 9(1) en 15(2) ELTIFR.
³⁸ See Art. 4(1)(Aj) AIFMD; Art. 1(2) UCITSD.
³⁹ Well-informed investors under Luxembourg law are investors that self-certify and either invest EUR 125,000 in an AIF or are by the AIFM or its delegate classified as an 'opt-in' professional investor.
⁴⁰ The EuVECAR/EuSEFR contain, for example, limited provisions in relation to (sub-threshold) AIFMs and depositaries, but extensive provisions in relation to 'product regulation', such as portfolio composition rules of these types of AIFs.

contractual phase, but also on a periodic basis. Sales regulation under EU fund law is also (partly) dependent upon the type of investor that invests in an AIF/UCITS. The 'default rule' is that more disclosure requirements are in place for retail investors and 'HNWI' investors than professional investors. The AIFMD, for instance, requires an annual report and 'Art. 23 AIFMD disclosure' for professional investors. For retail investors, however, the PRIIPSR[41] requires a 'key information document' and, for certain types of closed-end AIFs, a prospectus under the PR[42].[43]

23   The AIFMD and UCITSD only regulate the **'fiduciary governance'** within the 'investment triangle'. These requirements being imposed by both the AIFMD and UCITSD are to be found in the subscription/commitment agreements concluded between individual investors and AIFMs/UCITS ManCos, as well as, the service provider agreements, such as the depositary agreements concluded between AIFMs/UCITS ManCos and depositaries. Furthermore, the constitutive documents of the Fund Form employed constitute additional 'terms & conditions' of the subscription/commitment agreements concluded between individual investors and UCITS ManCos.

24   Both 'active' and 'passive' asset segregation that ensure the limited liability of investors and fund assets as a separate asset patrimony that is insulated from the assets of the AIFM/UCITS ManCo, depositary and individual investors is not being regulated by the AIFMD and UCITSD. The Fund Forms of AIFs and UCITS under the AIFMD and UCITSD Member State implementation laws thus have to cater for these two specific elements.

25   Intermediary, product and sales regulation under the AIFMD are thus the three 'communicating vessels' upon which EU investment law is built and which are complemented by 'Fund Forms' on the Member State level.

C. The Impact on Fund Managers (AIFMs & UCITS ManCos)

26   In the short and medium term, it is expected that EU *fund governance* will evolve due to DLT rather than be disrupted. To that end, Parts C – E of this chapter will focus on how DLT impacts the relationship between AIFM/UCITS ManCos, depositaries and investors; and 'manager', 'product' and 'sales/marketing regulation' that seeks to protect them.

Part C analyses the impact of DLT on fund managers (AIFMs & UCITS ManCos). For that purpose, it first explains the differences between 'Full AIFMs' and 'Small AIFMs' (→ paras. 27–28), as 'Small AIFMs' are, depending upon the laws of individual Member States, subject to less stringent rules than 'Full AIFMs'. It continues by addressing the duties of fund managers under the AIFMD & UCITSD (→ para. 30 et seq.). The chapter then discusses the impact of DLT on the 'core services' of AIFMs and UCITS ManCos, namely investment management, administration and marketing (→ paras. 47 et seq., 51 et seq., 60 et seq.). It concludes by discussing whether the 'portfolio management services' under the (proposed) Regulation of the EU Parliament and of the Council on Markets in Crypto-assets ('**MiCAR**') (should) fall under the AIFMD & UCITSD (→ para. 114 et seq.).

---

[41] Regulation (EU) No 1286/2014 on key information documents for packaged retail and insurance-based investment products (PRIIPs), OJ L 352, 9.12.2014 p. 1–23, as amended ('PRIIPR').

[42] Regulation (EU) 2017/1129 on the prospectus to be published when securities are offered to the public or admitted to trading on a regulated market, and repealing Directive 2003/71/EC, OJ L 168, 30.6.2017 p. 12–82, ('PR').

[43] Art. 23(3) AIFMD.

I. 'Full AIFMs' versus 'Small AIFMs' – De-minimis Exemption

1. De-minimis Exemption

Contrary to the UCITSD, the AIFMD diverges between 'Small AIFMs' and 'Full AIFMs'. 'Small AIFMs' managing and/or marketing AIFs do not have to obtain an authorisation as AIFM if they fall within the scope of the AIFMD **de-minimis exemption**. The AIFMD allows Member States to merely subject small AIFMs to registration with the Competent Authorities of their home Member States.[44] These AIFs are not subjected to the full AIFMD as the activities of these type of AIFMs are considered not to individually give rise to systematic risks.[45] Small AIFMs upon registration are required to report relevant information to Competent Authorities, including the main instruments they are trading and the principal exposures of the AIF in question.[46] The AIFMD only allows Member States to exempt AIFMs whose assets under management directly or indirectly do not exceed:[47] EUR 100 million; or EUR 500 million.[48] The latter threshold is only applied, provided that the portfolio(s) under management of the AIFM concerned are not leveraged and that investors in their respective AIFs have no redemption rights exercisable for a period of five years. 27

The AIFMD provides an opt-in procedure for small AIFMs falling within the *de minimis* exemption that wish to be authorised in order to benefit from the EU management and marketing passports.[49] The managers wishing to opt-in, however, need to comply with the full AIFMD.[50] 28

2. Implications DLT for Small AIFMs

The implications of DLT for AIFs managed by Small AIFMs have to be assessed on a Member State by Member State basis. Member States have taken various approaches as to the implementation of the AIFMD on this point. Some Member States only require Small AIFMs, in line with the AIFMD, to fulfil certain reporting duties. Other Member States require Small AIFMs to comply with certain degrees of the AIFMD. 29

In Member States that have not 'gold-plated' the 'de-minimum regime', 'Small AIFMs' have (slightly) more flexibility in relation to DLT. 'Small AIFMs', contrary to 30

---

[44] Art. 3(1)-(4) AIFMD.
[45] Recital 17 AIFMD.
[46] Art. 3(3) AIFMD.
[47] The term 'indirectly' refers to through a company with which the AIFM is linked by common management or control, or by a substantive direct or indirect holding, manage portfolios of AIFs. See Art. 3(3)(a) and (b) AIFMD.
[48] The 'de minimis exemption' has been implemented differently throughout Member States. Member States in general apply stricter requirements to retail AIFs than professional AIFs. Germany and the Netherlands are examples of Member States that decided to refrain from imposing stricter requirements that go beyond the de minimis exemption for AIFMs that are exclusively marketing AIFs to professional investors. See for Germany: Kamptner, 'Auswirkungen der AIFM-Richtlinie auf Spezialfonds' [2013] *Österreichische Bankwissenschaftliche Gesellschaft*, 127; See for the Netherlands: Groffen and Spoor, 'The Netherlands' in Van Setten and Busch (eds), Alternative Investment Funds in Europe – Theory and Practice; Austria, France and Ireland are examples of Member States that require small AIFMs managing retail AIFs to obtain a full authorization under the AIFMD. See Zetzsche, 'Fondsregulierung im Umbruch – ein rechtsvergleichender Rundblick zur Umsetzung der AIFM-Richtlinie' (2014) 26 *Zeitschrift für Bankrecht und Bankwirtschaft*, 22 (32).
[49] See Zetzsche and Veidt, 'The AIFMD's Third-Country Rules and the Equivalence Concept', in Zetzsche (ed) The Alternative Investment Fund Managers Directive – European Regulation of Alternative Investment Funds, 795.
[50] Recital 17 AIFMD.

'Full AIFMs', for example, do not have to obtain an authorisation to manage AIFs that invest in (non-financial instrument) crypto-assets, such as cryptocurrencies and stable-coins. Various Member States, however, have prohibited or restricted the marketing of such types of AIFs to (certain types of) investors. In the Member States in which the investment of AIFs managed by Small-AIFMs in cryptocurrencies and stable-coins is allowed, also any type of restriction with regards to depositaries are not in place. This is, however, only the case for those Member States that do not require a depositary to be appointed for AIFs managed by 'Small AIFMs'. Most DLT implications discussed for funds in this section, including developments discussed in terms of 'administration', 'distribution' and 'product regulation' apply to AIFs managed by 'Small AIFMs' and 'Full AIFMs' equally.

II. Duties of Fund Managers under the AIFMD & UCITSD

1. Overview

31   In principle, AIFMs and UCITS ManCos are not authorised under the AIFMD and UCITSD to carry on functions other than the **management of AIFs and UCITS**. The rationale for this restriction is that it protects investors by ensuring an optimum level of specialisation by ManCos and avoiding all risks of conflict of interests with other activities. For that reason, other regulated financial intermediaries at the EU level, such as credit institutions and insurance companies, may not obtain an authorisation as AIFM or as UCITS ManCo.

32   To that end, Art. 6(2) AIFMD requires external AIFMs not to engage in activities other than those referred to in Annex I AIFMD and the additional management of UCITS subject to authorisation under the UCITSD. Annex I AIFMD specifies that four types of functions are included in the activity of management of AIFs: (a) investment management, including portfolio management and risk management, (b) administration, (c) marketing and (d) activities related to the assets of AIFs. Similarly, UCITS ManCos shall under Art. 6(2) UCITSD not engage in activities other than the management of UCITS. Similar to the AIFMD, Annex II UCITSD specifies that three types of functions are included in the activity of collective portfolio management of UCITS: (a) investment management, (b) administration, and (c) marketing.

2. 'Core Services': Investment Management, Administration & Marketing

33   a) **Investment Management Function.** AIFMs and UCITS ManCos AIFMs and UCITS ManCos are under Art. 4(1)(w) and Annex I AIFMD and Annex II UCITSD charged with the AIF's '**investment management function**', i.e. the ManCos are responsible for the AIF's/UCITS' portfolio and risk management.

34   Portfolio management, in contrary to MiFID II, has not been defined in the AIFMD nor in the UCITSD. In the literature, however, it has been argued that the definition of portfolio management under the AIFMD has to be interpreted differently compared to MiFID II.[51] First, the investment policy is laid down in the constitutive documents for AIFs and UCITS. Second, the primary scope of MiFID II are portfolios that contain financial instruments.

---

[51] See Zetzsche and Eckner, 'Appointment, Authorization and Organization of the AIFM', in Zetzsche (ed) The Alternative Investment Fund Managers Directive – European Regulation of Alternative Investment Funds, 181.

Similar as to the UCITSD, portfolio management, therefore, has to be understood as 'collective investment', i.e. the decision to buy, hold or sell assets, including pre- and post-trade analysis of the investment decision on behalf of one or more investors. 35

Similar as for portfolio management, risk management has not been explicitly defined by the AIFMD nor the UCITSD. In the literature, (financial) risk management is defined as a mechanism and/or system to control and limit the chance of suffering a monetary loss, i.e. the possibility of negative schedule variances.[52] The literature seems, however, to suggest that risk management is broader than that and it seeks to:[53] 36
- control organisational, operational and procedural measures regarding the prevention and minimisation of risks;
- optimise the risk-return ratio of an investment; and
- enhance the governance of the intermediary by balancing risks and returns, beyond *eliminating* risks.

For that purpose, both the AIFMD and UCITSD require a risk organisation, i.e. an organisation that mitigates conflicts of interest by requiring 'operational' units (e.g. portfolio management, administration and distribution) to be functionally and hierarchically separate from the 'defensive' units of fund managers (e.g. internal control, compliance and risk management). Furthermore, the AIFMD and UCITSD require procedures to effectively measure risks, setting risks limits or requiring the portfolio manager to sell positions upon a trigger event. In accordance with these procedures, the risks are mathematically assessed (i.e. risk measurement). 37

Both portfolio and risk management are mostly digitised by developments in the artificial intelligence (automation and machine learning) and data analytics domain. This contribution therefore limits itself on highlighting whether fund managers in exercising their portfolio management decision may invest in tokenised assets (→ para. 47 et seq.). 38

b) Administration Services. AIFMs & UCITS ManCos are under the AIFMD and UCITSD allowed to perform the following **administration services**: 39
- legal and fund management accounting services;
- customer inquiries;
- valuation and pricing, including tax returns;
- regulatory compliance monitoring;
- maintenance of unit-/shareholder register;
- distribution of income;
- unit/shares issues and redemptions;
- contract settlements, including certificate dispatch; and
- record keeping.

In certain Member States, such as Ireland and Luxembourg, (part of) the administration duties is, usually, delegated to domiciliation and transfer agents. The adoption of DLT, as well as, smart contracts will have an impact on both fund administration and distribution. Its impact on fund administration will be discussed in more detail in → para. 51 et seq. of this contribution. 40

c) Marketing. Under Art. 4(1)(x) AIFMD, '**marketing**' means 'a direct or indirect offering or placement at the initiative of the AIFM or on behalf of the AIFM of units or shares of an AIF it manages to or with investors domiciled or with a registered office in the EU.' 41

---

[52] Zetzsche and Hanke, 'Risk Management', in Zetzsche (ed), The Alternative Investment Fund Managers Directive – European Regulation of Alternative Investment Funds, 315.
[53] Ibid.

42 The UCITSD does not contain an equivalent definition. Nevertheless, more or less the same should be understood for the 'marketing' activities of UCITS ManCos. Both the AIFMD and the UCITSD contain (passporting) rules that determine under what conditions and to what types of investors an AIFM/UCITS ManCo may market shares/units of AIFs and UCITS to a (potential) investor.

43 DLT does not have an impact on the 'marketing' of units/shares of AIFs/UCITS. With other words, in how fund managers contact (potential) investors to invest in their fund. Instead, tokenised units/shares of AIFs/UCITS have primarily an impact on the 'distribution process'. To that end, this contribution will focus more on the 'distribution process' than on 'marketing' itself (→ para. 109 et seq.).

3. 'Non-Core Services': MiFID II Portfolio Management Services

44 Both the AIFMD and UCITSD prohibit AIFMs and UCITS ManCos from obtaining an authorisation as investment firm under MiFID II. By way of derogation, both the AIFMD and UCITSD allow AIFMs and UCITS ManCos to carry on a few activities regulated by MiFID II that are exhaustively listed for AIFMs in Art. 6(4) AIFMD and for UCITS ManCos in Art. 6(3) UCITSD.

45 Both AIFMs and UCITS ManCos may be authorised, in addition to their primary function as a manager of AIFs and UCITS, to also perform **MiFID II portfolio management services** (i.e. individual discretionary portfolio management services) for professional, including pension funds, and retail clients, where such portfolios include one or more instruments, such as transferable securities, listed in Section B of Annex II MiFID II. The EU legislator allowed for this possibility in order to achieve significant economies of scale.

46 Along MiFID II portfolio management, both AIFMs and UCITS ManCos may under the AIFMD and UCITSD perform 'non-core services' comprising of investment advice[54] and/or the safekeeping and administration in relation to shares or units of collective investment undertakings.[55] AIFMs may, additionally, provide the non-core service of reception and transmission of orders in relation to financial instruments.[56] The term 'non-core service' indicates that these 'ancillary' MiFID II portfolio management services may only be performed provided that the AIFM and/or UCITS ManCo is authorised to perform the MiFID II portfolio management service. The AIFMD and the UCITSD prohibit that ManCos are merely authorised under the respective laws to perform the MiFID II portfolio management service and/or 'non-core services' on a 'stand-alone basis', *i.e.* without managing AIFs and/or UCITS.

47 Apart from this, authorised AIFMs may simultaneously also obtain a license as a UCITS ManCo and AIFMs 'by default' qualify as a PEPP provider that is under the PEPPR authorised to 'provide PEPPs', i.e. to manufacture and distribute PEPPs. No additional authorisation (no license extension) for the provision of PEPPs needs to be obtained for by the authorised AIFM. Instead, the authorised AIFM needs to obtain an authorisation for the PEPP itself.[57] In order to benefit from the PEPP 'product passport', i.e. to provide PEPPs to PEPP savers within the territory of a host Member State.[58]

---

[54] Art. 6(4)(b)(i) AIFMD; Art. 6(3)(b) UCITSD.
[55] Art. 64(b)(ii) AIFMD; Art. 6(3)(b) UCITSD.
[56] Art. 6(4)(b)(iii) AIFMD.
[57] Hooghiemstra, 'The Pan-European Pension Product Regulation – Europe's Solution to the 'Pensions Gap' (2020) available at http://dx.doi.org/10.2139/ssrn.3676918 (accessed 26.08.2021).
[58] Art. 15 PEPPR.

III. Investment Management

1. AIFMD – Limit on Types of Investment Strategy

Under Art. 8(4) AIFMD, Competent Authorities may limit the authorisation for AIFMs. The reason for this is that the AIFMD is 'manager regulation', i.e. it primarily regulated the fund manager and not the fund itself as a product. In this respect, Art. 12(1) AIFMD requires an adequate organisation. If an AIFM does not have the adequate organisation (for example, fit and proper key personnel) for all AIF investment strategies (ranging from securities over crypto assets), such a restriction enables the Competent Authority to grant a license limited to certain investment strategies.[59] Given that the AIFMD does not regulate **investment strategies**, Member States may rely on fund types established by domestic regulation for restricting the AIFM's license. Accordingly, an AIFM may be licensed as private equity or cryptocurrencies AIFs by receiving an AIFM license that is restricted with respect to all other investment strategies. 48

Depending upon the license of the AIFM, AIFs may, thus, in principal invest in any type of 'crypto asset'. In this respect, however, a 'look-through' or 'technology neutral' approach would need to be applied. In other words, the rights or assets represented by the crypto asset would need to be analysed to determine whether the AIFM is investing in conformity with its license (e.g. private equity or hedge fund strategies) and in accordance with the investment objective/policy restrictions, as set out in the constitutive documents of the AIFs it is managing. 49

AIFs managed by AIFMs licensed to manage certain types of investment strategies are, however, not completely free in investing in any type of 'crypto asset', i.e. rights or value represented by DLT. The EU legislator has by means of the EuVECA, EuSEF, ELTIF and MMFR adopted various 'product regulations' that AIFMs managing AIFs that comply with those have to respect when investing on behalf of them. Furthermore, various Member States have adopted 'product regulations' on the national level for AIFs.[60] AIFs that are not bound by any 'product regulation' are free to invest in any type of 'crypto asset', as long as it fits within the investment objective/strategies, as set out in the constitutive documents. 50

2. UCITSD – Limits by Product Regulation

Contrary to AIFMs, UCITS ManCos are not required to be licensed for certain investment strategies. Instead, the 'product regulation' approach frames the types of eligible assets that a UCITS ManCo may invest in on behalf of the UCITS it manages. In order to assess whether a UCITS may invest in a certain type of 'crypto asset', the UCITS ManCo needs to verify whether the 'crypto asset' represents an eligible investment under the UCITSD framework and whether such an investment respects the UCITSD diversification and concentration limits (→ para. 132 et seq.). 51

IV. Fund administration: The Impact of DLT & Smart Contracts

In general, DLT is not the only technology that fosters the digitisation of the asset management industry. Technological innovations, other than DLT, that will 52

---

[59] Zetzsche and Eckner, 'Appointment, Authorization and Organization of the AIFM 195', in Zetzsche (ed) The Alternative Investment Fund Managers Directive – European Regulation of Alternative Investment Funds, 178.

[60] See → para. 127 et seq.

have an impact on **fund administration** (and distribution) are, amongst others, automation and machine learning, APIs, data storage in the cloud, data and analytics. The scope of this contribution is, however, limited. It only analyses the extent to which DLT will help in digitizing investment funds. The area in which DLT directly will impact fund administration (and distribution) are in **account management** and order processing. To that end, first an overview of the typical EU fund distribution process will be provided, before an example of FundsDLT that is currently at the forefront of the administration and distribution process on the basis of DLT will be given. Finally, the digitisation of the account management and order process will be discussed.

1. Overview: The Current EU Fund Distribution Process

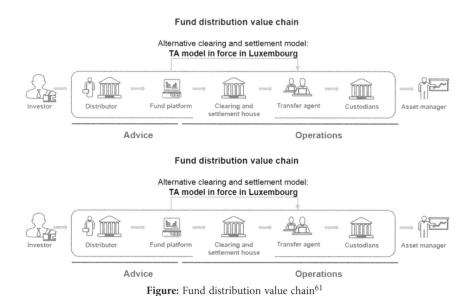

Figure: Fund distribution value chain[61]

53   Most fund managers in Europe sell their fund shares/units to, in particular, retail investors via **fund distributors**, such as (retail and private) banks, insurers, independent investment advisers, in the so-called Business-to-Business-to-Consumer ('**B2B2C**') model.[62] Under this model, (sub-)distributors, typically, perform AML/know-your-customer (KYC) checks under Anti-Money-Laundering (AML) law (→ § 10 para. 105), advise investors on (fund) products and sell those fund products. 'Fund platforms', such as 'Allfunds', functions, in practice, as the main distributor that works with a network of (sub-)distributors. They, amongst others:
– compute and collect inducements;
– sign and administer (sub-)distribution agreements;
– transmit fund documentation;
– advise on fund selection; and
– order routing, clearing and settlement.

---

[61] ALFI, 'Digital/Fintech White Paper – Digital Fund Distribution: Recommendations for the Luxembourg Fund Industry' (2018), 8, available at https://beck-link.de/2h7p7 (accessed 26.08.2021).
[62] Ibid, 8.

The clearing and settlement house performs so-called 'delivery vs payment' and the related clearing and settlement of transactions that involves both transfers of cash and securities.

Most funds issue registered shares. For such funds, a transfer agent is, usually, appointed that keeps the shareholder register and performs the following related services:
- performs AML/KYC checks on distributors or direct investors on behalf of the fund manager;
- collects orders;
- performs corporate actions and pays dividends.

Furthermore, the fund depositary safekeeps fund assets, collects cash from investors, makes payments performs reconciliations on transfer agent orders and performs oversight over fund flows. Finally, the fund manager (or delegated asset manager) invests cash received from investors, performs portfolio, risk management and compliance and develops new products.

2. The Impact of DLT on Distribution – Example: Funds DLT

In Luxembourg, **FundsDLT** that is currently being developed is a DLT based platform that is being built to not only accelerate distribution by streamlining the process described above. Furthermore, FundsDLT seeks to significantly reduce the administrative procedures relating to fund distribution, including KYC. To this end, it developed a platform in which the above-mentioned actors in the fund distribution chain can connect themselves to. It works as follows:[63]

In the first place, any distributors (in the case of B2B2C) or the fund manager ('**D2C**'); direct-to-customer model) would offer an account to investors that is connected to the digital infrastructure of FundsDLT. Through opening the 'app' on their smartphone, investors are able to see their personal information related to their account, including their AML/KYC status, investor classification according to MiFID II and the registered payment methods. Subsequently, investors can select the funds that are connected to the FundsDLT platform, access the specific fund details, including the UCITS key investor information document (KIID)/packaged retail and insurance-based investment products (PRIIPS)/key information document (KID), the prospectus or the PPM. All this information is made available by the FundsDLT Datahub. Upon selecting a specific fund, the price for units/shares and the desired amount can be inserted, and the order be confirmed. The order is then processed by FundDLT's DLT that is based upon Ethereum. The blockchain allows real-time access for all participations as to the status of the order being processed. The transfer agent can access the share register and the order book, the fund/asset manager can have a look at its real time cash flows and the cash central counterparty ('**CCP**') knows the status of the cash in the real-time process. The platform allows for a built-in AML/KYC process at the distributor or transfer agent level. These can access all the KYC documents that are stored in the KYC hub (AML/KYC repository) that is based upon a video onboarding process. After the AML/KYC process is fulfilled, the transfer agent can accept the order. On the cash CCP side, the payment upon subscription triggers a smart contract that converts the cash paid up by the regular payment method into cash-tokens. Subsequently, the smart contracts deliver the cash-tokens on the transfer agent's account. When the transaction is finalised, a smart contract updates the share register. On the fund/asset manager's

---

[63] The process description is (partially) based upon the official launch announcement of FundsDLT: available at https://beck-link.de/nz4xf (accessed 26.08.2021).

side, they have a complete overview of the cash flows. They have, amongst others, an overview of the share register and the settlement on the cash side. Furthermore, a smart contract converts, post-transaction, the cash-tokens back into regular Euro's held by the relevant fund's depositary cash accounts. On the investor's side, the account shows the investor's investment portfolio.

3. Conclusion: Impact on Account Management & Order Processing

59   In the context of payment, clearing, and settlement, FundsDLT shows that DLT enables fund managers to carry out transactions with simplified settlement and reconciliation processes that reduces the costs by streamlining back and middle office processes and a transparent record of transactions by verifying identity and validating transactions.[64] Furthermore, DLT allows the fund register to be distributed amongst distributors, asset managers, transfer agents and other fund service providers in a private network. The DLT network can process orders from investors and distributors while automatically updating the fund register. Fund units/shares can be directly issued on the DLT, whereas clearing and settlement of orders can be automatically triggered with an API (application programming interface) that connects the FundsDLT platform with (retail) investor banks.

60   To manage cash, tokenisation is used to reflect cash held at the bank of the platform. FundDLT can be linked to a fund account that publishes on the platform the net asset value ('**NAV**'), which triggers the confirmation of pending orders. At the same time, APIs communicate cash instructions to the bank. The DLT-based network allows for a layer of connectivity in order to receive orders and reporting; and data analytics can be plugged directly into the platform. FundsDLT allows large numbers of investor accounts to be managed while the investors are recorded in the fund register. This provides fund/asset managers with transparency and a high number of investor account and transactions is possible due to the digitisation and automation of the order process due to smart contracts. Furthermore, current labour-intensive reconciliation processes are not required anymore. In addition, digital interfaces can be plugged directly into the DLT network with APIs and the operational value chain is digitalised from front to back office. This allows to collect a large number of small amounts in the retail space, making D2C distribution or robo-advisors possible.

V. Marketing: The Distribution of Tokenised Fund Units/Shares

1. The Tokenisation of Fund Units/Shares & Distribution

61   **a) The Benefits of Tokenisation of Fund Units/Shares.** There are number of ways why the tokenisation of fund units/shares benefits investors and fund managers alike. First, tokenisation allows for the use of smart contracts that automates the process of settling a translation. This leads to larger trading volumes and increased liquidity on the secondary markets. In particular, for non-liquid AIFs this can be of benefit, as these shares/units are highly illiquid and investors have to wait for years to exit. Those fund units/shares are, usually, not listed and transfer of fund units/shares may take days or weeks. A pre-condition for this, however, is that the fund documentation of the respective funds allows for secondary transactions. Tokenised fund units/shares can be listed on an exchange or traded over-the-counter.

---

[64] ALFI, 'Digital/Fintech White Paper – Digital Fund Distribution: Recommendations for the Luxembourg Fund Industry' (2018), 34, available at https://beck-link.de/2h7p7 (accessed 26.08.2021).

Second, **tokenisation of fund units/shares** does not only enhance liquidity, but also is 62
attractive to investors due to the increased transaction speed and enhanced liquidity. It
could, if allowed by fund laws of individual Member States, open up illiquid funds to a
broader investor base. Tokenisation make illiquid asset classes liquid and the increased
'fractioning' element of tokenisation on the investor-fund side and at the level of the
investments could even lead to regulatory changes that would allow a large base of retail
investors. Regulators could, for instance, allow retail investors other than 'high-net-worth-
individuals' to invest in funds investing in traditional 'illiquid' asset classes, such as
private equity and real estate, thereby broadening the investor base. This, however, only
provided that the funds would have a minimum degree of (secondary market) liquidity.

Third, tokenisation allows smart contracts to track fund ownership and automatically 63
update all data. This helps fund managers complying with investor management and
corresponding reporting.

Finally, tokenisation of fund units/shares helps fund managers to establish a direct 64
relationship with investors by executing corporate transactions with no intermediaries
(→ para. 60 et seq.).

b) Legal Form Neutrality under the AIFMD and UCITSD. The scope of the 64
AIFMD and UCITSD are '**legal form neutral**'. The rationale behind this is that the
type of legal form in fund governance is, to a large extent, irrelevant from an investor
and market protection point of view.[65] Both the AIFMD and UCITSD, therefore, allow
Member States to regulate the legal forms for their funds in their national laws. Both the
AIFMD and UCITSD, however, indicate what legal forms may be regulated by Member
States. Recital 6 and Art. 2(2)(b) AIFMD state that for the scope of the AIFMD it is of
no significance '*whether the AIF is constituted under the law of contract, under trust law,
under statute, or has any other legal form*'. Similarly, the UCITSD also applies a legal
form neutral approach. Under Art. 1(3) UCITSD, UCITS may be constituted in
accordance with contract law (as common funds managed by management companies),
trust law (as unit trusts), or statute (as investment companies).[66] UCITS may thus be
established as a common fund, a unit trust and an investment company. The AIFMD, in
addition to the above-mentioned three legal forms, also allows other legal forms to be
employed. In practice, these are investment limited (liability) partnerships.[67] The scope
of the legal forms that Member States may use, is thus under the AIFMD broader than
under the UCITSD.

What legal forms are allowed to be employed for AIFs and UCITS depends upon the 65
AIFMD and UCITSD implementation laws of the individual Member States. Continental jurisdictions, such as Luxembourg, often offer all legal forms other than the unit
trust.[68] Member States with a common law tradition, such as Ireland and Malta,
(increasingly) offer all four legal forms.[69]

---

[65] Zetzsche 'Die Irrelevanz und Konvergenz des Organisationsstatuts von Investmentfonds' (2012) 111 *Zeitschrift für vergleichende Rechtswissenschaften*, 382.

[66] See also Recital 12 UCITSD that refers, with regard to portfolio management, to the management of unit trusts/common funds or investment companies.

[67] See, for example, in Liechtenstein for the Anlage-Kommanditgesellschaft ('investment limited partnership'): Art. 10 et seq. AIFMG and for the Anlage-Kommanditärengesellschaft ('limited liability partnership'): Art. 14 AIFMG; See for Luxembourg: Art. 1 SICAR Law.

[68] Common funds were developed in both German and Suisse law because the unit trust was not available. See Müller, Die Rechtsstellung der Depotbank im Investmentgeschäft nach deutschem und schweizerischem Recht (1969).

[69] Zetzsche and Veidt, 'The AIFMD's Third-Country Rules and the Equivalence Concept', in Zetzsche (ed.) The Alternative Investment Fund Managers Directive – European Regulation of Alternative Investment Funds, 32 et seq.

66 There are not only differences between Member States in what legal forms are available in their national laws, but also in the approach taken in how these are regulated. Contrary to most other Member States, legal forms in the Netherlands are, with some minor exceptions, mostly governed by private law. Dutch common funds are governed by contract law, investment companies (such as the Dutch N.V. and B.V), by corporate and the limited partnership by Dutch commercial law. EU Member States, such as Germany, France, Ireland, Liechtenstein and Luxembourg regulate their legal forms that are allowed to be employed by AIFs and UCITS fully or partially in the form of 'lex specialis' provisions in their fund legislation.[70] This 'lex specialis approach' is in line with the concept of legal form neutrality that is being applied by the AIFMD and UCITSD and, therefore, suits fund governance better. It, therefore, depends upon the laws of the individual Member States whether tokenisation of fund 'units' and 'shares' are allowed. Depending upon the Member State in question, this is regulated either in their fund legislation, the private/commercial law provisions to which the fund legislation makes reference or 'plain' private/commercial law.

67 c) 'Units' (and 'Shares') under the AIFMD and UCITSD. To determine whether the tokenisation of 'units' and 'shares' is possible, it worthwhile to first investigate what 'units' and 'shares' under the AIFMD and UCITSD are.

68 aa) 'Units' (and 'Shares') under the AIFMD. The terms 'units' and 'shares' are often referred to in the AIFMD and the AIFMR under various provisions. Both terms are, however, not under the AIFMD nor any other EU legislative documents defined. The reason for this is that the AIFMD is 'legal form neutral'. Art. 2(2) AIFMD not only confirms that the legal form 'shall be of no significance for the application of the AIFMD' but also that AIFs may be 'constituted under the law of contract, under trust law, under statute, or has any other legal form'. Under the AIFMD, collective investment undertakings may, thus, be set up as common funds, unit trusts, investment companies or 'any other legal form'. Limited partnerships, such as the Luxembourg SCSp, qualify as 'any other legal form'. The AIFMD leaves discretion to EU Member States to determine and retain the national requirements 'for AIFs with registered office in their territory'. Recital 10 AIFMD states that '[…] it would be disproportionate to regulate the structure or composition of the portfolios of AIFs managed by AIFMs at Union level and it would be difficult to provide for such extensive harmonisation due to the very diverse types of AIFs managed by AIFMs. This Directive therefore does not prevent Member States from adopting or from continuing to apply national requirements in respect of AIFs established in their territory […].' Recital 10 AIFMD, thus, confirms that the details of legal forms remain a national matter. Individual Member States may, thus, adopt national legislation in which they regulate legal forms. Apart from the indication that common funds, unit trusts, investment companies or 'any other legal form' are allowed, there are no restrictions. As there are no definitions of the terms 'units' and 'shares' under the AIFMD, individual Member States, thus, decide upon the specific features of the legal forms they allow AIFs to be established in, including what constitutes 'units' and 'shares' under national law. Any specific features determined, however, must comply with the material AIF definition and the requirements related to these 'units' and 'shares' under the AIFMD.

69 bb) 'Units' (and 'Shares') under the UCITSD. In contrast to AIFs, the UCITSD provides more guidance on what 'shares' and 'units' are. Under Recital 7 UCITSD 'units

---

[70] Hooghiemstra, 'Towards Modernization of the Luxembourg Legal Form 'Toolbox' for Funds' (December 2019), available at https://ssrn.com/abstract=3509731 (accessed 26.08.2021).

§ 15. Crypto Assets & Funds

of UCITS are considered to be financial instruments for the purposes of *MiFID2* [emphasis added by author].' Art. 1(3) UCITSD determines that 'units' of UCITS shall also include shares of UCITS. Both shares and units are, thus, qualifying as financial instruments under MiFID2. In addition, Art. 1(3) UCITSD determines that 'the undertakings referred to in paragraph 2 may be constituted in accordance with <u>contract law</u> (as common funds managed by management companies), <u>trust law</u> (as unit trusts), or <u>statute</u> (as investment companies) [...].' The legal forms of UCITS are, thus, under the national laws of the individual Member States restricted to common funds, unit trusts, and investment companies. Recital 12 UCITSD further determines that: '[...] where a management company distributes the units of its own harmonised unit trusts/common funds or shares of its own harmonised investment companies in [...].' 'Units' are, thus, related to unit trusts and common funds, whereas investment companies issue 'shares'. The specific features of the legal forms with respect to both AIFs and UCITS are being left over to the laws of the individual Member States.

d) The Issuance of Crypto Assets by AIFs/UCITS under the AIFMD and UCITSD. 70
aa) The Issuance of 'Crypto-Units' and 'Crypto-Shares' by AIFs & UCITS. Although the AIF definition in Art. 4(1)(a) AIFMD does not refer to 'units or shares', many other AIFMD provisions use the term. This concerns in particular to the term 'marketing'. Under Art. 4(1)(x) of the AIFMD 'marketing' means 'a direct or indirect offering or placement, at the initiative of the AIFM or on behalf of the AIFM of units or shares of an AIF it manages to or with investors domiciled or with a registered office in the EU Union.'

In delineating, AIFs from securitisation special purpose entities ('**SSPEs**'), the EU 71 Commission in its AIFMD Q&A has indirectly adopted a *formal approach* by referring to the equity characteristic of an AIF's 'shares or units'. The EU Commission notes that '[...] the term 'units and shares' [of an AIF] to be generic and inclusive of other forms of equity of the fund, i.e. a stock or any other security representing an ownership interest in the fund.'

Several Competent Authorities have both given guidance as to what legal/economic 72 features instruments issued by AIFs/UCITS need to have in order to qualify as 'ownership interests'.[71] Notes issued by SSPEs, in general, are falling outside of the scope of the AIFMD. Certain types of subordinated and/or variable interest notes having some 'ownership interest characteristics' may, however, qualify as 'units/shares' under the AIFMD.

In this respect, it is important to note that units/shares issued by AIFs (and UCITS) 73 qualify as financial instruments under MiFID2 that may under a pending proposal also be issued by means of DLT. It can thus be concluded that AIFs, at the minimum, need to issue units/shares that represent 'ownership interests' in the AIF. The same is to be assumed for UCITS.

bb) The Issuance of Crypto Assets other than 'Units' and 'Shares' by AIFs/UCITS? 74
The AIFMD nor the UCITSD explicitly prohibit AIFs and UCITS from issuing instruments other than 'units and shares'. The Member State laws that exclusively regulate the legal forms in which AIFs and UCITS may be established regulate what instruments the undertaking may issue. In practice, some AIFs also issue bonds.[72] Such

---

[71] Zetzsche and Hooghiemstra, 'Securitizations and SPVs under the STSR and AIFMD', in: Zetzsche (ed.), The Alternative Investment Fund Managers Directive – European Regulation of Alternative Investment Funds.
[72] Kremer and Lebbe, Collective Investment Schemes in Luxembourg – Law and Practice (Oxford University Press, 2nd edn, 2014), 314 et seq.

issues are allowed, provided that the AIF complies with restrictions in terms of employing leverage, as determined in the PPM or prospectus of the AIF concerned.

75 Although not explicitly prohibited by the AIFMD or UCITSD, most Member State laws regulating the legal form of UCITS and AIFs nor regulators for those funds requiring approval will allow crypto assets, such as utility or asset-referenced tokens, to be issued.

76 **e) Tokenised Fund 'Units' & 'Shares' under the Member State Laws.** EU Member States vary in the degree to which Fund Forms laid down in regulatory law substitute private law and, correspondingly, also whether the 'units' or 'shares' issued (on the DLT) by those Fund Forms are regulated by regulatory, private law or both. In the Netherlands, for instance, Fund Forms employed by AIFs and UCITS are solely laid down in commercial and corporate law. Dutch law only contains limited derogations from corporate law provisions for 'open-end investment companies' and (limited) regulation for 'independent management companies' (that are not AIFMs nor UCITS ManCos) acting on behalf of common funds. Consequently, whether Fund Forms in the Netherlands may issue **'crypto-units' or 'crypto-shares'** is fully determined by Dutch private and commercial law. At the other side of the 'spectrum' is Liechtenstein in which all Fund Forms, including unit trusts, investment companies, common funds and investment limited (liability) partnerships, are primarily regulated by Fund Forms laid down in 'fund law'. Furthermore, Fund Forms in Liechtenstein are only subject to private law to the extent that parties in their articles of association, trust deed or management regulations have not made use of their 'freedom to contract' with respect to the elements that the law requires them to do so.[73]

77 Similar to Luxembourg, France, Germany and Ireland take a position in between.[74] They regulate their Fund Forms for AIFs and UCITS in their fund laws, but make reference to certain private law rules, such as, for example, corporate law for investment companies. It goes beyond the scope of this contribution to analyse all the above-mentioned legal regimes in detail to answer the question whether 'units' or 'shares' of AIFs and UCITS in the above-mentioned Member States may be tokenised or not.[75]

78 The general message this section intends to convey is that the answer to this question depends upon the laws of in the individual Member States. Furthermore, it also depends upon the extent to which private/commercial law is derogated by regulatory law in the individual Member States whether regulatory, private/commercial law or both determine whether 'units' or 'shares' of Fund Forms in that Member States may be tokenised or not.

79 **f) Forms of Units/Shares.** In continental EU jurisdictions, units and shares, generally, can be issued in various forms. For common funds, the rights of units are, usually, in fund legislation 'by analogy' being determined in accordance with the rights for securities in private law.[76] For (limited) partnerships, fund legislation or partnership

---

[73] Zetzsche and Preiner, 'Das liechtensteinische AIFM-Gesetz: Die erste Umsetzung der europäischen AIFM-Richtlinie' (2013) 59 *Recht der internationalen Wirtschaft*, 265.

[74] Zetzsche 'Fondsregulierung im Umbruch – ein rechtsvergleichender Rundblick zur Umsetzung der AIFM-Richtlinie' (2014) 26 *Zeitschrift für Bankrecht und Bankwirtschaft*, 22 (32).

[75] See for an overview of these countries: Zetzsche, 'Fondsregulierung im Umbruch – ein rechtsvergleichender Rundblick zur Umsetzung der AIFM-Richtlinie' (2014) 26 *Zeitschrift für Bankrecht und Bankwirtschaft*, 22 (32); Wegman, Investor Protection. Towards Additional EU Regulation of Investment Funds? (2016).

[76] See, for example, for UCITS in Luxembourg established in the form of a common fund ('FCP'): Art. 10 Law of 17.12.2010 relating to undertakings for collective investment, as amended.

law, in general, refers to the rights and obligations of 'partnership interests' under the commercial laws of individual Member States. Apart from this, certain Member States, such as Luxembourg[77], allow (limited) partnerships also to issue securities.

Those units/shares allowed under the individual Member State laws to be issued in **80** the **forms of securities** may generally be (i) materialised securities or bearer securities, (ii) dematerialised securities or (iii) registered securities.[78]

aa) Materialised Securities or Bearer Securities. Materialised securities are also **81** known as bearer securities. They are issued by materializing the underlying rights. The rights and obligations of the securities were, in accordance with Savigny's incorporation theory[79], printed on the paper and the transfer of these rights was then made by delivery of the physical paper to the acquirer. Certain Member States, such as Luxembourg, issued immobilisation (or even dematerialisation) laws over the past few decades, which requires materialised securities to be deposited with a central securities depositary central securities depositary ('**CSD**') that creates a register entry for the securities holder. When immobilizing securities, a global certificate is deposited with a CSD and securities are transferred by way of crediting/debiting securities of the securities accounts held by 'account keepers' that have, in its turn, an account with the CSD in which the securities were originally issued.

Under the Regulation (EU) No. 909/2014 on improving securities settlement in the **82** European Union and on central securities depositaries ('**CSDR**')[80], current holders of paper securities, as long as they do not sell them through a regulated trading venue, will have the possibility to keep them in paper form until 2025.[81]

bb) Dematerialised Securities. Dematerialised securities have been introduced in **83** most EU Member States in the past few decades. In general, securities are issued through a CSD that enters the number of securities transferred to the security holder directly in a securities account. The 'dematerialised securities' are then – directly or indirectly – transferred by means of book-entry transfer between security accounts maintained by CSDs. In some Member States, security holders may directly hold a securities account with a CSD in other Member States security holders have an account with a custodian that, in its turn, holds an account with a CSD.

Over the past two years, various legislators in Europe, such as Luxembourg, Poland **84** and Germany, have (made plans to) put into place laws that clarify that securities account entries may also be made via DLT.[82] CSDs are – in most proposals/laws – still the primary constituency that is responsible for the issuance of dematerialised

---

[77] Partsch and Boyer, 'La Société en Commandite Simple – Constitution et Gouvernance', in: Boyer, Coribisier, Dusemon, Mischo, Panichi, Partsch, Pogorzelski, Schleimer, Schummer and Steichen (eds), Les Commandites en Droit Luxembourgeois.
[78] Bundesverband Investment und Asset Management e.V. (Federal Association of Investment and Asset Management), 'Stellungnahme des BVI zum Referentenentwurf eines Gesetzes zum Referentenentwurf eines Gesetzes zur Einführung von elektronischen Wertpapieren (eWpG)' (September 2020), available at https://beck-link.de/ycfv4 (accessed 26.08.2021).
[79] Von Savigny, System des heutigen Römischen Rechts (1840), 213.
[80] Regulation (EU) No 909/2014 on improving securities settlement in the European Union and on central securities depositaries and amending Directives 98/26/EC and 2014/65/EU and Regulation (EU) No 236/2012, OJ L 257, 28.8.2014 p. 1–72, as amended.
[81] Art. 76(2) CSDR.
[82] See for Germany: Auffenberg, 'Draft Legislation for Introduction of Electronic Securities – What will Be the Major Changes?' (2020), available at https://beck-link.de/c864a (accessed 26.08.2021); See for Luxembourg: EHP, 'Luxembourg's confirmation that securities can be held through DLT-like technologies, including blockchains!', (2019), available at https://beck-link.de/6tzvh (accessed 26.08.2021); See for Poland: Czarnecki, 'Dematerialisation of securities in Poland: Chaos or a brilliant plan?', (2020), available at https://beck-link.de/4pab8 (accessed 26.08.2021).

securities. It is, however, expected that, in line with the 'DLT Pilot Regulation'[83], the CSD's role in issuing the primary issuance of securities will be 'de-monopolised' and other entities, such as DLT MTFs and DLT securities settlement systems (→ para. 175 et seq.).

85   **cc) Registered Securities. Registered securities** are created by the issuer through the opening of a register of security holders. Contrary to dematerialised securities, the register can, generally, be held by the issuing company itself. Registered securities are transferred by inscribing the acquirer as the new holder into the securities register.

86   It depends upon the laws of the individual Member States whether issuing companies are free to provide for the issuance and transfer process in the statutory documents of the companies.

87   Various Member States, such as Luxembourg, allow for this.[84] Till now, most funds issuing tokenised shares/units were in the form of registered securities. Most likely, this is the case as shareholder registers under various Member State laws are already allowed to be issued/kept on DLT.

88   The issuance and transfer of registered securities through a 'token-based' shareholder register allows the fund manager to (i) keep track of their shareholders and (ii) allows to provide them for proof of ownership of the rights reflected by the registered securities. On top of this, shareholder registers held through DLT:
– saves transaction history on the blockchain;
– corresponding smart contracts linked to the DLT verify all transactions in which tokens are being transferred from one public address to the other and that are signed with a private key that is linked to the relevant wallets; and
– smart contracts with certain actions can be programmed (e.g. issuance/redemption of shares/units).

89   For that purpose, the register has to contain certain information with regard to the investors, including:
– The identity and details of the actual investors (holders of the transferable securities);
– The balance of the registered securities of each investors or holder of the transferable securities; and
– The transaction history.

90   In the investment fund context, the identity and details of the investors are often contained in a so-called whitelisting contract which ensures that only public keys of verified investors may receive tokens issued by a fund. In such cases, tokens serve no other purpose as to represent the balance of the registered securities held by such investors.

91   This so-called Whitelist ensures fund shares/units may only be distributed by the fund manager or other investors to investors that (i) have been identified/verified for KYC purposes, (ii) that meet the required investor classification ((semi-)professional investor) and (iii) have been classified for tax purposes.

92   The **Whitelist** is a register in which wallet addresses are being managed. This register is connected to a smart contract that monitors by technical means that tokenised units/shares only can be transferred to those Wallet addresses which are

---

[83] Proposal for a Regulation of the European Parliament and of the Council on a pilot regime for market infrastructures based on distributed ledger technology, Commission, 'Proposal for a Regulation of the European Parliament and of the Council on a pilot regime for market infrastructures based on distributed ledger technology' COM (2020) 594 final, ('DLT Market Infrastructure Regulation').

[84] Seidl, 'The True Value of Security Tokens Lies in their Proof of Ownership – An analysis of Luxembourg securities laws and how they may be applied to serve decentralized finance solutions without the need of major changes in the laws', available at https://stokr.io/ (accessed 26.08.2021).

included in the Whitelist. A wallet address of an investor is only included in the Whitelist when:
- it has been verified that the investor has the power of disposal over that wallet address;
- the investor has been, prior to the acquisition of the tokenised unit/share, identified/verified for KYC purposes by the fund manager, distributor or the transfer agent; and
- the investor has been classified for investor classification purposes.

93 Tokenised units/shares can only be transferred to investors to wallet addresses that are included in the Whitelist. Apart from the identification/verification of the identity of investors, the Whitelist function also ensures that tokenised units/shares are only distributed to investors that meet the investor classification requirements of the fund in question in case the fund only allows (semi)professional investors to invest in a certain fund.

94 The smart contracts as well as the Whitelist smart contracts used for tokenised units/shares are often based upon Ethereum or the Liquid Network. When investors are receiving tokenised units/shares, a smart contract verifies whether the investor wallet ('public key') is on the Whitelist. If this is not the case, the transaction is not being executed.

95 Upon **identification/verification** of an investor for AML purposes and upon classification of the status of the investor, the correspondent wallet address is being included on the fund's Whitelist. The fund manager (or transfer agent on behalf of the fund manager) may then mine (issue) a new tokenised share/unit and transfer this to the investor. The Whitelist function ensures that the investors receiving the tokenised units/shares are at all times identified. Furthermore, the Whitelist serves as a basis for the shareholders register that is being kept on the blockchain.

96 As only verified investors are entered into the Whitelist, any transfer of the tokens is visible to the fund manager or the transfer agent that holds the shareholders register on behalf of the fund manager. The permission-less blockchain allows to see the total transaction history relating to the specific registered securities. To comply with EU privacy legislation (e.g. GDPR[85]), personal and confidential data may be saved on a central secure server that is separate from the shareholders register on the blockchain. The transaction data may still be readout by the blockchain itself, but personal and confidential data may be simply connected via a whitelisting contract with the blockchain where the transactions are verified.

97 To execute a redemption order in the case of open-end funds, investors notify the depositary of their redemption request. The depositary informs the fund manager of the redemption request of the investor. Based upon the NAV calculation of the fund manager or its administrative agent on this behalf, the value of the tokenised units/shares to be redeemed is being determined. The depositary notifies the investor of the redemption Walletaddress to which he has to transfer the corresponding tokenised shares/units that he wants to redeem in order activate the forward pricing process.

98 After the tokenised units/shares have been transferred by the investor to the redemption **Walletaddress**, the investor will receive the corresponding amount on its bank account. At the same time, the depositary initiates a transaction through a smart contract in which the tokenised units/shares that are being transferred to the redemption Walletaddress are being 'burned'. Through this process, the tokenised shares/units that have been transferred to the 'redemption Walletaddress' will be 'deleted'.

---

[85] Regulation (EU) No. 2016/679 of the European Parliament and of the Council of 27 April 2016 on the protection of natural persons with regard to the processing of personal data and on the free movement of such data, and repealing Directive 95/46/EC, OJ L 119, 4.5.2016 p. 1–88, as amended ('GDPR').

99 Furthermore, the fund manager itself or a transfer agent on his behalf has the 'ownership function' over the smart contract. Due to this 'ownership function', the fund manager or the transfer agent on his behalf may, for example, enforce any court judgement. The shareholder register evidences that the token legally represents the shareholdings of the investors.

100 **g) Exclusion from the Scope of the (Draft) MiCAR.** When issuing tokenised shares/units of AIFs and UCITS, the question arises whether AIFMs, UCITS ManCos, AIFs or UCITS fall within the scope of the **MiCAR**. The MiCAR applies to entities engaged in the issuance of crypto assets and services related to crypto assets in the EU. Art. 2(3) MiCAR exempts certain entities and persons from its scope. These include the following entities and persons:
– the EU Central Bank and national central banks when acting in their capacity as monetary authority or other public authorities;
– insurance undertakings or undertakings carrying out the reinsurance and retrocession activities referred to in EMI 2[86] when carrying out the activities referred to in EMI 2;
– a liquidator or an administrator acting in the course of insolvency procedure, except for the purpose of Art. 42 MiCAR ('orderly wind-down');
– persons who provide crypto asset services exclusively for their parent companies, for their subsidiaries or for other subsidiaries of their parent companies;
– the EU investment bank ('**EIB**');
– the EU Financial Stability Facility and the EU Stability Mechanism; and
– public international organisations.

101 AIFMs, UCITS ManCos nor the AIFs and UCITS managed by them qualify as any of the entities and persons listed and are therefore not 'per se' exempted from its scope.

102 Furthermore, Art. 2(4)-(6) MiCAR contain various (partial) exemptions from obtaining a license and/or certain operational requirements under the MiCAR as an issuer of asset-referenced tokens[87], electronic money tokens and crypto asset service providers for credit institutions, investment firms or E-money institutions ('**EMIs**').

103 AIFMs, UCITS ManCos nor the AIFs and UCITS managed by them may obtain a license as a credit institution, investment firm or an E-money institution. Under the AIFMD nor the UCITSD, it is not allowed for any of these entities to obtain a parallel license as a credit institution under CRD V, an investment firm under MiFID2 or an E-money institution under EMD2.

104 Under Art. 2(2) MiCAR, however, the regulation also does not apply to 'crypto assets' that qualify as:
– financial instruments within the meaning of Art. 4(1)(15) MiFID2;
– electronic money within the meaning of Art. 2(2) EMD2, except if they qualify as an electronic money token under this Regulation;
– deposits within the meaning of Art. 2(1)(3) of Directive 2014/49/EU ('**DGSD**');
– structured deposits within the meaning of Art. 4(1)(43) MiFID2; or
– securitisation within the meaning of Art. 2(1) of Regulation (EU) 2017/2402 ('**STSR**').

105 Art. 3(1) No. 2 MiCAR defines 'crypto assets' as
'a digital representation of value or rights, which may be transferred and stored electronically, using distributed ledger or similar technology'.

---

[86] Directive 2009/138/EC on taking up and pursuit of the business of Insurance and Reinsurance (Solvency II), OJ L 335, 17.12.2009 p. 1–155, as amended ('EMD2').

[87] Under Art. 3(1) No. 3 MiCAR, an 'asset-referenced token' means a type of crypto-asset that purports to maintain a stable value by referring to the value of several fiat currencies that are legal tender, one or several commodities or one or several crypto-assets, or a combination of such assets.

§ 15. Crypto Assets & Funds

106 Materially speaking, units/shares of AIFs and UCITS fall within the ambit of the definition of 'crypto assets'. In this respect, Recital 6 MiCAR clarifies that MiCAR excludes from its scope crypto assets that qualify as financial instruments. In the view of the EU legislator, EU financial service legislation should not give a particular technology an advantage over another. Crypto assets that qualify as 'financial instruments' or 'electronic money' should remain regulated under existing EU legislation, such as MiFID2 and EMD2, regardless of the technology used for their issuance or their transfer.

107 Both units and shares of AIFs and UCITS qualify as 'financial instrument' under Section C, Annex I MiFID2. No. 3, Section C, Annex I MiFID2 includes all 'units in collective undertakings'. Both AIFs and UCITS, indisputably, qualify as such under MiFID2.

108 AIFMs, UCITS ManCos, AIFs and UCITS when marketing tokenised units/shares of UCITS and AIFs to investors are thus all exempted from the scope of the MiCAR, as such units/shares qualify as 'financial instruments' under MiFID2.

2. Impact on Distribution – From a B2B2C to D2C Model

109 DLT will have a significant impact on fund distribution. As both fund administration and distribution are intertwined, a large part of the impact on distribution (process) has already been discussed in → para. 51 et seq.[88] Furthermore, fund distribution platforms often act as intermediaries between fund managers, their distributors and perform order touring, commission computation, as well as, other compliance and operational services.

110 In general, EU fund distribution chains consist of various commercial and operational intermediaries. Till now, the distribution model in Europe is primarily B2B2C (business-to-business-to-consumers. In other words, asset managers mostly distribute funds via distributors such as banks, financial advisers and insurance intermediaries.[89]

111 The **D2C (direct-to-consumer) model** is not as widespread in Europe as, for example, in the US.[90] Various reasons for that are that brand awareness is low in the EU retail market and fund manager often have strong connections with distribution partners with whom they do not want to directly compete. Furthermore, fund managers do not always have the fund administrative capacity of managing a large number of investor accounts and transactions.

112 It is, however, to be expected that DLT-based platforms, such as FundsDLT, will allow more and more fund managers to distribute their funds directly to investors. DLT fund distribution platforms achieve disintermediation by reducing the number of counterparties involved in the distribution process thereby reducing the cost of fund distribution. Furthermore, the D2C model has as its advantage that fund managers may be able to develop better products that are aligned with the right client segment and meet the needs of those investors (e.g. product governance).

113 The adoption of the D2C model also depends upon the success of robo-advisers, i.e. online platforms providing algorithm-driven asset allocation and financial planning services.[91] This would allow to facilitate the commercialisation of the D2C model which – by nature – targets middle- or low-wealth investors. The combination of DLT distribution

---

[88] ALFI, 'Digital/Fintech White Paper – Digital Fund Distribution: Recommendations for the Luxembourg Fund Industry', (2018), 8, available https://beck-link.de/2h7p7 (accessed 26.08.2021).
[89] Ibid.
[90] Ibid, 10.
[91] Ibid, 19.

model and the implementation of robo-advisors would lead to a radical reduction of costs allowing market players to offer more refined investment services.[92]

VI. 'Non-Core Services': (MiFID II &) MiCAR Portfolio Management Services?

114 As discussed in → para. 43 et seq., both the AIFMD and the UCITSD allow ManCos to perform certain additional 'MiFID II portfolio management services' in addition to the management and marketing of AIFs and UCITS (as applicable). ManCos are restricted in the type of investment services/activities that they may perform. Under the 'same activity – same treatment' principle[93], a few additional rules are applicable to ManCos assuming the additional MiFID2 portfolio management services under the AIFMD and UCITSD, mainly prompted by the desire of the EU legislator to protect individual investors.[94] The recent MiCAR proposal allows investment firms to provide certain crypto asset services without obtaining an additional license. The question is whether AIFMs and UCITS ManCos may also provide crypto asset services without obtaining an additional license that are under MiCAR deemed equivalent to the MiFID2 portfolio management services they may provide under the AIFMD and UCITSD.

115 In principle, AIFMs and UCITS ManCos are not exempted from the scope of MiCAR. Under Art. 2(6) MiCAR, **investment firms** authorised under MiFID2 are not required to be authorised as a 'crypto-service provider'[95], where they provide one or several crypto asset services equivalent to the investment services and activities for which they are authorised under MiFID2. For that purpose, *inter alia*, the following services allowed to be performed as 'ancillary services' by AIFMs and UCITS ManCos, in addition to portfolio management, are deemed equivalent by MiCAR:
- 'the **reception and transmission of orders for crypto assets** on behalf of third parties' under Art. 3(1) No. 11 MiCAR are deemed to be equivalent to 'the reception and transmission of orders in relation to one or more financial instruments under point (1) of Section A of Annex I MiFID2' ('**MiCAR RTO**');[96] and
- 'the **advice on crypto assets**' under Art. 3(1) No. 17 MiCAR are deemed to be equivalent to 'investment advice' under point (5) of Section A of Annex I MiFID2.

116 With respect to the above, the MiCAR, the AIFMD nor the UCITSD clarify whether AIFMs (and UCITS ManCos) authorised to provide investment advice and the reception and transmission of orders in relation to one or more 'financial instruments' are also allowed to provide these services with respect to 'crypto assets'.

117 In the first place, it is clear that AIFMs nor UCITS ManCos would be allowed to provide any 'crypto assets service' other than these two. The text of the AIFMD, the UCITSD nor the MiCAR provides for this. Apart from that, AIFMs and UCITS ManCos are not qualifying as 'investment firms authorised under MiFID2'. They, however, are subject to all MiFID2 rules applying to the above-mentioned two services. In this respect, it would be consistent to consider, in particular, AIFMs to be materially qualifying for this. AIFMs may, in principle, invest in any type of

---

[92] Ibid, 20.
[93] Kremer and Lebbe, Collective Investment Schemes in Luxembourg – Law and Practice (Oxford University Press, 2nd edn, 2014), 314.
[94] Ibid, 315.
[95] Art. 3(1) No. 8 MiCAR.
[96] Art. 2(6)(e) MiCAR.

asset class, provided that they are authorised for that type of asset class. It would be a consistent approach of the EU legislator to allow AIFMs to also provide these services under the MiCAR.

118 A second question would be whether AIFMs (with or without UCITS ManCo license) would be deemed to be equivalent to an 'investment firm authorised under MiFID2' or would need to obtain a separate license as 'crypto asset service provider'. Given that AIFMs (and UCITS ManCos) are subject to all MiFID2 rules of the services that are deemed to be equivalent, it would logical if the EU legislator would allow AIFMs to perform those two services under MiCAR without obtaining an additional authorisation under that regulation.

119 This approach would be consistent with Recital 54 MiCAR that states that some firms are subject to high regulatory standards under EU financial services regulation and, therefore, should be allowed to provide crypto asset services without authorisation under MiCAR. In this respect, Recital 54 MiCAR mentions credit institutions and investment firms authorised under MiFID2 that should be allowed to provide such services across the EU, where they are authorised to provide one or several investment services under MiFID2 which are similar to the crypto asset services they intend to provide.

120 Similar to investment firms, however, they would need to be required to comply with the 'lex specialis' provisions under Art. 72 MiCAR (for 'reception and transmission of orders related to crypto assets') and Art. 73 MiCAR ('advice on crypto assets'). In practice, this would mean that they would need to 'top-up' their policy documents to the extent that they diverge from MiFID2. For providing AIFMs providing MiCAR RTO in relation to 'crypto assets' that would imply that AIFMs:[97]
- would have to establish and implement procedures and arrangements which provide for the prompt and proper transmission of client's orders for execution on a trading platform for crypto assets or to another crypto asset service provider;
- shall not receive any remuneration, discount or non-monetary benefit for routing clients' orders received from clients to a particular trading platform for crypto assets or to another crypto asset service provider;
- shall not misuse information relating to pending clients' orders, and shall take all reasonable steps to prevent the misuse of such information by any of their employees
- For AIFMs providing investment advice with respect to crypto assets, this would imply that they would need to comply with the following requirements:[98]
- AIFMs will have to assess the compatibility of such crypto assets with the needs of the clients and recommend them only when this is in the interest of the clients ('demand and needs') and request information, inter alia, regarding the (prospective) client's knowledge and financial situation;
- AIFMs will ensure that natural persons giving advice or information about crypto assets or a crypto asset service on their behalf possess the necessary knowledge and experience to fulfill their obligations ('suitability requirement'); and
- AIFMs will have to issue a warning to (prospective) clients that the crypto assets or crypto asset services are inappropriate for them and issue them a warning when they do not provide the AIFM with the information requested by the AIFM and clients have to acknowledge that they understood the warning issued by the AIFM.

---

[97] Art. 72 MiCAR.
[98] Art. 73 MiCAR.

121 Allowing AIFMs authorised for portfolio management services to provide the MiCAR RTO and crypto asset advice services would be consistent with the AIFMD and UCITSD, at the one, and the MiCAR, at the other hand.

D. Product regulation: Investing in Tokenised Assets

I. The Benefits of Investing in Tokenised Assets for Funds

122 Often overlooked is that tokenisation is not something in itself that leads to the (r)evolution of the asset management industry. It is one of the factors, amongst artificial intelligence, the use of APIs, data storage in a cloud and data analytics, that are a driving force behind the digitisation of the asset management industry.

123 Although there are many benefits associated with **tokenised assets**, the most important ones for illiquid assets, such as real estate and any other hard assets, are the 'fractionalisation' that leads to more liquidity and the development of secondary markets, and digitisation of the process involving transfer of ownership. In this respect, 'fractional ownership'[99] of illiquid and hard assets is not new. Over the past few decades, debt claims, for instance, have been transferred to securitisation special purpose vehicles to make them more tradable. In real estate, all types of 'fractional ownership', such as time shares, joint ownership and syndication, have emerged over the years.[100] What is new is that through tokenisation a new generation of fractional ownership structures employing DLT and, in some cases, centralised, regulated exchanges emerge.

124 So far, some claim the tokenisation of illiquid and hard assets and the emergence of more liquid secondary markets to be disappointing.[101] One of the reasons for that is that, legally speaking, the ownership of hard and illiquid assets is typically transferred by means of a public register or assignment. The adoption of governments of public registers on the DLT is in its infancy.[102] Indeed, hard and illiquid assets could be made liquid and secondary markets could involve. Governments would, however, first need to legally allow for the transfer of their ownership through DLT in order to facilitate this.

125 Till then, illiquid and hard assets will be, as currently is the case, typically, held through SPVs. Currently, various EU Member States, such as Germany, Liechtenstein and Luxembourg, allow for or consider to allow registered and dematerialised securities to be issued and held through the DLT. EU initiatives, such as the DLT Market Infrastructure Regulation are likely to have a big impact on the real time settlement of securities. Other than initially expected, DLT is likely to improve the clearing and settlement of securities for investors, such as investment funds, before it will be – more broadly – adopted for other types of assets as well. An explanation for this current development could be that securities (on the public markets) are, by their nature, already standardised, fungible and transferable, which make the broad adoption of standardised DLT technology easier.

---

[99] A method in which several unrelated parties can share in, and mitigate the risk of, ownership of a high-value tangible asset, usually a jet, yacht or piece of resort real estate.

[100] University of Oxford, 'Tokenisation: the future of real estate investment?', available at https://beck-link.de/e3zpx (accessed 26.08.2021).

[101] See Wibbeke, 'Security-Token im Sachwerte-Segment – Virtuelle Vehikel verändern die Fondswelt', (Börsen-Zeitung, 21.10.2020), 8, available at https://beck-link.de/m6c6k, (accessed 26.08.2021).

[102] An exception to the rule is Liechtenstein with its Law of 3.10.2019 on Tokens and TT Service Providers ('Token and TT Service Provider Act; TVTG' → § 20).

It is evident that the more legal systems will allow assets to be tokenised, the more investors of funds will benefit from corresponding digitisation benefits, such as the employment of smart contracts.

II. AIFs

The AIFMD applies to all types of assets and investment strategies. Although this is not explicitly specified in the AIFMD itself, the application to all investment strategies follows from Art. 4(1)(a) AIFMD which does refer or restrict AIFs to certain **investment strategies**.[103] The AIFMD, therefore, allows investments in a broad range of asset classes, including, amongst others, funds investing in securities, commodities, art, wine, patents/intellectual property, private equity and venture capital investments, ships, airplanes, real estate and derivatives.[104] AIFs may, thus, in principle invest in any type of (crypto-) asset (e.g. cryptocurrencies or stable coins) provided that (i) the manager's authorisation is authorised for the type of investment strategy that the asset covers and (ii) if the AIF is authorised under a EU or national product law, such product law allows for investments in such assets.

The types of crypto assets in which AIFMs may invest, furthermore, depends upon the eligible assets requirements under the EU fund product laws, i.e. MMFR, EuVECAR, EuSEFR and ELTIFR, and national fund product laws.

In this respect, it should be noted that the AIFMD itself does not regulate the AIF as a 'product'.[105] Instead, it allows Member States itself to impose requirements in addition to those applicable under the AIFMD.[106] In Luxembourg, SICARs[107], may, for example, only invest in accordance with the notion of risk capital. In accordance with this notion, an investment by a SICAR in crypto assets must be (i) a high risk, (ii) have as an intention to develop a target entity issuing the digital asset and (iii) an investment in risk capital. A crypto asset qualifies as eligible asset under the SICAR law, provided that it fulfils these criteria.

Apart from this, the EU legislator has after the adoption of the AIFMD, for various reasons, adopted specific fund product laws. The ELTIFR was, for example, adopted to promote investments in 'long-term investments' and, allows, apart from that, also investments in UCITSD assets (which includes financial instruments), whereas the EuVECAR was adopted to stimulate the EU venture capital industry and restricts investments in financial intermediaries and listed undertakings. Furthermore, various Member States, including Luxembourg have adopted laws for AIFs restricting the eligible assets in which AIFs may invest.

The eligible assets, diversification and concentration criteria under both EU and national fund product laws have to be assessed with view to a 'substance-over-form approach'. With other words, most crypto assets (other than cryptocurrencies) are not *per se* not eligible as an investment. Instead, the assets need to be assessed based upon their substance, i.e. the underlying rights and obligations have to be assessed, to determine whether the asset in question is eligible under a EU or national product law or not.

---

[103] Zetzsche and Preiner, 'Scope of the AIFMD', in Zetzsche (ed) The Alternative Investment Fund Managers Directive – European Regulation of Alternative Investment Funds, 61.

[104] Ibid; ESMA names six categories of investment strategies, whereas the sixth category is a fallback provision, see ESMA 2012/117, No. 31.

[105] Recital 10 AIFMD.

[106] Recital 10 AIFMD.

[107] Société d'Investissement en Capital à Risque.

III. UCITS

132 UCITS are under the UCITSD restricted to invest in certain categories of eligible assets set forth by law. These include under Art. 50 UCITSD, amongst others:
- transferable securities and money market instruments admitted to or dealt in on a regulated market;
- units/shares of UCITS;
- deposits with credit institutions; and
- financial derivative instruments.

133 UCITS may either directly invest in tokenised assets, provided that qualify under any category of the above-mentioned **eligible assets**. Payment and utility assets do not qualify as such and therefore are not eligible for direct investment by UCITS.

134 Assets represented on the DLT may qualify as transferable securities for the purpose of their eligibility assessment by UCITS provided that: they present features similar to those of shares in companies, bonds, other securitised debts, or of any other securities giving the right to acquire or sell any such transferable securities, and they meet all criteria set forth by the EAD[108]. This relates to, amongst others, the maximum potential loss not exceeding the amount paid in, liquidity, valuation, available information, negotiability, etc. If these criteria are met, security tokens could, in principle, be eligible for direct investment by UCITS.

135 UCITS are, in principle, also allowed to gain indirect exposure to crypto assets. Within the UCITSD framework, they could, for example, use (delta 1) certificates or financial derivative instruments (on indices).[109] This possibility is by various regulators accepted with respect to commodities.

136 Certificates on digital assets may qualify as eligible assets for investment by a UCITS if, in addition to meeting the criteria for the qualification as transferable securities under the UCITSD:
- physical delivery of the underlying crypto assets has been excluded, and
- the dependence of the certificate on the crypto assets must be structured as a 1:1 relation (delta 1).

137 In such case, a certificate on crypto asset could qualify as an eligible asset for investment by a UCITS under the UCITSD.

138 Alternatively, financial derivative instruments (on financial indices) on crypto assets can be eligible assets for investment by UCITS under the UCITSD, provided that such indices:
- are sufficiently diversified;
- represent an adequate benchmark for the market to which they refer;
- are published in an appropriate manner; and consist of different crypto assets, i.e. they are not entirely composed of the same crypto assets.

139 Various Competent Authorities, such as Luxembourg, however, have restricted or prohibited the direct and indirect investment in risky crypto assets, such as stable coins and cryptocurrencies.[110]

---

[108] Commission Directive 2007/16/EC of 19.3.2007 implementing Council Directive 85/611/EEC on the coordination of laws, regulations and administrative provisions relating to undertakings for collective investment in transferable securities (UCITS) as regards the clarification of certain definitions, OJ L 79, 20.3.2007 p. 11–19, ('EAD').

[109] LHoFT, 'A Guide through the common Features of Digital Asset Generating Events', (2019), available at https://beck-link.de/t2emv (accessed 26.08.2021).

[110] CSSF, 'Warning against Cryptocurrencies' (2018), available at https://beck-link.de/mxc4f (accessed 26.08.2021).

E. Depositary Regulation

I. The Depositary under the AIFMD & UCITSD

The most important legal provisions with respect to depositories under the AIFMD/ UCITSD that will be affected by DLT include provisions with respect to (i) eligible entities, (ii) the safekeeping function, (iii) controlling duties, (iv) delegation and (v) liability.

1. Eligible Entities

a) **UCITSD.** Under the UCITSD, central banks, credit institutions and 'other legal entities' complying with additional prudential, organisational and capital requirements to provide sufficient guarantees are allowed to be eligible as UCITS depositaries, to the extent allowed under the laws of the individual Member States.[111]

b) **AIFMD.** Under the AIFMD, **eligible entities** may be (1) a credit institution; (2) an investment firm; (3) an eligible 'UCITSD depositary'; (4) a prime broker[112] or, for non-EEA AIFs (5) an equivalent non-EEA entity.[113]

Furthermore, many Member States under an AIFMD Member State option authorise AIFMs to allow EEA-AIFs to appoint a person or entity as depositary (e.g., a lawyer, trustee, notary or registrar) not belonging to the eligible entities as discussed above.[114]

This option is designed for closed-ended AIFs, such as private equity, venture capital and real estate funds, that generally do not invest in financial instruments. Credit institutions and investment firms have little expertise in safekeeping such assets as real estate, partnership shares, ships and physical assets (e.g., pure gold). Moreover, these assets cannot be held in bank accounts. As this option requires significant private law and corporate law expertise, the AIFMD allows specialists to carry out the safekeeping of these types of assets.

The reason why the eligible entities between the AIFMD and UCITSD vary is that under the UCITSD all UCITS are required under UCITSD product regulation to invest their assets in (listed) liquid assets that are (mostly) to be held in custody, whereas all types of funds fall within the scope of the AIFMD, including liquid, illiquid and highly-leveraged AIFs. The latter types of funds do not always invest in assets that can be held in custody.

c) **The Impact of DLT on Eligible Entities.** The adoption of DLT by the AIFMD and UCITSD will – very likely – not have an impact on the types of entities eligible as a depositary under the AIFMD and UCITSD. CRD V and MiFID2 covers most of the above-mentioned eligible entities. The recently proposed MiCAR intends to introduce a 'MiFID II-like' license for 'crypto asset service providers', which are performing services in relation to non-financial instrument crypto asset services. It is, therefore, likely that any future changes under the AIFMD, UCITSD and MiFID2 will require 'eligible entities' to adapt their organisational structure to cater for the

---

[111] Art. 23(2) UCITSD.

[112] Hooghiemstra, Depositaries in European Investment Law – Towards Harmonization in Europe (2018), 237 et seq.

[113] A prime broker can also be appointed as a depositary and is, in particular, subject to the requirements of Art. 21(4) AIFMD. See Zetzsche, 'Prime Brokerage under AIFMD', in Zetzsche (ed), The Alternative Investment Fund Managers Directive – European Regulation of Alternative Investment Funds, 545.

[114] Art. 21(3)(c) subpara. 3 AIFMD.

2. Safekeeping

147 **Safekeeping the assets** of an AIF/UCITS is the *raison d'être* of a depositary. The AIFMD and UCITSD seek to clarify the understanding of this safekeeping duty by making reference to the type of assets held by the AIF/UCITS. In doing so, it makes a distinction between 'financial instruments that can be held in custody', on the one hand, and 'other assets', including financial instruments that cannot be held in custody, on the other.

148 a) **Financial Instruments that 'Can be Held in Custody'.** Depending on the type of assets, the depositary's safekeeping functions can take the form of custody, for **financial instruments that can be held in custody**, or record-keeping for other assets.[116] According to the AIFMD and UCITSD, the depositary shall hold in custody all *financial instruments* that[117]:
- can be registered in a financial instruments account opened in the depositary's books; and
- all financial instruments that can be physically delivered to the depositary.

149 Financial instruments, which cannot be physically delivered to the depositary, fall within the scope of the depositary's custody obligation when they are either: (1) transferable securities, or (2) capable of being registered or held in an account directly or indirectly in the name of the depositary. The definition of transferable securities includes certain types of derivatives[118], money market instruments and units of collective investment undertakings.[119] Any crypto assets that qualify as financial instruments that can be held in custody fall within the depositary's custody obligations under the AIFMD and UCITSD.

150 The **custody obligation** includes financial instruments that are provided to a third party, or by a third party to the AIF/UCITS as collateral, as long as they are owned by the AIF/AIFM or UCITS/UCITS ManCo on behalf of the AIF/UCITS.[120] This is also valid for financial instruments for which the AIFM/UCITS ManCo has given its consent to the depositary to reuse as long as the right of reuse has not been exercised.[121]

151 The definition of financial instruments is designed to capture all financial instruments the depositary is in a position to control and retrieve. Following the AIFMD and UCITSD (Commission) Regulation,[122] this excludes all securities that are directly registered with the issuer itself or its agent (i.e. a registrar or a transfer agent) in the

---

[115] Arts. 7 and 8 Market Infrastructure Regulation.
[116] Art. 21(8)(b) AIFMD; Art. 22(5)(b) UCITSD.
[117] Art. 21(8)(a); Art. 22(5)(a) UCITSD.
[118] These derivatives have to be in accordance with Art. 51(3) UCITSD. See Art. 88(1)(a) Commission Delegated Regulation (EU) No 231/2013 supplementing Directive 2011/61/EU with regard to exemptions, general operating conditions, depositaries, leverage, transparency and supervision, OJ L 83, 22.3.2013 p. 1–95, as amended ('AIFMD (Commission) Regulation')) and Art. 12(1)(a) Commission Delegated Regulation (EU) 2016/438, supplementing Directive 2009/65/EC with regard to obligations of depositaries, OJ L 78, 24.3.2016 p. 11–30, as amended ('UCITSD (Commission) Regulation')).
[119] Art. 88(1)(a) AIFMD (Commission) Regulation and Art. 12(1)(a) UCITSD (Commission) Regulation.; See on the status of derivate contracts and holdings in collective investment undertakings: ESMA/2015/850, 22.
[120] Recital 100 AIFMD (Commission) Regulation; Recital 12 UCITSD (Commission) Regulation.
[121] In contrast to ESMA/2011/379, 158, the final text of Art. 88 AIFMD (Commission) Regulation and Art. 12 UCITSD (Commission) Regulation brings more uncertainty with respect to the issue of collateral provided by the AIF or AIFM on behalf of the AIF.
[122] Recital 100 AIFMD (Commission) Regulation; Recital 12 UCITSD (Commission) Regulation.

§ 15. Crypto Assets & Funds

name of the AIF/UCITS. This applies except in the situation where financial instruments can be physically delivered to the depositary[123] or are registered/held in an account directly or indirectly in the name of the depositary (through a subsidiary or sub-custodian).[124]

Instruments that do not comply with the requirements above for satisfying the definition of 'financial instruments', such as crypto assets under MiCAR that are by definition not financial instruments that can be held in custody, should be considered 'other assets' within the meaning of the AIFMD/UCITSD and are subject to record-keeping duties.[125]

b) 'Other Assets'. All assets that do not fall under the definition of financial instruments constitute '**other assets**'.[126] These include:
- physical assets (non-financial assets) that do not qualify as financial instruments or cannot be physically delivered to the depositary (e.g. real estate, commodities, ships);
- financial instruments that can neither be held in book-entry form nor be physically delivered to the depositary (e.g. financial contracts), such as (OTC) derivatives other than those embedded in the transferable securities definition within Art. 21(8)(a) AIFMD and Art. 22(5)(a) UCITSD, in particular, derivatives are other assets that are important for prime broker settings;[127]
- cash deposits;[128]
- financial instruments issued in nominative form and registered with an issuer or a registrar.[129]

The last category refers to assets that are not intermediated and where the ownership derives from direct registration in the register held by the issuer itself (or a registrar agent acting on its behalf). Examples include investments in privately held companies, or participation interest in funds with a capital call structure, such as real estate or private equity funds. Also, assets of the AIF/UCFTS provided as collateral in general will be subject to safekeeping duties related to 'other assets'.[130]

The depositary should have a comprehensive overview of all assets that are not financial instruments to be held in custody.[131] These assets are subject to the obligation of the depositary to verify that the relevant 'other assets' effectively belong to the AIF/UCITS itself or to the AIFM/UCITS ManCo acting on behalf of the AIF/UCITS ManCo.[132] The ownership verification must be based on information or documents provided by the AIF/UCITS or the AIFM/UCITS ManCo and, where available, external evidence.[133] External evidence could be a copy of an official document showing that the AIF/UCITS is the owner of the asset(s) or any formal and reliable evidence that the depositary considers appropriate.[134] If necessary, the depositary should request additional evidence from the AIF/UCITS or AIFM/UCITS ManCo or, as the case may be,

---

[123] Art. 88(3) AIFMD (Commission) Regulation; Art. 12(3) UCITSD (Commission) Regulation.
[124] Art. 88(1)(b) AIFMD (Commission) Regulation; Art. 12(1)(b) UCITSD (Commission) Regulation.
[125] Art. 21(8)(b) AIFMD; Art. 22(5)(b) UCITSD.
[126] Art. 21(8)(b) AIFMD; Art. 22(5)(b) UCITSD.
[127] Zetzsche, 'Fondsregulierung im Umbruch – ein rechtsvergleichender Rundblick zur Umsetzung der AIFM-Richtlinie' (2014) 26 *Zeitschrift für Bankrecht und Bankwirtschaft*, 22 (32).
[128] Recital 103 AIFMD (Commission) Regulation and Recital 14 UCITSD (Commission) Regulation. See also ESMA/2011/379, 161.
[129] Art. 88(2) AIFMD (Commission) Regulation and Art. 12(2) UCITSD (Commission) Regulation.
[130] ESMA/2011/379, 162.
[131] Financial instruments within the meaning of Art. 21(8)(a) AIFMD and Art. 22(5)(a) UCITSD.
[132] Art. 21(8)(b) AIFMD; Art. 22(5)(b) UCITSD.
[133] Art. 21(8)(b)(ii) and (iii) AIFMD; Art. 22(5)(b)(i) and (ii) UCITSD.
[134] Recital 104 AIFMD (Commission) Regulation. See also ESMA/2011/379, 162.

from a third party.¹³⁵ A broad range of evidence could potentially prove ownership. The parameters of the verification obligation are, however, uncertain. The official document clarifies whether this obligation covers both the legal and equitable or beneficial title. The verification obligation of the depositary is also unclear insofar as, for instance, the enforceability of derivatives or share borrowing contractual arrangements are concerned. A record of those assets shall be maintained and regularly updated.¹³⁶

156 c) The 'Custody' of Crypto Assets. aa) ESMA's Position. Currently, neither the AIFMD nor the AIFMD (Commission) Regulation provides for a legal definition of **'crypto assets'**.¹³⁷ Recently, ESMA used the term to refer to both so-called virtual currencies (e.g. 'cryptocurrencies') and digital tokens.¹³⁸ In particular, the so-called tokenisation of assets, i.e., a method that converts rights to an asset into a digital token, might be a potential long term trend that has the potential to create beneficial outcomes for both market participants and investors.¹³⁹ When it comes to crypto assets, an issue that arises is what constitutes safekeeping services. ESMA in its recent advice held that having control of **private keys** on behalf of clients might be regarded as safekeeping services and that rules to ensure the safekeeping and segregation of client assets should apply to the providers of those services.¹⁴⁰ Nevertheless, the 'holding of private keys on behalf of clients' may take different legal forms and therefore have different legal meanings. Furthermore, the question arises what crypto assets are to be regarded as 'financial instruments that can be held in custody', on the one hand, and 'other assets', on the other. Crypto assets qualifying as financial instruments that can be registered in a financial instruments account opened in the depositary's books will have to be held in custody. Based on the above, where crypto assets qualify as, for example, transferable securities and are traded on trading venues, their issuer, provided it is established in the EU, is obliged to arrange for such securities to be represented in book-entry form with an authorised CSD under Art. 2(1) CSDR. This is a clear example of crypto assets that qualify as financial instruments that can be held in custody. Yet, the delineation between the two will require further consideration and regulators should consider the content of the rules and the way in which they might be fulfilled in a DLT environment.

157 The custody provisions laid down in the (proposed) MiCAR seem to shed some light as to the future policy of the EU legislator as regards the safekeeping of crypto assets by depositaries of AIFs (and UCITS). It is highly likely that these provisions will inspire the EU legislator as regard depositaries, as the provisions itself are also highly consistent with the 'non-crypto' aspects of depositaries under the AIFMD and UCITSD that clearly served as an inspiration.

158 bb) Definition 'Crypto Assets that can be Held in Custody'. Issuers of asset-referenced tokens under the MiCAR have to ensure that reserve assets¹⁴¹ are held in custody at all times. Art. 33(2) MiCAR requires **reserve assets** that are 'crypto assets' within the meaning of MiCAR (that do not qualify as financial instruments) to be held in custody by 'crypto asset providers' that are authorised for 'the custody and admin-

---

¹³⁵ Recital 104 AIFMD (Commission) Regulation. See also ESMA/2011/379, 162.
¹³⁶ Art. 21 (8)(b)(i) AIFMD; Art. 22(5)(b)(i) UCITSD; Recital 105 AIFMD (Commission) Regulation and Recital 16 UCITSD (Commission) Regulation.
¹³⁷ ESMA, 'Advice – Initial Coin Offerings and Crypto-Assets', 9 January 2019 | ESMA50-157-1391, Appendix 1 – Glossary.
¹³⁸ Ibid.
¹³⁹ Ibid, 18.
¹⁴⁰ Ibid, 35.
¹⁴¹ Under Art. 3(1) Nr. 21 MiCAR, 'reserve assets' means the basket of fiat currencies, commodities or crypto-assets, backing the value of an asset-referenced tokens, or the investment of such assets.

istration of crypto assets on behalf of third parties'[142]. In this respect, the 'custody and administration of crypto assets on behalf of third parties' means the 'safekeeping or controlling, on behalf of third parties, crypto assets or the means of access to such crypto assets, where applicable in the form of private cryptographic keys.'

159 Reserve assets may be 'other assets', such as commodities, but also can be highly liquid financial instruments within the meaning of MiFID2 that qualify as 'financial instruments that can be held in custody'.[143] Both of these 'non-crypto assets' qualify as other types of reserve assets that have to be safekept by credit institutions. As the definition of 'reserve assets' includes crypto assets and non-crypto assets (that can be held in custody), the safekeeping definition included under Art. 21(4) MiCAR includes three different safekeeping definitions. It has copy-pasted the 'financial instruments that can be held in custody' definition and the 'other assets' definition of the depositary provisions under the AIFMD and UCITS. Apart from that, however, it includes new safekeeping tasks that refer to 'crypto assets that can be held in custody' for 'crypto assets'. It is very likely that the latter duties will be included by the EU legislator in the AIFMD and UCITSD depositary provisions as well. Therefore, it is worthwhile to consider this definition a bit deeper.

160 Art. 33(4)(c) MiCAR determines for 'crypto assets that can be held in custody' that the crypto asset service providers shall hold the crypto assets included in the reserve of assets or the means of access to such crypto assets, where applicable, in the form of private cryptographic keys.

161 For that purpose, crypto asset service providers shall open a register of positions in the name of the issuer of asset-referenced tokens for the purpose of managing the reserve assets, so that the crypto assets held in custody can be clearly identified as belonging to the reserve of assets in accordance with the applicable law at all times.[144]

162 From the above, it is clear that, most likely, the EU legislator will include new tasks for depositaries under the AIFMD and the UCITSD with respect to 'crypto assets that can be held in custody'. For that purpose, it will likely define this by using the 'custody and administration of crypto assets on behalf of third parties' definition under the MiCAR as an inspiration. In other words, the new safekeeping category would likely be defined as the 'safekeeping or controlling of crypto assets or the means of access to such crypto assets, where applicable in the form of private cryptographic keys.'

163 For this purpose, depositaries under the AIFMD and UCITSD are likely to be required to open a register of positions for the purpose of managing the 'crypto assets', so that these assets are clearly identified as belonging to the respective AIFs or UCITS that they are bought for.

3. Control

164 Besides the safekeeping of assets, the AIFMD and UCITSD impose on depositaries the additional duty to **control the AIF's/UCITS' compliance** with the applicable national laws and its rules or instruments of incorporation. To that end, the depositary shall:
– check whether the sale, issue, re-purchase, redemption and cancellation of units or shares of the AIF/UCITS are carried out in accordance with the applicable national laws and the AIF/UCITS rules or instruments of incorporation (subscriptions/redemptions);[145]

---

[142] Art. 67 MiCAR.
[143] Art. 33(4)(b) MiCAR.
[144] Art. 33(4) MiCAR.
[145] Art. 21(9)(a) AIFMD; Art. 22(3)(a) UCITSD.

- ensure that the value of the units or shares of the AIF/UCITS is calculated in accordance with the applicable national laws, the AIF/UCITS rules or instruments of incorporations and the procedures with regard to valuation (valuations of share/unit pricing);[146]
- duties relating to the carrying out of the AIFM's/UCITS ManCo's instructions (regulatory compliance);
- ensure that, in transactions involving the AIF's/UCITS' assets, any consideration is remitted to the AIF/UCITS within the usual time limits (timely settlement of transactions).[147]
- ensure that the income distribution is appropriate, and, where an error has been identified, ensure that the AIFM/UCITS ManCo takes the appropriate remedial action (distribution of income);
- conducting a review of the reconciliation procedures with respect to cash accounts opened and monitoring on an ongoing basis any discrepancies detected (cash management).

These tasks serve as to mitigate risks in relation to the loss of investor' assets caused by negligent or fraudulent practices.[148]

165 It is to be expected that DLT will increasingly play a role in the oversight tasks that are performed by depositaries. For funds with tokenised units/shares, for instance, it is quite easy for the depositary to verify that subscriptions/redemptions administrated by the fund manager or its fund administrator has been performed in accordance with the law. The same holds true for the valuation of the share/unit pricing. For both, smart contracts could play an increasing important role in performing this role. The ad-hoc checking with traditional or other digitised means is, however, still necessary as the DLT being applied is still a 'permissioned network' in which there is still room for fund managers and their delegated administrators to conduct fraud. Most possibly, the depositary's role will evolve and the oversight tasks will, for instance, extend to IT- and DLT-related matters used by the fund manager or its delegated administrator in performed the above-mentioned tasks. Such controls could include verifications as to the cyber security and IT measures in place and verifying whether a 'safe' protocol complying with certain minimum standards is being used for both the DLT and the smart contracts used. The extent to which DLT will be applied will also depend upon whether the 'cash-leg' of the transactions on the fund and investment level will be tokenised or whether a 'digital Euro' will be introduced that will allow for smoother DLT-based transactions.

4. Delegation under the AIFMD/UCITSD

166 **a) Delegation for AIF/UCITS Depositaries.** Delegation in the **depositary chain** concerns the appointment of a sub-custodian to which a depositary may delegate its safekeeping function (both custody and record keeping).[149] The AIFMD and the UCITSD allow a depositary to delegate neither its cash management[150] function nor its oversight duties[151] to third parties.

---

[146] For the AIF depositary this shall be compliant with the AIFMD valuation rules as laid down in Art. 19 AIFMD. See Art. 21(9)(b) AIFMD; see also Art. 22(3)(b) UCITSD.

[147] Art. 21(9)(d) AIFMD; Art. 22(3)(d) UCITSD.

[148] Hooghiemstra, Depositaries in European Investment Law – Towards Harmonization in Europe (2018), 223 et seq.

[149] Art. 21(11) AIFMD; Art. 22a UCITSD.

[150] Art. 21(7) AIFMD; Art. 22(4) UCITSD.

[151] Art. 21(9) AIFMD; Art. 22(3) UCITSD.

The appointed depositary remains at all times responsible towards the AIF/UCITS and the investor for the safekeeping task being delegated. This is also the case if a 'sub-custodian', in its turn, is delegating the safekeeping to another third party. The appointment of a sub-custodian is subject to numerous requirements.

A depositary may not delegate (or sub-delegate) safekeeping functions to a sub-custodian with the intention of avoiding the requirements of the AIFMD and UCITSD.[152] In other words, it may delegate its functions to the extent that it would become a 'letter-box entity'.

For the purpose of the AIFMD and UCITSD, all 'sub-custodians' are considered delegates of the AIF's/UCITS' depositary. Furthermore, the depositary has to be able to prove and/or provide documents to the Competent Authorities, if requested, to prove that the delegation structure is based on objective reasons.[153] Objective reasons could be that a certain depositary has expertise related to certain assets or a specific region. The depositary may only delegate to a third party its safekeeping function if it has exercised all due skill, care and diligence in the selection and appointment of the third party to whom it wants to delegate parts of its tasks, and continues to exercise such diligences on an ongoing basis.[154] This allows the depositary, at all times, to assess whether its sub-custodians and the risks related to delegation of the safekeeping tasks are acceptable or not.

b) **The Impact of DLT on Delegation.** In line with the AIFMD/UCITSD depositary delegation rules, depositaries will be required, as part of their ex-ante and ongoing due diligence duties, to verify whether any delegates have the appropriate infrastructure, such as IT systems and DLT with appropriate protocols in place. Credit institutions that are performing 'the custody and administration of crypto assets on behalf of third parties' within the meaning of MiCAR and crypto-service providers (including investment firms) that have obtained a license under MiCAR for that purpose, should be considered as fulfilling the delegation requirements for the custody of non-financial instrument crypto assets. In this stage, it is unclear whether depositaries may delegate crypto asset custody to the above-mentioned service providers if they do not fulfil the organisational requirements themselves to safekeep crypto assets. Most AIF/UCITS depositaries are credit institutions that, without obtaining a separate license, may perform 'the custody and administration of crypto assets on behalf of third parties' under MiCAR. Nevertheless, they will still need to fulfil the ongoing MiCAR requirements to be able to do so. In this stage, it is not clear whether depositaries would be allowed to delegate the custody of crypto assets if they do not have the appropriate means in place to perform this task themselves in the first place.

5. Depositary Liability under the AIFMD & UCITSD

a) **Liability under the AIFMD & UCITSD.** The AIFMD and UCITSD deviate between **liability of the depositary** for the loss of financial instruments that can be held in custody and other losses. The depositary is under the AIFMD and UCITSD liable to the AIF/UCITS or to the investors for losses of financial instruments held in custody either by the depositary itself or sub-custodians to whom custody has been delegated.[155] Upon a loss, the depositary shall return a financial instrument of identical

---

[152] Art. 21(11) sub-para. 2(a) AIFMD; Art. 22a(2) (a) UCITSD.
[153] Art. 21(11) sub-para. 2(b) AIFMD; Art. 22a(2) (b) UCITSD.
[154] Art. 21(11) sub-para. 2(c) AIFMD; Art. 22a(2) (c) UCITSD.
[155] Art. 21(12) AIFMD; Art. 24(1) UCITSD.

type or the corresponding amount to the AIF/UCITS, or the AIFM/UCITS ManCo, without undue delay.[156] The depositary shall not be liable if it can prove in a private law case that the loss has arisen as a result of an external event beyond its reasonable control, the consequences of which would have been unavoidable despite all reasonable efforts to the contrary.[157] This strict liability regime is not applicable to real estate and any other assets than financial instruments that can be held in custody. With regard to losses for these assets, the depositary is liable to the AIF/UCITS, or the investors of the AIF/UCITS, if the loss is the result of the depositary's negligent or intentional failure to properly fulfil its obligations under the AIFMD/UCITSD.[158] Determining liability will, regarding these assets, solely be based upon the private law standards of the individual Member States. In civil law jurisdictions claims are likely to be based upon a breach of contract or a general tort law provision.[159] The AIFMD and UCITSD does not assign for these losses the burden of proof to the depositary, but to the AIF/UCITS, the AIFM/UCITS ManCo or investors involved.

172 **b) The Impact of DLT on the Depositary's liability.** In this stage, it is unclear whether 'crypto assets held in custody' would be subject to the strict liability regime currently applicable to 'financial instruments that can be held in custody' under the AIFMD and UCITSD or to the 'negligence type of liability' for 'other assets'. Similar as to the **AIFMD depositary liability regime**, France has adopted a strict liability regime that imposes an obligation to 'crypto asset custodians' to return lost crypto assets.[160]

173 Should the EU legislator follow France's approach, as it has done under the AIFMD and UCITSD, the liability regime explained above for AIFMD/UCITSD depositaries shall be expected to be introduced for lost crypto assets for depositaries under the AIFMD and UCITSD.

II. 'Crypto asset Custodians' under the EC's 'Digital Finance Package'

174 Most depositaries for both AIFs and UCITS are credit institutions (or investment firms). In this respect, it should be noted that the recently proposed 'Digital Finance Package' of the EU Commission contains three initiatives that will impact CSDs and both financial instrument and 'non-financial instrument' '**crypto asset custodians**', namely the DLT Market Infrastructure Regulation, the MiCAR, and a directive amending, amongst others, MiFID2. These three initiatives are relevant for credit institutions and investment firms. All of these initiatives either allow credit institutions (and investment firms) to act as a DLT market infrastructure (i.e. a 'DLT CSD'), to act as a 'crypto-custodian' for DLT financial instruments and DLT non-financial instruments, or both. These options allowing AIF/UCITS depositaries that are credit institutions (or investment firms) to perform these types of 'DLT CSD services' and 'crypto asset custody' will be subsequently discussed, as they will have an impact on their role as an AIF/UCITS depositary as well.

---

[156] Riassetto, 'L'obligation de restitution du dépositaire d'OPC en droit Luxembourgeois' (2013) 94 *Journal des Tribunaux Luxembourg*, 167.

[157] Art. 21(12) AIFMD; Art. 24(1) UCITSD.

[158] Riassetto, 'Responsabilité de la société de gestion et du dépositaire d'un OPC envers les actionnaires d'une société cible, note sous Cass. com. fr. 27 mai 2015', (2015) 16 *Revue de Droit Bancaire et Financier*, 65.

[159] See, e.g. in the Netherlands: Art. 6:162 and Art. 6:74 BW.

[160] Art. 722-1 6° of the AMF General Regulation; AMF, 'Questions & Answers on the Digital Asset Service Providers Regime', (AMF Position DOC-2020-07, 22.9.2020), 16, available at https://beck-link.de/38e6a (accessed 26.08.2021).

§ 15. Crypto Assets & Funds

1. DLT Market Infrastructure Regulation

In order to allow for the development of crypto assets that qualify as financial instruments and DLT, while preserving a high level of financial stability, market integrity, transparency and investor protection, the EU legislator currently proposes with the **DLT Market Infrastructure Regulation** a pilot regime for DLT market infrastructures. 175

The use of DLT, with all transactions recorded in a decentralised ledger, can expedite and condense trading and settlement to nearly real-time and could enable the merger of trading and post-trading activities.[161] However, the current rules envisage the performance of trading and settlement activities by separate market infrastructures. The CSDR requires that financial instruments admitted to trading on a trading venue within the meaning of MiFID2 to be recorded with a CSD, while a distributed ledger can be used as a decentralised version of such a depository. 176

To that extent, the DLT Market Infrastructure Regulation allows 'DLT market infrastructures' to be temporarily exempted from some specific requirements under the CSDR that could otherwise prevent them from developing solutions for the trading and settlement of transactions in crypto assets that qualify as financial instruments. In this respect, DLT market infrastructures are either 'DLT multilateral trading facilities' (**'DLT MTFs'**) or 'DLT securities Settlement systems'. In this respect, 'DLT MTFs' are 'MTFs' within the meaning of MiFID2 that are operated by an investment firm or a market operator, that only admits to trading DLT transferable securities. Furthermore, 'DLT securities settlement systems' are securities settlement systems operated by a 'CSD' authorised under the CSDR that settles transactions in DLT transferable securities against payment. 177

The piloting regimes allows both types of DLT market infrastructures to operate a DLT securities settlement system that only admits to trading or record DLT transferable securities on their distributed ledger.[162] DLT transferable securities should be crypto assets that qualify as 'transferable securities' within the meaning of MiFID2 and that are issued, transferred and stored on a distributed ledger. In order to allow innovation and experimentation in a sound regulatory environment while preserving financial stability, the DLT Market Infrastructure Regulation is limited to a certain category of transferable securities, that is – shares of market capitalisation of less than EUR 200 million and bonds of an issuance size of less than EUR 500 million. 178

a) DLT MTFs. DLT MTFs are under Art. 2(3) DLT Market Infrastructure Regulation allowed to ensure the initial recording of DLT transferable securities, the settlement of transactions in DLT transferable securities and the safekeeping of DLT transferable securities. More specifically, 'safekeeping' is further defined as providing 'safekeeping services in relation to DLT transferable securities, or where applicable, to related payments and collateral, provided using the DLT MTF'. 179

'Safekeeping', thus, refers to the function of a DLT market infrastructure as a 'crypto asset custodian' (or a **'DLT Investor CSD'**) and the other two mentioned functions to the DLT market infrastructure as a 'DLT CSD' or a **'DLT Issuer CSD'**. 180

In this respect, Recital 31 and Art. 6(5) DLT Market Infrastructure Regulation clarify that where the business plan of a DLT market infrastructure would involve the safekeeping of client' assets, the DLT market infrastructure should have adequate arrangements in place to safeguard their clients' assets. In this respect, client' assets may be client' funds, such as cash or cash equivalent, or DLT transferable 181

---

[161] Recital 9 DLT Market Infrastructure Regulation.
[162] Recital 11 DLT Market Infrastructure Regulation.

securities, or the means of access to such DLT transferable securities, including in the form of cryptographic keys.

182 To that end, the organisational requirements in place should prevent DLT market infrastructures from using clients' assets on own account, except with prior express consent from their clients. Furthermore, the DLT market infrastructure should segregate clients' funds or DLT transferable securities, or the means of access to such assets, from its own assets or other clients' assets. Finally, the overall IT and cyber arrangements of DLT market infrastructures should ensure that clients' assets are protected against fraud, cyber threats or other malfunctions.

183 **b) DLT Securities Settlement System – 'Investor CSDs'.** Similar to 'custodians' under MiFID2, CSDs may under the CSDR operate as a so-called 'Investor CSD'. In other words, it may maintain securities accounts in relation to the **settlement service**, collateral management and other ancillary services.[163] CSDs are under this ancillary service allowed to open 'lower tier' securities accounts, either in direct holding systems or by acting as an 'investor CSD' by maintaining securities accounts for its customers for securities issued in 'issuer CSDs'. The investor CSD is, thus, similar as a custodian. For cross-border transactions, investors can access securities in an issuer CSD by using either a custodian bank or an investor CSD that has an account with an issuer CSD. CSDs may also perform the same ancillary services as custodians.

184 The DLT Market Infrastructure Regulation (temporary) exempts 'Investor CSDs' from a number requirements that prevents such CSDs from acting as a 'crypto asset custodian'. De facto, 'Investor CSDs' that fulfill the DLT Market Infrastructure Regulation requirements with respect to 'DLT securities settlement systems' may, thus, also 'provide safekeeping services in relation to DLT transferable securities, or where applicable, related payments and collateral'.

185 In this respect, the DLT Market Infrastructure Regulation clarifies that DLT Securities Settlement Systems are required to have the same organisational requirements in place as DLT MTFs.[164]

2. MiFID2 – (Financial Instruments) Crypto Asset Custodians

186 Under MiFID2, the provision of investment services or activities, with or without ancillary services, requires authorisation. Authorisation must be granted by the Competent Authority. Before authorisation may be granted, an investment firm must fulfil a number of conditions. *Inter alia*, the investment firm has to be a member of an authorised investor compensation scheme and fulfil own fund and capital requirements in accordance with the IFD[165] and IFR[166].[167]

187 The safekeeping and administration of financial instruments for the account of clients is an ancillary service under section B Annex I MiFID2. This implies that the safekeeping and administration of financial instruments for the account of clients is not an

---

[163] Annex – List of Services, S. B, n. 3 CSDR.
[164] This is implicitly confirmed by: Art. 7(1)(e) and Art. 8(2)(e) DLT Market Infrastructure Regulation.
[165] Directive 2019/2034/EU on the prudential supervision of investment firms and amending Directives 2002/87/EC, 2009/65/EC, 2011/61/EU, 2013/36/EU, 2014/59/EU and 2014/65/EU, OJ L 314, 5.12.2019 p. 64–114, ('IFD').
[166] Regulation (EU) No. 2019/2033 on the prudential requirements of investment firms and amending Regulations (EU) No. 1093/2010, (EU) No. 575/2013, (EU) No. 600/2014 and (EU) No. 806/2014, OJ L 314, 5.12.2019 p. 1–63, ('IFR').
[167] Recital 39 IFD specifies that all cross-references in, inter alia, the UCITSD and AIFMD, which no longer apply to investment firms from the date of application of the IFD and IFR, should be construed as references to the corresponding provisions in the IFD and IFR.

investment service or activity and can only be provided by credit institutions and investment firms in connection with investment services and activities, such as, amongst others, portfolio management and investment advice.[168]

Currently, the definition of 'financial instrument' in MiFID2 does not explicitly include financial instruments issued using a class of technologies which support the distributed recording of encrypted data ('DLT').[169] In this respect, the EU legislator considers that 'in order to ensure that such financial instruments can be traded on the market under the current legal framework, the definition in Directive 2014/65/EU should be amended to include them.' **188**

To that end, it proposed to replace the current definition of 'financial instruments' under Art. 4(1) point 15 MiFID2 by the following: **189**

'financial instrument' means those instruments specified in Section C of Annex I, including such instruments issued by means of distributed ledger technology.'

De facto, this means that any type of 'traditional custodian' that is a credit institution or investment firm under MiFID2 may safekeep DLT financial instruments as an 'ancillary service' under section B Annex I MiFID2. Contrary to the DLT Market Infrastructure Regulation and MiCAR, MiFID2, however, does not (yet) contain organisational requirements, in terms of cyber security and IT, that are adapted to DLT. **190**

3. MiCAR – (Non-Financial Instrument) Crypto asset Custodians

Under Art. 2(5) MiCAR, such AIF/UCITS depositaries are not required to obtain a license as a (non-financial instrument) custodian for performing the service 'custody and administration of crypto assets on behalf of third parties' under the MiCAR. Firms other than credit institutions appointed as AIF and UCITS depositaries are required to obtain a license as crypto asset service provider in order to provide crypto asset custody services for non-financial instruments. Credit institutions are, however, required to perform ongoing duties under the MiCAR when performing that service. **191**

The requirements applicable to crypto asset service providers that provide 'custody on behalf of third parties of crypto assets or access to crypto assets' under Art. 67 MiCAR show some highlights of what (amended) requirements AIFMD/UCITSD depositaries may be confronted with in the (near) future. **192**

Crypto asset service providers are required to include the following content in their agreements with clients that diverge from those to be included in the AIFMD/UCITSD depositary agreement:[170] **193**

- the means of communication between the crypto asset service provider and the client, including the client's authentication system; and
- a description of the security systems used by the crypto assets service provider.

Crypto asset service providers have to keep a register of positions, opened in the name of each client, corresponding to each clients' rights to the crypto assets.[171] Crypto asset service providers shall record as soon as possible movements following instructions from the client in his/her position register and shall organise their internal procedures in such a way as to ensure that any movement affecting the registration of the crypto assets is evidenced by a transaction regularly registered in the client's position register. **194**

---

[168] Annex I s. A MiFID II.
[169] Recital 6 Proposal for a Directive of the European Parliament and of the Council amending Directives 2006/43/EC, 2009/65/EC, 2009/138/EU, 2011/61/EU, EU/2013/36, 2014/65/EU, (EU) 2015/2366 and EU/2016/2341 ('Digital Financial Amendment Directive').
[170] Art. 67(2) MiCAR.
[171] Art. 67(3) MiCAR.

195 The custody policy of crypto asset service providers has to include internal rules and procedures to ensure the safekeeping or the control of such crypto assets, or the means of access to the crypto assets, such as cryptographic keys.[172] These rules and procedures shall ensure that the crypto asset service provider cannot lose clients' crypto assets or the rights related to these assets due to frauds, cyber threats or negligence.[173]

196 Where applicable, crypto asset service providers shall facilitate the exercise of the rights attached to the crypto assets. Any event likely to create or modify the client's rights shall be recorded in the client's position register as soon as possible.[174]

197 Crypto asset providers shall communicate, at least once every three months and at each request of their client, a statement of position of the crypto assets recorded in the name of the client.[175] The statement mentions the crypto assets concerned, their balance, their value and the transfer of crypto assets made during the period.

198 Crypto asset service providers shall also communicate, as soon as possible, information relating to operations on crypto assets requiring a response from the client.[176] Furthermore, they shall ensure the establishment of the necessary means to return as soon as possible the crypto assets or the means of access to the crypto assets held on behalf of their clients.

199 Crypto asset service providers are required to segregate holdings on behalf of their clients from their own holdings.[177] They shall ensure that, on the DLT, its clients' crypto assets are held on separate addresses from those on which their own crypto assets are held.[178]

200 Crypto asset service providers shall refrain from using the crypto assets or the cryptographic keys stored on behalf of their clients, except with the express prior consent of the clients.[179]

201 Crypto asset service providers are liable to their clients for loss of crypto assets as a result of malfunction or hacks up to the market value of the crypto assets lost.[180]

202 The elements discussed above in relation to crypto assets shows the relevant aspects of custodian/depositary law that are expected to be amended in line with the MiCAR.

III. Frictional Boundaries of 'Crypto asset Custody' under EU Financial Law

203 Due to the absence of any proposed initiative for AIFMD & UCITSD depositaries, there will be **frictional boundaries** between credit institutions (and investment firms) acting as AIFMD/UCITSD depositary, at the one, and DLT market infrastructure under the piloting regime, '**crypto asset custodian**' under MiFID2 and MiCAR, at the other hand. For the latter three, 'crypto asset custody' and the operational rules applicable to credit institutions (and investment firms) will be clarified, whereas the same entities acting as AIFMD/UCITSD depositary are dependent upon the merit of their respective Competent Authorities whether they make safekeep 'crypto assets' at all. This is odd given the fact that most depositaries will have already (in the near future) the

---

[172] Art. 67(4) MiCAR.
[173] Art. 67(4) MiCAR.
[174] Art. 67(5) MiCAR.
[175] Art. 67(6) MiCAR.
[176] Art. 67(6) MiCAR.
[177] Art. 67(7) MiCAR.
[178] Art. 67(7) MiCAR.
[179] Art. 67(7) MiCAR.
[180] Art. 67(8) MiCAR.

appropriate organisational structure in place to safekeep 'crypto assets'. It is, thus, important that the EU legislator will 'fix' this gap by proposing an amendment to the AIFMD, the UCITSD and its implementation legislation that is in line with MiFID2 and, in particular, MiCAR.

F. DLT and its Future Impact on Funds

Most discussions about DLT and investment funds are about the unlimited possibilities that DLT offer for illiquid investment funds, such as real estate and private equity.[181] In the short and medium-term – it is expected that DLT will, however, have mostly an impact on liquid funds (e.g. UCITS). In this stage, the tokenisation of units/shares of AIFs and UCITS is in its infancy. Only a limited number of Member States have recognised the possibility for AIFs and UCITS to tokenise their units and shares. Despite of this, it is expected that the adoption of DLT, tokenisation and the recognition thereof will first take place with respect to issuing DLT-securities. Therefore, it is logical that – in the short and medium-term – most notable digitisation and benefits thereof will take place in the administration, distribution and depositary domains of EU investment funds. This benefits UCITS and ETFs the most. Once most Member States recognise the possibility to tokenise units/shares, or securities issues in general, secondary markets will develop in which not only units/shares of (illiquid) investment funds, but also the SPVs with illiquid assets can be traded. Thus, the benefits for (illiquid) investment funds are likely to be seen in the medium-term. In the long term, it is not unthinkable that DAOs will play a larger role in (EU) investment funds. In particular, DAOs could revolutionise the alignment of fund managers and their investors in a unique manner. EU funds established as DAOs are – in this stage – in its infancy. Therefore, the market and its developments in this domain will first need to be carefully observed over a longer period of time in order to be able to analyse the benefits of DAOs for investment funds more accurately.

G. Conclusion

This contribution has made an attempt to give a high-level overview on the potential implications of asset tokenisation and the use of DLT for EU investment funds. Till now, DLT nor the tokenisation of EU fund units/shares is not yet widespread. This is, however, likely to change rapidly in the years to come. To that end, this contribution gave a high-level overview of EU *fund governance* and explained that the unique governance of EU investment funds consists of fund managers, investors and depositaries. Furthermore, it explained that DLT is likely to be first leading to an evolution, in which DLT will help to digitise the tasks of fund managers in terms of, in particular, fund administration and distribution/marketing, and the way how depositaries safekeep assets.

Due to the fact that it is easier for Member States to implement the use and recognition of asset tokenisation of (the ownership of) securities rather than (the property rights of) hard assets, it is expected that liquid EU investment funds, such as UCITS, will in the short- and medium-term benefit the most from asset tokenisation. The scalability of administration and new D2C distribution models will benefit those

---

[181] University of Oxford, 'Tokenisation: the future of real estate investment?', (2020), available at https://beck-link.de/e3zpx (accessed 26.08.2021).

funds the most. Upon the adoption of DLT on a larger scale, it is expected that secondary markets trading tokens will develop and that also the ownership of hard assets in relation to tokenisation will be clarified by Member State laws. This will in the medium-term also be of benefit for secondary markets for illiquid investment funds, such as real estate and private equity funds. In the long-term, the adoption of DAOs may have an impact on fund formation and on different models of aligning the interest of fund managers and investors for liquid and illiquid EU investment funds alike. The limited adoption of DAOs in the EU investment fund industry so far is to be allocated to legal restrictions. Developments in this domain will first need to be carefully observed over a longer period of time in order to be able to analyse the benefits of DAOs for investment funds more accurately.

PART C
COUNTRY REPORTS

§ 16
France

Literature: Autorité des Marchés Financiers (AMF), 'Liste des offres de jetons ayant obtenu un visa de l'AMF', available at: https://beck-link.de/3dc3c (accessed 01.12.2020); Autorité des Marches Financiers (AMF), 'Procédure d'instruction et établissement d'un document d'information devant être déposé auprès de l'AMF en vue de l'obtention d'un visa sur une offre au public de jetons'(June 2019), available at: https://beck-link.de/5z3sm; Barsan, 'Regulating the Crypto World – New Developments from France', (2019) 4 *Revue Trimestrielle de Droit Financier (RTDF)*, 9–30; Barsan, 'Public Blockchains: The Privacy-Transparency Conundrum', (2019) 2 *Revue Trimestrielle de Droit Financier (RTDF)*, 50; Bullmann, Klemm and Pinna, 'In search for stability in crypto assets: are stablecoins the solution?' (ECB, Occasion Papier Series, n° 230, August 2019), 39, available at: https://beck-link.de/h5ee3 (accessed 12.01.2020); Corbion-Condé, 'De la défiance à l'égard des monnaies nationales au miroir du bitcoin', (2014) *Revue de Droit Bancaire et Financier (RDBF)*, 1; Douet, 'Fiscalité des Initial Coin Offerings (ICO)', (2019) *Dalloz IP/IT*, 237; European Central Bank (ECB), 'Crypto assets: Implications for financial stability, monetary policy, and payments and market infrastructures', (Occasional Paper Series, ECB Crypto assets Task Force, No. 223, May 2019), 4–28, available at: https://beck-link.de/ft7rr (accessed 01.12.2020); European Securities Market Authority (ESMA), 'Advice: Initial Coin Offerings and Crypto assets' (January 2019), available at: https://beck-link.de/dm5hb (accessed 01.12.2020); Financial Action Task Force (FATF), 'Guidance for a risk-based approach – Virtual Currencies' (June 2015), available at: https://beck-link.de/7n5pz (accessed 01.12.2020). Financial Action Task Force (FATF), 'International Standards on Combating Money Laundering and the Financing of Terrorism & Proliferation' (June 2019), available at: https://beck-link.de/mpd7d (accessed 01.12.2020); François, 'Décret 'Blockchain' – Note sous décret numéro 2018-1226 du 24 décembre 2018 relatif à l'utilisation d'un dispositif d'enregistrement électronique partagé pour la représentation et la transmission de titres financiers et pour l'émission et la cession de minibons', (2019) 2 *Revue des sociétés*, 86 ; Hacker and Thomale, 'Crypto-Securities Regulation: ICOs, Token Sales and Cryptocurrencies under EU Financial Law', (2017) 15 *European Company and Financial Law Review*, 645–696 (2018); Lavayssière, 'Blockchain et titres financiers: décret minimaliste pour réforme ambitieuse', (2019) 144 *RLDA*, 4; Legeais, 'Une nouvelle catégorie de biens: les actifs numériques', (2019) *Revue trimestrielle de droit commercial et de droit économique (RTDCom)*, 191; Libchaber, 'L'argent entre matière et mémoire', (1998) 42 *Archives de Philosophie du Droit*, 115; Oudin, 'La régulation des ICOs Étude sous l'angle des droits français et européen', (2019) 50 *Revue Trimestrielle de Droit Financier (RTDF)*, 36; Roussille, 'Loi Pacte et ICO: réflexion tronquée, occasion manquée?', (2019) 48 *Revue de Droit Bancaire et Financier (RDBF)*; Vabre, 'Prestataires de services sur actifs numériques', (2019) 6 *Droit des sociétés*, 111; Zetzsche, Buckley, Arner, Föhr, 'The ICO Gold Rush: It's a Scam, It's a Bubble, It's a Super Challenge for Regulators' (2019) 60 *Harvard International Law Journal*, 267–316.

Outline

	para.
A. Introduction	1
I. Definition of Digital Assets	3
II. The Incentives	7
B. The Primary Market: Initial Coin Offerings (ICO)	10
I. Protection of Potential Investors	12
II. Sanctions	18
C. Digital Asset Service Providers	20
I. Services Provided on Digital Assets	21
II. Mandatory Registration	23
III. Voluntary License	27
D. Conclusion	32

A. Introduction

1   France was **one of the first countries** enacting legislation regulating Initial Coin Offerings (ICOs) and intermediaries dealing with crypto assets. Indeed, an *ad hoc* regulation was adopted on 22 May 2019[1] in the PACTE law.[2] The aim was, on the one hand, to regulate this very quickly evolving and borderless environment but, on the other hand, the regulation enacted needed to be sufficiently flexible and attractive given that the actors of this ecosystem are very mobile and can easily change jurisdictions. Further, regulating this continuously developing and still quite recent ecosystem too quickly and too harshly risked hampering its evolution and potential. Therefore, the legislator had to square the circle with an original piece of legislation in order to respond to these quite opposing objectives. This is precisely what France tried to achieve by a new genre of regulation. Ignoring the preferences of the European regulator who favoured a common response,[3] France decided to provide for an optional visa for Initial Coin Offerings and a mix of mandatory registration for some intermediaries coupled with a voluntary license for all intermediaries.[4] Indeed, the ubiquitous nature of blockchain and distributed ledger technology (DLT) raises the challenge to target the right actors. Unsurprisingly, France targeted the gatekeepers who allow physical and legal persons to access this environment as these service providers are easy to identify.

This piece of legislation combining a voluntary approach with constraining sanctions is a new type of regulation: neither totally soft law, nor a default rule, nor totally hard law. Service providers are lured to opt into their own compliance but once this option is exercised, there are constraining rules and potentially sanctions applying.

2   But France went beyond regulating ICOs and digital asset service providers. Indeed, France wanted to offer a quite comprehensive legal landscape to virtuous blockchain projects. Therefore, France also made quite a lot of progress in terms of accounting and tax rules applicable to crypto assets.[5] Overall, the first impression is that the French legal landscape seems quite accommodating towards virtuous blockchain projects. Unfortunately, the devil is in the detail and the primary requirements that smartly mixed a voluntary with a mandatory approach seem to be jeopardized by the constraints and requirements provided for by secondary legislation. One could therefore wonder if the initial idea is **overburdened by a set of regulations that make sense in a traditional financial environment** but might be too onerous for FinTech and blockchain start-ups. Indeed, one year after the adoption of the PACTE law and

---

[1] LOI n° 2019–486 du 22 mai 2019 relative à la croissance et la transformation des entreprises (PACTE).

[2] For a detailed comment of the law see Barsan, 'Regulating the Crypto World – New Developments from France', (2019) 4 *Revue Trimestrielle de Droit Financier (RTDF)*, 9–30, available also at SSRN: https://beck-link.de/xac7v or (accessed 30.11.2020).

[3] European Securities Market Authority (ESMA), 'Advice: Initial Coin Offerings and Crypto-Assets' (January 2019), 5, available at: https://beck-link.de/dm5hb (accessed 01.12.2020). European Central Bank (ECB), 'Crypto-Assets: Implications for financial stability, monetary policy, and payments and market infrastructures', (Occasional Paper Series, ECB Crypto-Assets Task Force, no. 223, May 2019), 4–28, available at: https://beck-link.de/ft7rr (accessed 01.12.2020).

[4] Vabre, 'Prestataires de services sur actifs numériques', (2019) 6 *Droit des sociétés*, 111; Roussille, 'Loi Pacte et ICO: réflexion tronquée, occasion manquée?', (2019) 48(3) *Revue de Droit Bancaire et Financier (RDBF)*; Legeais, 'Une nouvelle catégorie de biens: les actifs numériques', (2019) *Revue trimestrielle de droit commercial et de droit économique (RTDCom)*, 191.

[5] Barsan, ibid.

its decrees there have been only three ICOs that applied for and obtained the voluntary visa[6] and merely ten digital asset service providers registered with the French Financial Markets Authority (Autorité des Marchés Financiers, AMF). As of the time of writing there has been no voluntary license of digital asset service providers.

We are first going to outline the definition of digital assets (→ para. 3) before presenting the incentives that were thought to push issuers and digital asset service providers towards the regulator and opt into the proposed voluntary regime (→ para. 7). Next, we are going to present the regulation of the primary market with the voluntary visa for an ICO (→ para. 10) and the regulation applying to digital asset service providers (→ 20) before concluding in a final chapter (→ para. 32).

I. Definition of Digital Assets

The legislation started by defining what crypto assets are. It uses the term '*digital assets*' to designate tokens on the one hand and other digital assets on the other hand. Financial instruments[7] and loan certificates[8] are expressly excluded from this definition. This means that if a digital asset has the characteristics of a financial instrument or a loan certificate, it must comply with the relevant rules and cannot claim the application of the *ad hoc* rules on digital assets.

Tokens are defined as '*any intangible property representing, in digital form, one or more rights that may be issued, registered, retained or transferred by means of a shared electronic recording device enabling the identification, directly or indirectly, of the owner of said property*'.[9] The reference to a shared electronic device is a reference to a distributed ledger (DLT). Therefore, the tokens the law is targeting here are exclusively DLT powered tokens. The definition of tokens is relevant for ICOs. Indeed, issuers can apply for the optional visa, for the public issuance of tokens, no matter how these tokens are offered to the public.[10] But there is a caveat for issuances subscribed to by less than 150 offerees acting on their own account.[11] This threshold is clearly inspired by the same threshold provided for by the Regulation (EU) No. 2017/1129 (Prospectus Regulation) for the public offering of securities to fewer than 150 subscribers.[12] This is surprising on the one hand, as the visa is purely optional but, on the other hand, it betrays a general attitude of the legislator who seems to see this legislation as a first step towards something more constraining in the future.

With this definition, the French legislator particularly had **utility tokens** in mind.[13] But given the broad approach, other digital assets might be also caught by the definition. Indeed, securities are already totally dematerialized in France and are neither less nor more than intangible property representing a right in a company. And as France has already adopted an ordinance and a decree allowing for non-listed securities to be

---

[6] List of ICOs that have received the AMF Approval (May 2020), available at: https://beck-link.de/6af4w (accessed 01.12.2020).

[7] Under French law financial instruments is a category regrouping securities and derivatives, see Art. L. 211-1 of the French Monetary and Financial Code.

[8] Art. L. 223-1 of the French Monetary and Financial Code (FMFC).

[9] Art. L. 552-2 FMFC.

[10] Art. L. 552-3 FMFC.

[11] Art. L. 552-3 and Art. 711-2 Règlement Général de l'Autorité des Marchés Financiers ('RGAMF').

[12] Art. 1(4)(b) Regulation (EU) No. 2017/1129 of the European Parliament and of the Council on the prospectus to be published when securities are offered to the public or admitted to trading on a regulated market, and repealing Directive 2003/71/EC, OJ L 168, 30.6.2017 p. 12–82.

[13] Barsan, ibid, 12.

issued on a blockchain[14] one could wonder if such securities cannot be characterized as a token. If this were the case an issuer of tokenized securities could still not apply for a voluntary visa. Indeed, applying for a visa is not only optional but also subsidiary in nature. Hence, if an issuer wants to offer tokenized securities to the public, he or she will have to comply with the relevant rules[15] and particularly with those requiring a prospectus[16] or invoke one of the exemptions.

5   **Other digital assets** are defined as '*any digital representation of a value which is not issued or guaranteed by a central bank or a public authority, which is not necessarily attached to legal tender and which does not have the legal status of a currency, but which is accepted by natural or legal persons as a means of exchange and which can be transferred, stored or exchanged electronically*'.[17] This definition is a paraphrase of the same definition used by the Directive 2018/843/EU (5th AML/CFT Directive)[18] to define virtual currencies.[19] Unfortunately, other digital assets do not need to be DLT powered. It is sufficient if they can be transferred, stored or exchanged electronically. This means that even non-DLT or blockchain related digital items like in-gaming money might be caught by this broad definition.

6   Other digital assets are mainly defined negatively: they must not be '*issued or guaranteed by a central bank or public authority*', they must not necessarily be '*attached to a legal tender*' and they shall not have '*the legal status of a currency*'. The only positive elements are that they are '*accepted by natural or legal persons as a means of exchange*'[20] and they '*can be transferred, stored or exchanged electronically*'. Given that no reference is made to a DLT or a blockchain a lot of 'electronic' assets such as securities or e-money might be caught by this definition. It is very likely that the French legislator had **currency-like tokens** in mind but given the broad definition, these rules might catch other assets too. Indeed, the main difference between e-money and cryptocurrencies especially in the form of stable coins is the claim on the issuer or right to redemption.[21] Depending on how a stable coin is structured, there might be an overlap between the *ad hoc* provisions of the PACTE law and the e-money directive.[22]

---

[14] Ordinance n° 2017-1674 of December 8, 2017; decree n° 2018-1226 of December 24, 2018; François, 'Décret "Blockchain" – Note sous décret numéro 2018-1226 du 24 décembre 2018 relatif à l'utilisation d'un dispositif d'enregistrement électronique partagé pour la représentation et la transmission de titres financiers et pour l'émission et la cession de minibons', (2019) 2 *Revue des sociétés*, 86. Lavayssière, 'Blockchain et titres financiers: décret minimaliste pour réforme ambitieuse', (2019) 144 *RLDA*, 4 et seq.

[15] See also Hacker and Thomale, 'Crypto-Securities Regulation: ICOs, Token Sales and Cryptocurrencies under EU Financial Law;', (2017). 15 *European Company and Financial Law Review*, 645–696 (2018), available at SSRN: https://beck-link.de/fs42r (accessed 01.12.2020).

[16] See § 7 para. 31.

[17] Art. L. 54-10-1, 2° FMFC.

[18] Directive 2018/843/EU of the European Parliament and of the Council amending Directive (EU) 2015/849 on the prevention of the use of the financial system for the purpose of money laundering or terrorist financing, and amending Directives 2009/138/EC and 2013/36/EU, OJ L 156, 19.6.2018 p. 43–74.

[19] Art. 3(18) as amended by the Directive 2015/849/EU of the European Parliament and of the Council on the prevention of the use of the financial system for the purpose of money laundering or terrorist financing, amending Regulation (EU) No 648/2012 of the European Parliament and of the Council, and repealing Directive 2005/60/EC of the European Parliament and of the Council and Commission Directive 2006/70/EC, OJ L 141, 5.6.2015 p. 73–117.

[20] On the notion of money see Libchaber, 'L'argent entre matière et mémoire', (1998) 42 *Archives de Philosophie du Droit*, 115 et seq. Corbion-Condé, 'De la défiance à l'égard des monnaies nationales au miroir du bitcoin', (2014) *Revue de Droit Bancaire et Financier (RDBF)*, 1 et seq.

[21] See Art. 11 Directive 2009/110/EC of the European Parliament and of the Council on the taking up, pursuit and prudential supervision of the business of electronic money institutions amending Directives 2005/60/EC and 2006/48/EC and repealing Directive 2000/46/EC, OJ L 267, 10.10.2009 p. 7–17; see also Douet, 'Fiscalité des Initial Coin Offerings (ICO)', (2019) *Dalloz IP/IT*, 237.

[22] European Banking Authority (EBA), 'Report on crypto-assets (January 2019), 12 et seq., available at: https://beck-link.de/6ra3v (accessed 01.12.2020); Bullmann, Klemm and Pinna, 'In search for stability in

Further, as other digital assets do not need to be DLT or blockchain powered, the *ad hoc* provisions also apply to in-gaming money or other digital stickers, stars, gems etc. that social networks or other online platforms use to build loyalty with their clients.

II. The Incentives

As the new legislation is constructed as a voluntary opt into one's own compliance, we need to say a word about the incentives. Indeed, as compliance is always costly, why would any issuer opt for a voluntary visa and why would any digital asset service provider opt for a license he or she does not really need in order to do business. 7

Besides the reputational aspect, the French legislator smartly combined what can be called a carrot and stick technique.[23] Indeed, token issuers that obtained a visa and licensed or registered digital asset service providers obtain **access to a bank account**.[24] Practically speaking this is quite relevant for the crypto-asset ecosystem. If a credit institution refuses to open a bank account, the customer can appeal to the Autorité de Contrôle Prudentiel et de Résolution (ACPR) that will examine the request and provide an answer within two months.[25] This means that applying for a visa, registering with AMF or applying for a license gives issuers and digital asset service providers almost a certain access to a bank account.

But besides the luring promise of a bank account, the French legislator also provided for a negative incentive in order to protect potential investors. Indeed, offering digital assets becomes relevant in terms of direct solicitation.[26] Only token issuers who obtained a visa and digital asset service providers who obtained a license are entitled to **banking and financial canvassing**.[27] It should be noted that merely registered custodian wallet providers, providers of the exchange services or operators of a trading platform are not allowed to provide banking and financial canvassing. Only the voluntary license enables digital asset service providers to directly solicit clients. Any violation of these rules is criminally sanctioned.[28] One should note that banking and financial canvassing is defined quite broadly. '*Any unsolicited contact, by any means whatsoever, with a natural or legal person, with a view to obtaining an agreement on digital assets, constitutes an act of banking or financial canvassing*'.[29] Hence, without direct solicitation an issuer or a digital asset services provider cannot actively promote his or her services or products. 8

Finally, the French legislator also introduced a provision in the **Consumer Code**[30] prohibiting direct or indirect advertising by electronic means with the purpose of inviting a person, by means of a reply or contact form, to request or provide additional information or establish a relationship with the advertiser in order to obtain his or her consent to carry out a transaction in relation with the provision of digital asset services or an ICO. This prohibition of course does not apply if the transaction is to be concluded with an issuer who obtained a visa from the AMF or a digital asset service 9

---

crypto-assets: are stablecoins the solution?' (ECB, Occasion Papier Series, n° 230, August 2019), 39, available at: https://beck-link.de/h5ee3 (accessed 12.01.2020).

[23] Barsan, 'Regulating the Crypto World – New Developments from France', (2019) 4 *Revue Trimestrielle de Droit Financier (RTDF)*, 24 et seq.

[24] Art. L. 312–23 § 2 FMFC.

[25] Art. D 312–23 FMFC.

[26] Art. L. 341-1 § 1, n° 8 & 9 FMFC.

[27] Art. L. 341-3, n° 7 & 8 and 341-10, n° 6 FMFC.

[28] Art. L. 353-2 FMFC.

[29] Art. L. 341-1 FMFC.

[30] Art. L. 222-16-1 § 2 Consumer's Code.

provider that obtained a license. An infringement can be punished with an administrative fine of up to 100,000€.[31]

The aim of these provisions is clearly **investor protection**. A lot of potential investors do not understand the complexity and danger of cryptocurrencies. There have already been quite some scams[32] and a lot of issuers of ICOs do not necessarily give investors sufficient information.[33]

B. The Primary Market: Initial Coin Offerings (ICO)

10   The French legislator adopted a very **original piece of legislation** for issuers of tokens who would like to propose these tokens to the public through an ICO. Token issuers can but are not obliged to apply for such a visa. Once they obtained the visa, they need, however, to comply with certain rules and can even face sanctions.

11   The whole legal setup of the **voluntary visa** is subsidiary in nature. One can only apply for a visa if no other financial regulation applies to such issuance.[34] As stated above, there is a caveat for issuances subscribed to by less than 150 offerees acting on their own account[35] which is neither more nor less than an extension of the exemption that applies under the Prospectus Regulation to security issuances. This exemption is totally unnecessary as long as the visa remains optional as an issuer can always proceed with the issuance even without a visa. The exemption would only make sense if an issuer offering his or her tokens to less than 150 investors can solicit them directly, but this is not the case.

Applying for a visa implies for the issuer to give the investor a certain amount of information in order to protect him or her (→ para. 12). Here again the influence of already existing regulation applying to securities is very visible. But the AMF will not only examine the information document but also all promotional communication documents that will be addressed to the public after obtaining the visa. And once the investor opted into this voluntary setup, he or she faces sanctions in case of non-compliance with the new provisions (→ para. 18).

I. Protection of Potential Investors

12   The **information document** required to apply for the voluntary visa is neither more nor less than a simplified version of a prospectus.[36] It is aimed at giving a subscriber all necessary and useful information about the issuer and the offer.[37] But in reality, the information document required is something in between a key information document and a prospectus. Indeed, other countries such as Liechtenstein require token issuers

---

[31] Art. L. 222-16-1 § 3 Consumer's Code.
[32] Tomasicchio, 'Top 5 Cryptocurrency Scams' (June 2017), available at: https://beck-link.de/676m6 (accessed 01.12.2020).
[33] Zetzsche, Buckley, Arner, Föhr, 'The ICO Gold Rush: It's a Scam, It's a Bubble, It's a Super Challenge for Regulators' (2019), *Harvard International Law Journal*, Vol. 63, n° 2. University of New South Wales Faculty of Law Legal Studies Research Paper Series (UNSW) Law Research Paper No. 17–83, available at: https://beck-link.de/wyw2h (accessed 01.12.2020).
[34] Art. L. 552-1 FMFC.
[35] Art. L. 552-3 FMFC and Art. 711-2 RGAMF.
[36] AMF, 'Procédure d'instruction et établissement d'un document d'information devant être déposé auprès de l'AMF en vue de l'obtention d'un visa sur une offre au public de jetons' (June 2019), available at: https://beck-link.de/mfsp6 (accessed 01.12.2020).
[37] Art. L. 552-4 § 2 of the French Monetary and Financial Code.

not to provide a prospectus or something resembling a simplified version of a prospectus[38] but only a key information document.[39]

In order to be easily understandable, **the information delivered to the potential investor must be accurate, clear, not misleading and be sufficiently concise and understandable**.[40] The document must contain information on the issuer and the issuance.

Firstly, the issuer must be identified as well as the major stakeholders who took part in the design and development of the project.[41] The person who drafted the information document must also be identified.

Secondly, the project, the offer, the motivations for the offer and the project, as well as the intended use of the proceeds from the offer must be described.[42] The issuer must describe the offer in detail and indicate how many tokens are being issued, their price, any existing thresholds and caps and the conditions to subscribe to the offer.[43] There is no requirement to indicated if a presale or a private sale preceded the offer, nor how many tokens the founders and other stakeholders hold compared to the tokens being issued.[44] This, however, is quite sensitive information as in practice, the founders hold a very large chunk of tokens and might easily influence the token price on the secondary market.

Thirdly, subscribers must be informed of their rights and duties incorporated into a token as well as how they can exercise their rights.

Fourthly, the issuer must describe the means put in place to monitor and safeguard the proceeds of the offer.[45] The aim here is to ensure traceability of the proceeds from the offer. Therefore, the monitoring and safekeeping system put in place must be reliable and ensure operability and effectiveness.[46] It must ensure the security of the collected proceeds even if they are converted into euros, other fiat or cryptocurrencies. The proceeds must be deposited either in a bank account or a wallet dedicated to the offer. If the proceeds of the offer are transferred to another account or public key, the recipient and the account into which the proceeds can be transferred must be easily identifiable.

Finally, the subscribers must be informed of the risks related to the issuer, the tokens, the offer and the project.[47]

The **information document** can be published in any common language other than French provided that the issuer also delivers a summary in French.[48]

The content of the document and any promotional communications must be clear, precise and not misleading.[49] The information document must, further, indicate under

---

[38] Landesverwaltung Fürstentum Liechtenstein, 'Bericht und Antrag 54/2019 der Regierung an den Landtag des Fürstentums Liechtenstein betreffend die Schaffung eines Gesetzes über Token und VT-Dienstleister (Token- und VT-Dienstleister-Gesetz; TVTG) und die Abänderung weiterer Gesetze' (May 2019), available at: https://beck-link.de/5zd4m (accessed 01.12.2020).
[39] This key information document is inspired by Art. 5 Regulation (EU) 1286/2014 of the European Parliament and of the Council on key information documents for packaged retail and insurance-based investment products (PRIIPs), OJ L 352, 9.12.2014 p. 1–23.
[40] Art. 712-2 § 2 RGAMF.
[41] Art. 712-2 § 1 n° 6 RGAMF.
[42] Art. 712-2 § 1 n° 1 RGAMF.
[43] Art. 712-2 § 1 n° 3 RGAMF.
[44] Oudin, 'La régulation des ICOs Étude sous l'angle des droits français et européen', (2019) 50(1) *Revue Trimestrielle de Droit Financier (RTDF)*, 36.
[45] Art. 712-2 § 1 n° 5 and Art. 712-6 et seq. RGAMF.
[46] Art. 712-7 RGAMF.
[47] Art. 712-2 § 1 n° 7 and Art. 712-3 RGAMF.
[48] Art. L. 552-4 para. 3 FMFC.
[49] Art. L. 552-4 para. 4 FMFC.

what conditions annual information is given to the subscribers on how the funds collected are used.

Once the subscription period expired, the issuer must inform the subscribers of the **outcome of the ICO** at the latest two working days after the closing of the offer.[50] The closing occurs either when the maximum amount of the offer is reached or at the end of the subscription period of maximum six months.

15   The issuer shall further inform the subscribers if a **secondary market** will be organized.[51] But this does not amount to an obligation to organize such secondary market but rather to inform subscribers of a spontaneous development of a secondary market.[52]

Besides the information document, all **promotional communications** are also checked by the AMF.[53] Promotional information must be identified as such and the issuer must indicate the internet site on which the offerees can access the information document.[54] All promotional communications must give offerees sufficient information so that they can understand the risks of the offer and must not contradict the information given in the information document.

16   Before starting to assess the information provided by the issuer, the AMF will first confirm electronically within two days reception and completeness of the information received.[55] The AMF will then examine the documents and deliver or refuse the visa in a time frame of **20 days**. But, the twenty-working-day period only runs from the date the information requested and received by AMF is complete.

If the AMF is satisfied with the information provided and decides to grant the visa, it will inform the issuer electronically. Obtaining the visa implies for the issuer that he or she cannot amend the information document without obtaining the agreement of the AMF who will respond within seven days.[56] The same applies for promotional communication but such communication must be presented to the AMF five days prior to any dissemination.[57]

17   Surprisingly, the French legislator imposes a strict time frame of **six months** on any issuance.[58] This period cannot be extended.[59] It is not quite understandable why the French regulator provided for such a limited visa in time. There have already been ICOs that were open for a year.[60]

Upon the delivery of the visa, the issuer must publish the information document on his or her internet site at the latest at the beginning of the ICO.[61] The document will also be published on the AMF's internet site.[62]

The AMF will publish a list of all the ICOs it granted a visa.[63] As of the date of writing, the AMF has delivered three optional visas.[64]

---

[50] Art. L. 552-7 FMFC and Art. 714-1 RGAMF.
[51] Art. L. 552-7 FMFC.
[52] Art. 714-2 RGAMF.
[53] Art. 713-4 RGAMF.
[54] Art. 713-5 RGAMF.
[55] Art. 712-8 RGAMF.
[56] Art. 712-11 RGAMF.
[57] Art. 713-6 RGAMF.
[58] Art. 712-10 RGAMF.
[59] Art. 712-11 § 3 RGAMF.
[60] The EOS ICO lasted for a year.
[61] Art. 713-1 § 1 RGAMF.
[62] Art. 713-1 § 3 RGAMF.
[63] Art. 713-3 RGAMF.
[64] AMF, 'Liste des offres de jetons ayant obtenu un visa de l'AMF', available at: https://beck-link.de/3dc3c (accessed 01.12.2020).

II. Sanctions

Firstly, issuers who obtained a visa have to comply with **AML/CFT duties**.[65] Even if these duties are limited to the ICO and the subscribers of the tokens the costs are quite extensive. Indeed, an issuer must conduct a risk analysis, put in place internal procedures, and identify his or her subscribers. Thus, token issuers have duties issuers of securities do not have. Furthermore, even the Financial Action Task Force (FATF) does not require token issuers to comply with AML/CFT duties. FATF only targets intermediaries intervening in an ICO.[66] Thus, the question is whether this duty outweighs the benefits of the visa, as the costs will be high. This might be one of the explanations why there have only been three ICOs that applied for a visa. 18

Secondly, the law provides for a **withdrawal** of the visa and an injunction to cease all communication in relation to the ICO and the visa. This will be the case if the ICO does not comply with what is written in the information document, or the issuer is no longer established in France or does not comply with the requirement to set up means to monitor and safeguard the assets collected.[67] A withdrawal can be temporary or definitive. If the AMF wants to withdraw a visa, it must first inform the issuer in advance by registered letter with acknowledgement of receipt, providing reasons for the withdrawal. Once the issuer received the letter, he or she has at least three days to respond in writing.[68] The AMF must take the issuer's response into account when deciding to withdraw the visa and notify the decision to the issuer. If the visa is withdrawn, the issuer must inform the public and cease any communication with a reference to the visa. The AMF must also publish the decision to withdraw the visa on its internet site and hold a public list of all visa withdrawals.[69]

Obviously, if an issuer, whether he has applied or not for the visa, makes **false or misleading statements** with regards to the issuance of the visa, the AMF can make a public statement to set things straight[70]. 19

Finally, the AMF seems to be able to use its **regular sanctioning powers** against issuers who infringe rules on investor protection, market manipulation, insider trading or AML/CFT.[71] The arsenal of sanctions at the disposal of the AMF is very large. Notably the AMF can impose a fine of up to 100 million euros or five times the advantage that an infringement procured.[72]

C. Digital Asset Service Providers

The French legislator further regulated **intermediaries** that provide services on digital assets. The aim of this regulation was twofold. On the one hand, the regulator needed to transpose the 5th AML/CFT Directive. But as this Directive is a minimum 20

---

[65] Art. L. 561-2, n° 7ter FMFC.
[66] FATF, 'International Standards on Combating Money Laundering and the Financing of Terrorism & Proliferation' (June 2019), 70 et seq. and 127, available at: https://beck-link.de/mpd7d (accessed 01.12.2020).
[67] Art. L. 552-6 § 1 FMFC.
[68] Art. 715-1 RGAMF.
[69] Art. 715-2 RGAMF.
[70] Art. L. 552-6 § 2 FMFC.
[71] Art. L. 621-15, II, e) FMFC.
[72] Art. L. 621-15, III FMFC.

harmonization directive, national legislators are free to go beyond. This is precisely what France did on the other hand.

In order to transpose the 5th AML-Directive, France provided for a mandatory registration for two service providers – custodian wallet providers and digital to fiat exchange service providers. Through an ordinance adopted on 9 December 2020[73], the French legislator further submitted exchange service providers between different digital assets and operators of trading platforms to mandatory registration. Beyond this mandatory registration, all service providers who carry on digital asset intermediary activities described below can apply for an optional license. But before presenting the mandatory registration (→ para. 23) and the voluntary licence (→ para. 27) it is necessary to look first into the services that are actually targeted by the law (→ para. 21).

I. Services Provided on Digital Assets

21   The services that are regulated by the PACTE law come actually very close to regular financial services provided on financial instruments and regulated by Directive 2014/65/EU (MiFID 2).[74] The following services are targeted:
- **Custodian wallet providers** either safe keep the digital assets for their clients or safe keep the private cryptographic keys giving access to the digital assets. Custodian wallet providers are '*controlling, on behalf of a third party, the means of access to the digital assets registered in the shared electronic recording device and keep a register of positions, open in the name of the third party, corresponding to its rights over the said digital assets*'.[75] Given this definition, only DLT powered custodial wallets are targeted by the regulation. Furthermore, during the legislative process it clearly appeared that the mere provision of a wallet without any custodial safekeeping of the private key is not subject to these provisions.[76]
- **Exchange services between digital assets and fiat money**; this service is defined as '*the fact of concluding purchase or sale contracts on behalf of a third party relating to digital assets in legal tender, with, where appropriate, the interposition of the service provider's own account*'.[77]
- **Exchange services between different digital assets**; this service is defined as '*the conclusion of contracts providing for the exchange on behalf of a third party of digital assets for other digital assets, with, where appropriate, interposition of the service provider's own account*'.[78]
- The **operation of a digital asset trading platform**. Such a service provider will manage '*one or more digital asset trading platforms, in which multiple third-party*

---

[73] Ordinance n° 2020-1544 of 9 December 2020 strengthening the anti-money laundering and anti-terrorist financing framework applicable to digital assets.

[74] Directive 2014/65/EU of the European Parliament and of the Council on markets in financial instruments and amending Directive 2002/92/EC and Directive 2011/61/EU, OJ L 173, 349–496.

[75] Art. R. 54-10-2, 1° FMFC.

[76] National Assembly, 'Third Plenary Discussion of 28 September 2018',available at: https://beck-link.de/zd58t (accessed 01.12.2020), particularly the answer of the Secretary of State Delphine Gény-Stephann to Mme de La Raudière; see also the answer of the Secretary of State Agnès Pannier-Runacher, Rapport fait au nom de la commission spéciale chargée d'examiner, après engagement de la procédure accélérée, le projet de loi, modifié par le Sénat en première lecture, relative à la croissance et la transformation des entreprises (n° 1673), Tome II, Comptes rendus, 254, available at: https://beck-link.de/h54np (accessed 01.12.2020).

[77] Art. R. 54-10-2, 2° FMFC.

[78] Art. R. 54-10-2, 3° FMFC.

buying and selling interests in digital assets against other digital assets or in legal tender can interact in a manner that results in the conclusion of contracts'.[79]
- The **reception and transmission of orders** on digital assets on behalf of third parties;
- Portfolio management of digital assets on behalf of third parties; this service consists in *'managing, in a discretionary and individualized manner, portfolios including one or more digital assets within the framework of a mandate given by a third party'*.[80]
- **Investment advice** in digital assets consists in the provision of *'personalized recommendations to a third party, either at its request or at the initiative of the provider providing the advice, concerning one or more digital assets'*.[81]
- **Underwriting** of digital assets *'is the act of acquiring digital assets directly from a digital asset issuer in order to sell them'*.[82]
- **Guaranteed placement** of digital assets *'is the act of seeking purchasers on behalf of an issuer of digital assets and guaranteeing a minimum purchase amount by agreeing to acquire the digital assets not placed'*.[83]
- **Non-guaranteed placement** of digital assets *'is the act of seeking purchasers on behalf of an issuer of digital assets without guaranteeing an acquisition amount to the issuer'*.[84]

The first four service providers must **mandatorily register** with the AMF. **All** service 22 providers, including the ones that must mandatorily register, can apply for a **voluntary license**.

Taking into account the services targeted, there is a clear inspiration from MiFID 2 for the last seven services, whereas the exchange services are quite similar to foreign exchange services. And even the custodial wallet service can be assimilated to the safekeeping of financial instruments by depositaries. Overall, the French legislator simply adapted existing regulated financial services to a blockchain and crypto-currency environment.

II. Mandatory Registration

Custodian wallet providers, crypto/fiat and crypto/crypto exchange service providers 23 as well as trading platform operators must register with the AMF. In exchange, they obtain a **monopoly** for the activities that require such registration. This means that any person who infringes this monopoly (exercises the activity without registration) faces **criminal liability**. This part of the French law is clearly the transposition of the 5th AML/CFT Directive. Indeed, the 5th AML/CFT Directive required Member States to register some of these service providers and submit them to AML/CFT duties. The Directive had to be transposed at the latest by 10 January 2020.

The **5th AML/CFT Directive** itself reflects FATFs recommendations of 2015 advocat- 25 ing in favour of submitting exchange services between cryptocurrencies and fiat money to a license and to AML/CFT duties as they are the point of intersection between the crypto world and the traditional financial system.[85] The 5th AML Directive implemented this recommendation and broadened it to custodian wallet providers. In the meantime,

---

[79] Art. R. 54-10-2, 4° FMFC.
[80] Art. R. 54-10-2, 5-2° FMFC.
[81] Art. R. 54-10-2, 5-3° FMFC.
[82] Art. R. 54-10-2, 5-4° FMFC.
[83] Art. R. 54-10-2, 5-5° FMFC.
[84] Art. R. 54-10-2, 5-6° FMFC.
[85] FATF, 'Guidance for a risk-based approach – Virtual Currencies' (June 2015), 10 and 12, available at: https://beck-link.de/7n5pz (accessed 01.12.2020).

FATF revised its recommendations in October 2018[86] to include all intermediaries that exchange virtual currencies for other virtual currencies or fiat money, transfer virtual currencies on behalf of someone else, wallet providers and other intermediaries that provide financial services[87] in the case of an initial coin offering or for the sale of virtual assets.[88] FATF requires Member States to submit these intermediaries either to a license or to registration and in any case to oblige them to comply with AML/CFT duties.[89] This means that the European Union will have to adopt a 6th AML Directive in the near future.[90]

26 The AMF will, firstly, check that the directors and shareholders[91] of digital asset service providers are **fit and proper**.[92] Shareholders who hold directly or indirectly more than 25 % of the share capital or of the voting rights, those who have a *de facto* majority in the general assembly or those who are able to designate the majority of the board members must ensure the sound and prudent management of the service provider.

Secondly, the service providers must set up an **organization, procedures and internal control systems** to ensure compliance with AML/CFT rules.[93]

Once the AMF obtained all required information, it will take up to **six months** to deliver its response to the service provider. Obviously, the deadline only runs if the file is complete. In practice it is very likely that this time frame will be exceeded due to incomplete files.

Once a service provider has obtained the registration, he or she also needs to inform the AMF of any substantial changes with regards to the directors or beneficial owners.[94] But this requirement is quite classical for any regulated financial services provider. If the service provider does not comply with the rules of his registration any more the AMF can deregister him.[95] Deregistration can also intervene upon the request of the service provider.

Once deregistered, the service provider must inform the public of his or her deregistration the day after the notification. A custodian wallet provider must return the assets held on behalf of the clients immediately. If a client does not respond within a reasonable time frame, the deregistered custodian wallet provider must transfer the clients' assets to a registered service provider and inform his or her clients of the transfer.[96]

III. Voluntary License

27 All service providers including custodian wallet providers and fiat/crypto and crypto/crypto exchange service providers as well as trading platform operators can apply for a voluntary license if they want to provide **services on digital assets on a regular basis**.

---

[86] Ibid.
[87] Ibid, 70 et seq. and 127.
[88] Barsan, 'Public Blockchains: The Privacy-Transparency Conundrum', (2019) 2 *Revue Trimestrielle de Droit Financier (RTDF)*, 50 et seq.
[89] FATF, ibid, 15.
[90] See also the position of ESMA who advocates for broader AML/CFT duties of service providers, European Securities Market Authority (ESMA), 'Advice: Initial Coin Offerings and Crypto-Assets' (January 2019), 40, available at: https://beck-link.de/dm5hb (accessed 01.12.2020).
[91] Art. L. 54-10-3, n° 2 FMFC.
[92] Art. L. 54-10-3, n° 1 FMFC.
[93] Art. L. 54-10-3, n° 3 FMFC.
[94] Art. D. 54-10-5 FMFC.
[95] Art. D. 54-10-5, II FMFC.
[96] Art. D. 54-10-5, III FMFC.

§ 16. France

Although the license is voluntary, without a license, providers carrying on these services are not permitted to directly solicit customers in France, in brief, this means they cannot directly market to French customers. The requirements a service provider needs to comply with in order to obtain such license are either common requirements for all service providers or specific requirements depending on the service provided.

In order to apply for a license, a service provider must comply with the following common requirements:

- Provide **general information**[97] such as the name, corporate form, address and contact information.
- Provide the **list of services** for which approval is sought as well as the services that would be provided without approval.
- Provide **financial information** (provisional accounts, assumptions, forecasts etc.).
- Provide the same information on directors and beneficial owners (**fit and proper**) as that which is required for custodial wallet providers and crypto/fiat exchange service providers.[98]
- Provide the **identity of any shareholder** that holds at least 10 % of the capital or voting rights or has any other possibility of exercising a significant influence over the management of the service provider.[99] These shareholders must guarantee a prudent management of the service provider.
- Every service provider needs either **professional insurance** or sufficient **equity capital**.[100]
- Depending on the activity exercised **minimum capital** – and thus permanent equity capital – shall be either 50,000€ or 150,000€.[101]
- Ensure an adequate system of **internal control measures** and make sure that the **IT system is resilient and sufficiently secure**.[102] The AMF can also require the service provider to use a certified IT system or to provide an audit for the IT system.[103]
- Put in place a system to manage **conflicts of interest**.[104] Service providers must analyse their risks and manage them. If ever they arrive to the conclusion that in spite of all efforts there is still a conflict of interest, they must inform their clients of this.[105]
- Publish their **pricing policies** and any costs or fees incurred.[106]
- Establish and implement a policy for managing **customer complaints** and ensure prompt processing of those complaints.
- Comply with **rules of conduct**: act honestly, loyally and professionally, putting client's interests first.[107] Amongst others, service providers must conclude a written agreement with their clients containing a description of the essential rights and obligations of the parties, the nature of the services provided and the types of digital assets to which the service applies, the pricing of services and the method of

---

[97] Art. D. 54-10-6 FMFC.
[98] Art. D. 54-10-6, II FMFC.
[99] Art. D. 54-10-6, III FMFC.
[100] Art. L. 54-10-5, I, n° 1 FMFC.
[101] 50.000€ apply to crypto/fiat and crypto/crypto exchange service providers if they act as brokers, to trading platforms under certain circumstances, to RTO services, to investment advice and to unsecured investment. All other service providers, including exchange service providers that act as dealers need a minimum capital and permanent equity capital of 150.000€.
[102] Art. L. 54-10-5, I, n° 2 & 3 FMFC.
[103] Art. D. 54-10-7 para. 3 FMFC.
[104] Art. L. 54-10-5, I, n° 4 FMFC.
[105] Art. 721-9 RGAMF.
[106] Art. 721-12 RGAMF.
[107] Art. 721-13 RGAMF.

remuneration, the period of validity of the agreement, and the legal confidentiality obligations of the service provider.[108]
– Must comply with **AML/CFT rules**.

28   Besides these common requirements, there are specific requirements depending on the services provided.

Custodian wallet providers must establish a safekeeping policy and make sure that they put in place means to return digital assets as soon as possible or provide access to those assets held on behalf of their clients.[109] A custodian wallet provider can delegate the safekeeping of the assets but must make sure that the sub custodian complies with the obligations of the custodian but that does not excuse him from his liability.[110] Custodian wallet providers must further segregate their own assets from those of their clients. Finally, the custodian wallet provider must not use the digital assets or cryptographic keys held on behalf of their clients without their prior consent.[111]

29   **Providers of exchange services**, be it crypto/crypto or crypto/fiat, have to establish a non-discriminatory commercial policy and must publish a firm price or a method for determining the price of the digital assets they exchange. They must further publish the volumes and prices of the transactions they have carried out.[112] Finally, they must execute their clients' orders at the prices displayed at the time of receipt. The AMF's General Rulebook provides for further and very extensive requirements with regards to order execution[113] and price transparency.[114]

30   **Service providers who operate a trading platform**[115] must set operating rules for the exchange.[116] These rules must be written in French and can in certain cases be written in another language if the majority of the platform's customer's either reside outside France or are professionals.[117] Negotiation must be fair and orderly and they can only commit their own capital to the platform they manage under the conditions and within the limits set by AMF's General Rulebook. Finally, they must publish details of orders and transactions concluded on their platforms.[118]

31   **All other service providers**[119] must have a program of operations for each service provided. They must specify the conditions under which they will provide the service and indicate the types of services they intend to provide and inform customers about the structure of their organization. Once they establish their program of operations, they must also ensure that they have all the means at their disposal to implement such a program. If they engage in investment advice or portfolio management, they must obtain the necessary information from their customers in order to recommend digital

---

[108] Art. 721-14 RGAMF.
[109] Art. L. 54-10-5, II, n° 3 FMFC.
[110] Art. 722-2 RGAMF.
[111] Art. L. 54-10-5, II, n° 5 FMFC.
[112] Art. L. 54-10-5, III FMFC.
[113] Amongst others there are a lot of requirements concerning the grouping of orders and order execution. If these requirements make sense when applied to financial instruments, one can wonder how an order concerning crypto assets is transmitted by an intermediary to an exchange. It makes little sense to pay the fees of the intermediary if the service requires the owner to confirm the order on the exchange with his or her private key. Order transmission would only be relevant if the exchange service provider is also a custodian holding clients' assets and executes the off-chain orders for the clients.
[114] Art. 722-6 et seq. RGAMF.
[115] Art. L. 54-10-5, V FMFC.
[116] Art. 722-12 RGAMF.
[117] Art. 722-12 para. 2 RGAMF.
[118] Art. 722-15 RGAMF.
[119] Art. L. 54-10-5, VI, n° 1, 2, 3 FMFC.

assets adapted to their profile. The AMF General Rulebook provides for further requirements based on the service provided.[120]

D. Conclusion

The French legislator has invented a **new genre of regulation** combining a seemingly optional law with very strong incentives and prohibitions. In practice, there have been only three ICOs that applied for a visa and there are ten digital asset service providers that registered with the AMF. Seven out of the ten registered service providers did so very recently as the scope of registration was broadened through the ordinance of 9 December 2020. There are no licensed service providers at the time of writing. This shows that the French initiative is not a huge success even though the law is only a year old. Indeed, the overall impression is that the provisions added in the decree and especially AMF's General Rulebook impose such regulatory constraints on the actors that the **burden seems to outweigh the advantages**. This is in particular true for the license that is, as of now, optional in nature. The advantage of the bank account and direct solicitation do not seem to outweigh the burden of the regulation. Simply adapting MiFID 2 requirements to the crypto ecosystem is probably not the right choice to make. It would have been certainly more useful to provide for some indispensable hard law rules to protect investors but besides that leave the ecosystem space to breathe and continue developing. This is not the choice the French legislation made and unfortunately, MiCA seems to go into the same direction.

32

---

[120] Art. 722-16 et seq. RGAMF.

§ 17
Germany

Literature: Bialluch-von Allwörden, 'Zivil- und prospektrechtliche Aspekte des eWpG-E', (2021) 1 *Recht Digital (RDi)*, 13; Bialluch-von Allwörden, 'Initial Coin Offerings: Kryptowährungen als Wertpapier oder Vermögensanlage?', (2018) 45 *Wirtschafts- und Bankrecht (WM)*, 2118; Bitbond, 'Securities Prospectus of Bitbond for the public offering of qualified subordinated token-based bonds with a maximum total nominal amount of EUR 100,000,000.00' (January 2019), available at: https://beck-link.de/f83nc (last accessed 14.01.2021); Höhlein and Weiß, 'Krypto-Assets, ICO und Blockchain: prospektrechtliche Perspektive und aufsichtsrechtliche Praxis', [2019] *Recht der Finanzinstrumente (RdF)*, 116; Just, Voß, Ritz and Becker, Wertpapierhandelsgesetz (C.H. Beck, Munich, 2015), § 2; Kaulartz and Matzke, 'Die Tokenisierung des Rechts', (2018) *Neue Juristische Wochenschrift (NJW)*, 3278; Lehmann, 'Zeitenwende im Wertpapierrecht', (2020) 9 *Zeitschrift für Bank- und Kapitalmarktrecht (BKR)*, 431; Meier, 'Übertragung von elektronischen Wertpapieren nach dem eWpG-E', (2021) 1 *Recht Digital (RDi)*, 1; Matzke, 'Voraussetzungen der Prospekthaftung bei einem ICO', (2021) 1 *Recht Digital (RDi)*, 44; Müller, Wertpapierprospektgesetz (C.H. Beck, 2nd ed., 2017); Patz, 'Handelsplattformen für Kryptowährungen und Kryptoassets', [2019] *Zeitschrift für Bank- und Kapitalmarktrecht (BKR)*, 435; Preuße, Wöckener and Gillenkirch, 'Der Gesetzesentwurf zur Einführung elektronischer Wertpapiere' (2020) 11 *Zeitschrift für Bank- und Kapitalmarktrecht (BKR)*, 551. Saive, 'Einführung elektronischer Wertpapiere', (2020) *Zeitschrift Rechtspolitik (ZRP)*, 219.

Outline

	para.
A. Market Development and Regulatory Environment	1
I. Classification of Tokens	3
II. First Security Tokens Offering	7
III. Crypto Exchanges	12
IV. Bitcoin ATMs	14
V. Role of the Regulator	17
B. Important Court Cases	20
I. KG Berlin, Judgement of 25.9.2018 – (4) 161 Ss 28/18 (35/18)	20
II. LG Berlin, Judgement of 27.5.2020 – 2 O 322/18	24
C. Regulatory Development and Reform	30
I. Crypto Assets	30
II. Electronic Securities and Crypto Securities	34

A. Market Development and Regulatory Environment

1 In late 2019, the **German Government** issued, after a consultation phase, its '**Blockchain Strategy**'.[1] Under the title 'We Set Out the Course for the Token Economy', the Government identified the potential, various use cases and legislative measures it intends to pursue in the coming years: 'The Federal Government has set itself the goal of embracing the opportunities in blockchain technology and of advancing the areas of potential that it offers for the digital transformation'. Based on this document, the discussions in Germany surrounding blockchains has become more intense, in particular on a corporate and institutional level. Also, authorities have had to take the necessary measures to respond to the high demand, first and foremost the German

---

[1] Bundesministerium der Finanzen, 'Blockchain Strategy of the Federal Government' (March 2019), available at: https://beck-link.de/4dht8 (last accessed 14.01.2021).

Federal Financial Supervisory Authority (Bundesanstalt für Finanzdienstleistungsaufsicht, BaFin).

BaFin has certainly played an important part in the regulation of crypto assets in the European Union (→ below para. 18). Being the competent body for financial services in Germany (including financial services targeting to customers in Germany), BaFin came quite early in contact with many blockchain use cases, or other distributed ledger technologies. The reason is that Berlin has been one of the European 'blockchain capitals' for the last years. BaFin has seized this opportunity, has extended its know-how, has published many guidelines, has been open to discussions, but also strict on illegal actions, and thus has become one of the first addresses to approach for companies pursuing blockchain-related business in the European Union.

I. Classification of Tokens

Like most other regulatory bodies, BaFin differentiates between three different types of tokens: a **utility token**, a **payment or currency token**, and a **security token** (this term seems more common in Germany compared to 'investment token').[2] There might be another, fourth type, which combines elements of the other three types, which one could qualify as a **hybrid token**.

In practice, utility tokens take by far the most important role in Germany, followed, with growing potential, by security tokens. Payment tokens in terms of e-money have not yet been issued in Germany in a relevant manner, but there is some potential once the demand for stable coins increases, becoming attractive for banks and corporates.[3]

Tokens allowing access to certain services or products, similar to a ticket or voucher, are considered to be **utility tokens** in the view of BaFin. The utility token is typically a financial instrument in terms of § 1 para. 11 German Banking Act (Kreditwesengesetz, KWG). This makes some license requirements applicable, like investment brokerage. However, issuing a utility token, for example during an ICO, is permission-free and does not require an approved prospectus.

Payment or currency tokens, which are used as a means of payment, may be qualified as **e-money** and thus fall under § 1(2)(3) German Payment Services Supervision Act (Zahlungsdiensteaufsichtsgesetz, ZAG). The issuance of e-money requires a license as an e-money emitter, § 1(2)(1)(2) ZAG. Payment tokens which qualify as e-money have not really yet been issued to the public in Germany and are thus more a 'threat' to the emitters than an actual use case. The reason might lie in the high regulatory requirements applicable to e-money emitters. There are, nevertheless, many issuances of payment-like tokens which do not qualify as e-money because they are not accepted by third parties (!) as a means of payment, but only by the emitter itself. In that case, the requirements of e-money are not met. Examples for such a token include in-platform/in-game crypto currencies. Since the goods and services are only offered by the issuer of the token, those tokens should rather be referred to as utility tokens, although the differentiations are not yet very clear in practice.[4]

---

[2] BaFin, 'Zweites Hinweisschreiben zu Prospekt- und Erlaubnispflichten im Zusammenhang mit der Ausgabe sogenannter Krypto-Token' (August 2019), sec. V.b, available at: https://beck-link.de/4d27t (last accessed 14.01.2021).

[3] Deutsche Bundesbank, 'Globale Stable Coin-Initiative 'Libra'' (December 2019), available at: https://beck-link.de/cy8hr (last accessed 14.01.2021).

[4] Höhlein and Weiß, 'Krypto-Assets, ICO und Blockchain: prospektrechtliche Perspektive und aufsichtsrechtliche Praxis', [2019] *Recht der Finanzinstrumente (RdF)*, 116, 120.

6   **Security tokens** represent rights similar to shares or membership rights or a right of a debt nature. They are, as a rule, freely transferable.[5] The German legislator distinguishes between two different types of securities: *Wertpapiere* according to the German Securities Prospectus Act (Wertpapierprospektgesetz, WpPG) and *Vermögensanlagen* according to the German Asset Investment Act (Vermögensanlagegesetz, VermAnlG). The term Wertpapier is identical with Art. 2(a) Regulation (EU) 1129/2017[6] (see in more detail → § 7). An example for Wertpapiere are corporate shares, an example for Vermögensanlagen are loans, provided that they are not fungible/tradeable. Vermögensanlagen are typically not tradeable on financial markets in the broader sense.[7] If linked to a token, however, a loan becomes transferable and thus typically also tradeable and must, according to BaFin, be qualified as a Wertpapier sui generis.[8] This corresponds to the principle of 'substance over form' stipulated by the European Securities and Markets Authority (ESMA). According to this principle, only the material components of an instrument are decisive, not its title. Securities in the regulatory sense do not require the written form to be compliant with Art. 4(1)(44) MiFiD2 (→ para. 25).

II. First Security Token Offering

7   In January 2019, BaFin approved the first **securities prospectus** for a security token in Germany. The issuer, the Berlin-based Bitbond Finance GmbH, structured its investment instrument as a registered bond (Namensschuldverschreibung). This bond would be subject to § 1(2)(6) VermAnlG and would therefore be considered as a Vermögensanlage (→ para. 6). Because of its transferability and thus tradability on financial markets, it had to be qualified as a Wertpapier sui generis and Bitbond drafted a securities prospectus in accordance with the WpPG.[9] The Bitbond token is the first of about 20 security tokens in Germany.[10]

8   The main 'intended' activity of the issuer was to grant loans in cryptocurrencies such as Bitcoin or Stellar Lumens to various companies of different sizes and self-employed persons. The granting takes place over an online brokerage platform operated by Bitbond GmbH, on which potential borrowers were listed with the desired loan amount and the loan conditions like interest rate and term.

9   The tokens issued by **Bitbond** Finance GmbH in the ICO, the so-called BB1 tokens, were linked to bonds which grant the creditor a claim against the issuer for redemption of the invested capital at the end of the term and interest during the term. The investment agreement contains a qualified subordination clause according to which in the event of a bankruptcy of the issuer claims from any other creditor take precedence over the claims from the token investors. In other words, token investors are subject to much higher risks than other creditors, comparable to the ones of shareholders. These **qualified subordination** clauses have become standard in most security token offerings (STOs) in Germany. The reason is that

---

[5] BaFin, ibid, sec. V.b.
[6] Regulation (EU) No. 1129/2017 of the European Parliament and of the Council on the prospectus to be published when securities are offered to the public or admitted to trading on a regulated market, and repealing Directive 2003/71/EC, OJ L 168, 30.6.2017 p. 12–82.
[7] Höhlein and Weiß, ibid, 116 (119 et seq.).
[8] Weiß, 'Tokenisierung' (April 2019), available at: https://beck-link.de/tbsf7 (last accessed 14.01.2021).
[9] Bitbond, 'Securities Prospectus of Bitbond for the public offering of qualified subordinated token-based bonds with a maximum total nominal amount of EUR 100,000,000.00' (January 2019), available at: https://beck-link.de/f83nc (last accessed 14.01.2021).
[10] ITSA, 'Token Lists Title', 'Security Tokens in Germany', https://beck-link.de/cp2z4 (last accessed 10.03.2021).

without such a clause, receiving money from a respective loan would be considered as deposit business (Einlagengeschäft) under § 1(1)(2)(1) KWG with the consequence that the issuer would need to apply for a banking license to BaFin according to § 32 KWG.

Although the prospectus provided by Bitbond mentioned a maximum investment amount of 100 million Euros, the goal of the issuer was apparently to receive 3.5 million, of which, according to media, only 2.1 million were reached.[11] Given the enormous press coverage which this first public STO to retail investors in Germany with an officially approved prospectus generated, this result could be considered disappointing. On the other hand, being first mover also means developing a new market, and it appeared that there have not been sufficient investors who understood the advantages offered by the issued bond, or they weighed them lower compared to the risks this new instrument raised. 10

The numbers of STOs in Germany remains relatively low. This certainly relates to two reasons. First, STOs are not yet on the agenda of investors. Classical investors still seem reserved about blockchain technology in general, or rather focus on crypto currencies like BTC or ETH with higher trading volumes and market recognition. They also question the advantages of tokenizing bonds. Second, there are still regulatory challenges to be solved. For example, there is no express law regulating the 'security sui generis' (→ para. 7), it is legally still impossible to inextricably link a token to a right represented by that token (→ para. 35),[12] and there are no legally compliant trading venues for security tokens in Germany (→ para. 12). 11

III. Crypto Exchanges

Although there are many international crypto exchanges available for German investors (coinbase, kraken, etc.), there are still only very few located in Germany. All of them have very limited functionalities compared to the aforementioned (e.g., bitcoin.de operated by futurum bank AG). German projects which are discussed more intensively are the ones by the Stuttgart Stock Exchange (Börse Stuttgart), which has recently published a mobile application called 'Bison'. **Bison** can be used to buy and sell a selection of cryptocurrencies. Furthermore, Stuttgart Stock Exchange launched **BSDEX**, a crypto exchange where investors can trade Bitcoin (BTC), Ether (ETH), Litecoin (LTC) and Ripple (XRP). Since those cryptocurrencies are no securities under EU laws, the specific rules for securities trading do not apply (e.g., with regard to MTFs, Art. 18, 19 Directive 2014/65/EU (MiFID II Directive)[13]), which makes those exchanges way less complex from a regulatory point of view. Besides, according to its website,[14] BSDEX falls under § 2(12)(2) KWG, which stipulates some exceptions for companies operating regulated stock exchanges like the Stuttgart Stock Exchange does.[15] BSDEX claims to ensure transparency by open order books, which provide information about existing orders and the current market 12

---

[11] Hofer, 'Bitbond STO geschlossen – Was ist das Fazit?' (July 2019), available at: https://beck-link.de/mnf75 (last accessed 14.01.2021).
[12] Kaulartz and Matzke, 'Die Tokenisierung des Rechts', (2018) *Neue Juristische Wochenschrift (NJW)*, 3278.
[13] Directive 2014/65/EU of the European Parliament and of the Council of 15 May 2014 on markets in financial instruments and amending Directives 2002/92/EC and 2011/61/EU, OJ L 173, 12.6.2016, 349–496.
[14] See Börse Stuttgart. available at: https://beck-link.de/ae6bk (last accessed 14.01.2021).
[15] Patz, 'Handelsplattformen für Kryptowährungen und Kryptoassets', [2019] *Zeitschrift für Bank- und Kapitalmarktrecht (BKR)*, 435 (437 et seq.).

situation. Investors' orders are executed according to pre-determined, fixed rules, which are published in a rulebook. Compliance with the rulebook shall be reached by internal market surveillance.

13 The Stuttgart Stock Exchange has announced to launch an ICO platform where companies can tokenize investment products, as well as an exchange for security tokens.[16] Both projects are not yet available.

IV. Bitcoin ATMs

14 In September 2020, BaFin published an opinion clarifying that Bitcoin ATMs shall be forbidden in Germany unless their operators have a **proprietary trading** license (§ 1 (1a)(2)(4)(c) KWG) or a license for **financial commission business** (§ 1(1)(2)(4) KWG).[17] Operating Bitcoin ATMs without the necessary licenses shall be forbidden and thus would be sanctioned. BaFin, furthermore, clarified that persons involved in the operation of Bitcoin ATMs, for example by providing electricity or an area within a shop, may also be subject to administrative measures such as fines.

15 Due to the briefness of the BaFin publication, it remains unclear how the Bitcoin ATMs BaFin had in mind function, what the exact legal arguments are for applying the proprietary trading regime, and in what cases one can assume that operating Bitcoin ATMs is considered a financial commission business. It seems rather questionable that any implementation of **Bitcoin ATMs** must be considered as proprietary trading. This would require purchasing or selling financial instruments on someone's own account as a service for others (§ 1 para. 1a s. 2 no. 4 lit. c KWG). Bitcoins are without doubt financial instruments under German banking law (see below → para. 31),[18] and typically sold/purchased on the operator's own account because the operator bears the price risk. However, the operation of an ATM does not in all scenarios constitute a service for others, as required by the proprietary trading definition. According to the German Federal Administration Court (Bundesverwaltungsgericht, BVerwG), this requirement must be interpreted in a narrow sense.[19] According to the court, proprietary trading is regularly characterized by an imbalance between the proprietary dealer and the customer, with the proprietary dealer having better access to the market on which he operates, in particular in order to cover his business with the customer or to close the open position resulting from the customer transaction or to give the customer access to the market in the first place, which would otherwise remain closed to him. The German Federal Court of Justice (Bundesgerichtshof, BGH) clarifies[20] that the prerequisite for proprietary trading is therefore that a specific customer order for the purchase of a specific security – usually at an agreed fixed price – has been placed before the purchase. Both court rulings allow for an argument according to which a Bitcoin ATM which keeps Bitcoins on stock but does not itself execute orders at the market to satisfy customers' demands, could not be qualified as proprietary trading.

---

[16] Börse Stuttgart, 'Gruppe Börse Stuttgart schafft durchgehende Infrastruktur für digitale Assets' (August 2018), available at: https://beck-link.de/xf8ac (last accessed 14.01.2021); Heise-online, 'Börse Stuttgart plant Plattform für ICOs und Kryptogeldhandel' (August 2018), available at: https://beck-link.de/5wpb2 (last accessed 14.01.2021).

[17] BaFin, 'Aufstellen von Krypto-ATM: Erlaubnis der BaFin erforderlich' (September 2020), available at: https://beck-link.de/d33da (last accessed 14.01.2021).

[18] But not under German/EU securities laws, → § 7 para. 33.

[19] German Constitutional Court of Justice (*Bundesverfassungsgericht*) 27.02.2008-6 11.07, para. 31.

[20] German Federal Court of Justice (*Bundesgerichtshof*) 6.11.2003-1 StR 24/03, 2 *Zeitschrift für Bank- und Kapitalmarktrecht* 2004, 74 (78).

Thus, the legal situation remains unclear. Current Bitcoin ATMs in Germany are 16
offered by companies with a license for proprietary trading, in cooperation with
technology providers which have the necessary expertise and know-how to develop
and maintain the ATMs. Since this leads to higher costs, a clarification from a court
specifically relating to Bitcoin ATMs or a more sophisticated guideline from BaFin
would be highly welcome.

V. Role of the Regulator

BaFin takes a two-sided role in the crypto space. On the one hand, BaFin qualified 17
Bitcoins as financial instruments very early (in 2011[21]), making the entire German
Banking Act (Kreditwesengesetz, KWG) applicable to services regarding cryptocurrencies and other tokens, and thus allowing BaFin to regulate tokens.[22] In particular, BaFin
was able to go after companies and investment schemes which BaFin considered scams,
whose number is unfortunately rather high compared to ordinary businesses. By being
able to publish warnings online on their website,[23] BaFin has a very sharp sword in
fighting scams, and not only a few companies have been unfortunate to 'benefit' of such
measures,[24] with severe consequences.

On the other hand, BaFin has always shown a strong interest in cryptocurrencies and 18
crypto use cases. Many BaFin staff members have a surprisingly profound knowledge of
blockchain technology, and it is not uncommon that both BaFin staff members and
practising lawyers end up discussing new trends on the phone, when only calling each
other for specific cases. This rather positive attitude leads to some level of openness to
discuss new and innovative projects and to make things happen which had not been
possible before. To give an example (→ para. 7), BaFin has approved a prospectus[25] for
the first security token offering in Germany[26] and apparently also in the European
Union, introducing the concept of a security sui generis, a security which does not
require the written form, although expressly required by German laws.[27] This push by
BaFin has been well perceived, but does, of course, only help with regard to the
regulatory perspective of tokenized securities, and not on the private law side, due to a
lack of competence of BaFin: The question remains how tokens and the right which
they represent (e.g., rights resulting from a loan agreement) can be linked with each
other without the possibility of one being transferred without the other. The corresponding statutory provisions (§ 793 German Civil Code (Bürgerliches Gesetzbuch,
BGB)) only apply to paper deeds but not to tokens. In practice, STOs have faced and are

---

[21] BaFin, 'Hinweise zu Finanzinstrumenten nach § 1 Abs. 11 Sätze 1 bis 5 KWG (Aktien, Vermögensanlagen, Schuldtitel, sonstige Rechte, Anteile an Investmentvermögen, Geldmarktinstrumente, Devisen, Rechnungseinheiten, Emissionszertifikate und Kryptowerte)' (December 2011, updated February 2021), available at: https://beck-link.de/cn2bx (last accessed 14.01.2021).
[22] See also Barsan, 'Legal Challenges of Initial Coin Offerings (ICO)', (2017) RDTF, 54–65.
[23] BaFin, 'Warnungen & Aktuelles für Verbraucher' (November 2020), available at: https://beck-link.de/4m2cs (last accessed 14.01.2021).
[24] Wagenknecht, 'Update 10. Oktober) In eigener Sache: Stellungnahme zur BaFin-Veröffentlichung hinsichtlich einer möglichen Verletzung der Prospektpflicht' (Oktober 2019), available at: https://beck-link.de/h3yv3 (last accessed 14.01.2021).
[25] Bitbond, 'tokenbasierte Schuldverschreibungen' (January 2019), available at: https://beck-link.de/65m2v (last accessed 14.01.2021).
[26] Klee, 'BaFin genehmigt Deutschlands erstes Security Token Offering (STO)' (February 2019), available at: https://beck-link.de/ww8kp (last accessed 14.01.2021).
[27] Bialluch-von Allwörden/von Allwörden, 'Initial Coin Offerings: Kryptowährungen als Wertpapier oder Vermögensanlage? ', (2018) 45 *Wirtschafts- und Bankrecht (WM)*, 2118; German Regional Court of Berlin 27.05.2020-2 O 322/18, BeckRS 2020, 32005, para. 85.

still facing the risk that the token linked to a right becomes an empty hull if a token holder assigns the rights to a third party keeping the token, or transfers the token without transferring the right. This issue might be one of the reasons why STOs are still rare in Germany, which might, however, change once the draft law on crypto securities enters into force (→ para. 34). Considering those civil law issues, the progressive steps of BaFin towards a security sui generis should be even more appreciated.

19 All in all, it seems that the role of BaFin is in most cases very supportive of the crypto space. They promote promising projects, are open for discussions and eager to learn more about blockchain technology, while on the other hand trying to eliminate rotten apples which could harm the development of the blockchain sector in Germany. This role of BaFin is very well received by companies, and also attracts business from outside of Germany.

B. Important Court Cases

I. KG Berlin, Judgement of 25.9.2018 – (4) 161 Ss 28/18 (35/18)

20 The Higher Regional Court of Berlin (Kammergericht, KG) had to decide upon a penalty imposed upon a natural person responsible for a company operating a crypto trading platform. According to the findings of the regional court, i.e., the first instance, Bitcoins could be traded via this platform, whereby the defendant conducted brokering services between buyers and sellers. Buyers had to register and deposit a corresponding number of Euros into their account which could be used to acquire Bitcoins. Sellers could offer their Bitcoins via their account. The customers' payments were made to an account of the defendant's company. This company did not hold any licenses from BaFin.

21 The court had to decide whether these activities should be qualified as **investment brokerage** in terms of § 1(1a) (2)(1) KWG, which would require a BaFin license according to § 32 KWG. Brokerage activities without a license are a criminal offence with imprisonment up to five years or fines, even in case of negligent conduct (§ 54(1) (2) and (2) KWG).

22 Investment brokerage requires a brokerage of transactions concerning the acquisition and sale of financial instruments. So, the decisive question was whether Bitcoins had to be qualified as **financial instrument**. BaFin has always taken this position, which is understandable since it allowed BaFin to apply many license requirements of the KWG to Bitcoin-related businesses. Otherwise, most crypto asset activities would have been unregulated.

23 Surprisingly, the Higher Regional Court of Berlin did not take the same view as BaFin. Instead, it clarified that Bitcoins are no financial instruments, and therefore operating a trading platform does not require a brokerage license according to § 1(1a) (2)(1) KWG. Because of the judgement, the crypto community expected BaFin to adapt its view on the qualification of Bitcoins, which BaFin, however, has not done yet. The reason is not only that the Higher Regional Court of Berlin is not the Federal Court of Justice (BGH), but that the Higher Regional Court of Berlin ruled in a **criminal case**, not an **administrative case**. Since BaFin is an administrative authority and does not impose criminal law penalties, BaFin stuck to its view. Nevertheless, the consequence is a bit contradictory: Financial services relating to Bitcoin might be subject to administrative measures (including discontinuation measures or monetary fines), but not to criminal sanctions (in particular, imprisonment). In the meanwhile, the consequences of

the court ruling are very limited since the legislator introduced the definition of crypto assets in the KWG, which qualify as financial instruments (→ para. 31). Bitcoins are without doubt crypto assets and § 32 KWG therefore applies.

II. LG Berlin, Judgement of 27.5.2020 – 2 O 322/18

The Regional Court of Berlin (Landgericht, LG)[28] had to decide on liability claims which had been raised by an investor who had purchased tokens during an ICO. The investor's claims were mainly based on wrong and insufficient information provided to investors during the ICO, which obliged the court to state what prospectus and information obligations exist. The court ruled that German laws apply according to Art. 4(3) and Art. 12(2)(c) Regulation (EC) No. 864/2007 (Rome II Regulation)[29]:[30] The **Rome II Regulation** applies because the damage claims were based on '**culpa in contrahendo**', Art. 1(1), Art. 2(1) and Art. (12). The country with which 'the non-contractual obligation arising out of dealings prior to the conclusion of a contract is manifestly more closely' (Art. 12(2)(c) Rome II Regulation) is Germany because of the many references to Germany in the available documents surrounding the ICO.[31] The nationality and the place of the registered office of the parties did not play a role for the court; the same applies, because not presented at court, to the place of the damage.[32]

Very surprisingly, the court held that the token in question is no security under German securities laws with the argument that it is not embodied in a **paper deed**. This interpretation of the law is in conflict with both the prevailing legal literature[33] as well as the view of BaFin.[34] Besides, it has the potential to lead to an unclear legal situation, because issuers of tokens cannot be clear any longer under what regime they draft and publish prospectuses: If they comply with the requirements stipulated by BaFin, they run into liability issues caused by the court, and if they follow the opinion of the court, they will get in conflict with the regulator.[35] Hopefully, this decision of the court will be set aside by the next instance – it is, to that extent, simply unconvincing.

Besides, the court correctly concluded that even if no statutory securities prospectus obligations apply, issuers have an obligation resulting from general German civil law to provide investors with sufficient and correct information: The court considers the application of the principles of civil law **prospectus liability** to be necessary in the present case. These were developed in the case law of the Federal Court of Justice (BGH) for the continuation of the basic ideas of a liability based on trust, as it has been created for cases of fault in contractual negotiations in certain areas which were not foreseen by the legislator to be expressly regulated, but which need to be filled out.[36] On this basis, although the prospectus provided during the ICO did not have to meet the formal requirements imposed on securities prospectuses according to the German Securities Prospectus Act (Wertpapierprospektgesetz, WpPG), the issuer, nevertheless,

---

[28] German Regional Court of Berlin 27.05.2020-2 O 322/18, BeckRS 2020, 32005.
[29] Regulation (EC) No. 864/2007 of 11.7.2007 on the law applicable to non-contractual obligations (Rome II), OJ L 199, 31.7.2007 p. 40–49.
[30] See for questions of private international law → § 3.
[31] German Regional Court of Berlin 27.05.2020-2 O 322/18, BeckRS 2020, 32005, para. 77 et seqq.
[32] Ibid, para. 73 et seq., 81 et seq.
[33] Just, Voß, Ritz and Becker, *WpHG*, (2015), § 2, para. 44; Müller, *WpPG*, (2017), § 2, para. 2.
[34] BaFin, 'Hinweisschreiben: Gz.: WA11-QB4100-2017/0010' (February 2018), available at: www.bafin.de (last accessed 14.01.2021) and BaFin, ibid, sec. V.b.
[35] Matzke, 'Voraussetzungen der Prospekthaftung bei einem ICO', (2021) 1 *Recht Digital (RDi)*, 44 (45).
[36] German Federal Court of Justice (*Bundesgerichtshof*) 26.09.1980- I ZR 119/78, 337–349.

Part C. Country Reports

was obliged to provide potential investors with truthful and complete information about the risk of a possible investment.[37]

27   It is noteworthy that this civil law **prospectus liability** does not only apply to the issuer of tokens. Rather, companies and persons who belong to the actual management group responsible for issuing the prospectus or who otherwise belong to the relevant 'backers' of the issuer may be equally held liable.[38]

28   It is also important to understand that those requirements do not only apply to prospectuses named as such, but to any market-related written statement that contains or gives the appearance of containing information material to the evaluation of the offered investment.[39]

29   The court's explanations on prospectus liability are not surprising as they result from a diligent application of the law and of comparable non-blockchain court decisions. However, given that the court now expressly stated these requirements in its decision, one can expect that issuers and persons behind issuers will apply even more care in the future when drafting marketing materials. Furthermore, the number of claims against ICOs will certainly increase, in particular if the market value of the tokens emitted decreases.

C. Regulatory Development and Reform

I. Crypto Assets

30   Beginning in 2020, the German legislator modified the German Banking Act (Kreditwesengesetz, KWG) and introduced so-called '**crypto assets**' (Kryptowerte). Crypto assets in terms of § 1 para. 11 s. 4 KWG are defined as a digital representation of a value which has not been issued or guaranteed by any central bank or public body, and which does not have the legal status of a currency or of money, but which is accepted by natural or legal persons as a means of exchange or payment by virtue of an agreement or actual practice, or which serves investment purposes and which can be transferred, stored and traded by electronic means ('digitale Darstellungen eines Wertes, der von keiner Zentralbank oder öffentlichen Stelle emittiert wurde oder garantiert wird und nicht den gesetzlichen Status einer Währung oder von Geld besitzt, aber von natürlichen oder juristischen Personen aufgrund einer Vereinbarung oder tatsächlichen Übung als Tausch- oder Zahlungsmittel akzeptiert wird oder Anlagezwecken dient und der auf elektronischem Wege übertragen, gespeichert und gehandelt werden kann'). Tokens which can be qualified as e-money or are subject to § 2(1)(1)(10) and (11) German Payment Supervision Act (Zahlungsdiensteaufsichtsgesetz, ZAG) and do not qualify as crypto assets, see § 1(11)(5)(1) and (2) KWG.

31   Since crypto assets are financial instruments (Finanzinstrumente) and since many businesses providing **financial services** require a license according to the KWG (e.g., investment brokerage), many use cases involving tokens may henceforth be regulated under German law. The reasoning behind this legislative engagement is simply to get legal clarity: Although BaFin has, driven by the will to regulate Bitcoin, for quite a while qualified Bitcoins and many other cryptocurrencies as units of account

---

[37] German Regional Court of Berlin 27.05.2020-2 O 322/18, BeckRS 2020, 32005, para. 93; Palandt/Grüneberg, *BGB*, (2017) § 311, para. 68.

[38] German Regional Court of Berlin 27.05.2020-2 O 322/18, BeckRS 2020, 32005, paras. 93, 97 et seqq.; German Federal Court of Justice (*Bundesgerichtshof*) 26.09.1980- I ZR 119/78, 337, para. 18.

[39] German Regional Court of Berlin 27.05.2020-2 O 322/18, BeckRS 2020, 32005, para. 94.

(Rechnungseinheiten) in terms of § 1(11)(1)(7) alt. 2 KWG and thus financial instruments, this view has been subject to criticism (→ para. 23). For practitioners, it was difficult to establish a general rule which one could apply to cryptocurrencies and other tokens.

The legislator did not only establish a definition of crypto assets, but also introduced the **crypto custodian business** (Kryptoverwahrgeschäft) as a new financial service requiring a license from BaFin.[40] According to § 1(1a)(2)(6) KWG, the crypto custodian business is defined as the safekeeping, administration and storage of crypto assets or private cryptographic keys which serve to hold, store or transfer crypto assets, for others ('die Verwahrung, die Verwaltung und die Sicherung von Kryptowerten oder privaten kryptografischen Schlüsseln, die dazu dienen, Kryptowerte zu halten, zu speichern und zu übertragen, für andere'). The difference between 'cryptographic keys' and 'crypto assets' relates to the intention of the legislator to define the crypto custodian business very broadly, including, in particular, any pooling of crypto assets of customers under a public key of the service provider.[41] The criterion 'for others' clarifies that storing own crypto assets is not subject to a license requirement.

The term '**administration**' is more difficult to interpret. If read in conjunction with the deposit business (Depotgeschäft, § 1(2)(2)(5) KWG) and the corresponding guidance of BaFin,[42] the term 'administration' could also include the exercise of voting rights. Such a broad interpretation of the term 'administration' could even cover the provision of **staking services**, in particular to the extent the staking service providers exercise voting rights corresponding to the tokens which have been delegated to them (token holders delegate their tokens to staking service providers which use those delegations to validate transaction and potentially also exercise voting rights in a proof-of-stake consensus mechanism (→ § 1). This would be unreasonable, because exercising voting rights is only an ancillary service when providing staking service, and while reviewing the requirements BaFin has imposed to obtain the crypto custodian license,[43] it is rather obvious that none of them has been developed for the purpose of exercising voting rights, if, at the same time, neither public keys nor crypto assets of others are held. BaFin expressly states that, in any case, the decisive factor for the crypto custodian business is always the possibility of accessing the public addresses under which the crypto assets are stored in a decentralized manner (which is why manufacturers of **hardware wallets** are not within the scope of the provision[44]), whereby such access is provided by the custody of private cryptographic keys.[45] In a staking provider scenario where investors delegate their crypto assets (= stake) to the staking provider, those crypto assets stay with the investors and are not transferred to the staking provider. However, the topic is still controversial, and a clarification of the legislator would be highly welcome, in particular when bearing in mind the growing importance of staking services for the functioning of blockchains and blockchain ecosystems.

---

[40] BaFin, 'Merkblatt: Hinweise zum Tatbestand des Kryptoverwahrgeschäfts' (March 2020), available at: https://beck-link.de/3xxrd (last accessed 14.01.2021).
[41] German Act 19/13827 implementing the amended directive of the 4th EU money laundering directive, 109.
[42] BaFin, ibid.
[43] BaFin, 'Hinweise zum Erlaubnisantrag für das Kryptoverwahrgeschäft' (March 2020), available at: https://beck-link.de/pc85s (last accessed 14.01.2021).
[44] BaFin, 'Merkblatt: Hinweise zum Tatbestand des Kryptoverwahrgeschäfts' (March 2020), sec. I.3, available at: https://beck-link.de/3xxrd (last accessed 14.01.2021).
[45] Ibid, sec. I.3.

II. Electronic Securities and Crypto Securities

34 On 3 June 2021, the German Government published an act on **electronic securities** (Geset über elektronische Wertpapiere, eWpG), regulating electronic securities and at the same time introducing **crypto securities**.[46] At the beginning, it shall only apply to bearer bonds (Inhaberschuldverschreibungen), § 1 eWpG, but in the long run also other securities like in particular shares shall be in the scope of the act.[47] The eWpG came into force on 10 June 2021.

35 Up to now, the issuance of a paper deed has, typically, been common under German securities law.[48] This paper deed, when used as a **global deed** (Globalurkunde), had to be sent to the central securities depository (CSD) **Clearstream** in Frankfurt which kept it in its archive. The eWpG leaves this mechanism untouched, but introduces a second, digital way of issuing securities. The idea is not to abolish physical documents, but rather to ensure the coexistence of the different forms of issuance. To establish this equivalence, electronic securities are to be regarded as property under civil law, whereby the purchaser and holder of the security enjoy a comprehensive protection of their ownership. Under civil law, this dematerialization of the property and the equation of virtual assets with physical objects is new, breaking with civil law traditions older than 120 years: Since 1900, when the German Civil Act (Bürgerliches Gesetzbuch, BGB) entered into force, objects always had to be physical. With the eWpG, objects (initially only electronic securities) can also be virtual, nevertheless, applying the very same regime as it is applicable to physical objects.[49]

36 The transfer of **ownership** of an electronic security is affected by the parties' agreement and the registration of the new holder in a securities register.[50] Those registers, which are yet to be established, shall create the legal certainty necessary for the functioning of the (digital) securities market, including good faith protection. It shall be possible to rely on the contents of the register: Even if a security was acquired by a non-owner, the registered owner should remain the actual owner.

37 The act also changes the German Investment Act (Kapitalanlagegesetzbuch, KAGB) with the consequence that shares in investment funds can also be issued as electronic deeds. As a rule, the provisions of the eWpG apply mutatis mutandis to these electronic deeds.

38 The main reason for this draft act is, however, the regulation of securities issued based on blockchain technology or similar technologies (the act itself is technology-neutral). In this case, the register introduced with the electronic securities is mainly stored on a blockchain, and the newly created '**crypto securities registrar**' (Krypto-wertpapierregisterführer) – which requires a license from BaFin – is responsible for its

---

[46] Bialluch-von Allwörden, 'Zivil- und prospektrechtliche Aspekte des eWpG-E', (2021) 1 *Recht Digital (RDi)*, 13; Lehmann, 'Zeitenwende im Wertpapierrecht', (2020) 9 *Zeitschrift für Bank- und Kapitalmarktrecht (BKR)*, 431; Saive, 'Einführung elektronischer Wertpapiere Aufsatz', (2020) *Zeitschrift Rechtspolitik (ZRP)*, 219; Preuße, Wöckener and Gillenkirch, 'Der Gesetzesentwurf zur Einführung elektronischer Wertpapiere' (2020) 11 *Zeitschrift für Bank- und Kapitalmarktrecht (BKR)*, 551.

[47] Bundesregierung, 'Entwurf eines Gesetzes zur Einführung von elektronischen Wertpapieren' (December 2020), 41, available at https://beck-link.de/2bkzn (last accessed 10.03.2021).

[48] Bialluch-von Allwörden/von Allwörden, 'Initial Coin Offerings: Kryptowährungen als Wertpapier oder Vermögensanlage?', (2018) 45 *Wirtschafts- und Bankrecht (WM)*, 2118.

[49] Critical: Bialluch-von Allwörden, 'Zivil- und prospektrechtliche Aspekte des eWpG-E', (2021) 1 *Recht Digital (RDi)*, 13, 14 et seqq.

[50] Meier, 'Übertragung von elektronischen Wertpapieren nach dem eWpG-E', (2021) 1 *Recht Digital (RDi)*, 1.

(technical) functioning. In other words, Germany outsources the register together with its good faith protection to private parties, but requires them to comply with high financial, technical and legal requirements, and also burdens them with liability for incorrect entries in the register. Using a costly central securities depository, such as Clearstream in Germany, is no longer necessary – but still possible.

39 Securities can be purchased and transferred embodied in and represented by crypto assets. The use of so-called smart contracts enables countless new business models, as they can be used to program money and securities flows directly. Complex processes can be replaced by lean and few lines of code, which opens the door to decentralized finance (**DeFi**). The new act thus has the potential to drive digitalization in the financial sector quite significantly.

40 The eWpG has been perceived quite well in the market. The legislator is addressing the requests and wishes from the financial sector to further regulate blockchain technology in order to make its use accessible to a broader range of companies, even beyond its current application, particularly in start-ups. The act also fits in with the European Commission's digital finance strategy, under which the draft regulation on the regulation of crypto assets (**MiCA**) other than securities was presented in September 2020.

§ 18
United Kingdom

Literature: Agrawal and Nasser, 'Insider Trading in Takeover Targets' (2012) 18 *Journal of Corporate Finance*, 598–625; Anderson, 'Insider Trading and the Myth of Market Confidence' (2018) 56 *Washington University Journal of Law and Policy*, 1–16; Ante and Fiedler, 'Cheap Signals in Security Token Offerings' (2019) 1 Blockchain Research Lab Working Paper Series, available at https://beck-link. de/ph8mk (accessed 31.05.2021); Atkins, Gerber, Micheletti and Saunders, 'Directors' Fiduciary Duties: Back to Delaware Law Basics' (February 2020), available at https://beck-link.de/hhn26 (accessed 31.05.2021); Awwad, 'Shareholders' Preemptive Rights in Listed and Closely Held Corporations and Shareholders' Protection Methods'(February 2016), available at https://beck-link.de/t688n (accessed 31.05.2021); Baum, 'The Future of Real Estate Initiative' (January 2020), available at https://beck-link. de/5vk5r (accessed 31.05.2021); Black, 'The Principal Fiduciary Duty of Boards of Directors. Presentation at Third Asian Roundtable on Corporate Governance' (April 2001), available at https://beck-link. de/mb6h8 (accessed 31.05.2021); Bonbright, 'The Danger of Shares Without Par Value' (1924) 24(5) *Columbia Law Review*, 449–468; Buckley, W. Arner, Zetzsche and Selga, 'Special Feature: TechRisk' (2020) 35(1) *Singapore Journal of Legal Studies*, 35–62. Carsten, 'Derivative Actions under English and German Corporate Law – Shareholder Participation between the Tension Filled Areas of Corporate Governance and Malicious Shareholder Interference' (2010) 7 *European Company and Financial Law Review*, 81–115; Cohney, Hoffman, Sklaroff, Wishnick, 'Coin-operated capitalism' (2019) 119(3) *Columbia Law Review*, 591–676; David, 'From Block Lords to Blockchain: How Securities Dealers Make Markets' (2018) 44(1) *Journal of Corporation Law*, 29-64; Davies, 'The Board of Directors: Composition, Structure, Duties and Powers' (December 2000), available at https://beck-link.de/red2x (accessed 31.05.2021); Deng, Hui Huang, Wu, 'The Regulation of Initial Coin Offerings in China: Problems, Prognoses and Prospects' (2018) 19 *European Business Organization Law Review*, 465–502; Deloitte, 'Are Token Assets the Securities Tomorrow?' (February 2019), available at https://beck-link. de/h85hf (accessed 31.05.2021); Demott, 'Perspectives on Choice of Law for Corporate Internal Affairs' (1985) 48 Law and Contemporary Problems, 161–198; Financial Conduct Authority (FCA), 'Market Watch 63: Newsletter on Market Conduct and Transaction Reporting Issues' (May 2020), available at https://beck-link.de/5mv84 (accessed 31.05.2021); Financial Conduct Authority (FCA), 'Distributed Ledger Technology to define potential benefits and challenges of the underlying technology that facilitates ICOs' (April 2017), available at https://beck-link.de/4ecs3 (accessed 31.05.2021); Financial Conduct Authority (FCA), 'Guidance on Cryptoassets: Feedback and Final Guidance to CP 19/3' (July 2019), available at https://beck-link.de/86rff (accessed 31.05.2021); Financial Conduct Authority (FCA), 'Algorithmic Trading Compliance in Wholesale Markets' (February 2018), available at https://beck-link. de/4v6ps (accessed 31.05.2021); Financial Reporting Council (FRC), 'The UK Corporate Governance Code' (July 2018), available at https://beck-link.de/4b3b3 (accessed 31.05.2021); Financial Conduct Authority (FCA), 'Quid pro quo? What factors influence IPO allocations to investors?' (October 2016), available at https://beck-link.de/h5wd7 (accessed 31.05.2021); Gibbon, Peel, Garston and Salaman, 'Corporate Governance and Directors' Duties in the UK' (2017), available at https://beck-link.de/ mz4b2 (accessed 31.05.2021); Greenwich Associates, 'The Tokenisation of Financial Market Securities – What's Next?' (2019), available at https://beck-link.de/8h33w (accessed 31.05.2021); Haw, Hu, Vigeland and Zhang, 'Insider Trading Restrictions and Share Repurchase Decisions: International Evidence' (January 2015), available at https://beck-link.de/pwt65 (accessed 31.05.2021); Information Commissioner's Office (ICO), 'Guide to the General Data Protection Regulation' (August 2018), available at https://beck-link.de/72ewz (accessed 31.05.2021); Keijser and Mooney, 'Intermediated Securities Holding Systems Revisited: A View Through the Prism of Transparency (2019) *University of Pennsylvania, Institute for Law & Economics Research Paper Series* No. 19-13, available at https://ssrn.com/abstract=3376873 (accessed 31.05.2021); Kershaw, *Principles of Takeover Regulation* (1st Edition, Oxford University Press 2018); London Stock Exchange, 'Depositary Receipts: Guide to Depositary Receipts on London Stock Exchange' (2020), available at https://beck-link.de/48db8 (accessed 31.05.2021); London Stock Exchange, 'AIM Rules for Companies' (2018), available at https://beck-link.de/3xtss (accessed 31.05.2021); Mendelson, 'From Initial Coin Offerings to Security Tokens: A U.S. Federal Securities Law Analysis' (2019) 22(1) *Stanford Technology Law Review*, 52–94; Moran and Ido (2020), 'ICO vs. IPO: Empirical Findings, Information Asymmetry, and the Appropriate Regulatory Framework' (2020) 53(2) *Vanderbilt Journal of Transnational Law*, 525–614; Morrison, Mazey and Wingreen, 'The DAO Controversy: The Case for a New Species of Corporate Governance?' (May 2020), available at https://

beck-link.de/h5vww (accessed 31.05.2021); Nord, 'Blockchain Plumbing: A Potential Solution for Shareholder Voting?' (2019) 29 *University of Pennsylvania Journal of Business Law*, 706–710; Organization for Economic Co-operation and Development (OECD), 'Risk Management and Corporate Governance (2014), available at https://beck-link.de/w8x3k (accessed 31.05.2021); Pierce, 'Protecting the Voice of Retail Investors: Implementation of a Blockchain Proxy Voting Platform' (2018–2019) 14 (1) *Rutgers Business Law Review*, 9-38; Priem, 'Distributed Ledger Technology for Securities Clearing and Settlement: Benefits, Risks, and Regulatory Implications' (2020) 6 *Financial Innovation*, 1–25; Securities and Markets Stakeholder Group, 'Advice to ESMA: Own Initiative Report on Initial Coin Offerings and Crypto assets' (October 2018), available at https://beck-link.de/62sx6 (accessed 31.05.2021); Sinclair and Taylor, 'The English law rights of investors in Initial Coin Offerings' (2018) 4 *Journal of International Banking and Financial Law (JIBFL)*, 214–216; Smart Contract Alliance, 'Smart Contracts: Is the Law Ready?' (September 2018), available at https://beck-link.de/aep8d (accessed 31.05.2021); Transparency International UK, 'Beneficial ownership transparency; (2018), available at https://beck-link.de/t5crm (accessed 31.05 2021); World Economic Forum, 'Personal Data: The Emergence of a New Asset Class' (2011), available at https://beck-link.de/7s7cy (accessed 31.05.2021); Yermack, 'Corporate Governance and Blockchains' (2017) 21(1) *Review of Finance*, 7–31; Yeung, 'Regulation by Blockchain: The Emerging Battle for Supremacy between the Code of Law and Code as Law' (2018) 82(2) *Modern Law Review*, 207–239; Zetzsche, Buckley and W. Arner, 'The ICO Gold Rush: It's a Scam, It's a Bubble, It's a Super Challenge for Regulators' (2019) 60(3) *Harvard International Law Journal*, 267–315; Zetzsche, Buckley and W. Arner, 'The Distributed Liability of Distributed Ledgers: Legal Risks of Blockchain' [2018] 4 *University of Illinois Law Review*, 1362–1365.

Outline

	para.
A. Introduction	1
B. Security Tokens as a Financial Instrument in Law	3
C. IPO Market Conduct Rules as a Template?	4
I. Prospectus Regime	4
II. Regulating the Intermediaries	6
III. A Professional Investor Market	8
D. Company Law as a Framework	9
I. Overview	9
II. Par value and No-discount Rule	11
III. Valid Consideration for the Token's Issues	13
IV. Allotment of Tokens (s 517)	15
V. Token Buyback	17
VI. Pre-emption Right (section 561)	19
VII. Voting Right	21
VIII. Removal of Management	23
IX. Derivative action (ss 260–264)	25
X. Insider dealing	27
E. Shareholder Transparency and Data Protection	29
F. Recommendation	32
I. Protection of the New Market Space	32
II. Governance Right	34
III. New Value and Governance Right	35
G. Conclusion	37

A. Introduction

This chapter investigates the legal and regulatory issues relating to security token offering (STO), a regulated form of Initial Coin Offering (ICO).[1] A security token is a type of crypto asset which is a cryptographically secured digital representation of

---

[1] World Bank and Cambridge Center for Alternative Finance, 'Regulating Alternative Finance: Results from a Global Regulator Survey' (2019), available at https://beck-link.de/2nypw (accessed 31.5.2021).

contractual rights that uses distributed ledger technology (DLT) and can be transferred, stored or traded electronically.[2] ICO is a digital way of raising funds from the public using a crypto asset, such as cryptocurrency, tokens representing shares in a firm, prepayment vouchers for future services, or in some cases an offer of no discernible value.[3] After issuance, crypto assets may be resold to others in a secondary market on digital exchanges or other platforms. With these features, ICO has been regarded as a financing mechanism similar to Initial Public Offering (IPO) in which companies or firms issue shares to the investing public.[4]

2   Despite burgeoning ICO activities, the ICO space has not received wide and positive support from the UK regulators, and as a result, many ICOs are not conducted in a regulated or organised market that is recognised by the law.[5] One of the reasons for this is that the legal nature of many ICO tokens cannot be securely defined in law,[6] and this causes difficulties in regulating the relationships between the token holders and issuers,[7] and in setting the regulatory parameters for their conduct with respect to ICO activities such as whether a prospectus is required or whether a whitepaper qualifies as a prospectus.[8] STO is a more legally secured ICO in that the security, which is legally defined, is digitally tokenised and is capable of being offered and issued to investors on the blockchain.[9] The law needs to provide the bedrock on which the STO market can build investor confidence and financial innovation, and thus increase access to the financial market.[10] Consequently, we need to know what benefits STO can bring, what safeguards are in place to ensure the STO market's safety and integrity, and what protection can be given to participants, especially token holders. To this end, I will assess whether the current securities law, which was designed for an IPO,[11] is suitable for an STO, and identify any deficiencies for the STO market. This discussion will be followed by an analysis of the protection of token holders within an organisation, using current UK company law as a framework to demonstrate the possible risk of harm to token holders posed by management and other controlling powers. In doing so, I will propose ways in which the law can maintain token holders' autonomy in negotiating their terms of contracts, can reduce transaction costs, and mitigate other negative features. I will also reassess the monetary value of the tokens and the governance rights of token holders in the context of data economy and propose a new approach to this from the perspective of both securities and company law.

---

[2] UK FCA, 'Distributed Ledger Technology to define potential benefits and challenges of the underlying technology that facilitates ICOs' (April 2017), available at https://beck-link.de/4ecs3 (accessed 31.5.2021).

[3] Organisation for Economic Co-operation and Development (OECD), 'Initial Coin Offerings (ICOs) for SME Financing' (January 2019), available at https://beck-link.de/kzbn5 (accessed 31.5.2021).

[4] Securities and Markets Stakeholder Group, 'Advice to ESMA: Own Initiative Report on Initial Coin Offerings and Crypto assets' (October 2018), available at https://beck-link.de/62sx6 (accessed 31.5.2021).

[5] FCA, 'Customer Warning about the Risks of Initial Coin Offerings' (February 2019), available at https://beck-link.de/73nez (accessed 31.5.2021).

[6] UK Jurisdiction Taskforce, 'Legal Statement on Cryptoassets and Smart Contracts' (November 2019), available at https://beck-link.de/ckk4v (accessed 12.11.2020).

[7] Zetzsche, Buckley and W. Arner, 'The ICO Gold Rush: It's a Scam, It's a Bubble, It's a Super Challenge for Regulators' (2019) 60(3) *Harvard International Law Journal*, 267–315.

[8] Deng, Hui Huang, Wu, 'The Regulation of Initial Coin Offerings in China: Problems, Prognoses and Prospects' (2018) 19 *European Business Organization Law Review*, 465–502.

[9] FCA, 'Guidance on Cryptoassets: Feedback and Final Guidance to CP 19/3' (July 2019), available at https://beck-link.de/86rff (accessed 31.5.2021).

[10] Cohney, Hoffman, Sklaroff, Wishnick, 'Coin-operated capitalism' (2019) 119(3) *Columbia Law Review*, 591–676.

[11] Moran and Ido (2020), 'ICO vs. IPO: Empirical Findings, Information Asymmetry, and the Appropriate Regulatory Framework' (2020) 53(2) *Vanderbilt Journal of Transnational Law*, 525–614.

B. Security Tokens as a Financial instrument in Law

Security tokens, as a type of crypto asset, represent underlying assets such as shares, bonds (debt), commodities, units of investment and rights to deal in those assets, such as options and futures.[12] They may be issued by entities such as companies or firms, but also by an individual or an association of individuals or entities.[13] If security tokens were treated as securities,[14] it would bring them into the current legal and regulatory framework, and securities law would apply to the whole security trading cycle: issuing, trading, clearing and settlement.[15] The current securities law covers the entire operation of the securities market; it recognizes primary and secondary markets, and divides market players into infrastructure providers, issuers, intermediaries, institutional and retail investors, domestic and foreign participants.[16] Securities law broadly divides into the prudential aspect of regulation with a focus on systemic risk issues, and the conduct aspect with a focus on market integrity, investor protection, consumer protection, and market competitiveness.[17] In the UK, security tokens representing transferable securities or other financial instrument[18] are securities under the EU's second Markets in Financial Instruments Directive, Directive 2014/65/EU (MiFID2)[19].

C. IPO Market Conduct Rules as a Template?

I. Prospectus Regime

The FCA has issued a stark warning about the risks of ICOs because of the opaque process of this funding method.[20] Lack of governance and transparency in such an unregulated space affect investors' rights with respect to cash flow, liquidity, and governance. What ICOs do not have, if they are to meet the same level of governance as IPOs are: a prospectus issued for investors to make informed judgements about the issuers (Prospectus Directive, → § 7);[21] intermediaries to help issuers comply with the

---

[12] Deloitte, 'Are Token Assets the Securities Tomorrow?' (February 2019), available at https://beck-link.de/h85hf (accessed 31.5.2021).
[13] Ibid.
[14] Mendelson, 'From Initial Coin Offerings to Security Tokens: A U.S. Federal Securities Law Analysis' (2019) 22(1) *Stanford Technology Law Review*, 52–94.
[15] Priem, 'Distributed Ledger Technology for Securities Clearing and Settlement: Benefits, Risks, and Regulatory Implications' (2020) 6 *Financial Innovation*, 1–25.
[16] Baker McKenzie, 'Global Financial Services Regulatory Guide' (2020), available at https://beck-link.de/3kxwx (accessed 31.5.2021).
[17] FCA, 'Guidance on Cryptoassets: Feedback and Final Guidance to CP 19/3' (July 2019), available at https://beck-link.de/86rff (accessed 31.5.2021).
[18] The Financial Services and Markets Act 2000 (Regulated Activities) Order 2001 (RAO) specifies that types of activities and investments for the purpose of clarifying the scope of the Financial Services and Markets Act 2000 (FSMA).
[19] Directive 2014/65/EU of the European Parliament and of the Council of 15 May 2014 on markets in financial instruments and amending Directives 2002/92/EC and 2011/61/EU, OJ L 173, 12.6.2016, 349–496.
[20] FCA, 'Customer Warning about the Risks of Initial Coin Offerings' (February 2019), available at https://beck-link.de/73nez (accessed 31.5.2021); FCA, 'Distributed Ledger Technology to define potential benefits and challenges of the underlying technology that facilitates ICOs' (April 2017), available at https://beck-link.de/4ecs3 (accessed 31.5.2021).
[21] Directive 2010/73/EC of the European Parliament and of the Council amending Directives 2003/71/EC on the prospectus to be published when securities are offered to the public or admitted to

rules for safeguarding market integrity and safety (MiFiD2, → § 8, and Directive 2011/61/EU (AIFMD)[22], → § 15); and public and private enforcement proceedings available to sanction market participants and to provide redress to investors. Furthermore, there is no market surveillance infrastructure to ensure market integrity or investor protection against insider dealing and market manipulation.[23] For an STO market to develop successfully measures must be in place to avoid it becoming a fraudulent space where criminals can exploit investors through its opaqueness,[24] easy access to unsophisticated consumers, market volatility, and lack of a regulatory and legal enforcement mechanism at domestic and cross-border levels.[25] Hence, to avoid the mistakes learnt from the ICO market, the STO market should not rely on the unregulated, unstandardized, and unverified 'whitepaper' system used in the ICO[26] as a way to show party autonomy, to demonstrate a more economical way to secure transparency, or as a basis for a self-governing mechanism.

5   STOs have now been brought under the current legal and regulatory framework that applies to IPOs. Section 19 of FSMA 2000 provides that no person may carry on a regulated financial services activity in the UK unless they are authorised or exempt. Section 21 of FSMA 2000 further specifies that a person must not, in the course of business, communicate an invitation or inducement to engage in investment activity. Section 85 of FSMA 2000 also makes it a crime to offer transferable securities to the public in the UK or to request that they be admitted to trading on a regulated market situated or operating in the UK, unless an approved prospectus has been made available to the public before the offer. Hence, an STO is required to comply with the FCA's Handbook's Prospectus Rules, Disclosure and Transparency Rules, and Listing Rules. An STO issuer is required to produce a prospectus that provides the necessary information to enable investors to make an informed judgement. Depending on the market segment that the STO falls into, different rules become relevant on the appointment of financial sponsors to guide the issuers[27] as well as for accounting,[28] and codes of practice.[29]

---

trading and 2004/109/EC on the harmonisation of transparency requirements in relation to information about issuers whose securities are admitted to trading on a regulated market, OJ L 327, 11.12.2010 p. 1–12.

[22] Directive 2011/61/EU of the European Parliament and the Council on Alternative Investment Fund Managers and amending Directives 2003/41/EC and 2009/65/EC and Regulations (EC) No 1060/2009 and (EU) No 1095/2010, OJ L 174, 1.7.2011 p. 1–73.

[23] FCA, 'Guidance on Cryptoassets: Feedback and Final Guidance to CP 19/3' (July 2019), 13, available at https://beck-link.de/86rff (accessed 31.5.2021); Directive 2015/849/EU of the European Parliament and the Council on the prevention of the use of the financial system for the purposes of money laundering or terrorist financing, amending Regulation (EU) No 648/2012 of the European Parliament and of the Council, and repealing Directive 2005/60/EC of the European Parliament and of the Council and Commission Directive 2006/70/EC, OJ L 141, 5.6.2015 p. 73–117 (The Fourth Anti-Money Laundering Directive).

[24] Torpey and Solomon, 'Tokenisation 2019: The Security Token Year in Review' (December 2019), available at https://beck-link.de/a547e (accessed 31.5.2021).

[25] FCA, 'Guidance on Cryptoassets: Feedback and Final Guidance to CP 19/3' (July 2019), 13, available at https://beck-link.de/86rff (accessed 31.5.2021).

[26] Sinclair and Taylor, 'The English law rights of investors in Initial Coin Offerings' (2018) 4 *Journal of International Banking and Financial Law*, 214–216.

[27] FCA, 'The Sponsor Regime' (February 2020), available at https://beck-link.de/2pdn7 (accessed 31.5.2021).

[28] Regulation (EC) No. 1606/02 of the European Parliament and the Council on the application of international accounting standards, OJ L 243, 11.9.2002 p. 1–4.

[29] Financial Reporting Council (FRC), 'The UK Corporate Governance Code' (July 2018), available at https://beck-link.de/4b3b3 (accessed 31.5.2021).

II. Regulating the Intermediaries

Issuers can also decide the method of offering an STO, which can be by direct subscription without intermediaries, or through intermediaries. It can also target particular types of investor such as professional investors.[30] When an STO aims to access retail investors directly without the involvement of intermediaries[31], it is similar to a direct listing on the exchange.[32] But if it is not offered directly, an STO would need to rely on financial intermediaries to connect with the investing public. This process can involve institutional investors who gauge investors' interest in the STO through market sounding.[33] A number of rules designed to protect market integrity through a wall-crossing regime apply to institutional investors.[34] Under the Regulation (EU) No. 596/2014 on Market Abuse (MAR)[35],[36] any investors who are wall-crossed are prohibited from dealing in the securities of the issuer, including their relevant securities (share, debt and other derivatives) currently traded on the regulated markets.[37] 6

One of the advantages of using STO on the blockchain is pricing transparency during the securities allocation.[38] This provides information necessary for end investors to assess the reasonableness of the price paid for the tokens and the fees charged by their asset managers or broker-dealers.[39] Whether or not this function of transparency is used depends on the extent to which it reduces market competitiveness and on the willingness of financial intermediaries to underwrite the risks of the sale. It is also unclear if it is necessary to have market-makers in the STO's secondary market to provide liquidity. If the STO's secondary market is to be conducted by the end investors themselves (probably retail investors), broker-dealers may become redundant in this supply chain. There may be a need for asset management to continue using security tokens in their structured investment portfolios and if so, both the EU MiFID2 and AIFMD regimes would apply. Asset management funds would need to deposit security tokens with custodian banks to comply with client-asset segregation rules (CASS).[40] A 7

---

[30] Partner Vine, 'LSE's Definition of Professional Investors under MiFID II' (August 2020), available at https://beck-link.de/kd76e (accessed 31.5.2021).

[31] David, 'From Block Lords to Blockchain: How Securities Dealers Make Markets' (2018) 44(1) *Journal of Corporation Law*, 29.

[32] MemeryCrystal, 'Direct Listings – A Viable Alternative to the Traditional IPO?' (February 2018), available at https://beck-link.de/3ywk8 (accessed 31.5.2021).

[33] FCA, 'Market Abuse Regulation' (October 2020), available at https://beck-link.de/a4yzb (accessed 31.5.2021).

[34] FCA, 'Asset Management Firms and the Risk of Market Abuse' (February 2015), available at https://beck-link.de/ra6wc (accessed 31.5.2021).

[35] Regulation (EU) No. 596/2014 of the European Parliament and of the Council on market abuse (Market Abuse Regulation) and repealing Directive 2003/6/EC of the European Parliament and of the Council and Commission Directives 2003/124/EC, 2003/125/EC and 2004/72/EC, OJ L 173, 12.6.2014 p. 1–61.

[36] FCA, 'Market Abuse Regulation' (October 2020), available at https://beck-link.de/a4yzb (accessed 31.5.2021). FCA, 'Market Watch 63: Newsletter on Market Conduct and Transaction Reporting Issues' (May 2020), available at https://beck-link.de/5mv84 (accessed 31.5.2021).

[37] Norton Rose Fulbright, 'The Market Abuse Regulation: Key Considerations for UK Listed Issuers' (February 2016), available at https://beck-link.de/7dvmr (accessed 31.5.2021).

[38] FCA, 'Quid pro quo? What factors influence IPO allocations to investors?' (October 2016), available at https://beck-link.de/h5wd7 (accessed 31.5.2021).

[39] Norton Rose Fulbright, 'MiFID II/MiFIR Series: Transparency and Reporting Obligations' (April 2014), available at https://beck-link.de/pvs26 (accessed 31.5.2021).

[40] FCA, 'Handbook: CASS 7.13: Segregation of Client Money' (2015), available at https://beck-link.de/55vab (accessed 31.5.2021).

digital wallet provider or a digital exchange could act as a bank custodian and they would then need FCA registration for the money laundering law and to be authorised to conduct investment activities.[41] If they become significant within the system, they would also need to be approved and regulated by the Prudential Regulation Authority (PRA) of the Bank of England.[42] Since there may be no need for tokens to be cleared centrally, rules under Regulation (EU) No 648/2012 (EMIR) may not be applicable.[43] Nevertheless, as tokens would be settled on the private blockchain, many provisions under CSDR would still need to be observed and the UK senior manager's regime would apply to key individuals within the asset management firms.[44] Under the FCA's new rules, asset managers are prohibited from offering derivatives of security tokens to retail clients.[45]

III. A Professional Investor Market

8 A separate law and regulation has been designed for the professional investor market which does not provide access to retail investors. As a result, the disclosure requirement can be streamlined as in the Global Depository Receipts' professional investor market[46] and the London Stock Exchange's Alternative Investment Market (AIM).[47] If AIM is to accommodate an STO market in which only professional investors are allowed to participate, the FCA's listing rules would not apply. Instead, AIM's rules would apply with the London Stock Exchange acting as the UK listing authority.[48] But this would limit the ability of the STO market to reach retail investors?

D. Company Law as a Framework

I. Overview

9 In addition to securities law, company law governs the internal affairs of a corporate organisation.[49] The major issues arising are: capital maintenance for investor protection, particularly minority shareholders and outside creditors, governance of the organisation such as the decision-making process and the right to obtain redress, re-organisation and

---

[41] FCA, 'The Money Laundering, Terrorist Financing and Transfer of Funds (Information on the Payer)' (2017), available at https://beck-link.de/23e63 (accessed 31.5.2021).

[42] Chambers, 'Unstable Coins: Cryptoassets, Financial Regulation and Preventing Financial Crime in the Emerging Market for Digital Assets' (March 2020), available at https://beck-link.de/nyar4 (accessed 31.5.2021).

[43] Regulation (EU) No 648/2012 of the European Parliament and of the Council on OTC derivatives, central counterparties and trade repositories, OJ L 201, 27.7.2012 p. 1–59.

[44] Regulation (EU) No 909/2014 of the European Parliament od of the Council on improving securities settlement in the European Union and on central securities depositories and amending Directives 98/26/EC and 2014/65/EU and Regulation (EU) No 236/2012, OJ L 257, 28.8.2014 p. 1–72; Deloitte, 'Are Token Assets the Securities Tomorrow?' (February 2019), https://beck-link.de/h85hf (accessed 31.5.2021).

[45] FCA, 'PS20/10: Prohibiting the sale to retail clients of investment products that reference crypto assets' (October 2020), available at https://beck-link.de/wkrn8 (accessed 31.5.2021).

[46] London Stock Exchange, 'Depositary Receipts: Guide to Depositary Receipts on London Stock Exchange' (2020), available at https://beck-link.de/48db8 (accessed 31.5.2021).

[47] London Stock Exchange Group, 'Being an AIM' (2020), available at https://beck-link.de/2kp22 (accessed 31.5.2021).

[48] London Stock Exchange, 'AIM Rules for Companies' (2018), available at https://beck-link.de/3xtss (accessed 31.5.2021).

[49] Demott, 'Perspectives on Choice of Law for Corporate Internal Affairs' (1985) 48 Law and Contemporary Problems, 161–198.

dissolution of the organisation, and dispute resolution.[50] Modern company law accommodates various types of company, from closely-held to publicly-listed companies. Specific regimes have been created within the company law framework to service companies with different objectives and functions.[51] The aim is to ensure, on the one hand, that capital can continue to be aggregated efficiently through the collective effort of promoters, directors, shareholders, employees and creditors, and, on the other hand, that benefits can be shared equitably among them.[52] New methods, processes, and markets, have been developed to facilitate the aggregation of capital, including private placement,[53] direct listing,[54] initial public offering,[55] private equity,[56] and the newly emerged securities token offering (STO).[57] To ensure that benefits are shared equitably, various mechanisms have been introduced such as minority shareholder protection in closely-held companies, or corporate governance of listed and quoted companies. As well as these mechanisms, the takeover market has been developed as a way to monitor corporate performance rather than as a way to share the benefits of a company, mainly through the sale of the control premium to bidders.[58]

Including security tokens under the company law framework poses a manageable legal risk for uncertainty, but the problem is whether it would defeat the prime purpose of issuing asset tokens,[59] namely to ensure efficient capital aggregation and equitable sharing of benefits. In many STO projects, security tokens are offered on the open market to anyone who can access the internet; issue and purchase do not need the traditional financial intermediaries.[60] However, under the current company law framework, only certain companies can issue securities to the general public,[61] needing, for example, a clean three-year trading record.[62] Furthermore, the corporate governance rules in company law and the Corporate Governance Code place additional requirements on issuers who are often not able to afford the expense of governance services such as legal, compliance and auditing costs.[63] Although 'code-as-law' seems to be able

10

---

[50] Watson and McKenzie, 'Shareholders' Right in Private and Public Companies in the UK (England and Wales): Overview' (July 2019), available at https://beck-link.de/pp3mb (accessed 31.5.2021).
[51] Harvard Law School Forum on Corporate Governance, 'Principles of Corporate Governance' (September 2016), available at https://beck-link.de/3dnr2 (accessed 31.5.2021).
[52] Davies, 'The Board of Directors: Composition, Structure, Duties and Powers' (December 2000), available at https://beck-link.de/red2x (accessed 31.5.2021).
[53] Baum, 'The Future of Real Estate Initiative' (January 2020), available at https://beck-link.de/5vk5r (accessed 31.5.2021).
[54] Ben-Tzur and Evans, 'The Rise of Direct Listings: Understanding the Trend, Separating Fact from Fiction' (December 2019), available at https://beck-link.de/tsx4t (accessed 31.5.2021).
[55] Zullo, 'Can Tokenisation Fix the Secondary IPO Market?' (April 2020), available at https://beck-link.de/tp4dh (accessed 31.5.2021).
[56] Greenwich Associates, 'The Tokenisation of Financial Market Securities – What's Next?'(2019), available at https://beck-link.de/8h33w (accessed 31.5.2021).
[57] Deloitte, 'Are Token Assets the Securities Tomorrow? ' (February 2019), available at https://beck-link.de/h85hf (accessed 31.5.2021).
[58] Kershaw, *Principles of Takeover Regulation* (2018), 44.
[59] Comsure, 'Initial Coin Offerings: Issues of Legal Uncertainty Report' (November 2019), available at https://beck-link.de/yb53p (accessed 31.5.2021); Buckley, W. Arner, Zetzsche and Selga, 'Special Feature: TechRisk' (2020) 35(1) *Singapore Journal of Legal Studies*, 35-62.
[60] Ilic, 'Security Token Offerings: What are They, and where are They Going in 2019?' (March 2019), available at https://beck-link.de/m58t3 (accessed 31.5.2021).
[61] § 755 of Companies Act 2006 provides that 'a private company limited by shares or limited by guarantee and having a share capital must not; (a) offer to the public any securities of the company, or (b) allot or agree to allot any securities of the company with a view to their being offered to the public.'
[62] FCA, 'Listing Rules 6.3.1R', available at https://beck-link.de/kvez6 (accessed 31.5.2021).
[63] Organization for Economic Co-operation and Development (OECD), 'Risk Management and Corporate Governance (2014), available at https://beck-link.de/w8x3k (accessed 31.5.2021).

to mitigate some of these costs through automation,[64] many areas would still require human intervention, especially where cognitive judgement is required to interpret rules that are based on policy objectives, or where there are different acts to be balanced against one another.[65] The reason that STO is attractive to legitimate businesses is its ability to reach the entire internet community without infrastructure obstacles or national boundaries.[66] Bringing them under the current company law framework would compromise this benefit. As an example, the US's Howey test when applied to DAO (an STO project),[67] hinders development in security token finance, and encourages underground STO markets.[68] While many countries have created a specific legal and regulatory regime for STO and have provided trading platforms for the investment community, none has been successful.

II. Par Value and No-discount Rule

11   Under the UK Companies Act 2006, each share must have a face value, the so-called par value[69]. A share cannot be issued below its face value and cannot be issued at a discount. This no-discount rule is to ensure that both shareholders and creditors are protected as capital providers[70]. The amount raised must be kept in a separate account and be treated as capital in the balance sheet.

12   In an STO, a token can be issued without a face value and its value is determined purely through negotiation between the parties in the market i.e. the issuer of the tokens and the buyer. The capital raised, whether cash or another type of cryptocurrency or crypto asset, does not need to be put in a special account or to be treated as a non-distributable asset. This substantially reduces the protection offered to shareholders or creditors when a business becomes insolvent and there is no reserve available to investors[71]. Without this protection, any capital raised can also be more easily returned to the investors, thus creating a major risk of asset stripping. As there is no value attached tokens and repurchase can be through a one-to-one negotiation, the repurchase price can be higher than the issuing price, at the expense of other investors. There are jurisdictions, e.g. Delaware in the US, that do not require par value on a share,[72] but in this case shareholders are protected by stronger statutory claims against boards of directors.[73] As will be discussed later, there are no clear legal claims, procedures, or appropriate forums for token holders to hold the agents of an organisation legally accountable[74]. Par value

---

[64] Patrick and Bana, 'Rule of Law Versus Rule of Code: A Blockchain-Driven Legal World' (December 2017), available at https://beck-link.de/ykf8m (accessed 31.5.2021).

[65] Smart Contract Alliance, 'Smart Contracts: Is the Law Ready?' (September 2018), available at https://beck-link.de/aep8d (accessed 31.5.2021).

[66] Deloitte, 'Are Token Assets the Securities Tomorrow?' (February 2019), available at https://beck-link.de/h85hf (accessed 31.5.2021).

[67] Decision of the Supreme Court of the United States (27.5.1946) – *SEC v. W.J. Howey Co.*, 328 and 293.

[68] Ante and Fiedler, 'Cheap Signals in Security Token Offerings' (2019) 1 Blockchain Research Lab Working Paper Series, available at https://beck-link.de/ph8mk (accessed 31.5.2021).

[69] Section 540, Chapter 1 of the UK Companies Act 2006.

[70] Section 580, Chapter 1 of the UK Companies Act 2006.

[71] Organization for Economic Co-operation and Development (OECD), 'Initial Coin Offerings (ICOs) for SME Financing' (January 2019), available at https://beck-link.de/kzbn5 (accessed 31.5.2021).

[72] Bonbright, 'The Danger of Shares Without Par Value' (1924) 24(5) *Columbia Law Review*, 449–468.

[73] Atkins, Gerber, Micheletti and Saunders, 'Directors' Fiduciary Duties: Back to Delaware Law Basics' (February 2020), available at https://beck-link.de/hhn26 (accessed 31.5.2021).

[74] Jevremovic, '2018 In Review: Blockchain Technology and Arbitration' (January 2019), available at https://beck-link.de/f7b4s (accessed 31.5.2021).

and the no-discount rule reduce the likelihood of management malpractice, reduce agency costs, and provide a benchmark for other safeguards on capital maintenance and investor protection.

III. Valid Consideration for the Token's Issues

The UK Companies Act 2006 also provides detailed rules on the considerations for shares issued by the companies.[75] For public companies, shares must be paid for with cash, while non-cash consideration, such as contract performance, must be evaluated and certified by auditors.[76] 13

In an STO, the organisation may argue that it is not a public company so the rules on consideration do not apply. It may argue that cryptocurrency is a cash consideration, and hence require no further evaluation or certified report by auditors.[77] This increases the risk of fraud, market manipulation, and misrepresentation in an STO. Investors could mistakenly believe that the process is transparent on the blockchain without knowing what is required of the issuers. Since the issuers can continue issuing more tokens on the blockchain, the participants could be misled into believing that the company has adequate assets, based on the capital raised through previous issuances. However, the participants cannot know whether the capital has been returned to the investors or whether the cash paid in with a type of cryptocurrency such as Bitcoin (an unstable coin) is of the same value as the consideration requested for the new issuance. This can lead to unfair and unequal treatment among shareholders who should be able to bring a claim based on S 994 of the Unfair Prejudice claim. However, shareholders may encounter several problems in accessing the appropriate forum and its remedies. For the latter, since there is no benchmark provided for the consideration, the buyout right provided by section 996 (2)(e) CA 2006 is not adequate to address losses. 14

IV. Allotment of Tokens (s 517)

Directors need powers to allot shares when authorised by shareholders at a general meeting. In UK companies, these powers must be renewed every year. In addition to the requirement of shareholder authorisation, directors must use their power of allotment solely for proper purposes.[78] 15

These property rights mean that shareholders are protected against share dilution that can affect their control rights (voting rights and economic right to receiving dividends) and residual rights if the company becomes insolvent. In some cases, company directors may allot shares to friends or family members who will support management moves to introduce measures that harm other existing shareholders, notably by reducing majority shareholders' control in the general meeting, entrenching management's position, or squeezing out minority shareholders. Hence, the power to allot shares must be specifically authorised by the existing shareholders, must be renewed with specifically authorised conditions, and must be exercised for a proper purpose that is subject to court scrutiny.

---

[75] Sections 593–597, Chapter 1 of the UK Companies Act 2006.
[76] Sections 580–592, Chapter 1 of the UK Companies Act 2006.
[77] Farras and Salmeron, 'From Barter to Cryptocurrency: A Brief History of Exchange' (May 2018), available at https://beck-link.de/zyb6f (accessed 31.5.2021).
[78] Bloomsbury Professional, 'Directors' Duties: Scope of the Proper Purpose Doctrine' (December 2015), available at https://beck-link.de/mr367 (accessed 31.5.2021).

16   In an STO, businesses can issue tokens without these restrictions thus removing both the ex ante (shareholder authorisation) and ex post (court scrutiny) protection given to existing token holders. The business can issue tokens to specific persons or groups without existing token holders controlling the amount and timing of the issuance. Furthermore, the management can issue tokens merely to gain more support in the consensus voting structure or to increase the demand for an asset class such as the cryptocurrency that is the required consideration for the issuance of the tokens.

V. Token Buyback

17   Under the UK Companies Act 2006, companies cannot buy back shares unless authorised to do so by the shareholders through a special resolution of a general meeting.[79]

These regulations make sure that there is no return of capital to shareholders and that companies do not use buyback to manipulate their market share price. There are also a number of safeguards in place against price manipulation and insider dealing in share buybacks that protect issuing companies, investors and the integrity of the market.

18   In an STO, the business can use buyback to return capital raised to investors. This can amount to unfair treatment of token holders who have not been offered the same chance to realise gains through the pre-emption right and it can also reduce the protection to creditors by decreasing the capital available to them if the business becomes insolvent. A buyback can also send the wrong signal to the market, especially to unsophisticated investors who may believe there is a demand for tokens issued by the business. A buyback programme can even be automated without adequate legal scrutiny on its procedures and purposes and, if its code is inaccessible to network participants, there is a real risk of fraud since funds raised by a new issuance can be used to buy back tokens of a previous issuance at no consideration or a much reduced one.

VI. Pre-emption Right (section 561)

19   A further protection mechanism for existing shareholders is contained in section 561 of the UK Companies Act 2006. Before a company may allocate new shares, it must first offer shares on the same or more favourable terms to each shareholder who holds ordinary shares in the company, in an equivalent proportion to the shares already held in the company. Without such a right, shareholders' effective shareholding in the company would be reduced by the issue of the new shares. The intention is to protect existing shareholders against dilution of their holdings[80]. Irrespective of any dilution of the asset substance, a capital increase can also reduce the chance of making a profit if the new shares do not lead to an increase in profit, and a profit that is the same or only slightly higher is distributed among more shareholders. This right gives existing shareholders priority in benefitting from the company's IPO through any subsequent sale in the secondary market to realise gains. Without such a right, investors would be less willing to take the initial risk involved in the early stages of the business. In addition, investors would have no ex ante protection against a deliberate dilution of their control right in the company by the management.

---

[79] Sections 658 to 659, Chapter 1 of the UK Companies Act 2006.
[80] Awwad, 'Shareholders' Preemptive Rights in Listed and Closely Held Corporations and Shareholders' Protection Methods'(February 2016), available at https://beck-link.de/t688n (accessed 31.5.2021).

In an STO, existing tokens do not have such a right to purchase newly issued tokens, either to take advantage of any demand for tokens in the secondary market, or against a potential abuse of power by the management. However, the pre-emption right can increase the cost of finance, particularly when a company needs immediate finance to take up a business opportunity, and also that its application can be time-consuming and costly. This increases the investment costs and risks to the initial token holders. Hence, under UK law there is new guidance on how such a right can be disapplied for public companies, along with restrictions on the frequency of disapplication and the number of new tokens that can be issued.

Do the benefits of disapplying a pre-emption right in an STO outweigh any additional costs and risks to existing token holders that the right may incur?[81] A pre-emption right enhances business transparency and empowers token holders to scrutinise and challenge the rationale of the issuance, and to take advantage of it, if outside investors benefitted at the expense of existing shareholders. For this reason, a right of first refusal should also apply to an STO and this benefit would be lost if the right were to be disapplied. However, it would be possible to integrate pre-emption rights into a smart contract which could speed up the current procedure since it would not be necessary to contact all the existing shareholders within a time limit. This would make offering pre-emption rights to existing shareholders more efficient, cheaper and less time consuming.

VII. Voting Right

One of the most important protection mechanisms for shareholders is their voting right because it involves them in important corporate decisions.[82] These rights significantly affect the value of the shares issued as well as the value of the company and its corporate governance rating. A block of controlling shares is worth more than the aggregate of the fractional minority shares. When there is a transfer of corporate control, the purchaser needs, usually through negotiation, to pay for a control premium, rather than for the aggregate value of the number of shares based on the current market price of each share. This explains why bidders in a takeover incrementally purchase shares in the target in order to reduce the cost of the purchase.

However, in an ICO, voting rights may not be attached to the tokens, and if they are attached, they can be modified after issuance, with the knowledge and agreement of the token holders. It can happen that the 'whitepaper' did not clearly state what voting rights can be exercised for, for example authorising a derivative claim, or how the rights are to be exercised, and whether a quorum is required. The lack of rules poses a major risk to investors who can mistakenly believe that they have the same level of the protection in an ICO as they do under current company law, and that the business they have invested in operates under the normal corporate governance framework. Token holders may not have the proper forum to challenge management decisions or the validity of decisions taken by consensus. Even if it is assumed that voting rights would be automated according to a pre-determined code,[83] there is also the possibility of faults in the design of the code and this means that token holders may wish to challenge the validity of decisions reached under the consensus rules.

---

[81] Ibid.
[82] As a right of membership, the right to vote forms an ancillary component of the membership and cannot be separated from it; see Heider, in: *Münchner Kommentar zum Aktienrecht* (2019, 5th Edition, Verlag C.H. BECK München), § 12 AktG, para. 6.
[83] Yeung, 'Regulation by Blockchain: The Emerging Battle for Supremacy between the Code of Law and Code as Law' (2018) 82(2) *Modern Law Review*, 207-239.

VIII. Removal of Management

23   The removal of directors is a corporate governance tool designed to ensure shareholder democracy and investor protection in a corporate business by giving shareholders the means to remove the management. The UK Companies Act 2006 provides a statutory regime through which shareholders can remove their board of directors.[84] For listed companies, further protection is given to shareholders by the requirement that the appointment of directors must be renewed annually.[85] This increases board accountability and reduces the agency costs incurred by mismanagement, board malpractice, or illegal behaviour by the board.

24   An STO company needs clear rules on how its management can be held accountable and can be replaced. While some STO organisations emphasize a democratic and autonomous mechanism of governance,[86] exactly how their management will be brought to account or replaced remains unclear. Hence, the claim that the autonomous mechanism of governance is value-enhancing is in reality a regulatory vacuum. Without an effective mechanism to enable removal of those who act as agents of the token holders, there is a high risk of incurring agency costs by the organisation. The only option then left to token holders is the exit right – selling their tokens in the network. In the less transparent market of the blockchain network and without the support of trustworthy financial intermediaries to discover the price of the tokens, there might not be ready buyers who will offer a fair price to the token holders. Token holders may find themselves selling to the management and those in control at a value substantially below what they originally paid, either because the value of the organisation has gone down or, worse, through fraud.

IX. Derivative action (ss 260–264)

25   Derivative action is a procedural regime provided by the UK Companies Act 2006 to empower shareholders, particularly non-controlling shareholders, to hold the board to account and to obtain redress for the company through judicial assistance.[87] Shareholders can bring a derivative claim for breach of duties against the board of directors or against a third party implicated in the breach, or both.[88] However, in order to do so, shareholders must pass a resolution at a general meeting or make a claim on the basis that there is a fraud on the minority if a general resolution of a shareholder meeting cannot be secured.

26   In an STO, since there is no clear structure for initiating such an action, minority token holders are at grave risk of investment loss because judicial assistance is not available to them to hold the board to account and obtain redress such as compensation, account of profits, and other injunctive reliefs. There might not even be a legal person on whose behalf the token holders can bring claims against the board of

---

[84] Section 168 of the UK Companies Act 2006.
[85] Watson and McKenzie, 'Shareholders' Right in Private and Public Companies in the UK (England and Wales): Overview' (July 2019), available at https://beck-link.de/pp3mb (accessed 31.5.2021).
[86] Morrison, Mazey and Wingreen, 'The DAO Controversy: The Case for a New Species of Corporate Governance?' (May 2020), available at https://beck-link.de/h5vww (accessed 31.5.2021).
[87] Section 260 of the UK Companies Act 2006.
[88] Carsten, 'Derivative Actions under English and German Corporate Law – Shareholder Participation between the Tension Filled Areas of Corporate Governance and Malicious Shareholder Interference' (2010) 7 *European Company and Financial Law Review* (ECFR), 81, 87.

directors. Whereas a shareholder resolution is one of the pre-requisites to initiating a claim under the Companies Act 2006, there is no forum for STO token holders to discuss and pass a resolution to bring such a claim. Even if this might have been predetermined in the STO programme under the code-as-law, token holders may not have the knowledge or know-how to initiate it on the blockchain network or networks. The accountability of the board relies solely on the market as a monitoring mechanism. This gives opportunities for the board to extract rent for themselves through misuse of business opportunities or insider dealing at the expense of investors.

X. Insider dealing

Company directors have constant contact with price-sensitive information that is not disclosed to investors or the public, and they can profit from trading in the company's securities using such information[89]. For this reason, insider dealing is deemed a criminal offence under UK law as it harms both the company and the market. It is also immoral to engage in insider dealing behaviour such as dealing, encouraging others to deal, and disclosing insider information without authority. There are also compliance requirements in place to prevent management from misusing corporate information for its own benefit in an IPO, a share buyback,[90] a takeover or a merger.[91] 27

In an STO, there is a greater risk that the management or insiders can profit from price sensitive information that is not known to other investors or the public. Unless dealing in tokens with inside information is made a criminal offence, and unless systems and controls to prevent such an offence are introduced, the STO market will be tainted.[92] To increase the level of market integrity and investor confidence, it is imperative that insider dealing is eliminated from STO markets.[93] However, in the decentralised business structure proposed in DAO, it would be difficult to implement traditional systems and controls that have been designed for a centralised organisational system. It would also be difficult to identify a non-public inside source within a decentralised/distributed organisation. 28

E. Shareholder Transparency and Data Protection

Transparency of shareholder ownership aims to combat money laundering[94], and can be achieved more effectively in an STO market that relies on a private or hybrid blockchain. With distributed ledger technology, shareholder ownership data can be recorded, allowing those with permission to access the information. The information is 29

---

[89] Gibbon, Peel, Garston and Salaman, 'Corporate Governance and Directors' Duties in the UK' (2017), available at available at https://beck-link.de/mz4b2 (accessed 31.5.2021).

[90] Haw, Hu, Vigeland and Zhang, 'Insider Trading Restrictions and Share Repurchase Decisions: International Evidence' (January 2015), available at https://beck-link.de/pwt65 (accessed 31.5.2021).

[91] Agrawal and Nasser, 'Insider Trading in Takeover Targets' (2012) 18 *Journal of Corporate Finance*, 598–625.

[92] Zetzsche, Buckley and Arner, 'The Distributed Liability of Distributed Ledgers: Legal Risks of Blockchain' [2018] 4 *University of Illinois Law Review*, 1362–1365.

[93] Anderson, 'Insider Trading and the Myth of Market Confidence' (2018) 56 *Washington University Journal of Law and Policy*, 1–16.

[94] Transparency International UK, 'Beneficial ownership transparency; (2018), available at https://beck-link.de/t5crm (accessed 31.5 2021); Department for Business Innovation & Skills, 'Transparency & Trust: Enhancing the transparency of UK Company ownership and increasing trust in UK business' (April 2014), available at https://assets.publishing.service.gov.uk/government/uploads/system/uploads/attachment_data/file/304297/bis-14-672-transparency-and-trust-consultation-response.pdf (accessed 30.11.2020).

both current (almost real time) and historical, and is immutable once input into the system. Even if it is not tamper-proof, it is tamper-evident. This enhances compliance with anti-money laundering law that requires companies to maintain a register of information about persons with significant control (PSC)[95] – i.e. who own 25 % of the shares or votes[96] – or who can exercise real and actual control in the company.[97] In addition to fulfilling this legal requirement, the blockchain and smart contract technology can also facilitate effective e-voting.[98] This enables a company to collect information on investors' voting patterns on issues such as the election and re-election of directors, directors' remuneration, issuance of new security tokens, approval of dividends to be distributed, or the acquisition and sale of major businesses assets[99]. Investors' behaviour on corporate governance issues will also be evident and this can reveal whether institutional investors are fulfilling their stewardship obligations to clients[100], or if they are consistent in their commitment to corporate governance. Such information can be important for existing and future investors when deciding to purchase tokens, exercise their governance rights, or deciding to exit the company.

30   Personal information stored on the blockchain, be it personal or behavioural data, can be of value to data companies, public authorities, researchers, market competitors, tech companies, and the issuing companies' management. Although personal data should belong to the data subject according to Regulation (EU) 679/2016 (General Data Protection Regulation; GDPR)[101] which gives data subjects a number of rights in relation to their data, securities law and company law have not yet systemically recognised the data right of investors. For instance, platform providers can process data to provide further algorithm-based products and services which might be discriminatory to investors,[102] prejudicial to STO issuers, or damaging to market integrity.

31   Even though there are FCA rules regulating algorithm trading,[103] the current laws do not address the issues of Big Data which aggregates different types of personal information. Trading data used to develop algorithms often does not give rise to personal data protection issues because the current member-based trading and intermediated securities market structure enables privacy protection.[104] In a disintermediated STO market, data becomes not only an asset in itself[105] but its protection is relevant to

---

[95] Section 21A of the UK Companies Act 2006.
[96] PCS schedule 1A Part 1 and 2 of the UK Companies Act 2006.
[97] PCS schedule 1A Part 1 and 2 of the UK Companies Act 2006; section 790K of the Companies Act 2006
[98] Nord, 'Blockchain Plumbing: A Potential Solution for Shareholder Voting?' (2019) 29 *University of Pennsylvania Journal of Business Law*, 706–710; § 333 of the UK Companies Act 2006.
[99] Pierce, 'Protecting the Voice of Retail Investors: Implementation of a Blockchain Proxy Voting Platform' (2018–2019) 14(1) *Rutgers Business Law Review*, 9.
[100] Yermack, 'Corporate Governance and Blockchains' (2017) 21(1) *Review of Finance*, 7, 23.
[101] Regulation (EU) 679/2016 of the European Parliament and of the Council on the protection of natural persons with regard to the processing of personal data and on the free movement of such data, and repealing Directive 95/46/EC (General Data Protection Regulation), OJ L 119, 4.5.2016 p. 1–88.
[102] Art. 21 of the Charter of Fundamental Rights.
[103] Art. 17 MiFID II; FCA, 'Algorithmic Trading Compliance in Wholesale Markets' (February 2018), available at https://beck-link.de/4v6ps (accessed 31.5.2021).
[104] Keijser and Mooney, 'Intermediated Securities Holding Systems Revisited: A View Through the Prism of Transparency (2019) *University of Pennsylvania, Institute for Law & Economics Research Paper Series* No. 19-13, available at https://ssrn.com/abstract=3376873 (accessed 31.5.2021); see also Directive (EU) 2017/828/EU of the European Parliament and of the Council amending Directive 2007/36/EC as regards the encouragement of long-term shareholder engagement, OJ L 132, 20.5.2017 p. 1–25.
[105] World Economic Forum, 'Personal Data: The Emergence of a New Asset Class' (2011), available at https://beck-link.de/7s7cy (accessed 31.5.2021); Martin, 'AI-Blockchain Platform Creates Digital Assets From Personal Data' (July 2020), available at https://beck-link.de/6s22e (accessed 31.5.2021).

investors' political and governance rights. Investors, as data subjects, should be able to decide who can control and process their data, and how. In law, the company, as a legal person, can hold investors' data. But, it may only do so with the consent of the investors and only process the data for legitimate purposes. It may not use data to gain profits or other benefits without the investors' consent. Internally, the management cannot use the data to manipulate the voting process and should not disclose information about individual shareholders' voting behaviour to majority shareholders without their consent.[106] If the management gives advice to specific shareholders based on their past corporate governance activities, e.g. voting behaviour, they would owe a number of fiduciary duties to them such as the duty to act in their best interest, the duty to avoid conflicts of interest, and the duty to act in good faith.[107] By using their data, the management also owes a duty to exercise reasonable care, skill and diligence.[108] How should such duties be translated into law for the protection of token holders in the STO market? Investor's data should be treated as an economic right (like a dividend) if the company benefits from the dataset (making profits or reducing cost). And in addition, the governance code for STO issuers should specifically include investors' data-based governance rights.

F. Recommendation

I. Protection of the New Market Space

As discussed, the current securities law can be made to apply to the STO market through extending the scope of 'security' to include security tokens. And if so, securities market laws that were designed to protect investors and to ensure market integrity must also be made apply to the STO market. The Prospectus regime and the continuing disclosure obligations, that are designed to address asymmetric information should also apply to the STO market. As security tokens are recognised as a security under both UK and EU laws, there is no major difficulty in applying market conduct rules to the STO market but the question is whether bringing STO into a regulatory framework that has been designed for an intermediated securities market and which relies on financial intermediaries to perform the market gatekeeping role, would still serve the objective of access to finance that the STO market wishes to achieve. Financial intermediaries provide advice on the processes of the IPO, recommend the price of the securities issued after exercises such as 'market sounding', and are involved in the wholesale underwriting and retail broker-dealing markets. Because the structure of the current securities law has been shaped by this intermediated market space, the law emphasises the function of intermediaries as market gatekeepers for liquidity, safety, integrity, and functionality. In addition to regulating issuers, the conduct of intermediaries is the focus of regulation through detailed rules in MiFID2, AIFMD, EMIR, CSDR, and MAR. These rules are necessary to protect clients' interests as well as the interest of the market intermediaries. The cost of compliance with these rules makes it less likely for smaller businesses to be able to access the investing public. While the disclosure regime is aimed at protecting

32

---

[106] Art. 6(1)(a) GDPR.
[107] Black, 'The Principal Fiduciary Duty of Boards of Directors. Presentation at Third Asian Roundtable on Corporate Governance' (April 2001), available at https://beck-link.de/mb6h8 (accessed 31.5.2021).
[108] Information Commissioner's Office (ICO), 'Guide to the General Data Protection Regulation' (August 2018), available at https://beck-link.de/72ewz (accessed 31.5.2021).

33 Whether the disclosure regime should be aimed at protecting end investors or issuers, or at covering the costs of financial intermediaries, needs to be investigated further. But, for an STO on the blockchain aiming at accessing the investing public directly, the current securities markets law and regulation are inappropriate. Current law is adequate to protect the investing public, but an unintended consequence of the cost of compliance, is to hinder financial inclusion to issuers and the investing public. Start-up companies do not have the means to go through the IPO process, and the majority of the investing public (retail investors) cannot afford shares in the IPO. STO issuers should comply with a disclosure regime in order to address the asymmetric information problem, but they should do so through a specific enabling regime that allows them access to a public who can invest with confidence. This does not imply that no intermediary could act as a trusted third party to facilitate the processes and provide safeguards because trusted third parties are able to provide a more streamlined process using the available technologies such as smart contract, blockchain, algorithms analytics, and automation in order to reduce transaction costs. Market supervision could also be included using technology to guard against market manipulation.

II. Governance Right

34 Current company law protects investors against potential risks to their economic (monetary) and political rights, and security token holders need to be given equivalent protection if the STO market is to develop successfully. In devising such protection, we need to be clear about the purpose of these legal interventions. Is it to provide an organisational structure that reduces the time of negotiation between token holders and management? Is it to provide a structure that encourages innovation so that the STO market can compete with more traditional markets? Is it to reduce the negative way other stakeholders can be affected by dealings in the STO market? Is it to create a power balance within organisations and associations to reflect a political ethos? Or do we see STO issuers as state sanctioned entities, carrying with them a wider state responsibility? The answers to these questions must be agreed if the law is to provide the default position for parties to develop their own structure and to stipulate what laws should be mandatory, and what enforcement mechanisms and consequential remedies to breaches of the laws are suitable for protecting token holders' interests. The analysis given here suggests that current company law should not apply to STO entities, even though a company wishing to issue tokenised securities on the blockchain may find it easy to do so in terms of compliance. The technology available should make compliance more cost-effective and should have a transformative effect on the legal model. Corporate law scholars have been debating the legal nature of corporation and shares, and STO provides us with an opportunity to think anew about connecting with the disconnected and the excluded. This is reminiscent of the time when the corporate limited liability principle was introduced into the UK, enabling capital to be amassed in a way that broke the trade monopoly of the land-owning class. The fourth industrial revolution that we are now experiencing allows new types of entity to re-create capital and distribute wealth in a way that competes with multinational companies who use mergers and acquisitions to drive out market competition. Is it desirable to see merger and acquisition activities in the STO market similar to those that modern company law has been facilitating? This forces us to re-think the relationship between token holders and the issuing entity. Should token holders be the legal owners of the entity and should the

management owe direct duties to them? What is the process for dissolving the entity? There is also the opportunity to make the issuing entity a nexus of contract, bringing excluded stakeholders such as the employees, consumers, and interested community stakeholders into the network.

III. New Value and Governance Right

Traditionally, data protection law stands outside capital market regulation and company law. Capital market law focuses on investor protection, market integrity, and market safety to ensure market confidence, while company law focuses on economic rights (liquidity right, credit right and dividend right) and political rights (right to vote, right to information, and right to redress). Data protection law relates to an individual investor's personal information and the issuers' responsibility with respect to information about investors and former investors. Personal information is not to be treated as a company asset and is protected by the duty of confidentiality that is owed by a company to individual investors. Software has been developed that identifies beneficial shareholders in a company using publicly available data. This can help achieve the objective of transparency about shareholder ownership and is able to combat money laundering. STO on the blockchain can make such data readily available not only to companies, but also to other participants such as token holders in the same entity or to third parties. However, although personal data is an asset belonging to individuals, when aggregated impersonally it can create valuable Big Data. Individual identity information and behavioural data can be useful for developing analytics that allow an issuing entity or management to target particular kinds of people in order to raise capital, to understand their voting behaviour, and to know when they are likely to exit an organisation or project. This means that data rendition, data surplus, surveillance capitalism and behavioural manipulation constitute risks in the STO market.

Yet, the current capital markets law and company law do not focus on data issues because, under the current intermediated financial market structure, personal data rests with the intermediaries at different layers. Issuing companies do not necessarily have full knowledge of the identity of their shareholders, while intermediaries, such as trust banks or asset managers, often hold securities (shares) as legal owners on behalf of their immediate clients who, in turn, may also hold securities as an intermediary for their clients. Hence, data is not considered as an asset and an investor's data is not included within investor protection in securities market law. Since a personal data right is not attached to a share as recognised by company law, investors cannot take dividends derived from it. It is also conceivable that voting information could be used to analyse investor behaviour and to provide proxy advisory services. If so, misuse of that data can amount to an interference with the investors' governance right. This is an area that company law needs to address.

G. Conclusion

The chapter discusses the importance of embedding security tokens in the law in order to provide investor confidence. However, current law and regulation should not apply to the STO market if it is to achieve its intended purpose of increasing access to finance. An STO is not an IPO on a smaller scale. To have a transformative effect, the STO market needs to emphasise its decentralised and disintermediated market structure that distinguishes it from the IPO market. Despite this, current law and regulation regime for IPOs remains a useful tool to examine market structure, to identify market risks involved and the ways in which those risks can be mitigated. Company law helps to identify risks to investors' economic and political rights, and the discussion of UK company law given here provides benchmarks for the development of smart contracts in self-governing organisations. Finally, an investor's data right should be recognised as both an economic and a political right. Data dividends should be distributed to security token holders and data governance should consider the power aspect of the decision-making process. Centralised management should no longer be allowed monopolise information.

§ 19
Switzerland

Literature: Enz *Kryptowährungen im Lichte von Geldrecht und Konkursaussonderung* (Zürich, 2019), 315–351; Committee on Payments and Market Infrastructures,'G7 Working Group on Stablecoins, Investigating the impact of global stablecoins' (October 2019), available at: https://beck-link.de/rar6f (accessed 24.01.2021); Commercial Register Office Zug, 'Merkblatt über die Liberierung mit einer Kryptowährung' (June 2018), available at: https://beck-link.de/y3vff (accessed 24.01.2021); Schweizerische Nationalbank (SNB), 'Die Schweizerische Nationalbank regelt den Zugang für Fintech-Unternehmen zum Swiss Interbank Clearing' (January 2019), https://beck-link.de/tt52b (accessed 24.01.2021); Kramer, Oser and Meier, 'Tokenisierung von Finanzinstrumenten de lege ferenda' (May 2019), available at: https://beck-link.de/7k38e (accessed 24.01.2021); Seiler B. and Seiler D., 'Sind Kryptowährungen wie Bitcoin (BTC), Ethereum (ETH) und Ripple (XRP) als Sachen im Sinne des ZGB zu behandeln?' (2018) *sui generis* 149–163; Schönknecht, 'Der Einlagebegriff nach Bankengesetz' (2016) 3 *Gesellschafts-und Kapitalmarktsrecht (GesKR)*, 300–319; The Federal Council of Switzerland, 'Draft of 27 November 2019 (official English translation) of the Federal Act on the Adaptation of Federal Law to Developments in Distributed Ledger Technology' available at: https://beck-link.de/f3pda (accessed 24.01.2021); The Federal Council of Switzerland, 'Message of 27 November 2019 on the Federal Act on the Adaptation of Federal Law to Developments in Distributed Ledger Technology' (no official English translation available), available at: https://beck-link.de/2mt46 (in German), https://beck-link.de/cr5we (in French), https://beck-link.de/4f57z (in Italian) (accessed 24.01.2021); The Federal Council of Switzerland, 'Report: Legal framework for distributed ledger technology and blockchain in Switzerland – An overview with a focus on the financial sector' (Bern, December 2018), available at: https://beck-link.de/mhyx5 (accessed 24.01.2021); Truffer and Suppiah, 'RdZ-Länderreport Schweiz, Recht der Zahlungsdienste', (2020) 1 *Recht der Zahlungsdienste* 48–54. Zellweger-Gutknecht and Bacharach, *Cryptoassets in insolvency proceedings* (2021) (forthcoming; for the unedited version see https://beck-link.de/pxh4z; Zellweger-Gutknecht and Weber, 'Private Zahlungsmittel und Zahlungssysteme' (January 2021), available at: https://beck-link.de/c2e4w (accessed 20.01.2021; Zellweger-Gutknecht, 'Developing the right regulatory regime for cryptocurrencies and other value data, in: Green and Fox (eds.), *Private and Public Law Implications of Cryptocurrencies* (Oxford, 2019).

Outline

	para.
A. Introduction	1
B. Private Law	5
I. Property Law	5
II. Securities Law	7
III. International Private Law	9
C. Financial Market Law	11
I. Banking Act	12
1. Activity subject to authorisation	12
2. Exemptions	14
II. Financial Services Act (FinSA)	17
III. Financial Institutions Act (FinIA)	18
IV. Financial Market Infrastructure Act (FinMIA)	20
V. Intermediated Securities Act (FISA)	22
D. Anti-Money Laundering	24
E. Insolvency Law	27
I. Introduction	27
II. Debt Enforcement and Bankruptcy Act (DEBA)	29
III. Leges speciales	34

Part C. Country Reports

A. Introduction

1 Crypto assets can be designed in many different ways and used by very heterogeneous actors in a variety of business models. Accordingly, it must be assessed on a case-by-case basis whether they fall within the scope of various fields of Swiss law, e.g. private law, financial market law, insolvency law or anti-money laundering law. Insofar as they prove relevant to crypto assets in Switzerland, selected aspects of these legal areas will be discussed below, accompanied by references to potential case law.

2 Looking at the **market development**, the number of companies with main activities in the field of distributed ledger technology in Switzerland and Liechtenstein has increased rapidly– and likewise has the number of indirectly related actors such as specialised consultancies, law firms, NGOs, government entities and scholars.[1] In spring 2017, there were around 350 of these active companies; until the first half of 2020 their number has increased to over 900 (with 439 in Zug alone), employing more than 4700 people. Until mid-2018, five of the 15 largest ICOs took place in Switzerland.[2] In 2019, the Geneva-based Libra Association announced its project of a global stable coin, strongly reminiscent of a money market fund of potential global systemic relevance (thus inciting a barrage of opposition voiced by central banks and regulators).[3] Meanwhile, the Association has filed an application for a payment system licence on the basis of an updated whitepaper. The outcome and duration of the procedure remain open.[4] In the Swiss DLT industry, two areas in particular stand out: protocol layer projects and financial services, including two licensed crypto banks.[5] In 2020, one of the latter issued a Swiss Franc stablecoin which was used for a payment transaction with the leading Swiss online retailer with the help of a digital currency platform provider.[6] Already in September 2017, the Commercial Register Office of the Canton Zug registered in its Commercial Register a non-cash contribution in the cryptocurrency Bitcoin (BTC).[7] In 2020, a completely virtual, annual general meeting including the execution of corporate actions on DLT infrastructure was organised.[8] To end this list of randomly chosen events throughout the years with a glimpse to the future: From 2021 on, the cryptocurrencies Bitcoin and Ether can be used to pay taxes worth up to 100,000 Swiss francs in the whole Canton of Zug.[9]

---

[1] For example, CV VC Ldt., Inacta and PwC, 'Top 50 Report H1/2020' (2020), available at: https://beck-link.de/c5f4f (accessed 24.01.2021).

[2] PWC and Crypto Valley, 'Initial Coin Offerings – A strategic perspective' (June 2018) p. 3, available at: https://beck-link.de/a463y (accessed 24.01.2021).

[3] For example, Committee on Payments and Market Infrastructures, 'G7 Working Group on Stablecoins, Investigating the impact of global stablecoins' (October 2019), available at: https://beck-link.de/rar6f (accessed 24.01.2021).

[4] FINMA, 'Libra Association: FINMA licensing process initiated' (April 2020), available at: https://beck-link.de/fhbv7 (accessed 24.01.2021).

[5] See the regularly updated FINMA list of all authorised institutions and investment funds available at: https://beck-link.de/3bt3p (accessed 24.01.2021).

[6] Sygnum Bank AG, 'Coinify and Galaxus enable world's first e-commerce payment using Sygnum Bank DCHF stablecoin' (August 2020), available at: https://beck-link.de/vhbt4 (accessed 24.01.2021).

[7] In the meantime, further entries have been added. See Commercial Register Office Zug, 'Merkblatt über die Liberierung mit einer Kryptowährung' (*available only in German*) (June 2018), available at: https://beck-link.de/y3vff (accessed 24.01.2021).

[8] Daura, 'KYC Spider is the first company which handle its general assembly digitally via daura' (June 2020), available at: https://beck-link.de/bwv6y (accessed 24.01.2021).

[9] Bloomberg, 'Swiss Canton Takes Taxes in Bitcoin as Crypto Gains Traction' (September 2020) available at: https://beck-link.de/2xm8m (accessed 24.01.2021).

With the growing economic importance of the DLT industry and the consequently 3 created crypto assets, a legal framework to regulate this area is becoming increasingly urgent, while no landmark court decisions have yet been rendered.[10] In this regard, and mainly in terms of financial market law and anti-money laundering legislation, the classification of crypto assets according to their respective function plays an important role. The Financial Market Authority (FINMA) follows the principle of '**substance over form**' by concentrating on the economic function and purpose of a crypto asset (which may however change over time) while simultaneously respecting the principle of '**same risks, same rules**'. In a number of statements,[11] FINMA set out the key features of several categories of tokens: Payment tokens (synonymous with currency tokens or cryptocurrencies) are intended to be used as means of payment (for acquiring goods and services) or as a means of value or money transfer. However, above all, they do not give rise to any claim for their issuer. In contrast, asset tokens represent assets such as a debt or equity claim on the issuer and in some cases, they enable tangible assets to be traded on a blockchain or even represent rights in rem. These tokens are analogous to equities, bonds or derivatives. Utility tokens are intended to provide access to an application or service by means of a blockchain-based or similar infrastructure at the point of issue. Finally, hybrid tokens feature characteristics of several categories, so that the category-based regulatory requirements (for discussion, → para. 11 et seq. and → para. 24 et seq.) must be met cumulatively.

On 25 September 2020, Parliament adopted the Federal Act on the Adaptation of 4 Federal Law to Developments in Distributed Ledger Technology[12] (henceforth: **DLT law revision**).[13] It came fully into force on 1 August 2021 and was conceived as an umbrella decree: it implements selective amendments to ten existing federal laws[14] with the aim of improving the legal and regulatory framework and strengthen legal certainty in the crypto asset and DLT economy. Similarly, an umbrella decree will incorporate the necessary legislative amendments at ordinance level.[15] The individual changes are

---

[10] However, see. → fn. 47, fn. 52 and fn. 80. Rather of an anecdotal nature is the decision of the Swiss Federal Supreme Court of Justice (FSCJ) of 18 April 2019 – 6B_99/2019, noting (*obiter*) in consid. 2.3.2, that cryptocurrencies are not legally tender but merely a means of exchange. In the FSCJ decision of 14.05.2019 – 8C_102/2019, the FSCJ denied start-up aid for self-employers under social security law by dismissing established crypto-currencies and trading in specialised IT hardware because they were deemed purely speculative projects, presumably not generating a sustainable income.

[11] FINMA, 'FINMA is investigating ICO procedures' (September 2017) available at: https://beck-link.de/255ar (accessed 24.01.2021); FINMA, 'ICO Guidelines for enquiries regarding the regulatory framework for initial coin offerings (ICOs)' (September 2019) available at: https://beck-link.de/hmcs4 (accessed 24.01.2021); FINMA, 'Supplement [regarding stable coins]' (February 2018), available at: https://beck-link.de/hmcs4 (accessed 24.01.2021).

[12] Federal Council of Switzerland, 'Draft of 27 November 2019 (official English translation) of the Federal Act on the Adaptation of Federal Law to Developments in Distributed Ledger Technology' available at: https://beck-link.de/7rens. See also Federal Council of Switzerland, 'Message of 27 November 2019 on the Federal Act on the Adaptation of Federal Law to Developments in Distributed Ledger Technology' (no official English translation available), available at: https://beck-link.de/2mt46 (in German, French and Italian), (accessed 24.01.2021).

[13] The National Council (large chamber) made only a few changes, which were all approved by the Council of States (small chamber): See The National Council of Switzerland, 'Bundesgesetz zur Anpassung des Bundesrechts an Entwicklungen der Technik verteilter elektronischer Register' (August 2020), available in German only at: https://beck-link.de/8zrmx (accessed 24.01.2021).

[14] Thus, no further action was taken to enact a new law specifically for crypto assets, DLT based business models and the like. This could have compromised the principle of technologically neutral legislation, which can now largely be observed in the umbrella decree. But above all, the technology is still young and in flux. Therefore, the risk of being overtaken by further developments or, conversely, to prevent such developments by conservative legislation was considered too great.

[15] The consultation on the blanket ordinance in the area of blockchain ran until 2 February 2021. The ordinance amendments came into force on the same date as the amendments to the federal laws (1 August 2021). See press release of the Federal Department of Finance of 19 October 2020 (with links

pointed out directly in the relevant sections below. The revision only mentions ledger-based securities and (in insolvency law) crypto assets (called crypto-based assets in the official English translation). The former can only be asset or utility token, while the latter are used as an umbrella term for both ledger-based securities and payment token.[16] Thus, the revision ultimately still implements the three token archetypes (or at least does not contradict them).

B. Private Law

I. Property Law

5   The advancing digitalisation raises legal questions which the Swiss private law so far did not answer.[17] One of the issues concerns the **transfer of digital assets** in general and of crypto assets in particular: With regard to purely factual intangible assets such as cryptocurrencies, there exist no requirements – and accordingly no obstacles – for their transfer.[18] In contrast, the transfer of assets of a claim check-nature (representing a legal position such as a claim, membership or a right in rem) depends on the form or representation of the asset in question, i.e. the way it is made perceptible.[19] The handwritten declaration required for some of them conflicts with the needs of a progressively ever more digitised economy. Nevertheless, considerable resistance was to be expected if it had been tried to abolish or soften these formal requirements de lege ferenda.

6   Above all, however, it is debated in academia whether a **right in rem** (or rather: a right erga omnes or an absolute right) can exist de lege lata with respect to data. While the prevailing majority objects, there are scholars who nonetheless affirm the question with regards to crypto assets.[20] Some argue that the underlying technology gives the holder of the private key exclusive and non-rivalled control, thereby substituting the power over a tangible object.[21] However, the element of tangibility continues to be paramount for existing property law.

In order to keep these controversies out of the legislative process, an alternative route was chosen: Instead of adapting specific provisions on the form of transfer and

---

to German version of the Draft blanket ordinance, an explanatory report and further material), available at https://beck-link.de/6kwh3 (accessed 20.01.2021).

[16] Federal Council of Switzerland, 'Message of 27 November 2019 on the Federal Act on the Adaptation of Federal Law to Developments in Distributed Ledger Technology' (no official English translation available), 242 and 247, available at: https://beck-link.de/2mt46 (in German) (accessed 24.01.2021).

[17] For an overview: Federal Council of Switzerland, Ibid, para 6.2.4.

[18] See Federal Council of Switzerland, 'Report: Legal framework for distributed ledger technology and blockchain in Switzerland – An overview with a focus on the financial sector' (Bern, December 2018), para 6.2.4, available at: https://beck-link.de/mhyx5 (accessed 24.01.2021). Federal Council of Switzerland, 'Message of 27 November 2019 on the Federal Act on the Adaptation of Federal Law to Developments in Distributed Ledger Technology' (no official English translation available), para 1.2.1.1, available at: https://beck-link.de/2mt46 (in German) (accessed 24.01.2021).

[19] Zellweger-Gutknecht, 'Developing the right regulatory regime for cryptocurrencies and other value data, in: Green and Fox (eds.), *Private and Public Law Implications of Cryptocurrencies* (2019), 57–91, para 4.60 et seq. re uncertificated rights, uncertificated securities, certificated (bearer or order) securities and intermediated securities.

[20] A rich and structured overview of the positions can be found at Enz *Kryptowährungen im Lichte von Geldrecht und Konkursaussonderung* (2019), 315–351.

[21] See (with further references) Seiler B. and Seiler D., 'Sind Kryptowährungen wie Bitcoin (BTC), Ethereum (ETH) und Ripple (XRP) als Sachen im Sinne des ZGB zu behandeln?' (2018) *sui generis* 149–163, available at: https://beck-link.de/7cv48 (accessed 24.01.2021); Zellweger-Gutknecht, 'Developing the right regulatory regime for cryptocurrencies and other value data, in: Green and Fox (eds.), *Private and Public Law Implications of Cryptocurrencies* (2019), 57–91, para 4.80 et seq.

trying to integrate crypto assets into a relatively rigid and inflexible property law, the legislators decided to regulate selected crypto assets mainly in securities law (→ para. 7 et seq.). At the same time, they created liberal in rem-like restitution rights in insolvency law, which now – under certain conditions – give holders of all types of crypto assets almost similar privileges to those holders of rights in rem and the like enjoy (→ para. 27 et seq.).

II. Securities Law

The Art. 973d–i of the Code of Obligations (CO)[22] regulate a new type of security: the **ledger-based security** (Registerwertrechte).[23] For their creation Art. 973d CO requires the following: First, the right (pre-existing or new) has to be represented as ledger-based security, therefore being possible to be securitize and freely transferable. This comprises asset tokens (including e.g. stablecoins of a claim-check nature) as well as utility tokens and also includes individual, non-standardised rights that are not suitable for mass trade. However, it excludes all types of assets that do not consist of a right at all (e.g. fiat-like cryptocurrencies) or that are not open to securitisation by law due to restrictions set out under company law[24] or in the Swiss Civil Code (CC).[25] Second, the parties who are entitled and obliged by the right (called creditor and obligor) must agree to the registration (registration agreement; Begebungsvertrag). In addition, companies limited by shares wishing to issue shares as leger-based securities must comply with all regulations and requirements under company law.[26] Third, the rights must be recorded in an electronic register that meets requirements set forth in Art. 973d(2) CO. Last but not least, the rights may be exercised and transferred only via this ledger. 7

The requirements for the securities ledger are set out in Art. 973d (2) and (3) CO: In short, the provision regulates the power of disposal over the rights; the standards of integrity; what has to be recorded on the ledger or in linked accompanying data; the degree of transparency and the duties of the obligor concerning the ledger.

Like its predecessors (certificated and intermediated securities),[27] the ledger-based security (in practice called registered security) is a **qualified form of representation of a right**. So far, the key functions of securities (legitimation, transport and protection of 8

---

[22] The Federal Act on the Amendment of the Swiss Civil Code (Part Five: The Code of Obligations) of 30 March 1911, SR 220, available at: https://beck-link.de/3p843 (accessed 24.01.2021).

[23] Earlier drafts spoke of DLT uncertificated securities (*DLT-Wertrechte*), see Federal Council of Switzerland, Ibid, 28; and uncertificated registry securities (*Registerwertrechte*), see Federal Council of Switzerland, 'Message of 27 November 2019 on the Federal Act on the Adaptation of Federal Law to Developments in Distributed Ledger Technology' (no official English translation available), 259, available at: https://beck-link.de/2mt46 (in German) (accessed 24.01.2021), respectively.

[24] Federal Council of Switzerland, 'Message of 27 November 2019 on the Federal Act on the Adaptation of Federal Law to Developments in Distributed Ledger Technology' (no official English translation available), 277, available athttps://beck-link.de/xf7bk (in German) (accessed 24.01.2021). Currently, company law only permits securitization of membership for the company limited by shares (Art. 620 et seq. of the Swiss Civil Code (Part Five: Code of Obligations, 'CO') and the partnership limited by share (Art. 764 et seq. CO).

[25] Swiss Civil Code of 10 December 1907, SR 210, available at: https://beck-link.de/x4z25 (accessed 24.01.2021). A numerus clausus also applies in property law, since securitization of rights in rem is only possible for the mortgage certificate (Art. 842 et seq. CC) and bonds secured by a lien (Art. 875 CC).

[26] See especially Art. 622(1) CO requiring that the Art.Art. of association stipulate the issuance of shares in a qualified form of representation (i.e. leger-based or intermediated security). For further details, see e.g. Kramer, Oser and Meier, 'Tokenisierung von Finanzinstrumenten de lege ferenda' (May 2019) (in German only), available at: https://beck-link.de/7k38e (accessed 15.01.202124.01.2021).

[27] Art. 965 et seq. CO; Art. 1 et seq. of the Swiss Financial Services Act, 'FISA' (→ fn. 70).

traffic by bona fide acquisition) have depended to a large extent on the tangible embodiment of a right in a deed (security) or on the registration with a regulated custodian (intermediated security). With the fulfilment of the requirements of Art. 973d CO, ledger-based securities now also have these functions as specified in Art. 973e and 973f.[28] They are supplemented by further provisions on collateral (Art. 973g CO), cancellation in case of loss (Art. 973h CO) as well as information duties and the liability of the obligor (Art. 973i CO).

III. International Private Law

9   The legal issues arising under private international law in connection with the issue or transfer of tokens can largely be subsumed under the existing provisions, whereby the intended function of the token in question is decisive. For example, actions concerning a **membership** right embodied in a token are classified as disputes under company law. Therefore, jurisdiction of the Swiss courts is determined according to Art. 151 of the Federal Act on Private International Law (PILA).[29] The law applicable to companies according to Art. 154 et seq. PILA determines to what extent the embodiment of membership in a token is legally valid and to what extent the transfer thereof can be linked to the transfer of the token.

If the function of the token is to embody a co-ownership share or a claim secured by a pledge, Art. 97 and 98 PILA (jurisdiction of the Swiss courts) and Art. 100 et seq. PILA (applicable law) apply to disputes relating to the concerned **right in rem**. Foreign judgments in connection with tokens may be recognised in Switzerland under the conditions set forth in Art. 25 et seq. PILA.

10   Furthermore, the DLT revision provides legislative clarification with regard to the question of the law applicable to **the transfer of tokenised claims**. According to new Art. 145a PILA, the law of the State in which the registered office or, in the absence thereof the place of habitual residence of the issuer is located, determines whether the claim is represented in the token and can be transferred together with the token. The applicable law describes the procedure necessary for the transfer. Additionally, the amendments clarify that the provisions of the PILA regarding securities and title documents ('Warenpapiere') are also applicable for tokenised securities and tokenised title documents.[30]

C. Financial Market Law

11   Constitutional norms on the economic order in general and on the financial market in particular are set out in Art. 94 et seq. of the Federal Constitution (Const.).[31] Based on Art. 98 Const., the Confederation is **competent** to legislate on banking, stock exchanges and private insurance as well as financial services in other fields. It has done so in particular by enacting a number of financial market acts (discussed below), making selected activities subject to authorisation and setting up a financial market supervisory

---

[28] Federal Council of Switzerland, Ibid.
[29] Swiss Federal Act of 18 December 1987 on Private International Law, SR 291 (no official English translation available), available at: https://beck-link.de/zkfk6 (accessed 24.01.2021). International treaties like the Lugano Convention take precedence (Art. 1(2) PILA).
[30] Art. 105 (2) and 106 PILA.
[31] The Federal Constitution of the Swiss Confederation of 18 April 1999, SR 101, available at: https://beck-link.de/46pz8 (accessed 24.01.2021).

authority (FINMA).³² The latter is regulated by the Financial Market Supervision Act (FINMASA).³³

Currently, Art. 1 FINMASA lists nine financial market laws. Those with a particular relevance for crypto assets will now be explained in more detail, together with the Intermediated Securities Act.

I. Banking Act

1. Activity subject to authorisation

The most decisive connecting criterion for the scope of application of the Banking Act (BA) and the Banking Ordinance (BO)³⁴ is the **acceptance of deposits from the public**. Its meaning therefore clarified here in advance: According to Art. 5(1) BO, deposits from the public are developed if domestic or foreign money or crypto assets of a claim check nature (entitling the holder to repayment)³⁵ are obtained in such a way that the recipient acquires an absolute right to them (for objects: ownership) and undertakes their reimbursement later, whereby a conditional repayment obligation is sufficient. This is especially the case with the depositum irregulare, where the recipient mixes the accepted deposits with its own assets. Crypto assets of a fiat nature (such as virtual currencies) do not qualify as such deposits. This is because they are by definition expressed in their own denomination and do not establish any right for repayment or other claims against their issuer; the most prominent example is Bitcoin. However, if they are held for the account of a third party they also qualify as deposits. 12

Companies which operate primarily in the financial sector and intend to accept deposits from the public on a commercial basis (i.e. for more than 20 clients) or simply advertise such service to the public,³⁶ must prior to commencing their activities obtain a **banking licence**. The latter is subject to a considerable number of requirements.³⁷

Alternatively, a company can qualify under Art. 1b BA for a **fintech licence**³⁸ (actually: licence for safekeepers of means of payment)³⁹ with less stringent requirements,⁴⁰ if it accepts deposits from the public up to a value of CHF 100 million (or the 13

---

³² FINMA operates in accordance with the principles of subsidiarity and economic freedom, takes account of the international minimum standards and supports self-regulation (Art. 7(2) and (3) FINMASA). The interplay of laws, licensing and prudential supervision (i.e. control of compliance with the financial market acts) has the objective to protect creditors, investors, and insured persons as well as ensuring the proper functioning of the financial market.
³³ Federal Act of 22 June 2007 on the Swiss Financial Market Supervisory Authority, SR 956.1, available at: https://beck-link.de/n8zdf (accessed 24.01.2021).
³⁴ Federal Act on Banks and Savings Banks of 8 November 1934, SR 952.0 (no official English translation available), available at: https://beck-link.de/z4tym (accessed 24.01.2021). Swiss ordinance on Banks and Savings Banks of 30 April 2014, SR 952.02, (no official English translation available), available at: https://beck-link.de/b3s2k (accessed 24.01.2021).
³⁵ Schönknecht, 'Der Einlagebegriff nach Bankengesetz', (2016) 3 *Gesellschafts-und Kapitalmarktsrecht (GesKR)*, 300–319, 309.
³⁶ Art. 6(1) BO.
³⁷ In particular Art. 3 et seq. BA.
³⁸ In March 2020, YAPEAL, which plans to develop a digital bank based on blockchain technology (https://yapeal.ch), was the first financial institution to receive such license.
³⁹ See Zellweger-Gutknecht and Weber, 'Private Zahlungsmittel und Zahlungssysteme' (January 2021), (in German only) para 33–35, available at: https://beck-link.de/c2e4w (accessed 20.01.2021).
⁴⁰ See, e.g., Art. 1b and 3(2)d BA and 14a BO re legal forms, seat and administration, Art. 1b (3)b BA and 14f(2) to (4) BO re permitted use of deposits (bank or fintech account or HQLA), Art. 14f(3) re and 17a BO re minimum capital requirement (3 % of deposits from the public and at least CHF 300'000). The auditing requirements are somewhat lower than for banks; see FINMA, 'Circular 2013/03 Prüfwesen (2012), available at: https://beck-link.de/5fm34 (accessed 24.01.2021).

equivalent) and neither invests the accepted funds nor pays interest on them. However, it has to inform its customers in advance based on Art. 7a BO that deposits will not be privileged or immediately paid out under Art. 37a and 37b Banking Act in case of insolvency.[41] The above mentioned DLT law revision extends the scope of Art. 1b BA to the **acceptance of crypto assets** defined in more detail in Art. 5a BO (for reference and reasons, → para. 14 in fine).

Providers of crypto asset business models (payment services provider, depository of cryptocurrencies, crowdlender, ICO-issuer of liabilities with debt capital character etc.) are therefore subject to authorisation, if their activities involve either the acceptance of deposits from the public or crypto assets.[42]

2. Exemptions

14 However, no deposits materialise if customers **retain full rights** to their funds even though they are transferred to a recipient. This is generally deemed to be the case if a recipient holds funds for the account of a third party in a way where the law allows their surrender in case of the recipient's insolvency, i.e. if they do not fall in the bankruptcy estate (for details, → para. 27 et seq.).[43]

The DLT law revision allows the **privileged surrender** of crypto assets that are either kept separate from the recipient's own assets (whereby omnibus client segregation is sufficient) or recorded in its ledgers in such a way that it is at all times apparent which share of the assets is due to a specific client. This follows in general from the new Art. 242a DEBA and, in the case of banks and fintech licensees, from the revised Art. 16 BA. According to Art. 14f BO, fintech licensees must already hold all their client assets in one of these two ways and, moreover, they are subject to an ordinary audit under Art. 727 CO, if they opt for the described second way.

Consequently, with this newly granted privilege of surrender, segregated or distinguishable crypto assets are not of a deposit nature, so that their acceptance from the public would not be subject to authorisation under previous rules. In order to minimise the associated risks for customers and the Swiss financial market, the scope of application of Art. 1b BA has been extended to crypto assets as mentioned earlier (→ para. 13).[44] In addition, the FINMA may set a threshold in individual cases for crypto assets held by a bank or fintech licensee depending on their risk evaluation (new Art. 4sexies BA).

---

[41] Fintech licensees whose business model is essentially rooted in the area of Swiss franc payment transactions can be granted access to the Swiss Interbank Clearing (SIC) system, provided such admission does not entail any major risks for the system, see Schweizerische Nationalbank (SNB), 'Die Schweizerische Nationalbank regelt den Zugang für Fintech-Unternehmen zum Swiss Interbank Clearing' (January 2019), available at: https://beck-link.de/tt52b (accessed 24.01.2021).

[42] An example is the Sygnum Digital Swiss Franc (DCHF), a token issued by Sygnum, an authorised Swiss digital asset bank for settlement in a DLT-based environment. Since the DCHF is pegged to and convertible into CHF, its issuance requires in principle (and subject to exceptions discussed below) a banking license.

[43] Under general insolvency law, surrender is only carried out upon application (in German referred to as 'Aussonderung'), whereas under financial market law (generally referring to Art. 17 FISA) it is carried out ex officio (in German: 'Absonderung'). In Art.17 FISA, the latter is termed 'exclusion from … estate'. However, English translation of the draft of Art. 37d BA speaks of 'segregation'. This is not suitable as the term of segregation is used in practice to describe the type of custody (e.g., omnibus client segregation). Therefore, the definite official translation should rather use the established terminology, i.e., 'surrender' if carried out upon application based on Art. 242a DEBA and 'exclusion' (from estate) if done so ex officio.

[44] Federal Council of Switzerland, Ibid. This will apply in particular to payment tokens held in collective custody (as liabilities on the balance sheet of the licensee). The BO will define the requirements for the safekeeping of crypto assets held in collective custody.

There exist a number of further exceptions from the licensing requirement: First, under 15 the **Sandbox exception** of Art. 6 BO, companies are not deemed to act on a commercial basis and may therefore not need any authorisation, if they accept deposits from the public up to a value of CHF 1 million (or the equivalent) without paying interest on them. In addition, they have to inform their customers (in advance and in another way than via their general terms and conditions) that they are not prudentially supervised by the FINMA and that deposits will neither be privileged nor immediately paid out under Art. 37a and 37b BA in case of insolvency. Companies can then invest the received funds – but are prohibited from agreeing on a specific or determinable interest rate for such an investment since this would be considered a so-called interest rate differential business, which remains the privilege of the banks.[45] However, due to the low threshold, the Sandbox has remained without practical relevance since its introduction in 2017.

Second, Art. 5(3)(a) to (f) BO lists a number of cases in which the law stipulates that 16 **no deposit is created**:

(a) funds transferred as security or representing consideration under a contract for the transfer of property[46] or under a service contract. This may mainly apply in case of a purchase of utility tokens.
(b) funds invested in debt securities in the sense of Art. 2(b) FinMIA (→ para. 20)[47] and issued by a company subject to an ordinary audit (Art. 727 CO), if at the time of the offer a prospectus in the sense of Art. 64 FinSA (→ para. 17) and with the content set forth in Art. 5(3)b BO is published.[48]
(c) funds accepted and booked on client accounts exclusively for settlement purposes, if no interest is paid for it and the settlement takes place within 60 days.[49] This includes business models of a pass-through nature such as money transmitting, crowdfunding or debt collection, but not crypto currency traders. The latter are put on an equal footing with foreign exchange dealers.[50]
(d) funds received and inextricably linked to a life insurance contract, the occupational pension scheme or other recognised forms of social insurance schemes.
(e) funds used for a means of payment or payment system in amounts up to CHF 3'000 per person[51] for the sole purpose of obtaining future goods or services and for which no interest is paid. If compliance with the ceiling is ensured, cryptocurrencies in particular can benefit from this exception.

---

[45] See also FINMA, 'Circular 2008/3 Public deposits with non-banks' (September 2019), paras. 8–9, available at: https://beck-link.de/5fm34 (accessed 24.01.2021). The investment in shares, foreign exchange or crypto-currencies does not qualify as interest rate differential business, since the purpose of these investments is predominantly to achieve indeterminable income or price gains. The circular is only available in German, French and Italian also at: https://beck-link.de/e74s8.

[46] The Federal Administrative Court denied an exception under Art. 5(3)a BO for the 'sale' of tokens, even though tokens might (sic) qualify as chattels provided, they could be controlled and individualised (which was not the case here). Even then, however, an economic point of view would speak against a purchase and in favour of a deposit: Decision of the Swiss Federal Administrative Court (FAC) of 21.01.2019- B-6413/2017, para 5.

[47] This comprises standardised certificated and uncertificated securities, derivatives and intermediated securities, which are suitable for mass trading.

[48] An example was the crypto franc XCHF until the end of 2020 (since 2021, it has been secured by a bank guarantee according to Art. 5(3)(f) BO; see www.swisscryptotokens.ch (accessed 24.01.2021)

[49] This limited duration does not apply to securities firms in the sense of Art. 41 et seq. FinIA (→ para. 18).

[50] See FINMA, 'Ibid, para 16.2. Truffer, Suppiah, 'RdZ-Länderreport Schweiz, Recht der Zahlungsdienste', (2020) 1 *Recht der Zahlungsdienste*, 48, 53–54 and fn. 25 with further reference.

[51] Regarding the ceiling see FINMA, Ibid, para. 18; Decision of the Swiss Federal Supreme Court of 24 November 2015 – 2C_345/2015 (confirming the legality of this ceiling for e-money, because issuers in Switzerland are not subject to an authorization of its own kind).

(f) funds whose repayment and interest are guaranteed by a bank (default guarantee).[52] Such a solution is unlikely to be attractive for issuers of crypto assets, especially due to the resulting costs. Moreover, to the extent that they would act as competitors of banks, the latter would be reluctant to help out at all.

II. Financial Services Act (FinSA)

17 Crypto assets – and namely asset tokens – can qualify as securities. In this case, activities related to them may be subject to **authorisation and regulation**, particularly under the Financial Services Act (FinSA, → para. 17) but also under the Financial Institutions Act (FinIA, → para. 18) as well as the Financial Market Infrastructure Act (FinMIA, → para. 20). Again, the notion of security and related terminology has thus to be clarified first.

According to Art. 3(1)(b) FinSA (→ para. 17) (mirrored in Art. 2(b) FinMIA), **securities** are certificated and uncertificated securities, derivatives, intermediated securities and – since the DLT law revision – also ledger-based securities, provided they are standardised and suitable for mass trading.[53] They qualify as financial instruments under Art. 3(1)(a) FinSA – as do derivatives according to Art. 3(1)(a) (5) FinSA. Any transaction involving a financial instrument (including its issuance) is deemed to be a financial service pursuant to Art. 3(1)(c) FinSA. Consequently, persons qualify as financial service providers in the sense of Art. 2(1)(a) and 3(1)(d) FinSA, thus falling under the scope of FinSA if they provide financial services on a commercial basis in Switzerland or for clients in Switzerland. The criterion of a commercial basis is satisfied if an independent economic activity is pursued on a permanent profit-oriented basis.

With regard to **crypto assets**, FINMA has not treated payment and utility tokens as securities so far, provided that they have no investment purpose. In contrast, **asset tokens** are treated as securities if they are standardised and suitable for mass trading. The same applies during the pre-financing and pre-sale phases of an ICO to all type of token which confer claims to acquire tokens in the future.[54] As is shown below, the FINIG or the FinfraG can be applicable in these cases.

III. Financial Institutions Act (FinIA)

18 Self-issuance of securities on the **primary market** is essentially unregulated. However, pursuant to Art. 41 FinIA,[55] an authorisation as a securities firm or as a bank is needed if a person operating primarily in the financial sector either underwrites securities issued by third parties or creates derivatives[56] in the form of securities and offers these to the public on the primary market on a commercial basis (Art. 12 and 44 FinMIA).

---

[52] For an example, see fn. 49 and the guarantee of Credit Suisse of 18 February 2020 in favour of REKA (a private means of payment, albeit not crypto-based, limited to the use in the travel and leisure sector) for holdings per person exceeding the ceiling mentioned above under (e): https://beck-link.de/2xvww (accessed 24.01.2021).

[53] That means they are publicly offered for sale in the same structure and denomination or are placed with more than 20 clients and have not been created especially for individual counterparties (Art. 2(1) of the Financial Market Infrastructure Ordinance ('FinMIO') of 25 November 2015).

[54] FINMA, 'Supplement [regarding stable coins] (February 2018), para 4 et seq., available at: https://beck-link.de/hmcs4 (accessed 24.01.2021), see fn. 11).

[55] The Swiss Federal Act on Financial Institutions ('FinIA') of 15 June 2018, SR 954.1, Ibid.

[56] E.g., if no repayment of investment is due but a share in future company earnings or capital flows.

§ 19. Switzerland

The issuing can further result in prospectus requirements (and exemptions) which are governed exclusively by Art. 35–57 FinSA.[57]

Activities on the **secondary market** are likewise unregulated for people acting in a private capacity. In contrast, an authorisation as a securities firm pursuant to Art. 41 FinIA is again needed by whoever trades in securities on a commercial basis either as a client dealer (letter a; operating in its own name for the account of clients) or as a market maker (letter c) or for its own account on a short-term basis, primarily on the financial market and under further conditions (as set out in letter b).

The **DLT law revision** has extended the definition of what entities are deemed to be **securities firms** and thus require authorisation for their activities. Market participants can now also apply for a licence exclusively for the purpose of operating an organised trading facility (**OTF**) under Art. 42 FinMIA (as described below).[58] Hence, Art. 41(b)(3) FinIA now qualifies entities as securities firms if they commercially trade in securities for their own account on a short-term basis or operate primarily on the financial market and undertake an OTF. However, this status does not go as far as the one of securities firms under Art. 41(a) FinIA which requires trading in securities for the account of clients. In particular, the authorisation does not include the right to operate any other regulated financial market activity (Art. 6(2) FinIA). Likewise, the provisions on the protection of deposits and on dormant assets[59] do not apply.[60]

19

Finally, the provisions of the Collective Investment Schemes Act (CISA)[61] and the licencing requirement under Art. 7(1) CISA are only relevant if the funds accepted in the context of an ICO are managed by third parties.[62]

IV. Financial Market Infrastructure Act (FinMIA)

Licensing requirements may also arise because securities are linked to an activity within the financial market infrastructure. Until now, only **trading venues** in accordance with Art. 26 FinMIA[63] (stock exchanges, **SE**, and multilateral trading facilities, MTF) needed a specific authorisation as financial market infrastructure (Art. 4(1), 5 and 26–37 FinMIA). They offer multilateral trading in securities based on non-discretionary rules for prudentially regulated participants, whereby only stock exchanges list securities (Art. 34(2) FinMIA).

20

Entities that wished instead to operate a trading facility for bilateral trading or for financial instruments other than securities or based on discretionary rules or for not prudentially regulated participants (or a combination thereof) had to opt for an **OTF** according to Art. 42 et seq. FinMIA. This in turn required an authorisation as bank, securities dealer or trading venue. However, until now it has not been possible to obtain one of these licences if a company wanted to operate only an OTF (e.g. to offer trading services for crypto assets).

---

[57] Art. 35(1bis) FinSA and Art. 73d (1) in fine FinIA.
[58] Federal Council of Switzerland, 'Ibid.
[59] Art. 37a et seq. BA.
[60] Art. 67(2) FinIA e contrario.
[61] Swiss Federal Act on Collective Investment Schemes ('CISA') of 23 June 2006, SR 951.31, available at: https://beck-link.de/zbf5s (accessed 24.01.2021).
[62] FINMA, 'Supplement [regarding stable coins] (February 2018), para 4 et seq., available at: https://beck-link.de/hmcs4 (accessed 24.01.2021). (*See* fn. 11).
[63] Swiss Federal Act on Financial Market Infrastructures and Market Conduct ('FinMIA') in Securities and Derivatives Trading of 19 June 2015, SR 958.1, available at: https://beck-link.de/sd3sk (accessed 24.01.2021).

21   Therefore, the DLT revision introduced a new set up for the financial market infrastructure, requiring a licence: the **DLT trading facility** (Art. 2(a)(5a), 4(1) and 73a-73f FinMIA). It has to be a commercially operated[64] institution for multilateral trading of DLT securities[65] based on non-discretionary rules. DLT securities are either ledger-based securities according to Art. 973d CO or functionally equivalent securities held in DLT registers, e.g. established under foreign law (Art. 2(bbis) FinMIA). In addition, a DLT trading facility has either to admit non-regulated participants or offer post-trade services relating to DLT securities (limited services for central custody, clearing and settlement, thus excluding any central counterparty function) or both. This allows a clear differentiation from MTF.

Finally, further requirements are imposed to ensure that **DLT trading systems** are treated at arm's length with other financial market infrastructures.[66] Hence, a set of rules has been extended to DLT trading systems.[67] In turn, just like trading venues, DLT trading systems may also operate an OTF.[68] Where appropriate, however, specific provisions have been created, particularly concerning the admission of participants and their duties (Art. 73d FinMIA), the easing of requirements for small DLT trading facilities (Art. 73f FinMIA) and the admission of DLT securities and other assets (Art. 73e FinMIA). With regard to the latter, the DLT trading facility must issue regulations and set out in particular the requirements to be met by the DLT securities and the issuers or third parties in connection with the admission (Art. 73e (1) FinMIA. Additional requirements may be defined at ordinance level (Art. 73e (2) FinMIA).

V. Intermediated Securities Act (FISA)

22   The Intermediated Securities Act[69] introduced a new category of assets to the Swiss legal system: the **intermediated securities**. Similar to certificated securities (including global certificates), intermediated securities are a qualified form of representation that makes a right, i.e. an asset of a claim-check nature, perceptible in a particularly trustworthy way. Its creation presupposes that the right in question is securitisable and of a fungible nature (Art. 3(1) FISA) and must first come into existence in the form of certificated securities in collective custody, global certificates or uncertificated rights according to Art. 973a–c CO. This form of representation is then immobilised as described in Art. 6 FISA, serving henceforth as underlying,[70] and intermediated securities of a corresponding value are credited to a securities account by a custodian. Only selected regulated financial intermediaries are authorised to operate as custodians (Art. 4 FISA). This is the reason why intermediated securities benefit from privileged functions (described in more detail in the rest of the act) similar to the ones of certificated securities and now also ledger-based securities (as mentioned above → para. 9 et seq.).

---

[64] The criterion requires an independent economic activity pursued on a permanent, for-profit basis: Art. 73a(2) FMIA.
[65] This criterion still allows DLT trading systems to also trade non-DLT securities (e.g., payment tokens, such as Bitcoin, or utility tokens) as ancillary services: also Federal Council of Switzerland, Ibid.
[66] See especially Art. 73b FinMIA regarding the applicability of certain requirements for trading venues.
[67] See Art. 16(2) FinMIA re restricted use of selected terms such as DLT trading systems etc.; Art. 22(2) FinMIA re systemic importance; Art. 89(1) and (2) FinMIA re system protection; and Art. 142, 143, 154 and 155 FinMIA re insider trading and market manipulation.
[68] Art. 43(1) FinMIA and Art. 41(b) FinIA; Federal Council of Switzerland, Ibid.
[69] Swiss Federal Act on Intermediated Securities ('FISA') of 3 October 2008, SR 957.1, available at: https://beck-link.de/y57x6 (accessed 24.01.2021).
[70] This prevents the same right from circulating simultaneously in several forms of representation.

If a DLT trading facility pursuant to Art. 73a et seq. FinMIA immobilises crypto assets in form of (fungible) ledger-based securities and holds them in central custody, its business model does not differ significantly from one of a traditional custodian under Art. 4 FISA. Consequently, the **DLT law revision** included such DLT trading facilities in the list of custodians (Art. 4(2)(g) FISA).

This inclusion required in turn the **adjustment of other provisions**. For example, Art. 5(h) FISA now defines the notion of ledger-based security. Art. 6(1)(d) and (3) FISA regulates the creation of intermediated securities based on ledger-based securities in three steps. (The transfer of the latter to a DLT trading facility acting as custodian, the immobilisation in its securities ledger in the sense of Art. 973d (2) CO and the crediting of the respective rights to one or more securities accounts of the custodian.)

A reverse conclusion from the reformulated Art. 7 FISA makes it clear that an underlying ledger-based security can neither be converted by the issuer into another form of underlying, nor converted into certificated securities upon request by the account holder (both would be possible with regard to certificated securities in collective custody, global certificates or uncertificated securities – unless otherwise provided by the terms of issue or the issuer's Art. of association).

According to Art. 9(1) FISA the rules on sub-custody in Switzerland and abroad now also apply to ledger-based securities. Art. 11 FISA requires custodians to prevent a potential shortfall by holding a (further specified) quantum of available securities. Under this definition now also fall qualify ledger-based securities which the custodian holds directly. Finally, Art. 17–19 FISA on exclusion and shortfall apply if a DLT trading facility acting as custodian is subject to proceedings for compulsory liquidation. In particular, in order to transfer intermediated securities credited to securities accounts maintained by the DLT trading facility for its account holders to these account holders, the liquidator has to exclude from the custodian's estate a corresponding number of securities as defined in Art. 17(1) FISA – among them now ledger-based securities which are then transferred to the account holder (Art. 17(1)(b) and (4)(c) FISA).

D. Anti-Money Laundering

The provisions on anti-money laundering[71] in general only apply to **financial intermediaries** pursuant to Art. 2 AMLA.[72] These comprise regulated financial entities (Art. 2(2) AMLA – among them since the DLT law revision DLT trading facilities[73]) and any other person who – on a professional basis[74] – accept or hold assets or assist in the investment or transfer of such assets (Art. 2(3) AMLA). They include in particular persons who carry out credit transactions, provide payment (among them the issuance

---

[71] Swiss Federal Act of 10 October 1997 on Combating Money Laundering and Terrorist Financing (Anti-Money Laundering Act, 'AMLA'), SR 955.0, official English translation available at: https://beck-link.de/edy6n; in addition, there exist further regulation on ordinance level, e.g. (without official English translation) the Swiss Federal Council Ordinance of 11 November 2015 ('AMLO'), SR 995.01.' the FINMA Ordinance of 3 June 2015 (AMLO-FINMA), SR 955.033.0 and the FINMA Circular of 20 October 2010 (FINMA-RS 2011/1) available at: https://beck-link.de/5fm34 (accessed 24.01.2021).

[72] Dealers outside the financial industry are only subject according to Art. 2(1)(b) and Art. 8a AMLA.

[73] See new letter d^{quater} in Art. 2(2) AMLA, referring to Art. 73a FinMIA.

[74] See Art. 7 AMLO: one or more out of four criterion has to be met per year: gross profit > CHF 50'000; > 20 contractual relationships with 20 clients, power of disposition over third party assets > CHF 5 million, turnover > CHF 2 million.

of means of payments), engage in trading, make investments as investment advisers, hold securities on deposit or manage securities.[75]

This gives rise to a range of due diligence and reporting requirements including the duty to establish the identity of the beneficial owner (Art. 3 et seq. AMLA) and to either affiliate to a FINMA-approved self-regulatory organisation (SRO; Art. 14(1) AMLA)[76] or to be supervised directly by FINMA or other official authorities (Art. 17 AMLA). The obligations relating to the FATF travel rule are dealt with in Art. 10 AMLO-FINMA.

25   With regard to crypto assets[77] in the form of **asset tokens**, the AML provisions do not apply to their issue at all and to their trading only if it is carried out by securities firms (Art. 5(2) AMLO). However, they apply in full to persons who hold on deposit or manage asset tokens while acting on a professional basis (Art. 2(3)(g) AMLA in conjunction with Art. 6(1)(a) and (c) AMLO).

In the case of **utility tokens** (and hybrids with utility element), AML regulation is not applicable if the payment or investment function of a token is of accessory nature only (Art. 2(2)(a)(3) AMLO) and the main reason for issuing the tokens is to provide access rights to a non-financial DLT application.[78]

26   Operations with **payment tokens** usually trigger an application of the AML legislation. On the one hand, this applies to payment services such as the issuance of means of payments or their management (e.g. as a custody wallet provider, as an escrow agent or as an operator of a closed or open payment system);[79] the electronic transfer of liquid assets on behalf of third parties;[80] and the remittance of funds.[81] On the other hand, the trade with payment tokens is usually also subject to AML legislation. This includes foreign exchange (with all combinations of fiat money and/or cryptocurrencies).[82] Exemptions are rare,[83] among them the issue for only bilateral use as a voucher (Art. 4(1)(b) AMLO) and trading in the form of money exchange on an accessory basis (Art. 5(III) AMLO). The latter is not given if transactions in the (total) amount of more than CHF 5'000 are offered or if more than 10 % of the gross profit per calendar year are generated by exchange transactions.[84] It must be clear in any case that the exchange is bilateral, else the transaction qualifies as a remittance.

---

[75] Art. 2(3)(a) to (g) AMLA, specified in Art.3 to 6 AMLO. Exemptions: Art. 2(4) AMLA and Art. 2(2) AMLO.

[76] As an alternative, e.g., an ICO organiser could have funds accepted via a financial intermediary who is already subject to the AMLA in Switzerland and who exercises on behalf of the organiser the corresponding due diligence requirements: Swiss Financial Market Authority ('FINMA'), 'FINMA Roundtable on ICOs' (March 2018), 23, available at: https://beck-link.de/bxwe7 (accessed 24.01.2021).

[77] FINMA, 'FINMA Roundtable on ICOs' (March 2018), 23, available at: https://beck-link.de/bxwe7 (accessed 24.01.2021) p. 18 et seq.

[78] FINMA, Ibid, 7 with further reference and more detailed 21.

[79] Art.2(3)(b) AMLA, Art.4(1)(b) AMLO: means other than cash whose value is fixed at the time of issue and which allow the transfer of monetary value. Art.2(3)(b) AMLA was held applicable with regard to non-accessory post-paid settlement service offered by telecommunication enterprise Swisscom and executed via short messages services (sms) for night surcharges on public transport tickets: Decision of the FSCJ of 12.03.2020 – 2C_488/2018, para. 4.4.2 and 5.2.

[80] Art.2(3)(b) AMLA, Art.4(1)(a) AMLO, see FINMA-RS 2011/1 para. 58.

[81] Art.2(3)(b) AMLA, Art.4(1)(c) and (2) AMLO: transfer of value by accepting liquid assets and delivering an equivalent amount of tangible liquid assets or allocation thereof via a payment or settlement system. See also Art.11 to Art.12, Art. 52, Art. 56(4) and (5) and Art. 61(1) AMLO-FINMA regarding related duties.

[82] Art.2(3)(c) AMLA and Art.5(1)(a) AMLO; FINMA-RS 2011/1 para. 84 et seq24.01.2021.

[83] For further exemptions of specific duties see, e.g., Art.11 AMLO-FINMA.

[84] FINMA-RS 2011/1 para. 84–87.

E. Insolvency Law

I. Introduction

Enforcement against the estate of an insolvent debtor is governed by the Debt Enforcement and Bankruptcy Act (DEBA).[85] Upon the bankruptcy of a debtor, all assets regardless of their location form the bankruptcy estate ('Konkursmasse'). This estate is then used to appease the claims of all creditors (Art. 197 DEBA). Assets held by the debtor which are subject to a better right of a third party are not part of the bankruptcy estate. They are to be surrendered (for terminology, → fn. 43) by the bankruptcy administration on request (Art. 242 DEBA). So far, such preferential third party-claims were in principle restricted to tangible objects which are regulated by property law.[86] Moreover, privileged rights of third parties are also regulated in a number of financial market acts. Usually, these acts implement the exclusion from the bankruptcy estate as effected ex officio (for discussion, → para. 34).[87] DEBA assumes a fundamental distinction between **rights in rem** and **contractual rights**: while rights in rem permit upon request the surrender of the chattel concerned from the bankruptcy estate, contractual rights are satisfied only pro rata jointly with the other creditors[88] in the order of the creditors' priority in the liquidation procedure (Art. 219 DEBA). 27

As mentioned, there is no consensus on whether crypto assets are subject to property law and can thus be classified as property (or other rights *in rem*, → para. 6). The courts have not yet decided upon the **surrender of crypto assets**. The Federal Council has recognised that there is a real practical need for the surrender of crypto assets – especially in the context of third-party safekeeping of crypto assets by wallet providers. Therefore, the DLT revision introduces the new Art. 242a DEBA in order to provide legal certainty on this matter. However, it does not explicitly classify crypto assets as chattel. Thus, it remains unclear if crypto assets are for example covered by movable property law, so that they could be seized like chattel. The same can be said for the pledge of crypto assets that do not qualify as ledger-based securities (while in relation to the latter, pledging, special lien and other types of collateral are newly governed by Art. 973g CO). However, from the viewpoint of insolvency law crypto assets are mostly treated like chattel. 28

II. Debt Enforcement and Bankruptcy Act (DEBA)

Whether an asset is part of the bankruptcy estate or not is primarily determined by who has custody of the asset. The objective of Art. 242 DEBA is to ultimately assign an asset to its beneficial owner, even if the legal ownership at the time of bankruptcy may 29

---

[85] Swiss Federal Act of 11 April 1889 on Debt Enforcement and Bankruptcy ('DEBA'), SR 281.1 (no official English translation available), available at: https://beck-link.de/6zxt2 (accessed 24.01.2021).

[86] Property Law, which regulates ownership and possession, other rights in rem, and the Land Register is set out in Art. 641 CC.

[87] An exception is the surrender (Aussonderung) pursuant to Art. 29(3) FISA in the bankruptcy of a person under a duty to make restitution of intermediated securities because of an unjust enrichment.

[88] Contractual claims are privileged in case of bankruptcy only if explicitly provided for by a special statutory provision as for example Art. 401 CO. This provision grants the principal the right to demand the release of chattels which the (bankrupt) agent had received in his own name and for the account of the principal from third parties (but not from the principal). If the agent acting on the principal's behalf has acquired claims in his own name against third parties, such claims pass to the principal, provided he has fulfilled all his obligations toward the agent with regard to the agency relationship.

30 If the debtor has **exclusive direct and factual control** ('Gewahrsam') over the claimed tangible object, for example if he holds chattels in sole Gewahrsam or if real estate is registered in the land registry in the name of the debtor, the legal presumption states that the debtor is the beneficial owner. The assets are therefore included in the bankruptcy estate. Consequently, and in accordance with Art. 242(2) DEBA, a third party who wishes to claim the chattel must prove to have a better right in court. This procedure of surrender is referred to as 'Aussonderung'.

Conversely, if the debtor only has **factual joint control** ('Mitgewahrsam') of the chattels together with the third party or if the third party holds sole Gewahrsam the chattels in question are not included in the bankruptcy estate. If the bankruptcy estate claims a better right in this case, it is for the bankruptcy administration to sue for inclusion ('Admassierung') according to Art. 242(3) DEBA. Only if successful, the chattel in question is included into the bankruptcy estate.

31 According to the new **Art. 242a DEBA**, the same principles apply to crypto assets (while access to other data is now provided for in a new Art. 242b DEBA). Again, upon request, the bankruptcy administration may issue an order for the surrender of crypto assets or (if it does not consider the claim to be justified) set a period of 20 days within which the third party can claim for surrender in court (paras. 1 and 3). To avoid problems of delineation, the provision's application scope covers **all crypto assets**, i.e. all crypto-based token-categories ('kryptobasierte Vermögenswerte'). However, instead of direct and factual control, the criterion of exclusive power of disposal ('Verfügungsmacht') is decisive – and supplemented by the further criterions of availability and allocability:

32 The crypto assets are **included in the estate**, if, first, – on the date the debtor is declared bankrupt – the private key is known exclusively by the debtor, who thus is solely able to directly initiate a transaction on the ledger (Art. 242a (1) DEBA). Second, the debtor must have held the crypto assets of the type and amount received available at all times to the third party (para. 2 pr). Some of the crypto assets can for example be replaced as long as their required total number is maintained. This, in principle, means that for instance crypto assets cannot be used by a wallet provider for lending business without the third party losing the right to surrender in case of the wallet provider's bankruptcy. Third, the crypto assets must be allocated either individually to the third party (e.g. in an individual client account) or to community ownership (e.g. in an omnibus client account) where it remains clear which share is due to the third party (para. 2(a) and (b)). Contrary to what was originally intended in the early stage of the legislative process,[89] it was deemed sufficient that the allocation does not result directly from the ledger but, for example, from an internal register of the debtor. This change has been proposed in order to make collective custody possible without impacting the third party's right to surrender. Conversely, crypto assets either mixed with the debtor's own holdings or used by the debtor for transactions on his own account cannot be surrendered. Finally, whoever demands surrender bears the associated costs. The bankruptcy administration may demand an advance payment (para. 4).

33 If the **private key** is known exclusively to the third party who claims the assets, the assets are not included in the estate as the debtor does not have the power of disposal over the assets. In this case an order of surrender is neither possible nor necessary. If the

---

[89] Federal Council of Switzerland, Ibid, para. 5.2.2; Federal Council of Switzerland, Ibid, para. 1.2.2.

third party and the debtor have identical access keys and thus can both directly initiate a transaction on the ledger, the criterion is not met satisfactory if the power of disposal is shared.[90] This is usually the case if the debtor is in possession of a key that forms part of a multi-signature address – unless the setup is formed in a way that allows the debtor exclusively to initiate a transaction on the ledger (e.g. a '2 out of 3 multi-signature' with the debtor holding 2 of the 3 private keys).[91] In short: if the debtor is not able to independently initiate a transaction on the ledger, the crypto assets in question are not included in the estate and thus must be surrendered.

Art. 242a DEBA does not expressly specify whether there is an inclusion proceeding as the bankruptcy estate's right to inclusion originates from general rules.[92]

III. Leges speciales

In the course of time, a number of provisions have been enacted, particularly in financial market law, which under certain circumstances allow creditors a so-called exclusion from the bankrupt estate – i.e. a surrender ex officio. Among them, the **provisions of the FISA** are pivotal. In case a custodian of intermediated securities in the sense of Art. 4 FISA becomes insolvent, the client's assets are excluded pursuant to Art. 17–18 FISA. If they do not suffice to satisfy the clients fully, assets of the same kind held by the custodian for its own account are also excluded to the necessary extent (Art. 19(1) FISA). Remaining shortfalls are borne by depositors in proportion to the number of assets of the missing kind credited to the respective securities accounts (Art. 19(2) FISA). By reference to Art. 17 et seq. FISA this applies equally to banks and other financial institutions subject to Art. 16 in conjunction with Art. 37d BA.[93] Furthermore, these provisions also apply by analogy to fund management companies and securities firms according to Art. 67(1) FinIA. Further references to Art. 37d BA in connection with Art. 17–19 FISA are for example set out to some extent in Art. 88 FinMIA.

In the light of the aforementioned amendment to the DEBA, the DLT law revision has created the possibility of an exclusion of crypto assets in case of bankruptcy of banks or other financial institutions acting as depository of crypto assets. This required a corresponding adjustment in the bank insolvency law provisions set out in Art. 16 BA (defining so called custody assets, 'Depotwerte', which are excludable under Art. 37d BA in conjunction with Art. 17 and 18 FISA): In order to allow exclusion and in accordance to Art. 242a DEBA – the new amendment no. 1bis in Art. 16 BA requires that crypto assets ('kryptobasierte Vermögenswerte', i.e. all crypto-based token-categories) must be individually allocated to customers from an individual or collective portfolio (whereas it's again not required that the allocation does result directly from the ledger). Likewise, the bank must show efforts to keep the crypto assets of the type and amount received available at all times to the third party, which in principle means that those assets cannot be used for lending business.

---

[90] Federal Council of Switzerland, Ibid, 264–265.

[91] If both, the debtor and the third party, cannot directly initiate a transaction on the blockchain without the participation of the other (e.g., both hold 1 private key in a '2 out of 2 multi-signature'-setup), surrender is not possible. Instead, the third party might demand access to the debtor's private key via the procedure governed by new Art. 242b DEBA (access to data), see Federal Council of Switzerland, Ibid, 292.

[92] Federal Council of Switzerland, Ibid, 294.

[93] Zellweger-Gutknecht and Bacharach, *Cryptoassets in insolvency proceedings* (2021) (forthcoming).

§ 20
Liechtenstein

Literature: Diwok and Gritsch, 'Bitcoin, Geldbegriffe und Zahlungsmittel', [2020] 29 *Zeitschrift für Finanzmarktrecht (ZFR)*, 64; Financial Market Authority, 'Information for clients of TT service providers' (January 2021), available at: https://beck-link.de/n772k (accessed 1.2.2021); Financial Market Authority, 'Guidelines 2018/18 – License as an e-money institution' (January 2015), available at: https://beck-link.de/bdvt2 (accessed 18.11.2020); Financial Market Authority, 'Guidelines 2018/18 – License as a bank or an investment firm' (January 2015), available at: https://beck-link.de/3arvd (accessed 18.11.2020); Financial Market Authority Liechtenstein, 'Fact Sheet on virtual currencies' (July 2018), available at: https://beck-link.de/hh6zk (accessed 17.11.2020); Layr and Marxer, 'Rechtsnatur und Übertragung von "Token" aus liechtensteinischer Perspektive', (2019) *Liechtensteinische Juristen-Zeitung*, 11; Nagele and Bont, 'Tokenized structures and assets in Liechtenstein law', Trusts & Trustees, Volume 25, Issue 6, July 2019, 633; OECD (2021), 'Regulatory Approaches to the Tokenisation of Assets', OECD Blockchain Policy Series, https://beck-link.de/6v7md; Omlor, 'Digitales Eigentum an Blockchain-Token – rechtsvergleichende Entwicklungslinien' (2020) 119 *Zeitschrift für Vergleichende Rechtswissenschaft (ZVglRWiss)*, 41; Raschauer and Silbernagl, 'Grundsatzfragen des liechtensteinischen "Blockchain-Gesetzes" – TVTG', (2020) 3 *Zeitschrift für Finanzmarktrecht (ZFR)*, 11; Silbernagl, 'Zivilrechtliche Regelungen des liechtensteinischen Blockchaingesetzes (TVTG) – Möglichkeiten für Österreich?' (2020) 7 *Zivilrecht aktuell (Zak)*, 10; Sild, 'Blockchain Regulation made in Liechtenstein: Das Fürstentum als Vorreiter?' (2020) 45 *Spektrum der Rechtswissenschaft (SPWR)*, 45; Tichmann and Falker, 'Liechtenstein – Das TVTG und Risiken der Blockchain-Technologie' (2020) 62 *Innovations- und Technikrecht (InTeR)*, 62; Wurzer, 'Practical Applications According to the Law on Tokens and TT Service Providers (Token- and TT Service Provider Act; TVTG)' (2019) *Spektrum der Rechtswissenschaft (SPWR)*, 221.

Outline

	para.
A. Introduction	1
B. Business Models and Market Structure	2
C. Legal Framework	6
I. The Liechtenstein TVTG	6
1. Concept and Regulatory Approach	6
2. Service Providers	10
3. Registration and Regulatory Requirements	14
II. Token	18
1. Transfer of Token and Transfer of Rights	19
2. Generation of Token, Tokenization and Public Offer	23
3. Basic Information and Prospectus Requirement	25
III. Anti-Money Laundering Legislation	28
D. Legislative Initiatives and Regulatory Guidance	31
E. Conclusion and Outlook	32

A. Introduction

1 Liechtenstein is a financial centre with a tradition in private wealth management, a strong banking sector and traditionally international client base. In recent years it has become an attractive jurisdiction for Fintech and DLT service providers. Liechtenstein market participants, start-ups as well as established firms, have quickly adopted and developed business models relating to crypto assets and digital financial services. As a member of the European Economic Area (EEA) Liechtenstein regularly implements secondary EU legislation in the field of financial regulation and anti-money laundering.

A number of activities relating to crypto assets and blockchain business are subject to harmonized European regulation and prudential supervision as discussed in Part 2 of this book. These legal acts and concepts are, however, not exhaustive from a regulatory perspective and do not cover questions of private law. With the enactment of the Law of 03 October 2019 on Tokens and TT Service Providers (the so-called Token and TT Service Provider Act, 'TVTG')[1], Liechtenstein was one of the first jurisdictions to introduce a specific regulatory model for business and products not regulated under the harmonized EU financial markets framework to capture tokenization and transactions in crypto assets.

While scope and application of EU regulation are covered in the second part of this book (chapters 3–15), Liechtenstein's national particularities and efforts are at the center of this chapter. Section B. (→ para. 2 et seqq.) of this chapter tracks the market structure and development in Liechtenstein as it relates to business models and concepts relating to crypto assets and DLT. Section C (→ para. 6 et seqq.) examines national legislation and regulation in more detail, introducing and explaining national legal concepts and the legal framework that is in place since 1 January 2020. Section D (→ para. 31 et seqq.) describes the approach of the regulator and section E (→ para. 32) concludes.

B. Business Models and Market Structure

Liechtenstein service providers operating in the 'crypto-sphere' show a wide variety of business models. Usually organized as limited stock companies, they are predominantly offering services that are subject to financial regulation or to registration under the TVTG. Some are or do have an affiliation with established market participants, while others are standalone startups. One of the main challenges for Liechtenstein's service providers was and still is the lack of a European passport for services that are not harmonized by EU law, the lack of legal certainty in both, EEA and non-EEA jurisdictions and the management of associated cross-border risks. As the scope of financial regulation, as it relates to crypto assets and business models, is difficult to navigate, the Liechtenstein Financial Markets Authority ('FMA'), known for its accessibility and cooperative approach, assumed an important role in building an understanding and providing legal certainty for market participants from the outset. 2

As in other jurisdictions, the early market and public discourse in the context of crypto assets focused on and around **currency tokens** and **initial coin offerings** ('ICOs'). 3

Bitcoin and other **currency tokens** are not accepted as **legal tender** or official currency in Liechtenstein as they are not issued by a central bank or other official authority. This means that a creditor is not legally required to accept it as a payment. Nevertheless, if the parties agree to, currency tokens may be traded or used and accepted in payment transactions as a means of payment.[2] As many other regulatory bodies in Europe, the FMA has warned consumers from using 'cryptocurrency' as a means of payment or investment, pointing out the risks of price fluctuations and cybercrime. The FMA recommends that investors only hold a small part of their overall assets in crypto.[3]

---

[1] Gesetz vom 3. Oktober 2019 über Token und VT-Dienstleister (Token- und VT-Dienstleister-Gesetz).
[2] See from the perspective of the Austrian Civil Code, Diwok and Gritsch, 'Bitcoin, Geldbegriffe und Zahlungsmittel', [2020] 29 *Zeitschrift für Finanzmarktrecht (ZFR)*, 64 (68 et seqq.).
[3] FMA, 'Fact Sheet on virtual currencies' (July 2018), available at: https://beck-link.de/hh6zk (accessed 26.08.2021).

4   Liechtenstein has seen a lot of activity in the field of **ICOs** and **security token offerings** ('STOs'). The first ICOs were conducted in 2017. Due to the close relationship of the jurisdictions Switzerland and Liechtenstein, Liechtenstein ICOs have often been conducted through foundation structures and based on a basic token classification system (utility token, virtual currency and security token), which was inspired *inter alia* by guidance issued by the Swiss regulator FINMA in February 2018: FINMA described payment tokens as virtual currency without further functionality or associated project, and utility token as token, which grant access to a digital service or interface. Lastly a security token was defined as a token that represents assets like stakes in companies or a claim for dividends or interest payments (for details, → chapter 19).[4] Although Liechtenstein law itself does not explicitly refer to these categories, they are still referenced by Liechtenstein's legislator and by the FMA.[5]

Since Liechtenstein is a member state of the EEA, the qualification of an asset or instrument as financial instrument under Directive 2014/65/EU ('MiFiD2') is not subject to national discretion. Guidance by the European Securities and Markets Authority ('ESMA') and the European Banking Authority ('EBA'), but also the legal clarification proposed by the European Commission, according to which *"financial instrument' means those instruments specified in Section C of Annex I [MIFID2], including such instruments issued by means of distributed ledger technology"*[6] must be taken into account.

5   Liechtenstein market participants have adapted the business model early on and moved to launch **STOs**, leading to the approval of the first approved prospectus for an STO in August 2018.[7]

Also, in other areas of financial regulation, Liechtenstein market participants proved to be early adopters: The first actively managed regulated **alternative investment fund** ('AIF') investing in crypto assets was launched in Liechtenstein in 2018, with a Liechtenstein bank acting as depositary.[8]

In the field of banking, in particular smaller private banks have embraced DLT and crypto assets early, offering *inter alia* trading and **custody services**. One bank, in addition to its banking license, is registered as token issuer, token generator, TT identity service provider and TT token depositary under the newly enacted TVTG. In total six TT token depositaries are registered under the TVTG, one of them is also registered as TT key depositary.[9]

When it comes to '**crypto exchanges**' there is no single definition or legal framework under Liechtenstein law. Depending on the type of service provided, different licensing

---

[4] Swiss FINMA, 'Wegleitung für Unterstellungsanfragen betreffend initial coin offerings (ICO)' (16. Februar 2018), available at: www.finma.ch (accessed 26.08.2021).

[5] See BuA 2019/54, 141 and FMA, 'Wegleitung 2018/7 – Allgemeine und branchenspezifische Auslegung des Sorgfaltspflichtrechts' (only available in German) (2018), 66 (Fn. 33), available at: https://beck-link.de/b35ne (accessed 26.08.2021) ('FMA Instruction 2018/7').

[6] European Commission, 'Proposal for a Directive of the European Parliament and of the Council amending Directives 2006/43/EC, 2009/65/EC, 2009/138/EU, 2011/61/EU, EU/2013/36, 2014/65/EU, (EU) 2015/2366 and EU/2016/2341, COM/2020/596 final' (September 2020), ar. 6 par. 1 amending Art. 4 (1) point 15 MIFID II, available at: https://eur-lex.europa.eu (accessed 26.08.2021).

[7] All approvals are documented on the FMA's website. Those for prospectuses at that time in the 'Register of published prospectuses until 20 July 2019', available at: https://beck-link.de/6hks6 (accessed 26.08.2021).

[8] Wulf, 'Postera Fund – Crypto I Aufsicht in Liechtenstein genehmigt ersten Krypto-AIF', Private Banking Magazin 05.03.2018, available at: https://beck-link.de/tpr7y (accessed 26.08.2021).

[9] For an overview of registered providers, see the *FMA-Register*, available at: https://beck-link.de/h5a3f (accessed 26.08.2021).

or registration requirements apply. Exchanges regarding tokens that do not qualify as financial instruments may be regulated under the Liechtenstein TVTG, depending on the service provided. There are currently six service providers registered as **TT exchange service provider** under the TVTG and two service providers registered as TT identity service provider. Recently, the launch of a crypto exchange that shall be licensed as a **multilateral trading facility** under MIFID2 has been announced, which is expected to take up business in 2021.[10]

Liechtenstein so far has not seen a registration as physical validator, TT protector or TT verifying authority.[11]

C. Legal Framework

I. The Liechtenstein TVTG

1. Concept and Regulatory Approach

The Token and TT Service Provider Act or TVTG of January 2020 is specifically tailored for regulating dealings in crypto assets both under Liechtenstein private law and supervisory law. The concept of the law is relatively broad and based on a technology neutral approach, as it seeks to capture the various applications and use cases for tokens and their transfer in the so-called 'token economy'.[12]

The abbreviation TT stands for '**trustworthy technology**', a concept that draws on the specific nature of relevant DLT systems without using the term 'blockchain' in order to remain 'technology neutral'.[13] TT is a technology 'through which the integrity of tokens, the clear assignment of tokens to TT identifiers[14] and the disposal of tokens'[15] are ensured. At the heart of this definition stands the notion that the integrity of the ledger is assured by technology and not by a central intermediary or organization.[16]

The law seeks to establish a legal framework for systems based on trustworthy technology.[17] A trustworthy technology system ('**TT system**') pursuant to Art. 2(1)(b) TVTG is a transaction system that allows for the 'secure transfer and storage of tokens' by means of trustworthy technology as well as the provision of services based thereupon. The law does not define the TT system further and deliberately[18]

6

7

---

[10] Franke, 'Europas erste Handelsplattform für Blockchain-Derivate in Vaduz', Volksblatt Liechtenstein 10.10.2020, available at: https://beck-link.de/8fbry (accessed 26.08.2021).
[11] For an overview of registered providers, see the *FMA-Register*, available at: https://beck-link.de/h5a3f (accessed 26.08.2021).
[12] State Administration Principality of Liechtenstein, 'Bericht und Antrag 54/2019 der Regierung an den Landtag des Fürstentums Liechtenstein betreffend die Schaffung eines Gesetzes über Token und VT-Dienstleister (Token- und VT-Dienstleister-Gesetz; TVTG) und die Abänderung weiterer Gesetze' (May 2019), 6, available at: https://beck-link.de/5zd4m (accessed 26.08.2021) ('BuA 2019/54').
[13] BuA 2019/54, 55.
[14] Pursuant to Art. 2(1)(d) TVTG an identifier that allows for the clear assignment of tokens, it is equivalent with a 'public key'.
[15] Art. 2(1)(a) TVTG.
[16] BuA 2019/54, 56.
[17] Art. 1 (1) TVTG.
[18] State Administration Principality of Liechtenstein, 'Stellungnahme der Regierung an den Landtag des Fürstentums Liechtenstein zu den anlässlich der ersten Lesung betreffend die Schaffung eines Gesetzes über Token und VT-Dienstleister (Token- und VT-Dienstleister-Gesetz; TVTG) und die Abänderung weiterer Gesetze aufgeworfenen Fragen' (September 2019), 17 et seq, available at: https://beck-link.de/b2tt5 (accessed 26.08.2021) ('BuA 2019/93').

does not specify minimum requirements for a system that is eligible as TT system under the TVTG.[19]

8   A **token** as a third central concept of the law is defined in Art. 2(1)(c) TVTG as 'a piece of information on a TT system', which may represent claims or membership rights, rights to property or other absolute or relative rights and which may be assigned to one or more TT identifiers ('public keys'). It has been suggested that the term token only refers to tokens that technically *can* represent claims or rights and does not encompass mere 'cryptocurrency'.[20] However, the legal materials, specifically clarify that the scope of the TVTG encompasses virtual currencies and 'empty tokens'.[21] The law does not distinguish between various token types, although it is apparent that certain concepts only refer to tokens that e.g. represent claims or rights,[22] while other provisions only apply to tokens that do not qualify as financial instruments.[23]

9   The TVTG aims to ensure trust in digital transactions, in particular in the financial and economic sector, the protection of users in TT systems and to create an innovation-friendly and technology-neutral framework for rendering services relating to TT systems.[24] The TVTG introduces various legal concepts relating to tokens, the tokenization of rights and the transfer of tokens under Liechtenstein private law as well as the supervision of service providers subject to the TVTG.[25] It can be divided into two main parts, one addressing tokens and dealings with tokens under Liechtenstein private law and from an international private law perspective, including questions of property law and the faith of tokens in case of insolvency, the other of a regulatory nature, addressing the registration and supervision, rights and obligations of service providers using TT systems. Deviating from the sequence of topics provided by the law, this section of the chapter first discusses the regulatory part of the TVTG, introducing the most important market participants and concepts.

2. Service Providers

10   The TVTG defines a number of **service providers** that are expected to be established in the context of a rising token economy along the value-chain from the generation event and issuing of tokens to the custody and exchange of tokens for fiat currency.

The **token generator** generates one or more tokens on a professional basis for third parties using an existing TT system or based on a self-created TT system. For example, in the case of the tokenization of a right, it has to ensure that the right is correctly represented over the course of the token's lifetime, that the disposal of the token directly results in the disposal of the represented right and that a competing disposal of the represented right is prohibited.[26] The **token issuer**, who may or may not be the token generator, is a natural or legal person that offers tokens to the public in its own name or in the name of a third party (client) on a professional basis.[27] The law in this context

---

[19] For criticism, see Raschauer and Silbernagl, 'Grundsatzfragen des liechtensteinischen 'Blockchain-Gesetzes' – TVTG', (2020) 3 *Zeitschrift für Finanzmarktrecht (ZFR)*, 11; also Sild, 'Blockchain Regulation made in Liechtenstein: Das Fürstentum als Vorreiter?' (2020) 45 *Spektrum der Rechtswissenschaft (SPWR)*, 45 (48).

[20] Omlor, 'Digitales Eigentum an Blockchain-Token – rechtsvergleichende Entwicklungslinien' (2020) 119 *Zeitschrift für Vergleichende Rechtswissenschaft (ZVglRWiss)*, 41.

[21] BuA 2019/54, 61; BuA 2019/93, 8; see also Sild, Ibid, 45.

[22] See also Art. 3(3) TVTG, whereas Art. 4 to 6 and 9 only apply correspondingly to tokens that do not represent rights.

[23] Art. 31(1)(d) in connection with Art. 30(a) and (b) TVTG.

[24] Art. 1(2) TVTG.

[25] Art. 3(1) TVTG.

[26] Art. 17 TVTG.

[27] Art. 2(1)(k) TVTG.

conflates the terms 'issuing' and 'public offer', whereby the registration requirement for the issuer is linked to the public offer.[28] Liechtenstein issuers[29] who issue and publicly offer tokens in a *non-professional* capacity must apply for a registration, if they intend to issue tokens in the amount of CHF 5 million or more within a period of twelve months. The token issuer must observe a number of statutory obligations, in particular information duties. These are discussed below (→ para. 23 et seqq.).

The Liechtenstein legislator has exerted great care to the regulation of custodianship. Due to the significant risk emerging from loss of keys and therefore assets for an individual,[30] the legislator expects that a number of professional service providers will emerge in order to enhance comfort and security.[31] The TVTG distinguishes between the custody of (private) keys and the custody of tokens. 11

A **TT key depositary** is defined as a natural or legal person who safeguards (private) TT keys[32] on behalf of clients.[33] This includes situations, where a client transfers the key to a service provider in order to prevent misappropriation or misuse or in order to facilitate transactions executed by service providers.[34] The TT key depositary is interpreted to include all service providers that have access to private keys of a third party in performing their services.[35] However, the mere safe deposit service of storing physical wallets on behalf of clients without having access to the keys, is not covered by this definition.[36] The TT key depositary is a 'custodian wallet provider' as defined[37] in Art. 3 (19) of the 5th Anti-Money-Laundering Directive ('AMLD5', for details → chapter 10).[38] As the TVTG applies to a broader range of tokens than AMLD5, the definitions are, however, not identical.[39]

The TT key depositary per se does not have the power to dispose of the token or to execute transactions on behalf of the client.[40] However, such additional powers may be agreed on by the parties. TT key depositaries are for example wallet providers that store TT keys for clients, offline storage providers, but also 'crypto exchanges' or asset managers that directly execute transactions for a client as a service and in this context hold the clients' keys.[41]

As opposed to the TT key depositary, the **TT token depositary** safeguards tokens in the name and for the account of others.[42] Tokens are transferred to a **TT identifier** (public key) managed by the depositary.[43] This implies that the service provider may allocate tokens of various clients to one or more TT identifiers and disposes over the

---

[28] According to the legal materials a sale without an offer to the public does not trigger a registration requirement for the issuer, see BuA 2019/54, 227.
[29] A token issuer with registered office or place of residence in Liechtenstein, see Art. 12(2) TVTG.
[30] Tichmann and Falker, 'Liechtenstein – Das TVTG und Risiken der Blockchain-Technologie' (2020) 62 *Innovations- und Technikrecht (InTeR)*, 62 (63); Wurzer, 'Practical Applications According to the Law on Tokens and TT Service Providers (Token- and TT Service Provider Act; TVTG)' (2019) *Spektrum der Rechtswissenschaft (SPWR)*, 221 (238).
[31] See BuA 2019/54, 39.
[32] TT keys are defined as keys that allow for disposal of tokens.
[33] Art. 2(1)(m) TVTG in connection with Art. 2(1)(e) TVTG.
[34] BuA 2019/54, 76.
[35] FMA Instruction 2018/7, 67.
[36] 'FMA Instruction 2018/7', 66 et seq.
[37] '[…] an entity that provides services to safeguard private cryptographic keys on behalf of its customers, to hold, store and transfer virtual currencies'.
[38] Directive 2015/849/EU.
[39] See BuA 2019/54, 154.
[40] Sild, Ibid, 45 (56).
[41] BuA 2019/54, 76 et seq.
[42] Art. 2(1)(n) TVTG.
[43] BuA 2019/54, 76.

identifier.[44] A registration as TT token depositary is already required if tokens are only held for a short period of time, e.g. if a service provider buys tokens on behalf of a client and transfers them to the client.

12   A **TT protector** holds tokens on TT systems in its own name on behalf of a client.[45] As this is deemed to be a trust service, the TT protector not only requires a registration under the TVTG, but also a trustee license under the Liechtenstein Law of 8 November 2013 concerning Professional Trustees and Fiduciaries (Trustee Act, 'TrHG').

13   A **TT exchange service provider** is a natural or legal person who exchanges legal tender for tokens and vice versa as well as tokens for tokens on their own account. An 'exchange', which (instead of settling a transaction against its own book) brings together buying and selling interests from a number of participants or, which operates a platform or interface that functions like a bulletin board[46] and which has no possibility to interfere with the transactions, will not qualify as TT exchange service provider, but as a **TT price service provider** pursuant to Art. 2(1)(s) TVTG, when furnishing TT system users with aggregated price information on the basis of purchase and sale offers or completed transactions.[47] If the service provider holds or manages tokens or TT keys for its clients, it will qualify as TT key or token depositary.[48]

Other regulated TT service providers are the newly introduced TT agent, the **physical validator**, which is described in more detail below in the context of tokenization, the **TT verifying authority** that verifies the legal capacity and the requirements for disposal of a token and the **TT identity service provider** that identifies the person in possession of the right of disposal of a token and records it in a directory. The use of a TT identity service provider in a transaction is not obligatory.[49]

3. Registration and Regulatory Requirements

14   Service providers are subject to a **registration requirement** if they have a registered office[50] or place of residence in Liechtenstein and (aside from some issuers) act on a **professional basis** ('*berufsmässig*').[51] For acting on a professional basis (as opposed to acting on a commercial basis or '*gewerbsmässig*'), it is sufficient if a service provider carries out its activities for remuneration or intends to make its services available to the public.[52] The TVTG is, apart from recently introduced exemptions not applicable to **foreign service providers** that offer their services to consumers in Liechtenstein. This restriction of scope to local service providers is unusual from a regulatory perspective and was criticized in literature.[53] Consequently, the law was amended in 2021, by inserting the TT service provider category "TT agent". The TT agent is anyone who provides and/or distributes TT services on a professional basis in the name and for the

---

[44] BuA 2019/54, 76.
[45] Art. 2(1)(p) TVTG.
[46] „*Schwarze-Brett-Funktion*", see BuA 2019/54, 160.
[47] BuA 2019/54, 160.
[48] BuA 2019/54, 102; see also FMA Instruction 2018/7, 68.
[49] See also Sild, Ibid, 45 (58 et seq.) criticising the unclear role of the TT identity service provider in the TVTG.
[50] Registered office is defined under reference to Art. 113 PGR (BuA 2019/54, 11), and shall, unless otherwise provided for in the statutes, be at the place where the entity has the center of their administrative activities, subject to the provisions on the registered office in international relations.
[51] Art. 12(1) TVTG.
[52] BuA 2019/54, 214.
[53] Raschauer and Silbernagl, 'Grundsatzfragen des liechtensteinischen 'Blockchain-Gesetzes' – TVTG', (2020) 3 *Zeitschrift für Finanzmarktrecht (ZFR)*, 11. Silbernagl, 'Zivilrechtliche Regelungen des liechtensteinischen Blockchaingesetzes (TVTG) – Möglichkeiten für Österreich?' (2020) 7 *Zivilrecht aktuell (Zak)*, 10 (15); Sild, Ibid, 45 (49).

account of a foreign TT service provider in Liechtenstein. This shall prevent TT service providers domiciled in Lichtenstein from being at a competitive disadvantage compared to foreign providers with a physical presence in Liechtenstein. Further, foreign service providers that provide TT services by way of physical vending machines in Liechtenstein are now also subject to a registration requirement.

TT service providers must **register** with the FMA prior to the start of their business activity.[54] A registration is only possible if the service provider complies with the statutory requirements. These include professional reliability, fitness ('technical suitability'), appropriate minimum capital, suitable organizational structure, internal control mechanisms and further requirements, partially tailored to the type of service. 15

If the respective registration requirements are met, the applicant is registered the **VT Service Provider Register** pursuant to Art. 23 TVTG, albeit the FMA may impose conditions and requirements. The FMA decides within a statutory period of three months upon receiving a comprehensive application.

Following the registration, the TVTG does not stipulate a fully-fledged ongoing prudential supervision by the FMA or ongoing reporting requirements. The FMA, however, has the competence to take necessary supervisory measures if it becomes aware of compliance violations or deficits, and may also impose sanctions and fines.[55] These differences have recently prompted the FMA to draw attention to the fact that the level of client protection under the TVTG is not comparable to that under financial market law.[56] 16

The TVTG generally applies from 1 January 2020, however, service providers who have already been active as per 1 January 2020 benefit from a **grandfathering** clause. This means that they have been able to continue to provide their service in compliance with the TVTG, if having notified their activities to the FMA pursuant to Art. 28(1) TVTG and were registered by 1 January 2021 at the latest.

If the business model of a service provider includes services that are regulated under **general financial markets law** (for details, → chapters 3–15), for example because it provides services relating to financial instruments, it will be subject to **licensing requirements** in addition to the registration und the TVTG. The registration may be combined with a license issued by the FMA under the financial markets' regulation pursuant to Art. 5(1) FMAG[57], if such license is in place upon registration.[58] 17

II. Token

According to Art. 3(2) TVTG, Chapter II (relating to the qualification of tokens and their disposal on TT systems under Liechtenstein private law) applies if tokens are generated or issued by a Liechtenstein TT service provider[59] or if parties declare the TVTG to apply in a legal transaction over tokens. If Liechtenstein law applies, the token is considered to be an asset located in Liechtenstein. This shall ensure a legal venue at the location of the property.[60] This allocation is made regardless of whether the token 18

---

[54] Art. 12(1) TVTG.
[55] Art. 47 TVTG.
[56] FMA, 'Information for clients of TT service providers' (January 2021), available at: https://beck-link.de/n772k (accessed 26.08.2021).
[57] Law of June 18, 2004 on Financial Market Supervision (Finanzmarktaufsichtsgesetz; FMAG).
[58] Art. 13(1)(k) TVTG.
[59] A service provider with registered office or place of residence in Liechtenstein, see Art. 3(2)(a) TVTG.
[60] Art. 50(1) Act of December 10, 1912 on the Exercise of Jurisdiction and the Jurisdiction of the Courts in Civil Cases (Jurisdiktionsnorm, JN).

1. Transfer of Token and Transfer of Rights

19 The TVTG defines the legal nature of a token autonomously and clarifies that a token is not a physical object.[62] Rather, a token may represent or 'contain'[63] rights such as property rights or membership rights or may be 'empty' as in the case of bitcoin (→ para. 8). The Liechtenstein property law shall not be directly applicable. Instead, the TVTG introduces standalone rules of legitimation and transfer, drawing analogies to established property law concepts. A right represented by a token and associated legal implications remain unaltered, while the right at the same time is subject to the TVTG rules of legitimation and transfer.[64] While some TVTG-provisions of a private law nature, such as Art. 8 TVTG that regulates the effect of a disposal of a token on a represented right, primarily address issues relating to tokens that represent rights, the provisions on qualification and disposal of tokens and the acquisition of a token in good faith, apply analogously to all types of tokens.

20 Pursuant to Art. 6 TVTG, the **disposal** of a token may take place as a transfer of the right to dispose of the token or the creation of a security interest or usufruct right to a token. The disposal requires that (a) the transfer follows the rules of the respective TT system,[65] (b) a unanimous declaration of transferee and transferor that the right of disposal of the token shall be transferred or a right in rem shall be created and (c) that the transferor has the right of disposal. Art. 7 TVTG clarifies that a disposal of the token results in a disposal of the right represented by the token. The law stipulates that, if this legal effect is not provided for by law, the person obliged as a result of the disposal must ensure that the disposal of a token *directly or indirectly* results in the disposal of the represented right, and that a competing disposal of the represented right is excluded.[66]

The TVTG assumes that the holder of the private key has the power to dispose of a token and that such person also has the right to dispose of the token.[67] This assumption is rebuttable, and the law does distinguish between de-facto control over a token and the right of disposal by the rightful owner. If for example a TT key is copied, the rightful owner shall be able to contest transactions initiated by the copy owners.[68] A **TT verifying authority** may be used to verify the legal capacity and the requirements for disposal of a token on a case-by-case basis.

---

[61] See also Raschauer and Silbernagl, 'Grundsatzfragen des liechtensteinischen 'Blockchain-Gesetzes' – TVTG', (2020) 3 *Zeitschrift für Finanzmarktrecht (ZFR)*, 11 (13).

[62] This is noteable as Liechtenstein property law applies to physical objects, see Raschauer and Silbernagl, 'Grundsatzfragen des liechtensteinischen 'Blockchain-Gesetzes' – TVTG', (2020) 3 *Zeitschrift für Finanzmarktrecht (ZFR)*, 11 (12); Layr and Marxer, 'Rechtsnatur und Übertragung von 'Token' aus liechtensteinischer Perspektive', (2019) *Liechtensteinische Juristen-Zeitung*, 11 (12) and Silbernagl, 'Zivilrechtliche Regelungen des liechtensteinischen Blockchaingesetzes (TVTG) – Möglichkeiten für Österreich?' (2020) 7 *Zivilrecht aktuell (Zak)*, 10.

[63] So-called 'Token Container Model'; see Ministry of Finance of the Government of Lichtenstein, 'Vernehmlassungsbericht der Regierung betreffend die Schaffung eines Gesetzes über auf vertrauenswürdigen Technologien (VT) beruhende Transaktionssysteme (Blockchain-Gesetz; VT-Gesetz; VTG) und die Abänderung weiterer Gesetze' (available only in German) (November 2018), 43, available at: https://becklink.de/2f47s (accessed 31.08.2021).

[64] Ibid, 43.

[65] A limited in rem right in a token can also be created without effective transfer, if this is apparent to third parties and the time of the creation of the right in rem is clearly defined, see Art.6(2)(a) TVTG.

[66] Art. 7(2) TVTG.

[67] Art. 5 TVTG.

[68] BuA 2019/54, 66–67.

In the event of **insolvency** of a TT service provider, tokens shall be considered third-party assets and shall be segregated in favor of the customer. Tokens must be stored separately from the TT service provider's assets.[69] In the event of **enforcement proceedings** against the transferor of a token, the disposal shall be legally binding and effective, if the transfer has been initiated in the TT system prior to the commencement of the respective proceedings, or, if the transfer has been initiated afterwards, but executed on the day of their opening, if the recipient proves that he was not and should not have been aware of the opening of the proceedings.[70]

The legal framework and thus the legal certainty created by the TVTG is limited to Liechtenstein and, except in case of voluntary subordination pursuant to Art. 3(2)(b) TVTG, Liechtenstein tokens (→ para. 18). Legal restrictions with regard to a valid choice of law,[71] the international nature of transactions and a lack of enforceability of decisions issued by Liechtenstein's courts in potentially relevant jurisdictions may further reduce the relevance of the respective provisions in practice.[72]

2. Generation of Token, Tokenization and Public Offer

The generation and issuing of tokens and the respective service providers are subject to a specific legal framework provided by the TVTG. The regulation of the token generator and token issuer apply irrespective of the type of token generated, while the requirements associated with a public offer may, depending on the quality of the token, be subject to the TVTG or the European Prospectus Regulation ('PR')[73] as *lex specialis*.

When a token is issued, rights associated with the token must be recorded digitally to ensure their integrity and provide legal certainty.[74] The **token generator** is responsible for the correct implementation of a token and for safeguarding the synchronization of digital and non-digital disposals.[75] As outlined above, a token may represent a right or claim and therefore also a property right (→ para. 19). The function of the **physical validator** is directly linked to the so-called **tokenization** of assets, where a token represents a right in an asset. The physical validator shall, as a trusted third party intermediary,[76] prevent conflicts between the assignment of rights to the asset in the 'online' and 'offline' context and ensure the enforcement of rights represented in a token.[77] The physical validator will review the property rights and rights of disposal over the respective assets prior to tokenization. It will usually take the tokenized asset into custody, in order to be able to safeguard the integrity of the asset and to ensure that respective rights can be enforced accordingly.[78] The physical validator is liable, for example, if the object, which the tokenized right refers to, is lost.[79] The **token issuer** publicly offers tokens. Pursuant to Art. 30 TVTG, token issuers must report a token

---

[69] Art. 25 TVTG.
[70] Art.7(3) TVTG.
[71] BuA 2019/54, 178.
[72] See also Silbernagl, 'Zivilrechtliche Regelungen des liechtensteinischen Blockchaingesetzes (TVTG) – Möglichkeiten für Österreich?' (2020) 7 *Zivilrecht aktuell (Zak)*, 10 (11) and Sild, Ibid, 45 (59).
[73] Regulation (EU), No. 2017/1129 on the prospectus to be published when securities are offered to the public or admitted to trading on a regulated market.
[74] BuA 2019/54, 38–39.
[75] Art. 17(1)(b) TVTG; BuA 2019/93, 20.
[76] OECD (2021), 'Regulatory Approaches to the Tokenisation of Assets, OECD Blockchain Policy Series',https://beck-link.de/6v7md., 19 ('OECD') (accessed 31.08.2021).
[77] BuA 2019/54.
[78] BuA 2019/54, 73, OECD, 19; see also Nagele and Bont, 'Tokenized structures and assets in Liechtenstein law', Trusts & Trustees, Volume 25, Issue 6, July 2019, 633 et seqq.
[79] BuA 2019/93, 20.

issuance to the FMA and, if neither the Prospectus Regulation nor an exemption under Art. 31 TVTG is applicable, prepare and publish basic information under the TVTG in an easily accessible way in German or English language.

3. Basic Information and Prospectus Requirement

25   The PR is incorporated into the EEA Agreement and in force. It is therefore (as part of the EEA-acquis) directly applicable in Liechtenstein. If no exemptions apply, a public offering of tokens that qualify as **securities** pursuant to Art. 2(a) PR (a so-called securities token offering or 'STO') is subject to the prospectus requirement of Art. 3(1) PR. While drawing up a prospectus compliant with the Prospectus Regulation is onerous and costly for the issuer, it comes with the advantage of a 'passport' for a public offering in all EEA-member states (for details on the PR, → chapter 7).

26   If the tokens do not qualify as securities, the PR is not applicable and an EEA-harmonized framework and 'passport' for a public offering is not available. The TVTG governs the public offering of tokens in Liechtenstein that do not qualify as securities. Art. 30 TVTG stipulates an obligation to prepare and publish **basic information** and to notify the issuing to the FMA. The preparation and publishing of basic information is pursuant to Art. 31 TVTG in the context of an issuing/public offering not required, if (a) all recipients waive the receipt of basic information prior the acquisition of the token and this has been adequately documented, (b) the offer is addressed to less than 150 market participants or (c) the sale price of the total issue does not exceed CHF 5 Mio[80], or (d) there is another applicable law that requires the publishing of information, such as the PR. A public resale according to Art. 31(2) TVTG can be conducted without publishing additional information if basic information has been published in the course of the initial offering and the issuer or other responsible person has approved its use in writing. Although not explicitly required by law, the orderly publication of any supplement that is necessary in accordance with Art. 34 TVTG will also be mandatory in a public resale.

Similar to the PR, the TVTG-**basic information** must be written in a way that is easily understandable and facilitates analysis.[81] It is possible to publish the respective information in several documents if the token issuer additionally publishes a brief and easily understandable summary regarding the token issuer and the token.[82] New material facts and every material error or inaccuracy trigger the requirement to publish a supplement.[83] Art. 33 TVTG describes the required contents of the basic information, including risk factors and warnings, information on the responsibility for the contents and for the technical and legal functionality of the token and the name of the TT system that is used. If the issued token represents a property right, the basic information must further include evidence regarding the ownership for the respective property and a confirmation by the physical validator that the respective rights are enforceable in line with the basic information.[84]

27   The TVTG also contains specific provisions on liability regarding basic information, including a reversal of the burden of proof with regard to the observance of due diligence standards. Claims for damages are time-barred one year from the day on which the injured party has knowledge of the damage and of the person liable to pay compensation. Art. 38 TVTG stipulates an absolute limitation period of ten years. The

---

[80] Or the corresponding equivalent in another currency, see Art. 31(1)(c) TVTG.
[81] Art. 32(1) TVTG.
[82] Art. 32(2–3) TVTG.
[83] Art. 34 TVTG.
[84] Art. 33(1)(f) TVTG.

possibility to waive, exclude or restrict liability in advance are restricted for intent or gross negligence. Liechtenstein courts shall have jurisdiction for claims arising from the legal relationship between a Liechtenstein token issuer[85] and the transferee of the token.

The basic information is not based on a harmonized European framework and does not come with a permission to publicly offer the respective token within the EEA. Such offering in jurisdictions outside of Liechtenstein therefore bears enhanced compliance risks.

III. Anti-Money Laundering Legislation

As a second major piece of legislation, the Law of 11 December 2008 on Professional Due Diligence for the Prevention of Money Laundering, Organized Crime and Financing of Terrorism (Due Diligence Act, 'DDA') has been amended following the emergence of crypto assets and respective service providers in Liechtenstein. Even prior to the full implementation of AMLD5, the Liechtenstein DDA subjected TT service providers and certain dealings in crypto assets to anti-money laundering legislation. The DDA is applicable to TT service providers pursuant to Art. 2(1)(k) and (m) to (q) and (u) TVTG and thus to token issuers, TT key depositaries, TT token depositaries, TT protectors, physical validators and TT exchange service providers[86] and TT agents, to the extent they provide or distribute TT services for the aforementioned TT service providers. 28

The exchange of a token for legal tender or vice versa, which triggers due diligence requirements for TT exchange service providers, according to the legal materials shall only cover dealings in tokens that are fungible goods. It shall, however, not cover a trade relating to a so-called **non-fungible token** (NFTs).[87] Also, TT exchange service providers, which only operate physical exchange machines, benefit from an exemption from obligations under the DDA up to a certain transaction value.[88] In context of the DDA the TT exchange service provider must not be confused with a service provider carrying out forex transactions ('Wechselstubenbetreiber' under the DDA).

Other service providers may be subject to the DDA, even if not regulated under the TVTG. These are in particular token issuers that are not subject to registration under the TVTG[89] and **operators of trading platforms for virtual currencies or token**.[90] The latter operate a platform through which customers exchange virtual currencies or tokens for legal tender or other virtual currencies or tokens and vice versa. In doing so, their activity thus goes beyond mere brokerage without any involvement in payment flows: operators interfere with the transactions.[91] However, unlike a TT exchange service provider, such platform operator will not execute the trades against their own book.[92] Furthermore, the operator will not hold tokens or TT keys for its customers, which would lead to a qualification as TT token or TT key depositary. These service providers must report the commencement of their activities to the FMA pursuant to Art. 2(1)(z^{ter}) DDA. 29

---

[85] A token issuer with registered office in Liechtenstein, see Art. 37 TVTG.
[86] Art. 3(1)(r) DDA.
[87] BuA 2019/93, 10.
[88] Art. 5(2)(h) DDA; FMA Instruction 2018/7, 68.
[89] Art. 3(1)(s) DDA.
[90] Art. 3(1)(t) DDA.
[91] BuA 2019/54, 103.
[92] As defined in Art. 2(1) DDA. In essence, this definition is coherent with the definition provided in Art. 3(1)(r) DDA in connection with Art. 2(1)(q) TVTG, nevertheless the FMA has clarified that the definition in Art.2(1) (lbis) DDA for the purposes of AML laws is *lex specialis*, see FMA Instruction 2018/7, 68.

The requirements of the DDA explicitly apply to dealings with tokens *or* virtual currency. **Virtual currency** in Liechtenstein's DDA in compliance with Art. 3 No. 18 AMLD5 is defined as 'a digital representation of value that is not issued or guaranteed by a central bank or a public authority, is not necessarily attached to a legally established currency and does not possess a legal status of currency or money, but is accepted by natural or legal persons as a means of exchange and which can be transferred, stored and traded electronically'.[93] The definition of a **token** in the DDA is identical with the definition provided by Art. 2(1)(c) TVTG and thus wider than the term 'virtual currency'. While stable coins for example do not fall under Art. 3 No. 18 AMLD5, they do qualify as a token under the TVTG. Corresponding to the TVTG, the DDA is thus applicable to dealings with all types of tokens.

30   The specific due diligence obligations depend on the type of TT service provider, business activity and risk assessment and will thus vary on a case-by-case basis. A physical validator for example will *inter alia* need to produce a business profile and identify and verify the beneficial owner and origin of the assets that shall be tokenized. Tokenization in this context is according to the FMA not an 'occasional transaction' but rather an ongoing business relationship.[94] In line with the considerations outlined in recitals 8 et seqq. of AMDL5, the FMA deems crypto currencies and tokens to be vulnerable to money laundering, primarily due to the lack of intermediaries and the **(pseudo-)anonymity** of the market.[95] At the same time, the FMA acknowledges that the specific features of the crypto assets and the possibility to verify the history and 'technical origin' of an asset also allow for additional options to combat money laundering and terrorist financing.[96] Consequently, in the case of business relationships or transactions with increased risks, the DDA requires a '**chain analysis**' by using a system that allows a review of the transaction history.[97] Generally the FMA urges caution and tends to assign higher risks to transactions in tokens.[98]

D. Legislative Initiatives and Regulatory Guidance

31   The Ministry of General Government Affairs and Finance is responsible for legislative initiatives. The government program 2017 to 2021 includes a commitment to develop the 'Digital Agenda Liechtenstein', which has been published in March 2019 and includes the establishment of legal security for the so-called 'token economy'. This commitment has been tackled by introducing the TVTG and by an adjustment of the wider legal framework and administrative practice for digital business models and service providers. Measures also included the establishment and strengthening of the FMA 'regulatory laboratory' in order to guide market participants in licensing and registration procedures. Furthermore, Liechtenstein committed to create an efficient basic infrastructure for digital business models and inter alia facilitating the use of digital identities.[99] Similar, digitalization of financial services and administrative practice

---

[93] Art.2(1) (z^{bis}) DDA.
[94] FMA Instruction 2018/7, 67.
[95] Ibid, 65.
[96] Ibid, 65.
[97] Art. 21(2) Ordinance of February 17, 2009 on Professional Due Diligence for the Prevention of Money Laundering, Organized Crime and Financing of Terrorism (Due Diligence Ordinance, 'DDO'); see also FMA Instruction 2018/7, 72.
[98] FMA Instruction 2018/7, 69.
[99] Government of the Principality of Liechtenstein, 'Digital Agenda Liechtenstein' (German), available at: https://beck-link.de/ds3xh (accessed 31.08.2021).

as well as technology-neutral and innovation-friendly regulation are a central pillar of the financial market strategy for Liechtenstein published in February 2020.[100]

The Liechtenstein FMA is competent not only for the supervision of financial market participants, services and products, but also for the supervision of services and service providers under the TVTG. The FMA is known for its accessibility and service orientation. In the course of the 'Digital Agenda Liechtenstein' the 'regulatory laboratory' as internal competence team has been set up, to facilitate handling of a growing number of inquiries and increasingly complex issues relating to innovative projects in the FinTech and crypto space. The FMA has issued a number of guidelines and instructions regarding licensing and registration procedures for financial services[101] and services regulated under the TVTG[102] and the relevant due diligence provisions.[103] For potential FinTech service providers, the FMA offers an online tool that allows a brief and rather superficial initial self-assessment,[104] and actively offers the answering of questions and 'constructive exchange' via email.[105] For a regulatory fee and upon formal 'subordination enquiry' pursuant to Art. 43(2)(b) TVTG, the FMA on an individual basis issues statements with regard to the scope of regulated activities in connection with the TVTG.[106]

E. Conclusion and Outlook

The TVTG is an ambitious first step to regulate services that are not yet covered by financial regulation and to address private-law considerations with regard to crypto assets and transactions. The TVTG will face two main challenges in the upcoming years: First, the theoretical concepts and the regulatory approach must pass the practical test. This mainly depends on the reception by courts and the acceptance of the complex concepts by market participants and the wider public. Second, the legal development on an international level may challenge the progress made. On 24 September 2020 the European Commission has released the so-called Digital Finance Package including new regulatory proposals for service providers and crypto assets not within the realm of financial regulation as well as for DLT Market Infrastructure. In its resolution of 8 October 2020,[107] the European Parliament stressed the necessity to regulate crypto assets not falling into the MIFID2 regime in a harmonized manner within Europe. It must be expected that Liechtenstein's

32

---

[100] Ministry of General Government Affairs and Finance, 'Financial centre strategy', available at: https://beck-link.de/a3scp (accessed 31.08.2021).

[101] FMA, 'Guidelines 2018/18 – License as an e-money institution' (January 2015), available at: https://beck-link.de/zv5xb (accessed 31.08.2021). FMA, 'Guidelines 2018/18 – License as a bank or an investment firm' (January 2015), available at: https://beck-link.de/3arvd (accessed 31.08.2021).

[102] FMA, Instruction 2020/1- Registration as a service provider under the TVTG' (January 2020), available at: https://beck-link.de/6vnhs (accessed 31.08.2021); FMA, 'Instruction 2020/2 – Enquiries under the TVTG' (January 2020), available https://beck-link.de/b35ne (accessed 31.08.2021); FMA, 'Instruction 2020/3 – Reporting and notification requirements under the TVTG' (January 2020), available at: https://beck-link.de/kkh78 (accessed 31.08.2021).

[103] FMA Instruction 2018/7.

[104] FMA, 'Does my Fintech need a registration or license?' (2019), available at: https://beck-link.de/zfm7b (accessed 31.08.2021).

[105] FMA, 'Legal Framework', available at: https://beck-link.de/tshh7 (accessed 31.08.2021).

[106] FMA, 'Instruction 2020/2 – Enquiries under the TVTG' (January 2020), available at: https://beck-link.de/b35ne (accessed 31.08.2021).

[107] European Parliament, 'Resolution of 8 October 2020 with recommendations to the Commission on Digital Finance: emerging risks in crypto-assets – regulatory and supervisory challenges in the area of financial services, institutions and markets' (2020/2034(INL)).

legislator will have to adjust the TVTG to European legislation despite the technology neutrality and general high-level nature of the TVTG with respect to types of crypto instruments. This is not only bad news: Market participants will benefit from a defragmentation and enhanced market access, while the legislator will be eager to use any provided leeway to further strengthen the unique profile and reputation that Liechtenstein has gained as a first mover in developing regulatory concepts for digital financial services.

§ 21
Russia[1]

Literature: Burke and Ogonyants, 'Die EU-Wirtschaftssanktionen gegen Russland und die russischen Gegensanktionen', (2016) 6 *Zeitschrift für Internationales Wirtschaftsrecht (IWRZ)*, 264; constituteproject.org, 'Russian Federation's Constitution of 1993 with Amendments through 2008' (2008), available at: https://beck-link.de/p7scz (accessed 12.02.2021); Goldsmith and Wu (eds), *Who Controls the Internet: Illusions of a Borderless World* (Oxford University Press, Oxford, 2006); ICORating, 'ICO market research Q1 2018' (2018), available at: https://beck-link.de/6sa65 (accessed 12.01.2021); Palshikar, Apte and Baskaran, Analytics for Detection of Money Laundering' (April 2014), available at: https://beck-link.de/hnv2f (accessed 12.01.2021); Steininger, 'Eine Zusammenfassung der wichtigsten Sanktionen der EU und der USA, Gegenmaßnahmen Russlands sowie der Lokalisierungspolitik' (2018) *Wirtschaft und Recht in Europa (WiRO)*, 46. Tatar, 'How Blockchain Is Revolutionary' (September 2020), available at: https://beck-link.de/pn87v (accessed 12.01.2021). The Russian Federation, 'National Money Laundering Risk Assessment 2017–2018: Key Findings' (2017), available (in yet unofficial translation in English) at: https://beck-link.de/ev56w (accessed 12.01.2021); Weidner, 'The Organisation and Structure of Central Banks' (2017), available at: https://beck-link.de/3rkw5 (accessed 12.02.2021). Wolf, *Initial Coin Offerings: Ökonomisch effiziente Regulierung kapitalmarktrechtlich und steuerrechtlich bedingter Aspekte von Marktversagen* (Dunker and Humblot, Berlin, 2020).

Outline

	para.
A. Market Development	1
I. Introduction	1
II. Russian Involvement in Initial Coin Offerings (ICOs)	2
III. Crypto and the Dark Web in Russia	5
IV. Russian Economy	6
B. Laws and Regulations	7
I. Current Legal Status of Crypto Assets	8
1. Legal Status Under Constitutional Law	10
2. Legal Status Under Regulatory Law	11
3. Legal Status Under Criminal Law	14
a) Money Laundering	16
b) Fraud	18
c) Illegal Use of Insider Information and Market Manipulation	19
II. Recent und Upcoming Changes in Regulatory Law	20
1. Media Confusion	21
2. The 'Digital Rights Law'	23
a) Object of the Digital Rights Law	23
b) Remaining Questions Concerning the Digital Rights Law	24
c) Is the Digital Rights Law Applicable to Crypto Assets?	25
3. Forthcoming: 'Digital Financial Assets Law'	26
III. International Aspects of Crypto Investments	31
1. Russian Law	32
a) Foundations of Russian Sanctions Law	32
b) Sanctions of Foreign Crypto Investments into Russia Under Russian law	34
c) International Crypto Transactions from Russia into foreign Countries	35
2. EU/US-Sanctions	38
C. The Central Bank of Russia as a Potential Regulator	40
D. Conclusion	43

---

[1] The author is grateful for helpful advice and market-insights to Vadim Konyushkevich, VK-partners Moscow.

A. Market Development

I. Introduction

1   Worldwide, the blockchain technology and especially the cryptocurrency Bitcoin have evolved quickly and revolutionized the global financial asset markets.[2] In the first quarter of 2018 most of the ICO-fundraising-projects have been aimed at providing financing in the fields of financial services ($ 233.8 million), banking and payments ($ 205.6 million) and blockchain infrastructure ($ 87.2 million). Most of the project funding is concentrated in Europe (46,6 %), the rest is divided between Asia (25,3 %) and North America (24,7 %).[3] Explaining **Russia's place in this global context** is a complex task. Although the country maintains a rather confusing regulatory framework[4] and Russian academic research on the issue is scarce, trading with cryptocurrencies (such as Bitcoin) has been very present in Russia since the beginning of the crypto boom[5]. Some websites even claim that Russia actually is the most important country when it comes to cryptocurrency trade and investments, with headlines like 'Why are there so many Russians in Crypto?'[6] and 'Meet the Russians Behind Your Blockchain'[7].

II. Russian Involvement in Initial Coin Offerings (ICOs)

2   Russia seems to play an especially important role in ICOs. **Trading** in crypto assets remains on a rather **low level within Russia itself** because the Russian state wishes to keep a tight grip on company financing and transactions. Russian companies, however, provide important technological services which are needed to implement and run ICO projects to companies worldwide, especially in Europe. Here a clear distinction should be made between the country in which a certain project is registered and offered, and the country where the actual project team is working.[8]

---

[2] Tapscott and Kirkland, 'How blockchains could change the world' (May 2016), available at: https://beck-link.de/hyyt8 (accessed 12.01.2021); Pollock, 'The fourth industrial revolution built on Blockchain and advanced with AI' (November 2018), available at: https://beck-link.de/7t8b6 (accessed 12.01.2020); Tatar, 'How Blockchain Is Revolutionary' (September 2020), available at: https://beck-link.de/pn87v (accessed 12.01.2021).

[3] ICORating, 'ICO market research Q1 2018' (2018), 29 et seq., available at: https://beck-link.de/6sa65 (accessed 12.01.2021).

[4] Alper, 'Russia's Crypto L aw is Taking a Confusing Shape' (November 2019), available at: https://beck-link.de/afwx6 (accessed 12.01.2021); Redman, 'Despite Russia's Confusing Crypto Laws, P2P Bitcoin Trade Volumes Soar' (June 2020), available at: https://beck-link.de/sv3rz (accessed 12.01.2021); Guznov, 'Director of the Central Bank's Department of Law: We are against institutions for organizing the issuance of cryptocurrency in Russia' (March 2020), available at: https://beck-link.de/3rawk (accessed 12.01.2021) *(translated from Russian)*.

[5] Redman, ibid; Gogo, 'Bitcoin Trading Is Booming in Uncertain Russia, with 350 % Spike in New Users on Paxful' (July 2020), available at: https://beck-link.de/kh2ac (accessed 12.01.2021); Partz, Updated: Russia Leads Global BTC Trading on LocalBitcoins in 2020' (June 2020), available athttps://beck-link.de/44prb (accessed 12.01.2021).

[6] Detrixhe, 'Why are there so many Russians in Crypto?' (May 2018), available at: https://beck-link.de/8nhbc (accessed 12.01.2021).

[7] Rapoza, 'Meet the Russian s Behind Your Blockchain (And Cryptocurrency, Too)' (April 2018), available at: https://beck-link.de/nvet2 (accessed 12.01.2021).

[8] ICORating, 'ICO market research Q1 2018' (2018), 32 et seq., available at: https://beck-link.de/6sa65 (accessed 12.01.2021).

In the first quarter of 2018, 13 ICO projects were started by Russian companies in Russia with a total volume of $ 20.8 million. This is a rather small number, as during the same period in North America, 68 projects with a total volume of $ 600.4 million have been initiated. By contrast, if one looks at the country of origin of the project teams involved, Russian citizens have participated in 45 projects totaling over $ 240.5 million in worth, which makes Russia one of the most important countries in this respect, behind only the USA, China, and Lithuania.[9]

Several studies have shown that developing an ICO project is quite affordable in Russia.[10] The Russian website 'Ratingratingov.ru' has created a list of over fifteen tech-companies which provide blockchain and crypto-services in this field.[11] The costs per ICO range from $ 3,378 to $ 44,583. The average cost per ICO amounts to approximately $ 21,505, or $ 53 per hour for the services offered.[12]

Just recently, a study was conducted which showed that the ICO-market has 'almost totally' disappeared. Instead of ICOs, now IEOs (Initial Exchange Offerings) are supposed to be the new trend.[13] The difference between ICOs and IEOs is that in the case of an ICO, the investor pays state-backed money to buy a token generated by the issuing company, whereas in the case of an IEO, both parties exchange different kinds of tokens. IEOs are believed to be a 'safer investment' with lower risk of abuse, as no party is subject to advance payment. Instead, company and investor buy (or rather: 'exchange') dynamic values in the form of tokens and are thereby bound to fulfil their contractual obligations as promised (mostly via smart contracts).[14]

III. Crypto and the Dark Web in Russia

Crypto trading in Russia goes beyond what is 'visible', such as Bitcoin trading. There is also a large 'dark web market' which offers crypto-based platforms for any kind of secret – or illegal – activity.[15] As published on the journal 'wired.com' in 2014, their journalists had an interview with 'Russia's favourite dark web drug lord'.[16] The phrasing of that headline surprises in various aspects: Firstly, it reveals that Russia obviously has multiple 'dark web drug lords', as the one in question is considered 'the favourite'. And secondly, it shows that the dark web and criminal activity (in this case: drugs) are associated with each other *per se* and cannot be separated.

The correlation between crypto and the dark web is not a specifically Russian phenomenon. Criminal activity is supposed to be responsible for a huge part of the dark web-traffic worldwide and because of their anonymity, blockchain technologies and cryptocurrencies seem to be major transaction tools in the criminal

---

[9] Ibid, 33.
[10] Tassev, 'Developing an ICO project in Russia Can Cost as Little as $ 1,500' (August 2018), available at: https://beck-link.de/7khfr (accessed 12.01.2021).
[11] Rating gov, 'Blockchain developers rating-experienced reliable', available at: https://beck-link.de/2z3s4 (accessed 12.01.2021) (*in Russian*).
[12] The foundation for these calculations is the numbers of the study by the rating agency "ratingratingov.ru"; Rating gov, ibid.
[13] Ana Alexandre, 'Studie: ICO-Markt fast vollständig zurückgegangen, Initial Exchange Offerings als neuer Trend' (May 2019), available at: https://beck-link.de/6sse6 (accessed 12.01.2021) (*in German*).
[14] Cryptonews, 'Initial Exchange Offering (IEO)?', available at: https://beck-link.de/nx34e (accessed 12.01.2021).
[15] Rubenking, 'The Evolution of Russia's Dark Web' (August 2019), available at: https://beck-link.de/s8aae (accessed 12.01.2021); Patterson, 'How much do you know about the Russian Dark Web?' (August 2019), available at: https://beck-link.de/2pphs (accessed 12.01.2021).
[16] Greenberg, 'An Interview with Darkside, Russia's Favourite Dark Web Druglord' (April 2014), available at: https://beck-link.de/mncf6 (accessed 12.01.2021).

world.[17] But in Russia in particular, financing criminal activities by using the dark web and cryptocurrencies seems rather common, as illustrated by the stark example an ICO with a volume of $ 146,000,000, which is 'almost certainly illegal': The issuing company under the pseudonym 'Hydra' was launched in 2015 and provides 'a marketplace for illegal goods such as drugs and their ingredients, counterfeit documents and money as well as hacking services.'[18] Another example that links criminal activity in Russia's dark web to cryptocurrencies is a case where Russian criminals exchanged $ 13,000,000 in cash for the same amount of a certain cryptocurrency – and the cash was found to be fake.[19]

IV. Russian Economy

6   A reason why a lot of Russians might be so interested in – non-criminal – cryptocurrency-trade could be the troubled state of the Russian economy. For decades, Russia's economy has been struggling because of several problems: There are no direct trade agreements beyond those with its immediate neighbours. It is dependent on foreign technology, has a rather weak infrastructure and just recently, the price for oil, a main source of income for the Russian economy, dropped heavily.[20] There are also the international sanction regimes against Russia.[21] Consequently, the Ruble, the official Russian currency, has decreased in value over the last years and has not been stabilized yet.

For these reasons, especially younger Russians are searching for alternative ways to invest their money. It may seem prudent to invest in foreign currencies but investing in dollars – for example – is connected to high transaction costs.[22] In fact, most of the money transfer services do not even support transferring money out of Russia.[23] As such, cryptocurrencies promise to be a new way of investing and saving money. Conversely, it is also a way of obtaining money from abroad for Russian projects.[24]

B. Laws and Regulations

7   Against this socioeconomic background, the following questions relating to crypto assets in Russia shall be elaborated in this chapter: First, are crypto assets generally legal in Russia (→ para. 8–19). Second, what changes have been made to civil law that could be relevant for the regulation of crypto assets in Russia (→ para. 20–30). Third, are there

---

[17] Sharma Rakesh, 'Litecoin Gains Ground on Bitcoin in The Dark Web' (June 2019), available at: https://beck-link.de/ye8pa (accessed 12.01.2021).
[18] Baydakova, 'Russia's Largest Darknet Market Is Hawking an ICO to Fund Global Expansion' (December 2019), available at: https://beck-link.de/m47yp (accessed 12.01.2021); Redman, 'Russia's Hydra Darknet Marketplace Plans $ 146 M Token Sale' (December 2019), available at: https://beck-link.de/xbw8x (accessed 12.01.2021); Ricca, 'Russian darknet marketplace ICO: expansion or exit scam?' (December 2019), available at: https://beck-link.de/fpa45 (accessed 12.01.2021).
[19] Partz, 'Russian Darknet Criminals Sell $ 13 M of Fake Cash for Crypto' (April 2020), available at: https://beck-link.de/zbmr4 (accessed 12.01.2021).
[20] Coface for Trade, 'Major Macro Economic Indicators (for Russia)' (May 2020), available at: https://beck-link.de/45xk5 (accessed 12.01.2021).
[21] See for the European Council's sanction strategy: European Council, 'EU restrictive measures in response to the crisis in Ukraine', available at: https://beck-link.de/zenp5 (accessed 12.01.2021).
[22] See for example: *ADVcash*, available at: (accessed 12.01.2021). https://beck-link.de/5v3eb
[23] See for example: *Currenc ytransfer.com*, available at: https://beck-link.de/x66ss (accessed 12.01.2021).
[24] Skalex, 'Cryptocurrency in Russia: A Useful History of a Love-Hate Relationship', available at: https://beck-link.de/edt3e (accessed 12.01.2021).

specific aspects of Russian sanctions law that one should be concerned about when using the crypto technology in Russia (→ para. 31–39).

I. Current Legal Status of Crypto Assets

According to most media sources, crypto assets are or will soon be almost entirely banned in Russia.[25] At the same time, there are also sources indicating the opposite.[26] Even state officials do not seem to be clear on the issue.[27] In any case a crucial development is the new 'Digital Financial Assets Law' coming into force in 2021 (→ para. 26–30).

To answer questions regarding the legality of crypto assets it seems sensible to first address whether crypto assets might already be forbidden in Russia today (→ para. 10–19), followed by whether it is likely that they *will be* banned in the nearer future (→ para. 20–30).

Regarding the first question, there are mainly three possibilities how crypto assets might already be banned in Russia. They could be banned directly by Russian criminal or regulatory law (b, c) or their use could be incompatible with constitutional law (a). As the constitution generally overrides the so called 'ordinary' law, this should be the primary point of examination.

1. Legal Status Under Constitutional Law

Article 75 of the Russian constitution states:

'The monetary unit in the Russian Federation shall be the Ruble. […] The introduction and issuance of other currencies in Russia shall not be permitted. Protecting and ensuring the stability of the Ruble shall be the principal function of the Central Bank of the Russian Federation.'

Based on the wording of this Article, it seems clear that in Russia cryptocurrencies – as special case of crypto assets – such as Bitcoin or Ethereum are generally banned. Despite the wording, there is an ongoing debate about whether cryptocurrencies are in fact banned in Russia or not. If Art. 75 of the constitution stipulates the illegality of cryptocurrencies *per se,* there would be no need for such discussions. This argument is further supported by the fact that there are several official drafts for bitcoin-regulating laws.[28] Also, transactions with foreign currencies such as Euro, Dollar or Yen are not banned but legal. In that context, it seems unlikely that the Russian constitution should singularly outlaw cryptocurrencies.

---

[25] Just a few: Zerelik, 'Crypto in Russia soon will be banned' (May 2020), available at: https://beck-link.de/w2s7k (accessed 12.01.2021); Baydakova, 'Russia Considering Draconian Rules for Illegal Crypto Operations' (September 2020), available at: https://beck-link.de/cakz5 (accessed 12.01.2021); Bambrough, 'Blow To Bitcoin as Russia Moves to Effectively Ban Crypto' (March 2020), available at: https://beck-link.de/3a3hn (accessed 12.01.2021); Gogo, 'Russia Proposes Law that criminalizes buying bitcoin with cash, offenders face 7 years in jail (May 2020), available at: https://beck-link.de/86rc3 (accessed 12.01.2021); Collin Brown, 'Russia: New law foresees total ban of Bitcoin and cryptocurrencies' (May 2020), available at: https://beck-link.de/crp4w (accessed 12.01.2021); Martin, 'Russia Proposes 2M Rub Fine and 7 Years in Jail for Illegal Crypto Use' (May 2020), available at: https://beck-link.de/wf5yd (accessed 12.01.2021).

[26] Frisco D'Anconia, 'Russia's Tax Authorities Recognize Bitcoin and Other Cryptocurrencies' (December 2016), available at: https://beck-link.de/xza7s (accessed 12.01.2021); Naumoff, 'Operations with Bitcoin in Russia Do Not Entail Punishment. Yet' (August 2016), available at: https://beck-link.de/p7m7w (accessed 12.01.2021).

[27] ICORating, 'ICO market research Q1 2018' (2018), 29, available at: https://beck-link.de/6sa65 (accessed 12.01.2021).

[28] Marley, 'The Bill 'On Digital Financial Assets' and Crypto Community' (March 2020), available at: https://beck-link.de/vr6hx (accessed 12.01.2021).

2. Legal Status Under Regulatory Law

11   Some observers rightfully state that Russia's crypto asset law took a 'confusing shape'.[29] A report stating that the Deputy Russian Finance Minister has claimed cryptocurrencies would be 'illegal'[30] has often been improperly shortened. His description of the legal situation was as follows (translated):

> 'As there is a legal 'vacuum' at the moment, it is hard to say whether it is legal or illegal to deal with cryptocurrencies. [...] Nevertheless, using cryptocurrency as a payment method is probably illegal.'[31]

12   Something which makes the debate about cryptocurrencies especially difficult is that there is 'no law at present that specifically allows cryptocurrencies.' Furthermore, there is no legal definition of cryptocurrencies at the moment (→ para. 26–30 for the new law on Digital Financial Assets). Nevertheless, there are some provisions that could be interpreted as cryptocurrency-bans. In addition to Article 75 of the constitution (→ para. 10), there is Chapter VI of the Federal Law on the Central Bank of Russia,[32] which also states that the Ruble is the only national currency and that the introduction of other currencies or even of currency surrogates is prohibited:[33]

> Organizing the Currency Cash Turnover
> Art. 27
> The official monetary unit (the currency) of the Russian Federation is the Ruble. [...] The introduction of other monetary units and the issue of monetary substitutes is prohibited.'

13   This Art. seems to only rephrase the corresponding constitutional provision (→ para. 10). As such, its applicability to cryptocurrencies should also be questioned. The argument that cryptocurrencies should be considered as *currency surrogates* seems generally reasonable but cannot be expressly validated either.[34]

Meanwhile, crypto assets have been declared as taxable property recently. In a bill, crypto assets are defined as 'a digital set of data that can be used as a payment method or investment tool for which no central party is responsible, 'except for the operator and (or) the nodes of such systems, which are only responsible for maintaining the issuance of the digital data and upending such a system.'

3. Legal Status Under Criminal Law

14   There has been a lot of discussion about whether dealing with crypto assets is illegal in Russia (→ para. 11). With regard to Russian criminal law, currently there is no statutory provision that punishes cryptocurrency-trade *per se*. Nevertheless, some events have occurred that might suggest cryptocurrency-trading is sanctioned by law in Russia.

Early in 2020 a draft bill proposed seven years of imprisonment for illegal crypto use. Although the announced changes of the criminal code have not yet been

---

[29] Otieno, 'Russia's Central Bank Will Ban Crypto Issuance and Trading in Upcoming 'Digital Financial Assets' Bill' (March 2020), available at: https://beck-link.de/xnhf2 (accessed 12.01.2021).

[30] ЭКОНОМИКА, 'Замминистра финансов РФ назвал незаконными расчеты в криптовалютах' (September 2017), available at: https://beck-link.de/zh4ky (accessed 12.01.2021).

[31] Wolf, *Initial Coin Offerings: Ökonomisch effiziente Regulierung kapitalmarktrechtlich und steuerrechtlich bedingter Aspekte von Marktversagen* (2020), 23 et seq.

[32] Federal Law NO. 86-FZ of July 10, 2002 on the Central Bank of the Russian Federation (The Bank of Russia), available (*translated in English*) at: https://beck-link.de/hm8fn (accessed 12.01.2021).

[33] Dmitriev and Kiseleva, 'Blockchain & Cryptocurrency Regulation 2020 in Russia', https://beck-link.de/cze6f (accessed 12.01.2021).

[34] In that direction: Dmitriev and Kiseleva, ibid.

codified, a consensus was reached about fines of up to 2,000,000 Rubles and seven years of imprisonment for individuals for dealing with cryptocurrencies. As a consequence, the Russian Association of Crypto-Economics has claimed that '[the Russian government] is proposing to build a new iron curtain in the digital economy with its own hands.'[35]

Also, the Russian Supreme Court ruled in February 2019 that crypto assets can be recognized as assets like money and property. The judgement was not meant to regulate cryptocurrencies and related only to lower courts' ability to condemn 'criminals' for dealing with crypto assets in terms of money laundering.[36] Nevertheless, as there are no provisions explicitly banning trading in crypto assets, the issue is whether some of the existing norms of criminal law could be seen as such. **15**

a) Money Laundering. First, a criminal offence that is often connected to crypto assets in Russia is money laundering.[37] It is regulated in Art. 174 of the Russian Criminal Code (RCC)[38]: 'The Legalization (Laundering) of Funds and Other Property Acquired by Other Persons Illegally'. It punishes the accomplishment of financial transactions and other transactions in monetary funds or other property knowingly acquired by other persons illegally for the purpose of bringing the appearance of legality to the possession, Art. 174 I 1 RCC. The fine is up to 120,000 Rubles or any other income of the convicted person for a period of up to one year calculated based on their wage or salary, Art. 174 I 2 RCC. Furthermore, the 'Federal Law No. 115 on Countering Money Laundering and the Financing of Terrorism'[39] allows for precautionary activities of the state in order to prevent money laundering.[40] In this regard, 'illegal earnings' are amounts of money or other property received as a result of committing an offence, Art. 3 Federal Law No. 115. As such, the offence of money laundry links to another criminal offence. The central indictment of the crime of money laundering is the so called 'legalization' of the illegal earnings, which means that the offender brings a legal appearance to the possession, Art. 3 Federal Law No. 115-FZ. **16**

Dealing with crypto assets is relevant for the criminal offence of money laundering if there is suspicion or evidence that the conversion of crypto assets into Rubles might be an act of bringing a 'legal appearance' to illegal earnings. As in the usual practice of identifying cases of money laundering, the Russian administration looks at specific transactions which are considered to be 'risky'.[41] For that purpose, there is a manual for identifying money laundering risks issued by the Central Bank of Russia (CBR).[42] This manual has been updated in February 2020 and includes cryptocurrency exchange **17**

---

[35] Martin, 'Russia Proposes 2M Rub Fine and 7 Years in Jail for Illegal Crypto Use' (May 2020), available at: https://beck-link.de/wf5yd (accessed 12.01.2021).

[36] Dmitriev and Kiseleva, ibid.

[37] Shevchenko, 'Russian Central Bank Links Crypto Transactions with Money Laundering' (February 2020), available at: https://beck-link.de/sbe5e (accessed 12.01.2021).

[38] Federal Law No. 63-FZ of June 13,1996-the Criminal Code of the Russian Federation, available (*translated in English*) at: https://beck-link.de/hm3x7 (accessed 12.01.2021).

[39] Federal Law No. 115-FZ On Countering Money Laundering and the Financing of Terrorism of the Russian Federation(2001 as amended 2004), available (translated in English at: https://beck-link.de/hah7v (accessed 12.01.2021).

[40] § 1 FL-No. 115-FZ.

[41] Oscar Canario da Cunha, 'AML Transaction Monitoring & Detection Scenarios' (December 2019), available at: https://beck-link.de/ab6kh (accessed 12.01.2021); Palshikar, Apte and Baskaran, Analytics for Detection of Money Laundering' (April 2014), available at: https://beck-link.de/hnv2f (accessed 12.01.2021).

[42] The Russian Federation, 'National Money Laundering Risk Assessment 2017–2018: Key Findings' (2017), available (*in yet unofficial translation in English*) at: https://beck-link.de/ev56w (accessed 12.01.2021).

transactions as high-risk-transactions: 'For cryptocurrencies, any activity that can be identified as buying or selling them will be considered a money laundering risk.'[43]

Although dealing with crypto assets *per se* is not considered money laundering, every exchange of virtual currency token is now considered to be of high risk of money laundering. This makes it harder and less attractive for market participants to use crypto assets. For some, it might seem that while crypto assets are not banned officially, they are in a practical sense.

18 **b) Fraud.** According to Art. 159 of the Russian Criminal Code (RCC), *fraud* is the stealing of other people's property or the acquisition of the right to other people's property by fraud or breach of trust. This criminal offence of swindling is considered to include fraud. The basic idea behind it is that there is an unjustified asset allocation which the offender managed to cause by a breach of trust or deceit.[44] The risk of committing such criminal activity is much higher when dealing with cryptocurrencies than dealing with the Ruble, as virtual currencies generally are not regulated and controlled by the state. As the case may be large amounts of money are stolen in the context of exchanging bitcoins for official payment currencies (such as dollars or Rubles).[45] But this does not equate to a ban of cryptocurrencies, although it does make them more likely objects of crime.

19 **c) Illegal Use of Insider Information and Market Manipulation.** Finally, in the context of virtual currencies, the criminal offence of the illegal use of insider information and market manipulation is important. This is stated in Art. 7 of the Federal Law No. 224 (as amended in 2016),[46] which provides that any individual or entity that has illegally used insider information and/or committed market manipulation shall be held accountable. In effect, market manipulation refers to '*actions causing the price, supply, demand or volume of trading in a financial instrument to materially change from what it would have been had such action not been taken.*' The illegal use of insider information means the usage of precise, material, non-public information that could influence the price of financial instruments, foreign currencies or commodities. Such illegal use could for example be carried out by disclosing insider information to the public.[47] Both of these criminal offences are especially relevant in the mostly volatile crypto assets market although, once again, they do not ban cryptocurrencies as such.

II. Recent und Upcoming Changes in Regulatory Law

20 Several statutory amendments have been made within the field of civil law which could have a direct or indirect influence on the market of crypto assets in Russia.

---

[43] Shevchenko, ibid; The Bank of Russia, 'The Central Bank of Russia updates its guidelines' (February 2020), available at: https://beck-link.de/ba4vc (accessed 12.01.2021). The standards of the US-Foreign Account Compliance Tax Act were used as a basis for Russian money laundering regulation, see also Foreign Account Tax Compliance Act (FATCA), available at: https://beck-link.de/anx8d (accessed 12.01.2021).

[44] Borodak, Financial crime in the Russian Federation (March 2020), available at: https://beck-link.de/5rwbc (accessed 12.01.2021).

[45] Partz, ibid, I.3.

[46] Federal Law No. 224-FZ dated July 27, 2010, of the Russian Federation on Countering the Illegal Use of Insider Information and Market Manipulation and on Amending Certain Legislative Acts of the Russian Federation (as amended on July 3, 2016), available (*translated in English*) at: https://beck-link.de/bk3tk (accessed 12.01.2021).

[47] Borodak, Financial crime in the Russian Federation (March 2020), available at: https://beck-link.de/5rwbc (accessed 12.01.2021).

§ 21. Russia

1. Media Confusion

As stated in the introduction to the related laws and regulations (→ para. 11), media sources have raised some doubts if bitcoin and other cryptocurrencies are legal in Russia.[48] On 21st May 2020, *Russia Today* reported that using cryptocurrencies could soon lead to imprisonment.[49] According to this article, members of the State Duma, Russian's Parliament, suggested punishment for the illegal use of digital assets and currencies. Some even say 'the proposed law amounts to a total ban on cryptocurrencies.' Nevertheless, according to *Russia Today*, Yuri Pripachkin, the president of the Russian Association of Cryptoeconomics and Blockchain (RACIB), explained that the proposed legislation would lead to a complete ban on cryptocurrencies in the country. Although these might be considered shocking news, it remains unclear whether the law proposes punishment for the use of cryptocurrencies for illegal activities or for any such usage *per se*. 21

Other media sources predict different changes to the crypto regulations in Russia: Some say there will be 'draconian rules for illegal crypto operations'[50], while others predict that cryptocurrencies will be banned as a means of payment, but it will be legal to possess, acquire and transfer cryptocurrencies if these actions are declared to the state.[51] 22

As it can clearly be seen, different media sources contradict in their reporting on the same legislature proposal. As of now no reliable statement can be made on how the Russian parliament and administration will decide about crypto assets regulations in the near future. However, the simple information that 'crypto in Russia soon will be banned' – as claimed by some media[52] – is at best imprecise, as it is not clear yet whether the proposed law will be so strict.

2. The 'Digital Rights Law'

a) Object of the Digital Rights Law. The Russian Federal Law No. 34-FZ which entered into force in October 2019, was the first Russian law regulating 'digital rights' specifically. It aims at simplifying electronic transactions and creating a basis for smart contracts.[53] Especially the last part is relevant for crypto assets, as smart contracts often share the Blockchain technology with crypto assets (→ § 1).[54] The central point of the law is to recognize 'digital rights' in the Russian Civil Code (new Art. 141), while it remains unclear how they can be defined or what could be examples for such digital rights.[55] 23

Nevertheless, the law does define who the holder of a digital right is: '*It is the person who, in accordance with the rules of the information system, has the opportunity to*

---

[48] Cointelegraph, 'Is Bitcoin Legal', available at: https://beck-link.de/z3yth (accessed 12.01.2021).

[49] RT, 'Prison for buying bitcoin? Proposed law could see Russians serving time for using cryptocurrencies' (May 2020), available at: https://beck-link.de/febz6 (accessed 12.01.2021); the article was a reaction to the draft law on criminal and administrative liability, the first version of which was attached to the draft law on Digital Financial Assets. There is now a separate draft law on amendments into the Criminal and Administrative liabilities Codes.

[50] Baydakova, ibid.

[51] Reuters, 'Russian lawmakers approve legal status for cryptocurrencies', but ban use as payment' (July 2020), available at: https://beck-link.de/zt7er (accessed 12.01.2021).

[52] Tokeneo, 'Crypto in Russia soon will be banned' (May 2020), available at: https://beck-link.de/rs7hw (accessed 12.01.2021).

[53] Gubanov and Shadrin, 'New law establishes conditions for digital rights in Russia' (May 2019), available at: https://beck-link.de/f4ynh (accessed 12.01.2021).

[54] Wolf, *Initial Coin Offerings: Ökonomisch effiziente Regulierung kapitalmarktrechtlich und steuerrechtlich bedingter Aspekte von Marktversagen* (2020), 45.

[55] Gubanov and Shadrin, ibid.

Denga

dispose of the right.' (Art. 141 para. 2 Russian Civil Code). This specification makes it possible to examine turnovers of digital rights, as there is now a definition of who the current holder of the right is.[56] Furthermore, according to the Central Bank of Russia, the aim of the digital rights law is, amongst other things, to codify provisions for 'attracting investments by offering utilitarian digital rights'. Utilitarian digital rights are defined to be the 'legal claim to the transfer of items or intellectual rights that are created and circulated in [an] IT system.'[57]

24 **b) Remaining Questions Concerning the Digital Rights Law.** As the Digital Rights Law itself is rather fragmentary[58], various key aspects of the issue remain unregulated. These include, for example, the formal requirements for transactions of digital rights. These are not set out, nor are provisions on which platforms are acceptable or what kind of digital signature is mandatory. The law also amends Art. 309 of the Russian Civil Code, which sets out requirements for the execution of contracts. This modification aims at facilitating smart contracts. The amendment allows for the transfer of ownership regardless of the parties' will. This supports the implementation of smart contracts, as their quintessence is the automated transfer of rights ('tokens') when specific factual conditions are met – regardless of whether the parties still agree on the contract at the time of its execution. The amendment legally supports the technical solution.

25 **c) Is the Digital Rights Law Applicable to Crypto Assets?** It is important to understand whether the Digital Rights Law is applicable to cryptocurrencies or crypto assets. First, the legal facilitation of smart contract execution seems perfectly applicable to crypto assets. In the field of blockchain technology and crypto assets, smart contracts are an important mechanism to automate payments and supply (→ generally, § 1). It is likely that the changes to the Russian Civil Code have been introduced with the intention of regulating cryptocurrencies.

The general applicability of the digital rights law to cryptocurrencies can also be demonstrated by the legislation process of the law: At first, the responsible members of the administration wanted to exclude 'digital money' and 'cryptocurrencies' from the area of application of the law, as they were sure that there would be an additional law explicitly regulating those sub-areas. The original idea was to only allow cryptocurrencies as a means of payment within the limits and regulation of such additional law. However, during the legislative process, the planned crypto-regulation was discarded. Therefore, the lawmakers of the digital rights law neither excluded cryptocurrencies and 'digital money' from the digital rights law, nor did they specifically include it.[59] This keeps the legal debate regarding the application of the digital rights law to crypto assets open.

3. Forthcoming: 'Digital Financial Assets Law'

26 The 'Digital Financial Assets Law'[60] (DFAL) comes into force on 1st January 2021. It contains a comprehensive regulatory regime ranging from basic definitions of digital

---

[56] Dianova (GRATA International), 'Russian law on digital rights' (2019), available at: https://beck-link.de/5ayw3 (accessed 12.01.2021).

[57] Bank of Russia, 'Russia introduces first law regulating digital rights' (August 2019), available at: https://beck-link.de/cv4ff (accessed 12.01.2021).

[58] Gubanov and Shadrin, ibid.

[59] Dianova (GRATA International), ibid.

[60] Федеральный закон от 31.07.2020 N 259-ФЗ "О цифровых финансовых активах, цифровой валюте и о внесении изменений в отдельные законодательные акты Российской Федерации" – Federal Law of July 31, 2020 N 259-FZ "On digital financial assets, digital currency and on amendments

financial assets and currencies (Art. 1 para. 2 f.), questions of validity of digital rights (Art. 2 para. 1, Art. 4 para. 5), information and organization duties of operators of information systems (Art. 5 f.), to trading rules (Art. 10 f.) and the prohibition of crypto currencies use as consideration in transactions (Art. 14). The law also modifies a wide range of other statutes, from the law on public companies to the bankruptcy act. It is important to stress that the DFAL does not apply to the circulation of non-cash funds, electronic funds, nor does it apply to the issuing, accounting and circulation of uncertified securities (Art. 1 para. 11).

Its underlying function, role and logic is that digital financial assets are issued by an issuer on an information system and can be purchased and traded through a trading agent. Both the operator of the information system and the trading agent have organizational and informational duties with regards to the Central Bank of Russia and other Russian authorities. The DFAL's main rules are the following.

Crypto assets fall under the definition of digital financial assets under Art. 1 para. 2: **27**

'digital rights, including monetary claims, the possibility of exercising rights under equity securities, the right to participate in the capital of a non-public joint stock company, the right to demand the transfer of equity securities, which are provided for by the decision on the issue of digital financial assets in the manner prescribed by law, the release, accounting and circulation of which is possible only by making (changing) entries in an information system based on a distributed register, as well as in other information systems'

Issuing digital financial assets implies quite exhaustive information duties, especially concerning the identity of the issuers which are accounted for on the information system (Art. 3 and Art. 4 para. 1). The DFAL only allows transactions with digital financial assets through 'digital financial asset exchange operators, which can be banks and exchanges, as well as other legal entities, provided they meet specific criteria.' In that way the Russian lawmaker creates a supervised intermediary for otherwise potentially anonymous transactions.[61] Art. 10 para. 3 of the law states that along with credit institutions, regulated and requiring authorisation under general Russian capital markets law, other organizations may issue digital financial assets if they (*inter alia*) have a nominal capital of 50 million Rubles and provide for a risk management system. The trade agent has to agree on its exchange rules with the Central Bank of Russia (Art. 11). If the trade agent is non-complaint with the DFAL, he is banned from trading in digital financial assets (Art. 11 para. 13 ff.).

The second intermediary under the DFAL is the operator of the information **28** system, who has to submit technical specifications of its system (technical specifications under Art. 6) to the Central Bank of Russia, which upon approval will include the operator in a public register of operators of information systems (Art. 7). Without inclusion into the public register, the operation of information systems in which digital financial assets are issued would be illegal (implied by Art. 5 para. 2). The operator of the information system maintains a register of its users (Art. 8) and is liable especially for loss of assets and breaches of the DFAL (Art. 9). It is obliged to provide the information contained in the records of the information system about digital financial assets belonging to their owner to public authorities (Art. 6 para. 3). It helps Russian authorities to impose trading bans (Art. 11 para. 13 ff.).

---

to certain legislative acts of the Russian Federation"; available (*translated in English*) at: https://beck-link.de/s82rt (accessed 12.01.2021).

[61] On the theory of regulation through intermediaries: Goldsmith and Wu (eds), *Who Controls the Internet: Illusions of a Borderless World* (OUP, 2006).

Art. 4 para. 5 provides that the rights certified by digital financial assets are transferred to the new owner in the moment the record is made in the information system of such a transition in accordance with the rules of the information system. As such the information contained in the information system is constitutive for the legal status of crypto token.

29 One central aspect of the law is to introduce a 'definition of digital currency that may not be a means of payment.' Under the very broad definition of Art. 1 para. 3, digital currencies are a

> 'set of electronic data (digital code or designation) contained in the information system, which are offered and (or) can be accepted as a means of payment that is not a monetary unit of the Russian Federation, a monetary unit of a foreign state and (or) an international monetary unit of account, and (or) as an investment and in respect of which there is no person obliged to each owner of such electronic data, with the exception of the operator and (or) nodes of the information system, which are only obliged to ensure compliance with the procedure for issuing these electronic data and their relation to actions to make (change) entries in such an information system to its rules.'

At the same time, the law states that the holding of digital currency, as well as the receipt and the transfer of digital currency holdings are only legal if so, declared by the Russian administration. As a rule, digital currencies are no legitimate consideration in transactions (Art. 14 para. 5).

30 The DFAL establishes a comprehensive system of state control for trade in crypto assets. In practice, everything will depend on the territorial scope of the law. If the Central Bank of Russia considers any transaction in crypto assets from or to Russia constitutes 'circulation of digital financial assets (...) in the Russian Federation' (cf. Art. 1 para. 1), all transactions outside of the DFAL will be illegal. However, the DFAL does not contain general[62] sanctions for that case – the immediate consequence being that transactions made outside of its system are deprived of legal protection and enforcement in Russia. It remains to be seen if this is incentive enough to establish a flourishing ecosystem for crypto trade under the rather strict state control.

III. International Aspects of Crypto Investments

31 Several aspects for crypto investments and transactions need to be taken into account in an international context. The following section of this chapter will cover possible sanctions and consequences because of investments or transactions using crypto technology that are carried out across Russian borders. For this purpose, the foundations of Russian sanctions law will first be illustrated (→ para. 32–33). Then the question of whether investments from foreign countries into Russia are allowed and how they might be sanctioned will be discussed (→ para. 34). Finally, it is important to examine which rules and regulations exist for crypto transactions and investments from Russia into foreign countries (→ para. 35–39).

---

[62] See Art.25 amending the Federal Law 'On the prohibition of certain categories of persons to open and have accounts (deposits), keep cash and valuables in foreign banks located outside the territory of the Russian Federation, own and (or) use foreign financial instruments' – with a prohibition for certain groups (of mostly public officials) only. Note also that there is also a draft for amending the Russian criminal code with regards to breaches of the DFAL.

§ 21. Russia

1. Russian Law

a) Foundations of Russian Sanctions Law. Sanctions law as it is understood in this context, encompasses all norms that establish penalties by Russian authorities for certain – mostly extremist or terrorist – illegal activities that are not exclusively governed by criminal law. The foundations of Russian sanctions law concern all legal measures available in order to impose a penalty on such crimes. In Russia, the relevant administrative authorities to impose sanctions are the government of the Federal Republic of Russia, the State Duma, the Security Council, the Federation Council of the Federal Assembly, various Ministries, and the Central Bank of the Russian Federation (CBR). Every sanction is firstly imposed by presidential orders, whereupon the sanctioned persons or legal entities are put on a sanctioned persons list. Sanctioned persons can be Russian citizens or foreign persons having domicile in Russia, sanctioned legal entities can be any legal entities established under Russian law. Once a person is put on the sanctioned persons list, its bank accounts can be suspended. For legal entities, the bank accounts of those persons of the legal entity may be suspended whose involvement in critical activities is supported by existing information. For non-monetary assets which the sanctioned persons possess, 'conditions are created under which the person will be practically deprived of the opportunity to dispose of the assets'.[63] The responsible authority for these actions is the Federal Financial Monitoring Service of Russia, the so called 'Rosfinmonitoring'.[64]

For certain transactions, persons and legal entities can get specific permissions issued by the Federal Service for Technical and Export Control or by the government directly. These allow them to carry out transactions and exports which would usually be sanctioned. The permissions can be issued for one-time-use as well as for continued use. In any case, it is important to ensure that the goods the permission is granted for are always under the control of the Russian legal entity which has been granted the permission. Permissions are exclusively granted to Russian legal entities.

If one person or legal entity has breached the conditions of the permit or conducted trading without such a permission, it can be held liable not only under civil law, but also under criminal law. The responsible legal authorities to investigate criminal offences are the Investigative Committee, the Ministry of Interior Affairs, and the Federal Security Service. In Russian criminal law, there is only personal liability. However, legal entities which have been involved in criminal offences should expect that goods would be confiscated and that banned products would be destroyed. Beyond that, they can be banned from further international trading.[65]

b) Sanctions of Foreign Crypto Investments into Russia Under Russian law. As stated above (→ para. 11–13, 20–30), the regulatory law is not comprehensive enough to conclude that using cryptocurrencies will be legal in Russia.[66] Thus, it is not easy to evaluate the possible consequences for foreigners investing in crypto in Russia or carrying out transactions in Russia using cryptocurrencies. Cryptocurrencies will be forbidden as a means of payment in the near future in Russia (under Art. 14 of the DFAL). However, holding crypto assets is not illegal and there are no specific signs that

---

[63] Mattila and Belotserkovskaya, Russia: Sanctions 2020, (ICLG, 2019), available at: https://beck-link.de/cb5n4 (accessed 12.01.2021).

[64] *Rosfinmonitoring*, available at: https://beck-link.de/6h3b6 (accessed 12.01.2021); Mattila and Belotserkovskaya, ibid.

[65] Mattila and Belotserkovskaya, ibid.

[66] Analytical Credit Rating Agency (ACRA), 'Cryptocurrency holdings concentration in Russia offsets risk for the national financial system' (June 2018), available at: https://beck-link.de/stws4 (accessed 12.01.2020).

it will be.⁶⁷ Founding a company that issues cryptocurrencies ('mining', → § 1) is not illegal for now but seeking legal advice from Russian lawyers in this regard is highly recommendable.⁶⁸ For now, only a few exchange tools and platforms exist that enable the purchase of crypto assets in Russia.⁶⁹ Holding cryptocurrency assets can be a high risk, as the regulatory laws can change quickly.⁷⁰

35 **c) International Crypto Transactions from Russia into foreign Countries.** Naturally, it is not only important to discuss whether investing in Russia in crypto as a foreigner is legal in Russia, but also to what extent Russian citizens or legal entities have the opportunity to legally invest in other countries in crypto. The relevant question here is if it is permitted for 'Russian money' to leave Russia via cryptocurrencies.

There are mainly two reasons why Russian citizens and legal entities would try to invest in crypto outside of Russia or why they would try to use cryptocurrencies to transfer Russian money out of Russia. Both have to do with the fact that in Russia, it is easy for the authorities to freeze bank accounts and to gain knowledge on the financial activities of bank account holders.⁷¹

36 When discussing whether investments in foreign countries (or transactions) are allowed out of Russia, it is important to look at the general rules that exist for exports out of Russia first. In Russia, exporting goods to other countries requires a specific permission which is issued by the customs authorities. Anyone who wishes to import or export into or out of Russia has to set up a legal entity which meets certain criteria set out by the Russian government and authorities. One of the requirements is that a trade license has been obtained from the Ministry of Industry and Trade in Russia, furthermore, there needs to be a specific permission for the traded goods.⁷² In any event, there are probably only a few instances where investing in crypto assets in foreign countries would fall under the scope of the general export regulations of Russia.

37 It is equally unlikely that such investments are a breach of certain federal laws which restrict investment possibilities in foreign countries, such as the Federal Law No. 127-FZ 'On Measures of Impact (Countermeasures) on the Unfriendly Actions of the United States of America and Other Foreign Countries'. This law has been passed to initiate countermeasures against the sanctions of the USA against Russia.⁷³ It is only applicable to certain goods and valuables, which do not include cryptocurrencies or other virtual currencies or assets.⁷⁴

Taking these regulations into account, it becomes clear that it is not illegal for Russian citizens or legal entities to invest in foreign countries' crypto projects, provided that they observe reporting duties under Russian tax law. However, one cannot expect

---

[67] Colin First, 'How to Buy Bitcoin in Russia?', available at: https://beck-link.de/8z4hn (accessed 12.01.2020).
[68] Lawyersrussia.com, 'Set Up a Cryptocurrency Company in Russia' (December 2018), available at: https://beck-link.de/ch6ct (accessed 12.01.2020).
[69] Colin First, 'How to Buy Bitcoin in Russia?', available at: https://beck-link.de/8z4hn (accessed 12.01.2020).
[70] Analytical Credit Rating Agency, 'Cryptocurrency holdings concentration in Russia offsets risk for the national financial system' (June 2018), available at: https://beck-link.de/stws4 (accessed 12.01.2020).
[71] Dixon, 'Russia freezes bank accounts of opposition leader Navalny – and the rest of his family, including 11-year-old son' (March 2020), available at: https://beck-link.de/wyk4h (accessed 12.01.2020).
[72] LawyersRussia.com, 'Importing and Exporting in Russia' (February 2020), available at: https://beck-link.de/t5yy3 (accessed 12.01.2020).
[73] President of Russia, 'Law on measures (countermeasures) against unfriendly actions of the United States of America and other foreign countries' (June 2018), available at: https://beck-link.de/hm2n3 (accessed 12.01.2020).
[74] Vodogreeva, 'The USA and other foreign countries sanctions law has come into effect' (June 2018), available at: https://beck-link.de/e5wkx (accessed 12.01.2020).

that the Russian government and authorities are endorsing such investments, as it is generally known that crypto transactions cannot be controlled as easily by the state than usual money transfers via bank accounts.[75] As the regulatory framework in Russia for cryptocurrencies is fragmentary, such investments and transactions are still *generally* allowed. However, that does not mean that indirect pressure would not be put on persons who carry out such investments or transactions.

2. EU/US-Sanctions

Crypto assets can be used to circumvent the EU- or US-sanctions against Russia – and also the Russian sanctions against the EU or USA. **38**

The EU and US-sanctions against Russia are implemented as export restrictions.[76] The general aim is to limit transactions of money in exchange for goods. This basic principle can be undermined by using cryptocurrencies, as it is not clear which consideration is paid for a token. The (alleged) anonymity of the blockchain technology and of cryptocurrencies makes it difficult for state authorities of any state to retrace transactions. As these kinds of currencies function by using a decentralized network (→ § 1 para. 7–15), there is no central server that could be located and seized. The network generally is not traceable and offers – if not complete anonymity at least – pseudonymity; for this reason, it is impossible to identify the participants and the traffic.

This naturally leads to the result that crypto transactions have the potential to circumvent these kinds of sanctions. The same applies to sanctions of Russia against the EU or US. Any kind of export or import restriction is hardly controllable if the exchange currency is virtual. Even as the use of cryptocurrencies in Russia as a payment tool is to be banned (see (→ para. 29), the question remains unanswered how authorities will locate users paying with crypto. In conclusion, cryptocurrencies make it hard to enforce international sanctions. **39**

C. The Central Bank of Russia as a Potential Regulator

Although it seems at least possible that there could be an additional committee or institution regulating crypto assets, the 'Bank Rossii', the Central Bank of Russia, is the main financial institution in the country. It is controlled by the state of Russia and succeeds the 'Central Bank of the Soviet Union'. Regarding the question of which Russian institution would fit best as a regulator of crypto assets, the CBR surely is the only *existing* institution in Russia which could fulfil this task. In this context, it seems appropriate to ask about the competences of the Central Bank of Russia (→ para. 41) and the tasks it might fulfil if it attains the status of a 'crypto assets regulator' (→ para. 42). **40**

The competences of the CBR are set out in Art. 75 of the Russian Constitution.[77] It states that the CBR is supposed to carry out the issuance of money exclusively and that it is not allowed to initiate the issuance of currencies other than the Ruble (→ also **41**

---

[75] Baydakova, 'Russian Activists Use Bitcoin, and the Kremlin Doesn't Like It' (July 2020), available at: https://beck-link.de/x8m5d (accessed 12.01.2020).

[76] For more detail Burke and Ogonyants, 'Die EU-Wirtschaftssanktionen gegen Russland und die russischen Gegensanktionen', (2016) 6 *Zeitschrift für Internationales Wirtschaftsrecht (IWRZ)*, 264; Steininger, 'Eine Zusammenfassung der wichtigsten Sanktionen der EU und der USA, Gegenmaßnahmen Russlands sowie der Lokalisierungspolitik' (2018) *Wirtschaft und Recht in Europa (WiRO)*, 46.

[77] Used translation: Constitute project, 'Russian Federation's Constitution of 1993 with Amendments through 2008' (2008), available at: https://beck-link.de/p7scz (accessed 12.02.2021).

Part C. Country Reports

para. 10). Furthermore, its central task is to protect and ensure the stability of the Ruble. Further status, goals, functions and power of the CBR are defined by the Federal Law No. 86-FZ 'On the Central Bank of the Russian Federation (Bank of Russia)'. Officially, the CBR is formally independent from the Russian government, whereas – as in many other jurisdictions – there is a certain tension arising from the fact that it is controlled by the government.[78]

42 One of the first tasks of a 'crypto-regulator' would surely be to *allow* or *not allow* certain virtual currencies such as Bitcoin or Ethereum. This is in line with DFAL, which provides for the Central Bank of Russia's supervision of the trading agents and information systems providers. Although the DFAL currently does not assign the task of legalizing a certain cryptocurrency to the CBR, it would be the only logical player to fulfil such task, as its main mission is to protect the stability of the Ruble as Russia's currency. Another important task for it would be to appoint trusted service providers for crypto holdings. Also, it could inform market participants about risks or possible crimes in connection with cryptocurrency-trading. Finally, there could be informational duties of the CBR (such as the duty to bring forward statistics) towards the State Duma or the Russian government. These could be helpful as these institutions have to regulate cryptocurrencies.

D. Conclusion

43 The situation of crypto assets in Russia is complex. While crypto assets are not a mass phenomenon, Russian entrepreneurs are an excellent source for services in connection with the establishment and layout of crypto asset infrastructure. The use of crypto assets in Russia seems often to be conflicting with politics, so that the Russian Duma's step to limit the use of cryptocurrencies and to introduce intermediaries into the trade of crypto assets under the new Digital Financial Assets Law is not surprising. The procedures for registering and trading for operators of information systems still need to prove their efficiency in the future and trade with non-registered operators from outside of Russia still seems possible for Russian citizens. Investors should be aware of the risk that quick changes in Russian law may impede the disposal of their crypto assets significantly, so it is advisable to monitor the market and the regulatory framework closely.

---

[78] Weidner, 'The Organisation and Structure of Central Banks' (2017), available at: https://beck-link.de/3rkw5 (accessed 12.02.2021).

§ 22
United States of America

Literature: Castellano, 'Towards a General Framework for a Common Definition of 'Securities': Financial Markets Regulation in Multilingual Contexts', (2012) 17 *Uniform Law Review*, 449, 457; Clayton, 'Statement on Cryptocurrencies and Initial Coin Offerings' (December 2017), available at https://beck-link.de/cs4n2 (accessed 19.5.2021); Coffey, 'The Economic Realities of a 'Security': Is There a More Meaningful Formula?', (1966) 18 *Case Western Reserve Law Review*, 367; Cox, Hillman and Langevoort (eds), *Securities Regulation, Cases and Matherials* (8th Edition, Wolters Kluwer, 2017); Debevoise and Plimpton, 'Securities Law Analysis of Blockchain Tokens' (December 2016), available at https://beck-link.de/f6pva (accessed 19.5.2021); De Martino, Brown and Silva, 'First SEC Enforcement Action Against Unregistered Digital Token Exchange' (November 2018), available at https://beck-link.de/3kayk (accessed 19.5.2021); Guseva, 'A Conceptual Framework for Digital-Asset Securities: Tokens and Coins As Debt And Equity', (2021) 80 *Maryland Law Review*, 166; Guseva, 'The Leviathan of Securities Regulation in Crypto-Offerings: A Cost-Benefit Analysis' (December 2020), available at https://beck-link.de/3p7dn (accessed 19.5.2021); Henderson and Raskin, 'A Regulatory Classification of Digital Assets: Towards an Operational Howey Test for Cryptocurrencies, ICOs, and Other Digital Assets', (2019) *Columbia Business Law Review*, 443; Hinman, 'Division of Corp. Fin., SEC, Remarks at the Yahoo Finance All Markets Summit: Crypto' (June 2018), available at https://beck-link.de/y3p8b (accessed 19.5.2021); Kaal and Dell'Erba, 'Blockchain Innovation in Private Investment Funds – A Comparative Analysis of the United States and Europe' (July 2017), available at https://beck-link.de/y3z8z (accessed 19.5.2021); Michael Del Castillo, 'SEC Launches Fintech Hub to Engage with Cryptocurrency Startups and More' (October 2018), available at https://beck-link.de/h2s66 (accessed 19.5.2021); Moffitt, 'The Fifty U.S. States and Cryptocurrency Regulations' (July 2018), available at https://beck-link.de/thb7p (accessed 19.5.2021); M. R. Albert, 'The Howey test turns 64: are the Courts grading this test on a curve?', (2011) 2 *William and Mary Business Law Review*, 1; Patti, 'Prodotti finanziari e contratti con i consumatori. Una recente pronuncia della Corte di giustizia a confronto con la *securities law* Americana', (2011) 5 *Giurisprudenza commerciale*, 1015; Peirce, 'Running on Empty: A proposal to fill the gap between regulation and decentralization' (February 2020), available at https://beck-link.de/e63md (accessed 19.5.2021); Shin, 'After Contact By SEC, Protostarr Token Shuts Down Post-ICO, Will Refund Investors' (September 2017), available at https://beck-link.de/3tas8 (accessed 19.5.2021); Vigna and Loder, 'SEC Rejects Nine Proposed Bitcoin Exchange-Traded Funds' (August 2018), available at https://beck-link.de/zdr2h (accessed 19.5.2021); Wilson, 'A Call to Clarify the Regulatory Scope of Money Transmitter Laws' (June 2013), available at https://beck-link.de/638tp (accessed 19.5.2021).

Outline

	para.
A. Introduction	1
B. The CFTC	2
C. The SEC	4
I. The Stages of Intervention	4
1. General Aspects	4
2. Increased activity in relation to digital tokens and cryptocurrencies	5
3. Identifying four main stages of intervention	6
II. First Stage: The DAO Report and ICO Tokens as Securities	7
1. The Howey Test	7
a) The Notion of 'Security' and a Fundamental Four-Prong Test	7
b) 'Security' as 'Investment Contract'	8
c) ICO tokens as 'Securities'	9
2. Investment of Money: A Broad Definition	10
3. Common Enterprise: Different Approaches the Different Circuits	11

　　　　4. Expectation of Profits... 12
　　　　　　a) United Housing Foundation, Inc. v. Forman 12
　　　　　　b) A Broad Spectrum of Return or Income 13
　　　　5. Managerial Efforts of Others: SEC v. Glenn W. Turner.............. 14
　　III. Second Stage: Going Beyond the Semantics of Phrases in the REcoin
　　　　and Munchee Cases... 15
　　　　1. Emergency Action to Charge REcoin and DRC.............................. 15
　　　　2. Munchee... 16
　　　　　　a) Confirmation of Previous Analysis (REcoin): Illegal
　　　　　　　　Unregistered Securities Offering 16
　　　　　　b) In re Tomahawk Exploration LLC 17
　　　　3. Recent Cases and Developments....................................... 18
　　　　　　a) In re Carriereq, Inc., d/b/a AirFox (AirFox) and In re Paragon
　　　　　　　　Coin Inc.. 18
　　　　　　b) William H. Hinman's 2018 Speech 19
　　　　　　c) The role of a Third Party 20
　　　　　　d) Beyond Howey: Gary Plastics 21
　　IV. Third Stage: Collaboration with 'Market Professionals, and
　　　　Especially Gatekeepers'... 22
　　　　1. The 'client-attorney' relationship 22
　　　　2. The endorsement of ICOs by celebrities 23
　　V. Fourth Stage: Infrastructures Supporting ICOs, Tokens, and
　　　Cryptocurrencies, Including Broker-Dealers and Digital Asset Hedge
　　　Funds 24
　　　　1. Digital tokens as 'securities' to extend the enforcement activity to
　　　　　　any related entity... 24
　　　　2. Online trading platforms... 25
　　　　3. EtherDelta.. 26
　　　　4. Crypto Asset Management LLP... 27
　　VI. Recent Regulatory Initiatives... 28
　　　　1. The Token Taxonomy Act... 28
　　　　2. Hester Peirce and Difficulties of Applying Howey to ICOs 29
　　　　3. The Securities Clarity Act and the Digital Commodity Exchange
　　　　　　Act 30
　　　　4. A 'Single Opt-in National Regulatory Framework for Digital
　　　　　　Commodity Trading Platforms'... 31
　D. Additional Initiatives by Other Authorities 32

A. Introduction

1　The architecture of American regulatory agencies supervising financial markets peculiarly divides responsibilities of the Securities and Exchanges Commission (SEC) and the Commodity Futures Trading Commission (CFTC). While the SEC is in charge of protecting investors, maintaining fair, orderly, and efficient markets, and facilitating capital formation, with a clear focus on 'securities', the mission of the CFTC is to foster open, transparent, competitive, and financially sound markets, in the context of 'commodities'. By working to avoid systemic risk, the CFTC aims to protect market users and their funds, consumers, and the public from fraud, manipulation, and abusive practices related to derivatives and other products that are subject to the Commodity Exchange Act (CEA). Therefore, as the CFTC has clarified, its 'jurisdiction is implicated when a virtual currency is used in a derivatives contract, or if there is fraud or manipulation involving a virtual currency traded in interstate commerce.'[1] Recent

---

[1] LabCFTC, 'A CFTC Primer on Virtual Currencies' (October 2017), available at https://beck-link.de/h6bxf (accessed 19.5.2021).

cases, including Telegram and Ripple, confirm the dual extended jurisdiction triggered by the two broad definitions of 'security' and 'commodity', that might be both relevant in the context of digital assets and cryptocurrencies. Courts have also noted the importance of overlapping regulatory regimes. Judge Jack B. Weinstein of the Eastern District of New York upheld the CFTC's determination that virtual currencies (including those with respect to which no futures contract is offered) are indeed commodities under the CEA. More importantly, Judge Weinstein confirmed that '[f]ederal agencies may have concurrent or overlapping jurisdiction over a particular issue.'[2] Multiple legal treatments result from regulators' efforts to apply the existing regulatory framework to new products, and do not lead to unreasonable overlaps. The multiple legal treatments derive from ICOs' multiple characteristics, and trigger different regulations corresponding to different kinds of protection and regulatory answers.

The following chapter reflects this dual dimension implicated in the context of digital assets, and will consider further initiatives by other authorities.

B. The CFTC

In 2014, former CFTC Chairman Timothy Massad decided that the agency could have jurisdiction over Bitcoin and more generally over virtual currencies, depending 'on the facts and circumstances pertaining to any particular activity in question,' and stated that derivative contracts based on a virtual currency represented 'one area within our responsibility.'[3] *Coinflip*[4] introduced a new era of 'Bitcoin' as a commodity, with the CFTC order stating that the CEA covers 'all services, rights, and interests in which contracts for future delivery are presently or in the future dealt in,' and further stated that the definition of "commodity' is broad… Bitcoin and other virtual currencies are encompassed in the definition and properly defined as commodities.'[5] Similar to the definition of 'security,' the definition of 'commodity' is very broad, encompassing a wide range of products: physical commodities, such as agricultural products or natural resources, as well as currencies and interest rates.[6] Further, the definition of 'commodity' encompasses 'all services, rights, and interests… in which contracts for future delivery are presently or in the future dealt in.'[7] The CFTC charged Coinflip with a violation of Sections 4c(b)[8] and 5h(a)(l)[9] CEA by 'conducting activity related to commodity options contrary to Commission Regulations and by operating a facility for the trading or processing of swaps without being registered as a swap execution

---

[2] United States District Court 6.3.2018 – Commodity Futures Trading Commission v. McDonnell, 287 F. Supp. 3d 213, 228 (E.D.N.Y. 2018).
[3] Massad, 'Testimony before the U.S. Senate Committee on Agriculture, Nutrition & Forestry' (December 2014), available at https://beck-link.de/82sav (accessed 19.5.2021).
[4] *In re* Commodity Futures Trading Commission 17.9.2015 – Coinflip, Inc., CFTC No. 15-29, 2015 WL 5535736, available at https://beck-link.de/hy7zc (accessed 19.5.2021).
[5] Ibid.
[6] Art. 1(a)(9) of the Commodity Exchange Act (CEA) and Art. 1(a)(9) of the U.S.Code (2012).
[7] Ibid.
[8] Art. 4(c)(b) CEA makes it unlawful for any person to 'offer to enter into, enter into or confirm the execution of, any transaction involving any commodity … which is of the character of, or is commonly known to the trade as, an 'option' …, 'bid', 'offer', 'put', [or] 'call' … contrary to any rule, regulation, or order of the Commission prohibiting any such transaction'.
[9] Art. 5(h)(a)(1) CEA forbids any person from operating 'a facility for the trading or processing of swaps unless the facility is registered as a swap execution facility or as a designated contract market …'.

facility or designated contract market.'[10] Specifically, Coinflip 'operated an online facility named Derivabit, offering to connect buyers and sellers of Bitcoin option contracts.'[11]

3   In October 2017, the CFTC issued a report indicating it was open to the possibility that virtual currencies and virtual tokens may trigger different regulation. In its document the CFTC expressed the position that the potential categorization of ICO tokens as securities would not be inconsistent with the CFTC's 'determination that virtual currencies are commodities and that virtual tokens may be commodities or derivatives contracts depending on the particular facts and circumstances.'[12] Similar to the definition of 'security,' the definition of 'commodity' is very broad, encompassing a wide range of products, *i.e.* physical commodities, such as an agricultural products or natural resources, as well currencies or interest rates. Further, the definition of 'commodity' encompasses 'all services, rights, and interests ... in which contracts for future delivery are presently or in the future dealt in.'[13]

C. The SEC

I. The Stages of Intervention

1. General Aspects

4   The identification of the main issues connected to ICOs and digital assets was a gradual process at the SEC. Certainly the creation of the Distributed Ledger Technology Working Group within the SEC was a first step, which was instrumental in developing a deeper understanding of the phenomenon and the risks connected to blockchain. In addition, the Working Group contributed to coordinated efforts between the different divisions and offices within the Commission. The creation of the Cyber Unit within the Enforcement Division of the SEC further demonstrates the intention of the SEC to fully enforce federal securities law in the cryptospace, due to the risks for both investors and market integrity emerging from virtual currency and blockchain technology.[14] The recent creation of the Strategic Hub for Innovation and Financial Technology ('Finhub') served to grant 'meetings and other assistance relating to FinTech issues arising under the federal securities laws,' as the SEC explained.[15] Finhub is a new portal, launched in

---

[10] *In re* Commodity Futures Trading Commission 17.9.2015 – Coinflip, Inc., CFTC No. 15-29, 2015 WL 5535736, p. 2.

[11] Ibid.

[12] LabCFTC, 'A CFTC Primer on Virtual Currencies' (October 2017), available at https://beck-link.de/h6bxf (accessed 19.5.2021).

[13] See Art 1(a)(9) CEA, 'The term 'commodity' means wheat, cotton, rice, corn, oats, barley, rye, flaxseed, grain sorghums, mill feeds, butter, eggs, Solanum tuberosum (Irish potatoes), wool, wool tops, fats and oils (including lard, tallow, cottonseed oil, peanut oil, soybean oil, and all other fats and oils), cottonseed meal, cottonseed, peanuts, soybeans, soybean meal, livestock, livestock products, and frozen concentrated orange juice, and all other goods and articles, except onions (as provided by section 13–1 of this title) and motion picture box office receipts (or any index, measure, value, or data related to such receipts), and all services, rights, and interests (except motion picture box office receipts, or any index, measure, value or data related to such receipts) in which contracts for future delivery are presently or in the future dealt in'.

[14] Stephanie Avakian, Co-Director, Division of Enforcement, 'The SEC Enforcement Division's Initiatives Regarding Retail Investor Protection and Cybersecurity' (October 2017), transcript available at https://beck-link.de/3xh6s (accessed 19.5.2021).

[15] US Securities and Exchange Commission, 'Request Form for FinTech-Related Meetings and Other Assistance', available at https://beck-link.de/tw3xb (accessed 19.5.2021).

October 2018, that should allow fintech entrepreneurs to create compliant platforms before the launch of their project, with efficiency benefits for both good faith entrepreneurs and the SEC.[16] These institutional improvements emphasize the role that technology is currently playing in reshaping the governance of regulatory agencies.

2. Increased activity in relation to digital tokens and cryptocurrencies

Starting in 2017, the SEC became increasingly active with regard to cryptocurrencies. **5** In March 2017, the SEC denied the authorization to the Winklevoss Bitcoin Exchange Traded Fund ('ETF').[17] The creators intended the Bitcoin ETF to be a common stock fund pegged to the price of Bitcoin, and it would have allowed investors to purchase Bitcoin without creating a personal wallet.[18] In rejecting the application, the SEC reasoned that the proposed fund was susceptible to fraud because of the unregulated nature of Bitcoin,[19] dismissing the proposed rule change that would have allowed the listing of the shares of the Winklevoss Bitcoin Trust.[20] The SEC's decision demonstrated its distrust towards the crypto asset class as a whole, especially funds attempting to trade digital currencies, and it foreshadowed future decisions disregarding ICOs as a non-regulated framework.[21] On subsequent occasions, the SEC confirmed the view expressed in the March 2017 Disapproval Order. On July 26, 2018 the SEC confirmed its July 2018 Disapproval Order,[22] in its response to the Winklevosses' petition for review of the March 2017 Disapproval Order. The SEC provided a consistent view with the March 2017 Disapproval Order, confirming its concerns about the bitcoin spot markets. The same risks of fraud and manipulation led the SEC to reject nine proposed ETFs backed by bitcoin future contracts,[23] highlighting concerns related to the exchanges where such ETFs would have been listed.[24]

3. Identifying four main stages of intervention

After the debate on Bitcoin ETFs approval, clearly identifiable steps opened the **6** season of the SEC enforcement strategy in cryptocurrencies. First, in July 2017, the SEC issued the DAO Report, which categorized ICOs as securities and applied securities laws to them. Second, in October and December 2017, the SEC defined 'security' with regard to ICOs, going beyond the semantics of phrases used in offering documents such as 'initial membership offer' and 'utility token,' as evidenced in the REcoin and Munchee

---

[16] Michael Del Castillo, 'SEC Launches Fintech Hub to Engage with Cryptocurrency Startups and More' (October 2018), available at https://beck-link.de/h2s66 (accessed 19.5.2021).

[17] SEC, 'Order Disapproving a Proposed Rule Change, Exchange Act Release No. 34-80206' (March 2017), available at https://beck-link.de/yfwm3 (accessed 19.5.2021). The SEC disapproved the proposed rule change that would have allowed the listing of the shares of the Winklevoss Bitcoin Trust.

[18] Brandom, 'The SEC Just Handed Bitcoin a Huge Setback' (March 2017), available at https://beck-link.de/tmas2 (accessed 19.5.2021).

[19] SEC, 'Order Disapproving a Proposed Rule Change, Exchange Act Release No. 34-80206' (March 2017), available at https://beck-link.de/yfwm3 (accessed 19.5.2021).

[20] Ibid, p. 2.

[21] Kaal and Dell'Erba, 'Blockchain Innovation in Private Investment Funds – A Comparative Analysis of the United States and Europe' (July 2017), available at https://beck-link.de/y3z8z (accessed 19.5.2021).

[22] SEC, 'Order Setting Aside Action by Delegated Authority & Disapproving a Proposed Rule Change, Exchange Act Release No. 34-83723' (July 2018), p. 5, available at https://beck-link.de/kktm2 (accessed 19.5.2021).

[23] Vigna and Loder, 'SEC Rejects Nine Proposed Bitcoin Exchange-Traded Funds' (August 2018), available at https://beck-link.de/zdr2h (accessed 19.5.2021).

[24] SEC, 'Order Disapproving a Proposed Rule Change to List and Trade the Shares of the ProShares Bitcoin ETF and the ProShares Short Bitcoin ETF, Exchange Act Release No. 34-83904' (August 2018), p. 2–3, available at https://beck-link.de/8v2nf (accessed 19.5.2021).

cases. Third, in January 2018, the SEC advocated for more collaboration with 'market professionals, and especially gatekeepers,' who have a duty to act responsibly and in accordance with the highest standards. Fourth, in March 2018, the SEC considered the infrastructure supporting ICOs, tokens, and cryptocurrencies; if coins and tokens are securities, the platforms for trading them may be subject to the securities laws applicable to exchanges. This was exemplified by the enforcement action against EtherDelta in November 2018 for being an unregistered digital token exchange. Furthermore, the recent creation of FinHub and the SEC's commitment to a 'path to compliance' expressed in two recent cases, *In the Matter of Carriereq, Inc., d/b/a Airfox* and *In the Matter of Paragon Coin Inc.*, may have opened an era of enhanced collaboration between the agency and market participants. In this environment, market participants can benefit from prior guidance provided by FinHub and opportunities to comply with the securities laws after a breach. The following paragraphs will consider this evolution.

II. First Stage: The DAO Report and ICO Tokens as Securities

1. The Howey Test

7   **a) The Notion of 'Security' and a Fundamental Four-Prong Test.** After the rejection of the Winklevoss ETF, the SEC issued the DAO Report in July 2017.[25] It was a stepping stone in the SEC's identification of a more structured regulatory framework for ICOs by characterizing ICO tokens as securities under the Securities Exchange Act. In the DAO Report, the SEC suggested the adoption of a case by case approach, considering that '[w]hether a particular investment transaction involves the offer or sale of a security – regardless of the terminology or technology used – will depend on the facts and circumstances, including the economic realities of the transaction.'[26] The SEC stated that the characterisation of ICOs' tokens as securities should be made taking into account the constitutive elements of the investment contract by applying the so-called *Howey* test, a four-prong test[27] based on the following parameters: 'investment of money,' 'common enterprise,' 'expectation of profits,' and '[profits] to come solely from the efforts of the promoter or a third party.'[28] The *Howey* test proved to be a useful tool, due to its incorporation of 'a flexible rather than a static principle, one that is capable of adaptation to meet the countless and variable schemes devised by those who seek the use of the money of others on the promise of profits.'[29] An immediate consequence of this extension of securities regulation to ICO tokens was that after requesting information from the SEC, a blockchain-based startup (Protostarr) opted to cancel its ICO and consequentially refunded its investors.[30]

Under American securities law, Section 2(a)(1) of the Securities Act of 1933 provides a definition of 'security'. Section 2(a)(1) of the Securities Act of 1933 contains 'a laundry

---

[25] SEC, 'Release No. 81207 – Report of Investigation Pursuant to Section 21(a) of the Securities Exchange Act of 1934: The DAO' (July 2017), available at https://beck-link.de/5pfa8 (accessed 19.5.2021).
[26] Ibid.
[27] Similar to the SEC, the Canadian Security Administration adopted a four-prong test. See CSA, 'CSA Staff Notice 46-307: Cryptocurrency Offerings' (August 2017), available at https://beck-link.de/ze6sm (accessed 19.5.2021).
[28] Scholars tend to separate the 'expectation of profits' from the 'efforts of the promoter or a third party.' See Coffey, 'The Economic Realities of a 'Security': Is There a More Meaningful Formula?', (1966) 18 *Case Western Reserve Law Review*, 367, 373.
[29] The US Supreme Court 27.5.1946 – SEC v. W. J. Howey Co., 328 U.S. 293, 299.
[30] Shin, 'After Contact By SEC, Protostarr Token Shuts Down Post-ICO, Will Refund Investors' (September 2017), available at https://beck-link.de/3tas8 (accessed 19.5.2021).

list of examples'[31], encompassing typical financial instruments qualified as 'security', ('*note, stock, treasury stock, security future, bond, [...], transferable share, investment contract*') and provides a circular definition of 'security'[32], as '*any interest or instrument commonly known as a 'security*'.[33,34]

b) 'Security' as 'Investment Contract'. To clarify the definition of 'security', the Supreme Court intervened by explicitly providing the definition of 'investment contract', one of the financial instruments listed as security pursuant to the Section 2(a)(1) of the Securities Act of 1933: '*an investment contract for purposes of the Securities Act means a contract, transaction or scheme whereby a person invests his money in a common enterprise and is led to expect profits solely from the efforts of the promoter or a third party*'.[35] In addition, the Supreme Court clarified that the notions of 'investment contract' and 'any interest or instrument commonly known as a 'security' were equivalent, making the definition of 'investment contract' the general definition of 'security'.[36]

8

---

[31] Cox, Hillman and Langevoort (eds), *Securities Regulation, Cases and Matherials* (8th Edition, Wolters Kluwer, 2017).

[32] Patti, 'Prodotti finanziari e contratti con i consumatori. Una recente pronuncia della Corte di giustizia a confronto con la *securities law* Americana', (2011) 5 *Giurisprudenza commerciale*, 1015. The author emphasizes the presence of the '*definiendum*' within the '*definiens*'.

[33] Art. 2(a)(1) of the Securities Act of 1933 (15 U.S.C. 77B(a)(1)) defines '*securities*' in these terms: "*The term "security" means any note, stock, treasury stock, security future, bond, debenture, evidence of indebtedness, certificate of interest or participation in any profit-sharing agreement, collateral-trust certificate, preorganization certificate or subscription, transferable share, investment contract, voting-trust certificate, certificate of deposit for a security, fractional undivided interest in oil, gas, or other mineral rights, any put, call, straddle, option, or privilege on any security, certificate of deposit, or group or index of securities (including any interest therein or based on the value thereof), or any put, call, straddle, option, or privilege entered into on a national securities exchange relating to foreign currency, or, in general, any interest or instrument commonly known as a "security", or any certificate of interest or participation in, temporary or interim certificate for, receipt for, guarantee of, or warrant or right to subscribe to or purchase, any of the foregoing*". In addition, a further definition of 'security' is provided by the Art. 3(a)(10) of the Securities Exchange Act of 1934, (15 U.S.C. 78C(a)(10)). The Supreme Court has often considered the two definitions identical: see The US Supreme Court 8.3.1982 – Marine Bank v. Weaver, 455 U.S. 551, 556 n.3; The US Supreme Court 16.1.1979 International Brotherhood of Teamsters v. Daniel, 439 U.S. 551, 556 n. 7; The US Supreme Court 16.6.1975 – United Housing Foundation, Inc. v. Forman, 421 U.S. 837, 847 n.12; The US Supreme Court 18.12.1967 – Tcherepnin v. Knight, 389 U.S. 332, 335–336, 342. The Uniform Securities Act (2004), sec. 102(28), provides an identical definition of '*security*' as the one provided by the Securities Acts.

[34] The American regulators opted for a definition of 'security' "*in sufficiently broad and general terms so as to include within that definition the many types of instruments that in our commercial world fall within the ordinary concept of a security*", H. R. Rep. No. 85, 73d Cong., 1st Sess. 11 (1933). The Supreme Court emphasized the approach of the Congress in adopting a broad definition of 'security': 'In defining the scope of the market that it wished to regulate, Congress painted with a broad brush…[and] enacted a definition of 'security' sufficiently broad to encompass virtually any instrument that might be sold as investment in painted with a broad brush in defining the scope of the market that it wished to regulate. Howey, 328 U.S. at 299. According to the interpretation of the Supreme Court, this definition 'embodies a flexible rather than a static principle, one that is capable of adaptation to meet the countless and variable schemes devised by those who seek the use of the money of others on the promise of profits'. Howey, 328 at 299. 'Congress therefore did not attempt precisely to cabin the scope of the Securities Acts. Rather, it enacted a definition of 'security' sufficiently broad to encompass virtually any instrument that might be sold as an investment.' The US Supreme Court 21.2.1990 – Reves v. Ernst & Young, 494 U.S. 56, 61. See M. R. Albert, 'The *Howey Test* Turns 64: Are the Courts Grading this Test on a Curve?', (2011) 2 *William and Mary Business Law Review*, 1. See also Cox et al, ibid supra ft. 31. On the need to combine flexibility and clarity with regard to the definition of 'security', see Castellano, 'Towards a General Framework for a Common Definition of 'Securities': Financial Markets Regulation in Multilingual Contexts', (2012) 17 *Uniform Law Review*, 449, 457.

[35] The US Supreme Court 27.5.1946 – SEC v. W. J. Howey Co., 328 U.S. 293, 298–299.

[36] In United Housing Foundation v. Forman, the Supreme Court stated that '*We perceive no distinction, for present purposes, between an 'investment contract' and an 'instrument commonly known as a 'security*"

9   c) **ICO tokens as 'Securities'.** The SEC qualified the ICO tokens as securities after assessing the constitutive elements of the investment contract, applying the so-called 'Howey' test, in order to ascertain the existence of the four main components characterizing a security, as elaborated by the American case law: the *'investment of money', 'common enterprise', 'expectation of profits to come solely from the efforts of the promoter or a third party'*.[37] The Howey test is a useful tool, due to its characteristic, as explained by the Court, of incorporating 'a flexible rather than a static principle, one that is capable of adaptation to meet the countless and variable schemes devised by those who seek the use of the money of others on the promise of profits'.[38]

2. Investment of Money: A Broad Definition

10   Regarding the prong of the 'investment of money', *Howey*, as well as the cases that followed it, defined an investment of money in a broad manner, encompassing a broad spectrum of cases, including goods services or promissory notes, in addition to the typical provision of capital, assets and cash.[39] Since the Tokens are generally distributed through a sale by the issuer to the buyers with a predefined price per token, the 'investment of money' is likely to be satisfied, even under the existence of a capped total amount raised and purchased.[40] In the DAO Report, the SEC confirmed that DAO Tokens were received in exchange for ETH and therefore such investment would qualify as a 'contribution of value', creating an investment contract under Howey.[41]

3. Common Enterprise: Different Approaches the Different Circuits

11   In relation to the second prong, the 'common enterprise', different definitions of 'Common Enterprise' have been elaborated by the different circuits, due to the different tests used to assess whether a common enterprise exists. Three approaches predominate: (i) horizontal; (ii) narrow vertical and (iii) broad vertical. According to the Third, Sixth and Seventh Circuit, the concept of 'common enterprise' shall be interpreted adopting the perspective of the 'horizontal commonality': a plurality of investors confers assets to the enterprise and participates to the distributions of dividends and losses, proportionally to the investment; the Fifth and the Eleventh Circuit adopted the 'vertical commonality', existing when the success of the investment depends on the ability of the promoter, even when it acts solely as an intermediary without participating to the entrepreneurial risk and receives a fee for its intermediation; according to the Ninth Circuit, the common enterprise should depend on the ability of the promoter and he participates to the entrepreneurial risk.[42]

(US Supreme Court 16.6.1975 – United Housing Foundation, Inc. v. Forman, (nt. 25), 852), consistently with the case of the US Supreme Court 22.11.1943 – SEC v C.M. Joiner Leasing Corporation 320 U.S. 344, 351, where the Court provided a more general definition of 'security' ('many documents in which there is common trading for speculation or investment').

[37] Scholars tend to separate the 'expectation of profits' from the 'efforts of the promoter or a third party'. See Loss Seligman, Securities Regulation (New York), II, 1998 (updated with the 2003 supplement). See also Coffey, 'The Economic Realities of a 'Security': Is There a More Meaningful Formula?', (1966–67) 18 *Case Western Reserve Law Review*, 367.

[38] The US Supreme Court 27.5.1946 – SEC v. W. J. Howey Co., 328 U.S. 293, 299.

[39] See, e.g., The US Supreme Court 16.1.1979 – International Brotherhood of Teamsters v. Daniel, 439 U.S., 560 n.12; The US Court of Appeals 23.2.1976 – Hector v. Wiens, 533 F.2d 429, 432–33 (9th Cir.); United States District Court for the Northern District of Ohio 5.9.1975 – Sandusky Land, Ltd. V. Uniplan Groups, Inc., 400 F. Supp. 440, 445.

[40] See Debevoise and Plimpton, 'Securities Law Analysis of Blockchain Tokens' (December 2016), available at https://beck-link.de/f6pva (accessed 19.5.2021).

[41] SEC, 'Release No. 81207 – Report of Investigation Pursuant to Section 21(a) of the Securities Exchange Act of 1934: The DAO' (July 2017), p. 11, available at https://beck-link.de/5pfa8 (accessed 19.5.2021).

[42] Loss & Seligman support this view.

Analyzing the tokens under the different approaches, the results may be strongly divergent. Adopting the perspective of the horizontal commonality, whether the reward for work is correlated to the reward received by other participant, tokens are likely to be qualified as a common enterprise, since the rewards received by the token holders may be considered correlated, although the issuer has some control over the protocol.[43] A different conclusion, in the sense of the non-existence of the common enterprise, would be likely to be reached under both the two other approaches.[44]

4. Expectation of Profits

a) United Housing Foundation, Inc. v. Forman. The third prong, the *'Expectations of profits'*[45], was better clarified in the case *United Housing Foundation, Inc. v. Forman*[46], when the Supreme Court emphasized that the term 'profits' shall be referred to an increase in the value of the initial investment (as in the case *SEC v. C.M, Joiner Leasing Corporation*) or as the profits participation.[47] The Supreme Court has also stated that "what distinguishes a security transaction [...] is an investment where one parts with his money in the hope of receiving profits from the efforts of others, and not where he purchases a commodity for personal consumption or living quarters for personal use".[48] The Supreme Court emphasized the relevance of the expectation of profits in connection to the passivity of the investor with regard to the investment: therefore an investment contract shall be qualified as a 'security' only if a return is associated with the passivity of the investor. In Reves v. Ernst & Young[49] the term 'profits' has been interpreted in a more restrictive way, excluding a fix economic return from such definition.[50] Further, in Edwards, the Supreme Court considered that '[P]rofits include 'dividends, other periodic payments, or the increased value of the investment'.[51]

b) A Broad Spectrum of Return or Income. In the context of the tokens, the expectation of profits may encompass a broad spectrum of return or income determined by the condition of being a token holder, and it shall be assessed whether the expectation of profits is associated with a passive (depending on the efforts of others) or rather an active approach to the investment.[52] The expectation of profits resulting from the purchase of a token would primarily relate to whether the token holder receives (i) rights and/or (ii) investment interests. A case by case analysis of the content of the rights may be helpful to ascertain the active or passive nature of the investment: if a token provides its holder with the rights to utilize, contribute or license the use of the system in many different ways, that would likely imply the qualification of the token holder rather as an active investor.[53] In the DAO Report, the SEC concluded that

---

[43] See Debevoise and Plimpton, 'Securities Law Analysis of Blockchain Tokens' (December 2016), p. 14, available at https://beck-link.de/f6pva (accessed 19.5.2021).
[44] Ibid.
[45] The 'Expectations of profits' is a distinctive feature of the Howey test, when compared with the 'risk-capital test', emphasizing on the contrary the risk to lose the initial investment. See the Supreme Court of California 18.5.1961 – Silver Hills Country Club v. Sobieski, 55 Cal. 2d 811, 361 P.2d 906.
[46] See the US Supreme Court 16.6.1975 – United Housing Foundation, Inc. v. Forman, 421 U.S. 837, 852.
[47] See the US Supreme Court 18.12.1967 – Tcherepnin v. Knight, 389 U.S. 332.
[48] See the US Supreme Court 16.6.1975 – United Housing Foundation, Inc. v. Forman, 421 U.S. 837, 858.
[49] The US Supreme Court 21.2.1990 – Reves v. Ernst & Young, 494 U.S. 56, 68 n. 4.
[50] See Gabaldon, 'A Sense of a Security: An Empirical Study', (1999–2000) 25 Journal of Corporation Law, 307, 336.
[51] See the US Supreme Court 13.1.2004 – SEC v. Edwards, 540 U.S. at 394.
[52] See Debevoise and Plimpton, 'Securities Law Analysis of Blockchain Tokens' (December 2016), p. 17, available at https://beck-link.de/f6pva (accessed 19.5.2021).
[53] Ibid.

investors who purchased DAO Tokens were engaged in a common enterprises, reasonably expecting to earn profits through that enterprise,[54] adhering to the definition of 'profits', provided by the Supreme Court in Edwards. The SEC concluded that investors who purchased DAO tokens were aware that The DAO was a 'for-profit entity whose objective was to fund projects in exchange for a return on investment', and that 'a reasonable investor would have been motivated, at least in part, by the prospect of profits on their investment of ETH in The DAO'.[55]

5. Managerial Efforts of Others: SEC v. Glenn W. Turner

14   Regarding the fourth prong of the Howey-test, 'the managerial efforts of Others', the Supreme Court in *SEC v. Glenn W. Turner*[56] considered that a key issues is 'whether the efforts made by those other than the investor are the undeniably significant ones, those essential managerial efforts which affect the failure or success of the enterprise'. From this starting point, the SEC concluded that the DAO's investors relied on the managerial and entrepreneurial efforts of the DAO promoters, founders and curators, for the management of the DAO and proposals capable to generate profits for the DAO investors.[57] In the context of 'the managerial efforts of Others', the existence of voting rights could play a role, although it is not determinant to qualify tokens as securities. This will be the case only if they correspond to a significant managerial control, the holder as the resources and expertise to make a meaningful contribution and he participates in management.[58] The SEC noted that DAO Token holders were granted limited voting rights, and DAO token holders substantially relied on the managerial efforts of the promoters.[59] In fact, DAO token holders could only vote on proposals decided by the curators, and had not sufficient information 'to make informed voting decisions'.[60] Further, according to the SEC, the characteristics of pseudonymity and dispersion of the DAO Token holders were an obstacle for them 'to join together to effect change or to exercise meaning control'.[61]

III. Second Stage: Going Beyond the Semantics of Phrases in the REcoin and Munchee Cases

1. Emergency Action to Charge REcoin and DRC

15   In October 2017, the SEC brought an emergency action to charge REcoin and DRC (Diamond Reserve Club), two ICOs launched by Maksim Zaslavskiy, with violating

---

[54] SEC, 'Release No. 81207 – Report of Investigation Pursuant to Section 21(a) of the Securities Exchange Act of 1934: The DAO' (July 2017), p. 11, available at https://beck-link.de/5pfa8 (accessed 19.5.2021).
[55] Ibid, p. 12.
[56] See the US Court of Appeals of 1.2.1973 – SEC v. Glenn W. Turner Enters., Inc., 474 F.2d 476, 482 (9th Cir.).
[57] See SEC, 'Release No. 81207 – Report of Investigation Pursuant to Section 21(a) of the Securities Exchange Act of 1934: The DAO' (July 2017), p. 12, available at https://beck-link.de/5pfa8 (accessed 19.5.2021).
[58] See Debevoise and Plimpton, 'Securities Law Analysis of Blockchain Tokens' (December 2016), p. 17, available at https://beck-link.de/f6pva (accessed 19.5.2021).
[59] See SEC, 'Release No. 81207 – Report of Investigation Pursuant to Section 21(a) of the Securities Exchange Act of 1934: The DAO' (July 2017), p. 13, available at https://beck-link.de/5pfa8 (accessed 19.5.2021). The SEC quoted in the decisions of the US Court of Appeals of 1.2.1973- SEC v. Glenn W. Turner Enters., Inc., and 9.8.1989 – Long v. Shultz, 881 F.2d129, 137 (5th Cir.).
[60] Ibid, p. 14.
[61] Ibid, p. 14.

securities law.⁶² This decision is particularly relevant because of the interpretation of the semantics that the SEC used, not formalistically but strictly connected to the economic reality of the underlying offer. In the whitepaper and on the website of REcoin, Zaslavskiy did not refer to the terms 'ICO' or 'securities,' adopting instead the semantics of 'Initial Membership Offering' ('IMO').⁶³ The complaints stated: 'In an attempt to skirt the registration requirements of the federal securities laws, Defendants Zaslavskiy and Diamond have refashioned the sale of the purported Diamond interests as sales of 'memberships in a club,' and the Diamond ICO as an 'Initial Membership Offering' or 'IMO.' In reality, the supposed 'memberships' are in all material respects identical to the ownership attributes of purchasing the purported (but, indeed, non-existent) 'tokens' or 'coins' and are securities within the meaning of the securities laws.'⁶⁴ In a Facebook post, REcoin stated that an IMO is different from an ICO or an IPO.⁶⁵ However, the SEC concluded that such a distinction was 'a sham,'⁶⁶ and REcoin certainly represented a case of 'illegal unregistered securities offerings and ongoing fraudulent conduct and misstatements designed to deceive investors in connection with the sale of securities in so-called 'Initial Coin Offerings.'"⁶⁷

2. Munchee

a) Confirmation of Previous Analysis (REcoin): Illegal Unregistered Securities Offering. The SEC confirmed this analysis in its December 2017 review of Munchee. The SEC stated that the offering of digital tokens to investors by a blockchain-based food review services company (Munchee) constituted an illegal unregistered securities offering.⁶⁸ In particular, the SEC challenged the view proposed by Munchee that the ICO tokens were 'utility tokens' instead of 'securities tokens.' The SEC took the view that although such tokens had a practical use at the time of the offering, this would not preclude the tokens from being construed as securities.⁶⁹ In its analysis, the SEC highlighted the relevance of 'the economic realities underlying a transaction.'⁷⁰ Because of these underlying realties, the SEC ordered Munchee to cease and desist pursuant to Section 8A of the Securities Act.⁷¹ The same day, SEC Chairman Clayton issued a statement on the risks of fraud and manipulation connected to ICOs (none of which registered with SEC), inviting investors to actively obtain information before deciding to invest.⁷²

b) In re Tomahawk Exploration LLC. The same extensive interpretation of ICO tokens as securities can be seen in the more recent case of *In re Tomahawk Exploration*

---

⁶² Regarding REcoin, Zaslavskyiy did not hire any professionals contrary to what he stated, and in addition, misrepresented the effective amount he raised, declaring an amount between 2 and 4 million dollars, instead of approximately 300,000 dollars in reality. With regard to DRC, Zaslavskiy bragged about non-existent relationships with diamond wholesalers that, through an arbitrage process, should have provided significant gains for his investors.

⁶³ Complaint at 7–8, the US District Court for the Eastern District of New York 20.9.2018 United States v. Zaslavskiy, WL 4346339 para. 2 (No. 17. Civ. 647).

⁶⁴ Ibid, para. 8.

⁶⁵ Ibid, para. 63.

⁶⁶ Ibid, para. 64.

⁶⁷ Ibid, para. 1.

⁶⁸ *In re* SEC, 'Munchee Inc., Securities Act Release No. 10445 at 36–38, File No. 3-18304' (December 2017) (order), available at https://beck-link.de/yd3ne (accessed 19.5.2021).

⁶⁹ Ibid, para. 35.

⁷⁰ Ibid.

⁷¹ Ibid.

⁷² Clayton, 'Statement on Cryptocurrencies and Initial Coin Offerings' (December 2017), available at https://beck-link.de/cs4n2 (accessed 19.5.2021).

LLC. In this case, the SEC confirmed that airdrops can also represent the sale of a security. Namely, distribution of securities in the form of tokens for promotional services serves two purposes, i.e. the function of advancing the issuer's economic objectives or creating a public market for the securities. According to the SEC, this distribution falls within Section 5 of the Securities Act, Section 10(b) of the Exchange Act, and Rule 10b-5.[73] This is consistent with SEC conclusions reached in relation to the free distribution of stocks in the 1990s.[74] These cases had the offering of a free instrument through a website in common, although the proponents never filed a registration statement, and no Form D was filed on the basis of an exemption from registration requirements of Section 5 of the Securities Exchange Act.

3. Recent Cases and Developments

18   a) **In re Carriereq, Inc., d/b/a AirFox (AirFox) and In re Paragon Coin Inc.** The two most recent cases, *In re Carriereq, Inc., d/b/a AirFox (AirFox)*,[75] and *In re Paragon Coin Inc.*,[76] opened a new, more collaborative way of enforcing the securities laws, a 'path to compliance with the federal securities laws ... even where issuers have conducted an illegal unregistered offering of digital asset securities.'[77] The SEC issued settled orders against the two companies in relation to the unregistered offering tokens. The orders provided that both companies should pay penalties, register the tokens as securities under Section 12(g) of the Exchange Act, and file periodic reports with the SEC.[78] Furthermore, the SEC required the compensation of investors 'who purchased tokens in illegal offerings if an investor elects to make a claim.'[79] The intention of the SEC was to ensure that 'investors receive the type of information they would have received had these issuers complied with the registration provisions of the Securities Act prior to the offer and sale of tokens in their respective ICOs.'[80] Finally, the SEC explicitly referred to its positive view of technological innovations capable of benefitting investors and capital markets. At the same time, the agency emphasized the importance for market participants to adhere to a 'well-established and well-functioning federal securities law framework when dealing with technological innovations, regardless of whether the securities are issued in certificated form or using new technologies, such as blockchain.'[81]

19   b) **William H. Hinman's 2018 Speech.** Despite the SEC's massive enforcement actions, the SEC Director of the Division of Corporation Finance, William H. Hinman,

---

[73] SEC, 'Tomahawk Exploration LLC., Securities Act Release No. 10530 at 35, Exchange Act Release No. 83839, File No. 3-18641' (August 2018) (order), available at https://beck-link.de/yb855 (accessed 20.5.2021).

[74] See, e.g., SEC, 'Joe Loofbourrow, Securities Act Release No. 7700, Exchange Act Release No. 41631, File No. 3-9934' (July 1999) (order), available at https://beck-link.de/datk2 (accessed 20.5.2021); SEC, 'Theodore Sotirakis, Securities Act No. 7701, File No. 3-9935' (July 1999) (order), available at https://beck-link.de/yetn5 (accessed 20.5.2021); SEC, 'Wowauction.com Inc. and Steven Michael Gaddis, Sr., Securities Act Release No. 7702, File No. 3-9936 July 1999) (order), available at https://beck-link.de/wmz25 (accessed 20.5.2021).

[75] SEC, 'Carriereq, Inc., Securities Act Release No. 10575 at 28–36, File No. 3-18898' (November 2018) (order), available at https://beck-link.de/4c8e7 (accessed 19.5.2021).

[76] SEC, 'Paragon Coin, Inc., Securities Act Release No. 10574 at 49–57, File No. 3-18897' (November 2018) (order), available at https://beck-link.de/rs6ry (accessed 19.5.2021).

[77] SEC, 'Statement on Digital Asset Securities Issuance and Trading' (November 2018), available at https://beck-link.de/ccmn3 (accessed 19.5.2021).

[78] Ibid.
[79] Ibid.
[80] Ibid.
[81] Ibid.

excluded an automatic characterisation of ICOs as 'securities' in a June 2018 speech.[82] In Hinman's view, Ether tokens at the launch of Ethereum did not necessarily fall under the notion of 'security' because of specific factual circumstances that are relevant when determining whether ICO tokens are securities.[83] In fact, the DAO Report lacked clarifications or indications around 'the facts and circumstances, including the economic realities of the transactions,' relevant to ascertaining 'whether a particular transaction involves the offer and sale of a security – regardless of the terminology used.'[84] Hinman's speech questions whether 'a digital asset offered as a security can, over time, become something other than a security,' and provides an illustrative but not exhaustive list of elements, helpful to take into account as 'facts and circumstances,' that are relevant in considering the applicability of the securities laws to ICO tokens.[85] This factual analysis is consistent with the Supreme Court's holding in *Howey* about the test's flexibility and adaptability to a broad range of schemes.[86] At the same time, Hinman provides a complimentary analysis by referring to *Gary Plastic Packaging v. Merrill Lynch, Pierce, Fenner, & Smith Inc.*[87] ('*Gary Plastics*'), as a relevant precedent, in particular when taking into account the role of the third parties and the secondary market. In this case the court held that although specific instruments (bank certificates of deposit) were not intrinsically a security (such as the oranges in *Howey*), such instruments may still be qualified as 'securities' and subject to the application of the securities law if such instruments 'animate a broader investment contract.'[88]

c) **The role of a Third Party.** In Hinman's analysis, the role of a third party in driving the expectation of a return and the 'economic substance of the transaction' are two relevant elements,[89] and for both of these elements, he provides a non-exhaustive list to illustrate the parameters. In relation to the first element, Hinman considers whether there is a person or a group that sponsored and created the sale of the digital offers and retained a stake or other interest in the digital asset. Furthermore, he considers whether the 'promoter raised an amount of funds in excess of what may be needed to establish a functional network,' and whether purchasers are 'investing…[or] seeking a return.'[90] A legitimate parameter that Hinman explicitly mentions is related to applications of the Securities Act protections and the specific function of securities laws in general to correct potential informational asymmetries that may exist between the promoters and potential purchasers/investors in the digital asset.[91] Regarding the second element, the 'economic substance of the transaction,' Hinman further considers specific parameters. Among them, Hinman considered whether the token creation relates to speculation and who sets the price (independent actor or secondary market influencing the trading), the clarity of the primary motivation related to purchasing

20

---

[82] Hinman, 'Division of Corp. Fin., SEC, Remarks at the Yahoo Finance All Markets Summit: Crypto' (June 2018), available at https://beck-link.de/y3p8b (accessed 19.5.2021).
[83] Ibid.
[84] Ibid.
[85] Ibid.
[86] See The US Supreme Court 27.5.1946 – SEC v. W. J. Howey Co., 328 U.S. 293, 299.
[87] Hinman, 'Division of Corp. Fin., SEC, Remarks at the Yahoo Finance All Markets Summit: Crypto' (June 2018), available at https://beck-link.de/y3p8b (accessed 19.5.2021) (citing Gary Plastic Packaging Corp. v. Merrill Lynch, Pierce, Fenner & Smith, Inc., 756 F.2d 230, 241 (2d Cir. 1985)).
[88] Concannon et al., 'The Yellow Brick Road for Consumer Tokens: The Path to SEC and CFTC Compliance', in GLOB. LEGAL INSIGHTS, BLOCKCHAIN & CRYPTOCURRENCY REGULATION 103 (Josias Dewey ed., 2019), at 1033.
[89] Hinman, 'Division of Corp. Fin., SEC, Remarks at the Yahoo Finance All Markets Summit: Crypto' (June 2018), available at https://beck-link.de/y3p8b (accessed 19.5.2021).
[90] Ibid.
[91] Ibid.

digital asset for personal use or consumption, the distribution of the tokens meeting users' needs, and whether the application is fully functioning or in early stages of development.[92]

21   **d) Beyond Howey: Gary Plastics.** On this basis, the *Howey* test is not the only relevant way to ascertain the characterisation of ICO tokens as security, but *Gary Plastics* analysis also comes into play. As Hinman explains,

> But this also points the way to when a digital asset transaction may no longer represent a security offering. If the network on which the token or coin is to function is sufficiently decentralized – where purchasers would no longer reasonably expect a person or group to carry out essential managerial or entrepreneurial efforts – the assets may not represent an investment contract. Moreover, when the efforts of the third party are no longer a key factor for determining the enterprise's success, material information asymmetries recede. As a network becomes truly decentralized, the ability to identify an issuer or promoter to make the requisite disclosures becomes difficult, and less meaningful.[93]

IV. Third Stage: Collaboration with 'Market Professionals, and Especially Gatekeepers'

1. The 'client-attorney' relationship

22   In addition to providing an extensive interpretation of the notion of 'security' (and extending the applicability of the securities laws to any activity connected to ICOs and more generally cryptocurrencies), the SEC has considered a revolutionary enforcement tool: the 'client-attorney' relationship. After a general remark about the importance for '[m]arket professionals, especially gatekeepers....to act responsibly and hold themselves to high standards,' SEC Chairman Jay Clayton explicitly referred to responsible legal advice in the context of ICOs, highlighting specific concerns and criticalities.[94] First, he considered the situation in which securities lawyers assist clients in structuring offerings of products sharing significant key issues with securities offerings, but claim that they do not represent securities products. Second, he refers to the '"it depends' equivocal advice' on the qualification of specific products as securities, instead of 'counselling their clients that the product they are promoting likely is a security.'[95] For all these situations, Chairman Clayton required 'the SEC staff to be on high alert for approaches to ICOs that may be contrary to the spirit of our securities laws and the professional obligations of the U.S. securities bar.'[96]

2. The endorsement of ICOs by celebrities

23   A complementary step is the position of the SEC regarding the endorsement of ICOs by celebrities.[97] As the SEC explained, ICO endorsements by celebrities and other social media users 'may be unlawful if they do not disclose the nature, source, and amount of any compensation paid, directly or indirectly, by the company in exchange for the

---

[92] Ibid.
[93] Ibid.
[94] Clayton, 'Statement on Cryptocurrencies and Initial Coin Offerings' (December 2017), available at https://beck-link.de/cs4n2 (accessed 19.5.2021).
[95] Ibid.
[96] Ibid.
[97] See, e.g., SEC, 'Two Celebrities Charged With Unlawfully Touting Coin Offerings' (November 2018), available at https://beck-link.de/rcm85 (accessed 19.5.2021).

endorsement,' since although they may appear unbiased, celebrity endorsement may be part of a paid promotion.[98] In addition, the SEC clarified that 'investment decisions should not be based solely on an endorsement by a promoter or other individual,' and '[c]elebrities…often do not have sufficient expertise to ensure that the investment is appropriate and in compliance with federal securities laws.'[99]

V. Fourth Stage: Infrastructures Supporting ICOs, Tokens, and Cryptocurrencies, Including Broker-Dealers and Digital Asset Hedge Funds

1. Digital tokens as 'securities' to extend the enforcement activity to any related entity

After providing an extensive interpretation of the notion of 'security,' a further consequential step towards a full enforcement approach by the SEC consists of extending the application of the federal securities law to those activities related to the securities, in particular online platforms for trading digital assets and exchanges, as well as broker-dealers and digital asset hedge fund managers. Regarding the former, in March 2018, the SEC considered that a vast majority of these platforms provide 'a mechanism for trading assets that meet the definition of a 'security' under the federal securities laws.'[100] The SEC concerns are mostly due to the appearance of online trading platforms as 'SEC-registered and regulated marketplaces' that are not registered or regulated by the SEC, including those referring to themselves as 'exchanges.'[101]

The consequence of a non-registration of these platforms with the SEC as securities exchanges is that the agency and self-regulatory organizations such as FINRA do not review any standards mentioned by the platforms when claiming that they 'use strict standards to pick only high-quality digital assets to trade.'[102] Similarly, in these circumstances the SEC has not reviewed any trading protocol implemented by the platforms: such protocols play a key function in determining the way orders interact and execute, as well as regulating access to a platform's trading services, which 'may not be the same for all users.'[103]

2. Online trading platforms

The SEC warned market participants operating online trading platforms that platforms trading securities and operating as an 'exchange,' in accordance with the definition provided by the Securities Exchange Act of 1934 ('1934 Act'), must be registered as a national securities exchange or operate under an exemption from registration, such as the exemption provided for Alternative Trading Systems ('ATSs') under SEC Regulation ATS.[104] However, even ATSs—as well as online trading platforms that may not meet the definition of an exchange under the federal securities laws—that directly or indirectly offer trading or other services related to digital assets that are securities are subject to specific regulatory requirements.[105]

---

[98] SEC, 'Statement Urging Caution Around Celebrity Backed ICOs' (November 2017), available at https://beck-link.de/tr2tp (accessed 19.5.2021).
[99] Ibid.
[100] SEC, 'Statement on Potentially Unlawful Online Platforms for Trading Digital Assets' (March 2017), available at https://beck-link.de/5zvah (accessed 19.5.2021).
[101] Ibid.
[102] Ibid.
[103] Ibid.
[104] Ibid.
[105] Ibid.

3. EtherDelta

26 In November 2018, the SEC charged EtherDelta, 'an online platform that allows buyers and sellers to trade certain digital assets – Ether and "ERC20 tokens' – with secondary market trading.'[106] As the SEC noted, 'From July 12, 2016 to December 15, 2017 … more than 3.6 million buy and sell orders in ERC20 tokens that included securities as defined by Section 3(a)(10) of the Exchange Act were traded on EtherDelta, of which approximately 92 % (3.3 million) were traded during the period following the DAO Report.'[107] For this reason, the SEC considered that EtherDelta met the criteria of an 'exchange' as defined by Section 3(a)(1)[108] of the Securities Exchange Act of 1934 and Rule 3b-16[109] and was not excluded under Rule 3b-16(b).[110] In fact, EtherDelta matched 'the orders of multiple buyers and sellers in tokens that included securities as defined by Section 3(a)(10) of the Exchange Act. The purchasers of such digital tokens invested money with a reasonable expectation of profits, including through the increased value of their investments in secondary trading, based on the managerial efforts of others.'[111] An important takeaway is that even a decentralized platform operating without a central infrastructure falls within the functional definition of the Securities Exchange Act.[112]

Consistent with this approach, in September 2018, the SEC charged TokenLot LLC and its owners for acting as unregistered broker-dealers in relation to the sale of digital tokens.[113] TokenLot was charged with soliciting investors. The platform 'actively and broadly solicited the general public to use the platform to purchase digital tokens,' and advertised digital tokens available on the platform through a broad range of channels (social media, forums, emailed newsletters).[114] Furthermore, TokenLot had received payment from digital token issuers for promoting the sale of

---

[106] SEC, 'Coburn, Release No. 84553, 2018 WL 5840155', para. 1 (November 2018) [hereinafter Coburn Release] (order initiating cease-and-desist proceedings), available at https://beck-link.de/77pe7 (accessed 19.5.2021).

[107] Ibid, para. 2.

[108] 15 U.S.C. § 78c(a)(1) (2018) ("[E]xchange' means any organization, association, or group of persons, whether incorporated or unincorporated, which constitutes, maintains, or provides a market place or facilities for bringing together purchasers and sellers of securities or for otherwise performing with respect to securities the functions commonly performed by a stock exchange as that term is generally understood, and includes the market place and the market facilities maintained by such exchange.').

[109] Rule 3b-16 provides: An organization, association, or group of persons shall be considered to constitute, maintain, or provide 'a market place or facilities for bringing together purchasers and sellers of securities or for otherwise performing with respect to securities the functions commonly performed by a stock exchange,' as those terms are used in section 3(a)(1) of the Act, (15 U.S.C. 78c(a)(1)), if such organization, association, or group of persons: **(1)**Brings together the orders for securities of multiple buyers and sellers; and **(2)**Uses established, non-discretionary methods (whether by providing a trading facility or by setting rules) under which such orders interact with each other, and the buyers and sellers entering such orders agree to the terms of a trade 17 C.F.R. § 240.3b-16(a) (2019). As the SEC explains, this rule 'provides a functional test to assess whether a trading system meets the definition of exchange under Section 3(a)(1) of the Exchange Act.'; see SEC, 'Coburn, Release No. 84553, 2018 WL 5840155', para. 24 (November 2018) (order initiating cease-and-desist proceedings), available at https://beck-link.de/77pe7 (accessed 19.5.2021).

[110] Art. 240.3b-16(b) 17 C.F.R (2019).

[111] SEC, 'Coburn, Release No. 84553, 2018 WL 5840155', para. 26 (November 2018) (order initiating cease-and-desist proceedings), available at https://beck-link.de/77pe7 (accessed 19.5.2021).

[112] De Martino, Brown and Silva, 'First SEC Enforcement Action Against Unregistered Digital Token Exchange' (November 2018), available at https://beck-link.de/3kayk (accessed 19.5.2021).

[113] SEC, 'SEC Charges ICO Superstore and Owners With Operating As Unregistered Broker-Dealers' (September 2018), available at https://beck-link.de/ep4ba (accessed 19.5.2021).

[114] SEC, 'TokenLot et al., Exchange Act Release No. 84075, 2018 WL 4329662', para. 7 (September 2018), available at https://beck-link.de/zrt78 (accessed 19.5.2021).

the issuers' tokens. In addition to solicitation, TokenLot facilitated initial securities offerings and transactions in secondary trading, acting as 'brokers or dealers in handling investor purchase orders.'[115]

4. Crypto Asset Management LLP

The same approach led the SEC to charge a hedge fund manager for failure to register an investment vehicle as an investment company, the basis of its investments in digital assets.[116] Crypto Asset Management LLP ('CAM') engaged in an 'unregistered non-exempt public offering and invest[ed] more than 40 percent of the fund's assets in digital asset securities.'[117] Therefore CAM caused the fund (Crypto Asset Fund, CAF) to not comply with the Investment Company Act. Section 3(a)(1)(C) of the Investment Company Act defines an 'investment company' as any issuer which 'is engaged or proposes to engage in the business of investing, reinvesting, owning, holding or trading in securities, and owns or proposes to acquire investment securities having a value exceeding 40 per centum of the value of such issuer's total assets (exclusive of Government securities and cash items) on an unconsolidated basis.'[118] As a consequence of the contacts with the SEC, CAM agreed to cease its public offering, offered buy backs to affected investors, and was ordered to pay a fine of $200,000.

VI. Recent Regulatory Initiatives

1. The Token Taxonomy Act

In the near future, the regulation of cryptocurrencies and digital tokens could drastically change, in particular, if the bipartisan initiative promoted by Congressmen Warren Davidson and Darren Soto, the Token Taxonomy Act, is passed. The Token Taxonomy Act would exclude digital tokens from the definition of 'security' and exempt 'transactions involving the development, offer, or sale of a digital unit' under specific conditions from the Securities Act.[119] In this way, the Token Taxonomy Act implements the view that digital tokens represent an alternative asset class and provides a definition of 'digital token' based on four main elements. This could affect the definition of both 'traditional' cryptocurrencies and stablecoins under existing securities laws.

2. Hester Peirce and Difficulties of Applying Howey to ICOs

In a recent speech, SEC Commissioner Hester Peirce emphasized the difficulties of applying the Howey test to ICOs. To address the uncertainty surrounding the application of securities laws to tokens, he proposed a safe harbor. This safe harbor would exempt network developers for a three-year grace period from ' (1) the offer and sale of tokens

---

[115] Ibid, para. 11.
[116] SEC, 'SEC Charges Digital Asset Hedge Fund Manager with Misrepresentations and Registration Failures', (September 2018), available at https://beck-link.de/v7y4d (accessed 19.5.2021).
[117] SEC, 'Crypto Asset Mgmt., LP et al., Securities Act Release No. 10544, 2018 WL 4374663', para. 8 (September 2018), available at https://beck-link.de/f675p (accessed 19.5.2021).
[118] Ibid. (quoting 15 U.S.C. § 80a-3(a)(1)(C) (2018)). In addition to the violation of Section 3(a)(1)(C) of the Investment Company Act, the SEC contested the violation of Sections 5(a), 5(c), and 17(a)(2) of the Securities Act, Section 206(4) of the Advisers Act and Rule 206(4)-8, and Section 7(a) of the Investment Company Act.
[119] Crimmins & Comstock, 'How Congress Could Change The Game for Digital Tokens', LAW360 (Jan. 10, 2019, 2:45 PM), https://www.law360.com/articles/1116952/how-congress-could-change-the-game-for-digital-tokens.

from the provisions of the Securities Act of 1933, other than the antifraud provisions, (2) the tokens from registration under the Securities Exchange Act of 1934, and (3) persons engaged in certain token transactions from the definitions of 'exchange,' 'broker,' and 'dealer' under the 1934 Act.'[120] In Commissioner Hester Peirce's view, the exemption from the registration requirements of federal securities laws would be a way to pursue 'the development of a functional or decentralized network,' making sure that new technologies can flourish while preserving investor protection.[121] In a past statement, Commissioner Hester Peirce discussed the difficulties related to applying the scheme of securities offerings to token offerings, mostly because of the decentralized nature of token offerings;[122] this was consistent with some commentators urges to reassess the *Howey* test.[123]

3. The Securities Clarity Act and the Digital Commodity Exchange Act

30   The Token Taxonomy Act is not the only initiative currently under discussion. In January 2019, Representative Tom Emmer proposed the Blockchain Regulatory Certainty Act that never passed the Committees at the House of Representative. In September 2020, the same Representative proposed two further texts, the Securities Clarity Act (SCA) and the Digital Commodity Exchange Act (DCEA). Both these proposed texts might have an impact on the ICO market. The SCA with a technology-neutral approach, introduces a new definition of 'investment contract asset' which refers to any asset, whether tangible or intangible, including assets in digital form, sold as part of an investment contract that would not be considered a 'security' but for its sale as part of an investment contract.

4. A 'Single Opt-in National Regulatory Framework for Digital Commodity Trading Platforms'

31   The DCEA seeks to create a 'single, opt-in national regulatory framework for digital commodity trading platforms' that will be regulated by the US CFTC. Under the DCEA, 'digital commodity' means any form of fungible intangible personal property that can be exclusively possessed and transferred person to person without necessary reliance on an intermediary, and which does not represent a financial interest in a company, partnership, or investment vehicle.

SCA and DCEA should help to better define the line between SEC and CFTC jurisdiction: pre-sale agreements will continue to be regulated by the SEC, but there

---

[120] Peirce, 'Running on Empty: A proposal to fill the gap between regulation and decentralization' (February 2020), available at https://beck-link.de/e63md (accessed 19.5.2021).

[121] Ibid. As Commissioner Peirce further explains, 'The initial development team would have to meet certain conditions, which I will lay out briefly before addressing several in more depth. First, the team must intend for the network on which the token functions to reach network maturity—defined as either decentralization or token functionality—within three years of the date of the first token sale and undertake good faith and reasonable efforts to achieve that goal. Second, the team would have to disclose key information on a freely accessible public website. Third, the token must be offered and sold for the purpose of facilitating access to, participation on, or the development of the network. Fourth, the team would have to undertake good faith and reasonable efforts to create liquidity for users. Finally, the team would have to file a notice of reliance'.

[122] Peirce, 'Regulation: A view from inside Machine' (February 2019), transcript available at https://beck-link.de/y7eyz (accessed 19.5.2021).

[123] See generally Henderson and Raskin, 'A Regulatory Classification of Digital Assets: Towards an Operational Howey Test for Cryptocurrencies, ICOs, and Other Digital Assets', (2019) *Columbia Business Law Review*, 443; see also Guseva, 'A Conceptual Framework for Digital-Asset Securities: Tokens and Coins as Debt And Equity', (2021) 80 *Maryland Law Review*, 16 and Guseva, 'The Leviathan of Securities Regulation in Crypto-Offerings: A Cost-Benefit Analysis' (December 2020), available at https://beck-link.de/3p7dn (accessed 19.5.2021).

will be less need for continued SEC wariness once the tokens are delivered and the network is live because the CFTC will be picking up the regulatory slack and supervising sales to the public upon network launch.

D. Additional Initiatives by Other Authorities

Token sales have also triggered the attention of other regulatory agencies. Among these are the Department of Justice, the Financial Crimes Enforcement Network ('FinCEN'), the Federal Trade Commission, the Financial Industry Regulatory Authority ('FINRA'), and the Internal Revenue Service ('IRS'). FinCEN noted that they may trigger the regulation provided for money services business. When issuing an interpretative guide in 2011, FinCEN stated that '[t]he definition of a money transmitter does not differentiate between real currencies and convertible virtual currencies. Accepting and transmitting anything of value that substitutes for currency makes a person a money transmitter under the regulations implementing the Bank Secrecy Act.'[124] More recently, FinCEN has confirmed that '[a] developer that sells convertible virtual currency, including in the form of ICO coins or tokens, in exchange for another type of value that substitutes for currency is a money transmitter and must comply.'[125] On this basis, token issuers may need to comply with anti-money laundering ('AML') and know-your customer ('KYC') rules. In addition, state money transmitter laws govern all activities related to 'money transmission.'[126] In the United States, each state has the authority to interpret its own money transmission laws and any state could take the position that the activity involving virtual currency is subject to regulation, especially if the services also involve the handling of fiat currency. In this respect, widely divergent positions may emerge.[127]

Virtual currencies may also raise concern as to their tax treatment. In a notice describing how existing general tax principles apply to transactions using virtual currency, the IRS treated virtual currency as property for federal tax purposes, and therefore transactions using virtual currency are subject to general tax principles applicable to property transactions.[128]

32

---

[124] Financial Crimes Enforcement Network, 'Application of FinCEN's Regulations to Persons Administering, Exchanging, or Using Virtual Currencies' (March 2013), available at https://beck-link.de/app2b (accessed 19.5.2021).

[125] Financial Crimes Enforcement Network, 'Letter to the Honorable Ron Wyden' (February 2018), available at https://beck-link.de/3e45e (accessed 19.5.2021).

[126] Wilson, 'A Call to Clarify the Regulatory Scope of Money Transmitter Laws' (June 2013), available at https://beck-link.de/638tp (accessed 19.5.2021). The author notes that in Maryland the applicable state law specifically covers the reception of any money for transmission 'by any means, including electronically or through the Internet.'

[127] Moffitt, 'The Fifty U.S. States and Cryptocurrency Regulations' (July 2018), available at https://beck-link.de/thb7p (accessed 19.5.2021).

[128] I.R.S. Notice 2014-21, available at https://beck-link.de/5nhse (accessed 19.5.2021).

§ 23
Singapore[*]

Literature: Koh, Jonas Lei, 'Crypto Conundrum Part I: Navigating Singapore's Regulatory Regime', (March 2020) 3 Singapore Academy of Law Practitioner ('SAL Prac'), available at https://beck-link.de/r2twh (accessed 25.11.2020); Koh, Pearlie, *Company Law* (3rd edition, LexisNexis, Singapore, 2017); Lau, 'Computerised Mistake and Proprietised Bitcoin – *B2C2 v Quoine Pte Ltd*' (December 2019), 35(1) *Banking & Finance Law Review*, 205; Lin, Lin, 'Regulating FinTech: The Case of Singapore' (2019) 35 *Banking and Law Review*, 93; Monetary Authority of Singapore, 'A Guide to Digital Token Offerings' (March 2020), available at https://beck-link.de/ex3x2 (accessed 25.11.2020); Monetary Authority of Singapore, 'Fintech Regulatory Sandbox Guidelines' (November 2016), available at https://beck-link.de/tv3tm (accessed 25.11.2020); Monetary Authority of Singapore, 'Sandbox Express Guidelines' (August 2019), available at https://beck-link.de/zw2ak (accessed 25.11.2020); Monetary Authority of Singapore & Temasek Holdings, 'Project Ubin Phase 5: Enabling Broad Ecosystem Opportunities' (July 2020) 3–6, available at https://beck-link.de/fd422 (accessed 25.11.2020). Tjio & Ying Hu, 'Collective Investment: Land, Crypto and Coin Schemes: Regulatory 'Property'' (2020) 21 *European Business Organization Review*, 171–198; Tjio, Hans, Yee Wan Wai and Hon Yee Kwok, *Principles and Practice of Securities Regulation in Singapore* (3rd edition, LexisNexis, Singapore, 2017).

Outline

	para.
A. Introduction	1
B. Regulation	3
I. Capital Markets Products	5
1. Securities	6
2. Units in a collective investment scheme	8
3. Derivative contracts	10
4. Licencing, criminal penalties, and civil liability	11
II. Commodities	14
III. Payment Services	15
1. E-money	16
2. Digital payment tokens	17
IV. Regulatory Sandbox	19
C. Developments	22
I. Recent Initiatives	22
II. Criminal Cases	24
III. Civil Cases	26
D. Conclusion	29

A. Introduction

1 New, complex, and rapidly changing, crypto assets are difficult to understand and even harder to regulate. The regulatory approach in Singapore, like other jurisdictions featured in this Volume, fall somewhere between the extremes of outright ban and full laissez-faire. The milestone Payment Services Act 2019 entered into force on 28 January 2020 and added a further layer to existing regulatory frameworks applicable to securities and commodities. With this development, the regulatory landscape is—at least on its

---

[*] I am grateful to Alan K Koh for comments on an earlier draft, and to Bryan Ong for research assistance. All errors are mine alone. The information in this chapter is accurate as of 30 September 2020.

face—more than ever a **patchwork of fragmented and overlapping rules**, although arguably alleviated for start-ups by a tailored set of regulatory sandboxes.

The local authorities have also taken a proactive approach to leading and coordinating initiatives on the technologies on which crypto assets are based. In July 2020, the central bank, the Monetary Authority of Singapore, and the state's most prominent investment arm, Temasek Holdings, announced the completion of a blockchain-based multi-currency payments network prototype. This marked the culmination of a four-year five-phase project with numerous foreign institutional partners ('Project Ubin') on the applications of blockchain and distributed ledger technology to clearing and settlement.

The two milestone events above make 2020 a particularly appropriate time to take stock of the crypto asset scene in Singapore. This Chapter aims to provide an **overview of recent changes** to Singapore's regulations on crypto assets, and to capture a snapshot of developments relevant to Singapore. It proceeds as follows: Part B (→ para. 3) explains the regulatory regime in Singapore applicable to crypto assets, depending on whether such assets are regulated as capital market products (e.g., securities), commodities, or payment services. Where full compliance with such complex regulations is difficult, businesses may consider launching their services under the regulatory sandbox operated by the Monetary Authority of Singapore (MAS). Part C (→ para. 22) explores the regulation of recent initiatives involving crypto assets, and how disputes involving crypto assets have been resolved in domestic courts. Part D concludes with a brief summary of criticisms of Singapore's regulatory regime on crypto assets.

B. Regulation

As of 2020, the regulatory regime applicable to crypto assets exists as a **patchwork of legislation, various licensing regimes, and informal guidance** issued by the primary regulator, MAS. The applicable regulations depend on whether the specific crypto asset is characterized as a (1) capital markets product within the scope of the Securities and Futures Act (SFA); (2) a commodity under the ambit of the Commodity Trading Act (CTA); or (3) a payment service falling within the regulated activities under the Payment Services Act (PSA). These three statutory regimes overlap in scope, and there is no statutory or other authoritative guidance as the relative priority of each of the three regimes over the others. It is thus possible, depending on how the asset is characterised, for these regimes to apply cumulatively and simultaneously to the same crypto asset. This list of relevant legislation is not exhaustive; it is possible for crypto assets to be characterised as other forms of property or services that may attract further regulation.[1]

Businesses providing financial services in Singapore are generally required to comply with domestic regulations for the **prevention of money laundering and countering the financing of terrorism (AML/CFT)**. The precise regulations involved depend on the type of licence held by the business under the SFA and other legislation, and the nature of the services provided.

Where compliance with such regulation is difficult – as is often the case for innovative financial services – providers can first launch their services under MAS's regulatory sandbox, which permits the relaxation of specific regulations subject to oversight from MAS. I address each of these potential sources of regulation in turn.

---

[1] For example, a person who provides financial advice in Singapore in relation to a crypto asset that is an investment product may be regulated under the Financial Advisers Act (Cap 110); see Monetary Authority of Singapore, 'A Guide to Digital Token Offerings' (March 2020), 6, available at https://beck-link.de/ex3x2 (accessed 25.11.2020).

Part C. Country Reports

I. Capital Markets Products

5   The SFA regulates the offer and sale of 'capital market products' including, *inter alia*, securities, units in a collective investment scheme, and derivative contracts, being the three most likely types of financial products that a crypto asset may be characterized as.[2]

1. Securities

6   The definition of **securities** in the SFA as includes, *inter alia*, 'shares, units in a business trust or any instrument conferring or representing a legal or beneficial ownership interest in a corporation, partnership or limited liability partnership; debentures; or any other product or class of products as may be prescribed'.

MAS has issued some guidance as to when a crypto asset may be considered as a share in a company; in its 'A Guide to Digital Token Offerings', MAS observes that a 'digital token' may be regarded a share where it 'confers or represents ownership interest in a corporation, represents liability of the token holder in the corporation,[3] and represents mutual covenants with other token holders ... *inter se*'.[4] It is notable that MAS's guidance does not emphasise other aspects of rights attached to shares, including the right to vote at a general meeting. Thus, in an arrangement where a crypto asset is 'structured to represent a share [in a company]', it is likely to fall within the ambit of the SFA.[5]

7   The definition of **debentures** under the SFA includes 'any debenture stock, bond, note and any other debt securities issued by or proposed to be issued by a corporation or any other entity, whether constituting a charge or not, on the assets of the issuer'.[6] Crypto assets may be considered debentures if the company has an obligation to repurchase the asset from the buyer, or to pay the buyer an amount in a specified currency.[7]

Consider a scenario where a company sets up a platform to invest in various start-ups. The company creates an entity as a vehicle to facilitate fund-raising; investors provide a loan to the entity, and the entity issues crypto assets to investors in return. Given that the crypto assets are offered to any person globally, including Singapore residents, the crypto asset may be regarded as a debenture regulated under the SFA.[8]

2. Units in a collective investment scheme

8   A succinct definition of **collective investment schemes** under the SFA by two local scholars is as follows:[9]

---

[2] The description under this part is not exhaustive, see generally Monetary Authority of Singapore, 'A Guide to Digital Token Offerings' (March 2020), 3, available at https://beck-link.de/ex3x2 (accessed 25.11.2020).

[3] The reference to 'liability' may be in respect of a company's right to make calls against a shareholder for the amount owing to the company for partly-paid or unpaid shares. Koh, Pearlie, *Company Law* (2017), 54.

[4] Monetary Authority of Singapore, Ibid, 3.

[5] Ibid, p. 11.

[6] Securities and Futures Act (Cap 289), s 2.

[7] Koh, Jonas Lei, 'Crypto Conundrum Part I: Navigating Singapore's Regulatory Regime', (March 2020) 3 Singapore Academy of Law Practitioner ('SAL Prac'), para. 9, available at https://beck-link.de/r2twh (accessed 25.11.2020).

[8] Monetary Authority of Singapore, Ibid, 13–14.

[9] Tjio, Hans & Ying Hu, 'Collective Investment: Land, Crypto and Coin Schemes: Regulatory 'Property'', (2020) 21 *European Business Organization Review*, 171, 176. The statutory definition in the SFA is considerably longer, see Securities and Futures Act (Cap 289), s 2.

[A] collective investment scheme ... has concurrent requirements that require delegation to a manager or the pooling of monetary contributions and profits (thus effectively excluding timeshares and club memberships), and the sharing of what appears to be profits in pecuniary form ('the profits or income from which payments are to be made to them are pooled' and 'profits, income, or other payments or returns') ... The long list of exclusions also relates to schemes that generate such financial returns.

Consider a scenario where crypto assets are offered for sale to raise funds for investment in a share portfolio. The offer is made to any person globally, including persons in Singapore.[10] The purchasers of the crypto assets do not have any powers over the day-to-day management of the arrangement, and profits from the share portfolio are pooled and distributed to the purchasers. In this scenario, MAS has given informal guidance that the arrangement would be considered a collective investment scheme, and the crypto asset would be a unit in said scheme.[11]

3. Derivative contracts

MAS has not provided any informal guidance on the types of arrangements involving crypto assets that could constitute a **derivatives contract** under the SFA. A local practitioner suggests that a crypto asset may be regarded as a derivatives contract in four scenarios:[12]

(a) The [crypto asset] is backed by fiat currency and/or a commodity, and such an [asset] is not considered a security;
(b) The said [crypto asset] is not a 'spot contract'[13] (i.e., delivery of the underlying thing is not pursuant to market convention;
(c) The said [crypto asset] is not a 'deposit' or 'contract of insurance' as defined under s 2 of the SFA; and
(d) The issuing entity of this [crypto asset] is under a 'contract or arrangement' to discharge all or any of its obligations to deliver the fiat currency or commodity underlying the [crypto asset] at some future time, and that the value of the contract is determined by the prevailing fiat currency or commodity value at that point in time.

4. Licencing, criminal penalties, and civil liability

Where a crypto asset is deemed to be a '**capital market produc**t', a business engaging in activities involving the crypto asset may require (1) a capital markets services licence[14] from MAS if it is 'dealing in capital market products';[15] and/or (2) a recognised market operator licence[16] if the business is operating an exchange that offers the crypto asset for sale, purchase, or exchange.[17] Failure to comply with **licensing requirements**

---

[10] If the offer is not made to any person in Singapore, the SFA will not apply: Monetary Authority of Singapore, ibid, 13.
[11] Monetary Authority of Singapore, Ibid, 12.
[12] Koh, Jonas Lei, ibid, para. 15.
[13] Securities and Futures Act (Cap 289), s 2 (definition of 'derivative contract' excludes 'spot contract', 'spot contract' is defined in the same section).
[14] Securities and Futures Act (Cap 289), s 82, read with Second Schedule, Part I (Regulated Activities).
[15] The statutory definition of 'dealing in capital market products' is broad, and 'means (whether as principal or agent) making or offering to make with any person, or inducing or attempting to induce any person to enter into or to offer to enter into any agreement for or with a view to acquiring, disposing of, entering into, effecting, arranging, subscribing for, or underwriting any capital markets products', Securities and Futures Act (Cap 289), s 2 , read with Second Schedule, Part II (Interpretation).
[16] Securities and Futures Act (Cap 289), s 7.
[17] Koh, Jonas Lei, ibid, para. 16.

may result in **criminal penalties**, including substantial fines for corporations,[18] and fines and/or imprisonment for business personnel.[19]

12   Contravention of the SFA may result in **civil enforcement actions** by MAS;[20] actions carrying civil penalties include market manipulation and insider trading.[21] MAS has supervisory and investigative powers under the SFA,[22] which includes the disclosure of the personal identities of natural persons involved in the acquisition or disposal of capital markets products.[23]

Another business activity that may fall under the ambit of the SFA is making a **public offer to sell crypto assets** to investors. Where such crypto assets are deemed to be 'securities', the offeror must comply with requirements under Part XIII of the SFA, including prospectus requirements.[24] Where the crypto asset is deemed to be a unit in a collective investment scheme, additional authorisation or recognition requirements may apply.[25] An offer may be exempt from the above requirements where the offer is (1) a small personal offer that does not exceed S$5 million in value within a 12 month period;[26] (2) a private placement offer made to no more than 50 persons within any 12 month period;[27] (3) only made to institutional investors;[28] or made to accredited investors.[29]

13   **False and misleading statements** made to investors in relation to an offer of sale carry **criminal penalties**[30] and **civil liability**,[31] subject to a due diligence defence.[32] Unlike other aspects of civil liability under the SFA, false and misleading statements are not within the scope of MAS's civil enforcement regime but can only be privately enforced by investors.[33]

II. Commodities

14   Crypto assets may be **backed by commodities** such as gold, silver, and other precious metals. Transactions involving such crypto assets may be regarded as 'spot commodity trading' within the definition of the CTA[34] where (1) a seller offers crypto assets backed

---

[18] Securities and Futures Act (Cap 289), s 7(12) (recognised market operator licence).

[19] Securities and Futures Act (Cap 289), ss 7(4) and 7(5) (recognised market operator licence), s 83(3) (capital markets services licence).

[20] Tjio, Hans, Yee Wan Wai and Hon Yee Kwok, *Principles and Practice of Securities Regulation in Singapore* (2017), 141–142.

[21] See generally Part XII (Market Conduct) of the Securities and Futures Act (Cap 289).

[22] See generally Part XI, Division 1 (Supervisory Powers) of the Securities and Futures Act (Cap 289).

[23] Securities and Futures Act (Cap 289), s 142.

[24] See Part XIII (offers of investments) of the Securities and Futures Act (Cap 289); Monetary Authority of Singapore, 'A Guide to Digital Token Offerings' (March 2020), 4, available at https://beck-link.de/ex3x2 (accessed 25.11.2020).

[25] Securities and Futures Act (Cap 289), ss 286–287; see also Part II of the Securities and Futures Act (Cap 289).

[26] Additional conditions may apply, see generally Securities and Futures Act (Cap 289), ss 227A and 302B.

[27] Additional conditions may apply, see generally Securities and Futures Act (Cap 289), ss 272B-302C.

[28] Securities and Futures Act (Cap 289), ss 274 and 304, read with s 4A(1)(c) (definition of institutional investor).

[29] Securities and Futures Act (Cap 289), ss 275 and 305, read with s 4A(1)(a) (definition of accredited investor).

[30] Securities and Futures Act (Cap 289), s 253.

[31] Securities and Futures Act (Cap 289), s 254.

[32] Securities and Futures Act (Cap 289), s 255; Tjio, Hans, Yee Wan Wai and Hon Yee Kwok, *Principles and Practice of Securities Regulation in Singapore* (2017), 469–470.

[33] Securities and Futures Act (Cap 289), s 254; Tjio, Hans et al., ibid, 142.

[34] 'Spot commodity trading' is defined as 'the purchase or sale of a commodity at its current market or spot price, where it is intended that such transaction results in the physical delivery of the commodity',

by a commodity for sale at its market price (or 'spot price') for sale; and (2) upon sale of the crypto asset, title of the underlying commodity is transferred from the seller to the buyer. If so, the crypto asset may be regulated by the CTA, and related notices issued by issued by Enterprise Singapore.[35]

III. Payment Services

The PSA regulates **payment services**, including (1) e-money issuance services; and (2) digital payment token services.[36] A provider of payment services must obtain a licence from MAS.[37] The two types of licences generally relevant for crypto assets are (1) a standard payment institution licence;[38] and (2) a major payment institution licence.

A standard payment institution **licence** is required where a business provides one or more of the regulated payment services.[39] A major payment institution licence is required where a business (1) provides one or more of the regulated payment services; and (2) the average, over a calendar year, of the total value of all payment services accepted, processed or executed by the business per month exceeds (a) S$3 million for any one payment service; (b) $6 million for 2 or more payment services.[40] Such a licence is also required where a business provides an e-money account issuance services, and the average, over a calendar year, of the total value in one day of all e-money issued by the business exceeds S$5 million.[41]

1. E-money

E-money is defined under the PSA as 'any electronically stored monetary value that: (a) is denominated in any currency or pegged by its issuer to any currency; (b) has been paid for in advance to enable the making of payment transactions through the use of a payment account; (c) is accepted by a person other than its issuer; and (d) represents a claim on its issuer'. This definition does not extend to 'any deposit[42] accepted in Singapore, from any person in Singapore'.[43]

Commodity Trading Act (Cap 48A), s 2. 'Physical delivery' is satisfied where there is transfer of title from the seller to the buyer; actual physical delivery of the commodity is not required. Koh, Jonas Lei, 'Crypto Conundrum Part I: Navigating Singapore's Regulatory Regime', (March 2020) 3 Singapore Academy of Law Practitioner ('SAL Prac'), para. 18, available at https://beck-link.de/r2twh (accessed 25.11.2020).

[35] Ibid, para. 17–19.

[36] The definition of 'payment services' in the Payment Services Act 2019 includes 7 services; the remaining 5 services are: (1) an account issuance service; (2) a domestic money transfer services; (3) a cross-border money transfer services; (4) a merchant acquisition service; and (5) a money changing services, Payment Services Act (2019), s 2, read with Schedule 1, Part 1. Services excluded from the definition of 'payment services' are provided in the Schedule 1, Part 2 of the Payment Services Act (2019).

[37] Payment Services Act (2019), s 5. The Act provides that specific services may be exempt from licensing requirements: Payment Services Act (2019), s 13.

[38] Payment Services Act (2019), s 6(2)

[39] Payment Services Act (2019), s 6(5).

[40] Payment Services Act (2019), s 6(5)

[41] Payment Services Act (2019), s 6(5)(b).

[42] Payment Services Act (2019), s 2 states that the definition of 'deposit' for the purposes of the Act is as provided under Banking Act (Cap 19), s 48B. 'Deposit' is defined by the Banking Act as ' (a) a sum of money paid on terms (i) under which it will be repaid, with or without interest or a premium, or with any consideration in money or money's worth, either on demand or at a time or in circumstances agreed by or on behalf of the person making the payment and the person receiving it; and (ii) which are not referable to the provision of property or services or to the giving of security; and (b) such other product as may be prescribed.'.

[43] Payment Services Act (2019), s 2.

Consider a scenario where a company offers **digital tokens** to any person in the world for US$1 per token. The company aims to ensure that the price of the token remains stable by pegging the token's price to the US dollar, and by only accepting payments for the token in the form of deposits of US dollars into the company's own bank account. Token holders can exchange the token for US dollars. In this scenario, it is possible for the token to be characterised as a debenture regulated by the SFA, or as e-money regulated by the PSA. If the token falls squarely within the definition of e-money, MAS has indicated that it will not regulate the token as a debenture under the SFA.[44]

2. Digital Payment Tokens

17 In sum, a crypto asset backed by fiat currency may be considered 'e-money'; if it represents a claim on the issuer, it may be considered a 'a debenture'. What about crypto assets that do not fall within either category? Such assets may be regarded as '**digital payment tokens**', which are defined under the PSA as 'any digital representation of value (other than an excluded digital representation of value) that (a) is expressed as a unit; (b) is not denominated in any currency, and is not pegged by its issuer to any currency; (c) is, or is intended to be, a medium of exchange accepted by the public, or a section of the public, as payment for goods or services or for the discharge of a debt; (d) can be transferred, stored or traded electronically; and (e) satisfies such other characteristics as [MAS] may prescribe.'[45] Given that this definition does not exclude any crypto asset backed by a commodity (e.g. gold), it is entirely possible that such a crypto asset might be simultaneously regulated under the Commodities Trading Act as a commodity and by the PSA as a digital token.[46] MAS has not issued any guidance on this legislative overlap.

18 A business will need to obtain a licence under the PSA if it (1) buys and sells digital payment tokens in exchange for money or any other digital payment token;[47] or (2) operates an exchange where users may buy or sell digital payment tokens in exchange for money on a centralised basis, and the exchange contemplates that the business will come into possession of digital payment tokens or money.[48] Thus, if a business sets up a crypto asset **exchange platform** that permits users to exchange crypto assets that do not constitute capital markets products regulated under the SFA, the payment may nevertheless be regulated as a digital payment token exchange under the PSA.[49]

IV. Regulatory Sandbox

19 To encourage and facilitate innovation in fintech, MAS operates a **regulatory sandbox** that allows participants to experiment with financial services for a defined duration. This regulatory sandbox was introduced in November 2016, shortly after the UK Financial Conduct Authority established a regulatory sandbox of its own.[50] Generally,

---

[44] Monetary Authority of Singapore, ibid, 19.
[45] Payment Services Act (2019), s 2.
[46] Koh, Jonas Lei, ibid, para. 28.
[47] This excludes '(a) facilitating the exchange of digital payment tokens; (b) accepting any digital payment token as a means of payment for the provision of goods or services; (c) using any digital payment token as a means of payment for the provision of goods or services. First Schedule; Part III of the Payment Services Act (2019).
[48] First Schedule; Part III of the Payment Services Act (2019); Koh, Jonas Lei, ibid, para. 29.
[49] Monetary Authority of Singapore, ibid, para. 15–16.
[50] Lin, Lin, 'Regulating FinTech: The Case of Singapore' (2019) 35 *Banking and Law Review*, 93, 97.

entrants to the sandbox are required to show that the proposed financial service uses innovative or emerging technology that either solves an existing problem, or benefits consumers or the industry as a whole. The entrant should also be able to deploy the proposed service in Singapore following its exit from the sandbox.[51]

MAS may, at its own discretion, relax specific legal and regulatory requirements while the participant remains in the regulatory sandbox.[52] Examples of legal and regulatory requirements that may be relaxed include minimum capital requirements, board composition (for companies), financial soundness, cash balances, and relative size. However, MAS has indicated that participants in the sandbox are generally expected to maintain compliance with requirements on confidentiality of customer information, 'fit and proper' criteria, handling of customer monies and assets by intermediaries, and AML/CFT.[53] Once a business exits the regulatory sandbox, it is expected to comply with all applicable regulations. It is possible for a business to apply for an extension of the exit date, but MAS clearly contemplates that participants cannot remain in the regulatory sandbox indefinitely, given that the regulatory sandbox is not intended to function as a mechanism for circumventing legal and regulatory requirements.[54]

MAS's regulatory sandbox seems to have been warmly received by **fintech start-ups** in Singapore, as it takes a more innovator-centric approach than the UK by focusing on lowering barriers to entry and emphasising industry benefits. However, the number of businesses that have successfully entered and exited the sandbox remains low. The relatively low number of participants is apparently consistent with MAS's own view of the sandbox as a last resort to facilitate innovation in fintech.[55]

MAS has also introduced an 'express' sandbox initiative to speed up the time taken for businesses to bring innovative services to the market, where the risks of such services are well-known, and relatively low. Eligible businesses enjoy expedited application procedures, and significant time and resource savings.[56] While the regulatory sandbox typically features customised constructs tailored to the needs of each participant, the 'express' sandbox uses pre-determined, standardised sandbox constructs on the assumption that the risks involved in eligible services can be reasonably covered by such constructs.[57] As of 2020, the 'express' sandbox covers businesses (1) carrying on business as an insurance broker; and (2) establishing or operating an organised market.[58]

C. Developments

I. Recent Initiatives

There are a variety of initiatives involving crypto assets in both the private and public sector. A significant number of **private sector initiatives** have been launched as a result of, or in conjunction with, MAS's regulatory sandbox. As of July 2018, the MAS's sandbox had provided guidance to more than 140 organisations.[59] MAS maintains a list

---

[51] Monetary Authority of Singapore, 'Fintech Regulatory Sandbox Guidelines' (November 2016), 5–6, available at https://beck-link.de/77533 (accessed 25.11.2020).
[52] Monetary Authority of Singapore, ibid, 3–4.
[53] Monetary Authority of Singapore, ibid, 10–11.
[54] Monetary Authority of Singapore, ibid, 5–7.
[55] Lin, Lin, ibid, 98–99.
[56] Lin, Lin, ibid, 100.
[57] Monetary Authority of Singapore, ibid, 4.
[58] Monetary Authority of Singapore, ibid, 3.
[59] Lin, Lin, ibid, 98.

Part C. Country Reports

of business that are currently operating within its sandbox; as of September 2020, there are two such participants. Propine, a Singapore-incorporated private limited company, is slated to remain in the sandbox from November 2019 to January 2021;[60] the company bills itself as 'the first end-to-end securities services firm built for digital securities from the ground up'.[61] The other business is HG Exchange, a Singapore-incorporated private limited company, that operates a private exchange for the trading of digital and non-digital capital market products based on blockchain technology.[62] The company's sandbox period is from June 2020 to December 2020.[63] Where a business graduates from the sandbox and obtains the necessary license(s) from MAS, restrictions that are imposed on sandbox participants, such as the size of issuances and number of users/investors, are removed. Examples of recent initiatives that have successfully graduated from the sandbox include capital markets platform iSTOX, which uses blockchain and smart contract technology in its platform.[64]

23   A high-profile initiative involving **public sector organizations** is Project Ubin, a collaboration between MAS, Temasek Holdings (Singapore's state investment firm), and various financial firms, including JP Morgan and Accenture. Project Ubin is a **multi-currency payment network** based on blockchain; it was initiated in 2016 by MAS to explore applications of **blockchain and distributed ledger technology** for the settlement of payments and securities. As of 2020, Project Ubin has successfully developed a prototype for a domestic multi-currency payment network and is moving beyond technical experimentation towards real-life implementation.[65]

II. Criminal Cases

24   **Criminal activities** involving crypto assets can be difficult to prosecute, especially when such activities are based in foreign countries and are fall outside the jurisdiction of MAS or the Singapore authorities generally.[66] Examples include **online investment scams** targeting Singapore residents that offer cryptocurrencies and other investment products.[67] The Singapore authorities have been more successful in targeting criminal activity based in Singapore, including a multi-level marketing scheme involving One-Coin, a purported cryptocurrency.[68] MAS has issued also strong warnings to potential bitcoin investors, advising them to act with 'extreme caution', and to understand the

---

[60] Propine's sandbox expiry date was extended from 7 August 2020 to 7 January 2021. Monetary Authority of Singapore, 'Sandbox' (June 2020), available at https://beck-link.de/phpf7 (accessed 25.11.2020).
[61] Propine, 'About Us', available at https://beck-link.de/ch5sb (accessed 25.11.2020).
[62] HG Exchange, 'About Us', available at https://beck-link.de/2ks3p (accessed 25.11.2020).
[63] Monetary Authority of Singapore (2020), ibid.
[64] iSTOX graduated in February 2020: Poh, 'Blockchain capital markets platform iSTOX graduates from MAS fintech sandbox', (Business Times, February 2020), available at https://beck-link.de/t7tpt (accessed 25.11.2020).
[65] Monetary Authority of Singapore & Temasek Holdings, 'Project Ubin Phase 5: Enabling Broad Ecosystem Opportunities' (July 2020) 3–6, available at https://beck-link.de/4k48s (accessed 25.11.2020).
[66] Such activities would fall under the jurisdiction of foreign authorities: see e.g. Ghosh, 'Singaporean man, 29, charged in US for sophisticated identity theft and wire fraud', (10 October *Straits Times* 2019), 29, available at https://beck-link.de/7835x (accessed 25 November 2020).
[67] Choo, Yun Ting, '$78k lost to bitcoin investment scams in last 3 months', (*Straits Times*, 6 December 2018), available at https://beck-link.de/xxe2k (accessed 25.11.2020).
[68] The scheme was investigated by the Commercial Affairs Department pursuant to the Multi-Level Marketing and Pyramid Selling (Prohibition) Act: Public Affairs Department, 'Two Men Charged for Promoting a Multi-Level Marketing Scheme Involving Cryptocurrency (OneCoin)' (*Singapore Police Force*, April 2019) , available at https://beck-link.de/dnf4s (accessed 25.11.2020).

substantial financial risks and potential for fraudulent schemes associated in such investments.[69]

As of September 2020, and to the best of the author's knowledge, there is no written or reported judgment addressing issues of **criminal liability** involving crypto assets for the statutory regimes discussed above. However, the Singapore authorities have been active in this area: a woman was charged with providing payment services without a licence under the Payment Services Act in June 2020. This marks the first time a person was charged with a criminal offence under the Act. The charge appears to have been brought on the basis that the woman had, on the instructions of an unknown person, used her bank account to receive S$3,000 in proceeds from online scams, which she then used to buy Bitcoin. The accused had allegedly carried out the transactions for a commission.[70]

III. Civil Cases

Quoine Pte Ltd v B2C2 Ltd[71] was a high-profile civil case involving **cryptocurrency trading** heard before the Court of Appeal, Singapore's apex court, in 2020. The case was on appeal from the Singapore International Commercial Court, a division of the Singapore High Court.[72] The significance of the case was underscored by the use of a *five* (instead of the usual three) judge panel, comprising two international judges,[73] two Singapore Judges of Appeal,[74] and the Chief Justice of Singapore.[75]

Quoine was a Singapore-incorporated company that operated a cryptocurrency exchange platform called 'QUOINExchange' that enabled users to trade cryptocurrencies for fiat currency or other cryptocurrencies.[76] B2C2 was a market maker that placed seven orders to sell Ethereum for Bitcoins at an exchange rate of about 10 Bitcoins for 1 Ethereum on 19 April 2017 (collectively 'the Disputed Trades'). This was approximately 250 times of the previous going rate of about 0.04 Bitcoins for 1 Ethereum.[77] The Disputed Trades were conducted between B2C2 and two margin traders (the 'Counterparties'), and were automatically settled by Quoine's platform.[78] The Disputed Trades were placed by B2C2 and executed by Quoine using computer systems executing predetermined trading algorithms; no human intervention was involved in the actual trades.[79] On 20 April 2017, Quoine discovered the Disputed Trades, and unilaterally cancelled all of them on the basis that the rates used were highly abnormal. Accordingly, Quoine reversed the settlement transactions for the Disputed Trades.[80] B2C2 commenced legal proceedings against Quoine for the unilateral cancellation of the Disputed Trades and the settlement transactions, alleging that Quoine's actions were in breach of

---

[69] Siow, Li Sen, 'MAS warns bitcoin investors to act with 'extreme caution', *Straits Times* (*Straits Times*, 20 December 2017), available at https://beck-link.de/by7nh (accessed 25.11.2020).
[70] Alkhatib, 'Woman first to be charged under new anti-money laundering law', (Straits Times, 24 June 2020), available at https://beck-link.de/ha58m (accessed 25.11.2020).
[71] *Quoine Pte Ltd v B2C2 Ltd* [2020] SGCA(I) 2, [2020] 2 SLR 20.
[72] *B2C2 Ltd v Quoine Pte Ltd* [2019] SGHC(I) 3, [2019] 4 SLR 17.
[73] Robert French IJ (a former Chief Justice of Australia) & Jonathan Mance IJ (a former Law Lord and Deputy President of the Supreme Court of the United Kingdom).
[74] Andrew Phang JA & Judith Prakash JA.
[75] Sundaresh Menon CJ.
[76] *Quoine Pte Ltd v B2C2 Ltd* [2020] SGCA(I) 2, [2020] 2 SLR 20 [9].
[77] *Quoine Pte Ltd v B2C2 Ltd* [2020] SGCA(I) 2, [2020] 2 SLR 20 [29].
[78] *Quoine Pte Ltd v B2C2 Ltd* [2020] SGCA(I) 2, [2020] 2 SLR 20 [2].
[79] *Quoine Pte Ltd v B2C2 Ltd* [2020] SGCA(I) 2, [2020] 2 SLR 20 [152].
[80] *B2C2 Ltd v Quoine Pte Ltd* [2019] SGHC(I) 3, [2019] 4 SLR 17 [4]-[5], *Quoine Pte Ltd v B2C2 Ltd* [2020] SGCA(I) 2, [2020] 2 SLR 20 [2].

contract and/or breach of trust.[81] A key aspect of Quoine's defence was that the contracts underlying the Disputed Trades were void or voidable for unilateral mistake, such that Quoine's cancellation of the trades was justified.

27　The Court of Appeal upheld the High Court's decision that Quoine was liable for **breach of contract.** First, there were no express or implied terms in the terms and conditions of the contract for the use of Quoine's platform that allowed Quoine to cancel the Disputed Trades.[82] Second, Quoine's defence of unilateral mistake was rejected. A key requirement for unilateral mistake is that one party must have been mistaken as to a fundamental term of the contract.[83] Quoine argued that the Counterparties were operating under a mistake as to the terms of the trading contract with B2C2, in that the Counterparties believed they were exchanging Ethereum for Bitcoin at prices that accurately reflected or did not significantly deviate from true market value.[84] The Court of Appeal (Mance IJ dissenting[85]) held that the Counterparties' mistake was not as to a *term* of the trading contract, but rather a mistaken *assumption* as to the circumstances under which the trading contract would be concluded.[86]

28　The Court of Appeal went on to consider if Bitcoin could regarded as a species of property that could be a subject of a trust, but did not come to any conclusion on this point, given that Quoine had only belatedly raised the issue on appeal.[87] This is unfortunate; there is little jurisprudence on the proprietary aspects of crypto assets in Singapore – and in the Anglo-Commonwealth as a whole.[88] While Singapore's statutory regime provides some guidance on the many ways in which crypto assets are regulated – as capital market products, commodities, and so on – such guidance is primarily directed towards whether crypto assets are subject to licencing requirements (→ para. 11), and not about the ***property rights*** associated with crypto assets. Without greater clarity on the proprietary aspects on the proprietary aspects of crypto assets, it is difficult to figure exactly how they should be treated under established areas of private law, such as personal property law and trust law. For example, should crypto assets be treated as a species of intangible property, as is the case for trademarks and patents?[89] This is a question that cannot be answered by Singapore's statutory regime as it now stands. The absence of judicial guidance on this issue creates considerable uncertainty over the validity of commercial arrangements between private parties, especially if these arrangements are not be directly regulated by Singapore's legislative patchwork.

D. Conclusion

29　Criticisms of Singapore's statutory regime on crypto assets can be summarised as follows. First, the current regime is fragmented, and potentially both over- and under-

---

[81] *Quoine Pte Ltd v B2C2 Ltd* [2020] SGCA(I) 2, [2020] 2 SLR 20 [2].
[82] *Quoine Pte Ltd v B2C2 Ltd* [2020] SGCA(I) 2, [2020] 2 SLR 20 [66].
[83] *Quoine Pte Ltd v B2C2 Ltd* [2020] SGCA(I) 2, [2020] 2 SLR 20 [80]. In the Anglo-Commonwealth, there are separate (but not entirely distinct) regimes for unilateral mistake at 'common law' and in 'equity'. This is a complex doctrinal regime that is not of immediate relevance to the treatment of crypto assets in Singapore and will therefore not be explained. in any detail.
[84] *Quoine Pte Ltd v B2C2 Ltd* [2020] SGCA(I) 2, [2020] 2 SLR 20 [112].
[85] *Quoine Pte Ltd v B2C2 Ltd* [2020] SGCA(I) 2, [2020] 2 SLR 20 [192]-[198].
[86] *Quoine Pte Ltd v B2C2 Ltd* [2020] SGCA(I) 2, [2020] 2 SLR 20 [115].
[87] *Quoine Pte Ltd v B2C2 Ltd* [2020] SGCA(I) 2, [2020] 2 SLR 20 [137].
[88] Lau, 'Computerised Mistake and Proprietised Bitcoin – *B2C2 v Quoine Pte Ltd*' (2019) 35(1) *Banking & Finance Law Review*, 205, 211–212.
[89] Lau, ibid, (205) 211–212.

inclusive. As Part B (para. 3); demonstrates, a crypto asset may be simultaneously regulated by more than one **statutory regime**, which may require compliance with more than one **licencing regime**. The lack of a clear distinction between various licencing regimes amplifies legal uncertainty, and saddles businesses dealing in crypto assets with substantial **compliance costs**.[90] Licencing requirements also makes it difficult for businesses to quickly alter their business model in response to dynamic commercial demands.

Second, it is not obvious if these complex regimes will protect Singapore residents and consumers in practice. Part C.II (para. 24) demonstrates that Singapore's authorities face serious difficulties in cracking down on fraudulent and criminal activities involving crypto assets because many of these schemes are based in foreign countries. While the recent introduction of the Payment Services Act may go some way towards deterring criminal activity, its practical utility (and public perception thereof) remains to be seen.

Finally, more regulation does not make for better regulation. While Singapore has **30** been proactive in introducing legislation and regulations that take an expansive view of crypto assets (e.g., the Payment Services Act), continuing this approach may only complicate and already fragmented and complex regulatory regime without offering any greater clarity or certainty to businesses and consumers. MAS's regulatory sandbox offers businesses some respite from regulatory compliance, but this respite – however welcome – must ultimately come to an end as MAS's position is that businesses must graduate from the sandbox. As a small, developed economy with efficient courts and regulators, neither Singapore's capacity nor political will to regulate crypto assets should be in doubt. Yet, the difficulties inherent in regulating crypto assets may pose substantial – and even insurmountable – challenges for its authorities.

---

[90] Koh, Jonas Lei, ibid, 38.

§ 24
Australia[*]

Literature: Baxt, Black and Hanrahan, *Securities and Financial Services Law* (9th edition, Routledge, 2016); Chambers, 'Budget 2020: Scott Morrison's $7bn digital fast-track push' (28 September 2018) *The Australian*, available at www.theaustralian.com.au (accessed 9.11.2020); Patrick, 'How to make and lose $2B' (28 December 2018-1 January 2019), The Australian Financial Review Weekend, available at: https://beck-link.de/nv73a, (accessed 9.11.2020), 12–13; Walker, 'Crowd-Sourced Funding, Cryptocurrencies and initial Coin Offerings in Australia and New Zealand' (2018) 36 *Company and Securities Law Journal (C&SLJ)*, 111–119; Xu, Xenos and Skevington, 'Blockchain Bites: Australian sentenced for Ripple theft, SEC enforcement action against Boon.Tech, New York greenlist and FedNow' (PiperAlderman Blog, 14.8.2020), available at: https://beck-link.de/2d7be (accessed 9.11.2020).

Outline

	para.
A. Introduction	1
I. Country Snapshot	1
II. Constitution	2
III. Legal System	4
IV. Securities Regulation	5
V. Consumer Usage of Cryptocurrency	6
B. Fintech Regulation	7
I. Regulator	7
II. Regulatory Policy Making	8
III. AML/CTF Legislation	9
IV. Digital Currencies	10
V. Tax Treatment of Cryptocurrencies	11
VI. Open Banking in Australia	16
VII. Crowd Sourced Funding	17
VIII. Peer-to-Peer Lending (P2PL)	18
IX. Abusive Conduct	19
C. Fintech Developments in Australia	20
I. Policy	20
II. Payments	21
III. Australian Securities Exchange	22
IV. Innovation Hub and International Co-operation on Innovation	23
V. Innovation: ASIC's Regulatory Sandbox	25
D. Crypto Asset Business Regulation	27
I. Overview	27
II. ASIC Guidance on Crypto Asset Trading	29
E. Initial Coin Offerings	39
I. Initial Coin Offerings of Digital Tokens	39
II. ASIC Guidance on ICOs	41
III. Definition of Security under the Corporations Act 2001	45
1. The Section 9 and Section 92 definitions	46
2. Definition of Security under Chapter 6D	49
a) First test: The scheme satisfies any one of the following	52
b) Second test	53
c) Third test	54
F. Summary	55

---

[*] This publication was made possible by the NPRP award NPRP 11 S-1119-170016 from the Qatar National Research Fund (a member of the Qatar Foundation). The statements made herein are the sole responsibility of the authors.

A. Introduction

I. Country Snapshot

Australia is a large island nation in the southern hemisphere. The **population** is approximately 25.5 million and **GDP** is around USD1.423 trillion. It is the 14th largest economy in the world and has the 10th highest per capita income. Australia rates highly on all relevant indices; it is a member of the OECD and has a first world education system. In 2019, Australia ranked 13th on the Network Readiness Index, a World Economic Forum framework which assesses the factors, policies, and institutions that enable a country to fully leverage information and communication technologies for inclusive, sustainable growth, competitiveness. Elsewhere, the Global Innovation Index 2019 ranked Australia at 22nd in the world and the Global Competitiveness Index ranked it at 16 out of 140 countries. In short, Australia has the requisite **infrastructure** and **human capital** to create Fintech businesses.

II. Constitution

Australia is a federation formed in 1901 from States which were British Colonies. The Commonwealth of Australia Constitution Act 1900 which contains the Australian Constitution, is an enactment of the British Imperial Parliament but the Constitution itself may be amended by a process involving the Commonwealth Parliament and a Referendum. The Commonwealth of Australia consists of six States (New South Wales, Queensland, South Australia, Tasmania, Victoria and Western Australia) and other Commonwealth Territories of which the two most important are the Northern Territory and the Australian Capital Territory.

Under the Commonwealth Constitution, specified legislative powers are assigned to the Commonwealth. Some of these powers are exclusive to the Commonwealth and others are exercisable concurrently with the States. The **Commonwealth** has **specific constitutional power** in respect of corporations formed in Australia and foreign corporations. Powers relating to interstate trade might also support securities laws. Each State has power under its own constitution to make laws for the peace, order and good government of that State. In the event of an inconsistency between Commonwealth laws and State laws, the State law is, to the extent of the inconsistency, inoperative. Australian laws (both Commonwealth and State) may operate extra-territorially in accordance with international law.

III. Legal System

The Australian legal system is derived from the United Kingdom. The final appellate court in Australia is the High Court of Australia. The principal legislation affecting Fintech is the **Corporations Act 2001.** Litigation relating to this Act may be brought in the first instance in the Federal Court or the Supreme Court of a State or Territory. Under rules of cross vesting a Court may decide to refer a matter to a more appropriate jurisdiction within Australia. Australian Courts follow rules of precedent, being bound by relevant appellate authority in their own jurisdiction and by decisions of the High Court (which is not bound by its own previous decisions). Other Australian decisions and decisions of the other common law jurisdictions such as the United Kingdom, New

Zealand and Canada are of persuasive authority. So, for example, the New Zealand High Court decision of 08.04.2020 in *Ruscoe v Cryptopia Limited (In Liq.)* HC 728 is of precedent value in Australia. The *Ruscoe* case considered whether crypto assets amount to property. The High Court in New Zealand relied on the United Kingdom Jurisdiction Taskforce, *Legal Statement on Cryptoassets and Smart Contracts* (2019) and case law from other common law jurisdictions.[1] The Court endorsed the 'classic statement' of the definition of 'property' in the UK House of Lords case, *National Provincial Bank Limited v Ainsworth*[2] [1965] AC 1175 at 1247–1248 per Lord Wilberforce. The High Court was satisfied that cryptocurrencies meet **all four of the requirements for 'property'** established by the *Ainsworth* case, viz.: identifiable subject matter, identifiable by third parties, capable of assumption by third parties, and some degree of permanence or stability. Decisions of United States' Courts on similar legislation are occasionally cited but tend to carry less weight in Australian courts. The Corporations Act 2001 provides some scope for class or representative actions. Under the Act any party having a recognized legal interest may generally initiate litigation.

IV. Securities Regulation

5   Securities legislation applied nationally from 1980 under co-operative arrangements between the Commonwealth and the States and the Northern Territory. In 1989, the Commonwealth asserted power to enact legislation covering the entire legislative field relating to corporations and securities. Some aspects of this legislation were challenged by several States and it was held to be invalid. Consequently, the Commonwealth, the States and Northern Territory entered into an agreement under which national legislation would be enacted effective to deal with the entire field relying on combined Commonwealth and State powers. This regime continued until 14 July 2001 when it was replaced by national statute law under power referred by the States. The current legislation – largely contained in the Corporations Act 2001 – was enacted by the Commonwealth pursuant to a referral of power from the States. As stated, the Corporations Act 2001 is the key statute affecting Fintech. Legislation on **taxation, AML/CTF and consumer protection** is also relevant.

V. Consumer Usage of Cryptocurrency

6   Cryptocurrency is used to some extent in the Australian consumer ecosystem. It is possible to buy cryptocurrency at the post office, through crypto ATMs, or via regulated Australian cryptocurrency exchanges. Australian crypto holders can use cryptocurrency in some **everyday transactions**. In June 2020, Coca-Cola Amatil entered into a partnership with digital asset integrator, Centrapay, that allows Australian and New Zealand crypto holders to exchange crypto for beverages at Coca-Cola vending machines. The legitimate use of cryptocurrency for everyday transactions is also speeding up in other Australian sectors. South Australian university students can now use Bitcoin to pay for

---

[1] The Court considered the case of the Singapore International Commercial Court 14.03.2019 – *B2C2 Ltd v Quoine Pte Ltd* 34 Singapore Law Reports (SLR) 2019, 17; decision of High Court of Justice (Business and Property Courts of England and Wales) 28.09.2018 – *Vorotyntseva v Money-4 Ltd*, 2596 (Ch.); decision of the Supreme Court of British Colombia – *Shair.Com Global Digital Services Ltd v Arnold*, 1512 and the decision of the High Court of Justice (Business and Property Courts of England and Wales) 13.12.2019- *AA v Persons Unknown* – 4 Weekly Law Reports (WLR) 2020, 35.

[2] Appeal case No. 1175 of the (Judicial Committee of the) House of Lords 13.05.1965 – *National Provincial Bank Limited v Ainsworth*, 1247–1248.

student housing or tuition, while homeowners can legally buy or sell property using cryptocurrency *in lieu of* Australian dollars.

The Australian legal system recently recognized cryptocurrency as a **valid security** for legal expenses. In March 2020, the New South Wales District Court approved a claimant's cryptocurrency account as security for court costs, which is normally taken as fiat payment into a trust account or as a bank guarantee. In 2020, a woman from Sydney was sentenced to two years in prison for the theft of 100,000 'Ripple' cryptocurrency which was valued at $400,000[3] at the time. The woman hacked into a 56-year-old man's cryptocurrency account and swapped the two-factor authentication to her mobile phone. She then transferred the large sum of cryptocurrency to an overseas exchange where it was traded for Bitcoin and shuffled into different wallets. The woman was one of the first Australians to be charged with the theft of digital assets in Australia.[4]

B. Fintech Regulation

I. Regulator

To a significant extent, the **Australian Securities and Investments Commission** (ASIC) is a 'one-stop shop' for crypto regulation in Australia. It is supported and assisted by various other government bodies and works alongside the **Australian Securities Exchange** (ASX, the largest securities exchange in Australia, itself a listed entity) which retains a strong relationship with ASIC and the **Reserve Bank of Australia**. Before the harmonization of corporate law across Australia, each state had its own National Companies and Securities Commission office. The Australian Securities Commission (ASC) was established on 1 January 1991 and later reincarnated as ASIC on 1 July 1998. ASIC's authority and remit are established under the Australian Securities and Investments Commission Act 2001. In 1998, the functions of ASIC were extended to include certain consumer protection matters including the regulation of some insurance and superannuation products. The Act confers various statutory powers on ASIC and directs it in performing its functions to strive to maintain, facilitate and improve the performance of the financial system and the entities within that system, in the interests of commercial certainty, reducing business costs, and the efficiency and development of the economy. It also seeks to promote the confident and informed participation of investors and consumers in the financial system, administer its functions with a minimum of procedural requirements and process and make available information to the public as soon as practicable. Finally, it must take whatever action it can to enforce the law.

7

II. Regulatory Policy Making

While the task of authoritatively interpreting the legislation is fundamentally that of the courts, ASIC, as the regulatory authority established under the 'Corporations Act 2001, issues a series of interpretative **Regulatory Guides**[5] which express a construction

8

---

[3] All references are made to the Australian Dollar.
[4] Xu, Xenos and Skevington, 'Blockchain Bites: Australian sentenced for Ripple theft, SEC enforcement action against Boon.Tech, New York greenlist and FedNow' (PiperAlderman Blog, 14.8.2020), available at https://beck-link.de/2d7be (accessed 9.11.2020).
[5] These guides as well as shorter Information Sheets can be viewed on the ASIC website: www.asic.gov.au.

of the law that it intends to adopt in its administration where doubts have arisen. ASIC guidance on blockchain and DLT appears in ASIC Information Sheet 219.[6] This information sheet refers prospective developers of DLT to the ASIC Innovation Hub which is designed to assist FinTech start-ups developing innovative financial products or services.

III. AML/CTF Legislation

9   The Anti-Money Laundering and Counter-Terrorism Financing Act 2006 (Cth) applies to entities that provide 'designated services' with an Australian connection. The Act catches any entity that engages in financial services or credit activities. Such entities must enrol with the Australian Transaction Reports and Analysis Centre (AUSTRAC). Obligations include reporting and due diligence.

IV. Digital Currencies

10   Early Australian policy work on aspects of digital currencies appears in a report of the Senate Economics Reference Committee on digital currencies, 'Digital Currency – Game Changer or Bit Player'.[7] This report contains extensive references to the **tax treatment of digital currencies** and notes that such currencies are not financial products for the purposes of the Corporations Act 2001. ASIC has also stated that digital currencies are not regulated by ASIC under the Corporations Act 2001.[8] In the result, a digital currency such as Bitcoin will not be caught by the provisions of the Corporations Act. Bitcoin can be characterized as a digital token which functions as a medium of exchange or a commodity. However, there are other types of digital tokens which may be characterized in Australia as securities or financial products in which case the Corporations Act 2001 may apply.

V. Tax Treatment of Cryptocurrencies

11   The Australian Tax Office's current views on the taxation treatment of cryptocurrencies are contained in four 2014 taxation determinations.

12   In **Taxation Determination 2014/25**, the commissioner expressed the view that Bitcoin is not foreign currency for the purposes of Division 775 of the Income Tax Assessment Act 1997.

13   In **Taxation Determination 2014/26**, the commissioner expressed the view that Bitcoin is a capital gains tax asset for the purposes of Section 108-5(1) of the Income Tax Assessment Act. This determination also sets out that:
– a disposal of Bitcoin may give rise to a capital gains tax if the capital proceeds exceed the cost base of the tokens. Capital proceeds can include the market value of other property given for the disposal. There appears to be a somewhat widespread misapprehension in the marketplace that disposals between various cryptocurrencies do not give rise to gains and that only conversion to fiat currency crystallises a gain – which is incorrect;

---

[6] ASIC, 'Information Sheet No. 219 – Evaluating distributed ledger technology' (March 2017), available at https://beck-link.de/awt2v (accessed 9.11.2020).
[7] The Senate Economics References Committee, 'Digital currency – game changer or bit player' (August 2015), available at https://beck-link.de/4;4mnc (accessed 9.11.2020).
[8] ASIC, 'Regulatory Guide 257 – testing fintech products and services without holding an AFS or credit license (withdrawn)' (August 2017), available at https://beck-link.de/p7ds2 (accessed 9.11.2020).

- if the first element of the cost base of a token is $10,000 or less and the token qualifies as a personal use asset, the gain may be disregarded under the personal use exemption; and
- in some cases, a gain on the disposal of cryptocurrency may be on income account (in which case the capital gain is disregarded). Taxpayers should refer to Taxation Ruling TR 92/3 for guidance on these points.

In **Taxation Determination 2014/27**, the commissioner expressed the view that Bitcoin held for the purposes of sale or exchange in the ordinary course of a business is trading stock for the purposes of Division 70. This determination also sets out that:
- Bitcoin held by a taxpayer carrying on a business of mining and selling Bitcoin or a taxpayer carrying on a Bitcoin exchange business will be considered trading stock; and
- Bitcoin received as a method of payment by any business that sells goods will also be considered to be trading stock of that business where the Bitcoin is held for the purpose of sale or exchange in the ordinary course of business.

In **Taxation Determination 2014/28**, the commissioner expressed the view that the provision of Bitcoin by an employer to an employee in respect of their employment is a property fringe benefit for the purposes of the Fringe Benefits Tax Assessment Act 1986. The determination also sets out that:
- Bitcoin is 'any kind of property other than tangible property' for Fringe Benefits Tax Assessment Act purposes. The provision of it to an employee is therefore a property fringe benefit; and
- Bitcoin will not be a property fringe benefit if it is salary or wages.

Fringe benefits are taxed differently than salary or wages.

VI. Open Banking in Australia

The Second Payment Services Directive (PSD2)[9] in EU legislation came into force on 13 January 2018. After that date, a managed roll-out was expected. **Open Banking (OB)** is the UK version of PSD2. PSD2 requires banks to open their data to third parties; OB requires them to do so in a standard format. OB in the UK was driven by the Competition and Markets Authority (CMA) with the intention of increasing competition and innovation in the market. In Australia, an important development for Fintech was the commencement of enabling legislation for OB in the Consumer Data Right Act 2019 on 1 October 2020. OB allows consumers to elect to share financial information held by one bank between other banks, non-bank financial institutions and fintech so-called, 'neo-banks'.[10] The sharing of financial information enables fintech organisations to onboard clients efficiently whilst more accurately calculating risk so they can offer competitive products. OB in Australia is part of a wider reform movement – not just the banking sector but also in the energy and telecommunications sectors.

VII. Crowd Sourced Funding

Fundraising laws are found in the Corporations Act 2001. So, for example, an initial public offering (IPO) must comply with the **disclosure obligations** contained in Chapter 6D of that Act unless an exemption applies. An exemption to enable crowd

---

[9] Directive 2015/2366/EU.
[10] Most Australia neo-banks do not have physical branches but instead offer online only savings accounts, FX accounts or mortgages. The neo-banks include: Up Bank; Volt Bank; 86400; Judo Bank; Revolut and Douugh.

sourced funding (CSF) by unlisted public companies came into force in Australia in September 2017 via a new Part 6D.3A of the Corporations Act 2001. ASIC has issued a Regulatory Guide that elaborates all requirements and is available on the ASIC website. For public companies, the **issuer cap** is $5 million, and the **retail investor cap** is $10,000 per company in a 12-month period. The assets and revenue test equals $25 million. The CSF intermediary is required to hold an **Australian Financial Services License** (AFS). Further development of CSF in Australia occurred via the Corporations Amendment (Crowd-sourced Funding for Proprietary Companies) Act, 2018 which enabled proprietary companies to raise up to $3 million in any 12-month period. ASIC Information Sheet 225, *Initial coin offerings and crypto-assets* (May 2019), examines the relationship between ICOs and crowd-sourced funding. It states 'ICOs are sometimes referred to by industry as a form of crowd funding. Crowd funding using an ICO is not the same as 'crowd-sourced funding' (CSF) regulated by the Corporations Act. Care should be taken to ensure the public is not misled about the application of the CSF laws to an ICO.'

VIII. Peer-to-Peer Lending (P2PL)

18   P2PL is known as marketplace lending in Australia and is operated by Fintech businesses via online platforms. Unlike New Zealand, there is **no specific legislative provision** for P2PL. Various legal structures are employed to facilitate P2PL in Australia as elaborated in ASIC Information Sheet 213 on peer-to-peer lending of March 2016.[11]

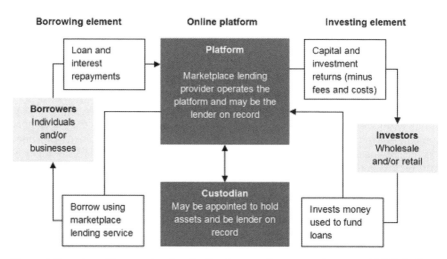

Figure 1: Overview of how marketplace lending is generally structured; source: ASIC Info Sheet 213, *Marketplace Lending (Peer-to-Peer Lending)*, March 2016.

IX. Abusive Conduct

19   During the COVID-19 pandemic in 2020, ASIC saw an increase in reports from consumers losing money in crypto-asset (or cryptocurrency) scams, particularly with

---

[11] ASIC, 'Information Sheet No. 213 – Marketplace lending (peer-to-peer lending) products' (March 2016), available at https://beck-link.de/ykxw8 (accessed 9.10.2020).

those using false celebrity endorsements. Reports of misconduct received by ASIC from March to May 2020 were up 20 % compared to the same period last year.[12]

C. Fintech Developments in Australia

I. Policy

Australia initially encouraged FinTech innovation by crafting a **national strategy** entitled 'Backing Australian Fintech' in 2016.[13] In 2019, a Senate Select Committee on Financial Technology and Regulatory Technology was formed to inquire into these areas and report in April 2021. In September 2020, the Senate Select Committee released an interim report.[14] Preliminary recommendations indicate a path to permanent reforms reflecting those passed in response to the COVID-19 pandemic.

The Committee's **preliminary recommendations** include:
- amendments to the Corporations Act 2001 to allow companies to decide the best format for holding annual general meetings and other prescribed meetings, including through virtual meetings, in-person meetings or a hybrid.
- amendments to the Corporations Act to allow companies to communicate with shareholders electronically by default, with shareholders having the right to request paper-based communications on an opt-in basis.
- amendments to the Corporations Act and other relevant legislation to allow for the execution of legal documents using electronic signatures.
- amendments to the relevant legislation to enable the witnessing of official documents via videoconferencing or other secure technological means.

The Digital Transformation Agency (DTA), a federal government entity, is developing a new digital ID system that will allow access to government services online: see dta.gov.au.[15] In response to the COVID-19 pandemic, the Australian government announced a AUD7 billion investment in the digital economy in the 2020 budget.[16]

II. Payments

The **New Payments Platform** (NPP) was launched in early 2018 as a collaboration between the Reserve Bank of Australia and Australian banks. The NPP is an upgraded payments infrastructure that benefits Fintech businesses as well as consumers and government agencies.

III. Australian Securities Exchange

The Australian Securities Exchange (ASX) is transitioning to a new **blockchain system** for the **settlement of trades**. In June 2020, the ASX announced it had decided

---

[12] ASIC, 'Scam alert: ASIC sees a rise in crypto scams', (June 2020), available at https://beck-link.de/7szkr (accessed 9.11.2020).
[13] Australian Government, The Treasury, 'Backing Australian FinTech' (18 March 2016), available at https://beck-link.de/w22sv (accessed 9.11.2020).
[14] Parliament of Australia, Select Committee on Financial Technology and Regulatory Technology, available at https://beck-link.de/r47db (accessed 9.11.2020).
[15] Australian Government, Digital Transformation Agency, dta.gov.au.
[16] Chambers, 'Budget 2020: Scott Morrison's $7bn digital fast-track push' (28 September 2018) *The Australian*, available at www.theaustralian.com.au (accessed 9.11.2020).

to delay the rollout of its DLT replacement for CHESS until April 2022, one full year behind the initial target launch date. Despite the delay, the ASX identified the following milestones which have been reached:

- The CHESS replacement application and the distributed ledger have been successfully deployed to several ASX technology environments across multiple data centres;
- A seventh software drop has been deployed on schedule into the customer development environment (CDE), which represents 89 % of the core clearing and settlement functionality used by customers and
- Thirty-four organisations have connected to the CDE, including software providers, brokers and share registries.

There are several Fintech companies listed on the ASX in the payments and consumer finance area. The most well-known is Afterpay Limited.[17] All cryptoasset exchanges are unlisted entities.

IV. Innovation Hub and International Co-operation on Innovation

23   In 2015, ASIC launched its Innovation Hub to help Fintech business navigate the regulatory framework without compromising investor and financial consumer trust and confidence. If an entity meets certain eligibility criteria, it can receive **informal guidance from ASIC** on its obligations under the financial services' regulatory framework; how ASIC will administer this framework (e.g. how to obtain an Australian financial services license); ASIC's thoughts on regulatory issues to consider in the establishment of the business. ASIC will not provide legal advice or financial assistance but encourages entities that have specific requests or questions about an ICO or crypto asset to contact the Innovation Hub.

24   ASIC and the UK Financial Conduct Authority (FCA) entered into an agreement in 2016 whereby they will **refer to one another those innovative businesses** seeking to enter the others' market. The regulators will provide support to innovative businesses before, during and after authorization to help reduce regulatory uncertainty and time to market.[18] On 18 October 2017, ASIC and the Swiss Financial Markets Authority (FINMA) entered a new agreement to cooperate on innovation in the financial sector. The agreement aims to encourage innovation in financial services in Switzerland and Australia and to support financial services innovators in meeting legal requirements when operating in each country.[19] To date, **FinTech referral and information-sharing agreements** have been entered with the Monetary Authority of Singapore, the UK Financial Conduct Authority, Ontario Securities Commission, Hong Kong Securities and Futures Commission, the Japan Financial Services Agency, Malaysia Securities Commission and Abu Dhabi Global Market Financial Services Regulatory Authority.

---

[17] Other ASX listed Fintech entities include EML Payments, Fintech Chain, Zip Co, Pushpay, Raiz, Digital X, Fatfish Blockchain and Wisr. The Australian crypto payments service provider, Banxa, established in 2014, chose to pursue listing on the Canadian TSX Venture Exchange instead of the ASX due to perceived hostility of the ASX towards crypto companies.

[18] ASIC, 'Media Release No. 16-088 – British and Australian financial regulators sign agreement to support innovative businesses' (March 2016), available at https://beck-link.de/63fcp (accessed 9.11.2020).

[19] ASIC, 'Media Release No. 17-364 – ASIC expands network of fintech cooperation agreements to Switzerland' (October 2017), available at https://beck-link.de/kn2mz (accessed 9.11.2020).

V. Innovation: ASIC's Regulatory Sandbox

To facilitate innovation, ASIC has introduced a **FinTech licensing exemption** which applies to specified products or services.[20] Innovative Fintech start-ups can rely on these exemptions where:
- there are existing statutory exemptions or flexibility in the Corporations Act 2001 and National Consumer Credit Protection Act 2009;
- the business can rely on ASIC's relief under ASIC Corporations (Concept Validation Licensing Exemption) Instrument 2016/1175 or ASIC Credit (Concept Validation Licensing Exemption) Instrument 2016/1176 for testing certain specified products and services or for other services, where ASIC grants individual relief.

On 29 May 2020, the Corporations (Fintech Sandbox Australian Financial Services Licence Exemption) Regulations 2020 and the National Consumer Credit Protection (Fintech Sandbox Australian Financial Services Licence Exemption) Regulations 2020 received royal assent. These regulations implement the **changes to the ASIC Fintech Sandbox** proposed under the Treasury Laws Amendment (2018 Measures No. 2) Act 2020. The key changes to the sandbox include: an increase in the length of the exemption from 12 to 24 months; broadening the range of financial services for market testing; empowering ASIC to attach conditions on the granting of exemptions and allowing the exemptions to apply to specific elements of an existing product or service. The enhanced regulatory sandbox is scheduled to commence on 1 September 2020. It supersedes and expands on the ASIC sandbox that was issued in December 2016, allowing for a longer testing period (up to 24 months) for a broader range of financial services and credit activities and for a wider range of businesses (including existing licensees). ASIC Information Sheet 248[21] covers the new regime and application process in greater detail.

D. Crypto Asset Business Regulation

I. Overview

The regulatory framework that applies to all Fintech businesses in Australia includes **financial services and consumer credit licensing, registration** and **disclosure obligations, consumer law requirements** and **AML/CTF law.** Entities that carry on financial service business or engage in consumer credit activities must hold an Australian Financial Services Licence (AFSL). Because the definitions of a financial service and financial product are wide, any investment or wealth management business, payment service, advisory business, trading platform must hold an AFSL, which will come with tailored conditions appropriate to the scope of the business. P2PL will require the holding of an Australian credit licence (ACL). Licensing applications for AFSL and ACLs, including the up-front and ongoing costs and the length of the application process should be considered when commencing a cryptoasset business in Australia.

As considered in ASIC Information Sheet 248,[22] there may be **exemptions for certain innovative financial services or credit activities** to operate without first obtaining an

---

[20] ASIC, 'Regulatory Guide 257 – testing fintech products and services without holding an AFS or credit license (withdrawn)', available at https://beck-link.de/dx28z (accessed 9.11.2020).
[21] ASIC, 'Information Sheet No. 248 – Enhanced regulatory sandbox' (August 2020), available at https://beck-link.de/xp525 (accessed 9.11.2020).
[22] Ibid.

Australian financial services (AFS) licence or an Australian credit licence by using the enhanced regulatory sandbox. Entities must meet eligibility criteria to test in the enhanced regulatory sandbox, including satisfying two new tests – the net public benefit test and the innovation test. There are also limitations on what financial services and products can be provided, and what credit activities can be engaged in. There is a $10,000 individual limit on the value of certain financial services that can be provided to retail clients, and an aggregate $5 million total exposure limit for all financial services provided to and credit activities engaged in with all clients.

II. ASIC Guidance on Crypto Asset Trading

29   When an entity needs a relevant license, ASIC Information Sheet 225[23] contains detailed information on crypto asset trading. The guidance must be treated with caution in the absence of judicial consideration. To better understand ASIC's views, we reproduce portions of this guidance in a restructured and abridged form for clarity of exposition:

30   What rules and restrictions govern the **exchange of fiat currency and cryptoassets**? Other than customary tax obligations and criminal law prohibitions, there are no specific restrictions governing the exchange of fiat currency and cryptoassets for users. Businesses providing the service of exchanging of fiat currency for cryptoassets and vice versa must comply with the Anti-money Laundering and Counter-Terrorism Financing (AML/CTF) Act 2006 and be registered as a digital currency exchange.

31   Where are investors allowed to **trade cryptoassets**? How are exchanges, alternative trading systems and **secondary markets for cryptoassets** regulated? There are no regulatory restrictions on where investors can trade cryptoassets. Exchanges, alternative trading systems and secondary markets for cryptoassets are regulated under the AML/CTF Act. If a cryptoasset is a financial product, an exchange or market operator must have an Australian financial services licence (AFSL) with suitable authorisation.

32   How are **cryptoasset custodians** regulated? Cryptoasset custodians are regulated only if the cryptoassets stored by the custodian entity are financial products, in which case the custodian must obtain an AFSL with appropriate custodial and depository authorisation in accordance with Australian Securities and Investments Commission (ASIC) Regulatory Guide 1 and Regulatory Guide 133.

33   How are **cryptoasset broker-dealers** regulated? Businesses that give advice, deal or provide other intermediary services for cryptoassets that are financial products must hold an AFSL. ASIC requires that broker-dealers interacting with these types of cryptoassets must comply with Regulatory Guide 36 ('Licensing: Financial product advice and dealing'). Where the broker-dealer is exchanging cryptoassets for fiat currency (whether Australian or not) or vice versa in the course of carrying on a digital currency exchange business, the broker-dealer must also apply for registration as a digital currency exchange with AUSTRAC and prepare a compliant AML/CTF programme.

34   What is the legal status of **decentralised cryptoasset exchanges**? There is no specific legislation or regulations which consider the legal status of decentralised exchanges. Depending on the characteristics of the decentralised exchange, it is likely to still be captured under the AML/CTF Act as a digital currency exchange which is required to be registered with AUSTRAC. A decentralised exchange is likely to be an unincorporated association, as would almost all decentralised autonomous organisations.

---

[23] ASIC, 'Information Sheet No. 225 – Initial coin offerings and crypto-assets' (May 2019), available at https://beck-link.de/t85ma (accessed 9.11. 2020).

What is the legal status of **peer-to-peer (person-to-person) transfers of cryptoassets**? There is no prohibition on the exchange of cryptoassets on a peer-to-peer basis. The operation of a peer-to-peer digital currency exchange will require an AFSL if the tokens on the exchange are financial products. An exchange business must also be registered as a digital currency exchange if it facilitates the transfer of cryptoassets for fiat currency.

Trading with anonymous parties. For individuals, there are no explicit legislative or regulatory restrictions on trading cryptoassets with anonymous parties. For businesses operating a digital currency exchange or providing another designated service, they must comply with the AML/CTF Act, which includes not providing a service to anonymous users. More than 250 global digital currency exchanges are registered in Australia.

Are **foreign cryptocurrency exchanges** subject to Australia's jurisdiction's laws and regulations governing cryptoasset exchanges? The AML/CTF Act provisions relating to digital currency exchanges apply to anyone that provides a registrable digital currency exchange service to users in Australia.

Under what circumstances may a citizen of your jurisdiction **lawfully exchange cryptoassets on a foreign exchange**? Subject to criminal laws prohibiting citizens from engaging in money laundering, terrorist financing or other criminal acts, there are no restrictions on a citizen participating in the lawful exchange of cryptoassets on a foreign exchange.

E. Initial Coin Offerings

I. Initial Coin Offerings of Digital Tokens

The compliance costs and liabilities placed on issuers for defective disclosure associated with an IPO means issuers usually seek to attract an exemption from full disclosure. Typically, however, an ICO seeks to avoid the application of the securities law altogether. The ICO fundraising mechanism is especially attractive for issuers for reasons such as: no business history required; no dilution of control; greatly reduced compliance costs; no formal prospectus required (although a Whitepaper containing key information will usually be promulgated) and the ability to reduce exposure to liability. There were a few Australian ICOs in 2018.[24] These ICOs all involved the **offering of utility tokens via unregistered managed investment schemes** (MISs). The tokens issued were then listed on crypto exchanges. Perhaps prompted by the launching of ICOs that were not registered as an MIS, on 19 April 2018, ASIC received delegated powers from the ACCC to take action under the Australian Consumer Law against misleading and deceptive conduct in marketing or selling ICOs, even if the ICO did not involve a financial product. In practice, this means that ASIC can move against the issuer of a Whitepaper that contains misleading and deceptive material but does not involve a financial product. This appears to have had a chilling effect on ICOs in Australia.[25]

---

[24] Walker, 'Crowd-Sourced Funding, Cryptocurrencies and initial Coin Offerings in Australia and New Zealand' (2018) 36 *Company and Securities Law Journal (C&SLJ)*, 111–119, for a brief discussion of the Power Ledger and other ICOs. For an in-depth account of the Power Ledger ICO and its aftermath, see Patrick, 'How to make and lose $2B' (28 December 2018-1 January 2019), The Australian Financial Review Weekend, available at https://beck-link.de/nv73a, (accessed 9.11.2020), 12–13.

[25] A crypto asset issuer in Australia would seek to avoid characterization of its tokens as a "financial product" where possible to avoid the disclosure provisions of the Corporations Act 2001.

40   The key legal issue arising from the ICO phenomenon in Australia is whether the digital tokens issued in an ICO fall within the definition of **'securities'** or a **'managed investment scheme'** for the purposes of securities regulation. As discussed above, a few ICOs have taken place in Australia. Digital tokens are neither shares nor debentures; however, they may be caught in Australia under the rubric of a managed investment scheme (MIS). In the United States, the SEC opined that the digital tokens issued by 'The DAO' were securities under the Securities Act 1933 and the Securities Exchange Act of 1934.[26] Under US law, an 'investment contract' is a security. The SEC applied the tests enunciated in SEC v WJ Howey Co., 328 U.S. 293 at 301 (1946)[27] to find that the tokens issued by the DAO amounted to an investment in an investment contract and were hence securities. In brief, the Howey test involves four factors: (1) the investment of money (glossed by the SEC as a 'contribution of value'); (2) a common enterprise; (3) a reasonable expectation of profit and (4) profit derived from the managerial efforts of others (for details, → § 22 paras. 7–14). There are **obvious parallels** between the concept of an investment contract under US law and a managed investment scheme under Chapter 7 of the Corporations Act 2001 in Australia.

II. ASIC Guidance on ICOs

41   ASIC provided guidance on Initial Coin Offerings in Information Sheet 225.[28] It provides basic guidance on the legal status of ICOs made available to investors in Australia regardless of where the ICO is created and whether offered from Australia or offshore. The Information Sheet seeks to answer a set of related questions. The salient questions and answers are reproduced below:

42   When could an ICO be a **managed investment scheme**? This involves a consideration of what rights or benefits are attached to the tokens. ASIC states that, '[i]f the value of the coin is related to the management of an arrangement the issuer of the ICO is likely to be offering an MIS.'

43   When could an ICO be an **offer of shares**? A share is usually understood as a bundle of rights relating to a company such as ownership rights, voting rights, an entitlement to share in future profits through dividends, and a residual claim in a winding up. Most ICOs will be structured in such a way that no question of share ownership will arise (e.g., a contribution to a Foundation). If shares are offered, however, then Chapter 6D will apply and a disclosure document must be prepared.

44   **Trading of coins on a financial market?** A financial market is a facility through which offers to acquire or dispose of financial products are regularly made. Anyone who operates a financial market in Australia must obtain a licence to do so or otherwise be exempted by the Minister. If an ICO token is found to be a financial product, then any platform that enables investors to buy or sell these coins may involve the operation of a financial market. If so, the operator of the platform may need to hold an Australian market licence.

III. Definition of Security under the Corporations Act 2001

45   To better understand the ICO matter, we now look more closely at the definition of a security. To place the ASIC guidance described in Information Sheet 225 in context, we

---

[26] SEC, 'Report of Investigation Pursuant to Section 21 (a) of the Securities Exchange Act of 1934: The DAO', Exchange Act Release No. 81207 (July 25, 2017); for more detailed discussion, → § 22 para. 7.

[27] Decision No. 843 of the U.S Supreme Court 27.05.1946 – *Securities and Exchange Commission (SEC) v. Howey Co.*, 293–301.

[28] ASIC, 'Information sheet No. 225, ibid.

now review the **various definitions of a security** appearing under the Corporations Act 2001.[29] As is well-known, the relevant statutory definitions in the Corporations Act 2001 are opaque and convoluted especially when compared to New Zealand. In this regard, Australia presents difficulties for ICOs.

1. The Section 9 and Section 92 definitions

46 The term, **'securities'** appears in s 9 which is the main interpretation section of the Corporations Act 2001. It states that, 'securities have the meaning given by section 92'. Section 92 (1) says that the term 'securities' means (in summary form):
- debentures, stocks or bonds issued or proposed to be issued by a government; or
- shares in, or debentures of, a body; or
- interests in a managed investment scheme; or
- units of such shares

but does not include a derivative as defined in Chapter 7.

Section 9 states that the terms, 'derivative', 'financial product', financial market', 'financial service' are defined in Chapter 7 of the Corporations Act 2001.

47 A **'managed investment scheme'** is defined in section 9 as a scheme that has the following features (in summary):
- people contribute money or money's worth as consideration to acquire rights (interests) to benefits produced by the scheme (whether the rights are actual, prospective or contingent and whether they are enforceable or not)
- any of the contributions are to be pooled, or used in a common enterprise, to produce financial benefits, or benefits consisting of rights or interests in property, for the people who hold interests in the scheme
- the members do not have day-to-day control over the operation of the scheme.

48 Section 92(3) states that in Chapters 6 to 6CA (inclusive), the term 'securities' is given a **slightly extended meaning**. However, s 92(4) says that in Chapter 6D (Fundraising) the term, 'securities' has the meaning given by section 700 and that, in Chapter 7, it has the meaning given by section 761A. Because an ICO involves a type of fundraising, the section 700 definition of a security is most important.

2. Definition of Security under Chapter 6D

49 Section 700 states that the term 'securities' has the **same meaning as it has in Chapter 7** excluding section 761A(e) or (f) or simple corporate bonds. It also states that Chapter 6D applies to offers of securities that are received in Australia regardless of where the issue occurs. The section 761A definition of a security is (to paraphrase):
- a share
- a debenture
- a legal or equitable right or interest in a security
- an option to acquire a security
- in Part 7.11, it also includes a managed investment product.

50 Typically, a digital token will not be caught by the section 761A definition. This is because none of the traditional indicia of a share will be present. Further, given the way ICOs are often legally structured, investors may not invest in a company and receive a share certificate and hence no shareholders rights (as commonly understood) will arise. A similar argument applies as regards debentures. The conclusion is that ICOs will not be caught by the Chapter 6D fundraising provisions. On the other hand,

---

[29] For an exhaustive analysis, see Baxt, Black and Hanrahan, *Securities and Financial Services Law* (9th edition, Routledge, 2016), Chapter 3.

there is a good reason to suggest that an **ICO can be characterized as a managed investment scheme** under Chapter 7. The argument runs as follows: while the section 92 definition catches a managed investment scheme, the section 761A definition does not except by reference to Part 7.11. Section 764A (appearing in Part 7) lists specific things that are financial products for the purposes of Chapter 7. These include a security, an interest in a registered scheme, *an interest in a managed investment scheme that is not a registered scheme* and a derivative [emphasis added]. Thus, section 764A(1)(ba) catches an interest in a managed investment scheme that is not a registered scheme. Section 765A goes on to list specific exclusions. In the result, Chapter 6D does not catch managed investment schemes but Chapter 7 does. Interests in all registered schemes and unregistered schemes under s 764A(1)(ba) are financial products for the purposes of Chapter 7. The relevance of the latter classification is that an ICO offering can be made via a managed investment scheme that was registered with ASIC under Chapter 5C or, via an unregistered scheme being operated in contravention of the registration requirement.[30] The practical upshot is that an ICO offering to Australian investors is **susceptible to characterization as an unregistered managed investment scheme absent registration or an exemption.** Such a characterization arises because of the section 9 statutory definition of a managed investment scheme and the registration requirement.[31]

51 As regards the section 9 definition of a managed investment scheme, the courts have stated that the different elements must be interpreted broadly.[32] A 'scheme' is simply a program or plan of action.[33] The contribution of money or money's worth would be satisfied by the contribution of a digital currency such as Bitcoin or Ethereum. The contribution would be pooled for the common enterprise and as consideration for the rights and benefits produced by the scheme – for example, the benefits attached to the digital token. Next, it is clear that at least some of the investors would not have day-to-day control. When considering these elements of the section 9 definition, it is important to closely scrutinize the actual legal structuring of an ICO. For example, if monies are pooled in a Foundation, the Foundation issues tokens and then sends monies to an operating company which allows token holders certain benefits, then the section 9 definition is met. The registration requirement applies where three tests are met:

52 **a) First test: The scheme satisfies any one of the following.**
- the scheme has more than 20-members;
- it was promoted by a person, or an associate of a person, who was, when the scheme was promoted, in the business of promoting managed investment schemes; or
- it is one of a number of schemes that ASIC has determined, in accordance with Corporations Act section 601ED (3) are related and that between them have more than 20 members.

All ICOs will have more than 20 'members' and so the first test will be met.

53 **b) Second test.** Interests in the scheme have been issued in circumstances that would have required the giving of a Product Disclosure Statement (PDS) under Part 7.9 Div.2 of the Corporations Act if the scheme had been registered when the issues were made

---

[30] 'A managed investment of the kind referred to in s 764A(1) (ba) might be unregistered because it is exempted from the registration requirement by s 601ED(2) or by ASIC exemption [under s 602QA] or because it is being operated in contravention of the registration requirement. An interest described in s 764A (1) (ba) is a financial product, but it is not a security.' Baxt, Black and Hanrahan, *Securities and Financial Services Law* (9th edition, Routledge, 2016), 134.
[31] There is an analysis of the statutory definition in Baxt, Black and Hanrahan, ibid, 121–131.
[32] Ibid, 121.
[33] Ibid, 126.

and the division applied to the interests at that time.[34] Here, a mere offering of tokens satisfying the section 9 definition in Australia would suffice to meet this test.

c) Third test. The scheme has not been granted an exemption from registration by ASIC under s 601QA of the Corporations Act.

As stated above, in April 2018 ASIC received delegated powers from the ACCC to take action under the Australian Consumer Law against misleading and deceptive conduct in marketing or selling ICOs, even if the ICO does not involve a financial product. This appears to have had a **chilling** effect on ICOs in Australia and there have been **no reported ICOs** since that time.

F. Summary

Australia has the required infrastructure to enable Fintech business. Not surprisingly, the majority of Fintech business established in Australia to date has been in the financial services sector where a well-established regulatory regime is in place and the coming of customer data sharing via Open Banking offers opportunities for Fintech non-bank financial intermediaries and neo-banks. Innovative fundraising by ICOs or similar devices are not allowed unless in compliance with existing financial market laws.

---

[34] S 601ED(b) of the Corporations Regulations 2001-REG 5C.11.05A.

§ 25
New Zealand*

Literature: Financial Conduct Authority (FCA), 'Regulatory Sandbox' (November 2015), available at: https://beck-link.de/hd2f5 (accessed 11.10.2020); Inland Revenue Department (IRD) – 'Public Ruling BR Pub 19/04: Income tax – application of the employee share scheme rules to employer issued crypto-assets provided to an employee' (December 2019), available at: https://beck-link.de/7nxf4 (accessed 12.11.2020); Sims, Kariyawasam and Mayes, 'Regulating Cryptocurrencies in New Zealand' (September 2018), The Law Foundation New Zealand, available at: https://beck-link.de/4yfhz (accessed 12.11.2020); The Government of New Zealand, 'Strategy for a Digital Public Service' (March 2020), available at: https://beck-link.de/wy65b (accessed 12.11.2020); Walker, 'Crowd-Sourced Funding, Cryptocurrency and Initial Coin Offerings in Australia and New Zealand' [2018] 36 (1) *Company and Securities Law Journal (C&SLJ)*, 111–119; Walker and Pekmezovic, 'Consumer Protection and Financial Products' in Tokeley (ed.), *Consumer Law in New Zealand*, (2nd ed., Wellington: Lexis Nexis, 2014), 409–461; Wilson, 'Consumer Information'. in Tokeley (ed.), *Consumer Law in New Zealand*, (2nd ed., Wellington: Lexis Nexis, 2014), 125–206.

Outline

	para.
A. Introduction	1
I. Country Snapshot	1
II. Constitution and Political System	2
III. Legal System	4
IV. Fintech Developments in New Zealand:	5
1. Equity Crowdfunding and Peer-to- Peer Lending:	6
2. Cryptocurrency	7
3. Initial Coin Offerings	8
4. Abusive Market Practices	9
5. Fintech Business	10
B. Regulators	11
I. Financial Markets Regulator	11
II. Reserve Bank of New Zealand, Department of Internal Affairs and Consumer Commission	12
C. Financial Market Regulation	14
I. Financial Markets Law	14
1. Financial Markets	15
2. Financial Service	16
3. Financial Markets Legislation	17
II. Financial Markets Participant	18
III. Financial Product	20
IV. Offering a Financial Product	21
V. Regulatory Approach	22
D. FMA Guidance on Cryptocurrency and Cryptoasset Services	23
I. FMA Guidance on ICOs	24
1. Types of financial products	27
2. Debt securities	28
3. Equity securities	30
4. Managed investment products	31
a) General	31
b) Are Utility Tokens Managed Investment Products?	32

---

* This publication was made possible by the NPRP award NPRP 11 S-1119-170016 from the Qatar National Research Fund (a member of the Qatar Foundation). The statements made herein are the sole responsibility of the authors.

    5. ICOs and wholesale or offshore offers 34
    6. ICOs and financial services 35
    7. ICOs that do not involve financial products or financial services . 36
    8. Can cryptoassets be offered through crowdfunding platforms? 37
  II. FMA Guidance on Financial Services 38
    1. Exchanges.. 38
    2. Wallets 39
    3. Broking 40
    4. Providing investment opportunities in cryptoassets 41
    5. AML/CFT obligations and cryptoasset related financial services ... 42
E. Judicial Interpretation 43
  I. General 43
  II. Cryptocurrency is Property 44

A. Introduction

I. Country Snapshot

New Zealand is an island nation in the Southwest Pacific Ocean comprising two main 1
islands (the North Island and the South Island) with a **population** of around 5 million.
Gross Domestic Product in 2020 is expected to be about USD196 billion. The biggest
industries are agriculture, fishing, and mining. Tourism is the biggest export industry at
about USD20 billion per annum but is adversely affected by the Covid-19 pandemic.
New Zealand is a member of the OECD and has a first world education system. In 2019,
New Zealand ranked 16th in the Network Readiness Index, a World Economic Forum
framework which assesses the factors, policies, and institutions that enable a country to
fully leverage information and communication technologies for inclusive, sustainable
growth, competitiveness, and well-being. New Zealand ranked 1st in the Network
Readiness Index 2019 for ease of doing business and e-commerce legislation.[1] Elsewhere, the Global Innovation Index 2019 ranked New Zealand at 25th in the world and
the Global Competitiveness Index ranked New Zealand at 19 out of 140 countries. As a
result, New Zealand has the requisite infrastructure to create Fintech businesses.

II. Constitution and Political System

New Zealand is a sovereign independent unitary State with a constitutional mon- 2
archy, responsible government, and a unicameral legislature. As with the United Kingdom, there is **no one document which embodies a national constitution**. The sources
of the constitution include Imperial legislation (principally the Imperial Laws Application Act 1988); New Zealand legislation (principally the Constitution Act 1986); the
common law (customary common law, judicial precedent and statutory interpretation);
customary international law; Letters Patent; the law and custom of Parliament and
convention. **The Constitution Act 1986** specifies the principal entities of the New
Zealand Constitution, namely, the Sovereign (represented by the Governor-General);
the Executive; the Legislature and the Judiciary. In recent decades, the **Treaty of
Waitangi 1840** made between indigenous Maori and the Crown has assumed increased
constitutional importance.

In 1963, New Zealand adopted a **proportional representation voting system** based 3
on the German model. From November 2008 to 2017, the Centre-right National Party

---

[1] See Networkreadingindex, available at: https://beck-link.de/ypx3e (accessed 19.11.2020).

led by Prime Minister John Key held power in New Zealand with support from minor parties. A General Election occurred in 2017 and the Centre-Left Labor Party led by Prime Minister Jacinda Ardern governed with support from the New Zealand First Party and the Greens Party. A General Election (delayed due to Covid-19) was scheduled for 18 October 2020. In the event, the Labour Party – again led by Jacinda Ardern – won an outright majority with 64 seats in parliament.

III. Legal System

4   New Zealand is a **common law** country. The legal system derives from United Kingdom origins. The court hierarchy comprises the District Court, the High Court, the Court of Appeal, and the Supreme Court. The principal sources of New Zealand financial market regulation are statutes. The leading statute is the **Financial Markets Conduct Act 2013 (FMC Act)** complemented by the Financial Markets Conduct Regulations 2014. **Case law** – decisions of the courts interpreting the provisions of the Act – is another source of law. Rules of precedent apply; New Zealand courts are bound by decisions of higher courts in the appellate hierarchy. Decisions of courts in other common law jurisdictions are of persuasive authority; for example, see the international citations in the High Court of New Zealand decision in *Ruscoe & Monroe v Cryptopia Limited (in liquidation)*[2] on the legal nature of cryptocurrencies. **Australian case law is especially persuasive** because New Zealand financial markets law is based on the cognate Australian law.

IV. Fintech Developments in New Zealand:

5   There is **no 'one stop' regulator** for Fintech related matters. Regulation is dispersed across relevant subject areas and is technology neutral. Most Fintech businesses fall under the purview of the Financial Markets Authority (FMA) as involving a 'financial product' or the offering of a 'financial service' as defined in the FMC Act.

1. Equity Crowdfunding and Peer-to-Peer Lending:

6   In 2013, New Zealand introduced two Fintech enabled fundraising innovations in the FMC Act: (1) equity crowd funding (ECF), and (2) peer-to-peer lending (P2PL). The FMC Act established a **licensing regime for ECF and P2PL providers**, with additional and more detailed requirements contained in the FMC Regulations 2014. As a result of these legislative changes, companies can make offers through licensed ECF and P2PL intermediaries' facilities without having to comply with the full regulatory disclosure requirements under financial markets legislation. In turn, this reduces compliance costs and enables investors to invest in early start-up financing which provides funds for fledgling companies with significant potential to growth. However, the ECF regime cannot be used for initial coin offerings.

2. Cryptocurrency

7   Early research on cryptocurrencies in New Zealand appears in Sims, Kariyawasam and Mayes, *Regulating Cryptocurrencies in New Zealand*.[3] The use of cryptocurrencies is

---

[2] *Ruscoe v Cryptopia Limited (in liquidation)* [2020] NZHC 728.
[3] Sims, Kariyawasam and Mayes, 'Regulating Cryptocurrencies in New Zealand' (September 2018), The Law Foundation New Zealand, available at: https://beck-link.de/4yfhz (accessed 12.11.2020).

permitted in New Zealand, but the adoption of digital assets by persons in New Zealand is **relatively low**. In 2019, the New Zealand Tax Authority, the Inland Revenue Department (IRD), approved the use of crypto payments as part of employee remuneration agreements, subject to a strict framework.[4] The IRD treats cryptocurrency as property for tax purposes and ordinary rules apply.

3. Initial Coin Offerings

There do not appear to have been any successful initial coin offerings (ICOs) or other offerings of digital assets via the regulated offer procedure in the FMC Act. Why is this the case? The **compliance cost** of a regulated primary market offer under the FMC Act is one deterrent. A second deterrent is the **fair dealing provisions** in the FMC Act (where a 'financial product' is concerned) which catch misleading statements and representations. A third deterrent is the provisions of **Fair-Trading Act 1986** which would apply to a Whitepaper where no financial product is involved. It is possible that some capital raising for Fintech businesses has occurred via the exemptions to the regulated offer regime in the FMC Act. The key commercial reason for little or no digital asset offerings appears to be the wide scope of the law regulating fundraising in the primary market in New Zealand and the vigilance of the regulator. As stated, the New Zealand equity crowdfunding regime in the FMC Act does not extend to digital assets. For these and other good reasons (such as the ease of international regulatory arbitrage), primary market activity for digital assets is minimal.

4. Abusive Market Practices

Of the **scam complaints** seen by the FMA from 2018–2020, the three most common subjects were cryptocurrencies, equity offers and foreign exchange.[5] If made aware of the scam, the FMA will issue a warning on its website.

5. Fintech Business

According to the industry group FinTech NZ, there are several FinTech businesses in New Zealand.[6] Most involve 'financial services' and include digital asset exchanges such as the **Digital Asset Exchange Limited (Dasset)** and other businesses in payments (Thankyou Payroll), investing, crypto micro-saving, robo-advice, equity crowdfunding (ECF) and peer-to peer lending (P2PL) among others.[7] The bank-owned entity, **Payments NZ**, has been working towards a national switch since 2018. The government has initiated a Digital ID project known as the Digital Identity Transition Program led by the Department of Internal Affairs in collaboration with the private sector and released its *Strategy for a Digital Public Service* (March 2020), which would likely rely on blockchain technology.[8]

---

[4] See Inland Revenue Department (IRD)- 'Public Ruling BR Pub 19/04: Income tax – application of the employee share scheme rules to employer issued crypto-assets provided to an employee' (December 2019), available at: https://beck-link.de/7nxf4 (accessed 12.11.2020).

[5] Boyes, 'Know the risks of unregulated investments' (Stuff, January 2020), available at: https://beck-link.de/rz53r (accessed 11.11.2020).

[6] *FinTechNZ*, https://fintechnz.org.nz. and *Crowdfundinsider* contain topical news and discussions of Fintech businesses in New Zealand. For *Crowdfundinsider*, see https://www.crowdfundinsider.com (last accessed 12.11.2020).

[7] Equity Crowdfunding and Peer-to-Peer Lending were enabled by the FMC Act and are well established: see Financial Markets Authority (FMA), 'Peer-to-peer Lending and Crowdfunding Sector Snapshot' (December 2019) available at: https://beck-link.de/7d4fm (accessed 11.11.2020).

[8] The Government of New Zealand, 'Strategy for a Digital Public Service' (March 2020), available at: https://beck-link.de/wy65b (accessed 11.11.2020).

B. Regulators

I. Financial Markets Regulator

11   On 1 May 2011, the Financial Markets Authority Act 2011 (FMA Act) came into effect. The new statute created the **Financial Markets Authority (FMA)**, a new market conduct regulator to replace the former Securities Commission and ushered in a new area of law for New Zealand's financial markets law.[9] The FMA supervises the offer of 'financial products', the provision of 'financial services', the licensing of financial advisers and enforces fair dealing rules. Whether a crypto asset is a 'financial product' will depend on the specific characteristics and economic substance of that crypto asset (→ para. 20).

II. Reserve Bank of New Zealand, Department of Internal Affairs and Consumer Commission

12   The Reserve Bank is responsible for:
- the supervision and prudential regulation of banks
- the supervision and regulation of non-bank deposit takers
- the supervision of insurers and
- the integrity of the financial system.

The Department of Internal Affairs (DIA) is responsible for **anti-money laundering and counter terrorism financing legislation** (AML/CTF) pursuant to the Anti-Money Laundering and Countering the Financing of Terrorism Act 2009. As such, the DIA is the lead AML contact for virtual asset service providers (VASPs). Financial services provided by VASPs fall within the existing definition of a 'financial institution' in the AML/CFT Act 2009. The definition includes: transferring money or value for, or on behalf of, a customer; issuing or managing the means of payment (for example, credit or debit cards, cheques, traveller's cheques, money orders, bankers' drafts, or electronic money) and money or currency changing.

13   The Commerce Commission is responsible for **competition law** under the Commerce Act 1986 and administers the Fair Trading Act 1986. The latter Act contains prohibitions on misleading and deceptive conduct that extend to misrepresentations. In the result, the Fair Trading Act could catch, for example, the Whitepaper of digital asset offerings or services that are not covered by the FMC Act.[10]

C. Financial Market Regulation

I. Financial Markets Law

14   In the second decade of the 21st century, securities regulation in New Zealand underwent a radical change. The term 'securities regulation ' is no longer apt and **'financial markets regulation'** is the better terminology although the terms are some-

---

[9] For an overview, see Walker and Pekmezovic, 'Consumer Protection and Financial Products' in Tokeley (ed.), *Consumer Law in New Zealand*, (2014), 409–461.

[10] See Wilson, 'Consumer Information' in Tokeley (ed.), *Consumer Law in New Zealand*, (2014), 125–206.

times used interchangeably. The change flowed from the shock of the global financial crisis (GFC) in 2007–2008 and the collapse of debt issuing finance companies in New Zealand which led to the establishment of a new market regulator in 2011 (the FMA), and new legislation covering the primary and secondary market enacted in September 2013 (the FMC Act). The new financial markets law rests upon three core definitions which appear in s 4 of the FMA Act.

1. Financial Markets

The first definition is **'financial markets'** which means the financial markets in New Zealand and includes markets in New Zealand for the provision of financial services and the capital markets of New Zealand.

2. Financial Service

Second, the term **'financial service'** is given the same meaning as in s 5 of the Financial Service Providers (Registration and Dispute Resolution) Act 2008. An operator of a 'financial service' must be registered. Section 5 defines the term expansively and includes:

> 5. Meaning of financial service
> (1) In this Act, financial service means any of the following financial services:
> (f) operating a money or value transfer service:
> (g) issuing and managing means of payment (for example, credit and debit cards, cheques, travellers' cheques, money orders, bankers' drafts, and electronic money)

Section 5(1)(f), 'operating a money or value transfer service' has a wide ambit. The words 'value transfer service' catch a digital asset exchange (fiat to crypto, crypto to crypto and crypto to fiat) and this term survives in Part 2A of the amending legislation, the Financial Services Legislation Amendment Act, 2019 (NZ) which comes into force in March 2021. Similarly, the words 'issuing and managing means of payment' in s 5(1)(g) catch an ICO and the operation of a digital exchange.

3. Financial Markets Legislation

Third, the meaning of the term 'financial markets legislation' is set out in Schedule 1 of the FMA Act. Schedule 1 is divided into two parts. Part 1 includes the Financial Advisers Act, 2008 and the Financial Service Providers Act 2008. Part 2 includes the Companies Act, 1993, Financial Reporting Act, 1993, Limited Partnerships Act, 2008, Trustee Companies Act, 1967 and Part 5C of the Reserve Bank of New Zealand Act, 1989.

The **significance of the division** between Part 1 and Part 2 of Schedule 1 of the FMA Act appears in s 9(1)(c), which sets out the FMA's functions and powers:

> (c) to monitor compliance with, investigate conduct that constitutes or may constitute a contravention of, and enforce–
> (i) the Acts referred to in Part 1 of Schedule 1 (and the enactments made under those Acts); and
> (ii) the Acts referred to in Part 2 of Schedule 1 (and the enactments made under those Acts) to the extent that those Acts or other enactments apply, or otherwise relate, to financial markets participants.

While the statutes listed in Part 1 of Schedule 1 fall under the FMA's jurisdiction directly, the statutes listed in Part 2 of Schedule 1 are indirectly covered. Hence, Part 1 sets out the core legislation for financial markets law while Part 2 delineates areas of law that constitute financial markets law in a broader sense. In this way, there are direct and indirect targets of financial markets law.

II. Financial Markets Participant

18   The FMA addresses one person in s 4, the **'financial markets participant'**, meaning a person (*inter alia*) who is, or is required to be, registered, licensed, appointed, or authorized under, or for the purposes of, any of the Acts listed in Part 1 of Schedule 1 or any of the enactments made under those Acts.

   This definition includes all the persons mentioned and covers related bodies and, very significantly, directors and senior managers. The comprehensive definition of 'financial markets participant' opens the door for the **personal liability of directors and managers** throughout the financial markets law. Equally significantly, it would catch an issuer within the meaning of section 4 of the Financial Reporting Act 1993 (NZ).

19   The FMA Act sets out in section 9 the **uniform objectives for the FMA** 'to promote and facilitate the development of fair, efficient, and transparent financial markets'. Hence, the new law creates a sole conduct regulator in charge of financial markets law bound to one single objective in the application of all the statutes listed in Schedule 1. This objective sets the baseline for financial markets law in general.

III. Financial Product

20   Section 7 of the FMC Act states that a **'financial product'** means a debt security, an equity security, a managed investment product or a derivative. These terms are further defined in sections 8–9. FMA commentary on these terms appears below.

IV. Offering a Financial Product

21   An offering of a financial product under the FMC Act must comply with Part 2 (Fair Dealing) and Part 3 (Disclosure of offers of financial products). Part 2 contains a set of provisions aimed at misleading and deceptive conduct and the making of unsubstantiated representations. Part 3 imposes disclosure obligations. Issuers of digital assets may seek to avoid the application of Parts 2 and 3 of the FMC Act for two reasons: the risks of non-compliance under Part 2 and the cost of compliance under Part 3.

V. Regulatory Approach

22   The FMA sees its role in facilitating innovation as central to its **objective of promoting fair, efficient, and transparent markets**. However, it states that new ideas and technologies often give rise to new risks, and investor interests still need safeguarding. The FMA considers it adopts a balanced approach when considering innovation. It recommends engaging early to determine if a product or service will be regulated and will consider scaling and modifying regulatory obligations to suit the proposal. This appears to be a less formalised take on the **Regulatory Sandbox** approach seen in other jurisdictions. The first formal Regulatory Sandbox is considered to have been created by the UK Financial Conduct Authority (FCA), which defines the sandbox as a 'safe space' in which businesses can test innovative products, services, business models and delivery

mechanisms without immediately incurring all the normal regulatory consequences of engaging in the activity in question.'[11] The concept was formally introduced in Australia by the equivalent regulator[12] and supported by an Innovation Hub.[13]

D. FMA Guidance on Cryptocurrency and Cryptoasset Services

The most recent guidance from the FMA on primary and secondary market activity involving cryptoassets was issued in March 2020.[14] To better understand the FMA's views, we reproduce portions of this guidance in a restructured and abridged form for clarity of exposition. The FMA uses the term, 'cryptoasset' throughout its guidance. This term should be regarded as a portmanteau term covering the full spectrum of cryptocurrency and digital assets. Further, the guidance must be treated with caution in the absence of judicial consideration.

I. FMA Guidance on ICOs

The FMA has stated:

Cryptoassets, also known as virtual assets, cryptocurrencies, digital coins, or tokens, are available online, for example via exchanges, initial coin offers (ICOs) and token events.

Initial coin offers (ICOs) are a form of fundraising where you receive cryptoassets (also known as virtual assets, cryptocurrencies, digital coins or tokens) that carry certain rights, such as providing access to a new product or service, or an interest in an underlying asset or project.
- If your ICO is offering a cryptoasset that is a **'financial product'** under the FMC Act, additional obligations will apply.
- ICOs may involve the financial service of 'operating a value transfer service'.
- ICOs may also involve the financial service of 'issuing and managing a means of payment'.

If you provide a **'financial service'** related to cryptoassets, you must comply with the fair dealing provisions in Part 2 of the FMC Act. These are broad principles that prohibit you from engaging in misleading conduct or making false, deceptive, or unsubstantiated statements. If the overall impression on your website, social media sites and promotional material is misleading, it will be in breach of the fair dealing requirements.

How an ICO is regulated in New Zealand depends on whether:
- the cryptoasset you are offering is a **'financial product'** under the Financial Markets Conduct Act 2013 (FMC Act). Cryptoassets that are financial products are also known as 'security tokens'. Whether a cryptoasset is a financial product will depend on the specific characteristics and economic substance of that cryptoasset. If your ICO is offering cryptoassets that are financial products, further obligations will apply.

---

[11] Financial Conduct Authority (FCA), 'Regulatory Sandbox' (November 2015), available at: https://beck-link.de/hd2f5 (accessed 11.10.2020).
[12] ASIC, 'Fintech regulatory sandbox' (October 2020), available at: https://beck-link.de/tfr87 (accessed 11.10.2020).
[13] ASIC, 'Innovation Hub: Practical support and informal assistance' (August 2020), available at: https://beck-link.de/tfr87 (accessed 11.10.2020).
[14] FMA, 'Cryptocurrency/Cryptoasset services' (March 2020), available at: https://beck-link.de/5reta (accessed 12.11.2020).

- you are in the business of providing a **'financial service'** (this will depend on the specific structure and features of the ICO)
- the person buying the cryptoasset is a member of the public (known as a **'retail investor'**) or a very experienced investor (known as a **'wholesale investor'**)
- the investor is **based in New Zealand** or overseas.

1. Types of financial products

27　The Financial Markets Conduct Act 2013 (FMC Act) sets out four types of financial products – debt securities; equity securities; managed investment products and derivatives.

2. Debt securities

28　A cryptoasset is a **debt security** if investors have a right to be repaid money or paid interest on money lent to, deposited with, or owed by a person, company, or unincorporated entity making a cryptoasset offer. For example, a cryptoasset linked to the value of a dollar or commodity could be a debt security if:
- investors can purchase a cryptoasset with money;
- investors holding the cryptoasset have the right to redeem that cryptoasset for money; and
- an investor holding the cryptoasset is not the beneficial owner of funds from which redemption proceeds are paid.

29　To make a regulated offer of debt securities, you must:
- register a product disclosure statement (PDS)
- appoint a licensed supervisor
- meet fair dealing requirements
- meet financial reporting obligations.

3. Equity securities

30　A cryptoasset is an **equity security** if investors buy, or have the option to buy, for example, a share in a New Zealand incorporated company or a body corporate incorporated outside New Zealand. A cryptoasset that provides an option to buy a share is an offer of both the cryptoasset and the equity share.

If you make a regulated offer of equity securities, you must:
- register a product disclosure statement (PDS)
- meet fair dealing requirements
- meet financial reporting obligations.

Investor interests and rights will be set out in the company's constitution. This means a trust deed is not required.

4. Managed investment products

31　a) **General.** For these products, an investor will:
- **contribute money or cryptoassets** to receive interests (cryptoassets) in a scheme (a structure or project that allows investors to pool their money).
- have a **'right to receive a financial benefit'** (as defined in the FMC Act) from the scheme – such as money, rights to a share in profits, cryptoassets, additional cryptoassets, or changes in the cryptoassets' value and these benefits are principally produced by someone else, and
- **not have day-to-day control** over the project or business (even if they have the right to be consulted or to give directions).

The manager of a managed investment scheme must be licensed by us to make a regulated offer to retail investors in New Zealand. The manager is the person, company, or unincorporated entity issuing the cryptoassets.

b) Are Utility Tokens Managed Investment Products? Utility tokens (sometimes called 'application tokens') typically give investors the right to access and/or use a company's platform, product, or service. They often grant holders rights similar to pre-payment vouchers. While each ICO must be looked at on an individual basis, utility tokens are **not considered managed investment products** simply because they can be traded on a cryptoasset exchange or other secondary market. *This is because any profits an investor receives by trading those utility tokens on a cryptoasset exchange are not 'rights to receive a financial benefit' under a managed investment scheme.*[15]

5. ICOs and wholesale or offshore offers

ICOs that offer cryptoassets that are financial products to wholesale investors, or to investors based outside New Zealand, will not be subject to full licensing, governance, and disclosure requirements under the FMC Act. However, fair dealing requirements under Part 2 of the FMC Act still apply.

6. ICOs and financial services

While each ICO must be looked at on an individual basis, most ICOs involve the financial service of 'operating a value transfer service'. ICOs may also involve the financial service of 'issuing and managing a means of payment'. If your ICO provides financial services, you must:
– Comply with the fair dealing requirements in Part 2 of the FMC Act. These requirements prohibit you from engaging in misleading conduct or making false, deceptive, or unsubstantiated statements in your white paper, website, or other promotional material.
– Register as a financial service provider if you are based in New Zealand. You must also pay the applicable fees and levies, for each category of financial service you are in the business of providing. If you offer financial services to retail clients, you must belong to a dispute resolution scheme.
– Comply with anti-money laundering obligations.

If you provide cryptoasset-related financial services in New Zealand in the ordinary course of your business, you will likely be captured as a 'financial institution' under the AML/CFT Act.

7. ICOs that do not involve financial products or financial services

Even if you are not providing a financial service or financial product, 'fair dealing' requirements still apply to white papers and other communications about your ICO under the Fair-Trading Act 1986.

---

[15] Emphasis added. This statement by the FMA must be treated with caution. The relevant section – section 9 (1) (b) states 'those interests are rights to participate in, or receive, financial benefits *produced principally by the efforts of another person under the scheme ...*". Suppose that utility tokens are issued, and the issuer subsequently arranges for the tokens to be quoted on a crypto exchange. The arrangement involves the efforts of another person (the issuer). Suppose further, the token appreciates in value on the exchange. The token holder now has the ability (right) to sell tokens. Is this ability to sell utility tokens at a profit, a right to "participate in, or receive, financial benefits produced principally by the efforts of another person under the scheme"? For an elaboration of this argument, see Walker, 'Crowd-Sourced Funding, Cryptocurrency and Initial Coin Offerings in Australia and New Zealand' [2018] 36 (1) *Company and Securities Law Journal (C&SLJ)*, 111–119. ASIC, 'Information Sheet No. 225 – Initial Coin Offerings and Cryptoassets' (May 2019) available at: https://beck-link.de/t85ma (accessed 12.11.2020).

We can designate cryptoassets to be a financial product if, based on their economic substance, this is necessary to promote fair and efficient financial markets in New Zealand or any of the other purposes of the FMC Act. For example, a cryptoasset giving investors voting rights and an interest in the company and its profits could be designated an equity security. A designation could be accompanied by an exemption to modify FMC Act disclosure and governance requirements.

8. Can cryptoassets be offered through crowdfunding platforms?

37   No, crowdfunding in the form of an ICO is not the same as crowdfunding covered by the FMC Act. We license crowdfunding platforms to provide an intermediary service via a facility, such as a website, where companies make offers of equity securities to retail investors. Equity crowdfunding under the FMC Act enables companies to raise up to $2 million in any 12-month period, without registering a PDS.

II. FMA Guidance on Financial Services

The FMA has stated:[16]

1. Exchanges

38   Exchanges issuing their own cryptoassets to facilitate trading fall within the financial service category of **'issuing and managing means of payment'**. Exchanges allowing cryptoasset trading fall within the financial service category of 'operating a value transfer service'. If you allow trading of cryptoassets that are financial products under the FMC Act you need to consider whether you are operating a financial product market. If so, you may need to be licensed.

2. Wallets

39   If you are a wallet provider storing cryptoassets or money on behalf of others, and you facilitate exchanges between cryptoassets or between money and cryptoassets, your services fall within the category of **'operating a value transfer service'**. If you hold money for depositors, you may be offering debt securities. However, if depositor funds are held in trust, your wallets may not be debt securities. Debt securities are financial products. They have additional regulatory requirements under the FMC Act.

3. Broking

40   If you arrange cryptoasset transactions, you are providing the financial service of **'operating a value transfer service'**. If you are providing safe-keeping or administration services in relation to cryptoassets, you are providing the financial service of keeping, investing, administering, or managing money, securities, or investment portfolios on behalf of other persons. If you provide transaction services in relation to cryptoassets that are financial products you may have obligations as a broker under the Financial Advisers Act 2008.

4. Providing investment opportunities in cryptoassets

41   If you are providing investment opportunities in cryptoassets (e.g., via a derivatives issuer providing cryptoasset options or via a managed investment scheme investing in

---

[16] FMA, ibid.

cryptoassets), you will be regulated in the same way as if you were providing investment opportunities in traditional assets or financial products.

5. AML/CFT obligations and cryptoasset related financial services

Cryptoassets are vulnerable to misuse by criminals to launder money and fund terrorism as they allow greater levels of anonymity and have global reach, making it easier for cross-border payments to be made, and they can be traded easily. 42

If you provide cryptoasset-related financial services in New Zealand in the ordinary course of your business, you will likely be captured as a 'financial institution' under the AML/CFT Act.

E. Judicial Interpretation

I. General

Various government and regulatory communications have outlined the New Zealand approach to cryptocurrency. In a common law jurisdiction, the application of these laws and regulations is rendered significantly stronger and clearer once judicially considered. As mentioned above, significant persuasive weight is given to judicial decisions in other common law jurisdictions such as Australia and the United Kingdom for these previously untested questions. 43

II. Cryptocurrency is Property

The decision of the High Court of New Zealand in *Ruscoe v Cryptopia Limited 2020 (in liquidation)*[17] considered the **legal nature of cryptocurrencies** for the first time in New Zealand. Cryptopia operated as a cryptocurrency trading exchange. All cryptocurrencies on the exchange were held in Cryptopia's hot wallets or cold wallets. Cryptopia's servers were hacked and about $30 million of cryptocurrencies were stolen. The company was put into liquidation in May 2019, at which point Cryptopia held cryptocurrencies worth around $170 million for itself and for its customers. The liquidators sought instructions from the Court as to the categorisation and distribution of Cryptopia's cryptocurrency assets. 44

The two issues were: 45
1. Is cryptocurrency 'property' as defined in section 2 of the Companies Act 1993 and, as a related issue, can cryptocurrencies form the subject matter of a trust?
2. Was Cryptopia holding cryptocurrency on trust for account holders through the provision of its storage and exchange services?

The High Court relied on United Kingdom Jurisdiction Taskforce, *Legal Statement on Cryptoassets and Smart Contracts* (2019) and case law from other common law jurisdictions.[18] The Court endorsed the 'classic statement' of the definition of 'property' in the 1965 House of Lords case *National Provincial Bank Limited v* 46

---

[17] *Ruscoe v Cryptopia Limited (in liquidation)* [2020] NZHC 728.
[18] The Court considered the case of the Singapore International Commercial Court 14.03.2019- *B2C2 Ltd v Quoine Pte Ltd* 34 Singapore Law Reports (SLR) 2019, 17; decision of High Court of Justice (Business and Property Courts of England and Wales) 28.09.2018- *Vorotyntseva v Money-4 Ltd*, 2596 (Ch.); decision of the Supreme Court of British Colombia – *Shair.Com Global Digital Services Ltd v Arnold*, 1512 and the decision of the decision of High Court of Justice (Business and Property Courts of England and Wales) 13.12.2019- *AA v Persons Unknown* – 4 Weekly Law Reports (WLR) 2020, 35.

Ainsworth[19] per Lord Wilberforce. The Court was satisfied that **cryptocurrencies meet all four of the requirements for 'property'** established by that case, viz.: identifiable subject matter, identifiable by third parties, capable of assumption by third parties, and some degree of permanence or stability.

The Court **dispensed** with the 'simplistic' argument that **cryptocurrencies are mere information**, primarily because 'the whole purpose behind cryptocurrencies is to create an item of tradeable value not simply to record or to impart in confidence information or knowledge'.

Cryptopia was found to be holding each type of cryptocurrency stored by it on a separate express trust for the relevant account holders. The Court reached this conclusion based on the inherent nature of the relationship between Cryptopia and each account holder. Account records, customer information, and marketing all strongly implied that Cryptopia was acting as a **'custodian' for account holders**. The subject matter of each trust was easily identifiable by reference to Cryptopia's structured query language (SQL) database, which recorded each account holder's details, including their account balance. The combined effect of the Court's decision on these two issues is that the cryptocurrencies stored by Cryptopia are held for the sole benefit of the relevant account holders and, so, are excluded from the pool of assets available to general creditors.

---

[19] Appeal case No. 1175 of the (Judicial Committee of the) House of Lords 13.05.1965 – *National Provincial Bank Limited v Ainsworth*, 1247–1248.

§ 26
Hong Kong

Literature: Cambridge Centre for Alternative Finance (University of Cambridge, Judge Business School), 'Global Cryptoasset Regulatory Landscape Study' (April 2019), 13, available at: https://beck-link.de/a3yhp (accessed 07.01.2021); CGAP, 'I-SIP Toolkit: Policy Making for an Inclusive Financial System' (November 2018), available at: https://www.cgap.org/sites/default/files/publications/Toolkit-ISIP-Nov-2018_1.pdf (accessed 07.01.2021); European Banking Authority, 'Report with advice for the European Commission on crypto assets' (January 2019), available at: https://beck-link.de/557eh (accessed 07.01.2021); FinTech Association of Hong Kong, 'Best Practice for Token Sales' (October 2018), available at: https://beck-link.de/byv8t (accessed 07.01.2021); Hong Kong Stock Exchange (HKEX), 'HKEX Strategic Plan 2019–2012', available at: https://beck-link.de/rh7h3 (accessed 07.01.2021); Huang, Yang and Loo, 'The Development and Regulation of Cryptoassets: Hong Kong Experiences and a Comparative Analysis', (2020) 21 *European Business Organization Law Review*, 319–347; Notification of the Bank of Thailand, 'TorPorTor ForNorSor 23 Wor 276/2561', available at: https://beck-link.de/e33xn (accessed 07.01.2021); Securities and Future Commission, 'Code of Conduct for persons Licensed by or Registered with the Securities and Futures Commission' (September 2020), available at: https://beck-link.de/5nke4 (accessed 07.01.2021); UNSGSA, 'Early Lessons on Regulatory Innovations to Enable Inclusive FinTech: Innovation Offices, Regulatory Sandboxes, and RegTech', available at: https://beck-link.de/z7x5c (accessed 07.01.2021); Zetzsche, Buckley, Barberis and Arner, 'Regulating a Revolution: From Regulatory Sandboxes to Smart Regulation', (2018) 13 *Fordham Journal of Corporate and Financial Law*, 70.

Outline

	para.
A. Introduction	2
B. The Regulatory Framework	6
I. Overview	6
II. Regulations on Crypto Assets Intermediation	12
1. The SFC Statement on Initial Coin Offerings	14
2. The SFC Statement on Virtual Asset Portfolio Managers, Fund Distributors, and Trading Platform Operators	17
a) Background	17
b) Virtual asset portfolio managers	19
c) Virtual asset fund distributors	21
d) Virtual asset trading platform operators	23
III. Self-regulatory Mechanism: Industry Standard Organization	25
IV. Innovative Regulatory Initiative: Regulatory Sandbox	27
V. Regulations on Crypto Asset Taxation	30
C. Conclusion	31

A. Introduction

In Hong Kong, regulators acknowledge the potential of **blockchain** technology in a number of ways; for instance, an initiative was launched by the Hong Kong Stock Exchange (HKEX) to utilize blockchain technology for post-trade allocations and processing.[1] Furthermore, in the HKEX's latest strategic plan (2019–2021), the key objectives include leveraging cutting-edge new technology such as artificial intelligence,

1

---

[1] Khatri, 'Hong Kong Stock Exchange Taps Digital Assets for Post-Trading Blockchain Trial' (October 2018), available at: https://beck-link.de/dftx5 (accessed 07.01.2021).

blockchain technology, etc.[2] In particular, the HKEX plan covers the use of blockchain in Stock Connect.[3]

2   Although there have been attempts to utilize such innovation in finance, the Securities and Futures Commission (SFC) of Hong Kong, which is one of three main monetary regulators in the territory, took a **cautious stance** on crypto assets and initial coin offerings (ICOs), as it feared that these could lead to negative or risky outcomes. To this extent, the action of the SFC against Hong Kong crypto exchanges, ICOs, as well as public warnings related to crypto asset market investment risks, reflect concern from the regulator in relation to these innovative products (→ para. 15).[4]

In contrast to the regulator's stance, in terms of the crypto asset **market**, in 2019, there was an increase in cryptocurrency trading volume.[5] It has been argued that the increase in the trading volume of digital assets positively correlates with the unrest and political uncertainty in Hong Kong.[6] Interestingly, even crypto assets are regarded as risky from the regulator's viewpoint; however, the increase in the trading of such digital assets can exhibit a different perspective from the market side. The BC Group's crypto subsidiary OSL is the first HKEX-listed digital asset trading platform that received tentative license approval from the Hong Kong's SFC,[7] which serves as an example of a clear regulatory stance for the digital asset trading business in the country (→ para. 21).

3   Apart from digital asset trading, the number of companies raising funds through **ICOs** in Hong Kong also increased rapidly from 2017 to the first quarter of 2018. Some researchers have stated that the increase in ICO activities in Hong Kong (and Singapore) are linked to a cautious approach in regulating the ICO mechanism in China, which resulted in the shutdown of a number of ICO platforms in the country.[8] This corresponds to an increasing number of enquiries with respect to ICO activities.[9] In particular, with respect to ICO transaction volume, in the last few years, ICOs have included those of Gatcoin, which successfully raised 14.5 million USD in January 2018, the OAX Foundation, which raised 18 million USD in July 2017,[10] as well as Block.one, which raised around 185 million USD (ETH 652,902) in the same year.[11]

The surge of ICOs as an alternative funding source in Hong Kong may reflect the less strict regulation and supervision in the country compared to other jurisdictions; however, it also leads to a number of **concerns** such as investor and systemic risks and

---

[2] HKEX, 'HKEX Strategic Plan 2019–2012', available at: https://beck-link.de/rh7h3 (accessed 07.01.2021).

[3] A unique collaboration between the Hong Kong, Shanghai, and Shenzhen Stock Exchanges that allows international and Mainland Chinese investors to trade securities in each other's markets through the trading and clearing facilities of their home exchange; see Stock Connect, available at: https://beck-link.de/rh5xk (accessed 07.01.2021).

[4] Blog Chain, 'Hong Kong Continues Taking Regulatory Actions, Hopes to Become International Blockchain Hub' (July 2018), available at: https://beck-link.de/b57ya (accessed 15.06.2021).

[5] Coin Idol, 'Hong Kong Cryptocurrency Trading Volume Sets All-Time High Record on Local Bitcoins' (October 2019), available at: https://beck-link.de/2xy3d (accessed 07.01.2021).

[6] Gundiuc, 'HONG KONG: Why have Bitcoin volumes hit a record high?' (October 2019), available at: https://beck-link.de/7rcbh (accessed 07.01.2021).

[7] Allison, 'How OSL Became the First Crypto Exchange to Win Over Hong Kong Regulators' (August 2020), available at: https://beck-link.de/3bd2t (accessed 07.01.2021).

[8] Liu, 'Forget China: Hong Kong, Singapore are the new kids on the blockchain', (April 2018), available at: https://beck-link.de/y8wad (accessed 07.01.2021).

[9] Fintech News Hong Kong, 'Hong Kong Remains ICO Crypto Hub Despite Regulator Skepticism' (April 2018), available at: https://beck-link.de/ycr3n (accessed 07.01.2021).

[10] Fintech News Hong Kong, ibid.

[11] Lee, 'Hong Kong company raises $185m in record-breaking initial coin coffering' (July 2017), available at: https://beck-link.de/wdp75 (accessed 07.01.2021).

the subsequent changing of regulators' stances.[12] Consequently, there is a decreasing number of ICOs in the country due to security concerns, as well as regulatory non-clarity.[13]

Accordingly, relevant **regulations** and **supervision** will be addressed in this chapter in order to explain such a phenomenon in the context of Hong Kong. Moreover, regulatory and supervisory risk should be analysed in order to comprehend the market's behaviour, as well as future trends. In short, the Hong Kong authority took actions intended to prevent any risks arising from crypto asset activities by issuing warnings, statements to extend the authorities' scope of supervision, and relevant policy documents.

B. The Regulatory Framework

I. Overview

In terms of the regulatory framework, in principle, the basic law of Hong Kong consists of **free market** principles that are important for the country to retain its position as an international financial hub. From this point of view, policy innovation aimed at market facilitation and other relevant initiatives include regulatory responses to FinTech development.

The **legal treatment** of crypto assets may depend on the main function or type of crypto asset being considered. Crypto asset categorizations are helpful for capturing the complexities of this asset class and in guiding regulatory responses to them. This chapter catalogues, compares, and evaluates the laws and regulations applicable to crypto asset in Hong Kong. For this purpose, a detailed analysis of crypto assets' complex features and unique functions is crucial to understanding possible implications in terms of risks and regulatory approaches.

In Hong Kong, crypto assets are primarily regulated by the territorial SFC. In principle, crypto assets or digital tokens fall under the regulatory scope of **the SFC**, as certain types of crypto assets or digital tokens may be considered 'securities' due to their characteristics or 'futures contracts' under the Securities and Futures Ordinance (SFO). It should be emphasized that the main authority charged with regulating and supervising crypto asset activities is the SFC. Furthermore, the main governing regulations are the SFC, statements, and a position paper issued by the institution.

Before the issuance of the statement by the SFC on the regulatory framework for virtual asset portfolios managers, fund distributors, and trading platform operators, which was designed to prevent the risks associated with virtual asset investment, certain types of crypto assets were regulated by existing securities **regulatory perimeters**. Before the issuance of the above-mentioned statement, as well as a position paper that was issued by the SFC in 2019, the SFC issued circulars in order to clarify its regulatory stances, including a statement on ICOs, the circular to licensed corporations and registered institutions on Bitcoin futures contracts, and cryptocurrency-related investment products in 2017.[14]

---

[12] Huang, Yang and Loo, 'The Development and Regulation of Cryptoassets: Hong Kong Experiences and a Comparative Analysis', (2020) 21 *European Business Organization Law Review*, 319–347, available at: https://beck-link.de/zrsz6 (accessed 07.01.2021).

[13] Asia Blockchain Review, 'ICO to STO: Hong Kong Represents the New Financial Wave in Asia' (July 2019), available at: https://beck-link.de/dzpa8 (accessed 07.01.2021).

[14] Securities and Futures Commission, 'Circular to Licensed Corporations and Registered Institutions on Bitcoin futures contracts and cryptocurrency-related investment products' (December 2017), available at: https://beck-link.de/ra743 (accessed 07.01.2021).

7   In addition, **the statement** on ICOs[15] clarifies that a digital token may constitute a security under the existing regulatory framework of Hong Kong. Furthermore, according to the statement on ICOs, the ICO's digital tokens may also constitute a share, a debenture or an interest in a collective investment scheme (CIS) depending on their features, as well as what the tokens represent. To exemplify this, if a digital token indicates ownership interest in a corporation, it will be considered a share. If such tokens are used to acknowledge a debt or liability, the tokens should be regarded as a debenture. In addition, tokens could be determined as having an interest in a CIS if they give token-holders a share in the returns provided by the project. To summarize, it is important to consider the rights attached to such digital tokens in order to determine which type of financial instruments they constitute.[16] It should be noted that in this regard, all possible types of financial instruments are considered 'securities' under the Hong Kong securities law.

8   However, cryptocurrencies are not **legal tender** in Hong Kong, with the Hong Kong Monetary Authority (HKMA) specifying three attributes of money. Firstly, cryptocurrencies are not widely accepted as a medium of exchange. This can be seen in the case of Bitcoin, which is a type of crypto currency whose value has been volatile. The fluctuation in the price of cryptocurrencies has the potential to prevent their use as a medium of exchange. The HKMA further noted that Bitcoin is 'a very inefficient means of payment' for many reasons, including its time-consuming validation process. Moreover, in a feature common to cryptocurrencies, its value has been solely a function of market demand and supply. This characteristic poses a challenge to relevant stakeholders in accepting such cryptocurrencies as a store of value or a unit of account. Moreover, from the addition specification that was proposed by the HKMA of 'moneyness,' cryptocurrencies are not scalable, and so do not meet the final qualification of constituting money or legal tender.

9   In general, this is in accordance with the way in which countries across the globe have considered the **legal status** of cryptocurrencies; for instance, the notification issued by the Bank of Thailand in 2018 to clarify that cryptocurrencies are not legal tender under Thai laws (the Currency Act B.E.2501 (1958),[17] or the policy document issued by Bank Negara Malaysia in order to declare that cryptocurrencies are not legal tender in the country.[18]

It should be noted that the HKMA primarily discusses the legal tender status of cryptocurrencies such as Bitcoin without mentioning other categorizations of crypto assets. Moreover, other types of crypto assets, for instance, stablecoins, may have different attributes that could potentially challenge the HKMA's analysis of the legal tender status of cryptocurrencies. At present, however, there is still no specific regulatory framework for **stablecoins**, even though a large number of people in Hong Kong recently used stablecoins to move their personal assets beyond the government's control following the implementation of Hong Kong's national security law.[19]

10 It is worth noting that the SFC initially issued a specific statement on the regulatory framework for virtual assets for portfolio managers, fund distributors, and trading

---

[15] Securities and Futures Commission, 'Statement on Initial Coin Offerings' (September 2017), available at: https://beck-link.de/vk5he (accessed 07.01.2021).

[16] Ibid.

[17] Notification of the Bank of Thailand, 'TorPorTor ForNorSor 23 Wor 276/2561', available at: https://beck-link.de/e33xn (accessed 07.01.2021).

[18] Bank Negara Malaysia, 'Bank Negara Malaysia issues policy document for digital currencies', available at: https://beck-link.de/pr8k3 (accessed 15.11.2020).

[19] Pan, 'Hong Kong Citizens Turn to Stablecoins to Resist National Security Laws', (July 2020), available at: https://beck-link.de/ybwr4 (accessed 07.01.2021).

platform operators aimed at mitigating potential risks. Given that a virtual asset in the context specified by the SFC (see '…A virtual asset is a digital representation of value, which is also known as 'cryptocurrency', 'crypto-asset' or 'digital token…') poses significant risks to investors. The risks could result from the characteristics of virtual assets and the operation of relevant stakeholders, such as the **intermediation** of virtual assets.[20]

Therefore, at present, in terms of crypto asset regulation, regulators have mainly focused on regulating and supervising the **related activities** of ICOs and crypto asset exchange.[21] In this regard, it is important to acknowledge that the SFC's approach is also relatively similar to those of other jurisdictions that focus on relevant intermediation. However, there are a number of approaches that must be taken into account when considering crypto asset regulation and supervision in Hong Kong.

II. Regulations on Crypto Assets Intermediation

In principle, crypto asset intermediation is regulated by the SFC through the **securities law** of Hong Kong (the SFO). However, the increasing public interest in virtual asset investment in recent years has led to the need for specific regulation for virtual asset trading platforms that are not subject to existing regulatory frameworks. To this degree, such existing regulations apply to the traditional offerings of securities or collective investment schemes. Accordingly, the SFC issued its position paper in 2019 to extend the scope of its supervision to include businesses or platforms dealing with non-security types of virtual assets or tokens.[22] In this regard, in order to comprehend regulations on crypto asset intermediation, the relevant regulations were catalogued, as presented below.

1. The SFC Statement on Initial Coin Offerings

The overview of the **regulatory framework** (→ para. 5) reflects the common approach to regulating crypto asset activities and intermediaries by the authority. In greater detail, there could be differences in regulations on crypto asset intermediation from country to country. In Hong Kong, in summary, the authority initially implemented existing securities laws with crypto assets that were regarded as securities based on their features and functions. Hence, the SFC issued a statement on ICOs to clarify that digital tokens could be considered securities. Therefore, because such tokens can be determined as securities, businesses or platforms that deal with securities may be regulated and must comply with requirements specified in the securities law, specifically the regulated activities prescribed in part 1 of schedule 5 of the SFO. In detail, 'regulated activities' in the SFO are categorized into 12 types, namely dealing in securities, dealing in futures contracts, leveraged foreign exchange trading, advising on securities, advising on futures contracts, advising on corporate finance, providing automated trading services, securities margin financing, asset management, providing credit rating services, dealing in OTC derivative products or advising on OTC derivative products and

---

[20] Securities and Futures Commission, 'Statement on the regulatory framework for virtual asset portfolios managers, fund distributors and trading platform operators' (November 2018), 13, available at: https://beck-link.de/t8cwb (accessed 07.01.2021).
[21] Cambridge Centre for Alternative Finance (University of Cambridge, Judge Business School), 'Global Cryptoasset Regulatory Landscape Study' (April 2019), 13, available at: https://beck-link.de/a3yhp (accessed 07.01.2021).
[22] Securities and Futures Commission, 'SFC adopts new approach to virtual asset trading platforms' (November 2019), available at: https://beck-link.de/2hhn4 (accessed 07.01.2021).

providing client clearing services for OTC derivative transactions. To be more relevant to crypto asset activities, regulated activities in this context can deal in digital tokens, advising on them and so forth.

13 Therefore, businesses that conduct **regulated activities** must comply with the requirements of the SFO; in general, entities that are not authorized financial institutions require a license in order to conduct regulated activities.[23]

Section 114(1) and (2) of the SFO further outlines restrictions on conducting business in regulated fields. In particular, subsection 1 provides general restrictions; however, it does not apply to an entity or individual specified in subsection 2 of Section 114. To this extent, Section 114(1) shall not apply to a corporation licensed under sections 116 and 117, an authorized financial institution registered under Section 119, or a person authorized under Section 95(2) to engage in the regulated activity.[24]

14 To this extent, in brief, corporations licensed under sections 116 and 117 are those that comply with licensing the requirements specified in Section 116. Moreover, this must be considered with Section 117, which prescribes additional specifications, such as a period of licensing in the case of a temporary **licensing arrangement**. For an authorized financial institution under Section 119, this covers institutions that deal with one or more regulated activities (other than type 3 and type 8 activities). In addition, the person authorized under Section 95(2) refers to one who is authorized by the authority to offer automated trading services. In summary, in case businesses wish to deal with specified regulated activities, Section 114(1) primarily prohibits them from carrying on their business operations unless they fall within the scope of Section 114(2), (5) and (6). In particular, in the case of crypto asset businesses, businesses shall obtain the operational license as prescribed in Section 116.

Considering the statement on ICOs, the statement provides a clearer picture of digital **token determination**. However, the regulatory aspects on businesses/intermediaries that are not within the scope of the Securities Law remain unexplored. This results in a lack of regulatory clarity on crypto asset intermediation that raises concerns; for instance, those related to risk management and compliance. This is also because the varied features of digital assets from security to non-security tokens can lead to complexities from a regulatory point of view.

2. The SFC Statement on Virtual Asset Portfolio Managers, Fund Distributors, and Trading Platform Operators

15 a) **Background.** The SFC issued a new statement in 2018[25] to include non-securities types of crypto assets under their jurisdiction. In this regard, it must be noted that the statement primarily focuses on regulating crypto asset **intermediation**.

With respect to the increasing transaction volume of both cryptocurrency trading and ICO activities in recent years, the SFC issued a statement on the regulatory framework for virtual asset portfolio managers, fund distributors, and trading platform operators (the 2018 statement) in 2018 in order to provide greater **regulatory clarity**. By comparison, the issue of regulatory clarity and risk mitigation are also currently being discussed in other countries. To exemplify this, concerns including market immaturity,

---

[23] Authorized Financial Institution means an authorized institution, as defined in Section 2(a) of the Banking Ordinance (i.e., a bank, restricted license bank or deposit-taking company).

[24] Securities and Futures Commission, 'Do you need a license or registration' (February 2019), available at: https://beck-link.de/cfwm8 (accessed 07.01.2021).

[25] Securities and Futures Commission, 'Statement on the regulatory framework for virtual asset portfolios managers, fund distributors and trading platform operators' (November 2018), available at: https://beck-link.de/t8cwb (accessed 07.01.2021).

market abuse, as well as security risks, are addressed in the report produced by the European Banking Authority.[26]

In the abovementioned 2018 statement, there are various **potential risks** addressed by the SFC, including market integrity, fraud, cybersecurity, money laundering, and terrorist financing, etc. In order to prevent all possible risks, the SFC considered regulating virtual asset portfolio management activities. Furthermore, the SFC proposed a conceptual framework for the potential regulation of virtual asset trading platforms.

In terms of this, the activities are categorized into three main types in accordance with the 2018 statement, namely virtual asset portfolio managers, virtual asset fund distributors, and virtual asset trading platform operators. Under the SFC licensing framework, virtual asset portfolio managers and virtual asset fund distributors are classified as a type 1 **regulated activity** (dealing in securities). Moreover, virtual asset portfolio managers must comply with the requirements according to type 9 regulated activity (asset management).

b) Virtual asset portfolio managers. The managers of funds refer to those investing in virtual assets and distributing in Hong Kong (type 1 regulated activity). Under the SFO, the term '**dealing in securities**' potentially includes many types of business due to the broad definition stated in the SFO.[27]

The statement also categorizes virtual asset portfolio managers as business entities dealing with type 9 regulated activity (**asset management**). This is in accordance with the definition specified in the SFO. In particular, asset management in this context is a service relating to securities and futures contracts portfolio management.

Also, in 2019, the SFC published the terms and licensing conditions for virtual asset fund managers (see the Terms and Conditions). Importantly, the SFC broadly defines virtual assets as referring to a **digital representation** of value. Virtual assets in the Terms and Conditions include both security and non-security types of assets. For example, the Terms and Conditions require a manager of virtual asset funds to ensure effective management, maintain financial resources as required by respective legal and regulatory requirements, ascertain effective risk management, and maintain compliance.[28]

c) Virtual asset fund distributors. For virtual asset fund **distributors**, the authority recognizes businesses that distribute funds to invest in virtual assets in Hong Kong as businesses dealing in securities. Accordingly, such businesses must comply with the SFO as well as the circular to intermediaries' distribution of virtual asset funds.[29] It should be noted that the SFC normally publishes a circular aimed at providing a better understanding of regulatory issues.

The circular to intermediaries regarding the distribution of virtual asset funds aims to provide guidance on the standards and practices for the distribution of virtual asset funds. The circular is helpful in many ways, particularly in preventing any potential or operational risks, as there are standards, assessments, and guidelines incorporated into it. In essence, the circular specifies **different standards** for firms (virtual asset funds) that are authorized or not authorized by the SFC. Both authorised and unauthorised

---

[26] European Banking Authority, 'Report with advice for the European Commission on crypto assets' (January 2019), available at: https://beck-link.de/557eh (accessed 07.01.2021).
[27] Securities and Future Ordinance No. 5 of 2002, available at: https://beck-link.de/4v33n (accessed 07.01.2021).
[28] Securities and Futures Commission, 'Proforma Terms and Conditions for Licensed Corporations which Manage Portfolios that Invest in Virtual Assets' (October 2019), available at: https://beck-link.de/m6x63 (accessed 07.01.2021).
[29] Securities and Futures Commission, 'Circular to Intermediaries Distribution of Virtual Asset Funds' (November 2018), available at: https://beck-link.de/k3ds6 (accessed 07.01.2021).

firms must comply with paragraph 5.2 of the Code of Conduct for Persons Licensed by or Registered with the Securities and Futures Commission (the Code of Conduct).[30] In terms of the Code of Conduct, the SFC has the authority to publish any codes of conduct to ensure consistency in the practices and standards of carrying out regulated activities. In this context, the Code of Conduct provides guidance concerning reasonable advice made by the licensed or registered person. In addition, in accordance with the circular, the unauthorized virtual asset funds must ensure compliance with additional requirements, such as sales restrictions, due diligence standards, and information disclosure requirements.

The SFC emphasizes that the distribution of virtual asset funds includes all types of virtual asset funds. Alternatively, the distribution of virtual asset funds falls under the scope of the circular, regardless of whether the virtual assets are security or **non-security** virtual assets.

21   **d) Virtual asset trading platform operators.** In summary, with regard to regulations on crypto/virtual asset intermediation, digital asset businesses are primarily regulated under the SFC **licensing framework**. Moreover, such digital asset businesses include a virtual asset trading platform.

Consequently, the SFC's position paper, which was issued in November 2019, aimed to provide a framework for the regulation of virtual asset **trading platforms**. In general, platforms that are intended to deal with only non-security types of digital assets or tokens are outside the regulatory and supervisory power of the SFC. In other words, the SFC has the power to grant a license in case such digital assets or tokens fall within the scope of 'securities' or 'future contracts' according to the SFO. In this respect, the SFO is the main regulator that should be taken into account when considering regulations on crypto asset trading businesses.

22   To conclude, financial intermediaries related to crypto/digital assets are regulated by the SFC through **the SFO**. From the scope of power of the SFC, the authority primarily regulates firms engaged in business relating to security-type assets or tokens. However, considering portfolio managers and fund distributors, the virtual assets associated with these actors may not be security-type assets/tokens.

For further details on the SFO, the SFC issued a statement on initial coin offerings in 2017 to clarify that digital tokens that are publicly offered or sold can be regarded as a security; accordingly, associated businesses must comply with the registration or licensing requirements specified by the SFC.[31]

III. Self-regulatory Mechanism: Industry Standard Organization

23   Essentially, the complexity and variety of structures of digital tokens make it difficult to design regulatory parameters. Accordingly, apart from the aforementioned approaches being used by the authority to regulate such crypto assets and related activities,

---

[30] Para. 5.2 of the Code of Conduct for Persons Licensed by or Registered with the Securities and Futures Commission *"...Know your client: reasonable advice. Having regard to information about the client of which the licensed or registered person is or should be aware of through the exercise of due diligence, the licensed or registered person should, when making a recommendation or solicitation, ensure the suitability of the recommendation or solicitation for that client is reasonable in all the circumstances..."* Securities and Futures Commission, 'Code of Conduct for persons Licensed by or Registered with the Securities and Futures Commission' (September 2020), available at: https://beck-link.de/5nke4 (accessed 07.01.2021).

[31] Securities and Futures Commission, 'Statement on initial coin offerings' (September 2017), available at: https://beck-link.de/vk5he (accessed 07.01.2021).

the FinTech Association of Hong Kong also issued **guidance** entitled 'Best Practices for Token Sales' in 2017 aimed at providing guidance in relation to digital token offerings focusing on the Hong Kong jurisdiction.[32]

To highlight significant practices in the Best Practices for Token Sales, the guidance begins with the terminology of tokens and other basic information. It further addressed **best practices** with respect to the various issues; for instance, the guiding principles, key factors in success, and key considerations for token sales. It should be noted that the Best Practices for Token Sales primarily focuses on relevant practices aimed at providing a clear picture for businesses that wish to launch an ICO in order to raise money. Therefore, all stakeholders should be aware that the guidance is a non-legally binding document. As a result, Best Practices for Token Sales has been updated to cover other aspects of digital token offerings, including security token offerings (STOs), airdrops, and the know your customer (KYC) process, etc.[33] Along with a **Hong Kong Blockchain Ecosystem Map** that was recently issued in 2019, these initiatives reflect the attempt by the association to support a robust digital ecosystem in the territory.[34]

In other words, it is the manifestation of a **self-regulation mechanism** that has been developed in a number of countries to respond to technologies, innovations, and new types of digital financial businesses. However, it should be noted that the approach might differ from those taken in countries that lack industry standard organizations. In brief, to clarify this issue, emerging economies in the Southeast Asia region can be seen as examples of countries still in the early stages of FinTech development, and therefore do not yet have an industry standard organization to regulate the crypto asset industry.

IV. Innovative Regulatory Initiative: Regulatory Sandbox

Apart from hard law measures and the self-regulatory mechanism, in Hong Kong, the SFC launched its **regulatory sandbox** in September 2017, aimed at promoting firms that offer innovative products and services.[35] More specifically, the sandbox initiative enables the SFC to closely monitor and examine firms' activities.

The outcomes of the use of a regulatory sandbox can include **evidence-based regulations** in the form of laws, regulations, and/or guidance (to supplement existing legislations). All sandboxes have common features as per their objectives. For example, an entry precondition requirement is that the first feature cover all stipulations, such as potential benefits of the proposed products and services to customers, as well as their adequate preparation. However, in order to consider these pre-entry requirements to be viable, i.e., to determine whether the proposed products or services are innovative, is also not an easy task for regulators.[36] Furthermore, it is common practice for regulators to assess the need for a sandbox. In addition, sandbox applicants must have made adequate preparations, as required by the regulators.[37]

---

[32] FinTech Association of Hong Kong, 'FinTech Association of Hong Kong Launches Best Practice Paper on ICOs' (December 2017), available at: https://beck-link.de/hr2nk (accessed 07.01.2021).

[33] FinTech Association of Hong Kong, 'Best Practice for Token Sales' (October 2018), available at: https://beck-link.de/byv8t (accessed 07.01.2021).

[34] FinTech Association of Hong Kong, 'Launch of Hong Kong Blockchain Ecosystem Map2.0' (November 2019), available at: https://beck-link.de/x56de (accessed 07.01.2021).

[35] Securities and Futures Commission, 'Circular to announce the SFC Regulatory Sandbox' (September 2017), available at: https://beck-link.de/2pywv (accessed 07.01.2021).

[36] Zetzsche, Buckley, Barberis and Arner, 'Regulating a Revolution: From Regulatory Sandboxes to Smart Regulation', (2018) 13 *Fordham Journal of Corporate and Financial Law*, 70, available at: https://beck-link.de/d25c4 (accessed 07.01.2021).

[37] Ibid, 71.

The entry precondition requirements are also linked to the sandbox's scope. The **design** of the sandbox in relation to the type of business that allows testing also falls under the purview of this subsection. A number of countries, such as the United Kingdom, Singapore, and Malaysia, do not restrict the sandbox scope to any particular type of business.[38] However, it may differ across jurisdictions, which limit sandboxes to certain business sectors, such as the authorized financial institution operating in the Hong Kong sandbox.[39] More specifically, the Hong Kong sandbox generally allows 'Tech Firms' to access it.[40]

26 On the basis of the abovementioned features (→ para. 25), the variation in the sandbox's design relies heavily on local **market conditions** and contexts. However, it was found that there are common issues in terms of the minimum requirements; conceptually, the following issues must be addressed in order to ascertain the effective and efficient establishment and implementation of sandboxes.

Given that the use of a regulatory sandbox also relates to the correlation between financial innovation and regulatory objectives, regulators should consider the interaction between these. There are a number of relevant factors that must be considered, such as financial stability, integrity, and consumer protection according to the **I-SIP toolkit**, as developed by the Consultative Group to Assist the Poor (CGAP).[41]

For the SFC sandbox, in particular, the circular for announcing the SFC regulatory sandbox specifies **standard features** of the sandbox, from eligibility requirements and licensing conditions, to relevant measures to protect investors, to the decision of the SFC to produce a guideline regarding exit from the sandbox.[42]

V. Regulations on Crypto Asset Taxation

27 In terms of **taxation regulations**, the relevant authority, namely Hong Kong's Inland Revenue Department, does not issue specific regulations concerning the taxation of crypto assets and relevant intermediaries. There is also no capital gains tax required from the sale of financial instruments; however, relevant crypto asset stakeholders may need to comply with the income tax and profits tax from cryptocurrency trading.[43]

C. Conclusion

28 To conclude, in Hong Kong, the authority is receptive to the utilization of crypto assets, which can be seen from the attempts of the authority, as well as the association. It is important to note that crypto asset-related policies and regulations in other countries could also influence domestic markets in other countries. The increase in ICOs in Hong Kong after their 2017 prohibition in China seems to best exemplify the case under discussion. Moreover, the cross-border features of crypto

---

[38] Ibid.
[39] Ibid.
[40] Hong Kong Monetary Authority (HKMA), 'FinTech Supervisory Sandbox (FSS)', available at: https://beck-link.de/rzbp4 (accessed 07.01.2021).
[41] CGAP, 'I-SIP Toolkit: Policy Making for an Inclusive Financial System' (November 2018), available at: https://beck-link.de/8mxk7 (accessed 07.01.2021).
[42] Securities and Futures Commission, 'Circular to announce the SFC Regulatory Sandbox' (September 2017), available at: https://beck-link.de/2pywv (accessed 07.01.2021).
[43] Library of Congress, 'Regulatory Approaches to Cryptoassets: Hong Kong' (December 2020), available at: https://beck-link.de/ksa27 (accessed 07.01.2021).

assets could necessitate the **international coordination** of crypto asset regulation. This is in accordance with the OECD calling for a more 'coordinated global approach' to reducing regulatory arbitrage.⁴⁴

---

⁴⁴ Organisation for Economic Cooperation and Develpment (OECD), 'Initial Coin Offerings (ICOs) for SME Financing' (2019), available at: https://beck-link.de/6f68k (accessed 07.01.2021).

§ 27
People's Republic of China

Literature: Baynakova, 'China's Crypto Miners Struggle to Pay Power Bills as Regulators Clamp Down on OTC Desks' (November 2020), available at: https://beck-link.de/2hrhs (accessed 28.01.2021); Bharathan, 'People's Bank Of China Draft Law Provides A Legal Basis For Digital Currency Electronic Payments (DC/EP) And Bans All Stablecoins Backed By Renminbi Reserves' (October 2020), available at: https://beck-link.de/d4hee (accessed 28.01.2021); Bossu, Itatani, Margulis, Rossi, Weenink and Yoshinaga, 'Legal Aspects of Central Bank Digital Currency: Central Bank and Monetary Law Considerations', IMF Working Paper, available at: https://beck-link.de/ktt5r (accessed 29.01.2021); Feng and Zhang, 'Explainer I What Xi Jin Ping's advocacy means for China – and the world' (November 2019), available at: https://beck-link.de/5b5c6 (accessed 28.01.2021); He, 'China wants to weaponize its currency. A digital version could help' (December 2020), available at: https://beck-link.de/m28yy (accessed 28.01.2021); Kharpal, 'With Xi's backing, China looks to become a world leader in blockchain as US policy is absent' (December 2019), available at: https://beck-link.de/zs6br (accessed 28.01.2021); Li, 'Bitcoin in China: An Insider's View' (August 2015), available at: https://beck-link.de/vzpa5 (accessed 28.01.2021); Pilarowski and Yue, 'China Bans Initial Coin Offerings and Cryptocurrency Trading Platforms' (September 2017), available at: https://beck-link.de/m5ka6 (accessed 29.01.2021); Rapoza, 'After Crackdwon, Neraly Every Chinese ICO Returns Cash to Investors' (September 2017), available at: https://beck-link.de/4b3dt (accessed 28.01.2021); Wenhao, 'China: Regulation of Cryptocurrency in China' (June 2020), available at: https://beck-link.de/yrsa7 (accessed 28.01.2021); Xiaochuan, 'Future Regulation on Virtual Currency Will Be Dynamic, Imprudent Products Shall Be Stopped for Now' (March 2018), available at: https://beck-link.de/d3fr5 (accessed 28.01.2021); Xie Xu, 'China to Stamp Out Cryptocurrency Trading Completely with Ban on Foreign Platforms' (February 2018), available at: https://beck-link.de/b35ne (accessed 28.01.2021); Yanfei, 'PBOC Inches Closer to Digital Currency' (October 2017), available at: https://beck-link.de/2fv3v (accessed 28.01.2021); Yujian, 'Bitcoin Exchanges Ordered to Formulate Non-Risk Clearance Plan and Shut Down by End of September' (September 2017), available at: https://beck-link.de/2anew (accessed 28.01.2021); Zhao, 'China's Supreme Court Calls for Better Protection of Digital Currency Rights' (July 2020), available at: https://beck-link.de/d736p (accessed 29.01.2021); Zhao, 'China's State Council Orders Faster Blockchain Technology' (May 2018), available at: https://beck-link.de/rmhn2 (accessed 28.01.2021); Zmudzinski, 'Chinese Social Media Giant WeChat Bans Crypto Transactions in Its Payment Policy' (May 2019), available at: https://beck-link.de/d86xs (accessed 28.01.2021).

Outline

	para.
A. Introduction	1
B. Regulatory Framework	7
I. Overview	7
II. Civil Code of the People's Republic of China	12
III. Regulatory Measures on Crypto Assets Activities	13
1. Regulatory Measures on Initial Coin Offerings (ICO)	13
2. Regulatory Measures on Trading Platforms	15
IV. Central Bank Digital Currency (CBDC)	19
V. Regulation of the Underlying Technology	25
C. Conclusion	30

A. Introduction

1   China is one of the countries providing strong support for **blockchain technology**. This could be heard in a recent speech by President Xi Jinping, who stated that blockchain is an 'important breakthrough in the independent innovation of core

technologies.'[1] This is in accordance with what has been addressed in the State Council's technology blueprint.[2]

The issuance of **the blueprint** is a significant move for the country to drive faster blockchain development with the support of local governance.[3] The orders issued by the state government in May 2018 to local authorities include the development and implementation of blockchain applications under existing regulatory frameworks to hasten the financial technologies' development in the country. However, the order related to a specific area, namely the Guangdong Pilot Free-Trade Zone.[4] Furthermore, it did not provide detailed information regarding the implementation process of blockchain within the free-trade zone.[5]

It should be noted that, in 2017, there was a rapid increase in the number of **Chinese blockchain startups**, according to the Ministry of Information and Technology. In addition, the Ministry recently published a new report, entitled '2020 China Blockchain Development: Situation Outlook' (中国区块链发展形势展望), which will be discussed in detail herein (→ para. 25).[6]

Apart from the country's strategies concerning blockchain technology, in terms of cryptocurrency, it should be pointed out that **crypto-related activities** are currently banned in China. This was apparent from the 2017 initial coin offering (ICO) crackdown in the country, which considered ICOs illegal in the country.[7] Following the crackdown, most ICO platforms in China returned around a billion dollars in total to their investors.[8]

Despite all relevant cryptocurrency-related activities seeming to be prohibited in China, cryptocurrency mining was not affected by the crackdown.[9] As a result, however, in 2020, stricter regulations on cryptocurrency exchanges and a crackdown on over-the-counter (OTC) brokers in China made it more difficult for crypto miners to pay for electricity.[10]

Prior to the crackdown, **Bitcoin** was also receiving public attention in China, as its price went up rapidly (with a 20,000-fold increase in three years). This was accompanied by a rapid increase in the number of ICOs in China in 2017, with a total 65 occurring and 394.6 million USD raised from 105,000 individuals.[11] These attracted both public attention and concerns from Chinese regulators.[12]

---

[1] Kharpal, 'With Xi's backing, China looks to become a world leader in blockchain as US policy is absent' (December 2019), available at: https://beck-link.de/zs6br (accessed 28.01.2021).
[2] Feng and Zhang, 'Explainer I What Xi Jin Ping's advocacy means for China – and the world' (November 2019), available at: https://beck-link.de/5b5c6 (accessed 28.01.2021).
[3] Zhao, 'China's State Council Orders Faster Blockchain Technology' (May 2018), available at: https://beck-link.de/rmhn2 (accessed 28.01.2021).
[4] 国务院关于印发进一步深化中国广东)，自由贸易试验区改革开放方案的通知 (*translation*: Notice of the State Council on Issuing the Plan for Further Deepening the Reform and Opening up of China (Guangdong) and Pilot Free Trade Zone), available at: https://beck-link.de/7crbp (accessed 28.01.2021).
[5] Zhao, ibid.
[6] China Banking News, 'Ministry of Industry Expects China's Blockchain Sector to Exceed 2 Billion Yuan in 2020' (March 2020), available at: https://beck-link.de/mw42f (accessed 28.01.2021).
[7] CNBC, 'ICO crackdown may just be the start: China is reportedly planning tighter cryptocurrency rules' (September 2017), available at: https://beck-link.de/rm46a (accessed 28.01.2021).
[8] Rapoza, 'After Crackdwon, Neraly Every Chinese ICO Returns Cash to Investors' (September 2017), available at: https://beck-link.de/4b3dt (accessed 28.01.2021).
[9] Kharpal, ibid.
[10] Baynakova, 'China's Crypto Miners Struggle to Pay Power Bills as Regulators Clamp Down on OTC Desks' (November 2020), available at: https://beck-link.de/2hrhs (accessed 28.01.2021).
[11] Reuters, 'China's regulators preparing new rules for digital coin offerings' (August 2017), available at: https://beck-link.de/artn8 (accessed 28.01.2021).
[12] Li, 'Bitcoin in China: An Insider's View' (August 2015), available at: https://beck-link.de/vzpa5 (accessed 28.01.2021).

Part C. Country Reports

To summarize the stances of Chinese regulators before going into detail on the regulatory perspectives, regulators implemented **strict measures** on crypto assets for the purposes of investor protection and financial risk prevention.[13]

B. Regulatory Framework

I. Overview

7   China has not passed any substantive legislation to regulate crypto assets and cryptocurrencies. However, as previously noted (→ para. 4), over the last few years, **regulatory measures** have been issued to crack down on cryptocurrency-related activities in the country, in accordance with the government's concerns over financial risks.[14]

The crackdown resulted in an order from a Chinese regulator prohibiting platforms that offer cryptocurrency exchange and facilitation services from their operations. As a result, such platforms relocated their businesses to other jurisdictions with more favourable regulatory regimes, such as the HKSAR and Singapore. Interestingly, it is not prohibited to hold cryptocurrencies in China.[15]

8   In light of these developments, it is important to determine **the status** of cryptocurrencies and other types of digital assets in China. Accordingly, this section will outline the government's circular and court decisions and further explain the taxonomy of such digital initiatives.

In terms of the legal status of cryptocurrencies, the Chinese banking system does not accept any as **legal tender**. Specifically, in 2013, in a 2013 circular, the government defined Bitcoin as **a virtual commodity**. However, the government also warned Chinese citizens to be aware of the associated risks.[16]

9   Specifically, with respect to the circular, in December 2013, five government offices, including the People's Bank of China, issued the 'Notice to Prevent the Risk of Bitcoin' (关于防范比特币风险的通知). This Notice not only classified Bitcoin as a virtual commodity but also clearly prohibited **financial institutions** from providing services to Bitcoin-focused businesses. It is also interesting to observe the part of the Notice that specified its objective as being to 'protect the status of the renminbi as the statutory currency, prevent risks of money laundering, and protect financial stability.' This means that, apart from the prevention of financial risks, China also aimed to protect its monetary sovereignty.[17]

10 In order to determine the legal status of Bitcoin (and other types of cryptocurrencies), further to the Notice issued by the authorities in 2013, Chinese **court decisions** will also be of interest in order to understand the interpretation of associated laws and regulations.

In 2019, the Hangzhou Internet Court ruled that Bitcoin is a virtual asset. The case centered on a dispute between an exchange platform and its users. Specifically, the Hangzhou Internet Court concluded that Bitcoin, due to its core characteristics,

---

[13] Xiaochuan, 'Future Regulation on Virtual Currency Will Be Dynamic, Imprudent Products Shall Be Stopped for Now' (March 2018), available at: https://beck-link.de/d3fr5 (accessed 28.01.2021).
[14] Xiaochuan, ibid.
[15] Wenhao, 'China: Regulation of Cryptocurrency in China' (June 2020), available at: https://beck-link.de/yrsa7 (accessed 28.01.2021).
[16] 中国人民银行 工业和信息化部 中国银行业监督管理委员会中国证券监督管理委员会 中国保险监督管理委员会关于防范比特币风险的通知,available at: https://beck-link.de/zppf8 (accessed 28.01.2021).
[17] Zhang, 'Regulation of Cryptocurrency: China' (December 2020), available at: https://beck-link.de/m86fx (accessed 28.01.2021).

constitutes a **virtual property**. Correspondingly, Bitcoin has value, scarcity, and disposability, and should accordingly be protected by Chinese property laws.[18]

In addition, an announcement was issued by the Shanghai Intermediate People's Court in May 2020 concerning the appeal of the Bitcoin case. In brief, the second court trial ruled that Bitcoin may be regarded as a **digital asset**.[19]

To conclude, Bitcoin has been determined to be a virtual asset or virtual property by the Chinese courts. However, the courts do not recognize its status as a **legal tender**. Therefore, it differs from the legal tender status of the PBOC's digital currency, which will be ascertained in the new draft Banking Law, and which is discussed herein.

Consequently, to supplement the courts' interpretative approaches, in July of 2020 the Supreme People's Court of China and the National Development and Reform Commission (NDRC) published a new guideline.[20] This guideline aimed to strengthen protections relating to ownership rights for virtual currencies – an umbrella term that includes digital assets, such as cryptocurrencies. Specifically, the guideline generally stipulated the need for **stronger protections** for new classes of property.[21] In term of laws and regulations concerning crypto assets in China, this chapter initially explores the Civil Code of the People Republic of China as the law that lays the foundation for the digital economy in a variety of ways.

II. Civil Code of the People's Republic of China

The New Civil Code of the PRC[22] promises to be a tool to boost the country's digital economy. According to a speech given by Liu Dongmin, head of the Centre for International Finance at the Institute of World Economics and Politics of the Chinese Academy of Social Sciences, there is no doubt that the New Civil Code represents an important step in advancing the Chinese **digital economy**. In particular, there are many key provisions according to the New Civil Code, such as Article 124, regarding the right of succession, which could be open to interpretation, along with other provisions to the extent that digital assets can be inherited. Moreover, Article 680 could also be used to prevent misconduct in the online lending industry (e.g., cyber loan sharks). Article 111 further states that the personal information of a natural person shall be protected by the law. Essentially, no person may illegally collect, use, process, transmit, trade, provide or publicise the personal information of others. This is significant for FinTech businesses, including digital asset intermediaries, as such businesses must normally process their customers' personal data.

---

[18] Kong, 'A Chinese "Internet Court" sanctifies Bitcoin as a virtual asset' (July 2019), available at: https://beck-link.de/mz6ff (accessed 29.01.2021).

[19] Faridi, 'Chinese Authorities Continue to Recognize Bitcoin (BTC) as A Digital Asset Entitled to Protection Under the Law in Latest Court Case' (May 2020), available at: https://beck-link.de/a85rr (accessed 28.01.2021).

[20] 最高人民法院国家发展和改革委员会关于为新时代加快完善社会主义市场经济体制提供司法服务和保障的意 (translation: The Supreme People's Court and the National Development and Reform Commission's opinion on providing judicial services and guarantees for accelerating the improvement of the socialist market economic system in the new era), available at: https://beck-link.de/saek3 (accessed 29.01.2021).

[21] Zhao, 'China's Supreme Court Calls for Better Protection of Digital Currency Rights' (July 2020), available at: https://beck-link.de/d736p (accessed 29.01.2021).

[22] Civil Code of the People's Republic of China (中华人民共和国民法典).

III. Regulatory Measures on Crypto Assets Activities

1. Regulatory Measures on Initial Coin Offerings (ICO)

13   In 2017, Chinese regulators, specifically the People's Bank of China (PBOC), the Cyberspace Administration of China (CAC), the Ministry of Industry and Information Technology (MIIT), the State Administration for Industry and Commerce (SAIC), the China Banking Regulatory Commission (CBRC), the China Securities Regulatory Commission (CSRC), and the China Insurance Regulatory Commission (CIRC), jointly issued the 'Announcement on Preventing Risks from Initial Coin Offerings' (关于防范代币发行融资风险的公告), which outlined their concerns regarding the potential risks of **ICO-related activities**.[23]

14   The Announcement prohibits ICO activities or the practice of raising funds from the public via the issuance of cryptocurrencies. The issuance of the announcement consequently resulted in **the closure** of cryptocurrency trading platforms in China. In particular, a number of cryptocurrency platforms, such as BTCChina, Houbi, OKCoin, and ViaBTC, notified their customers regarding the cessation of their operations.[24]

2. Regulatory Measures on Trading Platforms

15   The ICO Announcement further addresses **restrictions** on cryptocurrency trading platforms. Such platforms are prohibited from dealing with fiat-to-cryptocurrency exchange services. In addition, the platforms are barred from trading cryptocurrencies and providing other services. With respect to this, Chinese authorities have the power to shut down any websites and platforms' applications, as well as to suspend their licenses.[25]

16   Following the issuance of the ICO Rules in September 2017, senior executives of cryptocurrency trading platforms in China were reportedly summoned for 'chats' by regulators. In September 2017, for instance, the Beijing Internet Finance Risk Working Group summoned senior executives of cryptocurrency trading platforms to Beijing. The platforms were reportedly ordered to immediately cease new client registration and announce a deadline by which time they would cease all cryptocurrency trading.[26] As a result, the cryptocurrency trading platforms essentially **shut down** their trading businesses in the country.[27]

17   More recently, in February of 2018, the South China Morning Post reported that China was planning to **block websites** related to cryptocurrency trading and ICOs, including foreign platforms, in a bid to completely stamp out cryptocurrency trading.[28]

Consequently, in 2019, Chinese financial authorities took an active approach to **cracking down** on cryptocurrency trading again. The Notice issued by the Chinese

---

[23] 中国人民银行 中央网信办 工业和信息化部 工商总局 银监会 证监会 保监会关于防范代币发行融资风险的公告, available at: https://beck-link.de/8467x (accessed 29.01.2021).

[24] Pilarowski and Yue, 'China Bans Initial Coin Offerings and Cryptocurrency Trading Platforms' (September 2017), available at: https://beck-link.de/m5ka6 (accessed 29.01.2021).

[25] 中国人民银行 中央网信办 工业和信息化部 工商总局 银监会 证监会 保监会关于防范代币发行融资风险的公告, available at: https://beck-link.de/8467x (accessed 29.01.2021).

[26] Yujian, ' Bitcoin Exchanges Ordered to Formulate Non-Risk Clearance Plan and Shut Down by End of September' (September 2017), available at: https://beck-link.de/2anew (accessed 28.01.2021).

[27] Xie Xu, ' China to Stamp Out Cryptocurrency Trading Completely with Ban on Foreign Platforms' (February 2018), available at: https://beck-link.de/b35ne (accessed 28.01.2021).

[28] Ibid.

authorities, namely the Shanghai Internet Finance Rectification Agency and the Shanghai Bureau of the People's Bank of China in November 2019, ruled that Shanghai regulators were obliged to search for and inspect local cryptocurrency exchange services and report these to the Central Bank of People's Republic of China.[29]

In addition, regulators took **cautious stances** concerning cryptocurrency exchange or trading platforms. A ban was also enacted on anything related to cryptocurrency trading over online platforms such as Weido.[30] Furthermore, the prohibition of crypto-transactions in WeChat's payment policy exemplified the total ban of cryptocurrency trading activities in China.[31]

IV. Central Bank Digital Currency (CBDC)

Even though China took a strict approach to the regulation of cryptocurrency-related activities and businesses, the PBOC considered issuing their own digital currency. Specifically, China's national digital currency is considered to be the Digital Currency Electronic Payment (DECP). Conceptually, there are two relevant steps regarding this. First, the PBOC will be the sole authority that issues the **DECP**. Secondly, the DECP will be distributed by Chinese-backed financial institutions.[32]

The DECP differs from Bitcoin and other cryptocurrencies, as it is issued and backed by the PBOC. It should be noted that, as the DECP was designed to be similar to cash, this should negatively impact the market dominance of digital payment services, such as Alipay and WeChat Pay. Accordingly, as per its characteristics, the DECP should have a similar legal status to the **state currency** (Renminbi).[33]

The direct **benefit** of the DECP is its reduction of the costs associated with managing paper-based cash. Furthermore, its features make it more traceable. With respect to the latter point, the benefit from the DECP could be preventing its being used for money laundering or the financing of terrorism, etc.[34] Furthermore, some have opined that the attempt by China to issue its own digital currency is also due to its goal of competing with the U.S. as a major influencer of the global financial system. This is supplemented by their intention to supervise the spending behaviour of local users of the DECP.[35]

China recently began a **trial use** of the DECP in four cities, namely Xiongan, Shenzhen, Suzhou, and Chengdu. In a speech by the PBOC's governor, it was stated that more than 299.07 million USD has been spent using the new digital currency, with some four million transactions.[36]

---

[29] Zhao, 'China Is Poised for Another Crypto Trading Crackdown as Speculative Fever Returns' (November 2019), available at: https://beck-link.de/5nyhn (accessed 28.01.2021).
[30] Xie Xu, ibid.
[31] ZMudzinski, 'Chinese Social Media Giant WeChat Bans Crypto Transactions in Its Payment Policy' (May 2019), available at: https://beck-link.de/d86xs (accessed 28.01.2021).
[32] Reuters, 'Spending with China's digital yuan around $300 million, PBOC says' (November 2020), available at: https://beck-link.de/bnp3x (accessed 28.01.2021).
[33] Yanfei, 'PBOC Inches Closer to Digital Currency' (October 2017), available at: https://beck-link.de/2fv3v (accessed 28.01.2021).
[34] Murray, 'Understanding China's Digital (September 2020), available at: https://beck-link.de/87xyd (accessed 28.01.2021).
[35] He, 'China wants to weaponize its currency. A digital version could help' (December 2020), available at: https://beck-link.de/m28yy (accessed 28.01.2021).
[36] Reuters, ibid.

With respect to the legal status of the DECP, the draft Banking Law specifies that it[37] is to be considered a **legal tender**. Hence, the DECP is legally recognized as a means of settling a debt or meeting a financial obligation.[38]

22   Article 19 of the draft law specifies that the renminbi includes both physical and **digital forms**,[39] which differs from the laws in many jurisdictions that assigned legal tender status to only physical money in the form of coins or banknotes. In addition, the DECP is differs from so-called 'electronic money,' which is commonly defined as an electronic store of monetary value on a specific device. In contrast, in most jurisdictions electronic money does not have legal tender status.[40]

This is significant as a **legal foundation** for the DECP. Apart from the issue concerning the legal status of DECP, the draft law also prohibits any person from issuing digital tokens backed by the renminbi. Additionally, Article 65 of the draft law stipulates that the PBOC shall order the issuer to stop alleged activities and destroy tokens or cryptocurrencies, etc., in the case that such tokens are made, issued, or able to replace the renminbi.

23   To this, Article 22 added that 'No unit or individual may produce or sell tokens, coupons and digital tokens to replace the RMB in circulation in the market.' This is highly significant, as Article 22 potentially prohibits any digital tokens (**stable coins**) from being pegged to the renminbi.[41] It should be noted that this is to prevent associated risks from virtual currency in accordance with para. 3 of Article 22.

24   Moreover, in a speech, the head of the PBOC research unit stated that, 'WeChat and Alipay are just wallets, whereas the DECP is the money inside them.' This statement could also reflect the position and collaboration between the DECP and authorities, as well as private technology enterprises. However, after being trialled in four cities in China, the representative of the PBOC noted that a number of **concerns** arose, including the inaccessibility of underprivileged groups, privacy, and safety issues. However, the PBOC will resolve the inaccessibility concerns by developing a new digital yuan product and increase its oversight of relevant risks.[42]

V. Regulation of the Underlying Technology

25   In 2020, China enacted a **new law** on cryptography to pave the way for blockchain technology. Over the past few years, the government of China has taken several regulatory measures to crack down on activities related to various aspects of cryptocurrency, from the banning of ICOs and cryptocurrency exchanges, to discouraging Bitcoin mining.

---

[37] 中国人民银行关于《中华人民共和国中国人民银行法修订草案征求意见稿》》公开征求意见的通知 (*translation*: Notice of the People's Bank of China on Public Consultation on the "Law of the People's Republic of China on the People's Bank of China (Revised Draft for Solicitation of Comments), available at: https://beck-link.de/a4y3k (accessed 28.01.2021).

[38] Spangler, Wang and Schaffer, 'China to Legalize Digital RMB and Prohibit Competitors' (November 2020), available at: https://beck-link.de/dfr7c (accessed 28.01.2021).

[39] Bharathan, 'People's Bank Of China Draft Law Provides A Legal Basis For Digital Currency Electronic Payments (DC/EP) And Bans All Stablecoins Backed By Renminbi Reserves' (October 2020), available at: https://beck-link.de/d4hee (accessed 28.01.2021).

[40] Bossu, Itatani, Margulis, Rossi, Weenink and Yoshinaga, 'Legal Aspects of Central Bank Digital Currency: Central Bank and Monetary Law Considerations', IMF Working Paper, 6, available at: https://beck-link.de/ktt5r (accessed 29.01.2021).

[41] Bharathan, ibid.

[42] Tang, 'China moves to legalise digital yuan and ban competitors with new draft law' (October 2020), available at: https://beck-link.de/pbc4m (accessed 28.01.2021).

After years of public debate, on July 5, 2019, the Standing Committee of the National People's Congress of China issued a new draft **cryptography law** for public comment. The 2019 draft includes a range of issues, spanning cryptography classification and its usage to enforcement and penalties for non-compliance. This July 2019 draft also retained a number of items previously specified in the initial draft that was issued by the State Cryptography Administration (SCA) in 2017.

Late in October 2019, following President Xi Jinping's endorsement of blockchain technology, Xinhua-Chinese state media reported that China has passed its new law on cryptography,[43] which would become effective on January 1, 2020. In general, the new law regulates the use of cryptography in China by both the public and private sectors, facilitates business, promotes the industry, and aims to ensure the security of cyberspace and information.

The new law on cryptography is consistent with the country's plan to launch its own digital currency. In particular, the People's Bank of China (PBOC) plans to issue a Central Bank Digital Currency (CBDC) as legal tender. The **DECP**, which is a state-backed cryptocurrency, may have some similarities to Libra – the digital currency proposed earlier in 2019 by Facebook.

It is worth noting that the new cryptography law focuses on cryptography rather than any specific uses of it in cryptocurrencies such as Bitcoin or Litecoin. The new cryptography law outlines key points regarding the **definition** and **classification** of 'cryptography,' which are categorized as 'core and ordinary cryptography' and 'commercial cryptography.' Given that 'core and ordinary cryptography' is handled by the state, this type will be used to protect information that is regarded as state secrets and then subjected to strict regulatory requirements (Article 7). 'Commercial cryptography' in contrast, will relate to the protection of information that is not regarded as state secrets (Article 8).

As '**commercial cryptography**' is a type of cryptography used for protecting information that is not state secrets, the new law will further encourage the use of 'commercial cryptography' by any entities or individuals in accordance with the principle of non-discrimination. The applicable Article 21 binds the government at all levels. Furthermore, in the subcategory of 'commercial cryptography,' Article 28 conveys requirements pertaining to import and export control, with an exemption stated in para. 2.

It should be noted that, apart from the different restrictions for different types of cryptography, the new cryptography law includes **general provisions** that present overarching restrictions and background information that applies to cryptography in general. The general provisions include the prohibition of the use of cryptography for any kind to engagement in criminal activities that harm state security, public interests or the legitimate rights and interests of others (Article 12).

It is apparent that the general purpose of the new law is to clarify the regulatory framework relating to cryptography. On the other hand, the new law contains detailed principles regarding the public and private use cryptography. However, it is worth noting that some important areas will **require further clarification**, such as ambiguous exemptions as specified under Article 28, para. 2, in relation to the use of 'commercial cryptography' In particular, para. 2 specifies that the 'commercial cryptography' used in mass consumer products is not to be subjected to import and export control requirements.

---

[43] Xinhuanet, 'China Focus: China adopts law on cryptography' (October 2019), available at: https://beck-link.de/pcva6 (accessed 28.01.2021).

Although China still bans both ICOs and cryptocurrency exchanges, the new cryptography law aims to support the use of cryptography, which is generally referred to as a method for protecting the information that is used in cryptocurrencies.

C. Conclusion

30   To conclude, the Chinese financial authorities have taken intensified **regulatory measures** on crypto assets, including digital tokens and cryptocurrencies, in order to prevent associated risks; however, the country is advanced in the launching of its digital currency. To reemphasize the legal and regulatory framework, China has not issued substantive legislation to regulate crypto asset activities and businesses, although it has issued regulatory measures, including notices, announcements, and guidelines for their oversight.

As for the emergence of the country's digital currency and its distinct measures, it will be interesting to observe **future consequences** in the coming years. This is also because the Chinese government has expressed a positive view of blockchain technology. Furthermore, this can be seen from the attempts by the authorities to implement this technology and issue a regulatory framework to accommodate its use.

§ 28
Middle East and North Africa (MENA)*

Literature: Arslanian and Fisher, *The Future of Finance: The Impact of Fintech, AI, and Crypto on Financial Services* (Palgrave Macmillan, 2019); Financial Stability Board (FSB), 'Crypto assets regulators directory' (April 2019), available at: https://beck-link.de/p42hy (accessed 29.09.2020); Israel Tax Authority, 'Informing the public about possible risks inherent in distributed virtual currencies (such as Bitcoin)', available at: https://beck-link.de/ke3ap (accessed 01.06.2021) (in Hebrew); Israel Tax Authority, 'Circular No. 05/2018' (January 2018), §§ 3.1–3.3, available at: https://beck-link.de/5x43v (accessed on 01.06.2021) (in Hebrew); Mohamed and Ali, *Blockchain, Fintech and Islamic Finance: Building the Future in the New Islamic Digital Economy* (Walter de Gruyter, 2019); Nafis, Gupta and Zameni, *Fintech and Islamic Finance: Digitalization, Development and Disruption* (Palgrave Macmillan, 2019); Naifar, *Impact of Financial Technology (FinTech) on Islamic Finance and Financial Stability* (IGI Global, 2019); Oseni and Nazim Ali, *Fintech in Islamic Finance* (Routledge, 2019); Supervision and Control of Financial Institutions Division, 'Circular No. 6/2018 from 7 February 2018' (June 2018), available at: https://beck-link.de/es25h (accessed 29.09.2020).

Outline

	para.
A. Introduction	1
B. Early Adopters	4
I. Abu Dhabi	5
1. Digital Securities	8
2. Definition of Virtual Assets	9
3. Utility Tokens	11
4. Fiat Tokens	12
5. Additional Rules	13
II. Bahrain	23
1. Safeguards and Protections	29
III. Egypt	34
C. Cautious and Non-Adopters	35
D. Shar'ia Compliance	44
E. Conclusion	46

A. Introduction

This chapter addresses **crypto asset regulations across the MENA region**. The jurisdictions examined include the **Gulf States** (UAE, Saudi Arabia, Oman, Kuwait, Qatar, Iraq, Iran and Bahrain), the Levant (Lebanon, Jordan, Palestine and Israel) and North Africa (Egypt, Tunisia, Morocco and Algeria). Due to recent or on-going conflicts and the consequent lack of governmental authority and other difficulties, Yemen, Syria and Libya are not included.

Two extreme positions characterize the regulation of crypto assets in the MENA region. The first position, represented by jurisdictions such as Abu Dhabi and Bahrain, is one of **proactive regulation** informed by the potential represented by developments in the crypto asset space. This has translated into regulatory frameworks designed to support and attract fintech and regtech-related investments that leverage crypto asset

---

* This chapter was made possible by the NPRP Award NPRP 11S-1119-170016 from the Qatar National Research Fund (a member of the Qatar Foundation) (QNRF).

technology. The second position is **more cautious of the hype** and weary of potential crypto asset risks. These more cautious jurisdictions have imposed strict bans and restrictions pertaining to various types of crypto assets – mainly those policymakers deem cryptocurrencies. Interwoven into the fabric of the MENA crypto asset discourse is the ever-present and growing Islamic finance sector. *Shar'ia* **compliance** is therefore an additional unique dimension of regulatory consideration prevalent in MENA mirrored only in South East Asia.

3   Although the sweep of included jurisdictions examined in this chapter is broad, many of the above stated countries fall into common categories based on their respective regulatory postures. The clearest demarcation between jurisdictions is that between **early adopters** on the one hand and **cautious or non-adopters** on the other. The structure of this chapter, therefore, is along these lines.

B. Early Adopters

4   In the MENA region, a number of jurisdictions stand out as early adopters of crypto asset technology. A more appropriate name is 'early-believers' in that these jurisdictions have established **sophisticated regulatory frameworks** in the belief that such policy moves will instil confidence and attract investors and entrepreneurs into their respective regulatory environments. Particularly with the Gulf states, the crypto asset story forms part of a larger push to support regional fintech sectors – which are themselves part of long held **economic diversification** plans aimed at steering those economies away from a narrow dependence on the hydro-carbon fuel sector.

I. Abu Dhabi

5   Abu Dhabi is the richest emirate of the seven emirates making up the United Arab Emirates (UAE). It is also the home to the **Abu Dhabi Global Markets (ADGM) investment platform**. ADGM, like other similar regional financial centres, is a self-contained legal jurisdiction with a significant level of autonomy. It is within ADGM, and the ADGM regulatory framework, that relevant UAE crypto asset regulations exist. The most recent guidance on the regulations were issued in February 2020 seeing, among other things, a shift in the language used from 'Crypto Assets' to **'Virtual Assets'**. These regulations are binding on all firms registered and subject to the jurisdiction of ADGM. The initial introduction of these regulations was in in 2018. The regulations do not apply to entities operating in the ordinary jurisdiction of the UAE proper.

6   ADGM promotes its virtual asset regulatory credentials by claiming it is the:[1]

> ...first jurisdiction in the world to introduce a **comprehensive and bespoke regulatory framework for the regulation of spot virtual asset activities,** including those undertaken by multilateral trading facilities, brokers, custodians, asset managers and other intermediaries.

The main ADGM rule-making body responsible for overseeing virtual asset regulatory framework is the **Financial Services Regulatory Authority** (FSRA). The relevant rules are contained in the Financial Services and Market Regulations (FSMR). Three important documents, all updated this year, contain the relevant guidance:

---

[1] Virtual Asset Activities, 'A Leading Destination of Choice for Virtual Asset Players', available at: https://beck-link.de/d42ww (accessed 19.09.2020).

§ 28. Middle East and North Africa (MENA)

1. Guidance – Regulation of Virtual Asset Activities in ADGM (issued 24 February 2020)
2. Guidance – Regulation of Digital Security Offerings and Virtual Assets under the Financial Services and Markets Regulations (issued 24 February 2020)
3. Guidance – Regulation of Digital Securities Activities in ADGM (issued 24 February 2020)

These guidance documents are not binding on the FSRA although they do provide a detailed catalogue of regulatory expectations with respect to existing and binding regulations. The general posture of regulators in ADGM is permissive with respect to **Virtual Assets and the use of tokenization**. As stated in the *Digital Security Offerings* documents above:[2]

> To the extent that virtual tokens are used as a mechanism to enable or facilitate a Regulated Activity to be carried out, they are generally permitted. For example, subject to fit and proper safeguards, an authorized money remittance house may receive fiat currencies from Clients and use virtual tokens to securely remit an equivalent value overseas directly to a regulated foreign counterparty via the internet in real-time; the foreign counterparty can then pay out in fiat currencies to the intended end clients.

Any regulated firm engaging in a regulated activity that utilizes virtual tokens in this ancillary manner has the onus to prove that this use is 'fit-for-purpose' and not straying into other more direct virtual asset-related activities.

1. Digital Securities

With respect to Digital Securities, the FSRA will examine each fundraising activity that utilizes virtual tokens on a case-by-case basis and may, pursuant to section 58(2)(b)(4) of the FSMR, deem that virtual token a **'digital security'** for regulatory purposes. Regulators will treat such tokens no differently from ordinary issued securities.[3] The FSRA encourages issuers to engage with regulators early and note that they may be eligible for the ordinary exemptions that apply to offers directed at sophisticated clients etc. Any intermediaries, such as brokers and advisors, who deal with digital securities, will also be subject to exactly the same financial licensing rules as ordinary intermediaries.

This approach creates a level playing field in the corporate fundraising space, by distinguishing what is essentially corporate fundraising by another means, from the other **'Initial Coin Offering (ICO)'** activities. ICO activities that relate to Virtual Assets that do not conform to any stated virtual asset definitions are outside the regulatory ambit of the FSRA.

2. Definition of Virtual Assets

The regulations define 'Virtual Asset' as:[4]

A digital representation of value that can be digitally traded and functions as:
(1) a medium of exchange; and/or
(2) a unit of account; and/or
(3) a store of value but does not have legal tender status in any jurisdiction.

---

[2] Para. 2.2 of Guidance-Regulation of Digital Security Offerings and Virtual Assets under the Financial Services and Markets Regulations (issued 24 February 2020).

[3] Securities are defined under schedule 1 of the FSMR as including Shares (para. 87); Instruments creating of acknowledging indebtedness (para. 88); Sukuk (para. 89); Government and public Financial Instruments (para. 90); Instruments giving entitlements to investments (para. 91); Certificates representing certain Financial Instruments (para. 92); and Units in a Collective Investment Fund (para. 93).

[4] Financial Services Market Regulations, s 258 (1) 'Definitions'.

Part C. Country Reports

A Virtual Asset is –
(a) neither issued nor guaranteed by any jurisdiction, and fulfils the above functions only by agreement within the community of users of the Virtual Asset; and
(b) distinguished from Fiat Currency and E-money.

10   Within this formulation, the regulations define 'Fiat Currency' as government issued currency that its country of issuance designates as legal tender through government decree, regulation or law.[5] Whilst the regulations define **'E-money'** as any digital representation of Fiat Currency used to transfer electronically value denominated in Fiat Currency.[6] The regulations therefore treat Virtual Assets as commodities, rather than specific investments under the FSMR.[7] Even so, any person or entity engaging in any market activities dealing in Virtual Assets requires FSRA approval and must be the holder of a Financial Services Permission (FSP) (i.e. a financial services license). Moreover, in line with the approach of treating Virtual Assets as commodities, the regulations also treat derivatives of Virtual Assets, as commodity derivatives.[8]

The chart below represents the regulatory approach to the various forms of Virtual Assets.

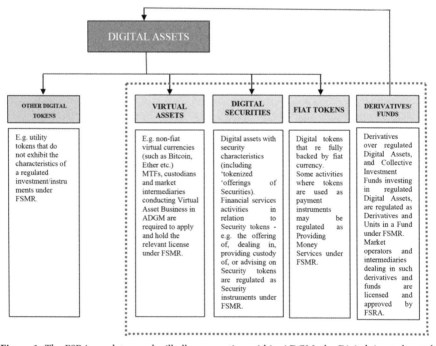

Figure 1. The FSRA regulates, and will allow operation within ADGM, the Digital Assets located within the dotted line.[9]

---

[5] Ibid.
[6] Ibid.
[7] Para. 4.2 of Guidance – Regulation of Digital Security Offerings and Virtual Assets under the Financial Services and Markets Regulations (issued 24 February 2020).
[8] Ibid, para. 4.5.
[9] Ibid, para. 5.2.

The representation of the regulations in the chart above is the 'Virtual Asset Framework (VAF)' used in ADGM.

3. Utility Tokens

The regulations do not intend that the VAF apply to **utility tokens**. Utility tokens are virtual tokens that provide other forms of benefit (i.e. software or platform access or use rights). The regulations deem utility tokens commodities.

4. Fiat Tokens

Regulators will deem **fiat tokens** (such as stablecoins fully backed by an underlying fiat currency) merely digital representations of that fiat currency. The regulation of Fiat Tokens is no different to the manner in which any other activity 'Providing Money Services' is regulated.[10]

5. Additional Rules

The Financial Services Regulatory Authority **Conduct of Business Rule Book** additionally requires operators to comply with some extra criteria pertaining to Virtual Assets. These additional criteria clarify that any Authorized Person conducting regulated activities in relation to Virtual Assets must comply with the:[11]
a) Conduct of Business Rulebook (COBS);
b) General Rulebook (GEN);
c) Anti-Money Laundering and Sanctions Rules and Guidance (AML);
d) Islamic Finance Rules (IFR); and
e) Rules of Market Conduct (RMC), made by the Regulator in accordance with section 96 of the Financial Services and Markets Regulations 2015.

In addition to these expectations, the Conduct of Business Rule Book 'retrofits' existing regulations in order that definitions capture dealings in Virtual Assets. For example,
a) 'Client Investments' in GEN shall be read as encompassing 'Virtual Asset' or 'Virtual Assets', as applicable; and
b) 'Financial Instruments' in RMC shall be read as references to 'Virtual Asset' or 'Virtual Assets', as applicable.

The Conduct of Business Rule Book also stipulates what are the categories of 'Accepted Virtual Assets' that are permissible in the ADGM jurisdiction.[12] The regulatory approach to determining whether a Virtual Asset is an **'Accepted Virtual Asset'** is a case-by-case basis where regulators will consider:[13]
a) maturity/market capitalisation threshold in respect of a Virtual Asset[14]; and
b) other factors that, in the opinion of the Regulator, are to be taken into account in determining whether or not a Virtual Asset meets the requirements to be considered

---

[10] Ibid, para. 5.1.
[11] Rule 17.1.4 of the Conduct of Business Rulebook (COB) must also comply with (a) Rule 3.4 (Suitability); (b) Rule 6.5 (Best Execution); (c) Rule 6.7 (Aggregation and Allocation); (d) Rule 6.10 (Confirmation Notes); (e) Rule 6.11 (Periodic Statements); and (f) Chapter 12 (Key Information and Client Agreement).
[12] Rule 17.2 COB.
[13] Rule 17.2.2 COB.
[14] Para. 24 of Guidance – Regulation of Virtual Asset Activities in ADGM (issued 24 February 2020). The criteria used are to determine maturity/market capitalisation are set out in the Guidance and include: the market capitalisation of the Virtual Asset (not determined in any prescribed way although considering certain recognised sources, as may be available from time to time), the sufficiency, depth and breadth of Client demand, the proportion of the Virtual Asset that is in free float, and the controls/processes to manage volatility of a particular Virtual Asset.

appropriate for the purpose of an Authorised Person conducting a Regulated Activity in relation to Virtual Assets.

16 **Capital requirements** for an Authorised Person to engage in a Regulated Activity in relation to Virtual Assets are to be equivalent to 6 months of operating expenses estimated according to International Financial Reporting Standards (IFRS).[15]

In regards to international tax reporting obligations, Authorised Person engaging in a Regulated Activity in relation to Virtual Assets are to comply with the Fair and Accurate Credit Reporting Act (FACTA) in accordance with the 2015 intergovernmental agreement between the United States and the UAE.[16] This specific reporting obligation is in addition to other reporting requirements set out in ADGM Common *Reporting Standard Regulations* 2017.

17 The Conduct of Business (COB) Rules in ADGM also require that specific technological services provided within the ADGM platform proscribe detailed procedures relating to such technologies.[17] For Virtual Asset Wallets,[18] for example, **procedures** should cover all aspects of the service such as creation, management and controls of the wallet, and additionally:
a) wallet setup/configuration/deployment/deletion/backup and recovery;
b) wallet access privilege management;
c) wallet user management;
d) wallet rules and limit determination, review and update; and
e) wallet audit and oversight.

18 For **private key services**,[19] the creation, management and controls procedures should specifically include:
a) private key generation;
b) private key exchange;
c) private key storage;
d) private key backup;
e) private key destruction; and
f) private key access management.

19 Technical systems should also provide the capability of determining the origin of an incoming Virtual Asset transaction, or the destination of an outgoing Virtual Asset Transaction.[20] Operators are also required to have in place **security plans**[21] that address:
a) the privacy of sensitive data;
b) architecture of networks and systems;
c) cloud based services;
d) physical facilities; and
e) documents, and document storage.

20 As with ordinary business operations, Virtual Asset activities are also subject to various market and operational risks. A detailed **risk management plan** that outlines the potential impact (high or low) of a risk transpiring, and any mitigation strategies are to be included in the plan.[22] A non-exhaustive list of considerations provided within the relevant regulations include:
a) operational risks;
b) technology risks, including 'hacking' related risks;

---

[15] Para. 3.2.2. of the Market Infrastructure Rule Book of Abu Dhabi (MIR) [VER05.240220].
[16] Rule 17.4.1(a) COB.
[17] Rule 17.5 COB.
[18] Rule 17.5(a) COB.
[19] Rule 17.5(b) COB.
[20] Rule 17.5(c) COB.
[21] Rule 17.5(d) COB.
[22] Rule 17.5(e) COB.

c) market risk for each Accepted Virtual Asset; and
d) risk of Financial Crime.

Given the novel nature of Virtual Asset transactions, the FSRA has made it obligatory for any Authorised Person conducting a Regulated Activity in relation to Virtual Assets to provide clients with a clear and non-misleading schedule of associate material risks involved an initial transaction.[23] A non-exhaustive **list of risks** provided within the relevant regulations include[24]:

a) Virtual Assets not being legal tender or backed by a government;
b) the value, or process for valuation, of Virtual Assets, including the risk of a Virtual Asset having no value;
c) the volatility and unpredictability of the price of Virtual Assets relative to Fiat Currencies;
d) that trading in Virtual Assets may be susceptible to irrational market forces;
e) that the nature of Virtual Assets may lead to an increased risk of Financial Crime;
f) that the nature of Virtual Assets may lead to an increased risk of cyber-attack;
g) there being limited or, in some cases, no mechanism for the recovery of lost or stolen Virtual Assets;
h) the risks of Virtual Assets being transacted via new technologies, (including distributed ledger technologies ('DLT')) with regard to, among other things, anonymity, irreversibility of transactions accidental transactions, transaction recording, and settlement;
i) that there is no assurance that a Person who accepts a Virtual Asset as payment today will continue to do so in the future;
j) that the nature of Virtual Assets means that technological difficulties experienced by the Authorised Person may prevent the access or use of a Client's Virtual Assets;
k) any links to Virtual Assets related activity outside ADGM, which may be unregulated or subject to limited regulation; and
l) any regulatory changes or actions by the Regulator or Non-ADGM Regulator that may adversely affect the use, transfer, exchange, and value of a Virtual Asset.

The rules applied to financial trading exchanges are also 'retrofitted' to apply to 'Multilateral Trading Facilities in relation to Virtual Assets.[25] Indeed the regulations embody the same approach with respect to custodial services as regulations that are to apply to ordinary financial intermediary custody services pertaining to Virtual Assets.[26]

It is important to note that the ADGM VAF operates only within the ADGM jurisdiction and against the backdrop of strong cryptocurrencies warnings by the Central Bank of the UAE and the UAE Securities and Commodities Authority (SCA) in 2017.[27]

II. Bahrain

The Kingdom of Bahrain is another jurisdiction in the MENA region that has sought to embrace the opportunities presented by crypto assets. The **Central Bank of Bahrain**

---

[23] Rule 17.6.1 COB.
[24] Rule 17.6.2 COB.
[25] Rule 17.7 COB; for example, Rule 17.7.5 COB provides that terms in the Market Infrastructure Rulebook (MIR) such as 'Recognised Body' and 'Financial Instrument' are to be read as 'Authorised Person' and 'Virtual Asset' respectively.
[26] Rule 17.8 COB.
[27] Diaa, 'UAE Central Bank warns against cryptocurrencies-again' (February 2018), available at: https://beck-link.de/v5cez (accessed 28.10.2020).

(CBB) is the main financial regulator and in 2019 released its directives covering 'regulated crypto asset services'.

Policymakers published the draft directives in December 2018 with a one-month feedback window before finalization and release in February 2019. The regulations were introduced under volume 6 (Capital Markets) of the CBB Rulebook. The title given to this collection of new rules the **'Crypto asset Module (CRA)'**. These regulatory efforts form part of a broader initiative to promote the fintech sector in the island kingdom. The establishment of Bahrain FinTech Bay (powered by FinTech Consortium) underscores this policy focus. Applications for the CBB sandbox foreshadowed the need for a crypto asset regulatory framework given that 40 % of applicants were in the crypto asset space.

24　Unlike ADGM that has in its latest iteration of rules adopted the language of 'Virtual Assets', CBB regulations continue to use the term 'crypto assets'. Regulators in Bahrain define 'crypto assets' as virtual, digital assets or tokens operating on a blockchain platform protected by cryptography.[28]

The **CRA** is more detailed and extensive than the ADGM regulations and covers in depth the broad spectrum of activities and risks relating to crypto asset activities. These include[29]:

1. CBB licensing (CRA-1), licensing conditions (CRA-2);
2. Minimum capital requirements (CRA-3);
3. Client safeguards (CRA-4);
4. Technology standards (in particular cyber security) (CRA-5);
5. Risk management (CRA-6);
6. AML obligations (CRA-7);
7. Reporting obligations, notification and approval obligations (CRA-10);
8. Conduct of business obligations (CRA-12);
9. Market abuse and manipulation rules (CRA-13); and
10. Enforcement powers under the CBB Law for inspection and access (CRA-11 and CRA-14).

25　In total, **CRA** is 189 pages in length. Although many of the provisions relating to risk management, reporting, conduct of business etc., are not unique and do not need exposition, there are several important elements that should be highlighted.

The CRA applies to both the undertaking of activities, as well as the marketing of regulated crypto asset services within Bahrain.[30] This would include the solicitation of clients in Bahrain[31] and or even operating or incorporating any company in Bahrain with the words (or equivalent in any language) 'crypto', 'digital', 'currency' or 'asset' in combination with 'exchange', 'manager', 'advisor', 'investment' or 'portfolio'.[32] All such activities require a valid license.

26　Regulators have carved out certain activities that are specifically **not 'regulated crypto asset activities'**. These include[33]:

1. The creation or administration of crypto assets;
2. The development, dissemination or use of software for the purpose of creating or mining a crypto asset; or
3. A loyalty program.

---

[28] Goud,' Central Bank of Bahrain Issues Regulations governing Crypto-Asset Services' (April 2019), available at: https://beck-link.de/cn3sm (accessed 28.10.2020).
[29] Para. B.1.2 CRA.
[30] Para. 1.1.1 CRA.
[31] Para. 1.1.5(c) CRA.
[32] Para. 1.1.3 CRA.
[33] Para. 1.1.7 CRA.

In contrast to these exemptions, **'regulated crypto asset services'** are defined to include:[34]

1. Reception and transmission of orders relating to accepted crypto assets;
2. Execution of buy/sell orders on behalf of clients in relation to accepted crypto assets;
3. Dealing on one's own account in relation to accepted crypto assets;
4. Managing a portfolio of accepted crypto assets on behalf of a client;
5. Custodianship of accepted crypto assets[35];
6. Investment advice in relation to accepted crypto assets;
7. Operating a crypto asset exchange dealing in the conversion of accepted crypto assets into fiat currency or into other accepted crypto assets.

Based upon these 'regulated crypto asset services', the CRA provides four **licensing categories** applying to persons seeking to engage in such activities:[36]

Category	Nature of Activity	License Obligation	Minimum Capital[37]
Category 1 (CRA-1.1.9 – CRA 1.1.10)	Receiving and communication orders Providing investment advice for accepted crypto assets	Must not hold client assets or money May not receive fees or commissions from non-clients Must not operate crypto asset exchange	BHD 25, 000 (apx. USD 66,500)
Category 2 (CRA-1.1.11 – CRA 1.1.12)	Trading in accepted crypto assets *only* as an agent Crypto asset investment advice and/or portfolio management Crypto asset custody	May hold client assets or money but may not deal in crypto assets transactions as a principal Must not operate crypto asset exchange	BHD 100, 000 (apx. USD 266,000)
Category 3 (CRA-1.1.13 – CRA 1.1.14)	Trading in accepted crypto assets *both* as principal or agent Crypto asset investment advice and/or portfolio management Crypto asset custody	May hold client assets or money and may also deal in crypto assets themselves transactions as a principal Must not operate crypto asset exchange	BHD 200, 000 (apx. USD 532,000)

---

[34] Para. 1.1.6 CRA.
[35] Para 8.1 CRA.
[36] Licensees may combine two or more regulated crypto-asset services given that all services fall within the list of permitted activities and do not create a conflict of interest, para. 1.1.23 CRA.
[37] Para. 3.1.2 CRA.

Part C. Country Reports

Category	Nature of Activity	License Obligation	Minimum Capital[38]
Category 4	Operate a licenses crypto asset exchange	May hold client assets or money	BHD 300, 000 (apx. USD 798,000)
(CRA-1.1.15 – CRA 1.1.17) (additional requirements in CRA 4.12)	Crypto asset custody	Must execute client orders against proprietary capital or engage in matched principal trading.	

Any entity seeking to obtain any one of the **crypto asset licenses** noted above must be either a Bahraini Joint Stock Company, or a branch resident in Bahrain of a company duly incorporated in its home jurisdiction.[39] If they are a branch office, the licensee is required to maintain a registered office on Bahrain with a local management present.[40]

1. Safeguards and Protections

29 In order to **safeguard** against money laundering or other risks that may undermine customer safety, the CRA imposes several **requirements** on clients of crypto asset services. These include[41]:
1. All clients must be registered with the licensee;
2. Clients may not be agents acting on behalf of other organizations
3. Charites, sporting, social, professional religious or cooperative societies may not register as clients;
4. All transactions with clients are to be by digital transfer and not in cash; and
5. All clients must have a designated account with a local licensed Bahraini bank, or an acceptable licenses overseas retail bank.

30 Furthermore, any person seeking to undertake a 'controlled function'[42], within the operations of a licensee must first obtain approval from the CBB and be designated an **'Approved Person'**.[43] The CBB must also be satisfied that any 'substantial shareholders'[44] do not pose any significant risk to the licensee or their operations.[45]

31 In addition to standard disclosures required of financial intermediaries, crypto asset licensees have further obligation to inform clients of all **material risks** associated with crypto asset transactions. This **disclosure** must be in both Arabic and English and communicated in a clear, conspicuous and legible manner.[46] Specifically, licensees must disclose the following information to potential customers:
a) a crypto asset is not a legal tender and is not backed by the government;
b) legislative and regulatory changes or actions at national level or international level may adversely affect the use, transfer, exchange, and value of crypto assets;
c) transactions in crypto assets may be irreversible, and, accordingly, losses due to fraudulent or accidental transactions may not be recoverable;

---

[38] Para. 3.1.2 CRA.
[39] Para. 2.1.1 CRA.
[40] Para. 2.2.1 CRA.
[41] Para. 7.1 CRA.
[42] Defined as: Director, CEO or GM, Head of function, Chief Information Security Officer, Compliance Officer, Money Laundering Reporting Officer (MLRO), para. 1.1.2 CRA.
[43] Para. 1.7.1 CRA.
[44] Defined as shareholders that own or controls no less than 5 % of the votes in the licensee, para. 2.3.2 CRA.
[45] Para. 2.3.1 CRA.
[46] Para. 4.5.8 CRA.

§ 28. Middle East and North Africa (MENA)

d) some crypto asset transactions may be deemed to be made when recorded on a public ledger, which is not necessarily the date or time that the client initiates the transaction;
e) the value of crypto assets may be derived from the continued willingness of market participants to exchange fiat currency for crypto asset, which may result in the potential for permanent and total loss of value of a particular crypto asset should the market for that crypto asset disappear;
f) the volatility and unpredictability of the price of crypto assets relative to fiat currency may result in significant loss over a short period of time;
g) the nature of crypto assets may lead to an increased risk of fraud or cyber-attacks;
h) the nature of crypto assets means that any technological difficulties experienced by the licensee may prevent the access or use of a client's crypto assets; and
i) any investor protection mechanism.

Additionally, licensees must also inform clients of the **specific risks of the products or services** provided.[47] Moreover, licensees must disclose and clarify to their potential and current clients: 32

a) the client's liability for unauthorized crypto asset transactions;
b) the client's right to stop payment of a preauthorized crypto asset transfer and the procedure to initiate such a stop-payment order;
c) under what circumstances the licensee will disclose information concerning the client's account to third parties;
d) the client's right to receive periodic account statements and valuations from the licensee;
e) the client's right to receive a confirmation note or other evidence of a transaction;
f) the client's right to prior notice of a change in the licensee's Rules or policies; and
g) such other disclosures as are customarily given in connection with the opening of client accounts.

The CRA is well developed and quite sophisticated in terms of its approach to the regulation of technology – including things such as procedures for system upgrades and the opening of new APIs.[48] Licensees must also have specific controls including with respect to crypto asset wallets, private keys, origin and destination of transactions, cybersecurity and other **risk management exposures**.[49] Cybersecurity is also designated a central part of corporate governance expectations imposed upon licensees.[50] This includes cybersecurity issues pertaining to outsourcing[51] and the reporting and notification of any breaches.[52] The CBB has also adopted comprehensive rules relating to custodianship allowing both third party and self-custodianship so long as licensees inform clients of all related material risk.[53] 33

III. Egypt

The most recent jurisdiction to implement a supporting regulatory framework for financial technology is Egypt. In late September 2020, the President of Egypt ratified 34

---

[47] Para. 4.5.9 CRA.
[48] Para 5.2 CRA. This includes audit trails for source code changes.
[49] Para. 5.1.2 CRA. Exemptions are available where the CBB is satisfied that the nature, scale and complexity of a business does not require such technology governance or cyber security measures: Para. 5.1.3 of the CRA.
[50] Paras. 5.8 and 6 CRA (Risk Management). Para. 9 CRA corporate governance Code must be met.
[51] Paras. 6.6.20 – 6.6.40 CRA.
[52] Para. 10 CRA.
[53] Para. 8 CRA.

a new banking law that has been in the works for several years.⁵⁴ Although the law mainly deals with reforming the banking system on a structural level, it does contain in chapter 4 provisions for regulating payment services and new digital financial innovations. This includes the establishment of a **fintech and regtech sandbox**.⁵⁵

In 2017, the Central Bank of Egypt (CBE) issued an extremely strong warning highlighting the unregulated nature of **cryptocurrencies** such as bitcoin and their unpredictability and volatility. It instructed Egyptians to use 'extreme' caution when engaging in any related trading activities.⁵⁶ The new 2020 banking law however does soften this position by allowing for the issuing, trading and dealing in cryptocurrencies but only under a license issued by the Central Bank board.⁵⁷ As of early 2021, the CBE has not released any licensing procedure or conditions.

C. Cautious and Non-Adopters

35   Other than Abu Dhabi, Bahrain and the recent legal reforms in Egypt, no other jurisdiction in MENA has adopted regulations supportive of crypto asset activities. The scope of treatment afforded to crypto assets in the region ranges from **warnings**, **bans** in response to the surge in **Bitcoin** prices of recent years, to policy guidance, and attempts to retrofit existing regulations, particularly in relation to taxation.

36   In the absence of policy guidance or regulations otherwise, the bans issued by authorities on bitcoin, and cryptocurrencies more broadly, are herein understood as **jurisdictional limitations** on all crypto assets. Those countries discussed below that have banned or warned against cryptocurrencies have generally not distinguished between types or classes of digital or Virtual Assets. It is important that observers not see central bank warnings as a permanent ban on such assets. In jurisdictions such as Egypt and Abu Dhabi, where crypto asset regulations are now emerging, they also started their path under the shadow of cautious central bank warnings.⁵⁸

37   Largest and most influential amongst the Gulf States, Saudi Arabia, through its Ministry of Finance officially warned its citizens and residents in 2019 against engaging in any dealings involving **'virtual currencies'**.⁵⁹ Currently, there are no regulations directly targeting crypto assets in Saudi Arabia. The **Saudi Arabian Monetary Authority (SAMA)**, however, does enjoy a mandate to assess the exposure of financial institutions under its supervision in a manner that includes crypto assets and supervise their operations relating thereto.⁶⁰

38   The smaller Gulf Sultanate of Oman has also recently issued warnings relating to cryptocurrencies through the **Central Bank of Oman (CBO)**:⁶¹

---

⁵⁴ Law of Egypt No. 194/2020 on The Egyptian Central Bank and Banking System (issued on September 2020).

⁵⁵ Art. 201, Law 194/2020.

⁵⁶ Central Bank of Egypt, 'A Warning Statement of the Central Bank of Egypt', available at: https://beck-link.de/n6nxa (accessed 29.09.2020).

⁵⁷ Art. 206, Law 194 of 2020.

⁵⁸ Debusmann Jr., 'UAE Central Bank warns against Bitcoin', Arabian Business (October 2017), available at: https://beck-link.de/ez42r (accessed 29.09.2020).

⁵⁹ Saudi Gazette, 'Ministry of Finance warns against dealings in virtual currencies', (August 2019), available at: https://beck-link.de/8b4n5 (accessed 29.09.2020).

⁶⁰ Financial Stability Board (FSB), 'Crypto-assets regulators directory' (April 2019), available at: https://beck-link.de/p42hy (accessed 29.09.2020).

⁶¹ Arabian Stories, 'Central Bank of Oman warns public against dealing with cryptocurrencies' (July 2020), available at: https://beck-link.de/as686 (accessed 29.09.2020).

...the Central Bank of Oman has not given any license/authorisation to any entity for dealing in cryptocurrencies or similar products. Hence, using, holding and trading of cryptocurrencies and similar products are neither guaranteed by the Central Bank of Oman nor protected by the Banking Law 114/2000 as a Central Bank money... Members of the public are cautioned that users, holders and traders of cryptocurrencies and similar products may be exposed to potential financial, operational, legal, and security related risks, in addition to the lack of customer protection. Anyone dealing in such cryptocurrencies and similar products will be doing so at their own risk and responsibility.

The State of Qatar has taken a similar approach to Oman with a 2018 central bank circular similarly warning against and limiting the ability of citizens and residents to engage in cryptocurrency trading and other related activities.[62] The **Qatar Financial Centre Regulatory Authority (QFCRA)**, the main financial regulator in the Qatar Financial Centre, reiterated this position by announcing a ban on any activities relating to 'Virtual Assets' in late 2019.[63] In the case of Qatar, however, several reports pertaining the QFCRA banning announcement note that the ban does not include security tokens.[64] 39

Kuwaiti authorities, through the central bank, have also banned bitcoin and other cryptocurrencies.[65]

Both the Central Bank of Iraq[66] and Iranian authorities[67] have also issued bans on bitcoin and cryptocurrency-related activities. This is despite the fact that many have noted the utility of cryptocurrencies specifically for Iran in their efforts to combat crippling US-imposed sanctions. 40

Likewise, in North Africa, no single jurisdiction (apart from Egypt) has allowed the use of or trading in cryptocurrencies. Although in 2019 rumours in Tunisia abounded of it launching a world-first **Central Bank Digital Currency (CBDC)**, Tunisian authorities have not implemented any specific crypto asset regulations nor are there any plans for a CDBC. Similarly, Algeria[68] has also banned cryptocurrency activities – as has Morocco[69].

Countries in the Levant region (Lebanon, Palestine, and Jordan) generally adhere to the same regulatory posture – that being warnings with no regulatory framework.[70] Indeed, the Central Bank of Jordan, has been warning of the risks associated with cryptocurrencies since 2014[71] and has continued to do so since. The fledgling State of Palestine has announced in recent years plans to launch its own virtual currency – the 41

---

[62] Supervision and Control of Financial Institutions Division, 'Circular No. 6/2018 from 7 February 2018' (June 2018), available at: https://beck-link.de/es25h (accessed 29.09.2020).
[63] Hamilton, 'Qatar Bans All Cryptocurrency in QFC', (June 2020), available at: https://beck-link.de/336e3 (accessed 29.09.2020).
[64] Goncalves, 'Qatar bocks crypto asset services', (January 2020), available at: https://beck-link.de/evbe4 (accessed on 29.09.2020).
[65] Sundarajan, 'Kuwait's Ministry of Finance Says It Does Not Recognize Bitcoin', Coindesk (December 2017), available at: https://beck-link.de/c3fzf (accessed on 29.09.2020).
[66] Central Bank of Iraq, (December 2017), available at: https://cbi.iq/news/view/512 (accessed on 29.09.2002).
[67] Financial Tribune, 'Iranian Financial Institutions Barred from Using Crypto-Currencies', (April 2018), available at: https://beck-link.de/7xcv8 (accessed on 29.09.2020).
[68] Art. 117 of the Law No. 17-2011, available at: https://beck-link.de/7mdt5 (French).
[69] Jenkinson, 'Morocco Outlaws Cryptocurrencies' (November 2017), available at: https://beck-link.de/8tsha (accessed on 29.09.2020).
[70] Hajdarbegovich, 'Lebanon's Central Bank Issues Bitcoin Warning', (January 2014), available at: https://beck-link.de/6cm3n (accessed on 29.09.2020).
[71] Southurst, 'Central Bank of Jordan Blocks Financial Companies from Bitcoin', (February 2014), available at: https://beck-link.de/mz3c4 (accessed on 29.09.2020).

Palestinian Pound – in order to **address limitations** on its monetary autonomy.[72] To date no such plans have progressed and no clear regulations exist.

Lebanon has been experiencing a financial and banking crisis for many years. Both internal and external commentators[73] have noted the potential benefits from cryptocurrencies by decoupling money from the state and sidestepping the weak and unstable Lebanese banking system. No official steps to legalize or regulate such activities, **cryptocurrencies** or crypto assets have materialized.

Israel is further down the track of crypto asset regulation than most of its neighbours – although it has yet to adopt a specific crypto asset regulatory regime.

42 Despite the issuing of the customary warning by the Bank of Israel (the central bank) in 2014 pertaining to the dangers of virtual currencies[74], regulations have still slowly evolved. Presently, Israeli authorities have designated **virtual currencies** as 'financial assets'.[75] Consequently, any dealings involving virtual currencies require a financial services license from the national financial regulator.[76] Tax authorities in Israel have also sought to apply capital gains tax standards to cryptocurrency transactions by treating them the same as other commodities.[77] Despite the 'start-up nation' moniker often applied to Israel, its regulatory regime for crypto assets lags somewhat behind the more sophisticated frameworks seen in other MENA jurisdiction – notably Abu Dhabi and Bahrain. In September 2020, all three states signed a normalization agreement (the so-called 'Abraham Accords') that opens up trade and markets between them – this will likely extend to regulatory co-operation in the crypto asset space. The direction of investment will likely be Israeli firms setting-up in the clearer and more certain crypto asset-friendly regulatory jurisdictions of ADGM or Bahrain.

Israeli banks have been cautious in their approach to virtual currency dealings. Two important cases are relevant in this regard. In 2015, *Bank Leumi LeIsrael Ltd* issued a ban and blocked the activities of an Israeli crypto-currency exchange – *Bits of Gold Ltd*. These actions followed the 2014 Bank of Israel circular noted above.[78] The company successfully obtained a temporary injunction from the District Court of Tel Aviv (in 2017)[79] and subsequently the Israeli Supreme Court (in 2018), preventing the bank from blocking their activities until a competent court decided the legality of the actions taken. In 2019, the Israeli Supreme Court decided in favor of *Bits of Gold* and ordered the bank to restore all account functionality to the company.[80]

---

[72] Cryptus, 'Palestinian Authority: Cryptocurrency will Bring Economic Freedom', Bitcoinist (July 2019), available at: https://beck-link.de/kv4zk (accessed on 29.09.2020).

[73] Azhari, 'Distrust in Lebanese Banks Spurs Bitcoin Boom', (February 2020), available at: https://beck-link.de/kyf5m (accessed on 29.09.2020).

[74] Israel Tax Authority, 'Informing the public about possible risks inherent in distributed virtual currencies (such as Bitcoin)', available at: https://beck-link.de/ke3ap (accessed 01.06.2021) (in Hebrew).

[75] Art. 11 subpara. 7 of the Law No. 5776/2016 on the Supervision on Financial Services (Regulated Financial Services).

[76] Art. 12 subpara. 7 of the Law No. 5776/2016 on the Supervision on Financial Services (Regulated Financial Services).

[77] Israel Tax Authority, 'Circular No. 05/2018' (January 2018), §§ 3.1–3.3, available at https://beck-link.de/5x43v (accessed on 01.06.2021) (in Hebrew); Income Tax Ordinance (New Version), 1961, 1 Laws of the State of Israel [LSI] (New Version) 1967 & Value Added Tax Law, 5736-1975, 30 LSI 46 (1975/76), both as amended.

[78] In fact, the circular was a joint statement by the Bank of Israel, the Capital Market, Insurance and Savings Department, the Israel Tax Authority (ITA), the Israel Securities Authority (ISA), and the Israel Money Laundering and Terror Financing Prohibition Authority.

[79] Decision CA 6389/17 of the Supreme Court of Israel of 25. February 2018 – *Bits of Gold Ltd. v. Bank Leumi LeIsrael Ltd* (in Hebrew).

[80] Haan, 'Israili Supreme Court Orders Bank Leumi to Restore Banking to Bits of Gold Cryptocurrency Exchange' (June 2019), available at: https://beck-link.de/tr2bt (accessed on 29.09.2020).

§ 28. Middle East and North Africa (MENA)

As noted by Daniels and Zivan[81], Israeli Courts have been reluctant to give banks free reign to impose a blanket ban and block all activities by companies that have some connection with crypto-currencies.[82] Moreover, the court has held that banks should allow companies with bank accounts subject to bank-imposed risk-based restriction an opportunity to provide evidence elaborating on their specific risk profiles.[83]

As explained by Daniels and Zivan, the official Israeli position was recently (March 2020) clarified through an *amicus brief* filed by the Attorney General of Israel in the case of *Roey Arev and Yifat Arev v. Bank Mercantile Discount (51757-08/18A, Court: Tel Aviv – Java District Court)*. The brief was prepared in conjunction with all major Israeli regulators, and it represents the official government position. The principles outlined in the brief identify when and how a bank may deal with the bank accounts of crypto asset market participants. The criteria set out in the brief as to what considerations banks should examine as part of their decision-making process pertaining to blocking or banning certain accounts are:

1. Limited risk transactions – similar to the common practice in 'regular' fiat accounts, the smaller the amount of the transactions the less the bank views those transactions as high risk. Accordingly, should the transactions in the account in question be limited in amount and scope, the bank should not automatically designate the account as high risk.
2. Virtual Assets derived directly from mining activities – if the Virtual Assets were derived directly from mining activities (and the account holder can provide suitable documentation attesting thereto) then the risk level can be lessened as the bank has a clear idea whence the virtual asset came from.
3. Virtual Assets transferred to/from a single virtual wallet – in the event that the account holder uses a single **virtual wallet** for the transfer of Virtual Assets, it can be considered by the bank as indicative of the account as having limited risk. It should be clarified that this criterion is subject to the aforementioned transactions taken by the virtual wallet have taken place in jurisdictions considered low risk for money laundering and on reputable exchanges.
4. approval of the tax authorities that capital gains tax was paid – while the payment of taxes in and of itself is not indicative of risk levels, the payment of taxes can be combined with one of the above factors in the bank's determination whether or not to classify the actions of an account as high risk.

D. Shar'ia Compliance

Beyond risk management and systemic financial stability, the crypto asset space in the MENA region also encompasses, for many players, a consideration of the morality and religious permissibility of such activities. In recent years, the **Islamic Finance** sector has received a proverbial 'shot in the arm' from the emergence of fintech. Indeed, literature on **Islamic fintech** has flourished of late.[84]

---

[81] Daniels and Zivan, 'Developments in Israeli Banking and Crypto', (March 2020), available at: https://beck-link.de/8vy8r (accessed on 27.01.2021).

[82] Decision of the District Court of Tel-Aviv (Israel) of 17 March 2019 – *Israminers Ltd. v. United Bank Ltd (in Hebrew)*.

[83] *Toyga OnLine Ltd. et. al. v. Bank Mizrahi Tefahot* 262-04-17, Tel Aviv – Java District Court.

[84] Nafis, Gupta and Zameni, Fintech and Islamic Finance: Digitalization, Development and Disruption (2019); Arslanian and Fisher, The Future of Finance: The Impact of Fintech, AI, and Crypto on Financial Services (2019); Mohamed and Ali, Blockchain, Fintech and Islamic Finance: Building the Future in the New Islamic Digital Economy (2019); Naifar, Impact of Financial Technology (FinTech) on Islamic Finance and Financial Stability (2019); Oseni and Nazim Ali, Fintech in Islamic Finance (2019).

Part C. Country Reports

The debate about the permissibility of crypto assets has been an ongoing debate in the world of Islamic finance.[85] The main concerns arising in terms of Islamic finance and crypto assets arise from the perceived speculative nature of such instruments and their lack of connection with the real economy. One of the main philosophies underpinning Islamic finance is that of the economy being a means to an end and not an end in itself. Experts and Islamic scholars deem only those activities that satisfy religious requirements expected of Islamic commercial transactions as 'sharia-compliant'.

45 In 2017, a well-respected Egyptian Islamic Scholar opined that bitcoin was non-sharia compliant due to its speculative nature and similarity to gambling.[86] Rather than being an insurmountable obstacle to crypto asset regulation, the principles of Islamic finance have created a framework within which a sharia-compliant crypto asset market can emerge. The need for instruments to be tied to real world assets can be seen, for example, in the innovate **Onegram** project which seeks to link each crypto-token created to one gram of gold held and convertible by the company.[87] Another example is crypto-brokerage firm Rain[88] that notes on its official website that the Shar'ia Review Bureau, a body that the Central Bank of Bahrain licenses to certify Islamic finance providers, has officially certified its operations.[89]

Most MENA states observe a general market distinction between conventional banking and finance on one hand, and *shar'ia* compliant Islamic financial products on the other. This means that irrespective of the *shar'ia* compliance status of crypto assets, there will still be a market for such innovations where regulators permit.

E. Conclusion

46 The regulation of crypto assets in the MENA region is mixed and multi-dimensional. There are economic, religious and even geo-political factors that animate this region. Even in the context of the bourgeoning crypto asset sector, regional political dynamics are both influencing and being influenced by the growth and promise of innovation in crypto asset business models. It is indeed telling that two of the first movers in the fintech and crypto asset scene in the Middle East (Bahrain and UAE) have also recently normalized relations with the fintech elephant in the room – Israel.

47 The religious dimension adds an extra layer of consideration for the crypto asset sector in parts of the MENA region. This has not prevented the growth in regulatory frameworks but rather purred innovation in business models that are *shar'ia* compliant.

As crypto assets and crypto asset-related activities become more mainstream, many of the animating factors flowing through MENA jurisdictions and influencing policy calculations will eventually have to yield to the necessity of informed and balanced crypto assets regulations.

---

[85] Yakubowski, 'Could Crypto be Compliant with Shariah Law? Expert Answer', (September 2019), available at: https://beck-link.de/ss7bp (accessed on 20.09.2020); Aljazeera , 'Islam and Cryptocurrency, halal or not halal?'(April 2018), available at: https://beck-link.de/mn4pe (accessed on 20.09.2020).

[86] Religious Decree No. 4205, 'The Status of Transactions in Bitcoins and other Cryptocurrencies under Islamic Law', (December 2017), available at: https://beck-link.de/adz26 (in Arabic), (accessed on 29.09.2020).

[87] *Onegram*, available at: https://onegram.org/ (accessed on 29.09.2020).

[88] RAIN, 'Information on Rain's Shari'a compliance certification, available at: https://beck-link.de/sa7d6 (accessed on 29.09.2020).

[89] *Shariyah Review Bureau*, available at: https://shariyah.com/ (accessed on 29.09.2020).

Index

A

Abu Dhabi
– digital securities **28** 8
– FACTA **28** 16
– fiat currency **28** 10
– fiat tokens **28** 12
– ICO **28** 8
abusive market practices
– New Zealand **25** 9
acceptance
– global **2** 47
accounting
– currency tokens **14** 5, et seqq
– further aspects **14** 39, et seqq
– hybrid tokens **14** 38
– initial measurement **14** 8, et seqq, 21, et seqq, 33, et seqq
– investment tokens **14** 14, et seqq
– measurement **14** 7, et seqq, 21, et seqq, 32, et seqq
– recognition **14** 5, et seqq, 14, et seqq, 26, et seqq
– subsequent measurement **14** 12, et seq, 25, 37
– utility tokens **14** 26, et seqq
acquiring of payment transactions **9** 90, et seqq
additional contractual obligatione **5** 48, et seqq
AIFM **15** 39, et seqq
airdrop **1** 84
allocation
– efficient **2** 80
– inefficient **2** 83
altcoin **1** 68
anonymity **6** 25
anti-money laundering **10** 1, et seqq
– administrative sanctions **10** 159, et seqq
– art market participants **10** 62, et seq
– Australia **24** 9
– banks **10** 66
– beneficial owner **10** 154, et seqq
– beneficial ownership **10** 116, et seqq
– book money **10** 8
– cash **10** 8
– competent authority **10** 30, et seq
– compliance officer **10** 74
– credit institutions **10** 66
– criminal offence **10** 165, et seqq
– criminal sanctions **10** 164
– crypto-to-crypto exchange **10** 45, et seqq
– custodian wallet provider **10** 50
– customer due diligence **10** 81, et seqq
– directives **10** 9
– e-money **10** 26, 64, et seq
– e-money agent **10** 65
– EU Regulation **10** 171
– EU regulatory framework **10** 9, et seqq
– FATF guidance **10** 168, et seqq
– fiat money **10** 8
– fiat-to-crypto exchange **10** 43, et seq
– financial intelligence unit (FIU) **10** 36, et seqq
– fines **10** 163
– group-wide policies **10** 69
– harmonisation **10** 11
– intermediaries **10** 42, et seqq
– internal controls **10** 73, et seqq
– issuers **10** 54, et seqq
– legislative proposal **10** 170, et seq
– Liechtenstein **20** 28, et seqq
– miners **10** 60
– money laundering **10** 165, et seqq
– money laundering reporting officer **10** 74
– obligations **10** 67, et seqq
– obliged entities **10** 42, et seqq
– persons trading in goods **10** 34, et seq, 61
– politically exposed persons (PEP) **10** 122
– providers of gambling services **10** 66
– public key **10** 158
– public register **10** 158
– registration / licensing **10** 39, et seqq
– risk assessment **10** 71, et seqq
– risk factors **10** 123, et seqq
– risk management **10** 70, et seqq
– risk-based approach **10** 68
– sanctions **10** 159, et seqq
– securities **10** 25
– superervision **10** 30, et seq, 172
– suspicious transactions **10** 103, et seq
– Switzerland **19** 24, et seqq
– territorial scope **10** 32, et seqq
– tokens **10** 12, et seqq
– training **10** 75
– transaction **10** 27, et seq
– transparency register **10** 154, et seqq
– tumblers **10** 53
– types of tokens **10** 23
– virtual asset service providers **10** 169
– virtual currency **10** 13, et seqq
– wallet provider **10** 49, et seqq
anti-money laundering directive **10** 9
art market participants **10** 62
– anti-money laundering **10** 62, et seq
– customer due diligence **10** 98, et seqq
– risk assessment **10** 79, et seq

Index

ASIC Innovation Hub
- Australia **24** 23, et seq

asset classes
- conventional **2** 6, et seqq

Australia
- abusive conduct **24** 19
- Australian Securities Exchange **24** 22
- constitution **24** 2, et seq
- consumer usage **24** 6
- digital currencies **24** 10
- fintech regulator **24** 7
- legal system **24** 4
- regulatory guides **24** 8
- regulatory sandbox **24** 25, et seq
- securities regulation **24** 5
- tax treatment **24** 11, et seq

authorisation
- initial capital endowment **8** 39
- management body **8** 40, et seqq

B

Bahrain
- blockchain **28** 24
- regulatory sandbox **28** 23
- risks **28** 29

banks *see credit insutitions*

behaviour
- irrational ~ **2** 15, et seq

beneficial ownership **10** 116, et seqq
- transparency register **10** 154, et seqq

Bitcoin
- China **27** 6
- core **2** 27
- dirty **2** 66

Bitcoin address **1** 17
Bitcoin blockchain **1** 3, 13, 14, 17, 31, 35, 38
Bitcoin Core **1** 2
blacklist **1** 104
block header **1** 15
block reward **1** 35, **2** 22, et seqq

blockchain
- categorization **1** 10, et seqq
- central ~ **6** 6
- chameleon hash function **6** 101
- client **1** 2
- data protection **6** 1, et seqq
- data protection compliance **6** 93, et seqq
- decentralized ~ **6** 7, **10** 7
- disadvantages **1** 67
- fork **1** 30
- incentive scheme **1** 33, et seqq
- initiation **1** 79
- participants **1** 7, et seqq
- peer-to-peer basis **1** 1
- permissioned ~ **1** 12
- permissionless ~ **1** 12
- private ~ **1** 10, et seq
- protocol software **1** 2

- pruning **6** 100
- pseudonymity **1** 102, et seq
- public **1** 10, et seq
- redactable ~ **6** 101
- source code **1** 2
- structure **1** 14, et seqq
- transaction **6** 14, et seqq

blockchain strategy
- Germany **17** 1

book money
- anti-money laundering **10** 8

broker **5** 24, et seqq

bubble
- archetype **2** 12, et seqq
- financial **2** 12, et seqq
- speculative **2** 12, et seqq
- speculative motives **2** 16

burning **1** 6, 73, 84

business relationship
- customer due dilligence **10** 90, et seqq, 120, et seq
- fiat-to-crypto exchange **10** 90, et seqq
- transction monitoring **10** 121

C

carbon dioxide **2** 87
- emission **2** 84

cascade effect **2** 16

cash
- anti-money laundering **10** 8
- tokens **10** 29

central bank digital currency (CBDC) **9** 40, 53

central blockchain
- data processing operations **6** 11
- data subjects' rights **6** 81
- GDPR **6** 17, 27
- lawfulness of processing **6** 56, 59, 62
- material scope **6** 17, 20
- processing on behalf **6** 71
- role of the participants under the GDPR **6** 33, 38, et seqq
- term **6** 6
- territorial scope **6** 27

central counterparty **2** 70
central entity **6** 33, 38
chameleon hash function **6** 101

China
- Bitcoin **27** 6
- blockchain **27** 25
- blockchain startups **27** 3
- collaboration **27** 24
- commercial cryptography **27** 28
- cracking down of websites **27** 17
- cryptocurrency trading platforms **27** 14, 15
- crypto-related activities **27** 4
- DECP **27** 27
- digital forms **27** 22
- ICO **27** 13

620

Index

- ICO rules **27** 16
- legal tender **27** 8, 21
- local governance **27** 2
- mining **27** 5
- Notice to Prevent the Risk of Bitcoin **27** 9
- regulatory measures **27** 7, 30
- stable coins **27** 23
- state currency **27** 20
- The Digital Currency Electronic Payment (DECP) **27** 19
- The New Civil Code of the PRC **27** 12
- the State Council's Technology Blueprint **27** 1
- the State Crytography Administration (SCA) **27** 26
- total ban **27** 18
- virtual property **27** 10

classification of tokens
- Germany **17** 3, et seqq

client **1** 2
cloud mining **1** 57
coin **1** 68
coinbase **2** 25
compliance
- term **10** 4

compliance officer
- anti-money laundering **10** 74

confiscation
- criminal confiscation **12** 23, 34, et seq
- criminal sanction **12** 43
- cross-border confiscation **12** 7
- extended confiscation **12** 26, et seqq, 36, 48, 51, et seq
- in specie confiscation **12** 8, 13, 16, et seqq, 21, 25, 53, 64
- measure sui generis **12** 43
- non-conviction based confiscation **12** 32, 34, 36, 43, 48, 51, et seq, 61
- proceedings in rem **12** 33, 36
- third party confiscation **12** 25, 48
- value confiscation **12** 13, 15, 17, et seq, 39, 53, 64

consensus building **1** 28
consensus mechanism
- cryptographic **2** 69

consent **6** 58, et seqq
consumer **5** 9
consumer protection
- consumer **4** 8, et seqq
- consumer rights directive **4** 2
- information obligations **4** 40, et seq
- MiCAR **4** 4
- trader **4** 11, et seqq

content data **6** 15, et seq, 57, 66, et seqq
contest **2** 82
- Tullock **2** 82
contractual partner **5** 38
controller **6** 33, 35, 38, 41, 43, 46, et seqq

counterfeit protection **2** 55
creative destruction **2** 90
credit institutions
- anti-money laundering **10** 66
- customer due diligence **10** 136, et seqq

crowd funding
- Australia **24** 17

crypto asset custodian
- DLT MTF **15** 223, et seqq
- DLT Securities Settlement System **15** 227, et seqq
- financial instrument **15** 230, et seqq
- non-financial insrument **15** 235, et seqq

crypto asset regulation
- Australia **24** 27, et seq

crypto assets **9** 51
- Germany **17** 30, et seqq
- legal nature **12** 15, et seq
- tracing **12** 9

crypto exchange **2** 65, **9** 81
- dealing on own account **8** 29
- execution of orders **8** 30
- Germany **17** 12, et seq
- MiCAR **8** 24, et seq
- multilateral trading facility **8** 18, et seqq
- organised trading facility **8** 26, et seqq
- regulated activities **8** 15, et seqq

crypto lending **1** 89
crypto securities
- Germany **17** 34, et seqq

crypto units
- issuance **15** 97, et seqq

crypto-shares
- issuance **15** 93, et seqq

crypto-to-crypto exchange **1** 92
- anti-money laundering **10** 45, et seqq

currency **2** 44, et seqq
- private **2** 60
- requirements **2** 45
- tokens **2** 45

currency token **1** 70
- accounting **14** 5, et seqq
- initial measurement **14** 8, et seqq
- measurement **14** 7, et seqq
- recognition **14** 5, et seqq
- subsequent measurement **14** 12, et seq
- tax exemption **13** 11, et seqq

custodian wallet provider
- anti-money laundering **10** 50
- customer due diligence **10** 96, et seq, 132, et seqq
- risk assessment **10** 77

customer due diligence **10** 81, et seqq
- art market participants **10** 98, et seqq
- beneficial owner **10** 116, et seqq
- business relationship **10** 90, et seqq, 120, et seq
- calculation of thresholds **10** 84, et seqq

- credit institutions **10** 136, et seqq
- custodian wallet provider **10** 96, et seq, 132, et seqq
- customer's identity **10** 108, et seq
- electronic identification **10** 115
- e-money **10** 102, 139, et seqq
- enhanced measures **10** 127, et seqq
- fiat-to-crypto exchange **10** 132, et seqq
- high-risk third countries **10** 129
- identification **10** 110, et seqq
- issuers **10** 135
- know-your-customer (KYC) **10** 108
- measures **10** 105, et seqq
- monitoring of busines relationship **10** 121
- occasional transactions **10** 95
- outsourcing **10** 144
- persons trading in goods **10** 98, et seqq
- politically exposed persons (PEP) **10** 122, 128
- refrain from applying ~ **10** 141, et seqq
- risk factors **10** 123, et seqq
- simplified measures **10** 125, et seq
- suspicion of money laundering **10** 103, et seq
- thresholds **10** 82, et seqq
- transction monitoring **10** 134
- unable to comply with ~ **10** 145
- user registration **10** 93
- verification of customer's identity **10** 113, et seqq

cyberattack **5** 35, et seqq, 62, et seqq

D

darknet **2** 62, 65
- Silk Road **2** 65

data processing on behalf **6** 32, et seq
data processing operations **6** 10, et seqq
- decentralized blockchain **6** 12
- trading platform **6** 13

data protection
- anonymity **6** 25
- consent **6** 58, et seqq
- controller **6** 35
- data processing operations **6** 10, et seqq
- data protection supervision **6** 89
- data subjects' rights **6** 79, et seqq
- homomorphic encryption **6** 97
- lawfulness of processing **6** 55, et seqq
- one-stop shop principle **6** 90
- processing on behalf **6** 36
- pseudonymity **6** 25
- zero-knowledge proof **6** 97

data protection authority **6** 89
data subject **6** 18, 33, et seq, 40, 53, et seq, 79
data subjects' rights
- blockchain **6** 99, et seqq
- central blockchain **6** 81
- decentralized blockchain **6** 82

- enforcement **6** 99, et seqq
- right of access **6** 83
- right to be forgotten **6** 86, et seqq
- right to erasure **6** 86, et seqq
- right to rectification **6** 84, et seq

debt token **1** 72
decentralized blockchain
- data processing operations **6** 12
- data subjects' rights **6** 82
- GDPR **6** 17, 27
- lawfulness of processing **6** 57, 60, 63
- material scope **6** 17, 21, et seq
- processing on behalf **6** 72, et seq
- role of the participants under the GDPR **6** 33, 44, et seqq
- term **6** 7
- territorial scope **6** 27

default risk
- counterparty **2** 76

depositaries
- eligible entities **15** 170, et seqq

desktop wallet **1** 25
developments
- current **2** 5, et seqq
- future **2** 3
- macroeconomic and political **2** 34
- market **2** 6, et seqq

digital content
- token **4** 30, et seqq

digital inheritance **5** 53, et seq
digital memory **2** 63
Directive 2014/42/EU **12** 11, et seqq, 21, et seqq, 34, 38, 41, 43, 51, 54, 61

disclaimer
- international jurisdiction **3** 11

disclosure obligations
- exemptions **11** 50, et seqq
- purpose **11** 42, et seqq

distribution
- B2B2C **15** 134, et seqq
- D2C **15** 134, et seqq
- fund distribution **15** 134, et seqq
- fund distribution process **15** 66, et seqq
- funds DLT **15** 70, et seqq

DLT Market Infrastructure Regulation
- DLT MTF **15** 223, et seqq
- DLT Securities Settlement System **15** 227, et seqq

double spending **1** 30, **2** 55, 68
durability **2** 63

E

e-commerce
- applicable law **3** 35
- E-Commerce-Directive **5** 4

economics
- basic aspects **2** 1, et seqq
- macroeconomic factors **2** 16

Index

Egypt
- cryptocurrency **28** 34
- regulatory sandbox **28** 34

electronic money *see e-money*

e-money **9** 10
- anti-money laundering **10** 26, 64, et seq
- customer due dilligence **10** 102, 139, et seqq
- Institution **9** 98, et seqq

e-money agent
- anti-money laundering **10** 65

energy consumption **2** 78, 84

equity token **1** 72

ERC-20 **1** 83

Ethereum blockchain **1** 13, 58, 63, 83, **2** 42

European Passport
- applicable law **3** 43, et seq

exchange rate
- fixed ~ **2** 75

exchanges *see crypto exchanges*

externalities
- negative ~ **2** 80, 87

F

fiat money **2** 56, **12** 5, 10, 17, 39
- anti-money laundering **10** 8

fiat-to-crypto exchange **1** 91
- anti-money laundering **10** 43, et seq
- business relationship **10** 90, et seqq
- customer due dilligence **10** 132, et seqq
- occasional transactions **10** 95
- risk assessment **10** 77

financial intelligence unit (FIU) **10** 36, et seqq
- tasks **10** 37, et seq

financial service providers
- applicable regulation **8** 2, et seqq
- authorisation **8** 37, et seqq

financial stability **2** 91

fine **6** 92

follow-up contracts
- applicable law **3** 34
- international jurisdiction **3** 31, et seq

forger **6** 39, 48, 52
- role of the participants under the GDPR **6** 33

fork **1** 30

framework agreement **5** 69

France
- digital asset service providers **16** 20, et seqq
- digital assets **16** 3, et seqq
- information document **16** 11, et seqq
- investor protection **16** 7, et seqq
- madatory registration **16** 23, et seqq
- sanctions **16** 18, et seq
- voluntary license **16** 27, et seqq
- voluntary visa **16** 10

freezing **12** 3, 37, et seqq, 47, et seqq, 54, 56, 61, et seqq

full node **1** 8
- role of the participants under the GDPR **6** 33, 39, 47, 52
- tasks **1** 29

fund forms
- legal form neutrality **15** 80, et seq

fund governance
- investment quadrangle **15** 19, et seqq
- investment triangle **15** 13, et seqq

fund managers
- investment management **15** 45, 61

funds **9** 20, et seqq

fungibility **2** 54

G

GDPR **6** 1, et seqq
- lawfulness of processing **6** 55, et seqq
- material scope **6** 17, et seqq
- territorial scope **6** 27, et seqq
- third country transfers **6** 74, et seqq

genesis block **1** 80

Germany
- ATMs **17** 14, et seqq
- blockchain strategy **17** 1
- classification of tokens **17** 3, et seqq
- crypto assets **17** 30, et seqq
- crypto securities **17** 34, et seqq
- exchanges **17** 12, et seq
- prospectus liability **17** 26
- staking **17** 33
- STO **17** 7, et seqq
- subordinated loans **17** 9

GTC-Directive **5** 9, et seqq

H

halving **2** 28

hardware wallet **1** 25

hash **1** 15

homomorphic encryption **6** 97

Hong Kong
- cautious stance **26** 3
- dealing in securities **26** 19
- different standards **26** 22
- digital representation **26** 20
- free market **26** 6
- fund distributors **26** 21
- guidance **26** 25
- HKEX **26** 2
- ICO **26** 4
- intermediation **26** 11, 17
- international coordination **26** 31
- legal tender **26** 9
- licensing arrangement **26** 16
- licensing framework **26** 23
- market conditions **26** 28
- potential risks **26** 18
- regulated activities **26** 15
- regulations **26** 5
- regulatory framework **26** 14

623

- regulatory sandbox **26** 27
- securities law **26** 12
- self-regulation mechanism **26** 26
- SFC **26** 7
- SFO **26** 24
- stablecoins **26** 10
- taxation regulations **26** 30
- the statement **26** 8
hybrid tokens **1** 74
- accounting **14** 38
- ICO **7** 69

I

ICO **1** 81, **2** 35, et seqq
- Abu Dhabi **28** 8
- abuse **2** 42, et seq
- adverse selection **7** 5, et seqq, 57
- advertisement **7** 1, 86, et seq, 102
- airdrop **1** 84
- allocational efficiency **7** 4, et seq, 42
- applicable law **3** 15, et seqq
- approval **7** 1, et seqq
- Australia **24** 39, et seq
- Autorité des Marchés Financiers (AMF) **7** 23
- bona fide acquisition **7** 24, 45, et seq
- Bundesanstalt für Finanzdienstleistungsaufsicht (BaFin) **7** 3, 24, et seqq, 29, 64
- business model **7** 7, et seqq, 42, 79
- Canadian Securities Administrators (CSA) **7** 15
- causation **7** 114
- China **27** 13
- choice of law **3** 16, et seqq
- consumer jurisdiction rules **3** 10, et seqq
- consumer protection PIL rule **3** 17, et seq
- cost of capital **7** 4, 6, et seq, 42
- country of origin **2** 41
- credence good **7** 4, 7
- crypto-asset **7** 89, et seqq
- crypto-asset white paper **7** 96, et seq, 98, et seqq
- crypto-assets, other than asset-referenced tokens or e-money tokens **7** 90, 95
- currency token **7** 14, 19, et seq, 22, 26, et seqq, 29, 36, 47, 65, et seqq, 69, 71, 76, et seq, 91, 94, 97
- debt **7** 25, 50
- distribution **2** 39
- efficient capital market hypothesis **7** 114
- Eidgenössische Finanzmarktaufsicht (FINMA) **7** 28, 29, 64
- equity **7** 25, 50
- European Securities and Markets Authority (ESMA) **7** 19, et seqq, 29
- financial claims **7** 27, 49, 50, et seq, 53
- Financial Conduct Authority (FCA) **7** 22

- financial instrument **7** 8, 19, et seq, 24, 31, 41, 46, 47, et seqq, 59, et seq, 61, et seq, 66, 70, 92, 95, 103
- financial rights **7** 25, 49, et seq
- financing function **7** 62, et seqq
- Finanzmarktaufsicht (FMA) **7** 3, 27, 29, 64
- fraud-on-the-market-theory **7** 114
- hard cap **1** 84
- Hong Kong **26** 4
- hybrid tokens **7** 69
- information asymmetry **7** 4, et seqq, 7, 10, et seq, 42, 48, et seq, 54, et seq, 56, et seq, 60, 61, et seq, 66, 68, 97, 102, 108
- international jurisdiction **3** 9, et seqq
- investment function **7** 27, 28, 29, 55, 57, 61, 63, 67, 69, 75, 79, 93
- investment information **2** 42
- investment token **7** 14, 17, et seqq, 22, et seq, 26, et seqq, 29, 34, et seq, 48, et seqq, 79, 91, et seq
- issuer **7** 1, et seqq, 4, et seqq, 8, et seqq, 21, 23, 34, 39, et seqq, 48, et seqq, 53, et seqq, 61, et seqq, 66, et seqq, 75, 77, 78, et seq, 81, et seqq, 86, et seq, 88, 93, 95, 96, et seq, 98, et seqq, 110, et seqq
- liability **7** 88, 104, 111, et seqq
- lock-up **7** 36, et seq
- management body **7** 100, 112, et seq
- market for lemons **7** 5
- marketing communications **7** 101, et seqq
- MiCAR / Regulation on Markets in Crypto Assets **7** 89, et seqq
- Monetary Authority of Singapore (MAS) **7** 18, 29
- monitoring practices **2** 43
- moral hazard **7** 55, 57
- negitiability **7** 25, 27, 33, et seq, 36, et seq, 44, et seqq, 47
- network effect **7** 9, 75
- New Zealand **25** 8
- objective connection to a national legal system **3** 20, et seqq
- payment function **7** 65
- Pre-ICO **1** 84, **2** 43
- primary market **2** 40
- principal-agent-relationship **7** 4, 7, 48, et seq, 55, 56, et seq, 60, 61, et seq, 66, 97
- private sale **1** 84
- profit right **7** 19, 48, et seq
- prospectus liability **7** 88
- public sale **1** 84
- raising capital **2** 36
- secondary market **2** 40
- Securities and Exchange Commission (SEC) **7** 2, 14, 29, 64
- Securities and Futures Commission (SFC) **7** 17, 29
- soft cap **1** 84

Index

- standardisation **7** 25, 28, 33, 38, et seqq
- transaction costs **7** 8, et seqq, 38, 42
- transferability **7** 25, 33, et seqq
- transferable security **7** 19, 24, et seqq, 27, 32, 33, et seqq, 44, 47, et seqq, 53, et seqq, 61, 63, et seq, 65, 67, et seq, 69, 71
- utility function **7** 63
- utilty token **7** 9, 14, 17, et seqq, 22, et seq, 26, et seqq, 29, 34, et seq, 47, 52, et seqq, 56, et seqq, 61, et seqq, 66, et seq, 75, 79, 91, 93, 95, 99, 108
- volume **2** 38, et seq
- voting rights **7** 14, 20, 50, et seq
- white paper **2** 42
illegal activities **2** 66
inflation **2** 24, 52
- costs **2** 24
- hyper- **2** 52, 63
Initial Coin Offering *see* ICO
insider dealing
- inside information **11** 31, et seqq
- prohibited conduct **11** 30, et seqq
- purpose **11** 28, et seq
interface provider **1** 27
intermediaries **2** 70
- anti-money laundering **10** 42, et seqq
- applicable law **3** 33, et seqq
- international jurisdiction **3** 28, et seqq
investment **2** 64
- over- **2** 78, 83
investment firm
- authorisation **8** 37, et seqq
- definition **8** 14
investment token **1** 71
- accounting **14** 14, et seqq
- initial measurement **14** 21, et seqq
- measurement **14** 21, et seqq
- recognition **14** 14, et seqq
- subsequent measurement **14** 25
- tax exemption **13** 27, 29
investor
- enthusiasm **2** 13, 16
Iraq
- cryptocurrency **28** 40
Israel
- cryptocurrency **28** 42
issuer **9** 15, et seqq
- anti-money laundering **10** 54, et seqq
- customer due dilligence **10** 135
- of asset-referenced tokens **9** 106
- of crypto assets **9** 101, et seqq
- of e-money tokens **9** 107, et seq
- of utility tokens **9** 105
- risk assessment **10** 78

K
know-your-customer (KYC) **1** 85, **10** 108
- electronic identification **10** 115

Kuwait
- cryptocurrency **28** 39

L
lawfulness of processing **6** 55, et seqq
legal tender **2** 57
Levant
- cryptocurrency **28** 41
- Jordan **28** 41
- Lebanon **28** 41
- Palestine **28** 41
Libra **9** 37, et seq
- Association **9** 37, et seq
- Diem **9** 37, et seq
- Diem-Association **9** 37, et seq
licensing
- anti-money laundering **10** 39, et seqq
Liechtenstein
- anti-money laundering **20** 28, et seqq
- initial public offering **20** 23, et seq
- market structure **20** 2, et seqq
- prospectus **20** 25, et seqq
- registration **20** 14, et seqq
- regulatory guidance **20** 31
- service providers **20** 10, et seqq
- transfer of tokens **20** 19, et seqq
- TVTG **20** 6, et seqq
light nodes **1** 9
lock-up **1** 84

M
managers' transactions
- disclosure obligations **11** 55, et seqq
- purpose **11** 53, et seq
- trading ban **11** 60, et seq
MAR
- competent authority **11** 13, et seqq
- disclosure obligations **11** 42, et seqq
- financial instrument **11** 7, et seqq
- geographical scope of application **11** 11, et seqq
- insider dealing **11** 28, et seqq
- key concepts **11** 1, et seqq
- managers' transactions **11** 53, et seqq
- market manipulation **11** 19, et seqq
- multilateral trading facility **11** 10
market
- black ~ **2** 62
- capitalization **2** 17, et seq
- intervention **2** 76
- mechanism **2** 86
- position **2** 18, et seq
market manipulation
- effects-based approach **11** 22
- prohibited conduct **11** 21
- purpose **11** 19, et seq
memoryless **2** 54
mempool **2** 19, et seq

MENA
- Bitcoin **28** 35
- central bank digital currency **28** 40

MiCAR
- authorisation **8** 46, et seq
- crypto asset services **8** 46, et seq
- crypto-asset custodian **15** 235, et seqq
- crypto-asset service provider **4** 14, 38
- disclosure obligations **11** 63, et seq
- geographical scope of application **8** 13
- insider dealing **11** 40
- issuer of crypto-assets **4** 14, 38
- key concepts **8** 7
- market abuse **11** 16, et seqq
- market manipulation **11** 41
- scope **15** 123, et seqq
- wallet custody **8** 36

MiFiD2
- competent authority **8** 8
- crypto ATM **8** 32, et seqq
- crypto exchange service **8** 31
- geographical scope of application **8** 8, et seqq
- key concepts **8** 6, et seq
- passporting **8** 11, et seq
- wallet custody **8** 34, et seq

miner **1** 38
- anti-money laundering **10** 60
- role of the participants under the GDPR **6** 33, 39, 48, 52

mining **1** 38, et seqq
- applicable law **3** 59
- international jurisdiction **3** 57
- tax exemption **13** 43, et seqq
- taxable transaction **13** 32, et seqq

mining pool **1** 40, et seqq, **2** 84
- applicable law **3** 60
- collaborative **1** 46
- forms of organisation **1** 53, seqq
- international jurisdiction **3** 58
- managed **1** 54
- modes of opertion **1** 45, et seqq
- non-collaborative **1** 49, et seqq
- peer-to-peer **1** 55
- pool blockchain **1** 55

minting **1** 58, et seqq
minting pool **1** 60
mixer **1** 106
mixing **12** 6, 10
mobile wallet **1** 25
monetary
- policy **2** 91
- theory **2** 2

monetary functions **2** 45, et seqq
- medium of exchange **2** 46
- primary **2** 46, et seq
- secondary **2** 49
- store of value **2** 46
- unit of account **2** 46

money laundering **10** 165, et seqq
money laundering reporting officer **10** 74
money remittance **9** 82, et seqq
money supply
- algorithmic **2** 77
multipools **1** 41

N
Nash equilibrium **2** 83
ne bis in idem **12** 50, 65
network effect **2** 51
New Zealand
- competition law **25** 13
- constitution and political system **25** 2, et seq
- Department of Internal Affairs **25** 12
- equity crowd funding/P2PL **25** 6
- Financial Markets Authority **25** 19, 22, 24, et seq, 38, et seq
- financial markets participant **25** 18
- financial markets regulation **25** 14, et seq
- financial markets regulator **25** 11
- financial product **25** 20, 21
- fintech regulator **25** 5
- judicial consideration of cryptocurrency **25** 44, et seq
- judicial interpretation **25** 43
- legal system **25** 4, et seq
- usage of cryptocurrency **25** 7

nodes **1** 7, et seqq
numéraire **2** 65

O
obliged entities **10** 42, et seqq
occasional transactions **10** 95
- fiat-to-crypto exchange **10** 95
off-chain **6** 41
Oman
- cryptocurrency **28** 38
on-chain **6** 42, et seq
one-stop shop principle **6** 90
online platform **5** 2
online wallet **1** 25
open banking
- Australia **24** 16
oracle **1** 64

P
P2B-Regulation **5** 68
paper wallet **1** 25
participants **6** 33, et seqq
payment
- micropayment **2** 21
- service providers **2** 21
- subsidized system **2** 22, et seqq
- system **2** 69
payment account **9** 77
payment institution **9** 98, et seqq
payment service providers **9** 97

payment services **9** 65, et seqq
payment token **1** 70
payment transaction **9** 27, et seq
payments platform
– Australia **24** 21
peer-to-peer lending
– Australia **24** 18
performance
– relative **2** 9, et seq
personal data **6** 18, et seqq
persons trading in goods **10** 34, et seq
– anti-money laundering **10** 34, et seq, 61
– customer due dilligence **10** 98, et seqq
– territorial scope **10** 34, et seq
platform agreement **5** 7, et seqq, 21, et seqq
– applicable law **3** 33
– international jurisdiction **3** 28, et seqq
platform token **1** 90
politically exposed persons (PEP) **10** 122
pool blockchain **1** 55
price increase
– exponential **2** 8, et seqq
privacy token **1** 108
private key **1** 18
proceeds of crime **12** 12, et seq, 25, 55
processing on behalf **6** 36, 39, 42, 52, 69, et seqq
– central blockchain **6** 71
– decentralized blockchain **6** 72, et seq
processing time **2** 20
product regulation
– AIFs **15** 153, et seqq
– UCITS **15** 158, et seqq
proof-of-stake **1** 58, et seqq, **2** 89
proof-of-work **1** 38, et seqq
prospectus
– approval **7** 81, et seqq
– content **7** 78, et seqq
– exemptions **7** 72, et seqq
– requirements **7** 31, et seqq
prospectus liability
– applicable law **3** 45, et seqq
– Germany **17** 26
– international jurisdiction **3** 39, et seqq
protocol software **1** 2
pruning **6** 100
pseudonymity **6** 25
public key **1** 16, et seq
– anti-money laundering **10** 158
purchasing power **2** 29, et seqq

Q
Qatar **28** 39

R
Regulation (EU) 2018/1805 **12** 57, 60, et seqq
Regulation on Markets in Crypto-assets (MiCAR) **9** 50, et seqq
remittances **2** 72

Reserve Bank
– New Zealand **25** 12
right against self-incrimination **12** 48
right of withdrawal
– currency token **4** 26
– distance contract **4** 16
– exceptions **4** 20, et seqq
– investment token **4** 25
– MiCAR **4** 36, et seqq
– utility token **4** 19, 28
right to information **5** 49, et seqq
right to private property **12** 46
ring signatures **1** 109
risk
– credit **2** 71
– liquidity **2** 71
risk assessment **10** 71, et seqq
– art market participants **10** 79, et seq
– custodian wallet provider **10** 77
– fiat-to-crypto exchange **10** 77
– issuers **10** 78
risk management **10** 70, et seqq
risk of liability
– liability risk **5** 17, et seqq, 71, et seqq
risk-based approach **10** 68
Russia
– constitutional law **21** 10
– criminal law **21** 14, et seqq
– digital financial assets law **21** 26, et seqq
– digital rights law **21** 23, et seqq
– economy **21** 6
– EU/US-sanctions **21** 38, et seq

S
sanctions
– disclosure obligations **11** 52
– insider dealing **11** 39
– managers' transactions **11** 62
– market manipulation **11** 25
– providing services without authorisation **8** 44, et seq
Saudi Arabi
– virtual currency **28** 37
Second Electronic Money Directive **9** 8, et seqq
Second Payment Services Directive **9** 65, et seqq
secondary market **5** 1
securities
– anti-money laundering **10** 25
security token **1** 72
security token offering *see STO*
seigniorage **2** 23, et seq
shareholder register
– DLT **15** 111, et seqq
Sharia **28** 2
– Islamic Finance **28** 44
– Islamic Fintech **28** 44

627

Index

Singapore
- blockchain **23** 1, et seq
- commodities **23** 1, et seq
- compliance **23** 30, et seq
- criminal activities **23** 24, et seq
- criminal liability **23** 25, et seq
- criminal penalties **23** 13, et seq
- digital payment token **23** 17, et seq
- digital token **23** 16, et seq
- distributed ledger technology **23** 1, et seq
- exchange platform **23** 18, et seq
- licence **23** 4, et seq
- multi-currency payment network **23** 23, et seq
- online investment scams **23** 24, et seq
- pament network **23** 1, et seq
- payment account **23** 16, et seq
- payment services **23** 2, et seq
- payment transactions **23** 16, et seq
- pbulic sector organisations **23** 23, et seq
- regulagory framework **23** 1, et seq
- regulatory approach **23** 1, et seq
- regulatory landscape **23** 1, et seq
- regulatory requirements **23** 20, et seq
- sandbox **23** 1, et seq
- securities **23** 1, et seq
smart contract **1** 62, et seqq, **5** 32
snapshot **2** 94
software wallet **1** 25
stable coin **1** 76, **2** 75, **9** 36, et seqq
- algorithmic stable coin **9** 36
- asset-backed stable coin **9** 36
- custodial stable coin **9** 36
staking
- Germany **17** 33
staking pools **1** 60
stealth address **1** 110, et seq
- view key **1** 111
STO **1** 81
- Germany **17** 7, et seqq
storage **2** 63
subordinated loans
- Germany **17** 9
superervision
- anti-money laundering **10** 30, et seq, 172
suspicious transaction report
- anti-money laundering **10** 103, et seq
Switzerland
- acceptance of crypto assets **19** 13
- anti-money laundering **19** 24, et seqq
- banking law **19** 12, et seqq
- banking licence **19** 12
- bankruptcy estate in general **19** 29
- bankruptcy of a bank or other financial institution **19** 35
- bankruptcy of a custodian of intermediated securities **19** 34
- classification on crypto assets **19** 3

- constitutional basis **19** 11
- crypto assets as part of the bankruptcy estate **19** 32
- deposits form the public **19** 12, et seq, 15
- DLT law revision **19** 4
- DLT trading facility **19** 21, 23
- exemptions from the licensing requirement **19** 14, et seqq
- financial institutions **19** 18, et seq
- financial market infrastructure **19** 20, et seq
- financial market supervisory authority (FINMA) **19** 3, 11, 14, 15
- financial services **19** 17
- fintech licence **19** 13
- intermediated securities **19** 22, et seq
- international private law **19** 9, et seq
- ledger based security **19** 4, 7, 8, 21, 23
- market development **19** 2, et seqq
- property law **19** 5, et seq
- securities law **19** 7, et seq
- transfer of digital assets **19** 5, et seq
- transfer of tokenized claims **19** 10
system
- decentralized **2** 60

T
territorial scope
- anti-money laundering **10** 32, et seqq
terrorist financing **10** 1, et seqq see also anti-money laundering
- Australia **24** 9
Tether (USDT) **1** 76
third countries **6** 74, et seqq
token
- (significant) asset-referenced token **9** 56, et seq
- (significant) e-money token **9** 58, et seqq
- accounting **14** 1, et seqq
- anti-money laundering **10** 12, et seqq
- asset-backed **1** 75
- burning **1** 6, 73
- cash **10** 29
- currency token **9** 34, et seq
- hybrid token **9** 46, et seqq
- input **1** 22
- investment token **9** 41, et seq
- output **1** 22
- purchase agreement **1** 85
- technical design **1** 68, et seq
- token-ATM **9** 75, et seqq
- utility token **9** 43, et seqq
- virtual currency **10** 13, et seqq
- volume growth **2** 27, et seqq
token ownership
- applicable law **3** 6, et seq
token property
- applicable law **3** 6, et seq

628

Index

token trading
- applicable law **3** 25, et seqq
- consumer protection PIL rule **3** 25, et seq
- international jurisdiction **3** 24

tokenisation **1** 72

tokenised fund 'units' & 'shares'
- benefits **15** 76, et seqq
- member state laws **15** 99, et seqq

tokenization **2** 92

tort law
- applicable law **3** 55
- international jurisdiction **3** 54

trading platform **1** 90, et seqq, **6** 40
- central **1** 97, et seq
- data processing operations **6** 13
- decentralised **1** 99, et seq
- GDPR **6** 17, 27
- lawfulness of processing **6** 56, 59, 62
- material scope **6** 17, 23
- off-chain **1** 96
- on-chain **1** 94, et seq
- role of the participants under the GDPR **6** 33, 40, et seqq
- territorial scope **6** 27

transaction **6** 14, et seqq
- amount **2** 20, et seq
- anti-money laundering **10** 27, et seq
- costs **2** 54
- fee **2** 21, et seqq
- international payment **2** 20
- number **2** 19, et seq
- volume **2** 19, et seq

transaction data **6** 15

transaction fee **1** 23, 36, **5** 30, 36
- breach of contract **5** 59, et seq, 65, et seq

transaction ID **1** 24

transaction recipient **6** 33, 40, 53, et seq

transaction sender **6** 33, 50, 53, et seq

transction monitoring **10** 121, 134

transparency register **10** 154, et seqq

trustee **5** 22, 34, 45

tumbler **1** 106
- anti-money laundering **10** 53

U

UAE
- Abu Dhabi **28** 2, 5, et seq
- Dubai **28**

unexplained wealth proceedings **12** 36, 61

unfair terms **5** 9, et seqq, 75

United Kingdom
- company law **18** 9, et seqq
- data protection **18** 29, et seqq
- financial instrument **18** 3
- governance rights **18** 34, et seqq
- intermediaries **18** 6, et seq
- prospectus **18** 4, et seq
- shareholder transparency **18** 29, et seqq

United States
- client-attorney relationship **22** 22
- CTFC **22** 2, et seq
- Howey test **22** 7, et seq
- Munchee case **22** 16, et seqq
- online trading platforms **22** 25
- ReCoin case **22** 15
- regulatory initiatives **22** 28, et seqq
- related entities **22** 24
- SEC **22** 4, et seqq
- The DAO Report **22** 7, et seqq

units & shares
- AIFMD **15** 84, et seqq
- dematerialised securities **15** 106, et seqq
- materialised securities **15** 104, et seqq
- registered securities **15** 108, et seqq
- UCITSD **15** 89, et seqq

utility token **1** 73
- accounting **14** 26, et seqq
- initial measurement **14** 33, et seqq
- measurement **14** 32, et seqq
- recognition **14** 26, et seqq
- redemption **4** 34
- subsequent measurement **14** 37

UTXO **1** 22

V

value
- fundamental **2** 15, et seq
- intrinsic ~ **2** 15, 56, et seq

value added tax
- currency token **13** 8, et seqq
- hybrid token **13** 30
- investment token **13** 23, et seqq
- platforms **13** 18
- utility token **13** 20, et seqq
- wallets **13** 15, et seqq

virtual account balance **5** 43, 46

virtual asset service providers **10** 169

virtual currency **10** 13
- means of exchange **10** 20, et seqq
- types of tokens **10** 23

volatility
- high **2** 8, et seqq

W

wallet **1** 25, et seqq, **9** 78
- desktop wallet **1** 25
- hardware wallet **1** 25
- mobile wallet **1** 25
- online wallet **1** 25
- paper wallet **1** 25
- provider **1** 27, **9** 79, et seq
- software wallet **1** 25

wallet provider **1** 27
- anti-money laundering **10** 49, et seqq

Index

white list
- AML **15** 118, et seqq
- GDPR **15** 119, et seqq
- Wallet addresses **15** 115, et seqq

white paper **1** 85
- international jurisdiction **3** 11

Z
zero-knowledge proof **6** 97